梦圆伶仃

DREAMS OVER LINGDING

港珠澳大桥岛隧工程画册

Album of the Island-Tunnel Project of Hong Kong-Zhuhai-Macau Bridge

中国交通建设股份有限公司 编
CHINA COMMUNICATIONS CONSTRUCTION COMPANY LIMITED

南方日报出版社
NANFANG DAILY PRESS
中国·广州

图书在版编目（CIP）数据

梦圆伶仃 / 中国交通建设股份有限公司编. — 广州：南方日报出版社，2019.3
（港珠澳大桥岛隧工程画册）
ISBN 978-7-5491-1987-5

Ⅰ. ①梦… Ⅱ. ①中… Ⅲ. ①跨海峡桥－桥梁工程－中国－图集
②水下隧道－隧道工程－中国－图集 Ⅳ. ①U4-64

中国版本图书馆 CIP 数据核字（2019）第 045117 号

GANG ZHU AO DAQIAO DAOSUI GONGCHENG HUACE · MENGYUAN LINGDING
港珠澳大桥岛隧工程画册·梦圆伶仃

编　　者：中国交通建设股份有限公司
设计排版：廣角品牌机构
出版发行：南方日报出版社
地　　址：广州市广州大道中 289 号
出 版 人：周山丹
责任编辑：杨柳青　曹　星
责任技编：王　兰
责任校对：裴晓倩
装帧设计：李文俊　田　红　吴　凯
翻　　译：刘风山　郭敬谊
经　　销：全国新华书店
印　　刷：雅昌文化（集团）有限公司
开　　本：635 mm×965 mm　1/8
印　　张：22
字　　数：404 千字
版　　次：2019 年 3 月第 1 版
印　　次：2019 年 3 月第 1 次印刷
定　　价：980.00 元 （全套 4 册）

编委会
Editorial Board

目录
CONTENTS

跬步千里
A SHORT STEP IS THE BEGINNING OF A THOUSAND MILES

闪耀伶仃
SHINING ON LINGDING BAY

画册索引
ALBUM INDEX

后记
POSTSCRIPT

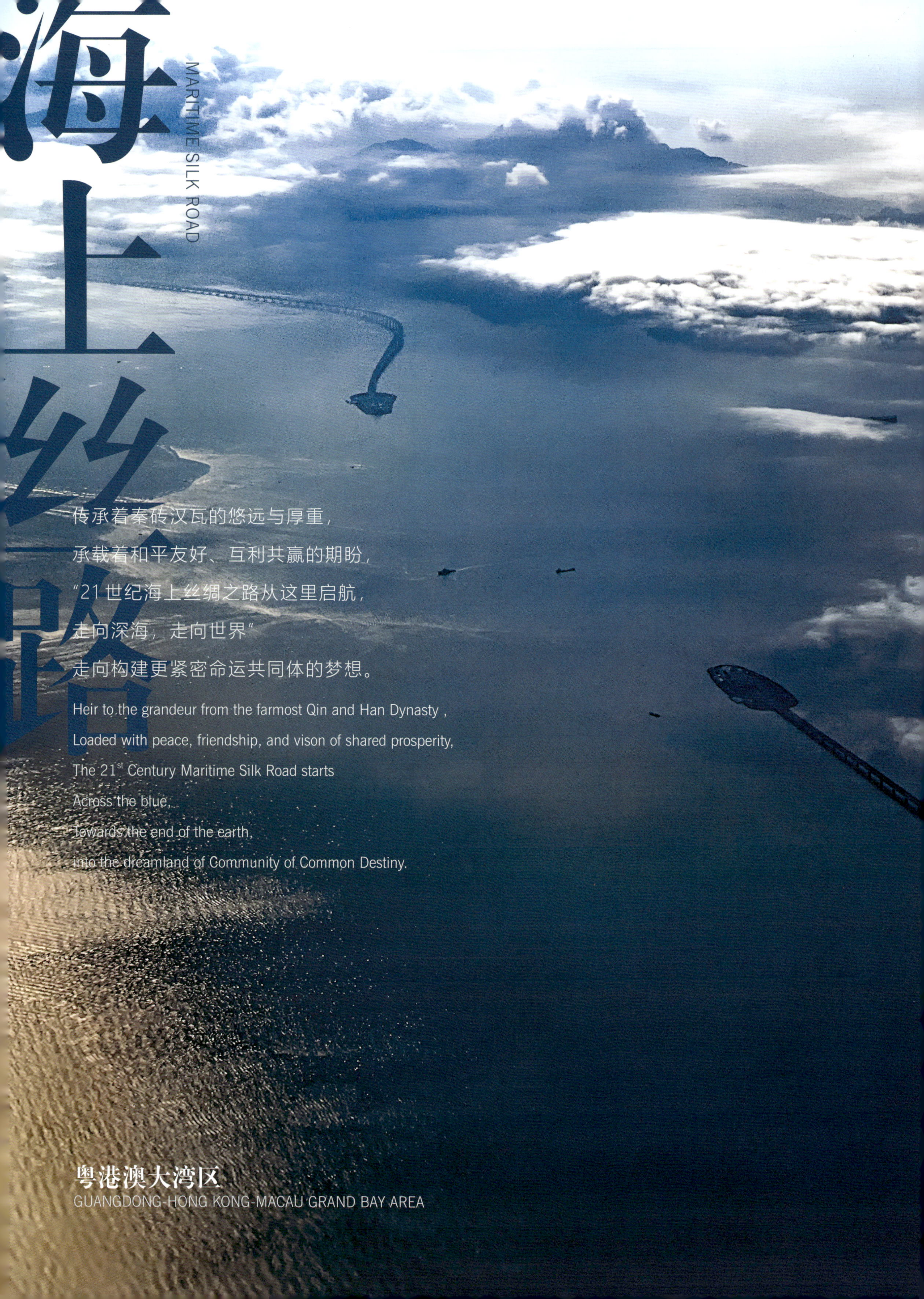

海上丝路

MARITIME SILK ROAD

传承着秦砖汉瓦的悠远与厚重，
承载着和平友好、互利共赢的期盼，
“21世纪海上丝绸之路从这里启航，
走向深海，走向世界”
走向构建更紧密命运共同体的梦想。

Heir to the grandeur from the farmost Qin and Han Dynasty ,
Loaded with peace, friendship, and vison of shared prosperity,
The 21st Century Maritime Silk Road starts
Across the blue,
Towards the end of the earth,
into the dreamland of Community of Common Destiny.

粤港澳大湾区
GUANGDONG-HONG KONG-MACAU GRAND BAY AREA

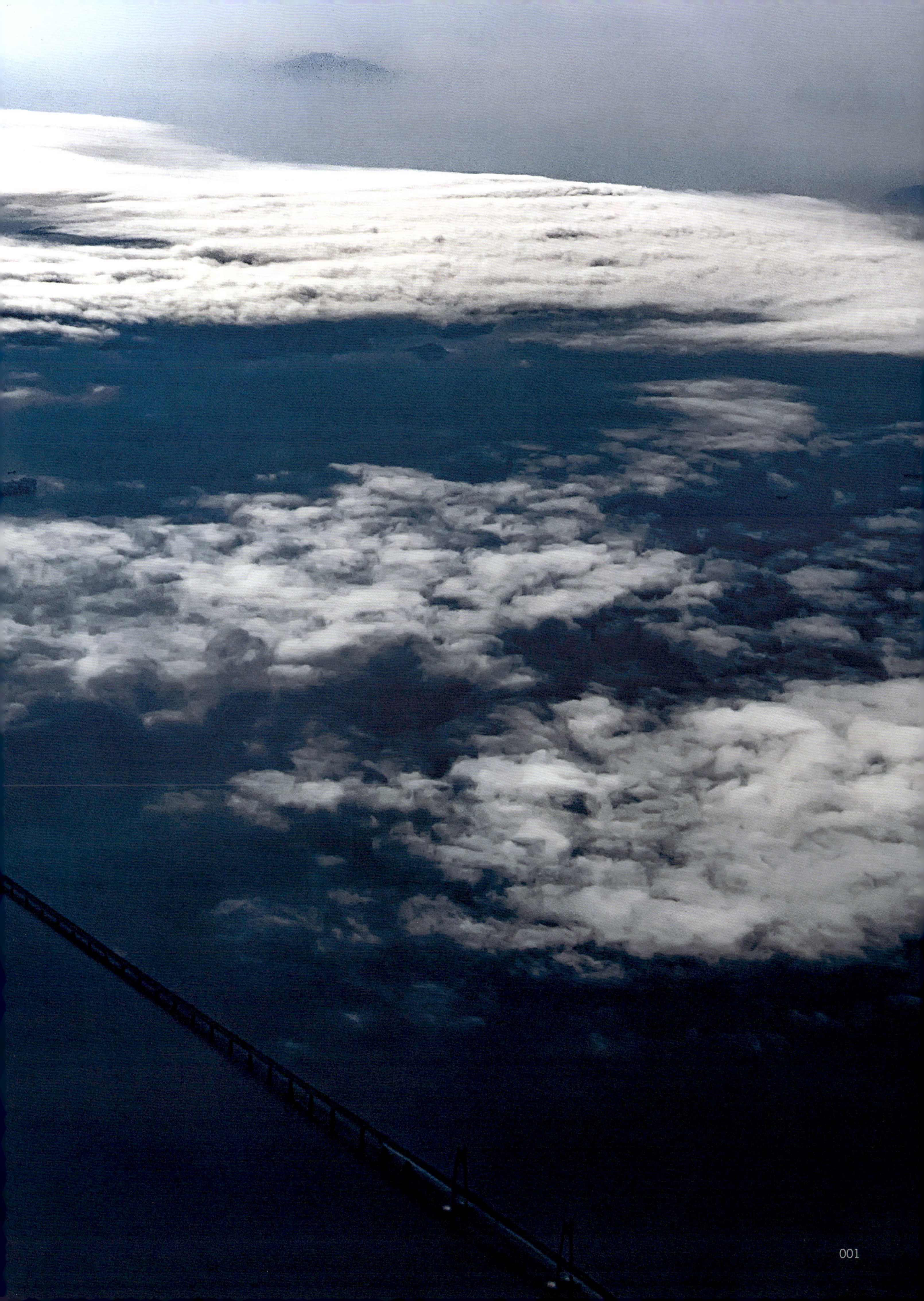

"21世纪海上丝绸之路"倡议构想于2013年提出，从中国东南沿海，经过中南半岛和南海诸国，穿越印度洋，进入红海，抵达东非和欧洲，成为中国与外国贸易往来和文化交流的海上大通道，增进同沿边国家和地区的交往，串起连通东盟、南亚、西亚、北非、欧洲等各大经济板块的市场链，以点带线，以线带面，发展面向南海、太平洋和印度洋的战略合作经济带，以亚欧非经济贸易一体化为发展的长期目标。

The concept of the 21st Century Maritime Silk Road was first conceived in 2013. It starts from the southeast coast of China, passes by Indo-China Peninsula and countries on the coasts of South Seas, across the Indian Ocean and the Red Sea, and finally reaches East Africa and Europe. It is an avenue on the seas connecting the countries and regions alongside, linking the markets of ASEAN, South Asia, West Asia, North Africa and Europe, facilitating the trades and cultural communications between China and the world. Beginning with one country, expanding into a region, it aims at building a community of economic cooperation among countries around South Seas, the Pacific Ocean and the Indian Ocean, integrating the economic entities in Asia, Europe and Africa.

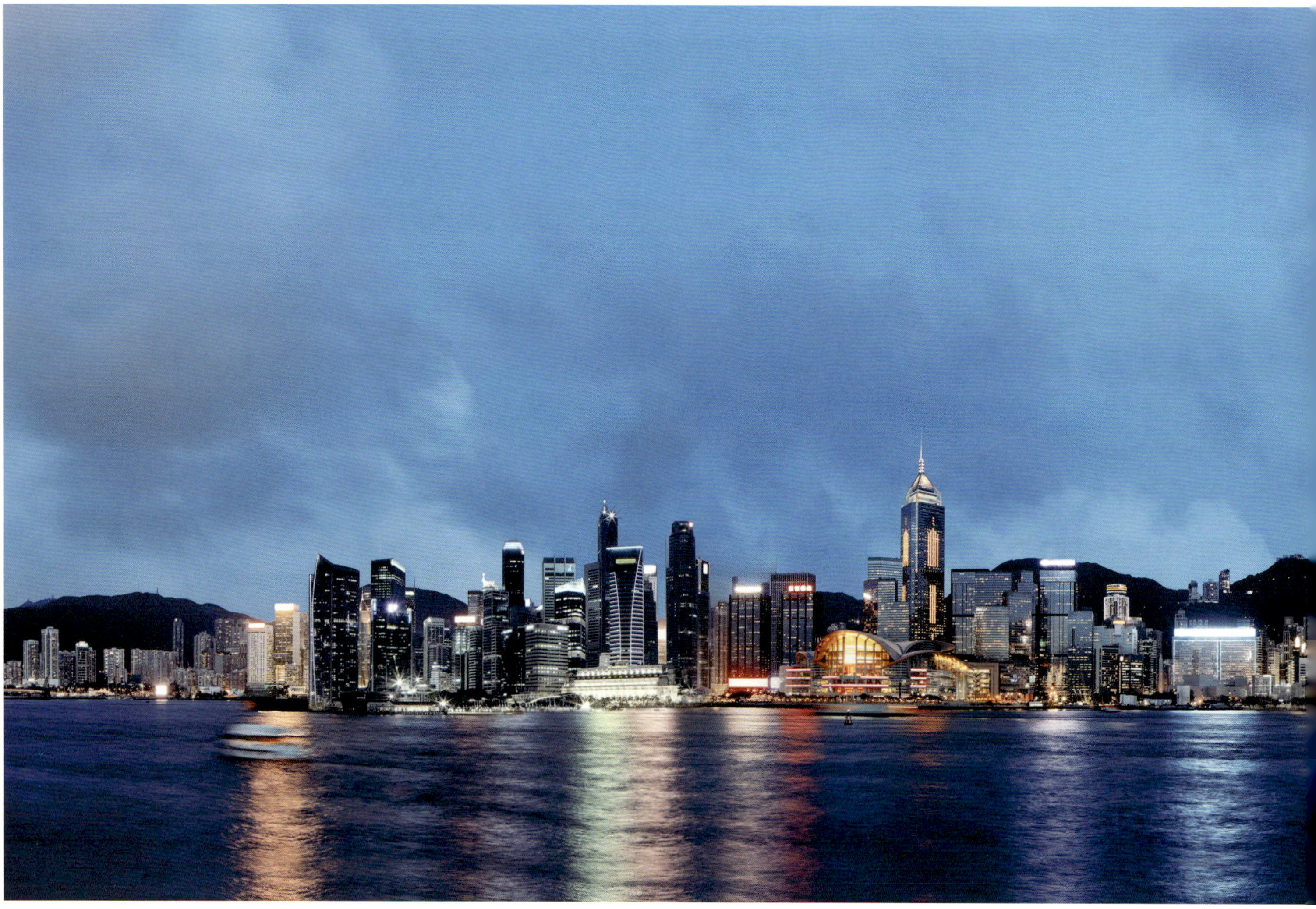

1. 港珠澳大桥位置图
Location Map of Hong Kong-Zhuhai-Macau Bridge

2. 香港
Hong Kong

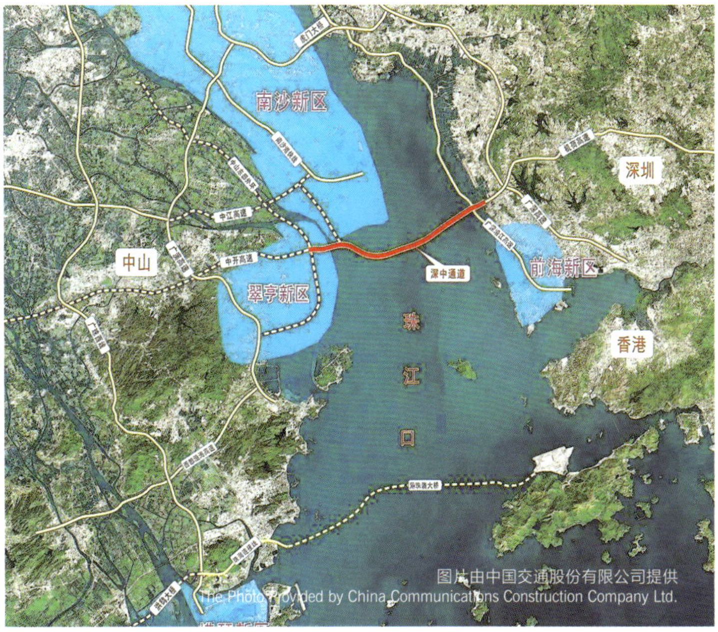

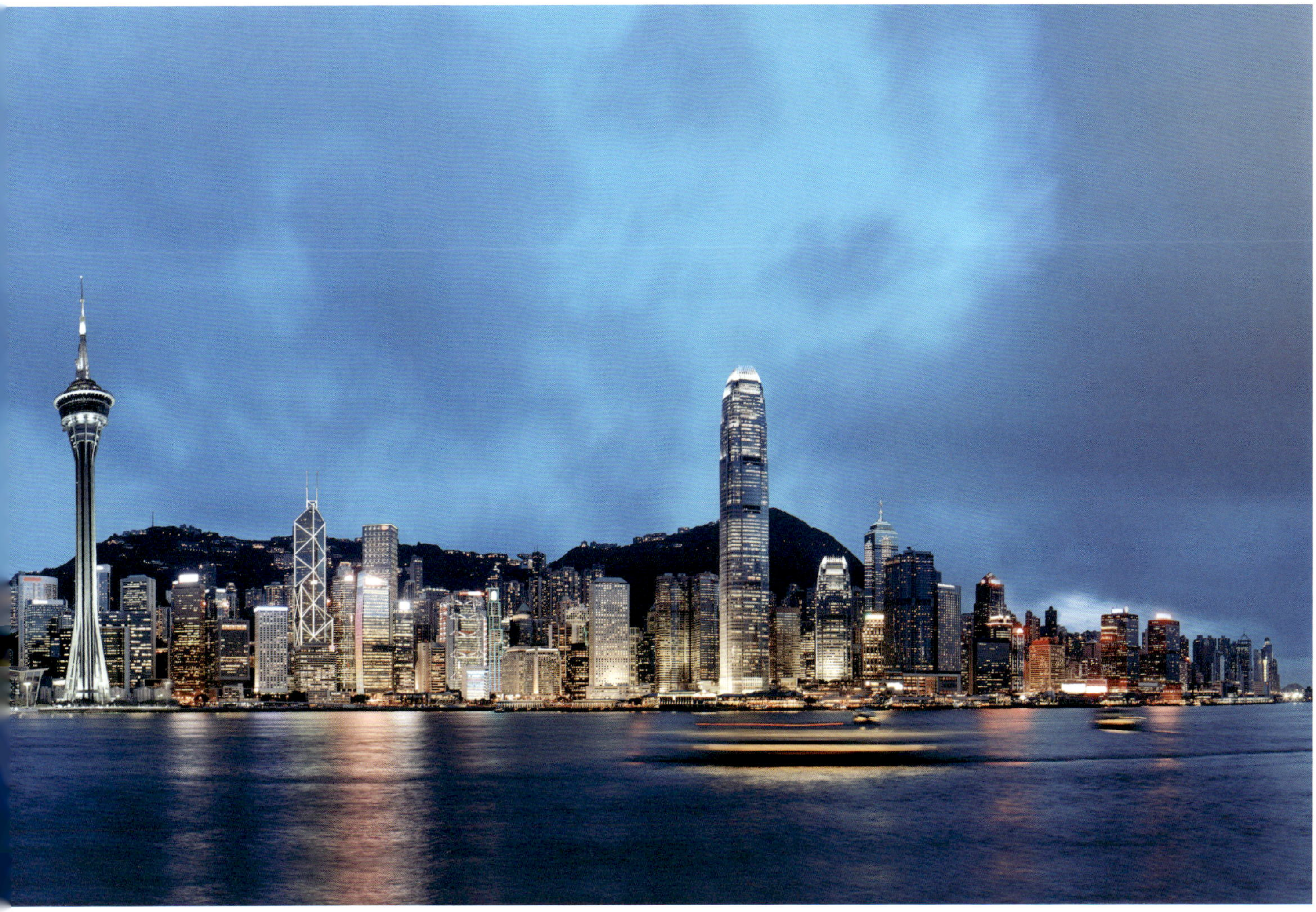

粤港澳大湾区作为"海上丝绸之路"的起点之一，以其特殊的历史文化、区位优势背景，承担着国家"一带一路"扩大对外开放的倡议重任。

香港、珠海、澳门，港珠澳大桥连接起来的三个关键点，将成为"21世纪海上丝绸之路"愿景的新支点。

Guangdong-Hong Kong-Macau Grand Bay Area, one starting point of the Maritime Silk Road with its special historical, cultural and geological advantages, takes as its duty the expansion of China's Belt and Road Initiative and China's opening up to the world.

Hong Kong, Zhuhai, Macau, the three links connected by the Hong Kong-Zhuhai-Macau Bridge, will be the pivots of the landscape waved by the 21st Century Maritime Silk Road.

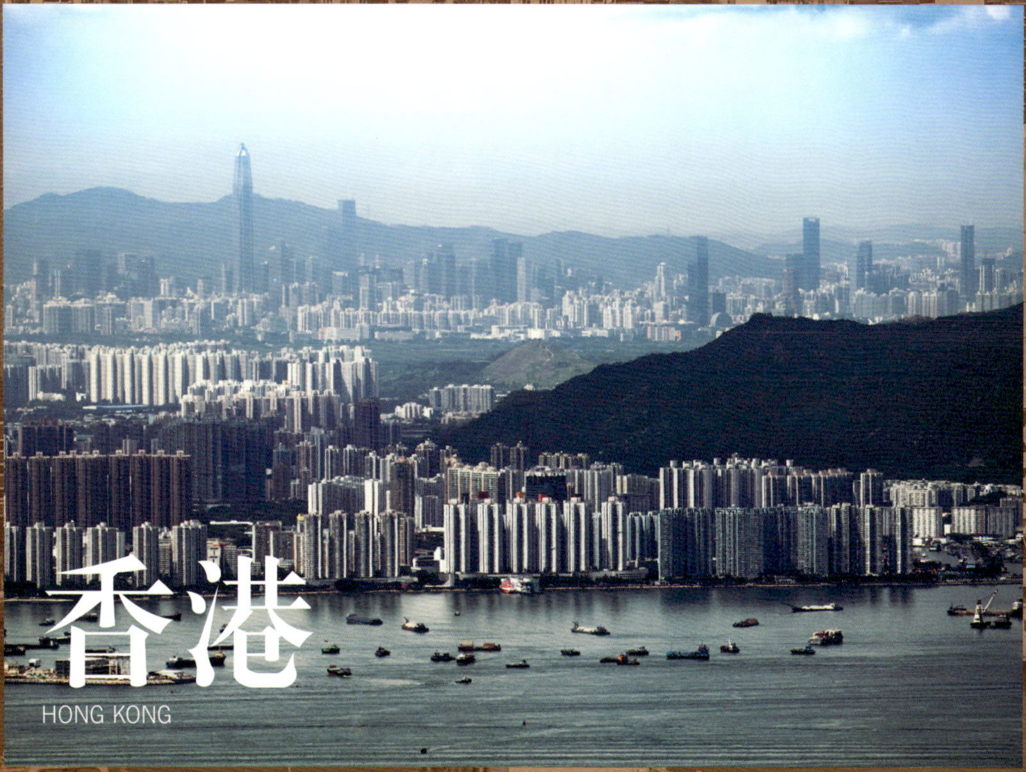

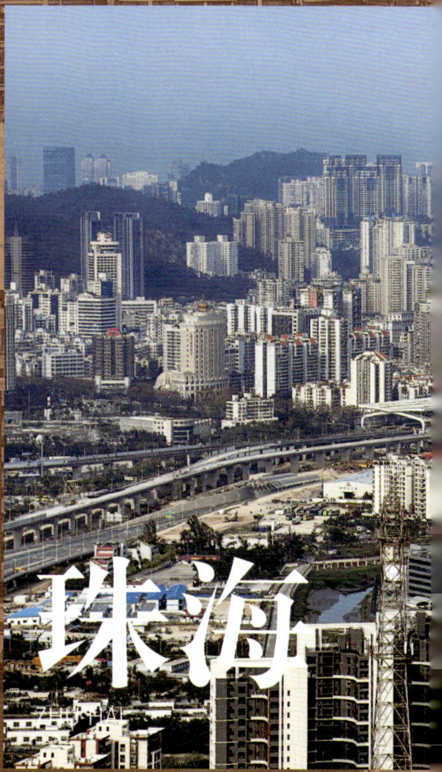

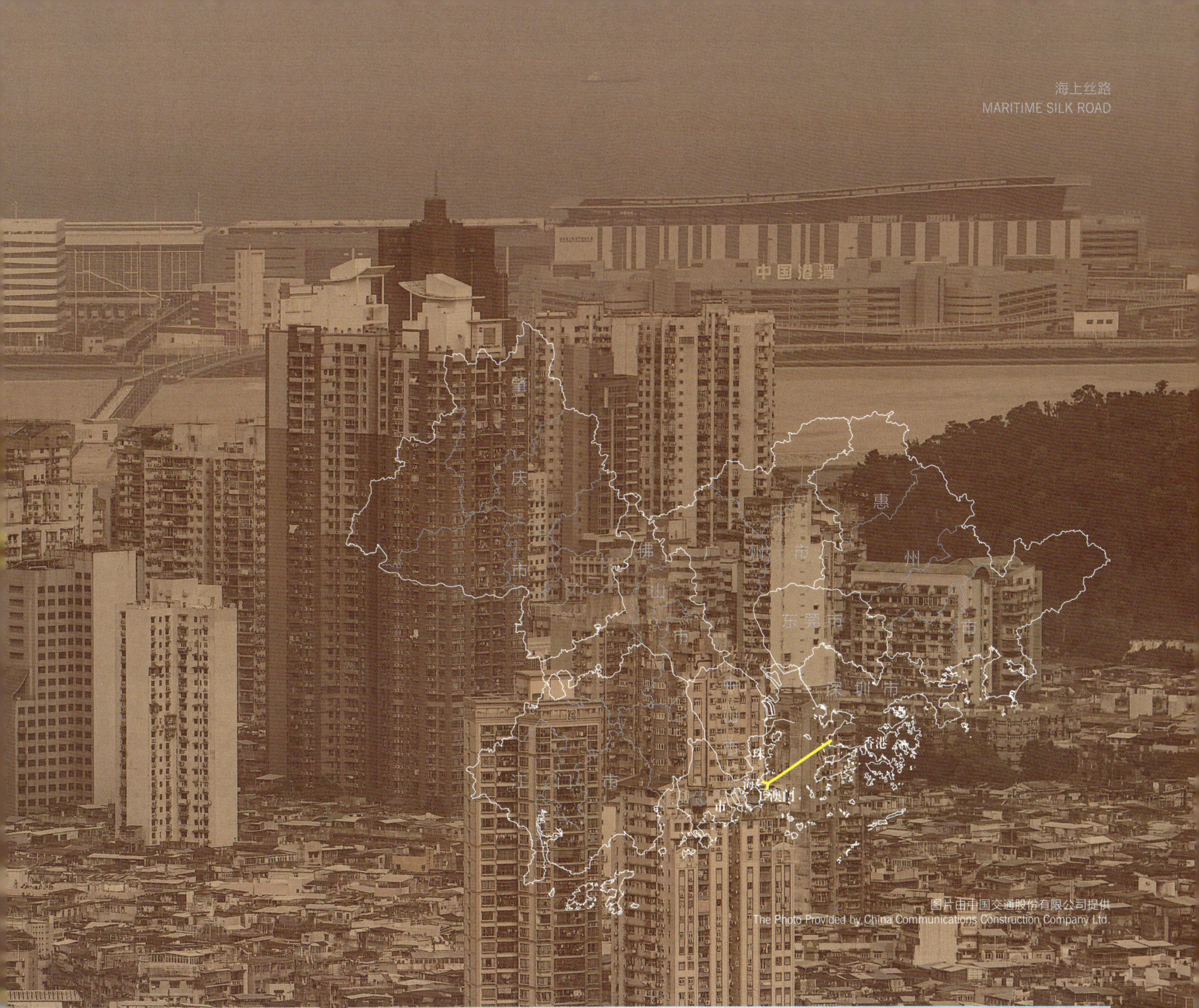

图片由中国交通股份有限公司提供
The Photo Provided by China Communications Construction Company Ltd.

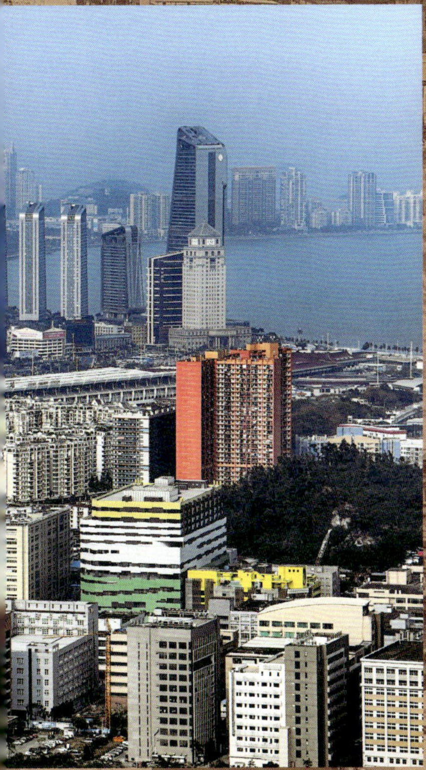

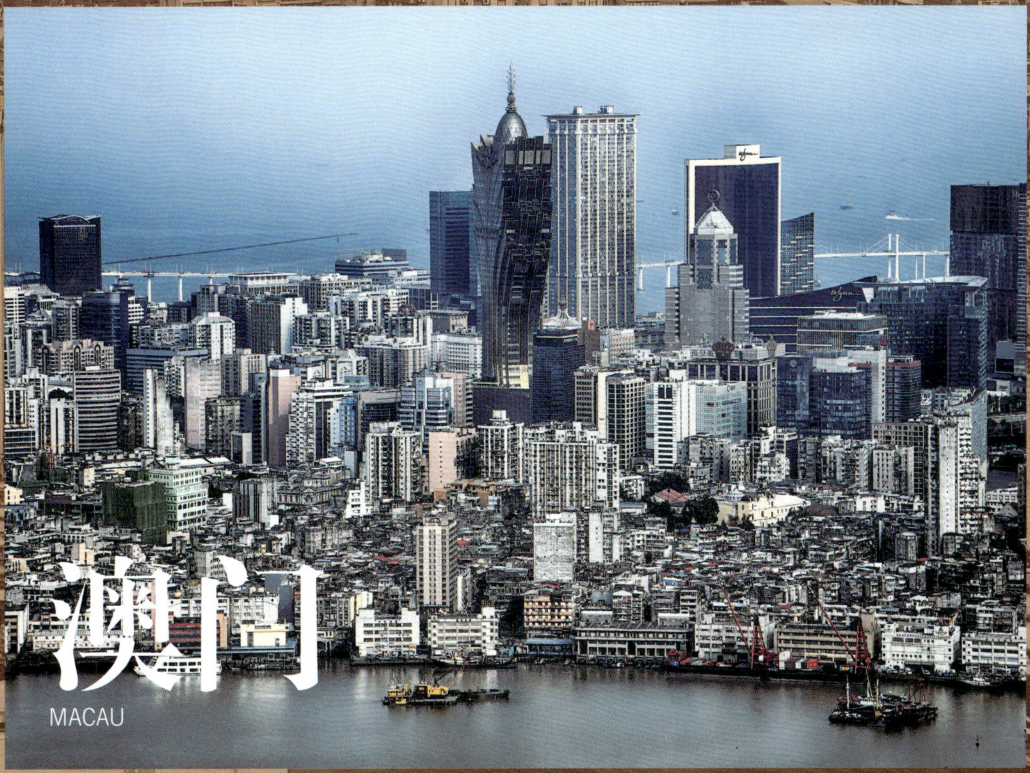

澳门
MACAU

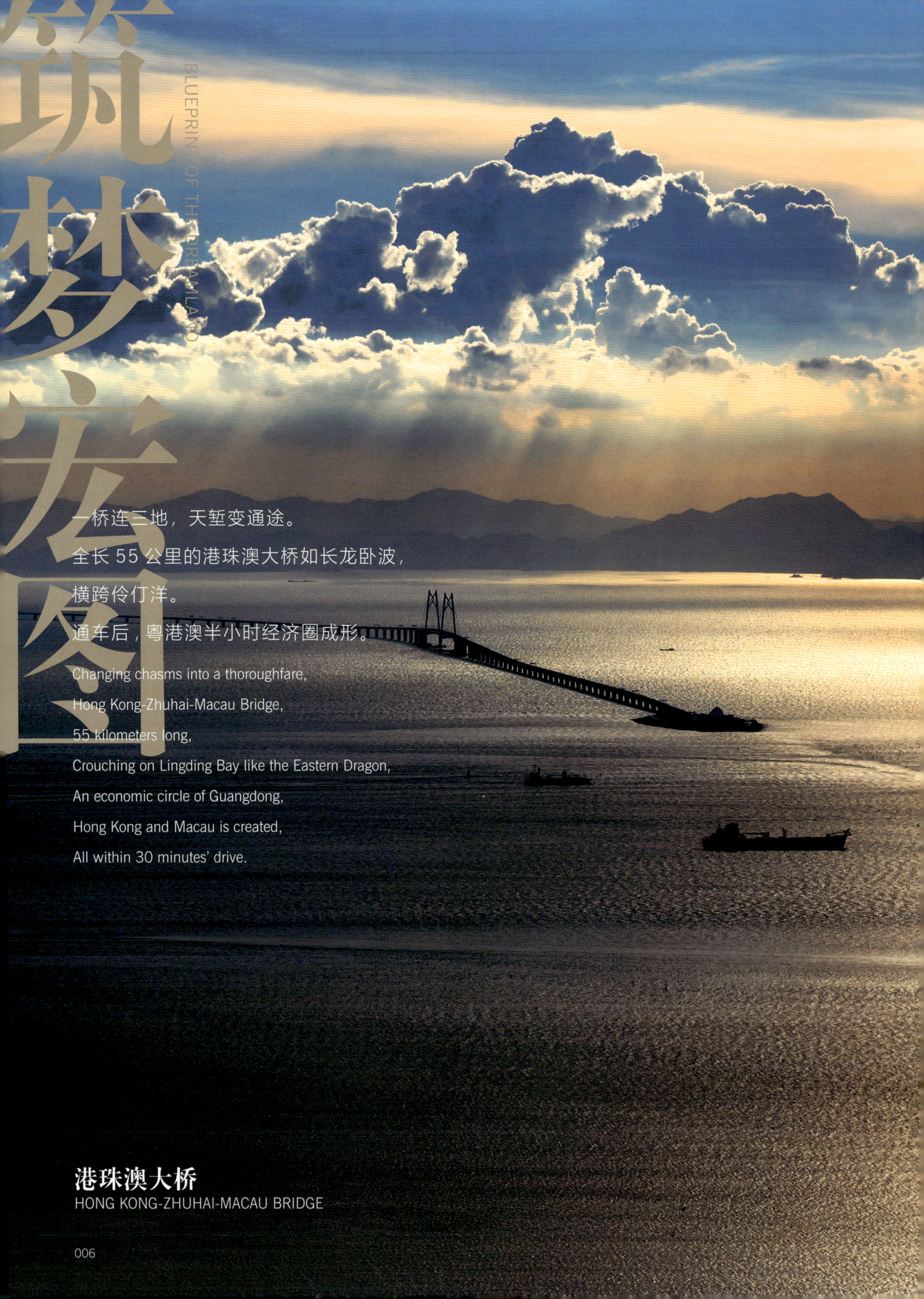

筑梦宏图

BLUEPRINT OF THE DREAMLAND

一桥连三地，天堑变通途。
全长 55 公里的港珠澳大桥如长龙卧波，
横跨伶仃洋。
通车后，粤港澳半小时经济圈成形。

Changing chasms into a thoroughfare,
Hong Kong-Zhuhai-Macau Bridge,
55 kilometers long,
Crouching on Lingding Bay like the Eastern Dragon,
An economic circle of Guangdong,
Hong Kong and Macau is created,
All within 30 minutes' drive.

港珠澳大桥
HONG KONG-ZHUHAI-MACAU BRIDGE

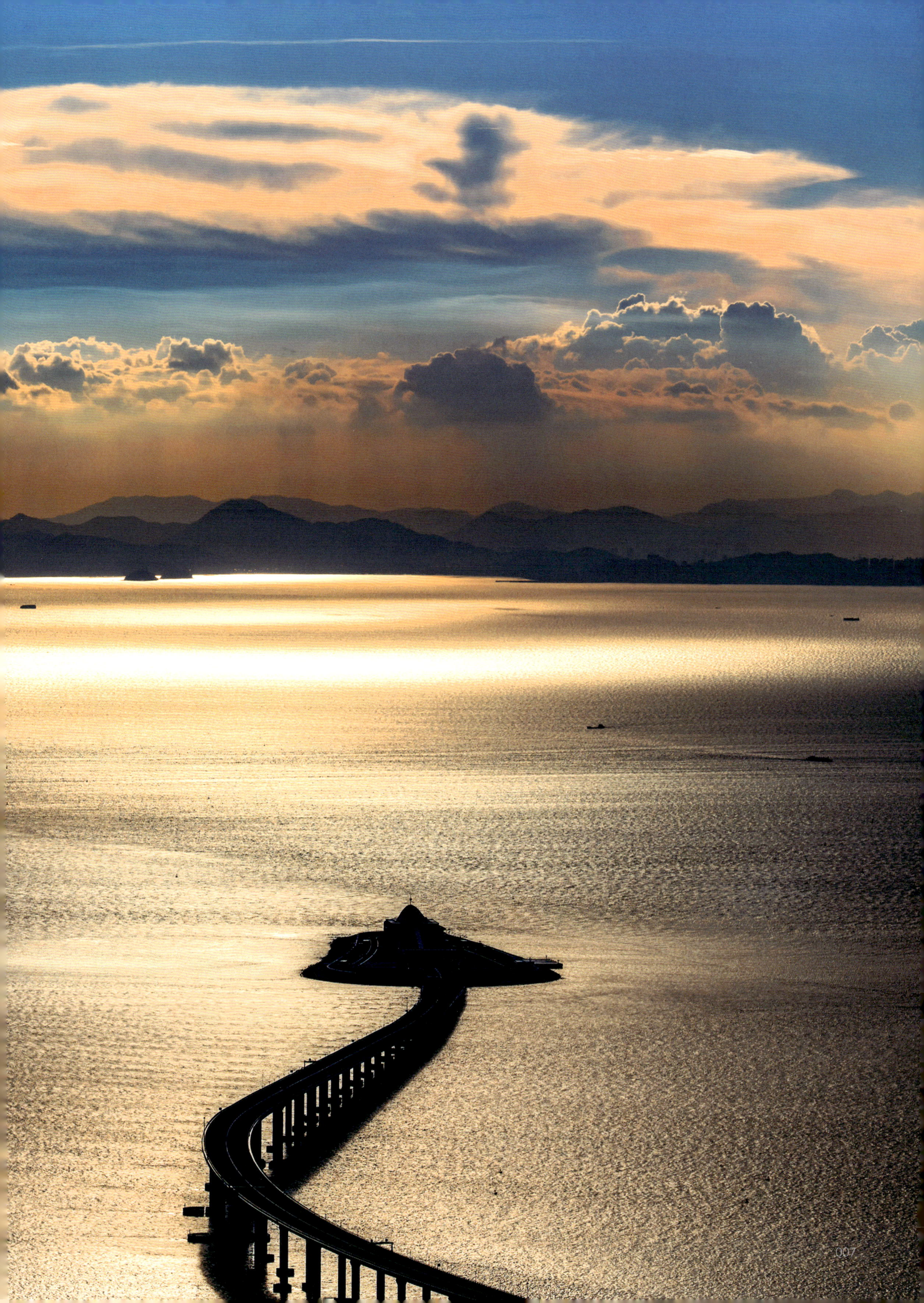

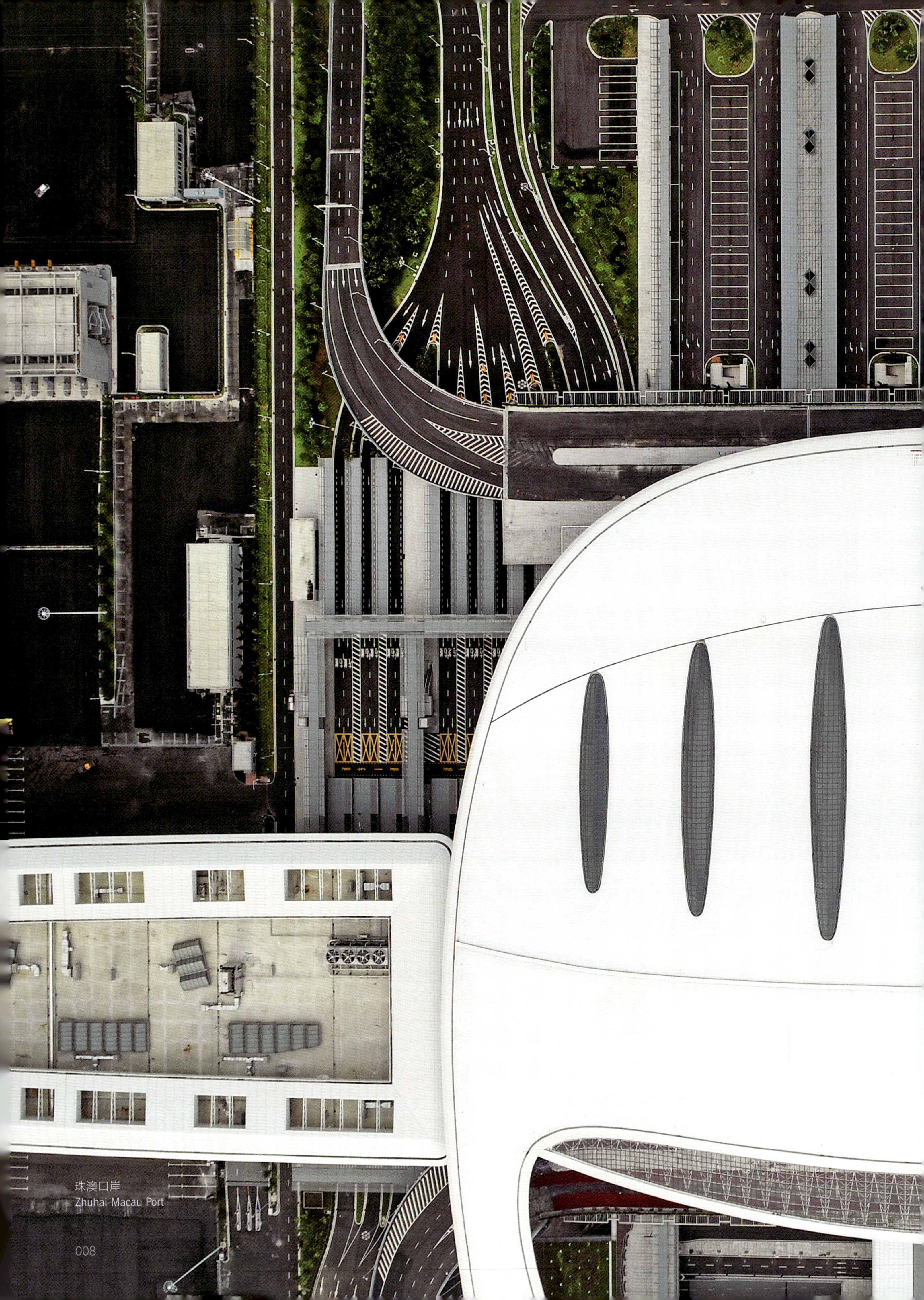

珠澳口岸
Zhuhai-Macau Port

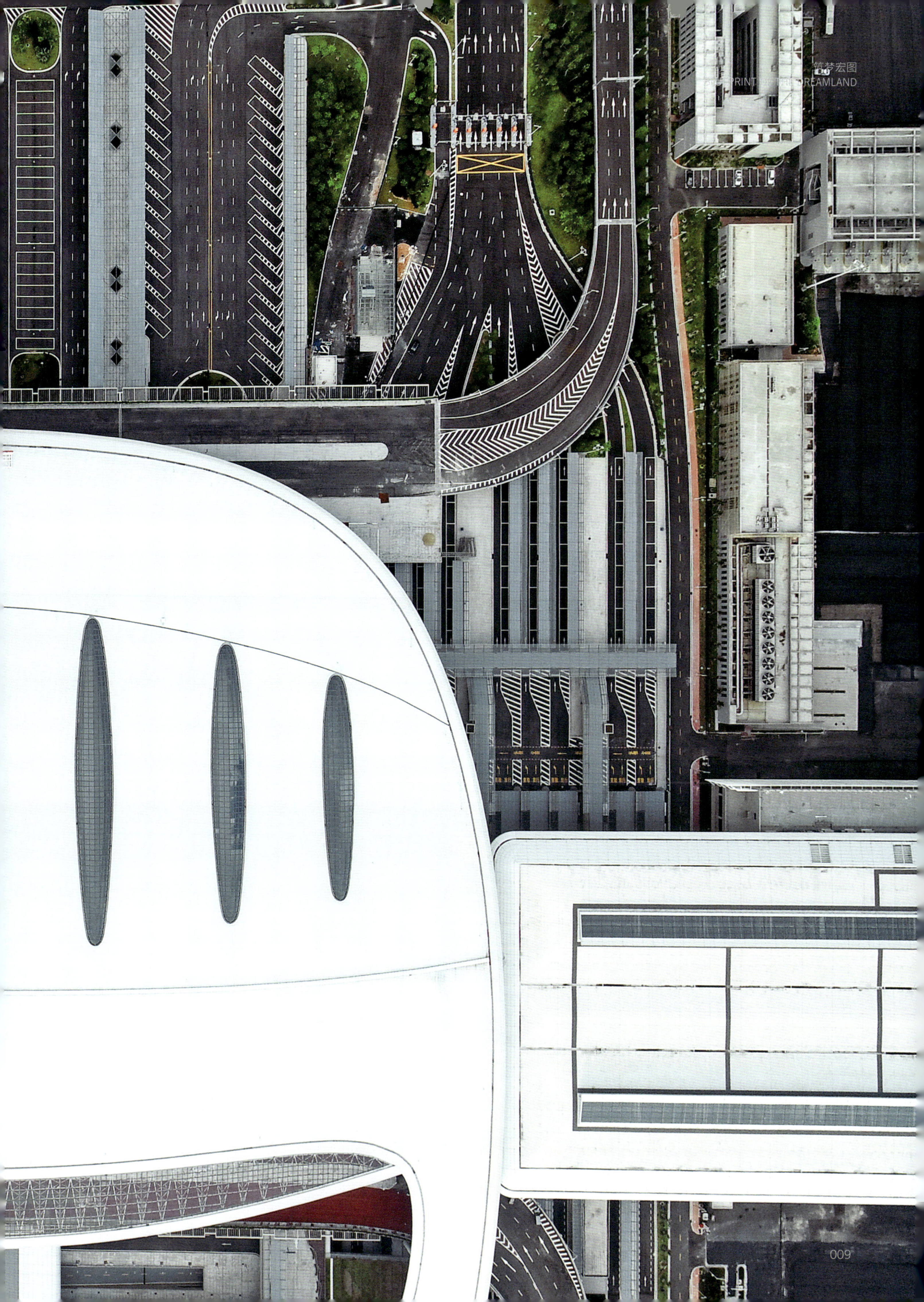

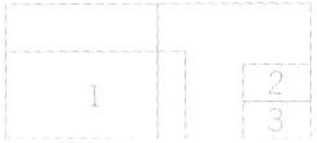

1. 珠澳口岸和大桥收费站
Zhuhai-Macau Port and the Hong Kong-Zhuhai-Macau Bridge Toll Gate

2. 珠澳口岸
Zhuhai-Macau Port

3. 港珠澳大桥收费站
The Hong Kong-Zhuhai-Macau Bridge Toll Gate

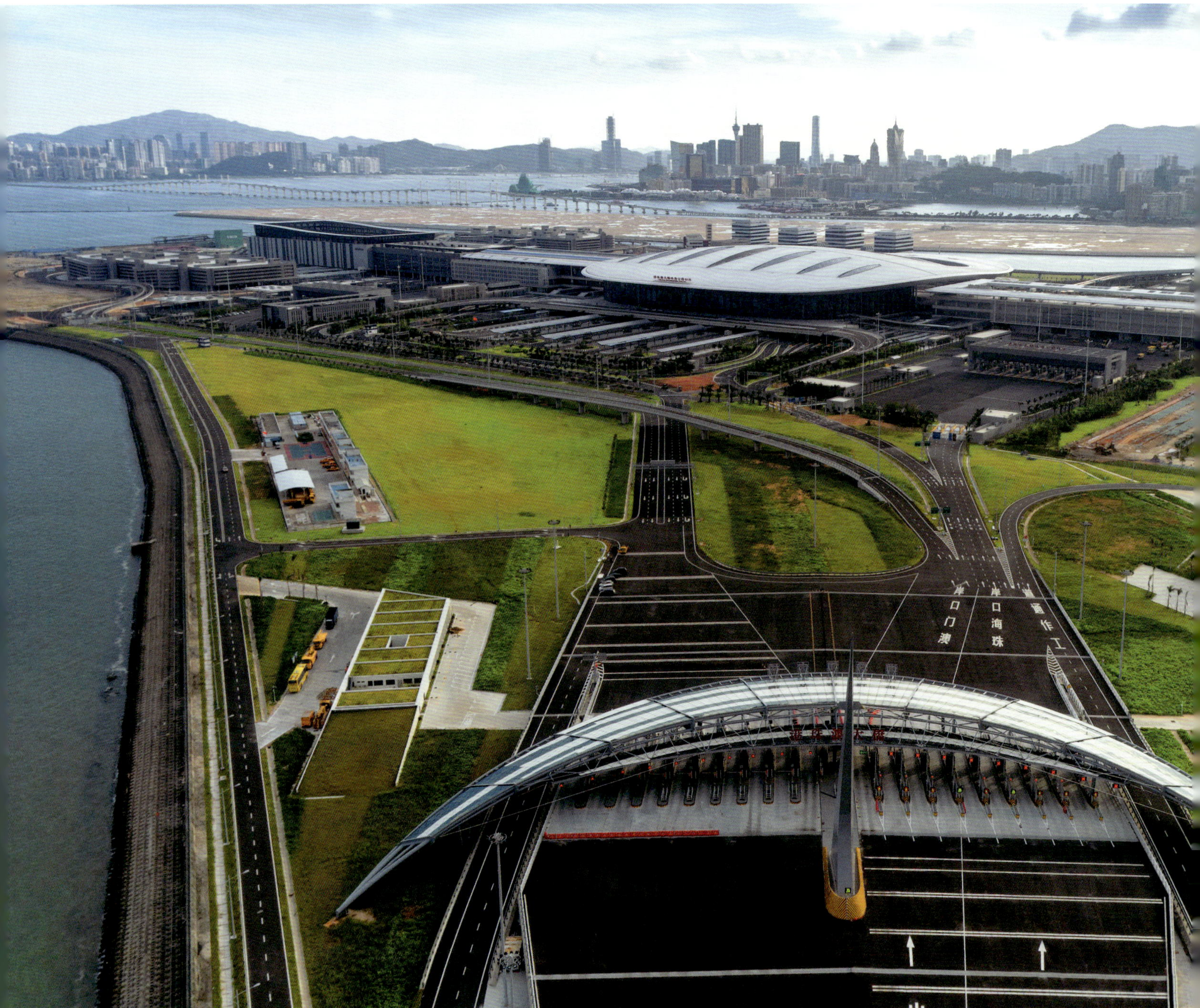

珠三角是中国最发达的经济区域之一，在面临产业转型升级的历史性时刻，与香港、澳门携手打造具有国际竞争力的城市群，成为中国经济新的增长极。

The Pearl River Delta, one of the most developed economic zones in China, works with Hong Kong and Macau to create a city group with considerable global competitiveness in the historic era of industrial transformation and upgrading, with an aim to be the new growth pole of China's economy.

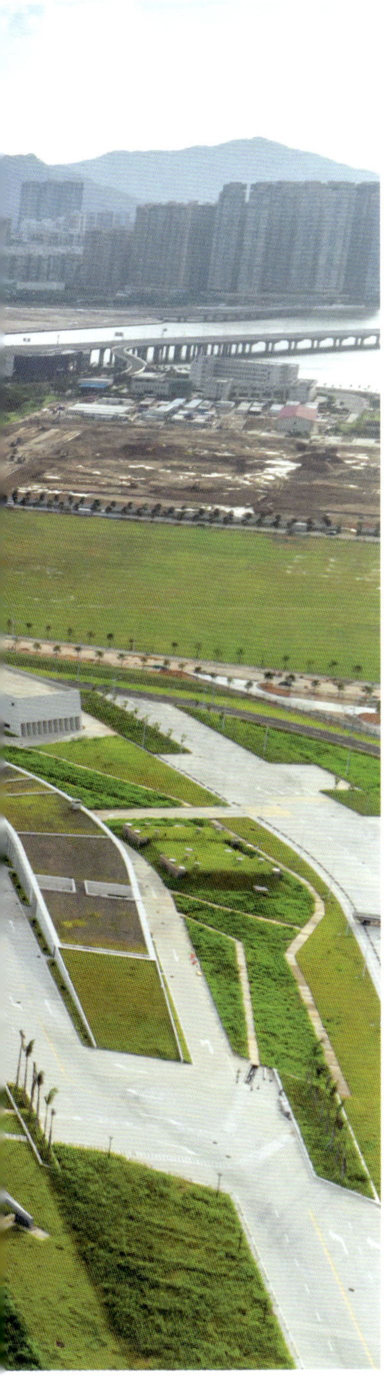

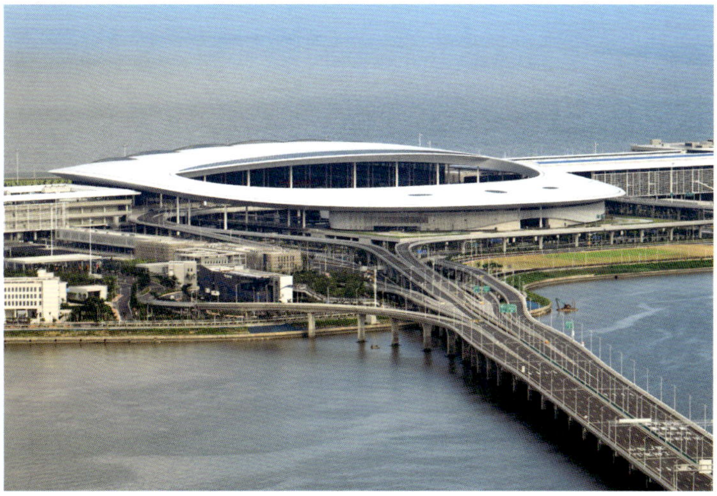

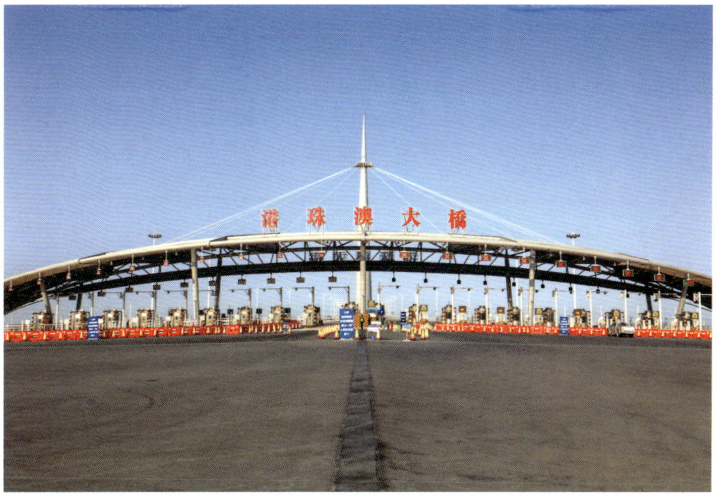

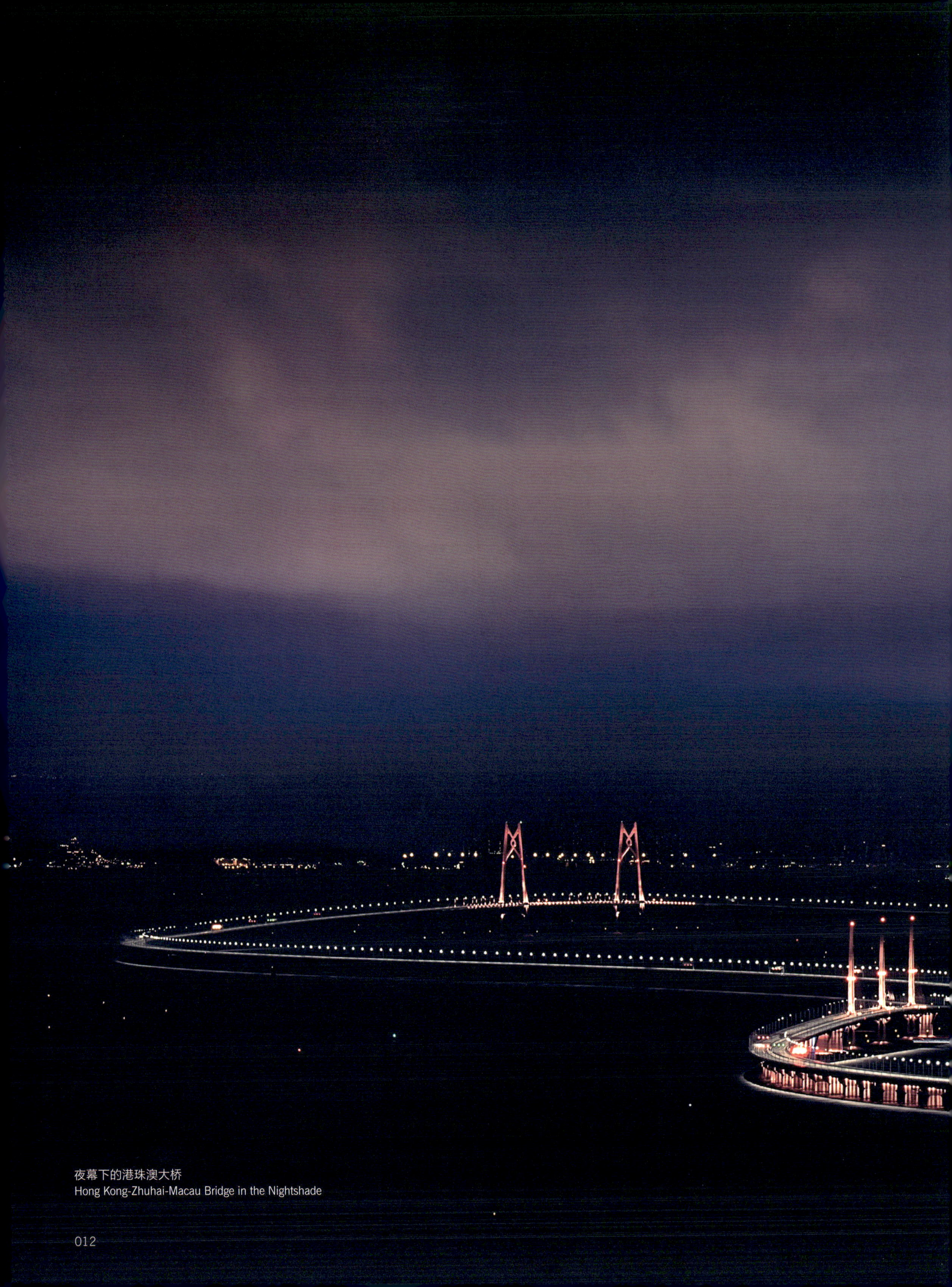

夜幕下的港珠澳大桥
Hong Kong-Zhuhai-Macau Bridge in the Nightshade

橘红色的灯光摇曳着港珠澳的独特风情，
蜿蜒的大桥延伸出对未来发展的美好愿景。

The orange lights shine the peculiar cityscapes of
Hong Kong, Zhuhai and Macau,
And the winding bridge
Over the sea pictures our hopes for a beautiful future.

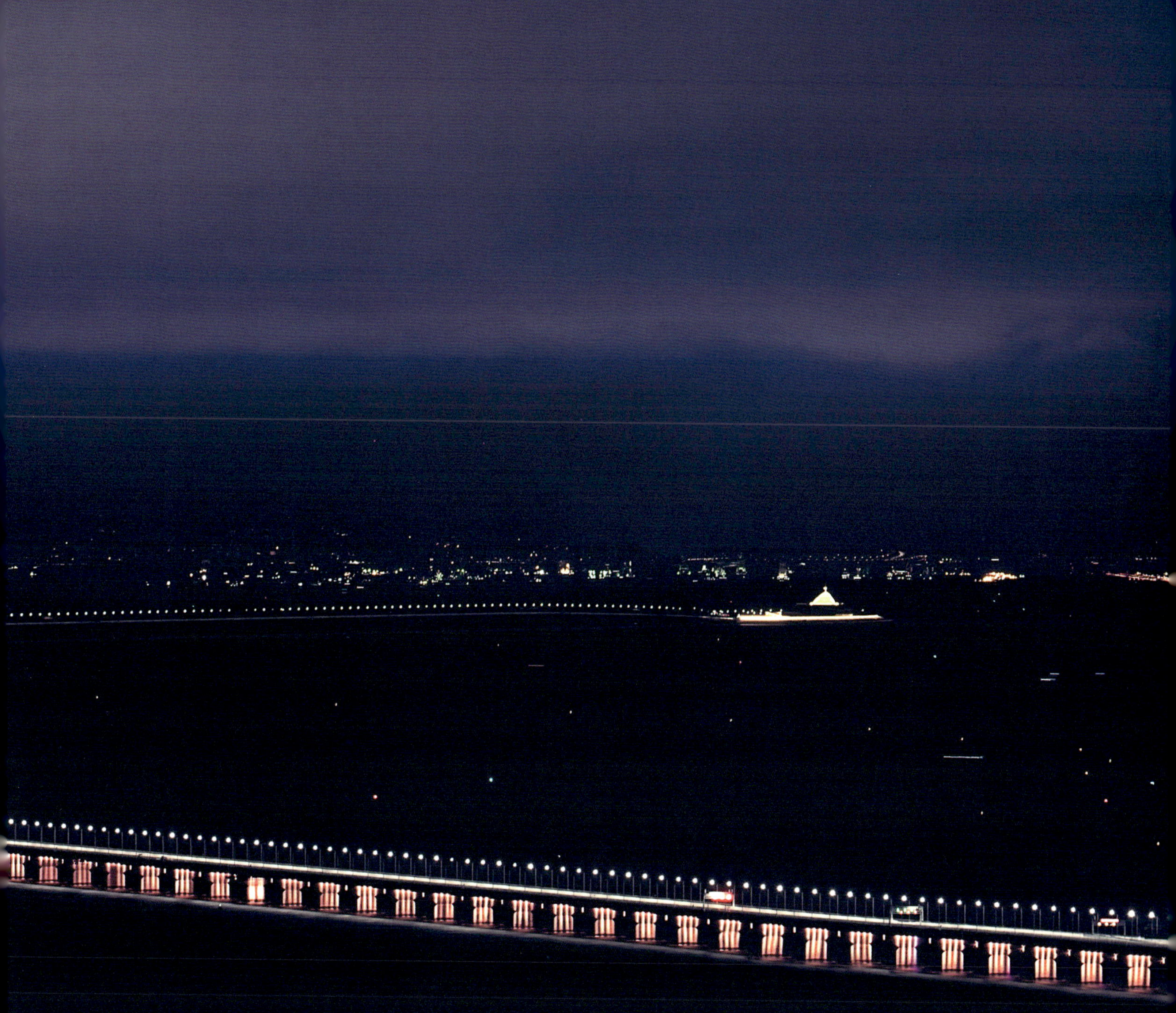

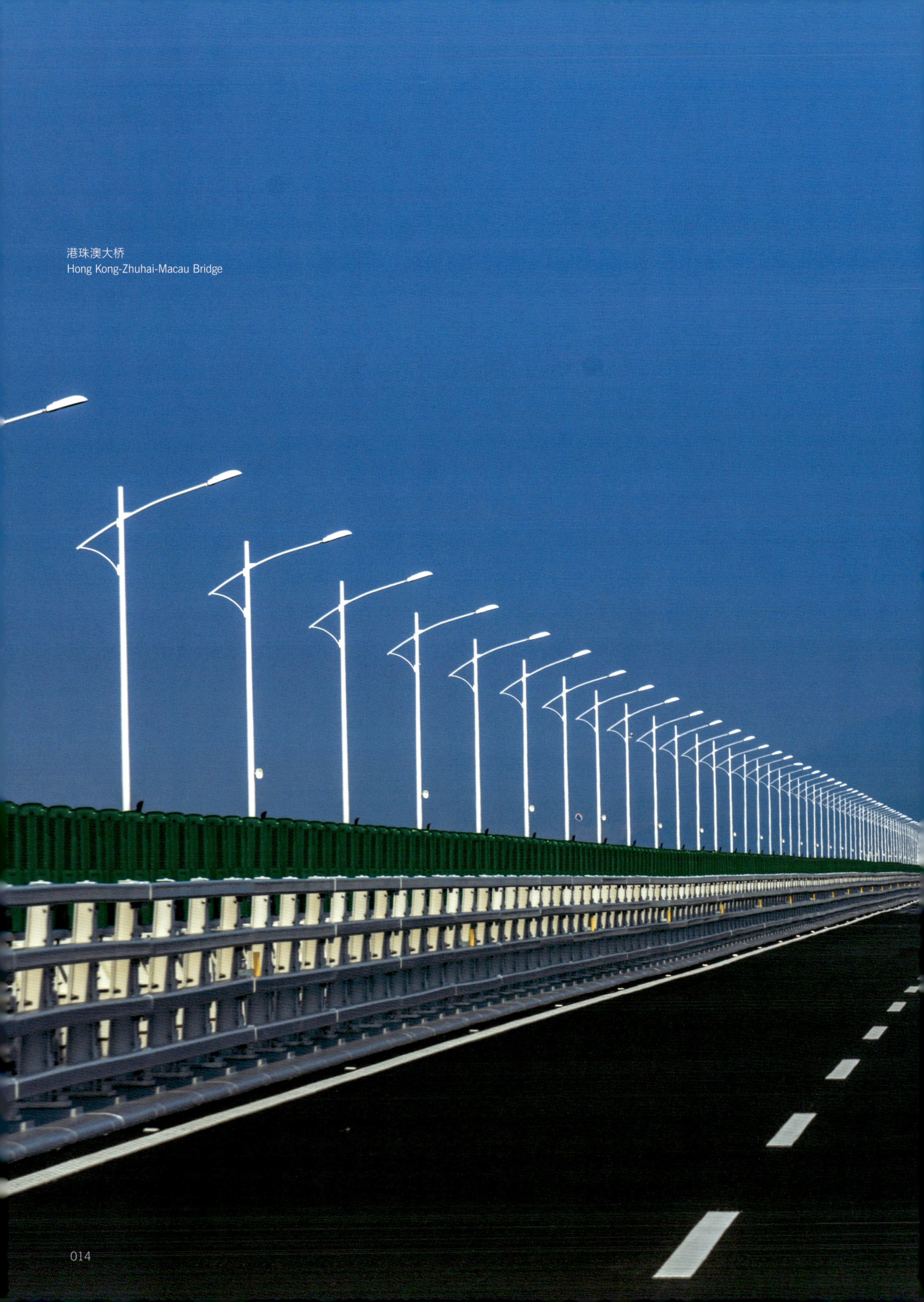

港珠澳大桥
Hong Kong-Zhuhai-Macau Bridge

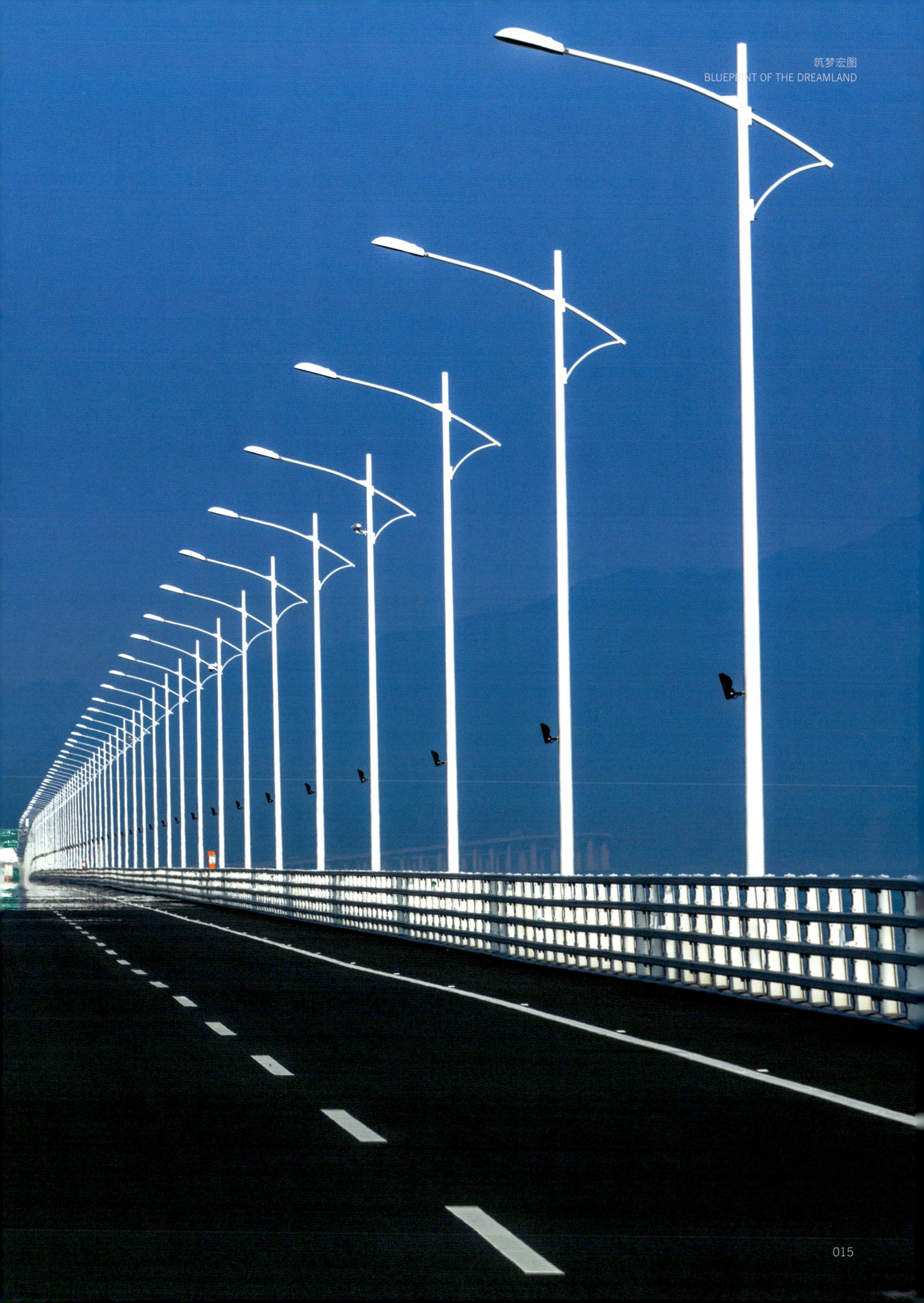

1	2

1. 江海航道桥
   Jianghai Channel Bridge
2. 九洲航道桥
   Jiuzhou Channel Bridge

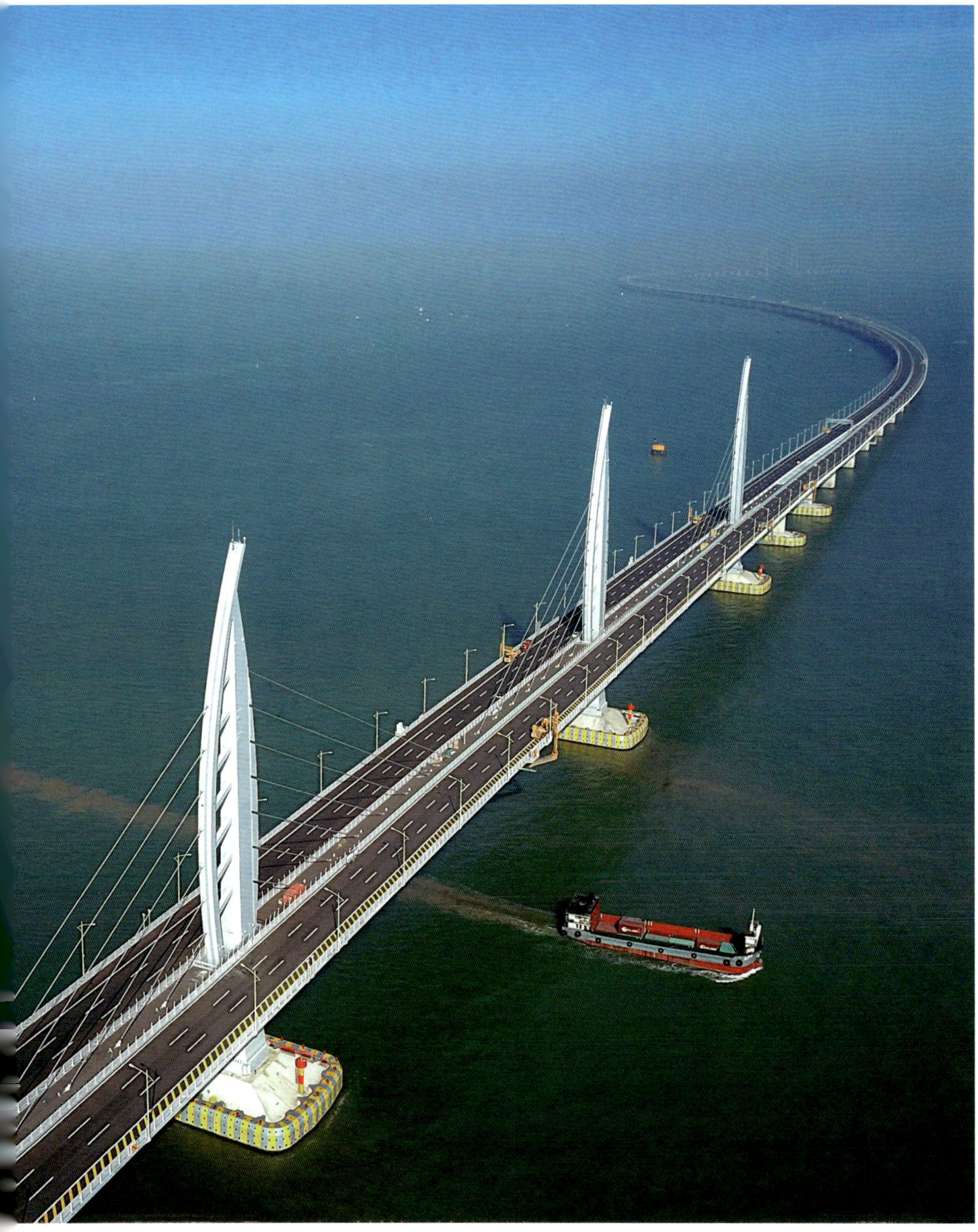

风出珠江口，帆起伶仃洋。
“风帆”造型的九洲航道桥预示着“第一湾”扬帆启航。

The winds rising in Pearl River Estuary,
Swell the sails across Lingding Bay.
The sail-shaped towers on Jiuzhou Channel Bridge speaks to the world the “First Bay” has swollen its sails.

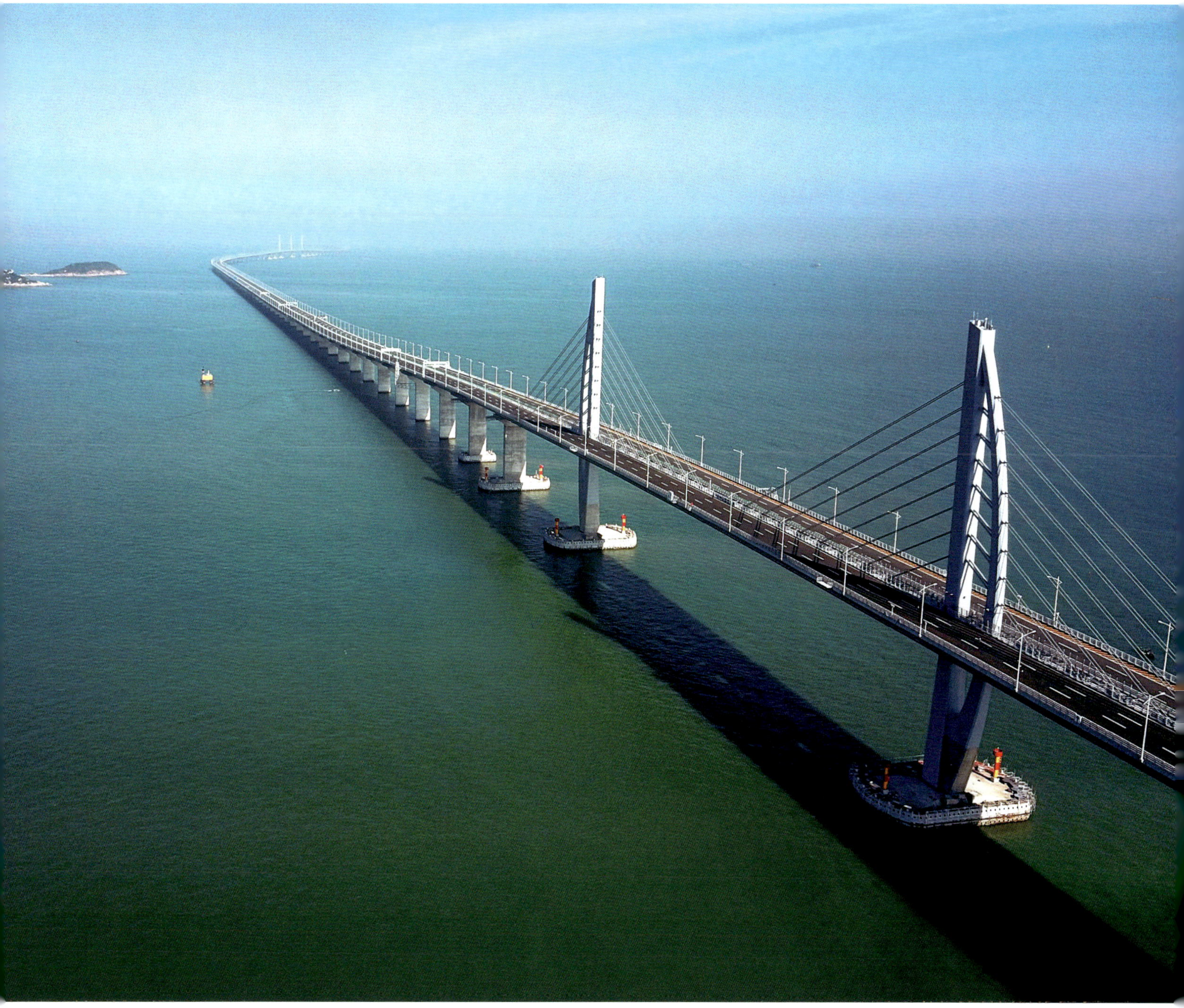

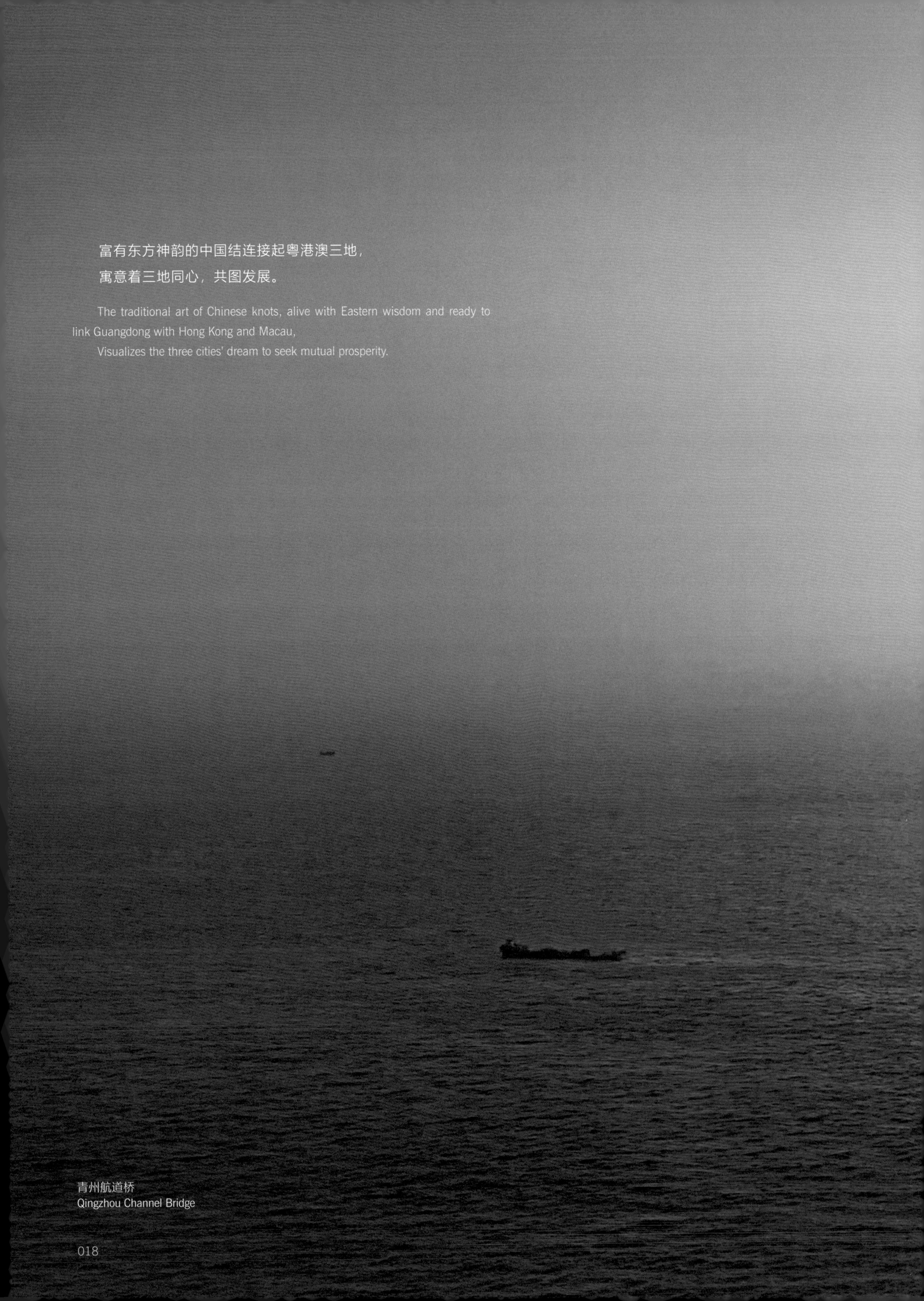

富有东方神韵的中国结连接起粤港澳三地，
寓意着三地同心，共图发展。

The traditional art of Chinese knots, alive with Eastern wisdom and ready to link Guangdong with Hong Kong and Macau,

Visualizes the three cities' dream to seek mutual prosperity.

青州航道桥
Qingzhou Channel Bridge

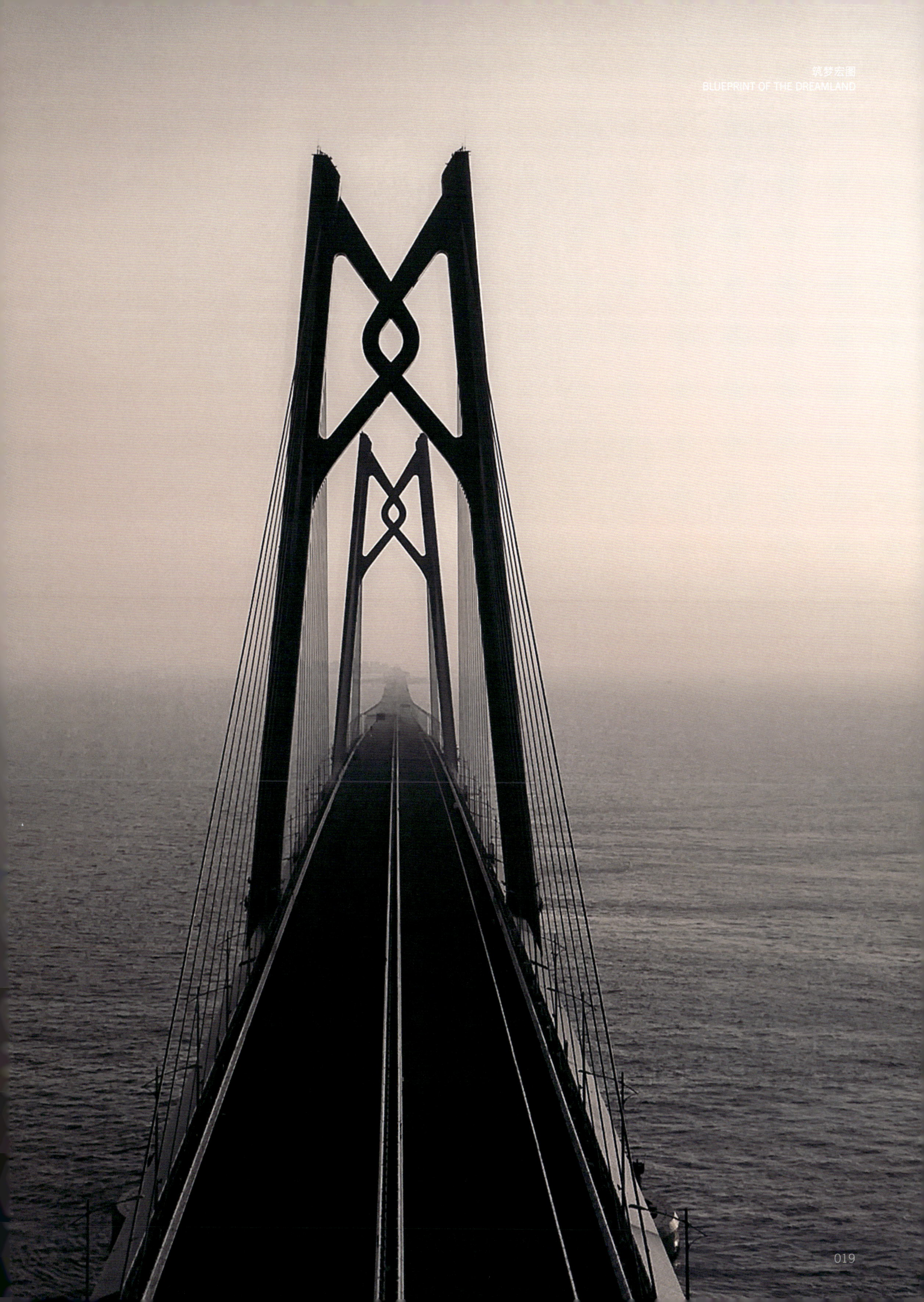

鸿蒙初辟

BIRTH OF A NEW WORLD

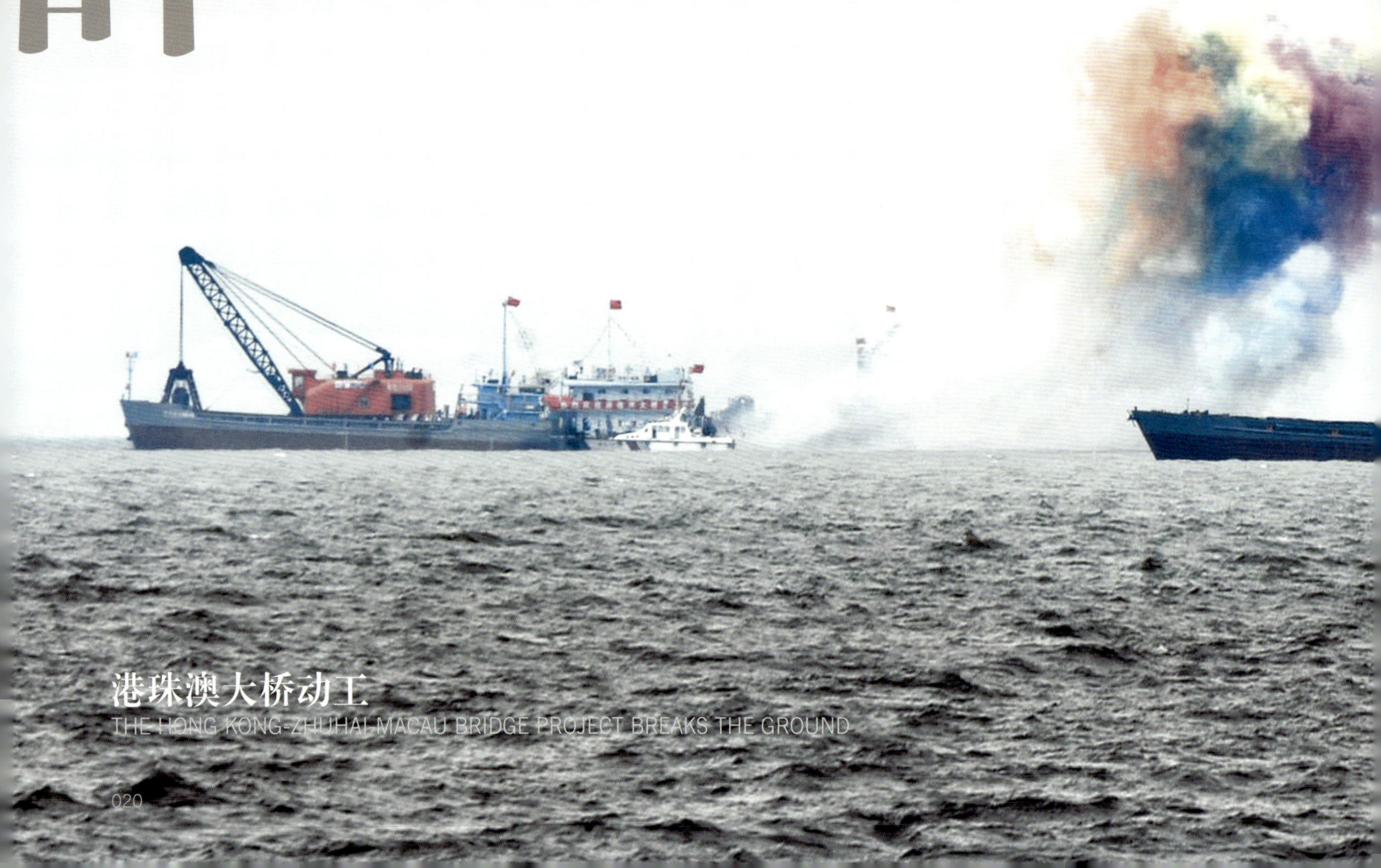

港珠澳大桥动工

THE HONG KONG-ZHUHAI-MACAU BRIDGE PROJECT BREAKS THE GROUND

6.7 公里海底隧道，

33 节超级沉管，

世界上最大沉管预制厂，

中国交建建设者毅然踏上七年筑梦之路。

An underwater tunnel, 6.7 kilometers long,

Composed of 33 super-sized immersed tubes,

Fulfilled the dream China Communications Construction Company,

The largest immersed tube precast factory in the world,

Strove for in the past seven years.

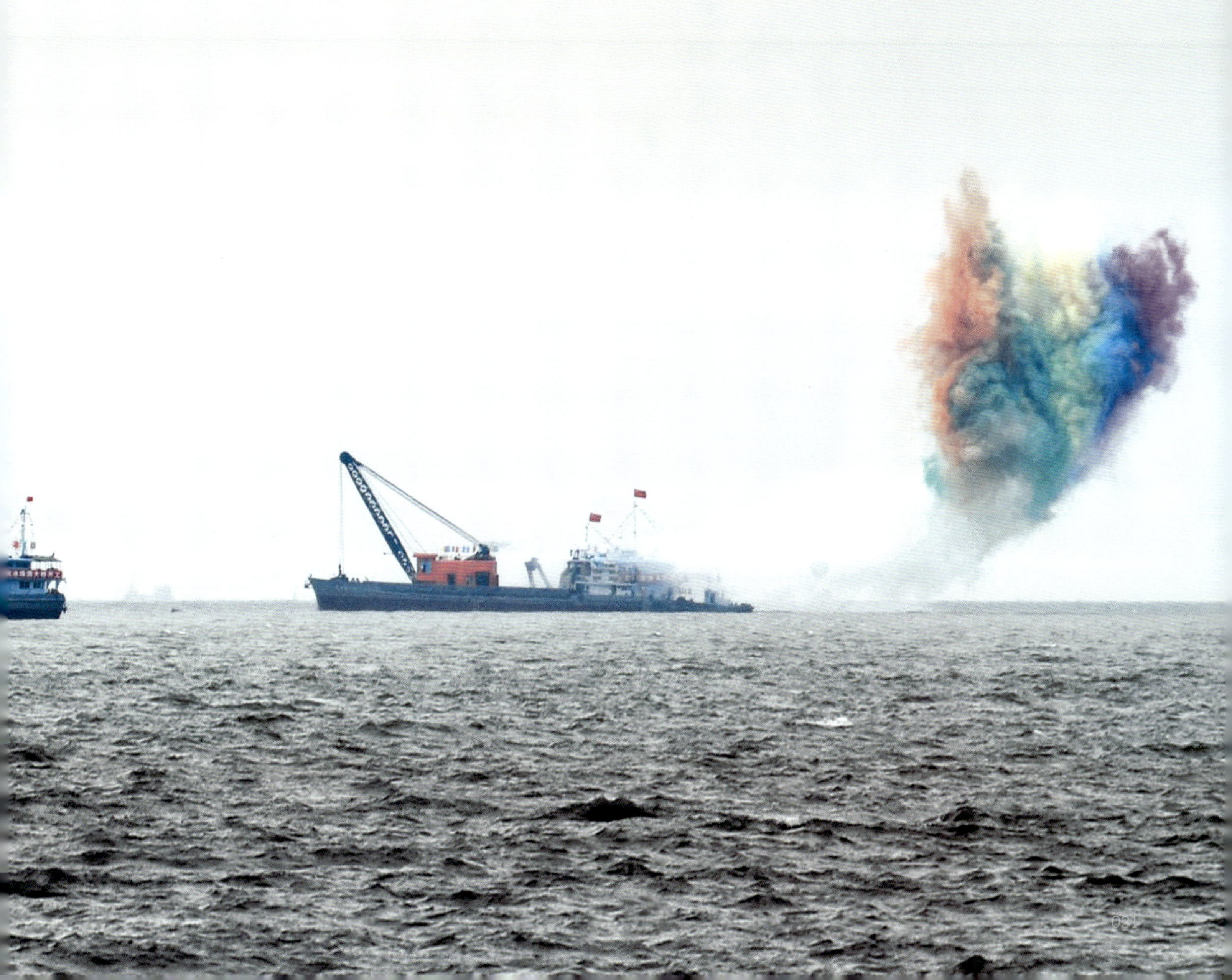

港珠澳大桥开工仪式

COMMENCEMENT CEREMONY OF
THE HONG KONG-ZHUHAI-MACAU BRIDGE PROJECT

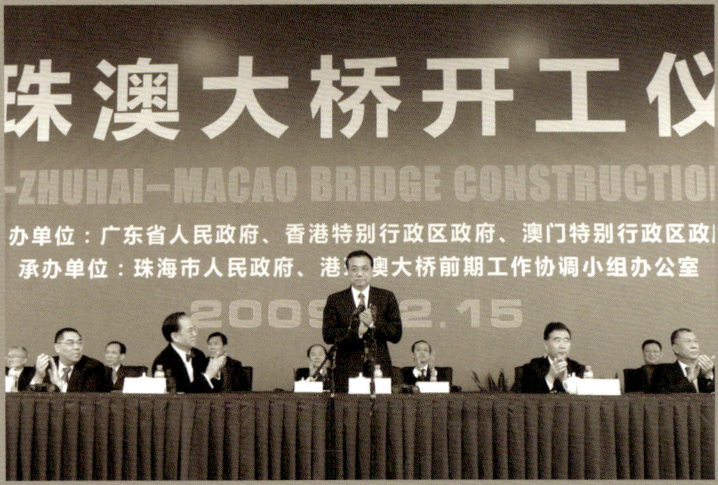

▲ 2009 年 12 月 15 日，港珠澳大桥开工

The Hong Kong-Zhuhai-Macau Bridge project was commenced on December 15, 2009

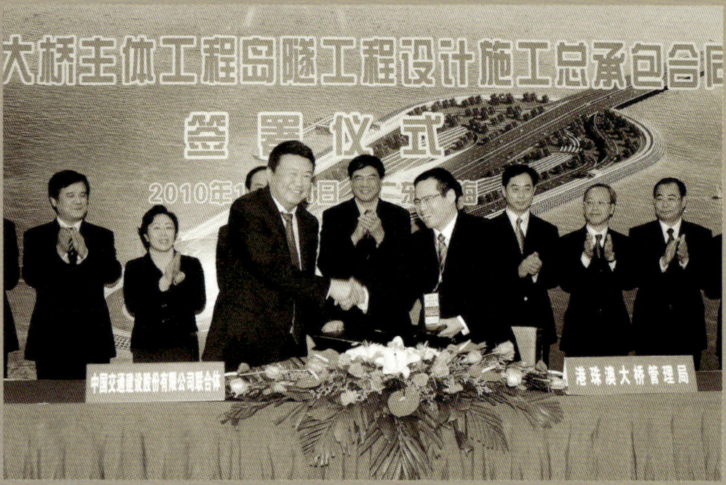

▲ 2010 年 11 月 25 日，中国交建联合体以设计施工总承包模式中标港珠澳大桥岛隧工程

China Communications Construction Company Ltd., as the general contractor, won the bidding for the design and construction of the island-tunnel project of Hong Kong-Zhuhai-Macau Bridge on November 25, 2010

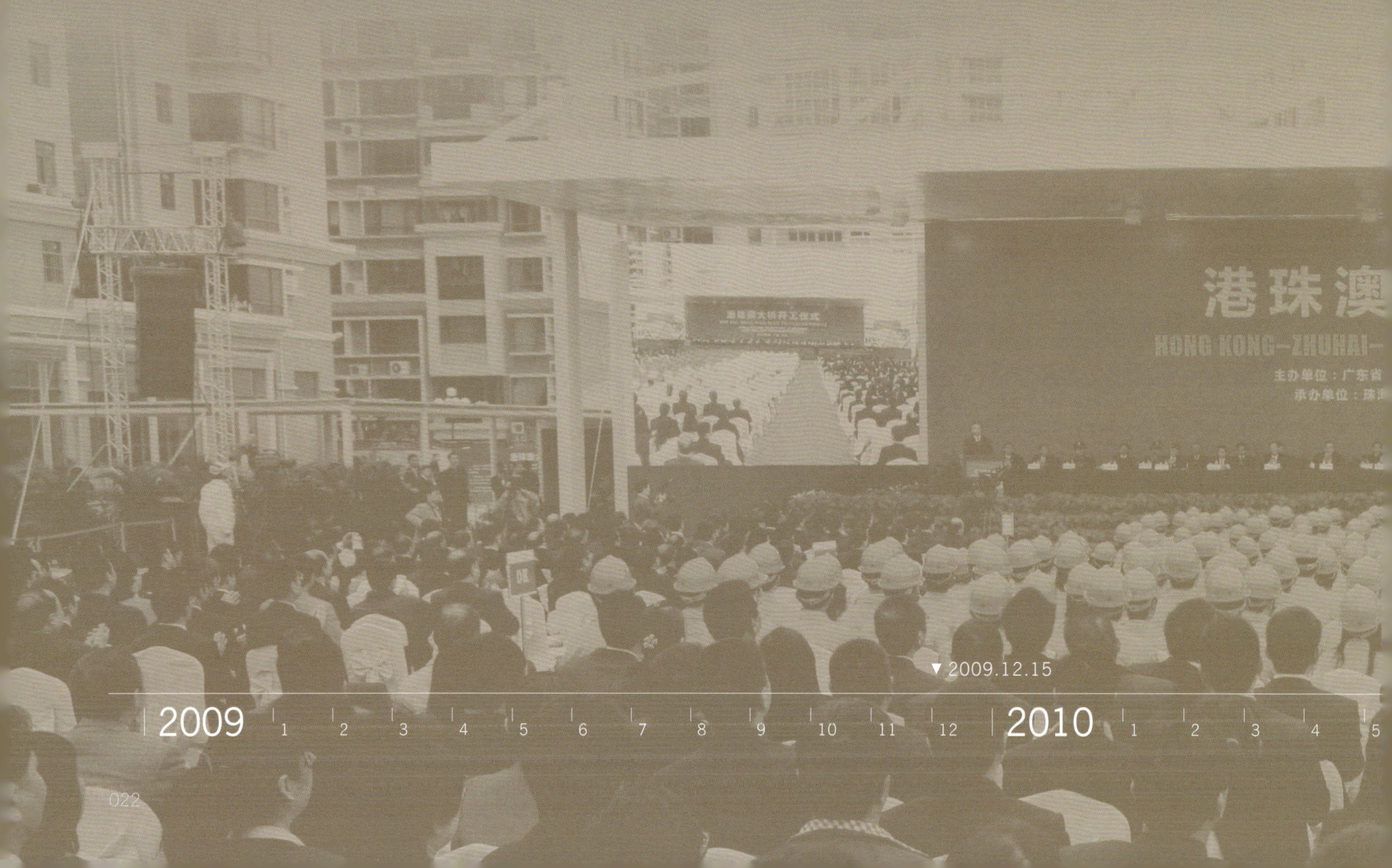

▼2009.12.15

2009 1 2 3 4 5 6 7 8 9 10 11 12 2010 1 2 3 4 5

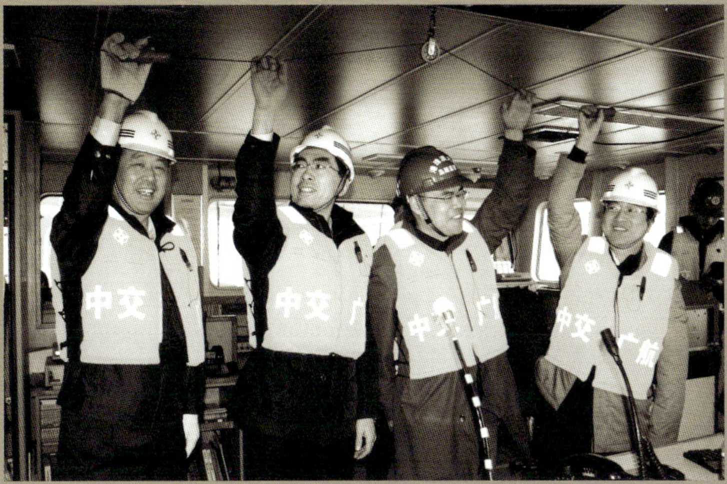

▲ 2011 年 1 月 4 日，港珠澳大桥西人工岛基础开挖动工鸣笛

The horns blew for the commencement of the excavation of the West Man-made Island base of Hong Kong-Zhuhai-Macau Bridge on January 4, 2011

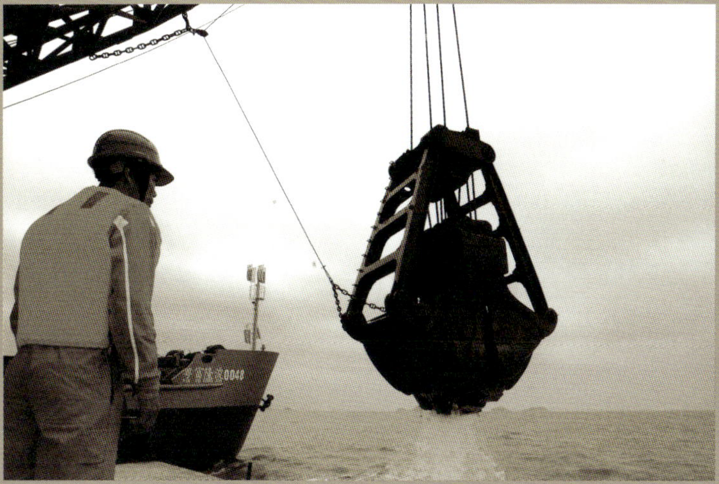

▲ 2011 年 12 月 30 日，沉管隧道基础开始精挖施工

The fine excavation of the base part of the immersed tube tunnel began on December 30, 2011

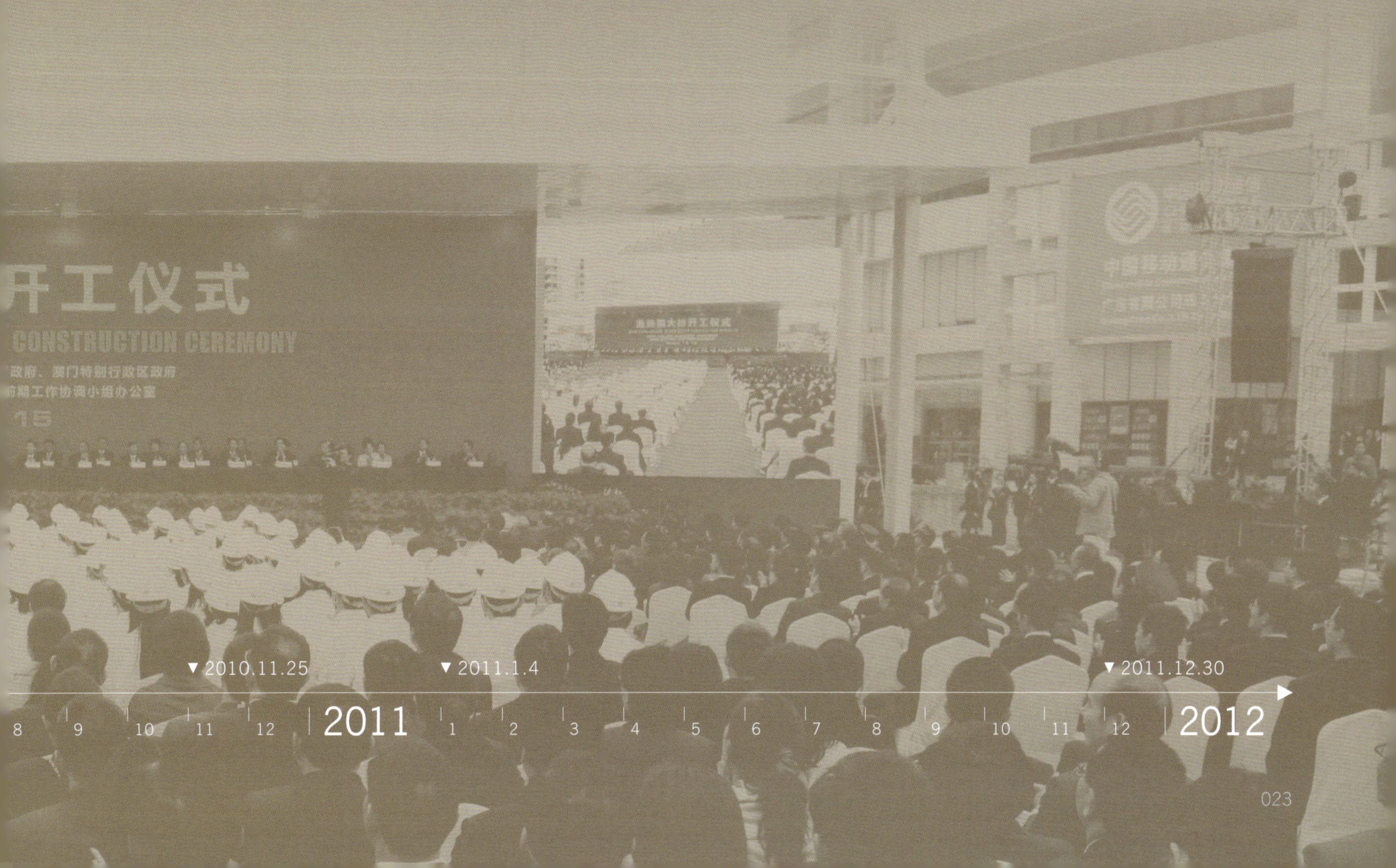

▼2010.11.25 ▼2011.1.4 ▼2011.12.30

8 9 10 11 12 2011 1 2 3 4 5 6 7 8 9 10 11 12 2012

总营地施工

GENERAL CONSTRUCTION CAMP WORKS

2011年9月28日上午9时，港珠澳大桥施工总营地举行了隆重的开营仪式。总营地包括码头、堆场、办公生活区三大功能区域。其中，岛隧工程营区于2010年12月24日开工，2011年6月24日主体施工完成，2011年9月6日交工验收。

At 9:00 am on September 28, 2011, the commencement ceremony was held in the general project camp of Hong Kong-Zhuhai-Macau Bridge. The general project camp is composed of the dock, the stockyard, the office area and the living quarters. The camp for the Island-Tunnel project began to be built on December 24, 2010, The main part was completed on June 24, 2011 and was delivered to use on September 6, 2011.

▼ 2011 年 9 月 28 日，岛隧工程施工总营地揭牌

The inauguration ceremony for the General Construction Camp of the Island-Tunnel Project was held on September 28, 2011

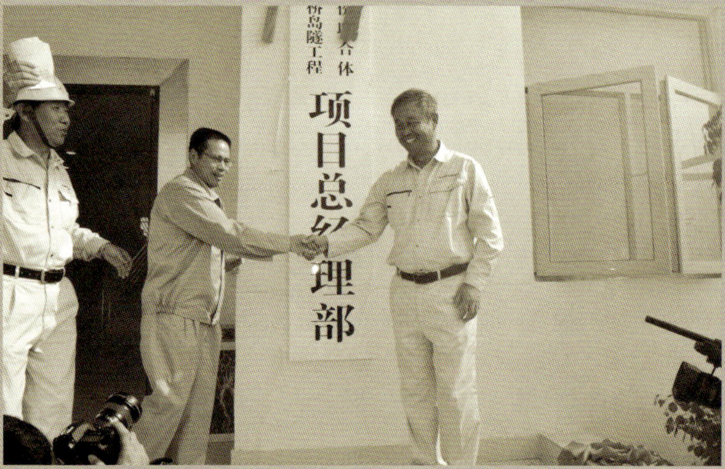

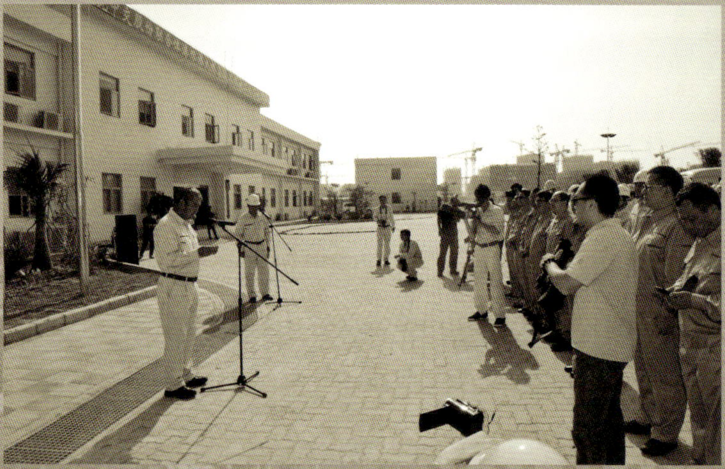

▲ 2011 年 9 月 28 日，港珠澳大桥施工总营地开营

The inauguration ceremony for the General Project Camp of the Hong Kong-Zhuhai-Macau Bridge Project was held on September 28, 2011

▶ 2011 年 5 月 13 日，港珠澳大桥施工总营地建设

The construction of the General Project Camp for the Hong Kong-Zhuhai-Macau Bridge Project was on process on May 13, 2011

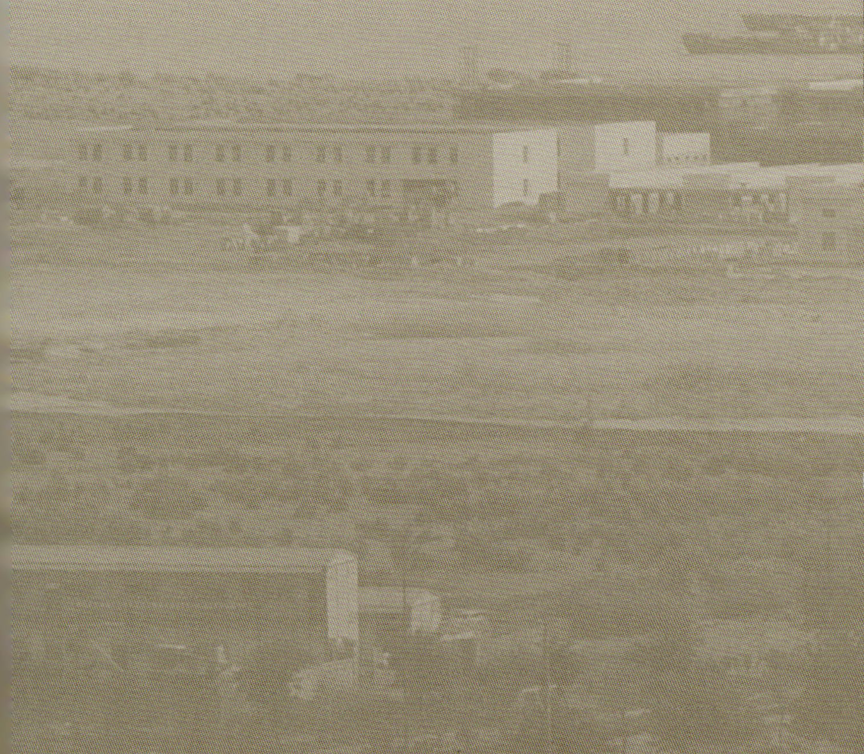

▼2011.5.13

2011 1 2 3 4 5 6

▼ 2011 年 9 月 28 日，港珠澳大桥施工总营地

On September 28, 2011, General Project Camp for the Hong Kong-Zhuhai-Macau Bridge Project

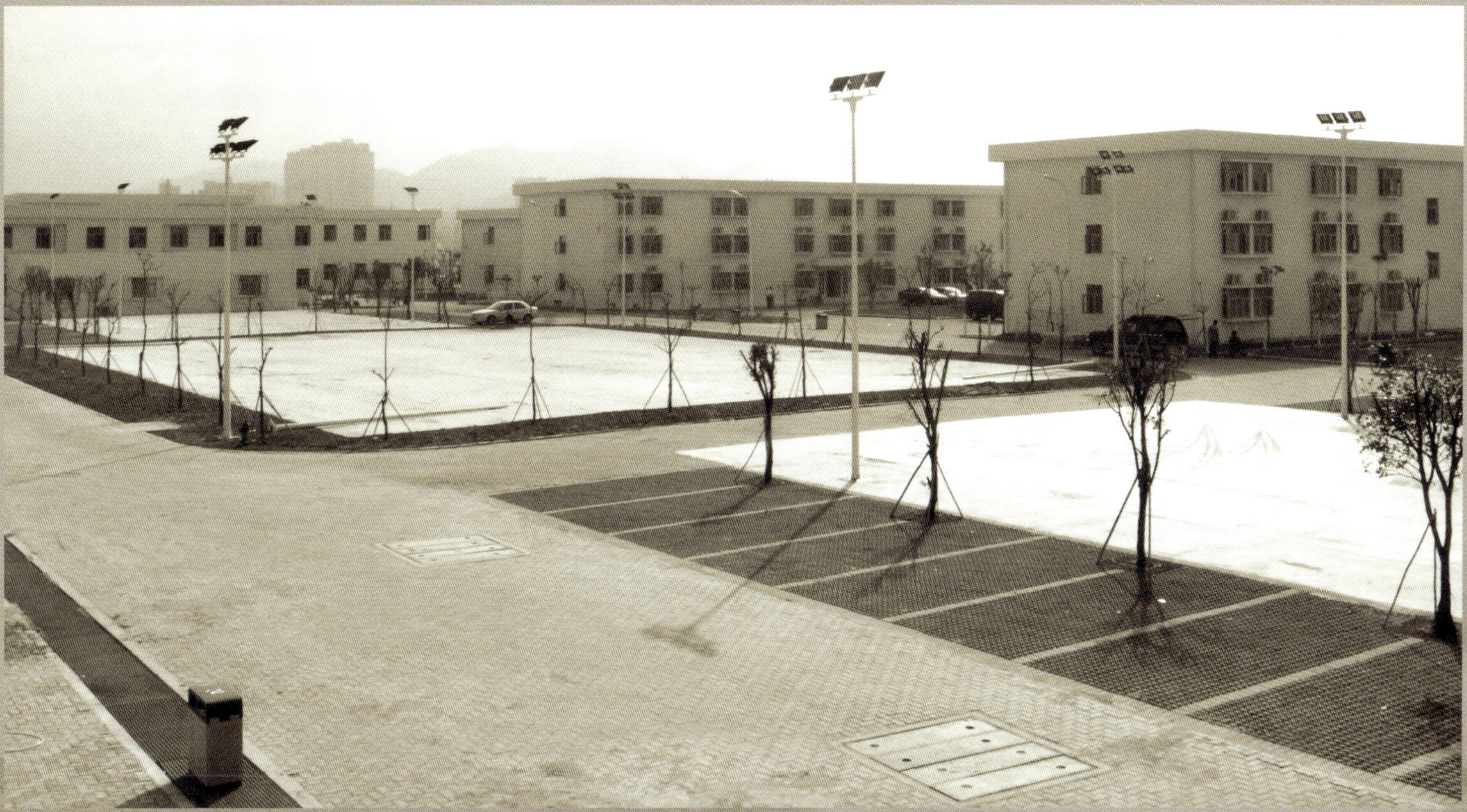

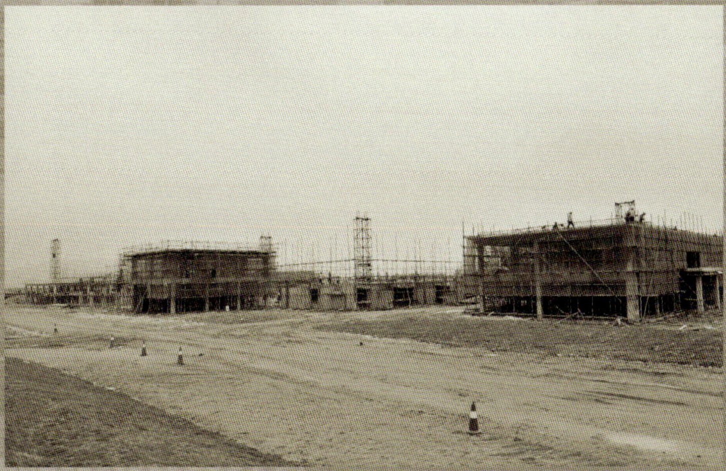

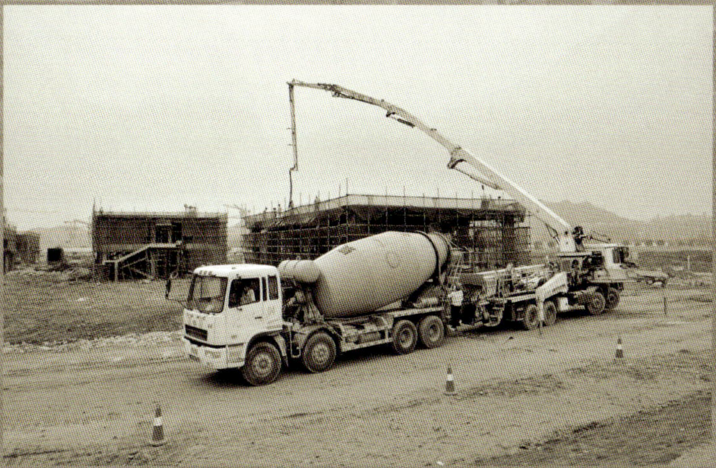

▼ 2011.9.28

7 8 9 10 11 12 2012

晨曦中的港珠澳大桥施工总营地
General Project Camp for the Hong Kong-Zhuhai-Macau Bridge Project at Dawn

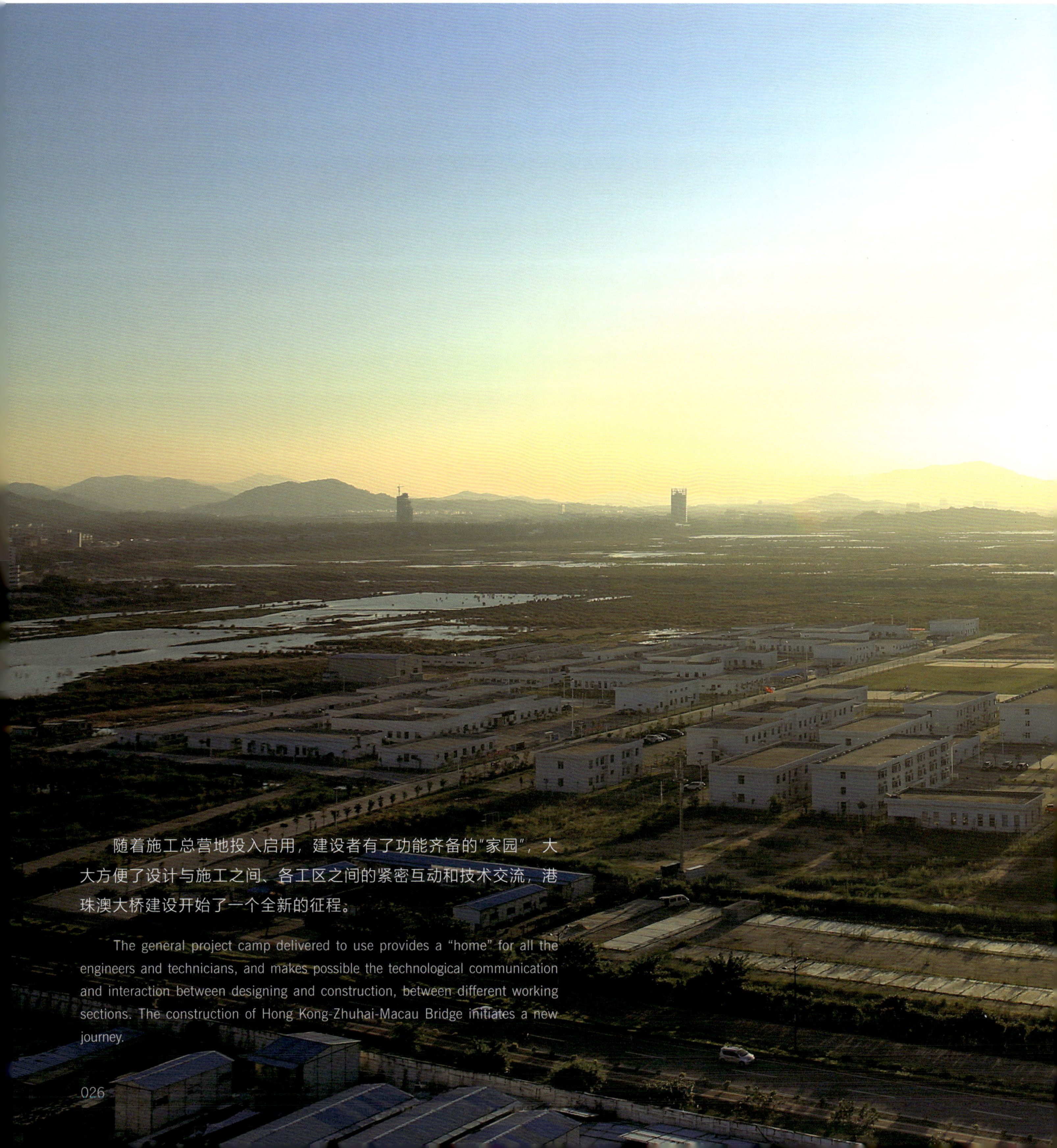

随着施工总营地投入启用，建设者有了功能齐备的"家园"，大大方便了设计与施工之间、各工区之间的紧密互动和技术交流，港珠澳大桥建设开始了一个全新的征程。

The general project camp delivered to use provides a "home" for all the engineers and technicians, and makes possible the technological communication and interaction between designing and construction, between different working sections. The construction of Hong Kong-Zhuhai-Macau Bridge initiates a new journey.

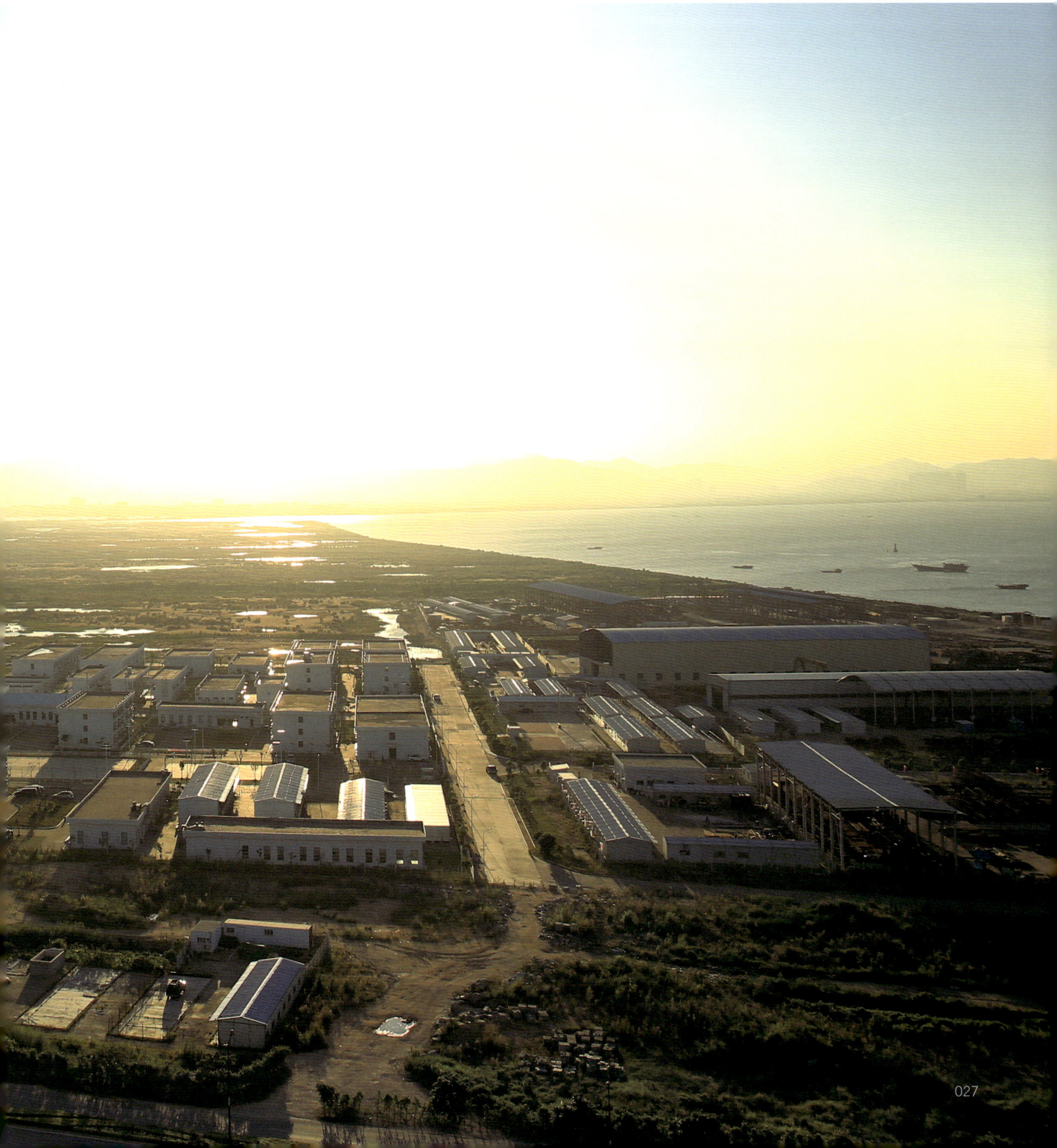

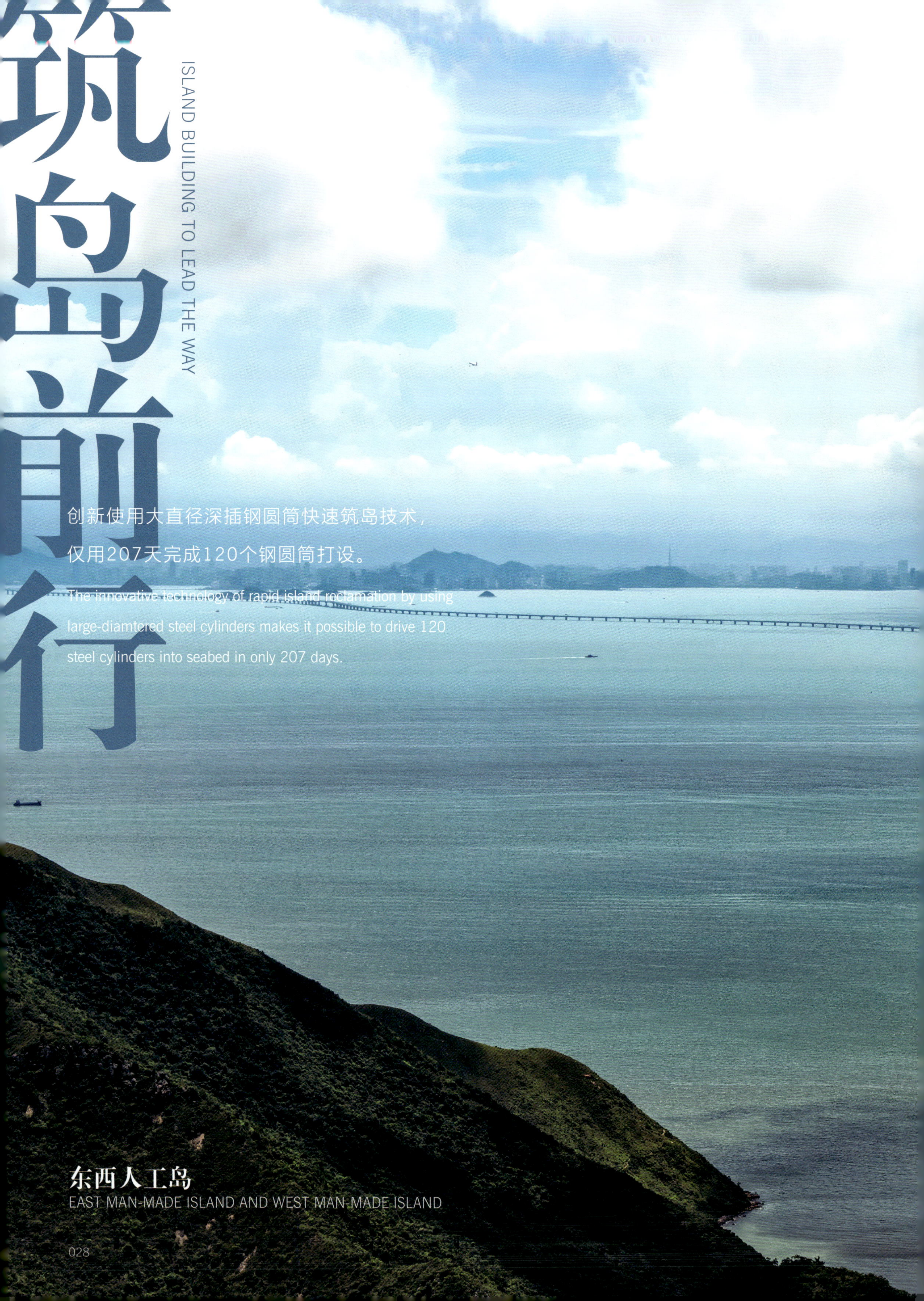

筑岛前行

ISLAND BUILDING TO LEAD THE WAY

创新使用大直径深插钢圆筒快速筑岛技术，
仅用207天完成120个钢圆筒打设。

The innovative technology of rapid island reclamation by using large-diamtered steel cylinders makes it possible to drive 120 steel cylinders into seabed in only 207 days.

东西人工岛

EAST MAN-MADE ISLAND AND WEST MAN-MADE ISLAND

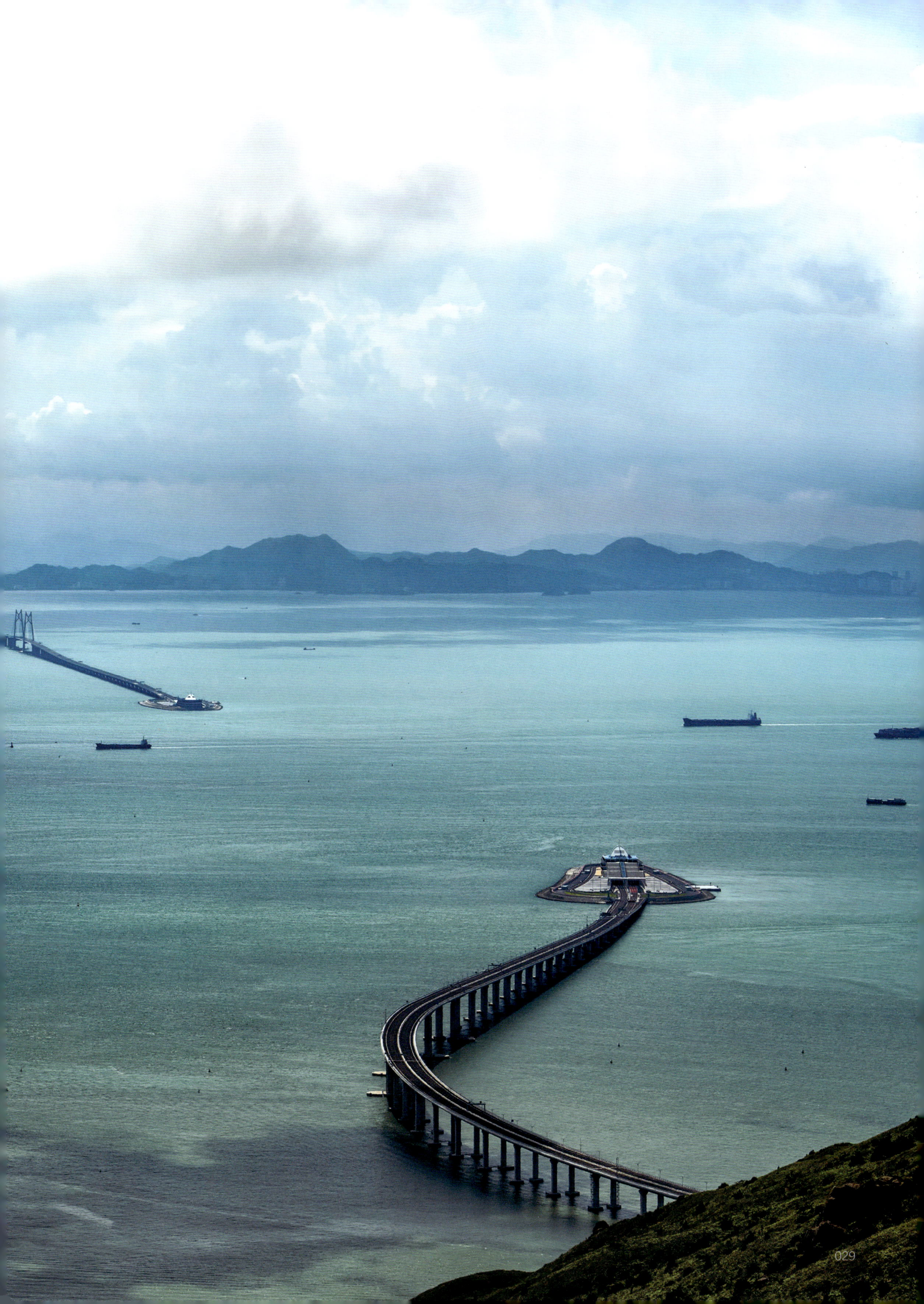

快速成岛
RAPID ISLAND RECLAMATION

西人工岛
WEST MAN-MADE ISLAND

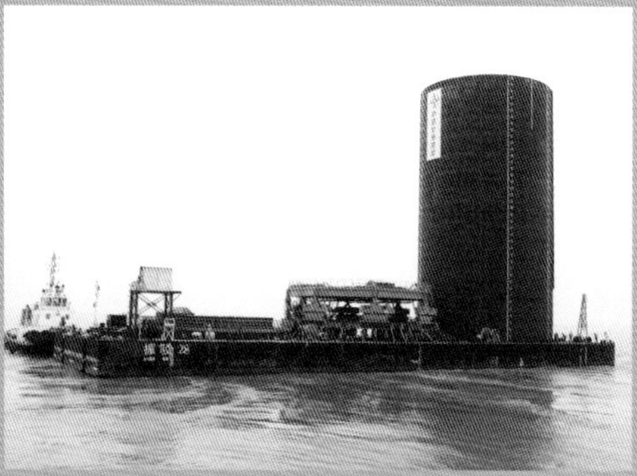

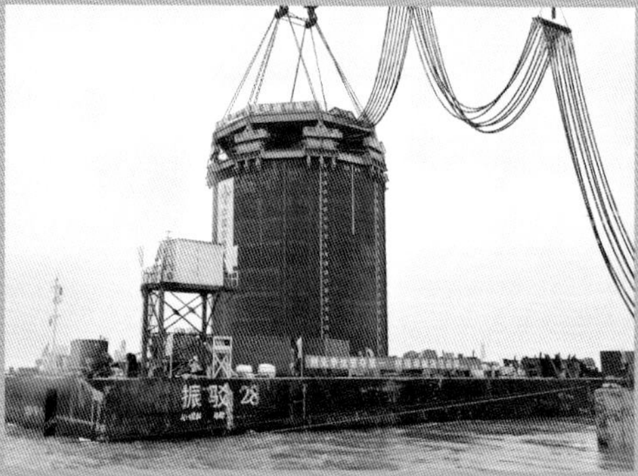

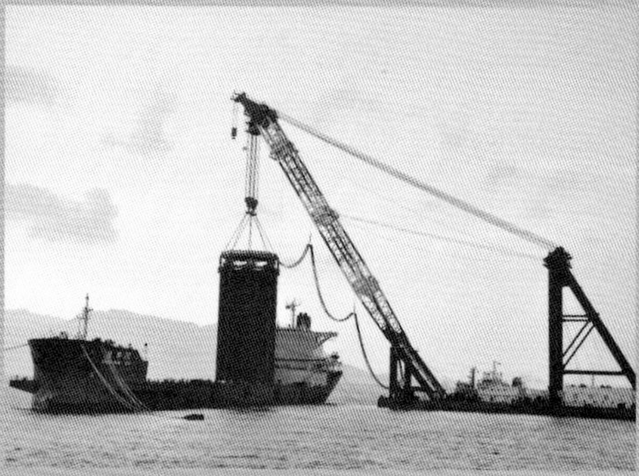

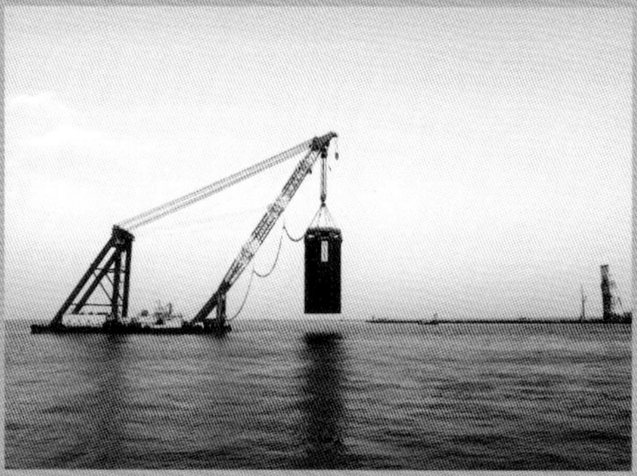

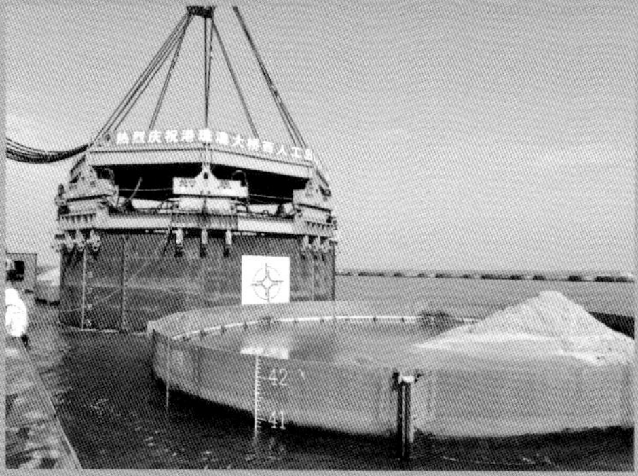

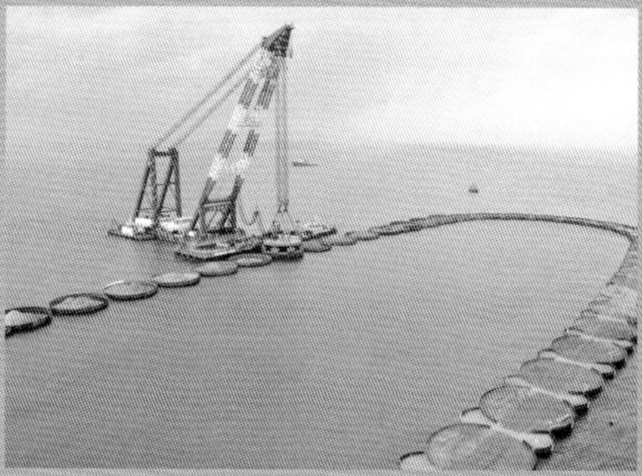

▲ 2011年5月15日—9月11日，西人工岛61个钢圆筒振沉完成，西人工岛成岛

From May 15 to September 11, 2011, the vibration of driving 61 steel cylinders on the West Man-Made Island was completed, and West Man-Made Island came into being

自2011年5月15日到12月7日，在7个月内建成了两个占地10万平方米的外海人工岛，减少泥沙开挖量近1000万立方米，节约工期两年半，创造了"当年开工，当年成岛"的工程奇迹。

Two offshore islands of 100,000 square meters were completed in 7 months from May 15 to December 7, 2011. About 10,000,000 cubic meters of sand was saved and the project was completed by 2.5 years in advance. This project created a constructional miracle by completing two man-made islands within one year.

▼ 2011.5.15

2011 | 1 | 2 | 3 | 4 | 5 | 6

东人工岛
EAST MAN-MADE ISLAND

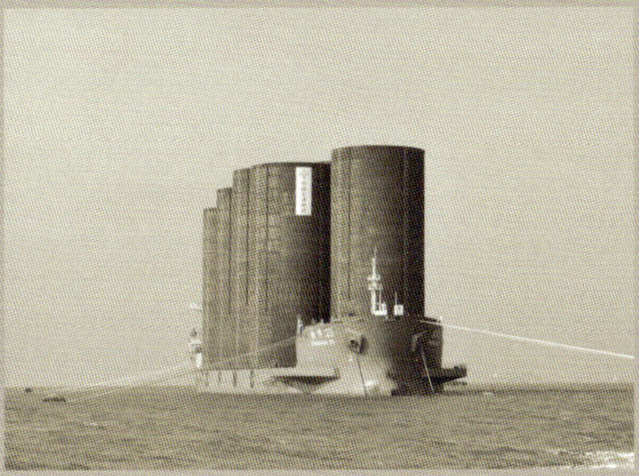
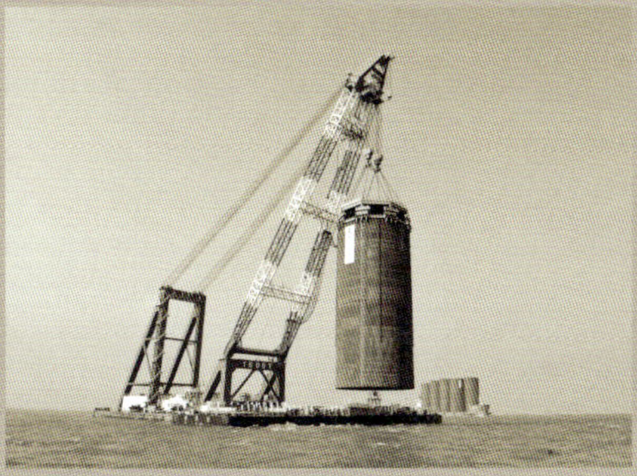
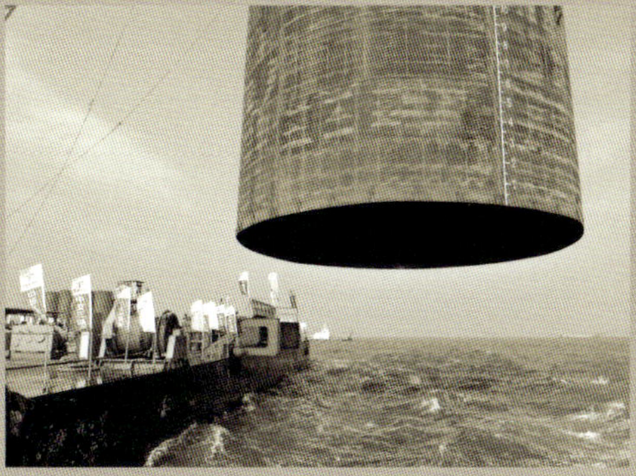
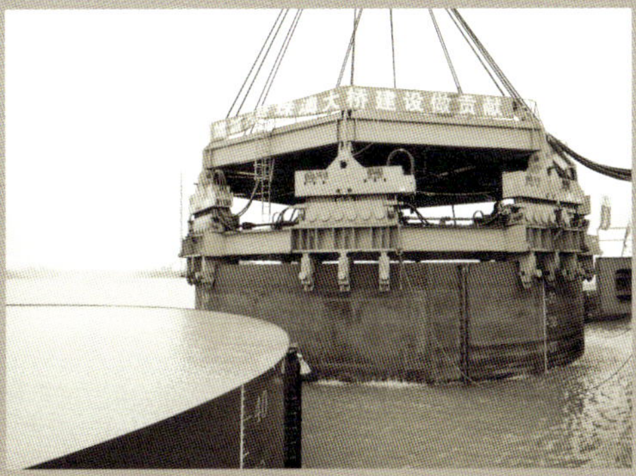
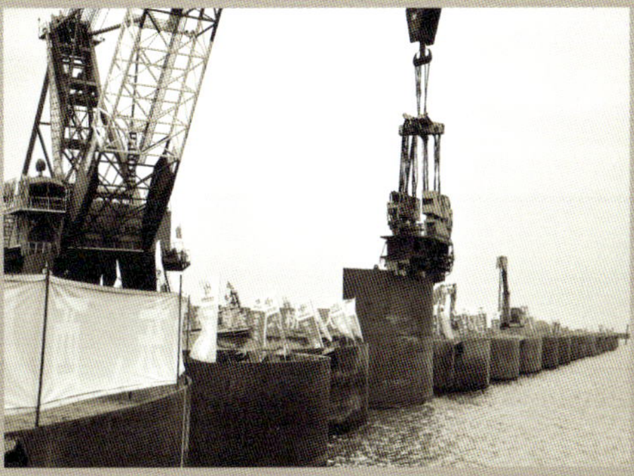
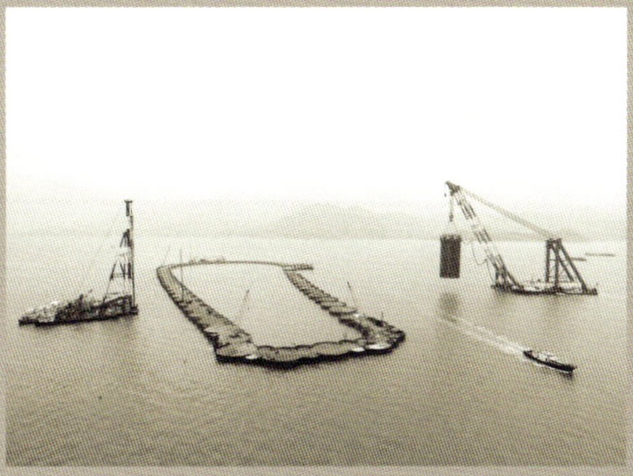

▲ 2011年9月22日—12月7日，东人工岛59个钢圆筒振沉完成，东人工岛成岛

From September 22 to December 7, 2011, 59 steel cylinders were driven into the seabed on East Man-Made Island, and East Man-Made Island came into being

▼2011.9.22

7 8 9 10 11 12 2012

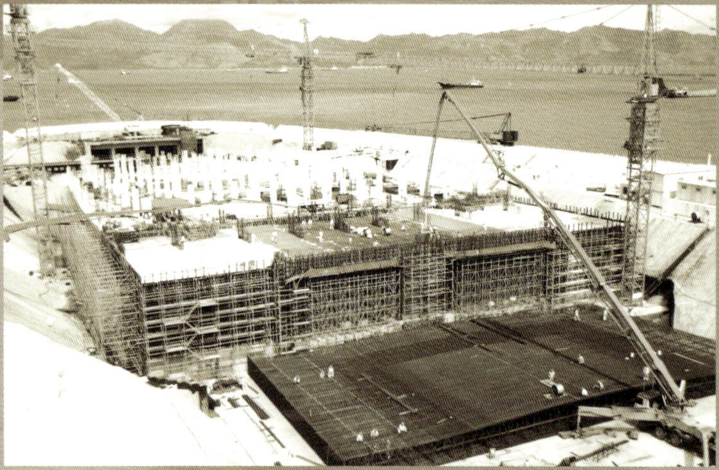

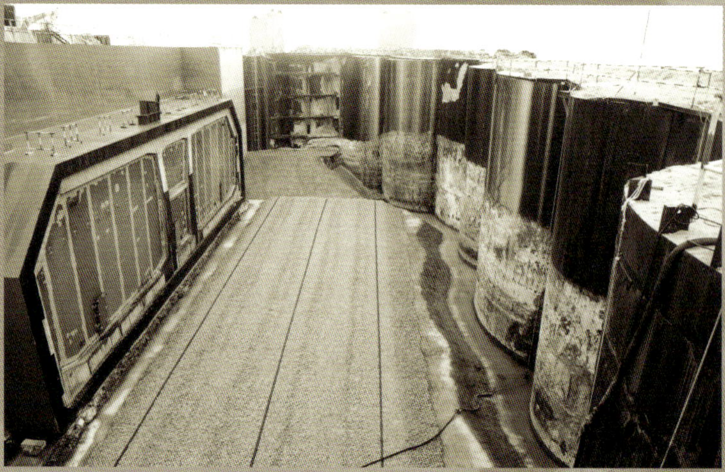

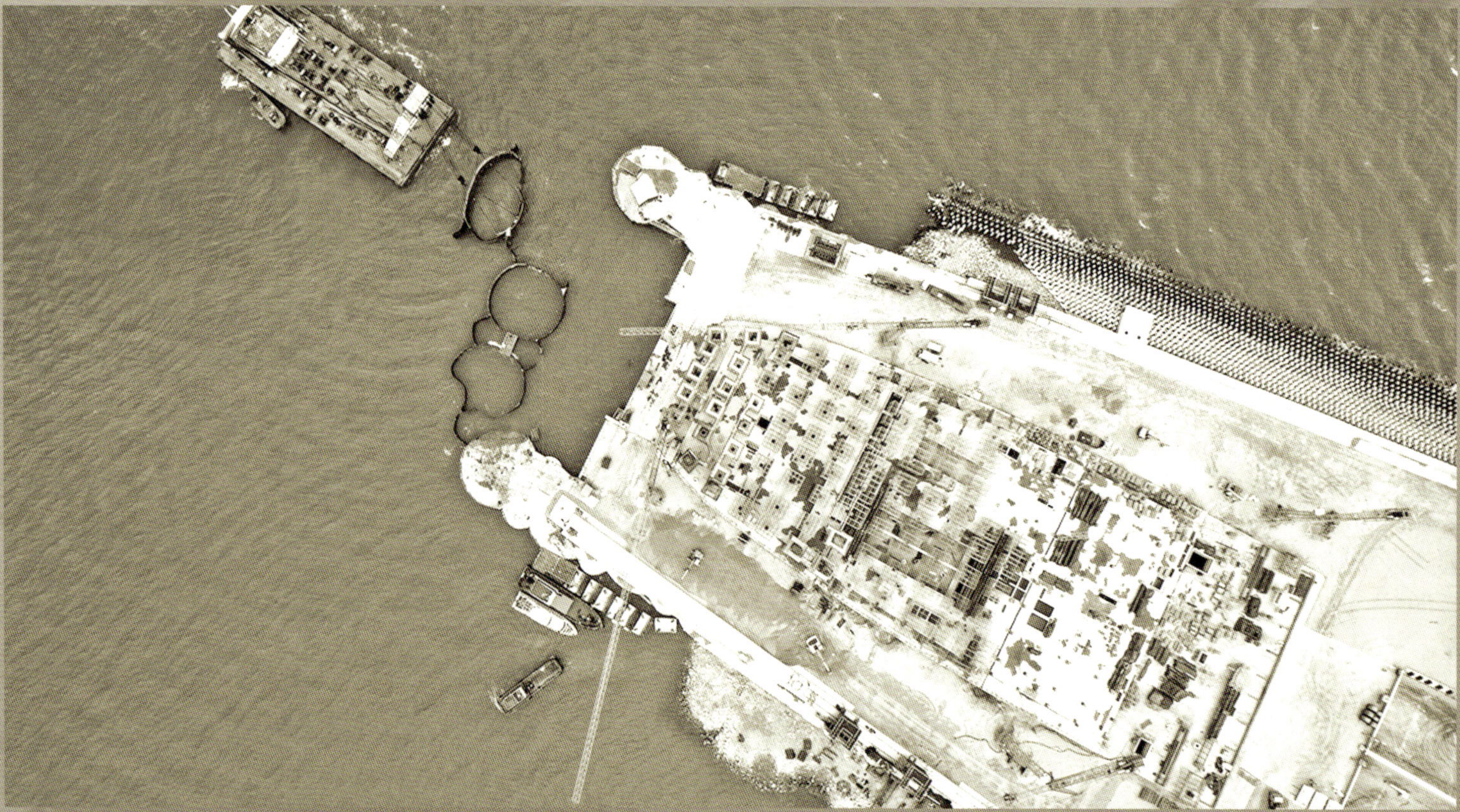

▲ 2016 年 5 月 19 日，东人工岛岛头钢圆筒、副格拆除

The steel cylinders and the connecting rails at the head part of West Man-Made Island were removed on May 19, 2016

▼2012.7.13 ▼2013.3.20

2012 1 2 3 4 5 6 7 8 9 10 11 12 2013 1 2 3 4 5 6 7 8 9 10 11

◀ 2012 年 7 月 13 日，西人工岛暗埋段施工

Construction of the Buried Section of the Tunnel on West Man-Made Island was done on July 13, 2012

◀ 2013 年 3 月 20 日，西人工岛正式具备外海岛、隧转换条件

West Man-Made Island was ready for offshore island-tunnel transition on March 20, 2013

▼ 2014 年 11 月 16 日，西人工岛敞开段行车道混凝土开工浇筑

The commencement of concrete placement for the driving lanes of the open section of the tunnel on West Man-Made Island was held on November 16, 2014

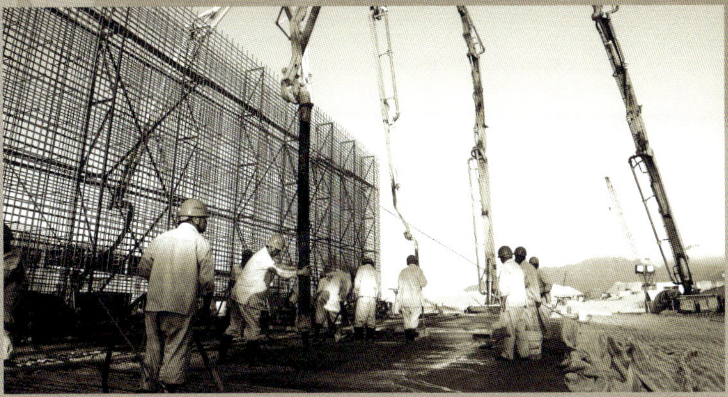

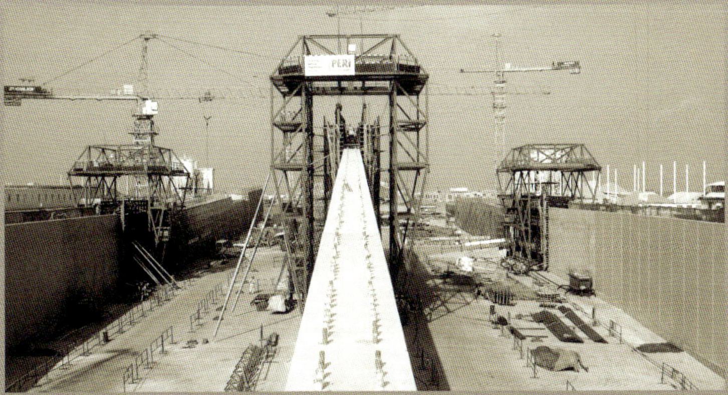

▲ 2015 年 9 月 25 日，东人工岛敞开段中隔墙清水混凝土浇筑

The commencement of fair-faced concrete placement for the partition wall of the open section of the tunnel on East Man-Made Island was held on September 25, 2015

隧道暗埋段长193米，浇筑完成后覆盖砂土，其上建设岛上建筑，用于人工岛的运营管理和观光旅游。

减光段与暗埋段相接，长110米，顶部设置光栅结构。

敞开段整体呈U形，长217米，分别与匝道、桥梁主体联通，形成岛上互通和岛桥过渡。

The buried parts of the tunnel under the man-made islands are 193 meters long. After its completion, the underneath tunnel was covered with sand and earth on which other facilitates were constructed for the island management or tourist purposes.

Light-reducing section that connects the buried section is 110 meters long with a grating structure installed on the top.

The U-shaped open section is 217 meters long, and connects the ramp and the main part of the bridge, providing access to the islands and the bridge.

▼2014.11.16 ▼2015.9.25

2 3 4 5 6 7 8 9 10 11 12 **2015** 1 2 3 4 5 6 7 8 9 10 11 12 **2016**

岛上结构物

CONSTRUCTION ON THE ISLAND

东、西人工岛上检修道盖板、路缘石、花盆、主体建筑大斜面台阶均采用清水混凝土工艺，实现了"工厂法预制，精细化安装"的目标。

The maintenance well covers, curbstones, flowerpots and the steps of the main buildings were all made of fair-faced concrete, which abided by the principle of "factory precasting plus precision installation".

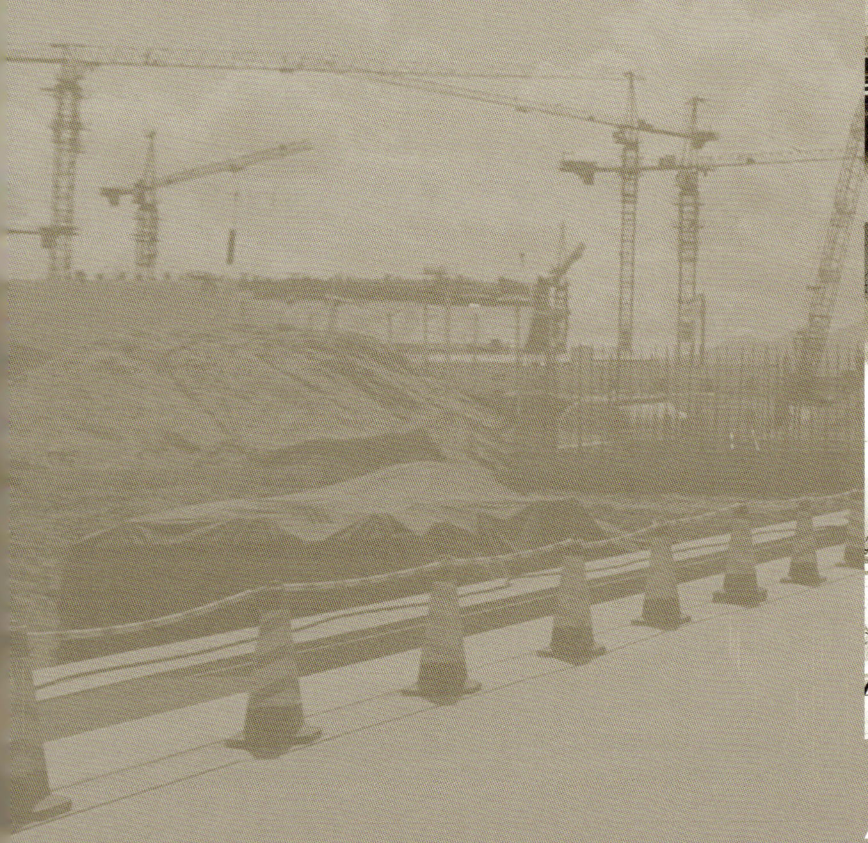

▼ 2014 年 11 月 25 日，东人工岛清水混凝土试验

Test of the fair-faced concrete on East Man-made Island was done on November 25, 2014

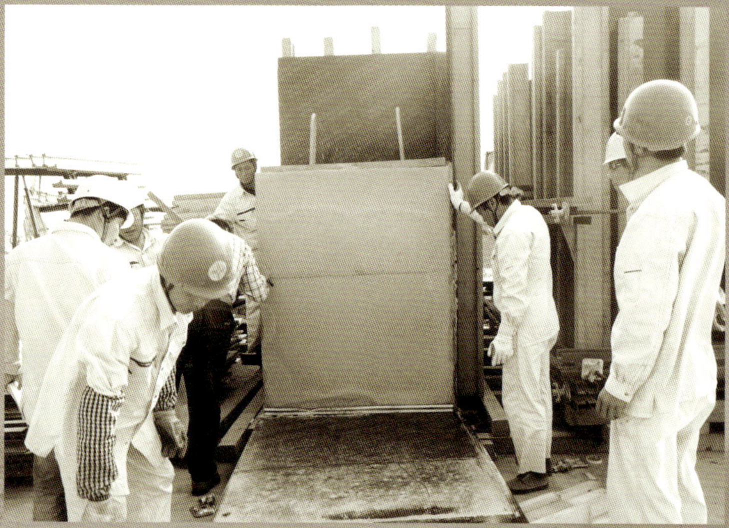

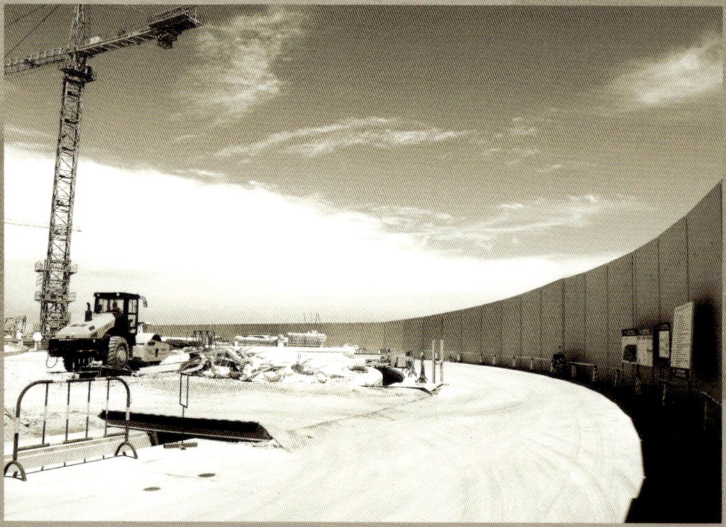

▲ 2017 年 8 月 25 日，西人工岛清水混凝土挡浪墙

Anti-wave wall made of fair-faced concrete on West Man-Made Island was done on August 25, 2017

▼2014.11.25 ▼2015.6.26

2014 1 2 3 4 5 6 7 8 9 10 11 12 2015 1 2 3 4 5 6 7 8 9 10 11

▼ 2015 年 6 月 26 日，东人工岛清水混凝土配合比优化试验

Optimal test on the fair-faced concrete ratio on East Man-Made Island on June 26, 2015

▼ 2016 年 1 月 25 日，东人工岛挡浪墙墙身混凝土浇筑

Concrete placement for the anti-wave wall on East Man-Made Island was done on January 25, 2016

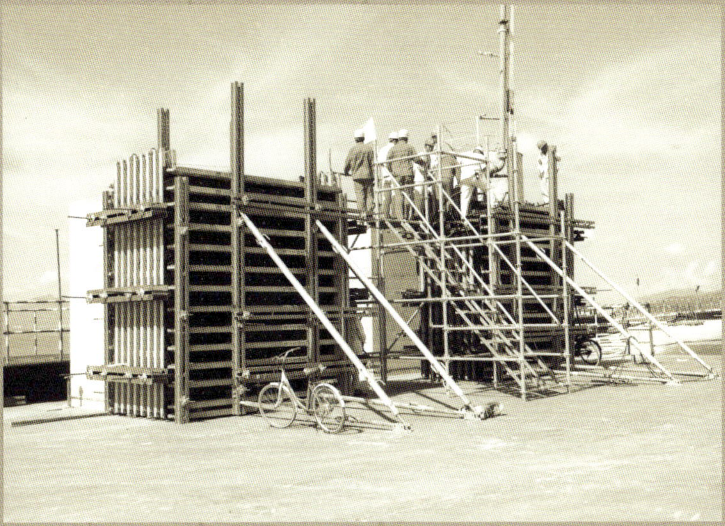

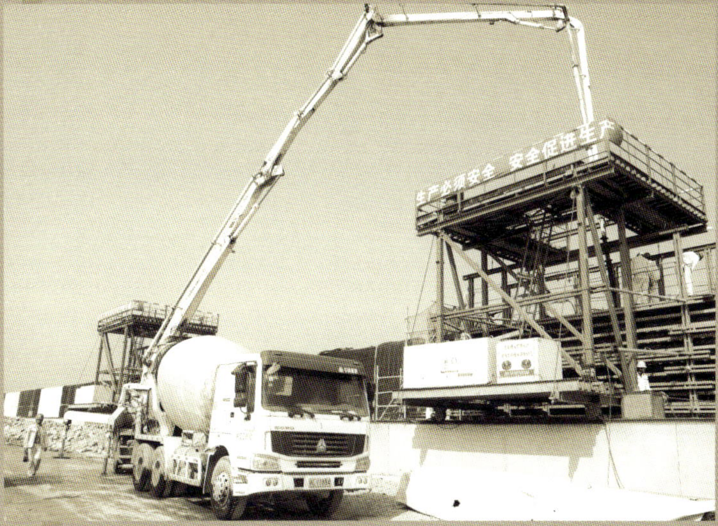

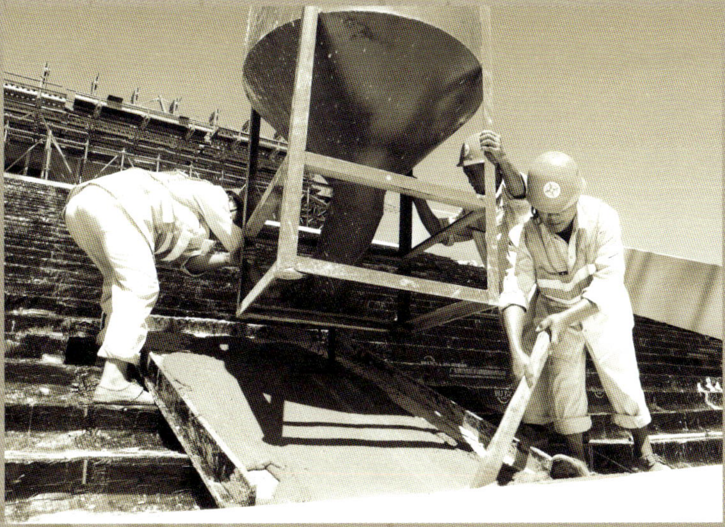

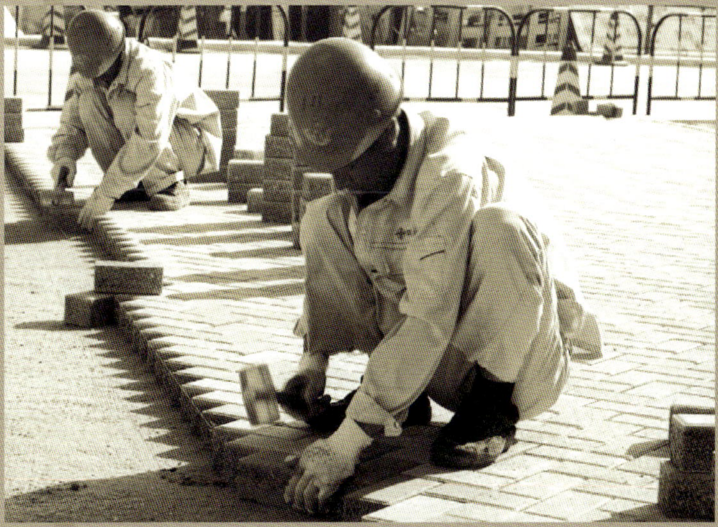

▲ 2017 年 8 月 29 日，东人工岛主体建筑大台阶基础浇筑施工

Concrete placement for the grand step of the main building on East Man-Made Island was done on August 29, 2017

▲ 2017 年 11 月 25 日，西人工岛广场透水路砖铺装施工

Placement of the water-permeable bricks on West Man-Made Island Square was done on November 25, 2017

016.1.25 ▼2017.8.25 ▼2017.8.29 ▼2017.11.25

2 3 4 5 6 7 8 9 10 11 12 2017 1 2 3 4 5 6 7 8 9 10 11 12 2018

东人工岛主体建筑为地下2层、地上4层的多层建筑，主要以商业、办公、展览为主。

西人工岛主体建筑为地下2层、地上3层的多层建筑，主要以办公、救援养护配套用房和设备用房为主。

The main building on East Man-Made Island is a 6-storeyed structure with 2 stories underground, mainly for commercial use or used as offices and exhibition rooms.

The main building on West Man-Made Island is a 5-storeyed structure with 3 stories above the ground, mainly used as offices, maintenance and emergency aid center or equipment rooms.

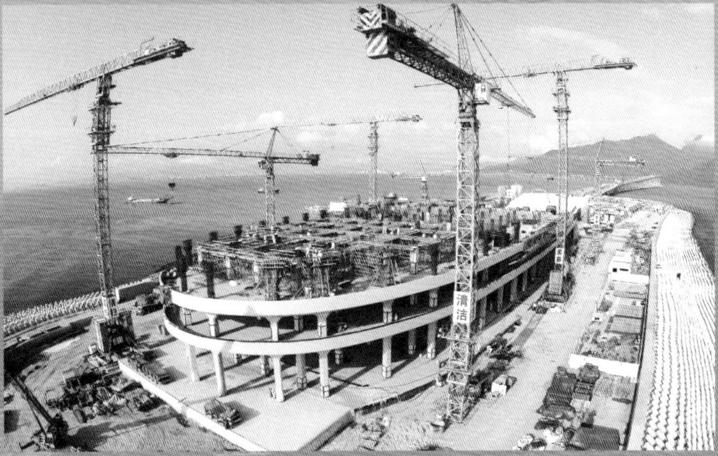

◀ 2016 年 5 月 31 日，东人工岛主体建筑第三层立柱钢筋笼绑扎施

Steel cage binding for the third layers of pillars of the main building on East Man-Made Island was done on May 31, 2016

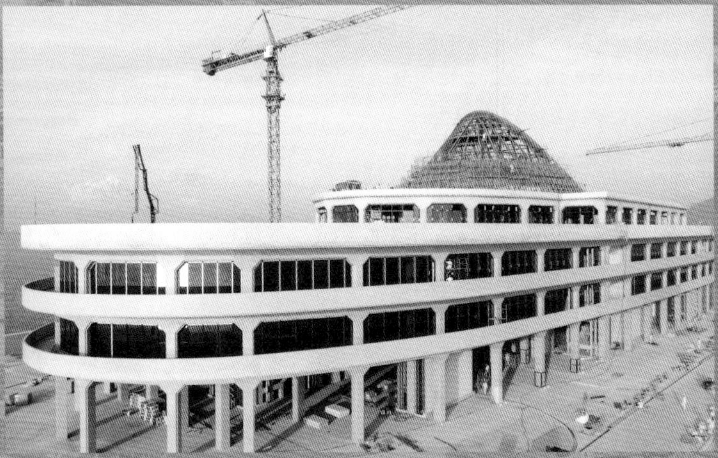

▲ 2017 年 8 月 26 日，东人工岛风帽结构施工

The construction of the wind cap structure on East Man-Made Island was done on August 26, 2017

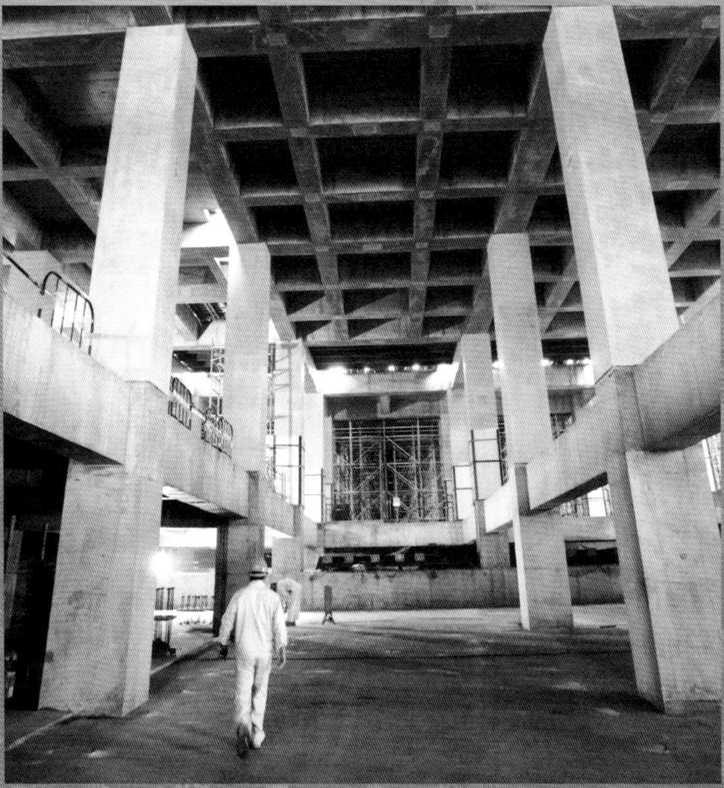

▲ 2017 年 3 月 25 日，西人工岛主体建筑负一层、一层楼板、立柱施工

On March 25,2017, the B-1 floor and the first floor of the mair building on West Man-Made Island were under construction

▼2016.5.31

2016 1 2 3 4 5 6 7 8 9 10 11 12

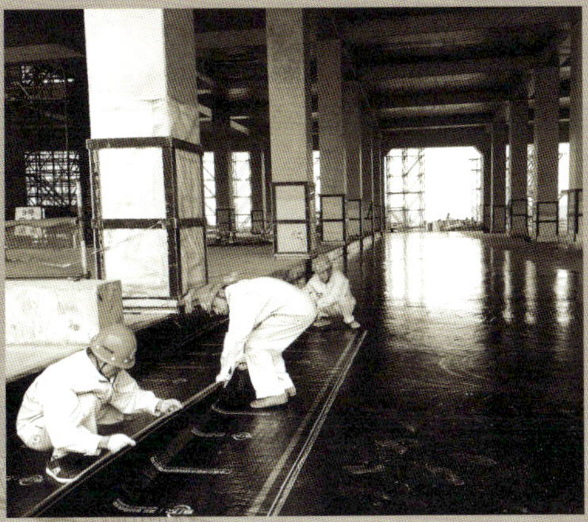

◀ 2017 年 2 月 25 日，西人工岛主体建筑首层行车道防水层铺设

The first layer of water-proof placement for the driving lanes of the main building on West Man-Made Island was done on February 25, 2017

▶ 2017 年 8 月 26 日，西人工岛主体建筑首层立柱浇筑

The concrete placement of the first layer of pillars of the main building on West Man-Made Island was done on August 26, 2017

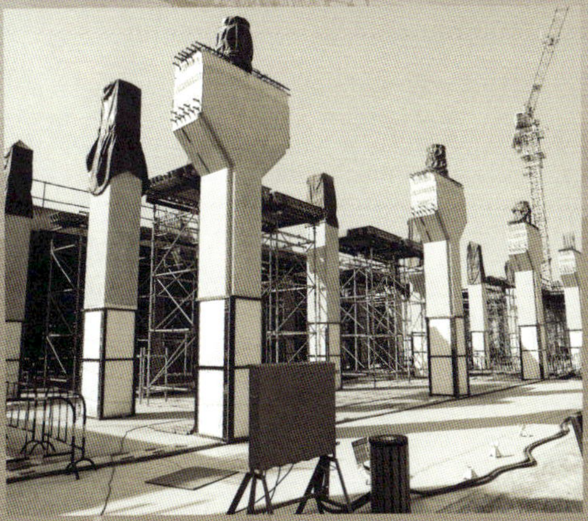

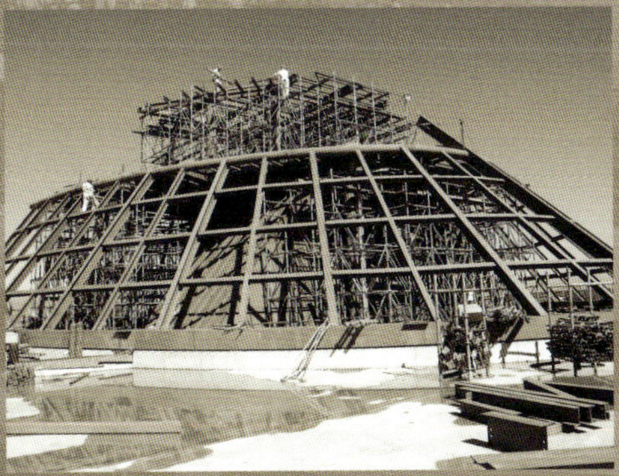

▲ 2017 年 8 月 14 日，西人工岛风帽风道板安装完成

The wind pipe plates of the wind cap on West Man-Made Island was completed on August 14, 2017

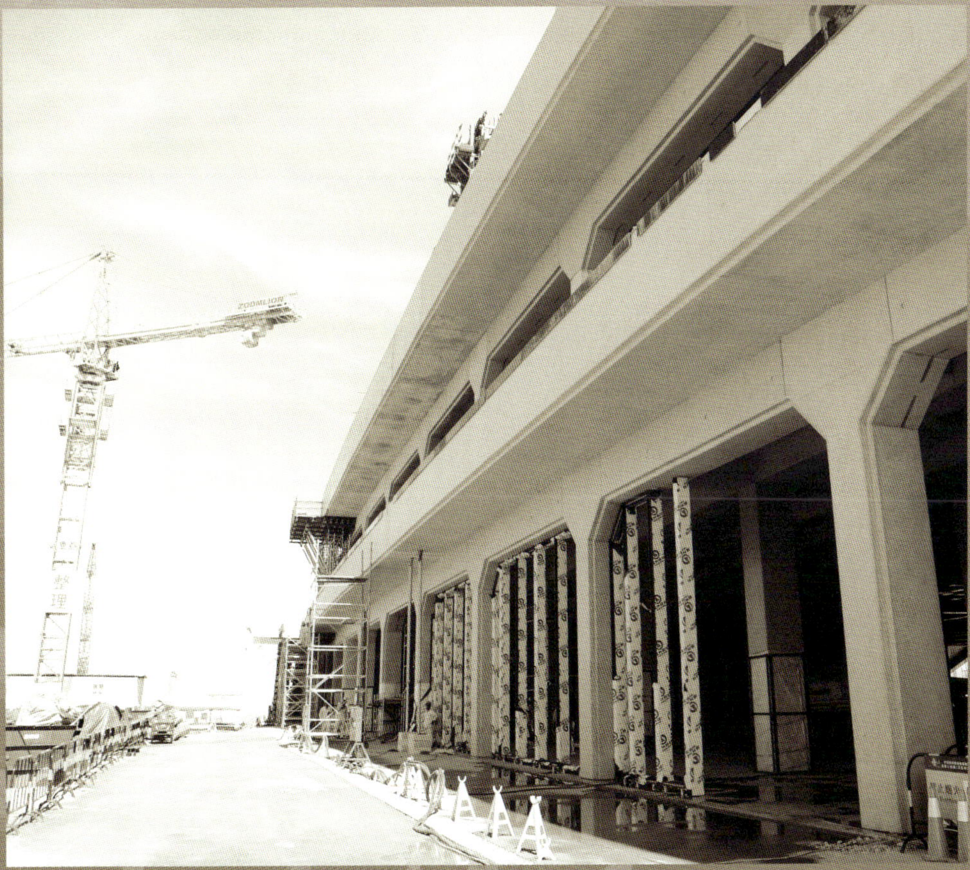

▲ 2017 年 6 月 25 日，西人工岛外侧廊道围栏施工

The construction of the protective rails for the outer gallery on West Man-Made Island was done on June 25, 2017

▼2017.3.25
▼2017.2.25
▼2017.6.25
▼2017.8.14
▼2017.8.26

1 2 3 4 5 6 7 8 9 10 11 12 | 2018

非通航孔桥

NON-NAVIGATION CHANNEL BRIDGE

▼ 2013 年 1 月 18 日，西人工岛非通航孔桥首套钢吊厢拼装

The first set of steel hoisted tanks for the non-navigation channel bridge on West Man-Made Island was installed on January 18, 2013

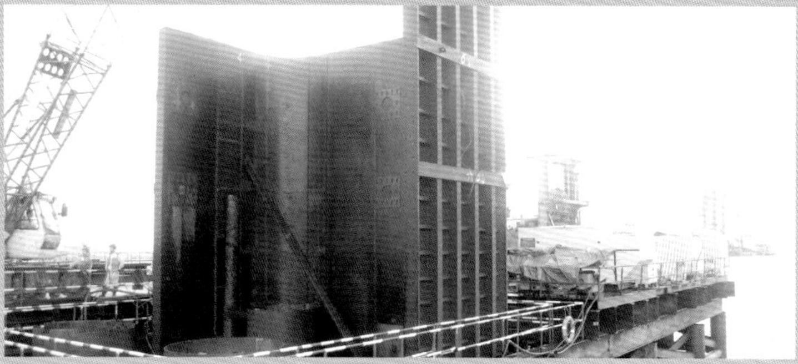

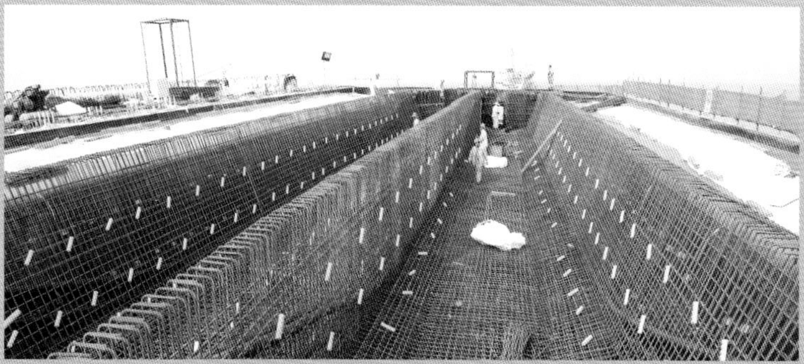

▲ 2014 年 9 月 3 日，西人工岛非通航孔桥箱梁第五施工段钢筋笼绑扎

Steel cage binding for the box girders in the fifth section of the non-navigation channel bridge on West Man-Made Island was done on September 3, 2014.

▶ 2015 年 1 月 10 日，东人工岛非通航孔桥临近粤港分界线一跨箱梁浇筑

Concrete placement for one spanning box girder of the non-navigation channel bridge near the dividing line of Guangdong and Hong Kong on East Man-Made Island was done on January 10, 2015

▼ 2014 年 6 月 23 日，东人工岛非通航孔桥第二联第二施工段模板拼装

The stencil plates in the second section of the second part of the non-navigation channel bridge on East Man-Made Island was installed on June 23, 2014

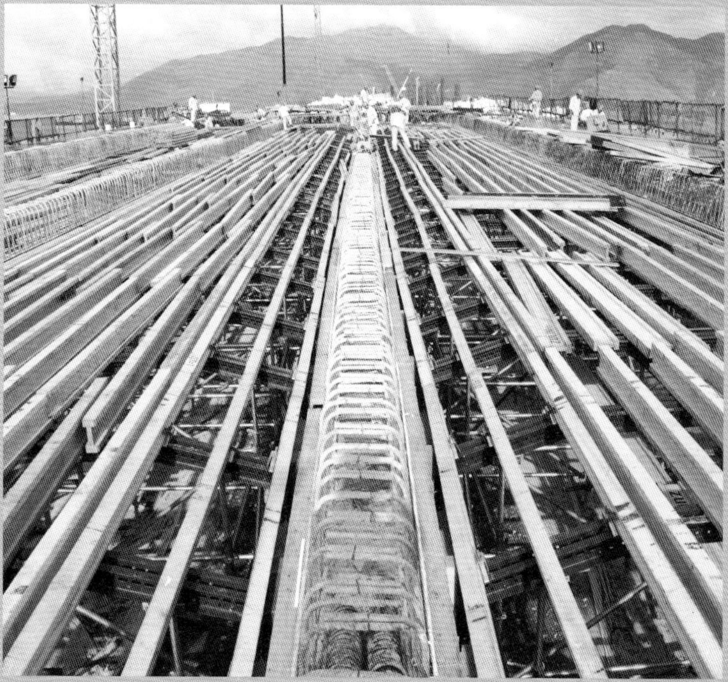

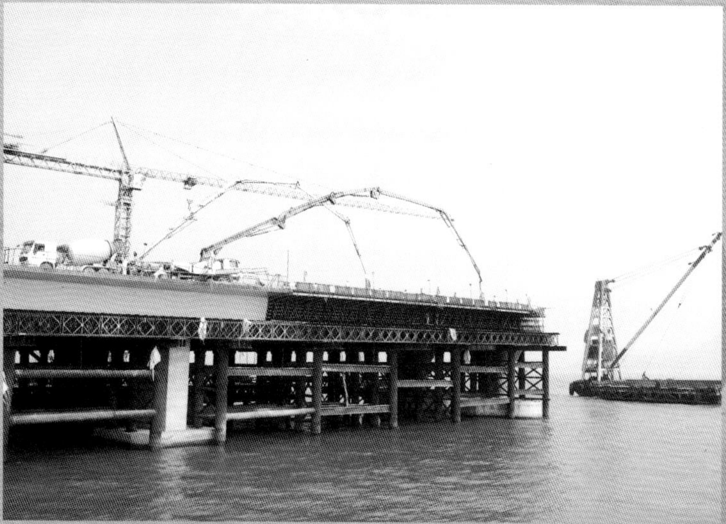

▼2013.1.18 ▼2014.6.23 ▼2014.9.3

2013 1 2 3 4 5 6 7 8 9 10 11 12 2014 1 2 3 4 5 6 7 8 9 10 11

东、西人工岛非通航孔桥为现浇预应力混凝土连续箱梁，全长639.75米。基础采用嵌岩钻孔灌注桩，桩基采用栈桥配合水上平台进行施工，上部箱梁采用少支架施工。

The non-navigation channel bridges on East and West Man-Made Islands are continuous cast-in-place pre-stressed concrete box girders with a total length of 639.75 meters. The base poles were made by pouring concrete into the sockets holed in the rock, the foundation of the poles was constructed by operation on the overwater platform and trestle, and the top box girders were built by operation on supporting scaffolds.

▼ 2015 年 10 月 28 日，东人工岛非通航孔桥管线槽安装

The cable tray of the non-navigation channel bridge on East Man-Made Island was installed on October 28, 2015

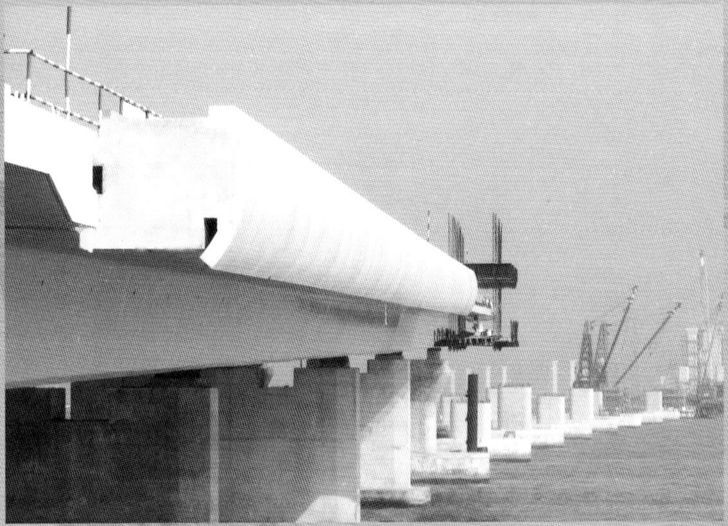

▼ 2016 年 2 月 25 日，东人工岛非通航孔桥管线槽安装完成

The installation of the cable tray of the non-navigation channel bridge on East Man-Made Island was completed on February 25, 2016

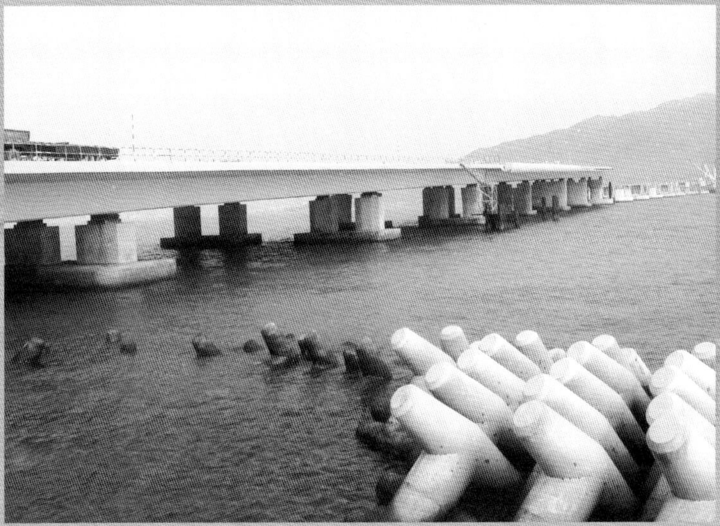

015.1.10 ▼2015.10.28 ▼2016.2.25

2 3 4 5 6 7 8 9 10 11 12 2016 1 2 3 4 5 6 7 8 9 10 11 12 2017

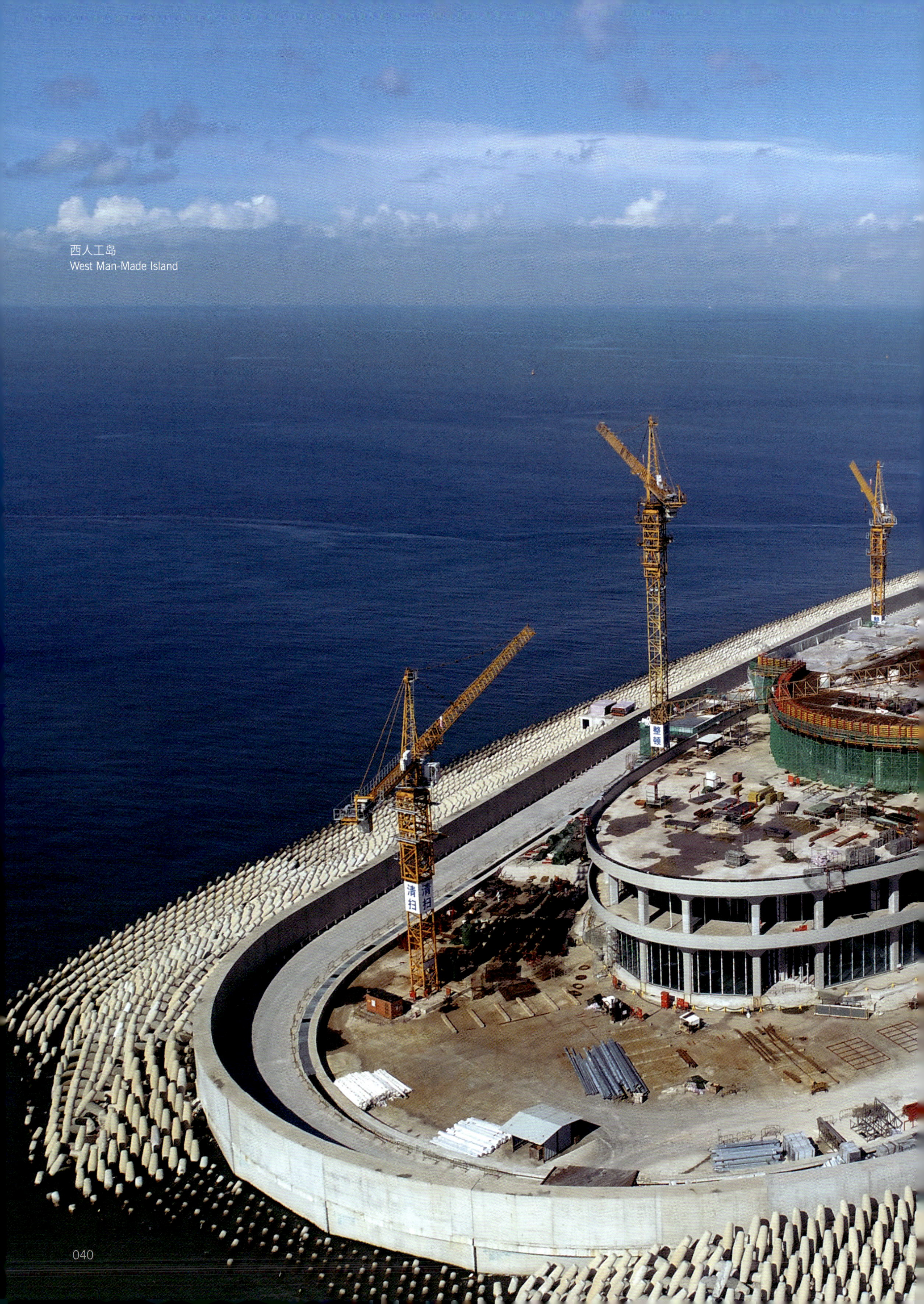

西人工岛
West Man-Made Island

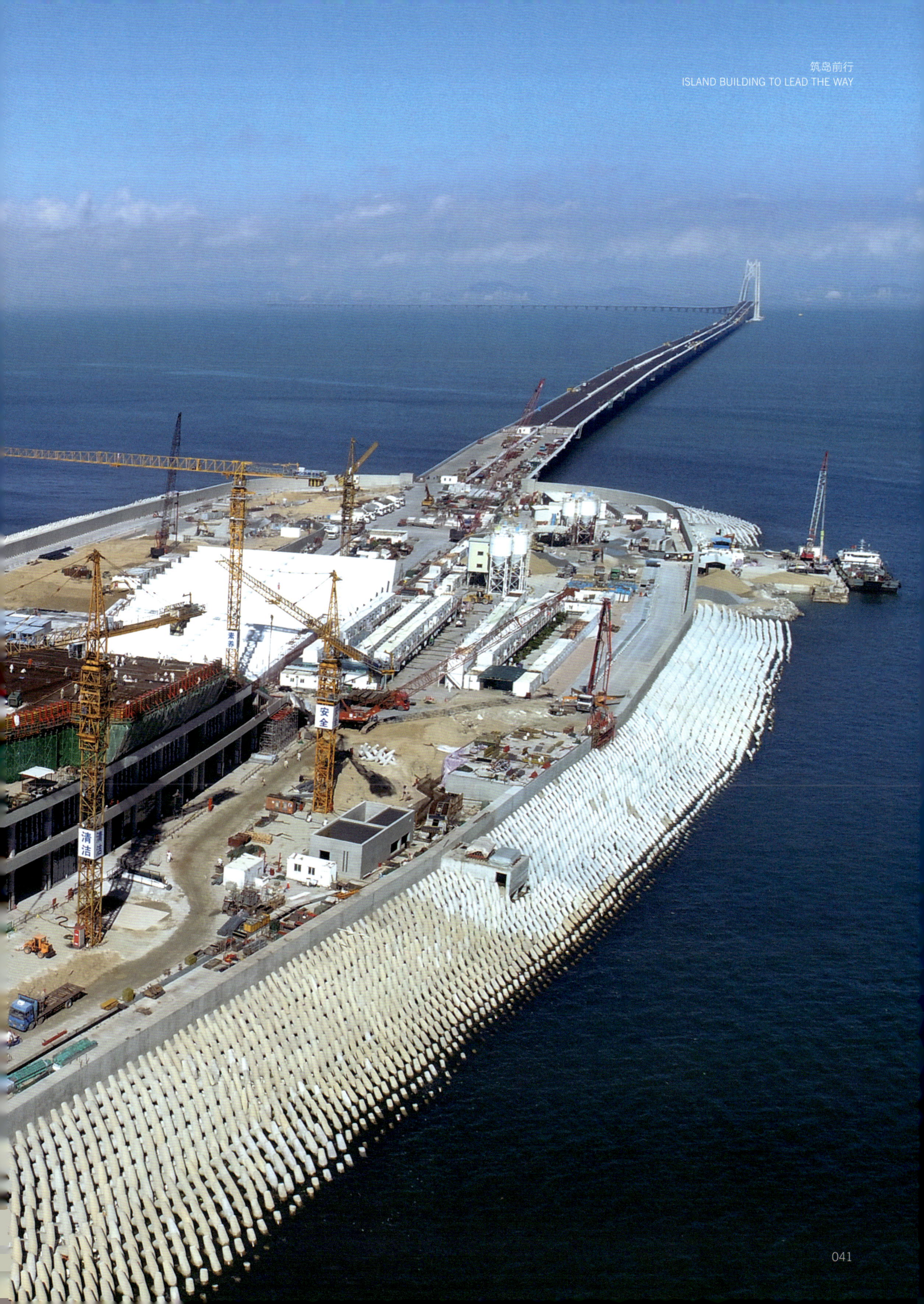
安全
清洁

建设中的东人工岛
East Man-Made Island under Construction

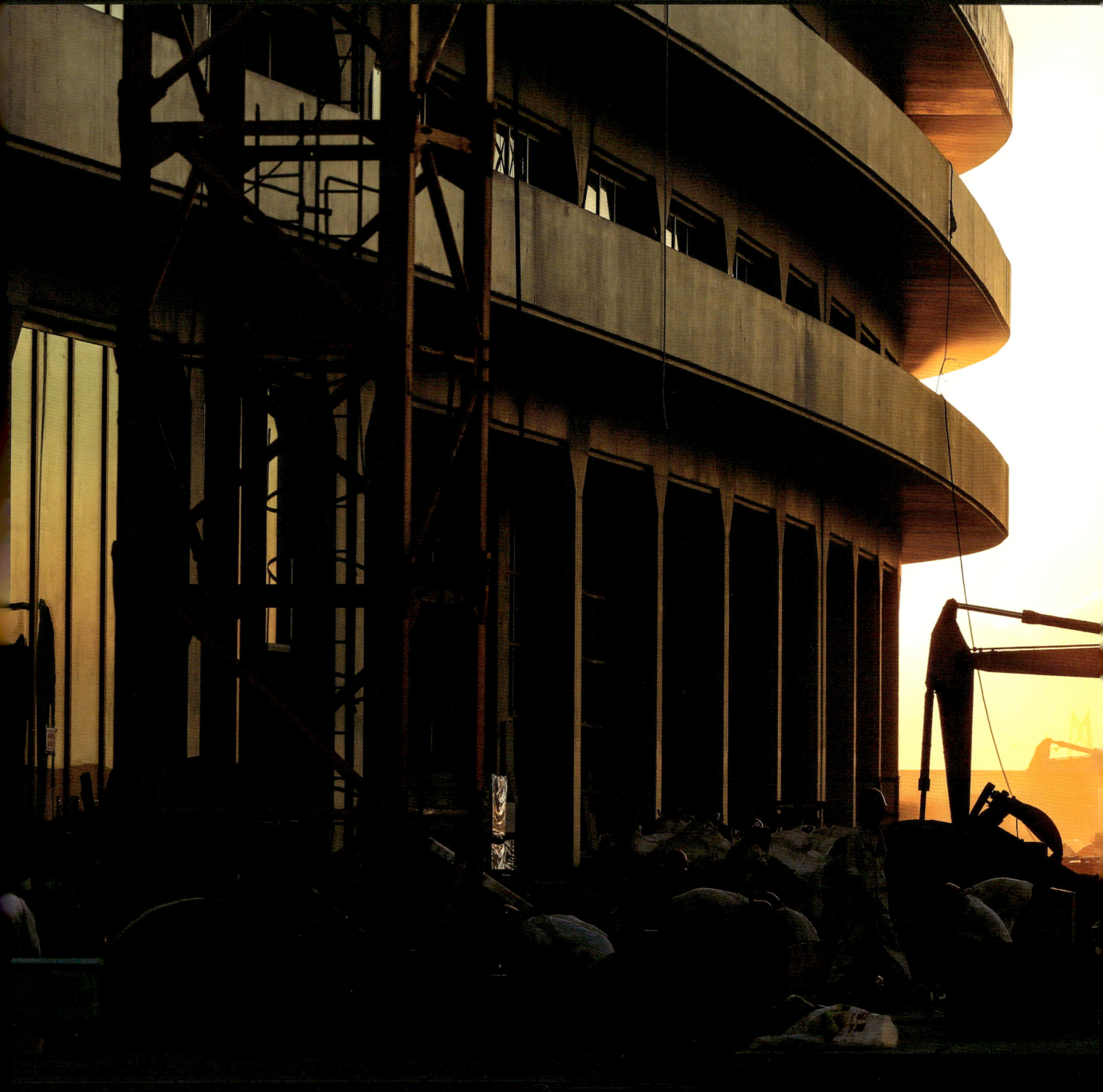

The roraing machines in the morning glow composed a vigorous symphony on East Man-Made Island.

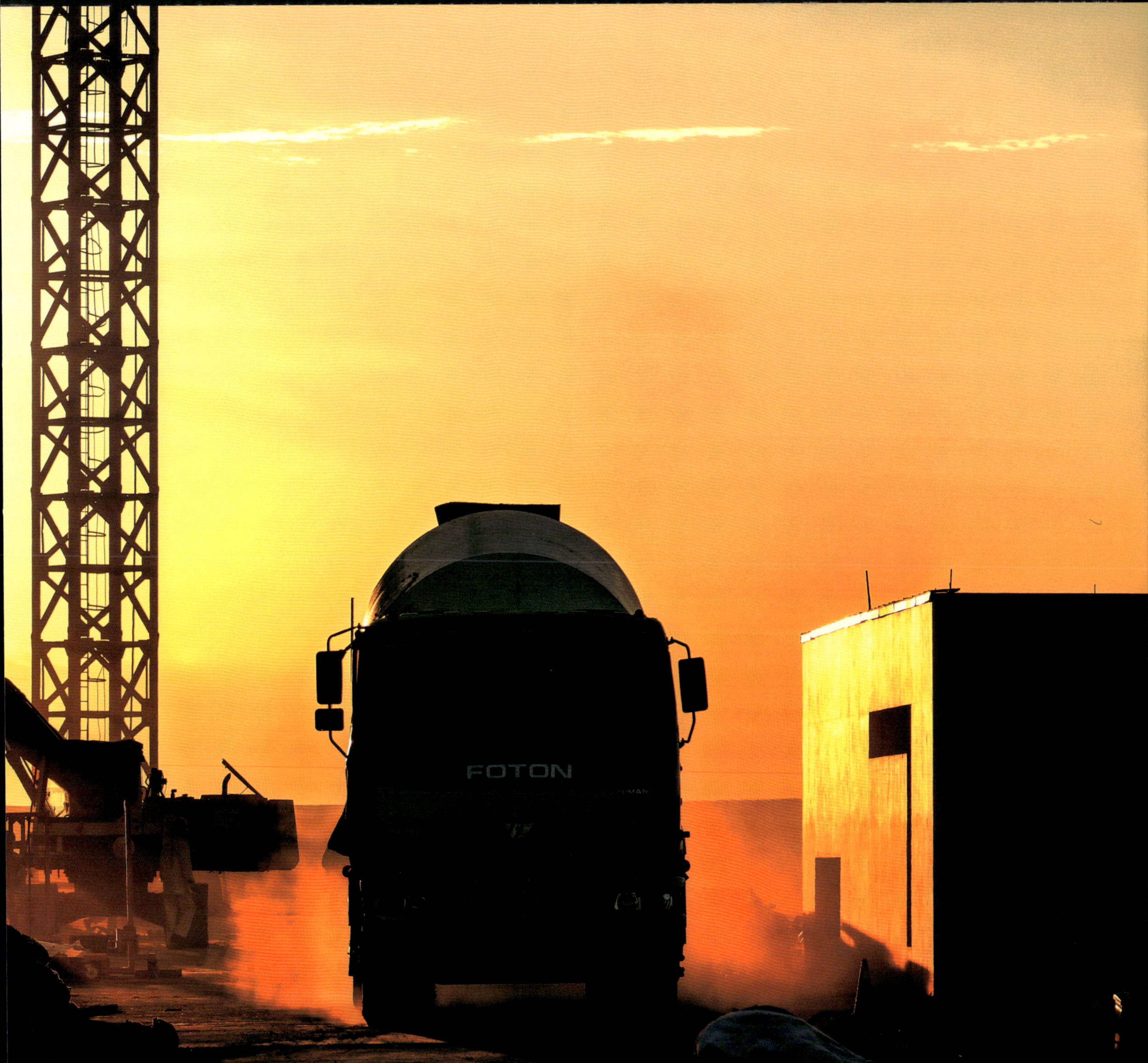

夜幕下的东人工岛主体建筑
Main Building on East Man-Made Island in the Nightshade

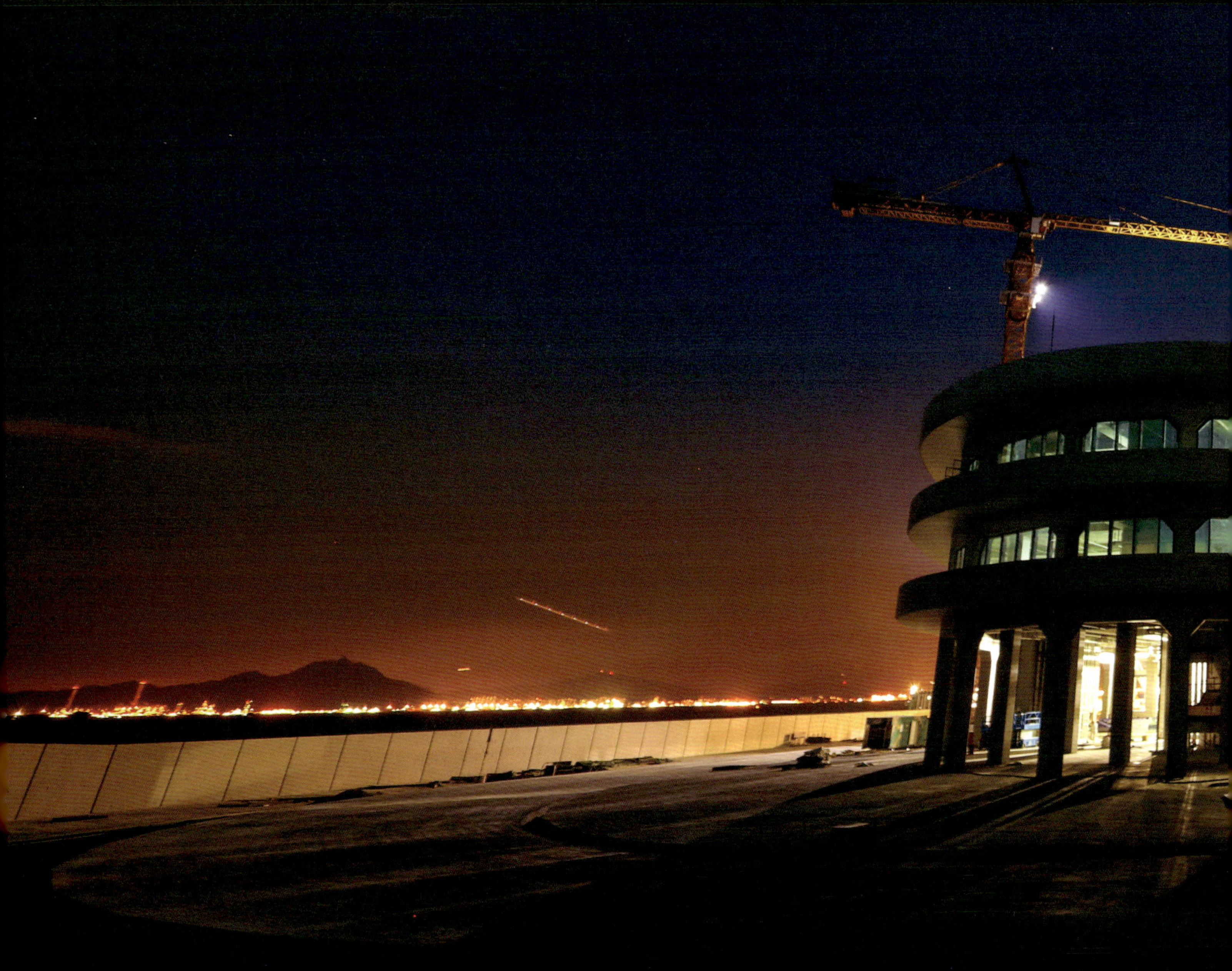

片刻的宁静，
只为积蓄更大的能量。
凌晨的东人工岛，
正默默迎接初升的朝阳和新一轮喧闹。

The momentary peace
Awaits the greater bustle.
East Man-Made Island at dawn
Welcomes the rising sun
And moment of clamor.

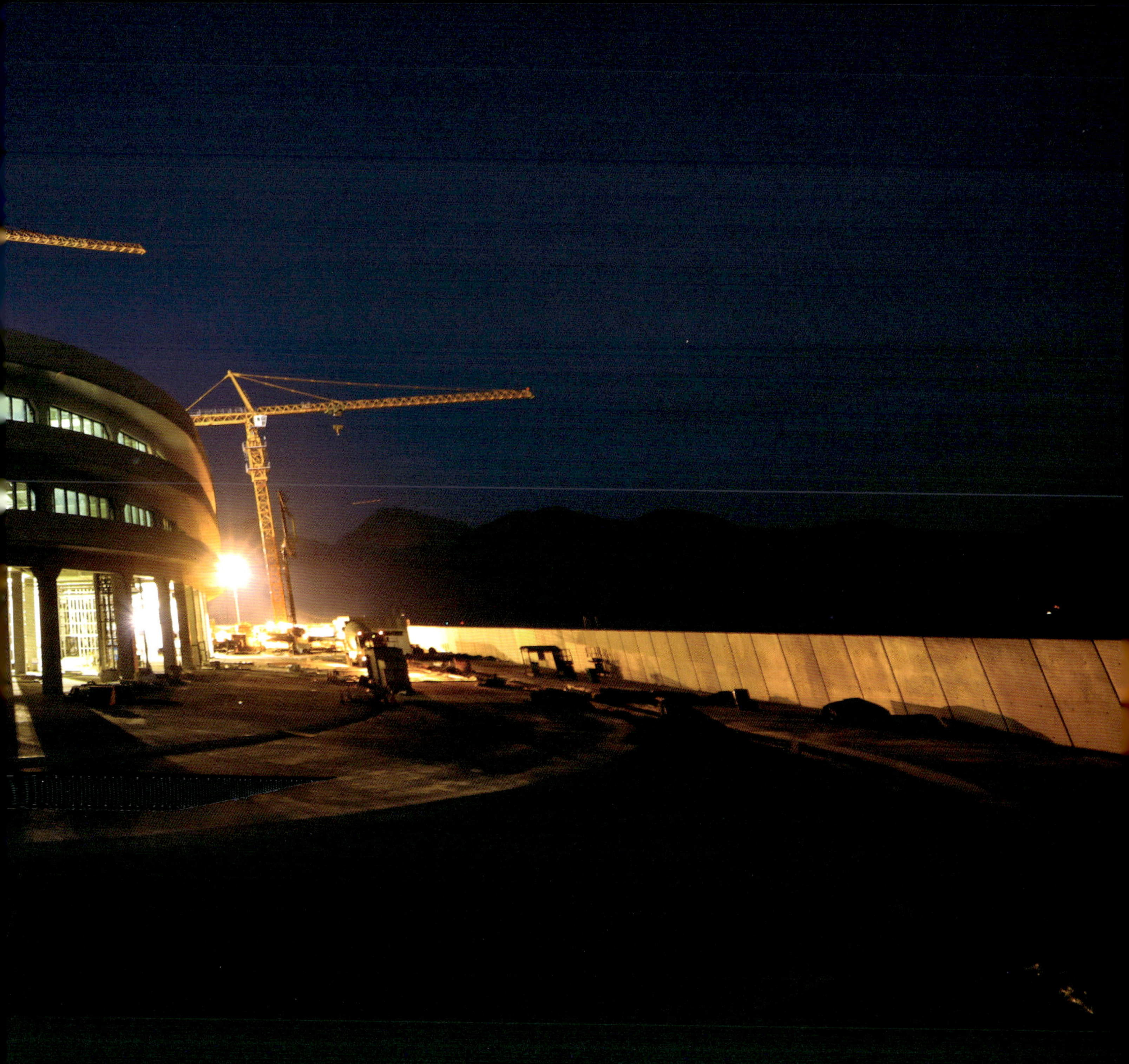

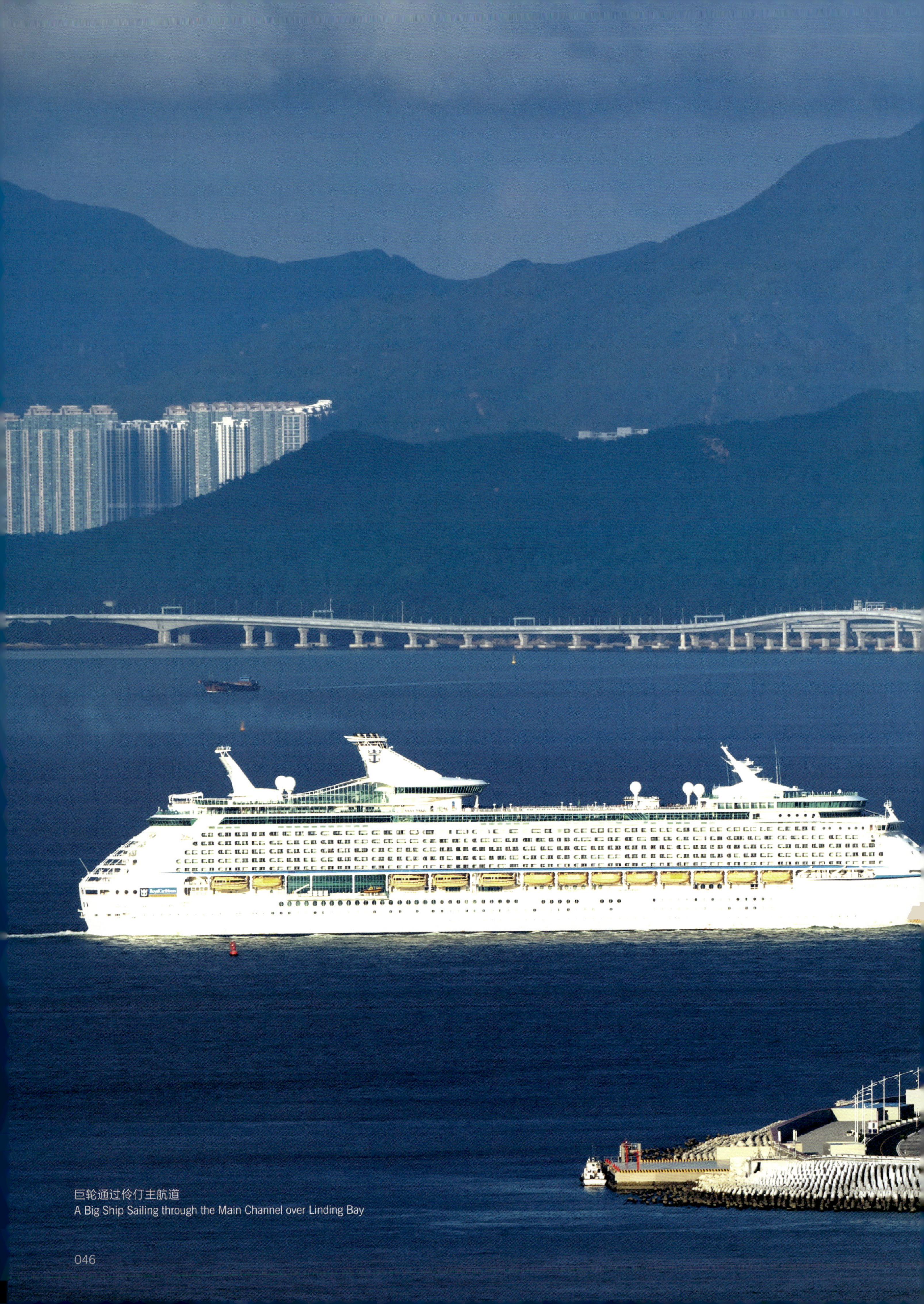

巨轮通过伶仃主航道
A Big Ship Sailing through the Main Channel over Linding Bay

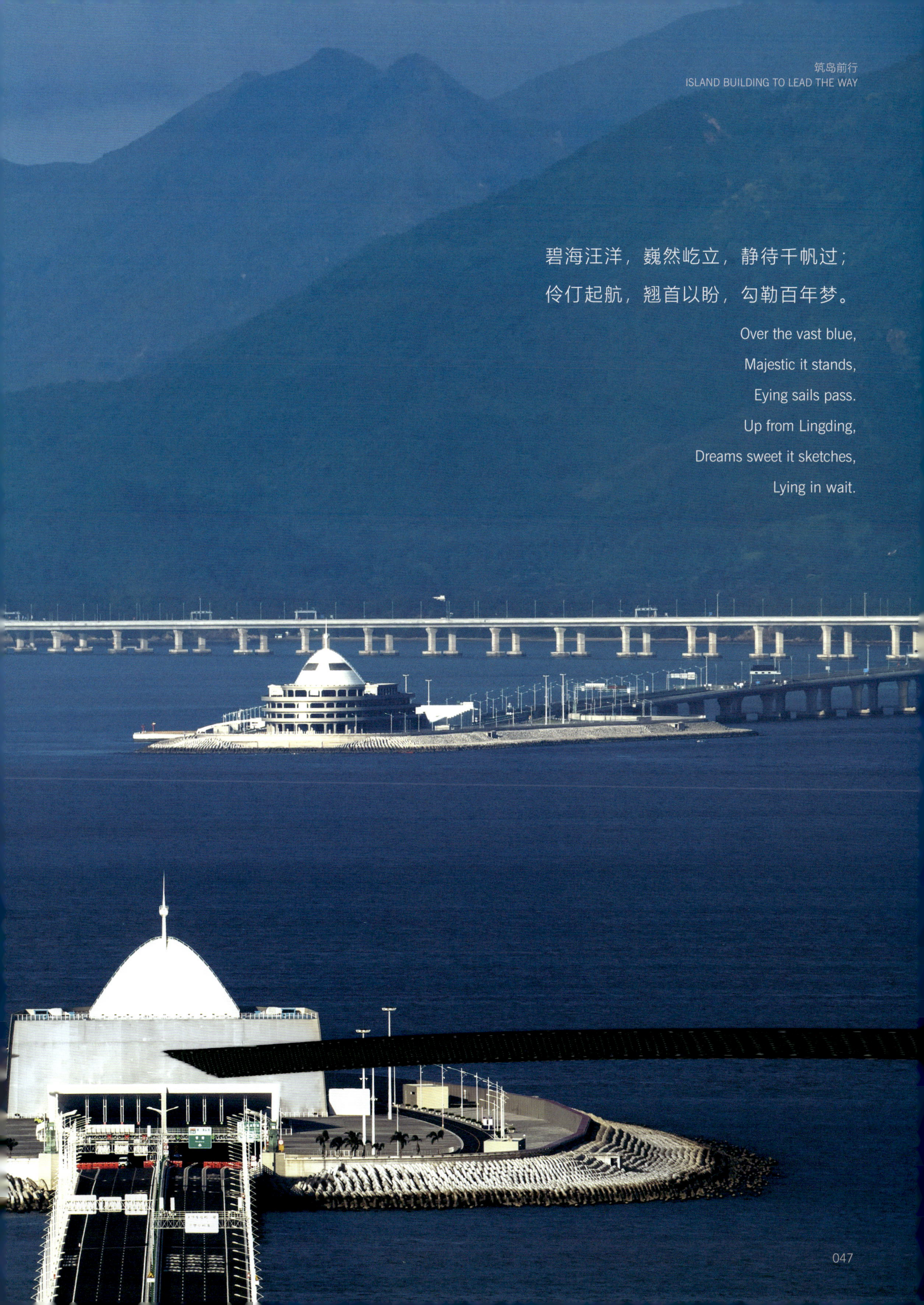

碧海汪洋，巍然屹立，静待千帆过；
伶仃起航，翘首以盼，勾勒百年梦。

Over the vast blue,
Majestic it stands,
Eying sails pass.
Up from Lingding,
Dreams sweet it sketches,
Lying in wait.

人工岛成品展示
DISPLAY OF MAN-MADE ISLAND PRODUCTS

1	2

1. 东人工岛
   East Man-Made Island
2. 西人工岛
   West Man-Made Island

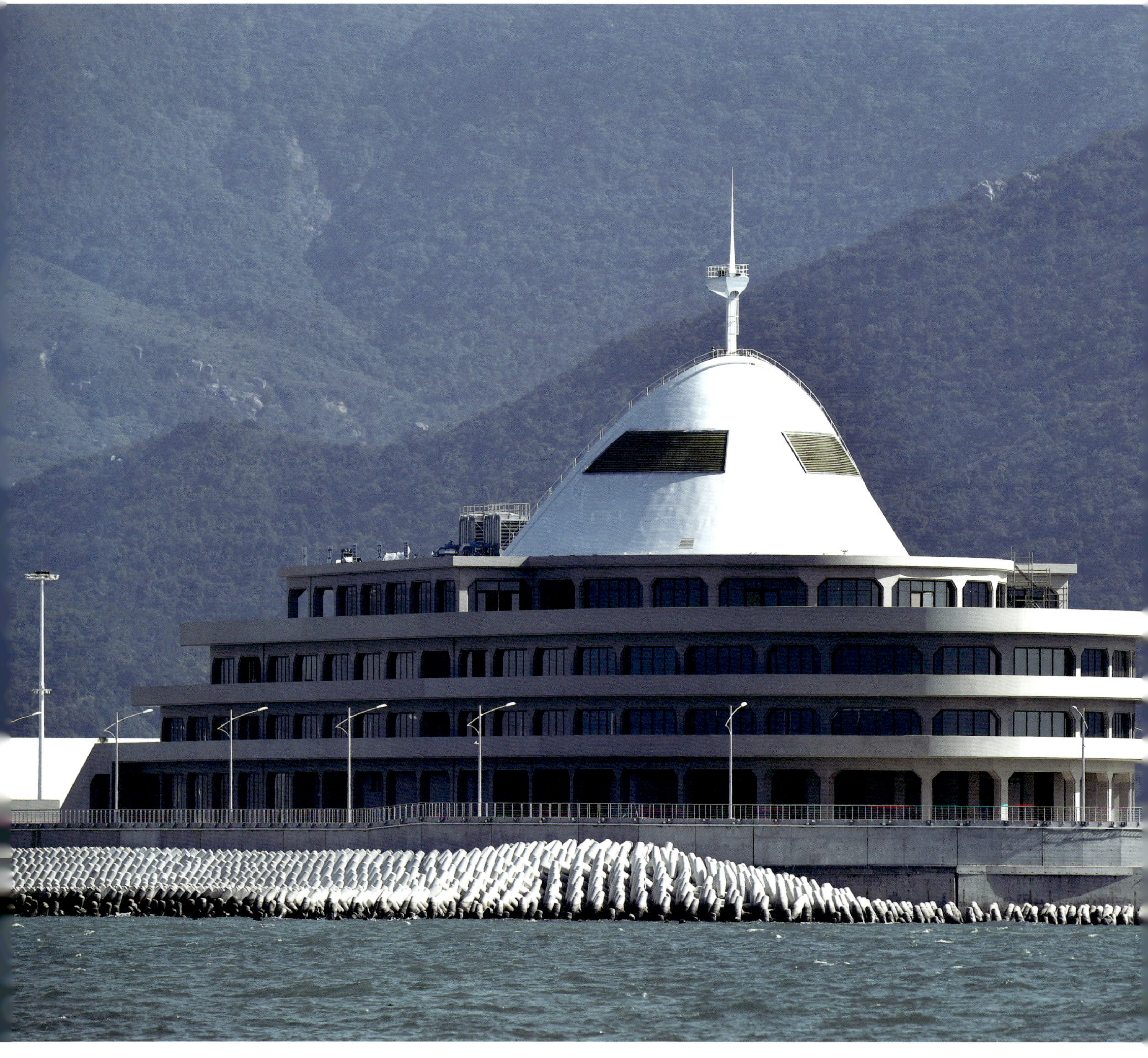

碧波之上，双贝辉映；世界之最，闪耀伶仃。

Over the green waves,
Dancing to the call of the Oysters,
The unprecedented human eyes may see Shines over the Bay.

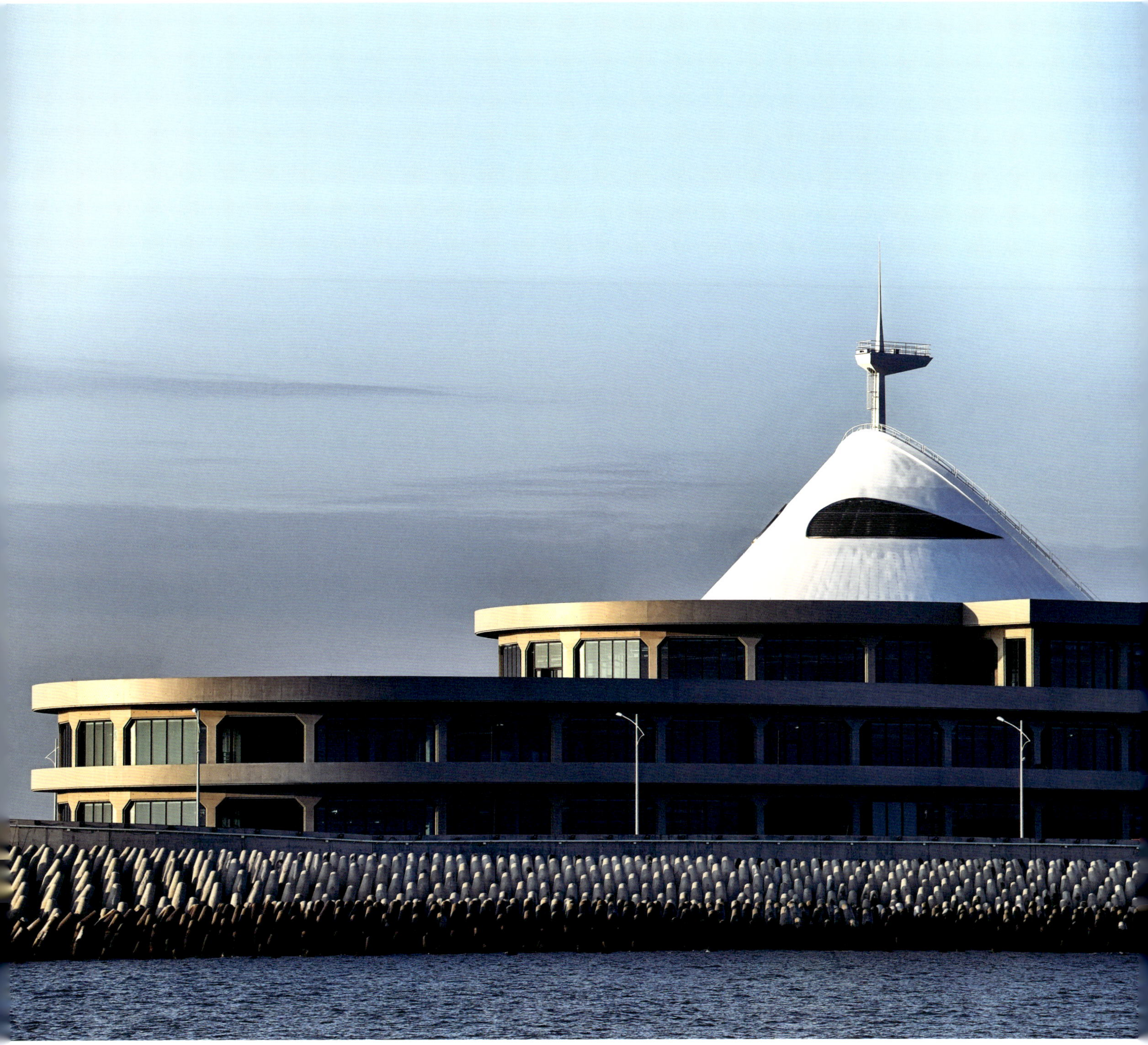

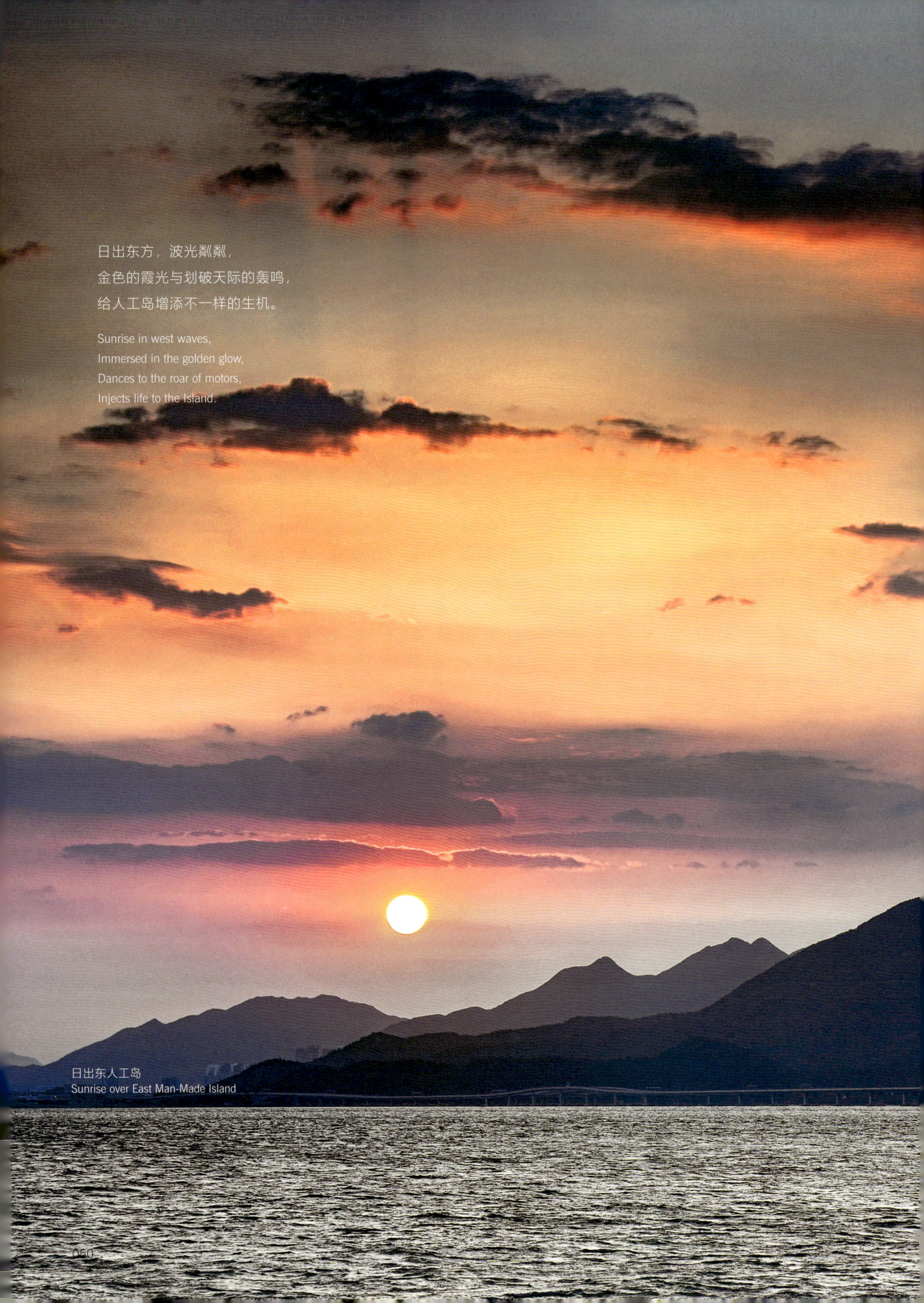

日出东方，波光粼粼，
金色的霞光与划破天际的轰鸣，
给人工岛增添不一样的生机。

Sunrise in west waves,
Immersed in the golden glow,
Dances to the roar of motors,
Injects life to the Island.

日出东人工岛
Sunrise over East Man-Made Island

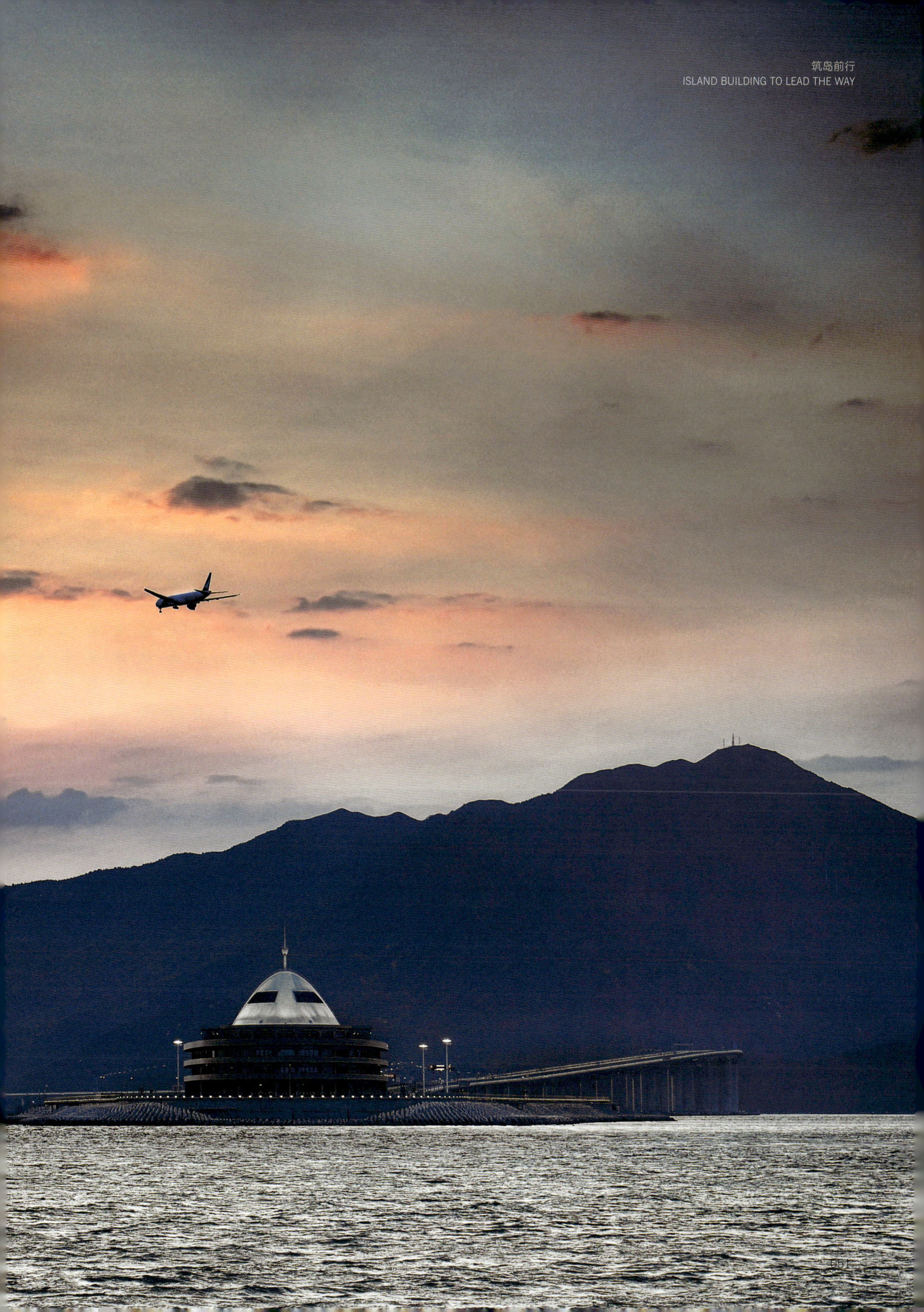

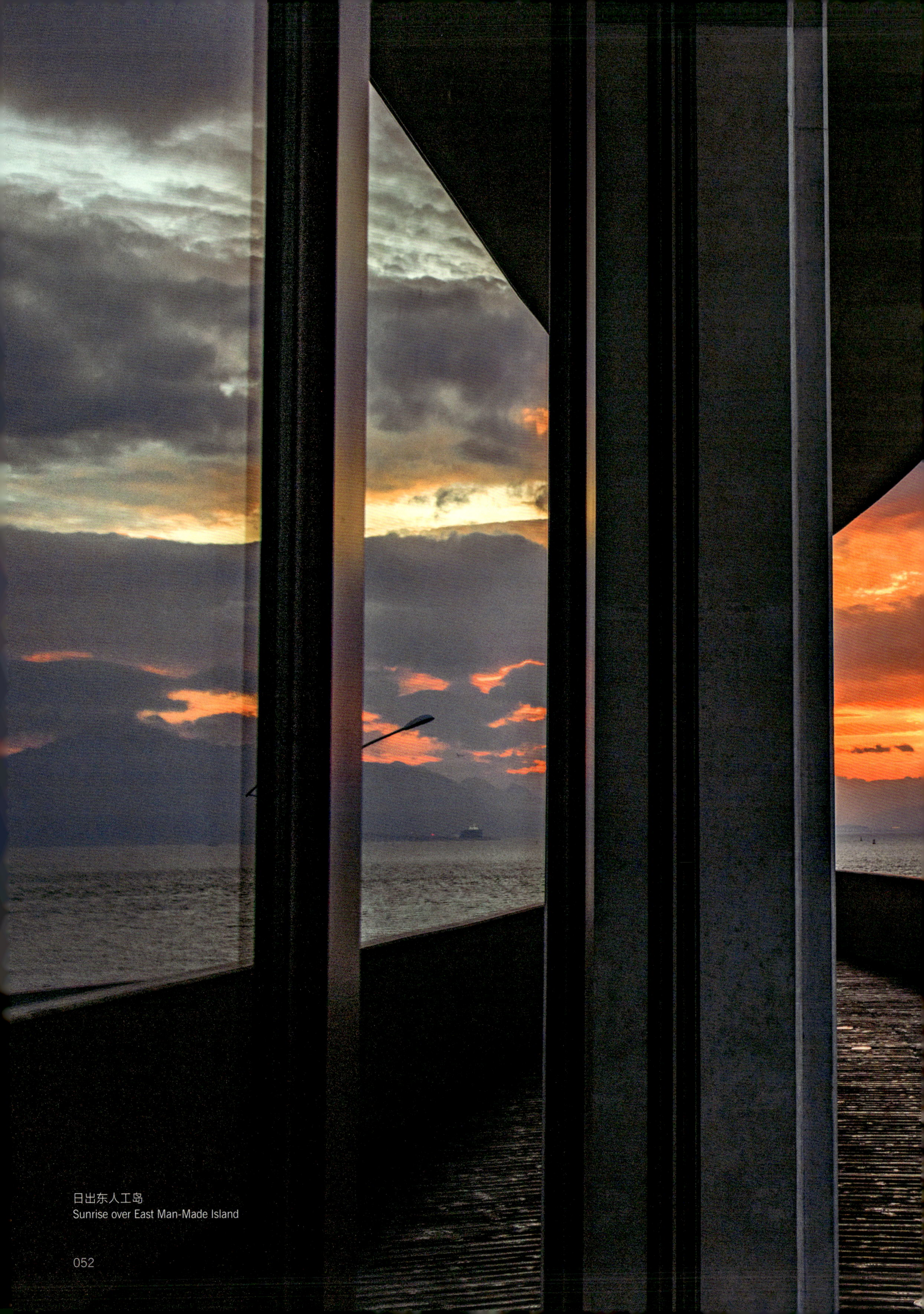

日出东人工岛
Sunrise over East Man-Made Island

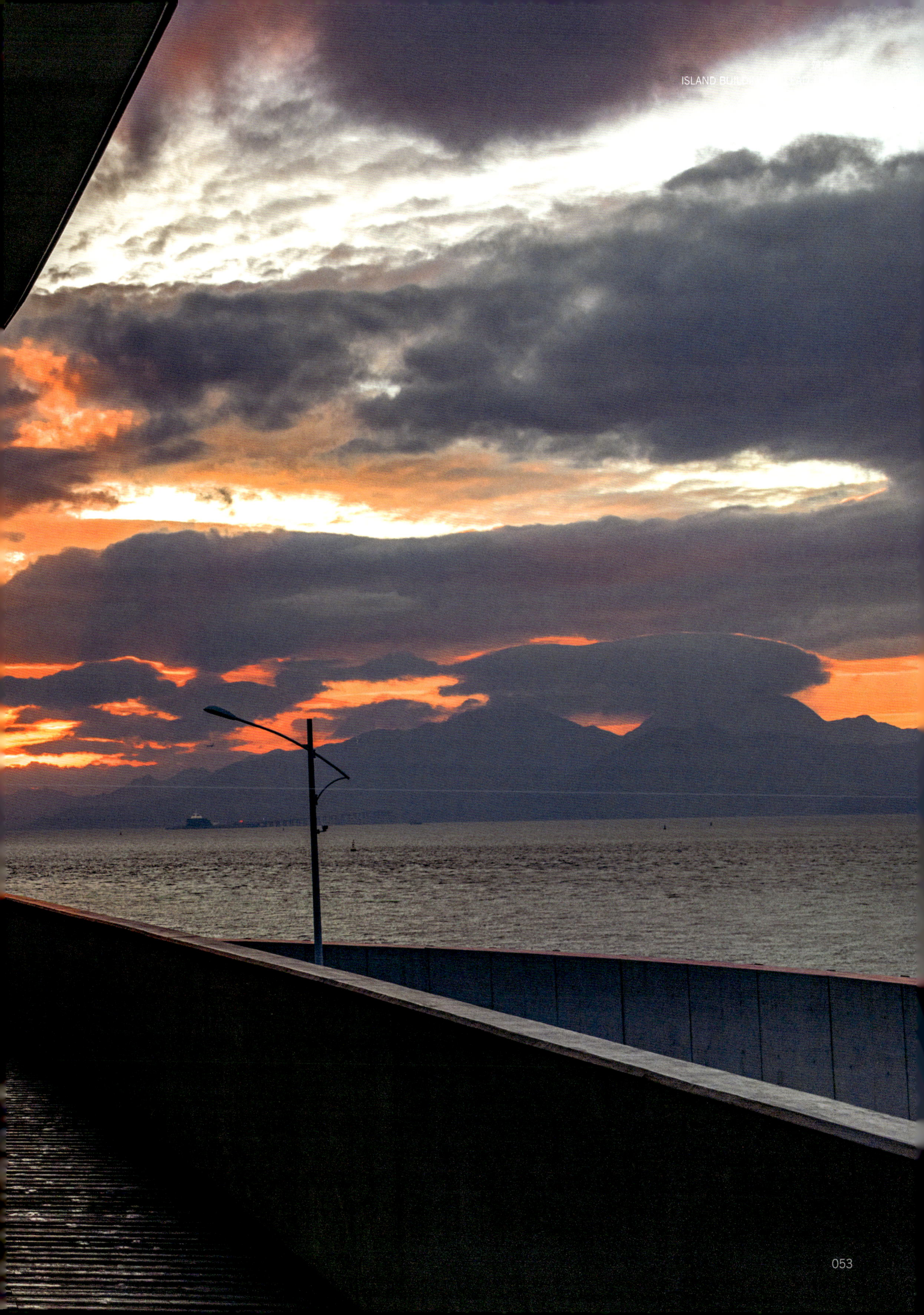

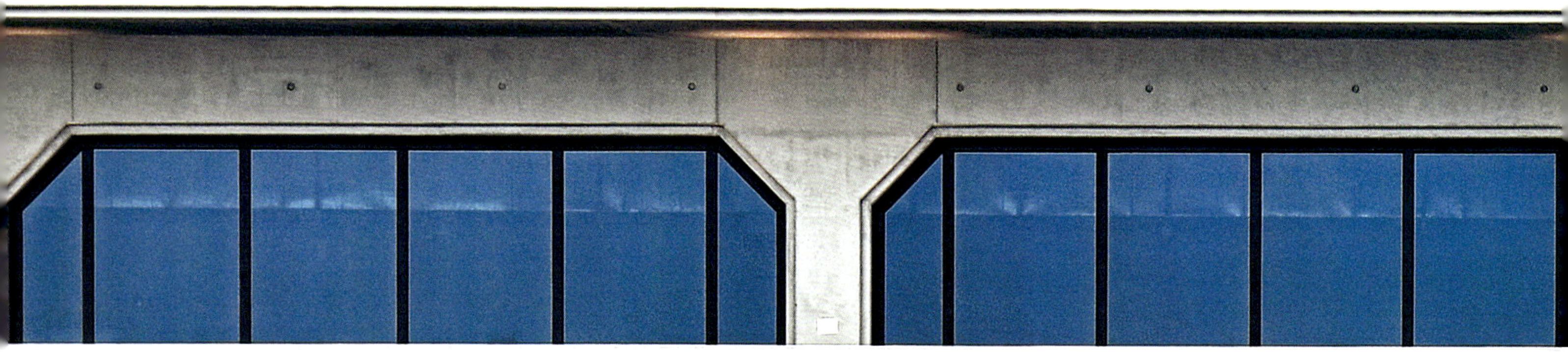

以这一刻的安详和静谧，
静待狂风巨浪随时而至的冲击。

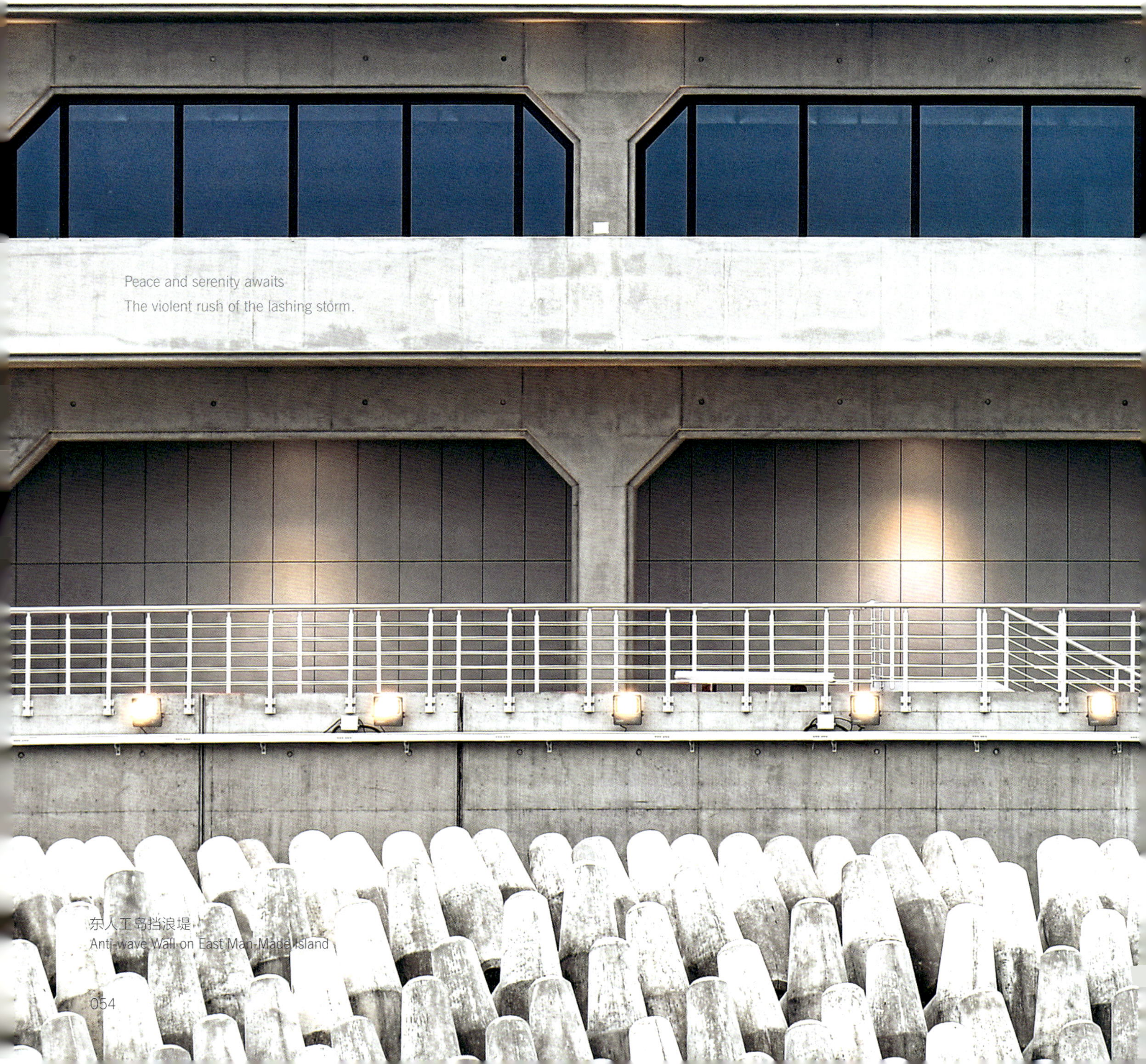

Peace and serenity awaits
The violent rush of the lashing storm.

东人工岛挡浪堤
Anti-wave Wall on East Man-Made Island

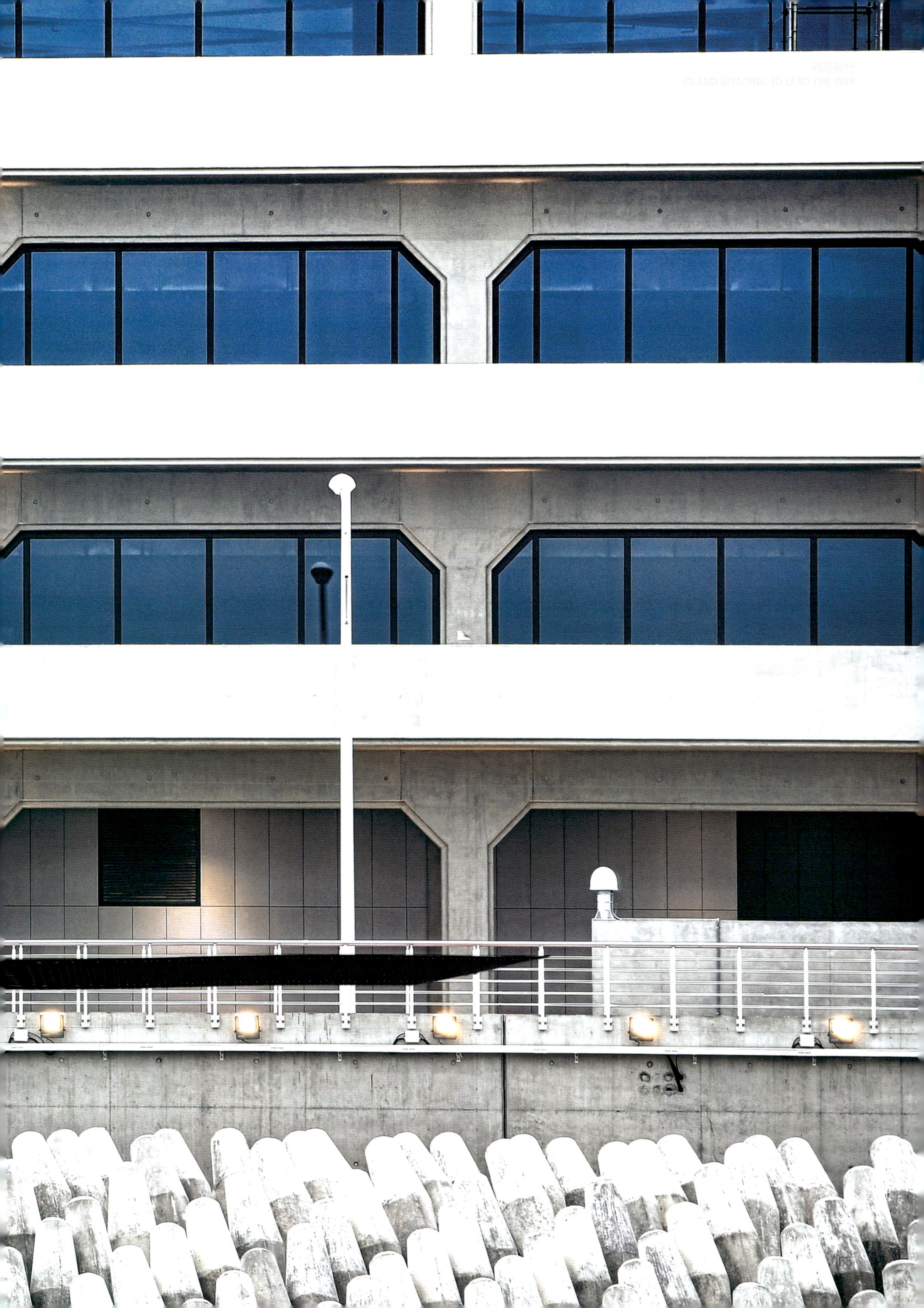

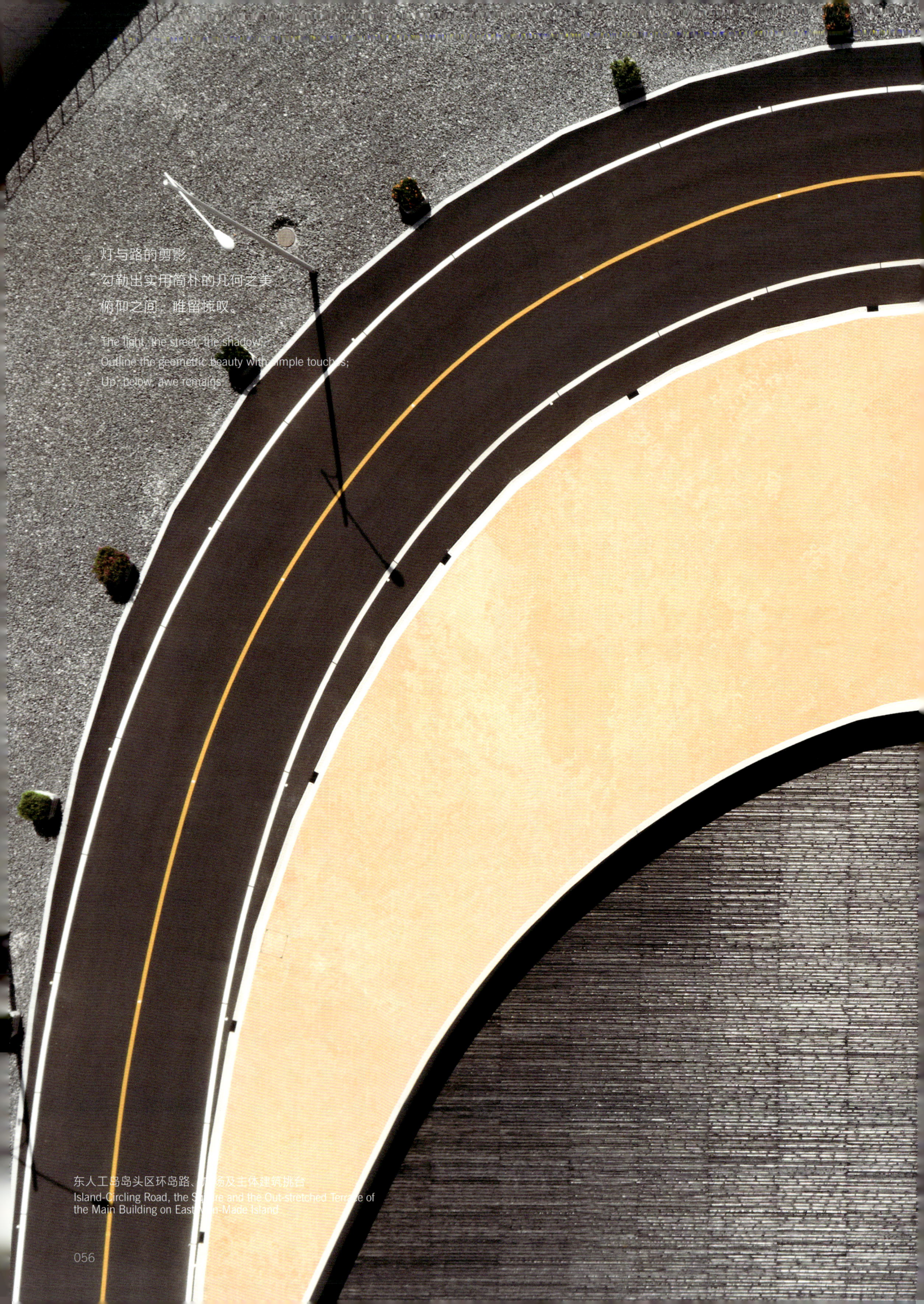

灯与路的剪影，
勾勒出实用简朴的凡何之美，
俯仰之间，唯留惊叹。

The light, the street, the shadow;
Outline the geometric beauty with simple touches;
Up, below, awe remains.

东人工岛岛头区环岛路、广场及主体建筑挑台
Island-Circling Road, the Square and the Out-stretched Terrace of the Main Building on East Man-Made Island

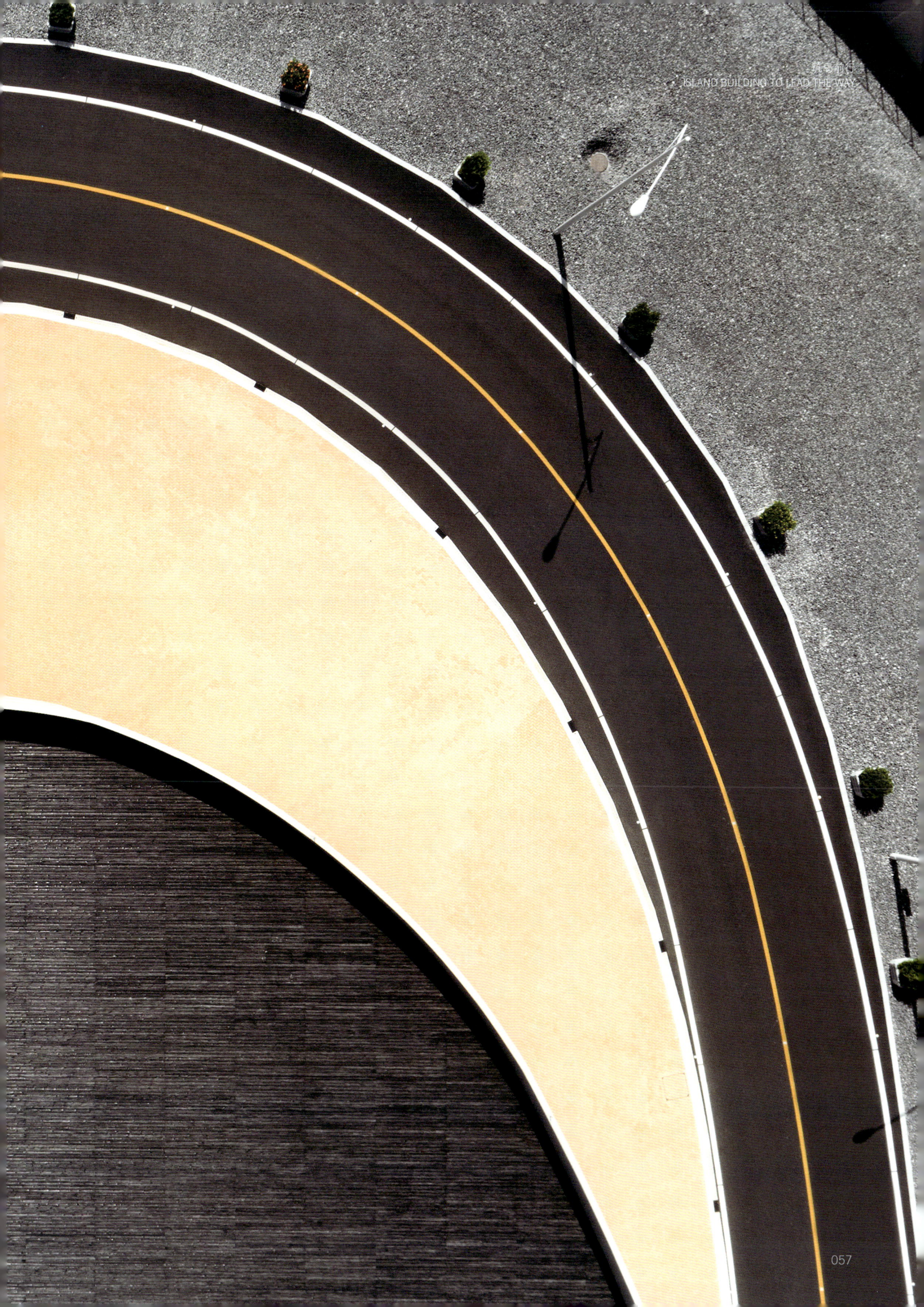

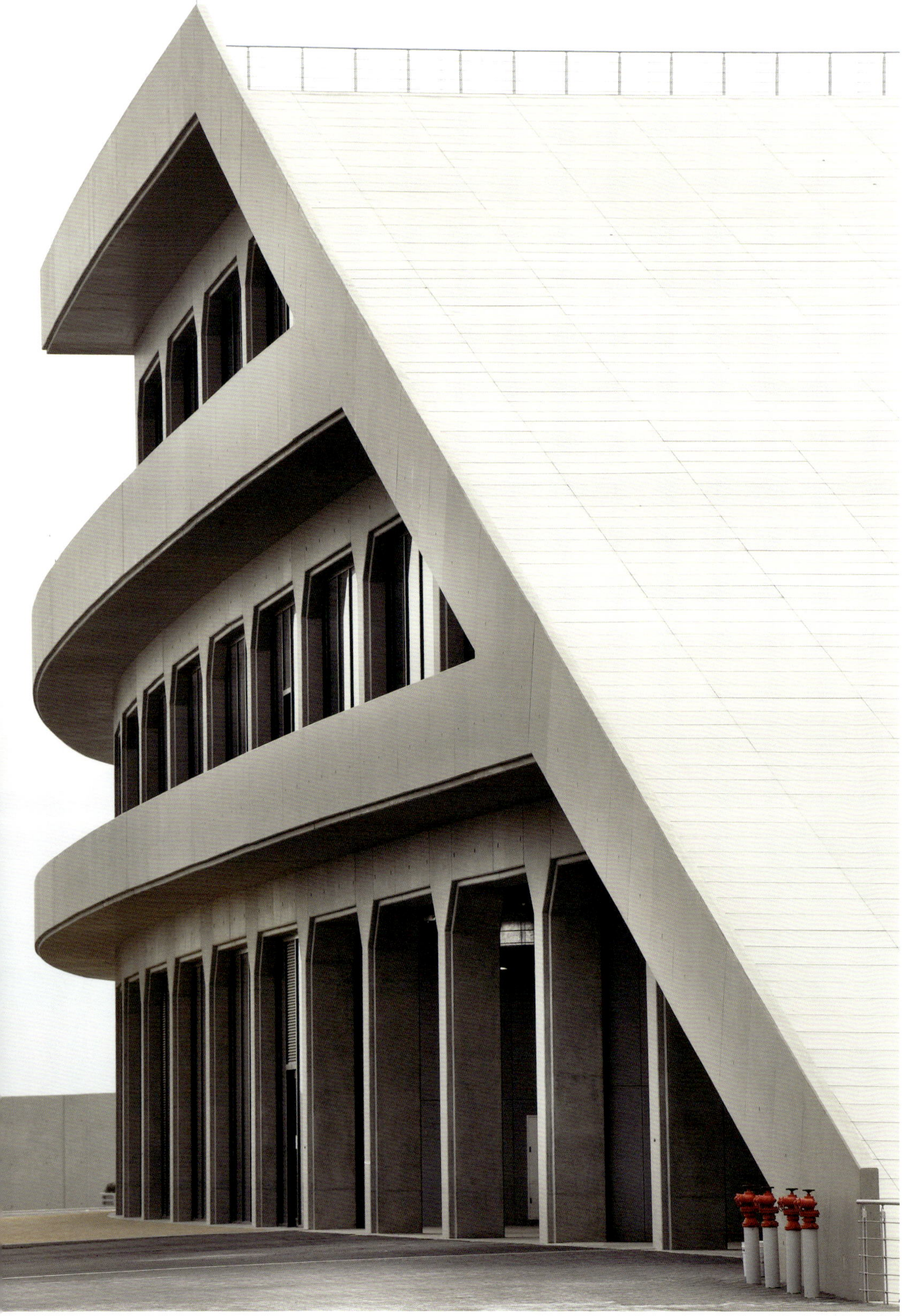

1. 西人工岛主体建筑大斜面
Big Slope of the Main Building on West Man-Made Island
2. 东人工岛主体建筑大台阶
Grand Step of the Main Building on East Man-Made Island

简朴的造型，营造了与生俱来的清雅；
极致的坚守，打造出返本溯源的无华。

Homely shapes awake homely elegance in-born;
Persistence obstinate traces simple beauty within.

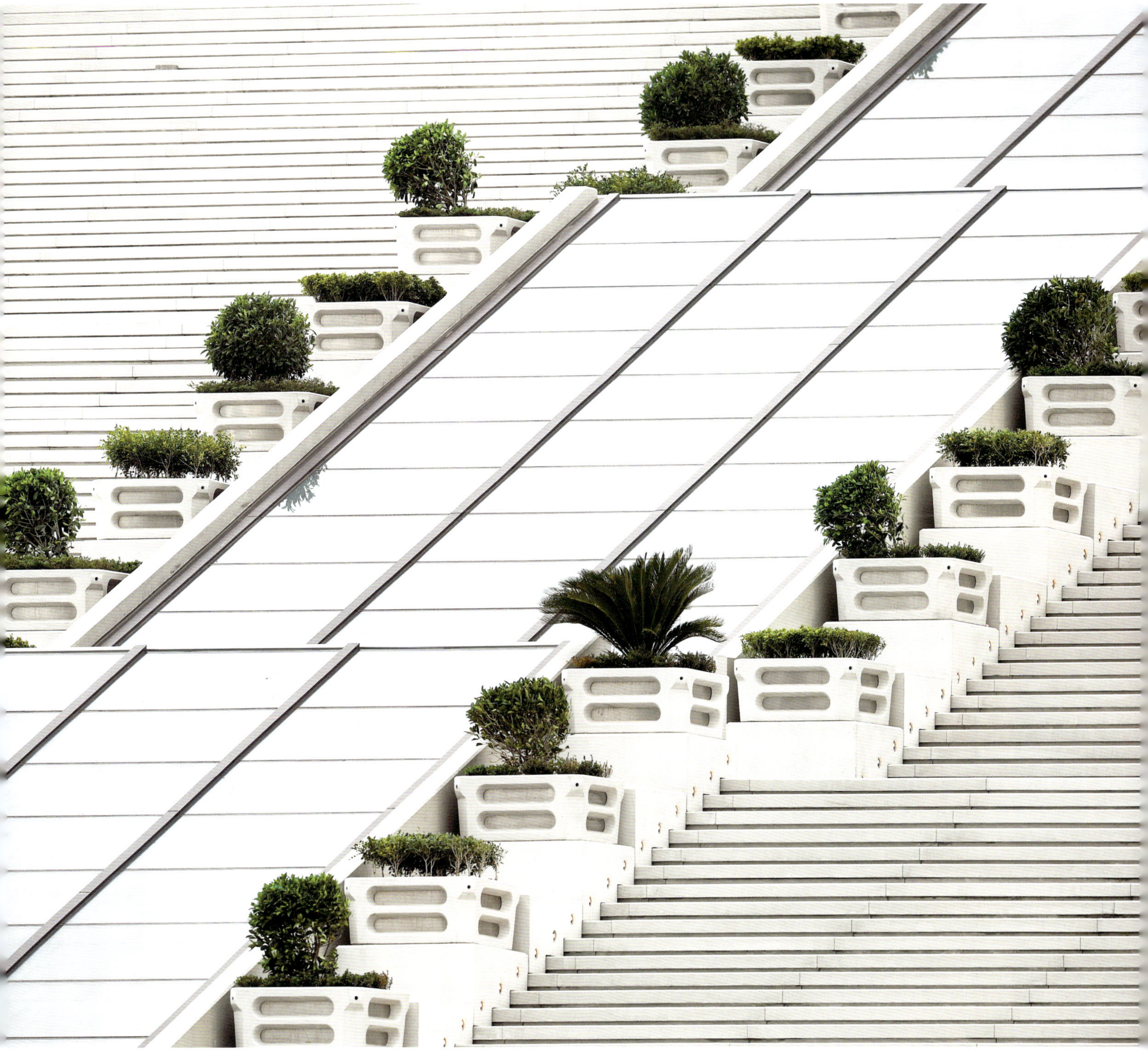

东人工岛主体建筑大台阶全貌
Global Overall View of the Grand Step of the Main Building on East Man-Made Island

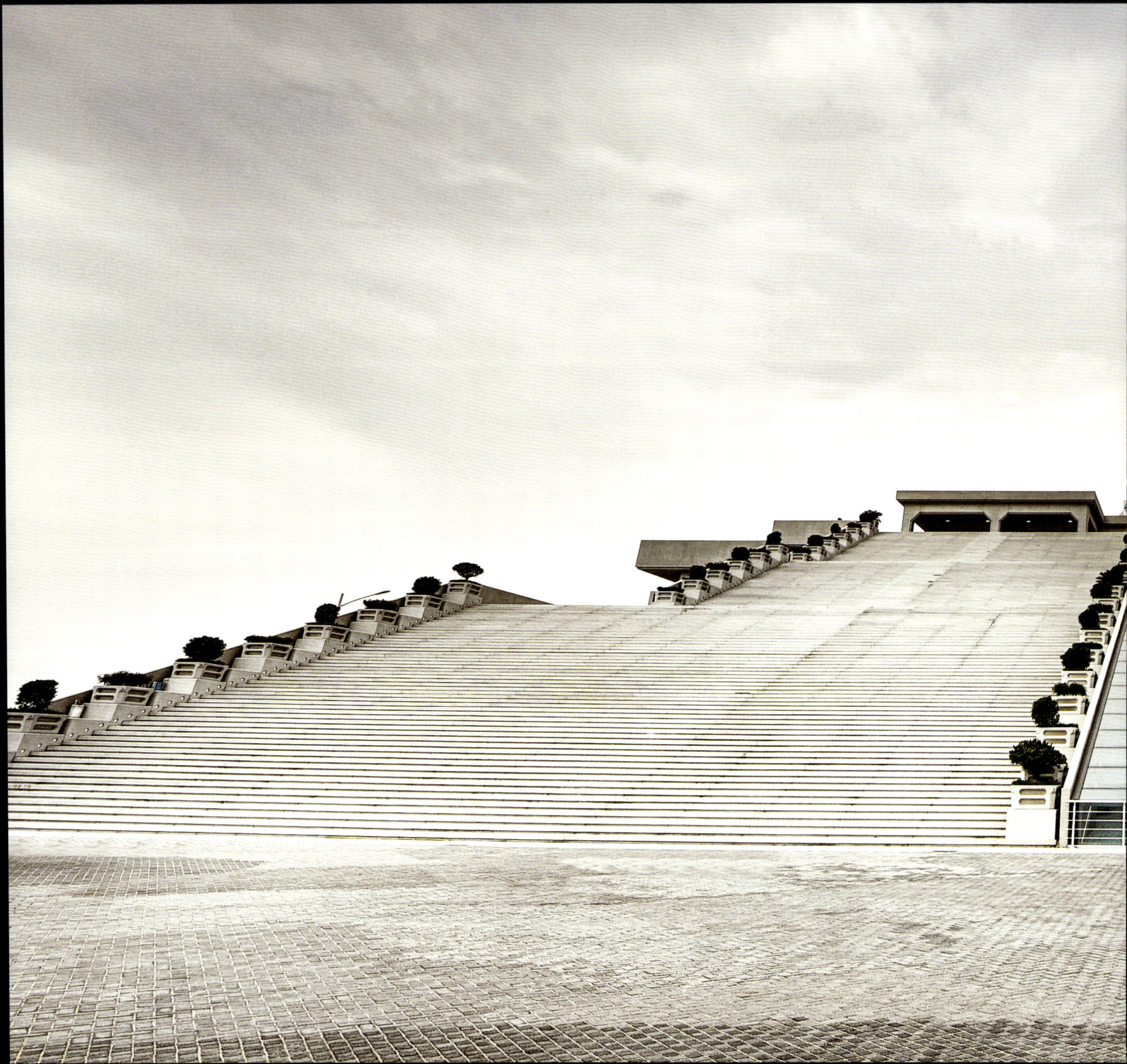

沿着大台阶拾级而上，感受着120年的厚重。

Standing on the grand steps, we harvest the grandeur of 120 years' in the past.

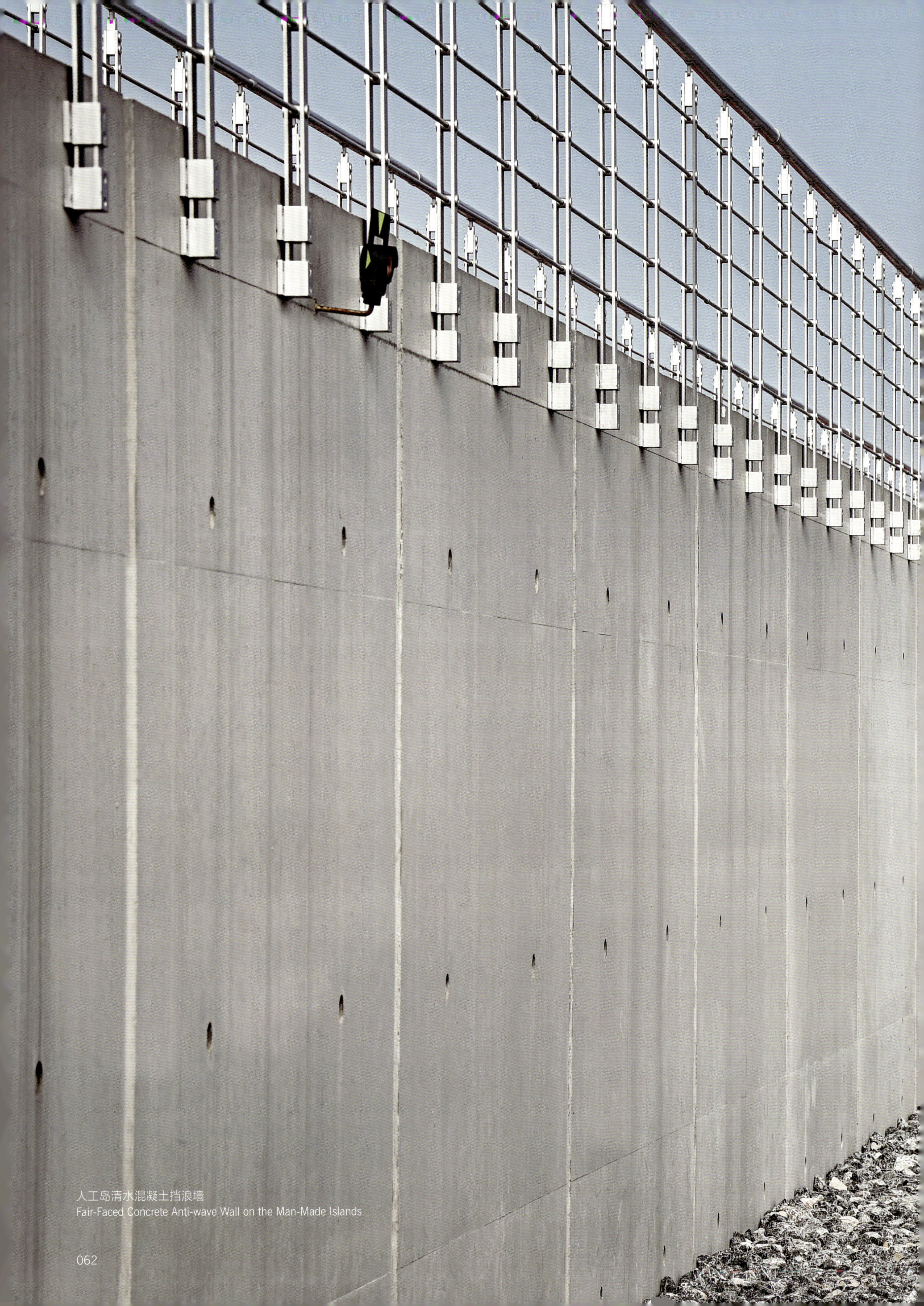

人工岛清水混凝土挡浪墙
Fair-Faced Concrete Anti-wave Wall on the Man-Made Islands

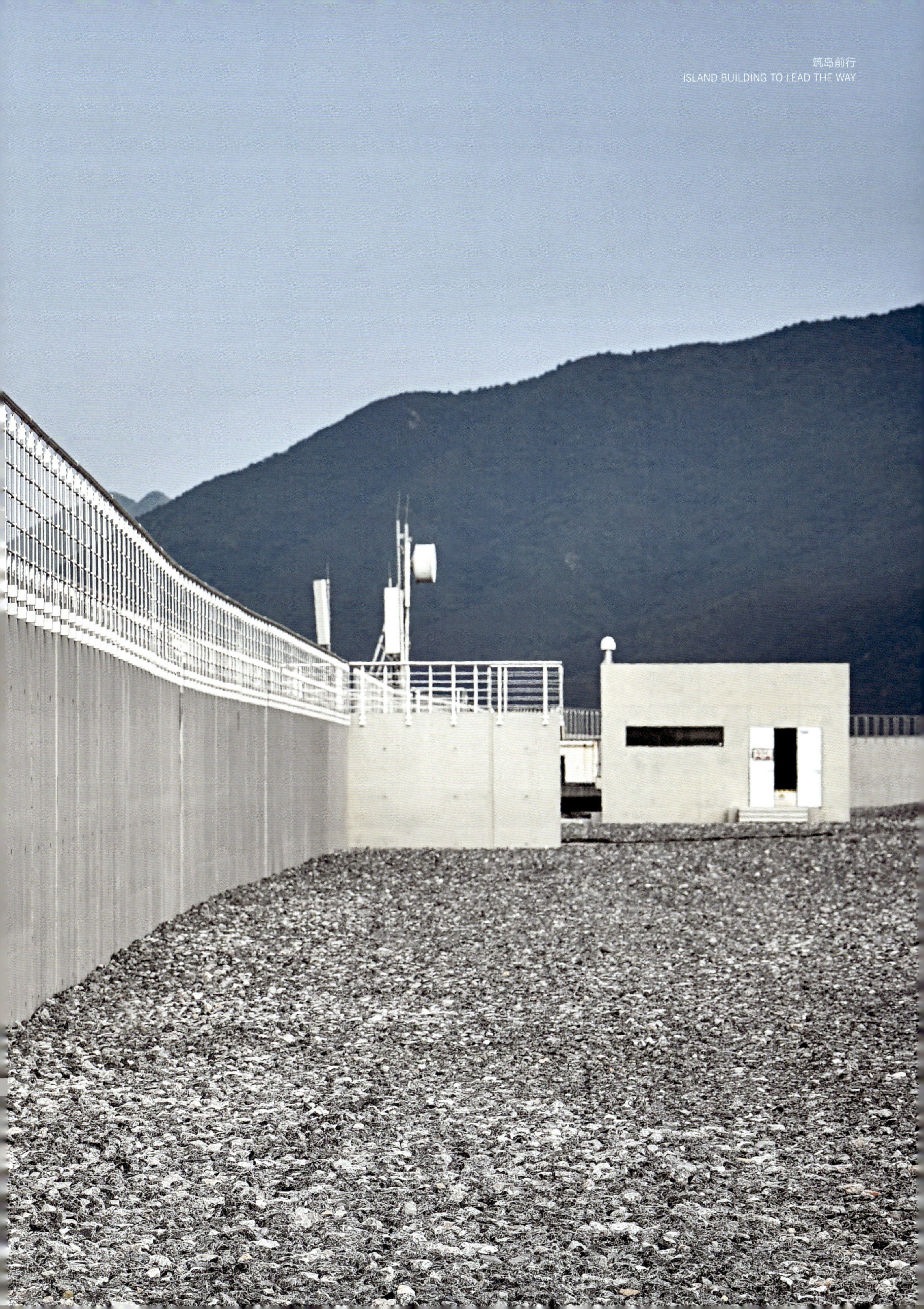

1. 人工岛越浪泵房
Pump Drainage Station on the Man-Made Islands
2. 清水混凝土景观花盆墩
Flower-Pot Pillar Cast with Fair-Faced Concrete

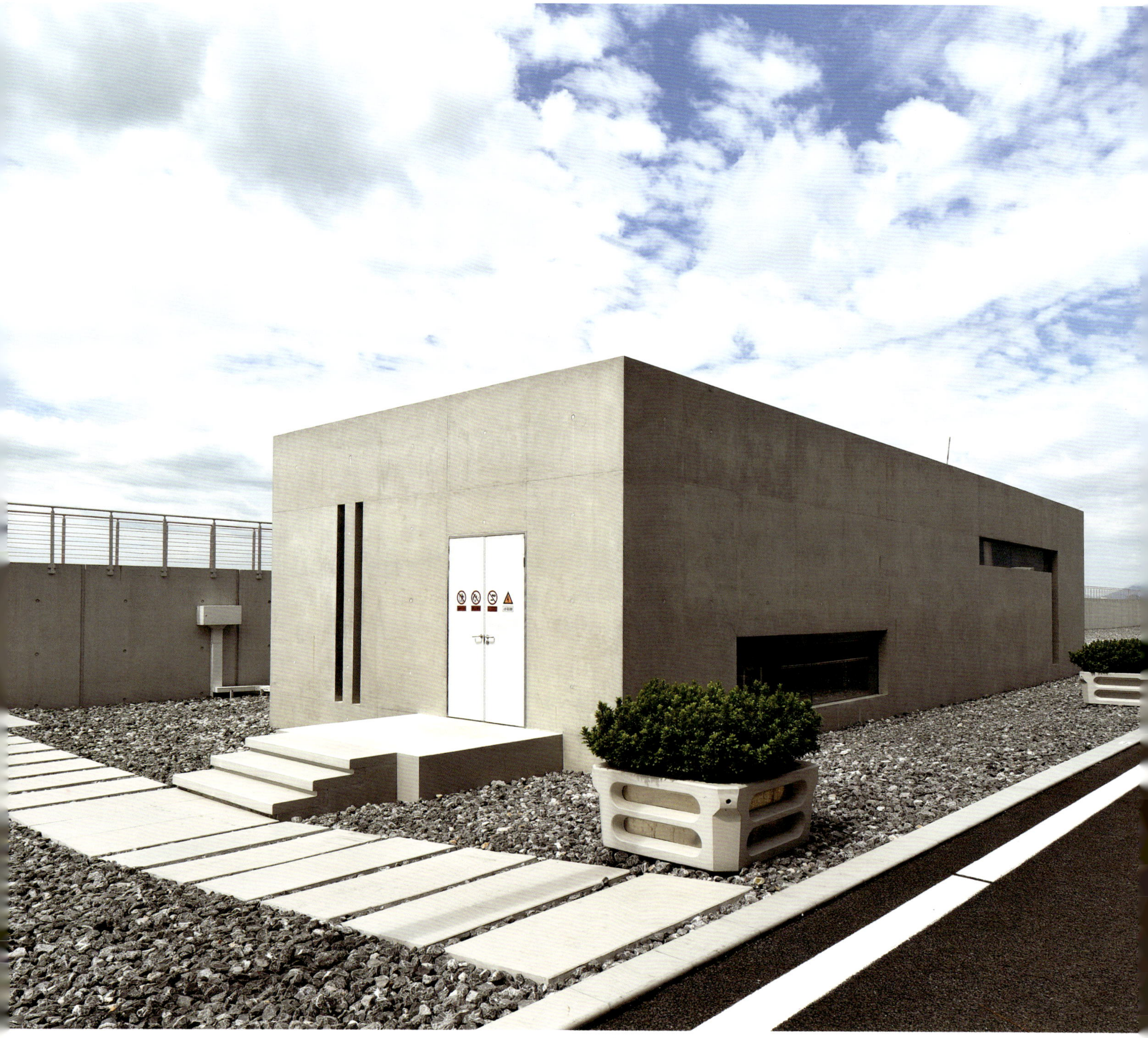

方寸之间，生机盎然。一道一台，尽显匠心。

Delicate but overflowing with life, a piece here and a piece there sketch human ingenuity.

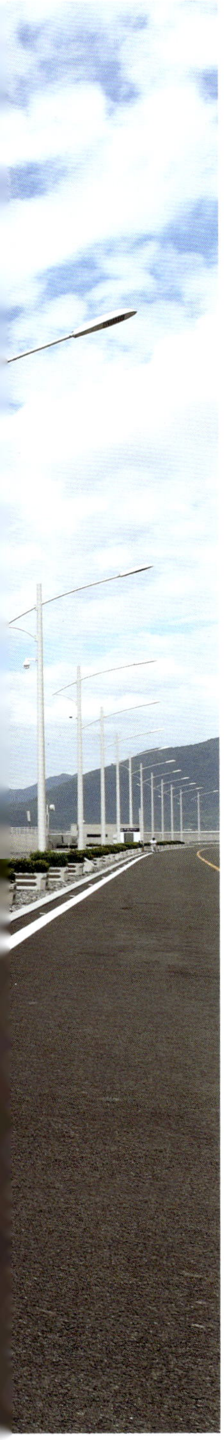

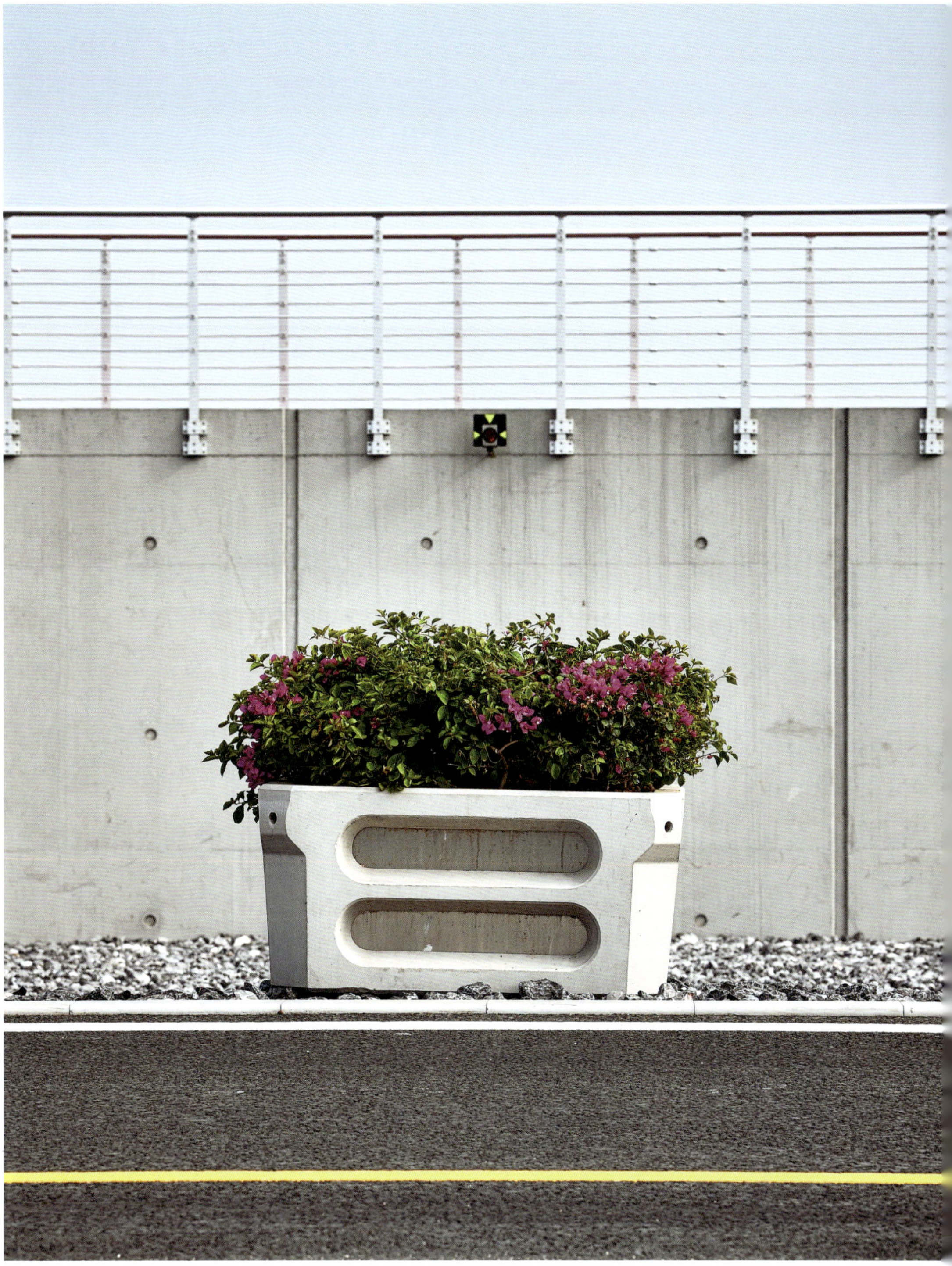

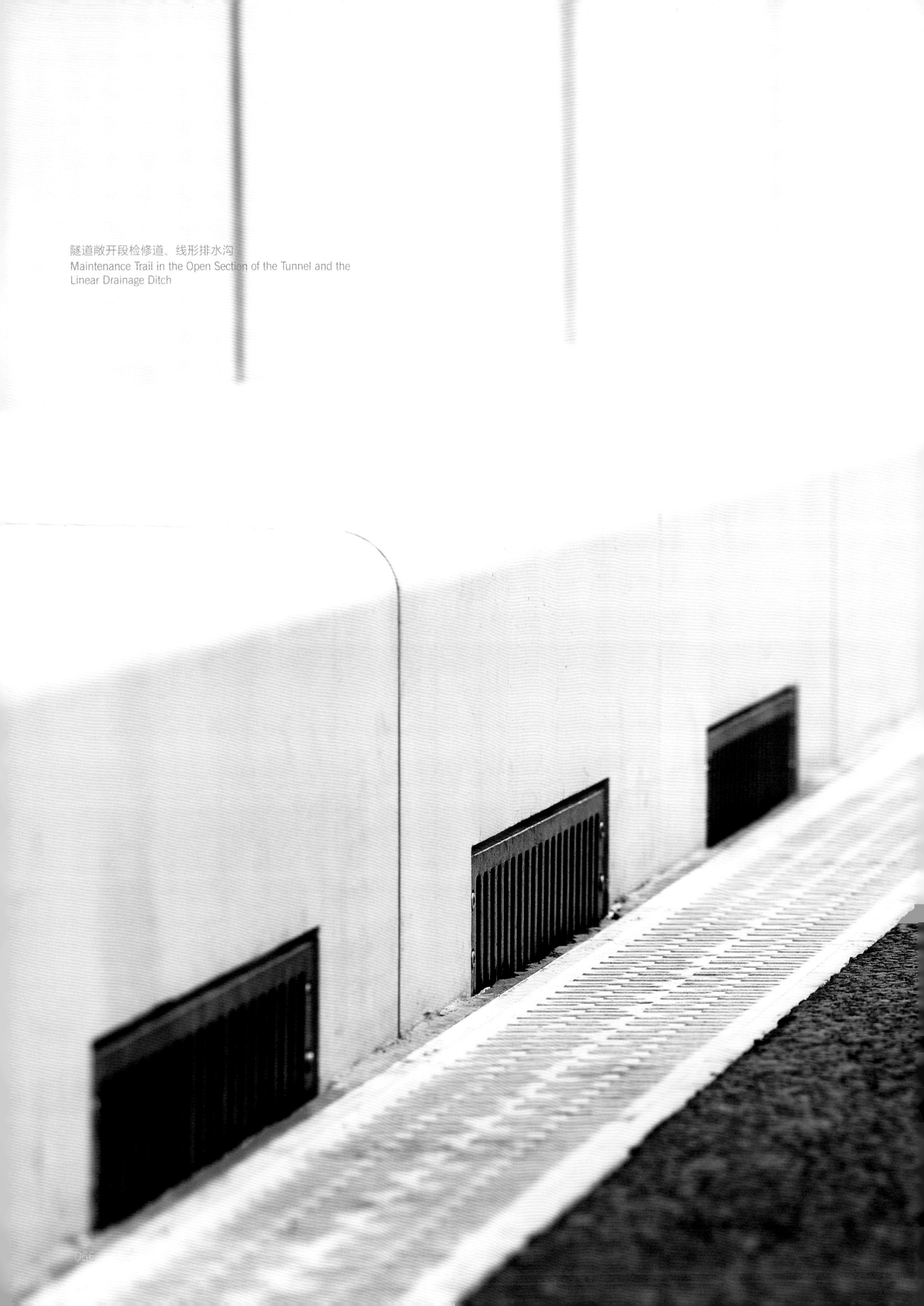

隧道敞开段检修道、线形排水沟
Maintenance Trail in the Open Section of the Tunnel and the Linear Drainage Ditch

一点、一面、一空间，

是深思细琢的佳作，是工程美学的极致追求。

The angle, the wall, the space are all children of minds pursuing the ultimate architectural beauty.

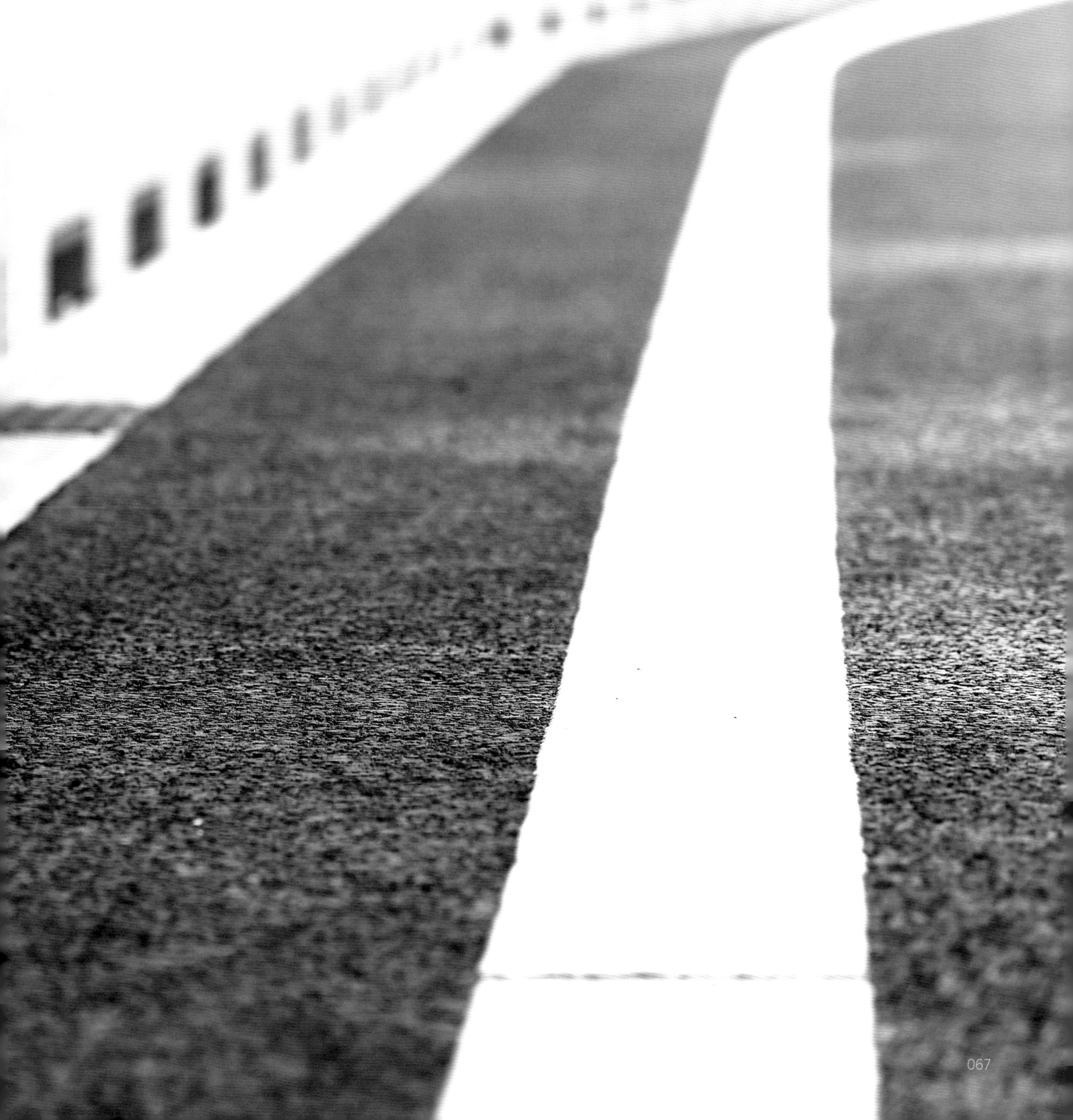

东人工岛救援码头
Rescue Dock on East Man-Made Island

桥岛相依，海山相连。
东人工岛岛桥结合部与香港新机场和大屿山近在咫尺。

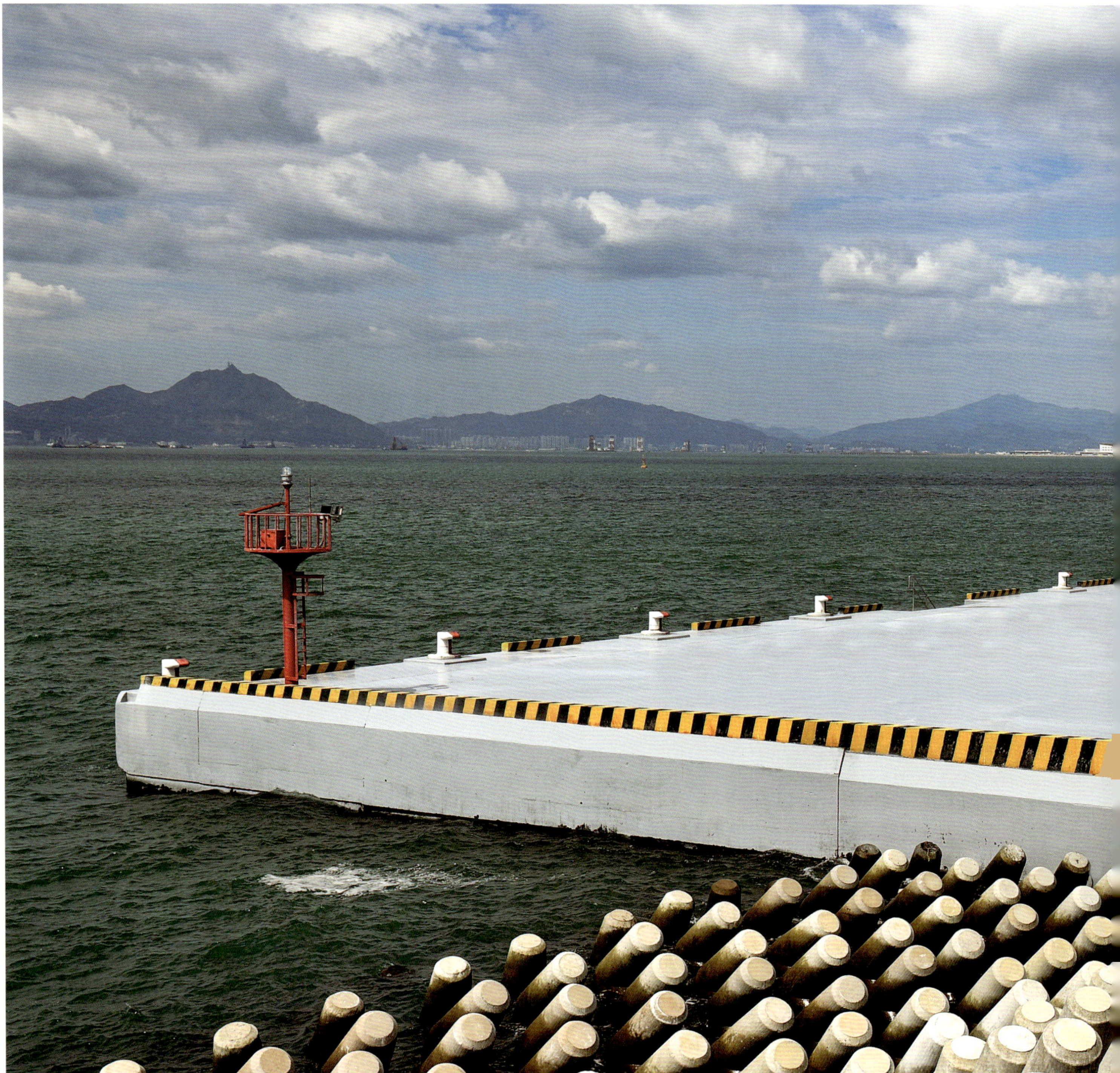

The island, the bridge, the mountain, and the sea.

East Man-Made Island where the Bridge runs into is not far from the new airport of Hong Kong and Lantau Island.

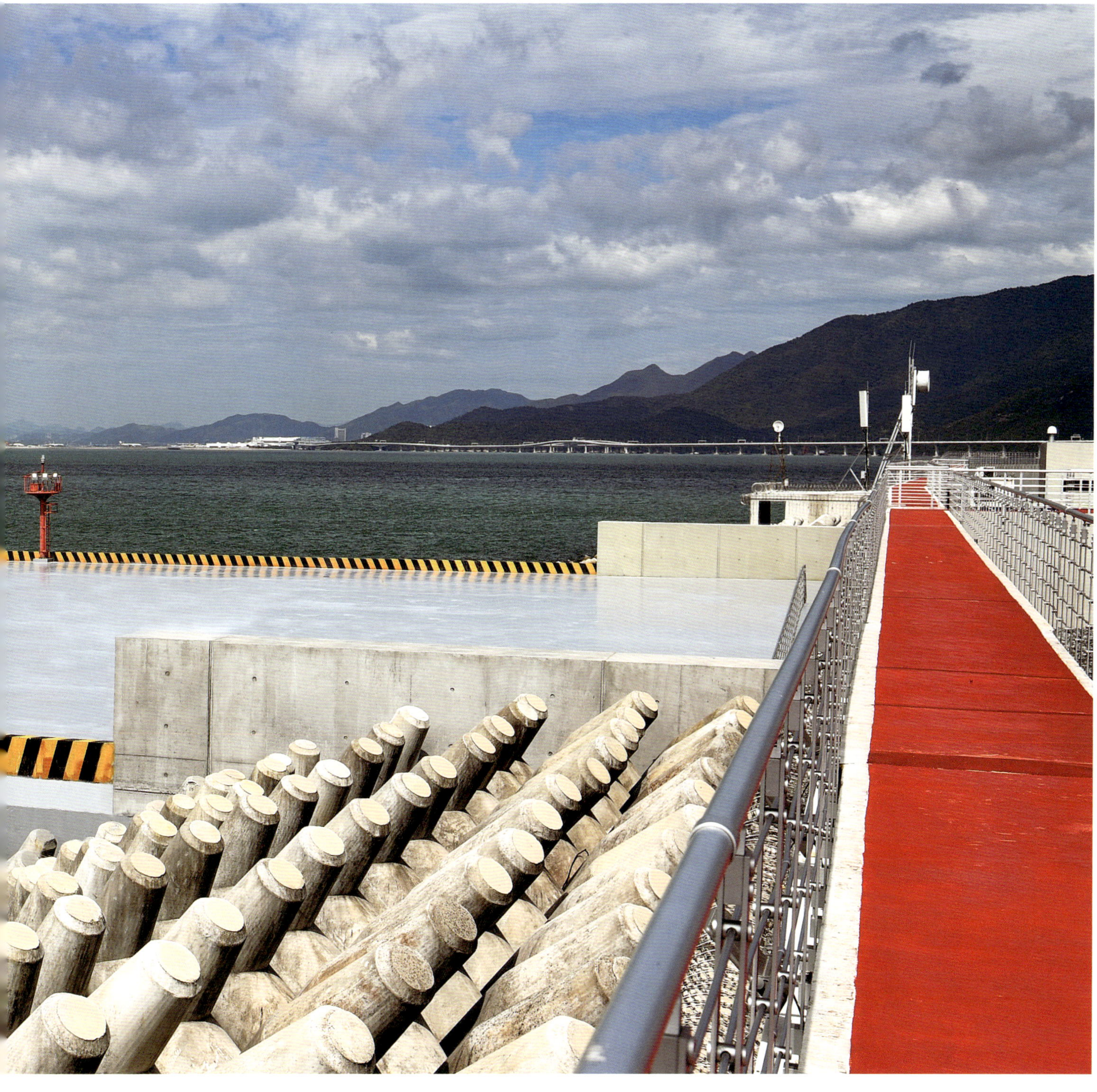

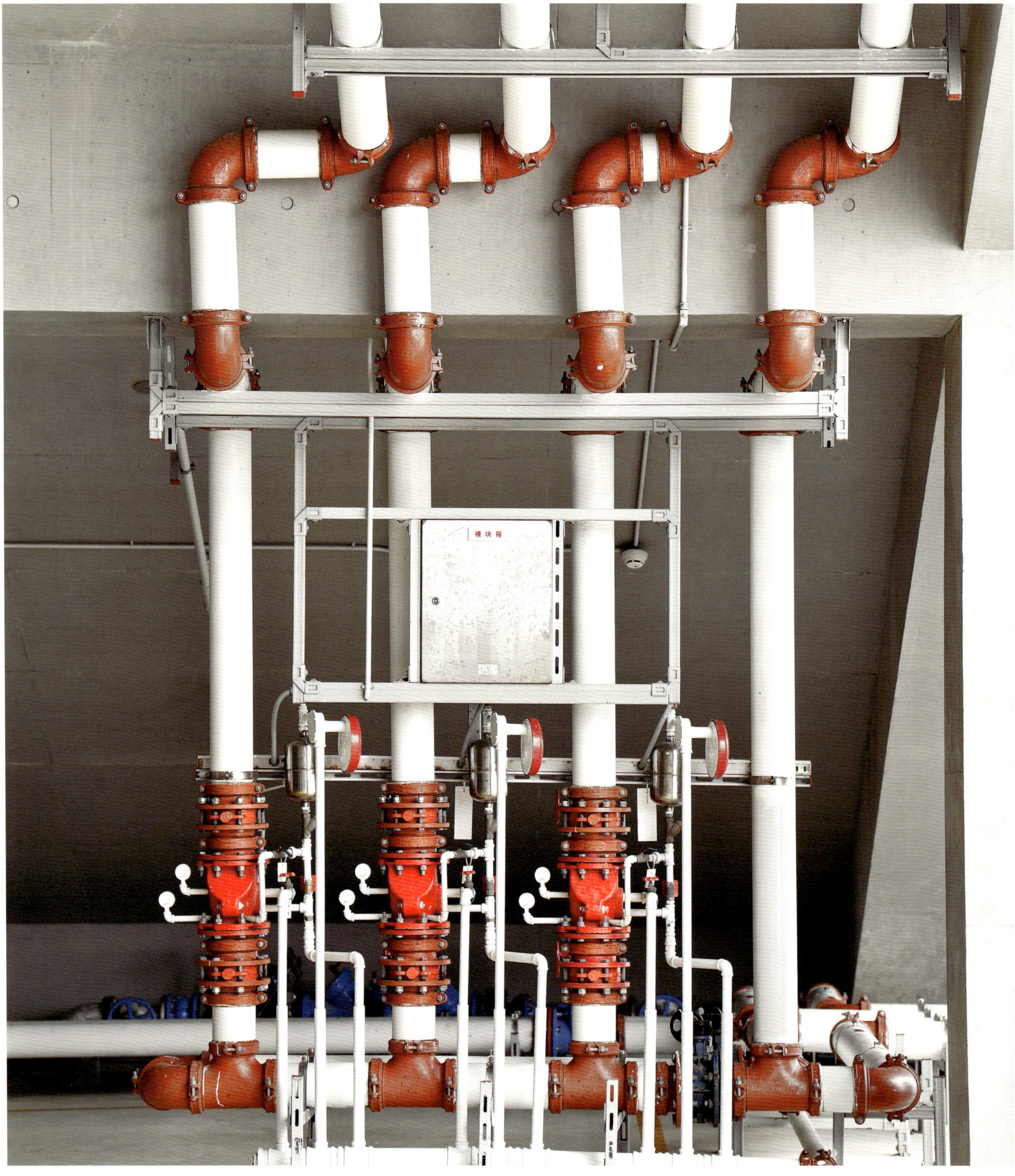
模 块 箱

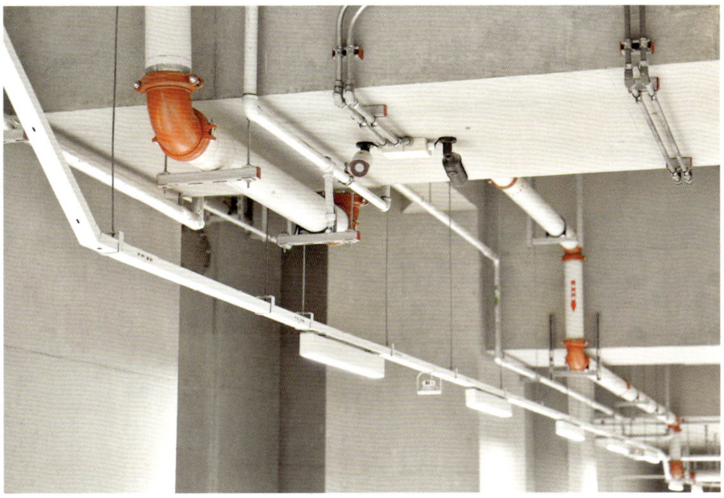

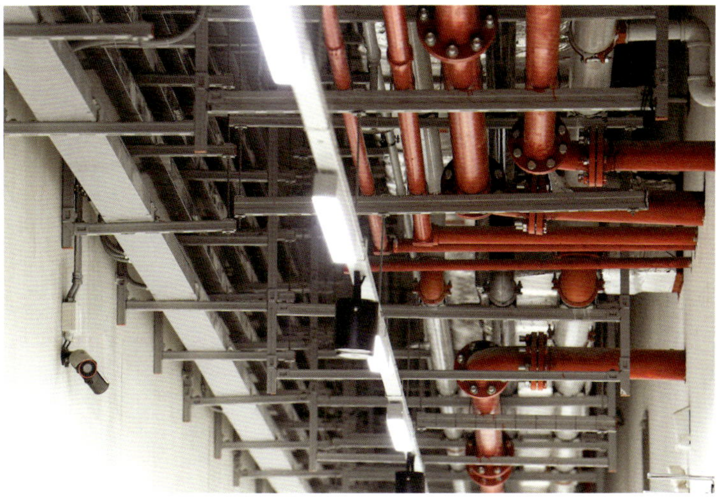

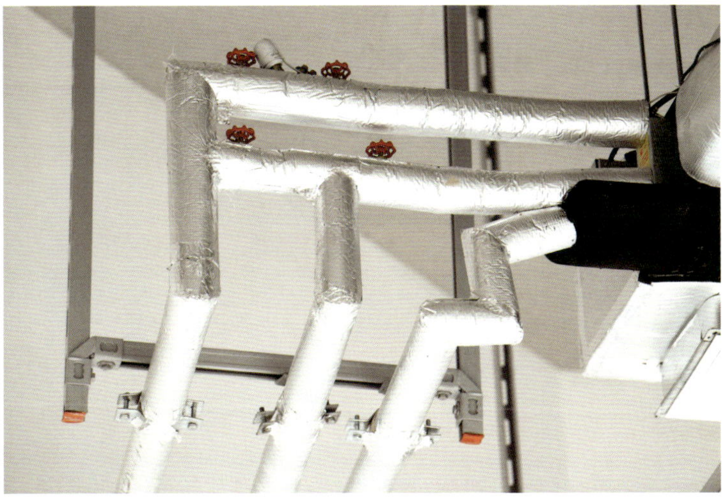

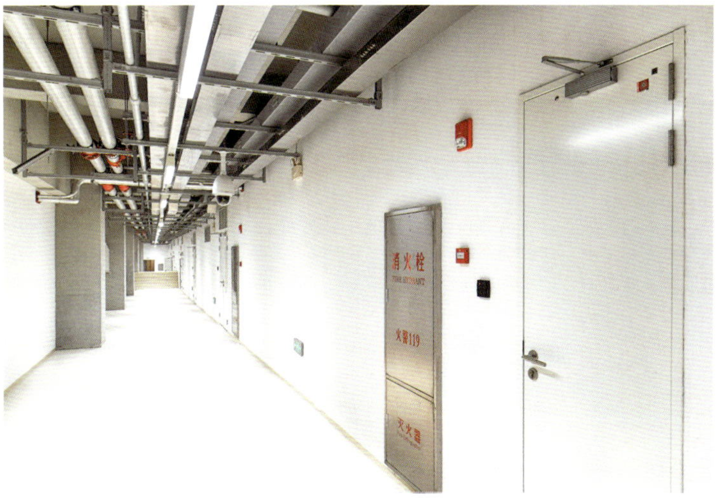

1	2	3
	4	5

1. 主体建筑消防管道
   Fire-Fighting Pipeline in the Main Building
2. 主体建筑室内照明设备
   In-door Lighting Equipment in the Main Building
3. 主体建筑室内消防管道及吊架
   In-door Fire-Fighting Pipeline and Hanging Bracket in the Main Building
4. 主体建筑室内空调管道
   In-door Air-Conditioner Pipeline in the Main Building
5. 主体建筑室内消防栓及防火门
   In-door Fire Hydrant and Fire-check Door in the Main Building

表里如一，精细依旧。
虽不是车行要道，
管线密布的综合廊道仍整齐划一，井然有序。

What we see is what it is, neat in order.
What we see is not the principal driving lane,
But the pipes and lines in the composite gallery neatly arranged.

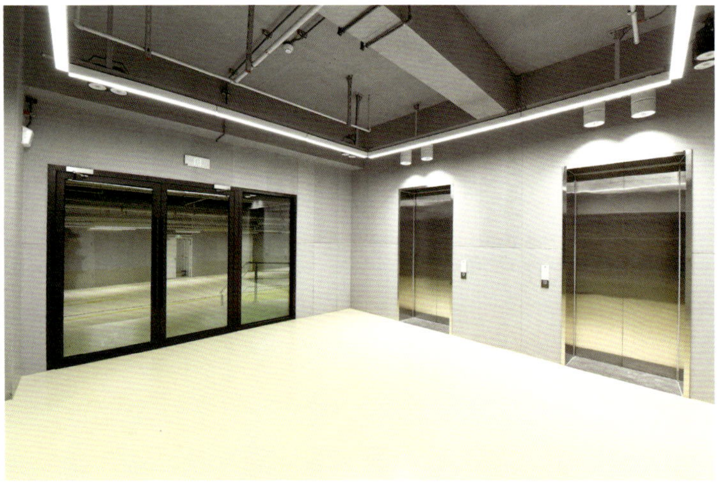

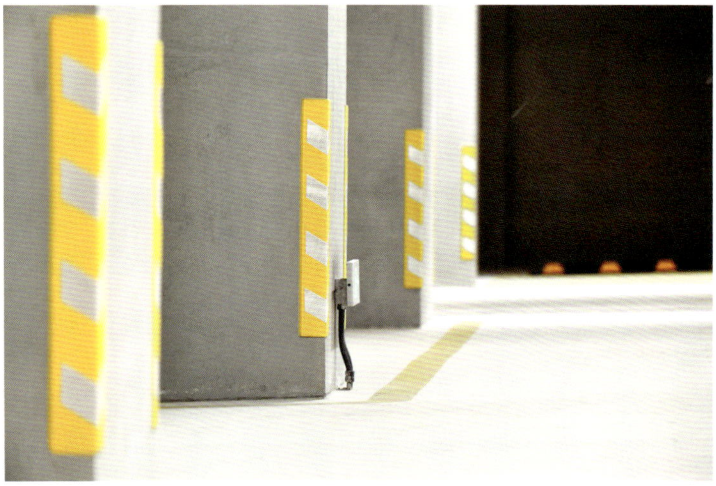

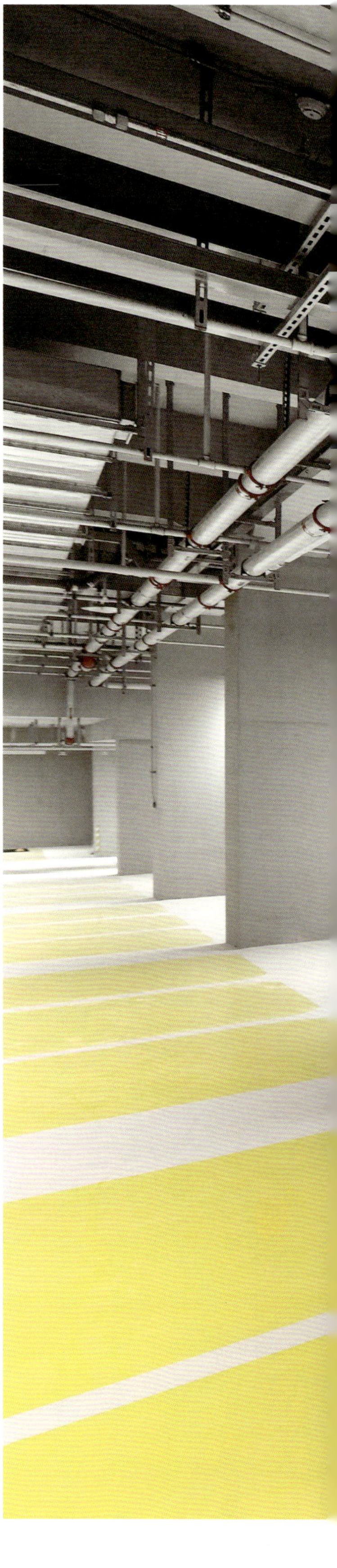

井井有条的管线，明净简洁的立柱，
细致入微的指示，彰显一片匠心。

The pipes orderly arranged,
Simple clean pillars,
Careful instructions,
All are signs of the builders' pursuit for perfection.

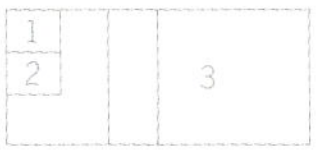

1. 主体建筑电梯间
   Elevator in the Main Building
2. 主体建筑负一层停车场立柱防撞角
   Anti-collision Bar of the Pillar in the Parking Lot on B1 Floor of the Main Building
3. 主体建筑负一层室内停车场
   Parking Lot on B1 Floor of the Main Building

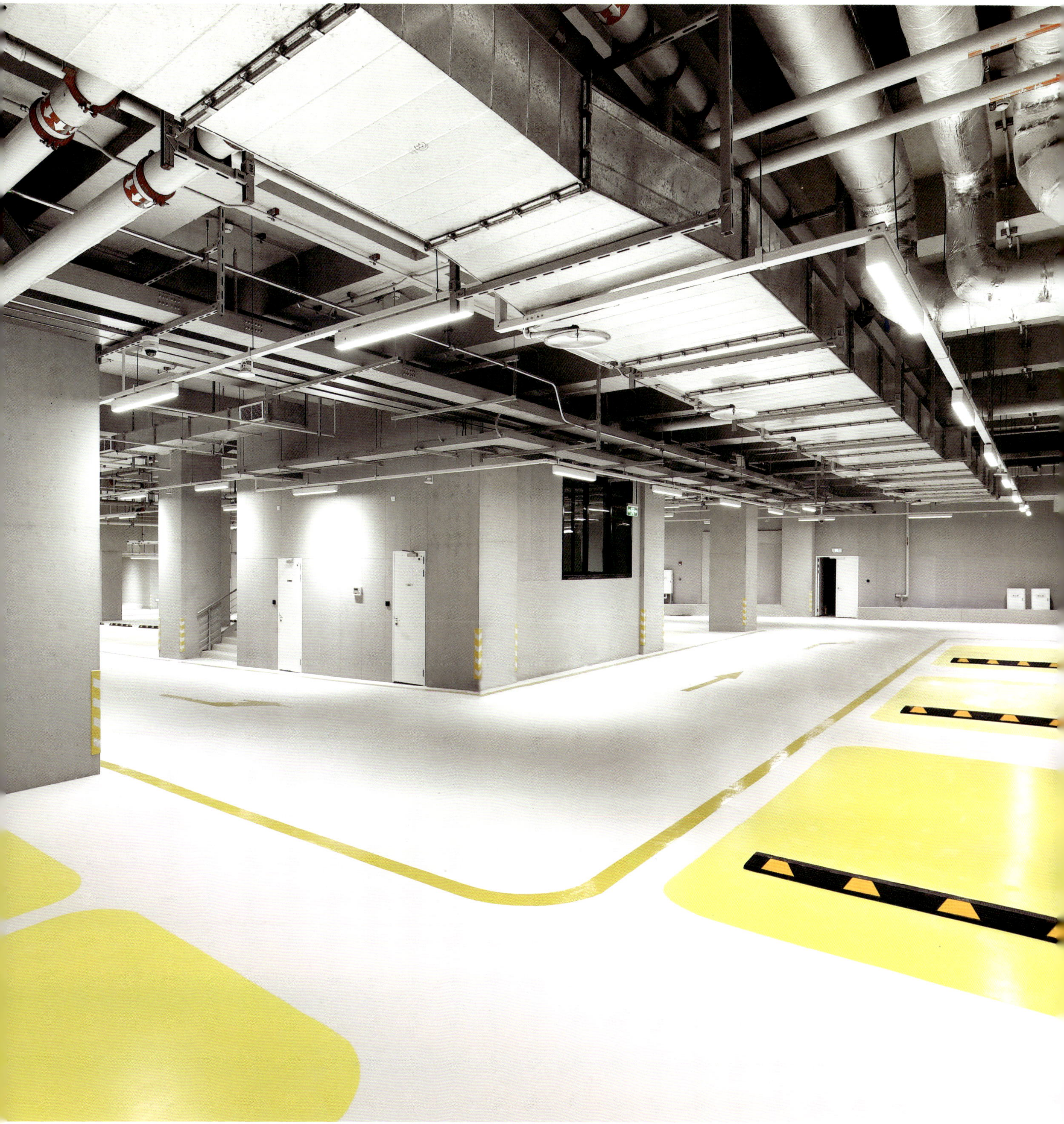

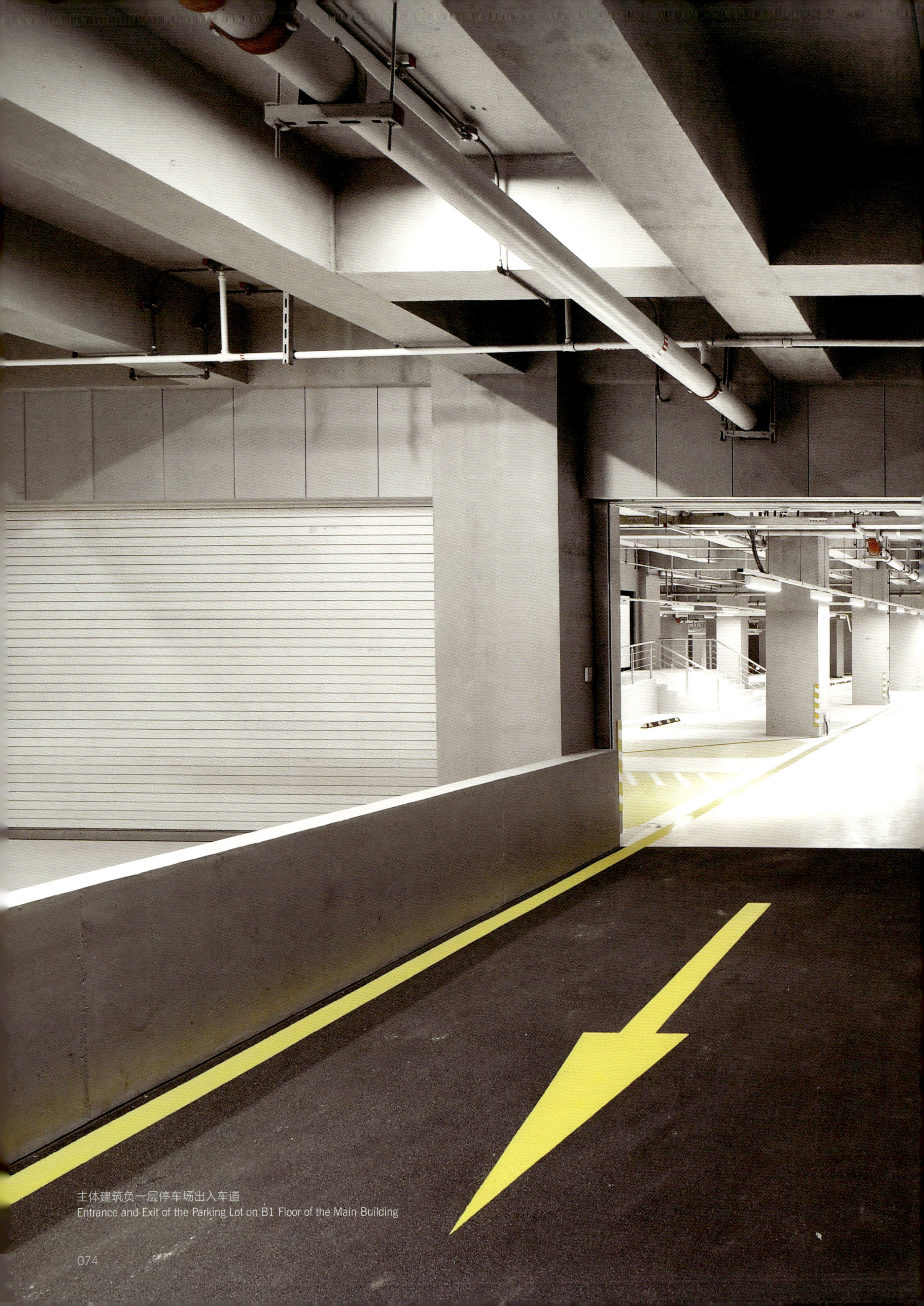

主体建筑负一层停车场出入车道
Entrance and Exit of the Parking Lot on B1 Floor of the Main Building

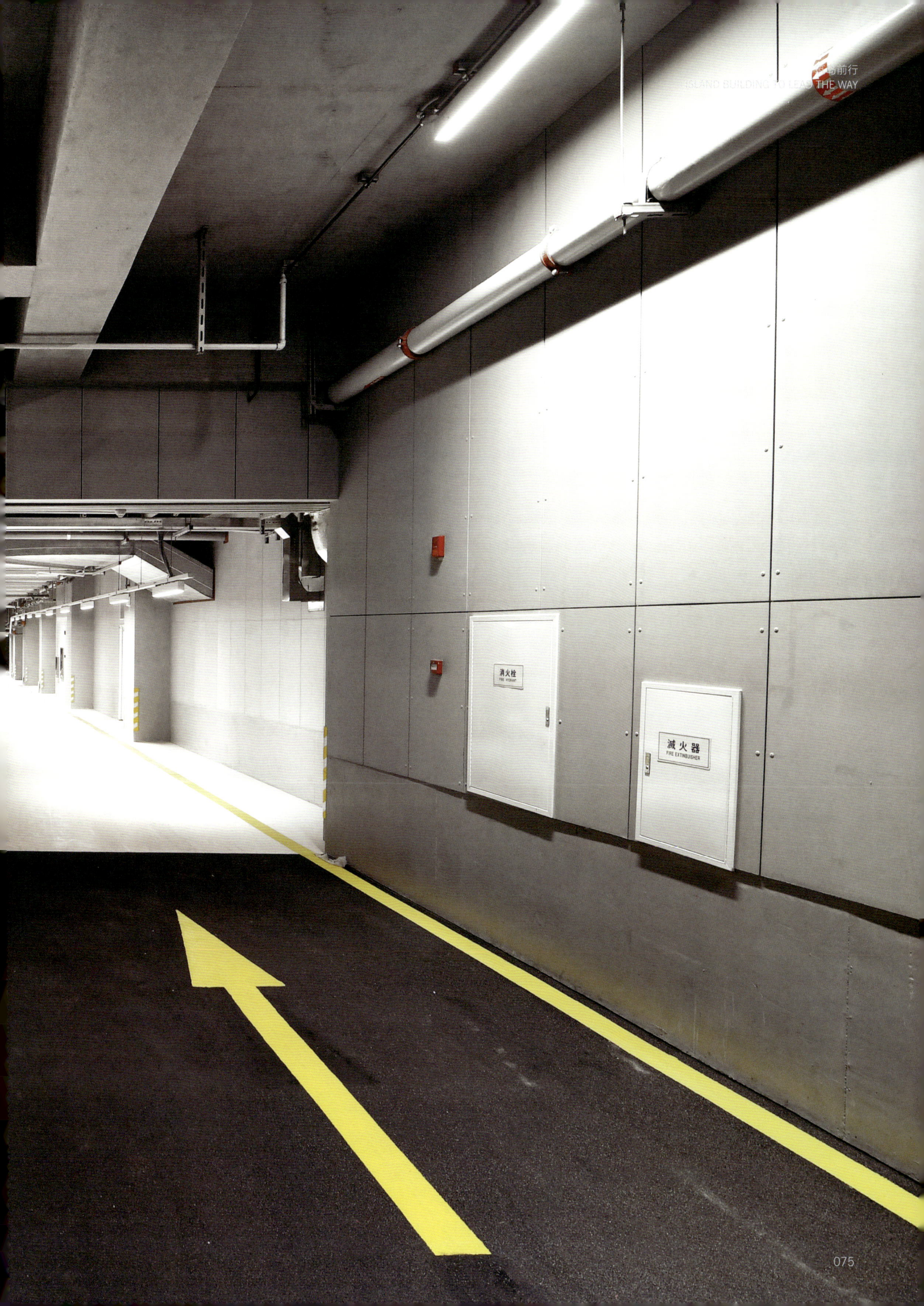
消火栓
FIRE HYDRANT
滅火器
FIRE EXTINGUISHER

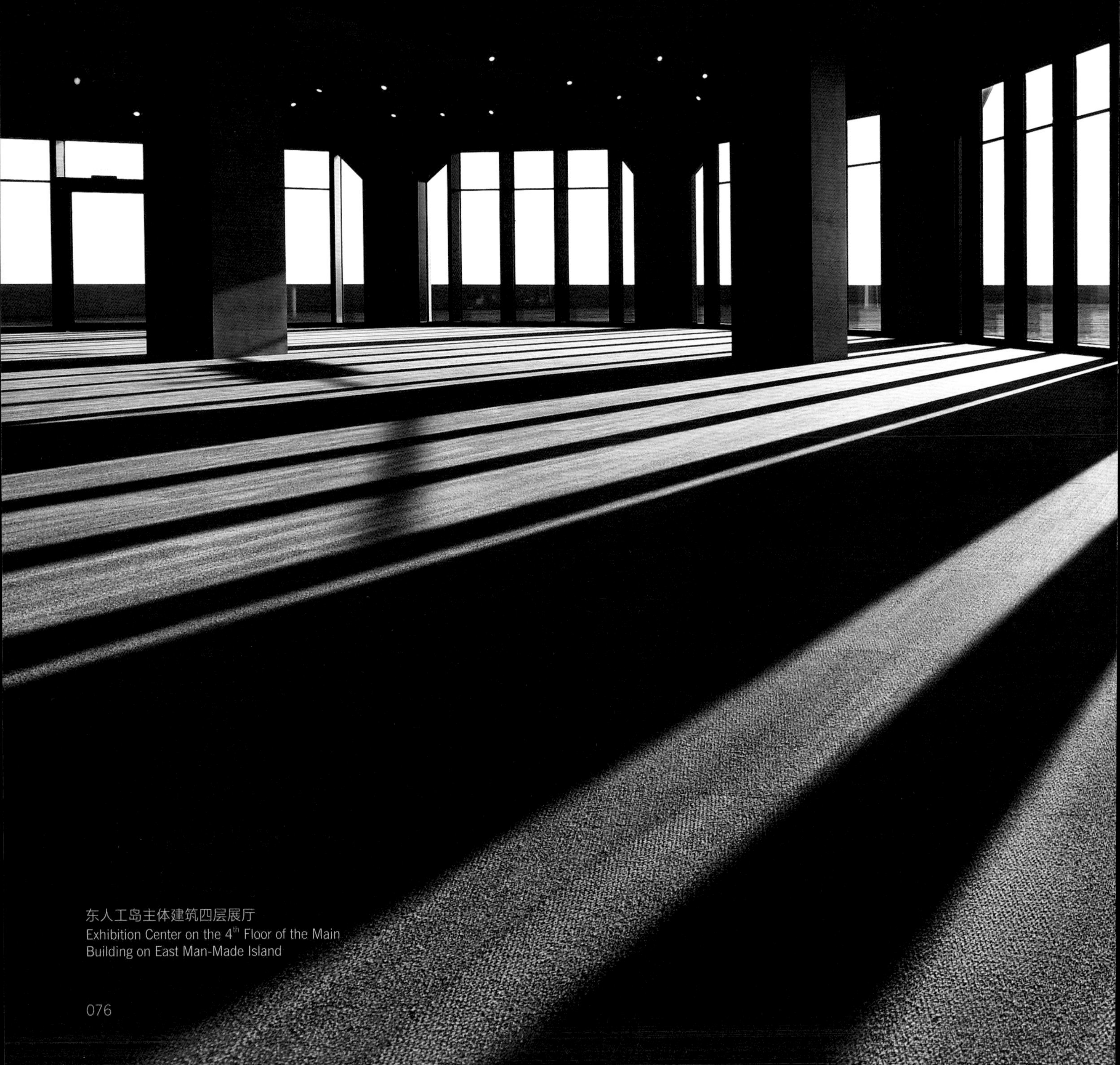

东人工岛主体建筑四层展厅
Exhibition Center on the 4th Floor of the Main Building on East Man-Made Island

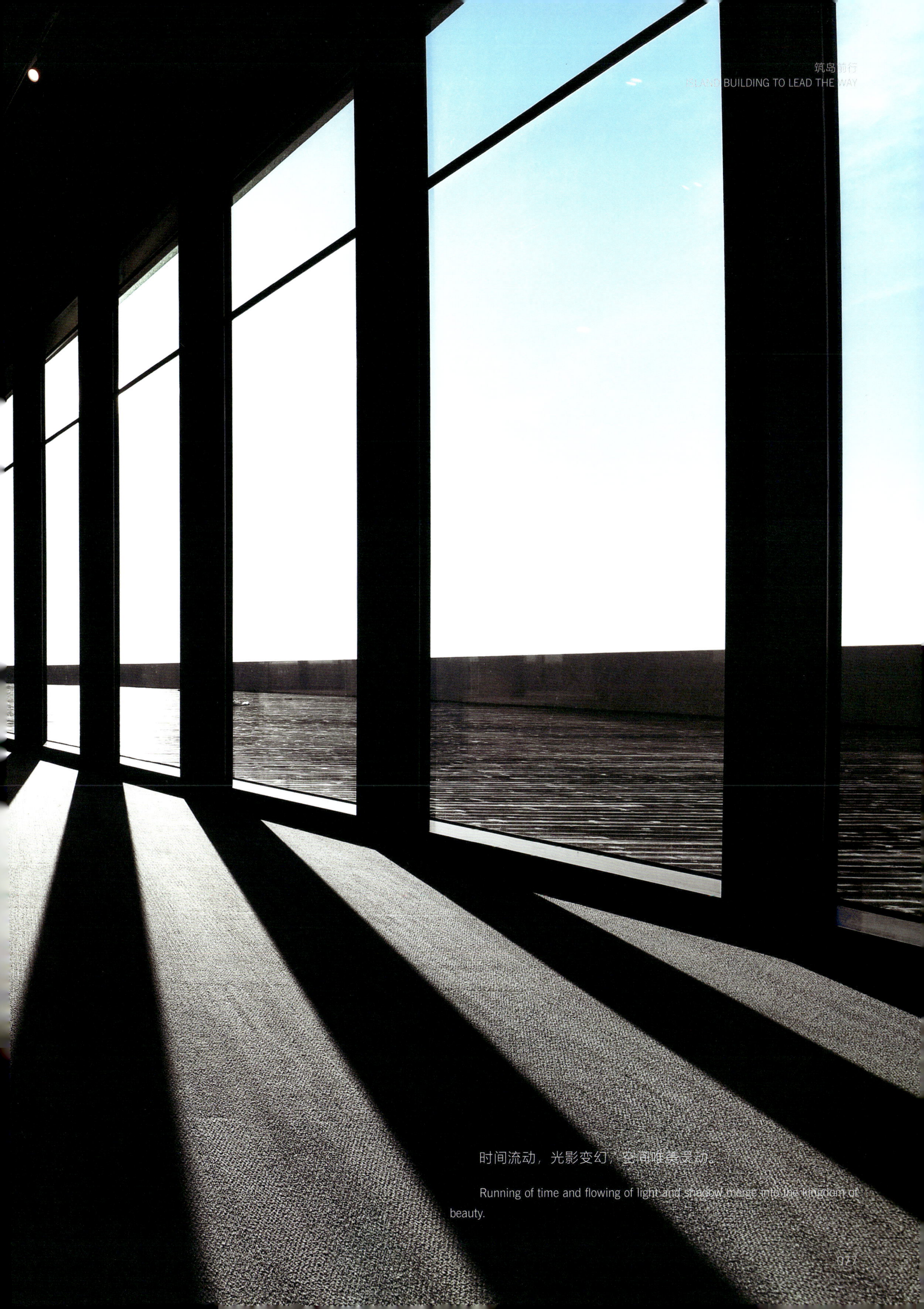

时间流动，光影变幻，空间唯美灵动。

Running of time and flowing of light and shadow merge into the kingdom of beauty.

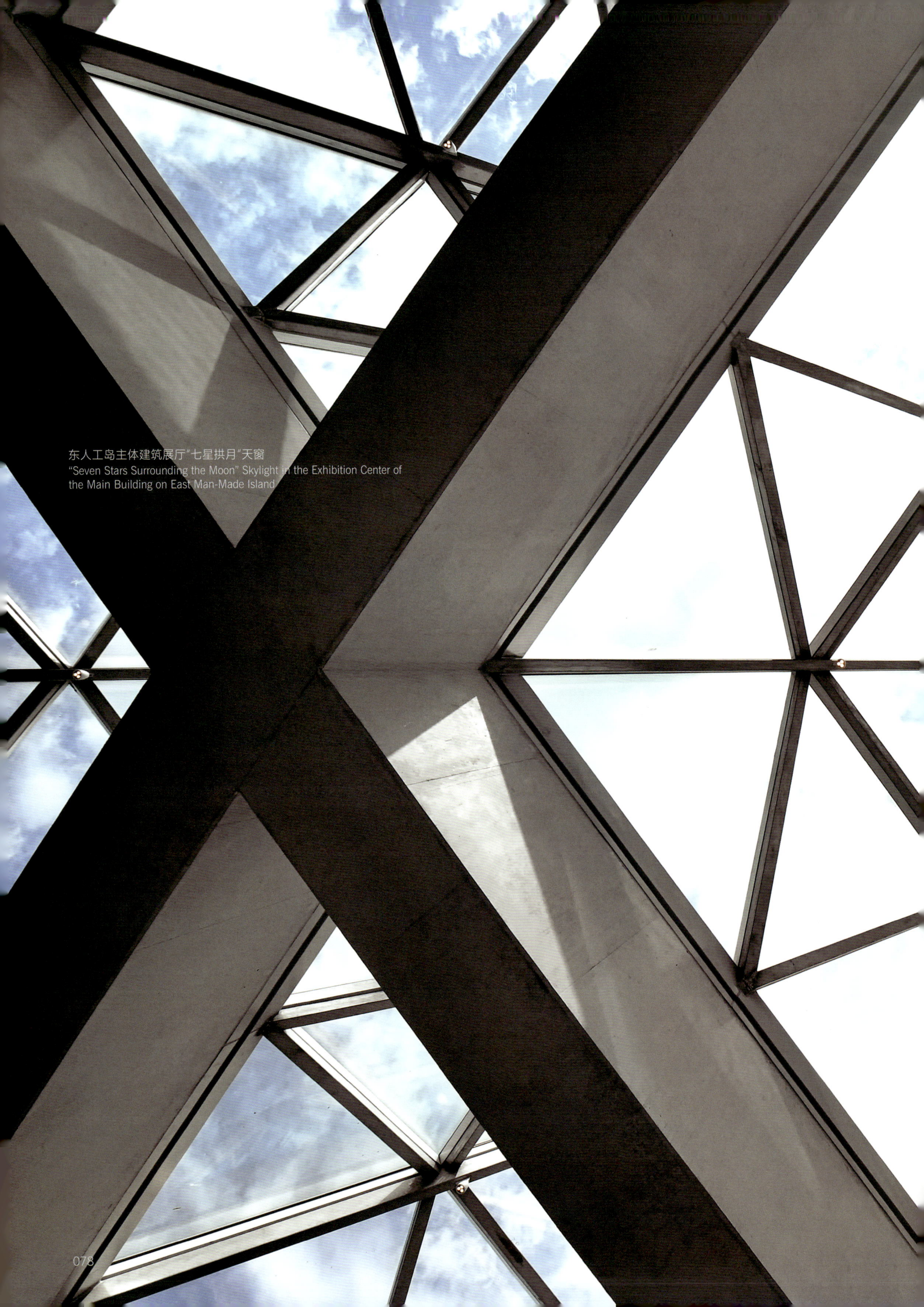

东人工岛主体建筑展厅"七星拱月"天窗
"Seven Stars Surrounding the Moon" Skylight in the Exhibition Center of the Main Building on East Man-Made Island

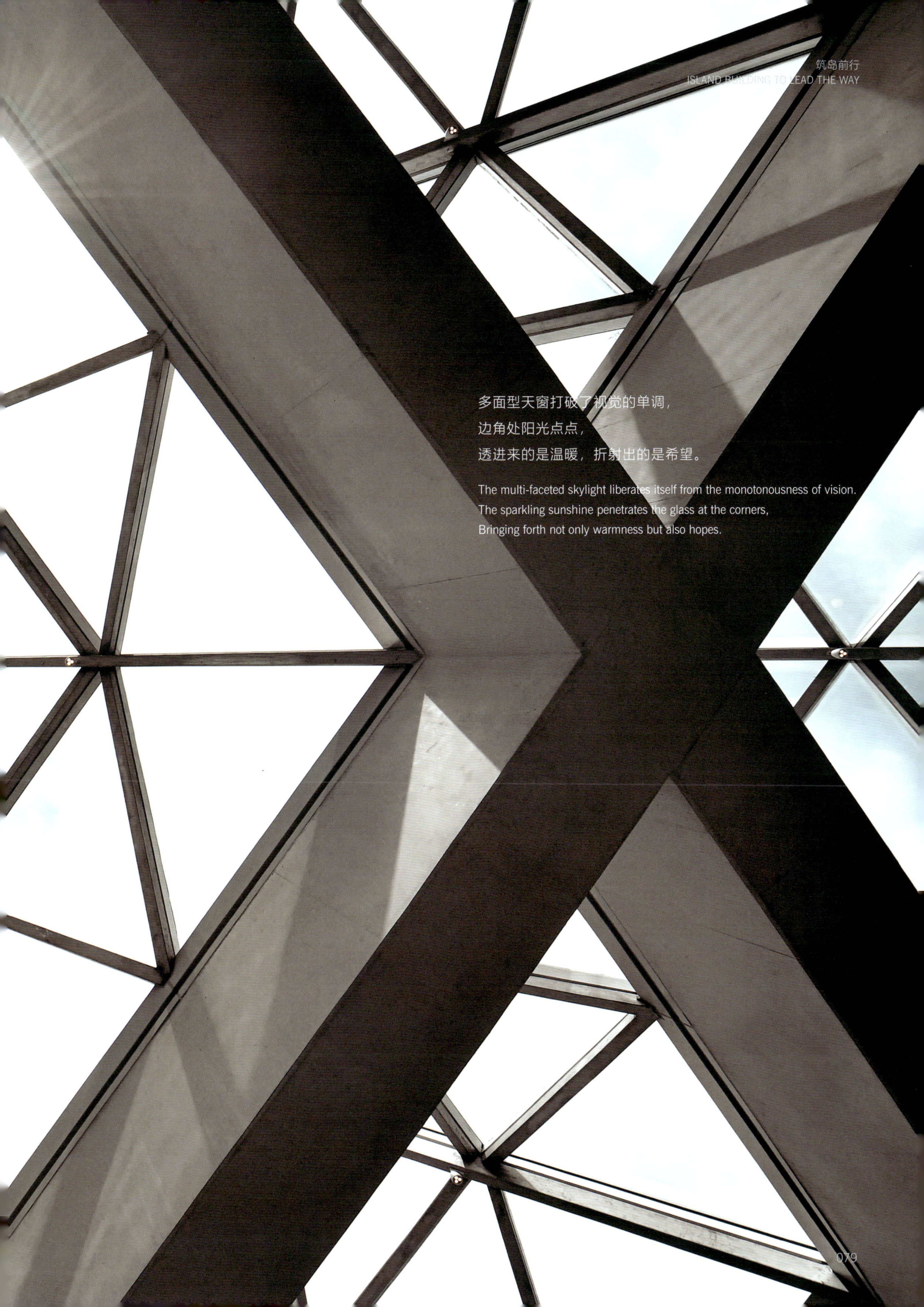

多面型天窗打破了视觉的单调，
边角处阳光点点，
透进来的是温暖，折射出的是希望。

The multi-faceted skylight liberates itself from the monotonousness of vision.
The sparkling sunshine penetrates the glass at the corners,
Bringing forth not only warmness but also hopes.

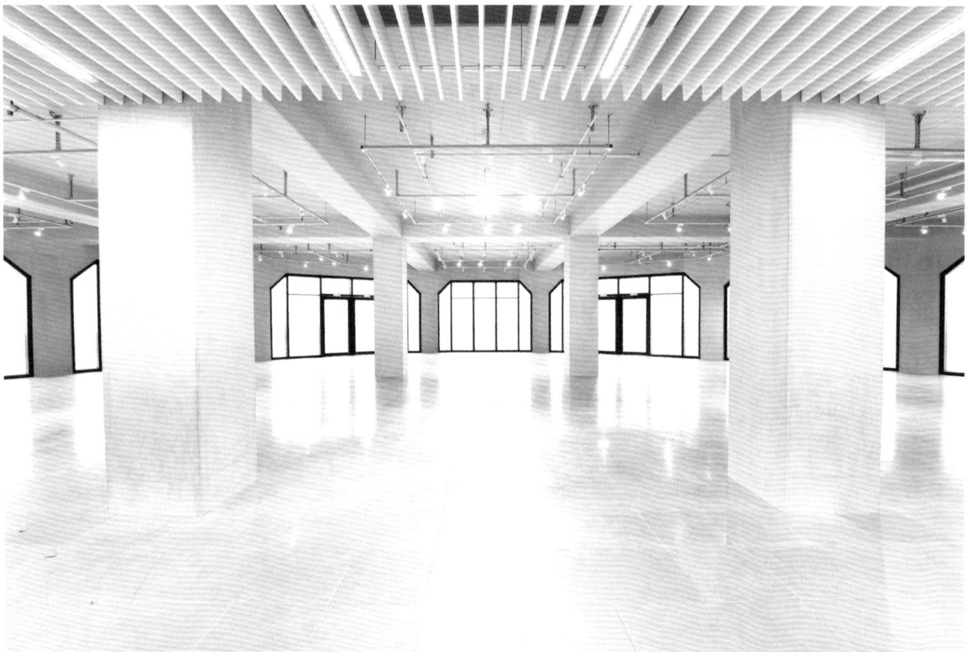

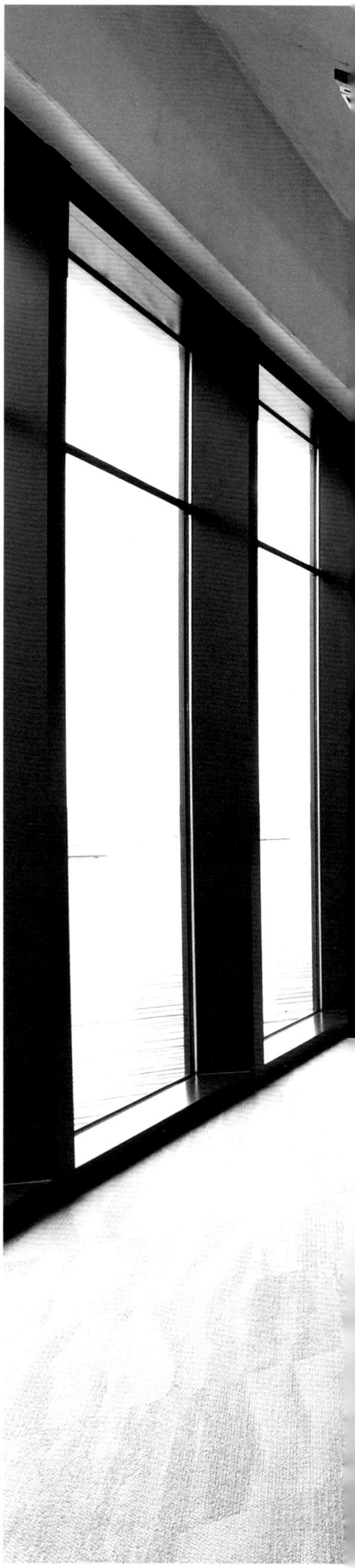

敞开式顶部与极简灯具，目之所及尽显工业之美，清简雅素，走向未来。

The open roof and the simple lights fill every place our eyes touch with the minimalist beauty.

1. 东人工岛主体建筑二层预留商场
Reserved Space for the Mall on the 2nd Floor of the Main Building on East Man-Made Island
2. 东人工岛主体建筑展厅防静电架空底板
Elevated Anti-electrostatic Soleplate in the Exhibition Center of the Main Building on East Man-Made Island

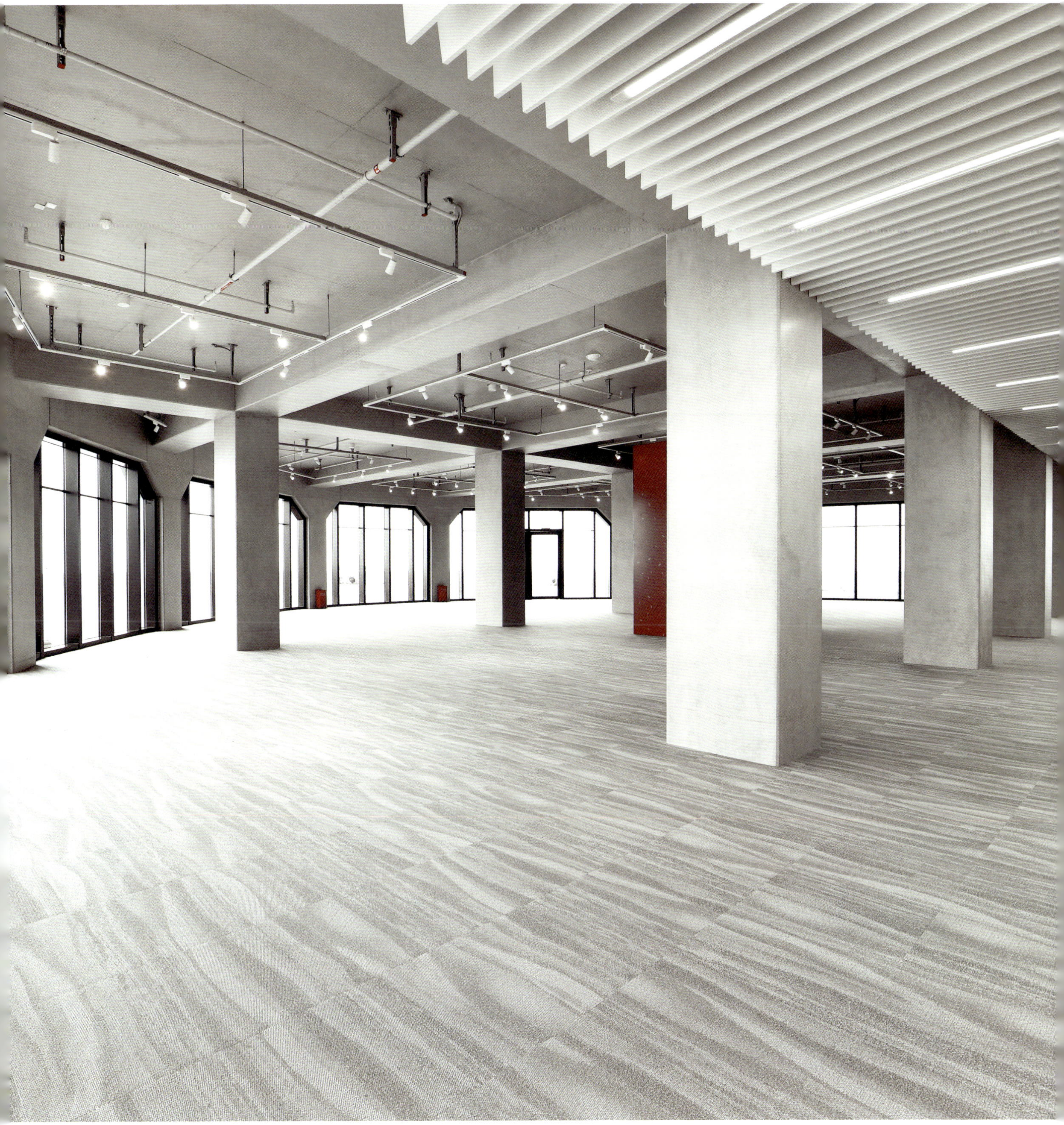

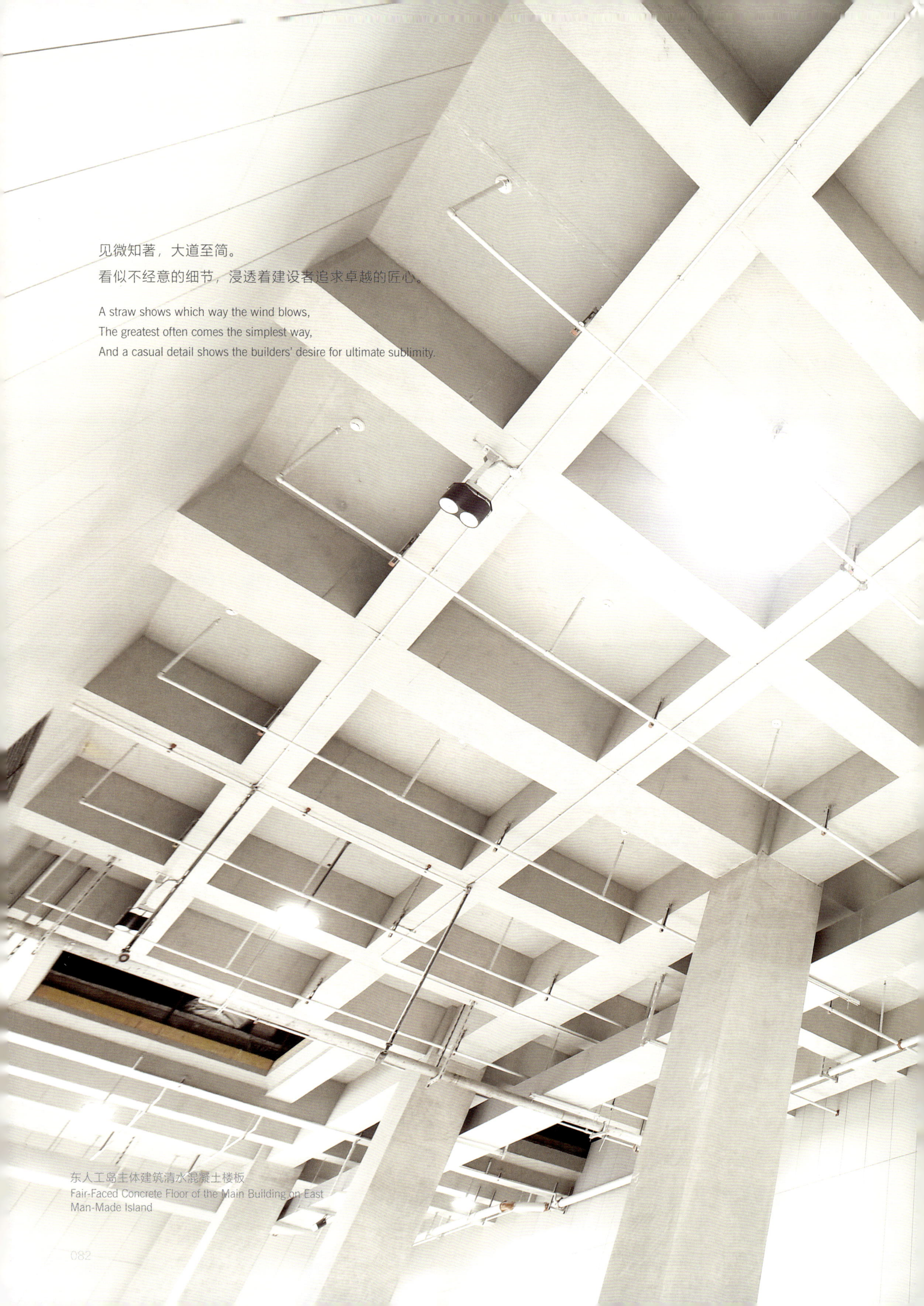

见微知著，大道至简。
看似不经意的细节，浸透着建设者追求卓越的匠心。

A straw shows which way the wind blows,
The greatest often comes the simplest way,
And a casual detail shows the builders' desire for ultimate sublimity.

东人工岛主体建筑清水混凝土楼板
Fair-Faced Concrete Floor of the Main Building on East Man-Made Island

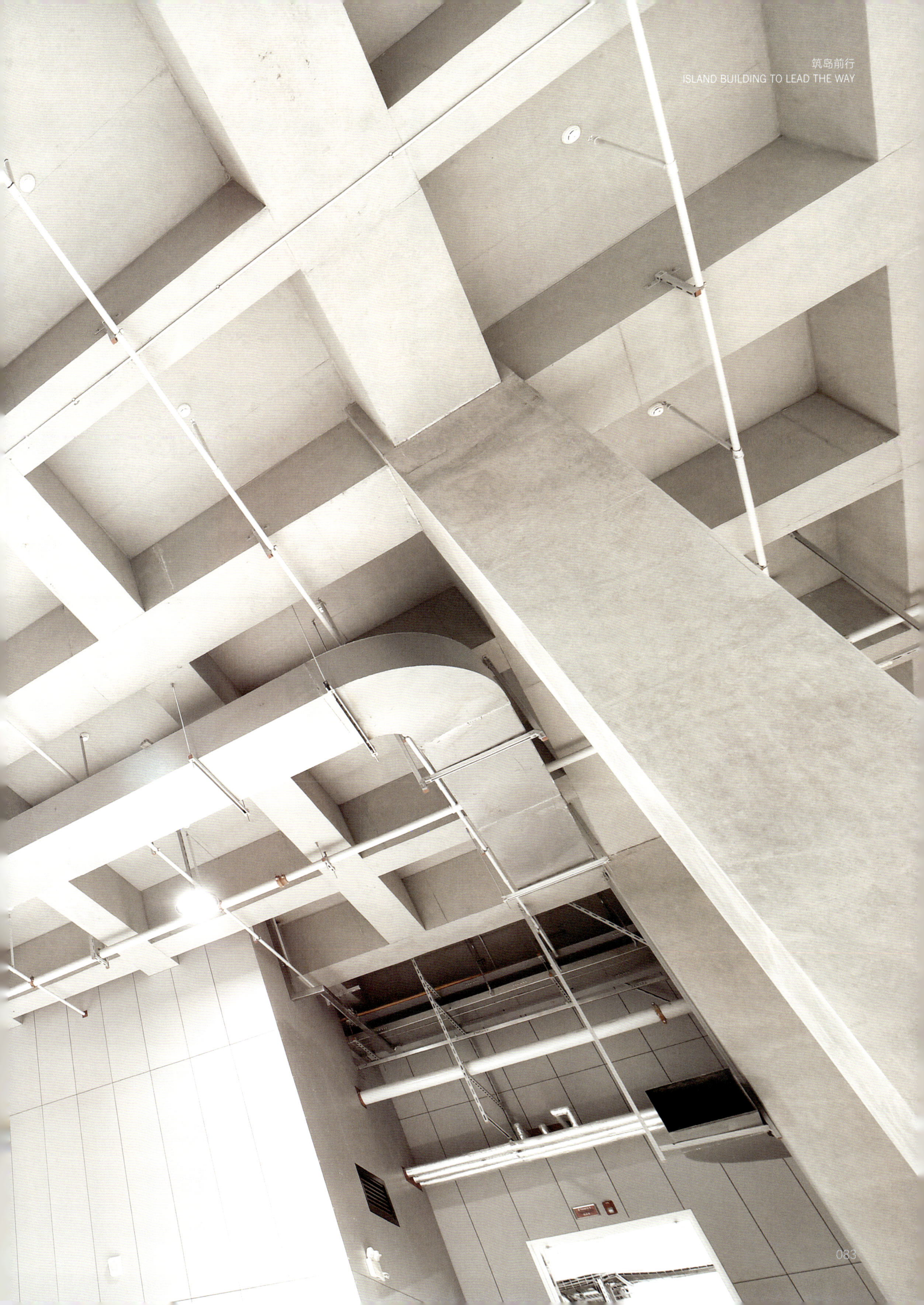

西人工岛办公区
Office Area on West Man-Made Island

通透明快的落地窗与简洁朴素的白色吊顶，
营造出明朗大气的现代风格；
简约静谧、似断非断的空间，打造了完美的办公环境。

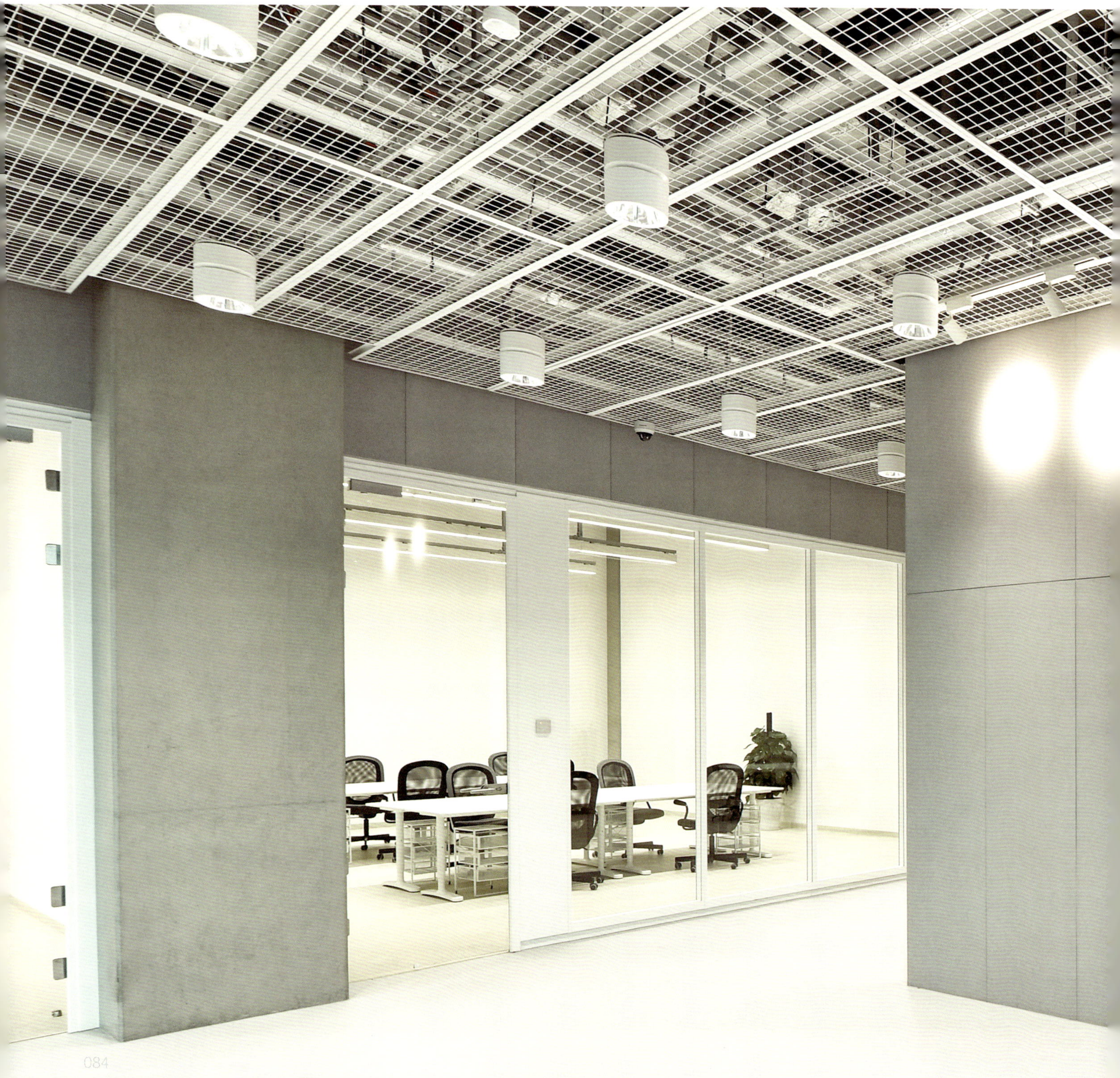

Bright windows, with homely white ceilings,
Create the modernist grandeur,
Simple, serene, expanding space,
Constructs perfect offices.

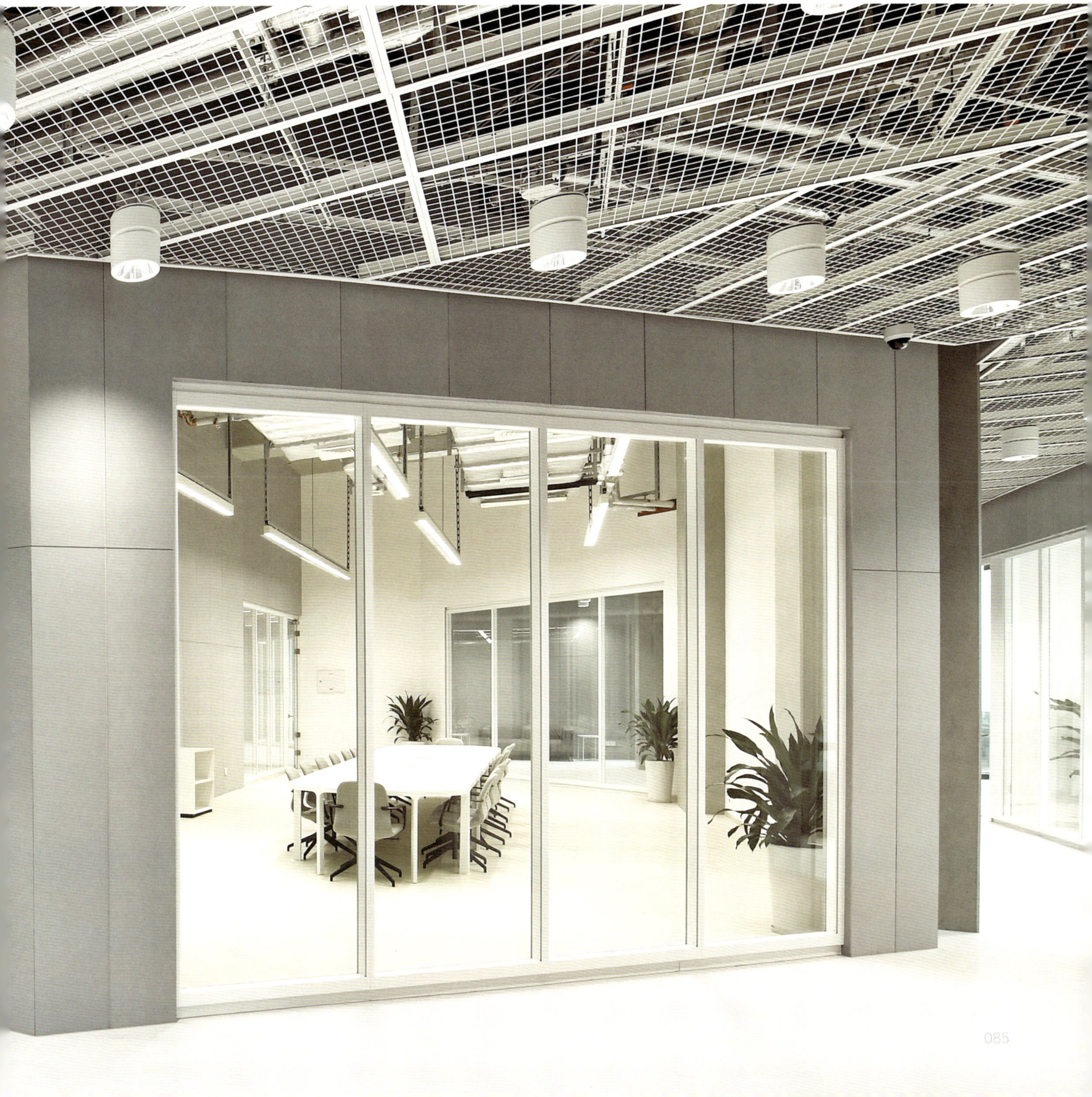

现代建筑巧妙融入中国元素，
七星拱月，红色宫灯，
实用美观，简洁精致，更显华贵大气。

Traditional Chinese cultural elements merge into modern architecture: Seven stars surrounding the moon, and red palace lanterns.

All are simplistic, delicate but elegant, magnificent.

1. 西人工岛主体建筑室内休息区
Lounge in the Main Building on West Man-Made Island
2. 西人工岛会议室
Conference Room on West Man-Made Island
3. 西人工岛职工食堂
Staff Dining Hall on West Man-Made Island

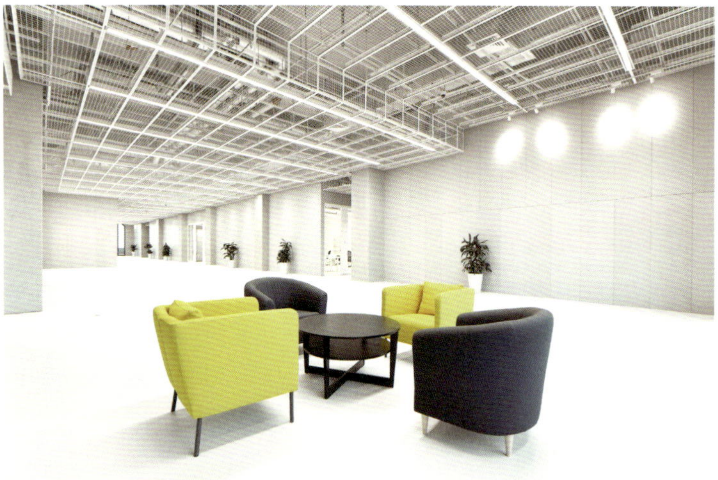

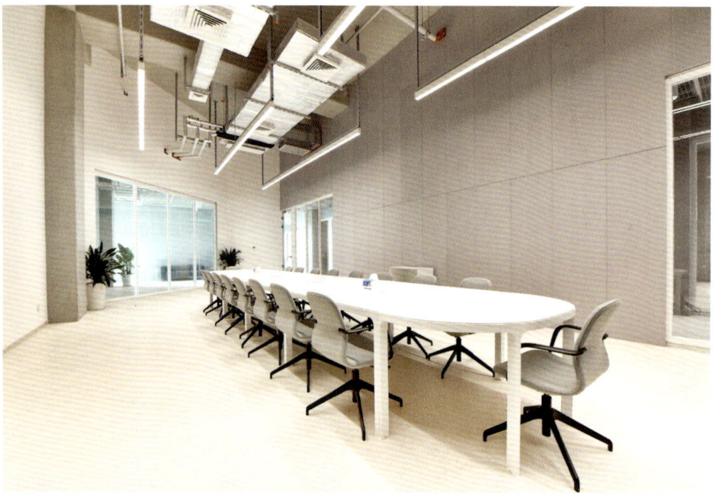

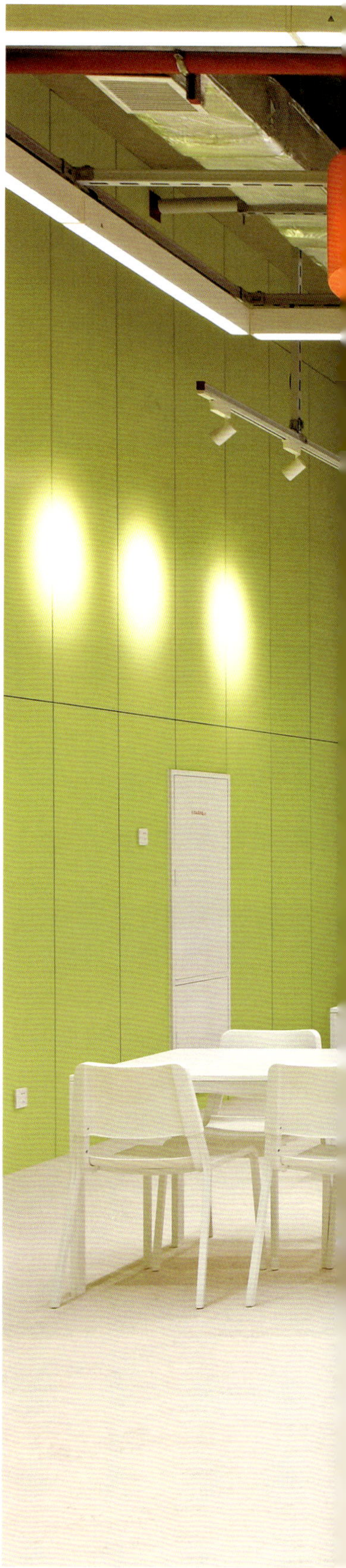

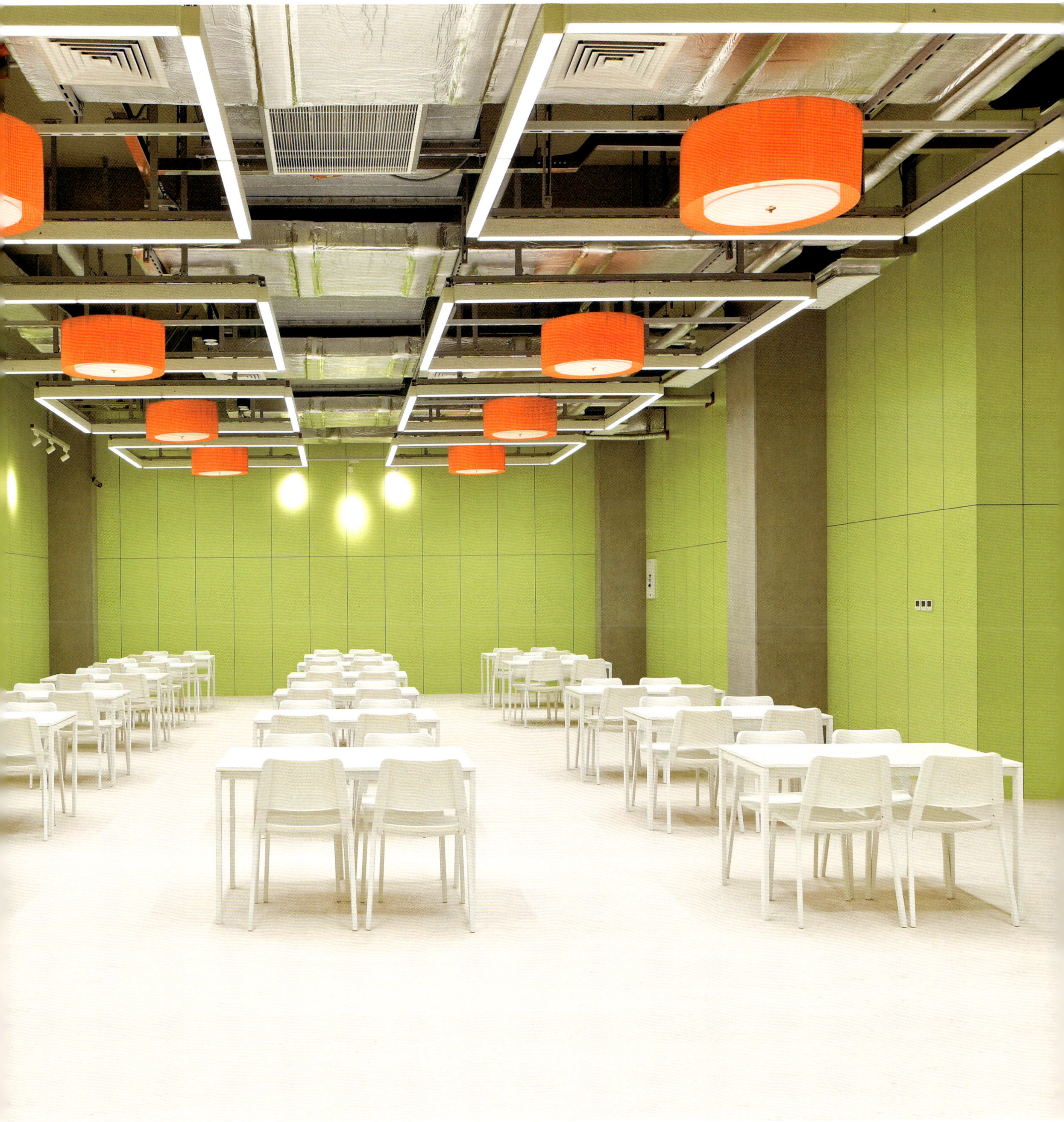

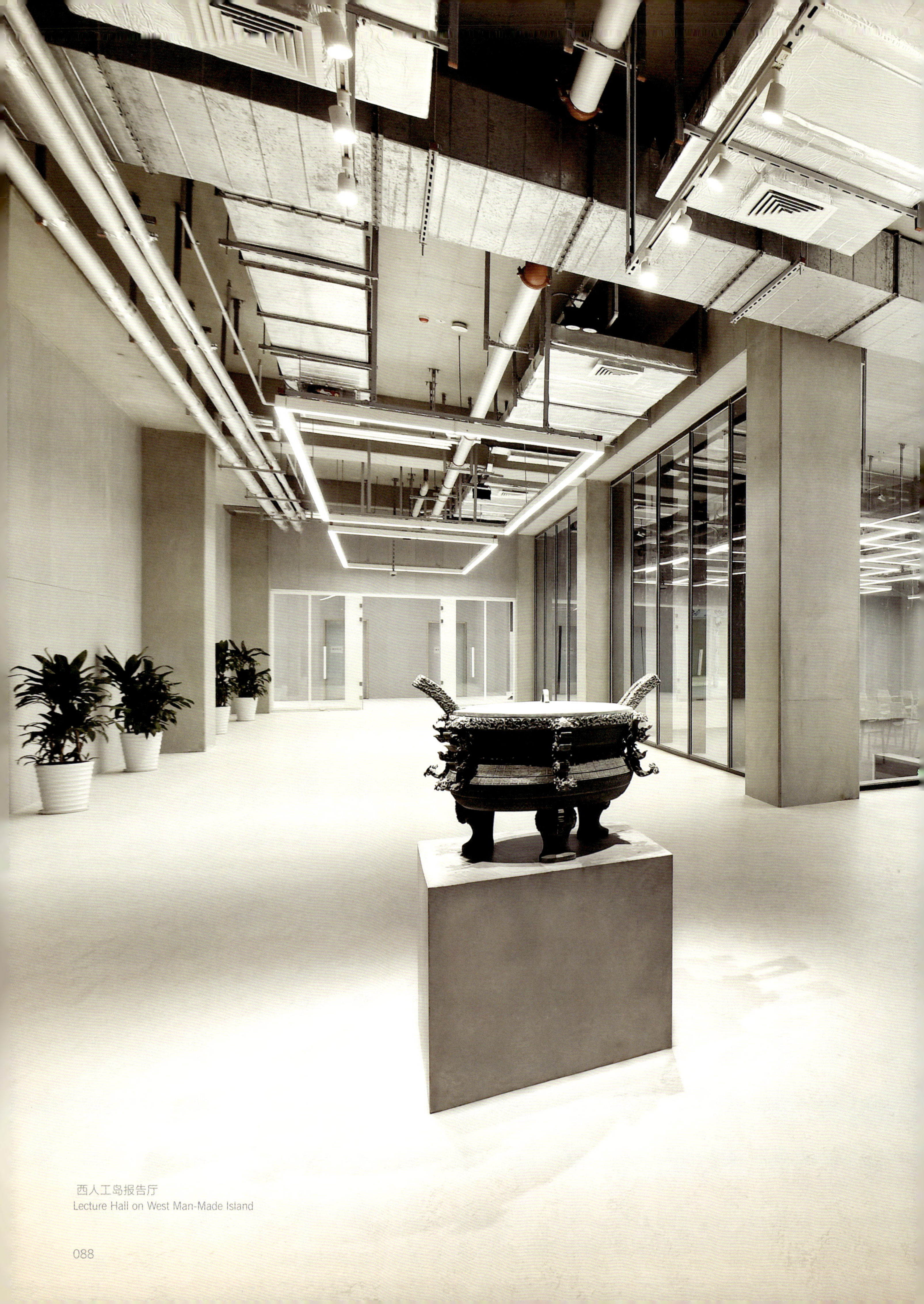

西人工岛报告厅
Lecture Hall on West Man-Made Island

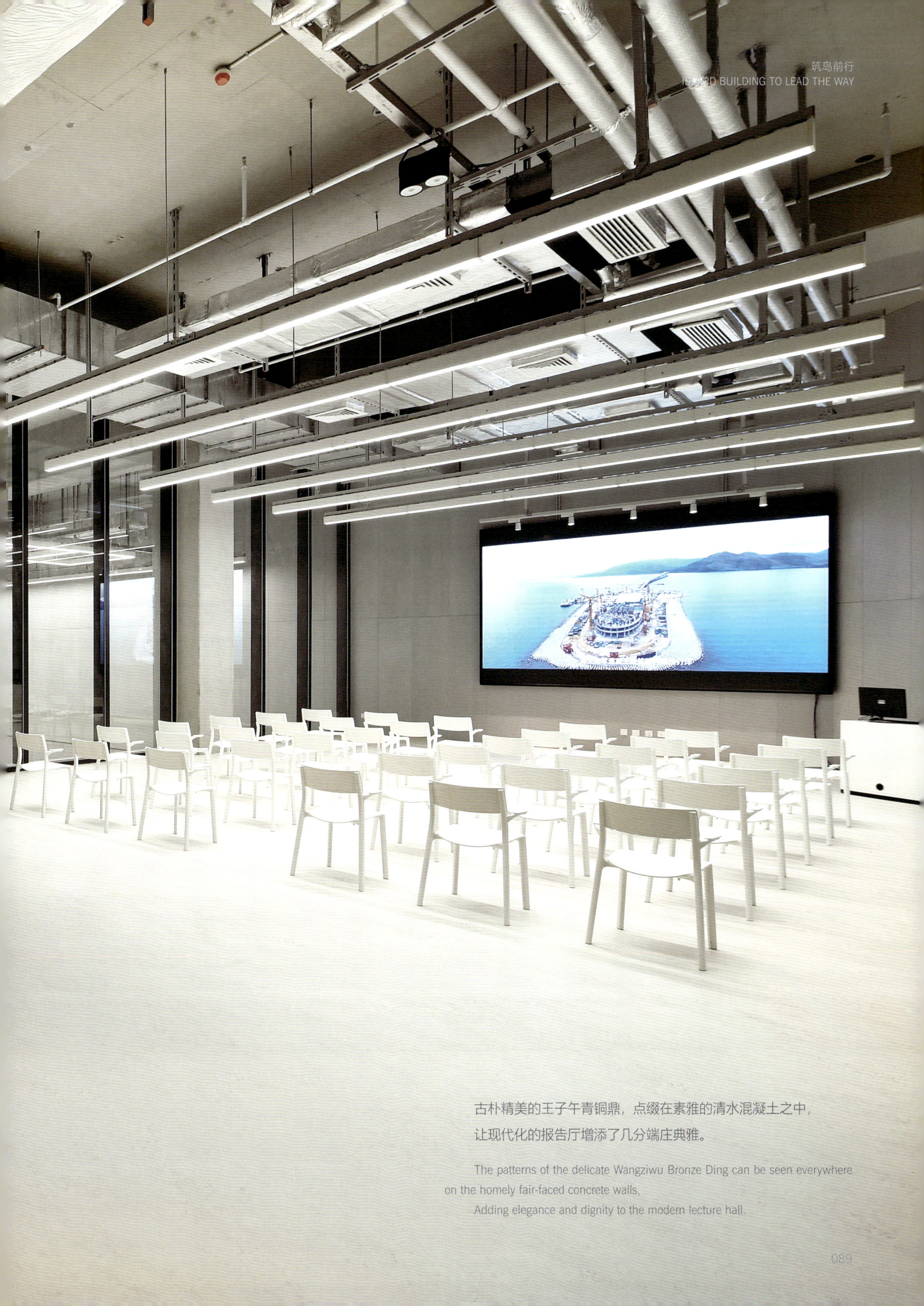

古朴精美的王子午青铜鼎，点缀在素雅的清水混凝土之中，
让现代化的报告厅增添了几分端庄典雅。

The patterns of the delicate Wangziwu Bronze Ding can be seen everywhere on the homely fair-faced concrete walls,
Adding elegance and dignity to the modern lecture hall.

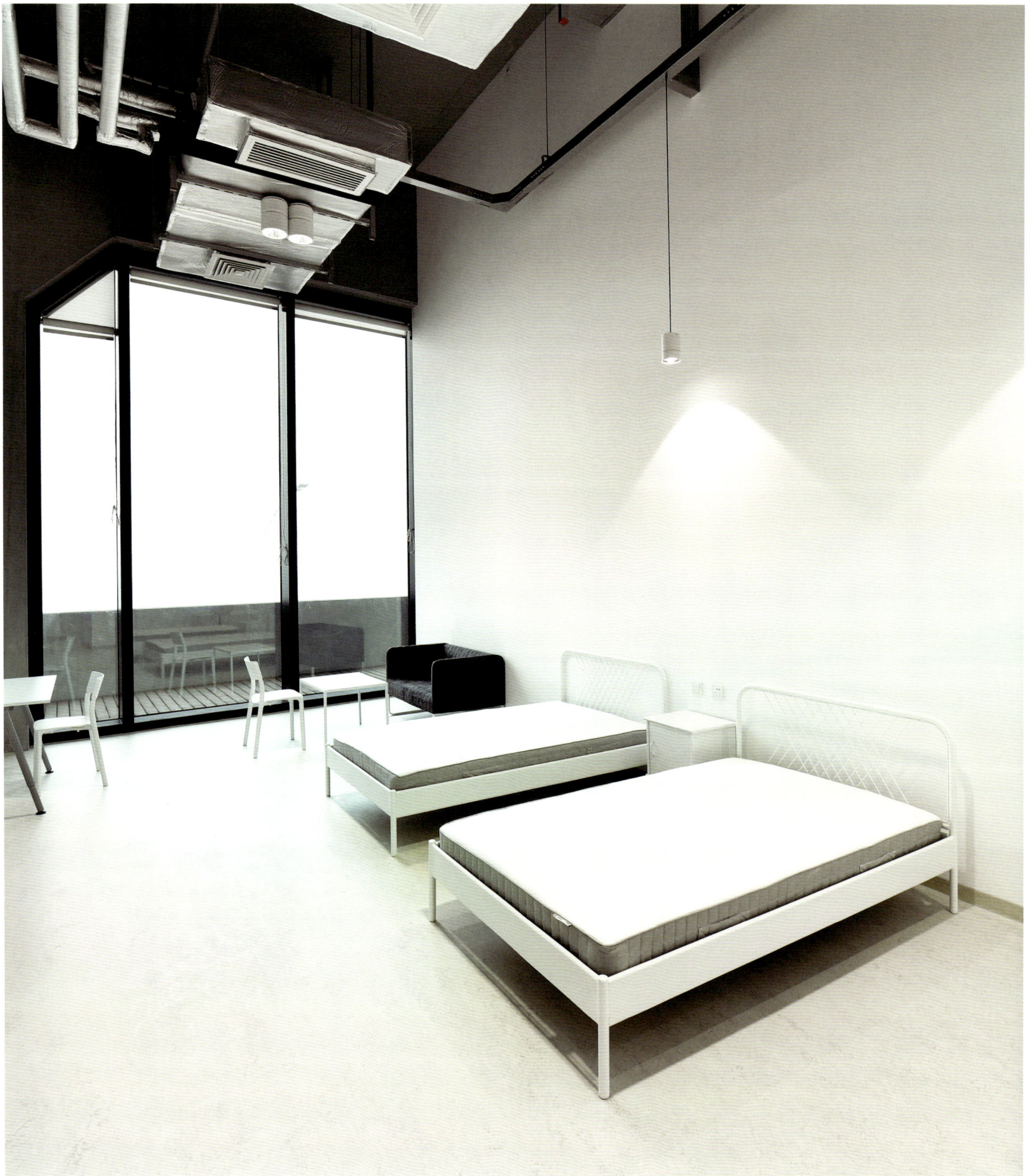

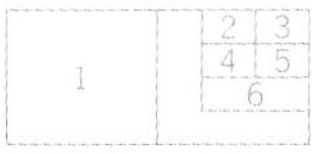

1. 西人工岛职工宿舍
   Staff Dormitory on West Man-Made Island

2—3. 人工岛主体建筑卫生间
   Toilet in the Main Building on the Man-Made Islands

4. 西人工岛职工宿舍
   Staff Dormitory on West Man-made Island

5. 人工岛主体建筑盥洗室
   Washroom in the Main Building on the Man-Made Islands

6. 西人工岛会客室
   Reception Room on West Man-Made Island

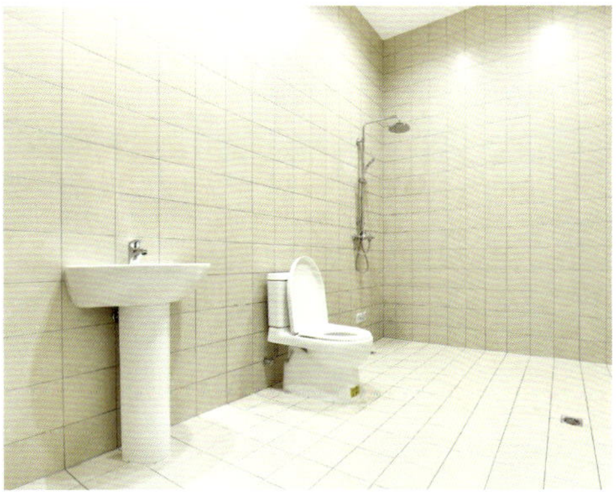

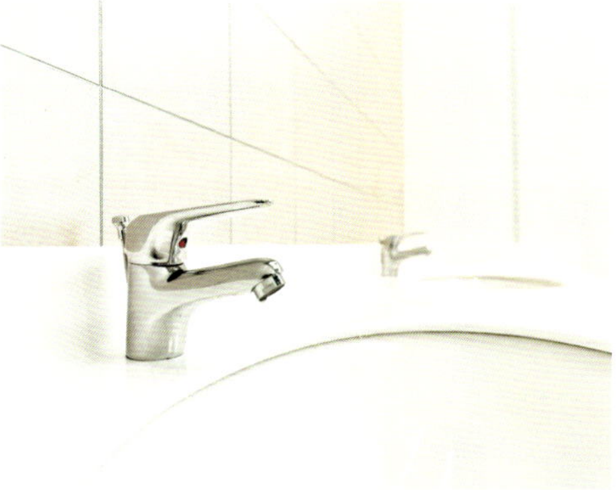

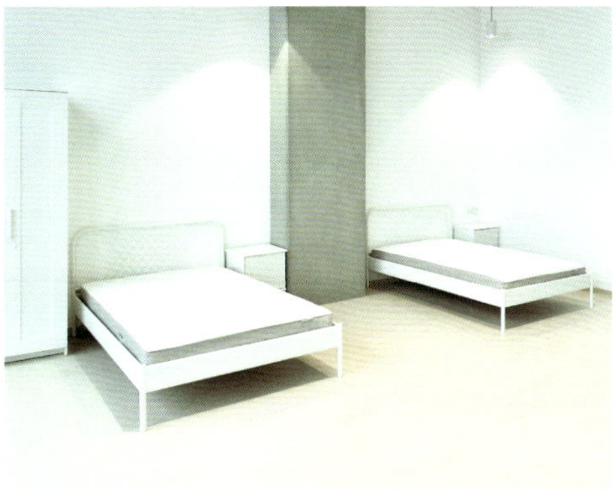

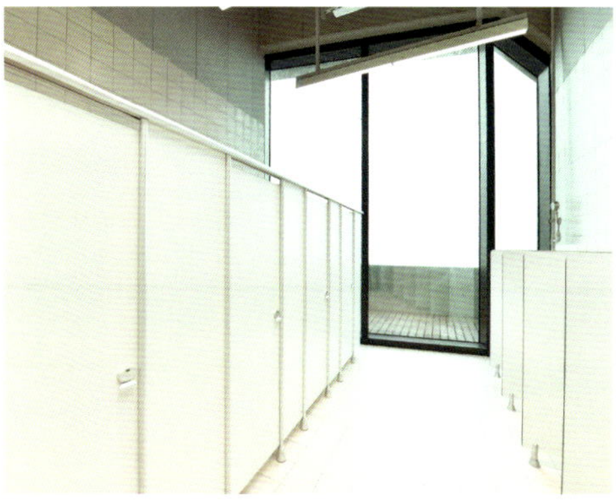

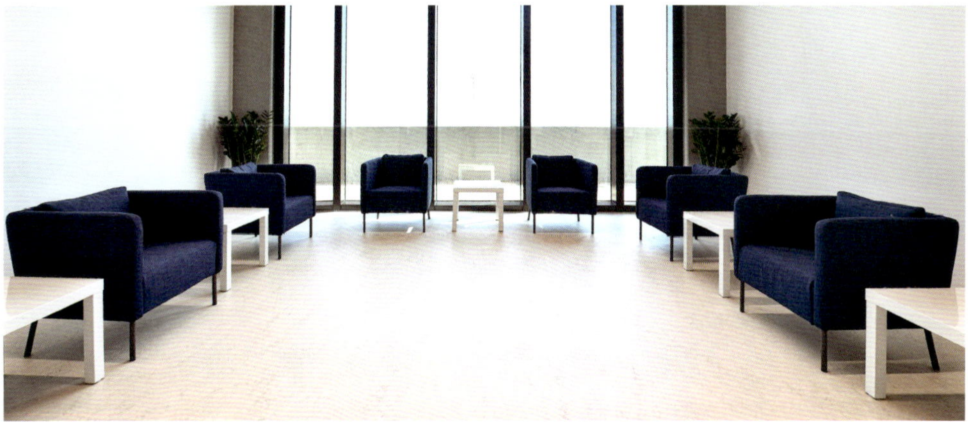

清水混凝土纤维板、地板胶、敞开式结构，营造出简约而舒适的环境。

The fair-faced concrete fiber board, the floor glue, and the open structure create a simplistic but comfortable environment.

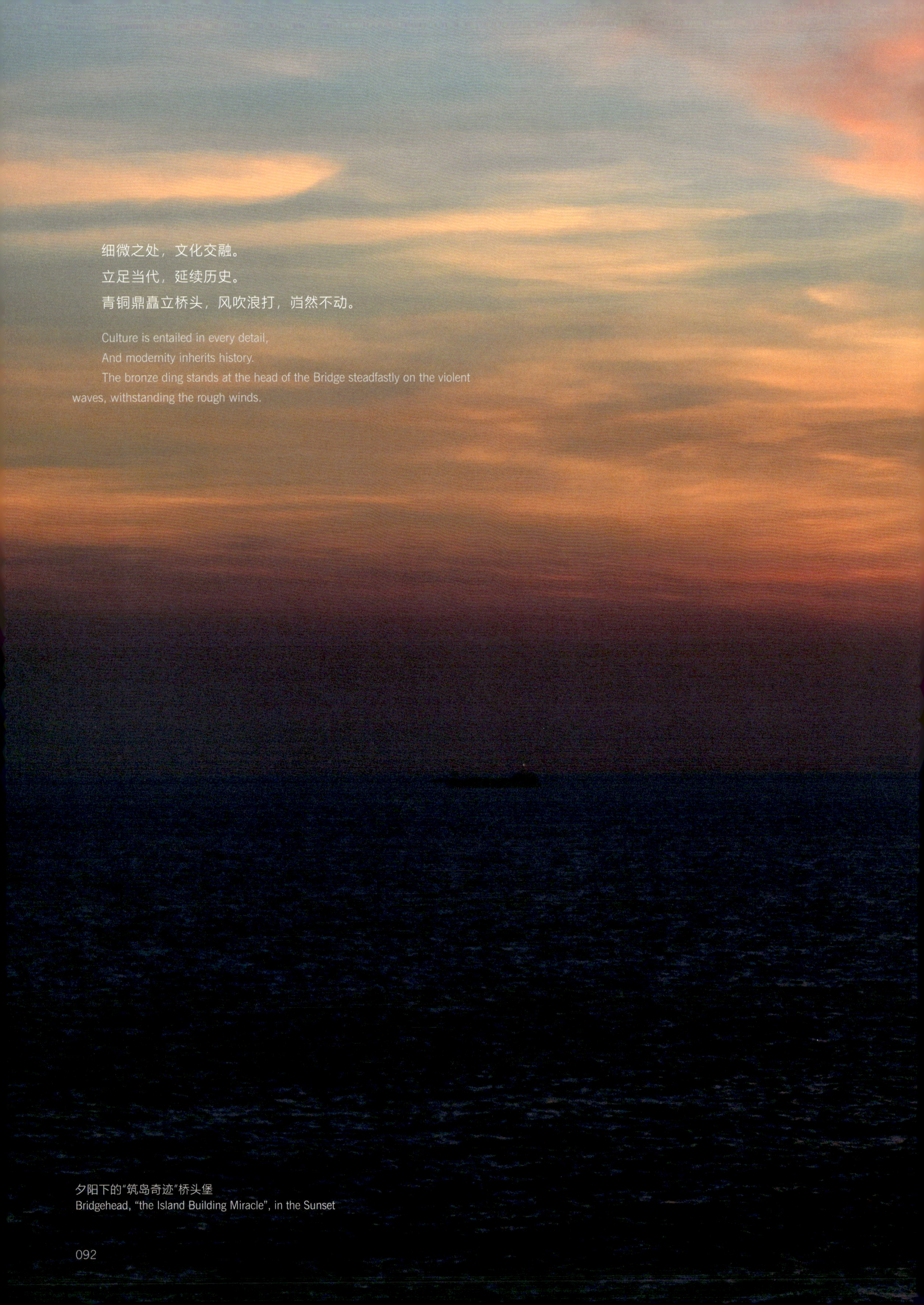

细微之处，文化交融。

立足当代，延续历史。

青铜鼎矗立桥头，风吹浪打，岿然不动。

Culture is entailed in every detail,

And modernity inherits history.

The bronze ding stands at the head of the Bridge steadfastly on the violent waves, withstanding the rough winds.

夕阳下的"筑岛奇迹"桥头堡

Bridgehead, "the Island Building Miracle", in the Sunset

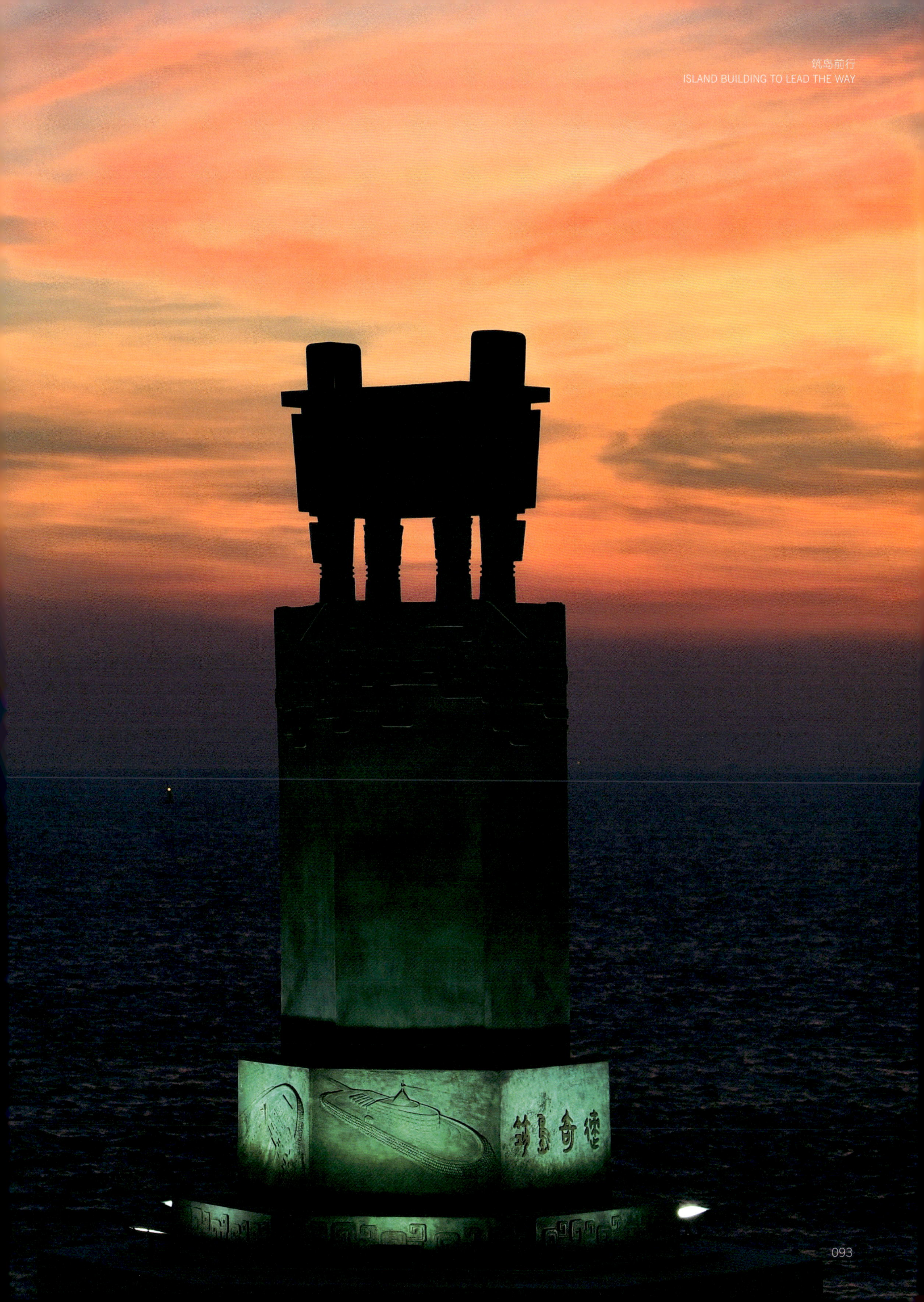

1. 青铜鼎龙形纹饰
Dragon-shaped Inscriptions on the Bronze Ding

2. 青铜鼎"隧道贯通"浮雕
"Closure of the Tunnel", Relief on the Bronze Ding

3. 青铜鼎"蛟龙出海"大篆
Ancient Chinese Words "蛟龙出海" (Dragon Rising from the Sea) Inscribed on the Bronze Ding

4. 东人工岛青铜鼎桥头堡
Bridgehead in the Shape of Bronze Ding on East Man-Made Island

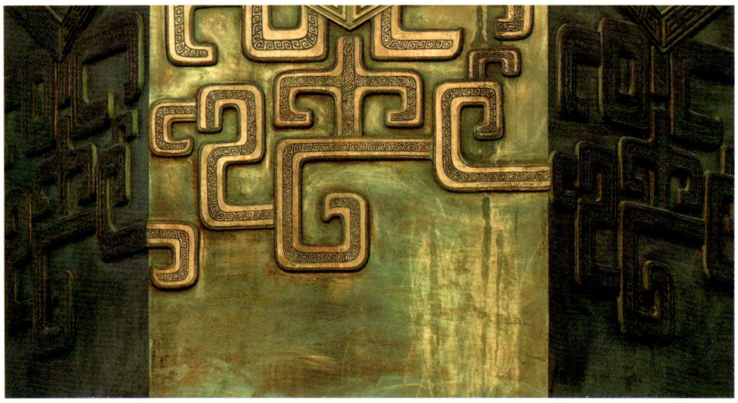

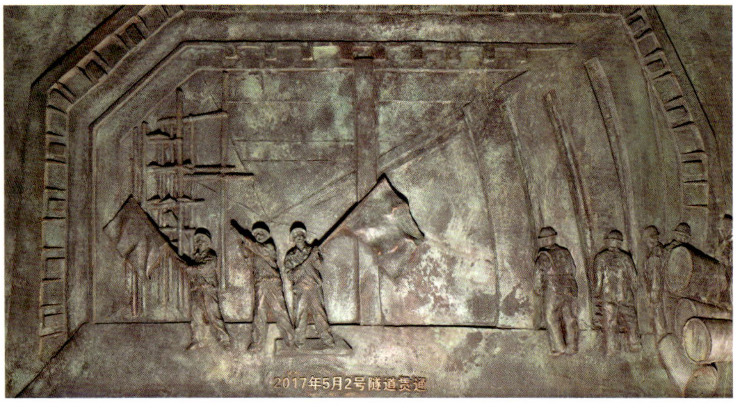

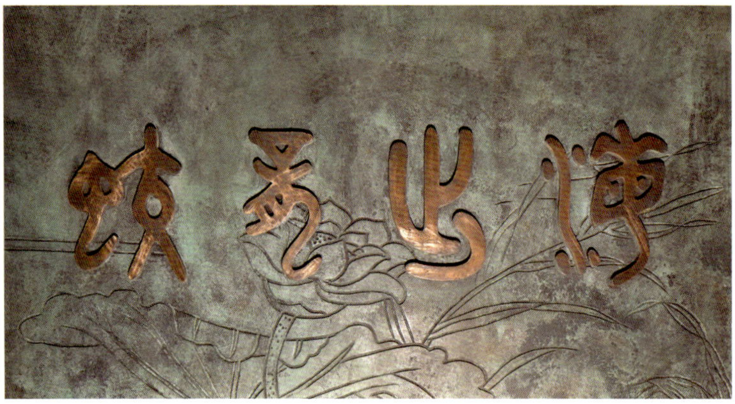

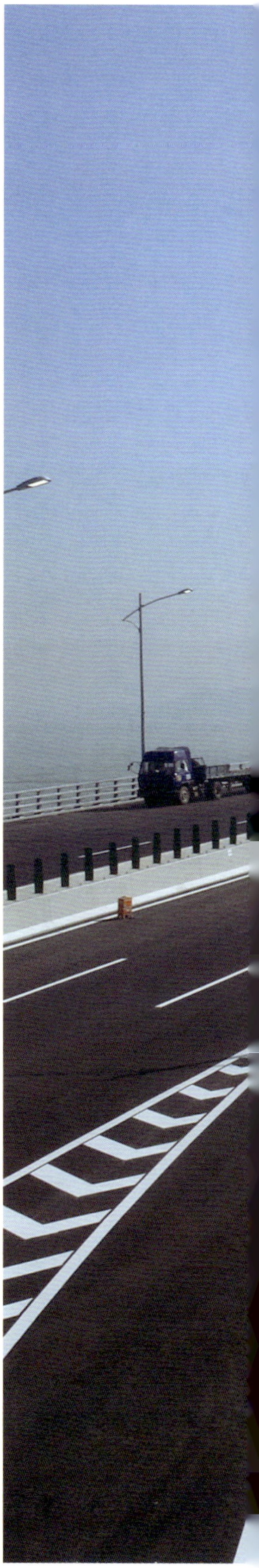

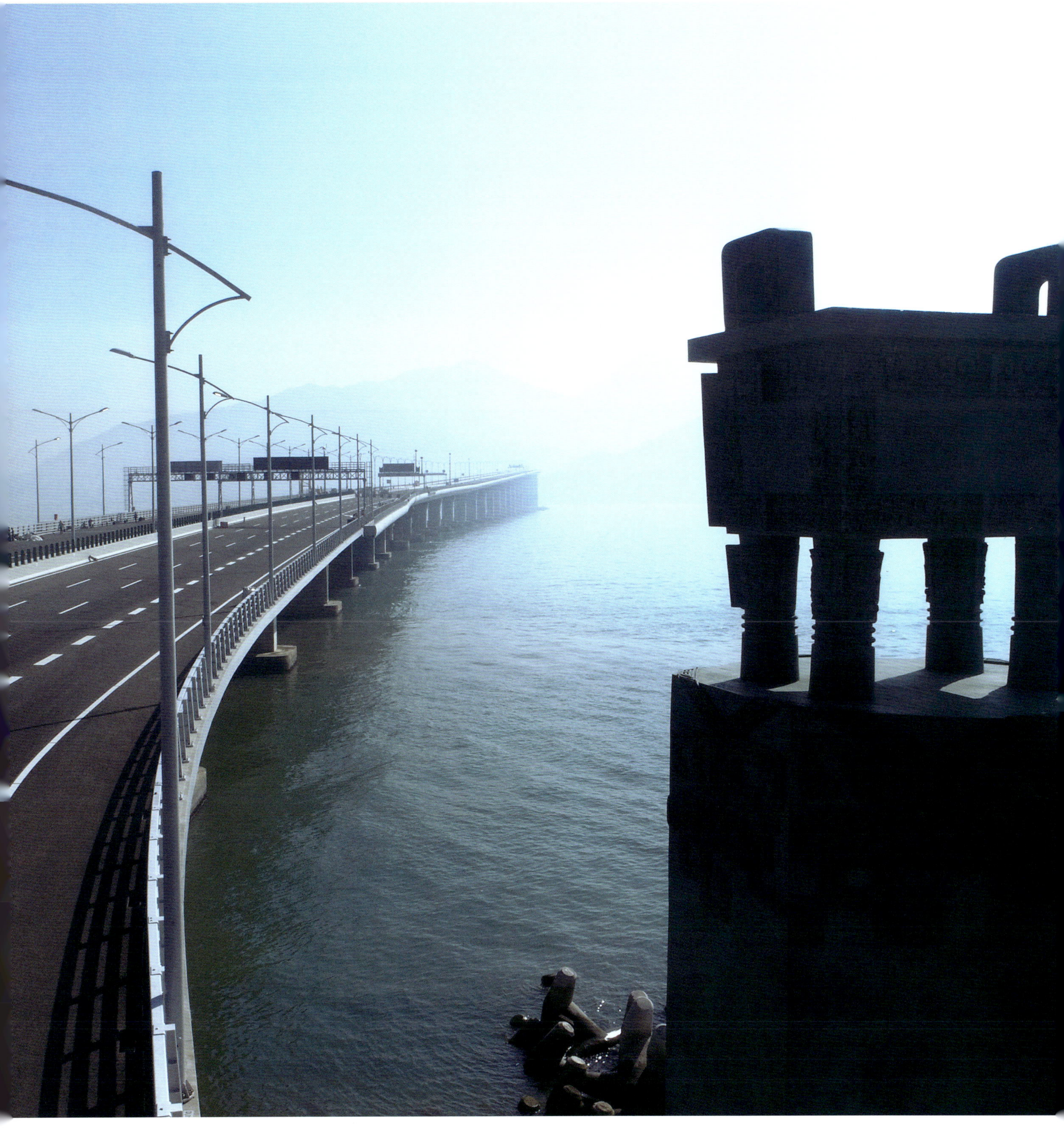

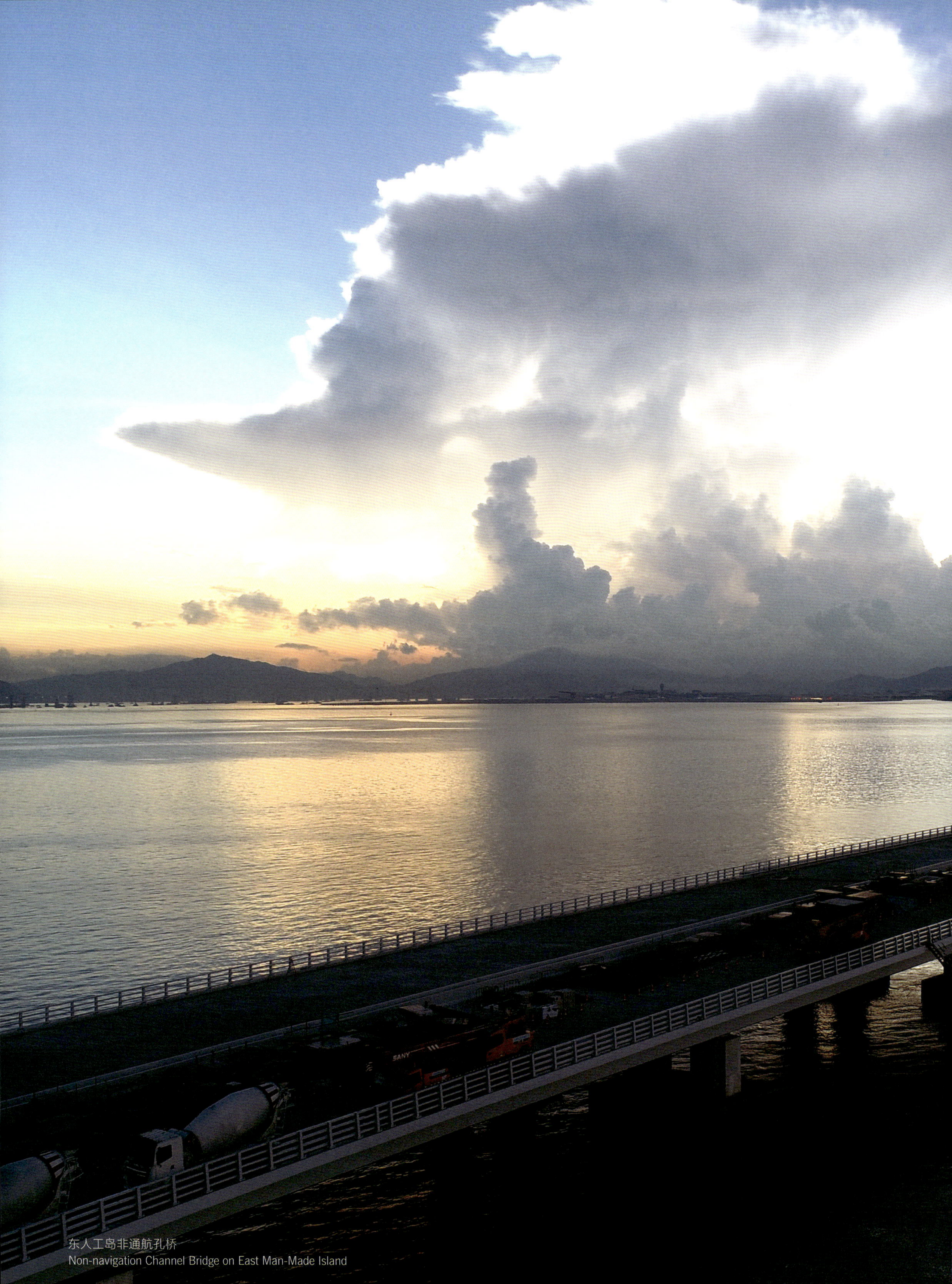

东人工岛非通航孔桥
Non-navigation Channel Bridge on East Man-Made Island

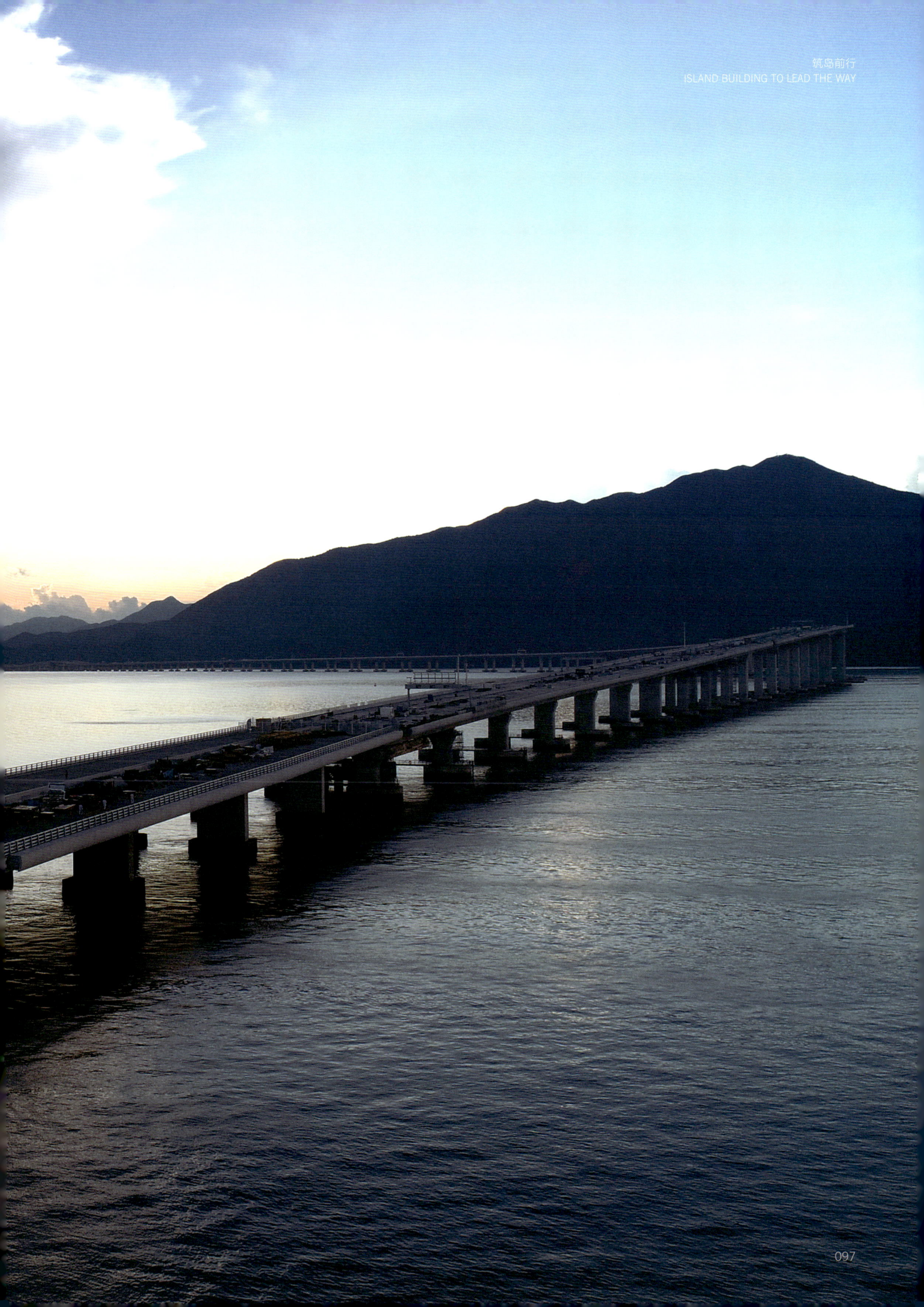

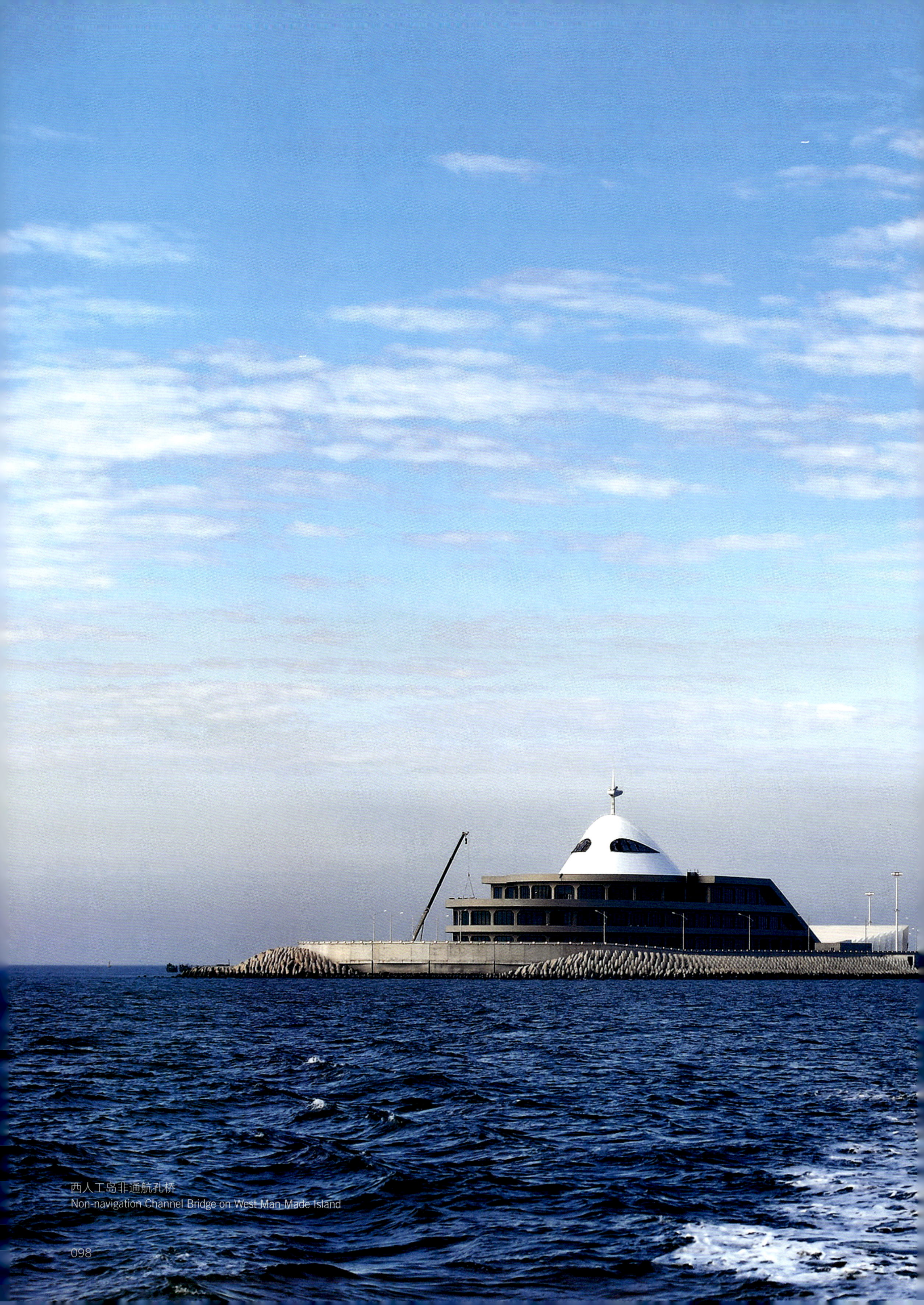

西人工岛非通航孔桥
Non-navigation Channel Bridge on West Man-Made Island

如战舰劈波斩浪，
如"航母"海中遨游，
造型优美的人工岛牵起海上长桥和海底隧道，
载着三地的希望驶向未来。

Like a battleship cleaving the waves,
Like the aircraft carrier roughing the seas,
The beautiful-shaped man-made island
Holds the long bridge over the sea in one hand, the underwater tunnel in the other,
And, loaded with hopes of the three cities, sails into the future.

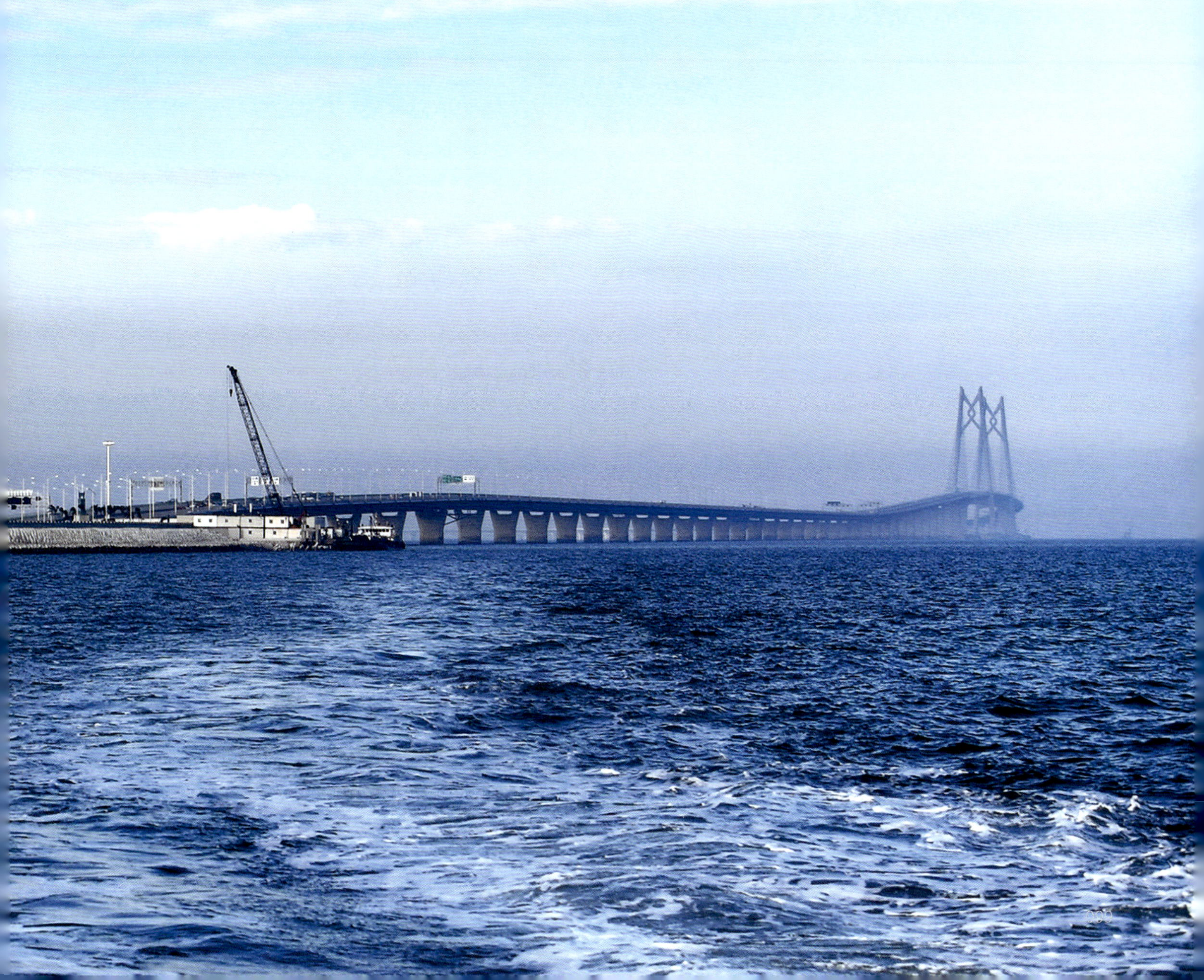

跬步千里

A SHORT STEP IS THE BEGINNING OF A THOUSAND MILES

6.7公里的海底沉管隧道，

彰显着中国沉管隧道跨越式发展的奇迹，

展现着工程建设者不畏艰难、勇于开拓的风采。

The immersed tube tunnel of 6.7 kilometers manifests

The miracle China has made in immersed tube tunneling

As well as Chinese engineers' courage and willpower.

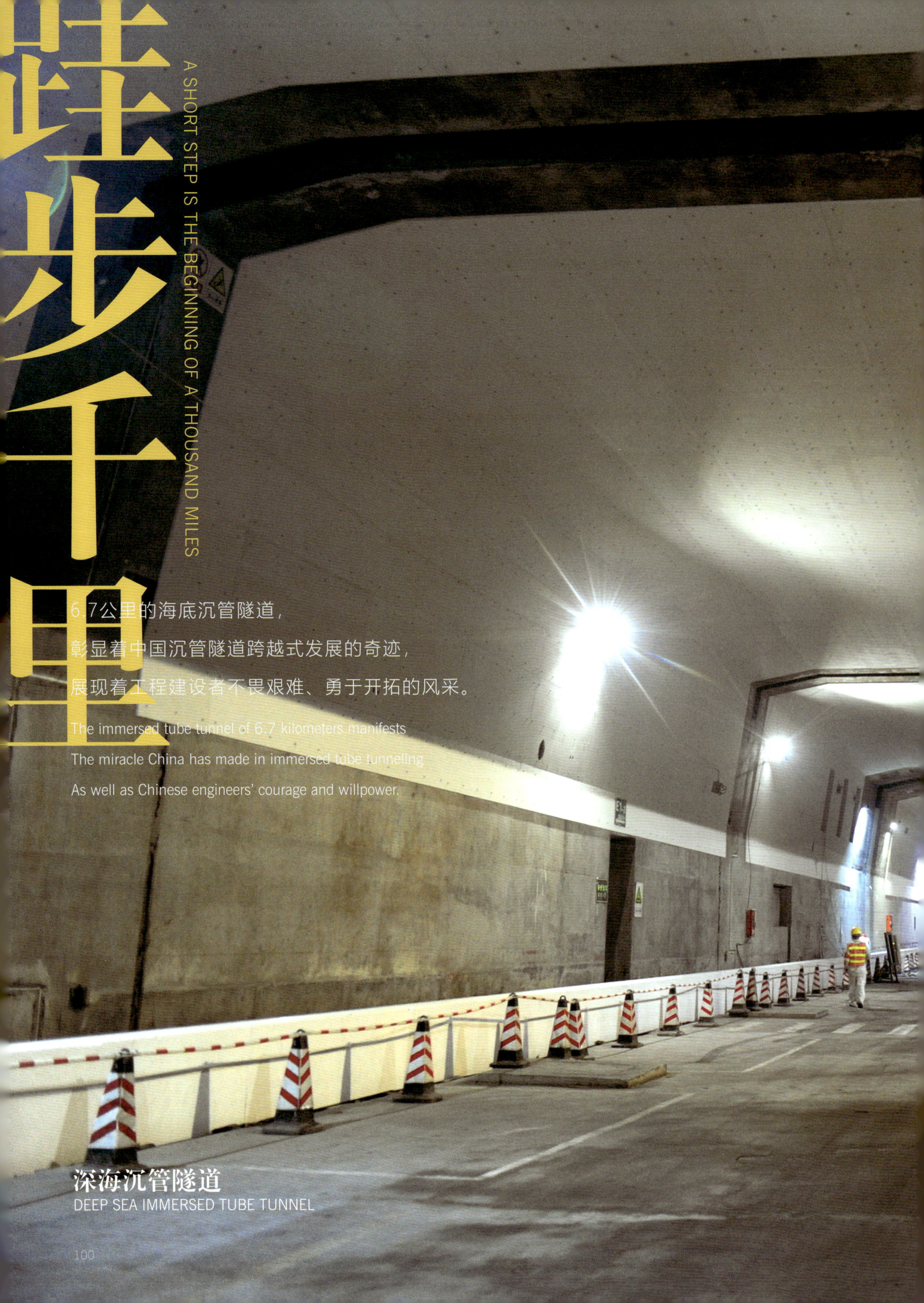

深海沉管隧道

DEEP SEA IMMERSED TUBE TUNNEL

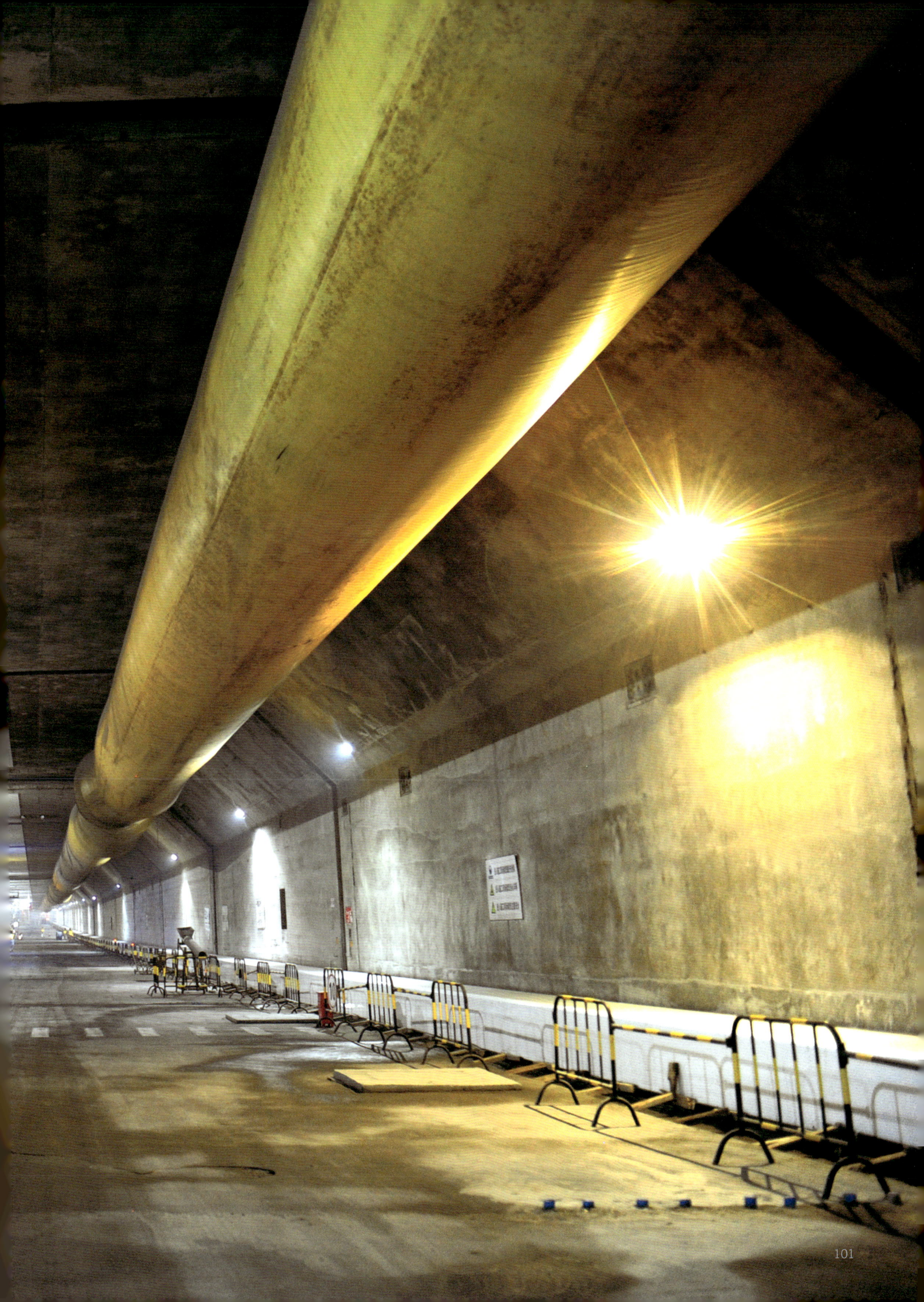

隧道基础

TUNNEL BASE

首创"碎石基床+复合地基"新工艺，夯实起6.7公里海底隧道的坚实基础。

The innovated technology of "rubble bedding + composite base" lays the solid foundation for the 6.7 kilometers-long underwater tunnel.

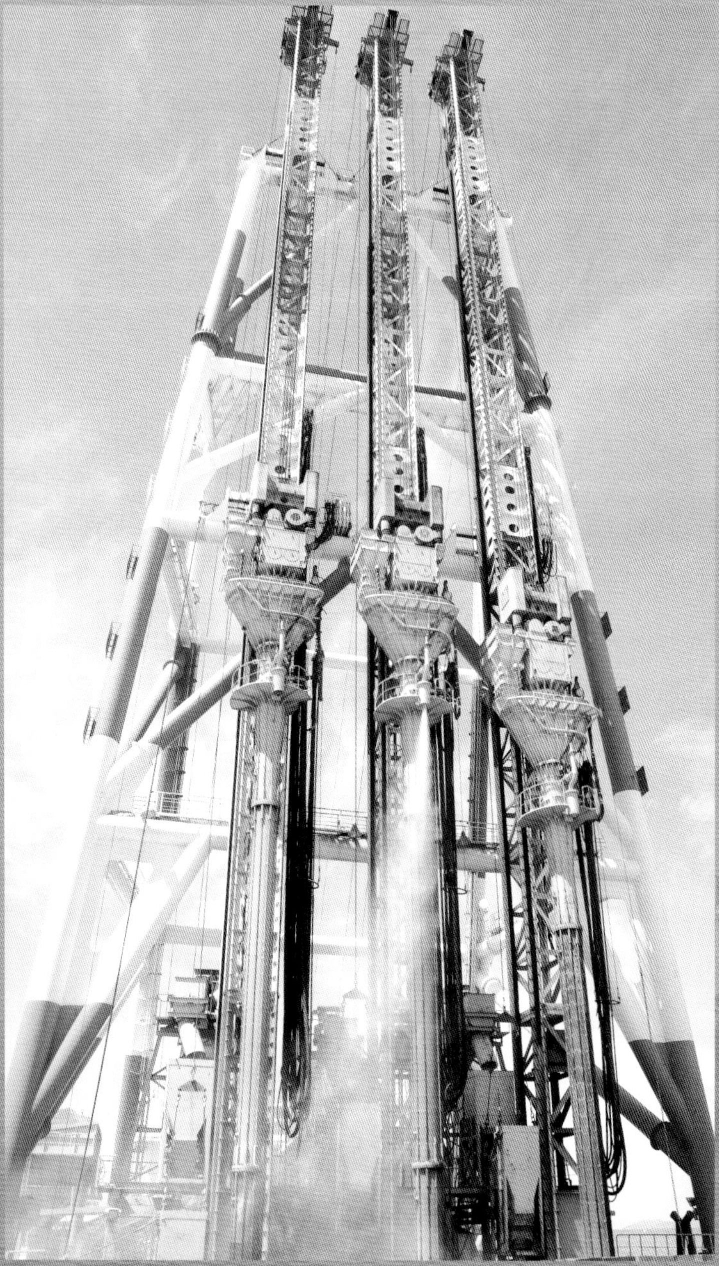

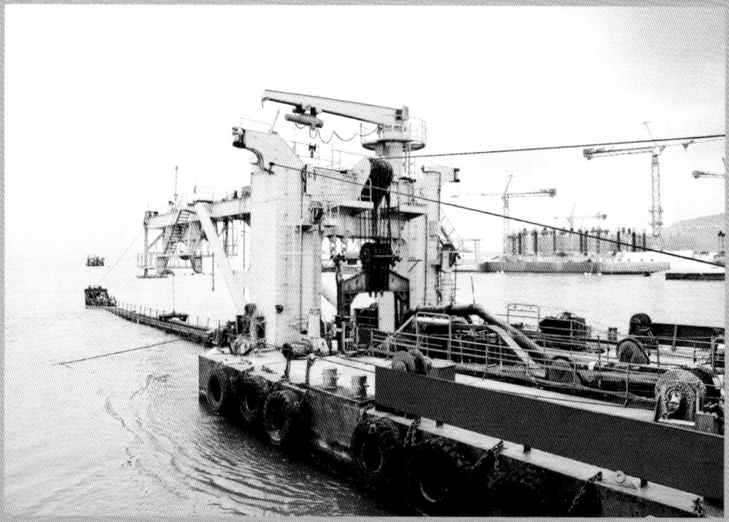

▲ 2012 年 11 月 25 日，"捷龙"清淤船进行隧道基础清淤作业

Dredger "Jielong" was cleaning the tunnel base on November 25, 2012

◀ 2011 年 8 月 14 日，"砂桩 6 号"SCP 施工船进驻西人工岛岛壁 C2 区，正式开始砂桩打设

SCP construction ship for Sand Pile #6 sailed to C2 Island Wall area on West Man-Made Island and began the sand pile drilling on August 14, 2011

▼2011.8.14 ▼2011.11.25 ▼2012.1.25

2011 1 2 3 4 5 6 7 8 9 10 11 12 2012 1 2 3 4 5

▼ 2011 年 11 月 25 日，"金雄"抓斗式挖泥船进行精挖施工

Grab dredger "Jinxiong" was conducting fine excavation on November 25, 2011

▼ 2012 年 1 月 25 日，"浚海 5"耙吸船进行基槽疏浚施工

Cutter suction dredger "Junhai 5" was cleaning the sediments on January 25, 2012

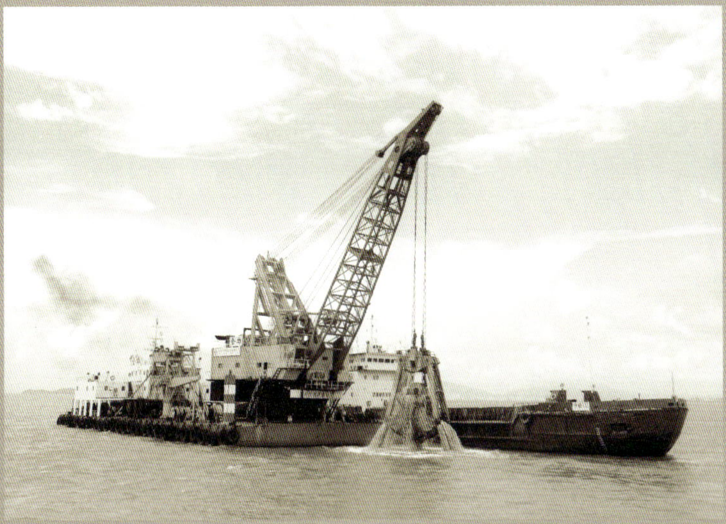

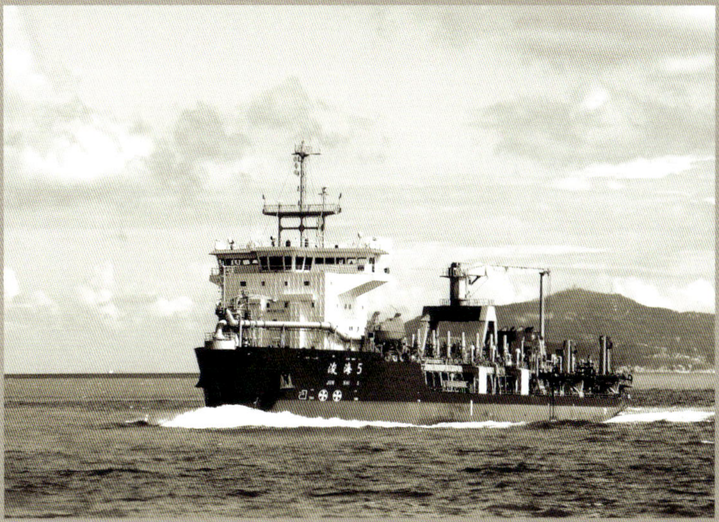

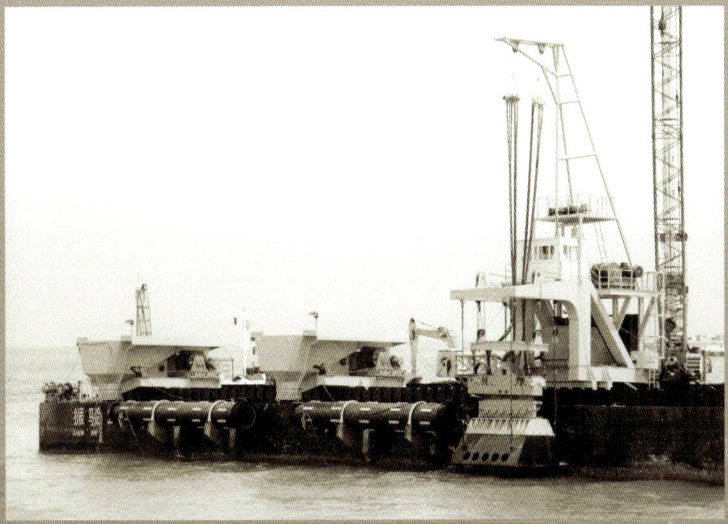

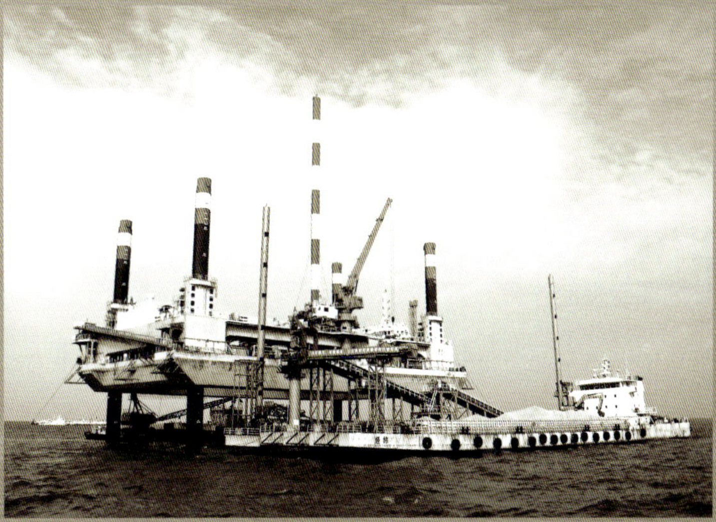

▲ 2012 年 10 月 25 日，"振驳 28"抛石夯平船进行抛石夯平施工

Barge "Zhenbo 28" was conducting rock filling, compacting and leveling on October 25, 2012

▲ 2013 年 4 月 25 日，"津平 1"碎石整平船进行基床整平施工

Barge "Jinping 1" was conducting rubble bed leveling on April 25, 2013

▼2012.10.25 ▼2012.11.25 ▼2013.4.25

9 10 11 12 2013 1 2 3 4 5 6 7 8 9 10 11 12 2014

沉管预制厂

PRECAST FACTORY OF THE IMMERSED TUBES

▼ 2010 年 12 月 19 日，沉管预制厂开工建设

Immersed tube precast factory began to work on December 19, 2010

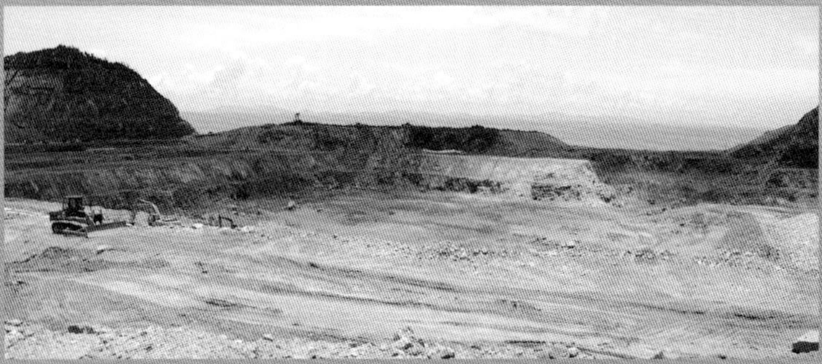

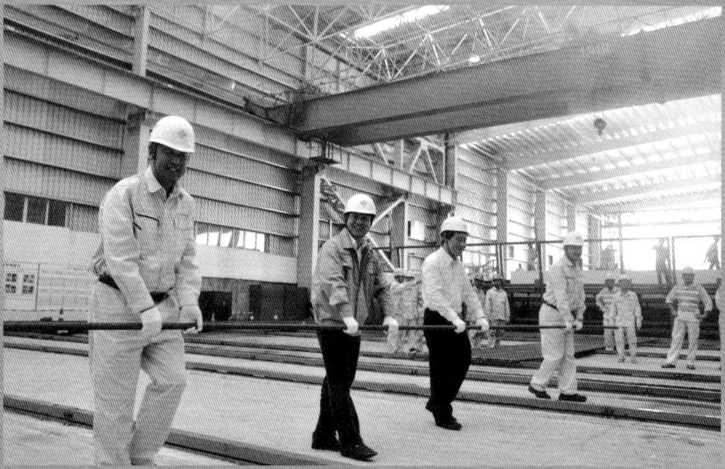

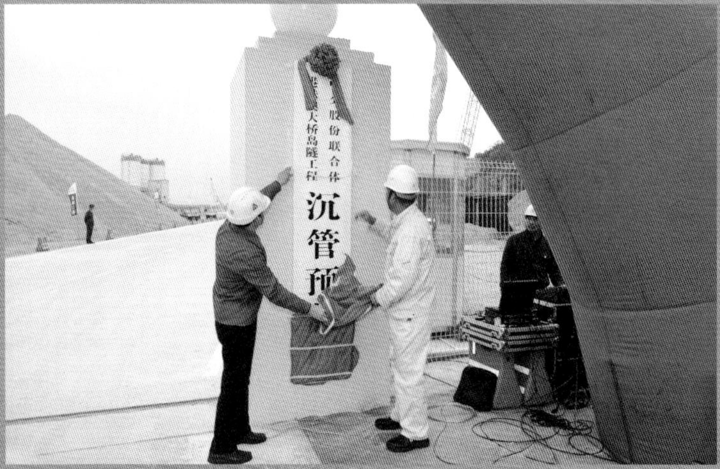

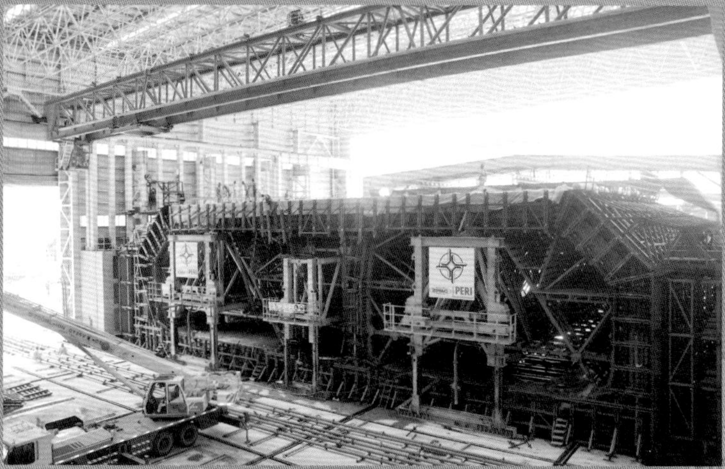

▲ 2012 年 2 月 27 日，沉管预制厂开厂

Opening ceremony of immersed tube precast factory was held on February 27, 2012

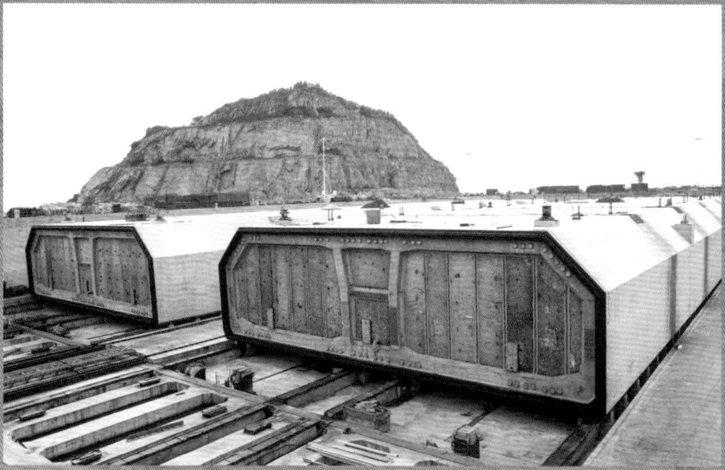

► 2016 年 6 月 15 日，首批曲线段沉管（E32、E33）一次舾装完成

The first fitting-out for the first set of curved immersed tubes (E32、E33) was completed on June 15, 2016

▼2012.4.29

▼2012.2.27 ▼2012.8.7

2012 1 2 3 4 5 6 7 8 9 10 11 12 2013 1 2 3 4 5 6 7 8 9 10 11 12 2014 1 2 3

56 万平方米的占地，2.6 万平方米的建筑面积，桂山预制厂是世界上最大的沉管预制厂。

Guishan Precast Factory, with a working place of 26,000 square meters on a land of 560,000 square meters, is the largest immersed tube precast factory in the world.

◀ 2012 年 4 月 29 日，港珠澳大桥海底隧道首节沉管投产

The first immersed tube for the underwater tunnel of Hong Kong-Zhuhai-Macau Bridge began to be constructed on April 29, 2012

◀ 2012 年 8 月 7 日，首节沉管节段 E2-S5 混凝土浇筑完成

The concrete placement for the first immersed tube E2-S5 was completed on August 7, 2012

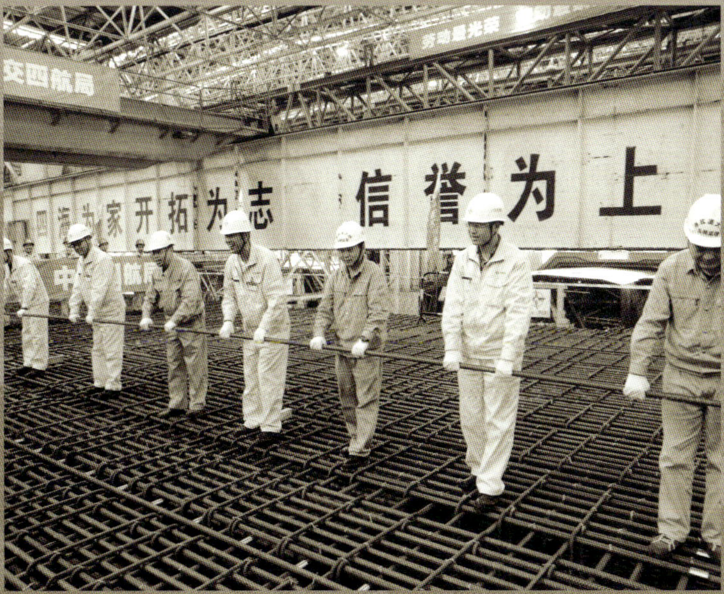

▲ 2016 年 12 月 20 日，最后一节沉管（E30-S1）钢筋笼绑扎完成

The steel cage binding for the last immersed tube E30-S1 was completed on December 20, 2016

▼ 2016 年 12 月 26 日，港珠澳大桥海底隧道沉管圆满预制完成

The landing of the immersed tubes of the underwater tunnel of Hong Kong-Zhuhai-Macau Bridge was successfully completed on December 26, 2016

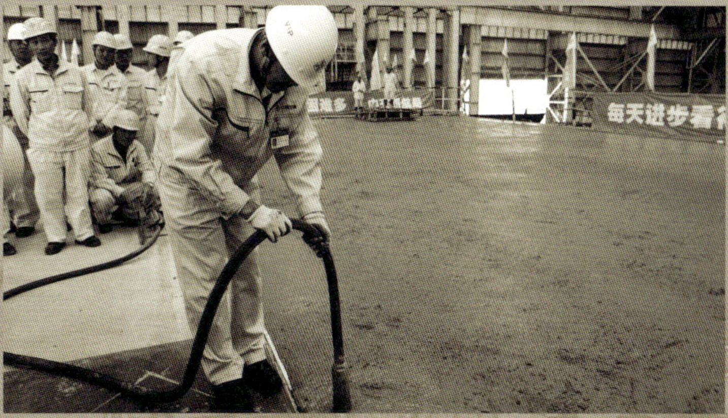

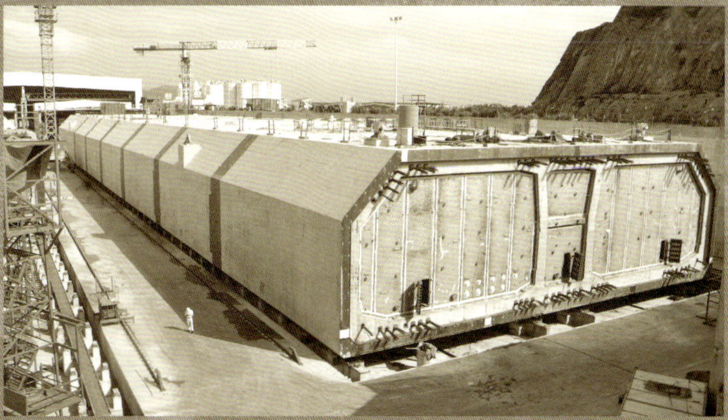

▲ 2017 年 1 月 1 日，港珠澳大桥最后一节沉管整体长距离顶推完成

The long-distance pushing of the last immersed tube of Hong Kong-Zhuhai-Macau Bridge was completed on January 1, 2017

▼2016.6.15 ▼2016.12.20 ▼2017.1.1

10 11 12 **2015** 1 2 3 4 5 6 7 8 9 10 11 12 **2016** 1 2 3 4 5 6 7 8 9 10 11 12 **2017**

沉管浮运安装

FLOAT CONVEYANCE AND INSTALLATION OF THE IMMERSED TUBE

▼ 2013 年 4 月 25 日，首批沉管一次舾装完成

The first outfitting of the first set of immersed tubes was completed on April 25, 2013

▼ 2016 年 3 月 16 日，最后一批直线段沉管（E27、E28）横移完成

The horizontal moving of the last set of immersed tubes (E27 and E28) for the straight section of the tunnel was completed on March 16, 2016

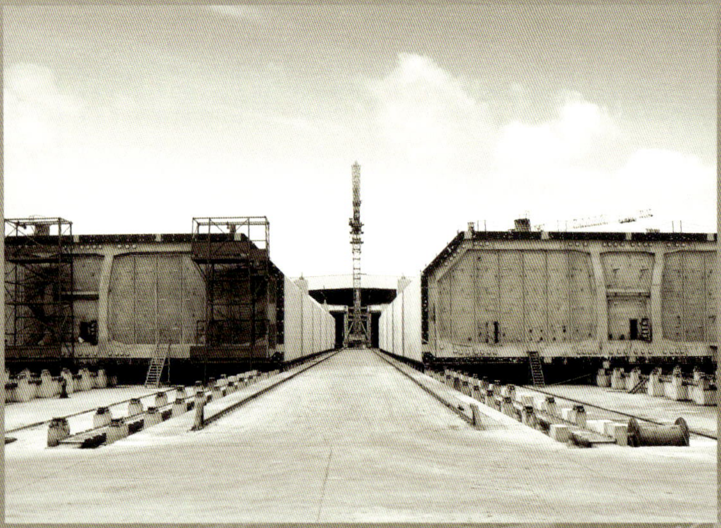

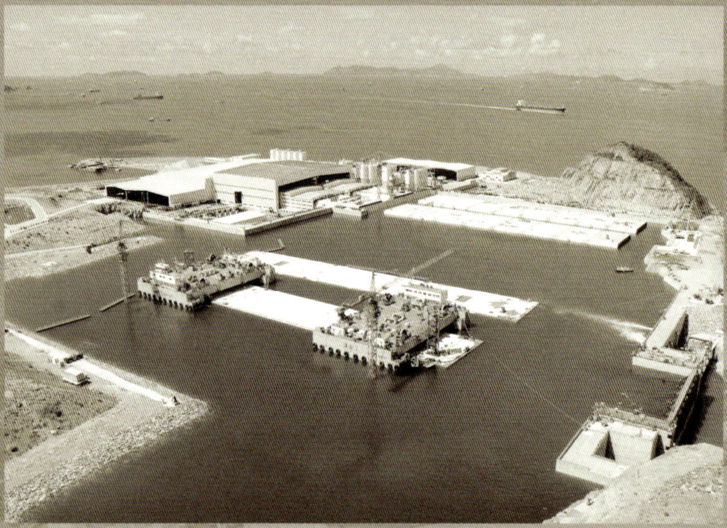

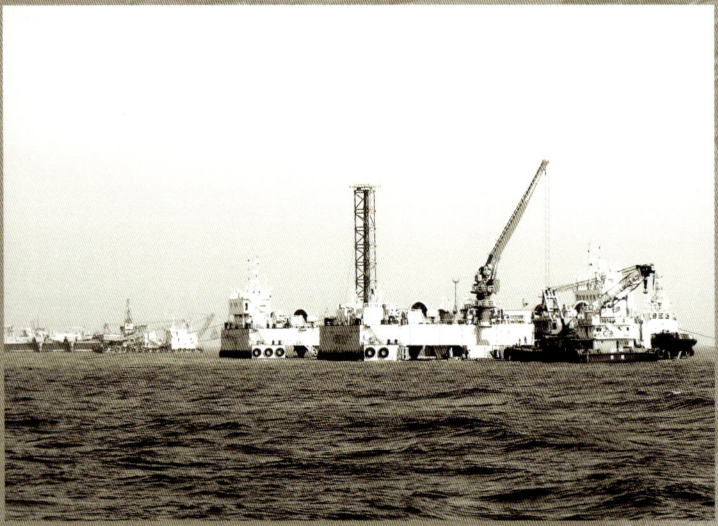

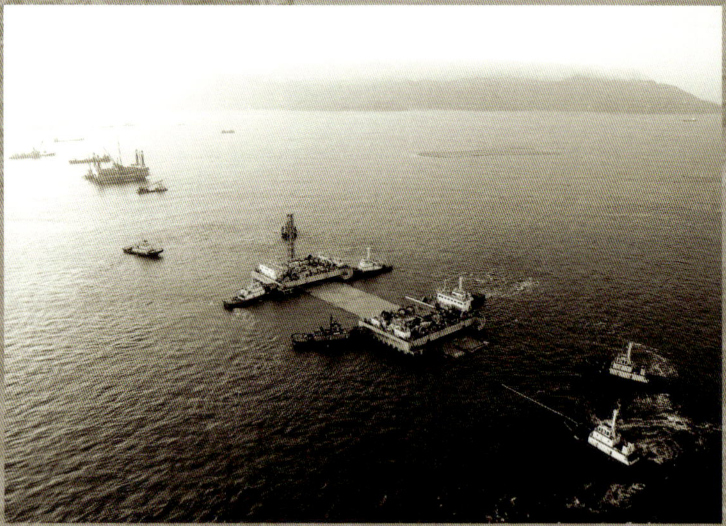

▲ 2013 年 5 月 2 日，首节沉管浮运安装

The float conveyance and installation of the first immersed tube was completed on May 2, 2013

▲ 2016 年 10 月 7 日，E33 沉管浮运至安装海域准备与东人工岛对接

Immersed tube E33 was moved to the installation site, ready to connect the tunnel on East Man-Made Island on October 7, 2016

▼ 2013.5.2

▼ 2013.4.25

2013 1 2 3 4 5 6 7 8 9 10 11 12 2014 1 2 3 4 5 6 7 8 9 10 11 12 2015 1 2 3

深水深槽、大径流、强回淤，复杂的海况条件，近 50 米水深的无掩护外海， 连续安装 33 节沉管，克服了一个个难关，创造了一年安装十节沉管的"中国速度"。

Deep water, deep trench, strong water flow, serious back silting, complicated oceanic environment, open seas of 50 meters deep without cover, and installation of 33 huge immersed tubes were all perfectly handled, and the "Chinese speed" won its fame by the installation of 10 immersed tubes in just one year.

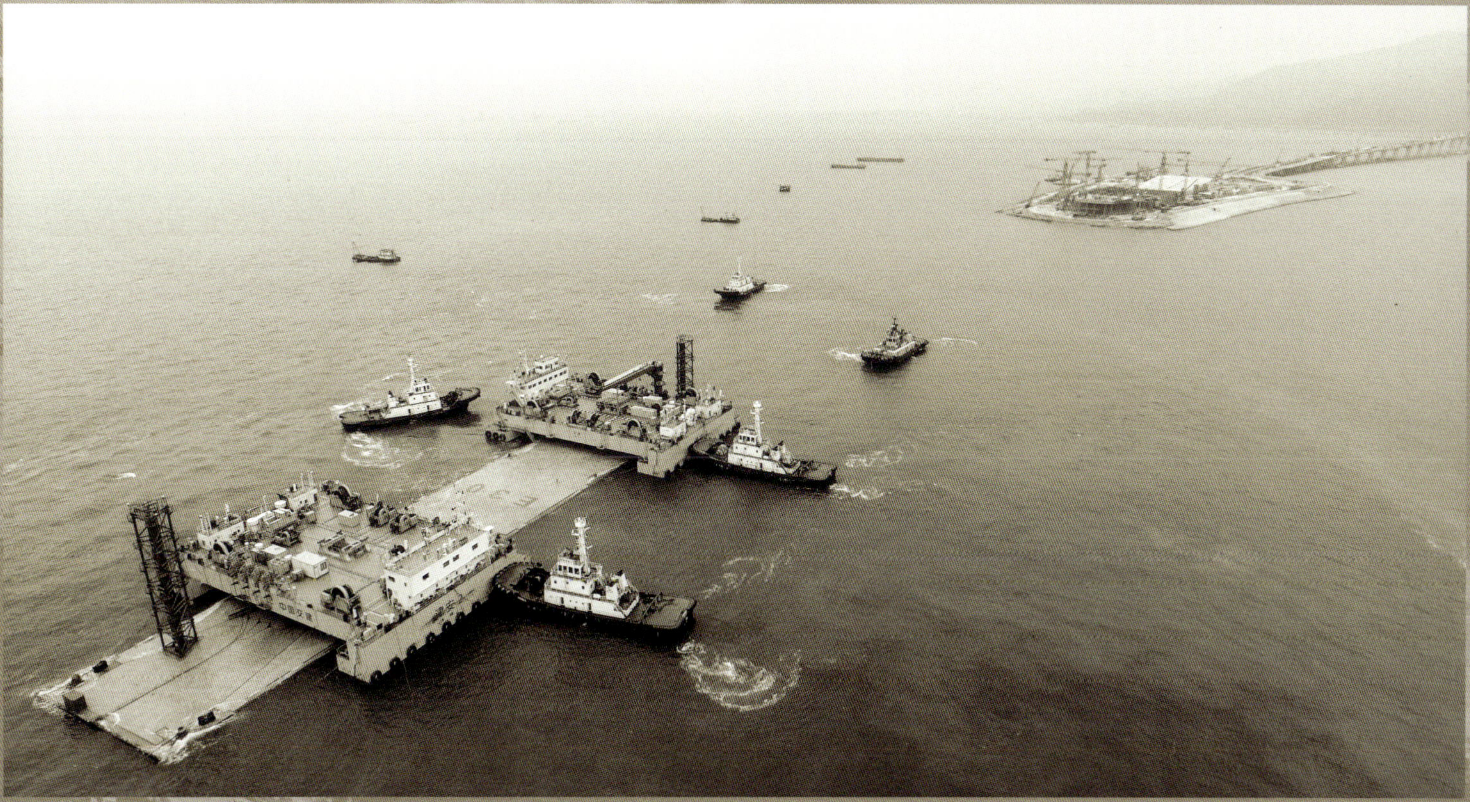

▲ 2017 年 3 月 6 日，最后一节沉管（E30）浮运安装

The float conveyance and installation of the last immersed tube E30 was completed on March 6, 2017

▼2016.3.16 ▼2016.10.7 ▼2017.3.6

10 11 12 2016 1 2 3 4 5 6 7 8 9 10 11 12 2017 1 2 3 4 5 6 7 8 9 10 11 12 2018

最终接头安装
INSTALLATION OF THE CLOSURE JOINT

“把功夫用在前面，成败取决于过程；一丝不苟于细节，风险防控至微末。”

铁打的团队，以拼搏的铁人精神、精细的工匠精神、严谨的科学精神，精心打造好每一个细节，铸就时代丰碑。

“If efforts lead, success comes in the process; if care prevails, risks lose trails.”

The iron-willed team, with the iron man spirit, with their ingenuity, with their scientific preciseness, never gives up a single detail to cast an epochal monument.

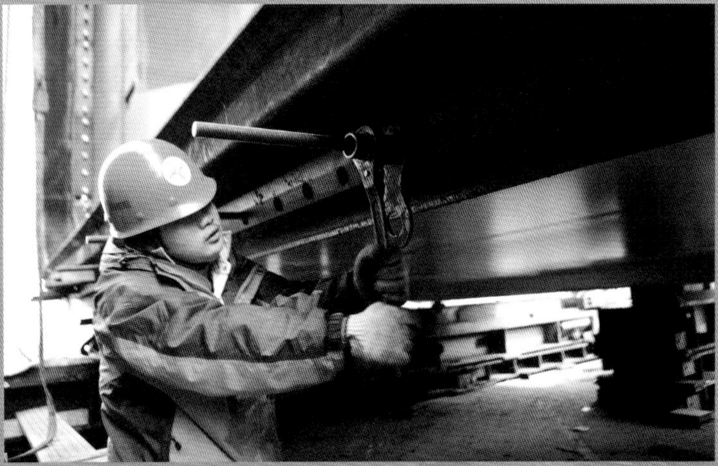

◀ 2017 年 2 月 24 日，最终接头 GINA 止水带安装

The GINA water-stop for the closure joint was installed on February 24, 2017

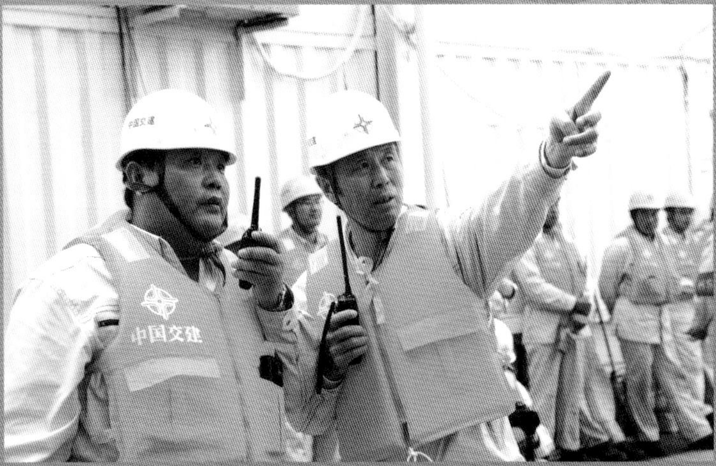

▲ 2017 年 4 月 2 日，最终接头试吊演练

Hoisting test of the closure joint was done successfully on April 2, 2017

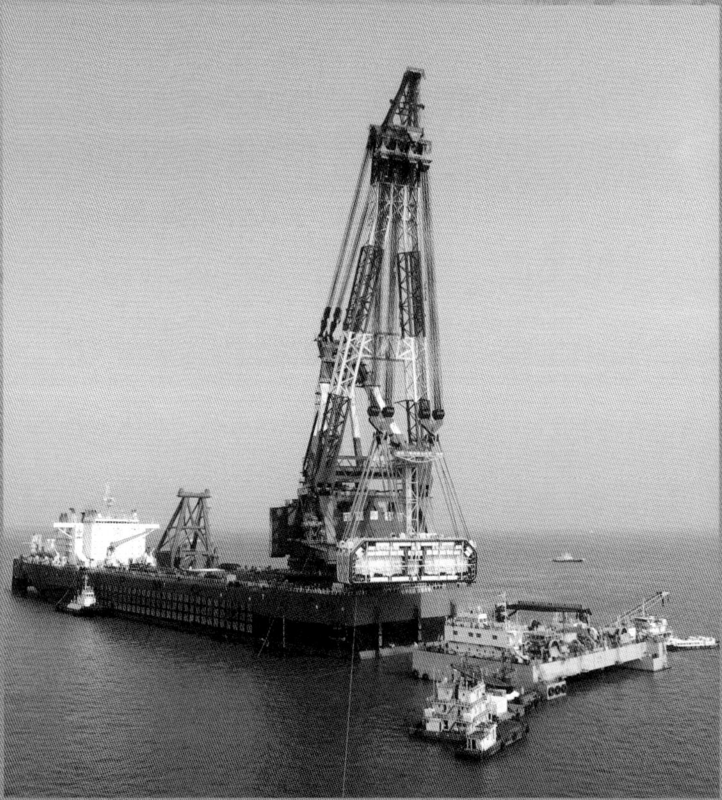

▲ 2017 年 5 月 2 日，最终接头安装起吊

The closure joint was hoisted up on May 2, 2017

▼2017.2.24 ▼2017.4.2 ▼2017.5.2

2017 1 2 3 4 5 6

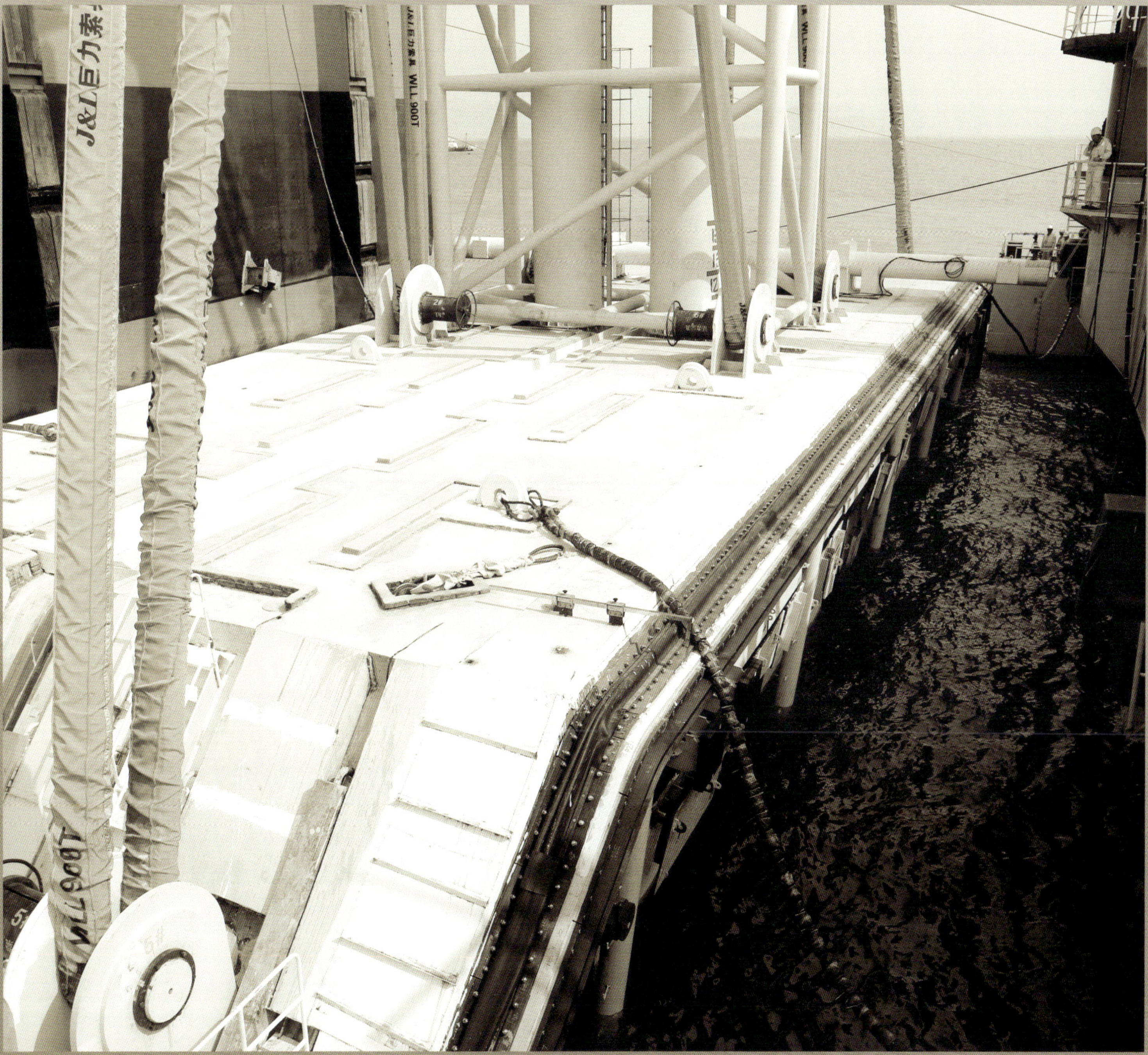

▲ 2017 年 5 月 2 日，最终接头沉放入水对接

The closure joint was landed underwater for the butt welding on May 2, 2017

深海隧道
DEEP SEA TUNNEL

隧道暗埋段减光罩
Light-Reducing Grating for the Buried Section of the Tunnel

遥遥在望的隧道口向未来延伸，
缕缕金线连接起绚丽的梦想之门。

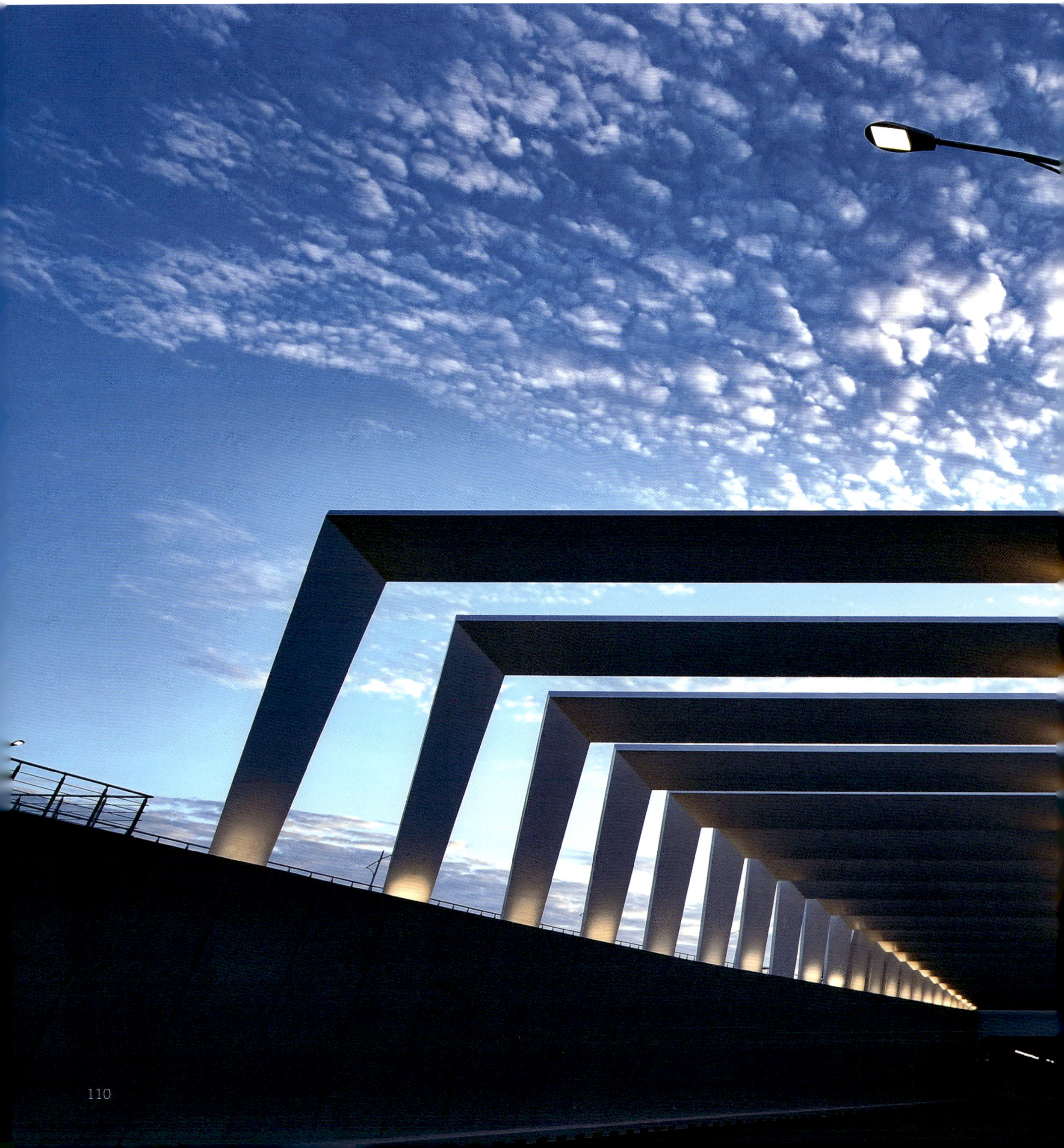

The portal of tunnel in the distance leads to the future, and the golden lines weave the gate to the beautiful dreamland.

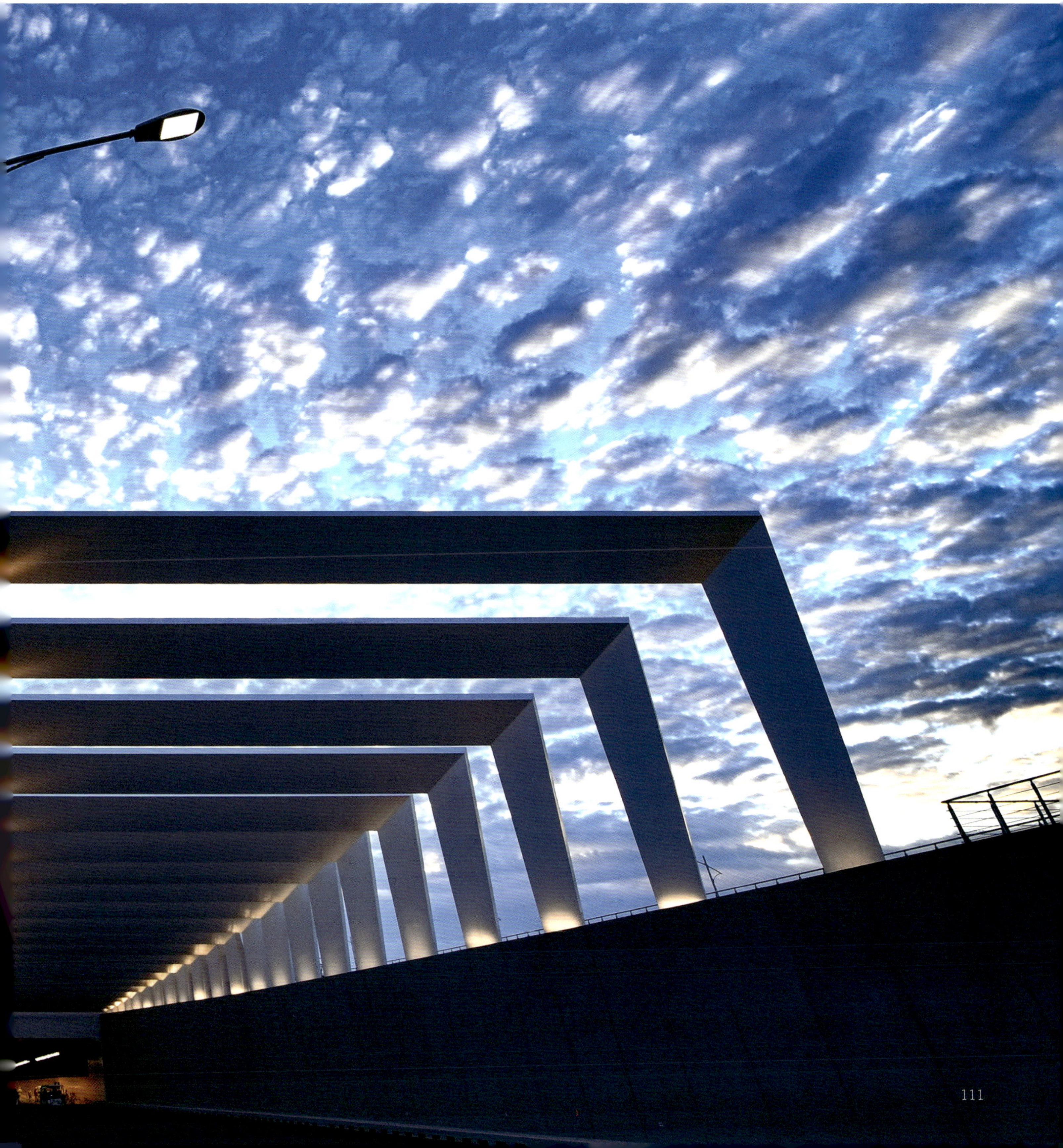

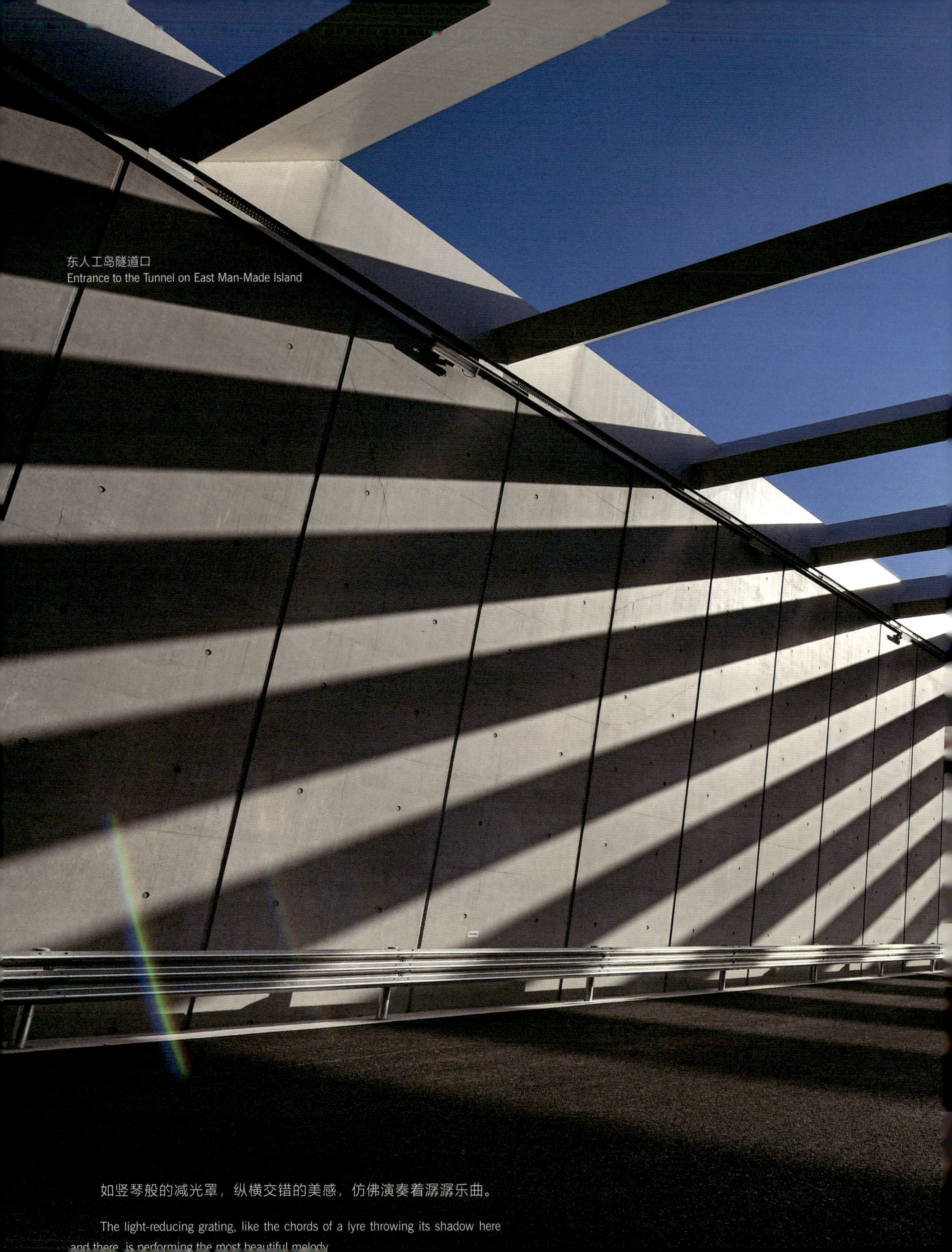

东人工岛隧道口
Entrance to the Tunnel on East Man-Made Island

如竖琴般的减光罩，纵横交错的美感，仿佛演奏着潺潺乐曲。

The light-reducing grating, like the chords of a lyre throwing its shadow here and there, is performing the most beautiful melody.

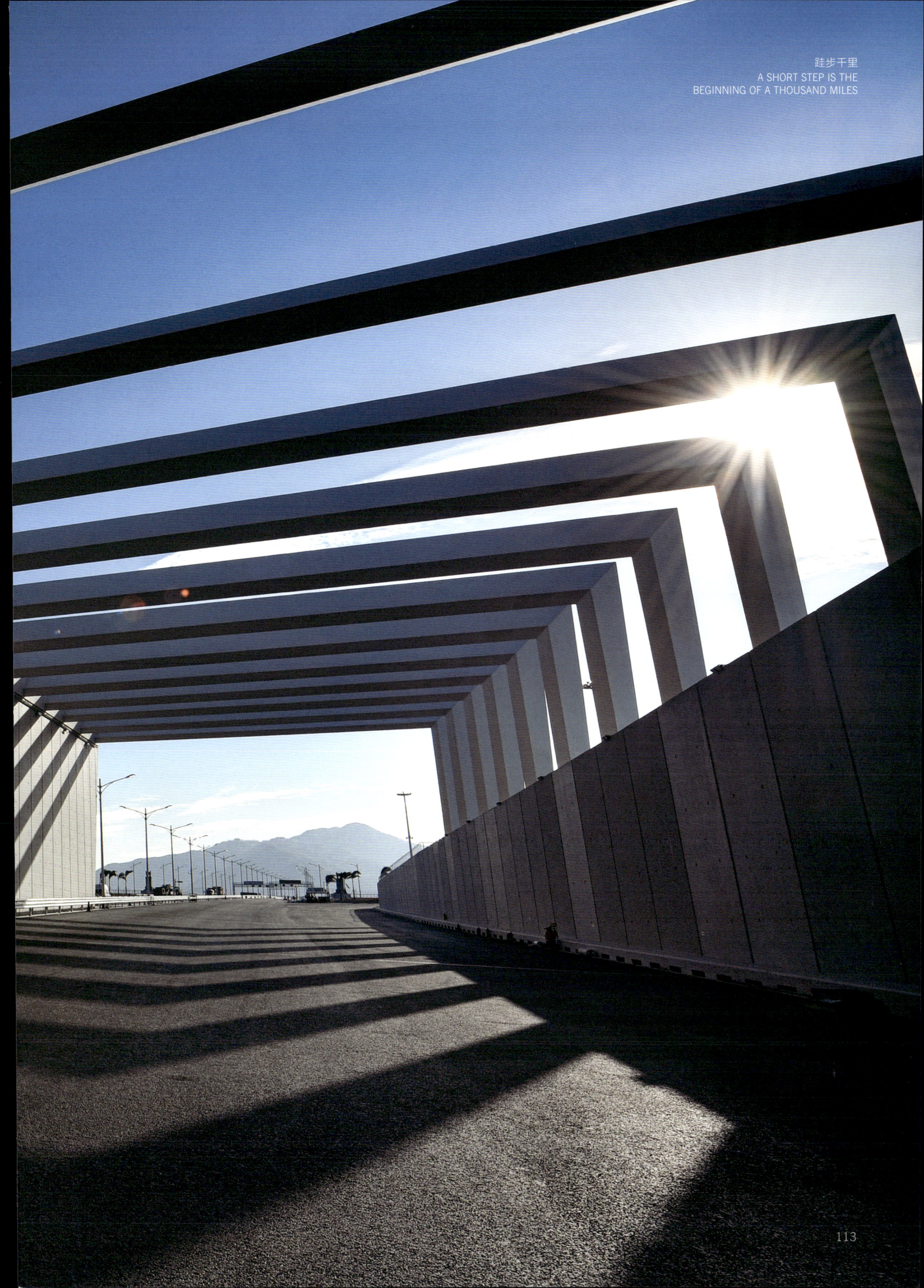

跬步千里
A SHORT STEP IS THE
BEGINNING OF A THOUSAND MILES

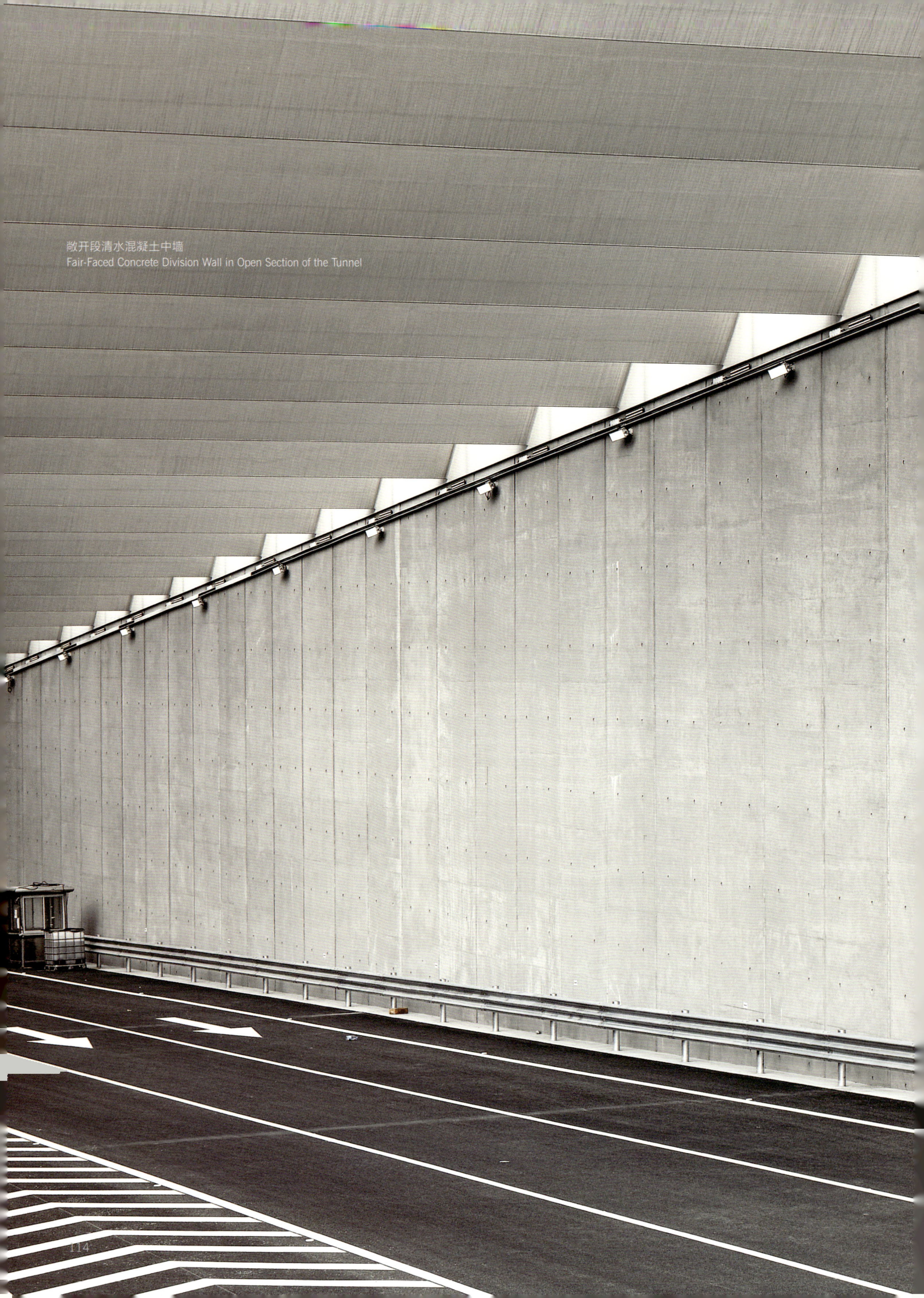

敞开段清水混凝土中墙
Fair-Faced Concrete Division Wall in Open Section of the Tunnel

跬步千里

A SHORT STEP IS THE BEGINNING OF A THOUSAND MILES

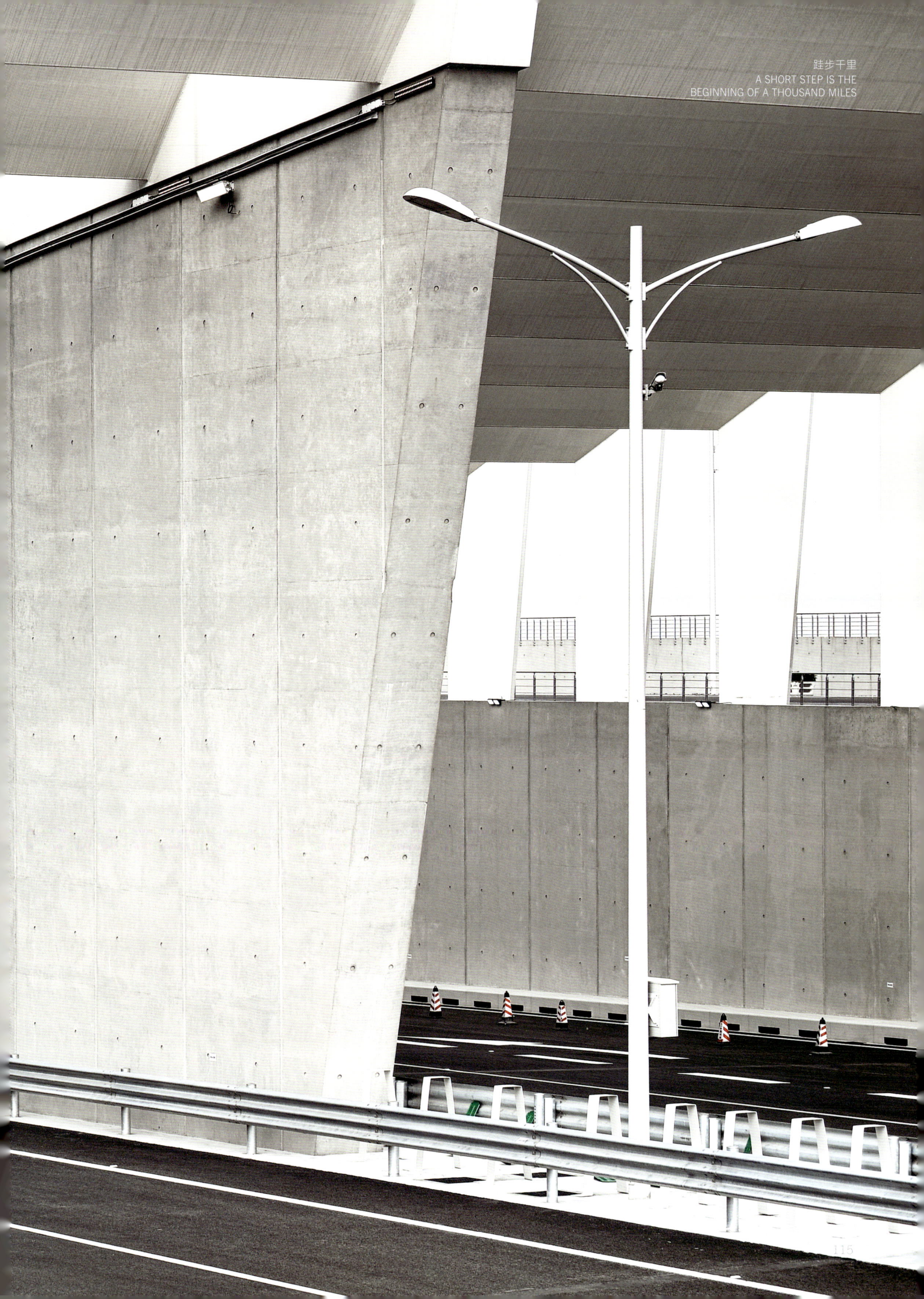

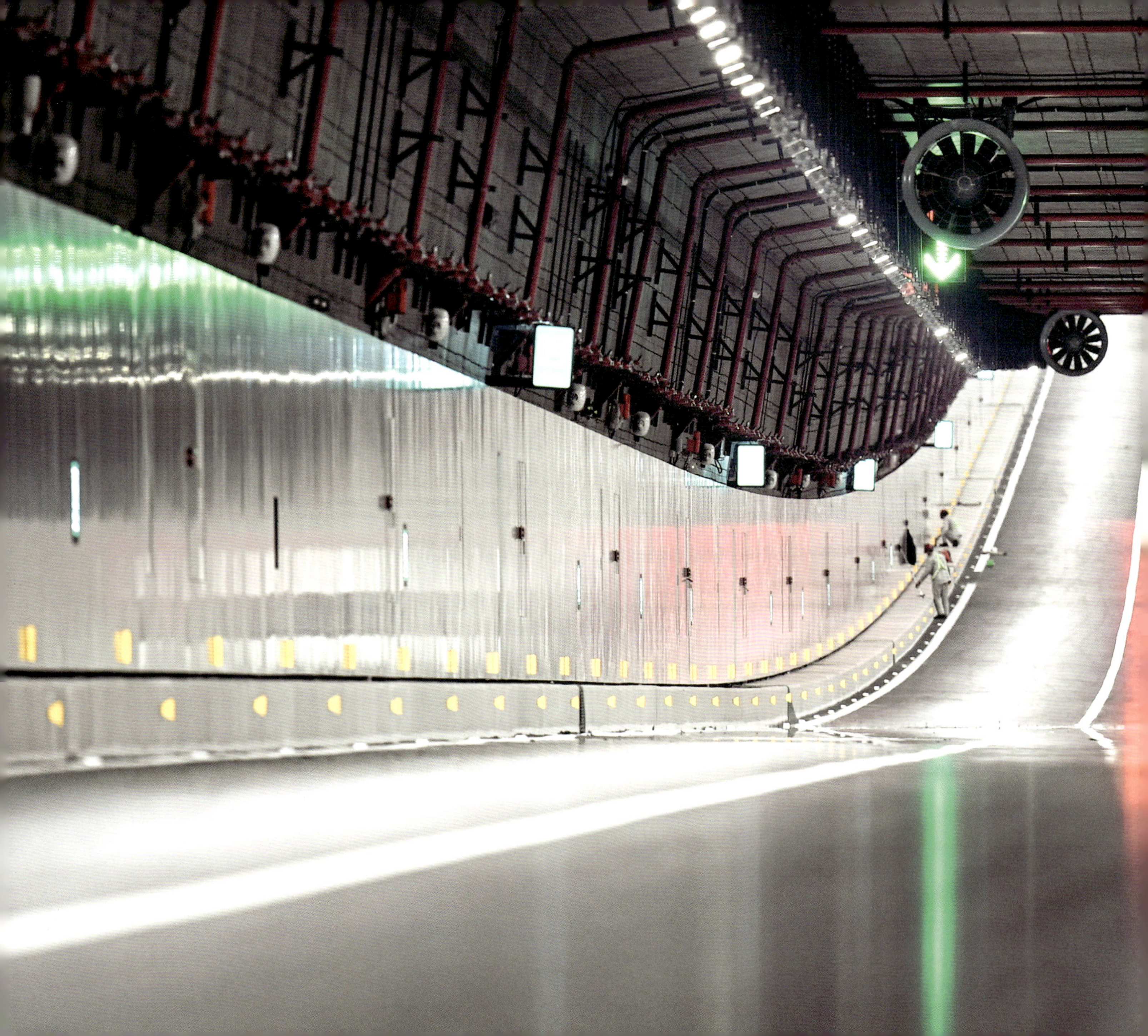

劈波筑路，踏浪架桥。6.7公里海底隧道穿过45米海底，连接三地通途，托起湾区梦想。

Taming the rough waves, the 6.7-kilometer tunnel breaks the seabed 45 meters underneath the sea, links the three cities, and lights up the dreams of those living around the Grand Bay.

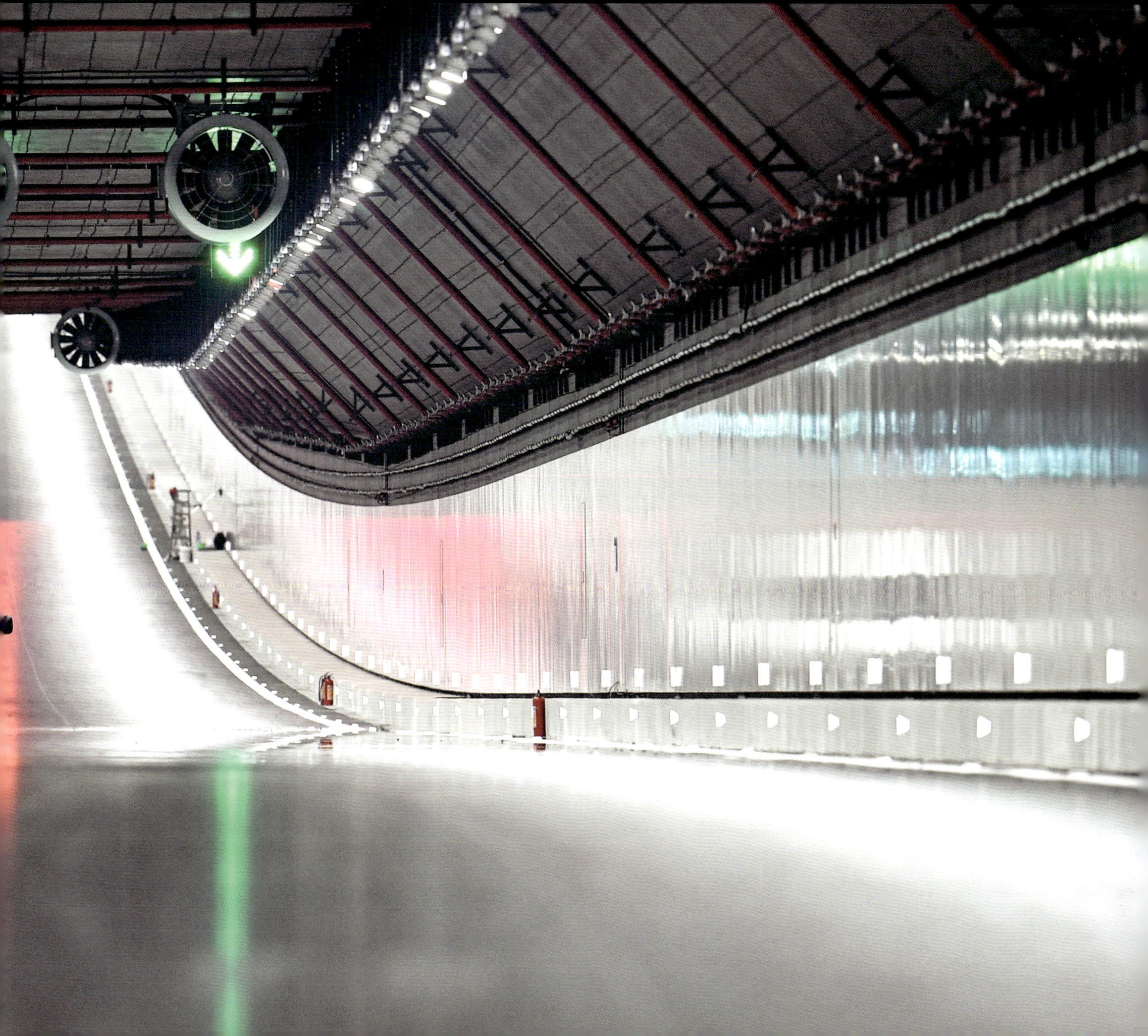

港珠澳大桥曲线段隧道
The Curved Tunnel of Hong Kong-Zhuhai-Macau Bridge

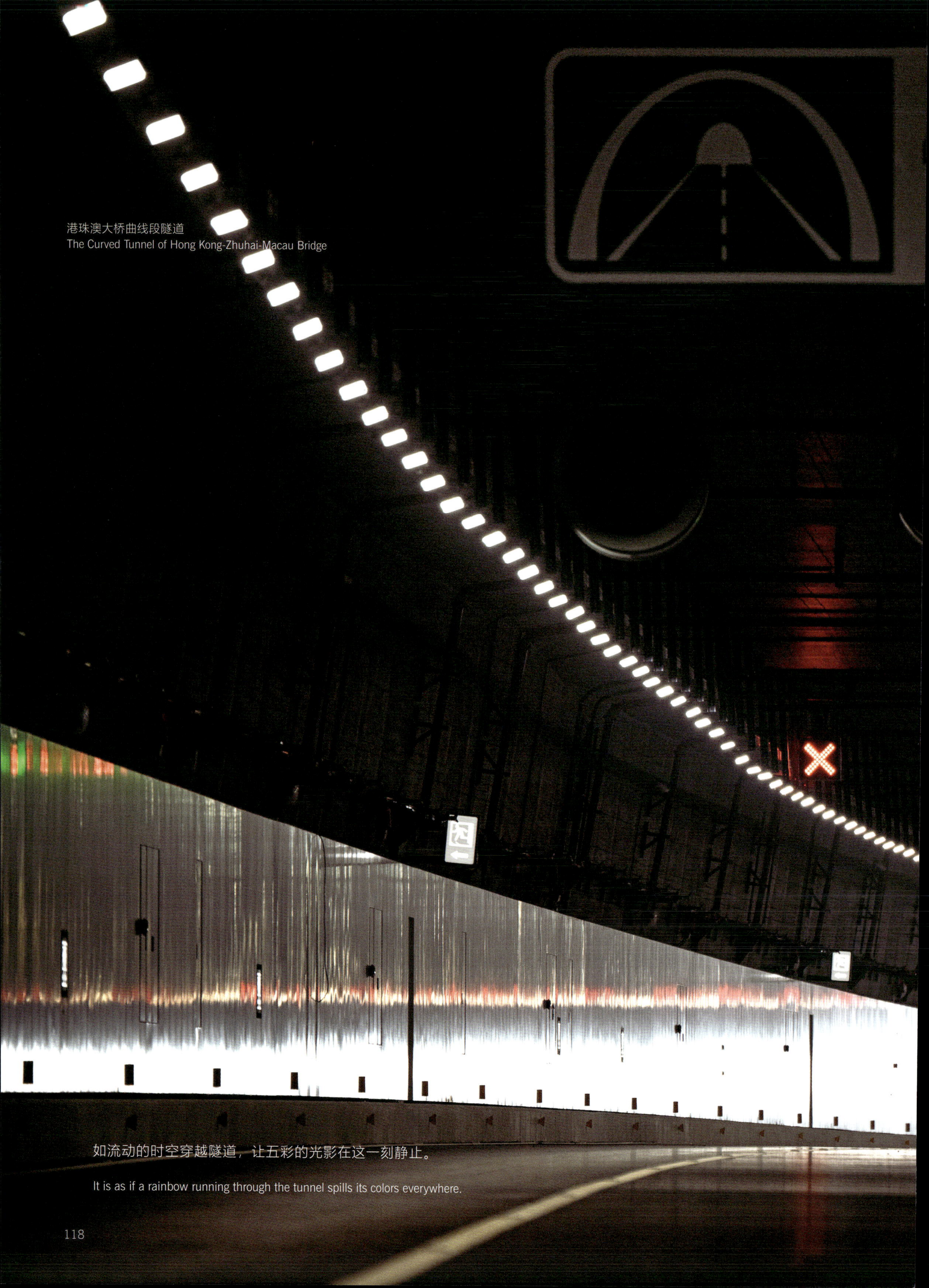

如流动的时空穿越隧道，让五彩的光影在这一刻静止。

It is as if a rainbow running through the tunnel spills its colors everywhere.

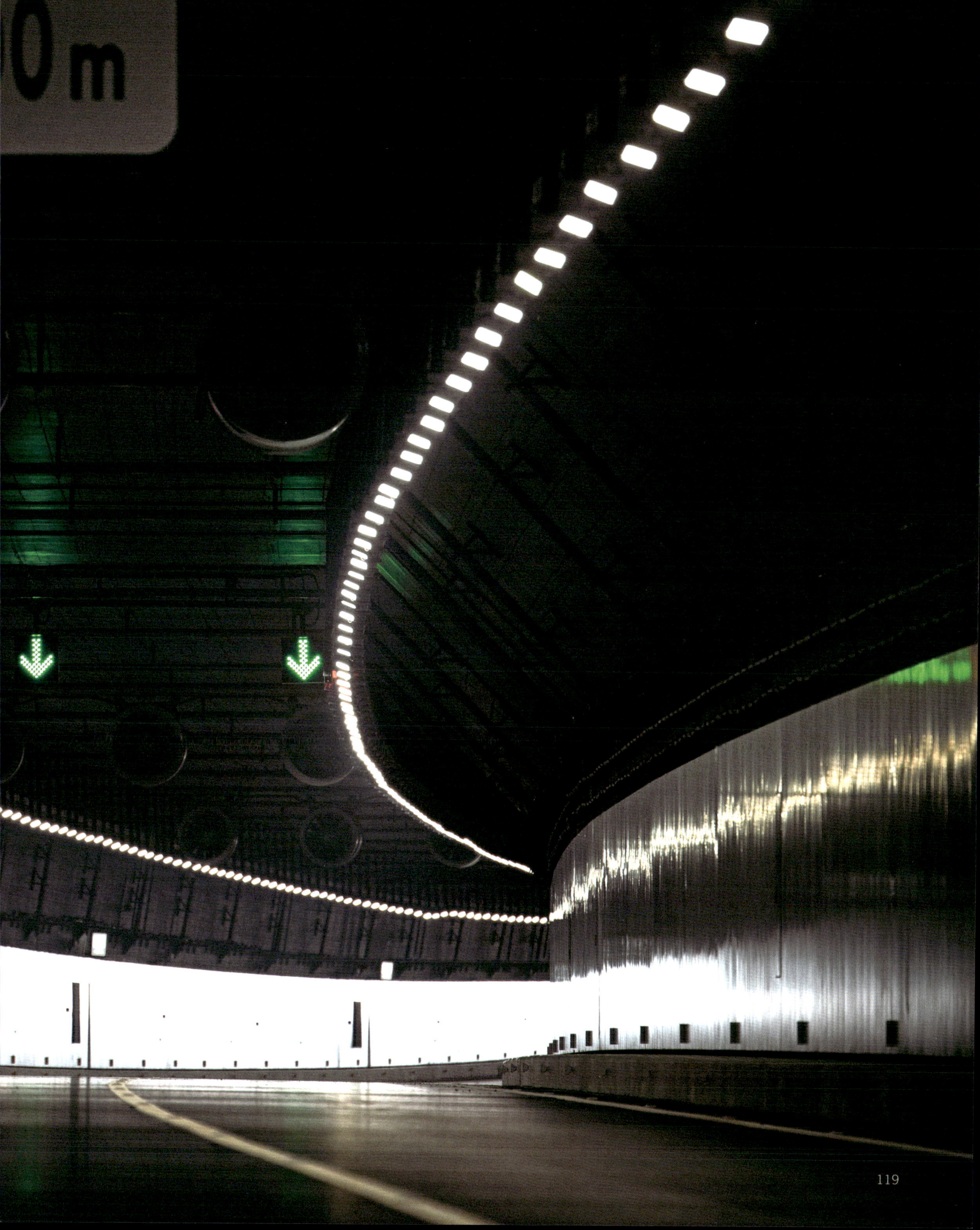
0 m

1. 港珠澳大桥隧道中廊道
Internal Pipe Gallery in the Tunnel of Hong Kong-Zhuhai-Macau Bridge

2. 隧道搪瓷钢板与检修道
Porcelain Steel Plate and the Maintenance Trail in the Tunnel

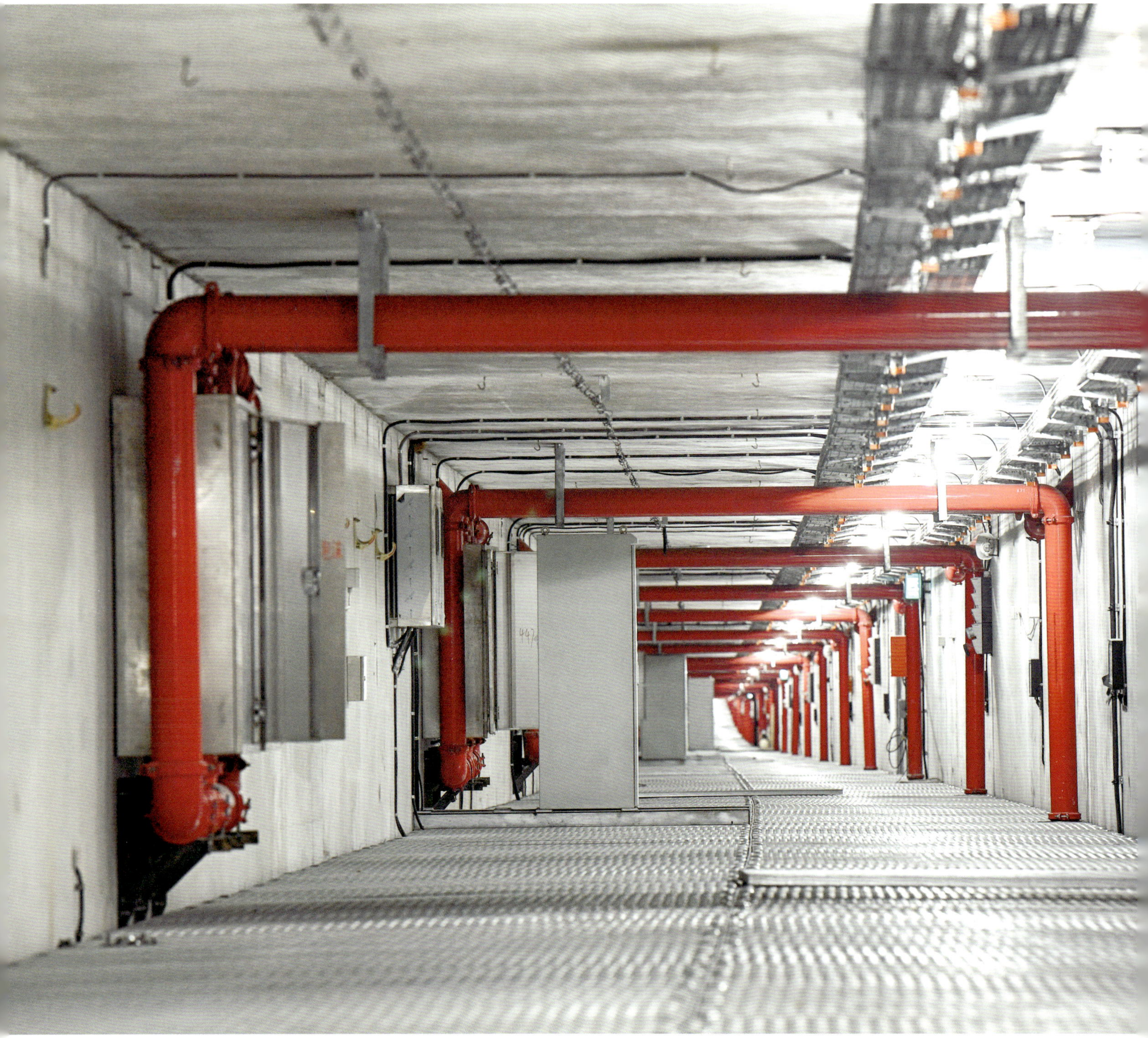

以最普通的材料，完成精湛的工艺，

步道整齐划一，每一道缝隙都完美相融。

The most common material creates the superb crafts,

Each step, each lane, and each gap, neatly made, merge harmoniously into each other.

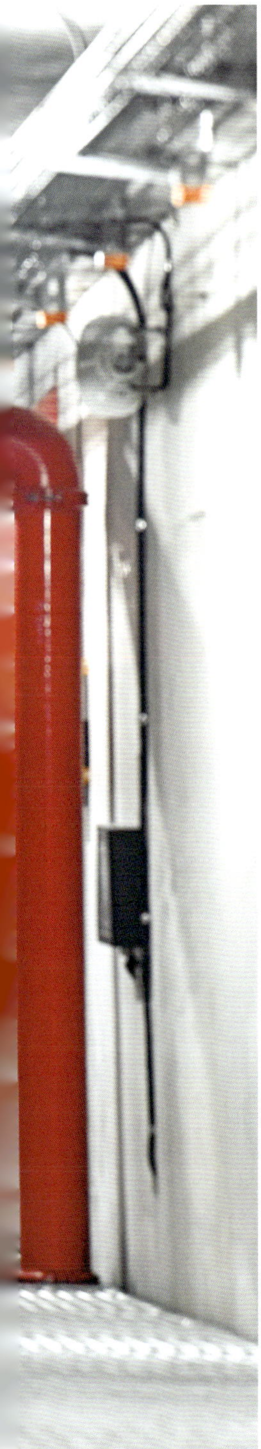

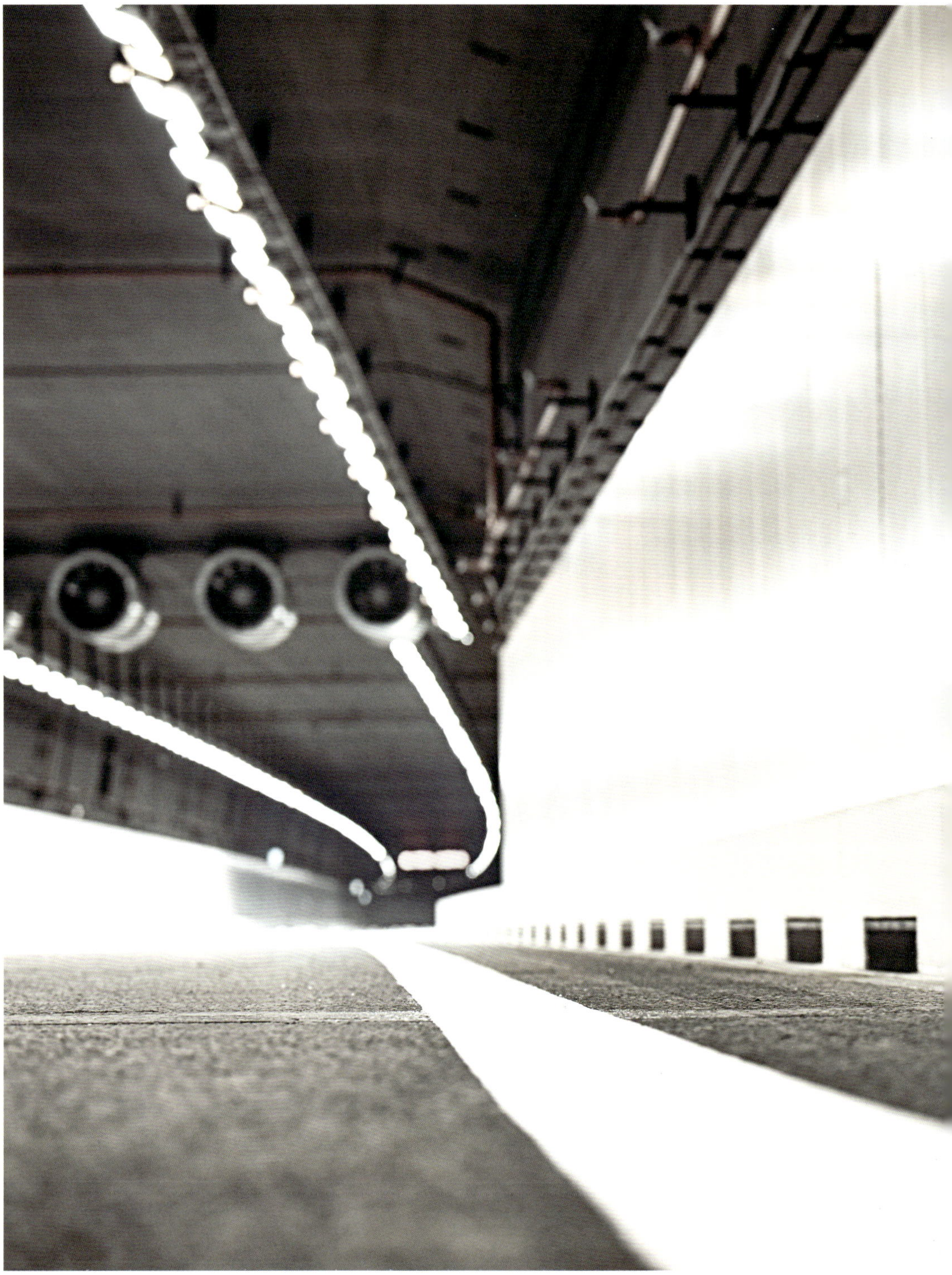

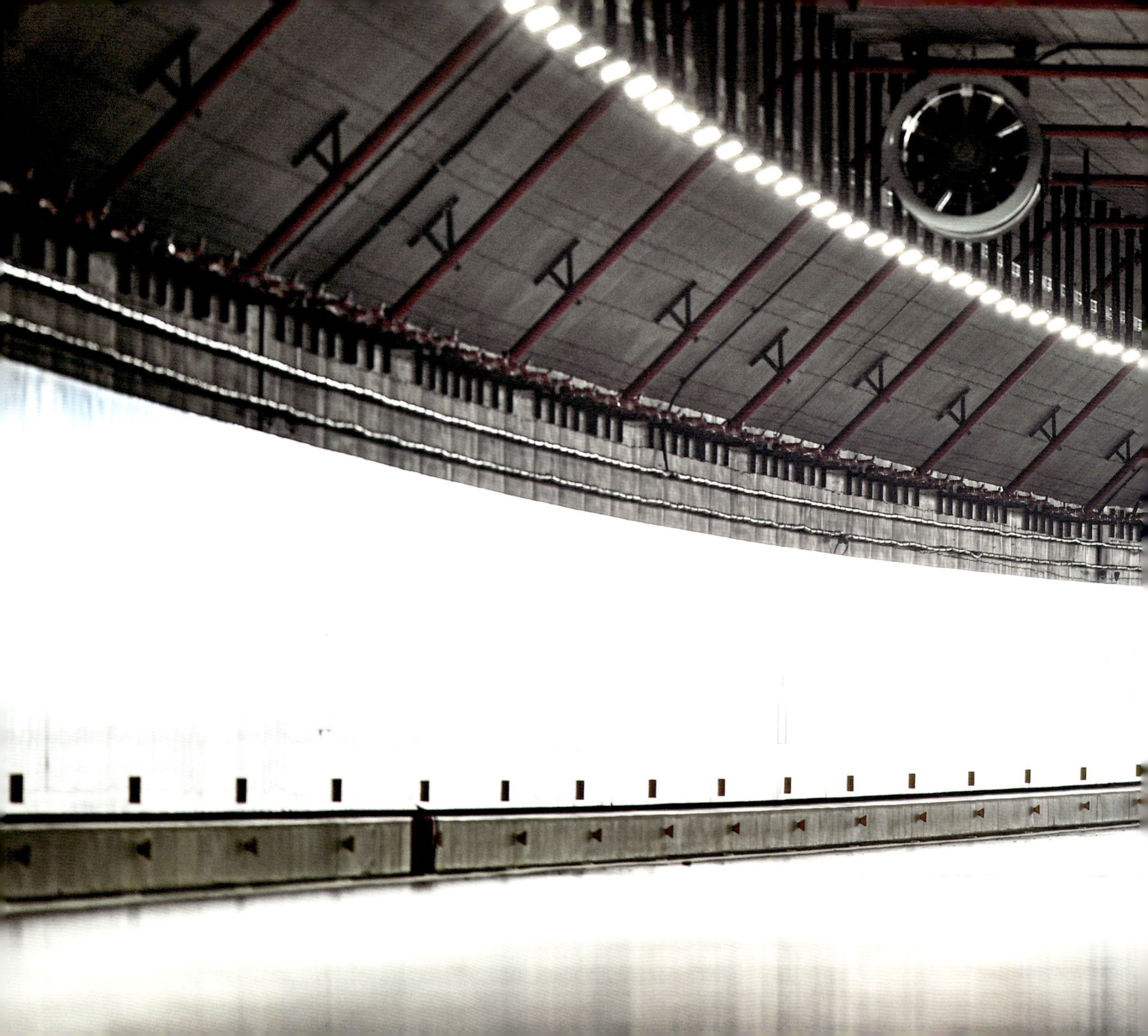

优雅的弧度，完美的造型，

世界首例"工厂法"曲线段沉管预制的结晶。

With the elegant arc, with the graceful shape,

It is a piece of art crystallized by the first try in human history to precast curved tubes in factories.

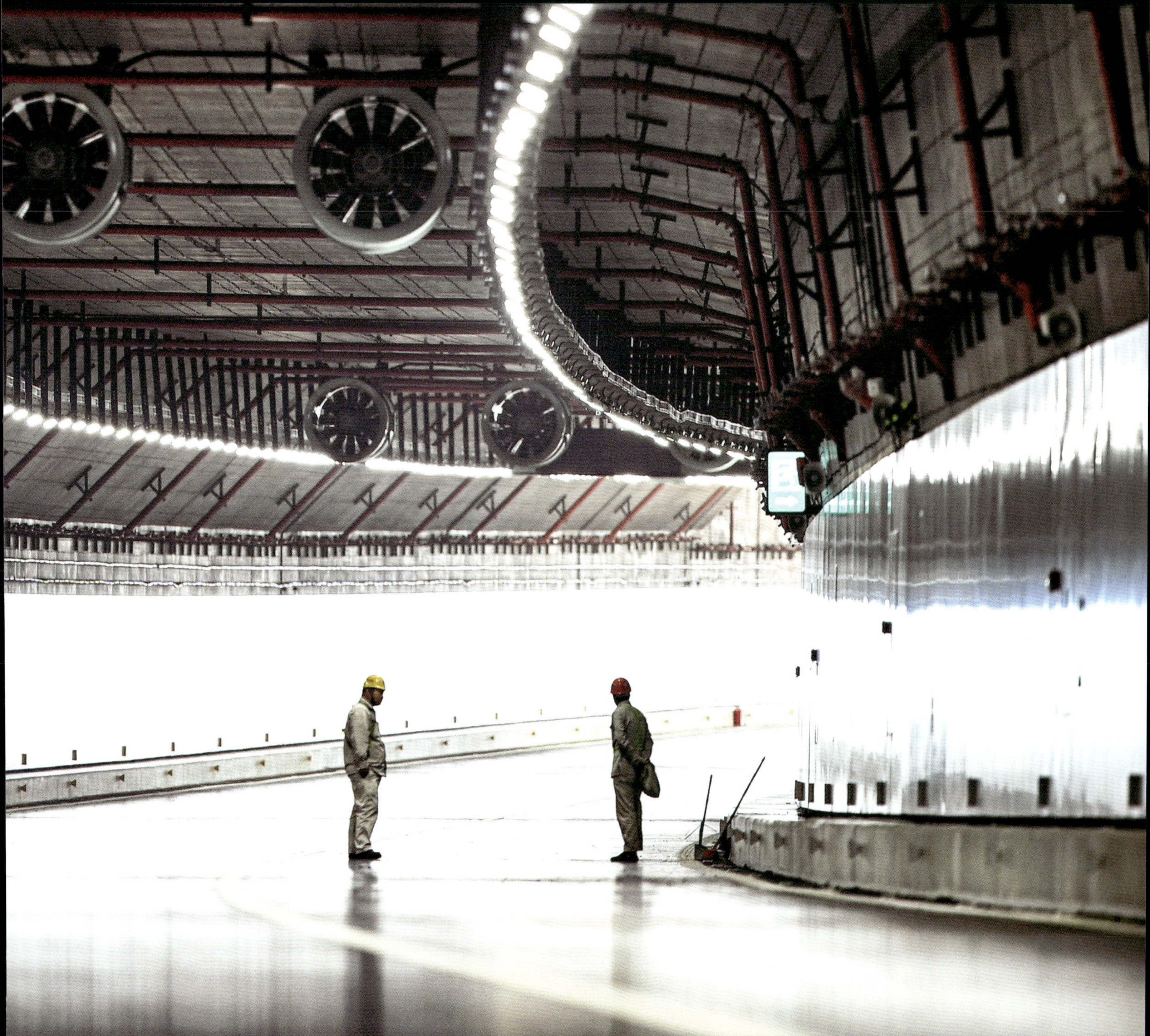

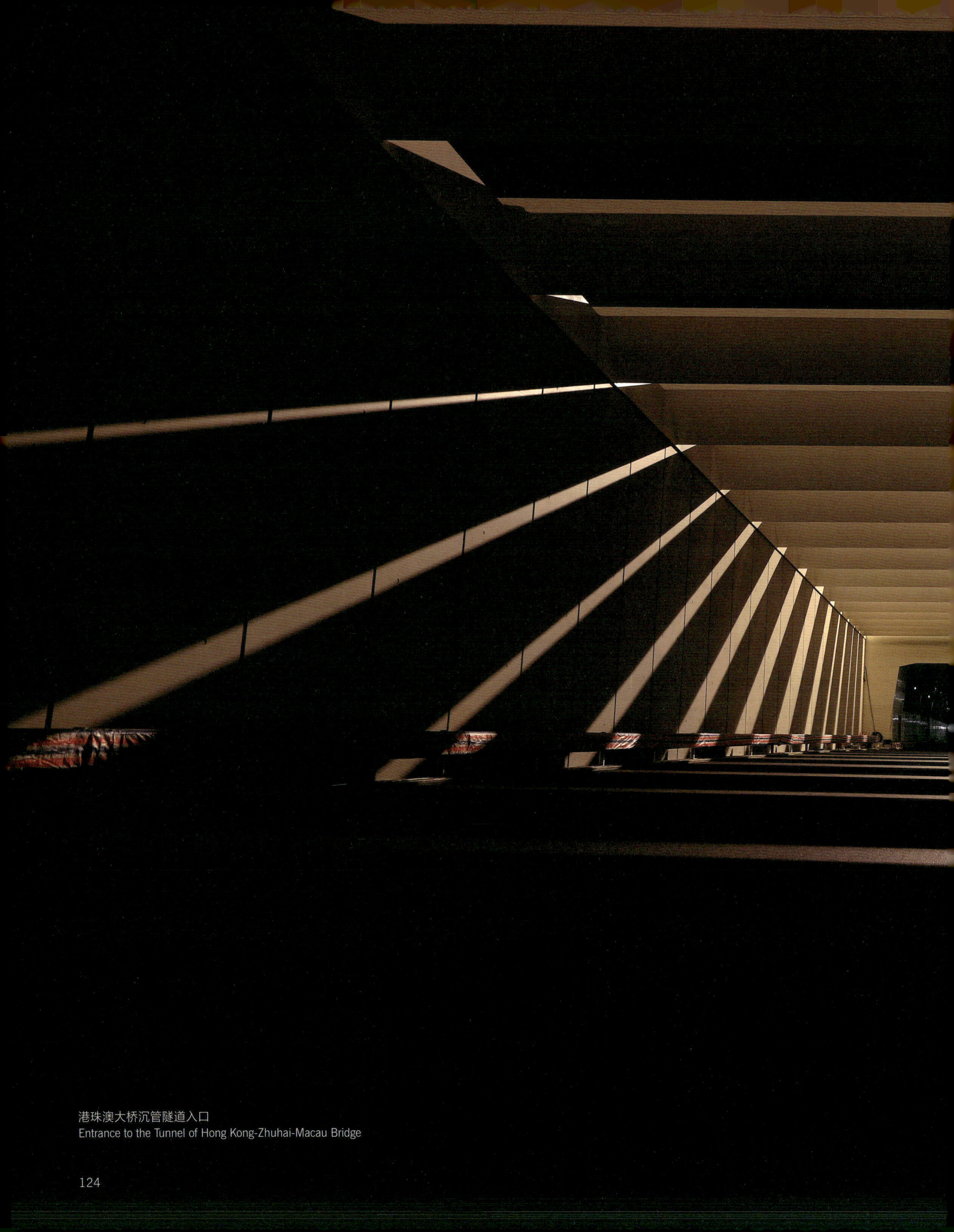

港珠澳大桥沉管隧道入口
Entrance to the Tunnel of Hong Kong-Zhuhai-Macau Bridge

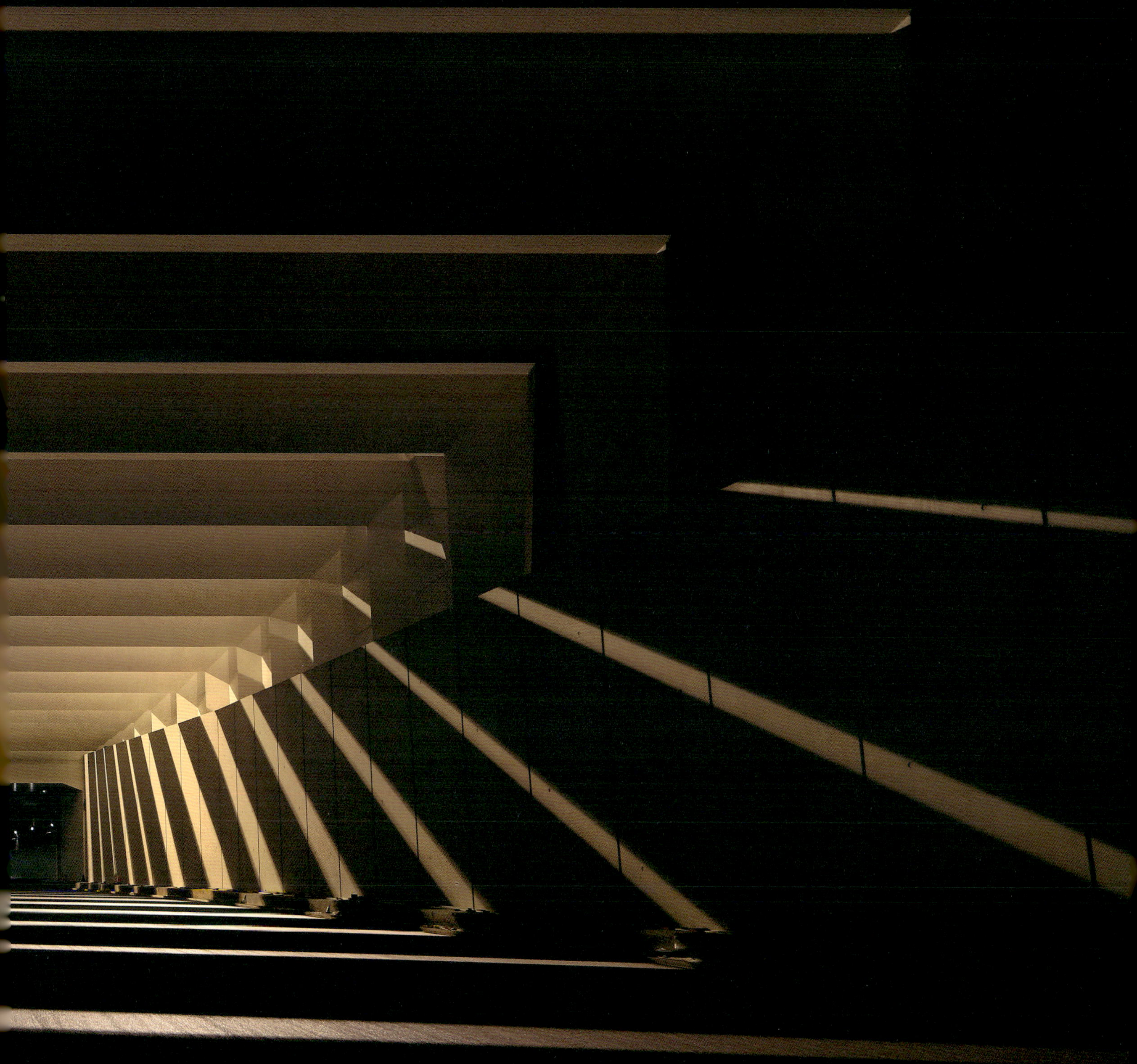

光影纵横，如梦如幻。

The interlacing light and shadow weave fantastic dreams.

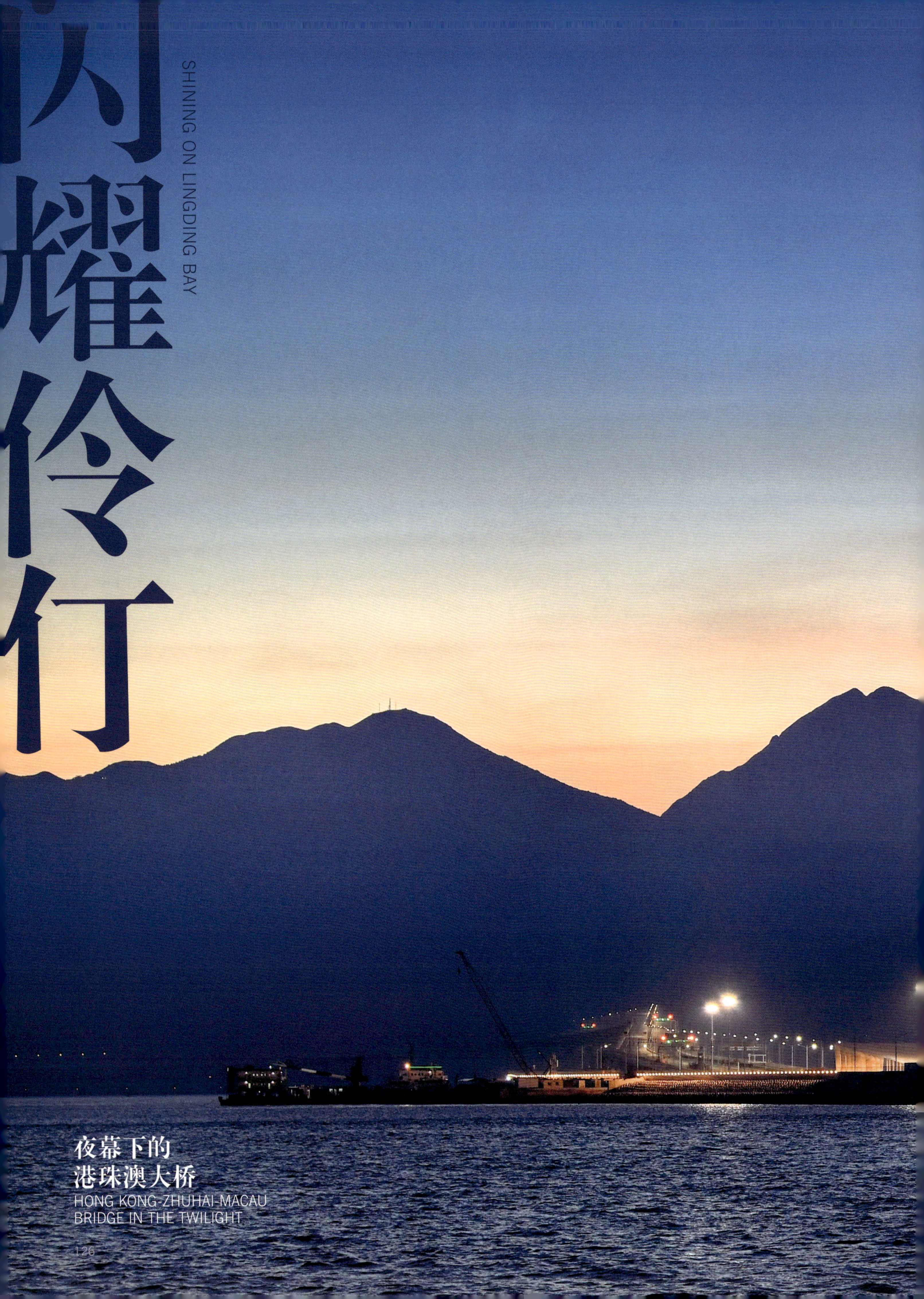

闪耀伶仃

SHINING ON LINGDING BAY

夜幕下的
港珠澳大桥
HONG KONG-ZHUHAI-MACAU
BRIDGE IN THE TWILIGHT

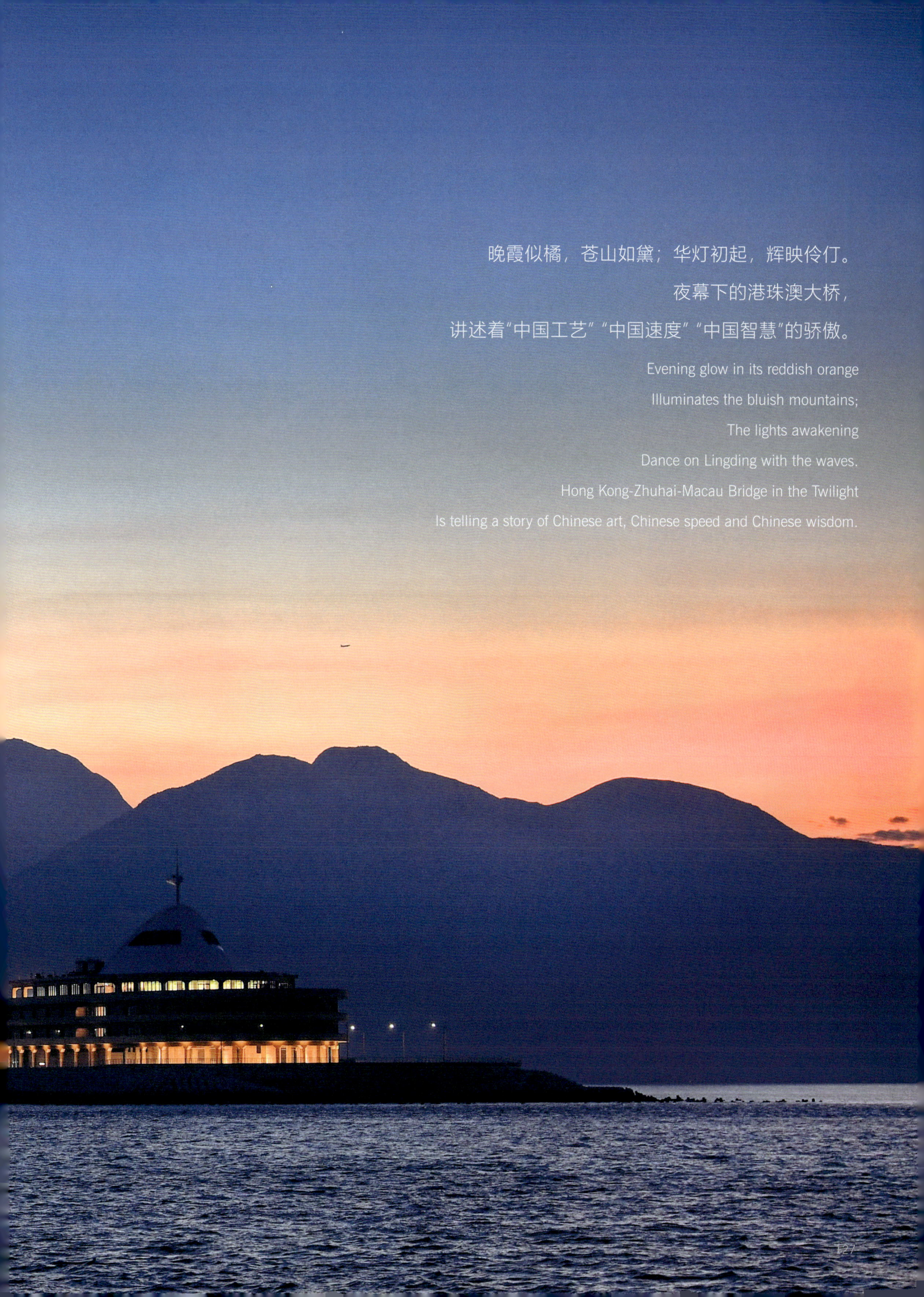

晚霞似橘，苍山如黛；华灯初起，辉映伶仃。
夜幕下的港珠澳大桥，
讲述着"中国工艺""中国速度""中国智慧"的骄傲。

Evening glow in its reddish orange
Illuminates the bluish mountains;
The lights awakening
Dance on Lingding with the waves.
Hong Kong-Zhuhai-Macau Bridge in the Twilight
Is telling a story of Chinese art, Chinese speed and Chinese wisdom.

1. 港珠澳大桥点亮仪式
Lighting-up Ceremony of Hong Kong-Zhuhai-Macau Bridge

2. 车队进入港珠澳大桥海底隧道
The cars entered the underwater tunnel of Hong Kong-Zhuhai-Macau Bridge

3. 车队进入港珠澳大桥西人工岛
The cars embarked on West Man-Made Island of Hong Kong-Zhuhai-Macau Bridge

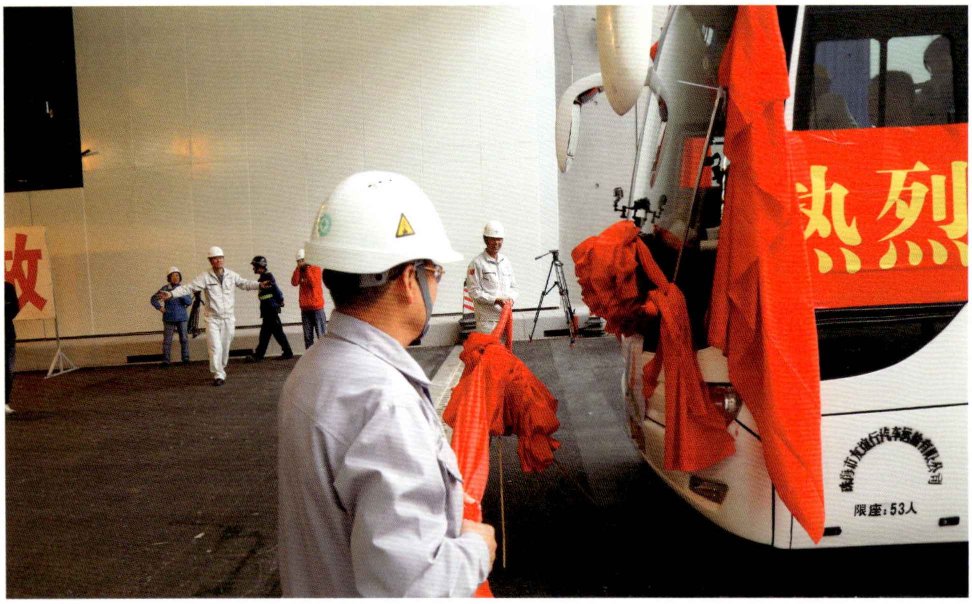

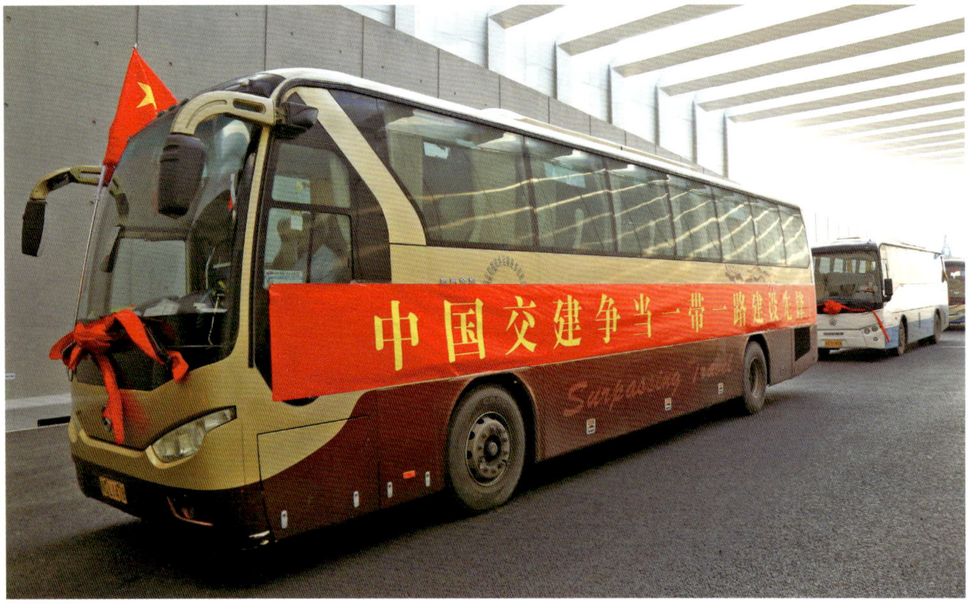

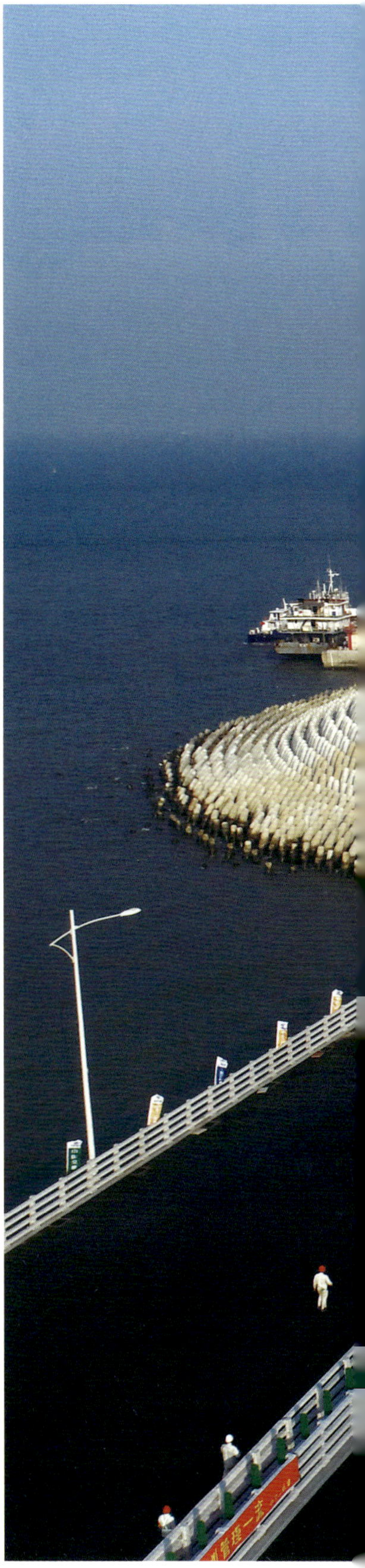

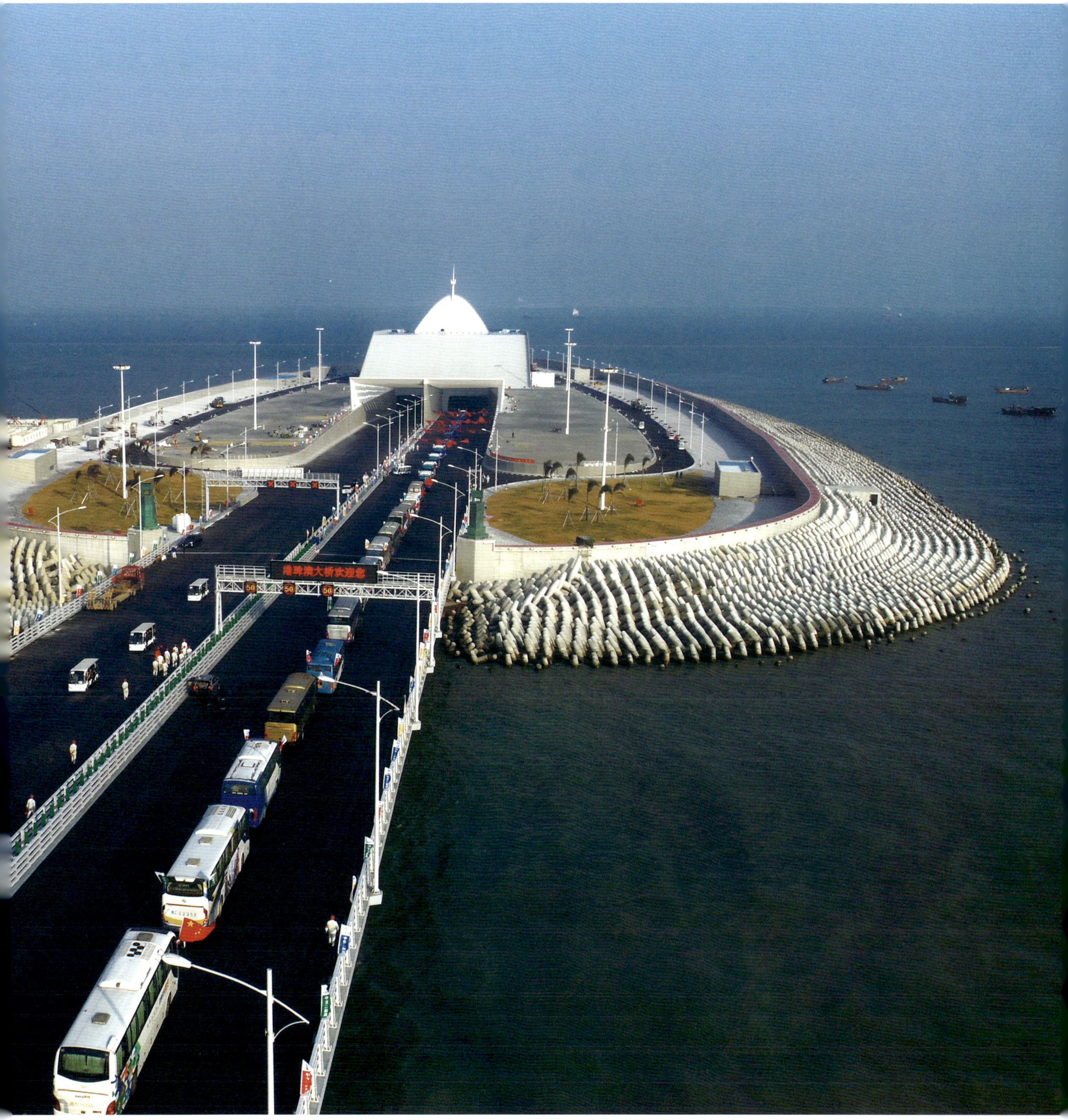
港珠澳大桥欢迎您
50
50
50

港珠澳大桥风帽亮灯
Lighting up the Wind Cap of Hong Kong-Zhuhai-Macau Bridge

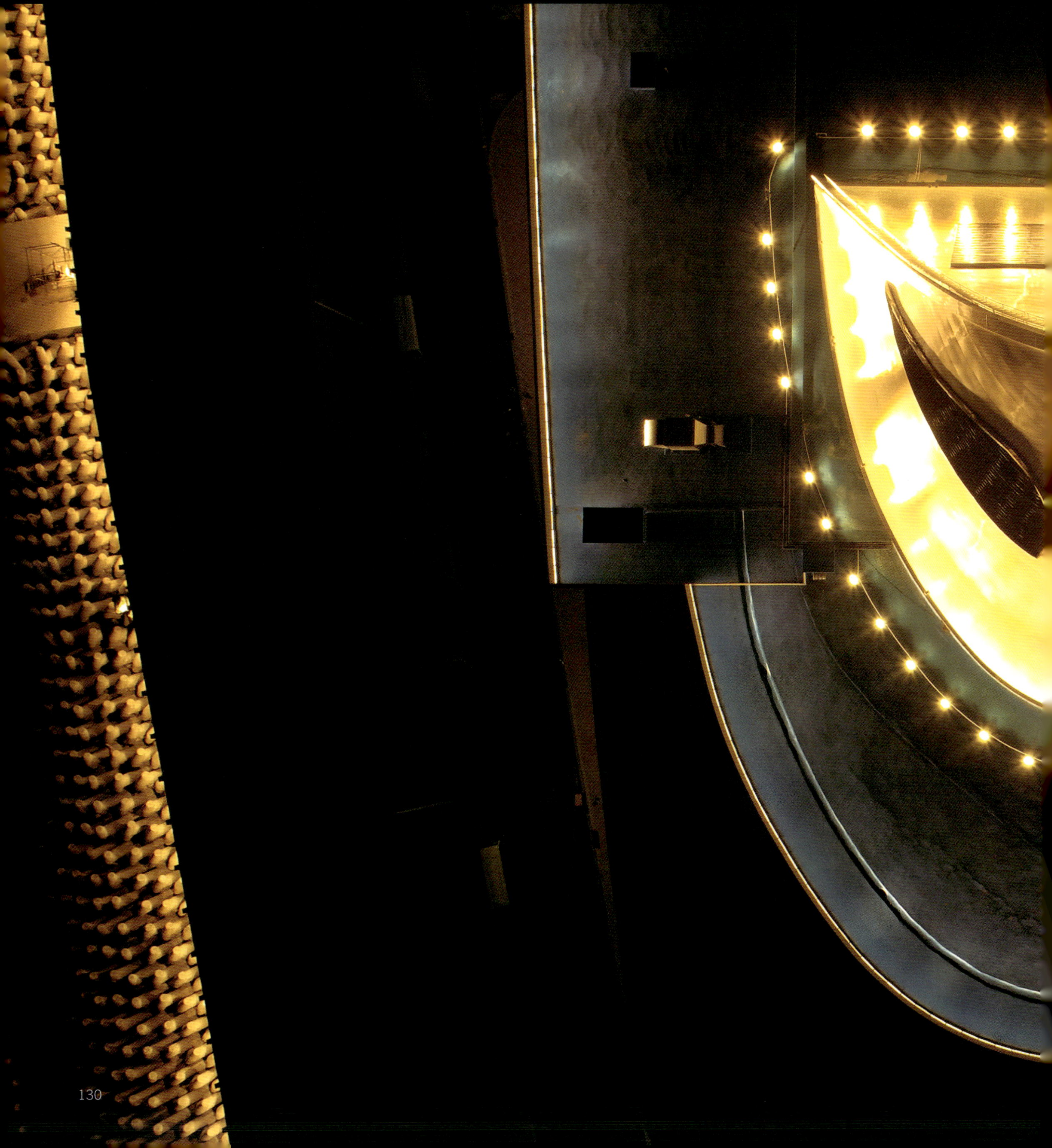

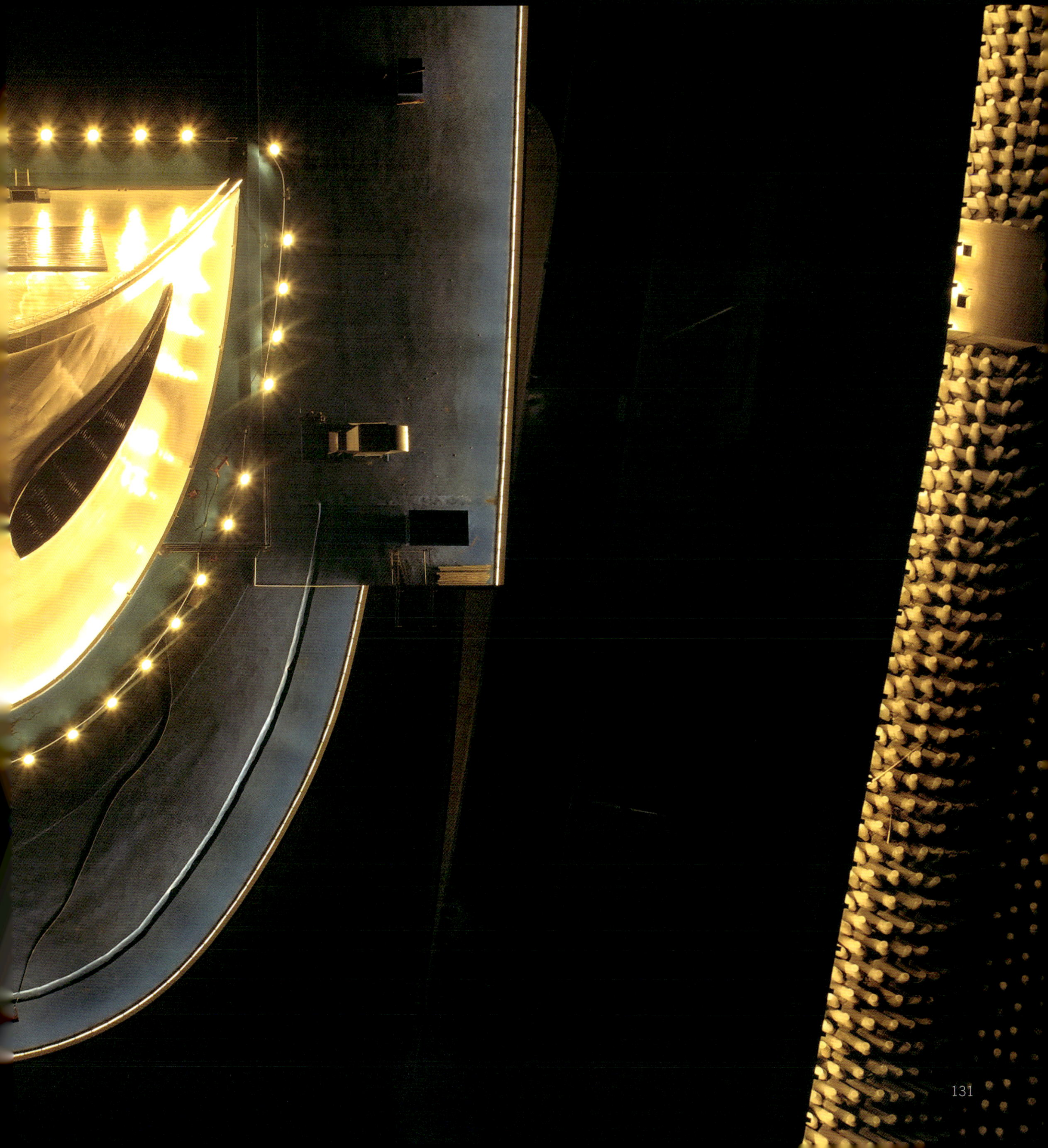

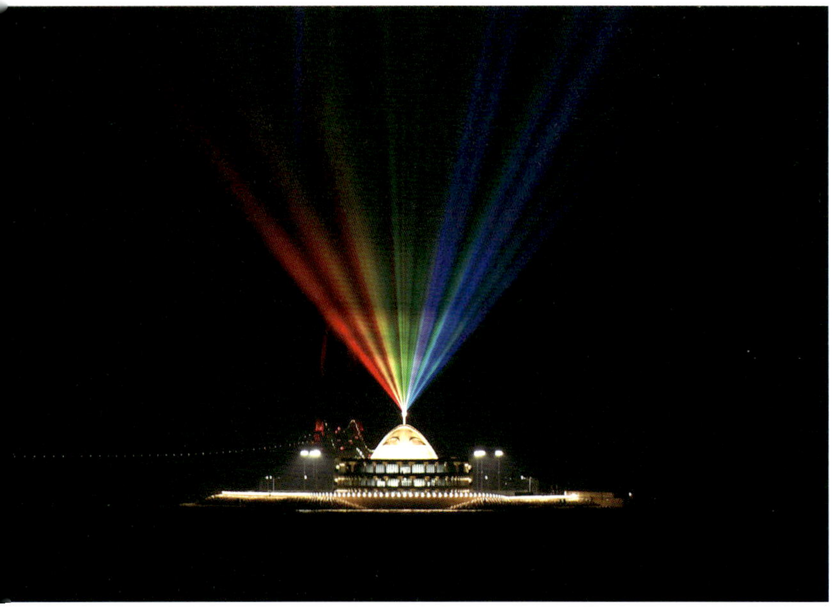

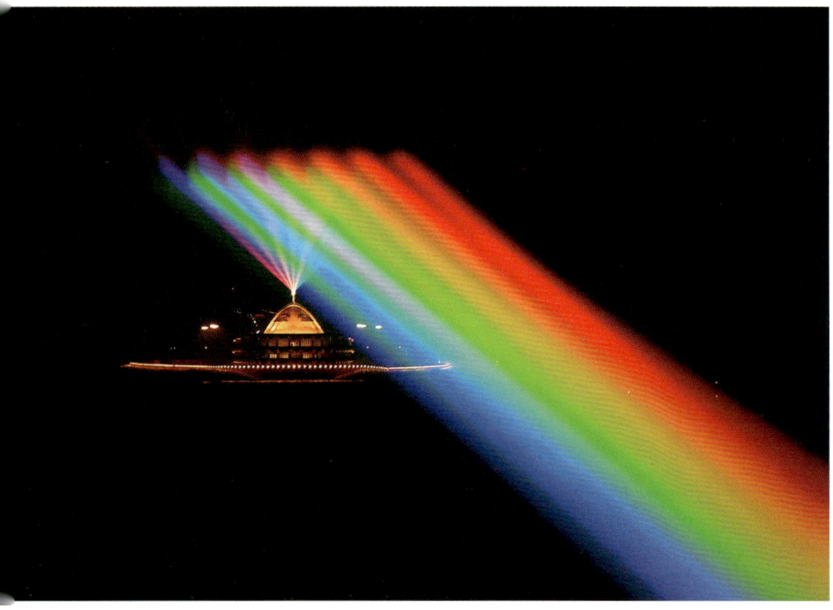

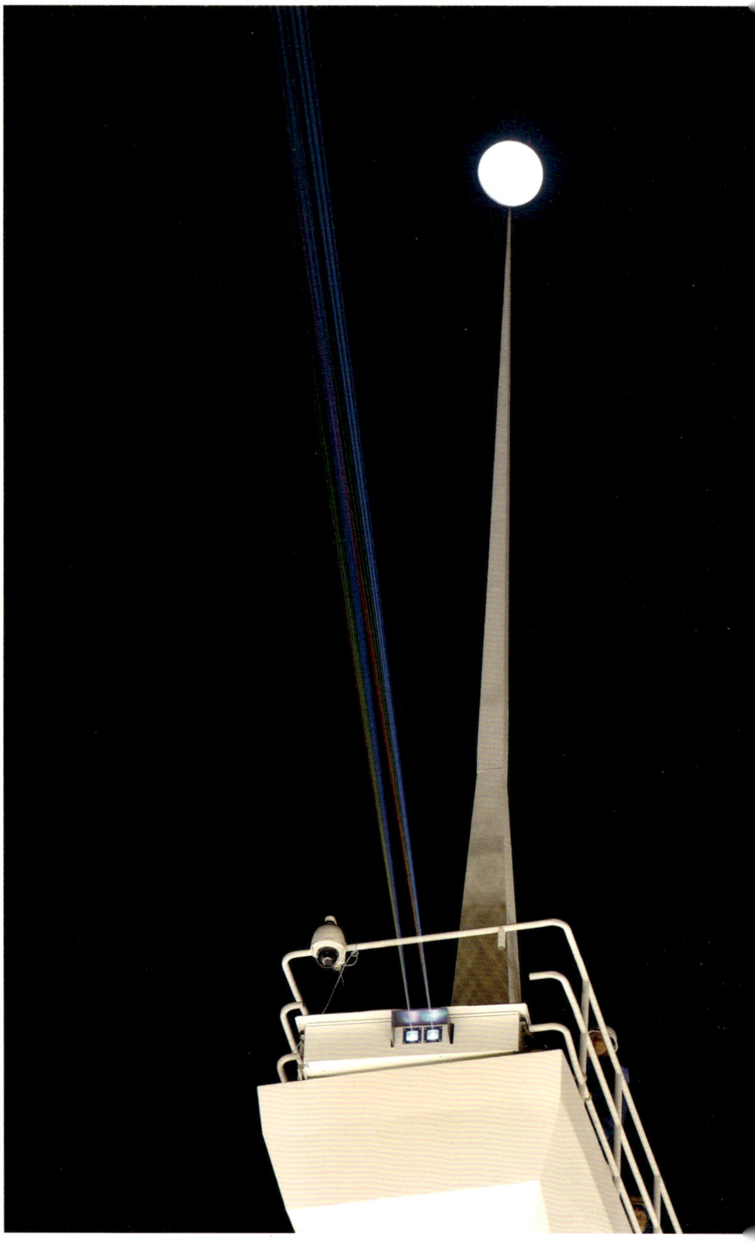

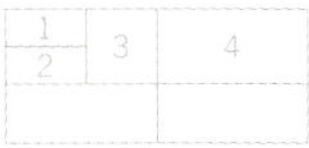

1—2. 激光束跨越伶仃
The laser beam spanned across Lingding Bay

3. 风帽避雷针亮灯
Lighting up the lightening rod on the wind cap

4. 东人工岛主体建筑亮灯
Lighting up the Main Building on East Man-Made Island

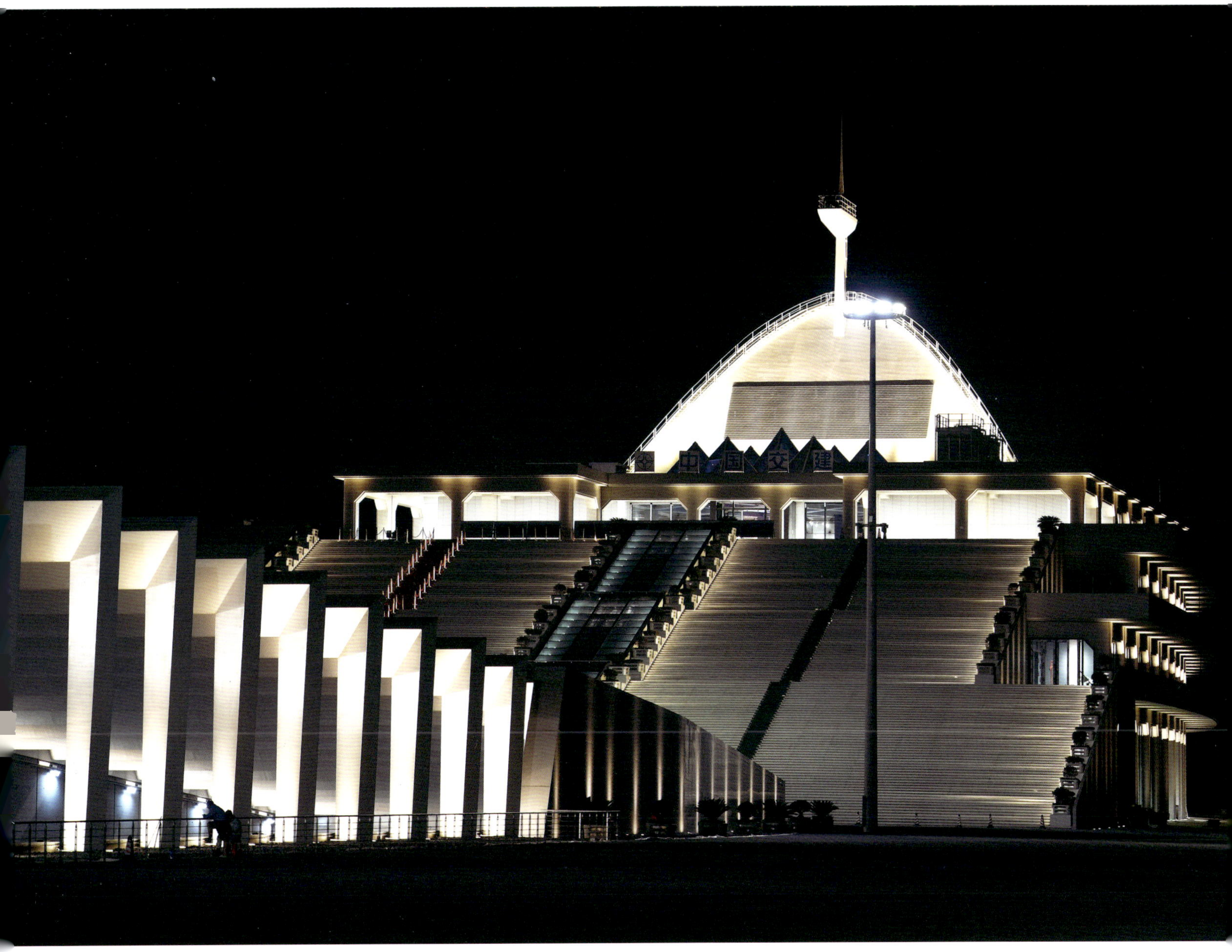

皓月当空，明灯璀璨。激光划开夜空，架起海上彩虹。
天上彩桥，海中隧道，光缠路绕，横跨伶仃。

The moon shines, and the lights twinkle.
The colored laser gashes the nightshade and weaves an arc of rainbow.
The tunnel, the rainbow swimming in the sea,
Entwines with light, spans Lingding Bay.

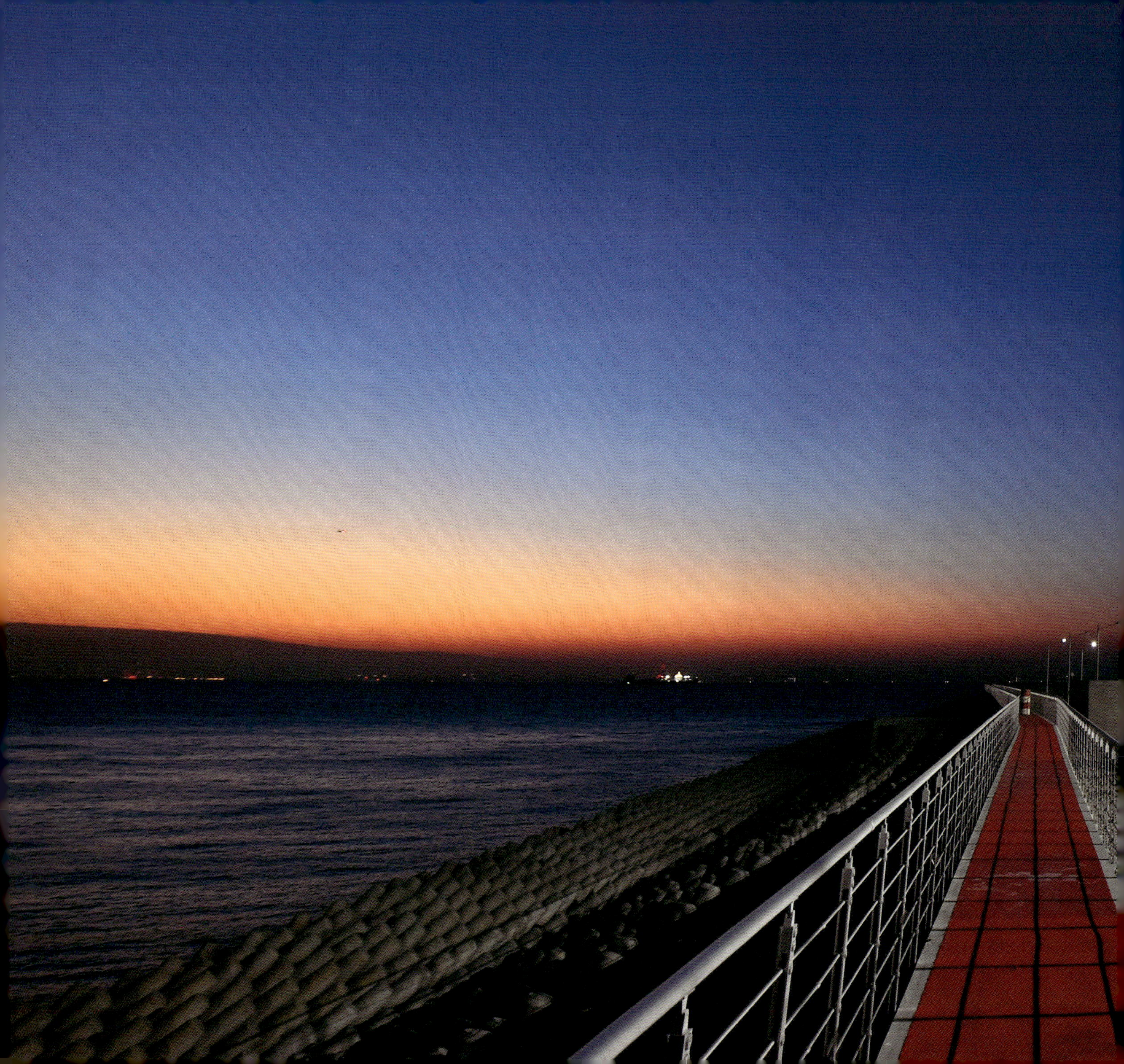

流连观光步道，眺望海中琼阁，赏瑰丽海景，听浪花私语。

Linger on the foot walk, gaze into sea, and we get lost in the beauty of the sea, eavesdropping on the murmuring waves.

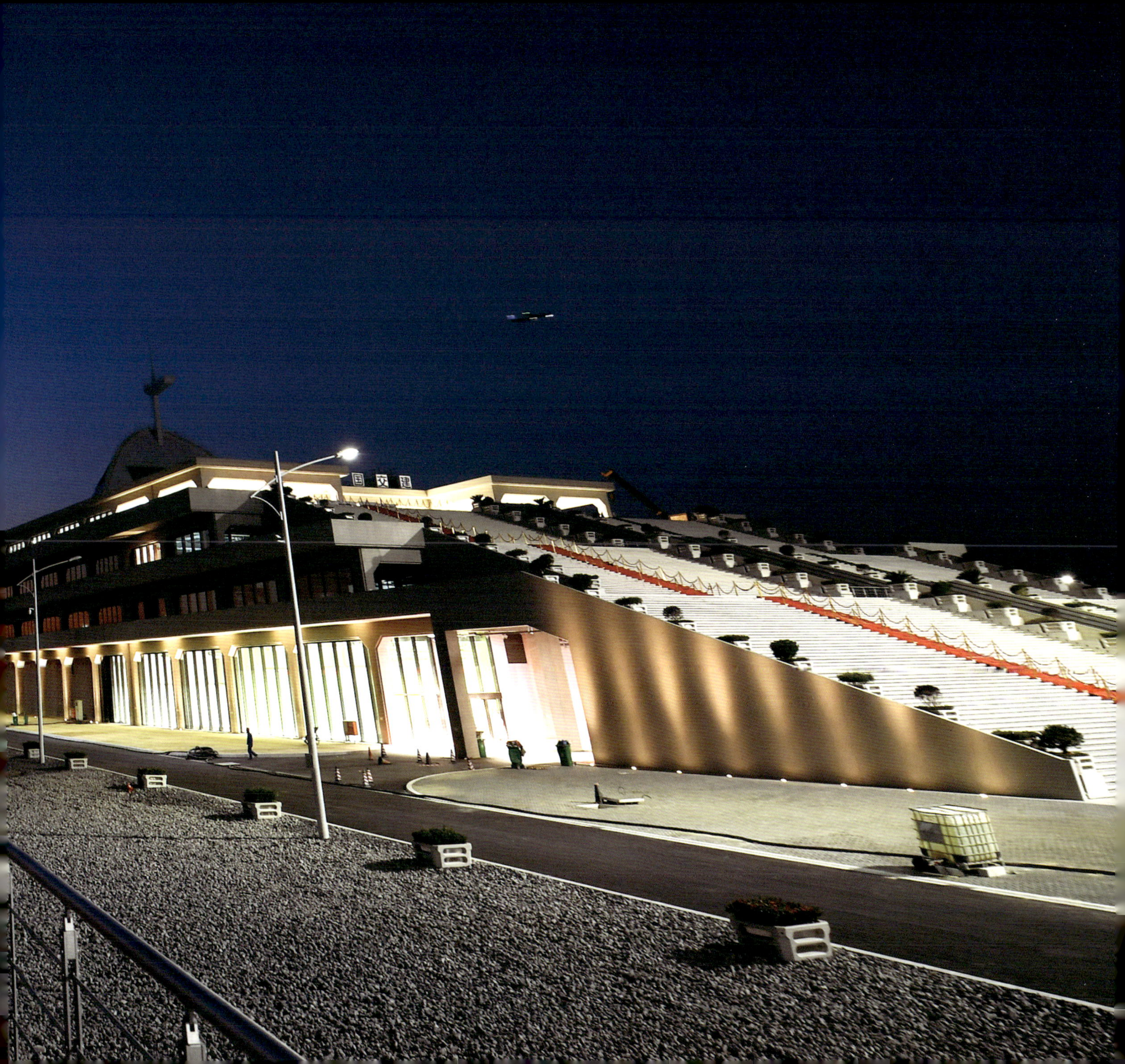

心血铸就历史，历史指引未来。
默默矗立的青铜鼎如一位敦厚的长者，
无声地传递着建设者的故事……

Painstaking efforts create a history leading to future.
The majestic bronze ding, an old man of wisdom,
Tells stories of its creator…

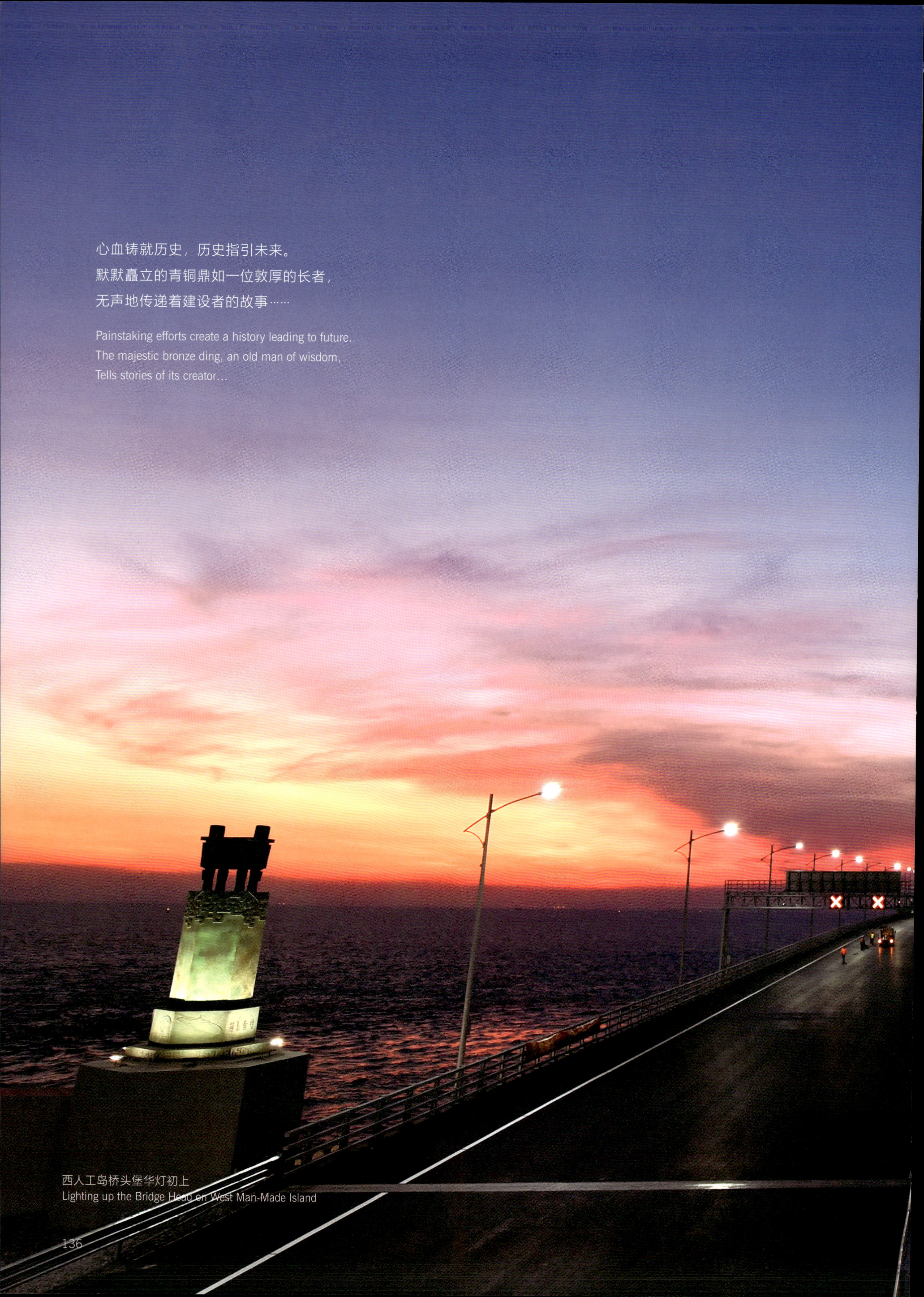

西人工岛桥头堡华灯初上
Lighting up the Bridge Head on West Man-Made Island

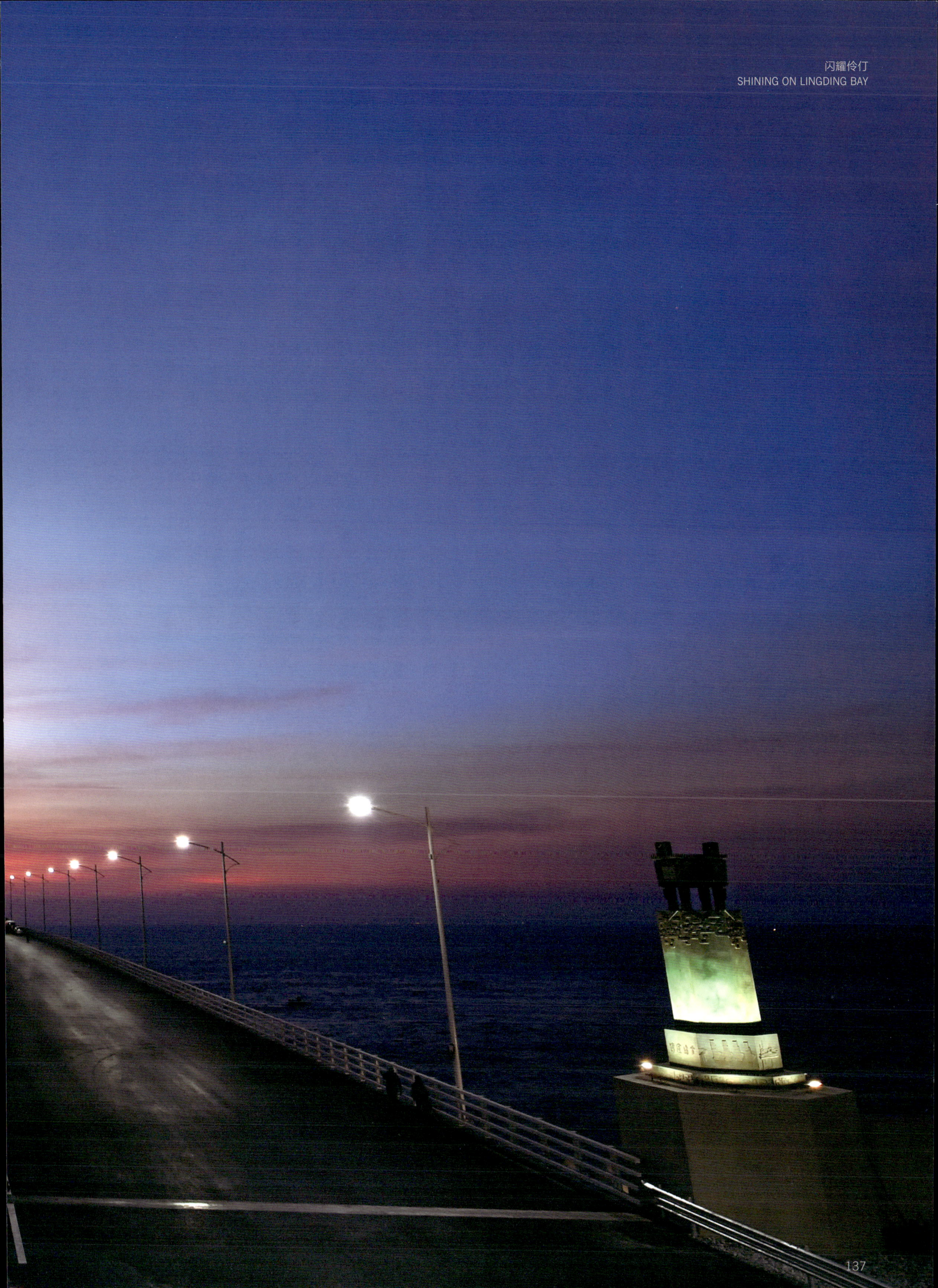

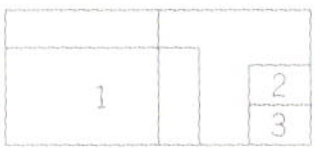

1. 东人工岛岛面大篆"华"形图案
Ancient Chinese Word "华" Inscribed on the Surface of East Man-Made Island
2. 西人工岛岛面大篆"中"形图案
Ancient Chinese Word "中" Inscribed on the Surface of West Man-Made Island
3. 东人工岛岛面大篆"华"形图案
Ancient Chinese Word "华" Inscribed on the Surface of East Man-Made Island

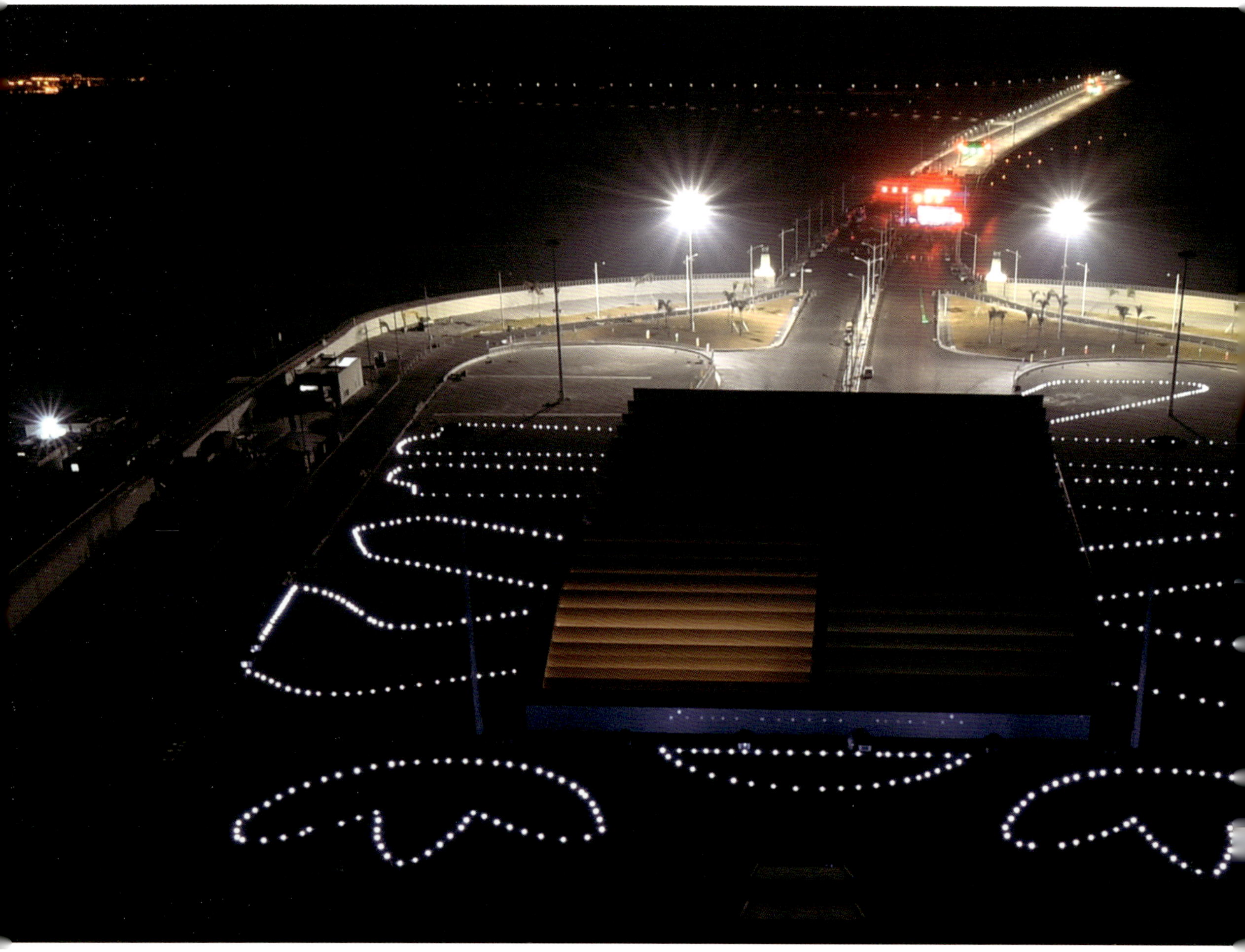

中华儿女情，世纪家国梦。
两个金文大字"中""华"镌刻在东、西人工岛的地面上，
在灯光的照耀下熠熠生辉。

China's love and China's Dream
Two ancient Chinese words " 中 " and " 华 ",
Inscribed on the faces of East and West Man-Made Islands,
Portray Chinese wisdom in the sparking light.

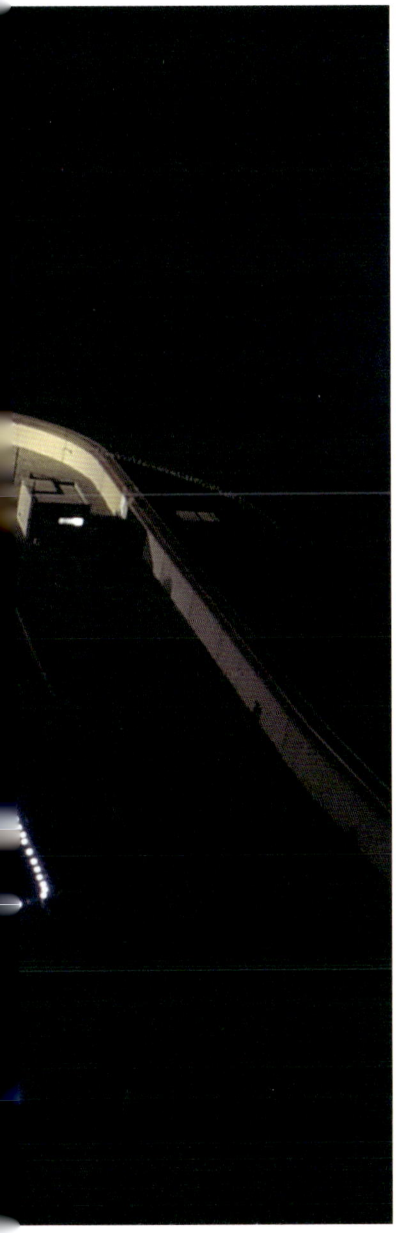

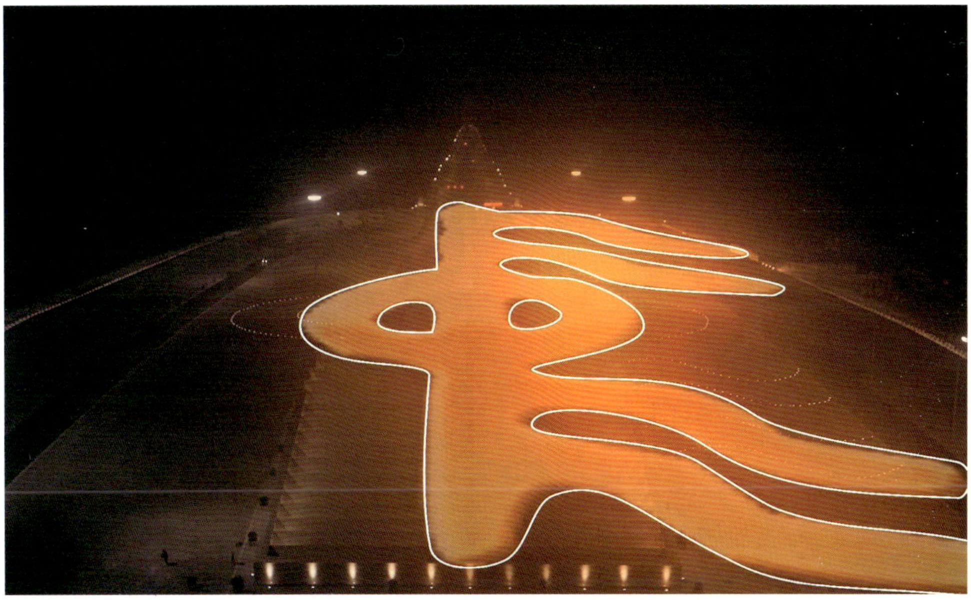

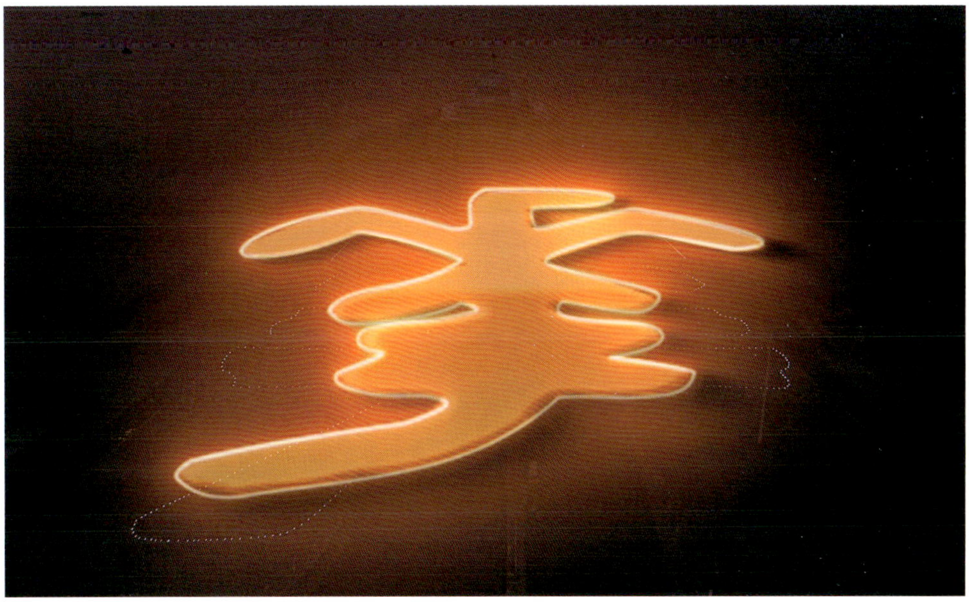

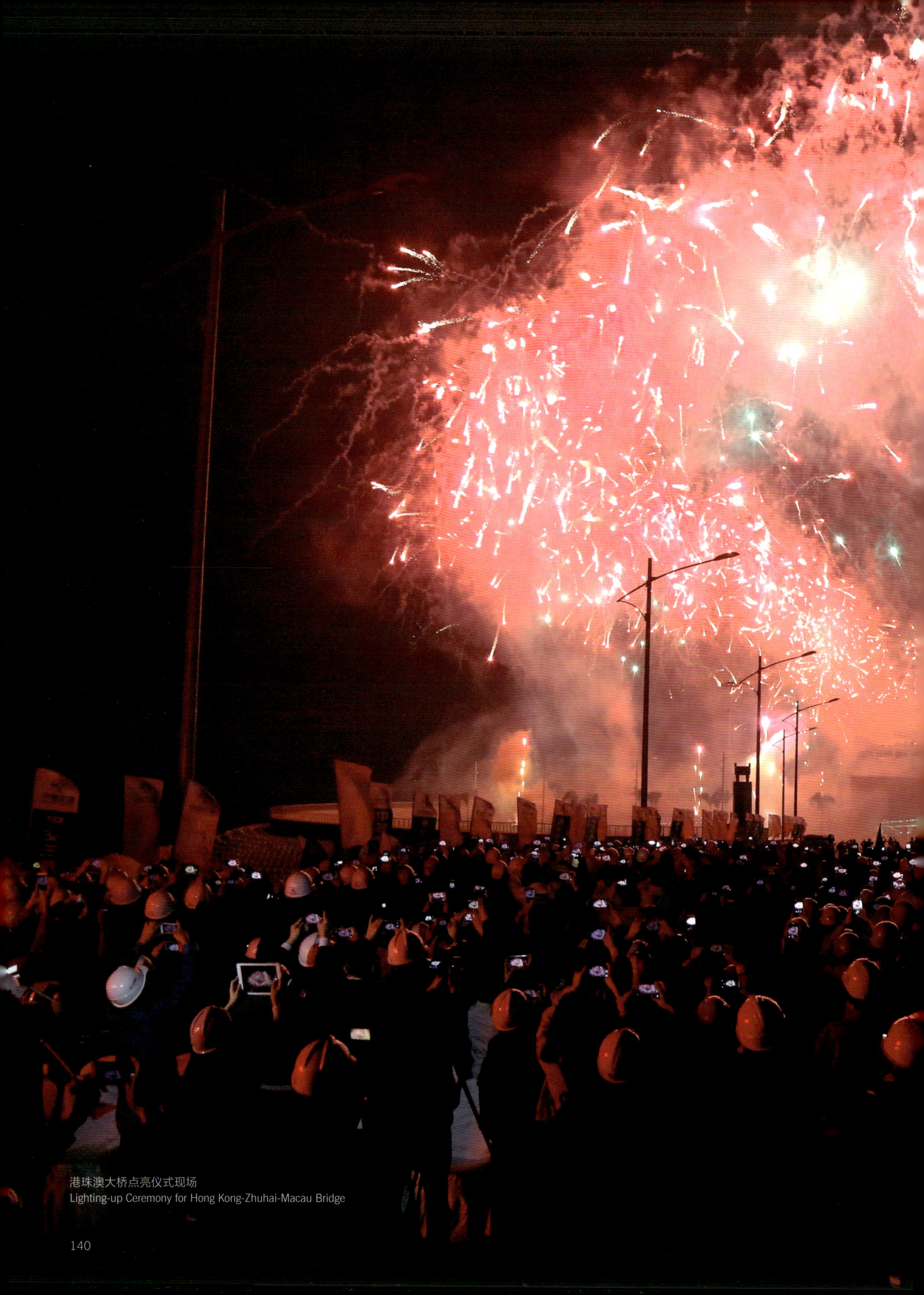

港珠澳大桥点亮仪式现场
Lighting-up Ceremony for Hong Kong-Zhuhai-Macau Bridge

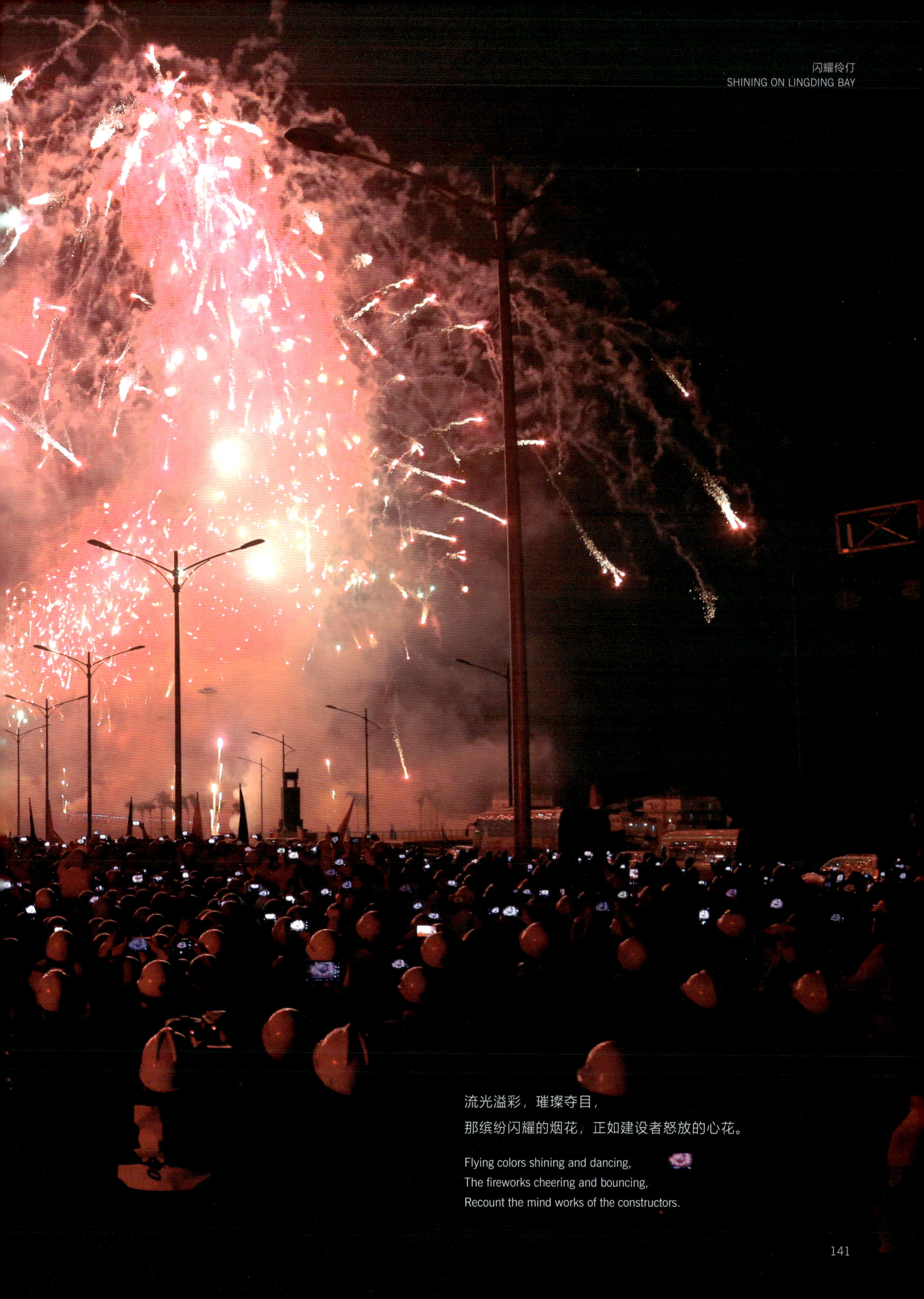

流光溢彩，璀璨夺目，
那缤纷闪耀的烟花，正如建设者怒放的心花。

Flying colors shining and dancing,
The fireworks cheering and bouncing,
Recount the mind works of the constructors.

落日熔金，远岛如黛。
日复一日的依依不舍，
守望着大湾区的金色未来。

Golden sunset, the remote islands of hazy blue
Welcome you day in and day out,
Embracing the golden dream of the Grand Bay.

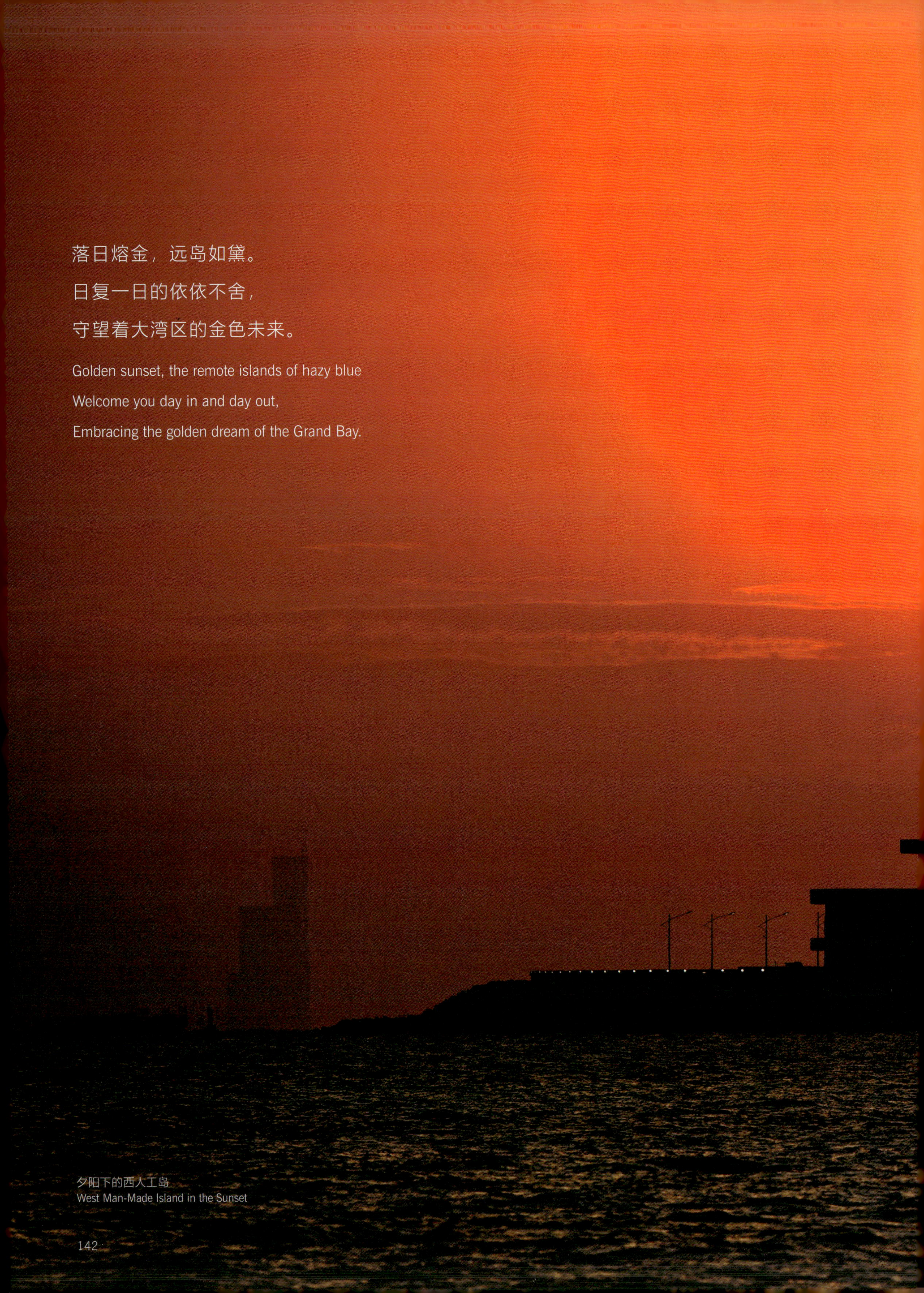

夕阳下的西人工岛
West Man-Made Island in the Sunset

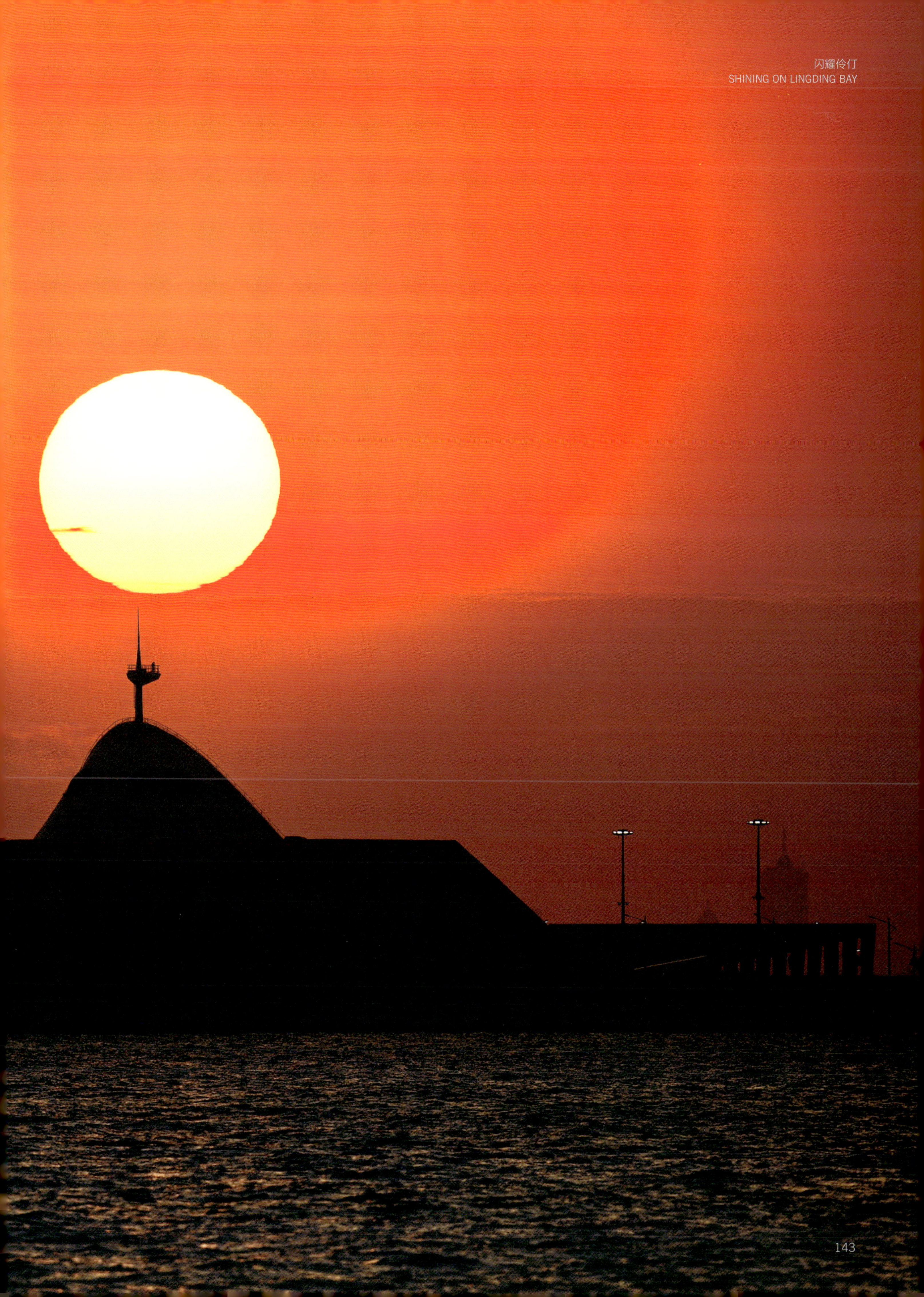

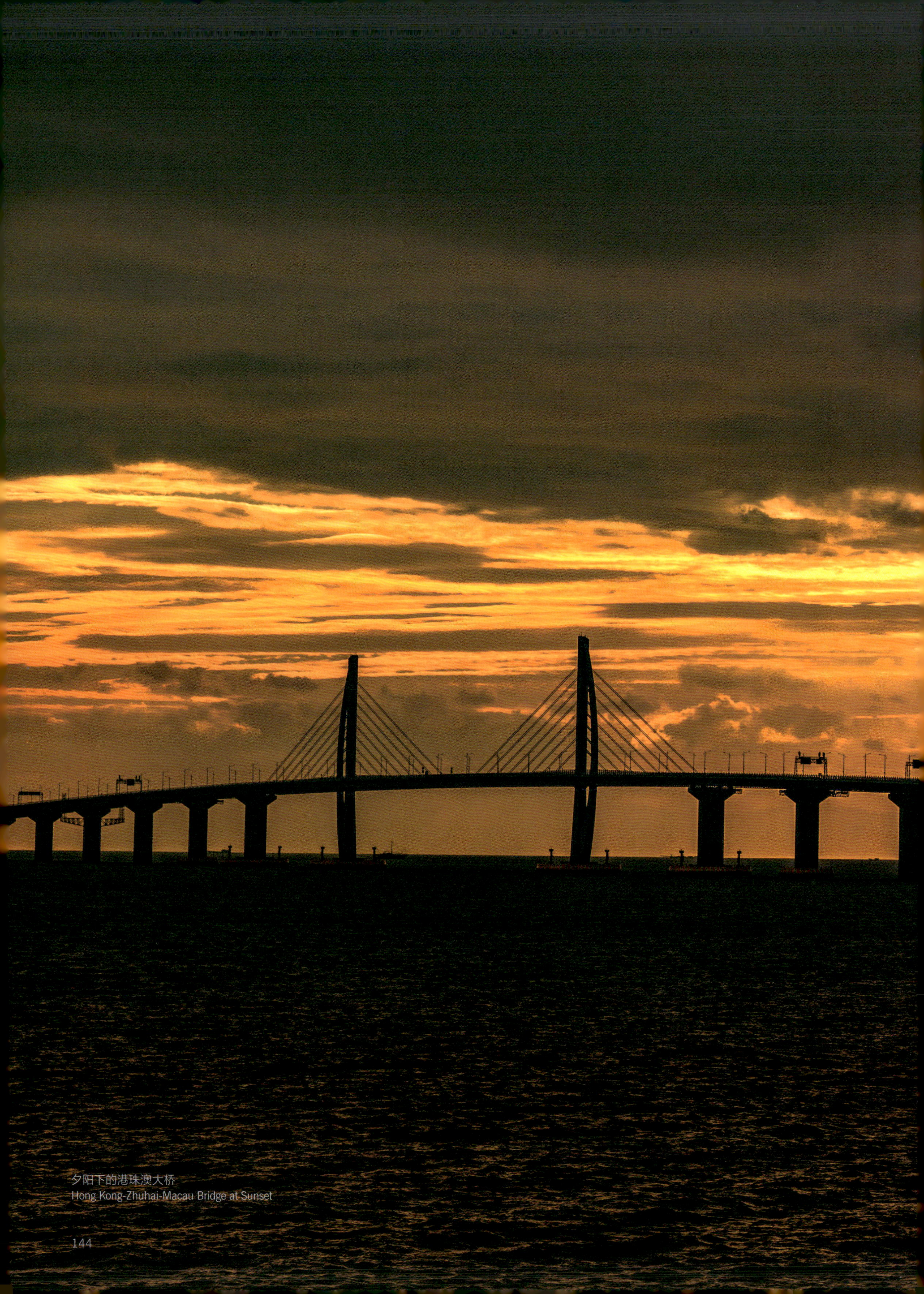

夕阳下的港珠澳大桥
Hong Kong-Zhuhai-Macau Bridge at Sunset

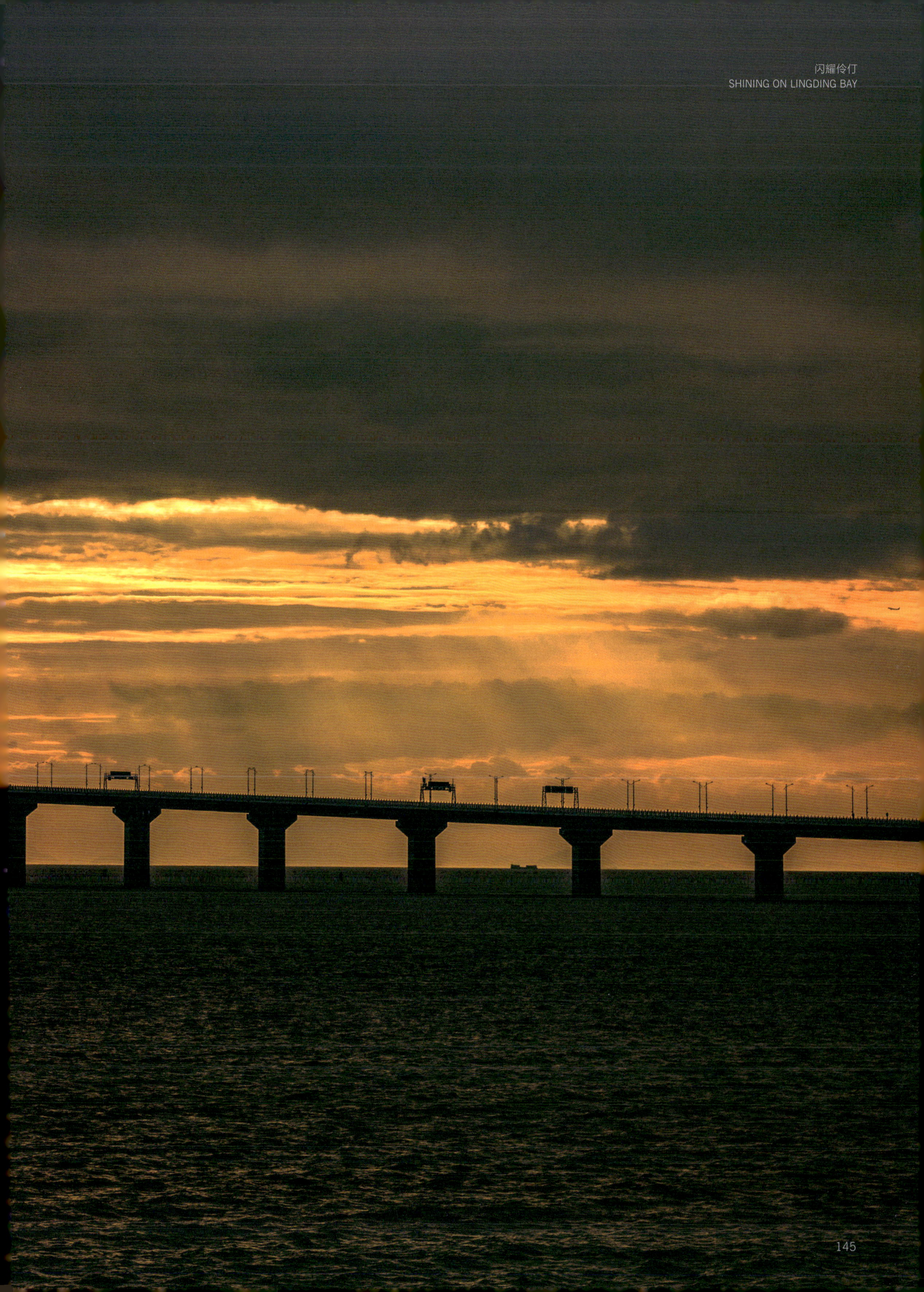

港珠澳大桥岛隧工程总结表彰大会建设者合影
Picture of the Honorary Constructors of Hong Kong-Zhuhai-Macau Bridge

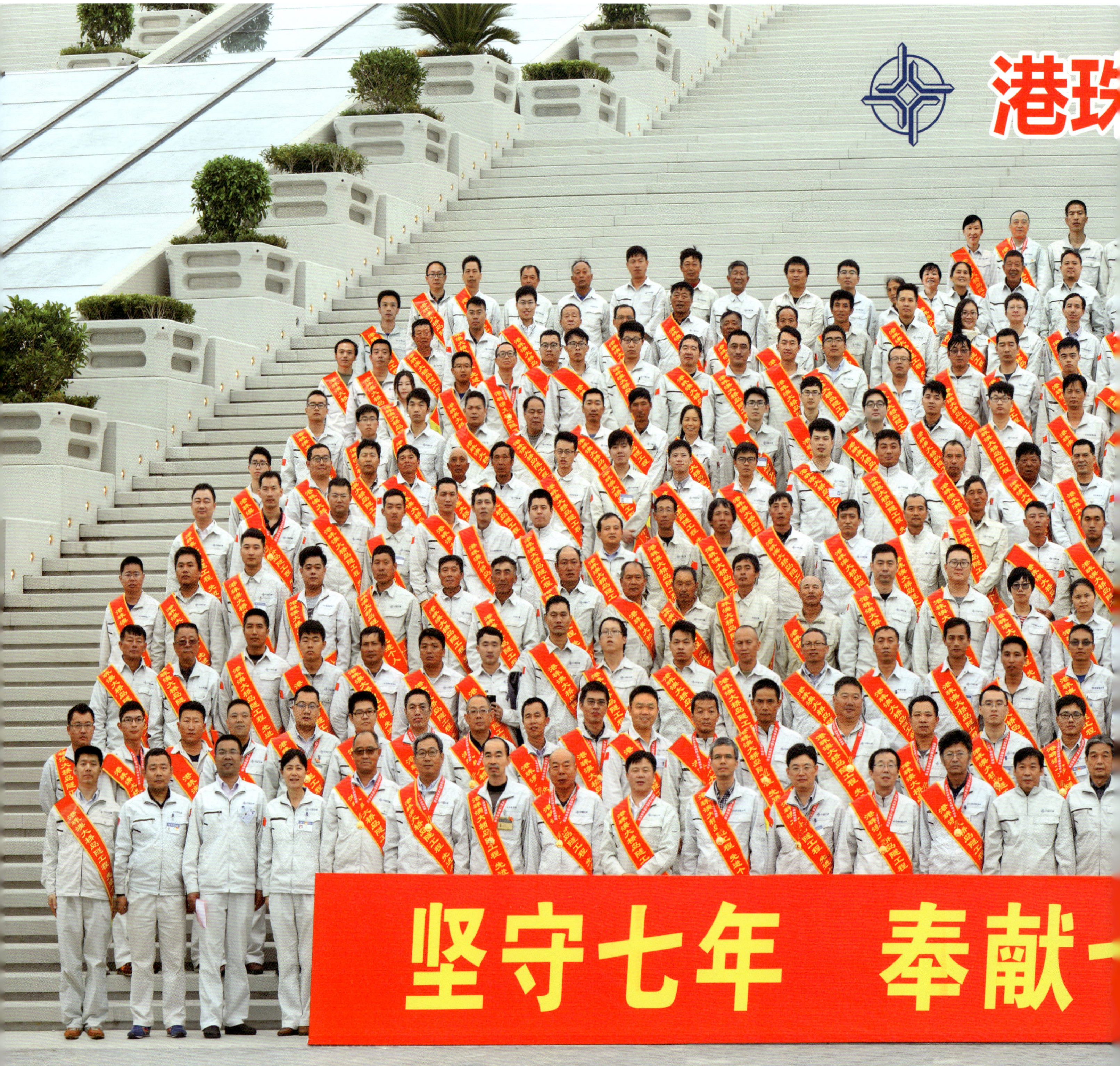

孙长树 Sun Changshu	靳　胜 Jin Sheng	杨润来 Yang Runlai	陈卫洪 Chen Weihong	林祥标 Lin Xiangbiao	陈耀金 Chen Yaojin	刘建港 Liu Jiangang	张　洪 Zhang Hong	孙　志 Sun Zhi
张怡戈 Zhang Yige	高　潮 Gao Chao	李　瀚 Li Han	郑根长 Zheng Genchang	叶长荣 Ye Changrong	彭晓鹏 Peng Xiaopeng	唐永国 Tang Yongguo	熊俊明 Xiong Junming	张秀振 Zhang Xiuzhen
李元庆 Li Yuanqing	冀　晋 Ji Jin							

第一排
First Row

王　琦 Wang Qi	林彦臣 Lin Yanchen	胡志远 Hu Zhiyuan	樊建华 Fan Jianhua	吴凤亮 Wu Fengliang	刘海青 Liu Haiqing	陈伟彬 Chen Weibin	黄维民 Huang Weimin	杨绍斌 Yang Shaobin
梁杰忠 Liang Jiezhong	高纪兵 Gao Jibing	刘晓东 Liu Xiaodong	尹海卿 Yin Haiqing	程　文 Cheng Wen	花田幸生 Hanada Yukio	张惠新 Zhang Huixin	吴利科 Wu Like	曾宪洲 Zeng Xianzhou
曹湘波 Cao Xiangbo	段国钦 Duan Guoqin	江晓霞 Jiang Xiaoxia	曹根祥 Cao Genxiang	李　江 Li Jiang	方　磊 Fang Lei	吴维忠 Wu Weizhong	林　鸣 Lin Ming	朱永灵 Zhu Yongling
李竞伟 Li Jingwei	吴　洪 Wu Hong	苏　毅 Su Yi	陈　越 Chen Yue	高星林 Gao Xinglin	戴利云 Dai Liyun	王汝凯 Wang Rukai	罗　冬 Luo Dong	谢臣伟 Xie Chenwei
刘亚平 Liu Yaping	卢永昌 Lu Yongchang	王彰贵 Wang Zhanggui	董　政 Dong Zheng	宿发强 Su Faqiang	孟凡利 Meng Fanli	冯颖慧 Feng Yinghui	陈　林 Chen Lin	陈向阳 Chen Xiangyang
孟令月 Meng Lingyue	秦大兵 Qin Dabing	何　波 He Bo	张宝兰 Zhang Baolan	李建宇 Li Jianyu	林　巍 Lin Wei	陈三洋 Chen Sanyang	曾小娟 Zeng Xiaojuan	

港珠澳大桥岛隧工程项目大事记

CHRONICLE OF IMPORTANT EVENTS OF THE HONG KONG-ZHUHAI-MACAU BRIDGE PROJECT

2009-12-15 港珠澳大桥开工

The Hong Kong-Zhuhai-Macau Bridge project was commenced on December 15, 2009.

2010-11-25 中国交通建设股份有限公司港珠澳大桥岛隧工程联合体中标大桥控制性工程。

November 25, 2010: China Communications Constuction Co. Ltd., together with the Hong Kong-Zhuhai-Macau Bridge project union, won the bidding for the construction of the main part of the Bridge.

2010-12-22 港珠澳大桥岛隧主体工程开工动员大会在珠海隆重举行，港珠澳大桥主体工程建设正式启动。

December 22, 2010: The commencement assembly to start the construction of the main part of Hong Kong-Zhuhai-Macau Bridge was held in Zhuhai, and the project was launched.

2010-12-19 沉管预制厂土建施工正式启动。

December 19, 2010: The immersed tube precast factory began its civil construction.

2011-01-04 西人工岛及隧道基槽开始粗挖施工。

January 4, 2011: The construction of West Man-Made Island and the deep excavation of the foundation trench for the tunnel began.

2011-03-10 首批钢圆筒在上海振华长兴岛基地开工制造。

March 10, 2011: The first set of steel cylinders began to be constructed in Changxing Island Base of Shanghai Zhenhua Port Machinery Company Limited.

2011-05-08 首个钢圆筒和八锤联动振沉系统顺利运抵珠海。

May 8, 2011: The first steel cylinder and Eight-hammer vibratory-driving devices were transported to Zhuhai.

2011-05-15 西人工岛首个钢圆筒顺利振沉，港珠澳大桥岛隧工程人工岛围护结构正式开始施工。

May 15, 2011: The first steel cylinder was successfully driven into the seabed on West Man-Made Island, and the fending structure of the island-tunnel project of the Bridge began to be constructed.

2011-05-24 港珠澳大桥岛隧工程海上补充地质勘察外业工作全部完成。

May 24, 2011: The supplementary maritime geological survey for the island-tunnel project of the Bridge was completed.

2011-08-16 沉管预制模板拼装正式启动。

August 16, 2011: The precast plate for the immersed tubes began to be assembled.

2011-09-11 西人工岛61个钢圆筒振沉完毕，西人工岛成岛。

September 11, 2011: 61 steel cylinders were driven into the seabed on West Man-Made Island, and West Man-Made Island was formed.

2011-09-22 东人工岛首个钢圆筒振沉。

September 22, 2011: The first steel cylinder was driven into the seabed on East Man-Made Island.

2011-09-28 港珠澳大桥主体工程施工总营地隆重举行开营仪式。

September 28, 2011: Inauguration ceremony for General Construction Camp of the main part of the Bridge was held.

2011-12-05 沉管预制模板安装全部完成，提前进入预制准备阶段。

December 5, 2011: Installation of the precast plates for the immersed tubes was completed and the precast of the immersed tubes started.

2011-12-07 东人工岛59个钢圆筒振沉完毕，东人工岛成岛。

December 7, 2011: 59 steel cylinders were driven into the seabed on East Man-Made Island, and East Man-Made Island was formed.

2011-12-21 东人工岛副格全部振沉完毕，创造了"当年开工，当年成岛"的奇迹。

December 21, 2011: All the steel connectors on East Man-Made Island were landed, and by then the miracle "completing the island building in one year" was created.

2012-02-10 沉管预制足尺模型S1段混凝土浇筑完成。

February 10, 2012: The concrete placement for the precast of full-sized model S1 of the immersed tube was completed.

2012-02-27 沉管预制厂举行开厂仪式。

February 27, 2012: Inauguration ceremony of the immersed tube precast factory was held.

2012-03-15 世界最大的深水抛石整平船"津平 1"正式下水。

March 15, 2012: "Jinping 1", the largest barge in the world that conducted deep water rock filling and leveling entered into service.

2012-03-31 沉管预制厂钢筋加工、绑扎区胎架制造及现场安装全部完成，具备生产条件。

March 31, 2012: The reinforcing steel bar processing, the manufacturing of the molding bed for binding operation and installation were all done, ready for the immersed tube production.

2012-04-28 沉管隧道过渡段堆载预压抛石施工全面展开。

April 28, 2012: Surcharge, pre-compression, and rock filling for the transitional section of the immersed tube tunnel were all completed.

2012-04-29 港珠澳大桥岛隧工程首节沉管预制正式启动。

April 29, 2012: The precast of the first immersed tube for the island-tunnel project of the Bridge started.

2012-04-30 足尺模型 S2 段混凝土浇筑完成。

April 30, 2012: Concrete placement of the full-sized model S2 was completed.

2012-05-08 外海沉管安装成套技术方案初稿形成。

May 8, 2012: Technical solution for offshore immersed tube installation was approved.

2012-06-01 沉管预制厂深坞坞门完成首次起浮关闭，深坞土建工作全部完成。

June 1, 2012: The gate of the deep dock in the precast factory of the immersed tube was lifted and closed for the first time, and the civil construction of the dock was completed.

2012-06-27 自主研发并建设的分离式双体沉管安装船"津安 3"正式下水。

June 27, 2012: "Jinaan 3", the separable twin-barge for the installation of the immersed tube developed by the project union entered into service.

2012-07-08 西人工岛隧道现浇止推段CW1段开始进行底板钢筋绑扎，止推段结构施工正式拉开序幕。

July 8, 2012: The steel binding for the bottom plate in the cast-in-place thrust CW1 section began and the construction of the thrust structure commenced.

2012-08-07 首节沉管节段E2-S5混凝土浇筑完成，世界最大沉管正式投产。

August 7, 2012: The concrete placement of the E2-S5 section of the first immersed tube was completed, and the biggest immersed tube in the world began to be constructed.

2012-08-23 西人工岛全部高压旋喷桩打设完成。

August 23, 2012: The drilling of all the high-pressure jet-grouted piles on West Man-Made Island was completed.

2012-09-04 东人工岛壁区挤密砂桩全部完成。

September 4, 2012: The dense sand piles for the fending wall on East Man-Made Island were all completed.

2012-09-10 沉管预制厂深浅坞蓄水达到+15.35米标高，历时17天的深浅坞蓄水试验完成。

September 10, 2012: The water level at the deep and shallow docks of the immersed tube precast factory reached +15.35 meters, and the test of the deep and shallow dock impoundment that lasted 17 days was finally completed.

2012-09-29 西人工岛过渡段挤密砂桩全部完成。

September 29, 2012: The dense sand piles in the transitional section of the tunnel on West Man-Made Island were all completed.

2012-10-19 世界最大的深水抛石整平船"津平1"抵达港珠澳大桥岛隧工程施工现场。

October 19, 2012: "Jinping 1", the largest barge in the world used for deep water rock filling and leveling moved to the working site of the island-tunnel

2012-11-28 沉管安装船"津安3""津安2"顺利抵达港珠澳大桥岛隧工程施工现场。

November 28, 2012: The immersed tube installation barges, "Jinaan 3" and "Jinaan 2" moved to the construction site of the island-tunnel project of the Bridge.

2012-12-02 西人工岛隧道现浇止推段混凝土浇筑全线告捷。

December 2, 2012: The cast-in-place thrust concrete placement on West Man-Made Island was all completed.

2012-12 港珠澳大桥岛隧工程项目总部在世界范围首次创新提出"半刚性"沉管新结构体系方案，解决了深埋沉管的结构难题。

December, 2012: For the first time in the world, the project center of the island tunnel project of the Bridge proposed the technical solution of "half-fixed" immersed tube structure and solved the problems involved in the deep burial of the immersed tube.

2013-01 首批管节（E1、E2）安全横移至深坞系泊，沉管一次舾装工作顺利完成并圆满通过密水"大考"；2 月，世界最大的首个 180 米标准管节预制成功；当年完成 11.25 节沉管预制和 10 个管节舾装施工，单个节段预制周期缩短到 8.5 天。

January, 2013: The first set of immersed tubes E1 and E2 were safely transported to the deep dock; the first fitting out of the immersed tubes was successful and passed the linkage tests.
February, 2013: The first largest standard 180-meter tube in the world was successfully precast. 11.25 immersed tubes and the outfitting of ten tubes were completed in the same year, and the time duration for the precast of each tube was as short as 8.5 days.

2013-01-25 岛隧转换的关键结构西人工岛隧道暗埋段CW1段顺利通过验收。

January 25, 2013: The key structure of the island-tunnel transition, the buried tunnel section CW1 on West Man-Made Island, passed the test.

2013-01-28 西人工岛岛壁结构挤密砂桩施工完成。

January 28, 2013: The dense sand piles for the fending wall of West Man-Made Island were completed.

2013-03-01 西人工岛岛头钢圆筒顺利拆除完毕，首次实现了外海条件下人工筑岛的岛、隧转换。

March 1, 2013: The steel cylinders at the head part of West Man-Made Island were successfully removed. For the first time in the world, the island-tunnel transition on offshore man-made island was completed.

2013-01-29 ～04-27 岛隧工程项目总部先后举行四次沉管浮运系泊演练。

January 29, 2013 to April 27, 2013: The project center of the island-tunnel project conducted 4 tests on the float conveyance and anchoring of the immersed tubes.

2013-05-06 首节外海深埋沉管E1安装成功，与西人工岛顺利对接，历时96小时完成“深海初吻”。

May 6, 2013: The first offshore deep-buried tube E1 was successfully installed, and successfully connected with West Man-Made Island. After 96 hours' hard work, the "first deep-sea kiss" of Tube E1 and West Man-Made Island was completed.

2013-07-30 首节180米、重约8万吨标准沉管E3浮运安装成功，沉管安装顺利走向深海。

July 30, 2013: The first standard 180-meter immersed tube E3, weighing 80,000 tons, was transported and installed. It proved that the immersed tube installation could be done in deep waters.

2013-07-11 -- 12-12 东、西人工岛综合救援码头顺利通过验收，国内首次在软土地基上采用高置换率挤密砂桩进行地基处理的沉箱重力式码头建成投入使用，开创了我国在软土地基绿色、环保、高效建设重力式码头的新工法。

July 11, 2013 to December 12, 2013: The composite rescue center on East and West Man-Made Island passed the test. For the first time in China, the technique of high-replacement-ratio dense sand piling on soft earth was used to deal with the tunnel base in the construction of caisson-gravity dock. It was the first case in the world that China constructed the gravity dock on soft earth base effectively.

2013-08-04 历时两年，东人工岛过渡段挤密砂桩施工全部完成。

August 4, 2013: After two years' hard work, the dense sand piles in the transitional section on East Man-Made Island were all completed.

2013-12-08 E7管节浮运安装取得圆满成功，世界规模最大的跨海大桥沉管隧道建设突破1000米大关。

December 8, 2013: Tube E7 was safely transported to the working site and successfully installed. The first 1000 meters of the longest undersea immersed tube tunnel of the world had been successfully constructed.

2014-01-07 E8 沉管浮运安装完成。

January 7,2014: Tube E8 was transported to the working site and installed.

2014-02-24 E9沉管浮运安装完成，安装水深突破40米关口。

February 24, 2014: The flat conveyance and installation of Tube E9 were completed. The depth record of 40 meters was broken.

2014-03-23 E10 沉管浮运安装完成。

March 23, 2014: The flat conveyance and installation of Tube E10 were completed.

2014-07-16 历时两年，西人工岛隧道现浇暗埋段主体结构浇筑完成。

July 16, 2014: After two years hard work, the cast-in-place concrete placement of the main part of the buried section of the tunnel on West Man-Made Island was completed.

2014-07-21 E11沉管顺利安装。水深超过45米，槽深超过30米，深水深槽沉管安装工艺技术攻关取得阶段性成果。

July 21, 2014: Tube E11 was successfully installed. The water depth was 45 meters and the depth of the foundation trench was over 30 meters. The technique of deep water immersed tube installation in deep trench was original.

2014-08-10 西人工岛敞开段OW1段第一步混凝土浇筑完成，敞开段首次大体积混凝土浇筑告捷。

August 10, 2014: The first stage of concrete placement for the open section of the tunnel OWI on West Man-Made Island was completed. The first trial of large-volume concrete placement in open section was successful.

2014-08-16 “工厂法沉管预制厂建设集成技术研究”通过国家水运建设行业协会科技成果鉴定。

August 16, 2014: The composite technique of immersed tube precast in factories passed the technological test of the National Water Transportation Construction Association.

2014-08-19 E12沉管浮运安装完成，工程建设顺利推进至隧道最深处，已建隧道总长突破2000米。

August 19, 2014: The float conveyance and installation of Tube E12 were completed. The construction of the project had come to the most critical part, and the total length of the tunnel completed was more than 2000 meters.

2014-09-20 E13沉管浮运安装完成，隧道建设顺利变坡上升。

September 20, 2014: The float conveyance and installation of Tube E13 were completed. The Tunnel construction had come to the slope part.

2014-10-09 西人工岛非通航孔桥主体工程顺利完工，为港珠澳大桥桥隧转换奠定了坚实基础。

October 9, 2014: The non-navigation channel bridge on West Man-Made Island was completed, which lay a solid foundation for the transition of the Bridge project from the bridge part to the tunnel part.

2014-10-18 E14 沉管浮运安装完成，已安装隧道总长累计达 2385 米。

October 18, 2014: The float conveyance and installation of Tube E14 were completed, and the total length of the tunnel completed so far was 2385 meters long.

2014-11-18 E15 沉管首次安装遭遇异常回淤，平安返回沉管预制厂深坞。

November 18, 2014: The installation of Tube E15 encountered the problem of abnormal back silting, but was safely moved back to the precast factory.

2015-01-10 东人工岛非通航孔桥主体工程顺利完工，大桥建设顺利抵达“一国两制”分界线。

January 10, 2015: The non-navigation channel bridge on East Man-Made Island was completed, and the bridge had come to the "one-country-two-systems" dividing line.

2015-02-01 项目总经理部申报的“外海深槽沉管安装保障系统研究与开发”正式通过交通运输部科技计划项目立项评审，成为 2015 年科技计划重点项目。

February 1, 2015: The research program "Studies and Development of the Support System for Offshore Deep Trench Immersed Tube Installation" proposed by the project management center passed the technological evaluation of the Ministry of Transport and won its financial support as the one of the key technological research projects in 2015.

2015-02-25 E15 沉管第二次安装遭遇边坡滑塌，再次返回沉管预制厂等待合适时机再行安装。

February 25, 2015: The installation of the Tube E15 suffered slope collapse and the tube was returned to the precast factory for the second time.

2015-03-26 中国交建建设团队攻克回淤难题，历经历时 150 天的 ”三次浮运、两次回拖”曲折，完成 E15 沉管浮运安装。

March 26, 2015: China Communications Construction Company Ltd. solved the problem of back silting. After three times of float conveyance and two times of returning to precast factory in the past 150 days, Tube E15 was finally installed.

2015-04-13 E16 沉管安装完成，继 3 月 26 日实现 E15 沉管对接之后，历史性地在半个月内完成了又一节沉管安装施工。

April 13, 2015: The installation of Tube E16 was completed. Following the butt welding of Tube E15, in only half a month, another immersed tube was successfully installed on March 26.

2015-06-10 E17 沉管浮运安装成功。

June 10, 2015: The float conveyance and installation of Tube E17 were finished.

2015-06-27 E18沉管浮运安装成功，港珠澳大桥沉管隧道已突破3000米。

June 27, 2015: The float conveyance and installation of Tube E18 were completed, and 3000 meters of the immersed tube tunnel had been completed.

2015-07-25 E19沉管浮运安装完成，港珠澳大桥海底隧道已建总长达到3285米。

July 25, 2015: The float conveyance and installation of Tube E19 were completed, and the total length of the tunnel completed was 3285 meters.

2015-08-24 E20沉管浮运安装完成。

August 24, 2015: The float conveyance and installation of Tube E20 were completed.

2015-09-15 东人工岛暗埋段正式“封门”，为E33沉管与东人工岛对接奠定了基础。

September 15, 2015: The buried section of the tunnel on East Man-Made Island was finally completed, which lay foundation for the connection of Tube E33 with East Man-Made Island.

2015-09-23 E21 沉管浮运安装完成。

September 23, 2015: The float conveyance and installation of Tube E21 were completed.

2015-11-05 E22 沉管浮运安装完成。

November 5, 2015: The float conveyance and installation of Tube E22 were completed.

2015-11-19 E23沉管浮运安装完成，已建海底隧道总长突破4千米。

November 19, 2015: The float conveyance and installation of Tube E23 were completed, and the total length of the underwater tunnel was over 4,000 meters.

2015-11-28 “金雄”轮完成 E28沉管基槽精挖施工。历时近5年，港珠澳大桥沉管隧道基槽精挖施工全面收官。

November 28, 2015: The fine excavation of the foundation trench for Tube E28 by Barge "Jinxiong" was completed. After 5 years' hard work, the fine excavation of the foundation trench for the immersed tube tunnel of the Bridge was all completed.

2015-12-08 “津平1”碎石整平船清淤技改通过验收，世界唯一的平台式清淤整平船投入工程建设。

December 8, 2015: The dredging adjustment technology for Barge "Jinping 1" that was used for rubble bed leveling passed the test, and the first platform-based dredging and leveling barge entered into service.

2015-12-12 港珠澳大桥沉管隧道最终接头方案通过专家评审，历经两年多的研究，首创“新型整体安装沉管最终接头方案”。

December 12, 2015: The butt welding solution for the immersed tube tunnel of the Bridge passed the test of scholars. Two years' scientific research resulted in the innovation solution for the butt welding of the immersed tubes applicable for global installation.

2015.12.20 沉管隧道中管廊电缆通道隔墙典型施工段首段混凝土顺利浇筑完成，管内附属工程施工正式启动。

December 20, 2015: The concrete placement for the first section of the division wall of the cable rack in the internal pipe gallery in the immersed tube tunnel was completed, and the in-tube subsidiary construction began.

2015-12-21 E24沉管安装成功。2015年，中国交建建设者攻克深水深槽、基槽突淤、大径流等重大难题，一年安装十节沉管，创造世界沉管隧道建设史上的“中国速度”。

December 21, 2015: The installation of Tube E24 was completed. In 2015, the constructors of the China Communications Construction Company Ltd. solved the problems concerning deep water deep trench, trench silting and strong water flow. 10 tubes were installed in one year, which created the so-called "Chinese Speed" in world history of immersed tube tunneling.

2016-01-25 历时三年的沉管隧道基础块石抛填及夯平施工全部完成。

January 25, 2016: Three years' hard work witnessed the completion of the rock filling, compacting and leveling in the base part of the immersed tube tunnel.

2016-03-04 西人工岛主体建筑清水混凝土模板开始拼装。

March 4, 2016: The fair-faced concrete plates for the main building on West Man-Made Island began to be assembled.

2016-03-29 东人工岛岛头导流堤基础开挖圆满完成。

March 29, 2016: The excavation of the training dyke base at the head part of East Man-Made Island was completed.

2016-03-31 E25 沉管浮运安装完成。

March 31, 2016: The float conveyance and installation of Tube E25 was completed.

2016-04-16 首节曲线段沉管（E32）预制完成。

April 16, 2016: The precast of the first curved tube E32 was completed.

2016-05-14 E26沉管浮运安装完成，已建成隧道总长度达到4545米。

May 14, 2016: The float conveyance and installation of Tube E26 was completed, and the total length of the tunnel completed was 4545 meters.

2016-06-11 建设者战胜"龙舟水"、强对流天气等风险，顺利完成港珠澳大桥深槽区首个非标准管节——E27 沉管的安装，已建成隧道 4702 米，超过总体长度的 80%。

June 11, 2016: Overcoming such bad weather as "dragon boat rain" and strong convective weather, the constructors completed the installation of the first non-standard tube E27 in deep trench, and the total length of the tunnel completed was 4702 meters, more than 80% of the total length of the whole tunnel.

2016-07-12 E28沉管安装成功，直线段沉管全部安装完毕。

July 12, 2016: The installation of Tube E28 was completed, and all the tubes in the straight section of the tunnel had been installed.

2016-08-02 历时三年的攻关，港珠澳大桥沉管隧道最终接头方案通过专家评审，进入实施阶段。

August 2, 2016: After three years' hard work, the solution for the butt welding of the closure joint of the immersed tube tunnel of the Bridge won the approval of the scholars and began to be applied in the construction.

2016-09-26 E29 沉管浇筑完成，沉管预制厂一分厂圆满结束沉管预制任务。

September 26, 2016: The precast of Tube 29 was finally completed. The First Subsidiary of the Immersed Tube Precast Factory had completed all its tasks.

2016-10-08 首节曲线段 E33 沉管成功安装，实现与东人工岛的成功对接。

October 8, 2016: The installation of the first curved tube E33 was completed. The tunnel was successfully connected to East Man-Made Island.

2016-10-14 港珠澳大桥海底隧道最终接头钢壳正式投产。

October 14, 2016: The steel shield of the closure joint used in the underwater tunnel of the Bridge was put into production.

2016-11-23 E32 沉管浮运安装成功。

November 23, 2016: The float conveyance and installation of Tube E32 was completed.

2016-12-16 港珠澳大桥沉管预制钢筋绑扎施工全面告竣。

December 16, 2016: The steel bar binding for the precast of the immersed tubes of the Bridge was completed.

2016-12-24 东人工岛减光罩安装完成，与敞开段清水混凝土构成充满光影韵律的新景观，成为人工岛上又一标志性建筑。

December 24, 2016: The installation of the light-reducing grating was completed. The light-reducing grating, together with the fair-faced concrete, formed a special view of light and shadow, and thus was regarded as the landmark of East Man-Made Island.

2016-12-25 E31 沉管浮运安装完成。

December 25, 2016: The float conveyance and installation of Tube E31 was completed.

2016-12-26 港珠澳大桥33节沉管全部预制完成，在近6年的预制生产中，中国交建建设团队创造了百万方混凝土现浇无裂缝的奇迹。

December 26, 2016: The precast of the 33 tubes of the Bridge was finally completed. In the past seven years, China Communications Construction Company Ltd. created a miracle that millions of cubic meters' concrete cast suffered no cracks.

2017-01-09 成功完成E31～E32沉管接头基础注浆抬升施工，解决了该段沉管的差异沉降难题。利用管底注浆工艺实现已装沉管姿态调整尚属世界首次。

January 9, 2017: The grouting and raising of the base part of the closure joint between Tube E31 and E32 were completed, and the problem involved in the differential settlement was solved. Grouting into the tube base to adjust the position of the installed immersed tube was the first case in the world.

2017-02-08 港珠澳大桥岛隧工程风帽正式开工。

February 8, 2017: The construction of the wind cap for the island-tunnel of the Bridge began.

2017-02-19 E29沉管安装完成，为最终接头施工奠定了良好基础，距隧道贯通仅剩183米。

February 19, 2017: The installation of Tube E29 was completed, which lay solid foundation for the construction of the closure joint. There was only 183 meters of the tunnel to be constructed.

2017-02-27 港珠澳大桥沉管隧道最终接头在振华重工南通基地建成发运，整体为"三明治"钢—混结构。历经三年多攻关，世界首次提出可折叠主动止水的结构理念，发明整体式主动止水最终接头技术，开创了沉管隧道最终接头施工的新工法。

February 27, 2017: The closure joint of the island tunnel of the Bridge was completed at the Nantong Base of Zhenhua Port Machinery Company Ltd., ready to be transported. The closure joint employed the sandwich steel concrete structure. After three years' hard work, for the first time in the world, the technology of foldable active water-stop structure was proposed, the overall active water-stop technology was developed, and for the first time in construction history, the new craft for the closure joint construction in the immersed tube tunneling was developed.

2017-02-27 港珠澳大桥沉管隧道焊接合龙演练启动仪式在振华重工南通基地举行。

February 27 2017: Commencement ceremony for the butt welding drill in the island tunnel of the Bridge was held at Nantong Base of Zhenhua Port Machinery Company Ltd.

2017-03-07 港珠澳大桥海底隧道最后一节沉管（E30）安装圆满成功，33节世界最大沉管全部安装完毕。

March 7, 2017: The last immersed tube of the underwater tunnel of the Bridge E30 was installed successfully. By now the 33 largest tubes in the world were all installed.

2017-03-07 港珠澳大桥海底隧道最终接头顺利运抵桂山沉管预制厂。

March 7, 2017: The closure joint of the underwater tunnel of the Bridge was successfully transported to the immersed tube precast factory at Guishan.

2017-03-13 港珠澳大桥沉管隧道最终接头开始混凝土浇筑，国内首次大规模采用高流动性混凝土工法。

March 13, 2017: The concrete placement for the closure joint of the immersed tube tunnel of the Bridge started, and for the first time in China, the craft of large-scaled high-fluidity concrete placement was used.

2017-03-26 港珠澳大桥沉管隧道最终接头高流动性混凝土浇筑完成。形成了高流动性混凝土设计与施工从理论到具体实施环节的完整技术体系，填补了国内"三明治沉管结构"技术空白。

March 26, 2017: The high-fluidity concrete placement for the closure joint of the immersed tube tunnel of the Bridge was completed. The design and operation of high-fluidity concrete placement was proved feasible in real-life constructional practice. It was the first successful case to practice the technology of "sandwich immersed tube structure".

2017-04-24 港珠澳大桥沉管隧道最终接头试吊演练完成，充分验证了吊装方案的可行性和吊索的稳定性，为正式安装施工奠定基础。

April 24, 2017: The hoisting drill of the closure joint of the immersed tube tunnel of the Bridge was completed, which marked the feasibility of the solution of hoisting installation and the stability of the hoisting cable. All this provided support for the final installation of the closure joint.

2017-05-02 ~ 05-04 港珠澳大桥岛隧工程在全球首次实施整体式主动止水最终接头安装施工，经过精调，安装精度达到毫米级，实现了深水复杂环境下沉管隧道滴水不漏，在世界沉管隧道建设史上首次验证了最终接头施工方法"工序可逆"。随着最终接头的安装完成，历时四年的"第三战役"取得全面胜利。

May 2 to May 4, 2017: Global active water-stop closure joint installation in the island-tunnel project of the Bridge was for the first time in the world successfully conducted. By fine adjustment, the installation accuracy could be calculated by millimeters, and the welded tube was completely leak-proof in complicated deep water environment. And for the first time in the world history of immersed tube tunnel construction, it proved that the operation of the closure joint installation was reversible. The completion of the closure joint installation could be regarded as "the third battle" of the project that had lasted for four years.

2017-05-25 港珠澳大桥沉管隧道最终接头焊接合龙完成。经过 20 个日日夜夜的连续作业，最终接头与两端的 E29、E30 沉管焊接形成整体，港珠澳大桥 6.7 公里的沉管隧道永久结构胜利贯通，建设者攻克了沉管隧道建设的最后一道难关。

May 25, 2017: The butt welding of the closure joint of the immersed tube tunnel of the Bridge was completed. After 20 days' work, the closure joint successfully connected Tube E29 and Tube E30 into a whole. It meant the completion of the whole immersed tube tunnel that covered 6.7 kilo meters under the sea. The constructors had solved the last problem in the immersed tube tunnel construction.

2017-08-23 ~ 08-27 港珠澳大桥岛隧工程遭遇"天鸽"强台风正面袭击，东、西人工岛主体建筑经受住了 15 级强台风的严峻考验。

August 23 to August 27, 2017: Typhoon Hato attacked the construction site of the island-tunnel project of the Bridge. The main buildings on East and West Man-Mad Island withstood the attack of the typhoon measured 15 on the Beaufort Scale.

2017-08-31 东人工岛主体建筑结构正式封顶，与 7 月 28 日封顶的西人工岛主体建筑交相辉映，宛如伶仃洋上的两艘"超级航母"，成为珠江口的新地标。

August 31, 2017: The main building on East Man-Mad Island was topped out, echoing the main building on West Man-Mad Island that was topped out on July 28. They were like the super aircraft carriers sailing over Lingding Bay and became the new landmark of Pearl River Estuary.

2017-10-08 东西人工岛测量平台及临时码头钢管相继拆除完成，港珠澳大桥岛隧工程海上施工全面告竣，历时七年的海上施工画上了圆满句号。

October 8, 2017: The measurement platforms and the steel scaffolds for temporary docks on East and West Man-Made Island were removed, and the island-tunnel project of the Bridge was finally completed after 7 years' hard work.

2017-10-23 东人工岛风帽雷达塔尖吊装到位，港珠澳大桥人工岛风帽主体结构安装施工顺利完成。

October 23, 2017: The wind cap radar tower tip on East Man-Mad Island was installed, and the body structure of the wind cap of the man-made islands of the Bridge was completed.

2017-12-31 港珠澳大桥岛隧工程点亮仪式在东人工岛举行，港珠澳大桥主体工程具备通车条件。

December 31, 2017: The lighting-up ceremony of the island-tunnel project of the Bridge was held on East Man-Mad Island, and the traffic condition of the main part of the Bridge was satisfied.

2018-02-06 港珠澳大桥岛隧工程交工验收。历经七年多的紧张施工，港珠澳大桥的关键控制性工程正式具备通车试运营条件。

February 6, 2018: The Island-tunnel project of Hong Kong-Zhuhai-Macau Bridge was delivered. After 7 years' hard work, the critical part of the Bridge had reached the standard for traffic test.

画册索引
ALBUM INDEX

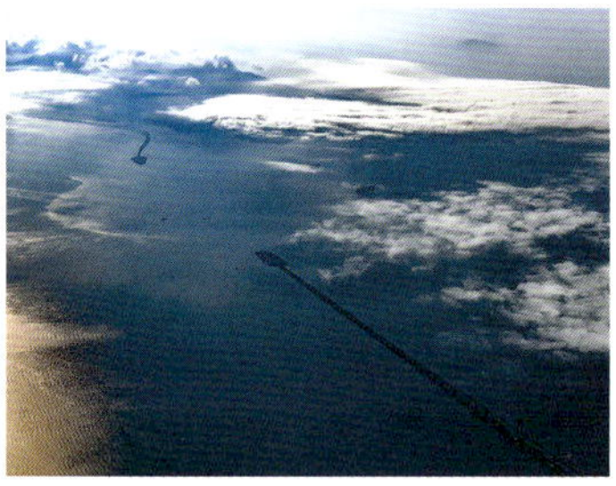

粤港澳大湾区
Guangdong-Hong Kong-Macau Grand Bay Area
001

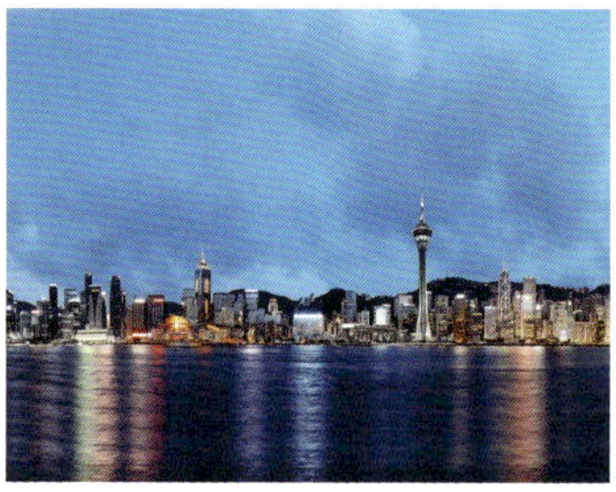

香港
Hong Kong
002

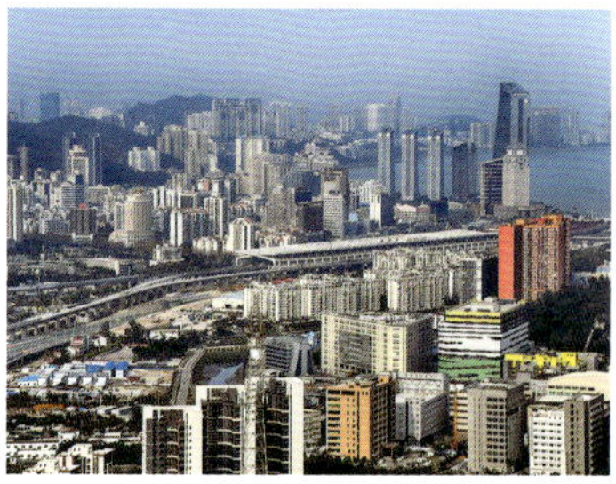

珠海
Zhuhai
004

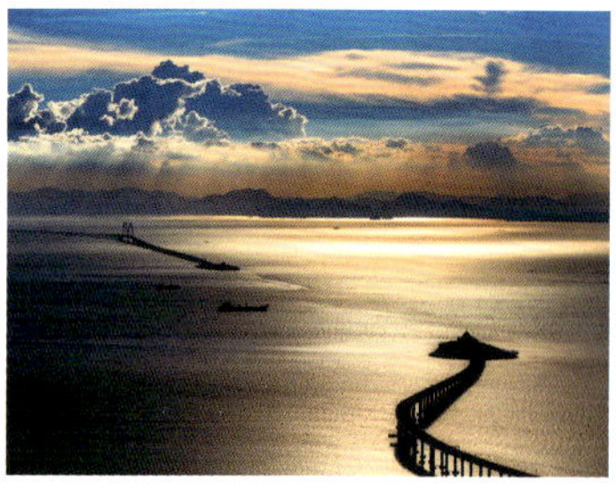

港珠澳大桥
Hong Kong-Zhuhai-Macao Bridge
006

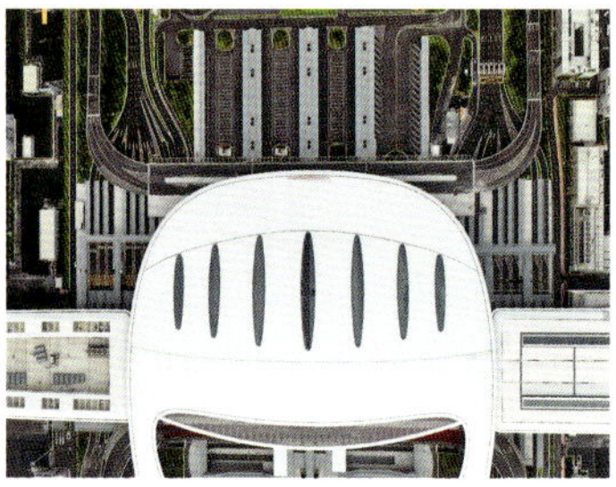

珠澳口岸
Zhuhai-Macau Port
008

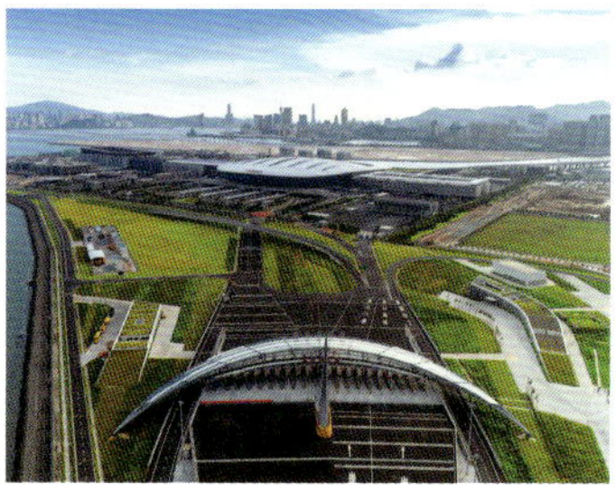

珠澳口岸和大桥收费站
Zhuhai-Macau Port and the Hong Kong-Zhuhai-Macau Bridge Toll Gate
010

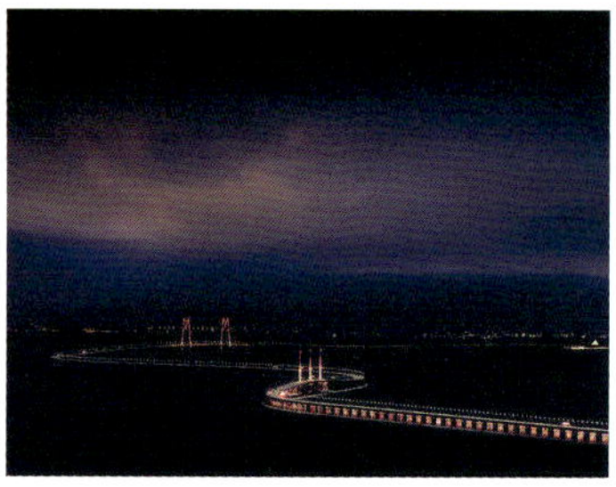

夜幕下的港珠澳大桥
Hong Kong-Zhuhai-Macau Bridge in the Nightshade
012

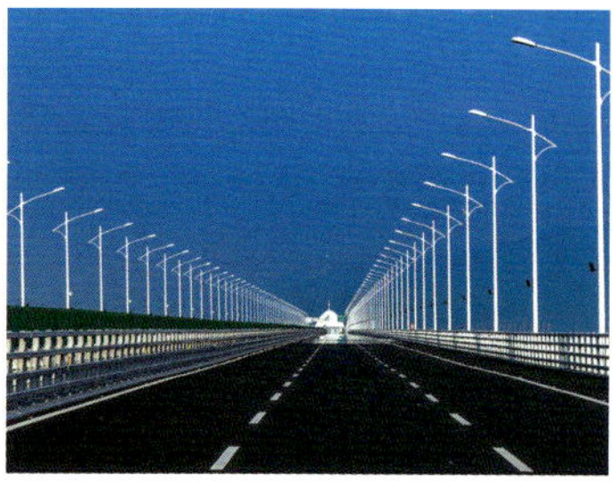

港珠澳大桥
Hong Kong-Zhuhai-Macau Bridge
014

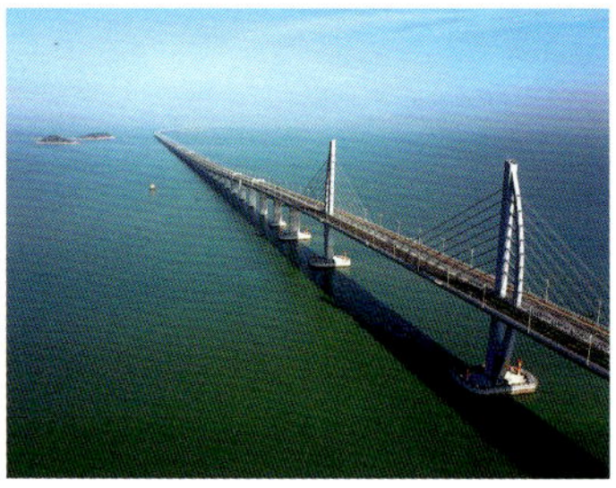

九洲航道桥
Jiuzhou Channel Bridge
017

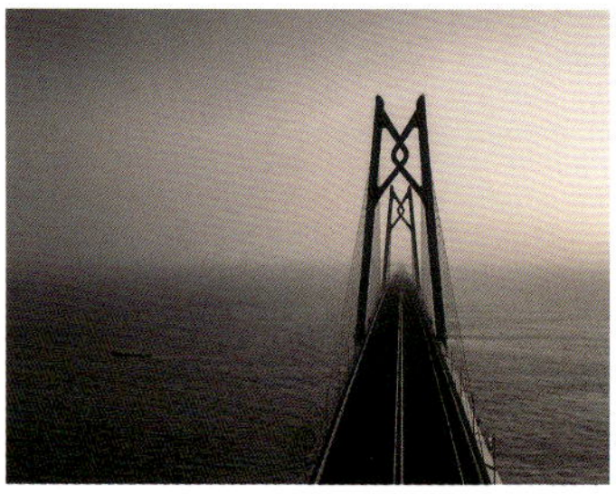

青州航道桥
Qingzhou Channel Bridge
018

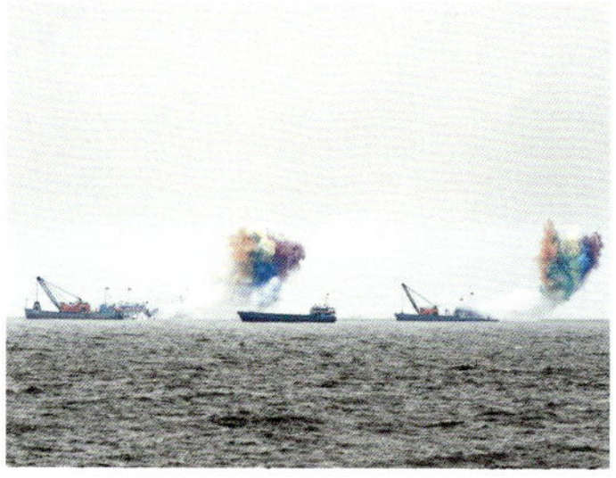

港珠澳大桥动工
The Hong Kong-Zhuhai-Macau Bridge Project Breaks the Ground
020

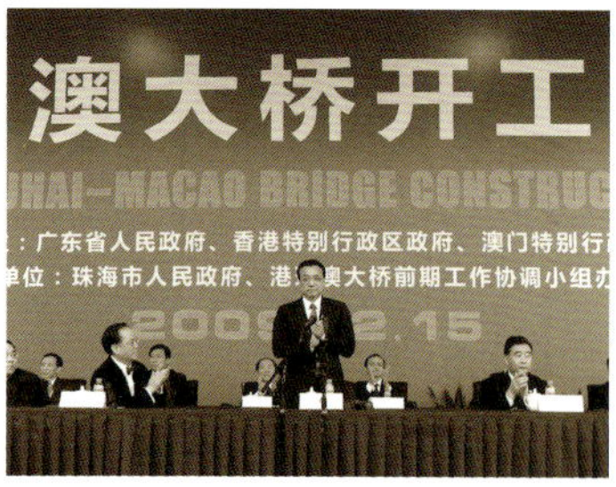

港珠澳大桥开工
The Hong Kong-Zhuhai-Macau Bridge Project was commenced
022

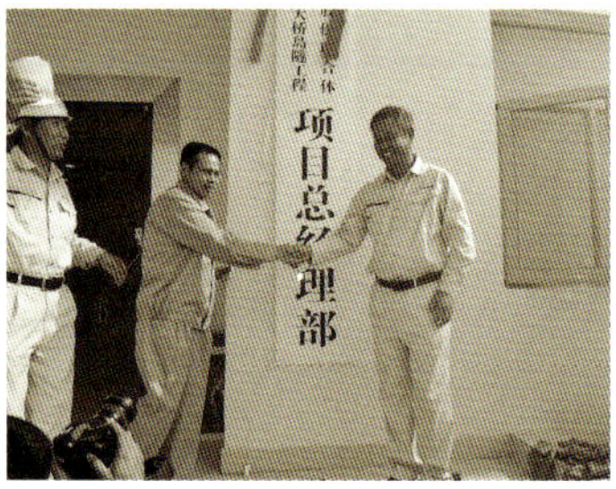

岛隧工程施工总营地揭牌
The Inauguration Ceremony for the General Construction Camp of the Island-Tunnel Project was held
024

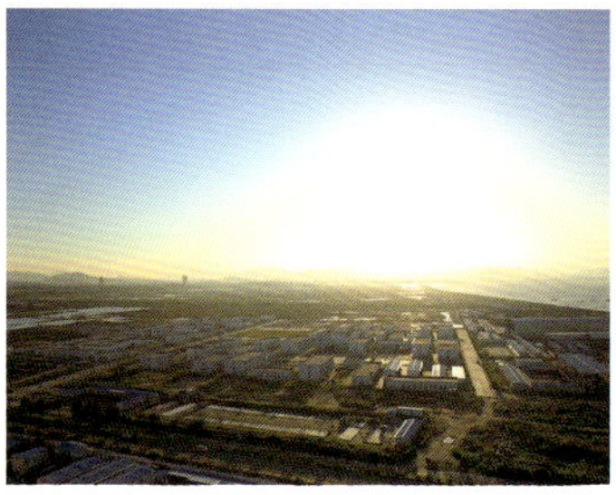

晨曦中的港珠澳大桥施工总营地
General Project Camp for the Hong Kong-Zhuhai-Macau Bridge Project at Dawn
026

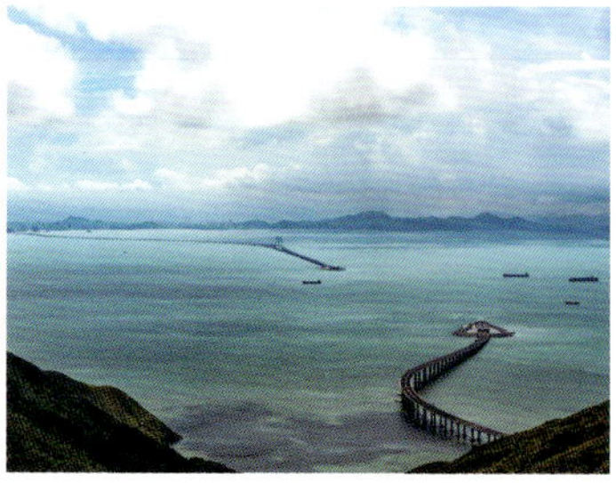

东西人工岛
East Man-Made Island and West Man-Made Island
028

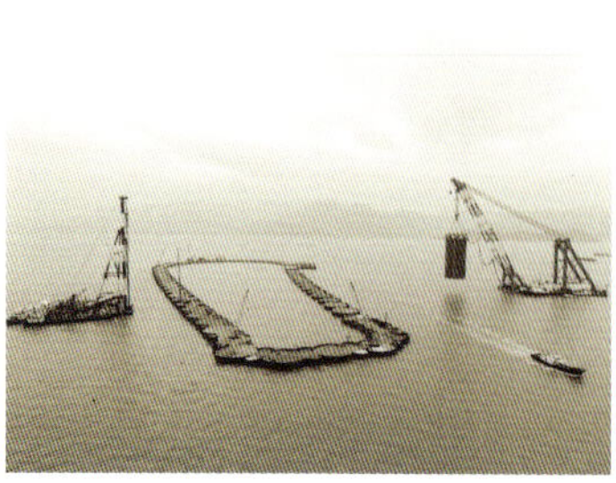

东人工岛 59 个钢圆筒振沉完成，东人工岛成岛
59 Steel Cylinders were Driven into the Seabed on East Man-Made Island, and East Man-Made Island Came into Being
031

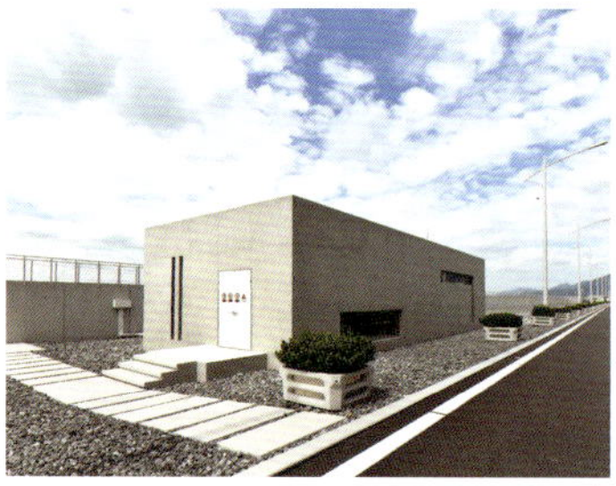

人工岛越浪泵房
Pump Drainage Station on the Man-Made Islands
064

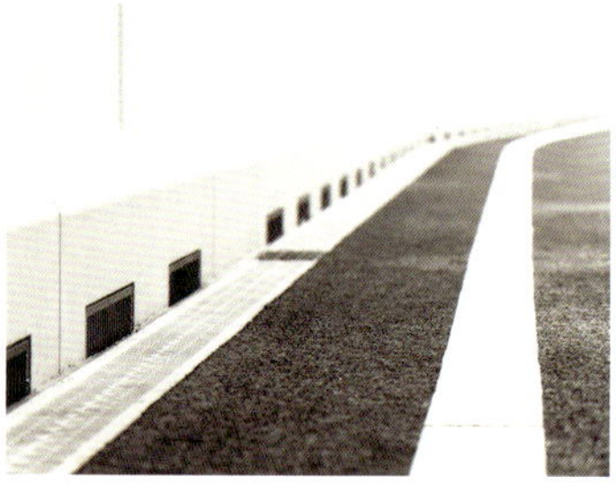

隧道敞开段检修道、线形排水沟
Maintenance Trail in the Open Section of the Tunnel and the Linear Drainage Ditch
066

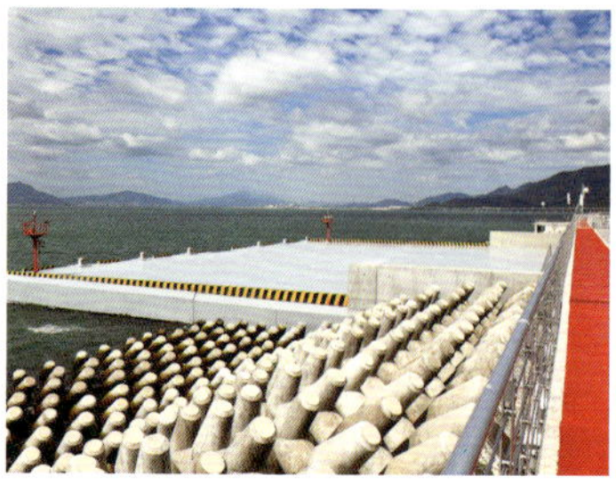

东人工岛救援码头
Rescue Dock on East Man-Made Island
068

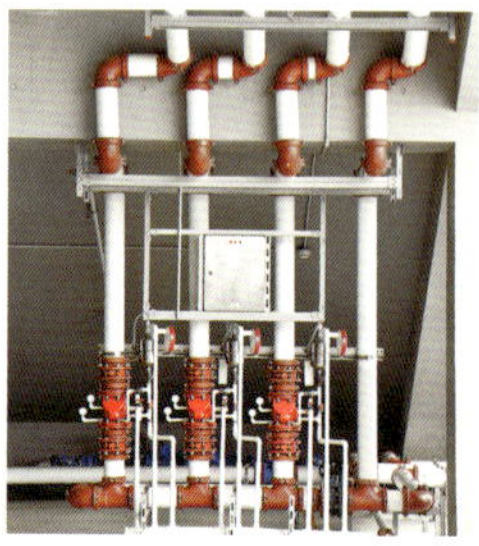

主体建筑消防管道
Fire-Fighting Pipeline in the Main Building
070

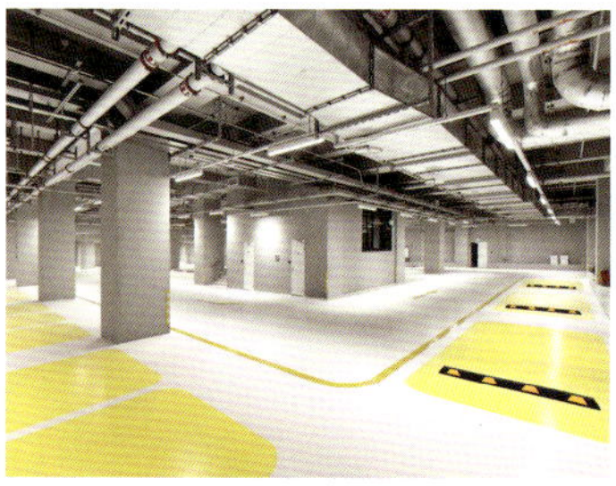

主体建筑负一层室内停车场
Parking Lot on B1 Floor of the Main Building
073

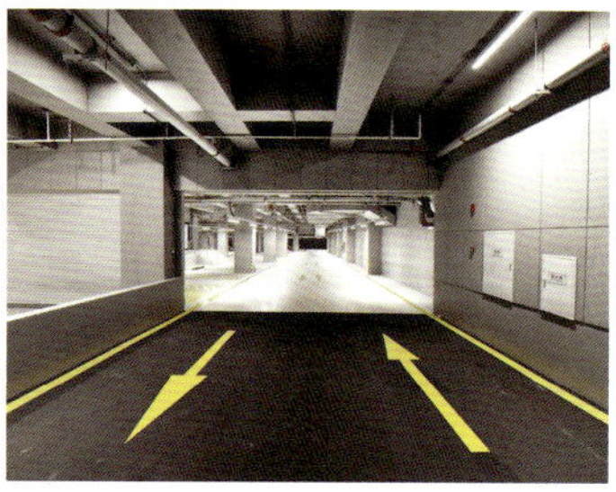

主体建筑负一层停车场出入车道
Entrance and Exit of the Parking Lot on B1 Floor of the Main Building
074

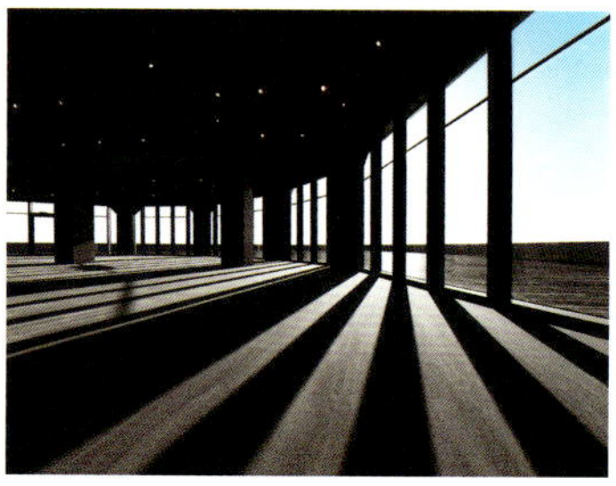

东人工岛主体建筑四层展厅
Exhibition Center on the 4th Floor of the Main Building on East Man-Made Island
076

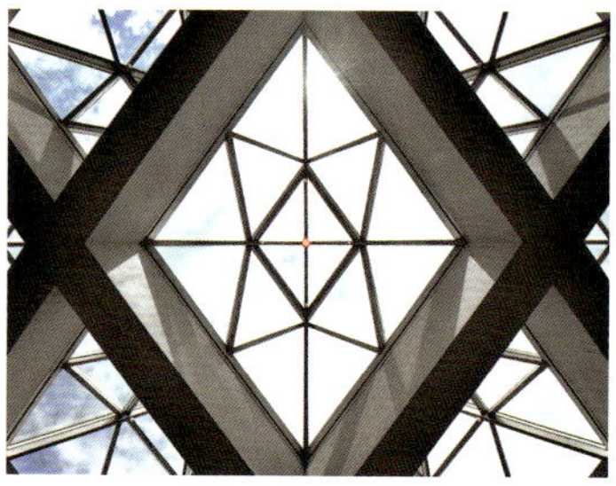

东人工岛主体建筑展厅"七星拱月"天窗
"Seven Stars Surrounding the Moon" Skylight in the Exhibition Center of the Main Building on East Man-Made Island
078

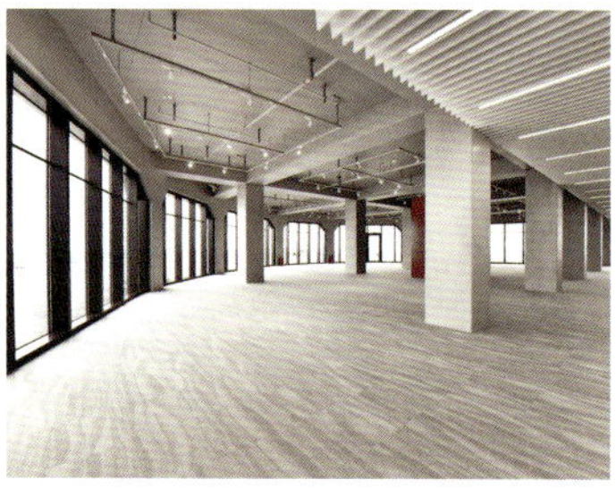

东人工岛主体建筑展厅防静电架空底板
Elevated Anti-electrostatic Soleplate in the Exhibition Center of the Main Building on East Man-Made Island
081

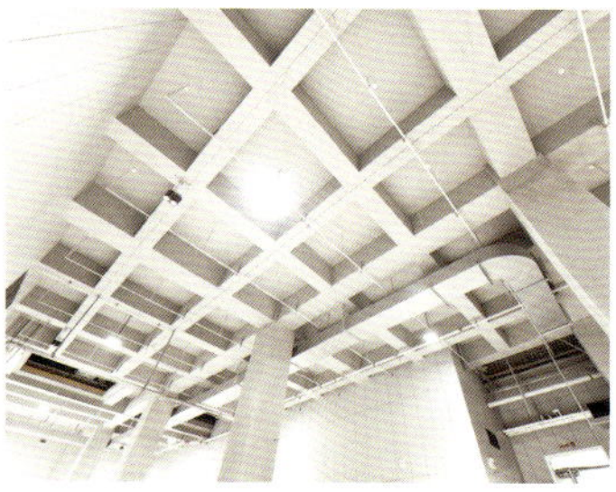

东人工岛主体建筑清水混凝土楼板
Fair-Faced Concrete Floor of the Main Building on East Man-Made Island
082

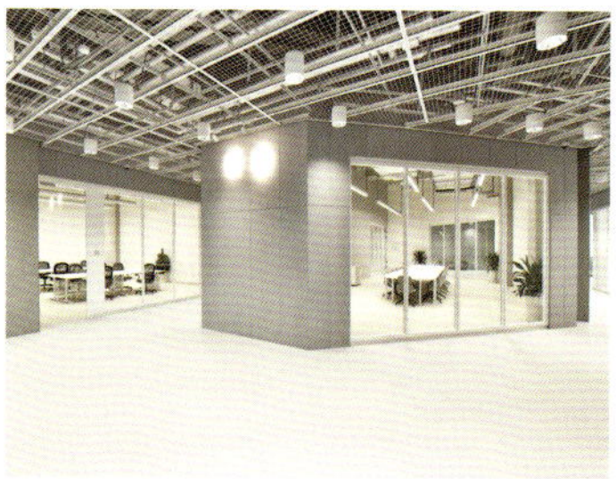

西人工岛办公区
Office Area on West Man-Made Island
084

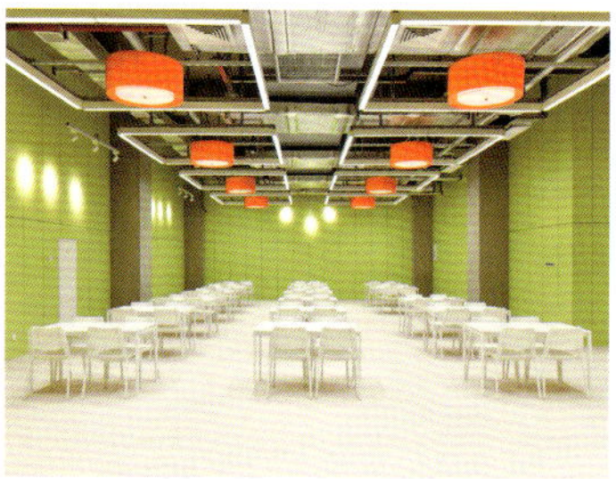

西人工岛职工食堂
Staff Dining Hall on West Man-Made Island
087

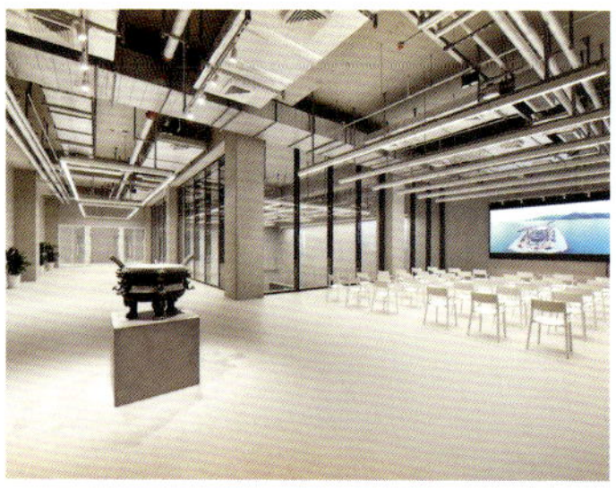

西人工岛报告厅
Lecture Hall on West Man-Made Island
088

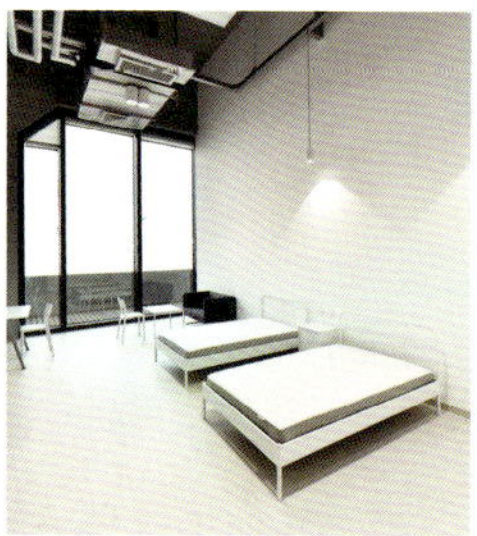

西人工岛职工宿舍
Staff Dormitory on West Man-Made Island
090

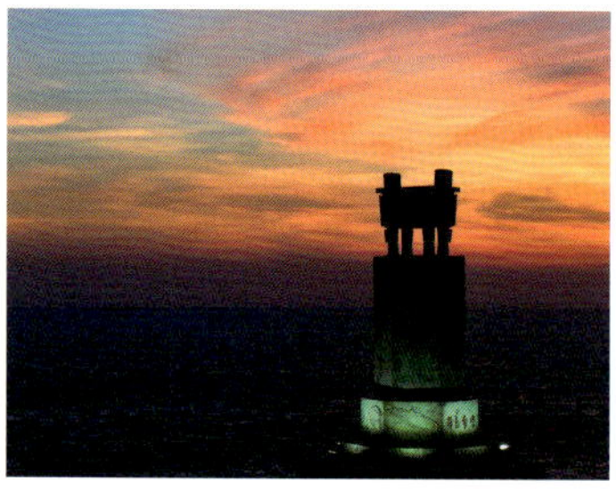

夕阳下的"筑岛奇迹"桥头堡
Bridgehead, "the Island Building Miracle", in the Sunset
092

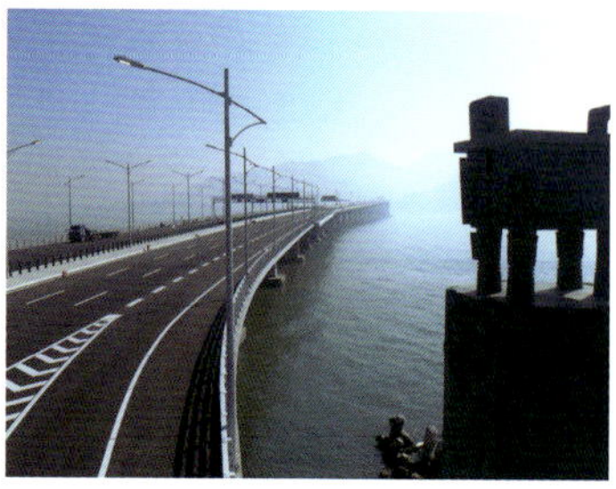

东人工岛青铜鼎桥头堡
Bridgehead in the Shape of Bronze Ding on East Man-Made Island
095

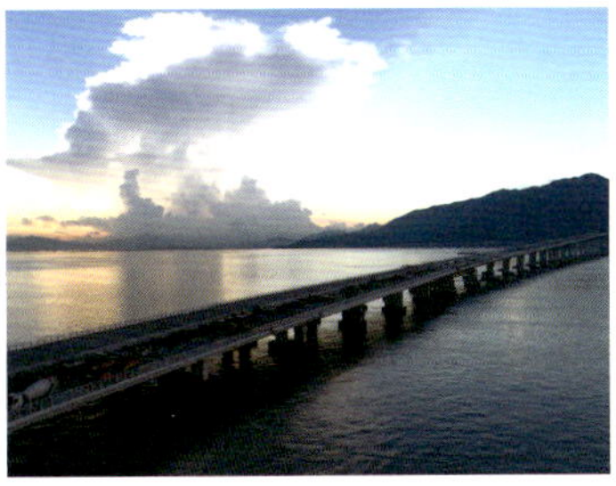

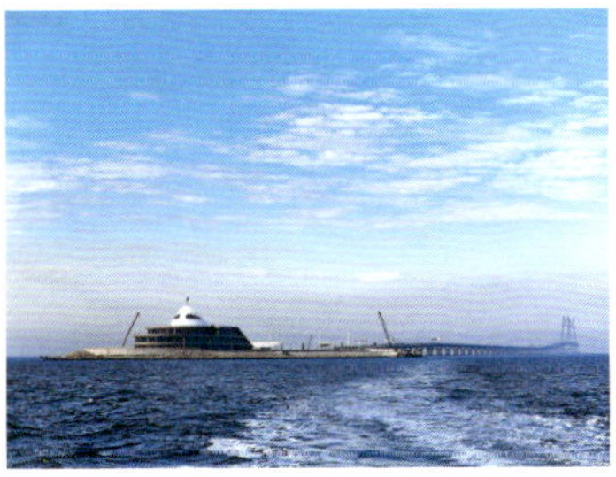

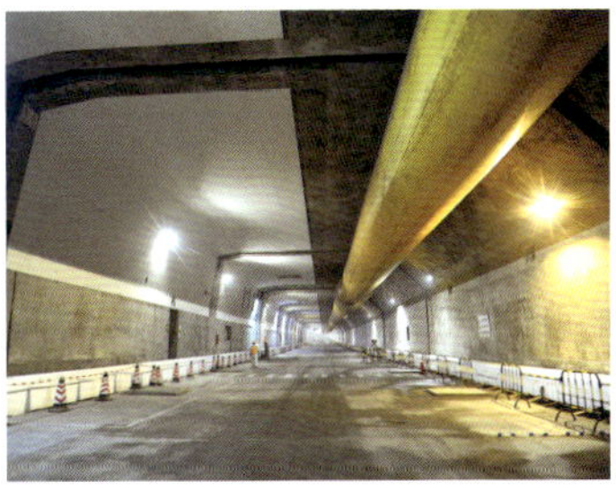

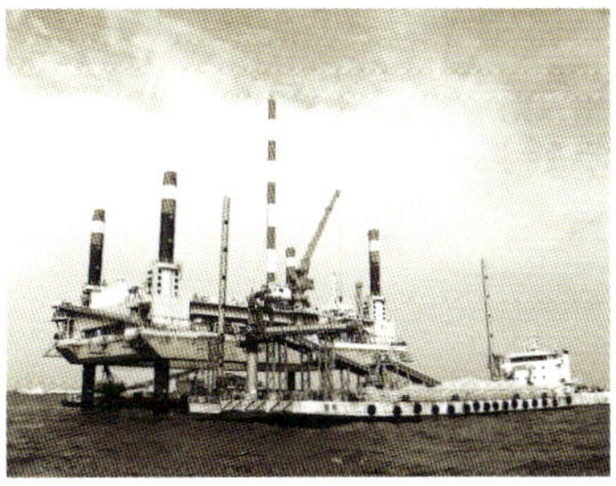

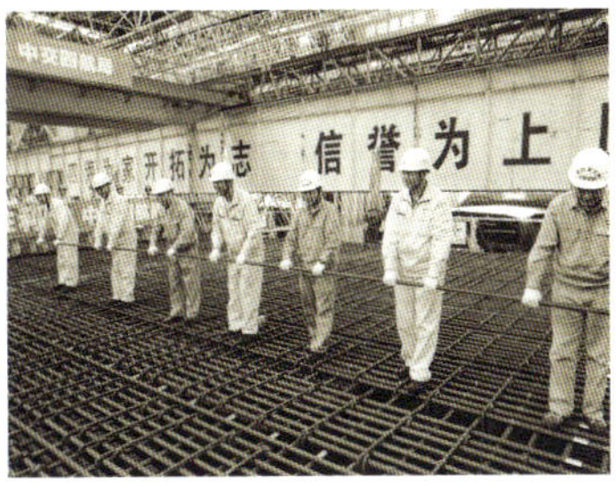

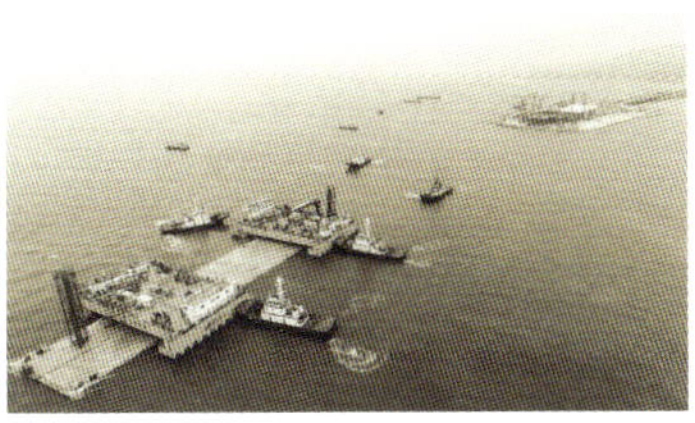

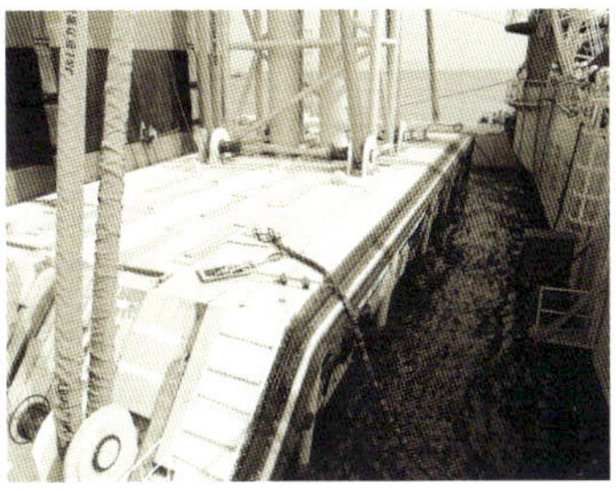

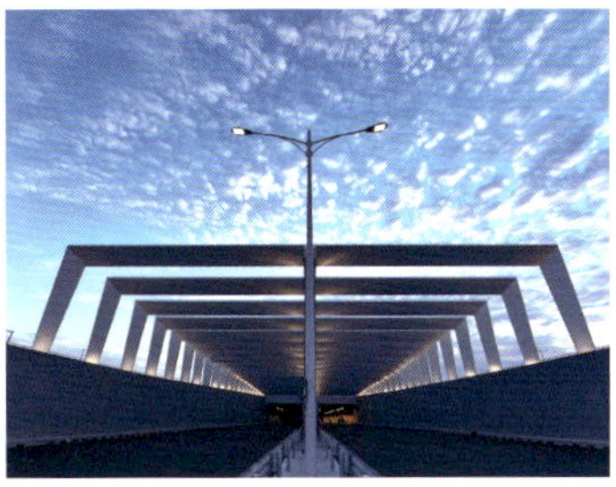

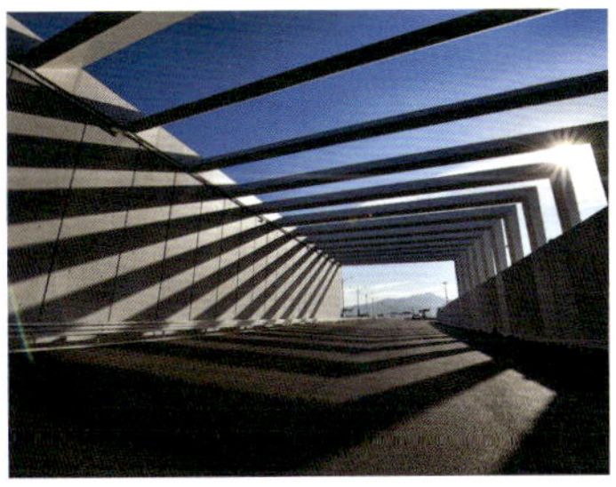

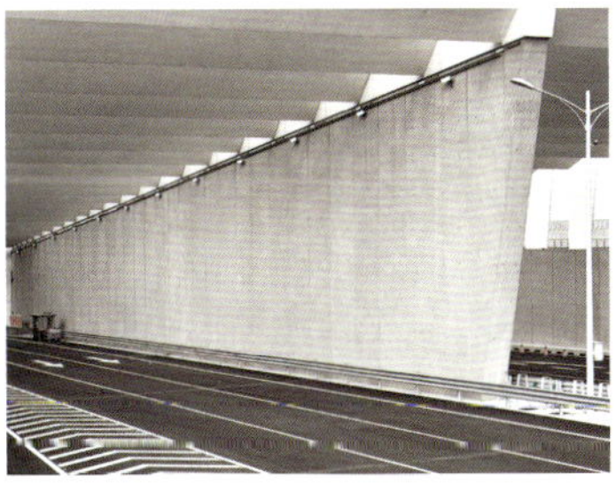

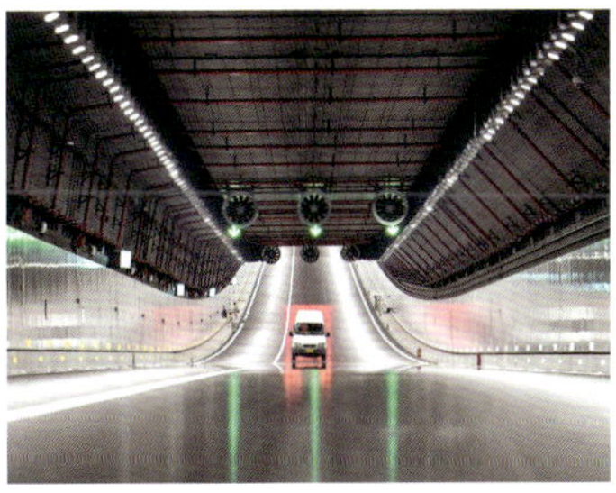

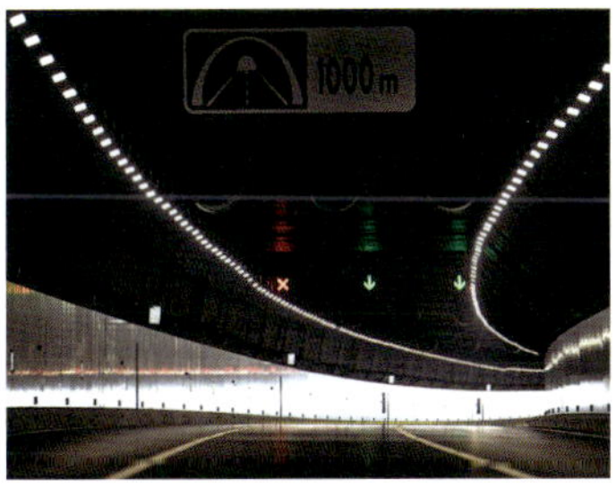
1000m

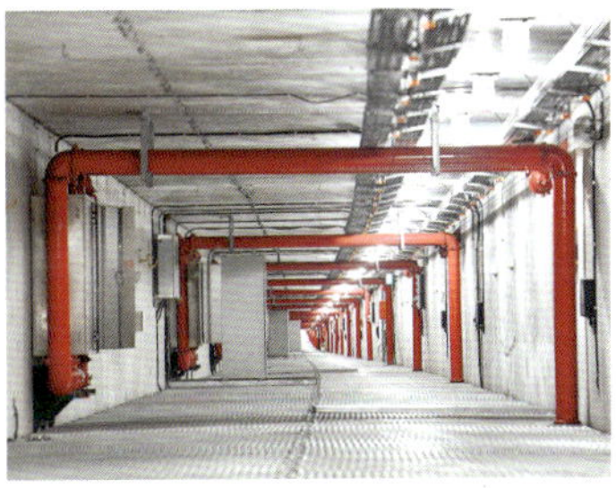

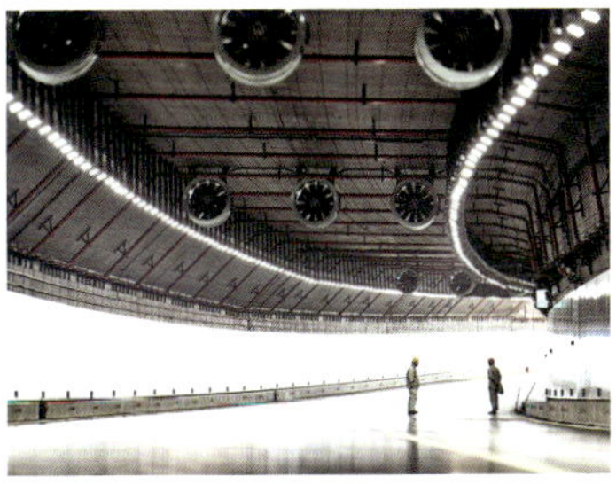

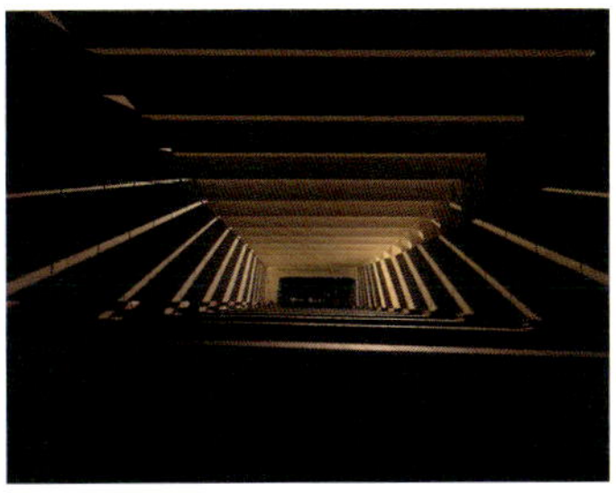

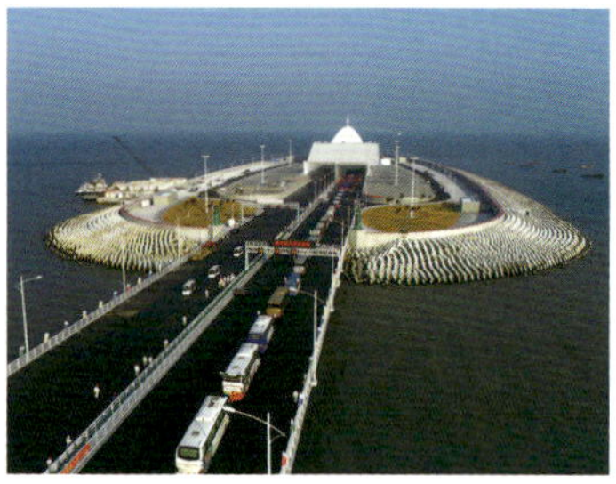

车队进入港珠澳大桥西人工岛
The cars embarked on West Man-Made Island of Hong Kong-Zhuhai-Macau Bridge
129

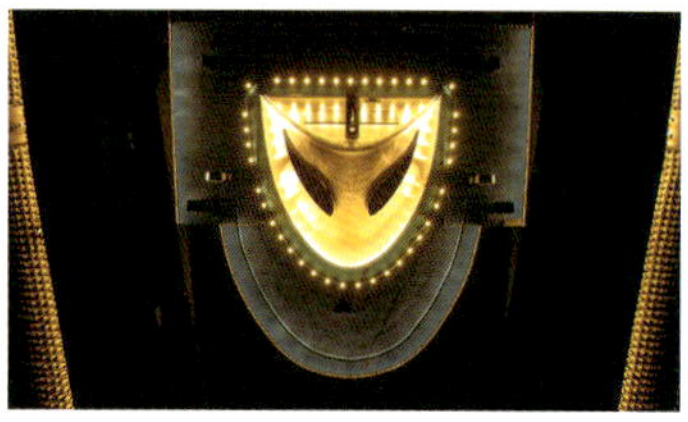

港珠澳大桥风帽亮灯
Lighting up the Wind Cap of Hong Kong-Zhuhai-Macau Bridge
130

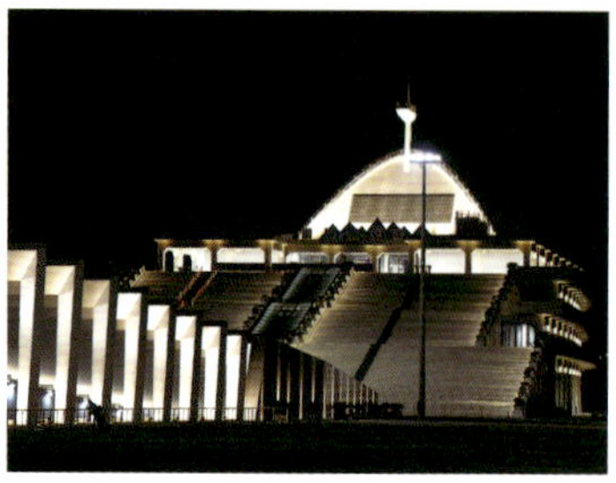

东人工岛主体建筑亮灯
Lighting up the Main Building on East Man-Made Island
133

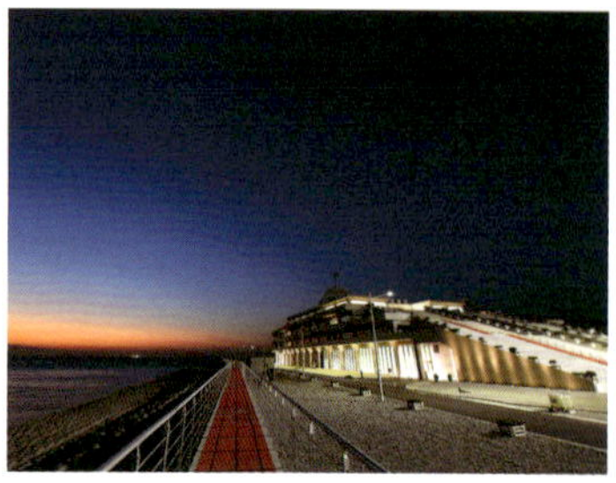

夜幕下的东人工岛主体建筑
Main Building on East Man-Made Island in the Nightshade
134

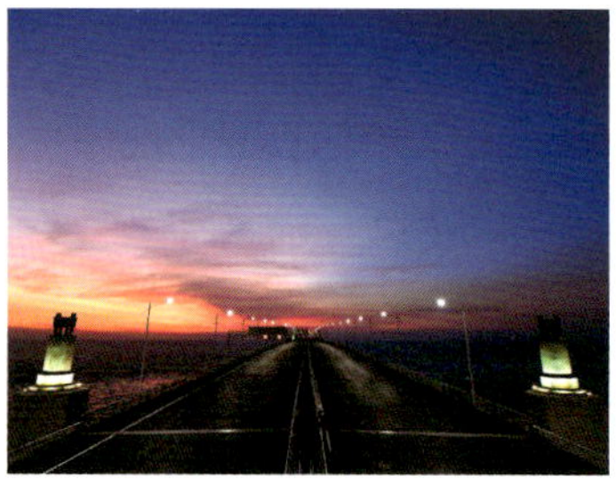

西人工岛桥头堡华灯初上
Lighting up the Bridge Head on West Man-Made Island
136

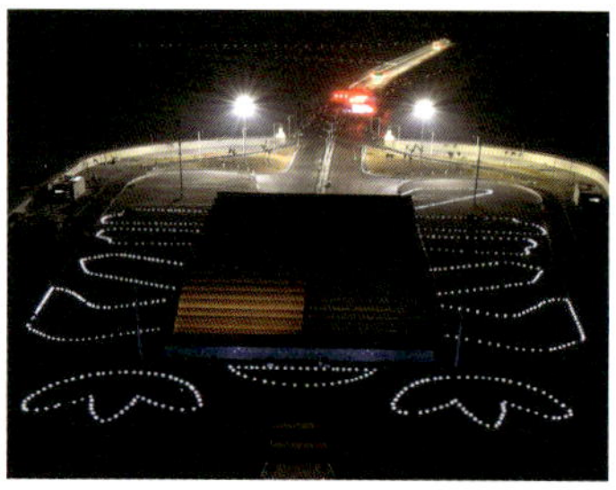

东人工岛岛面大篆"华"形图案
Ancient Chinese Word " 华 " Inscribed on the Surface of East Man-Made Island
138

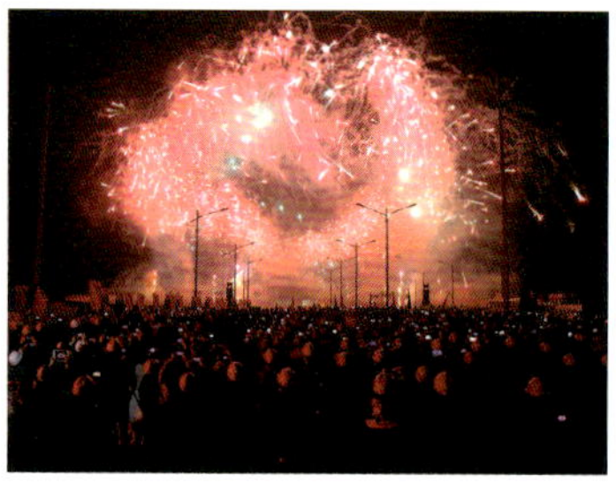

港珠澳大桥点亮仪式现场
Lighting-up Ceremony for Hong Kong-Zhuhai-Macau Bridge
140

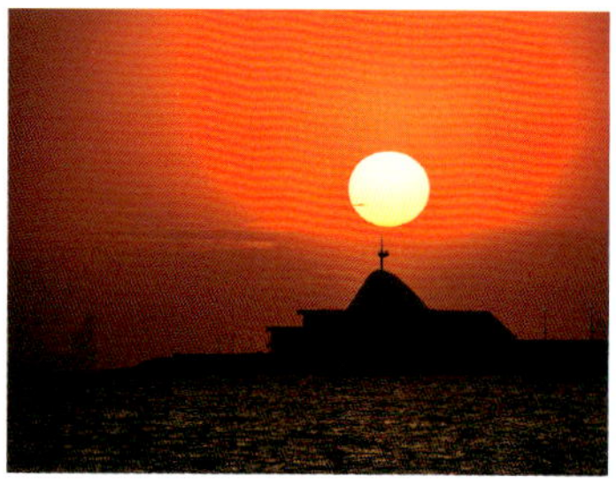

夕阳下的西人工岛
West Man-Made Island in the Sunset
142

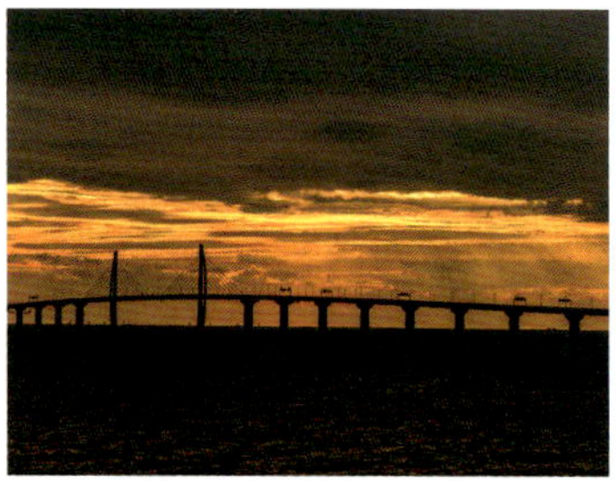

夕阳下的港珠澳大桥
Hong Kong-Zhuhai-Macau Bridge at Sunset
144

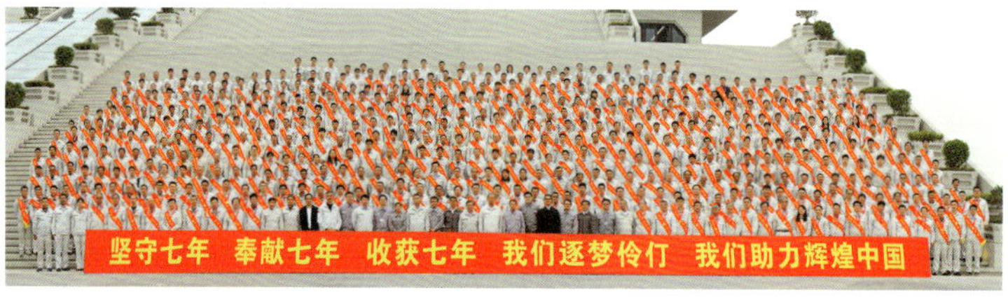

港珠澳大桥岛隧工程总结表彰大会建设者合影
Picture of the Honorary Constructors of Hong Kong-Zhuhai-Macau Bridge
146

后记

POSTSCRIPT

1983年，作为改革开放后最早投入内地建设的实业家，香港合和实业集团主席胡应湘从珠江口两岸经济发展的巨大差异中，前瞻性地提出在珠海和香港之间修建一座跨海大桥——内伶仃洋大桥。那时的珠海，刚刚从一个小渔村跃为中国第一批对外开放的四个经济特区之一，对大桥建设尚属有心无力。

1993年，珠海特区发展日新月异，为了缩小与珠江东岸同时起步的深圳特区之间的差距，珠海市市长梁广大从政府层面呼吁建设伶仃洋大桥，并先期投入建设伶仃洋大桥的前期工程——淇澳大桥。而当时的香港政府表示至少到2020年前没有这个需求，建设方案再一次搁浅。

2003年，珠三角已在改革开放的先机中实现经济腾飞，广州GDP已超越香港，广东省开始准备自己建设连接珠海到深圳的跨海通道。当时遭受亚洲金融风暴重创的香港，在深圳、上海港口的崛起中优势明显下降。

1997年，时任总理朱镕基明确提出支持修建粤港澳大桥。

2003年1月，时任香港特首董建华提出建设港珠澳大桥的意向。

2003年7月，国家发改委论证报告完成，确定兴建港珠澳大桥。

2009年底，港珠澳大桥历经26年的前期论证开工建设。历经7年的艰苦拼搏，一座粤港澳三地投资共建，集桥、岛、隧为一体的世界最大规模公路跨海通道，吸引了全世界的目光。被英国卫报评为"世界新七大奇迹之一"。

2017年5月2日，林鸣站在港珠澳大桥沉管隧道最终接头上，指挥12,000吨浮吊"振华30"轮，吊起重达6000吨的钢混组合结构，在空中旋转90°，插入水下28米深处与两端沉管实现精准合龙，精度控制在毫米级，实现了世界沉管隧道技术的新突破。

作为港珠澳大桥岛隧工程项目总经理，从梦始伶仃洋到圆梦港珠澳的经历让林鸣感慨万千：

一座桥的历史是一个时代的缩影。1994年中国的现代桥梁建设刚刚起步，在建桥的工艺、装备、技术水平方面我们都在向国际同行学习。2010年，中国交建承担了港珠澳大桥岛隧工程建设，让我们开始了挑战世界超级工程技术极限的追梦之旅。

我们到了离梦想最近的时代，这是一个充满机遇的时代，一个机遇大于挑战的时代，一个可以选择的时代。

中国桥梁已开启了超级工程建设的新阶段，过去有什么样的装备才能设计什么样的方案，现在想做什么样的工程就能造出什么样的装备。我国与世界桥梁建设的水平正在缩小，是跟跑、并跑、还是领跑，完全在于我们的视野和心态。

我们需要开阔的视野吸收世界最先进

的技术，站在巨人的肩膀上寻求突破；也需要更加开放的心态与世界交流，为世界桥梁技术的进步做出贡献，赢得的世界信任和尊重。

港珠澳大桥这样一个辉煌的工程是时代的需要，它将成为这个伟大时代的一个符号，承载着一代人的梦想永久屹立在伶仃洋上。

Early in 1983, Hu Yingxiang, the chair of Hopewell Holdings Limited at Hong Kong and the first entrepreneur who was devoted to the mainland construction after the implementation of the reform and opening up policy in China, noticed the great gap between the economies on the two sides of the Pearl River Estuary and for the first time proposed the construction of a cross-sea bridge that connected Zhuhai and Hong Kong—Inner Lingding Bay Bridge. Zhuhai at that moment was only a small fishing village who had just became one of the four economic zones that opened to the world and was not so confident about this project.

Zhuhai in 1993 had undergone tremendous changes as a special economic zone. In order to shorten the gap between Zhuhai and Shenzhen on the other side of Pearl River who started its economic development at the same time, Liang Guangda, the mayor of Zhuhai, as a member of the city government, proposed the construction of Lingding Bay Bridge, beginning with the construction of Qi'ao Bridge. Hong Kong government at that time claimed that they didn't have the desire to build this bridge before 2020. So, the plan aborted again.

By 2003, the Pearl River Estuary had achieved its economic prosperity by taking advantages of the reform and opening up policy. The GDP of Guangzhou had surpassed that of Hong Kong, and Guangdong Province began to prepare the construction of a cross-sea highway that connected Zhuhai and Shenzhen on its own cost. Hong Kong of that time suffered greatly in the Asian Financial Crisis and lagged far behind Shenzhen and Shanghai.

In 1997, the then Premier Zhu Rongji declared that the government would support the construction of a bridge connecting Guangdong, Hong Kong and Macau.

In January, 2003, Dong Jianhua, the then Chief Executive of Hong Kong, showed Hong Kong's intention to build Hong Kong-Zhuhai-Macau Bridge.

In July, 2003, National Development and Reform Commission completed the research and declared the construction of Hong Kong-Zhuhai-Macau Bridge.

After 26 years' research and discussion, the construction of Hong Kong-Zhuhai-Macau Bridge started in 2009. After 7 years' hard work, the largest cross-sea bridge in the world, financed by Guangdong Province, Hong Kong and Macau and combining bridge, island and tunnel into a whole, was completed and attracted the attention of the whole world. The Guardian of U. K. acclaimed it as "one of the new seven world wonders".

On May 2, 2017, Lin Ming, standing on the closure joint of the immersed tube of Hong Kong-Zhuhai-Macau Bridge, commanded Zhenhua 30, the hoisting barge of 12,000 tons, to lift the steel concrete structure of 6000 tons and land it 28 meters under the water after a 90° swerve in the air for the precise connection with the immersed tubes on the two ends. The installation precision is controlled within the limit of a few millimeters, and a new breakthrough in the world immersed tube tunneling was achieved.

The dream began with Lingding Bay Bridge and was realized finally by the completion of Hong Kong-Zhuhai-Macau Bridge. This experience moved Lin Ming, general project manager of the island-tunnel project of Hong Kong-Zhuhai-Macau Bridge into a speech:

The history of a bridge is the miniature of an era. China's modern bridge construction started in 1994, and we had to learn from other countries in crafts, equipment and technologies at that time. In 2010, China Communications Construction Company Ltd. won the bidding for the island-tunnel project of Hong Kong-Zhuhai-Macau Bridge, which initiated our journey to challenge the technological limit of a super-class project in the world.

Our dream has come true. And this is an age of opportunities, an age of opportunities giving way to challenges, and an age of making choices.

China's bridge engineering has come to its new stage. We depended on our facilities to make our plans in the past, but now we produce facilities by our plans. The gap between China's bridge construction and world's bridge construction has become smaller. Whether we follow the world, we advance side by side, or we lead the world depends on our horizon and determination.

We need a broad horizon to absorb the most advanced technologies of the world, and we need to stand on the shoulders of the giants for breakthroughs; we need to open our eyes and our heart to communicate with the world and devote ourselves for the advancement of the world's bridge engineering technologies to win the trust and respect of the world.

Hong Kong-Zhuhai-Macau Bridge is one of the grand projects the age needs. It will be a mark we leave on this great age, embracing our generation's dream to standing over Lingding Bay.

海底绣花

EMBROIDERY UNDERSEA

港珠澳大桥岛隧工程画册

Album of the Island-Tunnel Project of Hong Kong-Zhuhai-Macau Bridge

中国交通建设股份有限公司 编
CHINA COMMUNICATIONS CONSTRUCTION COMPANY LIMITED

南方日報出版社
NANFANG DAILY PRESS
中国·广州

图书在版编目（CIP）数据

海底绣花 / 中国交通建设股份有限公司编. — 广州：南方日报出版社，2019.3

（港珠澳大桥岛隧工程画册）

ISBN 978-7-5491-1987-5

Ⅰ. ①海… Ⅱ. ①中… Ⅲ. ①跨海峡桥－桥梁工程－中国－图集 ②水下隧道－隧道工程－中国－图集 Ⅳ. ①U4-64

中国版本图书馆 CIP 数据核字（2019）第 045103 号

GANG ZHU AO DAQIAO DAOSUI GONGCHENG HUACE · HAIDI XIUHUA

港珠澳大桥岛隧工程画册·海底绣花

编　　者：中国交通建设股份有限公司

设计排版：廣角品牌机构

出版发行：南方日报出版社

地　　址：广州市广州大道中 289 号

出 版 人：周山丹

责任编辑：杨柳青　曹　星

责任技编：王　兰

责任校对：王　燕

装帧设计：李文俊　田　红　吴　凯

翻　　译：刘风山　郭敬谊

经　　销：全国新华书店

印　　刷：雅昌文化（集团）有限公司

开　　本：635 mm×965 mm　1/8

印　　张：22

字　　数：418 千字

版　　次：2019 年 3 月第 1 版

印　　次：2019 年 3 月第 1 次印刷

定　　价：980.00 元（全套 4 册）

编委会
Editorial Board

目录
CONTENTS

沉管预制
PRECAST OF THE IMMERSED TUBES

画册索引
ALBUM INDEX

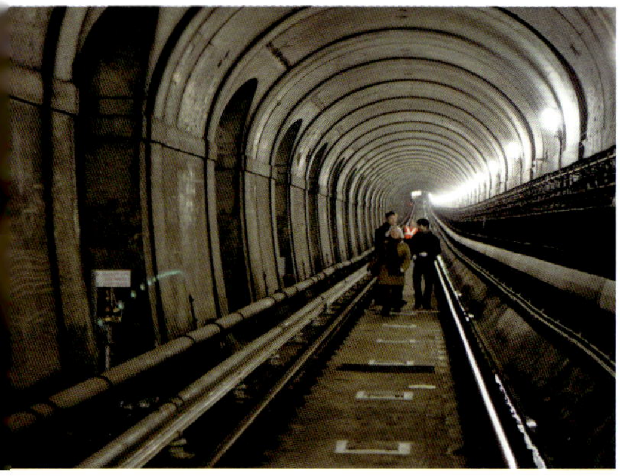

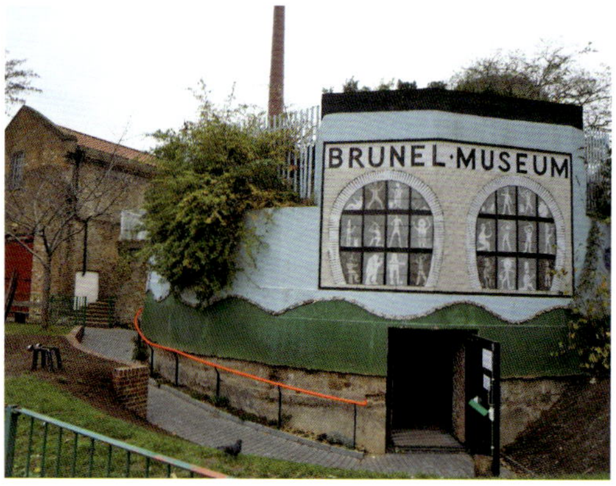

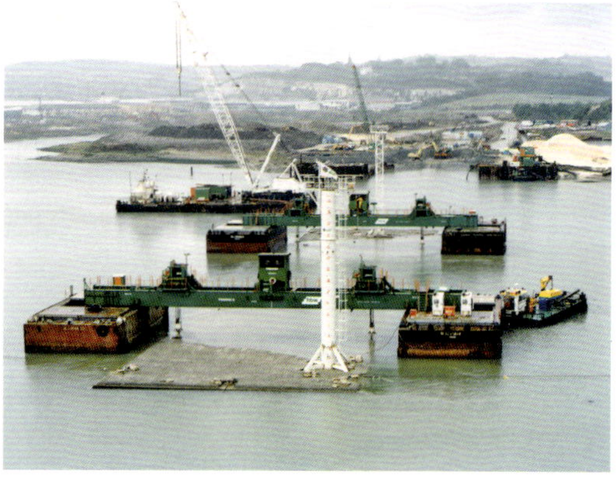

沉管隧道背景综述

PROFILE OF THE IMMERSED TUBE TUNNELING

沉管预制技术发展

DEVELOPMENT OF THE IMMERSED TUBE PRECAST TECHNOLOGY

1810 年，英国首次在伦敦进行了沉管隧道施工试验；19 世纪末期，沉管隧道施工工法获得进一步发展和完善；1910 年，美国在跨越加拿大和美国之间的底特律河上建造了世界第一条铁路沉管隧道，标志着沉管隧道技术的成功应用。经过 100 多年的发展，到 21 世纪初期，近 20 多个国家先后修建了 150 多条沉管隧道。

美国旧金山海湾水下隧道、土耳其博斯普鲁斯海峡沉管隧道、连接丹麦和瑞典的厄勒海峡沉管隧道、韩国釜山隧道以及被誉为"新世界七大奇迹"之一的中国港珠澳大桥沉管隧道是沉管隧道的代表，这些工程的成功建设为沉管隧道的发展提供了新的思路。

按照建成时间、结构特点和预制类型，可以把沉管隧道的发展划分为三个主要阶段：

第一阶段：20 世纪 20 至 40 年代。典型特征为：1 钢壳结构；2. 单个行车道内不超过两个车道；3. 造船厂预制沉管。

第二阶段：20 世纪 40 至 60 年代。典型特征为：1. 钢筋混凝土（或预应力）结构；2. 矩形断面；3. 干坞内或造船厂预制沉管。这个阶段沉管隧道以钢筋混凝土结构为主，在车道布置形式上更加灵活，满足了道路通行的基本要求。

第三阶段：20 世纪 60 年代后期。典型特征为：1. 节段管节；2. 混凝土结构自防水；3. 工厂法预制开始得以应用。第三阶段沉管隧道最大的技术进步当属混凝土预制水平提高，沉管自防水获得成功。

自 20 世纪 80 年代末以来，沉管隧道的防水重点为加强混凝土裂缝控制，通过节段式沉管和整体式浇筑尽可能地减少出现温度裂缝，使混凝土自身成为永久的防水屏障，不再使用外包材料进行辅助防水；而且可以根据浮运条件与设备能力制作较长的沉管管节。

从世界沉管隧道工程发展历史，大致可以看出世界沉管隧道技术发展趋势：

1. 单节沉管长度越来越长，车道越来越多。

2. 从单一用途向多用途发展。

3. 沉管隧道的地基适应性越来越复杂。沉管隧道可修建在较坚硬地基（河、海床）上，亦可修建在软弱地基（河、海床）上。

4. 制造材料逐步由钢筋混凝土取代，主要采用高性能混凝土。

5. 预制过程中，须采取多种混凝土裂缝控制措施，确保沉管质量，特别要防止出现贯穿裂缝。

6. 标准化防水体系日趋完善。

7. 沉埋沉管的浮运、沉放、连接等系统日趋科学、简便，以适应多变的外界施工环境。

8. 沉管设计计算逐渐趋于规范化。

In 1810, England conducted the first immersed tube tunnel construction test in London. Towards the end of the 19th century, the technology of the immersed tube tunneling was greatly improved. In 1910, the United States built the world's first immersed tube railway tunnel spanning the Detroit River between Canada and the United States, marking the successful application of the immersed tube tunneling technology. After more than 100 years of development, by the early 21st century, more than 150 immersed tube tunnels have been built in nearly 20 countries of the world.

The representative immersed tube tunnel projects in the world include the Transbay Tube under San Francisco Bay in the U. S., the Eurasia Tunnel underneath Bosphorus Strait of Turkey, the Oresund Strait Tunnel connecting Denmark and Sweden, the Busan-Geoje Tunnel of South Korea and the immersed tube tunnel of Hong Kong-Zhuhai-Macau Bridge known as "one of the New Seven Wonders of the World". The successful construction of these tunnels provides new prospects for the development of immersed tube tunneling.

According to their construction time, structural characteristics and prefabrication modes of the immersed tubes, the development of immersed tube tunneling can be divided into three main stages:

Stage One: 1920s to 1940s. The typical features of this stage include: 1. Steel-shelled structure; 2. No more than 2 driving lanes in one carriageway; 3. Tubes precast in the shipyard.

Stage Two: 1940s to 1960s. The typical features of this stage include: 1. Reinforced concrete (or pre-stressed) structure; 2. Rectangular cross section of the tunnel; 3. Tubes precast in the dry dock or shipyard. At this stage, the tube tunneling mainly employed steel-reinforced concrete structure; the layout of the driving lanes was more flexible and satisfied the basic requirements for road traffic.

Stage Three: the late 1960s. The typical features of this stage include: 1. Tube segments; 2. Automatic waterproofing concrete structure; 3. Factory-based prefabrication being applied. The biggest technical progress in immersed tube tunneling at this stage was the improvement of the quality of concrete placement and the success of automatic waterproof tubes.

Since the late 1980s, the key point of waterproofing for the immersed tube tunnel was to enhance the control of concrete cracks. Segmented immersed tubes and monolithic casting were adopted to reduce the occurrence of temperature-incurred cracking as much as possible, the concrete itself became the permanent waterproof device, and the external enveloping materials were no longer used as auxiliary waterproofing tools. In addition, longer immersed tubes could be fabricated according to the shipping conditions and relevant equipment's capacity.

Seen from the world history of the development of immersed tube tunneling, the development trend of the immersed tube tunneling technology of the world can be roughly concluded as the following:

1. One single segment of the immersed tube becomes longer and longer, and there are more and more driving lanes in the tunnel.

2. The immersed tube tunnel is proper for multiple uses.

3. The immersed tube tunnel has become

increasingly adaptable to more complex foundations. It can be built both on hard ground (or river bed and sea bed) and on soft ground (or river bed and sea bed).

4. Steel-reinforced concrete, mainly high-performance concrete, gradually becomes the dominate material.

5. During the prefabrication of the immersed tubes, different measures are used to avoid concrete cracking, especially the penetrating cracks, so as to guarantee the quality of the immersed tubes.

6. The standardized waterproof system is improving gradually.

7. The float conveyance, landing and butt joint of the immersed tubes become more and more scientific and easier to handle to adapt to the ever-changing external environment.

8. The design and calculation of the immersed tubes are increasingly standardized.

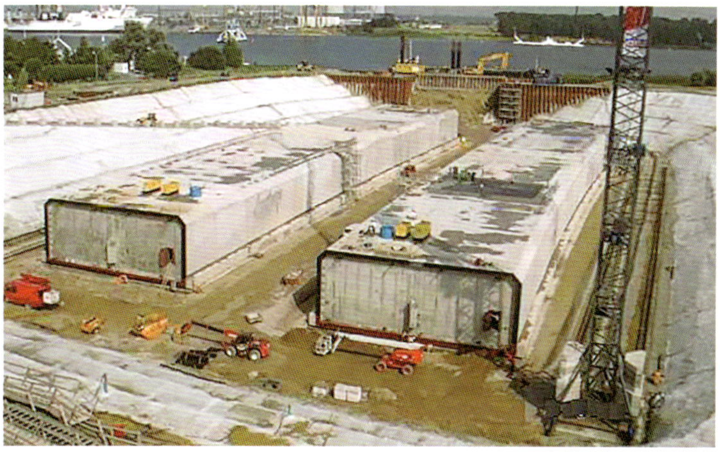

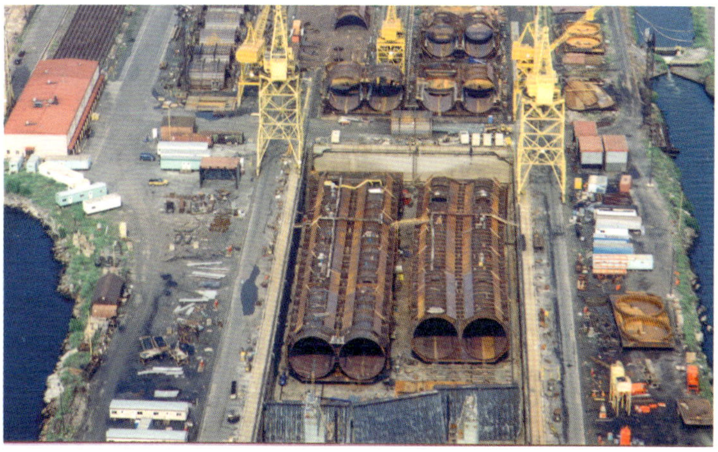

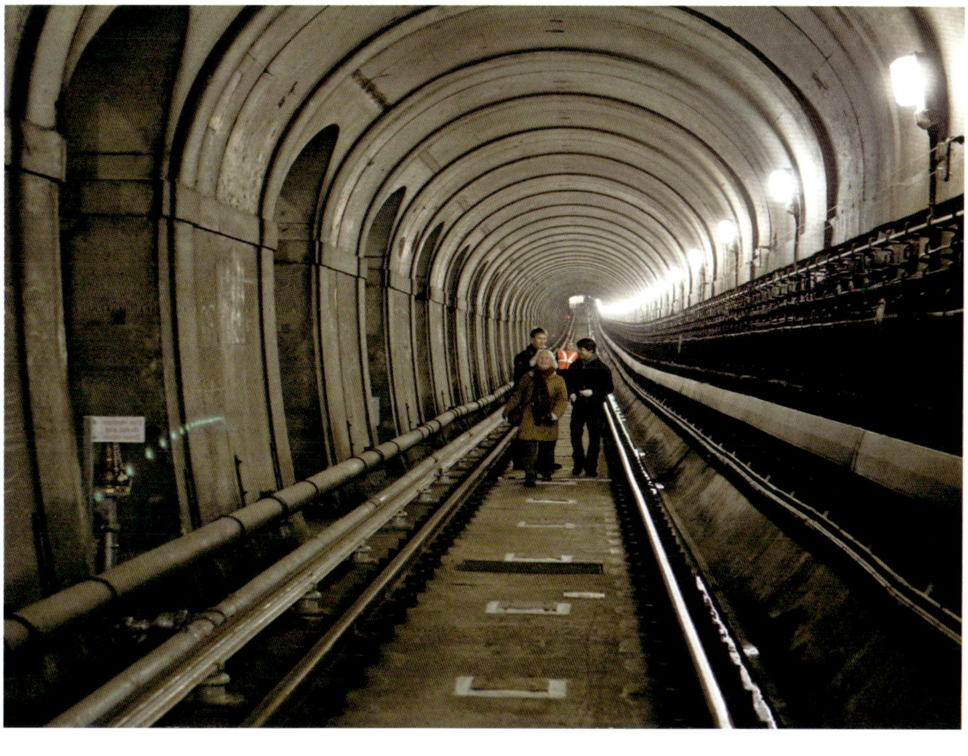

1. 德国瓦尔诺河隧道
   The Warnow Tunnel, Germany
2. 美国波士顿泰德·威廉姆斯隧道
   Ted Williams Tunnel, Boston, U. S. A.
3. 英国泰晤士河海底隧道
   River Thames Immersed Tube Tunnel, U. K.

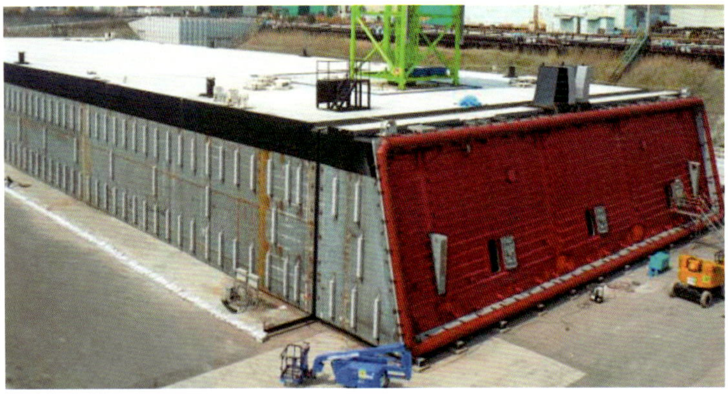

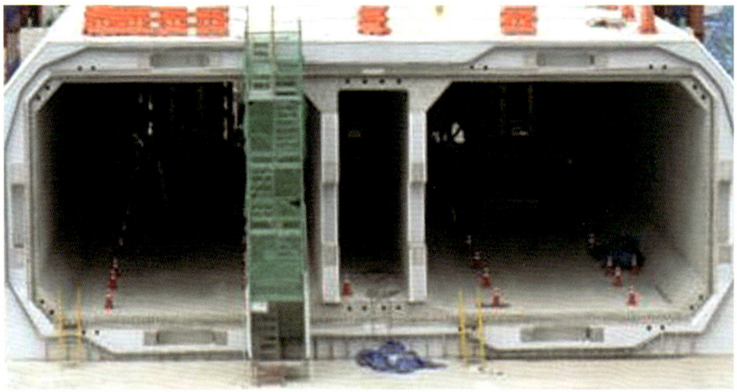

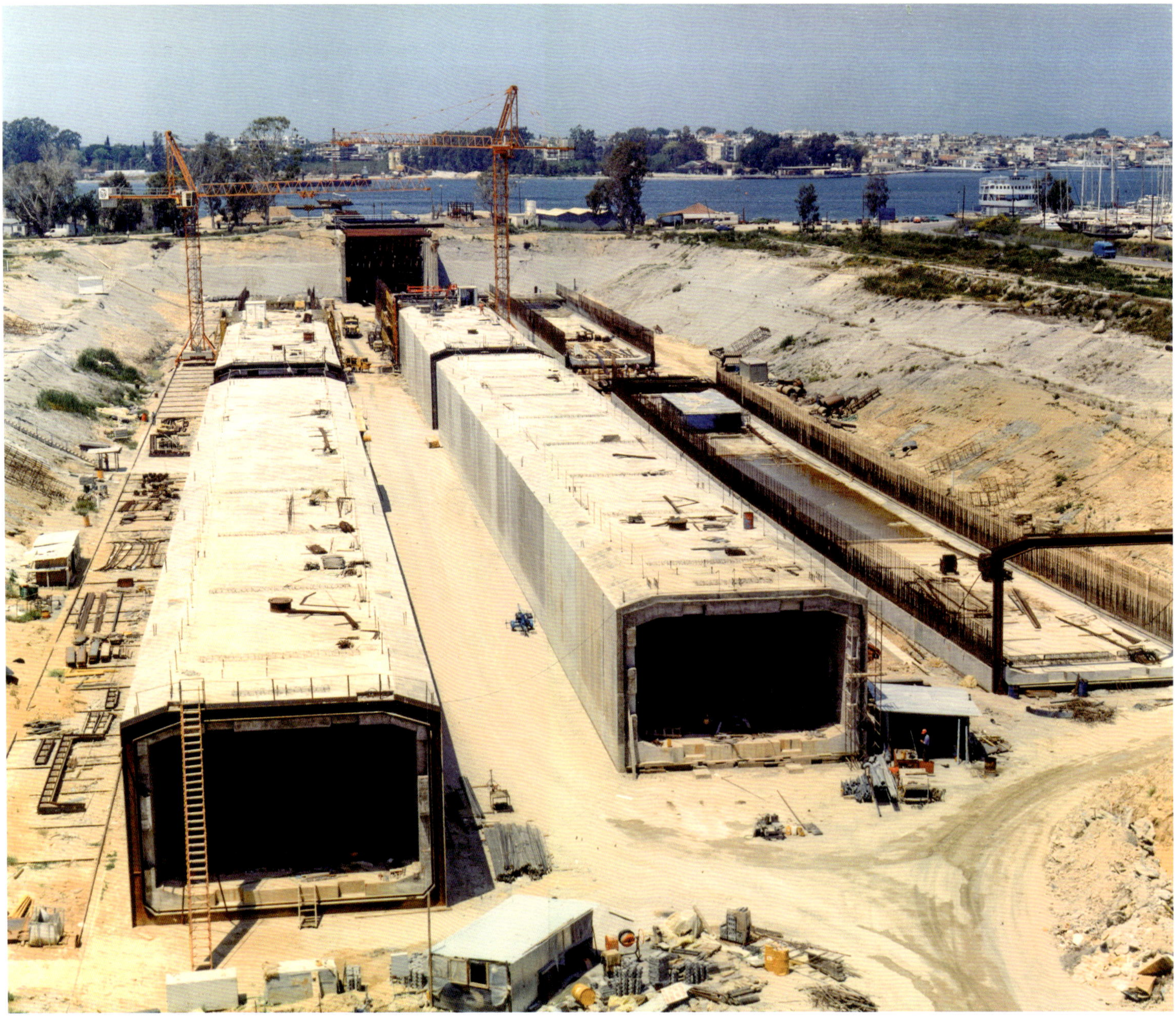

整体式沉管结构的纵向刚度大，在地基反力作用下，呈现"宁折不弯"的结构特性，其适应地基变形能力弱，沉管结构易产生较大的纵向内力，差异沉降变形会集中反应在沉管接头，沉管接头需要具有更高的传力能力和抗形变能力。

节段式沉管由若干个小节段通过临时预应力组合而成，每个小节段为刚性段，沉管受力变形时能利用更多的节段接头及时消化变形，吸收平衡内力。与整体式管节沉管相比较，其适应地基变形能力较强，呈现"以柔克刚"的结构特点。

沉管结构类型有钢筋混凝土结构、钢壳混凝土组合结构及预应力钢筋混凝土结构。

钢筋混凝土沉管使用最为广泛，技术十分成熟。既可以采用整体式沉管结构，以期得到更好的防渗漏功能；也可采用节段式沉管结构，获得更好的柔性以适应地基变形。

钢壳混凝土沉管分为全钢壳组合结构及单侧钢壳混凝土组合结构。全钢壳混凝土组合结构又称"三明治组合结构"，可分为单圆形、双圆形或矩形等断面，钢壳外包于混凝土的内外表面，能够让钢材更好地发挥结构效率，进而有可能获得断面尺度最经济的设计效果；单侧钢壳混凝土组合结构的钢壳外包于混凝土外侧表面，主体结构仍然采用钢筋混凝土结构，更好地发挥其防水功能。

钢壳混凝土沉管已有较长的历史，最大的优势是可以实现工业化制造，对现场干坞和临时工程的要求相对最低，在防渗、结构抗震方面具有优势，并且由于能够实现工业化制造，质量控制也有明显优势。其造价一般较高。

The monolithic immersed tube has great longitudinal rigidity, and under the pressure of the tunnel foundation's reaction, it exhibits a special structural feature, that is, it may fracture rather than bends. The tube has weak adaptability to the deformation of the foundation, and it's easy for the tube structure to generate an immense internal longitudinal force. Deformation resulting from differential settlement happens at the butt joint part of the tube, so the butt joint needs to have strong capacity to transmit the force and resist deformation.

The segmented immersed tube is made up of small segments connected by temporary pre-stressing force, and each segment features its rigidity. When the immersed tube deforms under pressure, the joints between different segments can absorb the deforming force to balance the internal forces. Compared with the monolithic immersed tube, the segmented tube demonstrates stronger capacity to adapt to the deformation of the tunnel foundation, that is, its good flexibility replaces its rigidity.

By structural features, the immersed tubes can be divided into reinforced concrete structure, steel-shelled composite concrete structure and pre-stressed reinforcement concrete structure.

The reinforced concrete immersed tube is widely used today, and the relevant technology is mature. The monolithic immersed tube can be used for its good anti-seepage capacity; the segmented immersed tube can be used for its better flexibility to adapt to the deformation of the tunnel foundation.

The steel-shelled concrete immersed tube is further classified into the whole-steel-shelled composite structure and the single-sided steel-shelled concrete composite structure. The whole-steel-shelled composite concrete structure, also known as the "sandwich composite structure", has either single-ringed cross-section, twin-ringed cross-section or rectangular cross-section. The steel shell is attached to both the inner and the outer surfaces of the concrete tube so as to exert its structural efficiency better for the best economic effect when the designing of the cross section is involved. For the single-sided steel-shelled composite concrete structure, the steel shell is attached only to the external surface of the concrete tube while the main structure still uses reinforced concrete structure, so as to exert the best waterproof function of the tube.

The steel-shelled concrete immersed tube has a long history. Its greatest advantage is that it can be industrially manufactured, and the requirements for the dry dock and the temporary works are relatively low. This kind of tube has very good anti-seepage capacity and good capability to withstand seismic vibrations. Since it is fit for industrial manufacture, the product quality can be better controlled, but its cost is also high.

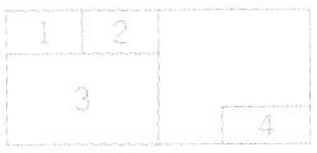

1. 钢壳混凝土组合结构沉管
Steel-Shelled Composite Concrete Immersed Tube
2. 钢筋混凝土结构沉管
Steel Reinforced Concrete Immersed Tube
3. 希腊普里维沙—阿克森沉管隧道干坞
Dry Dock of the Aktio–Preveza Undersea Tunnel, Greece
4. 钢筋混凝土结构沉管结构示意图
Structural Diagram of the Steel Reinforced Concrete Immersed Tube

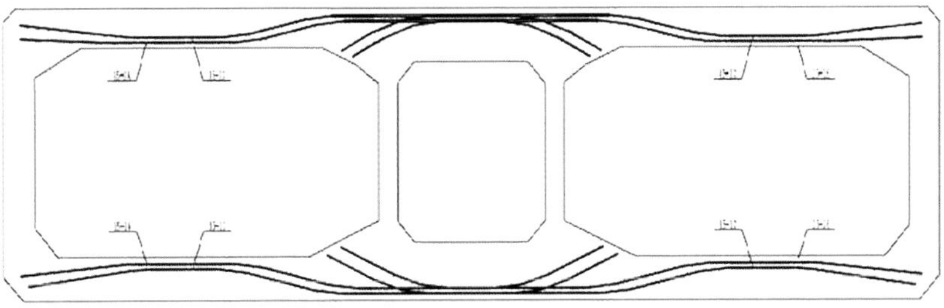

沉管预制方法

METHODS OF IMMERSED TUBE PRECAST

沉管预制方法总体可分为“工厂法”和“干坞法”两大类。

根据构造型式，干坞分为移动干坞和固定干坞两类。固定干坞又分为轴线干坞和另选址干坞。另选址干坞方案即在隧道轴线以外选择合适的位置建造干坞。该方案可实现岸上段结构、沉管制作和基槽开挖等关键性工序并行进行，最大限度节省工期。

“工厂法”属于另选址干坞方案中的一种沉管制造方法，即在工厂内采用流水线方式完成沉管预制，再浮运至现场安装。该法适用于钢筋混凝土节段式沉管及钢壳混凝土沉管的生产，可以在稳定环境下全天候作业，具有高效、标准化及流水线生产的特点。

采用“工厂法”生产钢筋混凝土沉管，先在室内进行钢筋流水线加工、绑扎，混凝土全断面浇筑，待浇段与前一已预制的节段匹配、浇筑，连续顶推，完成沉管主体结构生产。

厂区内设置浅坞和深坞两级坞系统，将预制沉管沿轨道顶推到浅坞（池底高于海平面），采用临时水平预应力将若干节段连接成沉管整体；注水将沉管起浮横移至深坞（池底与海平面的距离应大于沉管高度），等待出坞浮运至隧址沉放，实现沉管预制、沉管舾装和沉管浮运的流程化作业。

The methods of immersed tube fabrication are mainly divided into two types: “factory manufacturing” and the “dry dock manufacturing”.

By structure, dry docks are divided into two categories: moveable dry docks and fixed dry docks. Fixed dry docks are further divided into axial dry docks (built on the axis of the tunnel) and non-axial dry docks (built at any appropriate places rather than on the axis of the tunnel). The dry docks allow the simultaneous operation of such key projects as construction of the on-shore section, prefabrication of the immersed tubes and foundation trench excavation, which can save time of construction to the maximum.

The “factory manufacturing” is a kind of tube prefabrication method that belongs to the non-axial dry dock method. Namely, the tunnel element is prefabricated in the assembly line of the factory before the completed tube is transported to the construction site for installation. This method is suitable for the fabrication of the reinforced concrete segmental immersed tubes and the steel shelled concrete immersed tubes. The method ensures steady operation in the stable environment in any weather conditions and features highly-efficient, standardized, assembly-line production.

To produce steel reinforced concrete tubes by “factory manufacturing”, the steel bars need first to be processed and bound indoors in an assembly line, cross sectional concrete placement follows while the segment of the tube newly cast needs to match well with the precast segment, then continuous thrust is conducted, and by now the body part of the immersed tube is completed.

The factory is equipped with a shallow dock system and a deep dock system. The immersed tube usually goes through the following stages like precast, outfitting and transportation by float conveyance. First, the precast immersed tube segments are pushed along the sliding track to the shallow dock (whose bottom is above the sea level). Second, several segments are connected into a complete immersed tube by the temporary horizontal pre-stressing force. Third, water is pumped into the dock to float up the tube and the tube is moved horizontally to the deep dock (where the distance between the bottom of the dock and the sea level should be bigger than the height of the tube). Finally, the tube is moved out of the dock and is transported by float conveyance to the construction site to be landed underwater.

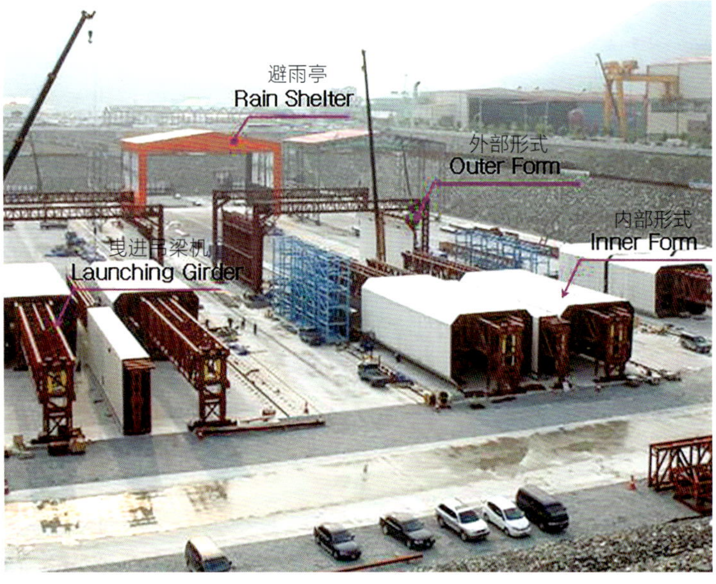

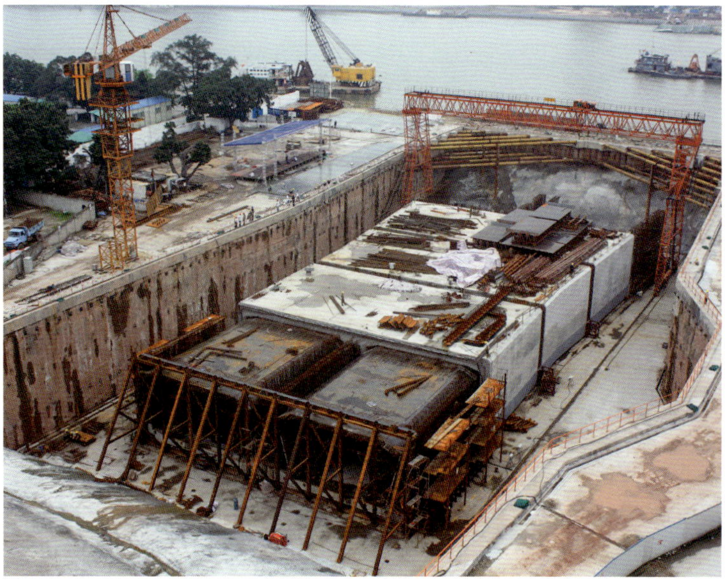

1. 韩国釜山隧道沉管预制厂
Immersed Tube Precast Factory for Busan-Geoje Tunnel

2. 中国广州沙洲咀跨江隧道预制
Precast Cross-River Tunnel at Sha Chau Tsui, Guangzhou, China

3. 荷兰厄勒海峡沉管隧道预制厂
Precast Factory for the Oresund Strait Tunnel, the Netherlands

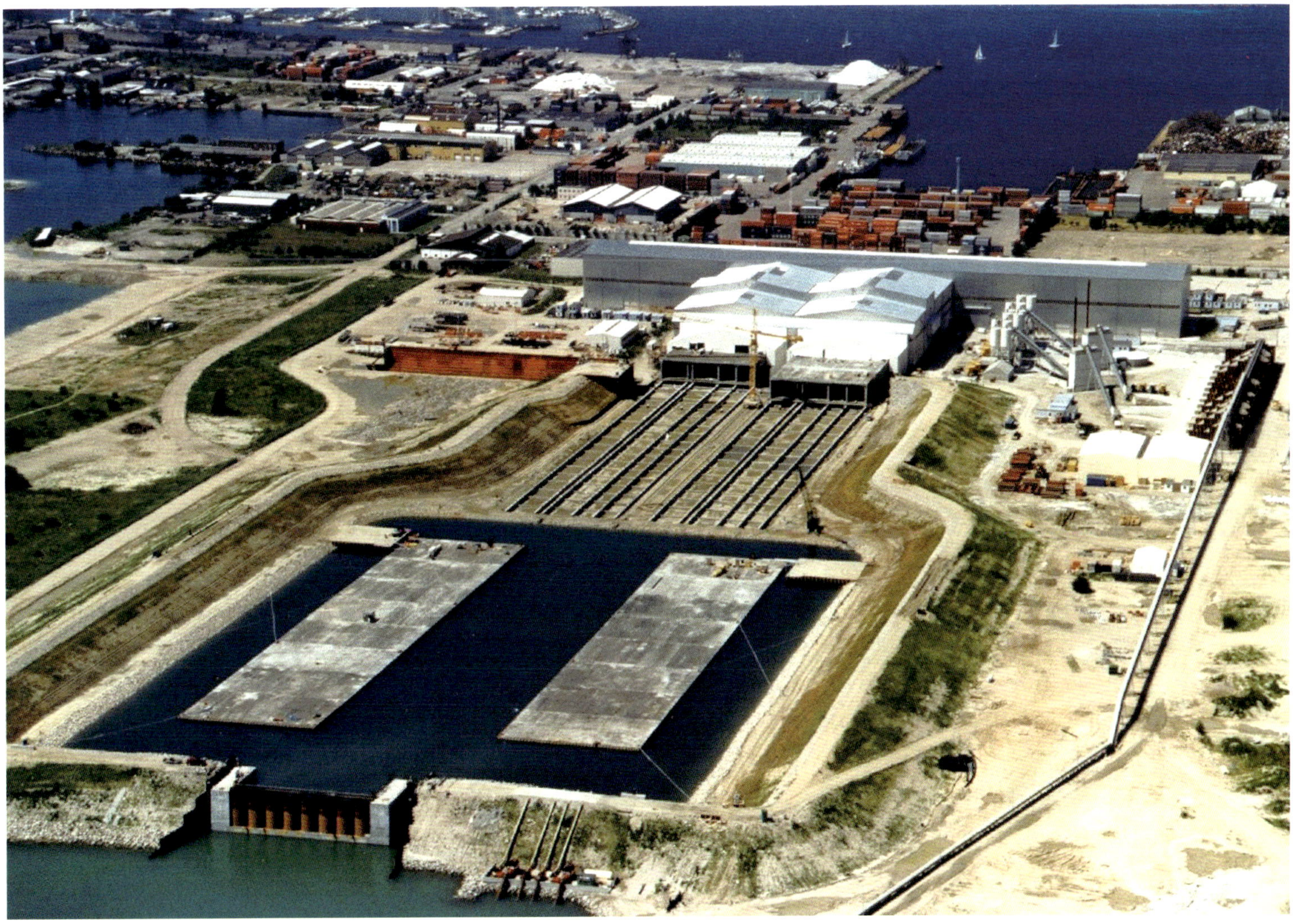

港珠澳大桥沉管概述

PROFILE OF THE IMMERSED TUBE OF HONG KONG-ZHUHAI-MACAU BRIDGE

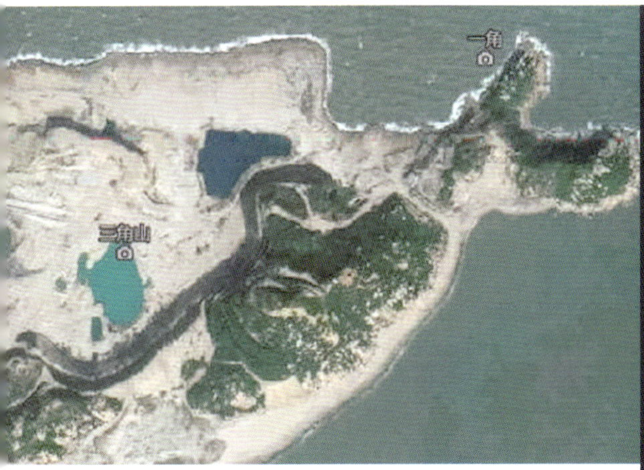
一角
三角山

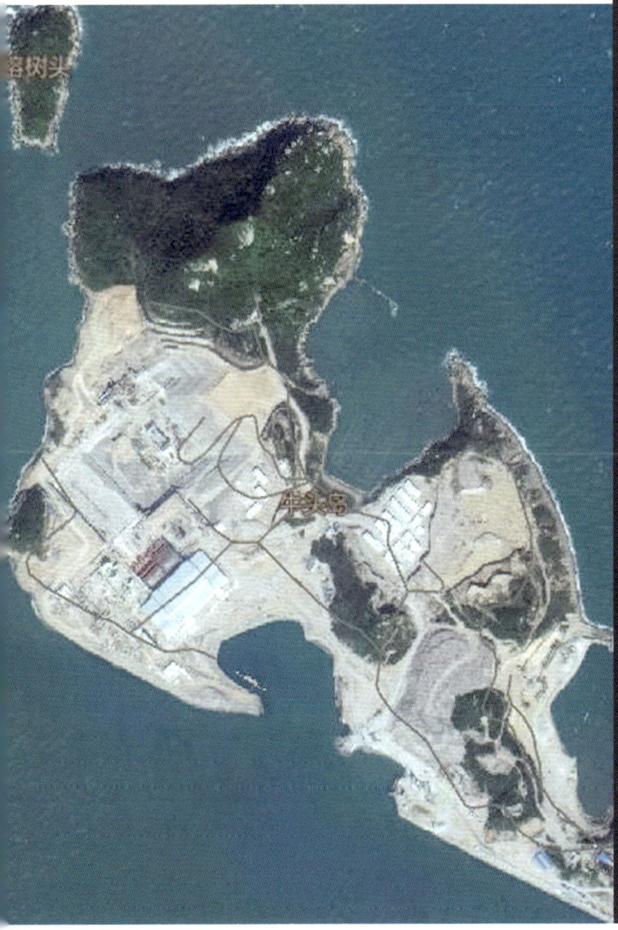

港珠澳大桥沉管预制综述

INTRODUCTION TO THE PRECAST OF THE IMMERSED TUBE FOR HONG KONG-ZHUHAI-MACAU BRIDGE

沉管预制是岛隧工程的关键线路之一。

港珠澳大桥隧道沉管段总长5664米，由33节沉管组成。每节标准沉管高11.4米，宽37.95米，长180米，重约76,000吨。全部沉管采用“工厂法”预制。这是中国首次采用工厂流水线预制工艺生产大型沉管，沉管预制数量、工厂规模、沉管尺寸均为世界之最。

港珠澳大桥沉管预制厂位于珠海万山海洋开发试验区牛头岛。

沉管预制厂分为钢结构厂房、浅坞区、深坞区、件杂货码头、粉料码头、砂石料码头、混凝土搅拌站、试验室、发电机房及办公生活区。厂内设置两条预制生产线，在流水线上标准化预制，约每75天生产两节标准沉管。

沉管设计使用寿命120年，对沉管保护层质量控制、节段水密性提出了严峻的挑战。

The precast of the immersed tube is one of the critical steps of the islands-tunnel project.

The immersed tube tunnel of Hong Kong-Zhuhai-Macau Bridge is 5664 meters long in total and consists of 33 immersed tubes. Each standard immersed tube is 11.4 meters high, 37.95 meters wide, 180 meters long and weighs about 76,000 tons. All the immersed tubes are prefabricated by “factory manufacturing”. This is the first time that China adopts the assembly line in the factory to produce the large-sized immersed tubes by precast technique. The project ranks first in the world in terms of the number of the immersed tubes manufactured, the scale of the factory and the size of the immersed tubes.

The factory that produces the immersed tubes used in the Hong Kong-Zhuhai-Macau Bridge project is located on Niutou Island, Wanshan Marine Experimental Development District of Zhuhai.

The immersed tube precast factory consists of the steel structure workshop, the shallow dock, the deep dock, the general cargo wharf, the powder wharf, the sand and stone wharf, the concrete mixing plants, the laboratory, the power generator station and the office and living area. Two precast assembly lines were set up in the factory for the standardized tube prefabrication; two standard immersed tubes were produced every 75 days.

The designed life span of the immersed tube is 120 years, which posed severe challenges to the quality control of the protective layer of the tube and to the water-proof quality of the segments.

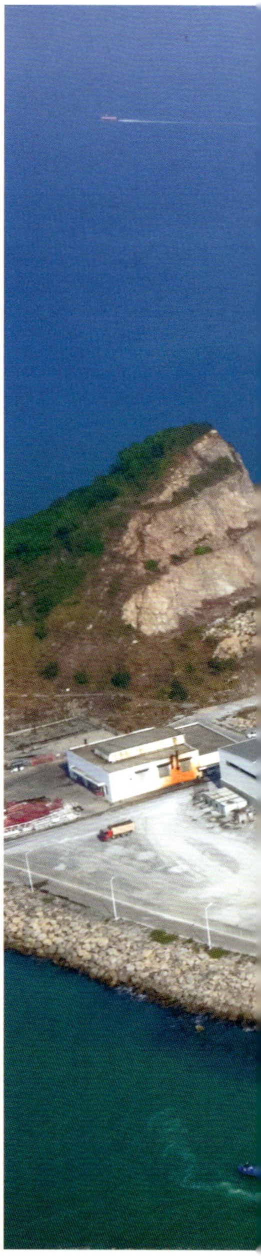

港珠澳大桥沉管预制厂厂区及坞区
Immersed Tube Precast Factory and Docks for Hong Kong-Zhuhai-Macau Bridge

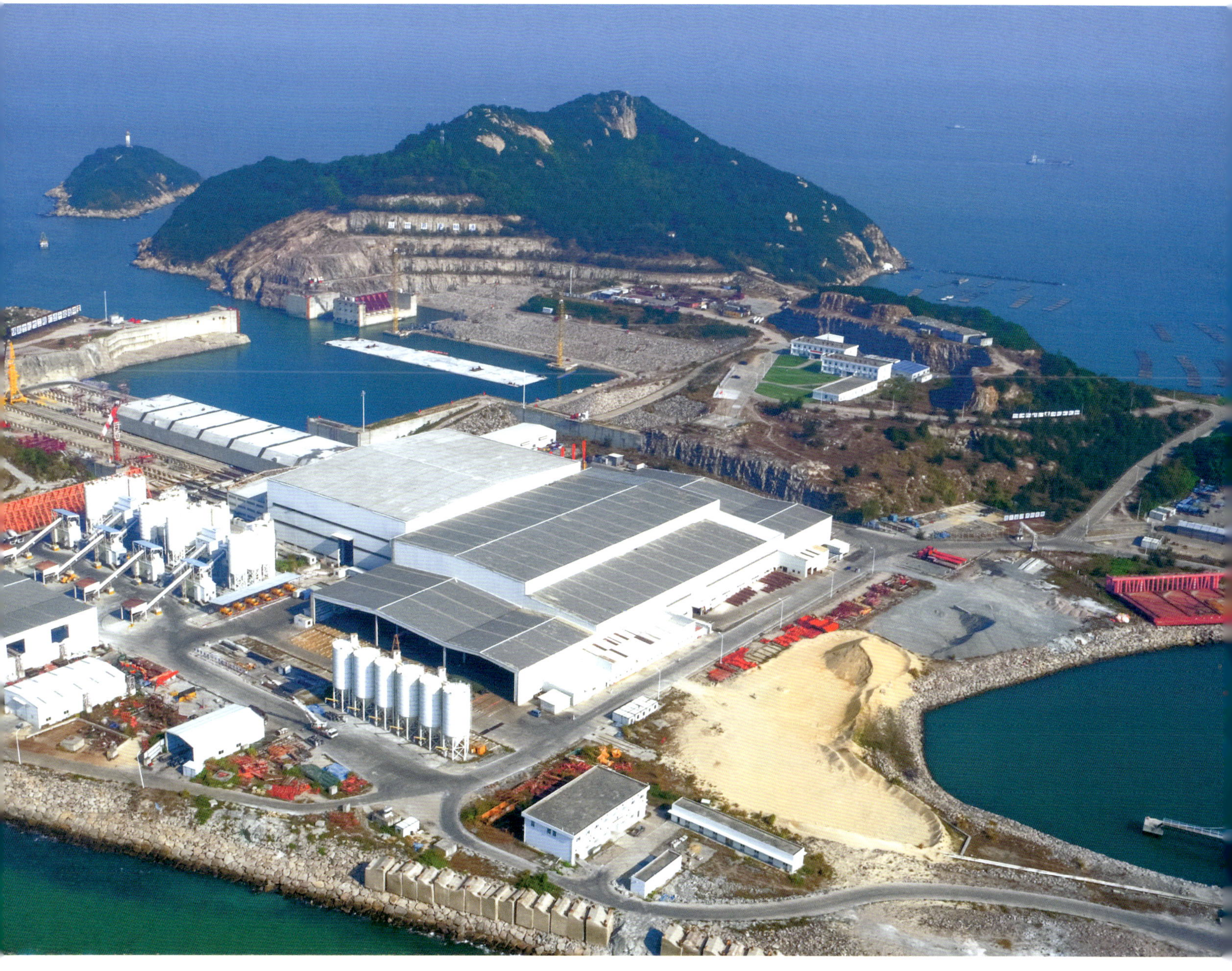

“工厂法”沉管预制厂选址

SITE SELECTION FOR THE IMMERSED TUBE PRECAST FACTORY

“工厂法”沉管预制选址须满足以下几项原则：离沉管隧道安放现场距离近；地质条件好，拥有适应开挖和沉管预制的良好地基条件；水深条件好，有良好的出坞航道和浮运航道，航道距离短；交通运输和材料来源、供水、供电可保证；陆域场地面积大，费用低，用地性质和使用功能合适、明确；有适合沉管寄放的水域；预制工厂征地拆迁建设工期短，满足隧道建设总体进度需要。

港珠澳大桥位于珠江口外，综合考虑沉管浮运风险最小等因素，预制厂选址主要在珠江口附近进行。

经对珠江口附近多个建设用地考察比对，结合场地与隧址关系，以及建设条件相关因素，初步选择万山群岛、中山横门、南沙港区及深圳大铲湾附近地块作为预制备选场地。

通过设计比选，南沙及牛头岛预制厂方案可达到最佳的工期及品质效果，满足港珠澳大桥总体施工要求。根据牛头岛天然岩基好、浮运距离短等因素及当地政府部门的良好合作意向，最终选择了在牛头岛建设沉管预制厂方案。

牛头岛距工程现场约 12 公里，地处香港、深圳、澳门和珠海陆地之间，西距澳门、香洲 17 海里，北距香港大屿山 3 海里。

The site selection for the "factory manufacturing" of the immersed tube precast factory should meet the following requirements: First, the factory should be close to the construction site where the tubes are supposed to be installed. Second, the factory should have good geological conditions for the excavation of the solid foundation and the immersed tube prefabrication. Third, the water depth is proper for the construction of undocking channels and float conveyance channels, and the channel should be short enough. Fourth, there should be convenient transportation, enough materials, good water supply and power supply. Fifth, the land area is large enough with low costs, and the land usage and the land function are properly and clearly defined. Sixth, there are water areas suitable for depositing the tunnel tubes. Seventh, the time for land expropriation and factory construction is short enough to match the overall progress of the tunnel construction.

Hong Kong-Zhuhai-Macau Bridge is located outside the Pearl River Estuary. With such factors as the minimum risks of float conveyance of the tunnel tubes taken into consideration, the immersed tube precast factory is decided to be built near the Pearl River Estuary.

Based on the investigation into and comparison between several construction sites near the Pearl River Estuary, by taking into consideration the relationship between the factory site and the tunnel site as well as the factors relevant to the tunnel construction, the areas around Wanshan Islands, Hengmen of Zhongshan, Nansha Port and Dachan Bay of Shenzhen were among the possible choices for the site of the precast factory.

After initial design and comparison, Nansha and Niutou Island can match the progress of the whole project and meet the requirements for project quality as well as the general requirements for the construction of Hong Kong-Zhuhai-Macau Bridge. Because of the solid natural batholite on Niutou Island and because it can guarantee short-distanced float conveyance, and also because of the local government's cooperation intention, Niutou Island was finaly chosen as the site of the immersed tube precast factory.

Niutou Island is about 12 kilometers away from the project site and is located between Hong Kong, Shenzhen, Macau and Zhuhai. Macau and Xiangzhou are 17 nautical miles away to the west of Niutou Island, and Lantau Island of Hong Kong is 3 nautical miles away to the north.

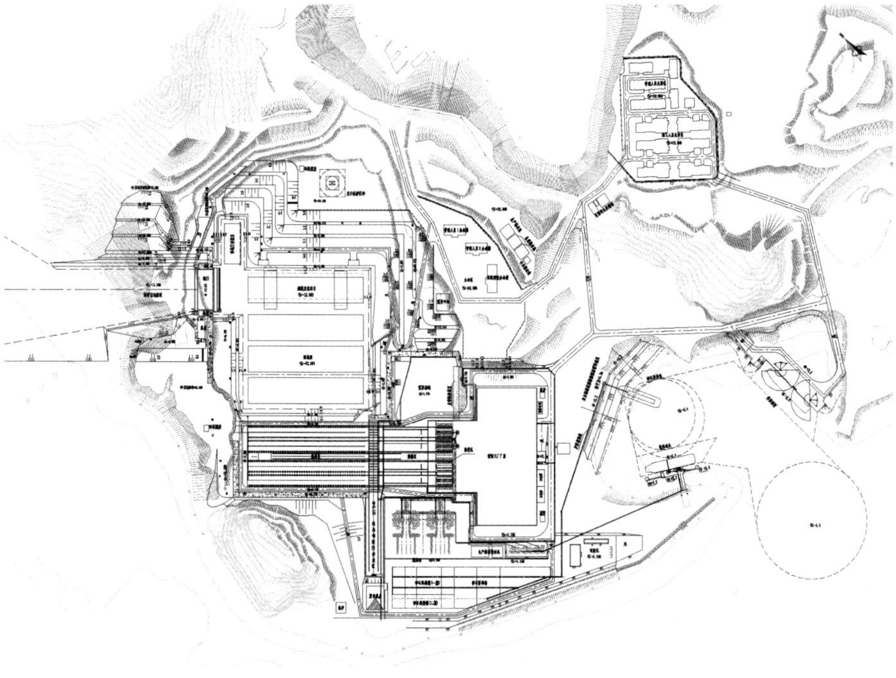

1. 牛头岛沉管预制厂布置图
   Layout of the Immersed Tube Precast Factory at Niutou Island
2. 牛头岛沉管预制厂位置图
   Site of the Immersed Tube Precast Factory at Niutou Island

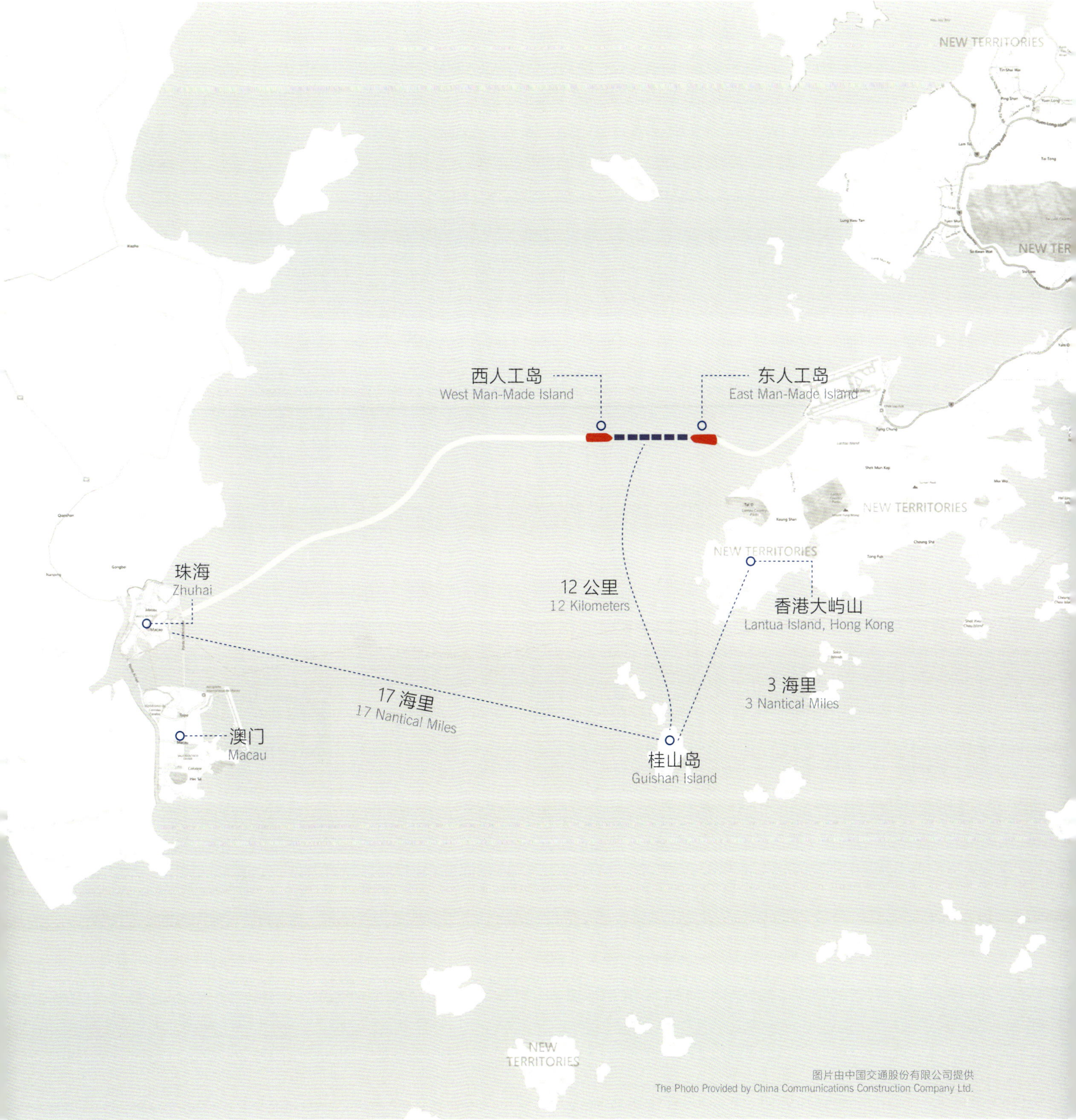

图片由中国交通股份有限公司提供
The Photo Provided by China Communications Construction Company Ltd.

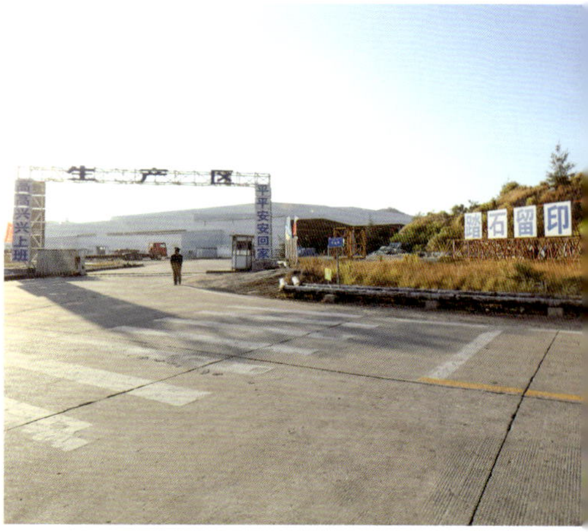

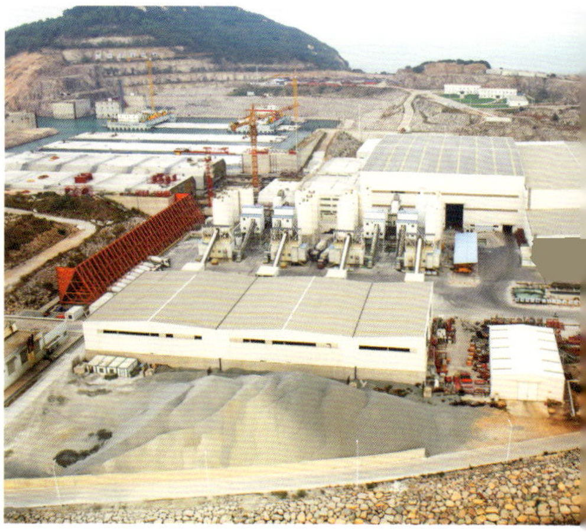

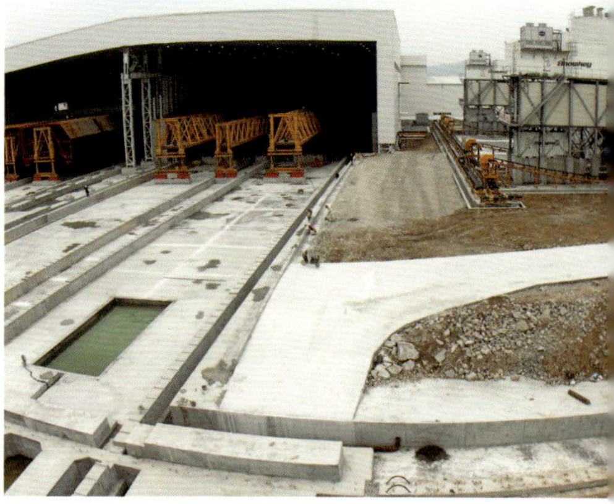

预制厂建设

CONSTRUCTION OF THE IMMERSED TUBE PRECAST FACTORY

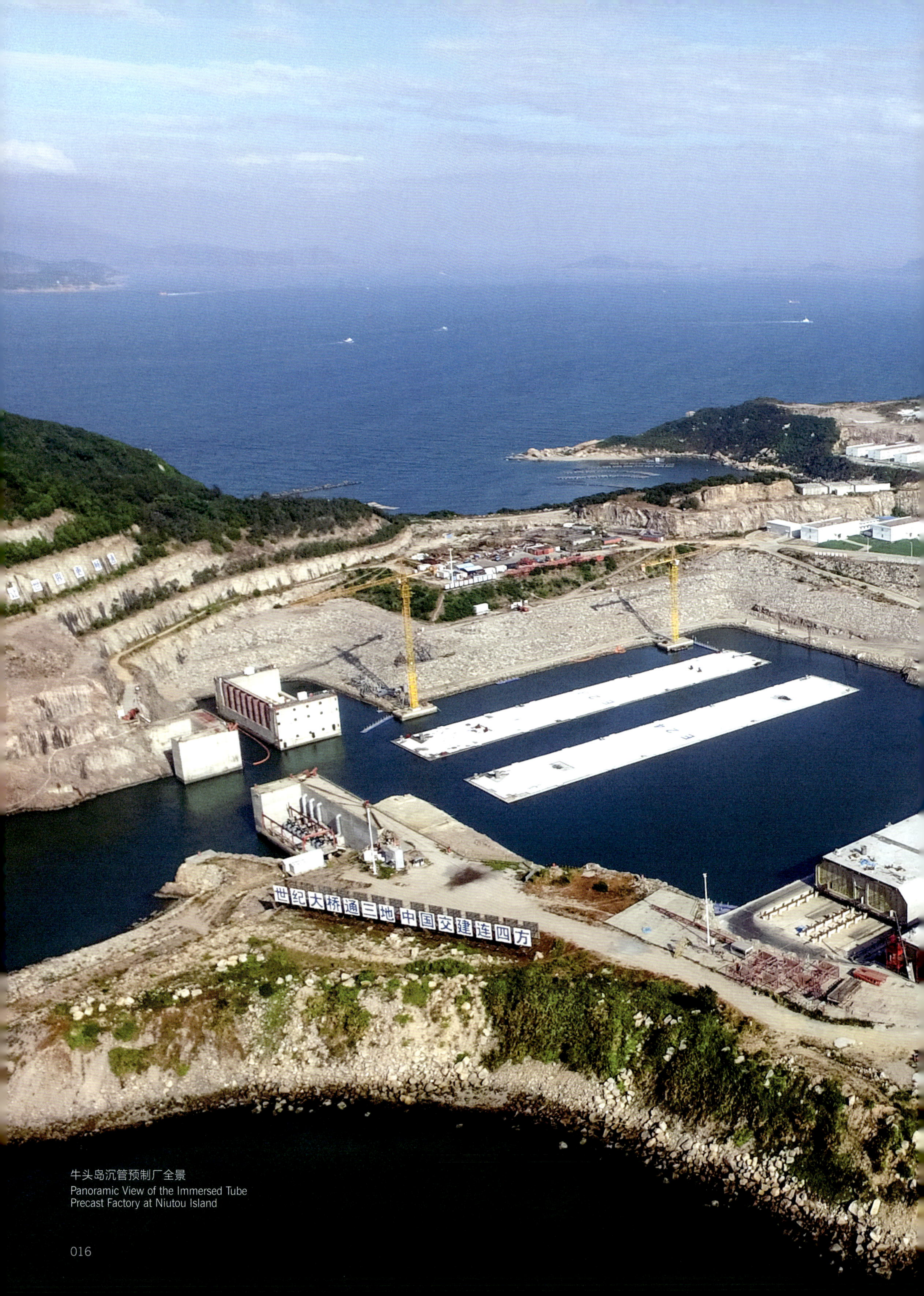

牛头岛沉管预制厂全景
Panoramic View of the Immersed Tube Precast Factory at Niutou Island

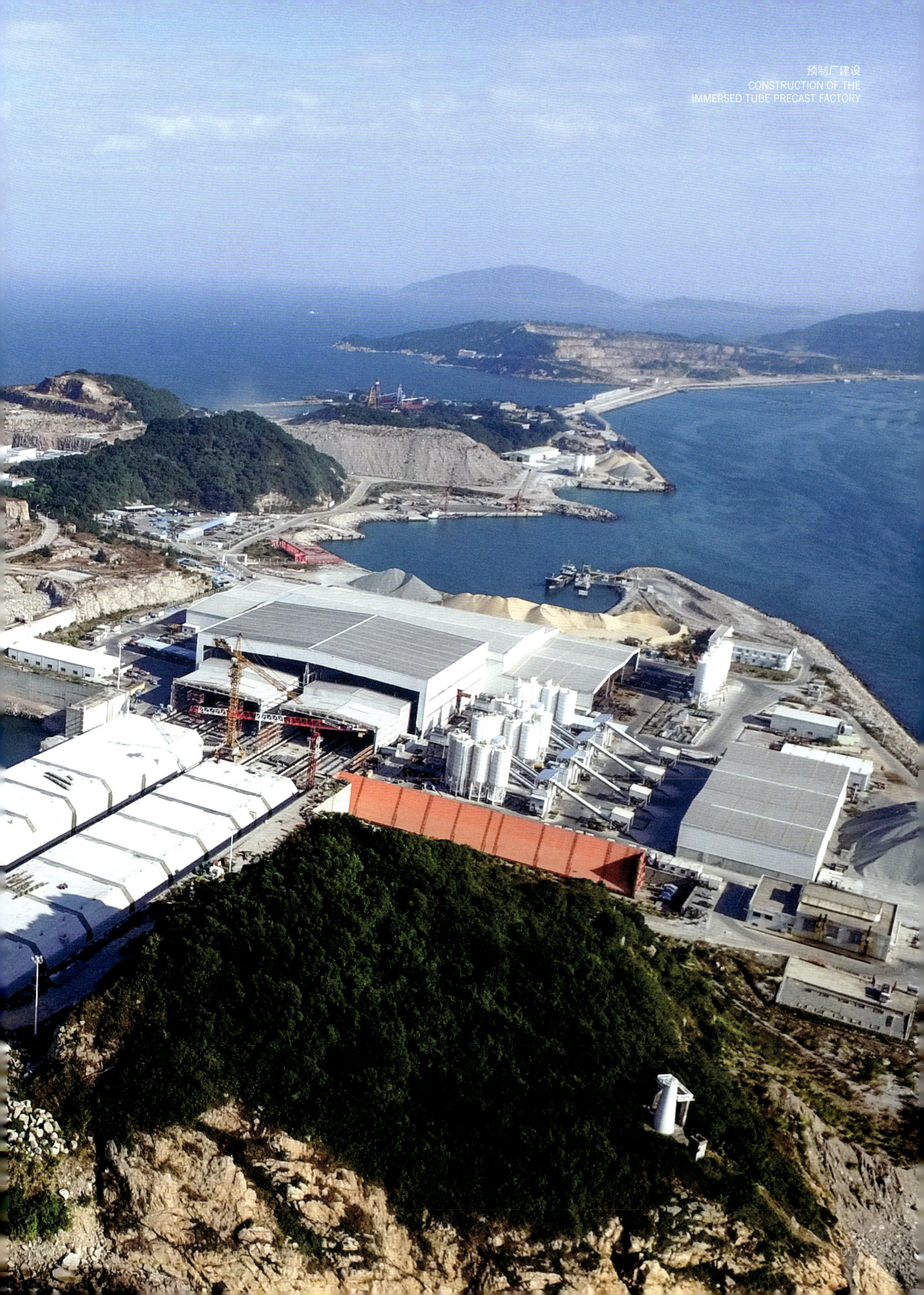

预制厂建设
CONSTRUCTION OF THE
IMMERSED TUBE PRECAST FACTORY

总平面布置原则

PRINCIPLES FOR THE GENERAL LAYOUT OF THE FACTORY

与传统的"干坞法"相比较，"工厂法"预制沉管不仅具有占地少、施工周期短、质量可靠性高、全天候施工等优点，而且能够大大降低工程成本，具有很高的环保优势。

根据牛头岛地形特点，项目总经理、总工程师林鸣提出，将深浅坞并列布置，用"L"型替代传统的"一"字型厂区布局，把纵向推动改为横向拉移，实现浅坞区和深坞区之间的沉管移动。

"L"型布局不仅解决了场地纵深不够的问题，而且巧妙利用原有的采石坑改为深坞，大大降低了开挖工程量。沉管寄放、舾装均在坞内，避免了风浪、台风等极端天气的影响，保证沉管的全天候安全。

牛头岛沉管预制厂占地约56万平方米。厂内设置沉管预制厂房、浅坞区、深坞区和配套的生产生活设施；厂房、浅坞和深坞"L"型布置，预制厂房至浅坞为直线分布，浅坞与深坞并排。

工厂西南侧为混凝土搅拌站、砂石料堆场及砂石料码头；场地北侧分开布置有生活区与办公区；工地实验室设置在搅拌站附近。

Compared with the traditional "dry dock manufacturing", the "factory manufacturing" of immersed tubes features the smaller space, short construction period, high quality and good conditions for around-the-clock construction, which can reduce considerably the project costs and is considerably environment-friendly.

Based on the topography of Niutou Island, Lin Ming, the general manager and chief engineer of the project, proposed to arrange the deep and shallow docks side by side, replacing the traditional straight line-shaped factory layout with the L-shaped layout and changing the longitudinal pushing to the horizontal pulling to move the immersed tubes between the shallow dock and the deep dock.

The L-shaped layout solves not only the problem of insufficient longitudinal depth of the working area, but also cleverly transforms the original stone pit into the deep dock which greatly reduces the excavation workload. The tubes are stored and outfitted inside the dock, which helps avoid the unfavorable influences of the extreme weather like strong waves or typhoons, and guarantees the around-the-clock safety of the immersed tubes.

The Immersed Tube Precast Factory at Niutou Island covers an area of about 560,000 square meters. The factory consists of the immersed tube precast workshop, the shallow dock and the deep dock, equipped with supporting production and living facilities. The workshop, the shallow dock and the deep dock are arranged in an L-shaped layout; the precast workshop is on a line with the shallow dock, and the shallow dock stands side by side with the deep dock.

In the southwest part of the factory are the concrete mixing plant, the sand-gravel yard and the sand-gravel wharf. The living and office areas are in the north part of the factory, and the laboratory is located near the concrete mixing plant.

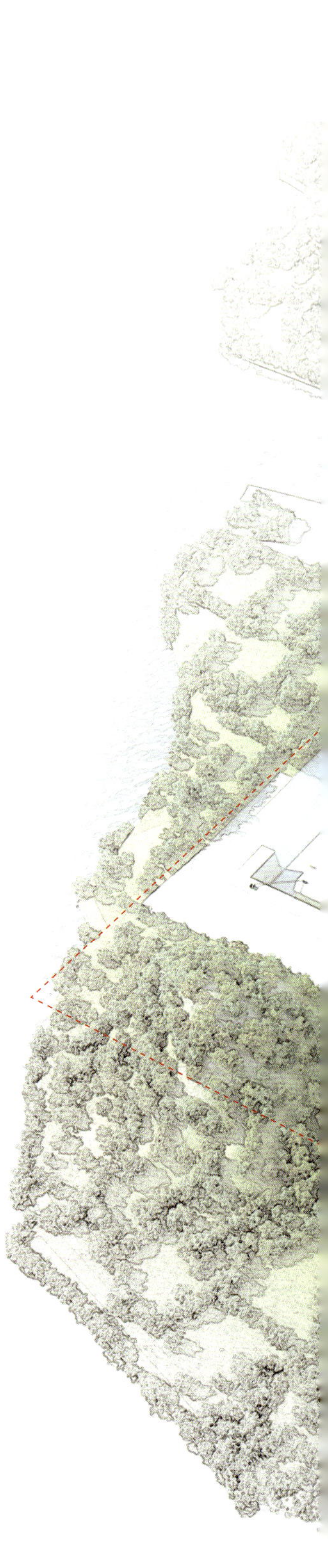

牛头岛沉管预制厂平面图
Plan View of the Immersed Tube Precast Factory at Niutou Island

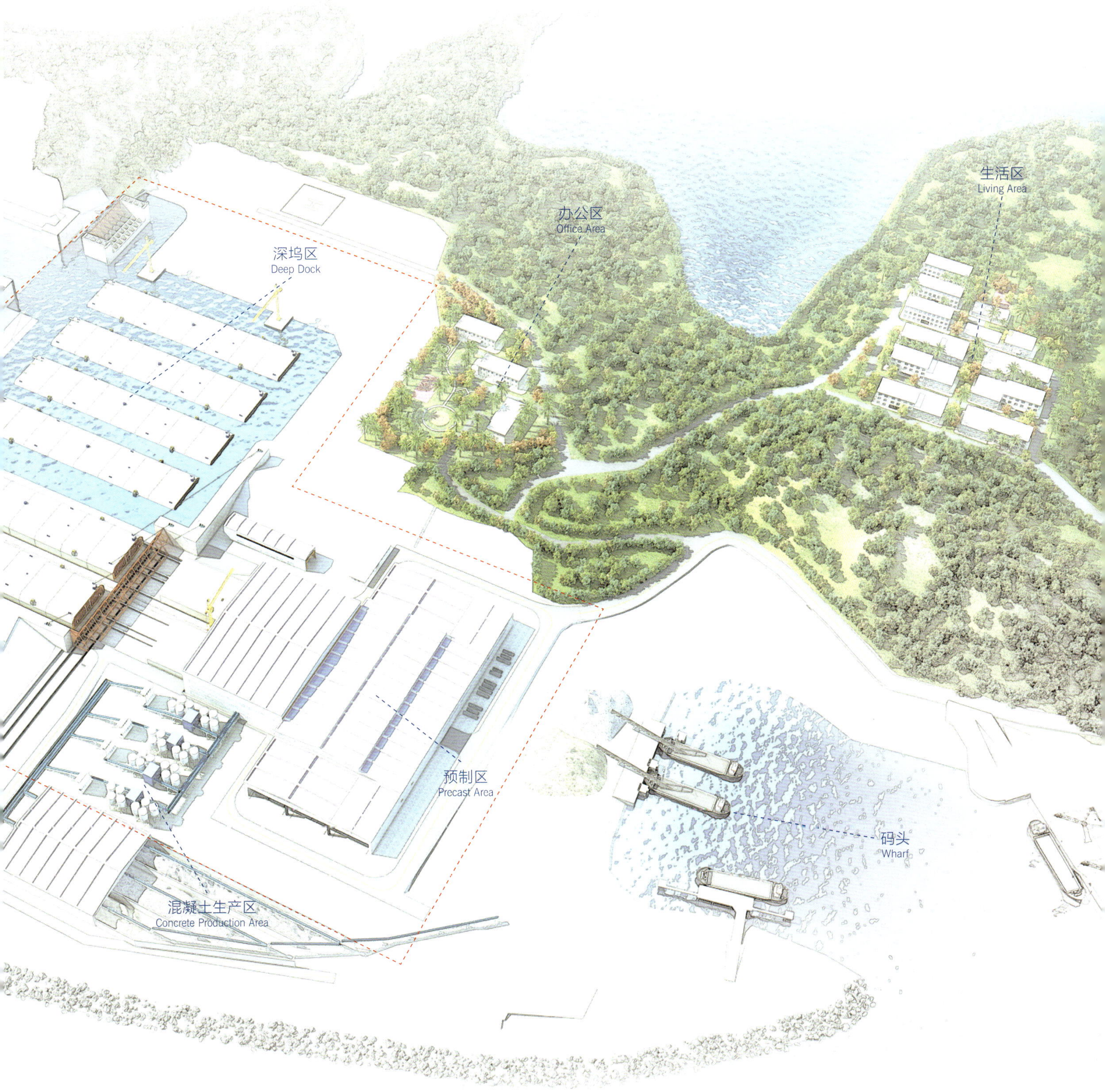
生活区
Living Area
办公区
Office Area
深坞区
Deep Dock
预制区
Precast Area
码头
Wharf
混凝土生产区
Concrete Production Area

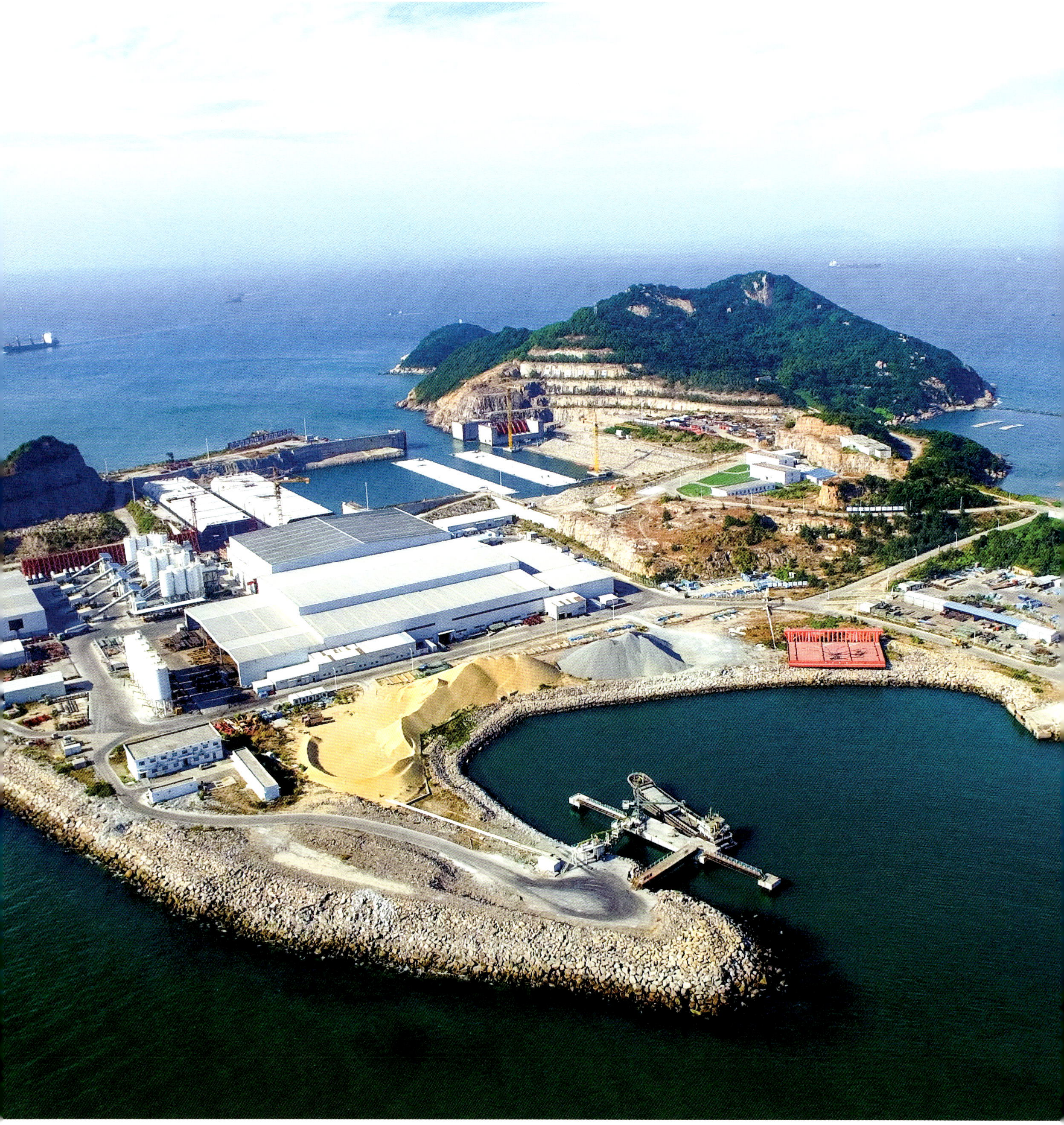

预制厂房和浅坞纵深约 500 米，设两条生产线，依次布置有底板、侧墙、顶板钢筋绑扎区、模板休整区和浇筑台座；钢筋绑扎区两翼均设有相应的钢筋存放加工车间。

浅坞区宽 104 米，净长度 196 米。浅坞周边建设坝体，蓄水后浅坞区水深满足沉管起浮要求。沉管浇筑台座至浅坞区设置 8 条通长无缝沉管滑移轨道，实现沉管从生产区到一次舾装区的移动。

办公及生活区为"砖混 + 框架"结构，按最高两层楼进行设计；食堂为单层建筑。

The longitudinal depths of the precast workshop and the shallow dock are all around 500 meters where two assembly lines are set up: the area for the bottom plate, side wall, top plate and steel binding, the area for formwork modification and the precast stand, and storing places for the steel formworks on the two sides of the steel binding area.

The shallow dock is 104 meters wide and 196 meters in net length. The shallow dock is surrounded by dams, and the impoundment meets the requirements for the floating of the immersed tubes. Eight seamless tracks leading from the tube casting stand to the shallow dock are constructed to move the tubes from the precast area to the initial outfitting area.

The buildings in the office and living areas are of brick-concrete formwork structures. These buildings are designed to be no more than two storeys, and there is only one storey in the dining hall.

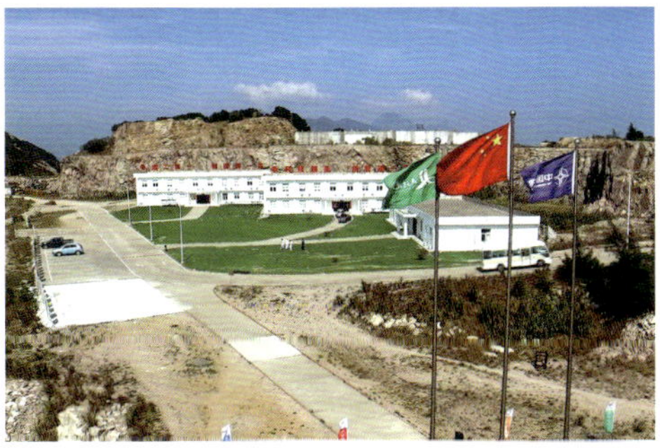

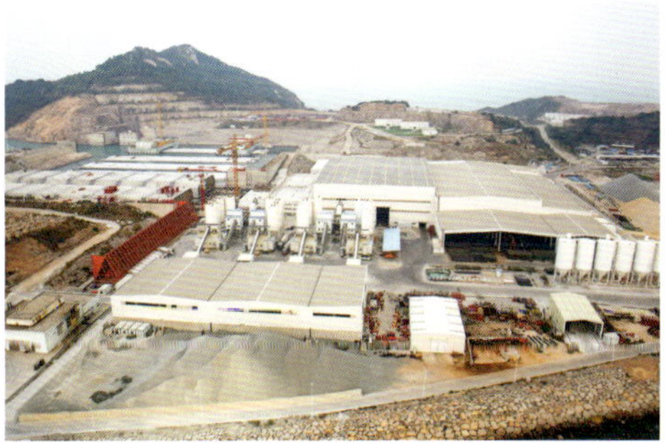

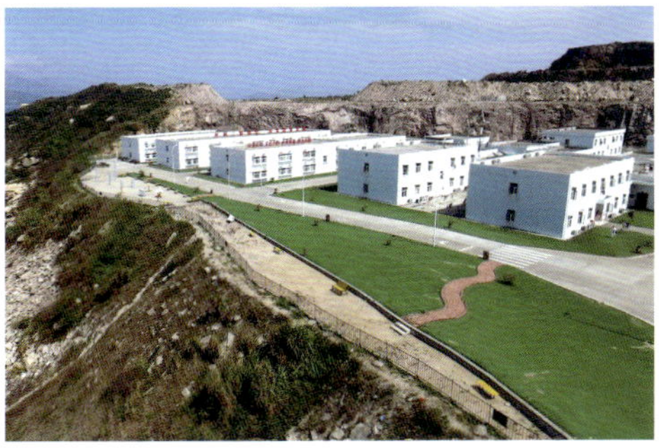

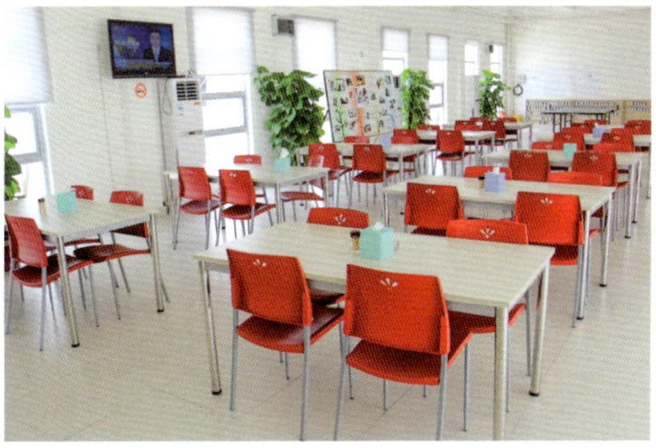

1. 牛头岛沉管预制厂
Immersed Tube Precast Factory at Niutou Island

2. 沉管预制厂办公区
Office Area of the Immersed Tube Precast Factory

3. 沉管预制厂厂区
Factory Area of the Immersed Tube Precast Factory

4. 沉管预制厂生活区
Living Area of the Immersed Tube Precast Factory

5. 沉管预制厂食堂
Dining Hall of the Immersed Tube Precast Factory

“工厂法”预制工艺规划

PRECAST PLANNING BY FACTORY-MANUFACTURING METHOD

沉管预制厂按照流水式生产进行工艺布置，所有生产均在厂房内完成。

标准沉管为180米，分为8个节段，每个节段长22.5米，节段在固定的台座上浇筑，养护达到顶推强度要求后，向前顶推22.5米，空出浇筑台座，下一节段与刚顶出的节段相邻匹配预制。

如此逐段预制逐段顶推，直至完成全部8个节段浇筑后，整体向前顶推至浅坞（顶推距离约132米）；临时预应力索张拉形成整体，完成一次舾装；然后关闭浅坞与预制工厂之间的滑动浅坞门，浅坞灌水，沉管起浮横移至深坞进行二次舾装，完成沉管浮运安装准备。

The layout of the immersed tube precast factory is designed for the assembly line production, and all the production activities are done inside the factory building.

The standard immersed tube is 180 meters long and is divided into eight 22.5-meter segments. Each segment is cast on the fixed casting stand. After maintenance, if it meets the required rigidity standard, it is pushed 22.5 meters forward, vacating the casting stand. The next segment should match completely the segment that is just pushed away.

In this way, all the segments are cast and pushed forward one by one until all the 8 segments are completed. Then as a whole the 8 segments together are pushed forward by about 132 meters to the shallow dock, where a temporary pre-stressed cable is used to weld them into one complete tube and then the initial outfitting is completed. Then

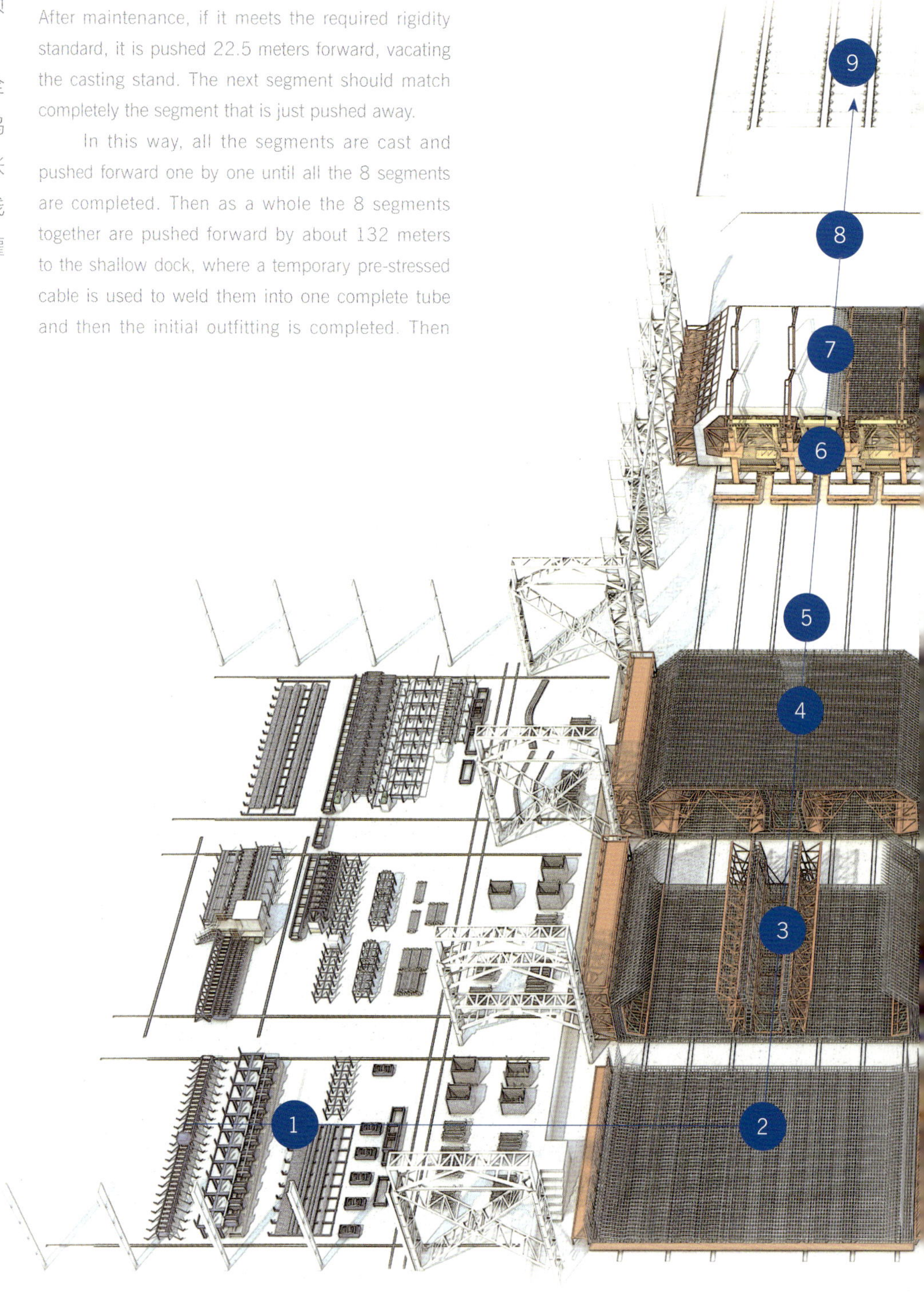

1. 钢筋加工
   Steel Bar Processing
2. 底板绑扎
   Bottom Plate Steel Binding
3. 侧墙、中隔墙绑扎
   Side Wall and Partition Wall Steel Binding
4. 顶板绑扎
   Top Plate Steel Binding
5. 钢筋笼顶推
   Pushing of Steel Reinforcement Cages
6. 液压模板安装
   Installation of the Hydraulic Formwork
7. 混凝土浇筑
   Concrete Placement
8. 沉管顶推
   Pushing of the Immersed Tubes
9. 长距离顶推至浅坞区
   Long Distance Pushing to the Shallow Dock

the sliding gate between the shallow dock and the precast factory is closed, and water is pumped into the shallow dock, so that the tube floats up and is moved horizontally to the deep dock for the secondary outfitting. By then the preparations for the float conveyance of the immersed tube are completed.

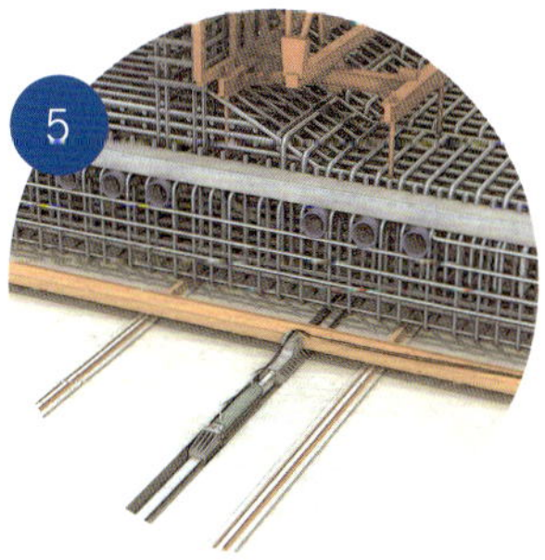

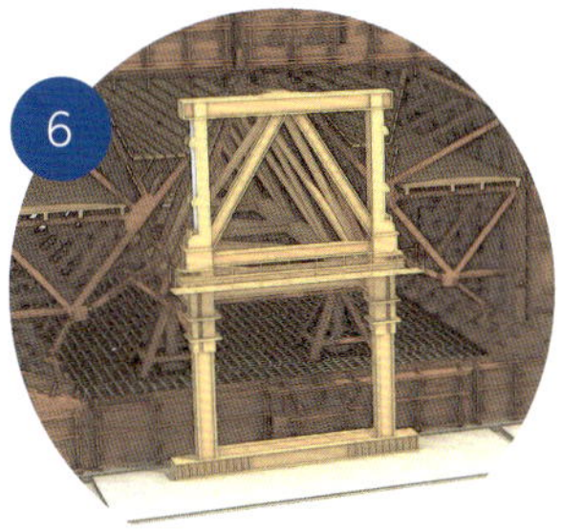

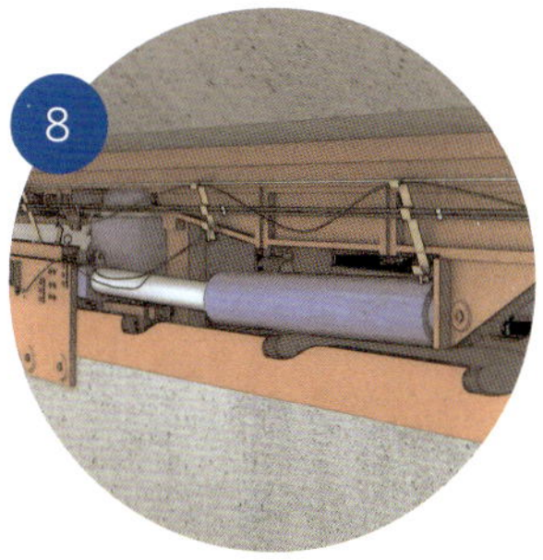

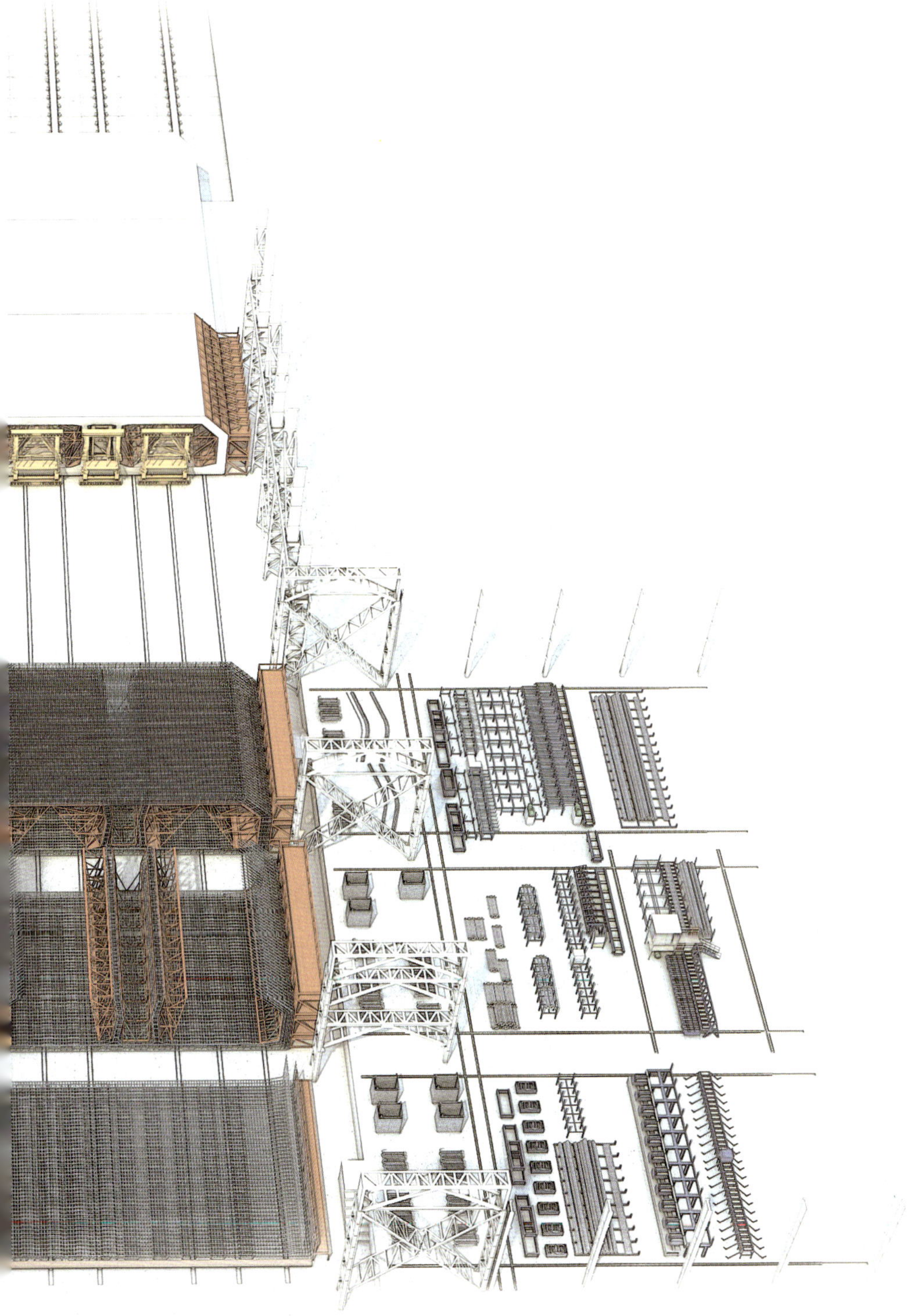

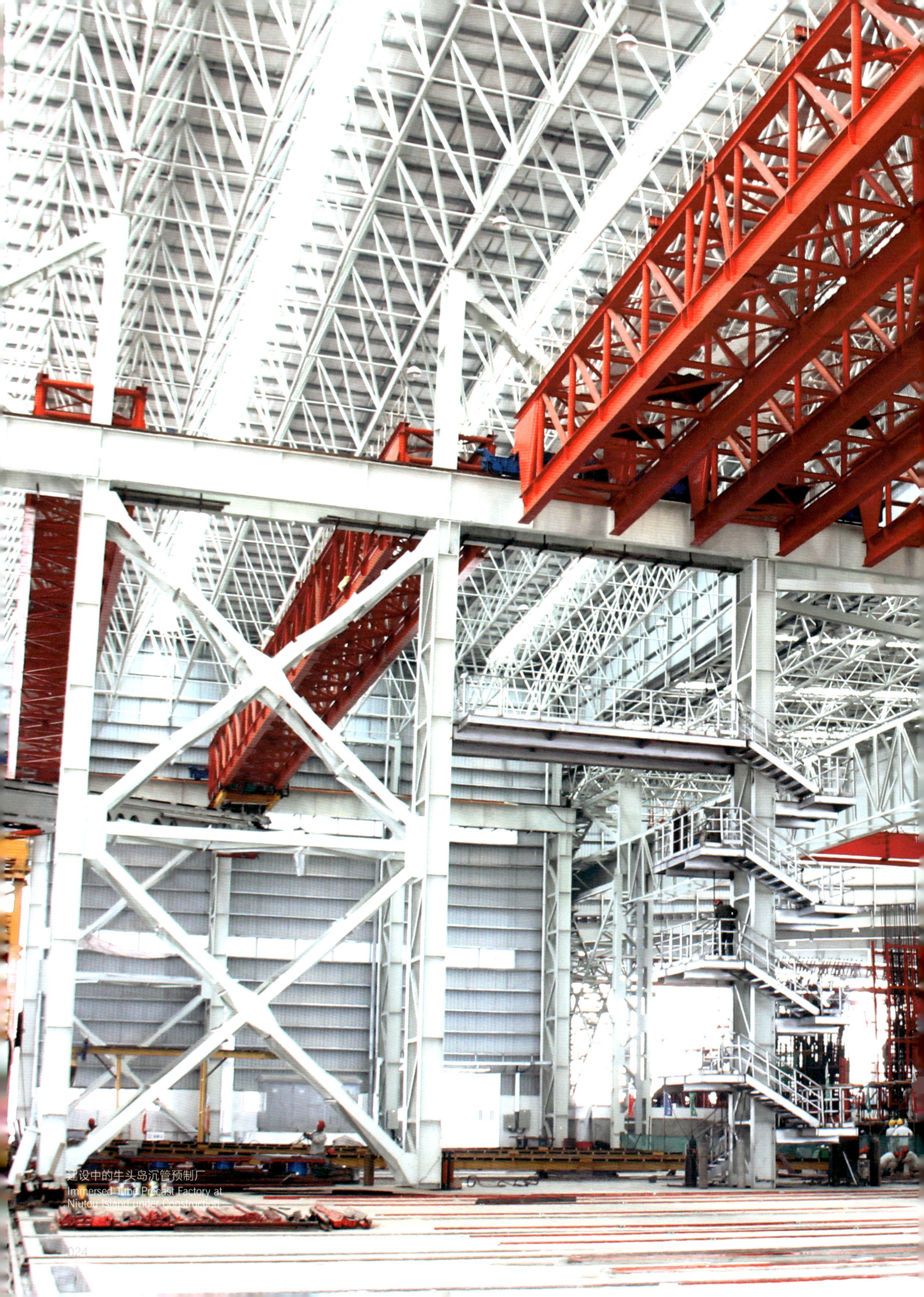

建设中的牛头岛沉管预制厂
Immersed Tube Precast Factory at Niutou Island under Construction

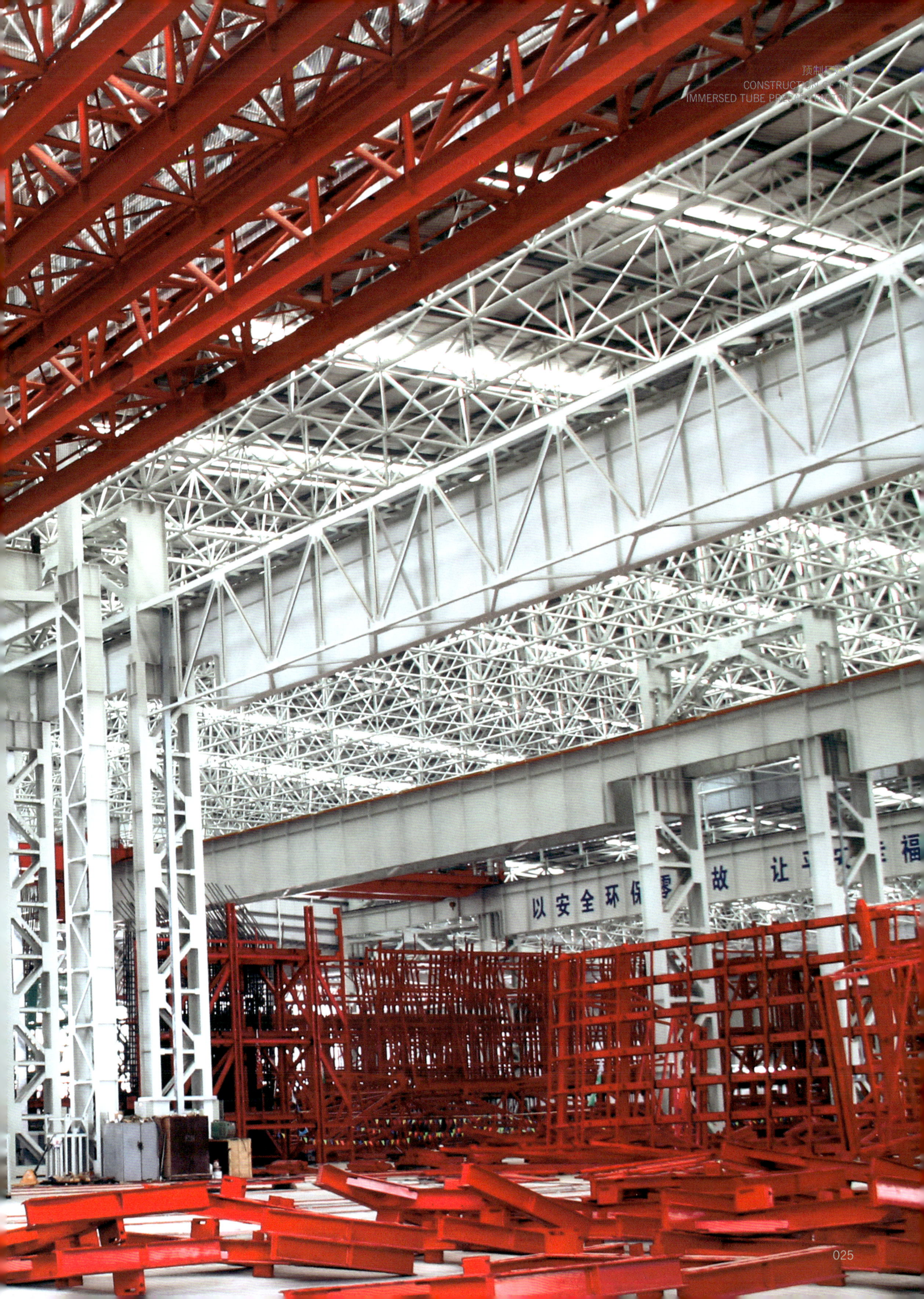
以安全环保
故 让
福

沉管预制厂建设

CONSTRUCTION OF THE IMMERSED TUBE PRECAST FACTORY

2010年底，中国交建建设团队在无水无电的牛头岛拉开了建设世界最大沉管预制厂的序幕，2012年2月建设完成。深坞、浅坞、预制生产区及坞口开挖总量达265.2万立方米，建设钢结构厂房20,000平方米，并完成件杂码头、骨料码头、粉料码头、搅拌站、实验室、办公区、生活区等配套设施建设及设备安装。

At the end of 2010, the constructors from China Communications Construction Company launched the construction project of the largest immersed tube precast factory in the world on Niutou Island where there were no electric power and water. The construction of the factory was completed in February 2012. The total excavation volume for the construction of the deep dock, the shallow dock, the precast area and the dock entrance amounted to 2,652,000 cubic meters. The steel structure workshops constructed covered 20,000 square meters. The construction and installation of the supporting facilities for general cargo wharf, formwork material wharf, powder wharf, concrete mixing plant, laboratory, office area and living quarters were all completed.

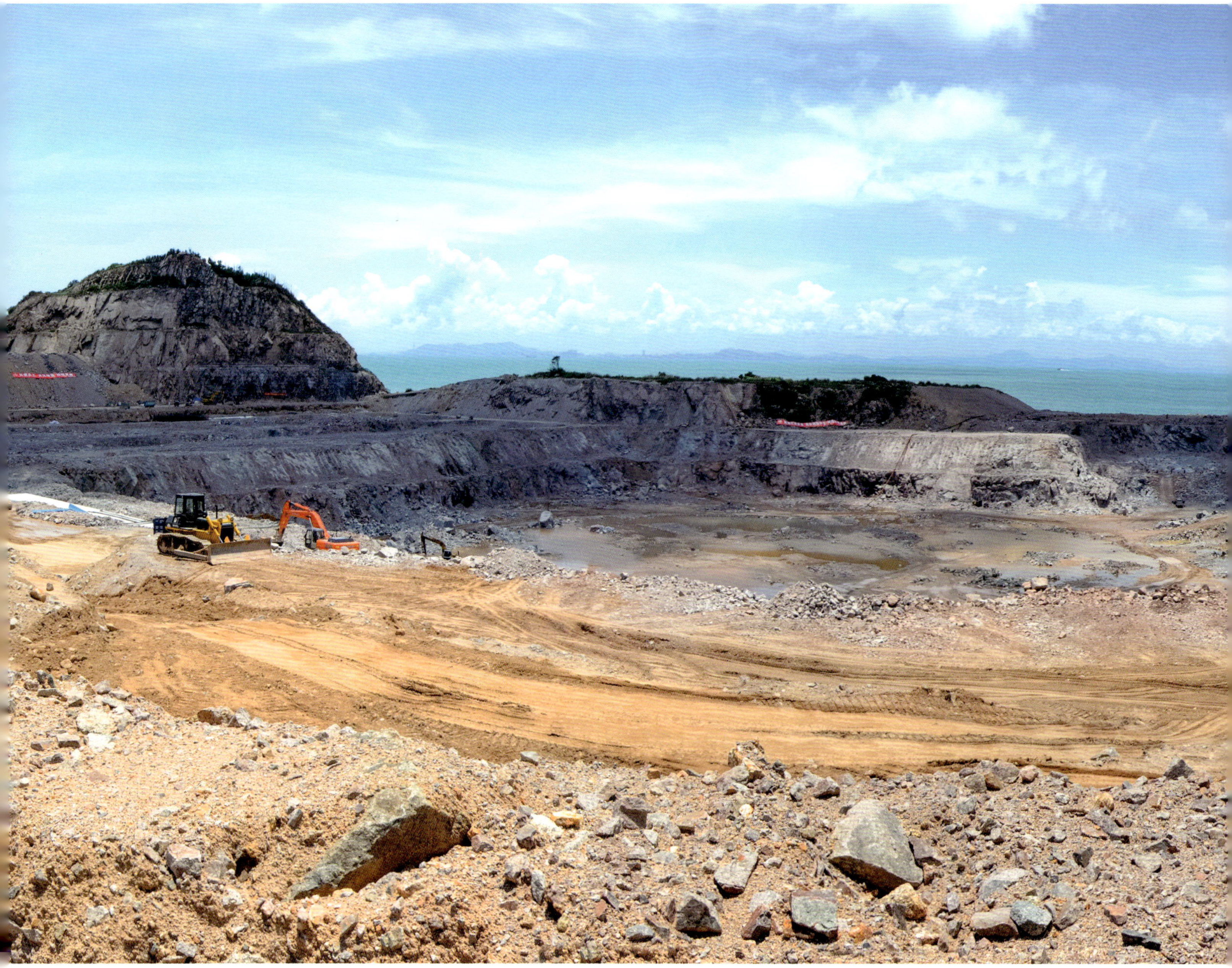

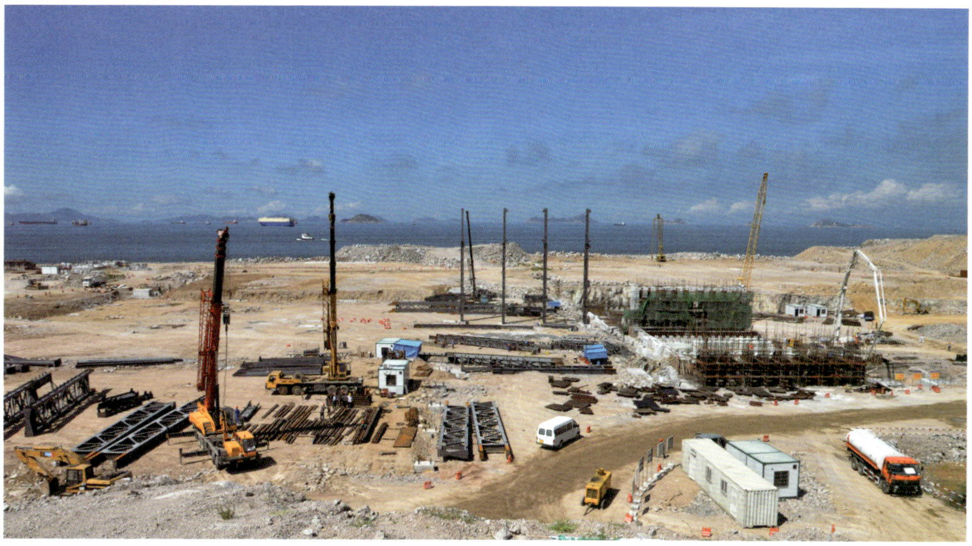

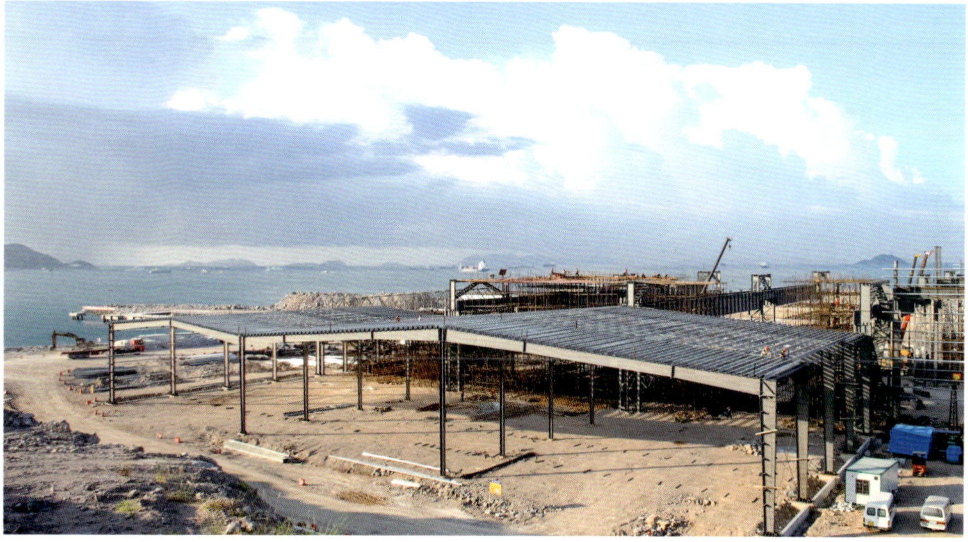

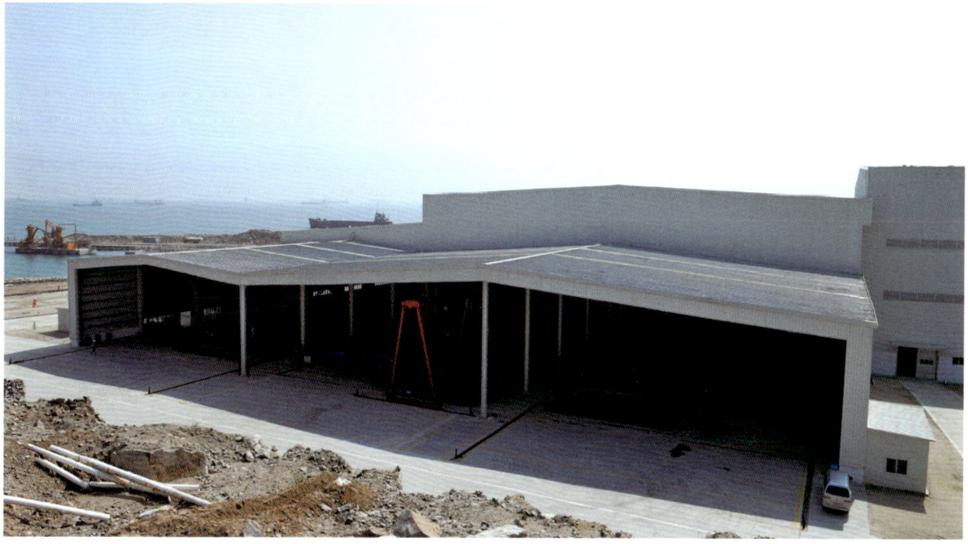

1. 牛头岛沉管预制厂初始风貌
Initial View of the Immersed Tube Precast Factory at Niutou Island

2—4. 牛头岛沉管预制厂厂房建设历程
Construction of the Workshops in the Immersed Tube Precast Factory at Niutou Island

反力墙、浇筑坑建设

CONSTRUCTION OF THE REACTION WALL AND THE CASTING PIT

反力墙位于模板系统侧模外侧，替代对拉螺杆为侧模稳定提供反力，消除采用对拉螺杆方案产生孔洞对沉管耐久性的影响。反力墙基础通过锚杆固定在岩基上。

浇筑坑为底模操作施工区，设计底标高为1.25米，设钢筋混凝土条形基础梁、顶推轨道梁及支墩等结构。

浇筑坑共设置256个钢筋混凝土支撑立柱，垂直于顶推滑移轨道方向共分为16排，每排16个。每排支撑立柱分为3组，由条形基础连为一体；条形基础断面宽0.6米，高0.6米，坐落于岩层上。在条形基础上设置支撑立柱，柱顶预埋螺栓，方便底模板支撑系统的安装和调平。

浇筑坑共设置18个针形梁支撑墩，沿顶推滑移轨道方向分为3列，每列6个。

The reaction wall is located on the outside of the side formwork of the formwork system, taking the place of the pulling screw to provide reaction force for the side formwork while avoiding the negative influence of the holes produced by the pulling screw solution on the durability of the immersed tube. The foundation of the reaction wall is fixed on the rock ground with anchor bolts.

The casting pit is an area for bottom formwork casting and the designed height for the bottom is 1.25 meters. It is equipped with a reinforced strip concrete foundation beam, a pushing track beam and a rest pier.

256 reinforced concrete support columns are set up in the casting pit, which are divided into 16 rows perpendicular to the pushing track with 16 columns in each row. The 16 columns in each row is divided further into 3 groups, which are connected into a whole by a strip foundation beam. The cross section of the strip foundation beam is 0.6 meters wide, 0.6 meters high, and is fixed on the rock stratum. Supporting columns with screw bolts embedded on the top are set on the strip foundation to facilitate the installation and leveling of the supporting system of the bottom formwork.

There are altogether 18 pointed-beam rest piers in the casting pit, which are divided into 3 columns alongside the pushing track, with 6 piers in each column.

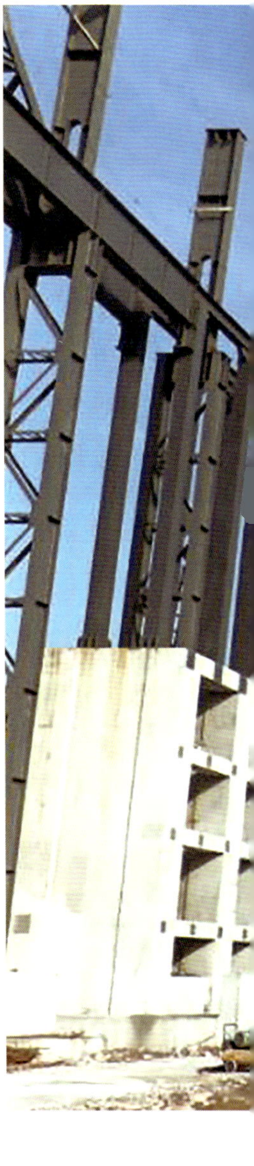

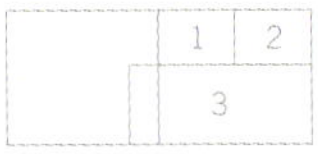

1. 浇筑坑支撑基础
   Supporting Foundation of the Casting Pit
2. 浇筑坑支撑立柱
   Supporting Column of the Casting Pit
3. 反力墙、浇筑坑施工
   Construction of the Reaction Wall and the Casting Pit

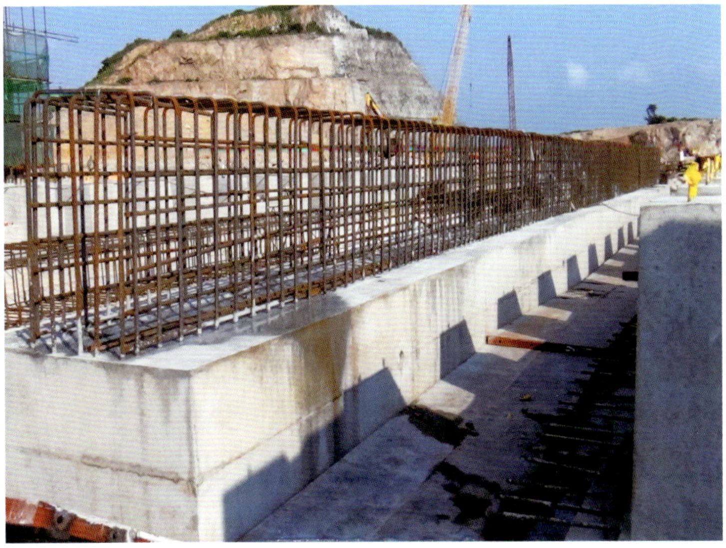

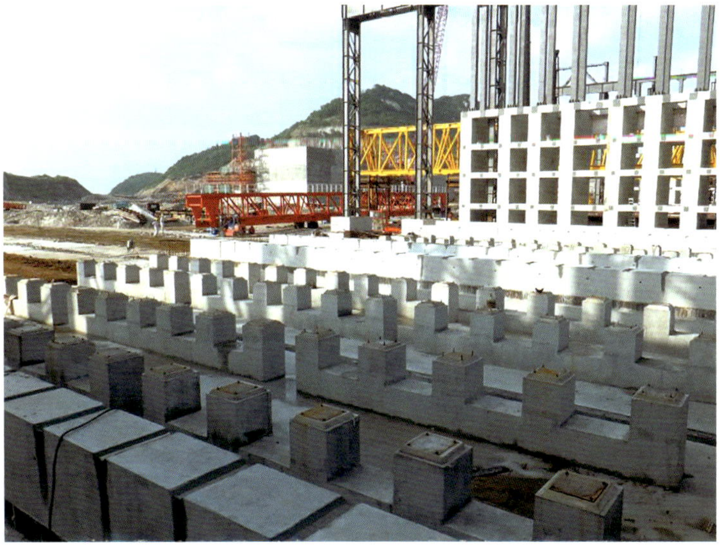

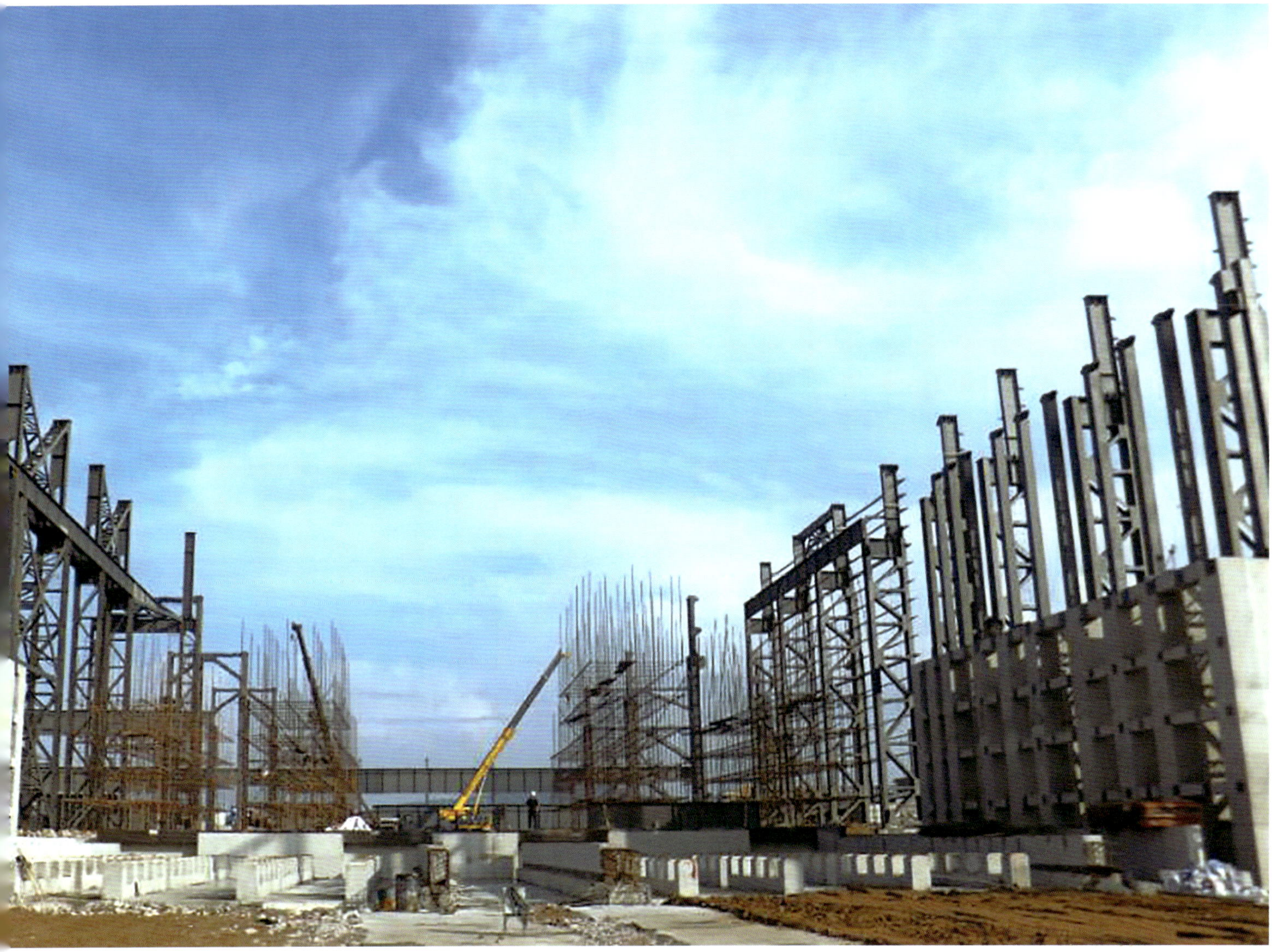

深浅坞建设

CONSTRUCTION OF THE
DEEP AND SHALLOW DOCKS

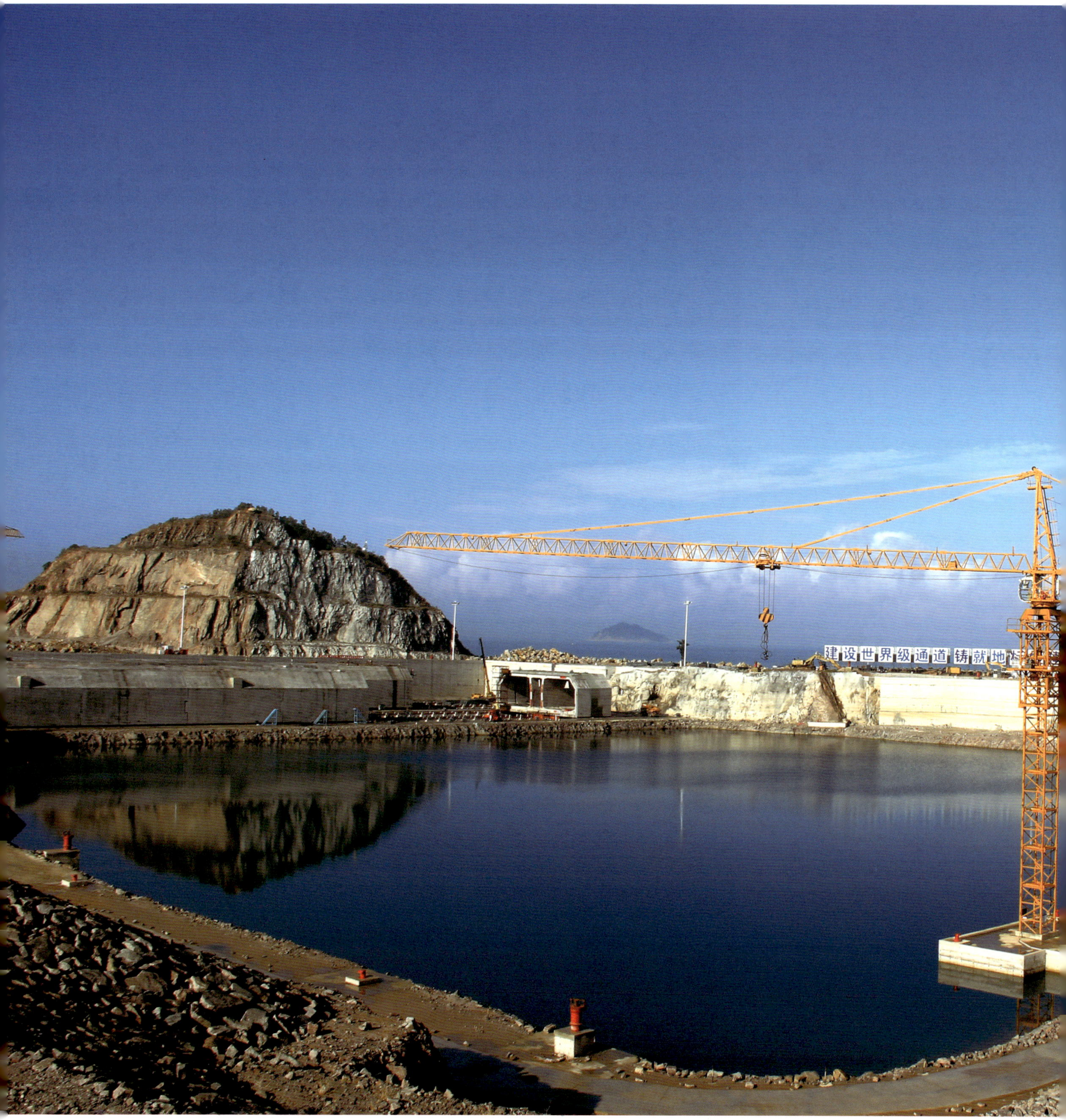

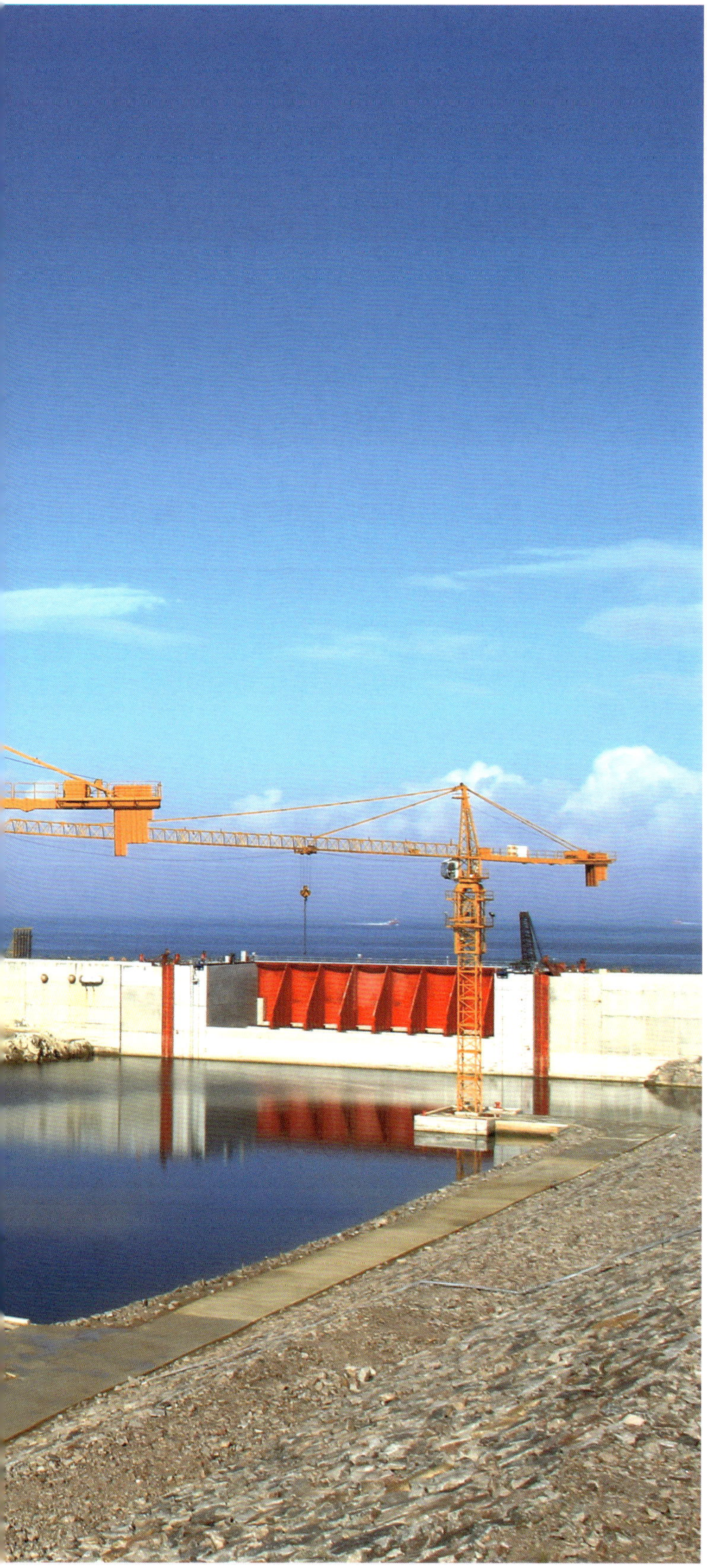

整个沉管预制厂坞区包括深坞区、浅坞区以及四周的拦水坝。

深、浅坞拦水结构多样，根据不同的位置与功能，综合采用了拦水坝沉箱挡水结构、浅坞钢闸门挡水结构、利用现有岩质山体挡水和浮坞门挡水结构。

The docks of the immersed tube precast factory consists of the deep dock, the shallow dock and the surrounding dams.

The water blocking structures for the deep and shallow docks are diversified. According to their different positions and functions, cofferdam structure, steel floodgate for the shallow dock, natural rock mountains, and floating dock gate are used for water blocking.

沉管预制厂坞区
Docks of the Immersed Tube Precast Factory

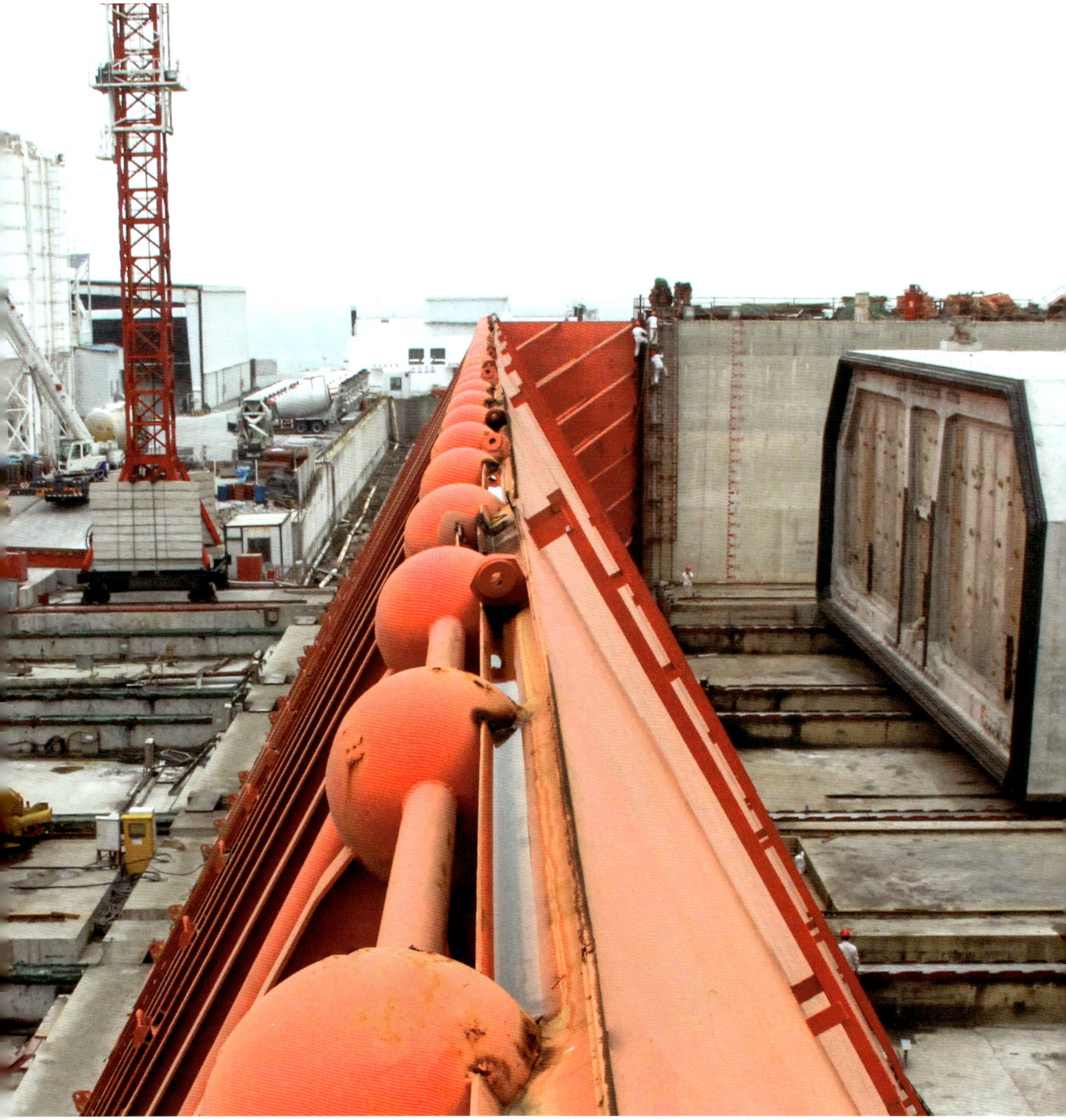

浅坞钢闸门总重约780吨，采用工字钢及钢管组合成的混合桁架结构形式，以三角钢架为基木受力单元，通过相互联系的撑杆形成整体受力结构。三角钢架由工字钢梁组成三角边，三角钢架间设置钢管系杆和斜撑，从而形成钢架整体受力体系。

整体钢架迎水面通过设置连续工字钢墙梁＋止水钢板形成横向挡水，端部则通过钢架悬挑＋外围止水板形成端部止水。

钢闸门采用卷扬机牵引，通过其在滑移轨道上的来回移动进行启闭。

The steel floodgate of the shallow dock weighs about 780 tons. It uses the hybrid truss structure composed of I-beams and steel pipes. The triangular steel frame is used as the basic force-bearing unit, and the general force-bearing structure is formed by interconnected struts. The whole triangular steel frame consists of the triangular edges composed of I-beams, and the steel tie rods and diagonal braces between the frames to bear the forces on the top.

I-beam wall beams and water-stopping steel plates are used on the side of the whole steel frame that faces the water for water blocking in the horizontal direction; water blocking at the top is realized by the hanging steel frame and outer water-stop plates.

The steel floodgate is driven by a windlass, opening and closing by moving back and forth on the sliding track.

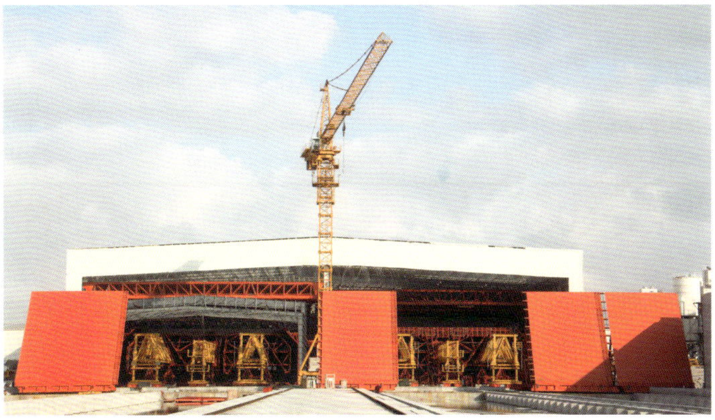

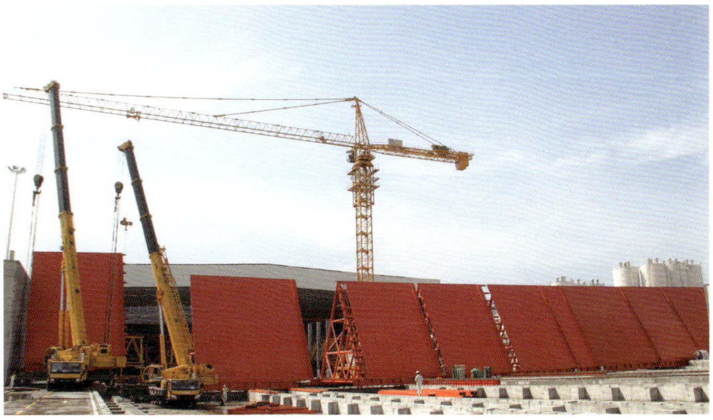

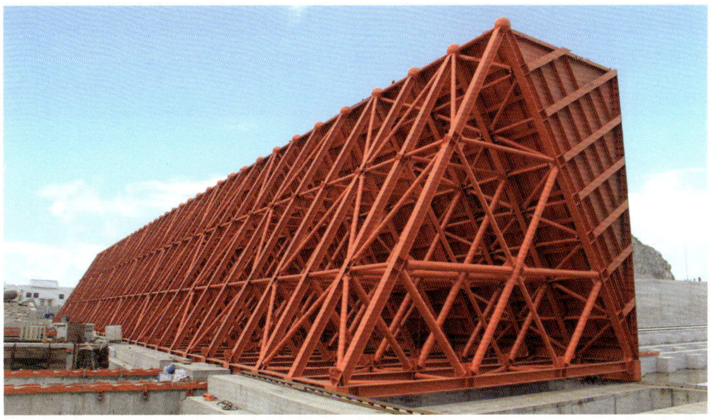

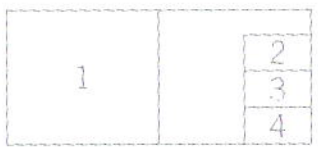

1. 浅坞钢闸门闭合
Closure of the Steel Floodgate of the Shallow Dock

2—4. 浅坞钢闸门拼装施工
Assembling of the Steel Floodgate of the Shallow Dock

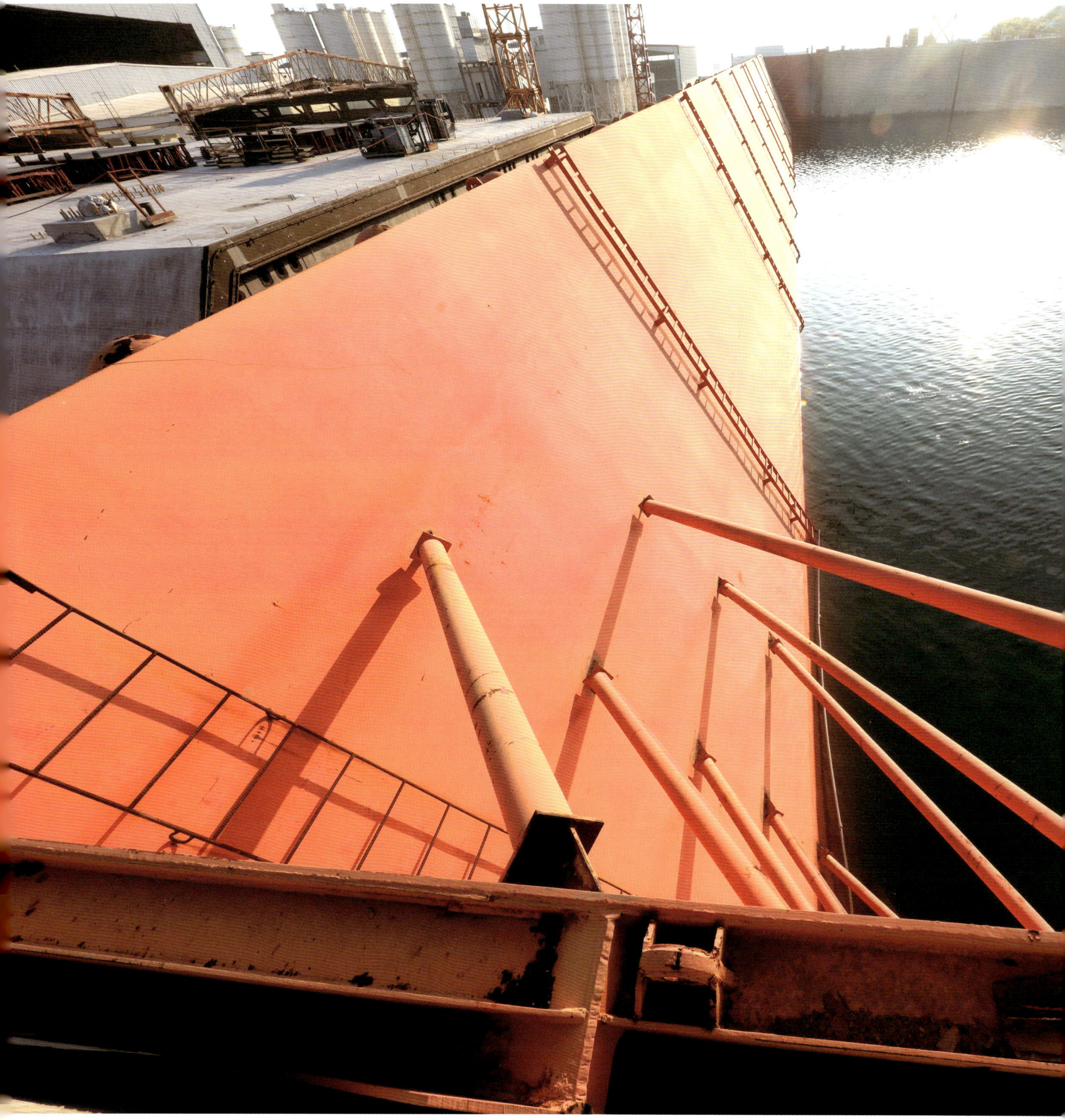

1. 坞内蓄水后的浅坞钢闸门
Steel Floodgate of the Shallow Dock after Impoundment

2. 浅坞钢闸门结构及受力示意图
Schematic Diagram of the Structure and Stress of the Shallow Dock Steel Floodgate

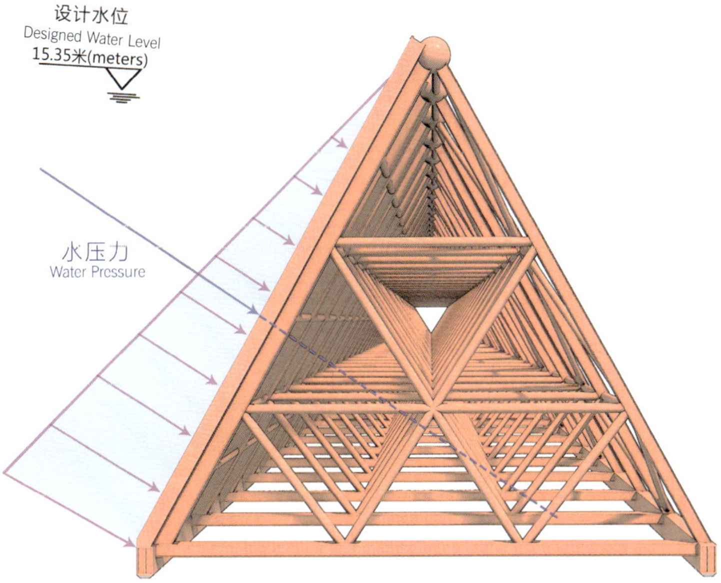

深坞门采用现浇钢筋混凝土重力式结构，分为坞门墩基础与坞门沉箱两部分。

坞门墩基础为倒直角梯形现浇素混凝土结构，现浇于开挖基岩面上。为增强素混凝土与开挖岩面的整体性，在开挖岩面上打设直径32毫米锚筋（间距1.5米×1.5米方形布置）与素混凝土基础连接。坞门墩沉箱内回填碎石土，顶部设置临时路面结构。坞门墩与相邻的沉箱拦水坝之间设置橡胶止水带。

深坞门采用复合沉箱结构，坞门沉箱长59米，宽25.2米，高29.1米，整个沉箱高度方向分为两个部分，标高-13.39～+5.3米内坞门由40个舱格组成；标高+5.3米以上坞门靠坞墩两侧舱格高出10.5米，高出的舱格之间靠海侧处设置挡水钢扶壁。

The deep dock gate adopts the cast-in-situ reinforced concrete gravity structure, consisting of the pier foundation and the caisson.

The pier foundation of the dock gate is an inverted right-angled trapezoidal plain concrete structure cast in place on the excavated bedrock. In order to enhance the integrity of the plain concrete and rock surface, anchor rods with a diameter of 32 millimeters, by the 1.5×1.5-meter spacing, are driven into the rock to connect the plain concrete foundation with the rock. The pier caisson is backfilled with gravel and earth, and a temporary road surface is built at the top. Rubber water-stops are used between the dock gate pier and the adjacent cofferdam.

The deep dock gate adopts a composite caisson structure. The caisson is 59 meters long, 25.2 meters wide and 29.1 meters high. The whole caisson is divided into two parts alongside the longitudinal direction: the internal dock gate between the altitudes of -13.39 and +5.3 meters are composed of 40 compartments, and the compartments on the two sides of the pier are 10.5 meters above the altitude of +5.3 meters. Water-blocking steel buttress is installed between these compartments above +5.3 meters on the seaward side.

	2	3	4
1	5		

1. 深坞门结构示意图
   Structural Diagram of the Deep Dock Gate
2. 深坞门沉箱
   Deep Dock Gate Caisson
3. 深坞门门墩垫块
   Pier Foundation Pad of the Deep Dock Gate
4. 深坞门挡水钢扶壁安装
   Installation of the Water-Blocking Steel Buttress of the Deep Dock Gate
5. 坞内蓄水后深坞门起浮作业
   Floating Operation of the Deep Dock Gate after Impoundment

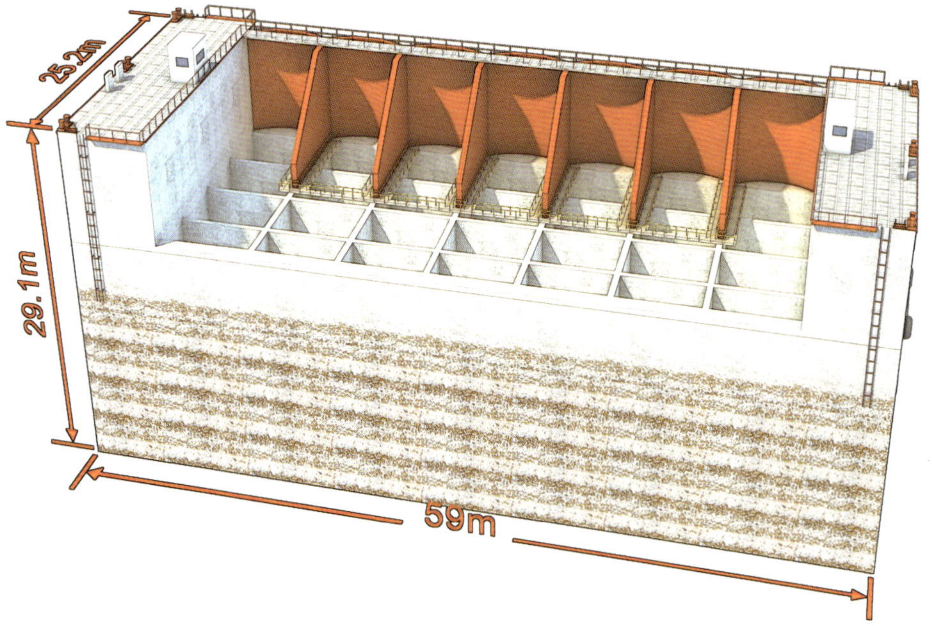

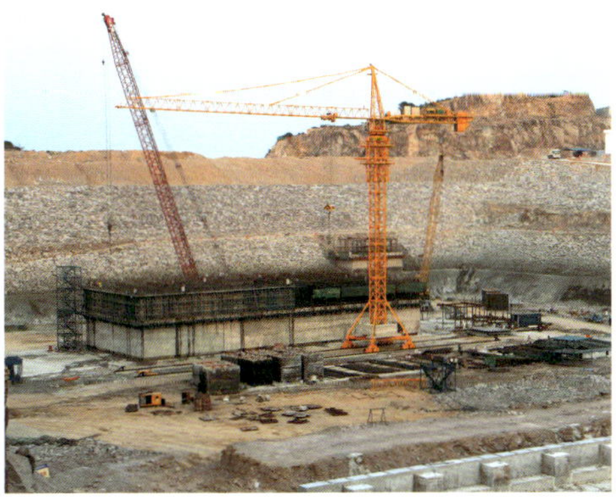

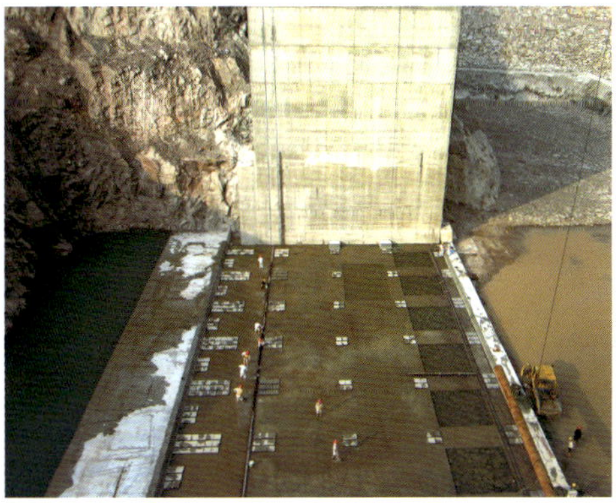

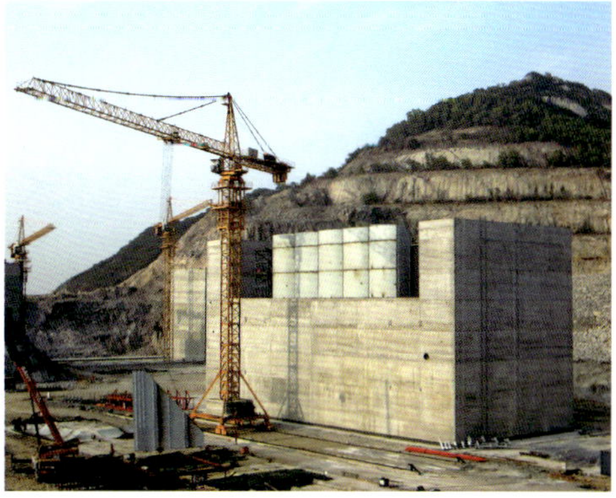

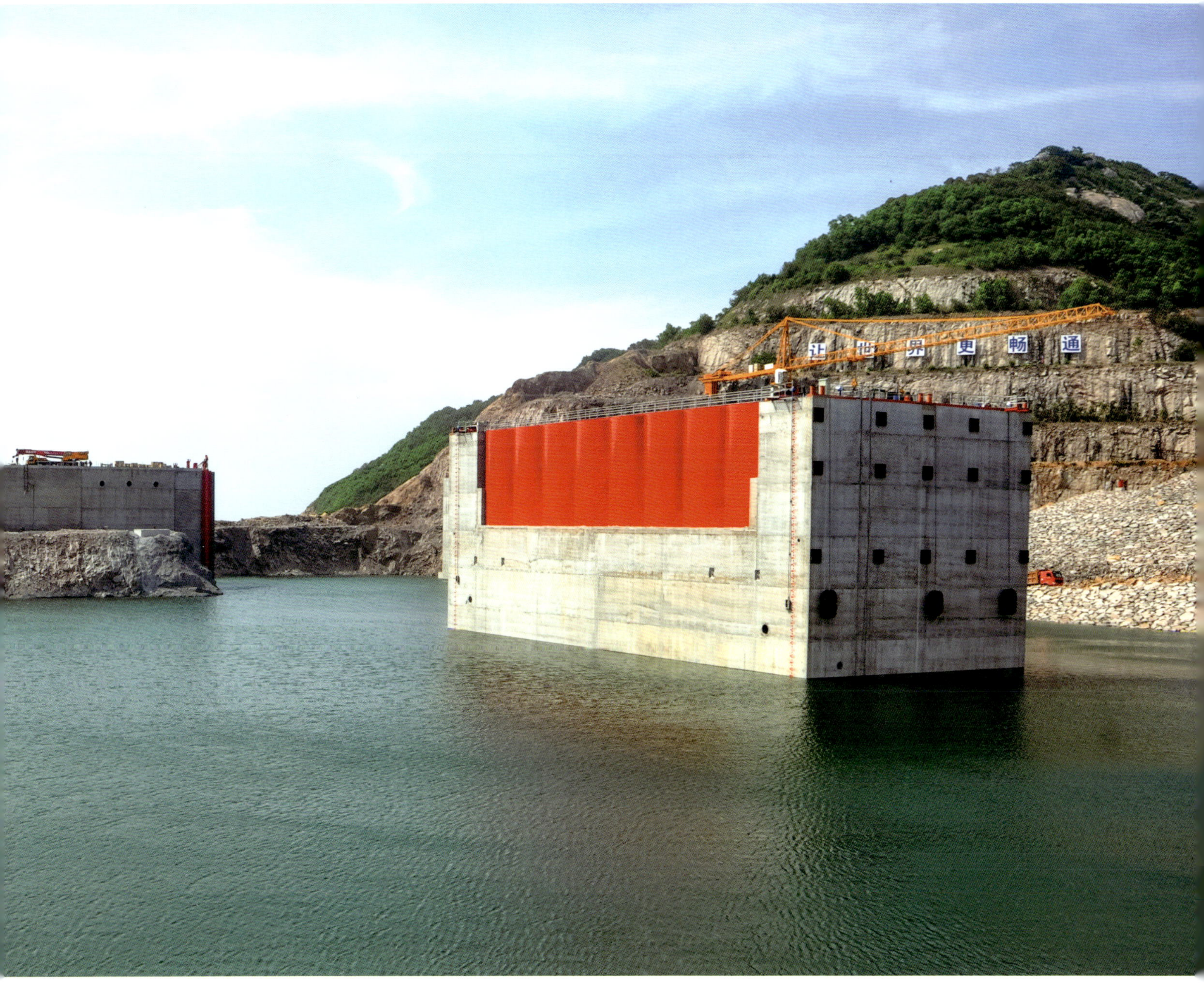
让世界更畅通

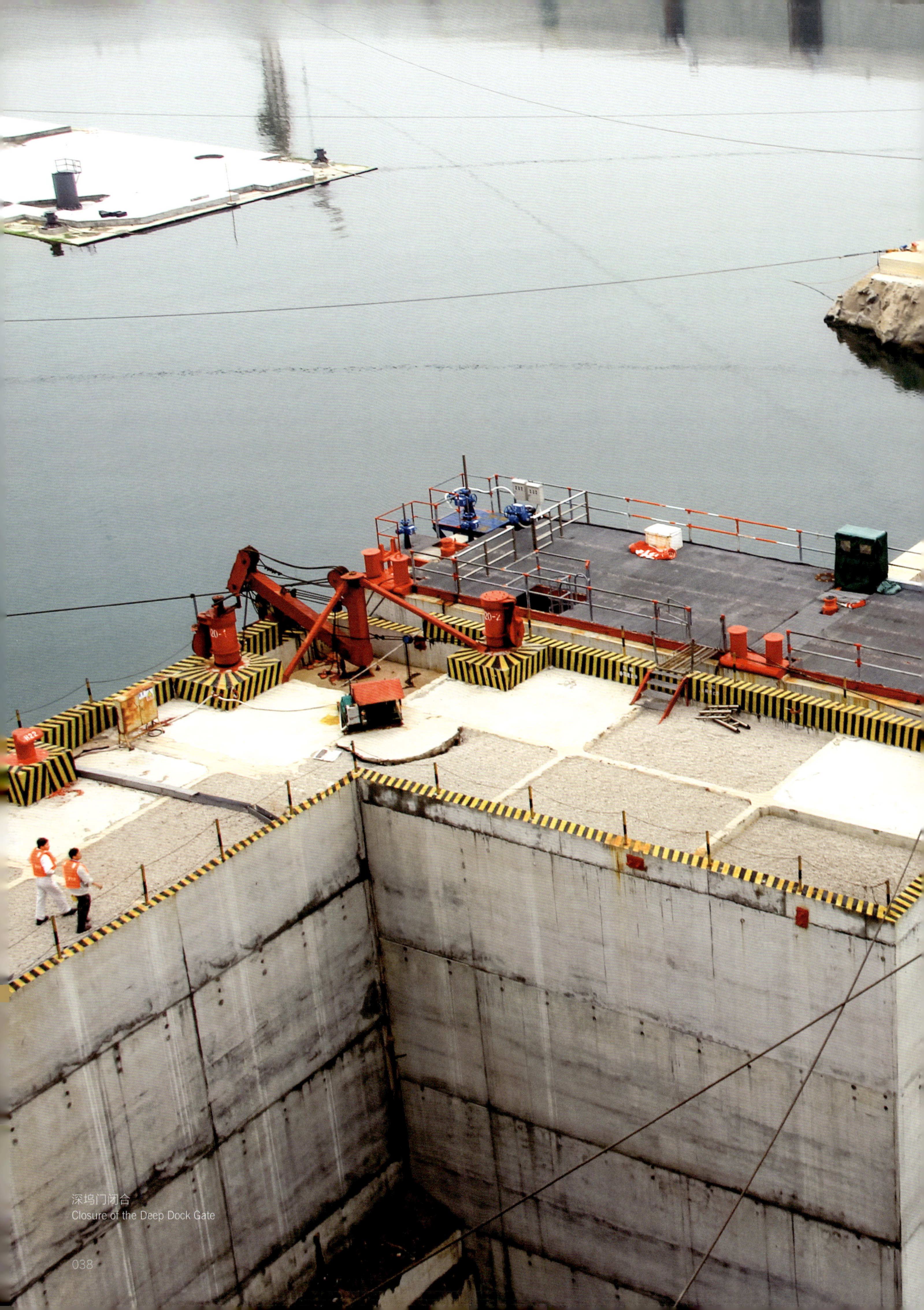

深坞门闭合
Closure of the Deep Dock Gate

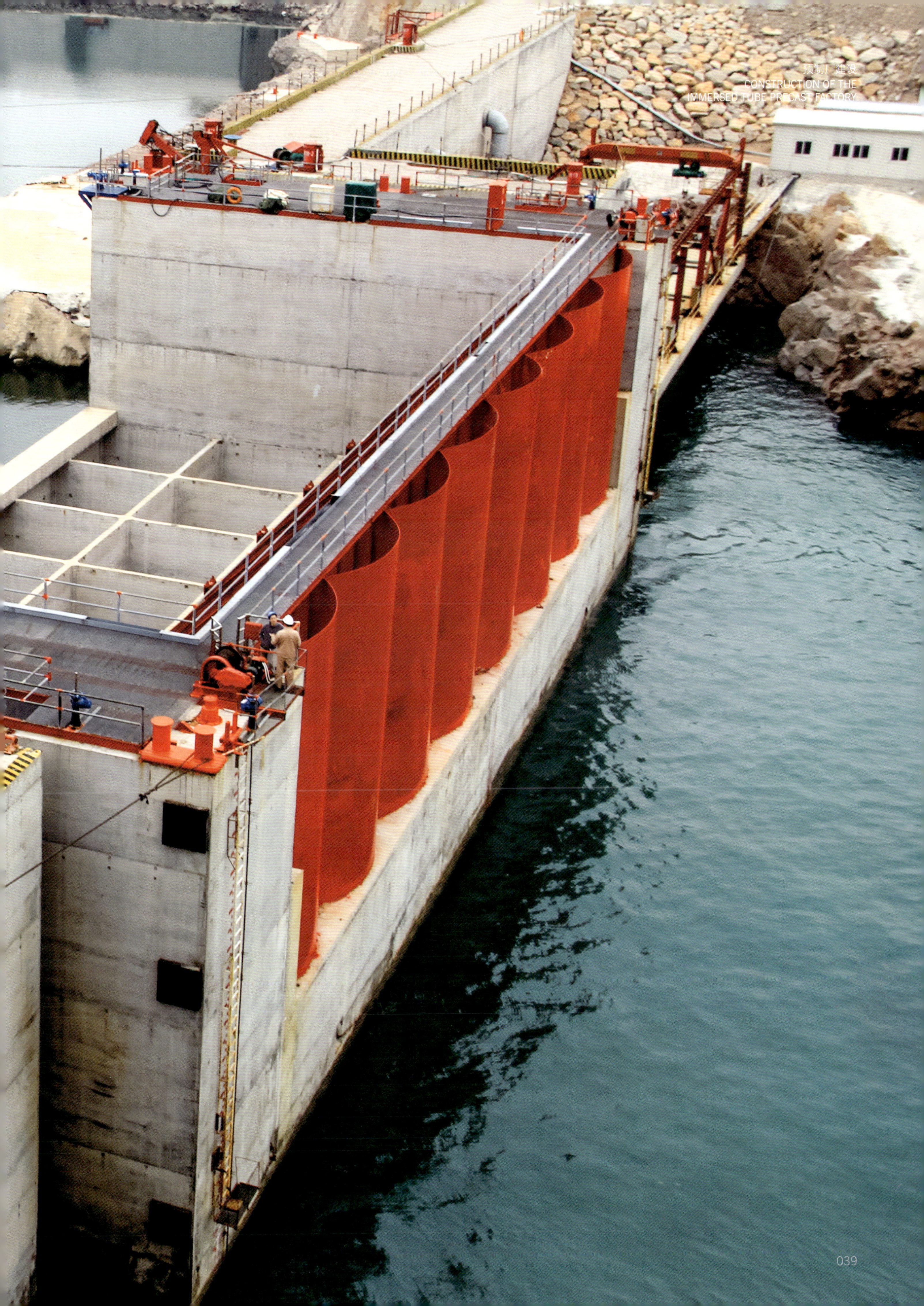

混凝土搅拌站

CONCRETE MIXING PLANT

搅拌区域共设 4 个搅拌站，三仓隔断砂石料棚、1000 立方米水池、6 个中间仓储料罐，总面积约 18,000 平方米，地面设计标高 6.5 米。

粉料的总储存量为：水泥 5600 吨，粉煤灰 3600 吨，矿粉 3600 吨；均可满足 6 个节段的混凝土生产用量。

每个搅拌站设两个 500 吨水泥罐，1 个 500 吨粉煤灰罐、1 个 500 吨矿粉罐和 1 个 500 吨备用储料罐。每两个搅拌站设 1 个冰库，冰库由水池、冷却水泵及冷却塔组成。

Four mixing plants are installed in the concrete mixing area, consisting a three-compartmented sand and stone material shed, a water tanker of 1000 cubic meters, and 6 intermediate storage tanks, covering a total area of around 18,000 square meters, with the designed elevation of 6.5 meters.

The total storage of powder materials includes 5600 tons of cement, 3600 tons of fly ash and 3600 tons of mineral powder, which can provide the concrete needed by the production of 6 tube segments.

Each of the concrete mixing plants is equipped with two 500-ton cement tanks, one 500-ton fly ash tank, one 500-ton mineral powder tank and one 500-ton spare storage tank. For every two mixing stations, one cooling station is built which contains pools, cooling water pumps and cooling towers.

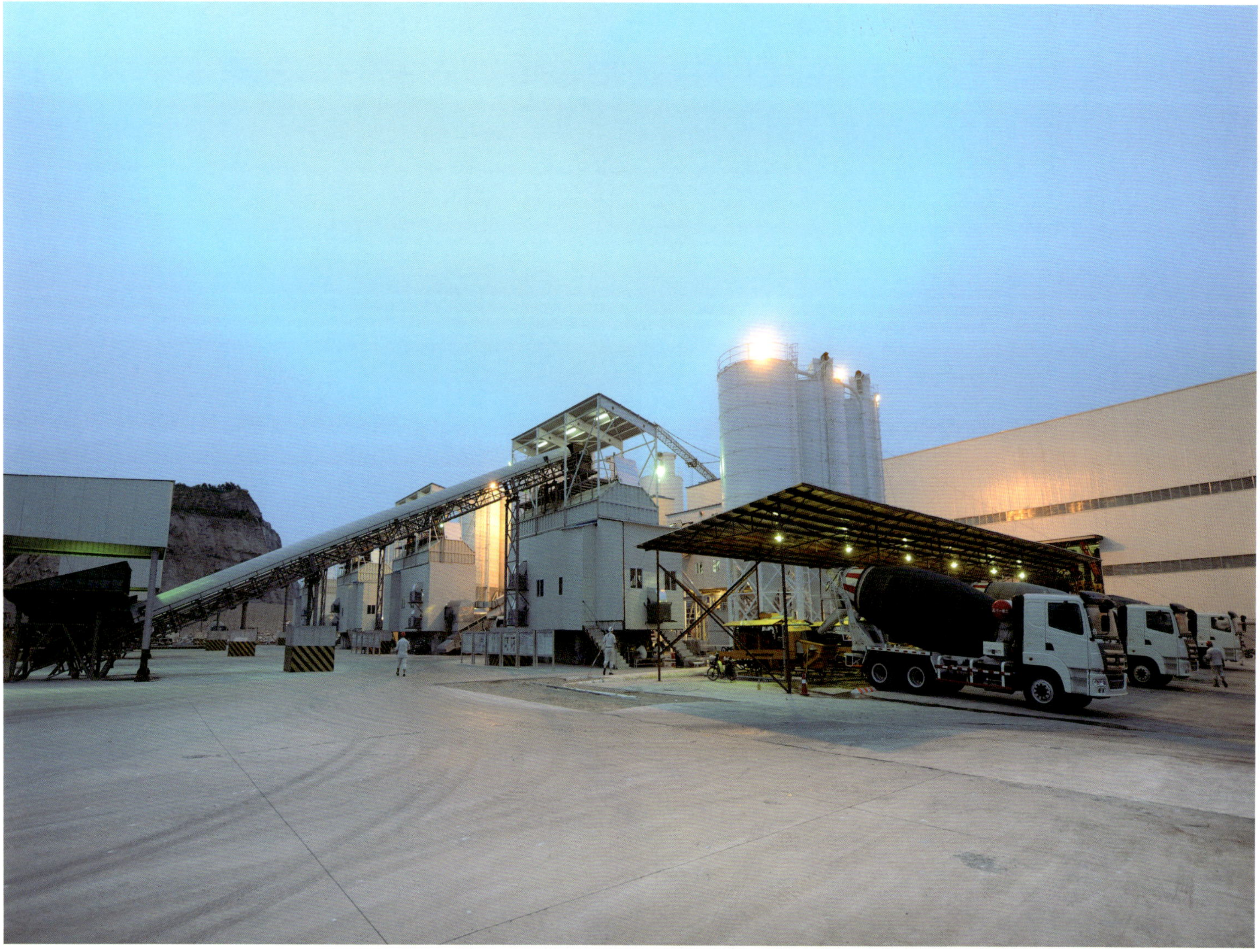

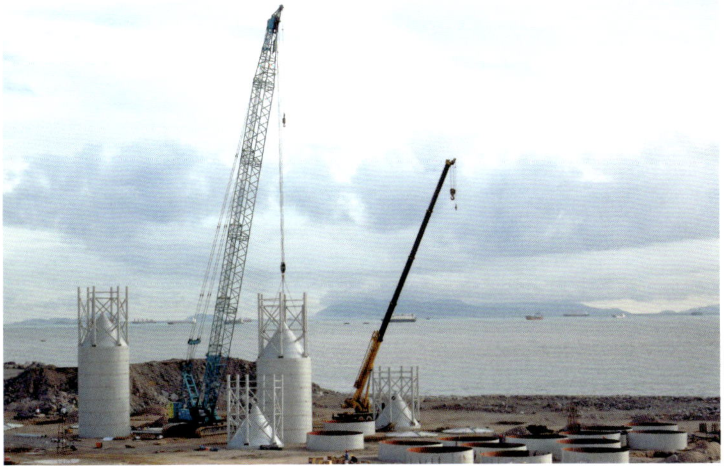

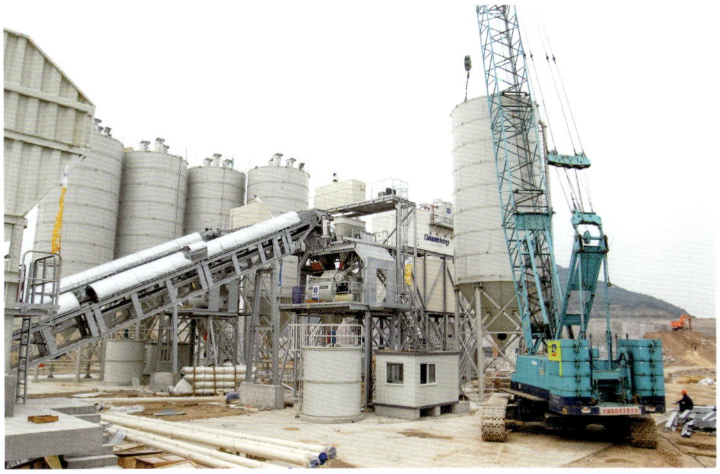

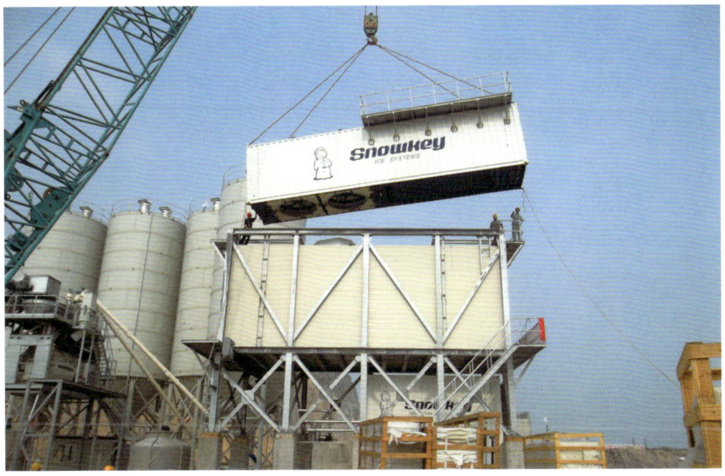

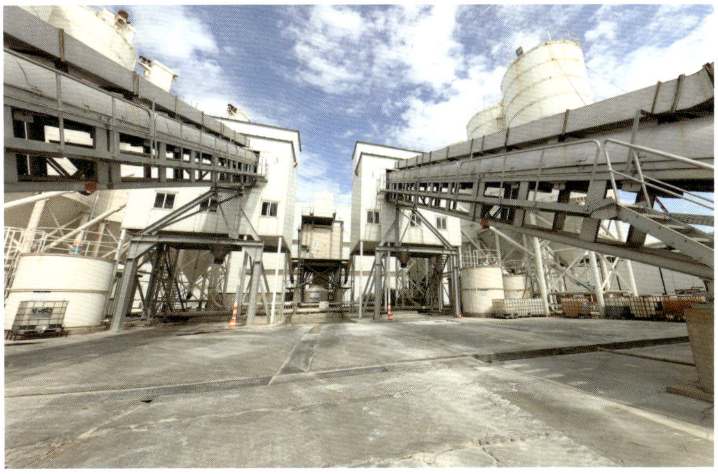

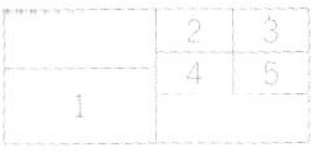

1. 沉管预制厂混凝土搅拌站
Concrete Mixing Plant in the Immersed Tube Precast Factory
2. 搅拌站粉料罐安装
Installation of the Powder Tank in the Concrete Mixing Plant
3. 拌合楼安装
Installation of the Batching Plant
4. 制冰机安装
Installation of the Ice Producing Machine
5. 安装完工后的拌合楼
Well-Installed Batching Plant

沉管预制厂混凝土搅拌站全景
Panoramic View of the Concrete Mixing Plant in the Immersed Tube Precast Factory

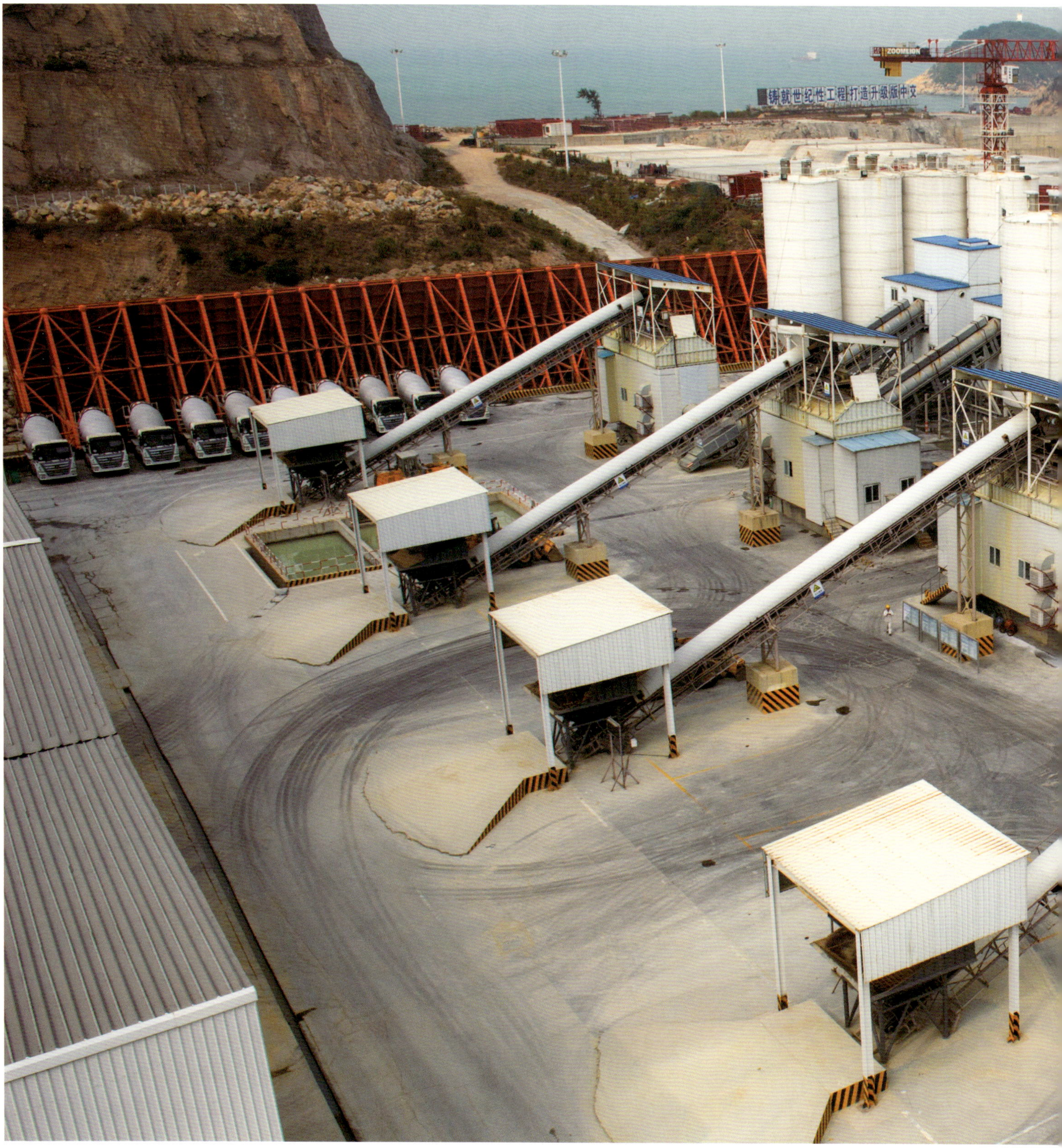

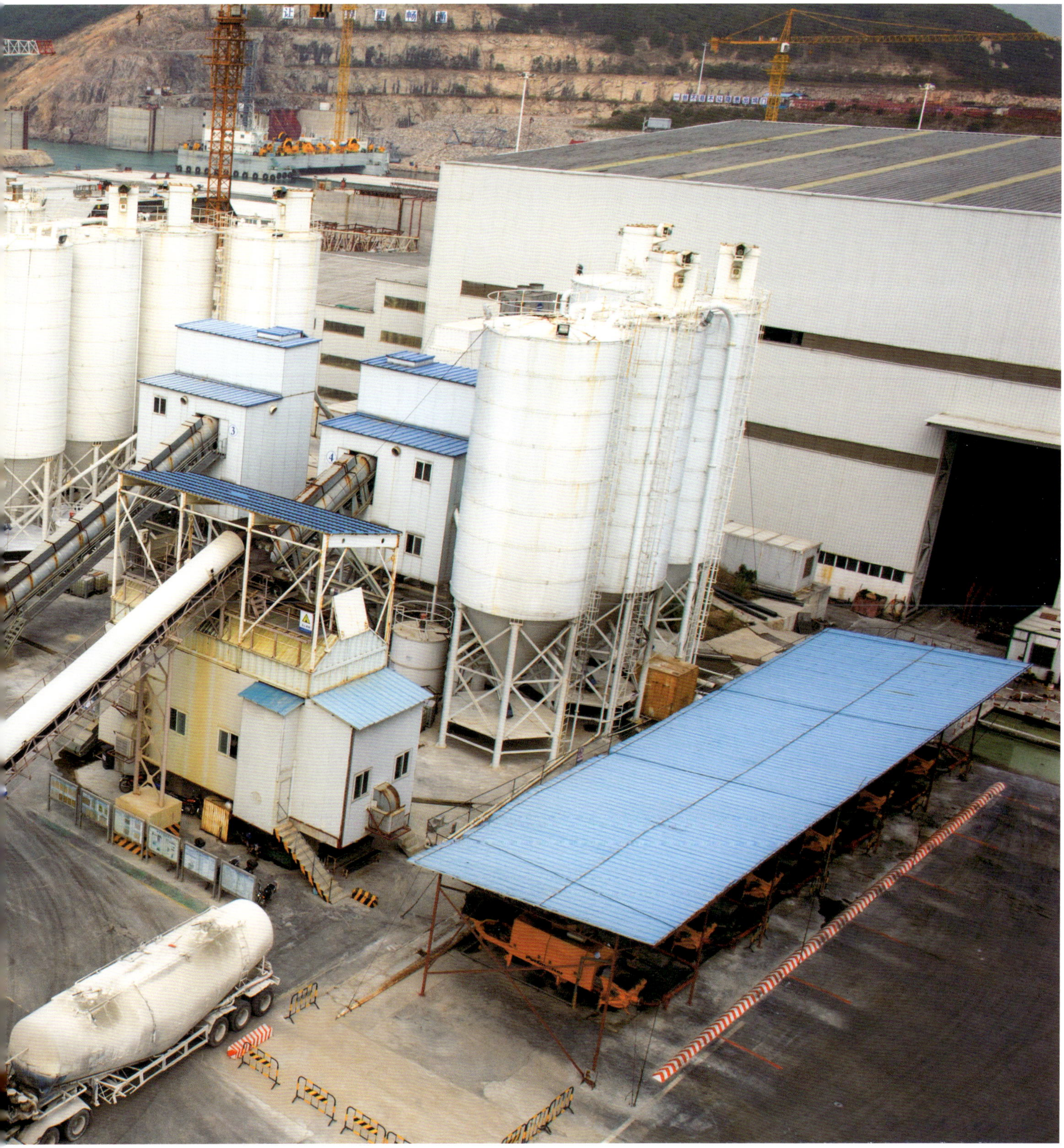

码头建设
WHARF CONSTRUCTION

码头位于预制厂东南侧的天然港湾崎沙湾，湾内风浪流均较小，水深及水域面积能满足交通船、砂石料船和散货船的靠泊要求，适合建设配套码头。

件杂货码头布置在崎沙湾东南侧，泊位长度110米，可停泊2000载重吨件杂货船；在码头端头布置10米斜坡段，后端回填至陆域，可停靠滚装船。

散料码头位于湾内西侧，为高桩码头。港池内侧护岸兼做砂石料码头，位于码头港池内湾北侧，沿原有岸线向后延伸50米的范围。施工材料通过装卸车运转至料仓，场地分两级边坡放坡至港池底。

The dock is located in Qisha Bay on the southeast side of the immersed tube precast factory, where the relatively slow current, the water depth and the size of the water area meet the requirements of the transportation vessels, sand and gravel carriers and general cargo carriers for mooring there, and is thus suitable for the construction of the docks.

The general cargo wharf is located on the southeast side of Qisha Bay, with a berth of 110 meters long. It can accommodate the berthing of the cargo ships with the DWT of 2000 tons. A 10-meter slope is constructed at head part of the wharf and the end part is connected to the land by backfilling, suitable for the anchorage of the roll-on-roll-off ships.

The balk cargo wharf is located in the west side of the bay and is built on high piers. The revetment of the inner side of the harbor dock can also serve as a sand and stone wharf, located at northern part of the harbor dock, extending 50 meters backward along the original coast line. All the construction materials are transferred to the material storehouse by the loaders. The two-leveled side slope extends to the bottom of the harbor dock.

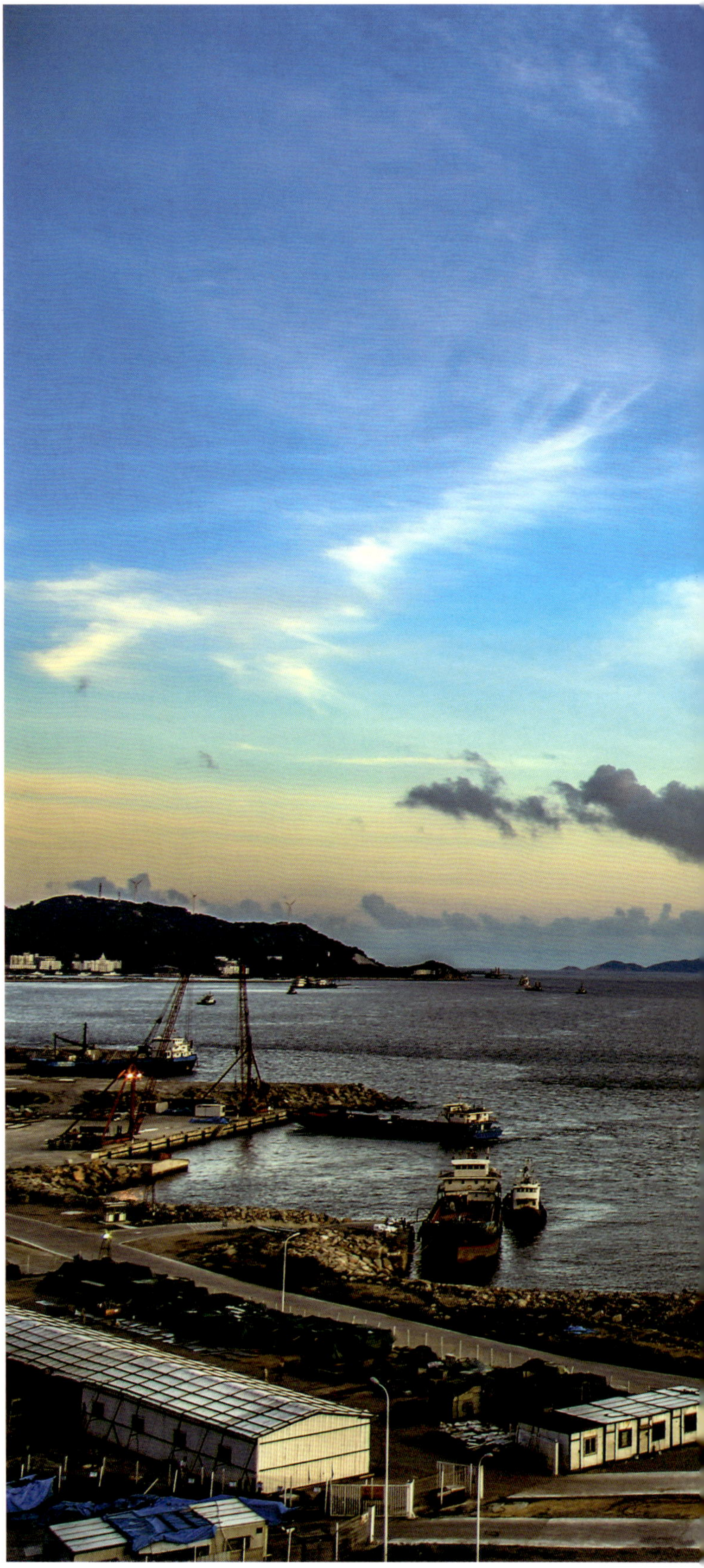

沉管预制厂码头
Docks of the Immersed Tube Precast Factory

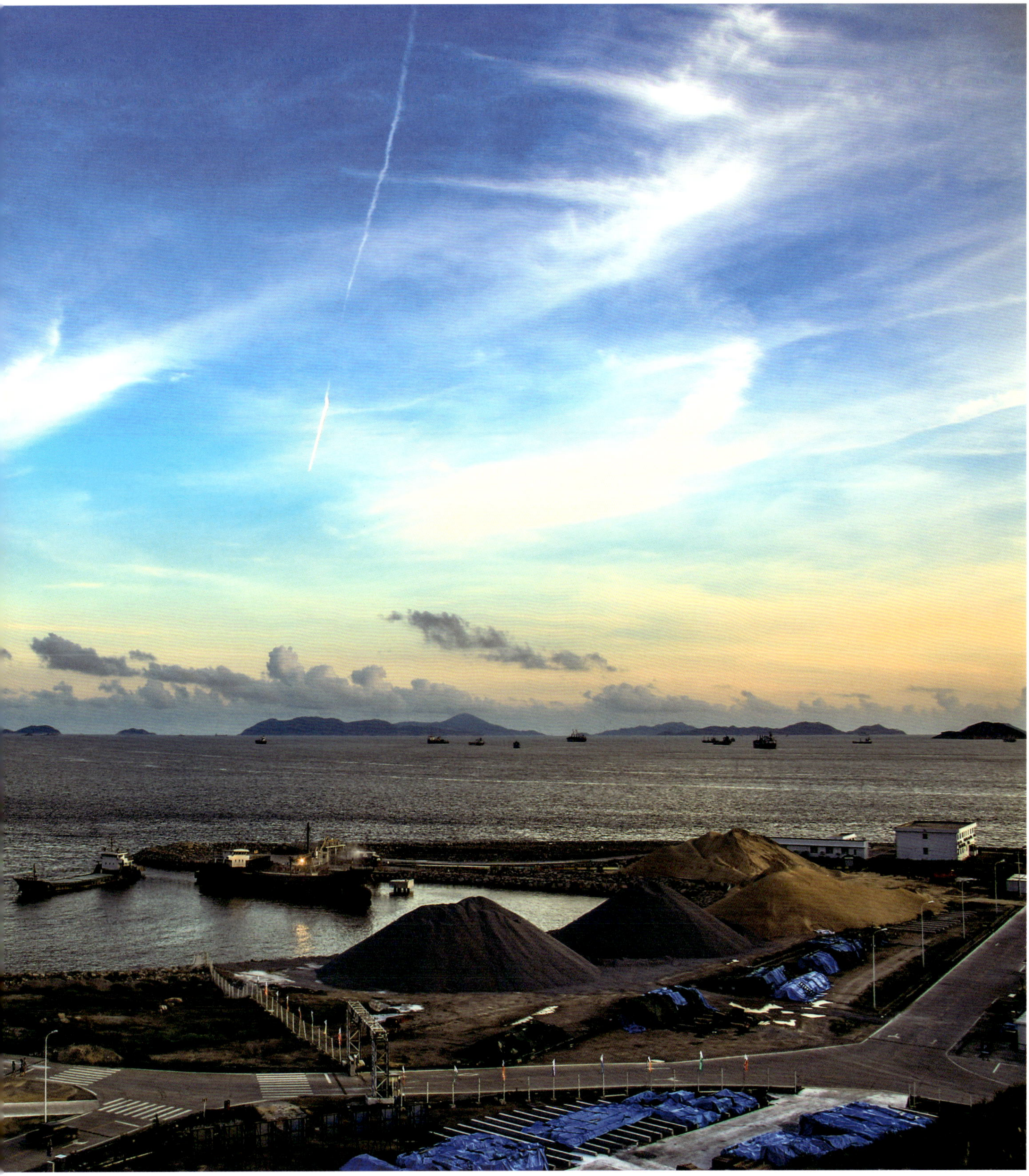

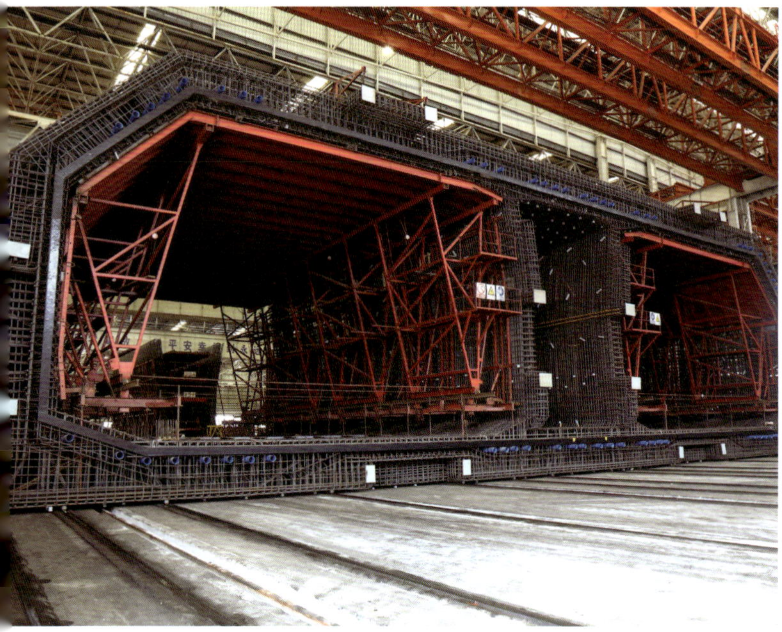

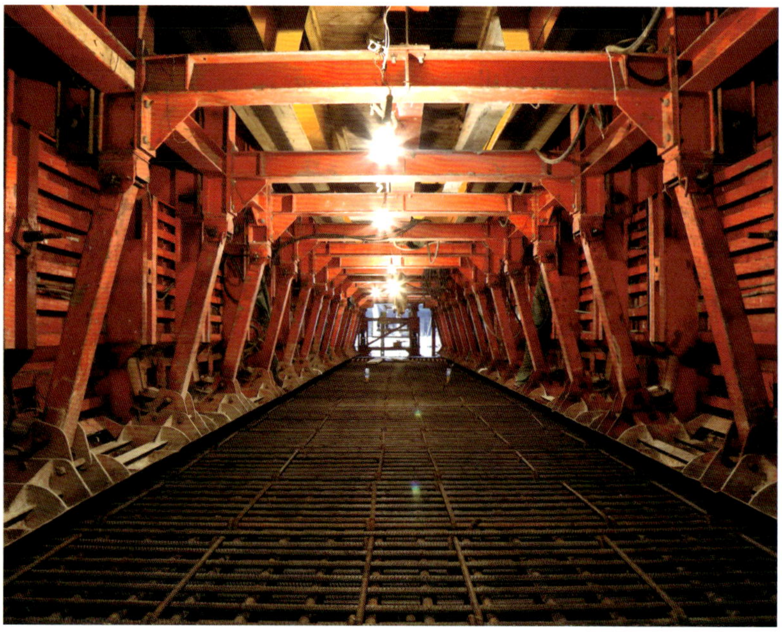

沉管预制

PRECAST OF THE IMMERSED TUBES

预制完成的沉管
Immersed Tube Precast

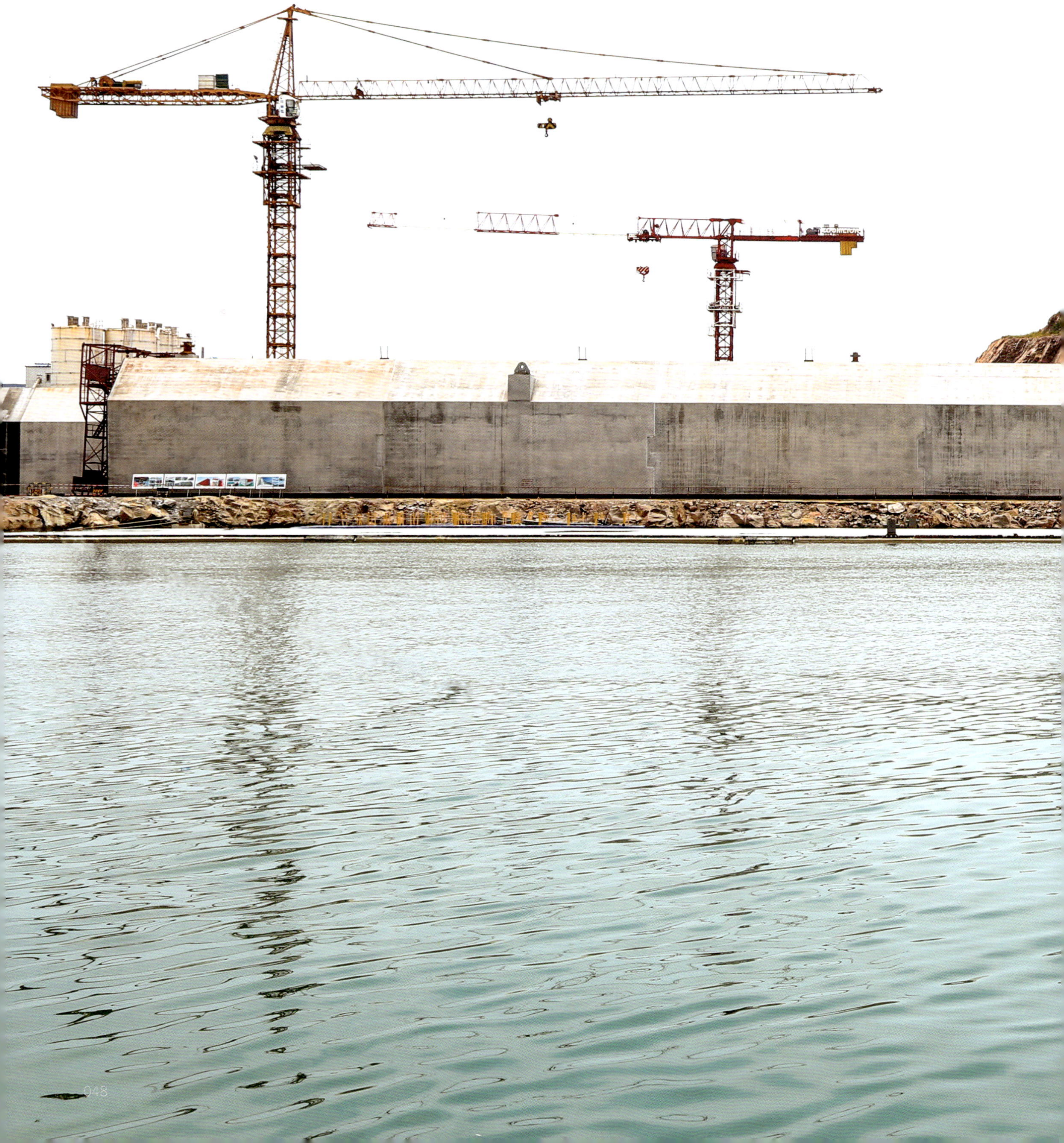

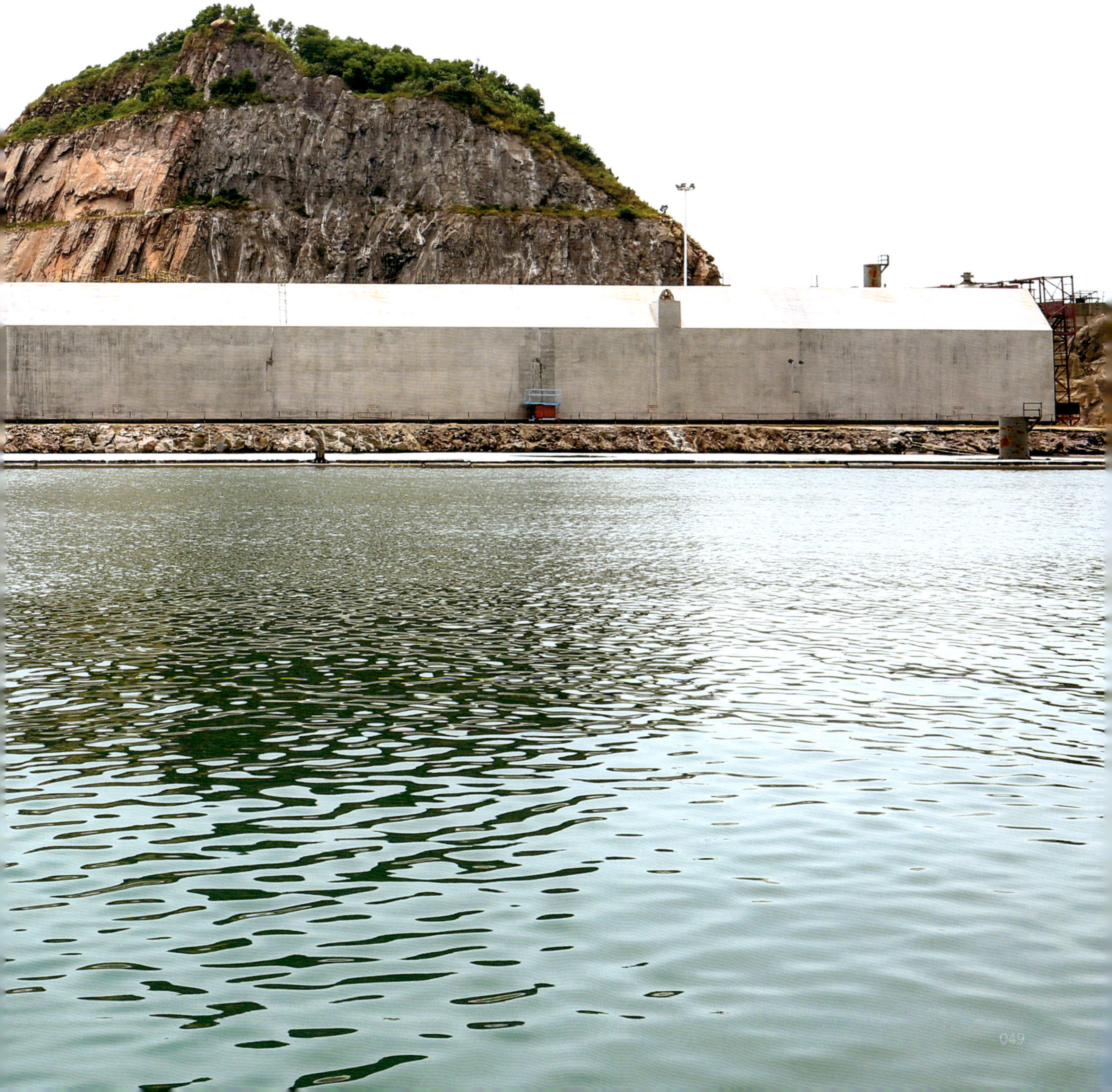

港珠澳大桥沉管介绍

INTRODUCTION TO THE IMMERSED TUBES OF HONG KONG-ZHUHAI-MACAU BRIDGE

沉管隧道由 33 节沉管连接而成，每个标准沉管长 180 米、宽 37.95 米、高 11.4 米，重 7.6 万吨，是世界上最大体量的沉管。

The immersed tube tunnel is made up of 33 immersed tubes. Each standard immersed tube is 180 meters long, 37.95 meters wide, 11.4 meters high and weighs 76,000 tons, the largest immersed tube in the world.

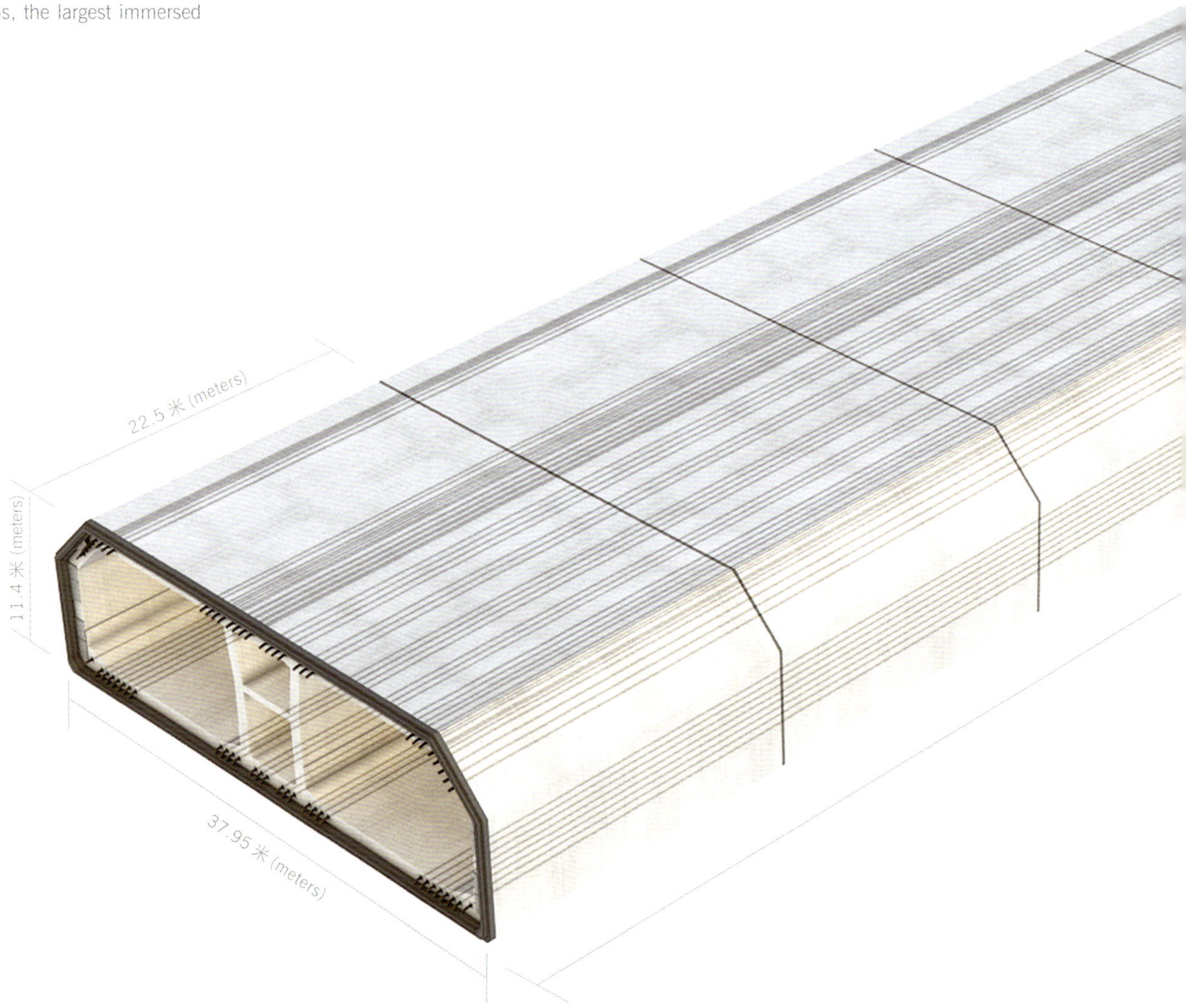

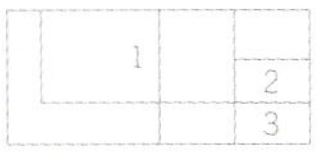

1. 沉管结构示意图
   Structural Diagram of the Immersed Tube
2. 沉管批次及长度参数表
   Batch Number and Length Parameter of the Immersed Tubes
3. 沉管长距离顶推
   Long-Distance Pushing of the Immersed Tube

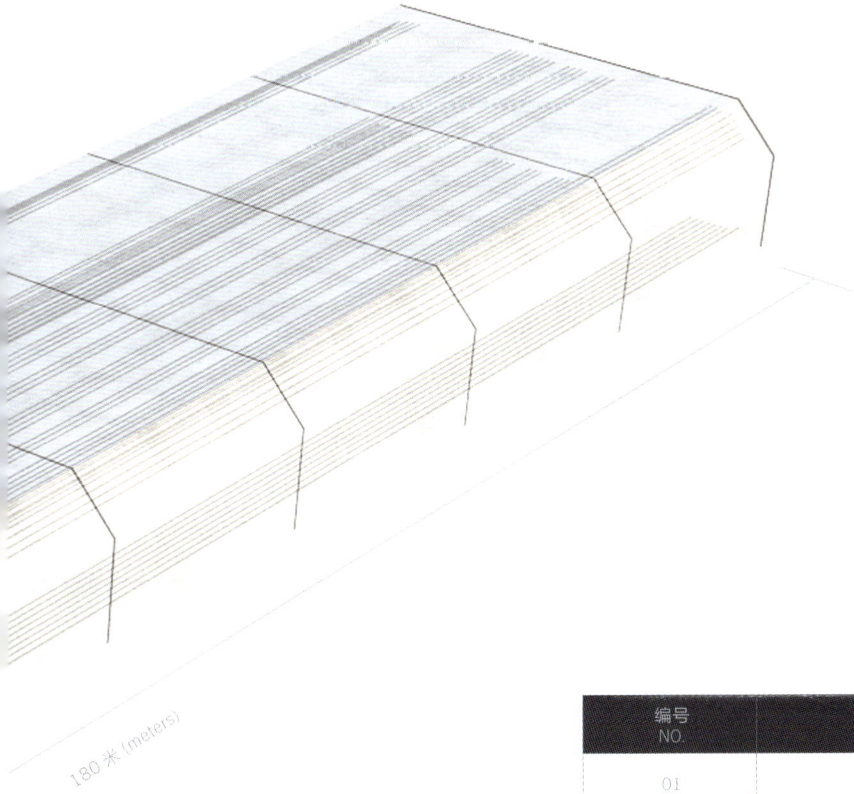

编号 NO.	管节名称 Tube Name	设计长度 Designed Length	管节线性 Tube Shape
01	E1、E2	112.5 米 (meters)	直线 Straight
02	E3~E28	180 米 (meters)	
03	E29-1	172 米 (meters)	曲线 Curved
04	E30+E29-2	175+5 米 (meters)	
05	E31	180 米 (meters)	
06	E32、E33	112.5 米 (meters)	

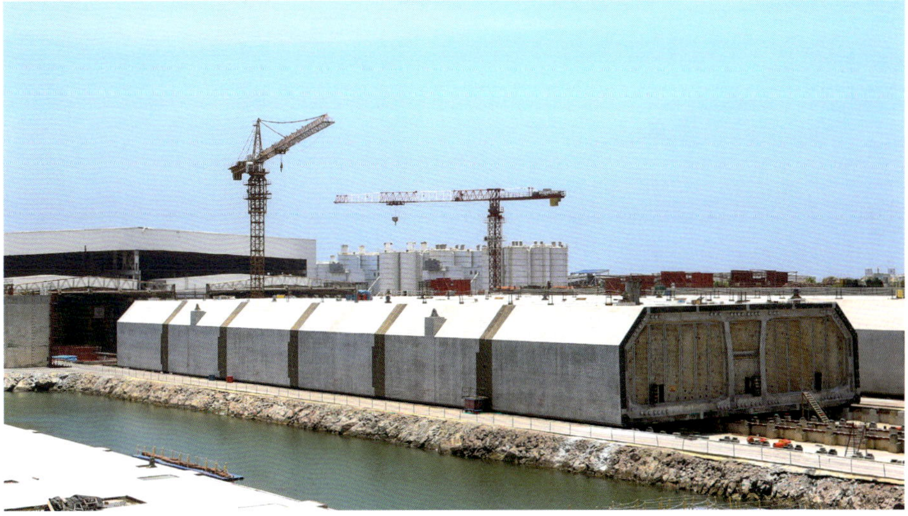

“半刚性”创新

INNOVATION OF SEMI-RIGID TUNNEL

1 2 3 4 5

1—3. 不同结构沉管受力原理示意图
Schematic Diagrams of the Stress of the Immersed Tube with Different Structures

4. 预应力筋穿束示意图
Schematic Diagram of the Pre-stressing Tendon Threading

5. 沉管预应力筋布置图
Layout of the Pre-stressing Tendons in the Immersed Tube

全世界已建成一百多条沉管隧道，按纵向结构可分为“刚性”结构和“柔性”结构。

为了预留珠江口远期航道，沉管隧道需深埋至海床面以下20余米。在超过浅埋沉管4~5倍荷载的情况下，无论采用传统的刚性结构或是柔性结构，沉管开裂与漏水的风险都会成倍增加。

沉管隧道抗震烈度要求高，沉管又深埋在水下46米的软弱地基上，地基不均匀沉降的处理难度大，单一采用纯粹的刚性结构或柔性结构都无法满足抗震和地基不均匀的沉降要求。

为此，项目总经理部委托六家研究团队同时进行“半刚性”理论分析和数值模拟计算，开展了相关试验研究，开发了“半刚性”沉管新结构，解决了深埋沉管的技术难题。

“半刚性”沉管节段之间通过剪力键连接并在接头处设置防水措施，浮运与沉放阶段通过临时纵向通长预应力筋保证整个沉管的纵向刚度，在沉放与回填之后预应力筋不剪断。利用预应力将节段接头压紧，从而产生一定的摩擦力与接头剪力键共同抗剪，更好地控制隧道节段接头的位移及张开量，从而提高接头水密性。

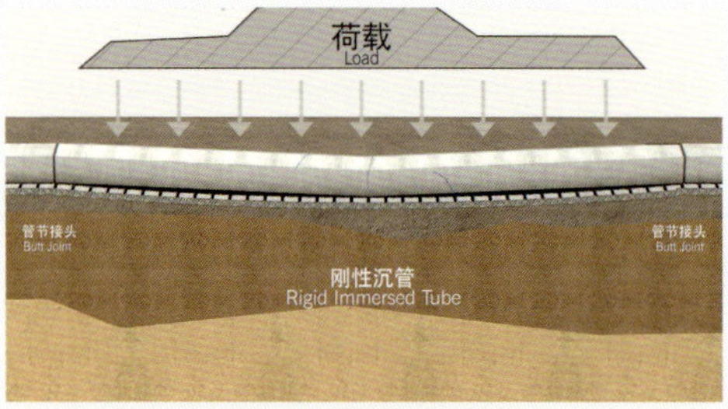

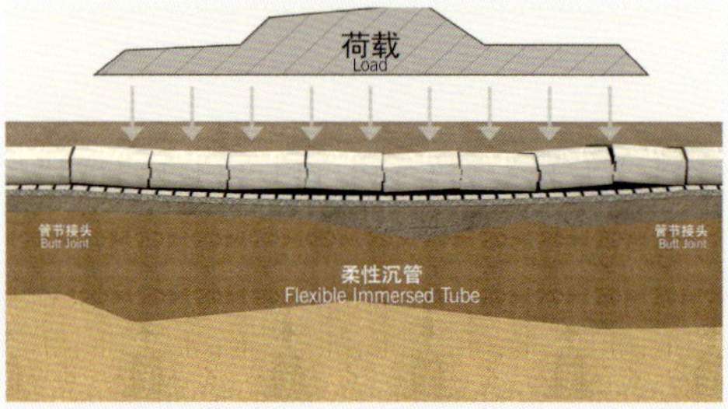

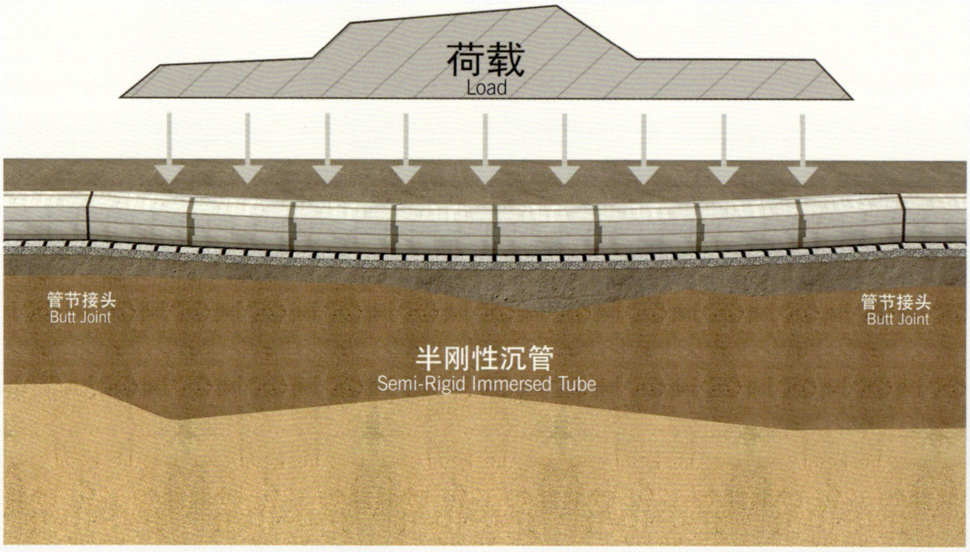

More than 100 immersed tube tunnels have been built around the world. By longitudinal structure, these tunnels can be divided into rigid- and flexible-structured tunnels.

In order to protect the long-term channels on the Pearl River Estuary, the immersed tube tunnel has to be buried more than 20 meters below the seabed. When the load on the deep-buried tunnel exceeds 4 or 5 times that of the shallow-buried immersed tube tunnel, the risk of crack and leakage of the immersed tube will multiply whether the traditional rigid structure or flexible structure is used.

Due to the high anti-seismic requirement of the immersed tube tunnel and the fact that the immersed tube is deep-buried on the soft foundation of 46 meters underwater, it is difficult to deal with the uneven settlement of the foundation. Neither the pure rigid structure nor the flexible structure can meet the requirements for coping with the seismic impact and the uneven settlement of the foundation.

To solve these problems, the project management center entrusted 6 research teams to simultaneously conduct experiments for theoretic analyses and relevant numerical simulating calculation of a "semi-rigid" structure. Based on the findings of these experiments, the innovative "semi-rigid" immersed tube structure was developed to cope with the technical challenge involved in the deep-burial of the immersed tubes.

The different sections of the "semi-rigid" immersed tube are connected by shear keys and waterproof devices are inserted at the joints. Temporary full-length longitudinal pre-stressing cables are used in the stages of float conveyance and landing to realize the longitudinal rigidity of the whole immersed tube, and the pre-stressing cables remain there after the landing and backfilling are completed. The pre-stressing force is used to compress tight the joints between the different segments so as to produce certain friction to jointly resist the shear force at the junction with the shear keys for better control of the displacement and opening of the joints, thus improving their water-stop effects.

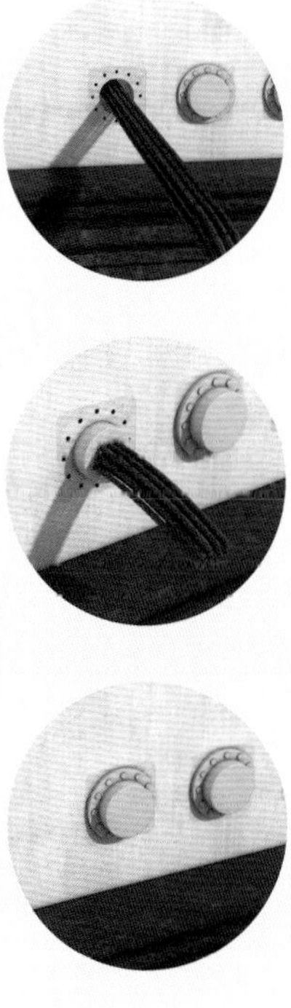

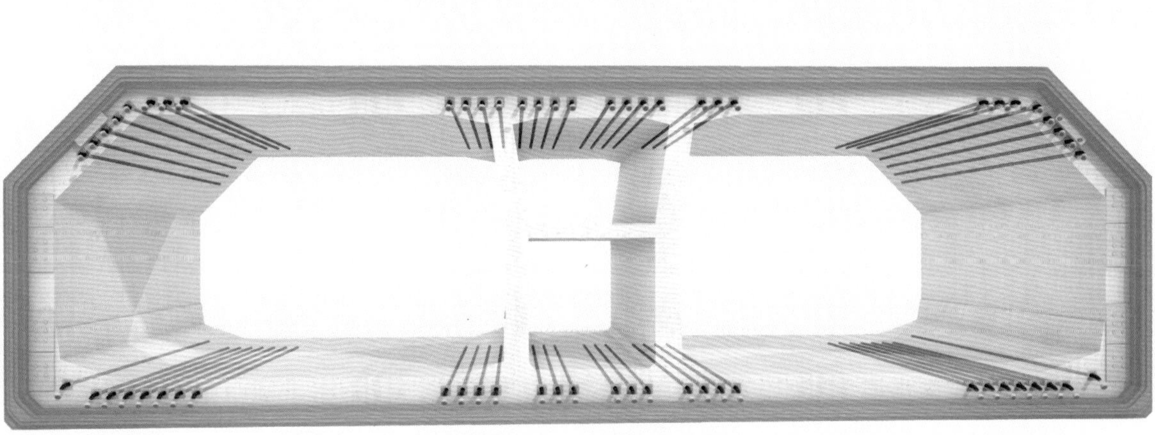

沉管预应力采用"半刚性"设计理论，即在节段接头区域 6 米范围采用无粘结预应力方案，其余采用有粘结预应力方案，确保沉管浮运安装及运行中的结构安全。

沉管断面顶板和底板共布置 60 个孔道，其中 56 个孔道需进行预应力张拉。

采用张拉应力和张拉伸长量双控，张拉控制应力为 1265 兆帕。张拉完成后对预应力孔道进行真空灌浆。

E1~E28 沉管为直线管节，预应力束布置为直线；E29~E33 沉管为半径 5500 米的曲线管节，预应力束在接头处缓和过渡。

钢绞线采用 Ryb=1860 兆帕的 Φ15.2 毫米低松弛钢绞线，锚具为防水密封锚具，在锚具后方设保护罩，保护罩与锚垫板间设铜垫圈止水，在 0.6 兆帕水压力下保持水密性。锚垫板为 QT400-18 球墨铸成，表面加热发蓝处理。保护罩经热镀锌处理，锌层厚度≥ 100 微米。

预应力钢绞线的穿束方法分为整束穿束和单根穿束，工艺成熟，但长达 180 米的预应力束仍较少使用。

预应力张拉分为沉管长距离顶推前预张拉和顶推到位后剩余预应力张拉两个阶段。沉管顶推到位后预应力张拉要求混凝土强度达到 28 天设计强度的 90% 以上。

采用 4 套 6000 千牛（或 4500 千牛）液压千斤顶两端同步张拉，并左右对称进行。

The immersed tube pre-stressing technique adopts the "semi-rigid" design theory, i.e. the non-adhesive-bonding pre-stressing solution is used in the area 6 meters within the junction between two segments while in the other places the adhesive-bonding pre-stressing solution is used, so as to ensure the structural safety of the immersed tube during transportation, installation and operation.

60 holes are arranged on the top and bottom plates of the cross section of the immersed tube, 56 of which need pre-stressing pulling.

Double controls of tension-pulling stress and tensioning elongation are used, with the controlled tensioning stress of 1265 MPa. After tension-pulling, the pre-stressing holes are vacuum-grouted.

The immersed tubes E1~E28 are straight tubes and the pre-stressing tendons are arranged in straight lines. The immersed tubes E29~E33 are curved tubes with a radius of 5500 meters and the pre-stressing tendons transit gradually at the junction.

The steel stranded wire is the Φ15.2 millimeter steel wire of Ryb=1860 MPa with low relaxation. The anchor is the sealed waterproof anchor with a protective cover in the back part; a copper gasket is set between the protective cover and the anchor pad to stop water, and water tightness is maintained under the water pressure of 0.6 MPa. The anchor pad is manufactured with QT 400-18 nodular cast, and its surface is heated and blued. The protective cover is hot-dip galvanized, and the zinc coating is ≥100 micrometers thick.

The threading of the pre-stressing steel stranded wires can be either multiple-wire threading and single-wire threading. It is a mature technique, but the pre-stressing tendons as long as 180 meters are rare.

Pre-stressing tensioning is divided into two stages: pre-tensioning before the long-distance pushing of the immersed tube and residual pre-stressing tensioning after the tube has been pushed to the designed position. The residual pre-stressing tensioning after the tube has been pushed to the designed position needs the concrete strength to reach more than 90% of the designed 28-day strength.

Four sets of 6,000-KN (or 4,500-KN) hydraulic jacks are used for simultaneous tensioning at both ends, and the tensioning should be conducted symmetrically on the left and the right sides.

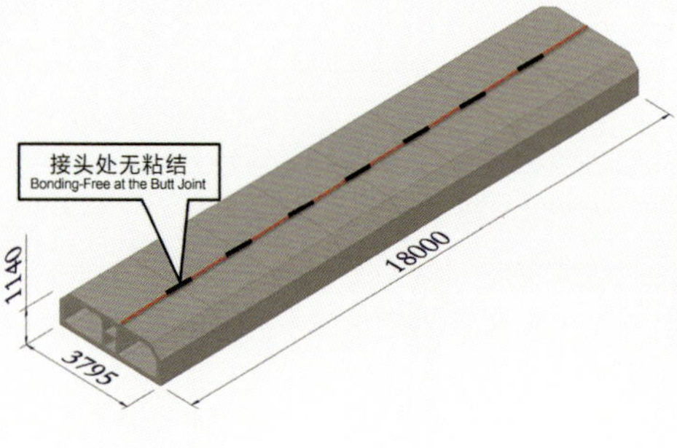

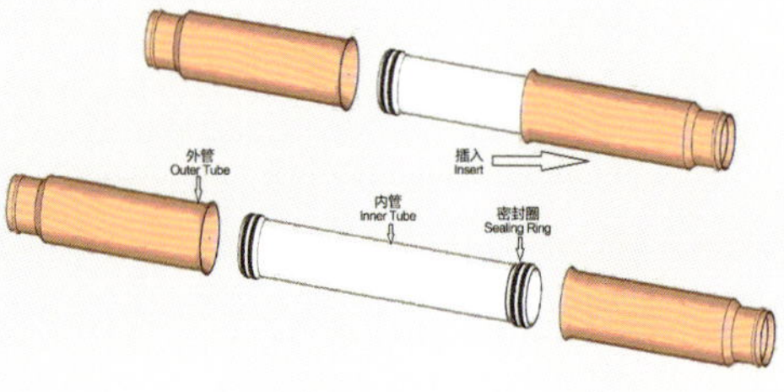

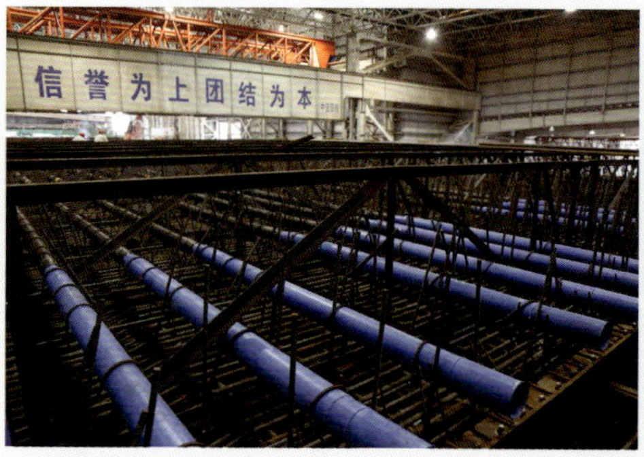

1. "半刚性"沉管预应力粘结方案示意图
Schematic Diagram of the Pre-stressing Bonding of the "Semi-Rigid" Immersed Tube

2. "半刚性"沉管预应力三件套
Three-piece Pre-stressing Set of the "Semi-Rigid" Immersed Tube

3. "半刚性"沉管预应力管
Pre-stress Duct of the "Semi-Rigid" Immersed Tube

4. 钢绞线穿束
Steel Stranded Wire Threading

5. 预应力张拉
Pre-stressing Tension

6. 预应力张拉完成
Pre-stressing Tensioning Completed

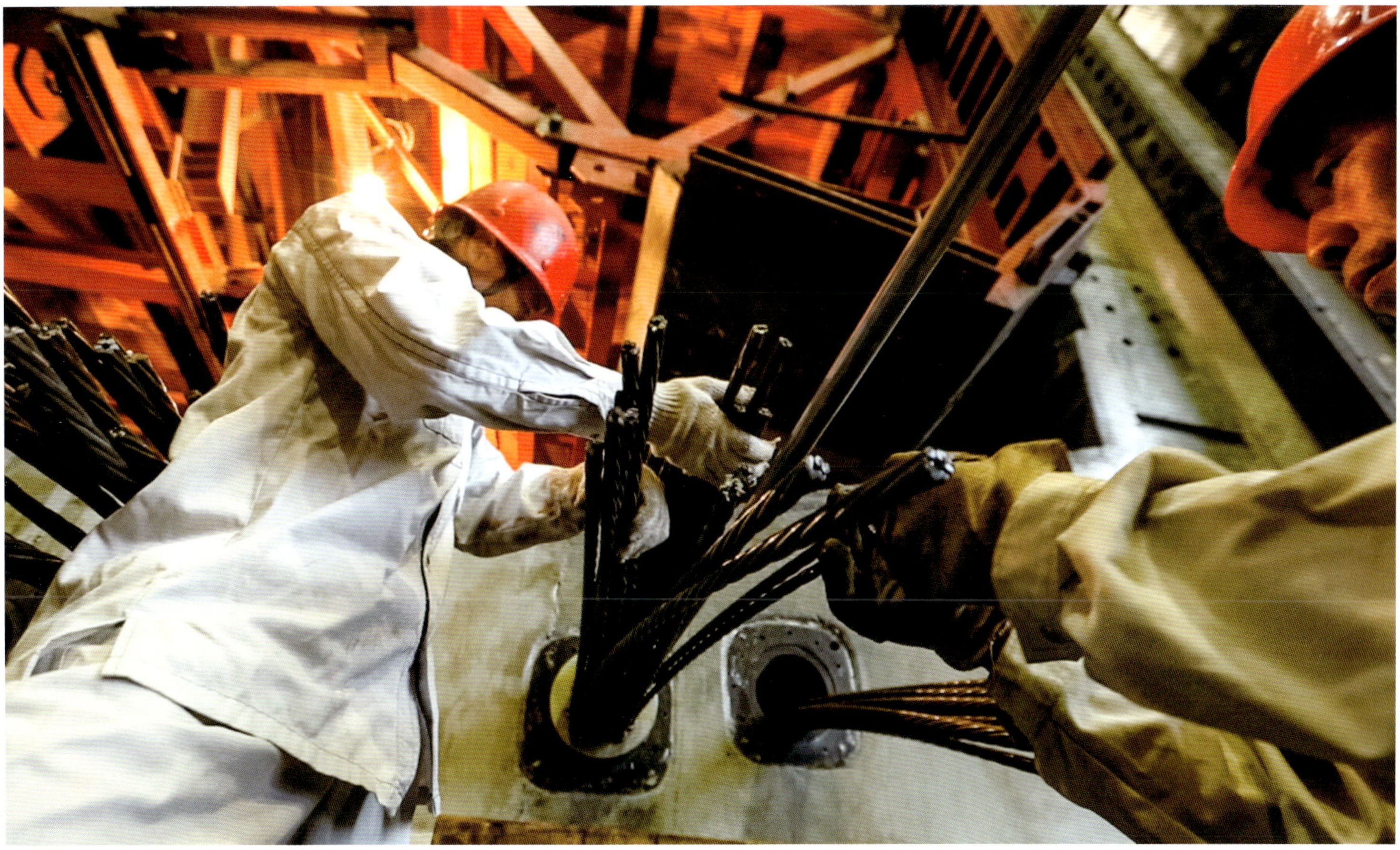

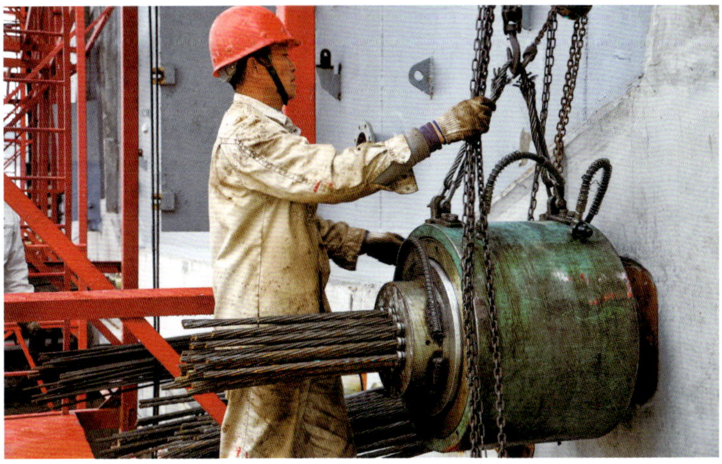

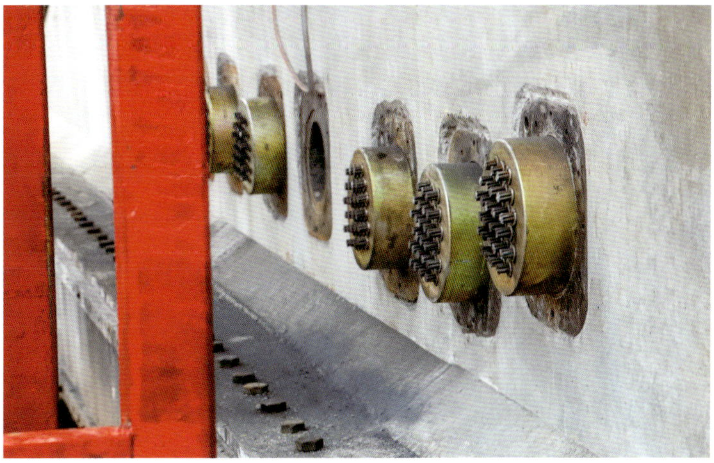

记忆支座
MEMORY SUPPORT

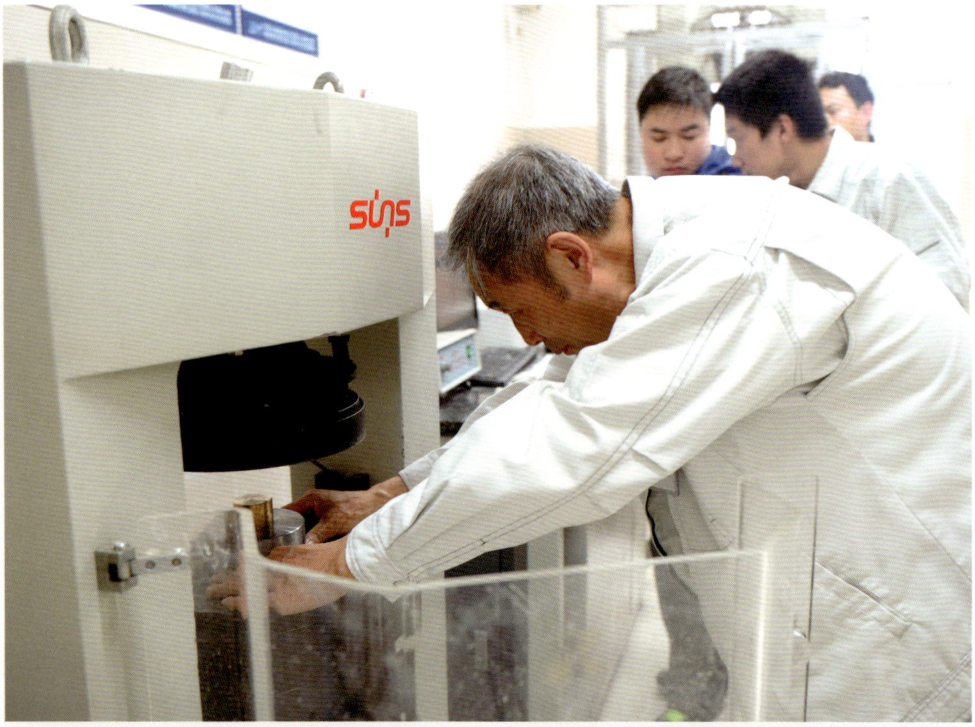

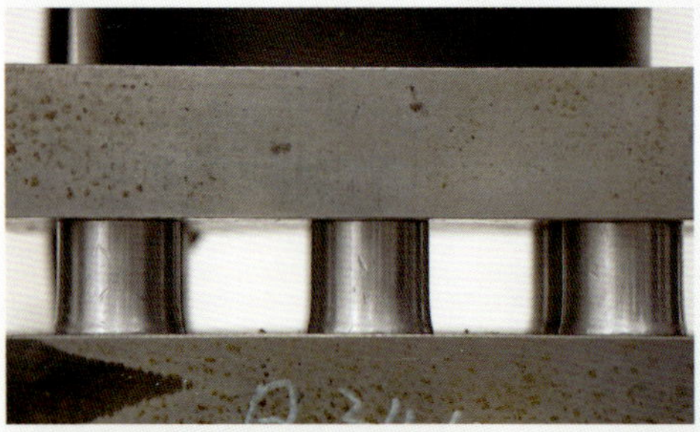

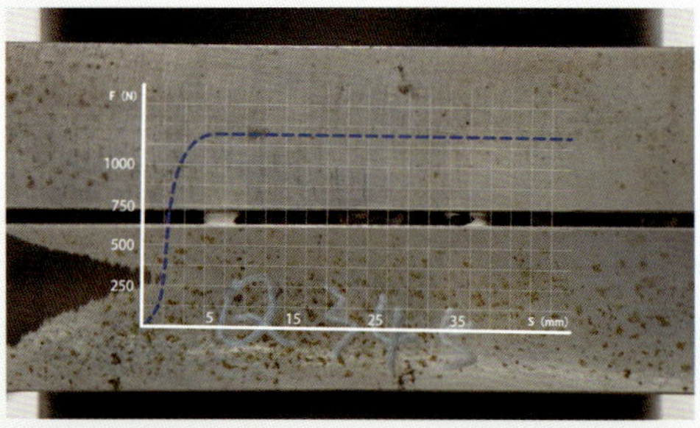

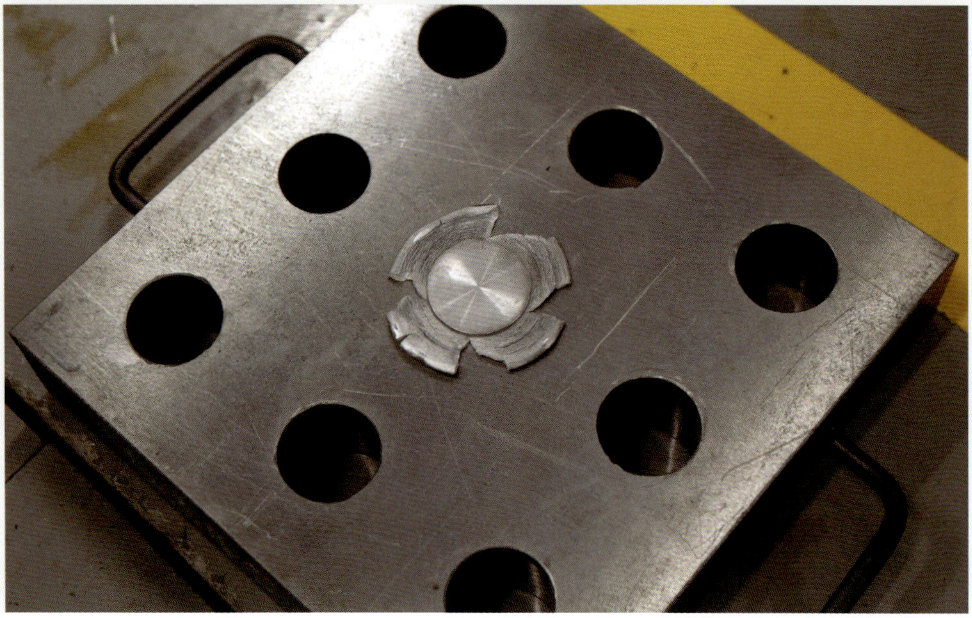

1. 记忆支座材料比选试验
Comparison and Selection Test for the Memory Support Material

2. 3. 记忆支座压力变化曲线图
Curve Diagram of the Pressure Variation on the Memory Support

4. 记忆支座材料比选试验合金块
Alloy Block in the Comparison and Selection Test for the Memory Support Material

5. 记忆支座结构图
Structural Diagram of the Memory Support

6. 记忆支座安装
Installation of the Memory Support

7. 记忆支座
Memory Support

8. 安装完成后的记忆支座
Well-Installed Memory Support

9. 记忆支座安装位置示意图
Schematic Diagram of the Installation Position of the Memory Support

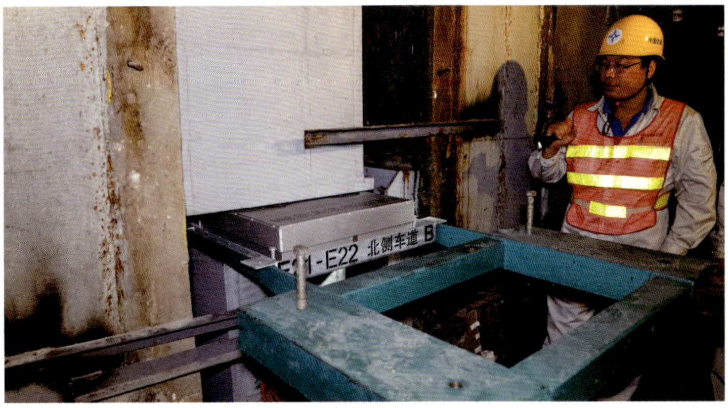

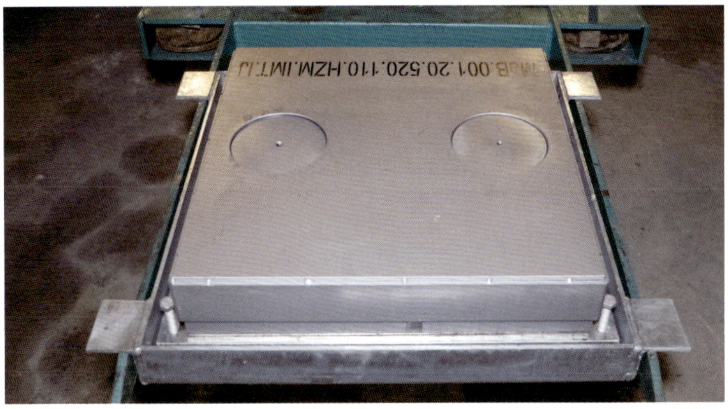

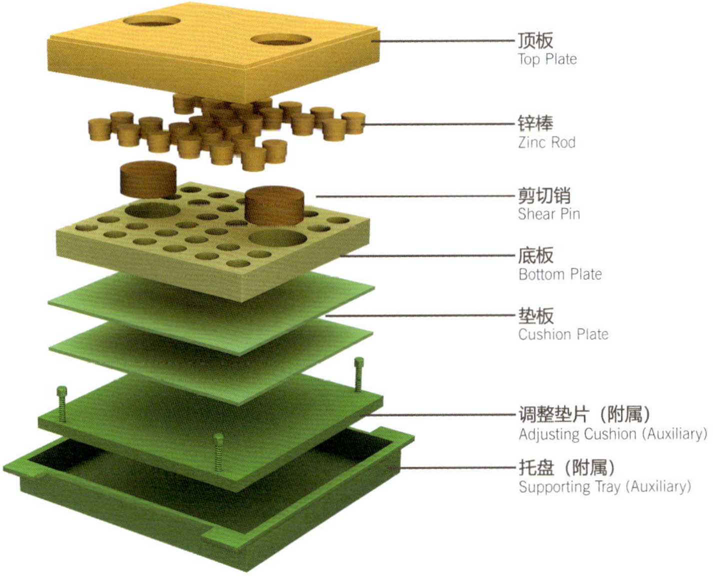

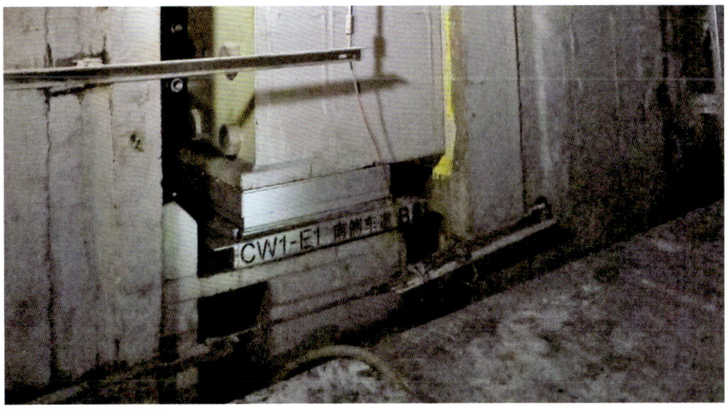

小尺寸模型试验
SMALL-SIZED MODEL TEST

足尺模型试验内容繁多，影响因素复杂，为提高对实际施工的指导作用，确保试验的可比性和可行性，在足尺模型试验之前还进行了数个小尺寸模型试验。

为充分考虑配筋及剪力键对混凝土浇筑质量的影响，检验混凝土的现场操作性能，并为混凝土坍落度的选择提供依据，按照沉管结构设计及配筋，从节段截面上选择可代表钢筋最密集区、剪力键区以及剪力键与节段结合部位开展了六次小尺寸模型试验。

通过小尺寸模型试验优选入围混凝土原材料，进行沉管混凝土配合比再优化及原材料适应性试验，验证配合比的可操作性，观察模型外观质量以及钢筋密布区、剪力键混凝土是否能够充分振捣密实；验证模型实体结构混凝土力学性能、耐久性能是否满足"工厂法"预制工艺要求；监测实体结构温度发展情况，为沉管温度应力仿真分析参数修正和调整以及沉管正式生产的温度参数控制指标、温控工艺确定提供依据。

The full-sized model tests are diversified and are subject to complicated factors. In order to provide useful guide for actual construction and to ensure the comparability and feasibility of the test, several small-sized model tests are conducted before the full-sized model test.

In order to fully grasp the influence of the auxiliary reinforcement and shear keys on the quality of concrete placement, to check the feasibility of the on-the-site performance of the concrete, and to provide references for the selection of concrete slump, by referring to the design of immersed tube structure and the auxiliary reinforcement, six small-sized model tests are conducted by casting models simulating relevant parts of the cross section of the segments, including the part where the steel reinforcement is most densely embedded, the shear keys area, and the joint of the shear keys and the tube segments.

By small-sized model tests, the best concrete materials are chosen; the concrete mix ratio for the immersed tube is re-optimized and the adaptability of raw materials is tested to verify the feasibility of the tested mix ratio; the outward quality of the model, and whether the concrete in steel intensive part and shear key part can be fully vibrated and compacted are also tested; whether the mechanical properties and durability of the concrete in the physical structure of the model and durability of the concrete of the models meet the requirements of the technique of "factory manufacturing" is tested; the temperature variation of the physical structure of the models is monitored to provide data for the correction and adjustment of the simulation analysis parameters for the immersed tube's temperature stress, as well as for the choice of the temperature parameter control indexes and temperature control methods proper for the formal production of the immersed tube.

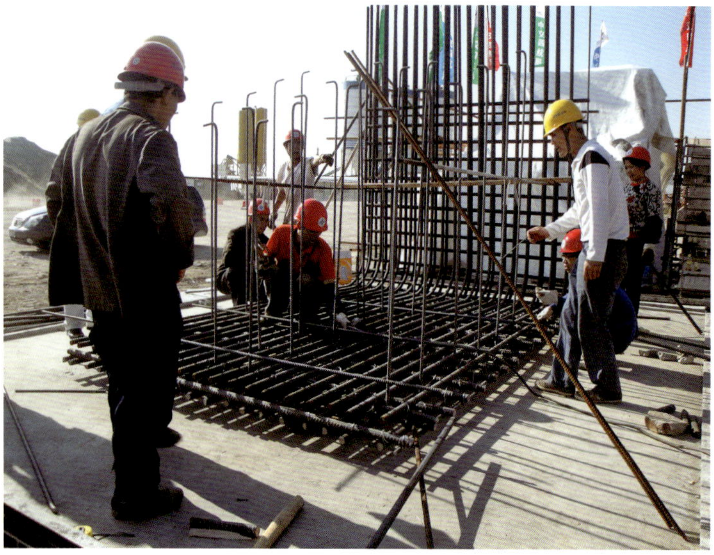

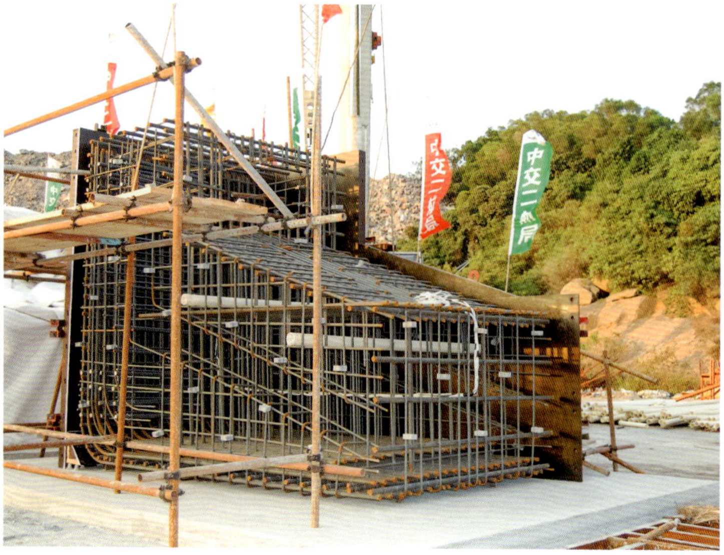

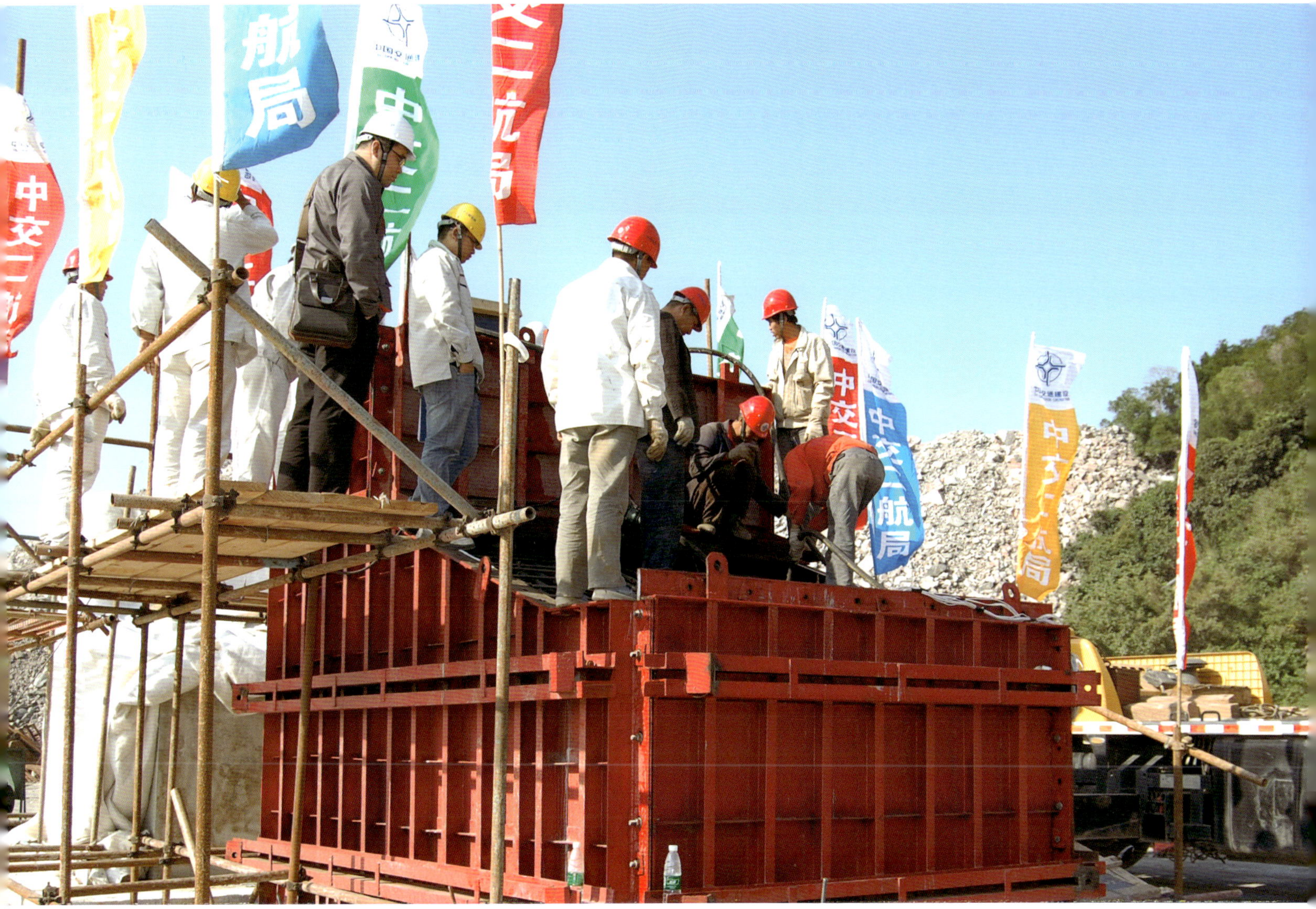

1. 小足尺模型钢筋绑扎
Steel Reinforcement Binding of the Small Full-Sized Model
2. 小足尺模型钢筋笼
Steel Reinforcement Cage of the Small Full-Sized Model
3. 小足尺模型浇筑
Casting of the Small Full-Sized Model

足尺模型试验

FULL-SIZED MODEL TEST

在正式预制之前，材料的选用、配合比设计、工艺的选择、设计的合理性需要通过大量的室内和室外试验进行验证。

模型构造设计：足尺模型按全断面进行预制，共浇筑两个小节段，纵向长度均为5.8米。两节段间设置节段接头，其中一节段外端头设置管节接头。

钢筋布置：两个小节段模型，一节按照浅埋区间进行钢筋布置，另一节按照深埋区间进行钢筋布置。

预留孔洞布置：主要验证排烟口、逃生门及消火栓三类预留洞室钢筋安装及混凝土浇筑工艺。

预埋件布置：沉管预埋件种类较多，布置较复杂。其中节段接头预埋件包括混凝土剪力键、中埋止水带预埋件、OMEGA止水带预埋件；管节接头预埋件包括预埋钢板、螺栓、端钢壳；舾装件包括端封门、压舱水箱、吊点、系缆柱、拉合支座。

临时预应力试验包括预应力张拉实验、预应力剪断试验。

Before formal prefabrication, the material selection, mix ratio, processing crafts and the rationality of the design need to be tested through a large number of indoor and outdoor experiments.

Model Construction and Design: The full-sized model is precast by the gross section, and two segments are cast with a longitudinal length of 5.8 meters each. A joint is placed between the two segments, and a joint is set at the outer end of one segment.

Steel Reinforcement Arrangement: For two model segments, in one the steel bars are arranged for shallow burial while the other for deep burial.

Layout of Reserved Holes: This is mainly to test the reinforcement installation and concrete placement crafts in three types of reserved cavities for smoke outlet, emergency exit and fire hydrant.

Layout of Embedded Items: There are many kinds of items needing to be embedded in the immersed tubes, so how to arrange these embedded items is a very complicate operation. The embedded items in the joint part of the segments include the concrete shear keys, internal embedded water-stop and OMEGA water-stop. The embedded items in the joint part of the tubes include embedded steel plates, bolts and steel end shells. Outfitting items include end sealing devices, ballast water tanks, hoist points, bollards and pull-in pedestals.

The temporary pre-stressing test includes pre-stressing tension test and pre-stressing shear test.

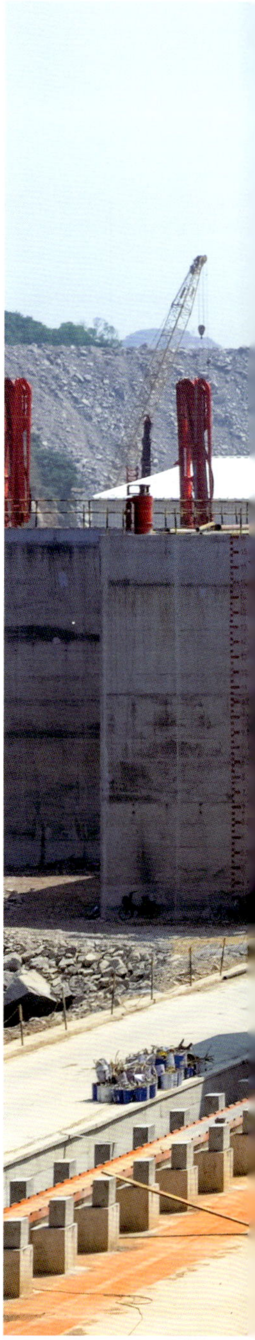

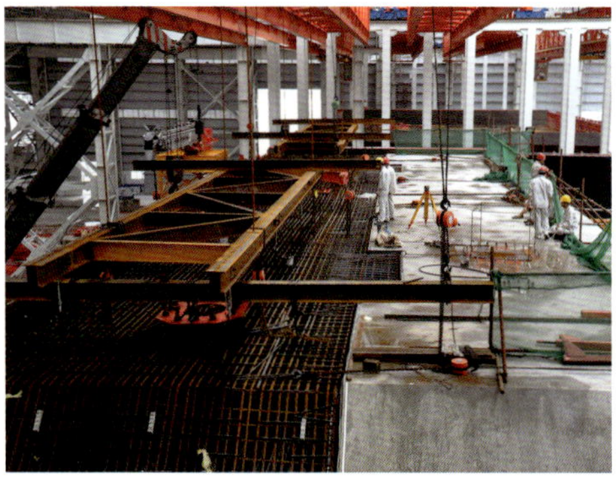

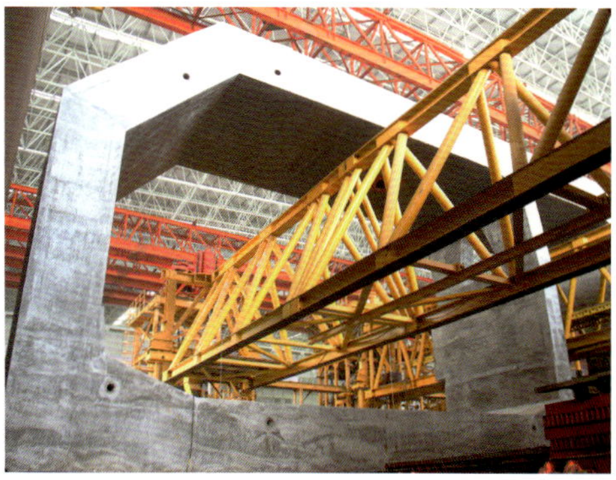

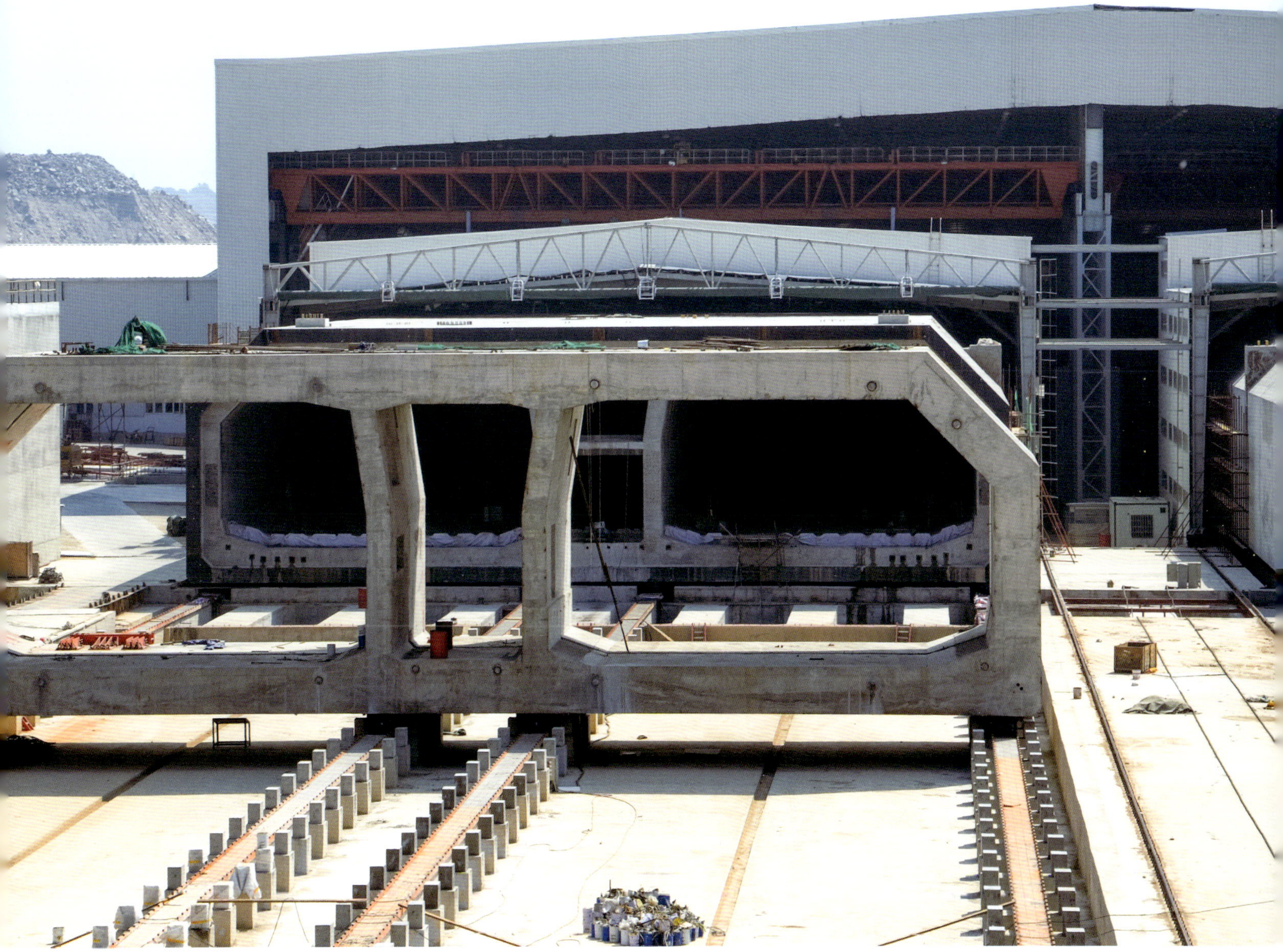

1. 足尺模型 S2 段浇筑
Casting of Section S2 of the Full-Sized Model

2. 浇注出模的足尺模型 S1 段
Well-Cast Section S1 of the Full-Sized Model

3. 足尺模型试验段顶推
Pushing of the Testing Section of the Full-Sized Model

皮带输送与泵压输送均是大型、高效并且广泛应用的混凝土浇筑输送方式，各有优缺点，适用于不同的施工条件。根据预制工厂场地条件以及功效方面的要求，选择合适的混凝土运输浇筑工艺，是沉管混凝土全断面浇筑必须解决的关键技术问题。

足尺模型按沉管标准节段的全断面尺寸预制，高 11.4 米、宽 37.95 米、长 5.8 米，分为 E0-S1、E0-S2 两节足尺模型。E0-S1 段试验采用皮带机输送、布料进行混凝土浇筑，E0-S2 段试验采用搅拌运输车 + 地泵方式联合输送、布料进行混凝土浇筑。

项目总经理部通过两次足尺模型试验，对材料、设备、施工工艺、功效等进行验证，对比皮带输送与泵压输送工艺的实际应用情况，确定采用泵送工艺进行沉管全断面浇筑。

Both belt conveying and pump conveying are powerful, efficient and widely used methods of concrete conveyance and casting. They each have their own advantages and disadvantages and are suitable for different construction conditions. According to the site conditions of the precast factory and the requirements for efficiency, appropriate concrete conveying and casting methods are chosen, which is the key technical problem that must be solved for the gross section casting of the immersed tube.

The full-sized model is prefabricated according to the size of the gross section of the standard immersed tube segments, 11.4 meters tall, 37.95 meters wide and 5.8 meters long, and two full-sized models of E0-S1 and E0-S2 are made. The cast of the E0-S1 section employs the belt conveyor to send and arrange the concrete, while the E0-S2 section is cast by using "mixing truck + ground pump" to send and arrange the concrete.

The project management center used two full-sized model tests to test the materials, equipment, construction technology and efficiency, made comparison between belt conveying and pumping conveying about their efficiency, and finally decided to adopt the pumping technology for the gross section casting of the immersed tube.

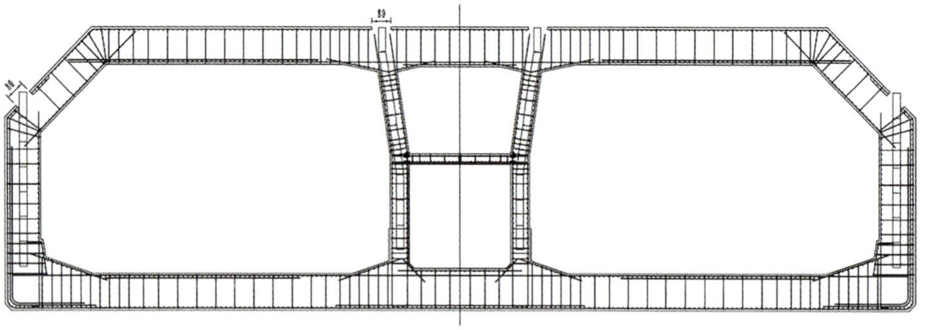

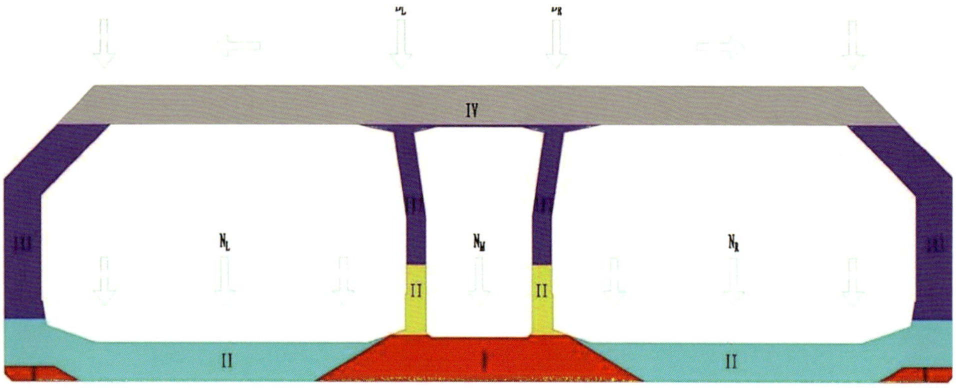

1. 足尺模型浇筑顺序示意图
Schematic Diagram of the Casting Sequence of the Full-Sized Model
2. 足尺模型 S1 段混凝土浇筑
Concrete Placement of Section S1 of the Full-Sized Model
3. 浇筑成型的足尺模型
Well-Cast Full-Sized Model

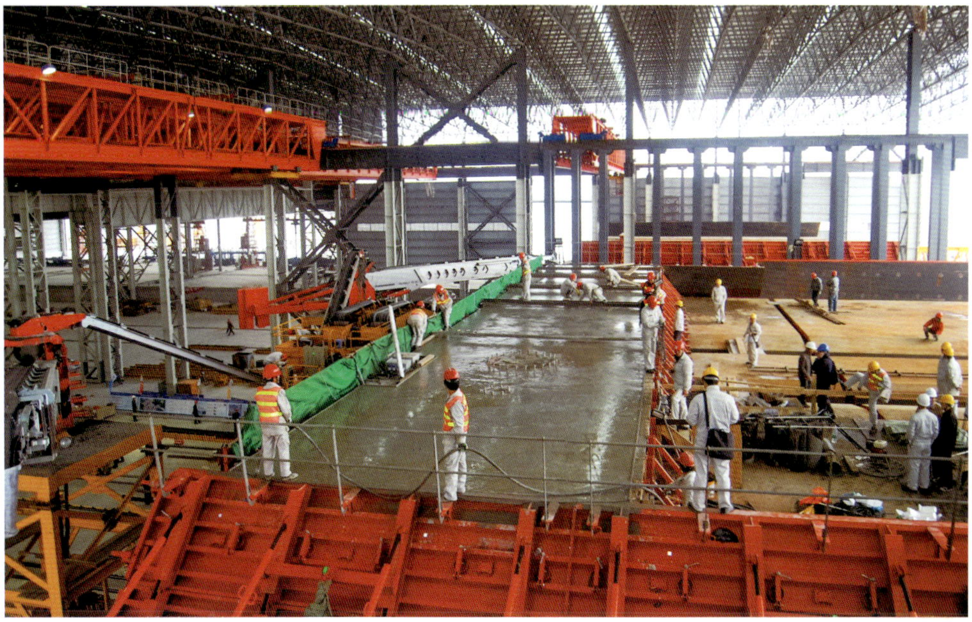

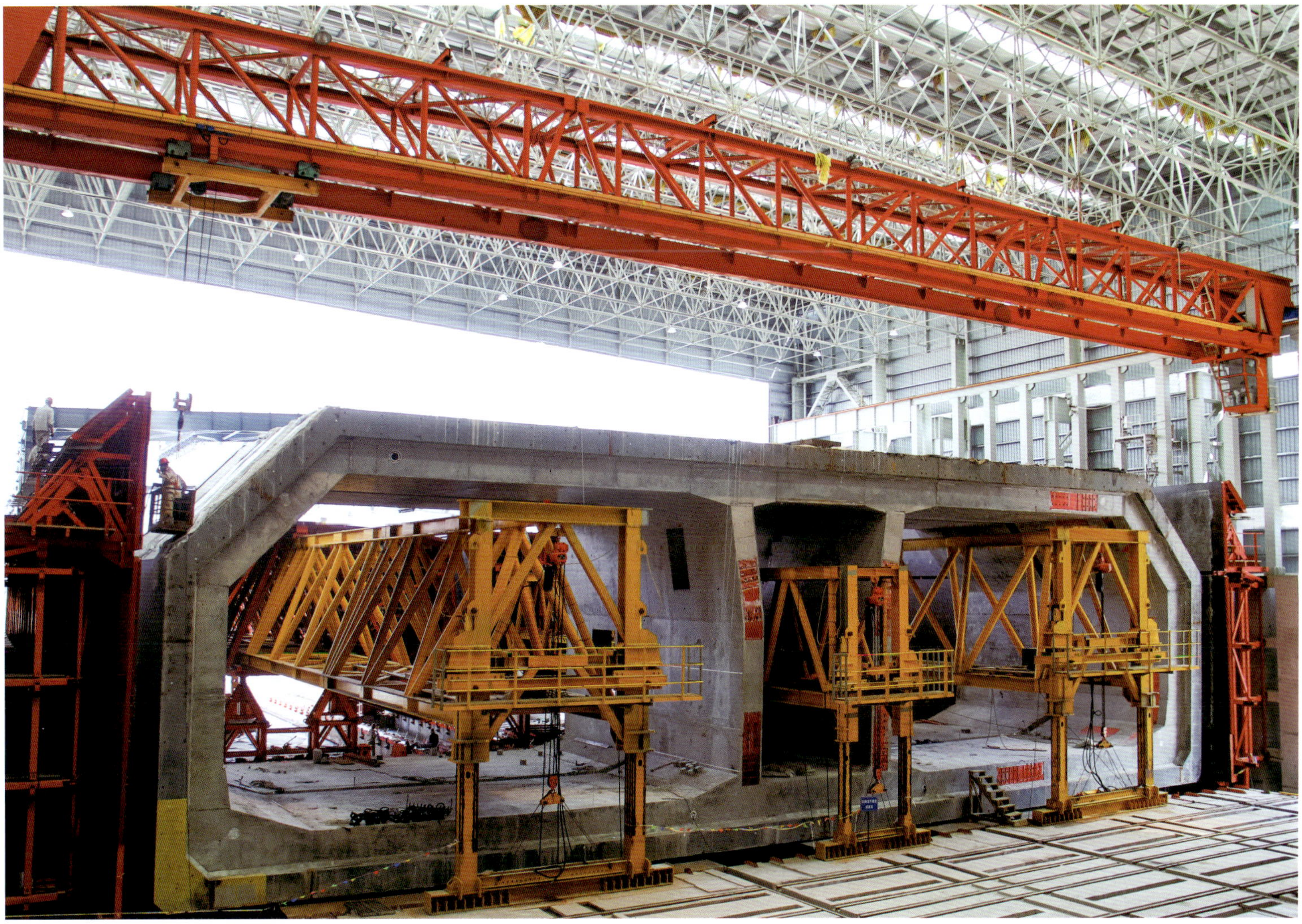

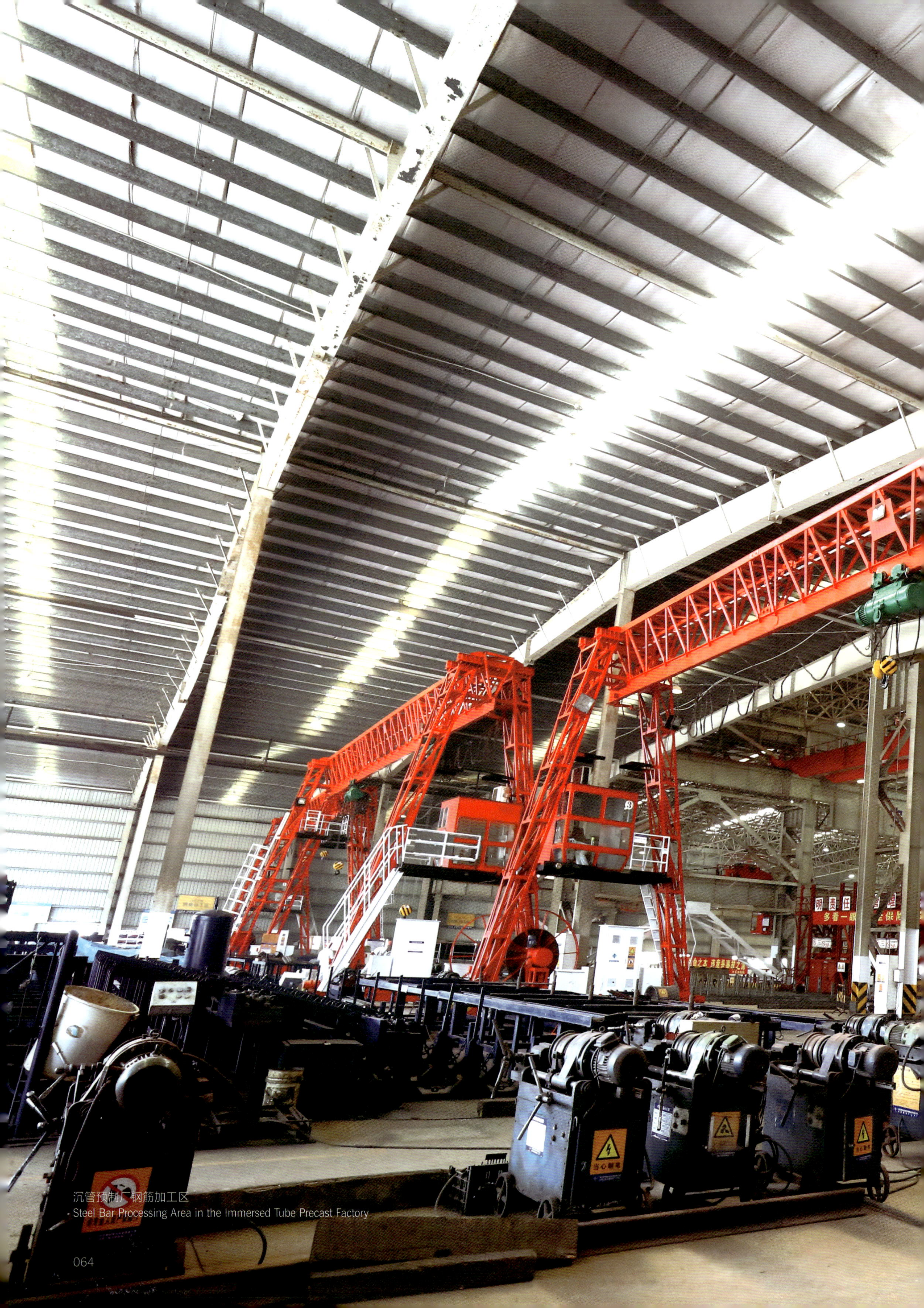

沉管预制厂钢筋加工区
Steel Bar Processing Area in the Immersed Tube Precast Factory

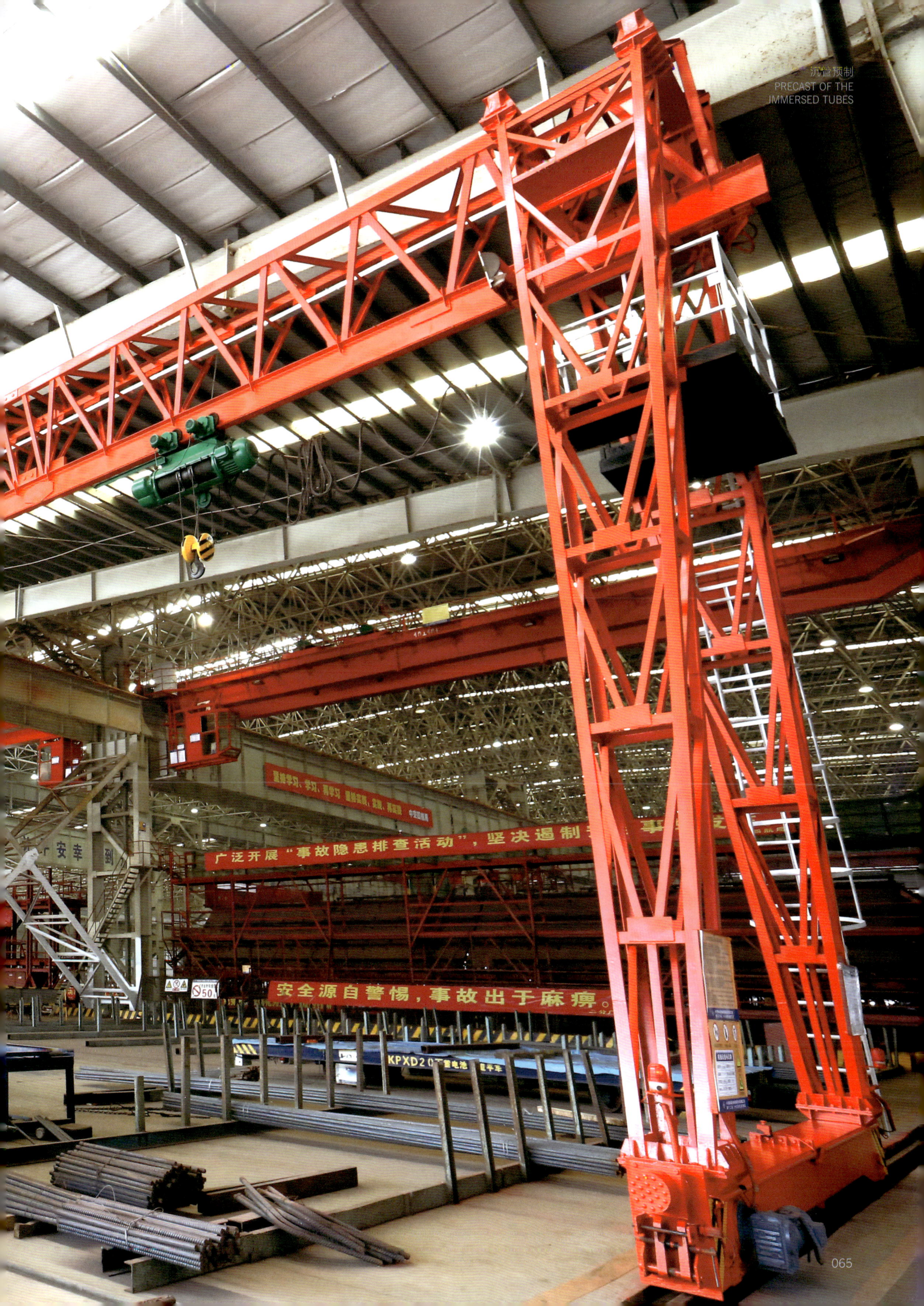
广泛开展“事故隐患排查活动”，坚决遏制
安全源自警惕，事故出于麻痹。
50

钢筋加工

STEEL REINFORCEMENT

每条生产线上设置3个钢筋绑扎区（即底板钢筋绑扎区、墙体钢筋绑扎区和顶板钢筋绑扎区）和4套钢筋绑扎胎架（每个钢筋绑扎区设置一套钢筋支撑胎架，另一套周转）。当底板钢筋完成后，移至墙体区绑，然后移至顶板区完成整个钢筋笼绑扎，形成流水生产线工厂化施工。

为满足沉管预制进度要求（生产高峰期7~8天/节段），按照节段钢筋用量1100吨计算，钢筋日加工能力需达到150吨/天以上。同时，为保证沉管120年使用寿命，断面钢筋形成精准闭合是混凝土保护层达标的关键，钢筋加工精度至关重要。

经足尺模型试验验证，购置普通钢筋加工设备，采用传统加工方法，钢筋加工精度、工效已无法满足要求。

通过广泛调研，沉管预制厂采用进口数控剪切、弯曲设备结合国产锯切、套丝设备和物料流水线，建成自动化、高精度、高效率的钢筋加工生产流水线。

每条钢筋生产线由原材料待检区、合格材料堆存区、钢筋加工区、半成品堆存区等四个区域组成，其中半成品堆存区与绑扎区域对应划分成底板、墙体、顶板三个区域。场内钢筋转运采用输送辊道或平移台车配合龙门吊进行转运，充分体现流水化和机械化的施工特点。

Each production line is equipped with 3 steel binding areas (namely the bottom plate binding area, the partition wall binding area and the top plate binding area) and 4 sets of steel binding jig frames (one set of jig frames are allocated for each steel binding area, with a surplus set waiting for emergency use). After the steel binding of the bottom plate is finished, the steel cage is moved to the partition wall binding area and then to the top plate binding area where the whole steel reinforcement cage is completed. This is the standard assembly line for the factory manufacturing of the immersed tube.

In order to follow the designed schedule for the fabrication of the immersed tubes (7~8 days per segment at the top speed of production), the daily processing capacity of steel bars should be more than 150 tons per day if calculated by the standard of 1,100 tons of steel bars for each segment. At the same time, in order to ensure the immersed tube's designed life span of 120 years, the critical point for the protective layer of the concrete to meet the standard is the accurate closure of the cross-section steel reinforcement, so that the accuracy of processing the steel reinforcement cage becomes very important.

Based on the results from the full-sized model tests, ordinary steel bar processing equipment and traditional processing methods can't satisfy the requirements for the accuracy and efficiency of steel bar processing.

Based on extensive investigation, the immersed tube precast factory built an automatic, high-precision and high-efficiency steel bar processing production line by using imported numerical-controlled cutting and bending equipment together with domestic sawing, threading equipment and domestic assembly lines for raw material processing.

Each steel bar processing line is composed of four areas: the raw material inspection area, qualified material storage area, steel bar processing area and semi-finished product stockpiling area. The semi-finished product stockpiling area matches the binding area and is correspondingly divided into three sub-areas for bottom plates, partition wall and top plates. The steel bars inside the factory yard are transported with the conveying rollers or translation trolleys together with gantry crane, which features the streamlined and mechanized construction.

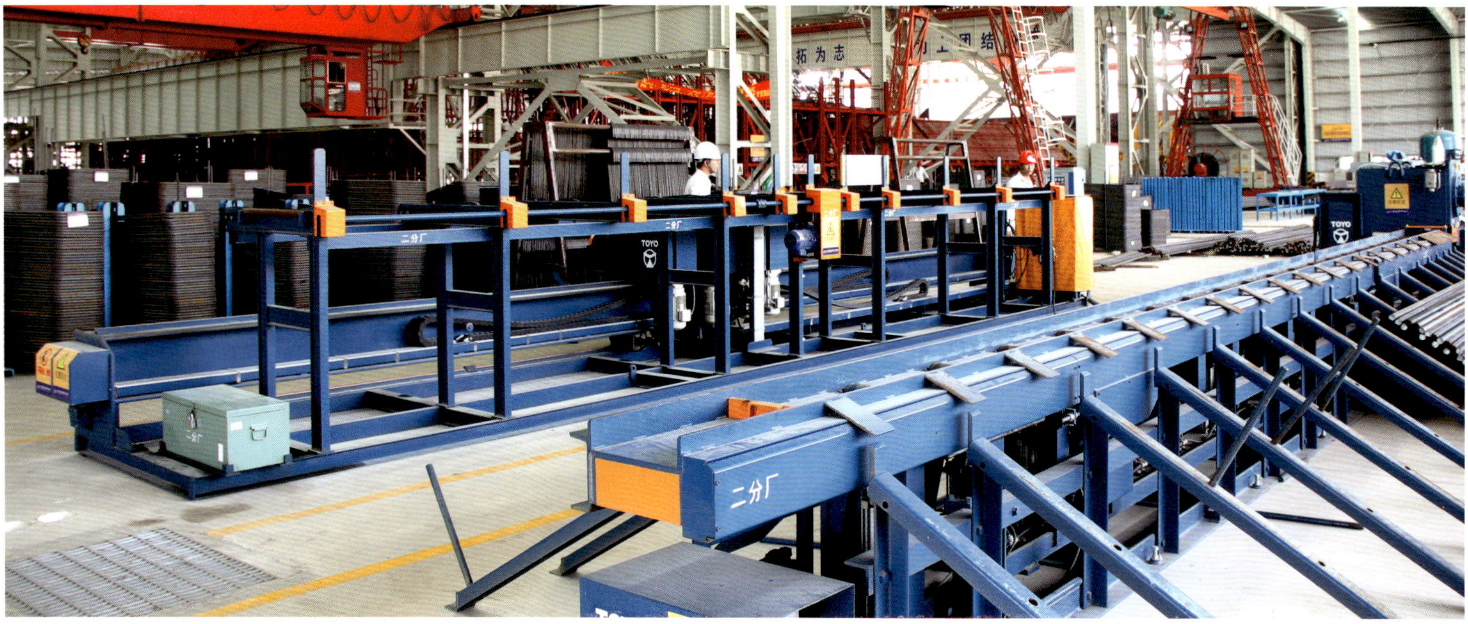

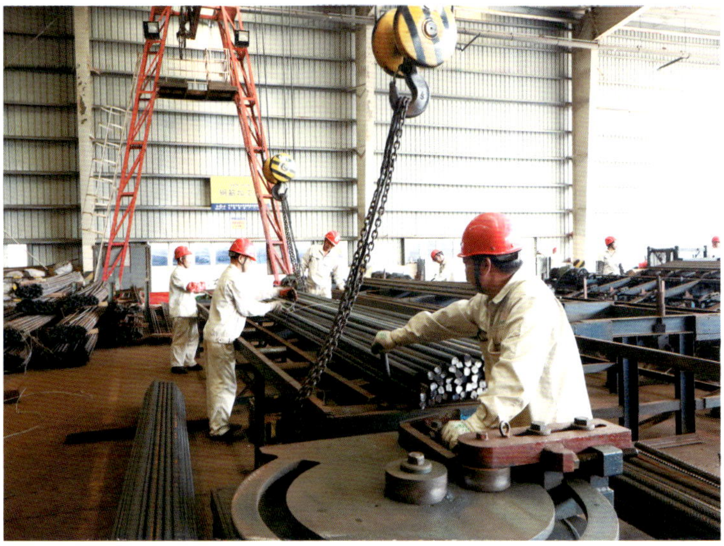

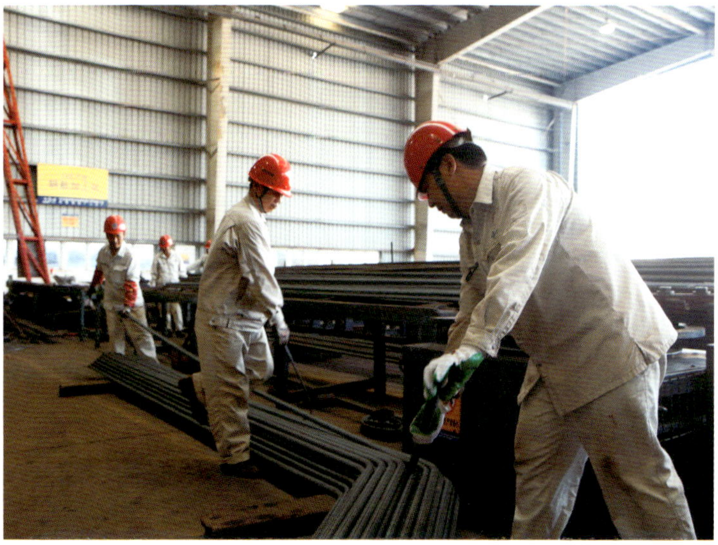

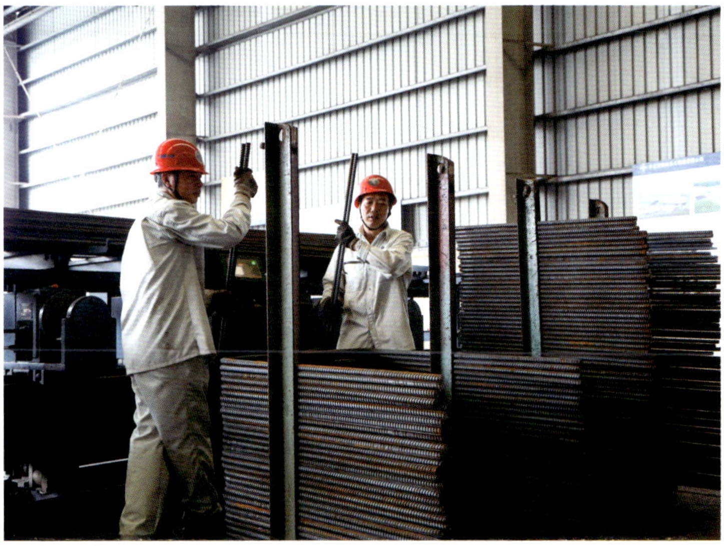

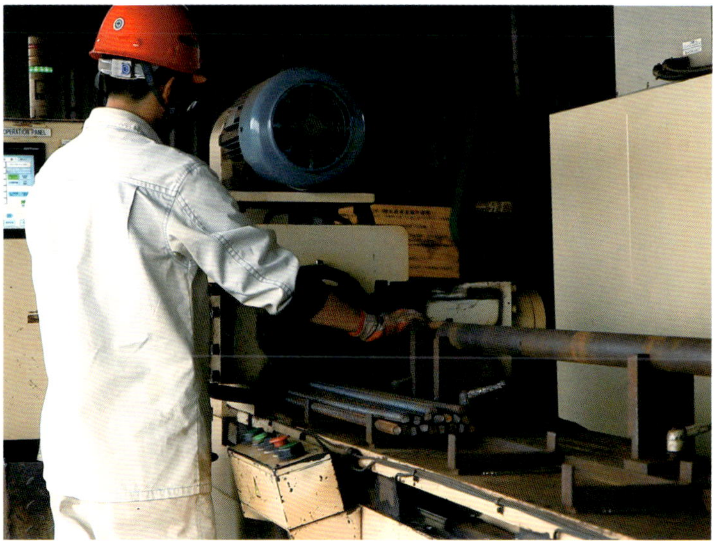

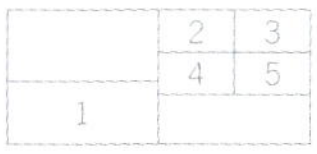

1. 钢筋加工设备
Steel Bar Processing Equipment

2. 钢筋转运
Steel Bar Transition

3. 钢筋弯曲
Steel Bar Bending

4. 架立筋加工
Supporting Steel Bar Processing

5. T 型拉勾筋加工
T-Type Steel Hoop Bar Processing

钢筋笼绑扎

STEEL REINFORCEMENT CAGE BINDING

钢筋笼分底板绑扎、墙体绑扎、顶板绑扎三步，分别在对应绑扎区进行绑扎，并根据需要分别设置顶板钢筋绑扎架、墙体钢筋绑扎架（包括中墙背架）、顶板钢筋绑扎架（包括顶板内胎架）。

钢筋笼在底板绑扎区完成底板绑扎后顶推至墙体绑扎区进行墙体绑扎，墙体钢筋绑扎完成后顶推至顶板钢筋绑扎，上一个钢筋笼顶推出去后立即在对应区域进行下一个节段钢筋笼绑扎，形成流水线绑扎作业。

The steel reinforcement cage binding consists of three steps: bottom plate binding, partition wall binding and top plate binding, all done in corresponding binding areas. If necessary, bottom plate binding jig frame, partition wall binding jig frame, and top plate binding jig frame are constructed.

After the bottom plate binding of the steel cage is finished at bottom plate binding area, it is pushed to the partition wall binding area for the partition wall binding, and then it is pushed to the top plate binding area for the top plate binding. After the steel cage fully bound is pushed out of the binding area, the binding of the new steel cage begins. This is the production line of the steel cage binding.

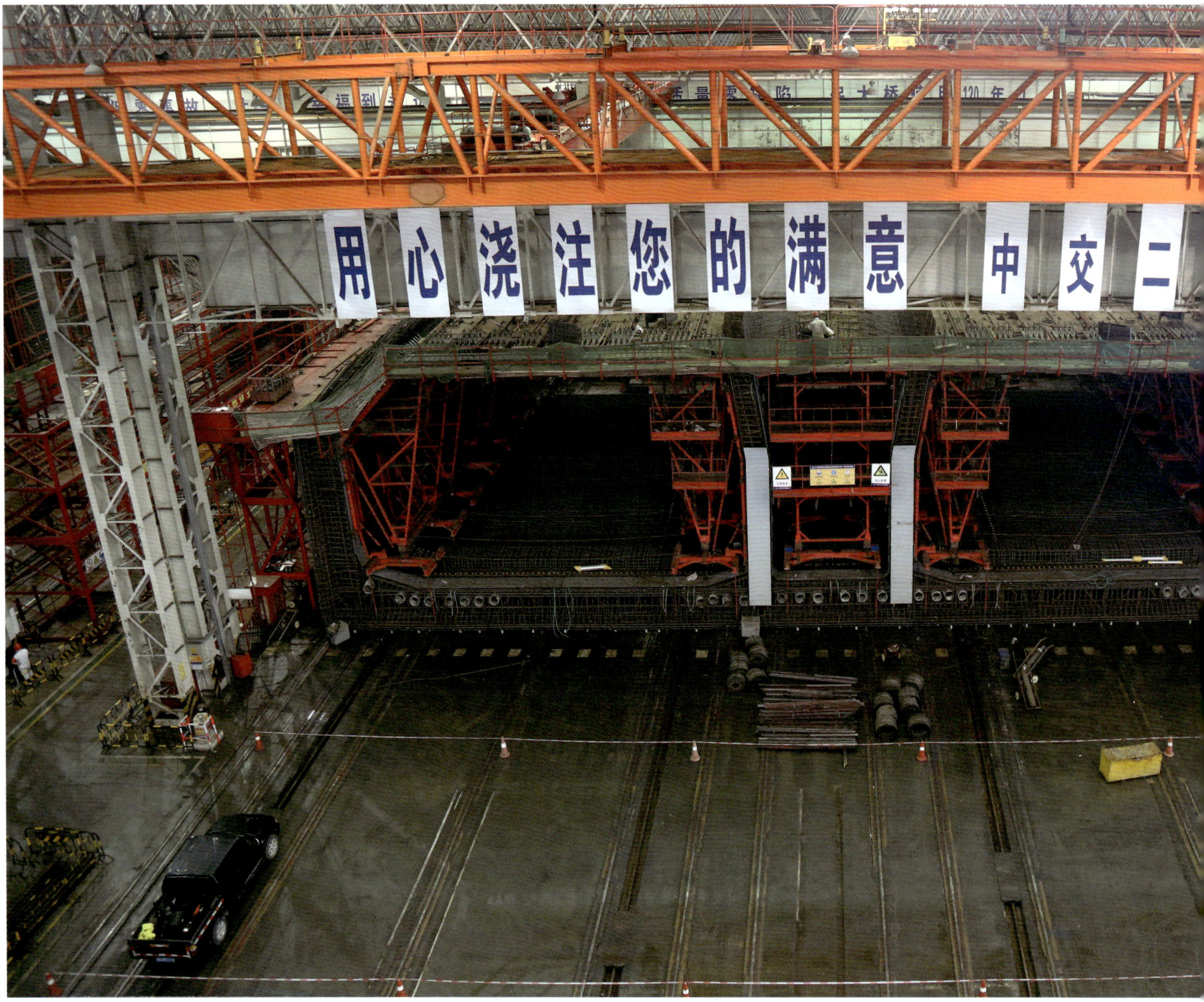

1. 顶板钢筋绑扎
Top Plate Steel Binding
2. 侧墙钢筋绑扎作业
Side Wall Steel Binding
3. 顶板倒角钢筋绑扎
Top Plate Chamfer Steel Binding

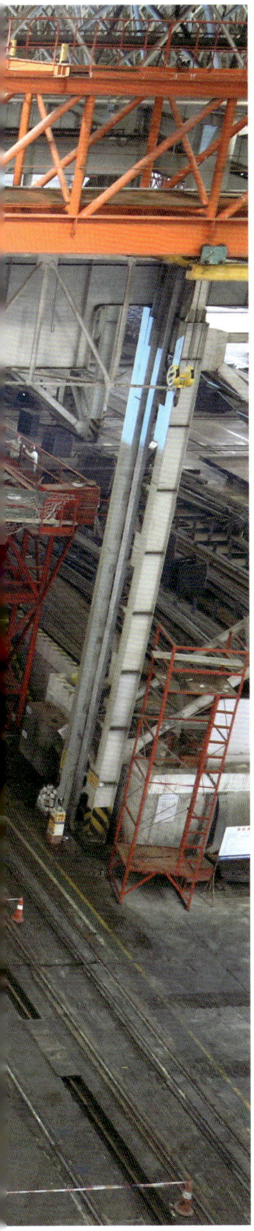

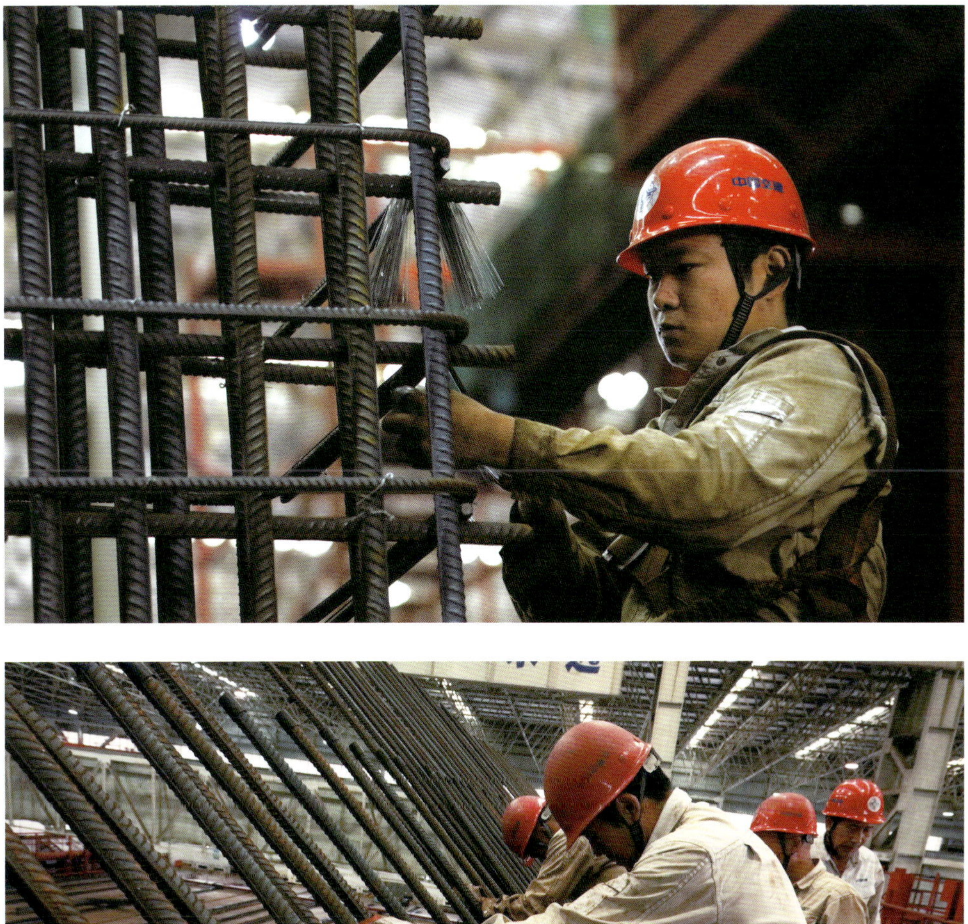

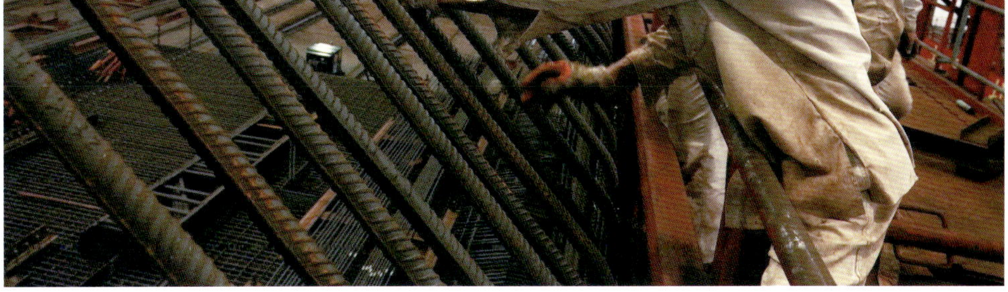

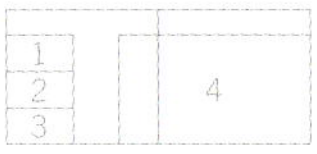

1. 底板首层钢筋铺设
Top Layer Steel Binding on the Bottom Plate
2. 底板架立筋安装
Supporting Steel Bar Installation on the Bottom Plate
3. 底板上层钢筋绑扎
Upper Layer Steel Binding on the Bottom Plate
4. 绑扎成型的底板钢筋笼
Bottom Plate Steel Reinforcement Cage Binding Completed

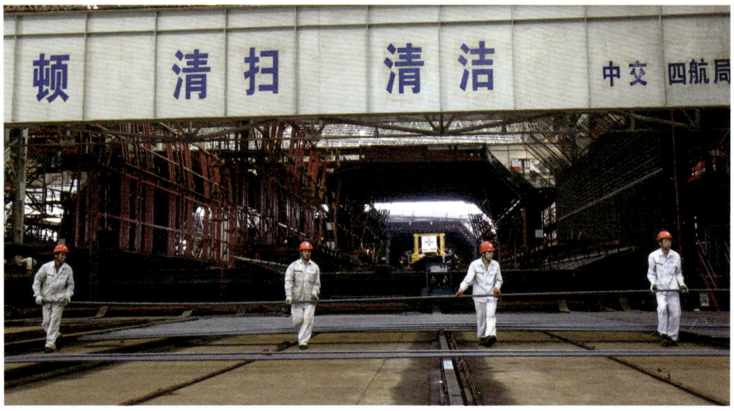

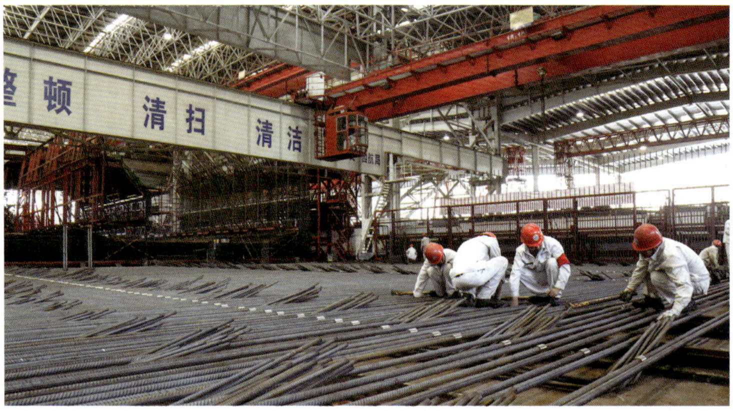

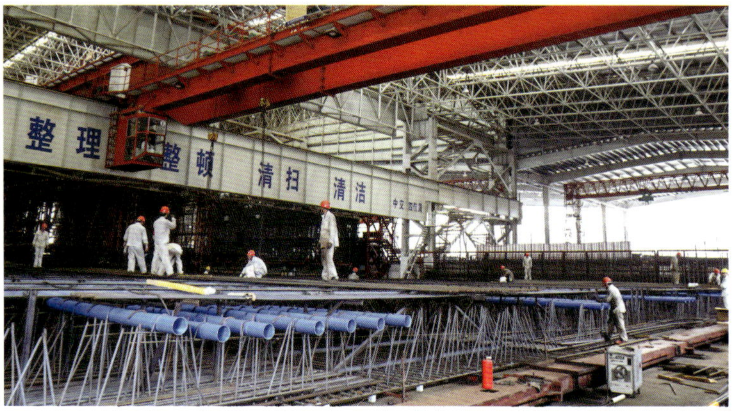

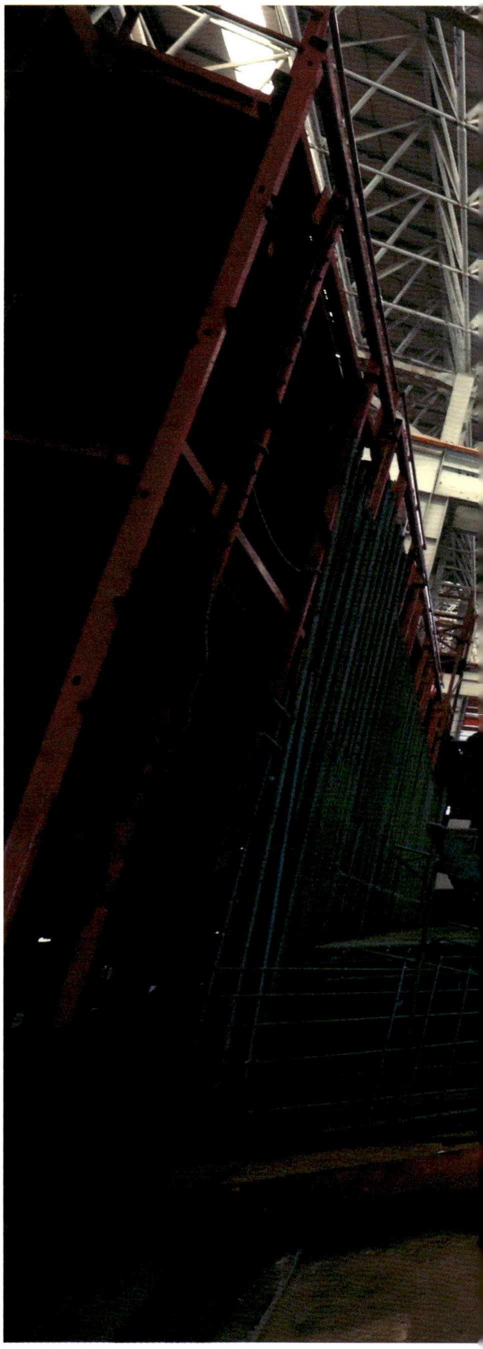

底板钢筋笼绑扎： 底板钢筋绑扎胎架由14条滑移轨道及侧面绑扎胎架组成。轨道及绑扎胎架设钢筋限位板，控制主筋钢筋绑扎间距。侧绑扎架可以进行水平横向调整。

Bottom Plate Steel Reinforcement Cage Binding: The jig frame for the bottom plate binding consists of 14 sliding tracks and a side binding jig frame. The tracks and the side binding jig frame are equipped with steel spacing boards to control the spacing of main steel binding. The side binding jig frame can be horizontally adjusted.

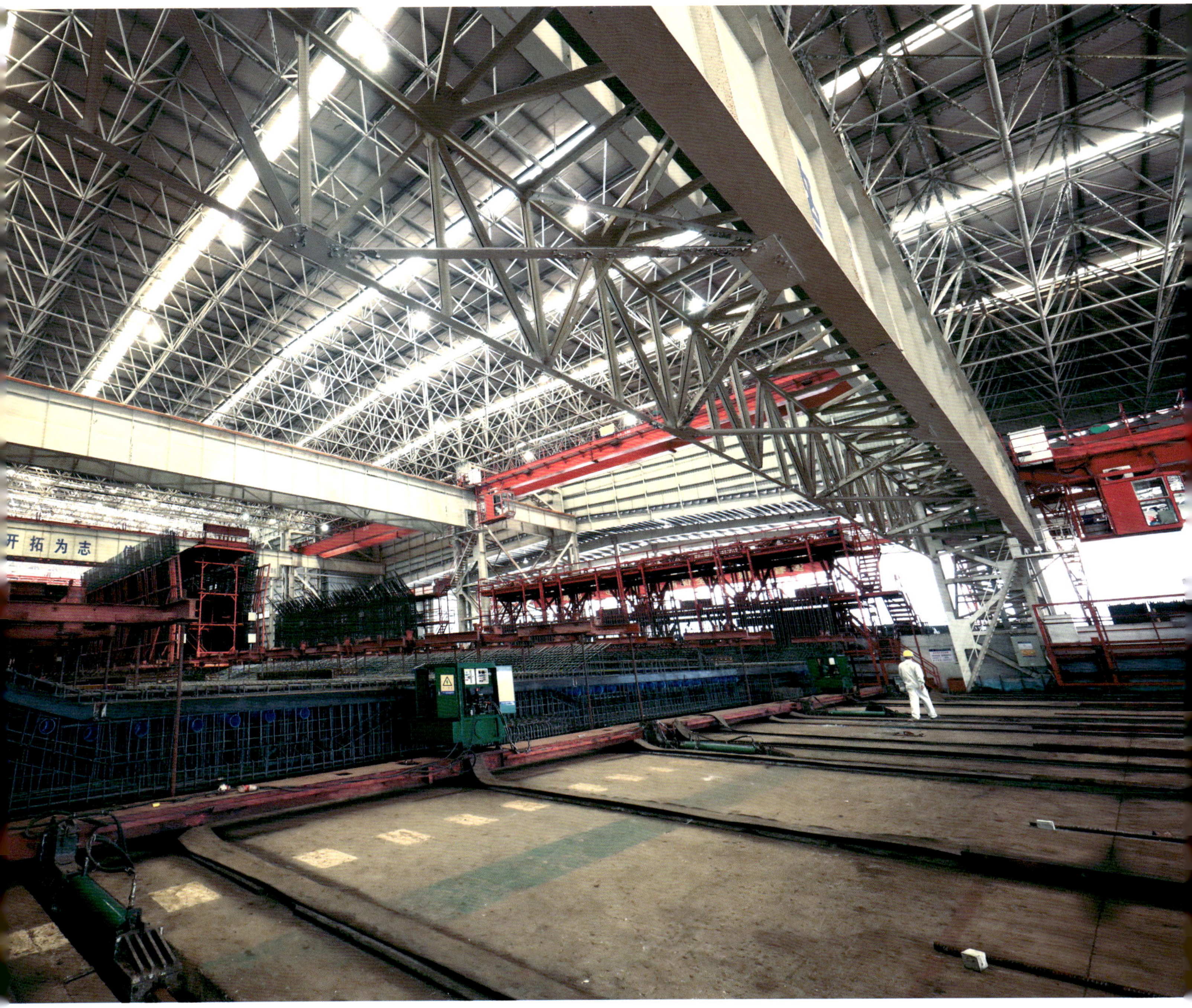

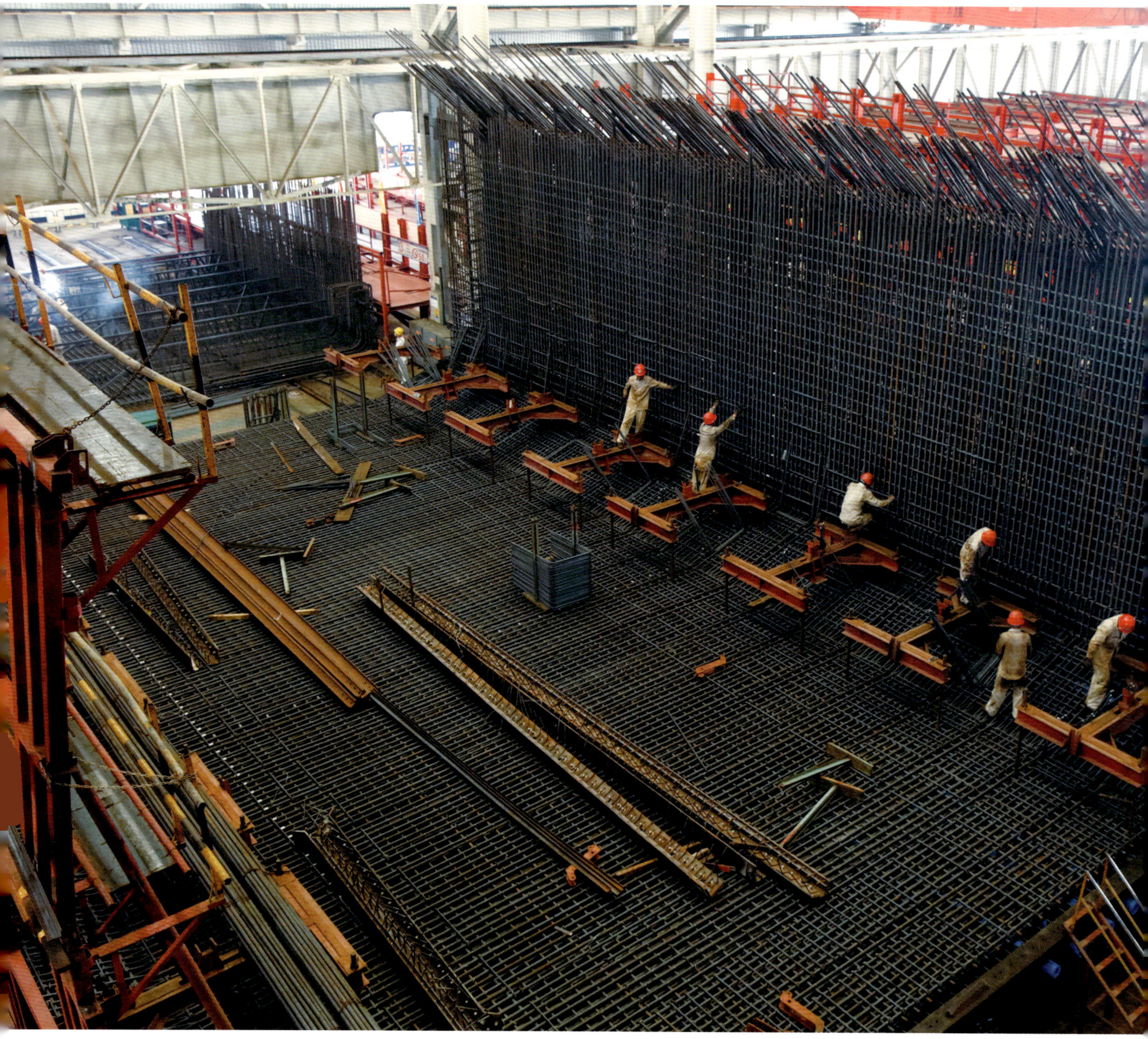

1. 侧墙钢筋绑扎
Side Wall Steel Binding

2. 侧墙架立筋安装
Supporting Steel Bar Installation on the Side Wall

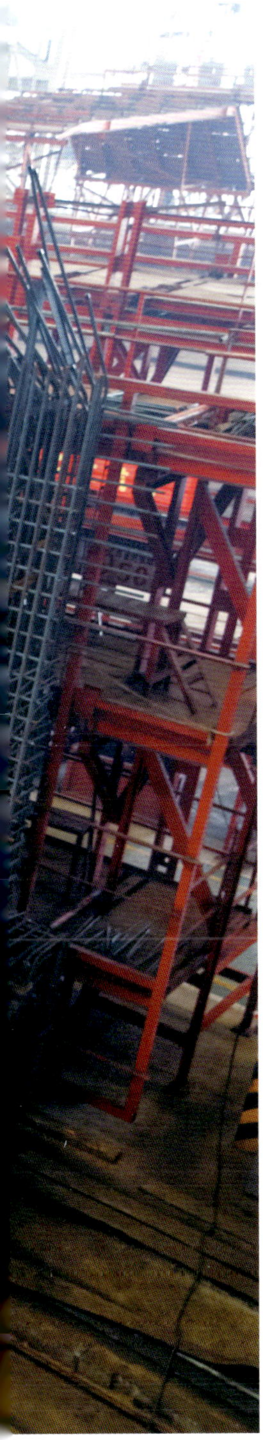

墙体钢筋笼绑扎：墙体钢筋安装胎架由侧面绑扎架和内墙可拆卸式胎架组成。侧墙内侧及中墙钢筋安装采用可快速安拆活动胎架，主要由胎架底座、固定及调节螺杆、贝雷架、操作平台和其他连接构件组成。底座结构由撑杆固定于滑移轨道上，通过调节螺杆和撑杆进行高度和角度调整。

侧墙钢筋绑扎胎架也通过调节螺杆进行侧墙绑扎胎架的边线调整。外墙绑扎架可以进行水平方向调整（-650~+400毫米）。内侧墙钢筋绑扎前，需进行可拆卸式绑扎胎架安装，并固定调整螺杆及工作平台。

Partition Wall Steel Reinforcement Cage Binding: The jig frame system for the partition wall steel reinforcement binding is composed of a side binding jig frame and a removable jig frame for the inner wall. The steel binding for the internal side of the side wall and the inner wall makes use of a movable jig frame which can be quickly installed and uninstalled. The movable jig frame is mainly composed of a jig base, fixing and adjusting bolts, the bailey truss, the operation platform and other connecting components. The base structure is fixed on the sliding track by struts, and the height and angle of the base structure are adjusted by adjusting the bolts and struts.

The jig frame for the side wall steel binding can also be adjusted by adjusting the bolts and the sidelines of the jig frames. The jig frame for the steel binding of the external wall can be adjusted horizontally (-650 millimeters~+400 millimeters). Before the steel binding for the internal side wall, the detachable steel binding jig frame shall be installed and the adjusting screw bolts and working platform shall be fixed.

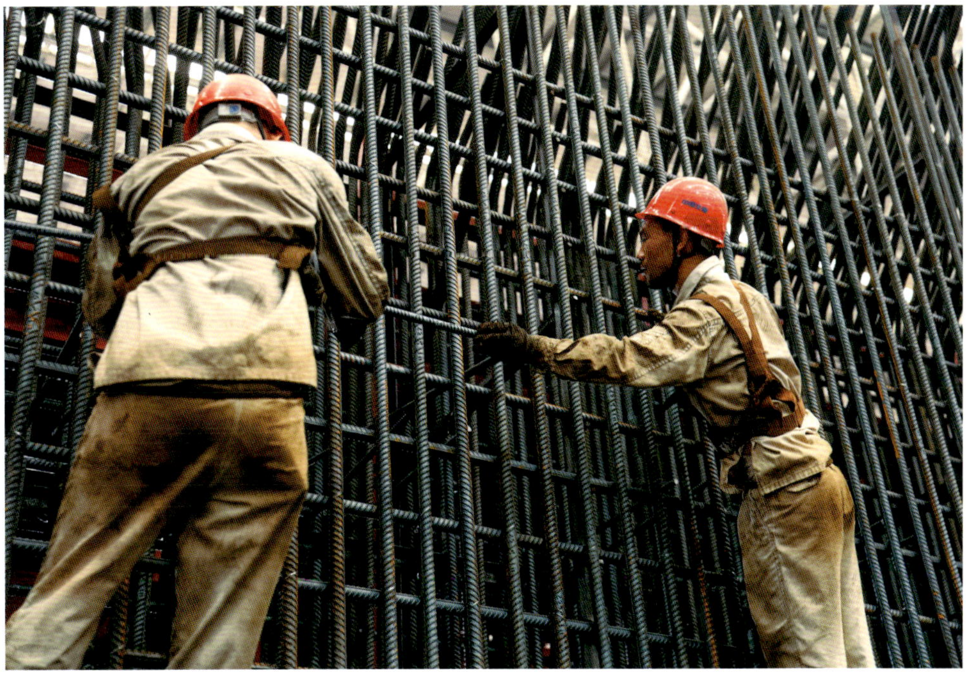

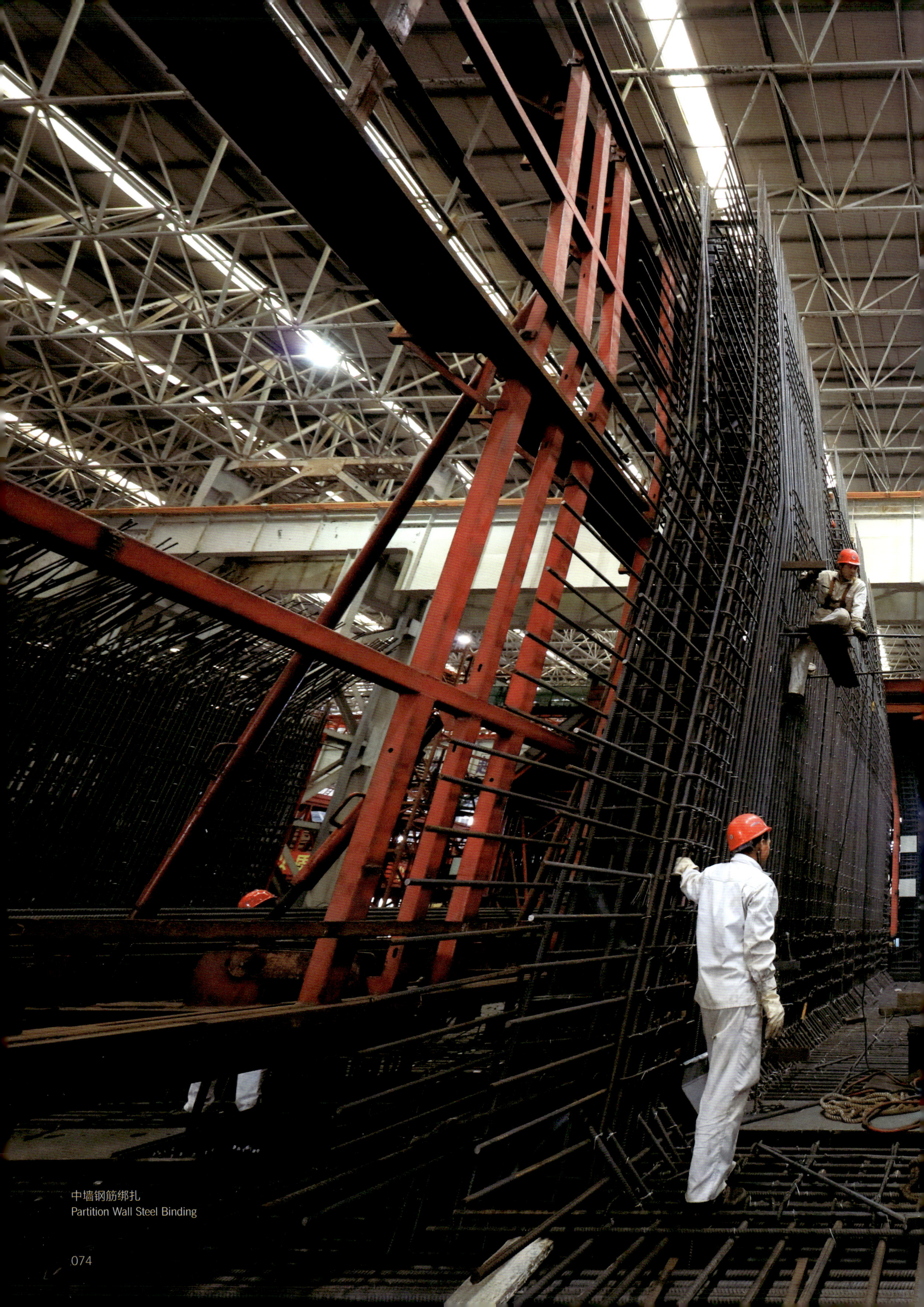

中墙钢筋绑扎
Partition Wall Steel Binding

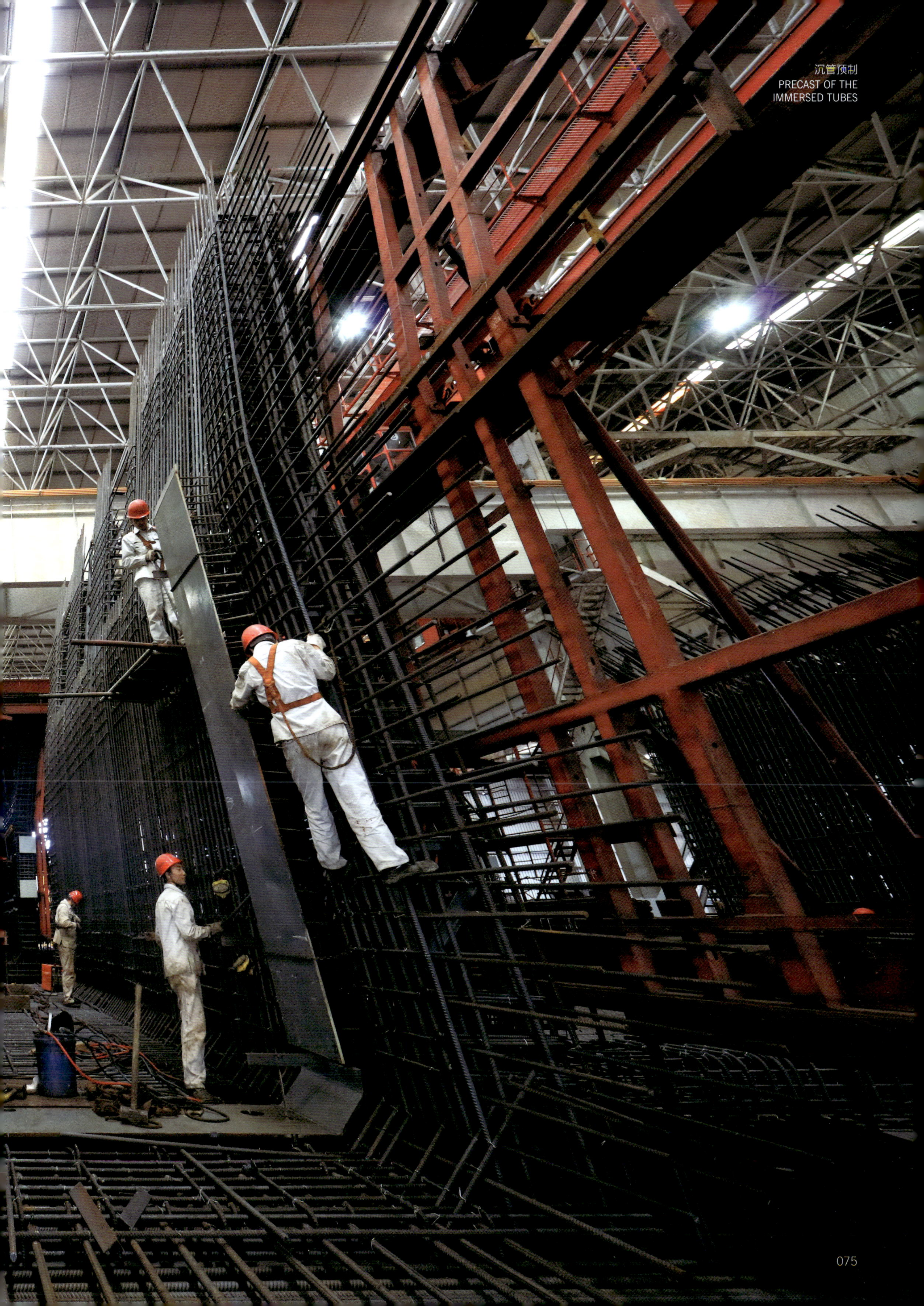

顶板钢筋笼绑扎：顶板钢筋绑扎胎架支撑在胎架底座上，下部设置调节螺栓作为顶升调节装置，以调节顶面标高和水平度。

Top Plate Steel Reinforcement Cage Binding : The jig frame for the top plate steel binding is set on the jig base, and the lower part is equipped with an adjusting screw bolt to adjust the elevation and levelness of the top surface.

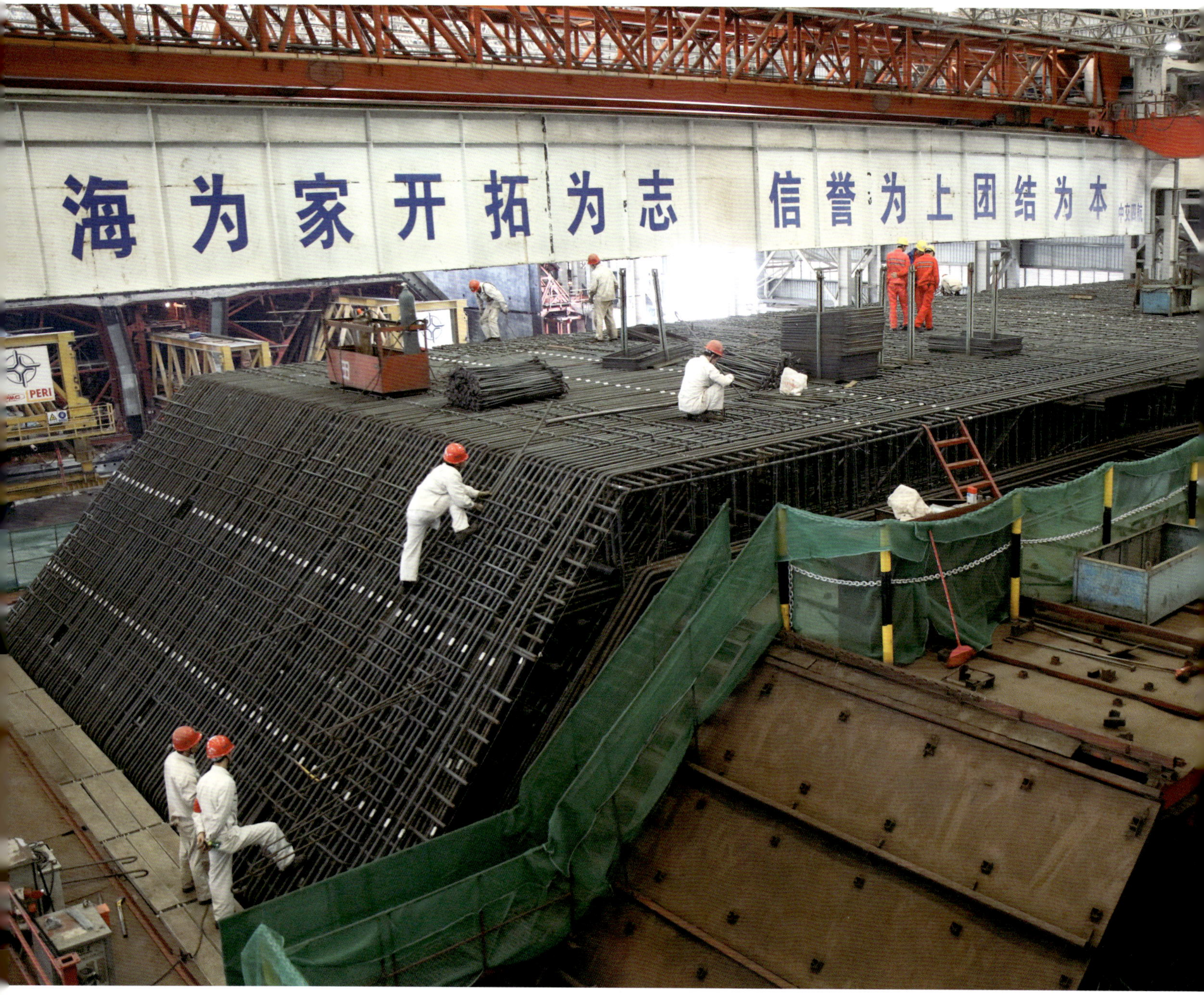

1. 顶板钢筋绑扎
Top Plate Steel Binding
2. 顶板底层钢筋铺设
Lower Layer Steel Binding on the Top Plate
3. 顶板倒角钢筋铺设
Top Plate Chamfer Steel Binding
4. 顶板架立筋安装
Supporting Steel Bar Installation on the Top Plate

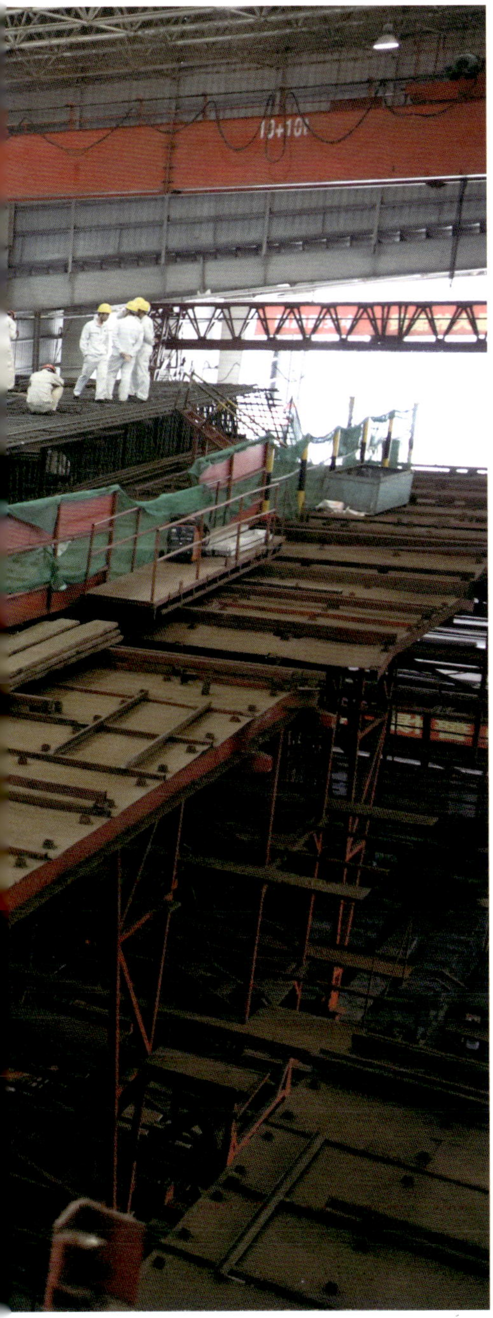

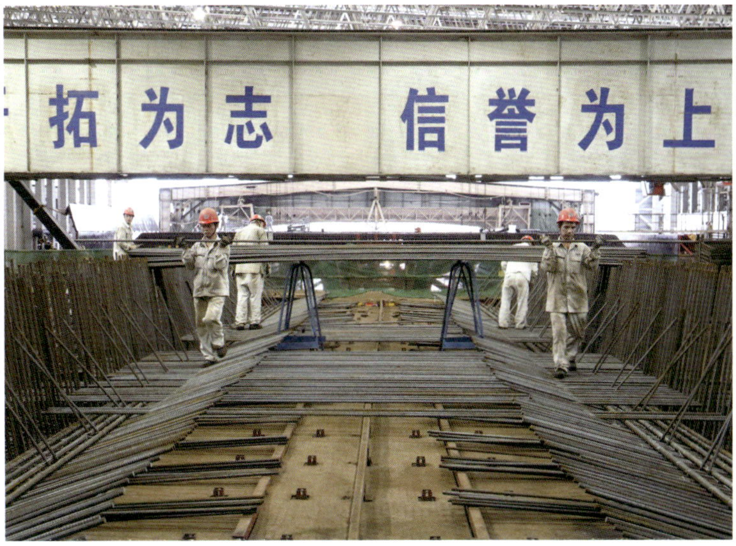

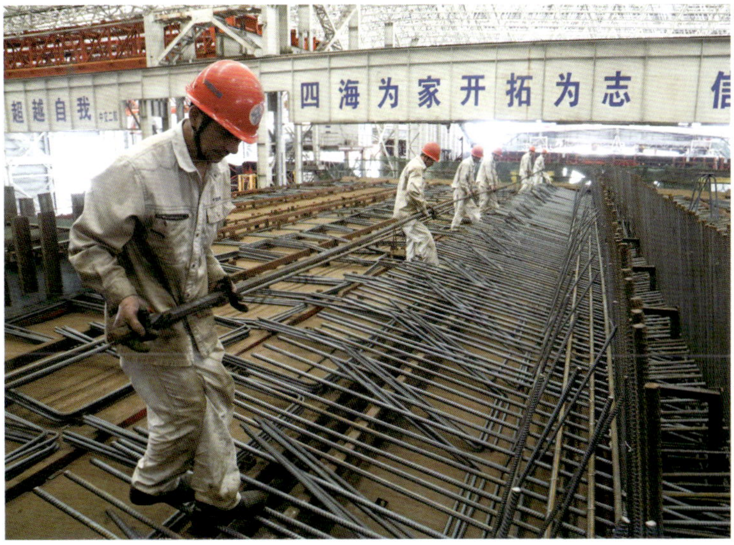

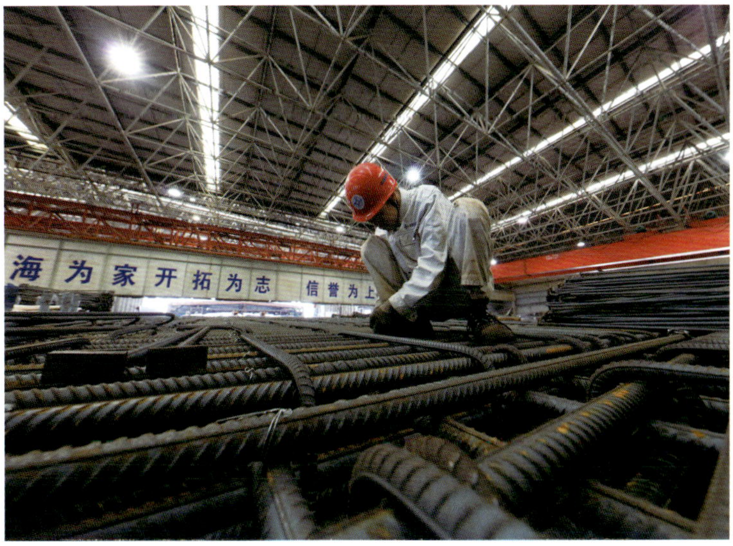

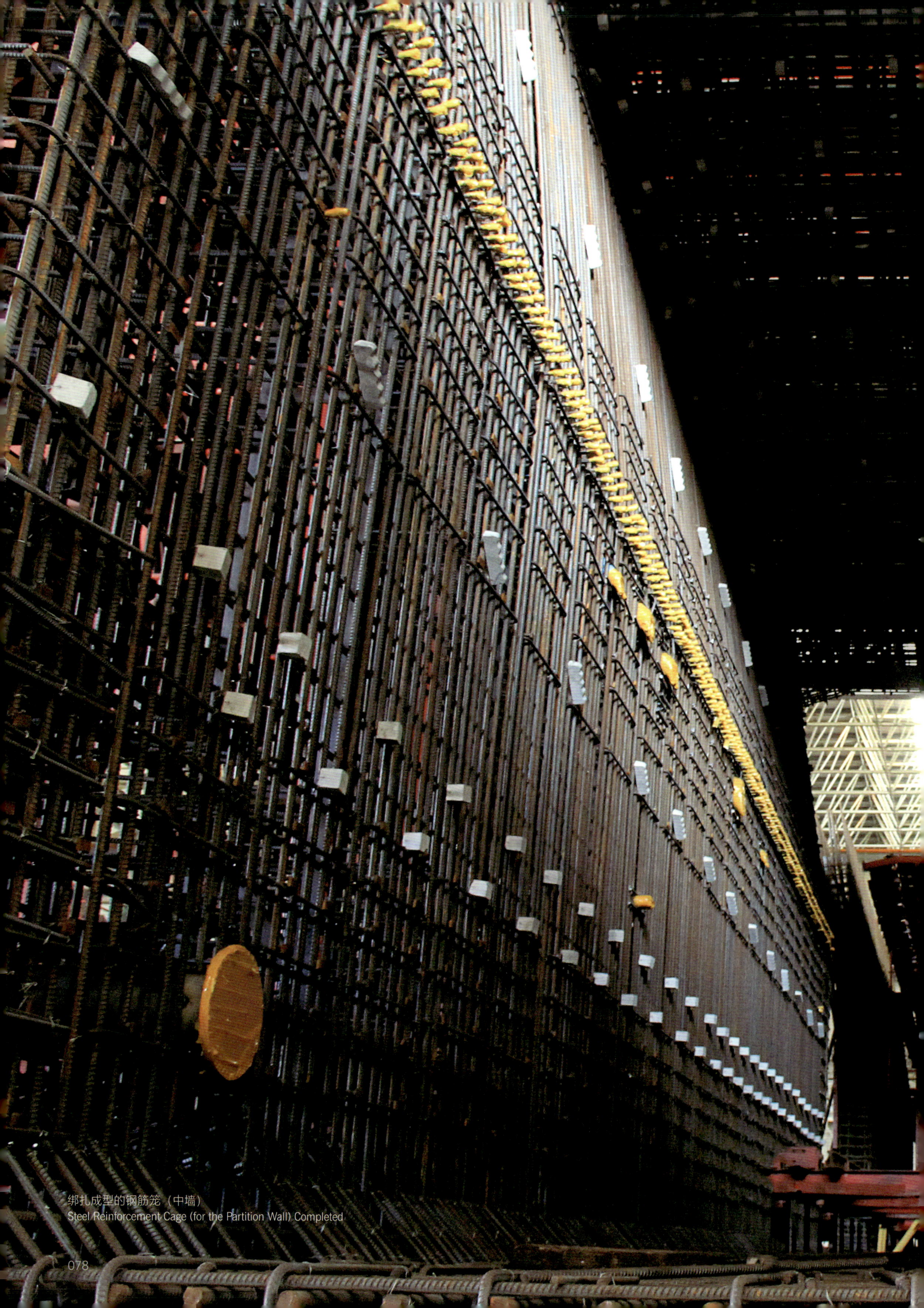

绑扎成型的钢筋笼（中墙）
Steel Reinforcement Cage (for the Partition Wall) Completed

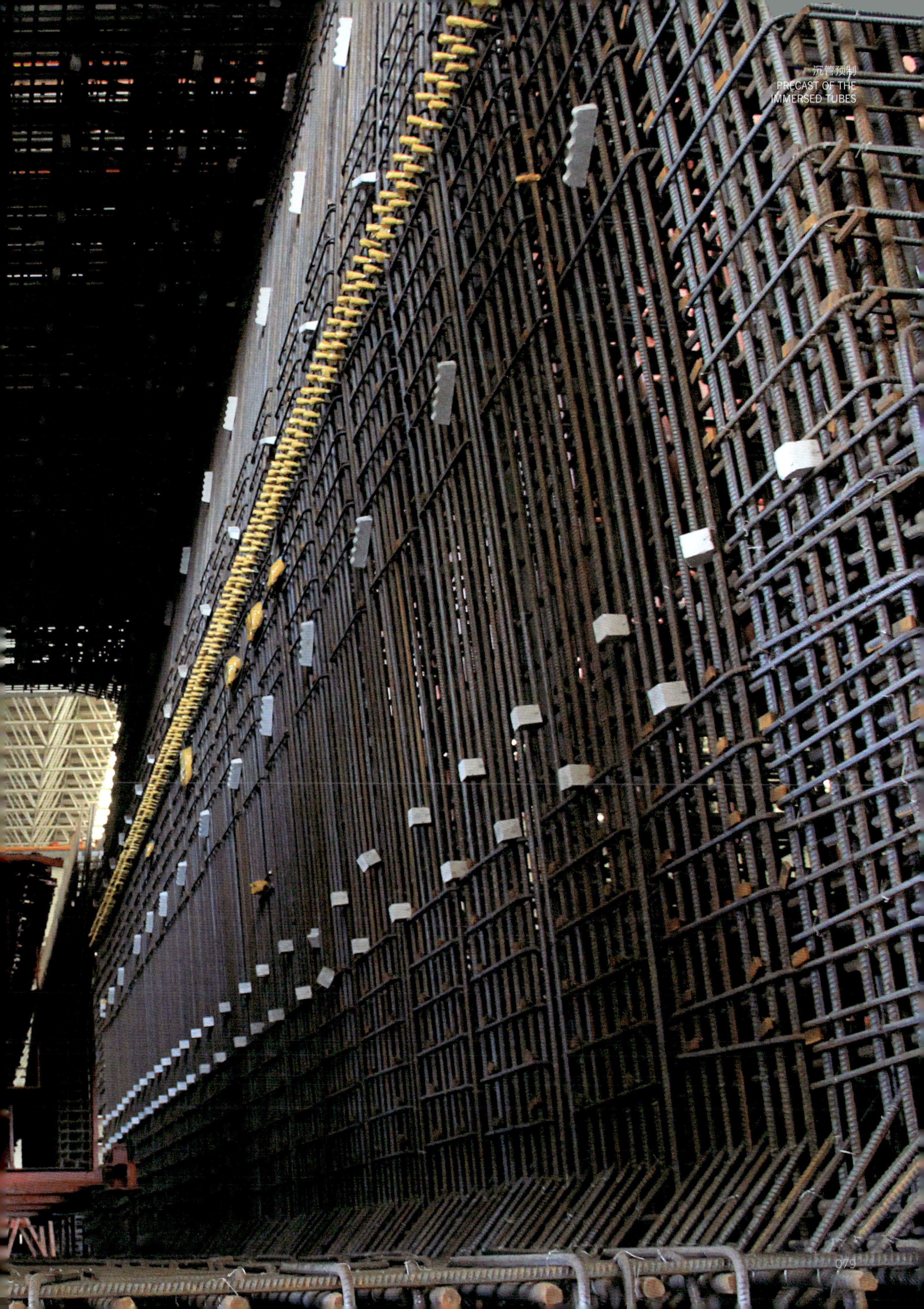

预设、预埋件安装
INSTALLATION OF PRESET AND EMBEDDED ITEMS

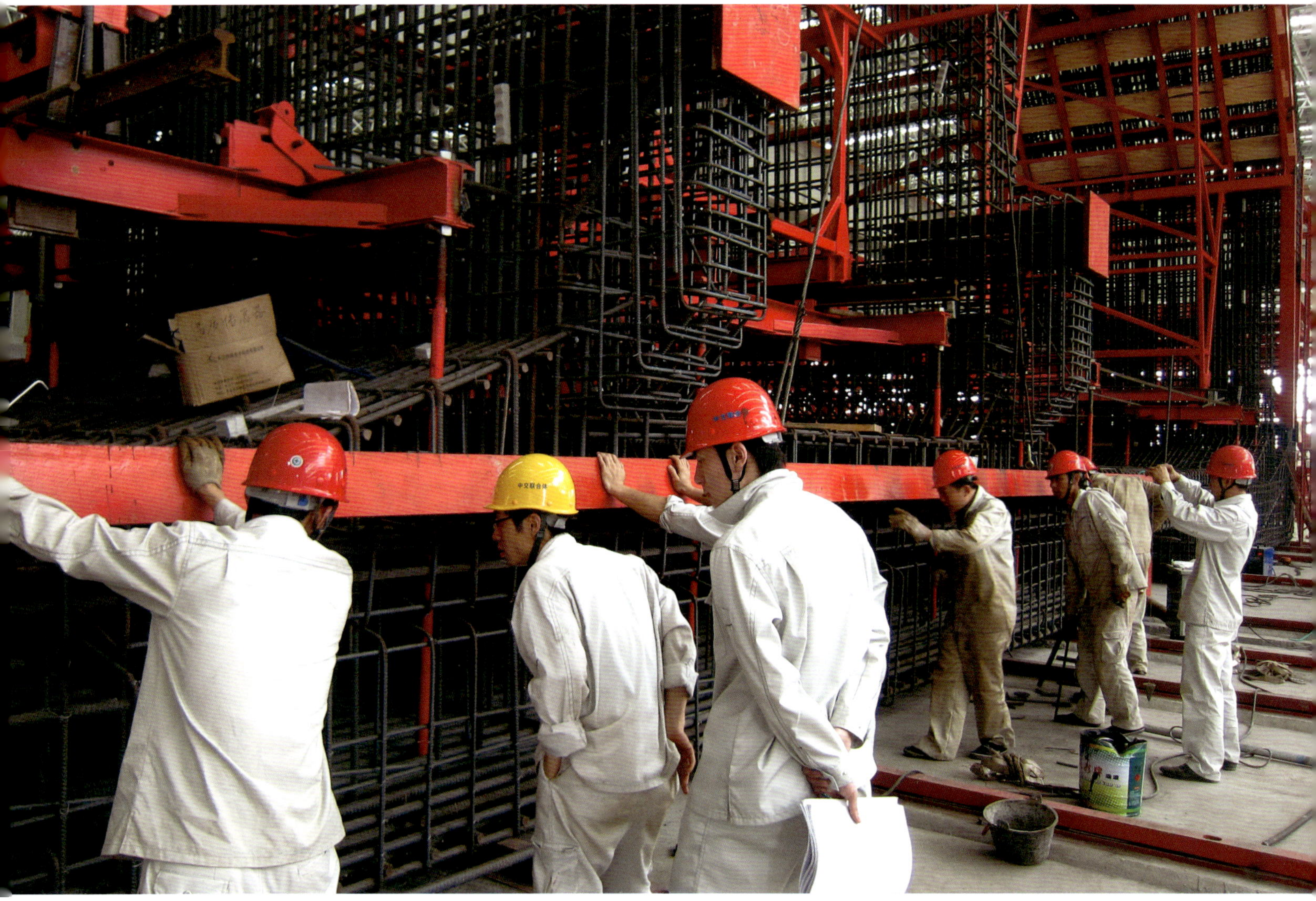

1. 钢端壳安装
Installation of the Steel End Shell
2. 沉管吊点牛腿安装
Installation of the Lifting Point Corbel of the Immersed Tube
3. 钢端壳牛腿安装
Installation of the Steel End Shell Corbel

预设、预埋件按照部位、使用功能主要分为接头预埋件、交通工程预留预埋设施和沉管安装辅助设施预埋件等三类。

预埋件大多为钢结构，根据所处的位置和环境，采用不同的防腐措施，较之其他工程而言，港珠澳大桥沉管预埋件种类和数量多，体量大，安装精度高。

根据预埋件的种类，预埋件集中在现场加工车间进行加工或委托钢结构加工厂生产。加工过程中必须严格控制精度及焊缝质量。

预埋件位置与钢筋位置冲突时，采取钢筋避让原则，在设计允许情况下，对切断的钢筋结构进行补强。沉管内预留、预埋孔洞等宜在墙体内侧开洞，并补强钢筋。预埋钢结构时，应按环境条件及设计使用年限，并按照相关技术规范采取防腐措施。

The preset and embedded items are mainly divided into three categories according to the places they are set or embedded and their functions: embedded items at the joint; embedded facilities reserved for traffic engineering and auxiliary embedded parts for the installation of the immersed tubes.

Most of the embedded parts are steel structures. According to their location and the environment, different anti-corrosion measures are adopted. Compared with other projects, the embedded items used in the immersed tube tunnel of Hong Kong-Zhuhai-Macau Bridge features diversified types, large quantity and high-precision installation.

By their types, the embedded items are collectively manufactured in the on-site processing workshops or manufactured by the entrusted steel structure processing factories. Precision and the welding quality need to be strictly controlled when they are manufactured.

When the position of embedded items conflicts with the position of the steel bars, the steel bar shall give way. Without violating the principles for the general designing, the steel bar that is cut short shall undergo additional reinforcement. The reserved and embedded holes in the immersed tube should be opened from inside the tube wall and this part of the wall should be reinforced with steel bars. When the steel structure is embedded, anti-corrosion measures shall be taken in accordance with relevant technical specifications as well as with environmental conditions and designed life span in service.

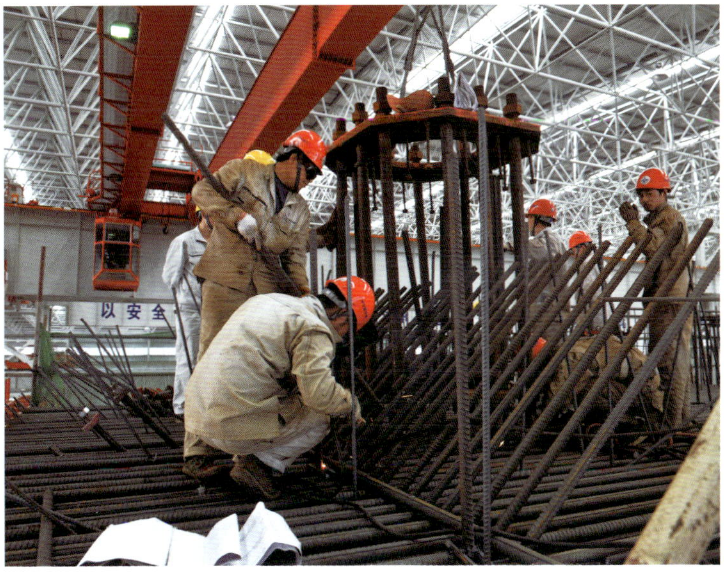

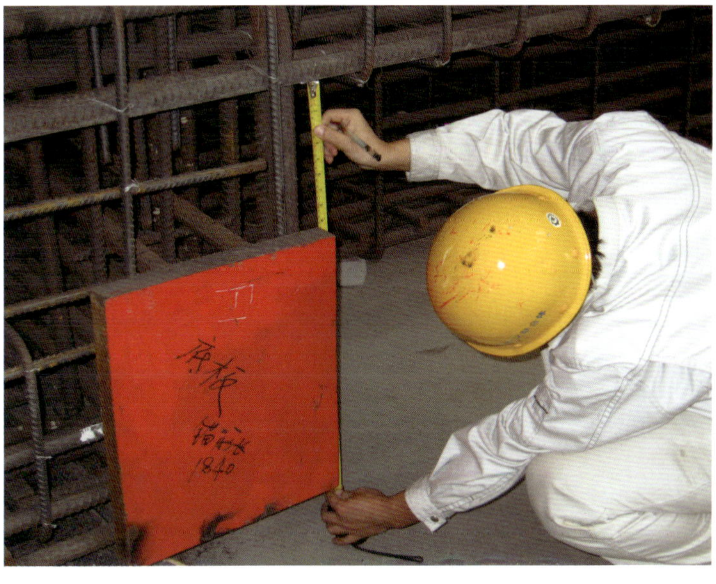

钢端壳安装：沉管隧道的各管节的连接接头中，钢端壳作为安装 GINA 止水带和 OMEGA 止水带的载体，是沉管隧道接头的重要组成部分，在沉管隧道建设中具有重要作用。

钢端壳呈环形，宽度 65 厘米，外包尺寸与沉管外包尺寸相同，由 24 毫米厚的钢板焊接成 L 形，并配有锚筋。钢端壳分为 A 型和 B 型两种，A 型用于沉管 GINA 端，B 型用于沉管非 GINA 端。沉管钢端壳采用一次性浇筑成型工艺，安装精度、标准化作业及施工工效均满足"工厂法"预制沉管的需求。

Steel End Shell Installation: Among all the butt joints of the different segments of the immersed tubes, as the carrier of GINA water-stop and OMEGA water-stop, the steel end shell is an important part of the butt joints of the immersed tube tunnel, playing an very important role in the construction of the immersed tube tunnel.

The steel end shell is made in the shape of a ring with a width of 65 centimeters. The size of its outer cladding is the same as that of the immersed tube. It is welded into the shape of L with the 24-millimeter-thick steel plate and is equipped with anchor rods. The steel end shells fall into two types of Type A and Type B. Type A is used for the GINA end of the immersed tube while Type B is used for the non-GINA end of the immersed tube. The steel end shell of the immersed tube employs the one-time casting process, and the installation accuracy, standardized operation and construction efficiency all meet the requirements for the factory manufacturing of the immersed tubes.

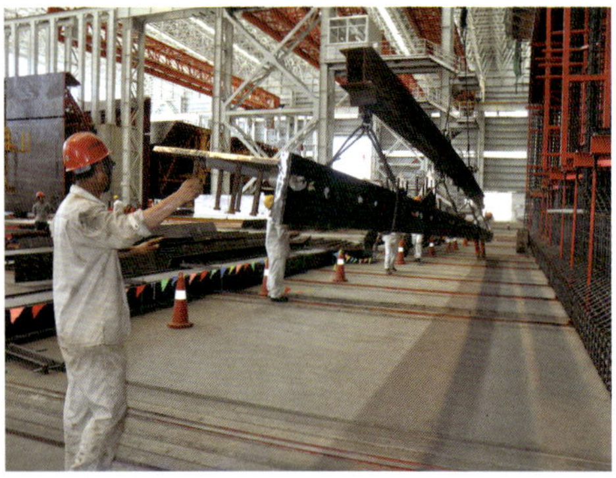

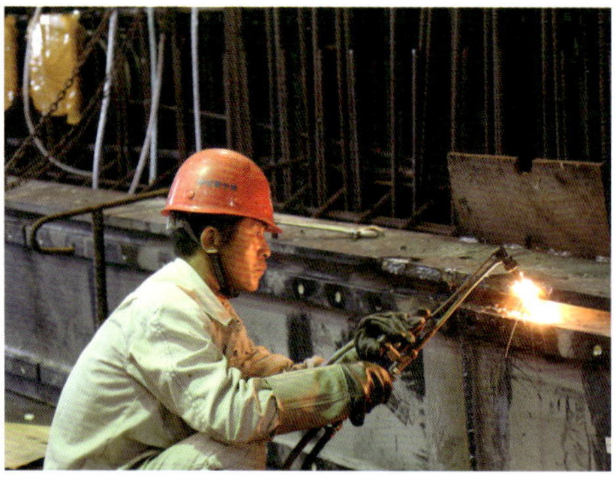

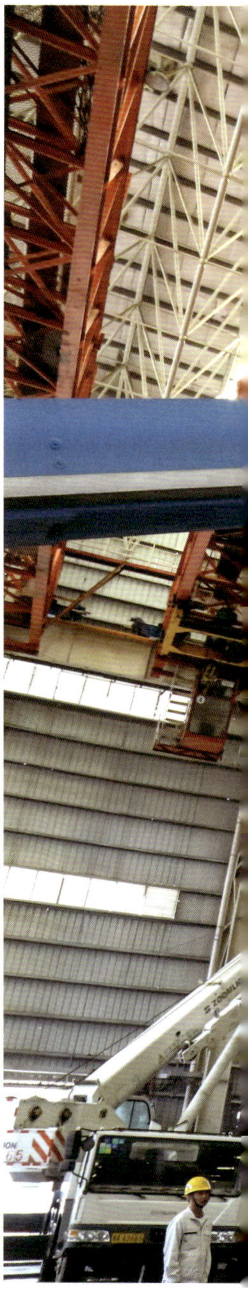

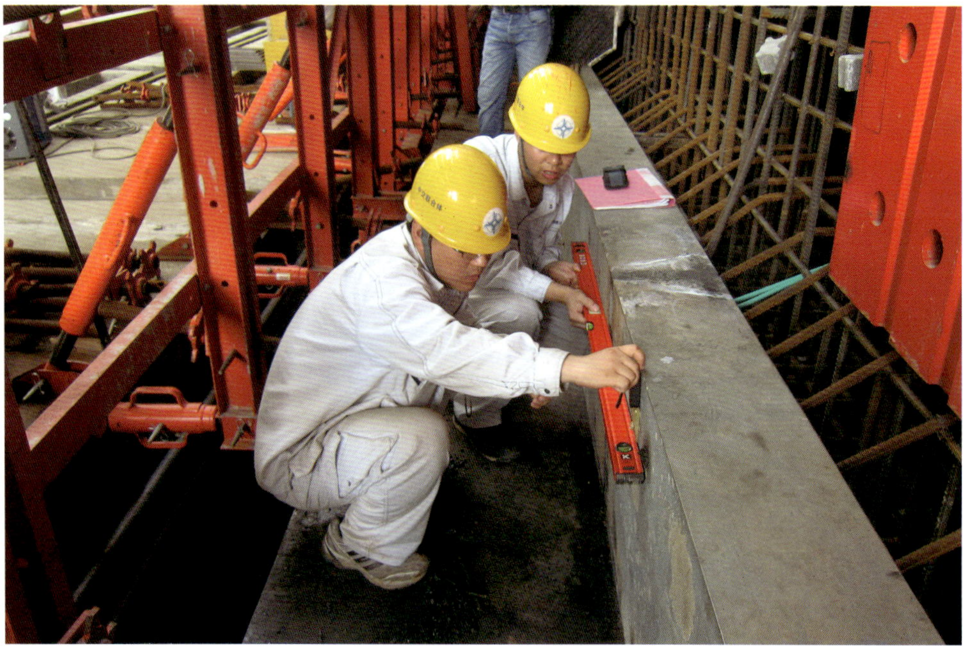

1. 钢端壳吊运
Steel End Shell Hoisting and Transportation

2. 钢端壳焊接
Steel End Shell Welding

3. 钢端壳安装精度测量
Accuracy Measurement for the Steel End Shell Installation

4. 钢端壳焊接
Steel End Shell Welding

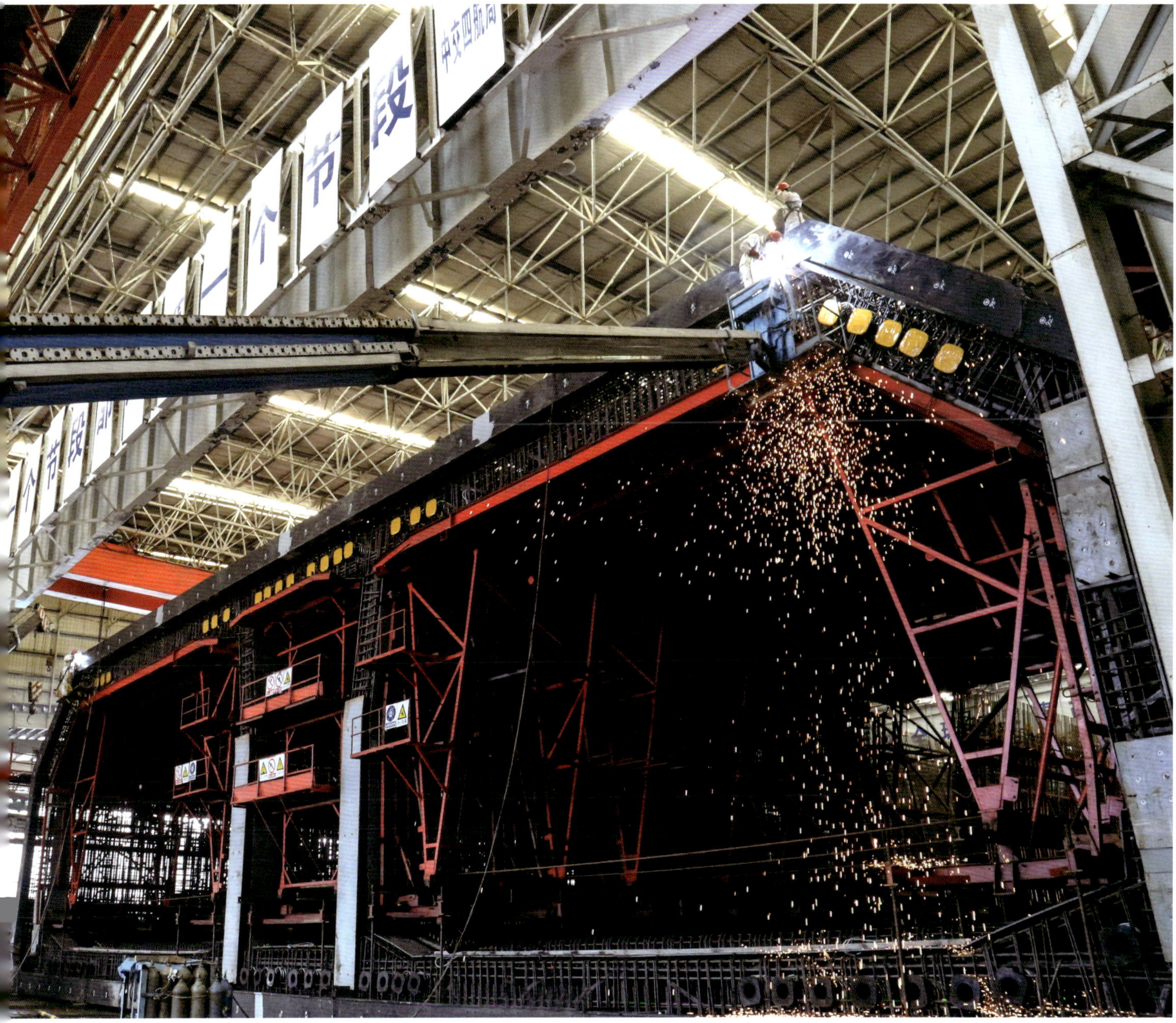

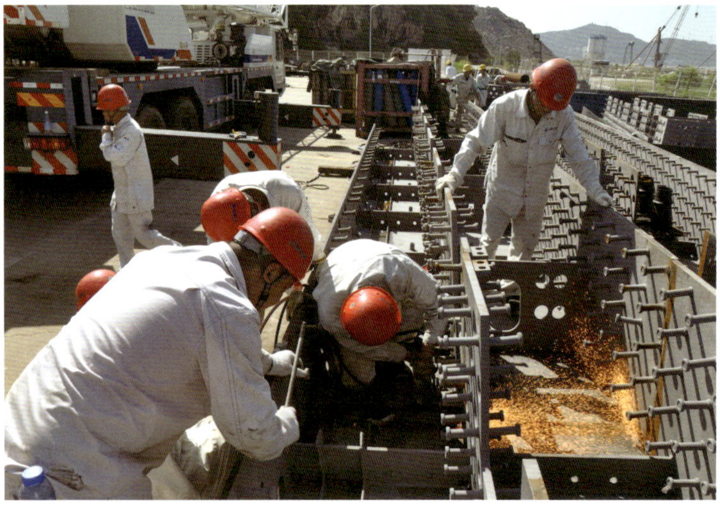

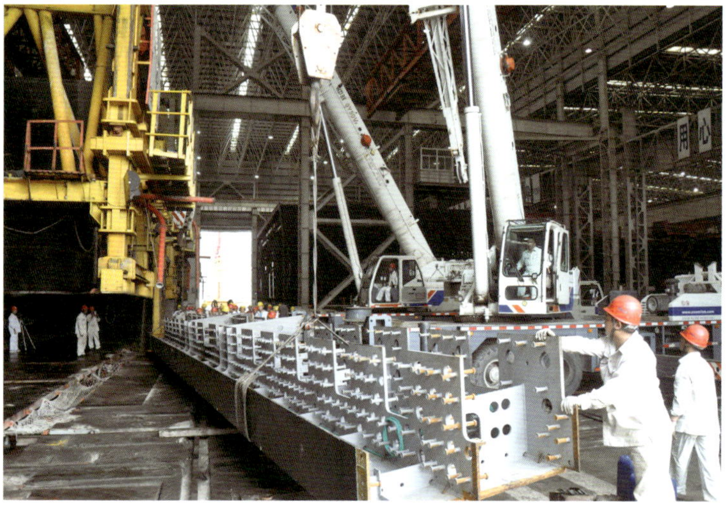

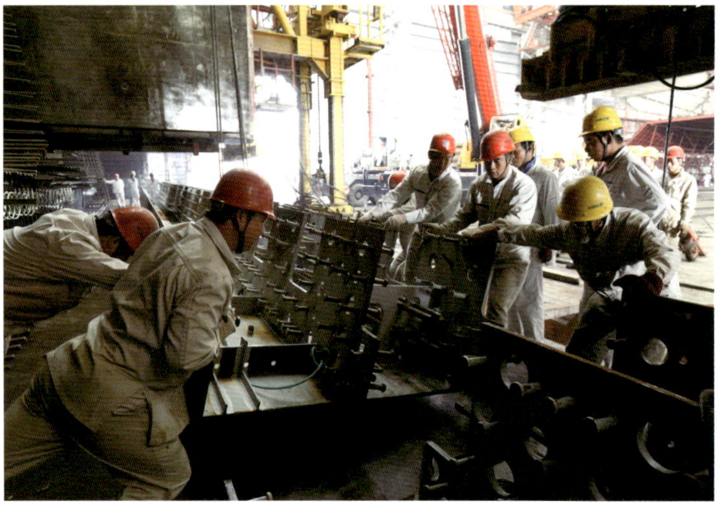

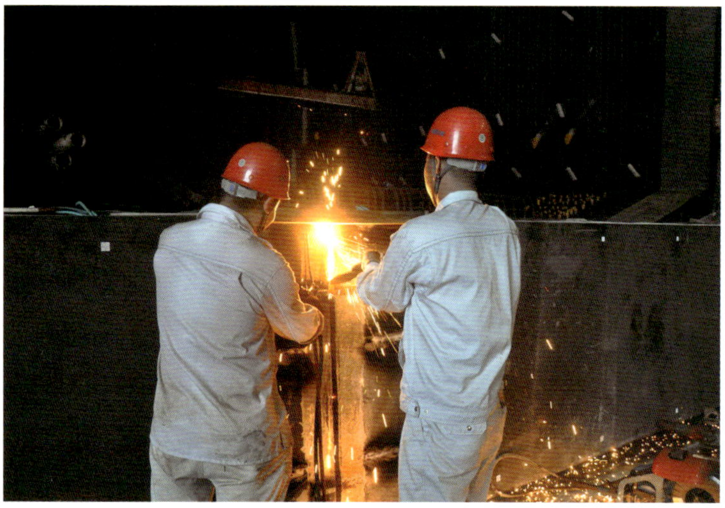

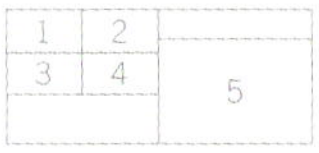

1. 钢帽预焊成型
   Steel Cap Pre-welded
2. 钢帽吊装
   Steel Cap Lifting
3. 钢帽安装
   Steel Cap Installation
4. 钢帽焊接
   Steel Cap Welding
5. 钢帽防腐处理
   Steel Cap Anti-corrosion

钢帽安装：钢帽分两种类型，分别位于E29-S8、E30-S1沉管端部，用于水下与最终接头的对接和密封。待最终接头安装就位后，E29-S8、E30-S1钢帽与最终接头两端的钢帽进行刚性连接，实现隧道贯通。钢帽长37.95米，宽11.4米，截面为E型结构，由翼缘板、加劲板、承压板、外伸腹板、止水钢片、焊钉、钢套等部件组成。每套钢帽重约80吨，分为12段在工厂内制造完成后，运输至沉管预制厂安装。

Steel Cap Installation: There are two types of steel caps, which are located at the end of E29-S8 and E30-S1, respectively. They are used for docking and sealing of underwater and final joints. When the final joint is installed in place, E29 S8 and E30-S1 steel caps are rigidly connected with the caps at both ends of the final joint for the final holing-through of the tunnel. The steel cap is 37.95m long and 11.4m wide. Its cross section is an E-shaped structure. It consists of the flange plate, stiffening plate, bearing plate, outrigger web, water stop steel sheet, welding nail, steel sleeve and other components. Each steel cap weighs about 80 tons and is divided into 12 sections. After being manufactured in the factory, it is transported to the immersed tube precast plant.

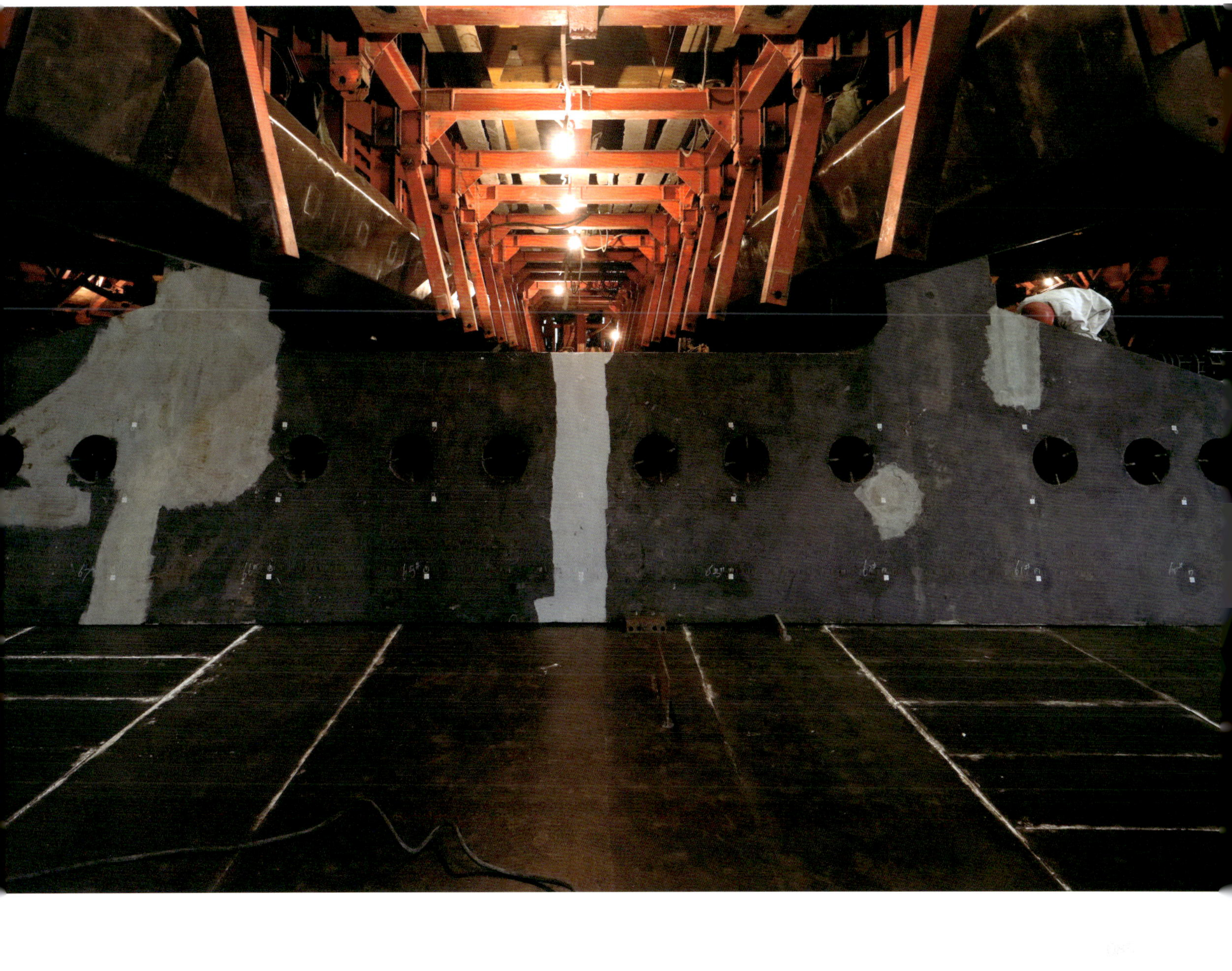

1 2 3	4

1. 中埋式止水带平面图
   Plan View of the Embedded Water-Stop
2. 中埋式止水带安装
   Embedded Water-Stop Installation
3. 中埋式止水带接驳
   Embedded Water-Stop Connection
4. 中埋式止水带安装
   Embedded Water-Stop Installation

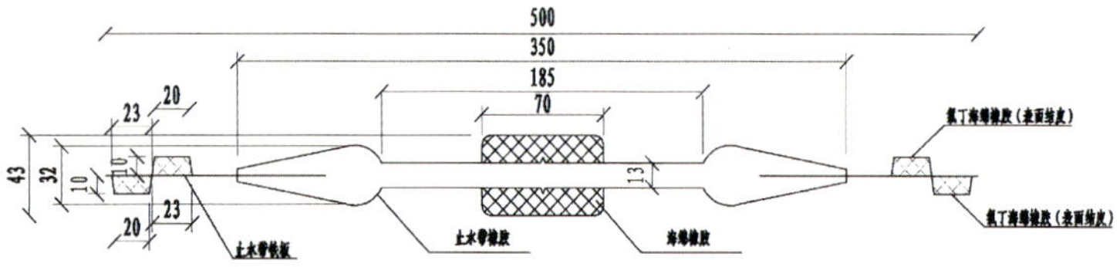

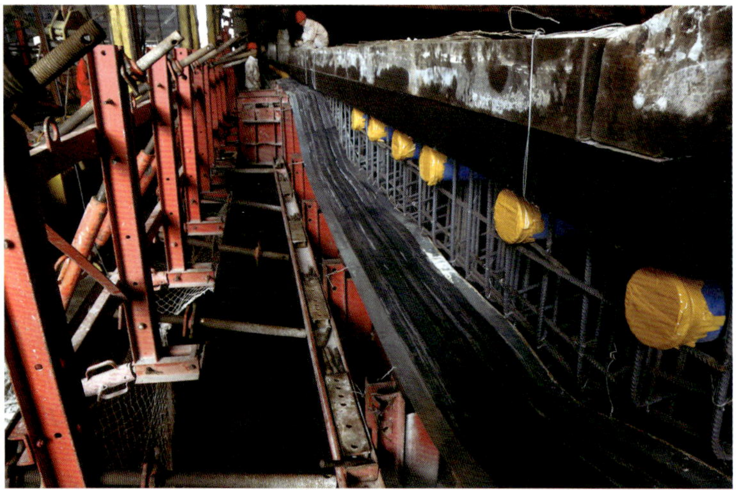

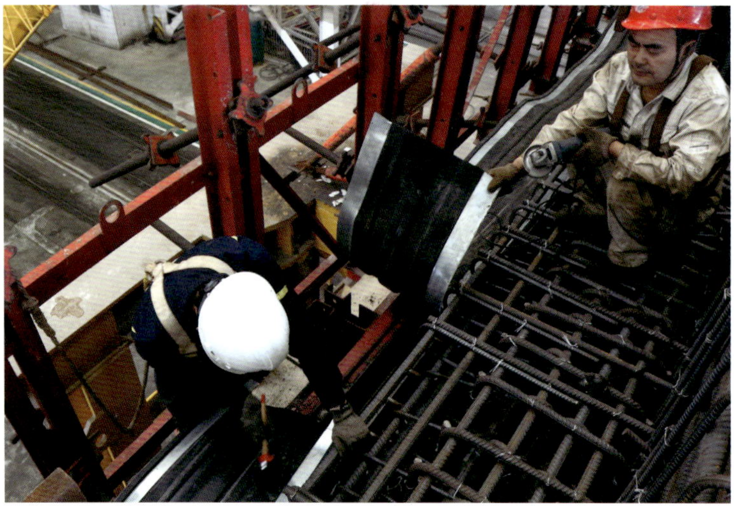

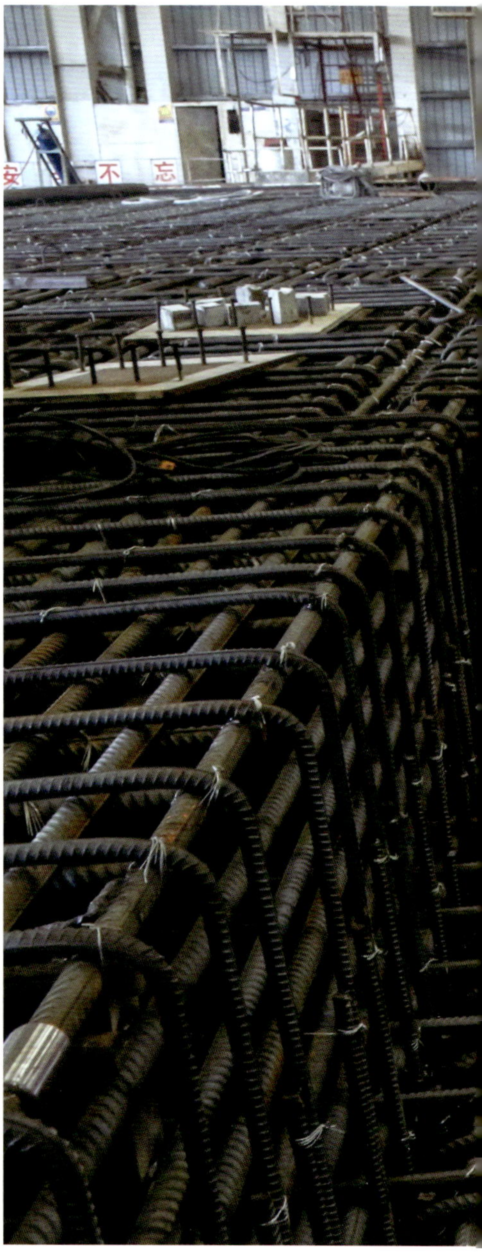

中埋式止水带安装：中埋式止水带嵌入两个节段之间，是沉管节段接头（施工缝）防水的重要组成部分，主要由橡胶带、不锈钢片、氯丁海绵橡胶条（注浆用）、注浆管等组成。居中设置于各节段接头（施工缝）。中埋止水带在下半部端模安装完成后进行，止水带接头设在行车道顶板中部，采用专用设备硫化对接。

Installation of the Embedded Water-Stops: The embedded water-stop is inserted between two tube segments and is the important part of the water-stop operation at the joints (construction joints) between the segments of the immersed tubes. It is composed mainly of the rubber seal, the stainless steel sheet, the neoprene sponge rubber strip (for grouting) and the grouting pipe. It is inserted in the middle part of the segment joints (construction joints). The embedded water-stop operation is conducted after the end formwork at the lower part is completed, and the butt joint of the water-stop is set in the middle part of the top plate of the driving lanes. Vulcanized butt welding is done by special equipment.

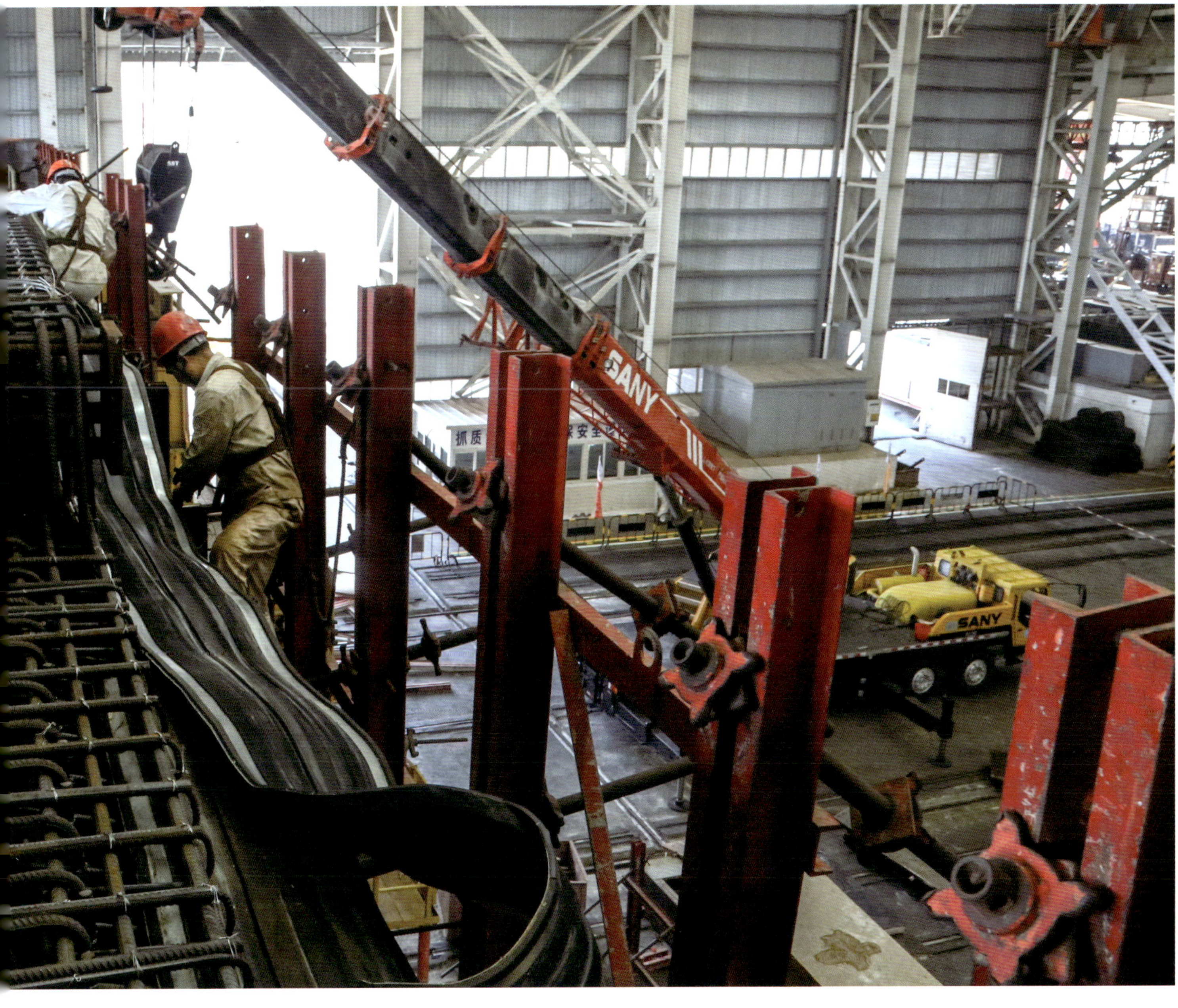

剪力键预埋件安装：沉管接头侧墙及中墙上设置钢剪力键，每道墙设置3个，交错布置。底板位置设置混凝土剪力键，沉管安装完成后在内部进行现场浇筑。

Installation of the Embedded Shear Keys: Steel shear keys are embedded on the side wall and the partition wall of the butt joint of the immersed tube. Three shear keys are embedded on each wall in staggered layout. Concrete shear keys are embedded in the bottom plate, which is cast on the site inside the tube after the installation of the immersed tube is completed.

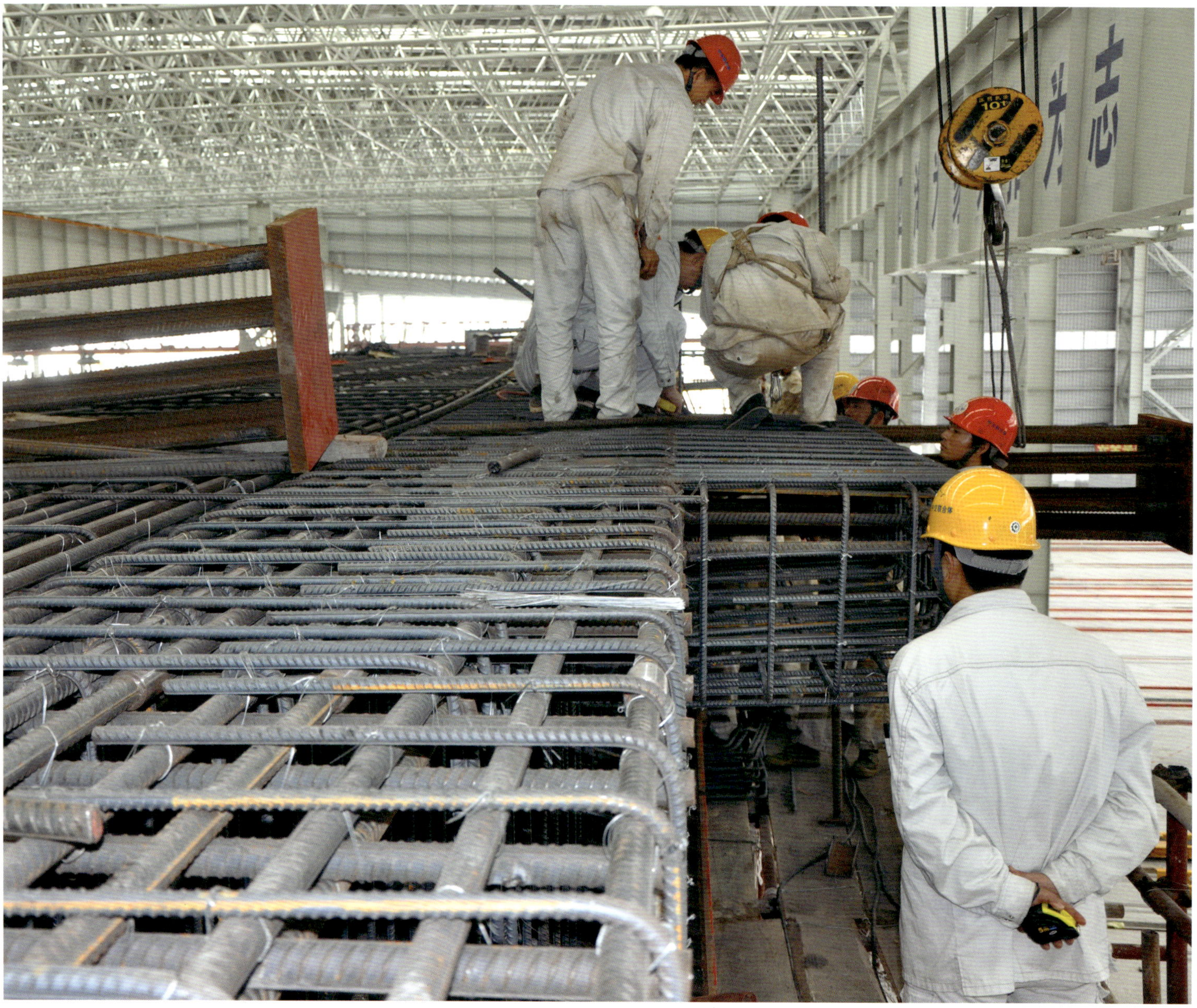

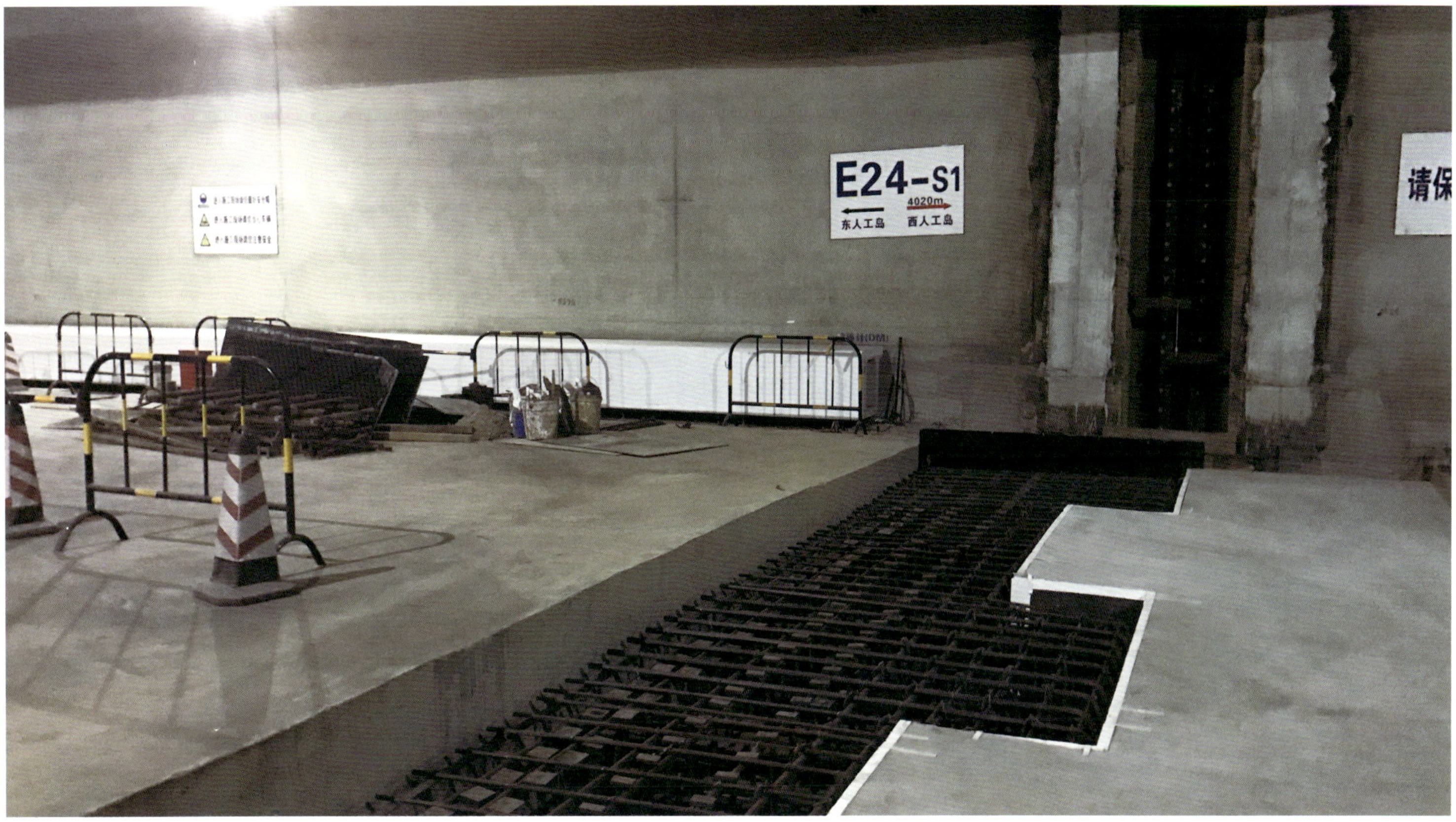

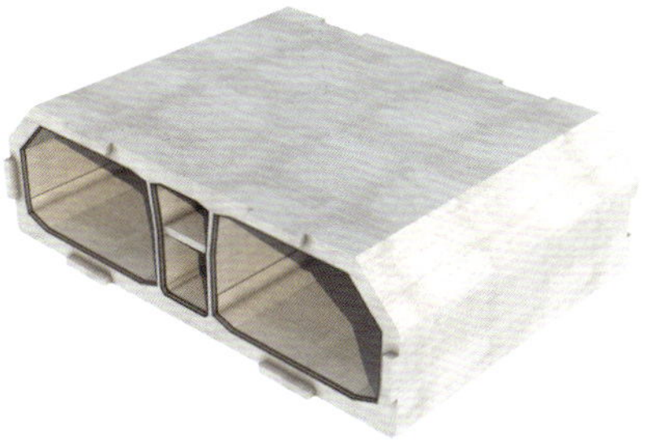

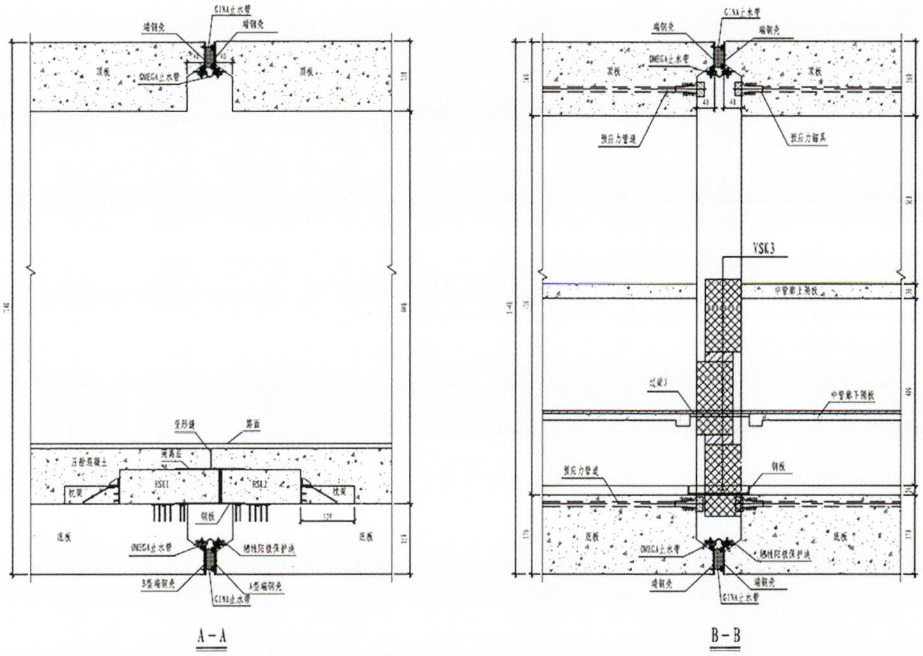

1	2
	3

1. 钢剪力键预埋件安装
Installation of the Embedded Items of the Steel Shear Key
2. 混凝土剪力键浇筑
Concrete Placement of the Shear Key
3. 剪力键分布图
Layout of the Shear Keys

钢筋笼顶推
PUSHING OF THE STEEL REINFORCEMENT CAGE

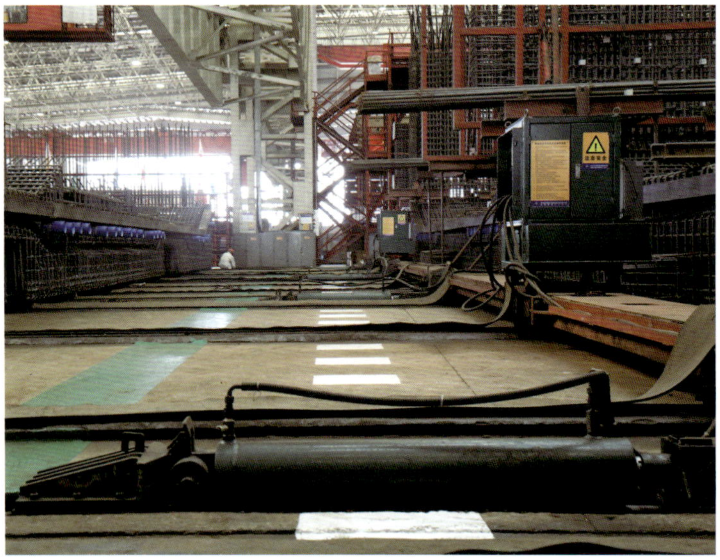

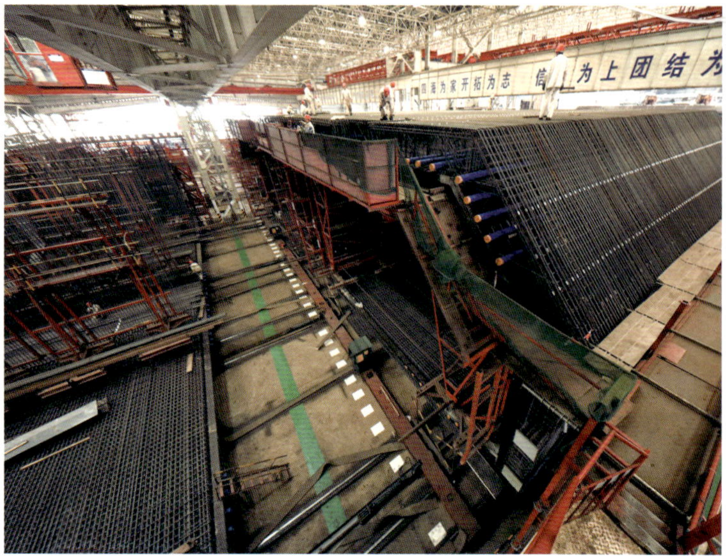

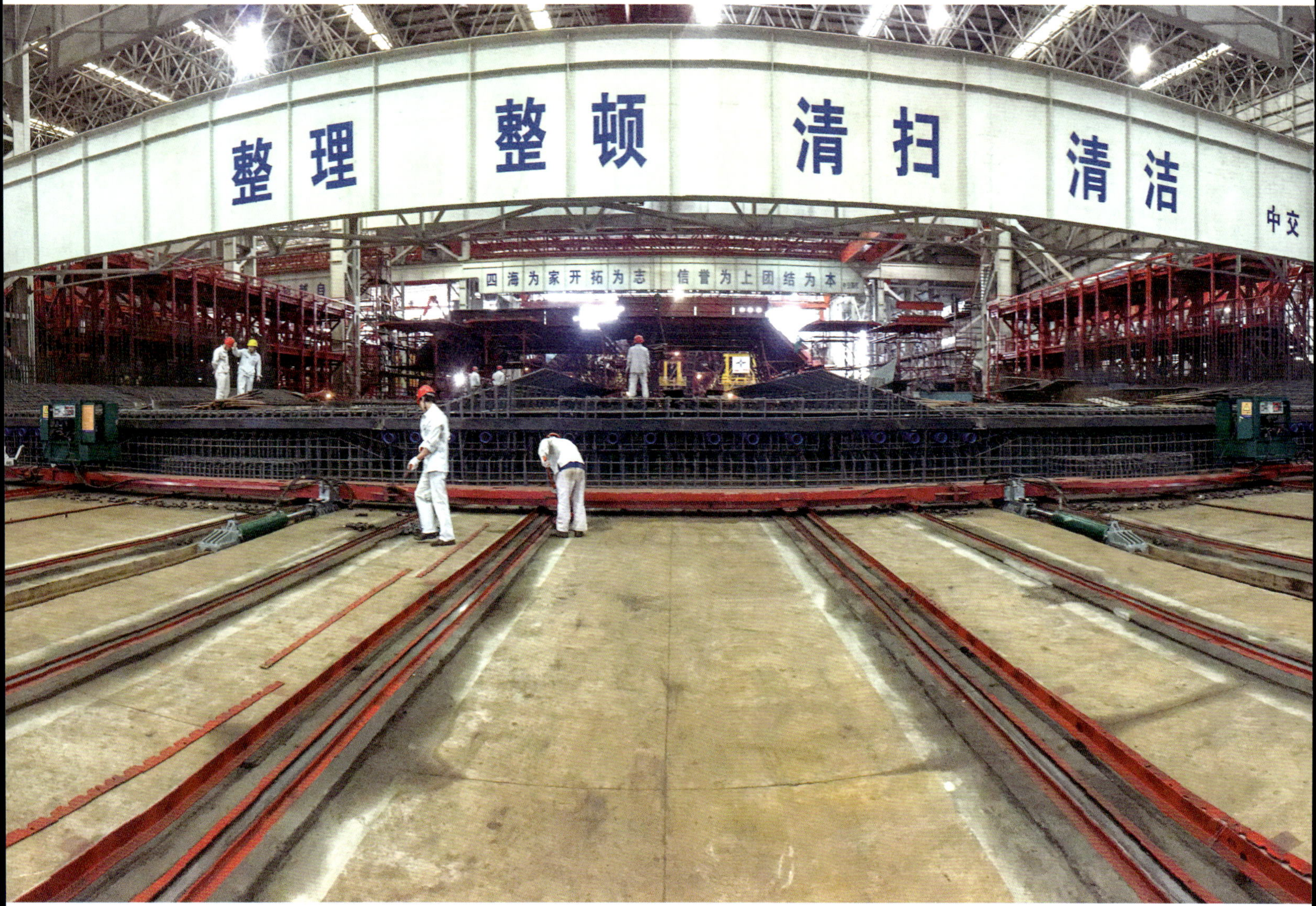

每个钢筋笼下方设置14条钢筋绑扎台车，完成钢筋笼各绑扎区域之间的移动。钢筋绑扎台车主要由滑移支撑面和滑移钢板组成。

钢筋笼移动步骤：

第一步，在底板绑扎区域绑扎完成后，安装顶推千斤顶，将绑扎成型的钢筋笼顶推至墙体钢筋绑扎区域；待墙体钢筋绑扎完成后，顶推至顶板钢筋绑扎区。

第二步，顶板钢筋笼在胎架上绑扎成型后，安装钢筋笼顶推千斤顶，整体移动钢筋笼与绑扎台车至浇筑区底模板上。

第三步，4台钢筋吊架悬挂钢筋笼顶板，移出钢筋绑扎胎架。

第四步，在钢筋笼底部安装充气胶囊，充气顶升钢筋笼，抽出底板台车，安装保护层垫层，卸载下落就位，完成体系转换。

14 steel reinforcement binding trolleys are set under each steel cage to allow the steel cage to move from one binding area to another. The trolley is mainly made up of the support sliding surface and steel sliding plates.

Stages of the Steel Cage Movement:

Stage 1: After the steel binding at the bottom plate binding area is completed, a pushing jack is installed to push the completed steel cage to the partition wall steel binding area. After the partition wall steel binding is completed, the steel cage is pushed to the top plate binding area.

Stage 2: After the top plate binding is completed on the jig frame, the pushing jack pushes the steel cage and the binding trolleys to the bottom formwork in the casting area.

Stage 3: Four hoisting frames hoist up the top plate of the steel cage and move the steel cage away from the jig frame.

Stage 4: Inflatable bag is installed at the bottom of the steel cage and the bag filled with air will push up the cage. Then bottom trolleys are taken away, followed by the installation of a protective cushion. Then the cage is lowered in the designed position and the system transition is completed.

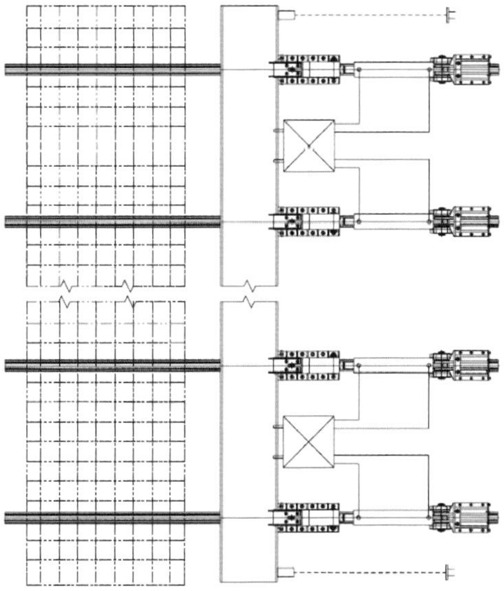

1. 钢筋笼顶推千斤顶
Pushing Jack for the Steel Reinforcement Cage
2. 钢筋笼顶推
Pushing of the Steel Reinforcement Cage
3. 钢筋笼顶推系统
Reinforcement Cage Pushing System
4. 钢筋笼顶推千斤顶分布图
Layout of the Steel Reinforcement Cage Pushing Jacks

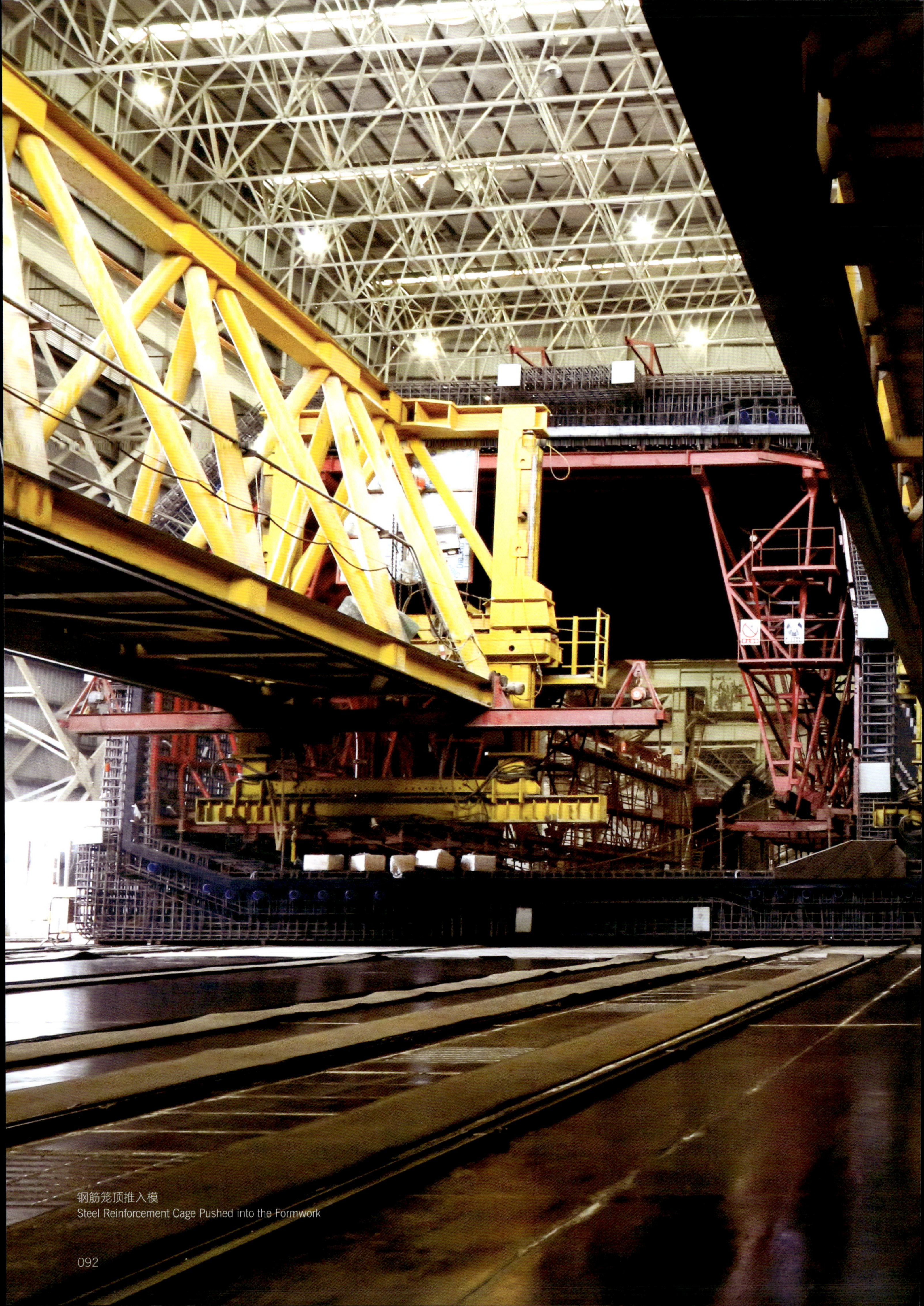

钢筋笼顶推入模
Steel Reinforcement Cage Pushed into the Formwork

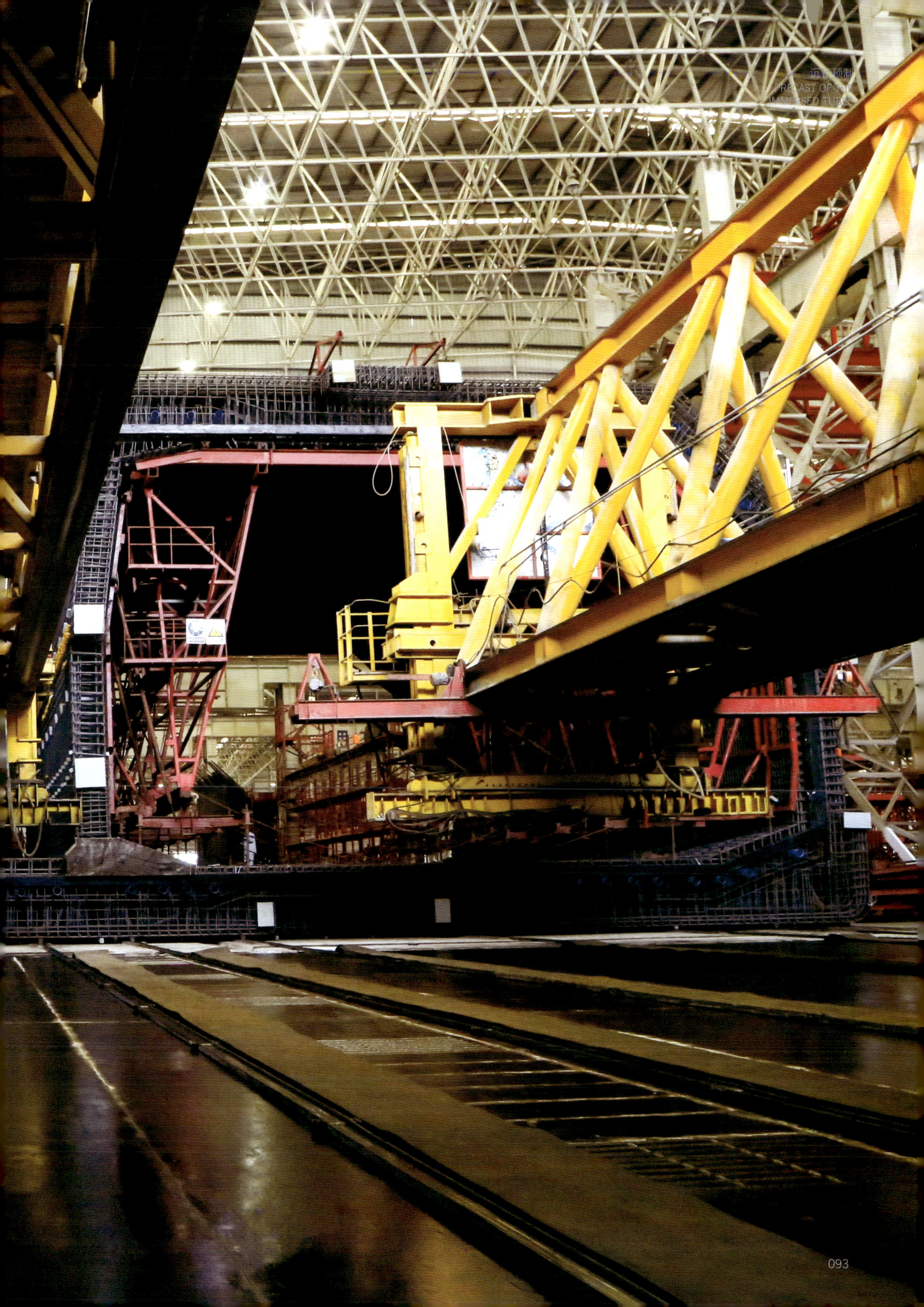

钢筋笼体系转换

SYSTEM TRANSITION OF THE
STEEL REINFORCEMENT CAGE

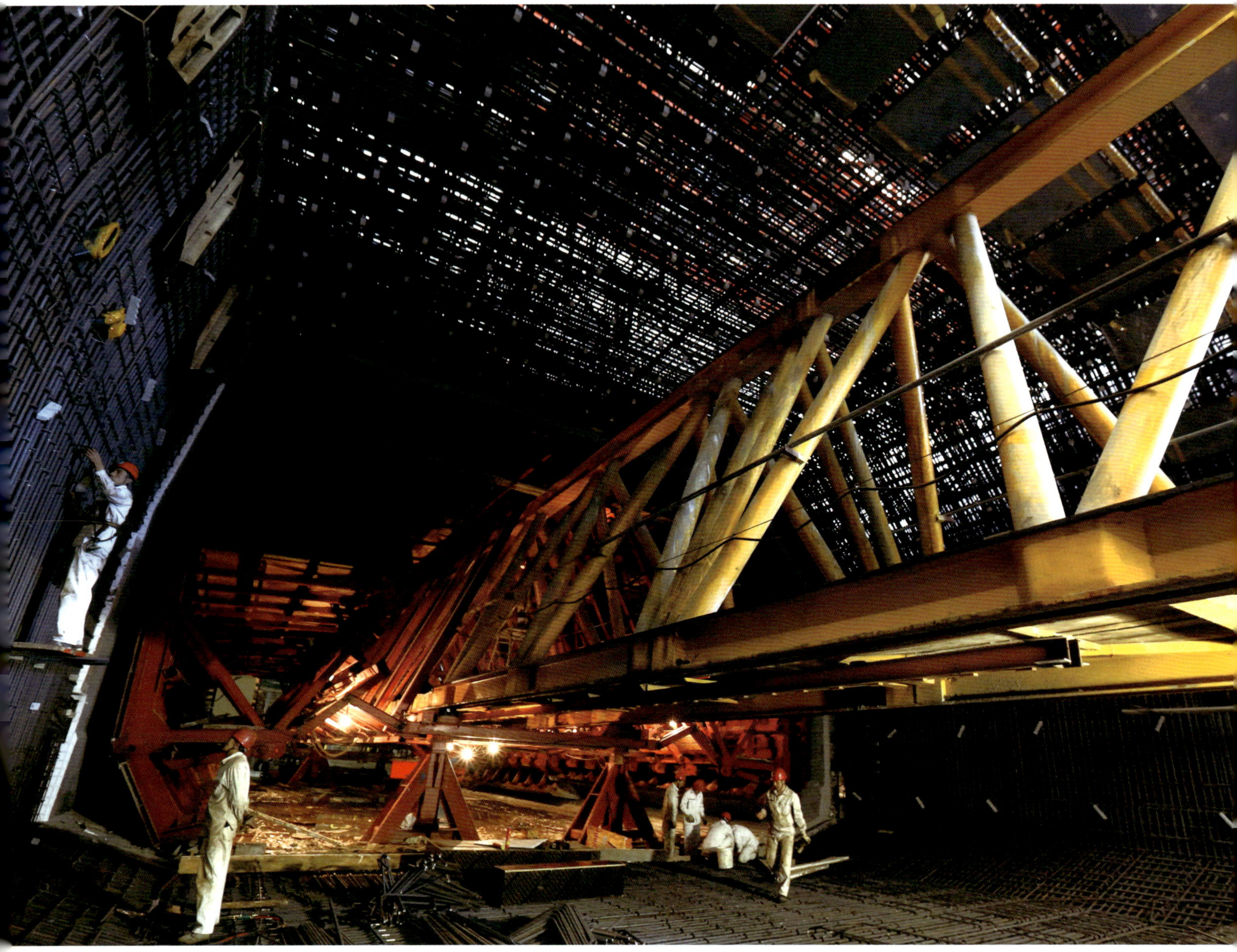

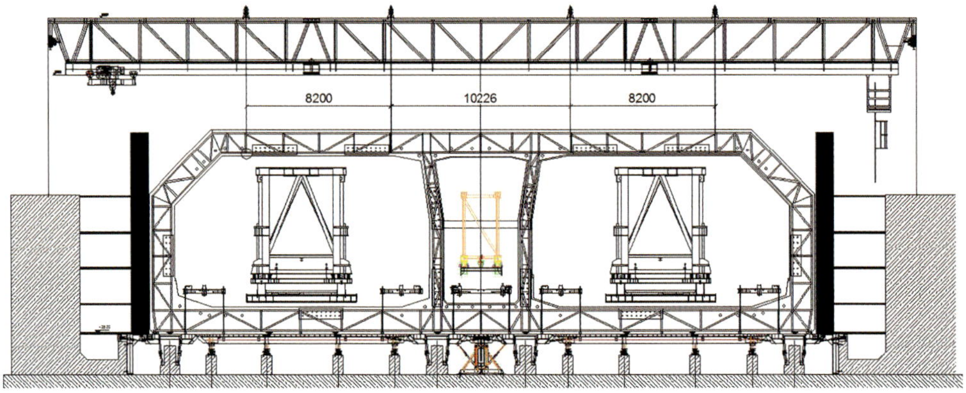

1. 钢筋笼体系转换
   System Transition of the Steel Reinforcement Cage
2. 钢筋笼体系转换顶部吊点分布图
   Layout of the Top Hoisting Points on the Steel Reinforcement Cage for System Transition
3. 钢筋笼体系转换工序示意图
   Schematic Diagram of the Process of System Transition of the Steel Reinforcement Cage

钢筋笼体系转换就是将钢筋笼的胎架支撑体系转换为模板支撑体系，实现出胎架受力向模板受力的转换。

1. 钢筋笼在向前推进的过程中始终是坐落在滑移台车上（滑移轨道），而为了最终能取出轨道，需要在钢筋笼顶推到位后将钢筋笼提升，故在钢筋笼下部插入若干气囊，为气囊充气使得整个钢筋笼平稳上升至合适高度，取出轨道，之后释放气压，让钢筋笼坐落在钢筋保护层垫块上，由底模支撑钢筋笼。

2. 体系转换借助顶部吊点，提升钢筋笼顶板，拆除顶板及侧墙钢筋绑扎胎架，完成内模板安装。

The system transition of the steel reinforcement cage means that the supporting system of the steel cage by jig frame is changed into the formwork supporting system, thus realizing the transition of the stress on the jig frame to the stress on the formwork.

1. The steel cage always sits on the sliding trolleys (skidding tracks) in the whole process of being pushed forward. To finally move the cage out the trolleys, it is necessary to lift up the steel cage after the cage is pushed to the designed position. Hence a number of air bags are inserted beneath the steel cage, and when the air bags are inflated, the steel cage will rise steadily to a suitable height. Then the trolleys are removed before the air in the bags is released to let the steel cage sit on the protective pad. Then the formwork below supports the steel cage.

2. The system transition is realized via the hoisting points on the top. Lift up the cage by the top plate, remove the steel binding jig frames for the top plate and the side wall binding, and the installation of internal formwork is completed.

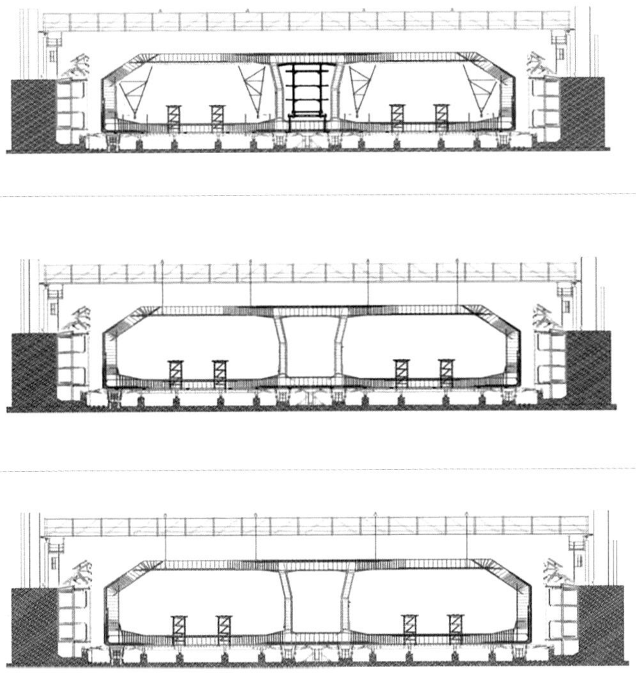

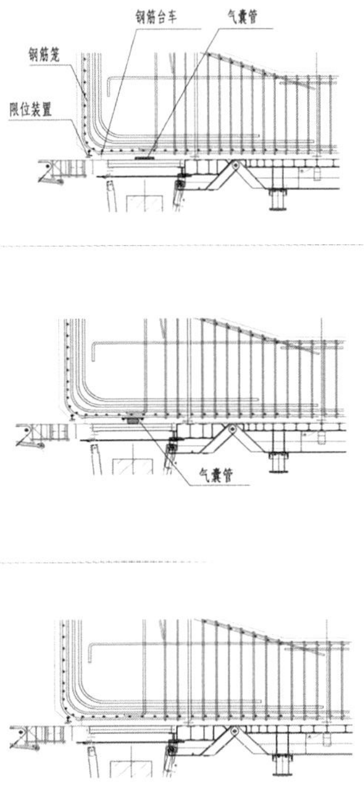

□ 钢筋笼在推入浇筑区前，在钢筋笼位置下方设置气囊管；
□ 将钢筋笼推入浇筑区位置。

Before pushing the steel reinforcement cage into the casting area, an air bag is put underneath the steel cage;
The steel cage is pushed to the designed place in the casting area.

□ 钢筋笼定位后，利用 4 台吊架将顶板钢筋悬挂起来； □ 拆除顶板钢筋胎架；
□ 气囊管充气，将钢筋笼顶升一定高度，抽出钢筋胎架。

After the steel cage is positioned, 4 hoisting frames lift the steel cage of the top plate;
The jig frame for the top plate is removed;
The inflated air bag raises the steel cage to a proper height, and the jig frame for the steel cage is taken away.

□ 气囊放气，将钢筋笼下放坐落在混凝土保护层垫块上； □ 抽出气囊；
□ 钢筋笼就位完毕，进入下一道工序。

The air in the air bag is released, and the steel cage is lowered onto the protective concrete cushion;
The air bag is taken away;
After the steel cage is landed on the designed place, the next stage begins.

钢筋笼体系转换流程图

Flow Chart of the System Transition for the Steel Reinforcement Cage

标准节段钢筋笼顶部设4台钢筋吊架，每台吊架上设2排，每排4个吊点，共计32个吊点，每个吊点提供70千牛吊力。吊点结构为顶部设置千斤顶，通过精轧螺纹钢连接钢筋笼，通过集中控制系统操作千斤顶，严格控制各吊点的受力均匀，实时可控。

3. 钢筋笼顶推至浇筑区后，32个吊点同时受力，顶板绑扎胎架分四级下降，每次下降5厘米，共20厘米。铺设顶板绑扎胎架行走轨道，拖出顶板绑扎胎架。

4. 卷扬机沿着行走轨道牵引顶板胎架，转运至下一节段使用。拖出过程中，须仔细观察胎架与钢筋笼是否有摩擦和挂住现象，并即时排除。

5. 气囊充气顶起钢筋笼，拖出滑移轨道，气囊放气，依次拖出气囊，底部保护层垫块支撑钢筋笼并坐落在底模上。

6. 顶板绑扎胎架、滑移方钢、滑移轨道、气囊卸除后，将内模推入钢筋笼，调整、定位，然后下降吊点，将顶板钢筋笼受力转换到内模上，并卸载吊点，即完成钢筋笼体系转换。

Four steel hanger frames are set on the top of the steel cage of each standard segments, with 2 rows for each hanger frame and 4 hoisting points in each row. Each of the 32 hoisting points can withstand the lifting force of 70 KN. The hoisting points are equipped with pulling jacks on the top and are connected with the steel cage by finish rolling steel rebars. The jacks are operated through a centralized control system to ensure that each hoisting point bears the pulling force evenly and is controllable.

3. After the steel cage is pushed to the casting area, 32 hoisting points are pulled at the same time, and the jig frame for the top plate binding lowers down in four stages, 5 centimeters each stage, 20 centimeters in all four stages. Then the sliding tracks to move the jig frame for the top plates binding are placed to pull the jig frame away.

4. A windlass pulls the jig frame for the top plate binding away along the sliding tracks, and the jig frame is transported to the next section for further use. In the process of pulling out the jig frame, care should be given to avoid the friction between the jig frame and the steel cage. Adjustment must be done to avoid any friction and scratching.

5. When the air bags are inflated to jack up the steel cage, the sliding trolleys should be pulled out. When the air in the air bags is let out, the air bags are pulled out. The protective cushion blocks at the bottom support the steel cage and let it sit on the bottom formwork.

6. After the jig frame for top plate binding, the sliding square steel bars, the sliding trolleys, and the air bag are removed, the internal formwork is pushed into the steel cage. After the adjustment and positioning of the formwork, the hoisting points are lowered and the stress moves from the top plate of the steel cage to the internal formwork. Uninstall the hoisting points, and the system transition of the steel cage is completed.

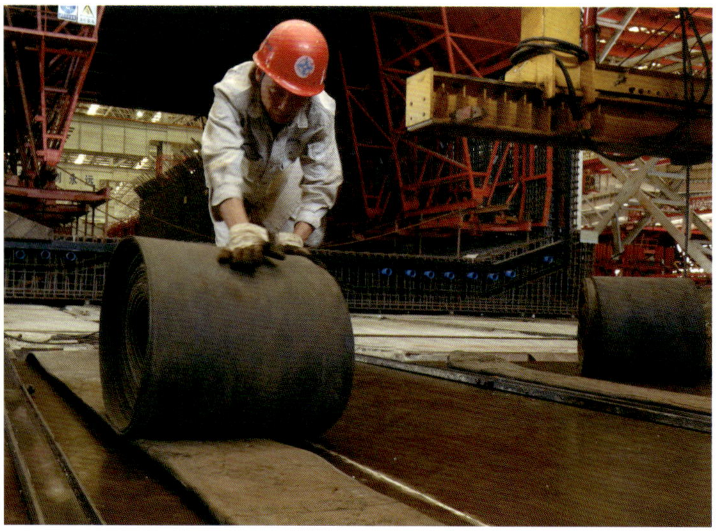

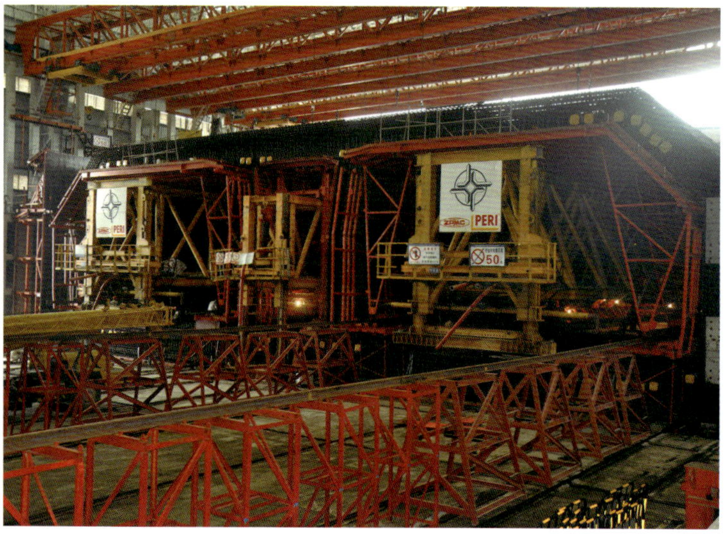

1. 移出钢筋笼顶升气囊
Removing the Airbag Used to Uplift the Steel Reinforcement Cage
2. 钢筋笼绑扎支架绞移出浇筑区
Moving the Jig Frame for the Steel Reinforcement Cage out of the Casting Area by Winches
3. 钢筋笼顶部吊架
Hanger on Top of the Steel Reinforcement Cage

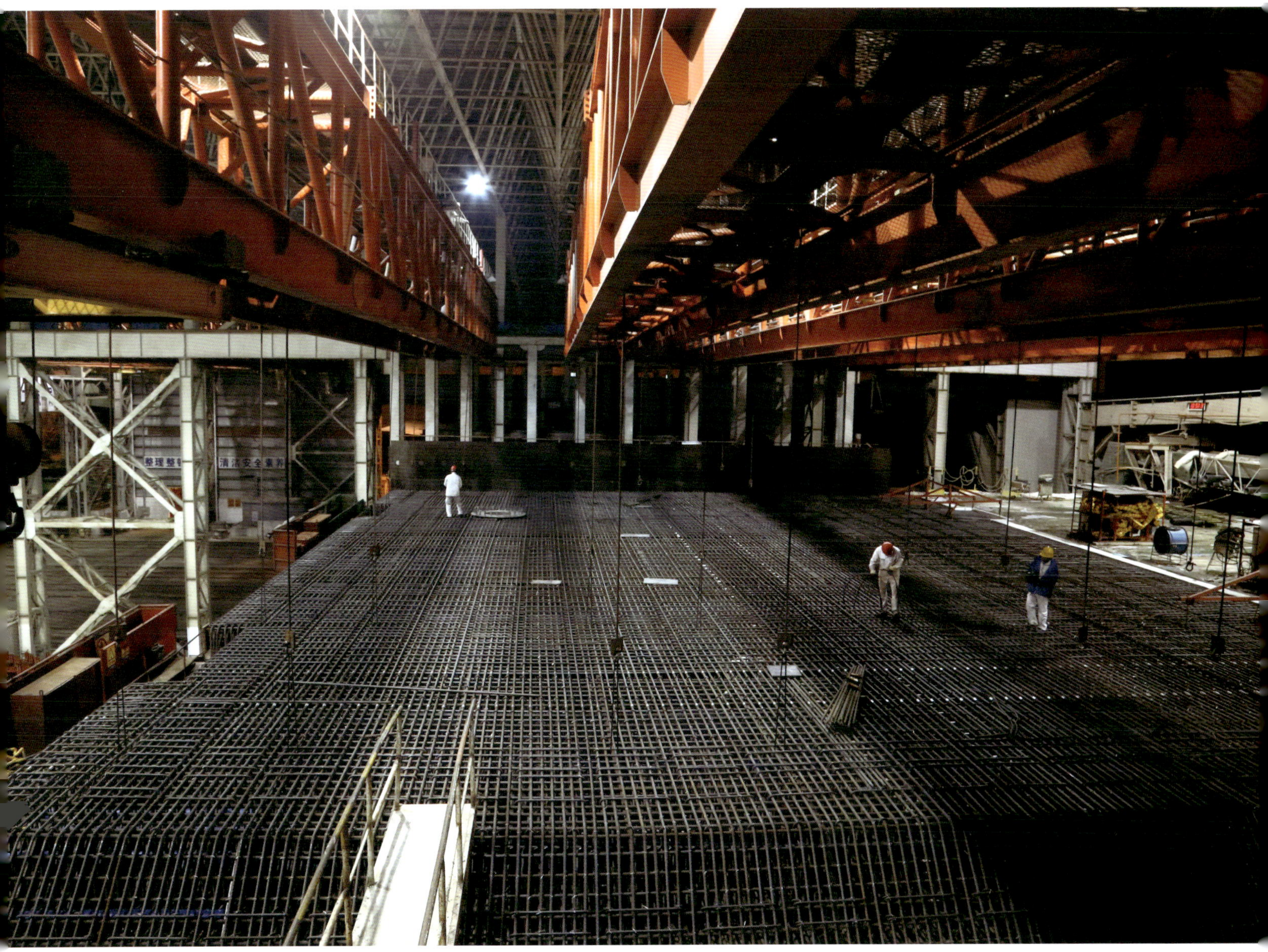

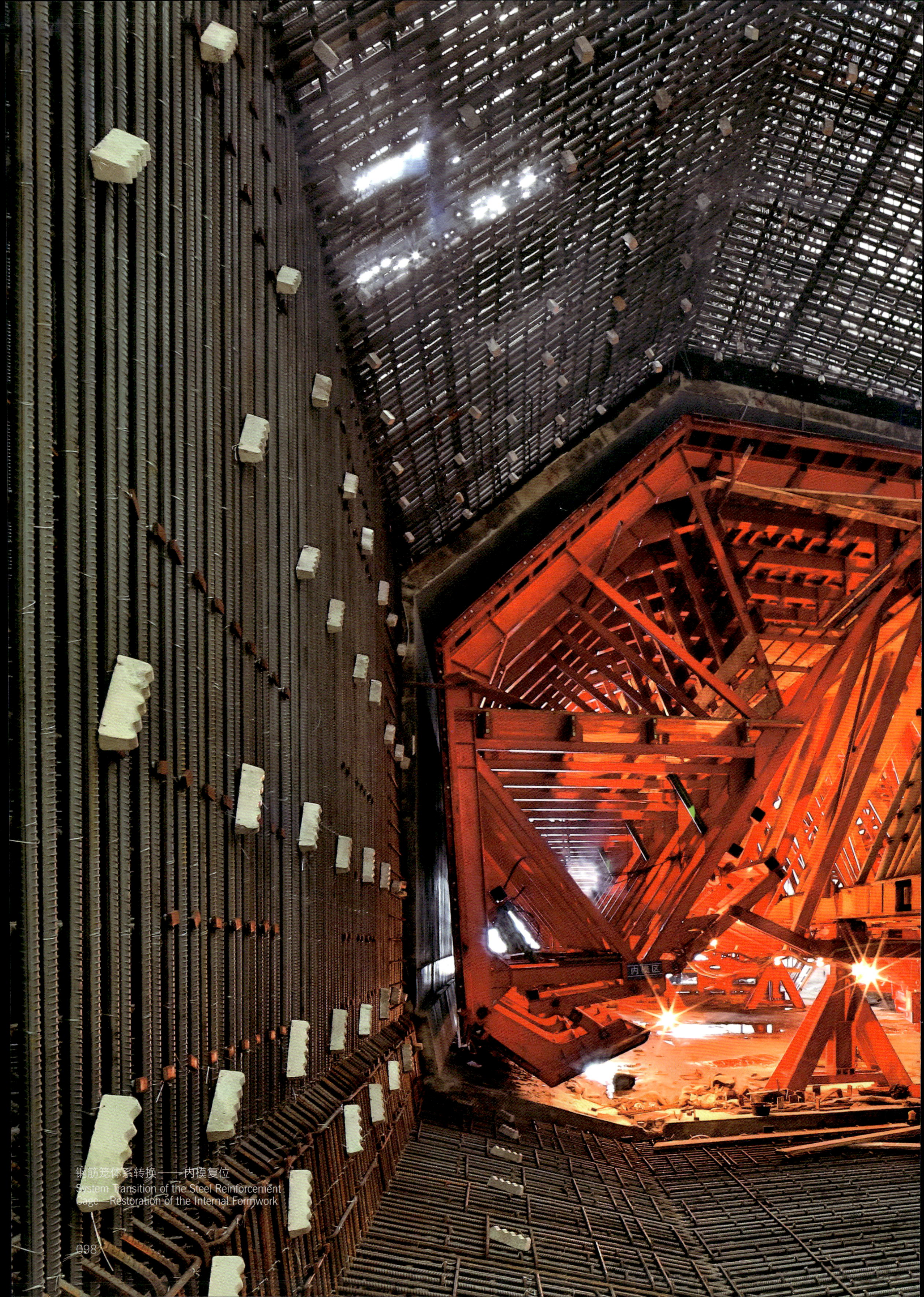

钢筋笼体系转换——内模复位
System Transition of the Steel Reinforcement Cage—Restoration of the Internal Formwork

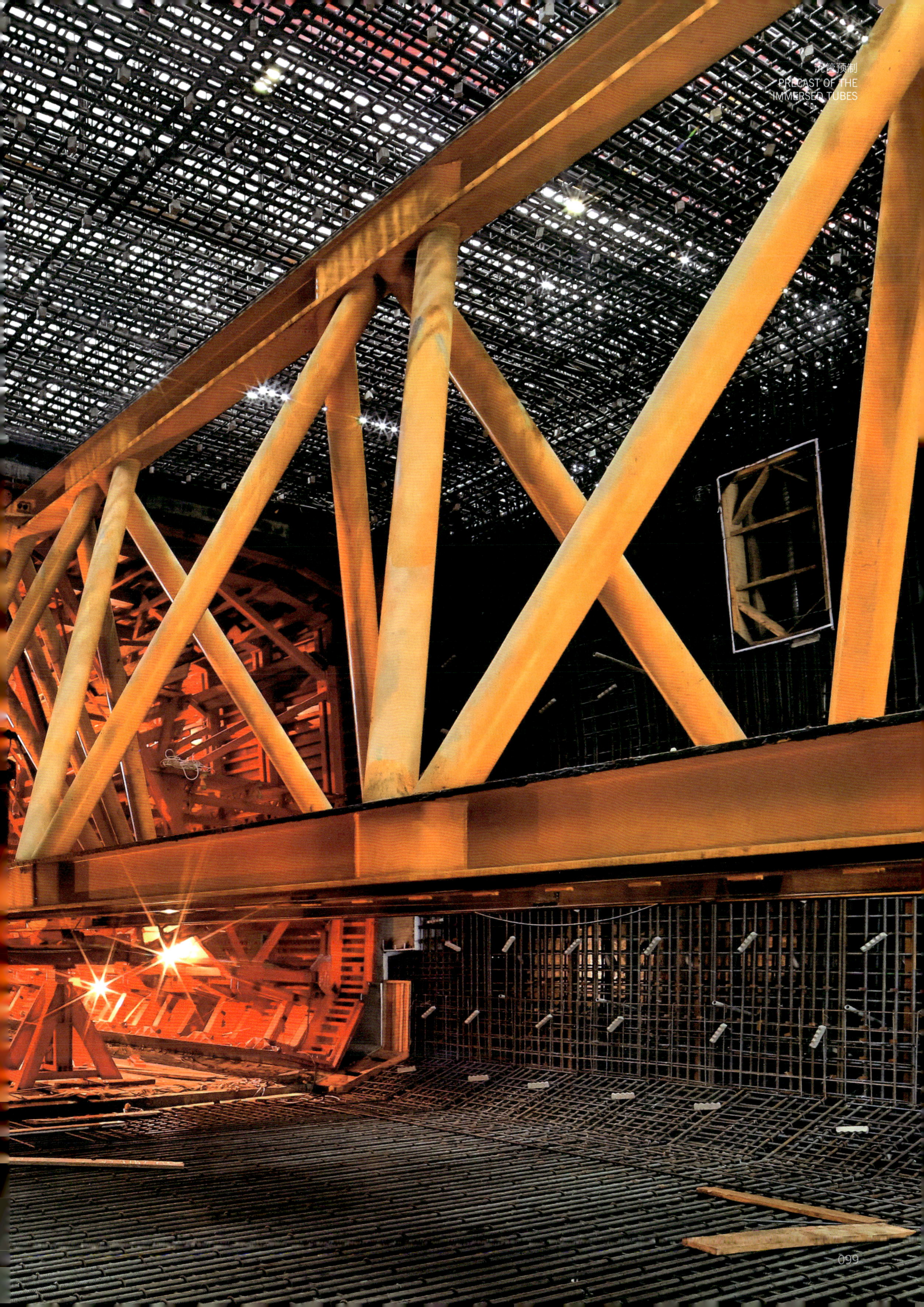

沉管预制模板系统

PRECAST FORMWORK OF THE IMMERSED TUBE SYSTEM

沉管预制模板由德国PERI公司设计，上海振华重工（集团）有限公司制造。主要分为底模、内模、侧模、端模和针形梁五大系统。底模、侧模、内模均为全液压钢模，仅端模为分块拼装式，每套模板总重约2000吨。

整体式全液压钢模相对传统拼装式模板有明显优势：1. 整体式钢模具有良好的整体性和刚度，没有明显的拼接缝，沉管外观质量好。2. 模板不会产生明显形变，涨模量小，有效保障沉管保护层厚度。3. 底模、侧模、内模采用全液压系统控制，操作简单、效率极高，是7~8天一个预制周期的关键保障因素之一。4. 动作、位置限位精准，经100多次周转使用无明显变化，仍然能精确保证沉管尺寸。5. 模板装拆人、机需求大幅降低，成本费用低。

The precast formwork of the immersed tube was designed by PERI of Germany and manufactured by ZPMC in Shanghai. The formwork system is mainly composed of five major sub-systems: bottom formwork, internal formwork, side formwork, end formwork and pointed beams. The bottom formwork, the side formwork and the internal formwork are monolithic hydraulic steel formwork and only the end formwork is an assemblage of more pieces. Each set of the formwork weighs approximately 2,000 tons.

The monolithic hydraulic steel formwork has obvious advantages compared with the traditional seams formwork.

1. The monolithic steel formwork shows sound integrity and rigidity without any conspicuous sealings, and the outward quality of the immersed tube is better.

2. The formwork will not easily deform and swell, which can effectively assure the thickness of the cover of the immersed tube.

3. The bottom formwork, the side formwork and the internal formwork are all controlled by the hydraulic system, so that the operation of the formwork is simple but highly efficient. This is one of the critical factors to ensure the production cycle of 7-8 days.

4. The monolithic steel formwork can accurately restrict the movement and location of the tube. There is no obvious change after over 100 periodic uses, and the dimensions of the immersed tube can still be accurately controlled.

5. The demand for hands and machine in the assembling and disassembling of the formwork is greatly reduced, thus the cost is reduced.

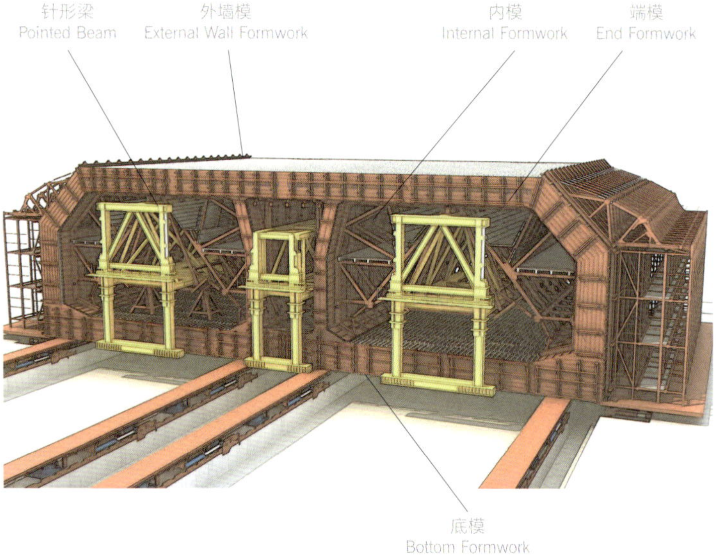

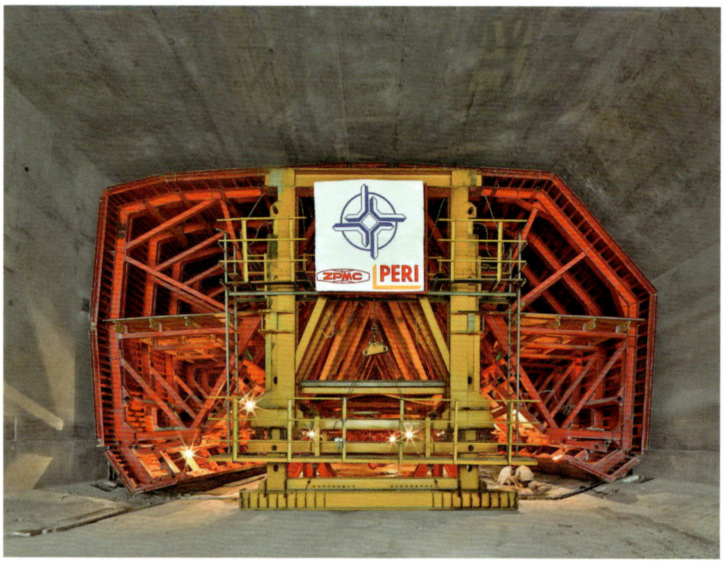

1. 沉管模板系统结构图
Structural Diagram of the Formwork System of the Immersed Tube

2. 内模
Internal Formwork

3. 沉管模板系统
Formwork System of the Immersed Tube

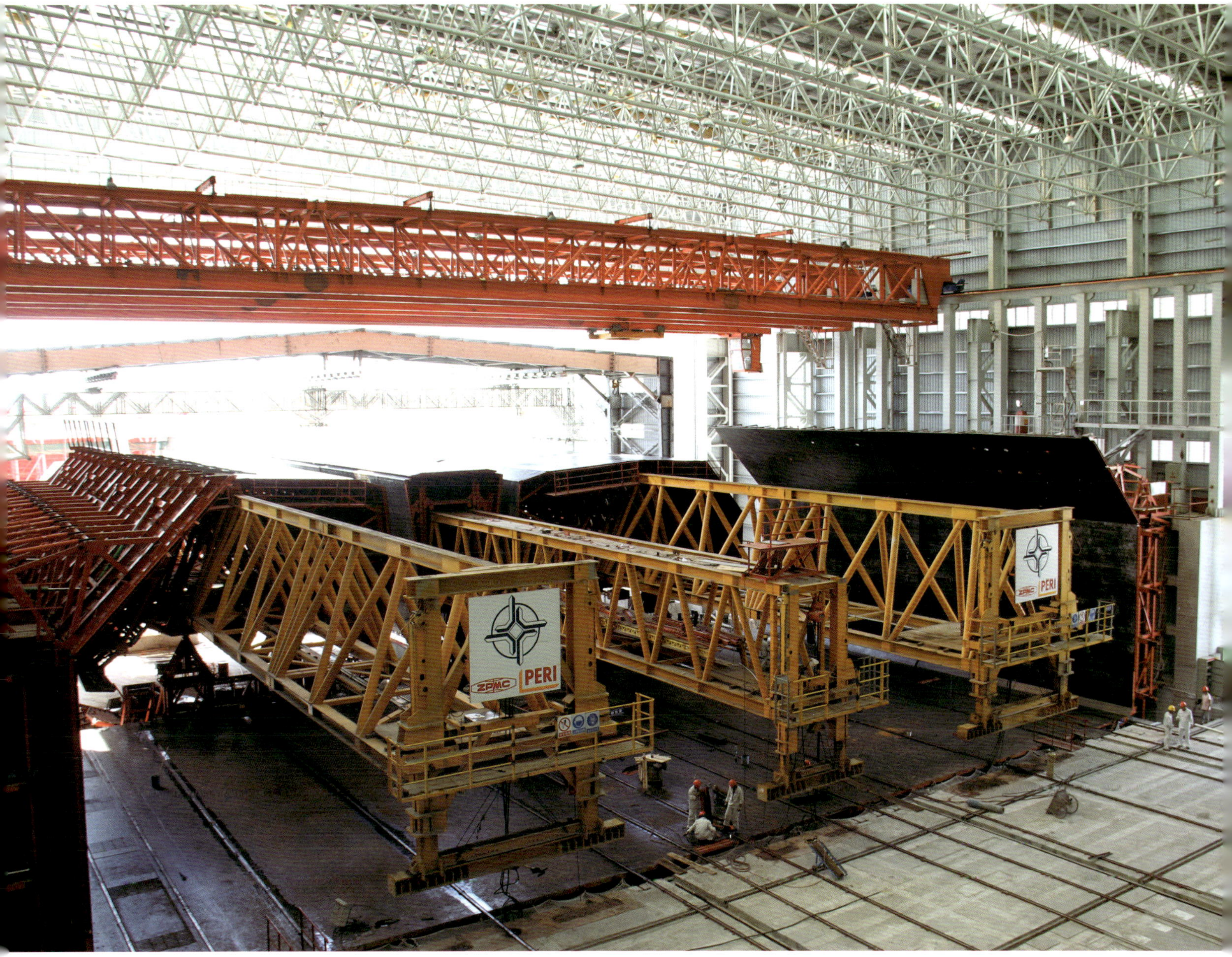

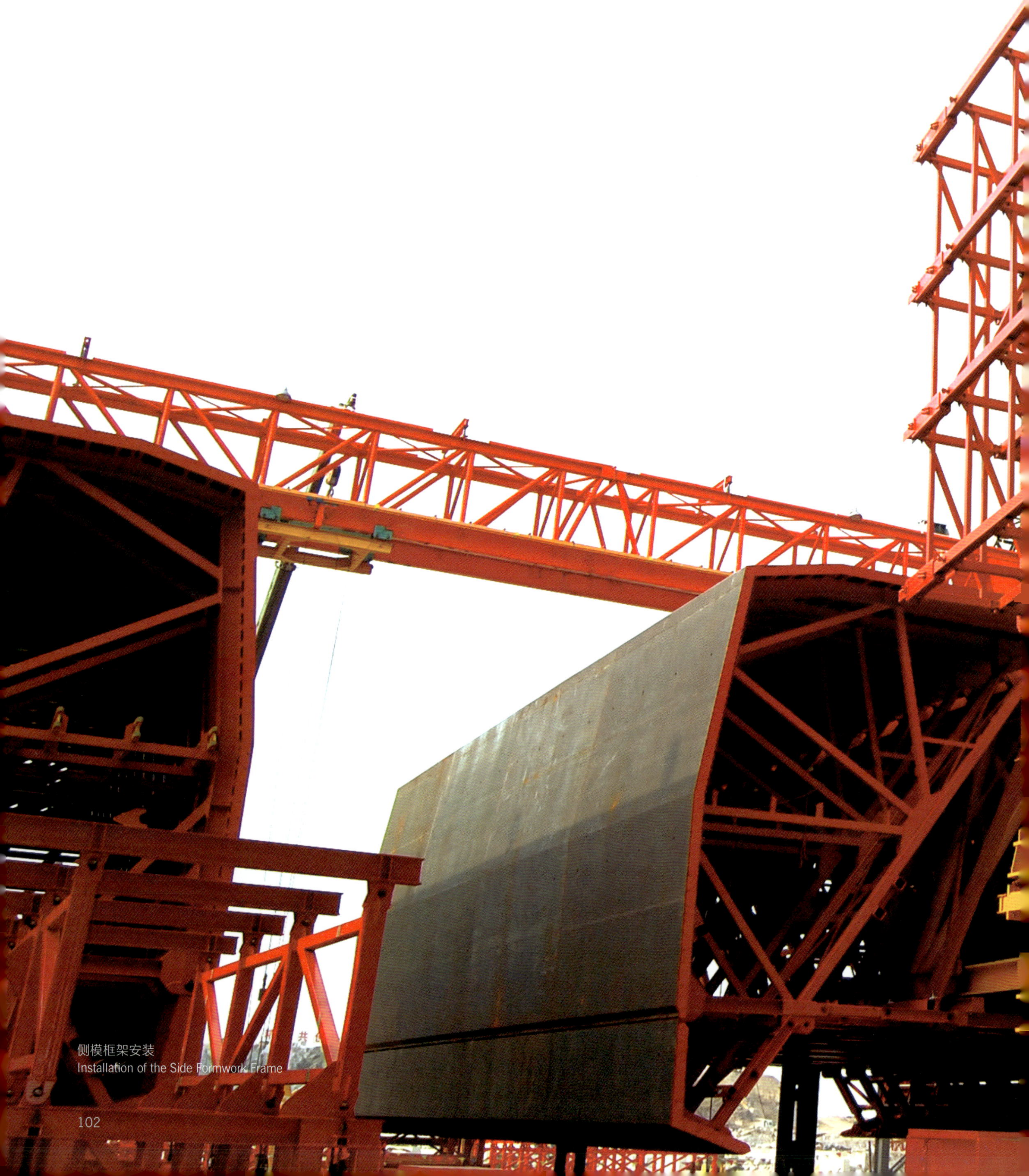

侧模框架安装
Installation of the Side Formwork Frame

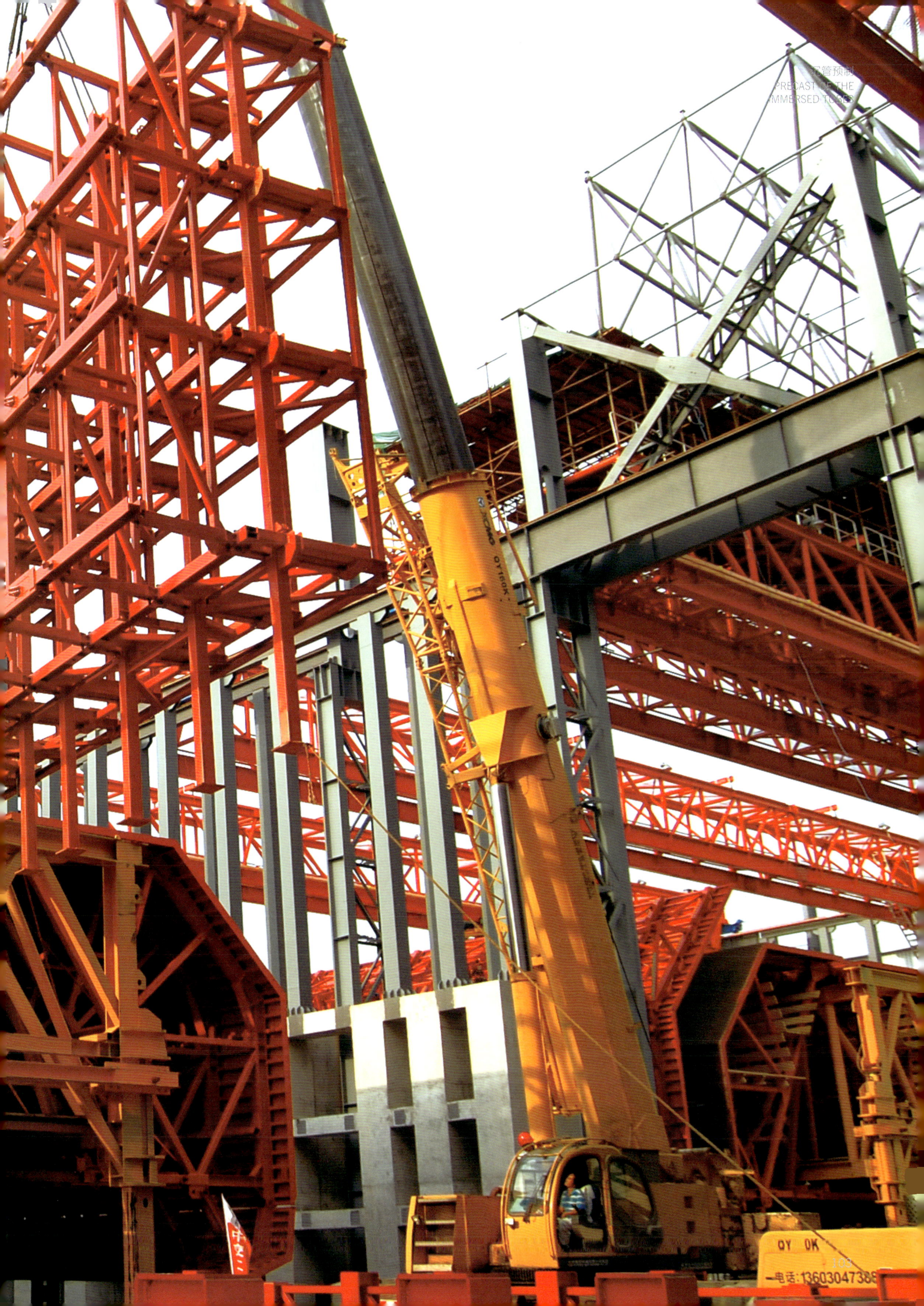

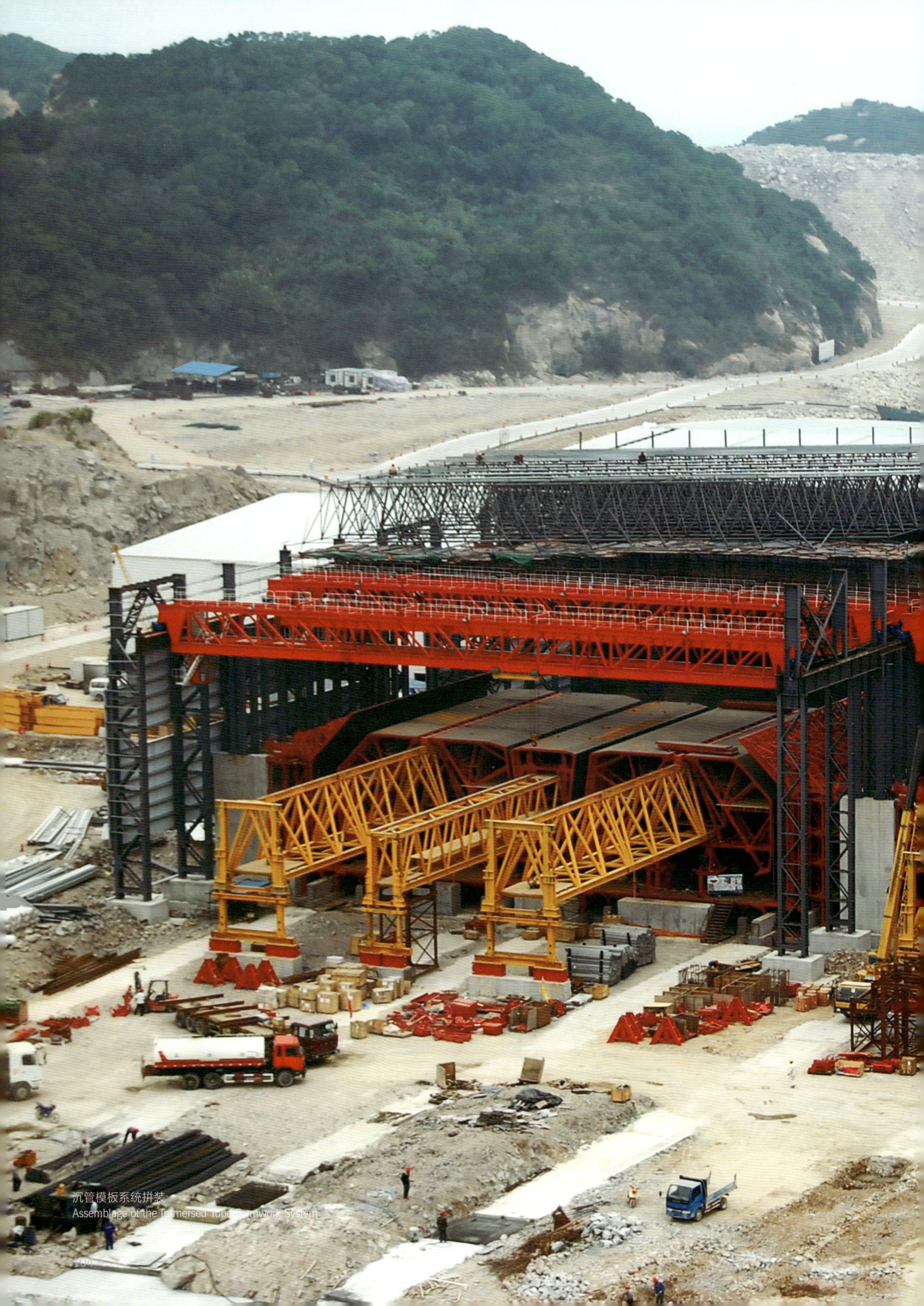

沉管模板系统拼装
Assemblage of the Immersed Tube Formwork System

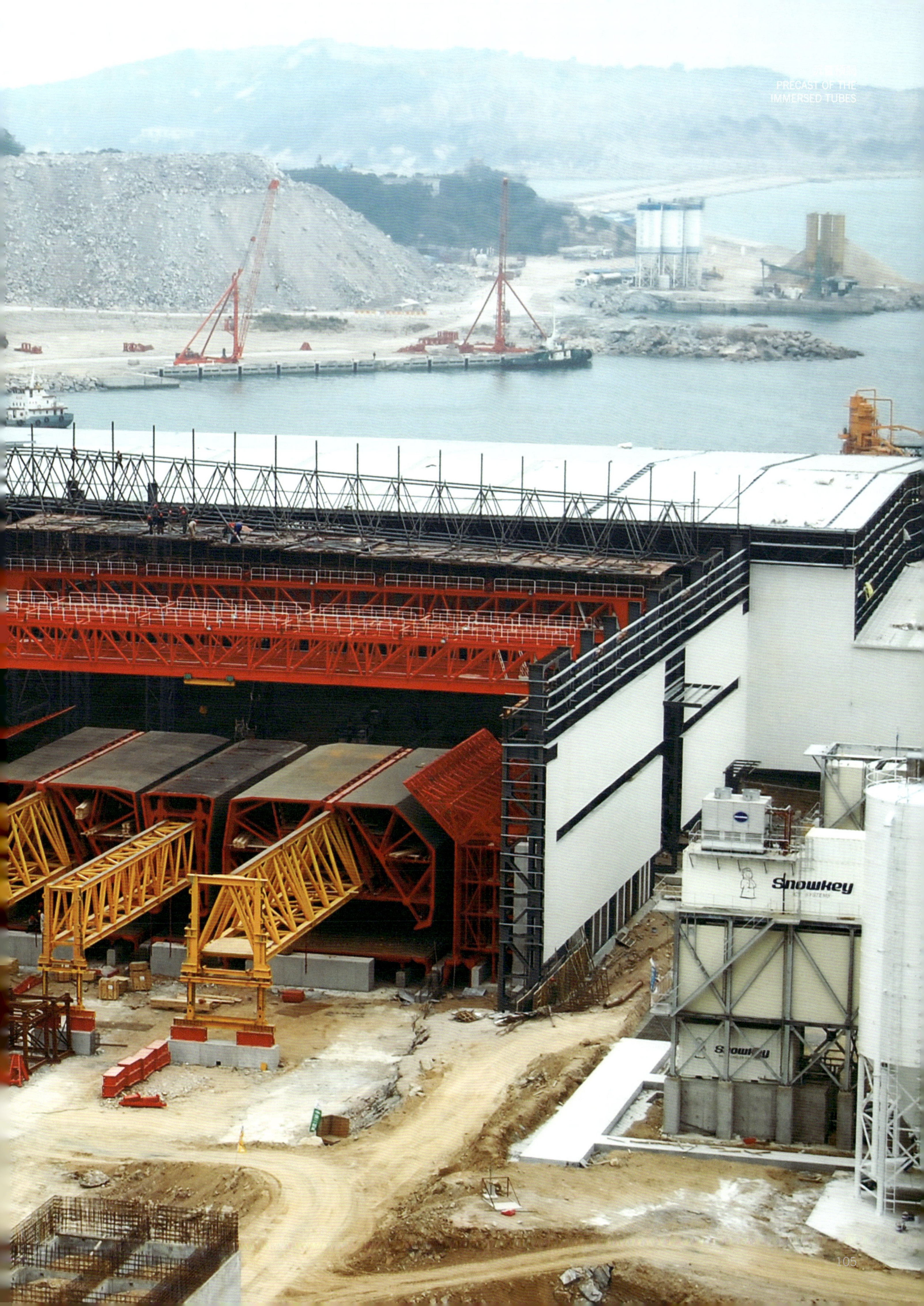
Snowkey
Snowkey

每套模板设置1套底模，固定于浇筑台座。底模通过底部千斤顶支撑系统实现合模和脱模，分为左、右行车道底模，廊道底模以及连接的翻折板；设计长23.92米，宽39米，布置横向支撑大梁和纵向分配梁，支撑大梁与支撑千斤顶相连接。底模支撑系统主要包括：自锁式液压千斤顶、楔形千斤顶、支撑关节和其他附属顶升液压装置。

Each set of formworks is equipped with 1 set of bottom formwork fixed on the casting base. The supporting jacks at the bottom of the bottom formwork are used for the bonding and separation of the formwork. The bottom formwork consists of the bottom formworks of the left and right driving lanes, the bottom formwork of the pipe gallery and the connecting turnover plate. The bottom formwork is designed to be 23.92 meters long and 39 meters wide, with horizontal supporting girders and longitudinal distribution girders, while the supporting girders are connected with the supporting jacks. The supporting system of the bottom formwork mainly includes self-locking hydraulic jacks, wedge jacks, supporting joints and other auxiliary hydraulic thrust devices.

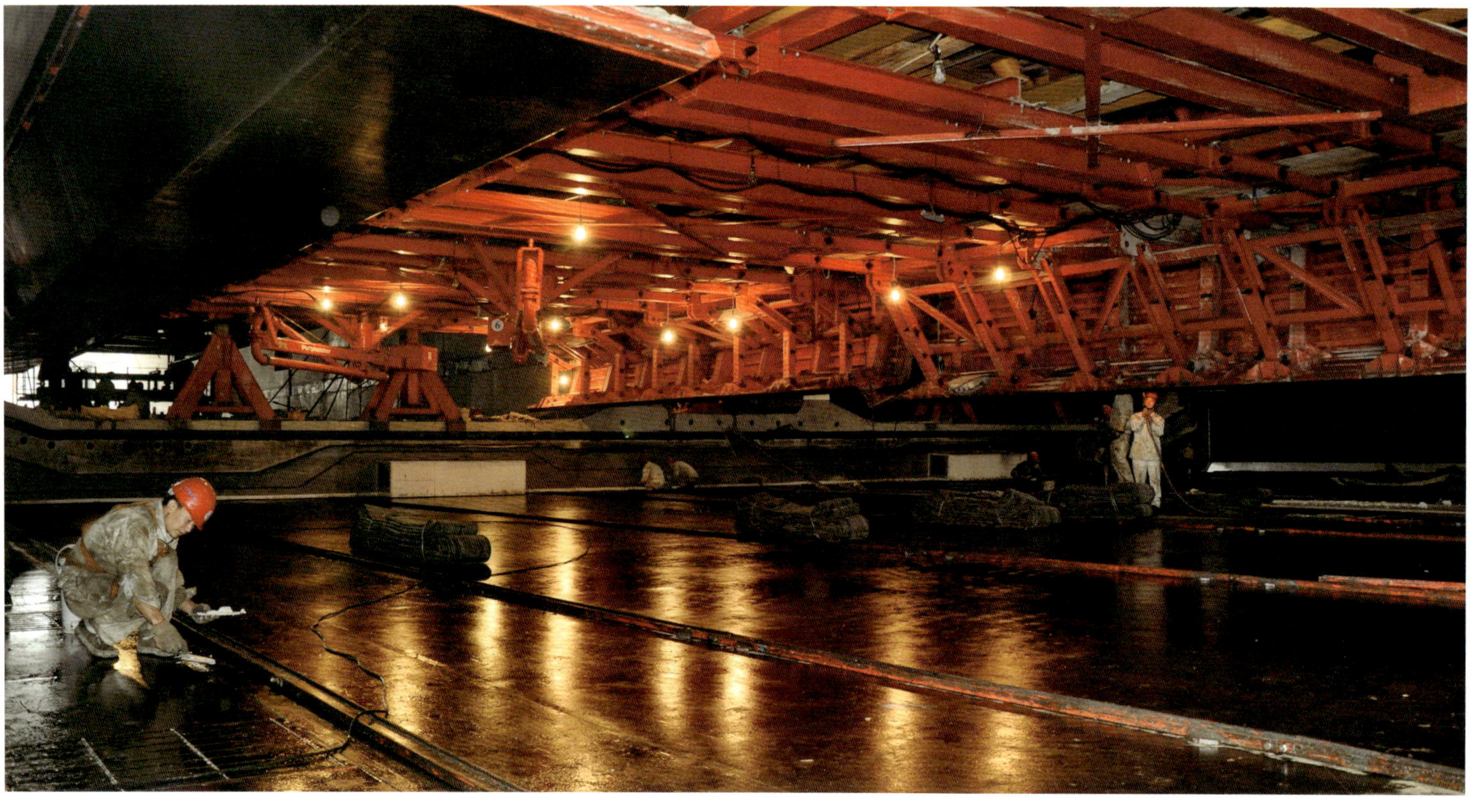

1. 底模养护
Maintenance of the Bottom Formwork

2. 底模支撑关节
Supporting Joint of the Bottom Formwork

3. 底模升降液压千斤顶
Hydraulic Jack for the Lifting of the Bottom Formwork

4. 底模及针行梁
Bottom Formwork and Pointed Beam

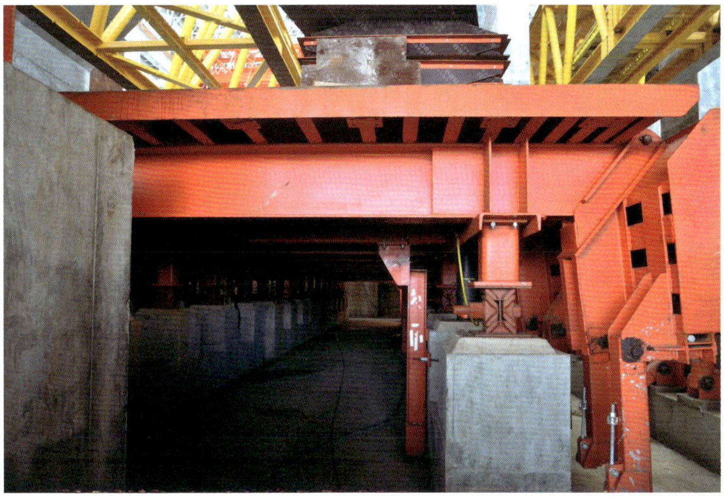

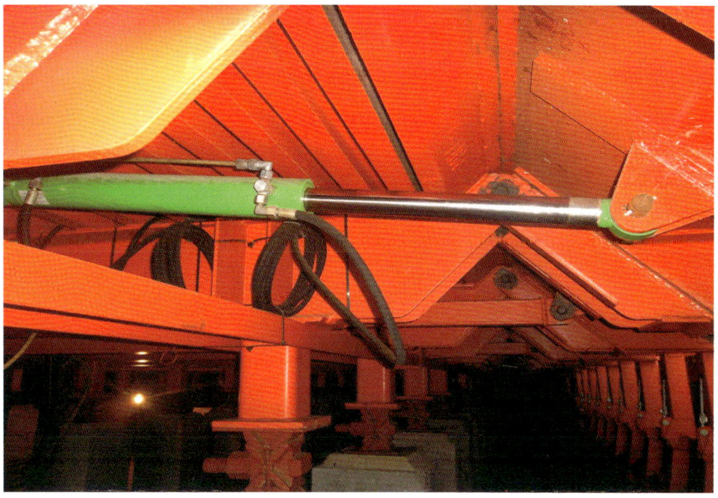

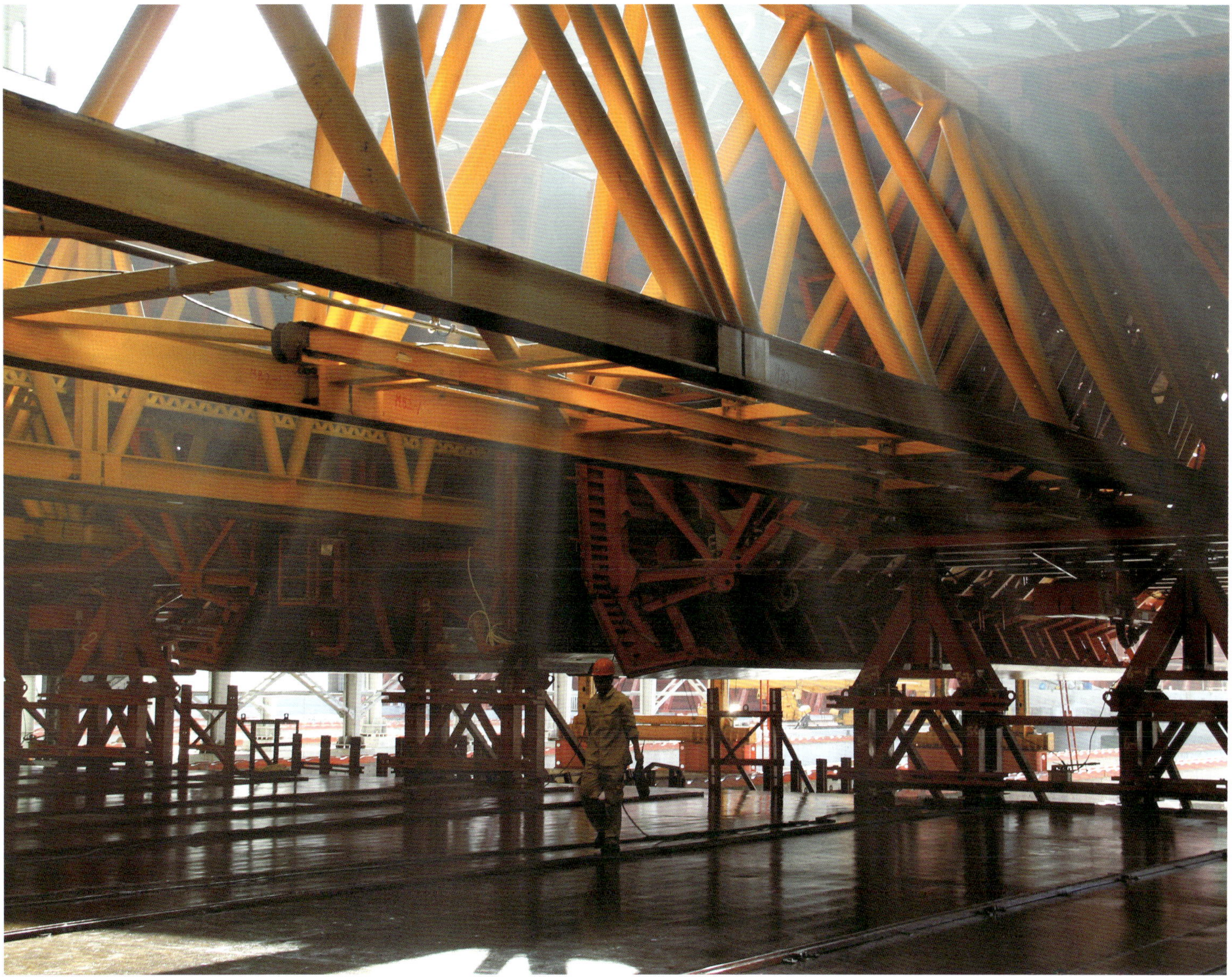

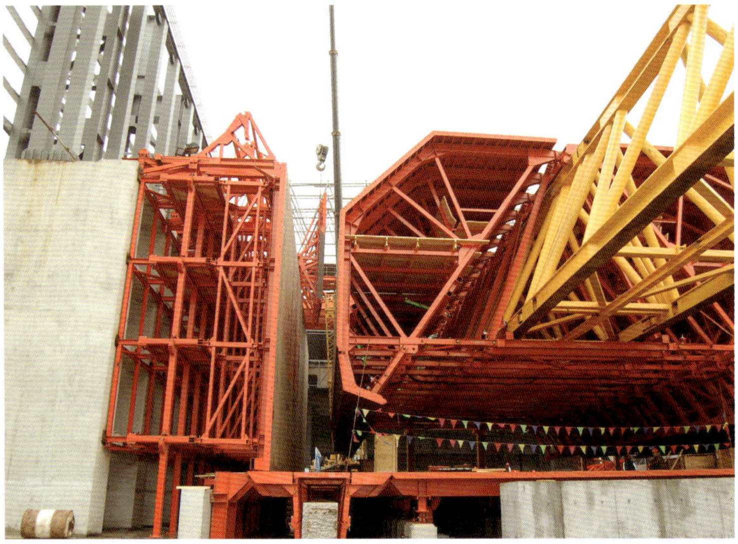

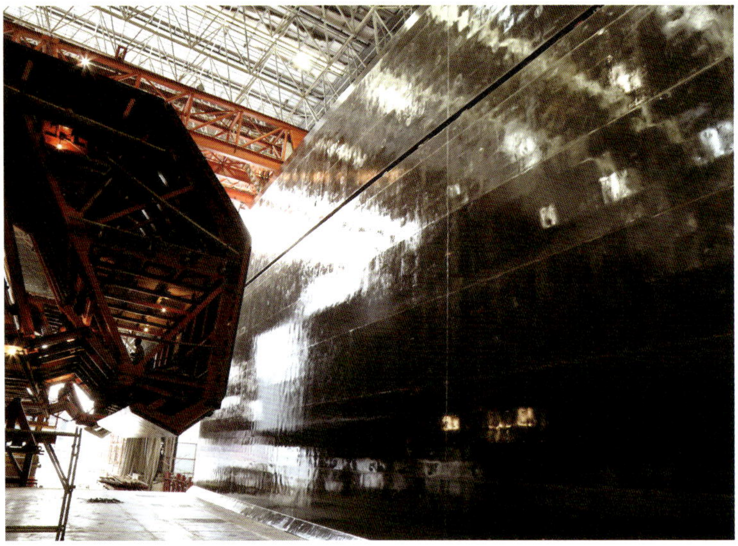

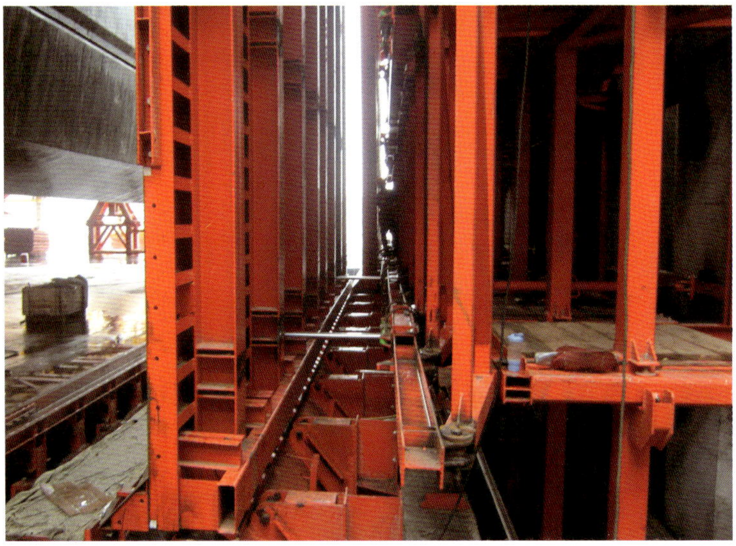

1		
2		4
3		

1. 侧模支架安装
   Installation of the Side Formwork Brackets
2. 侧模
   Side Formwork
3. 侧模复位
   Restoration of the Side Formwork
4. 侧模
   Side Formwork

每套模板设置左右 2 个侧模。单个侧模由 4 块 5.98 米 ×7.771 米、4 块 5.98 米 ×3.408 米、4 块 5.98 米 ×1.73 米模板组成，采用全液压驱动，整体安装、整体脱模、整体移动，可沿固定轨道水平进退 1 米。侧模支撑系统由可伸缩钢框架及反力墙构成。整个侧模采用插销、螺杆—螺栓配套连接，为方便混凝土振捣，侧模上端布置有 2 节可翻折模块，其上开设多排振捣孔。

每套模板设置 3 个穿入式移动内模，可做拆、合模动作和纵向移动。单个内模横向由 2 块组成，具有翻折功能；纵向由 4 段组成，每段长 5.8 米，总长 23.2 米。

Each set of formworks are composed of two side formworks, one on the left and one on the right. Each single side formwork is made up of four 5.980×7.771-meter formworks, four 5.980×3.408-meter formworks and four 5.980×1.730-meter formworks. All of them are fully hydraulic driven and proper for global installation, global demolding, and global movement, and all can move back and forth by 1 meter horizontally along the fixed track. The support system for the side formwork consists of a retractable steel frame and the reaction wall. The whole side formwork is connected into one integrated whole with latches, screw bolts and nuts. In order to facilitate concrete vibratory mixing, the upper end of the side formwork is equipped with two foldable modules with multiple rows of vibratory mixing holes in them.

Each set of formworks are also equipped with 3 infixing movable internal modules, which can be disassembled and assembled and can move longitudinally. Any single internal module consists of 2 pieces in the horizontal direction which can be folded, and four sections in the longitudinal direction, 5.8 meters long for each piece and 23.2 meters in total.

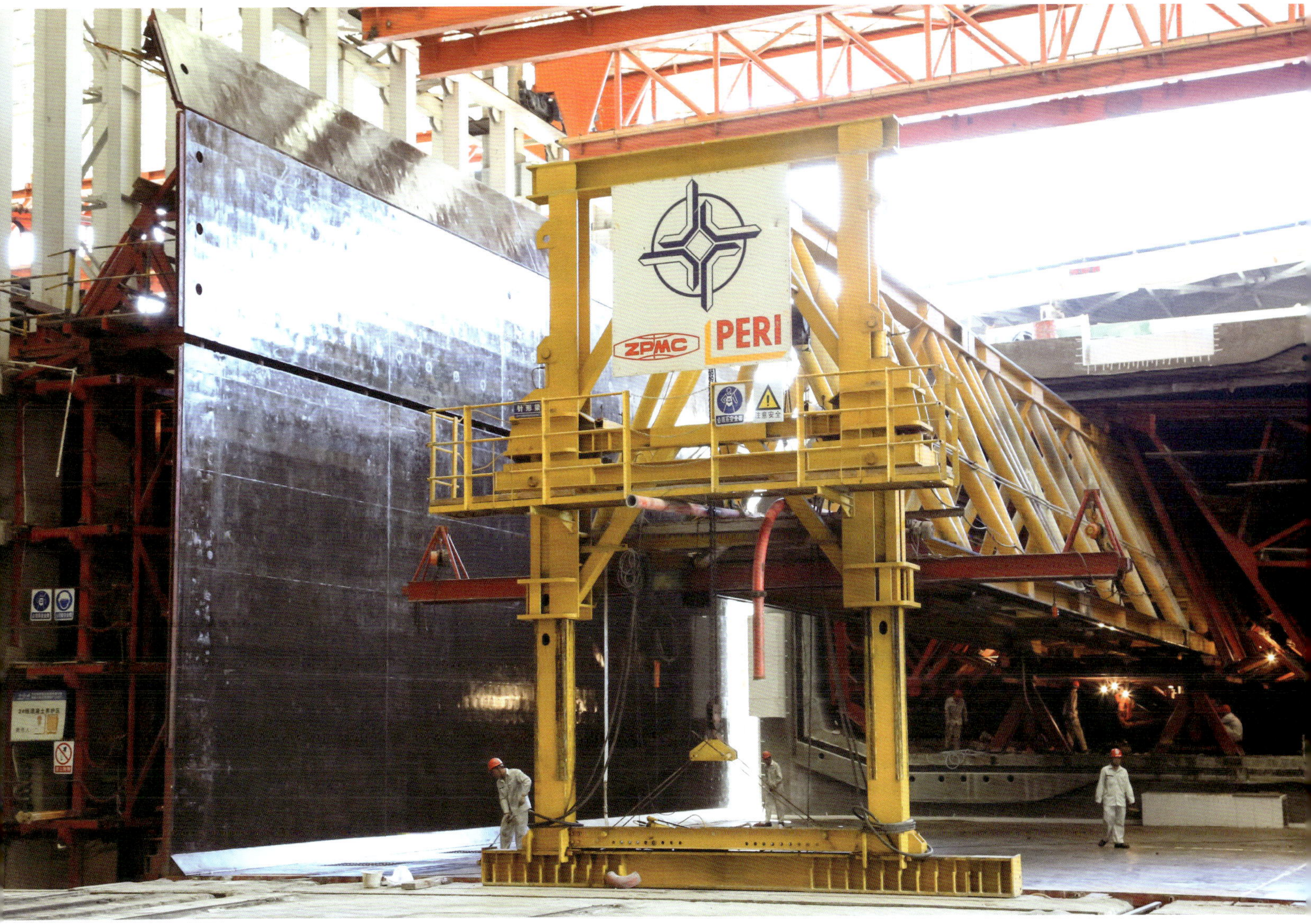

每套模板设置两套可拆卸式端模，分别为沉管端头EJ模板和节段端头SJ模板，利用桥式起重机安装和拆除。

Each set of formworks have two sets of removable end formworks: one is the EJ formworks for the ends of the immersed tube, and one is the SJ formworks for the ends of the tube segments. Bridge cranes are used for the installation and removal of the end formworks.

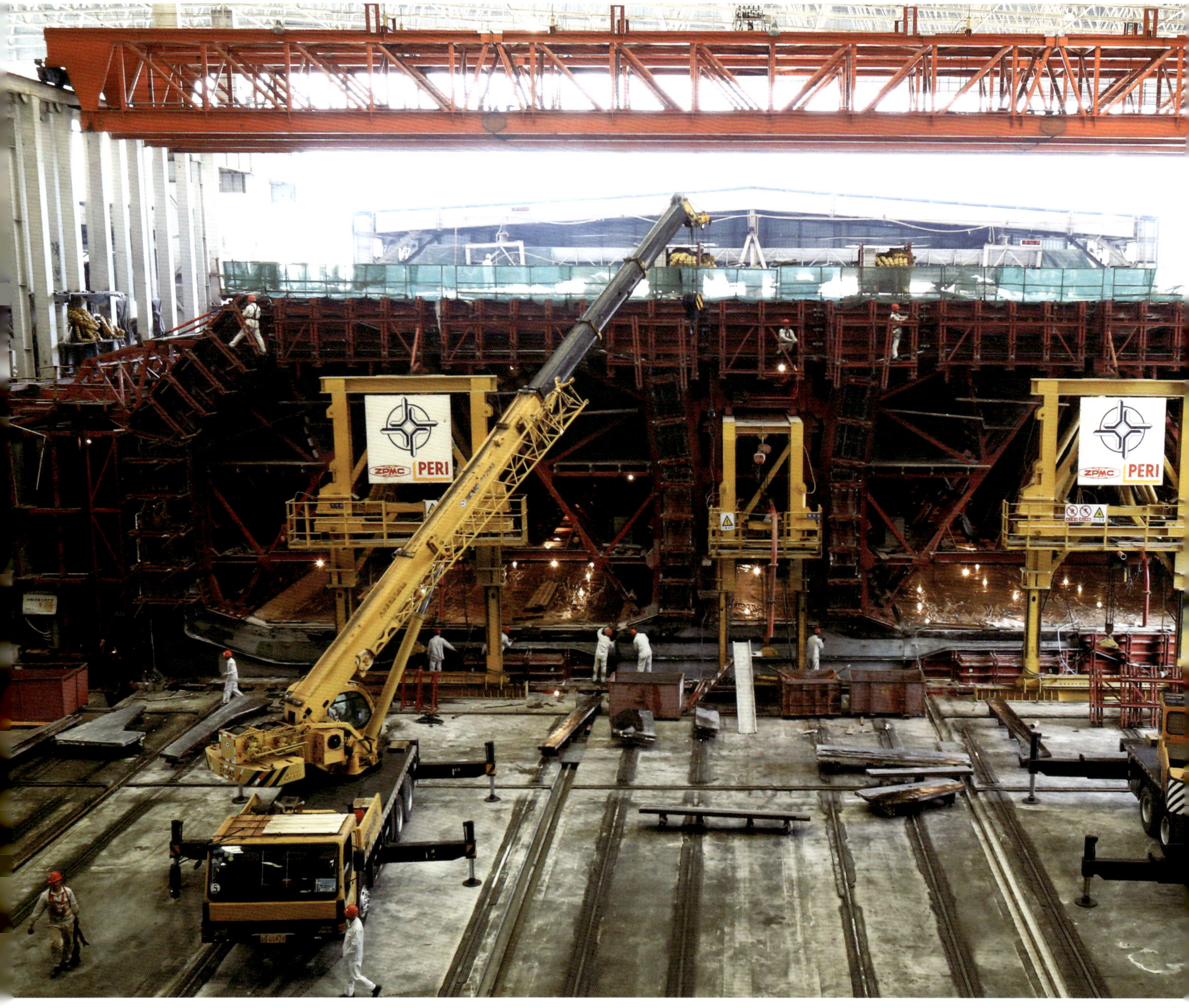

1. 端模安装
End Formwork Installation

2. SJ 端端模结构图
Structure of the End Formwork at the SJ End

3—5. 端模安装
End Formwork Installation

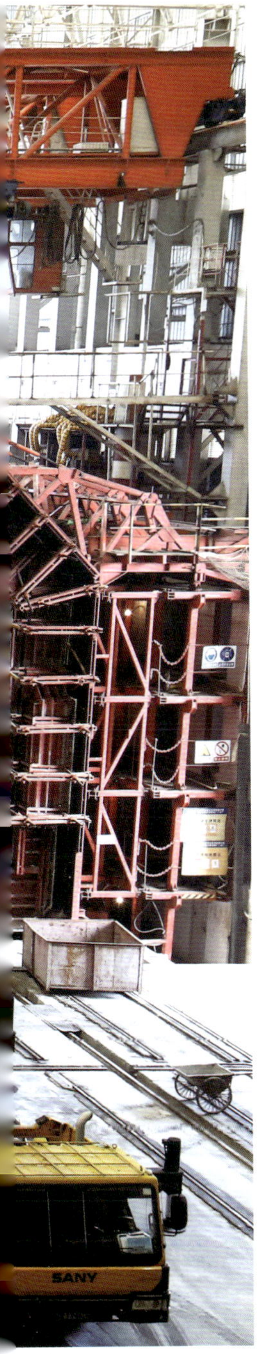

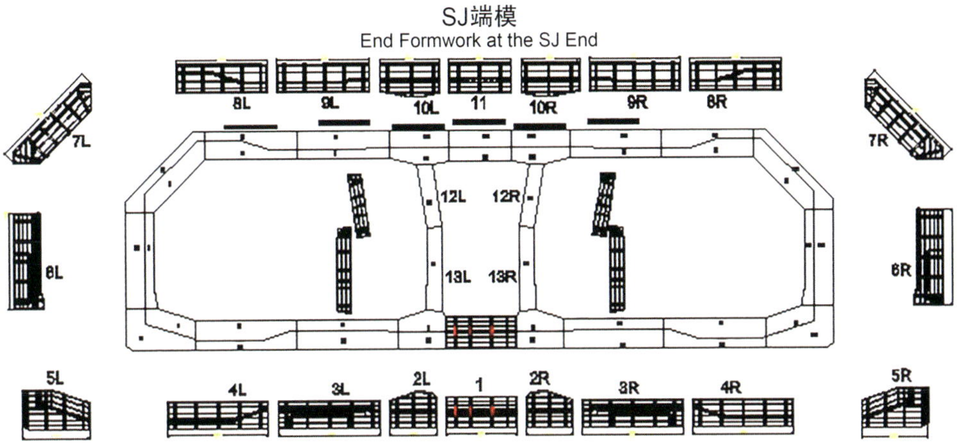

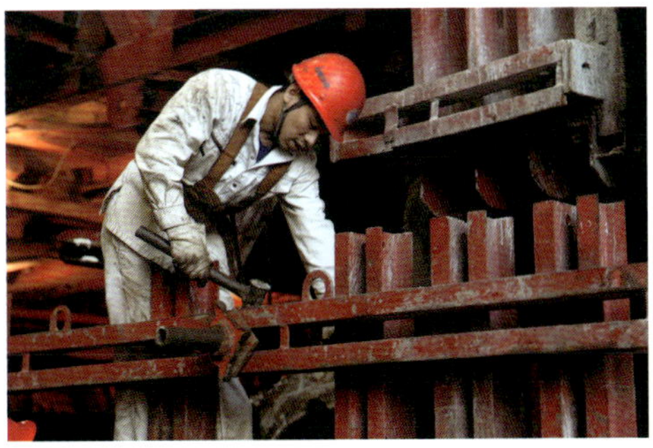

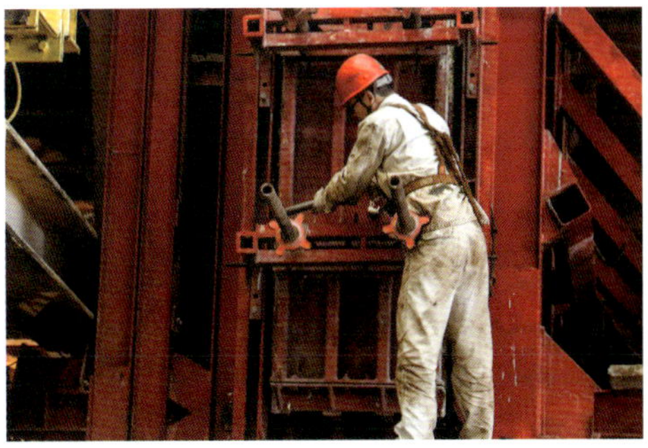

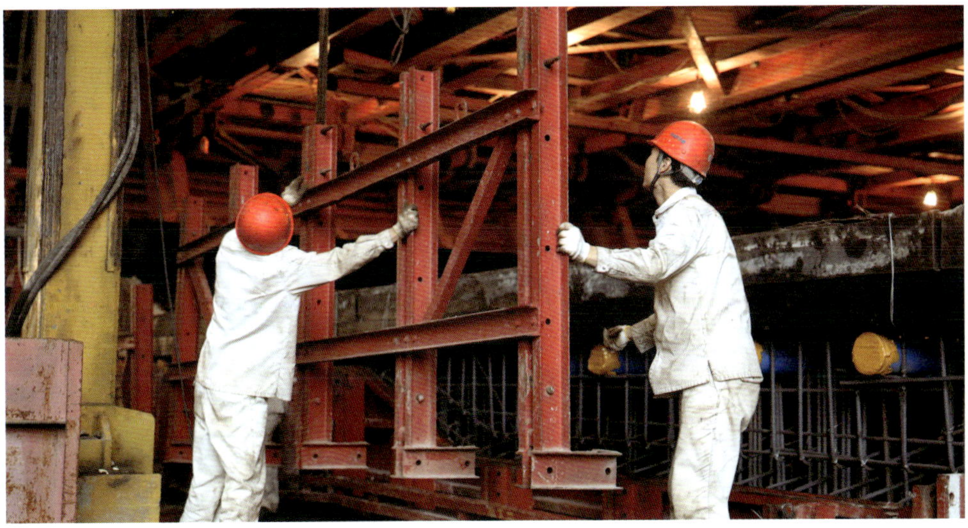

沉管 SJ 端端模安装全景图
Panoramic View of the End Formwork Installation at the SJ End of the Immersed Tube

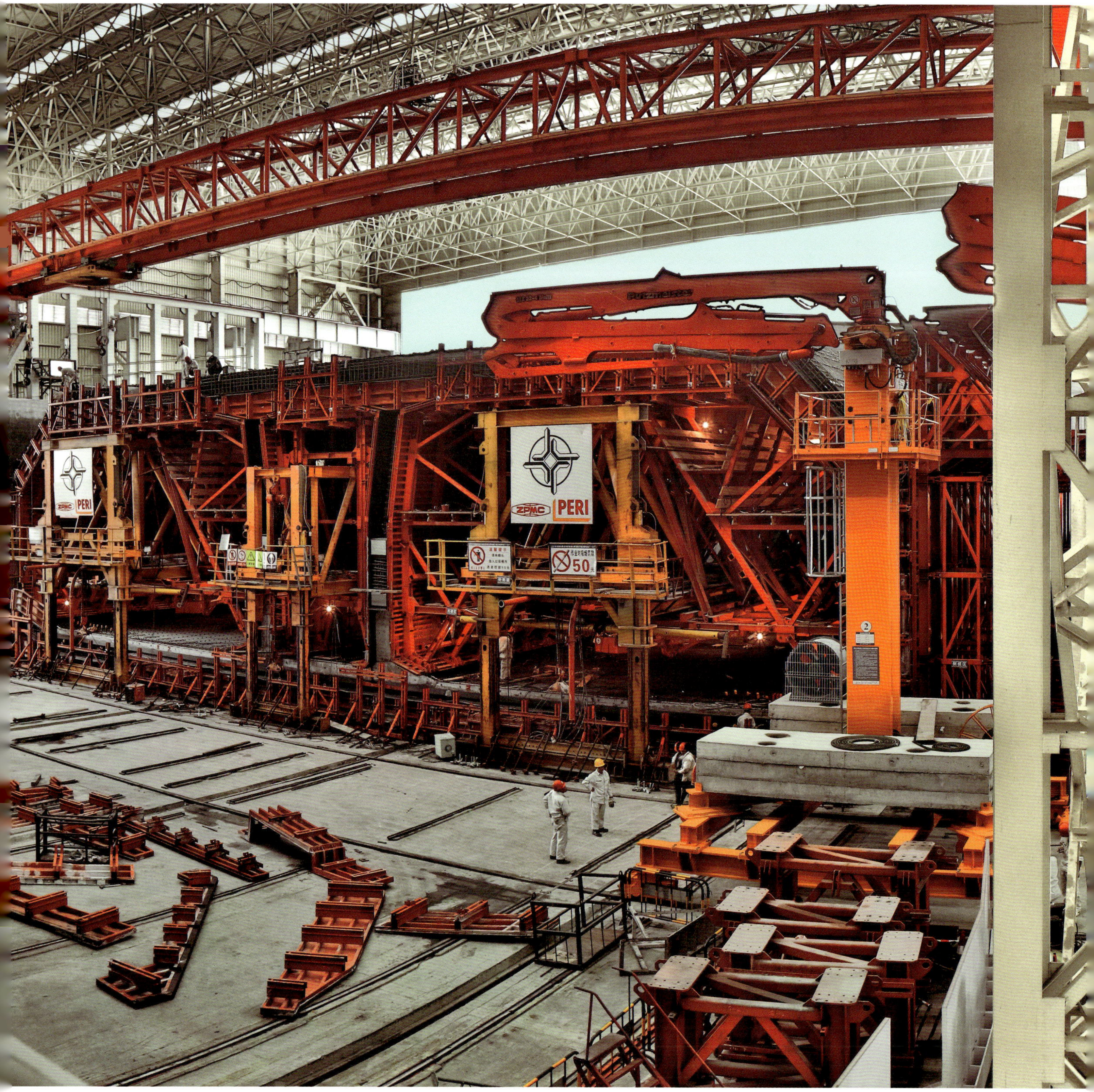

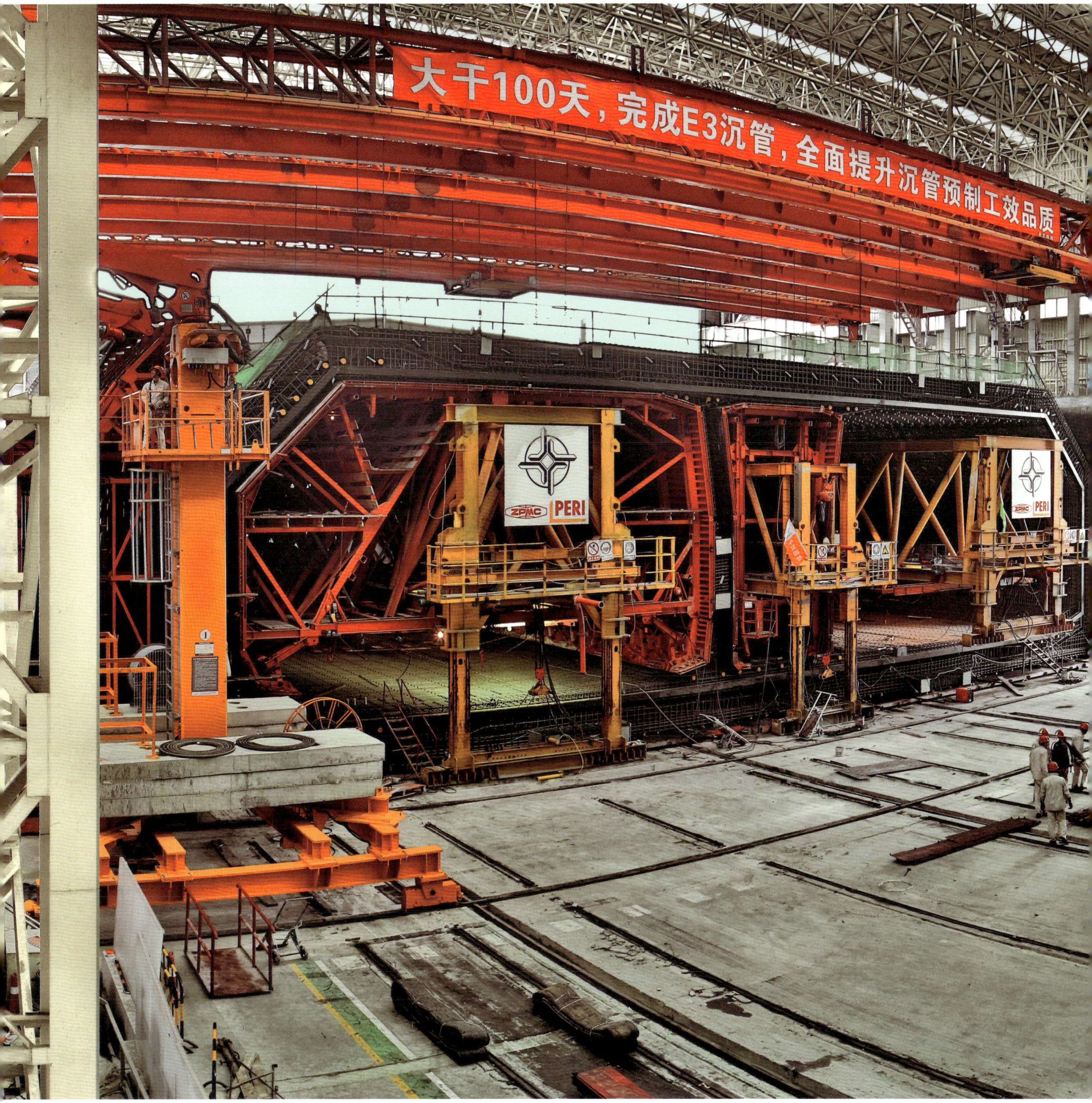
大干100天，完成E3沉管，全面提升沉管预制工效品质
ZPMC
PERI
ZPMC
PERI

混凝土生产和运输

CONCRETE PRODUCTION AND TRANSPORTATION

在厂区设置自动计量拌和系统生产混凝土，确保混凝土出站品质。

根据现场条件选择合理的混凝土输送方式，尽可能缩短输送距离和中间环节，减少混凝土在输送过程中的升温。

沉管预制厂采用混凝土罐车+混凝土泵车方式进行混凝土输送，共设置了4套混凝土拌和系统，每套系统每小时可生产60立方米混凝土；每两套系统配置一台制冰机，根据环境情况添加冰屑、冷水，控制混凝土夏天出机温度在20~22℃，冬季出机温度为20℃。

Automatic metering and mixing system is established in the factory for concrete production to ensure the quality of the concrete thus produced.

Proper concrete transportation mode is chosen according to the site conditions to shorten the transportation distance, omit intermediate steps, and reduce the risks of temperature rise of the concrete in the process of transportation.

The immersed tube precast factory uses "concrete tanker + concrete pump truck" to transport the concrete, and is equipped with four concrete mixing systems, each of which can produce 60 cubic meters of concrete per hour. An ice maker is allocated for every two systems, which can add ice chips and cold water to the system according to the environmental conditions to control the temperature of the concrete moved out of the system: 20℃ ~22℃ in the summer and 20℃ in the winter.

1. 混凝土入泵
   Concrete Put into the Pump
2. 混凝土布料系统
   Concrete Distributing System
3. 沉管混凝土浇筑工序图
   Procedures of the Concrete Placement for the Immersed Tube

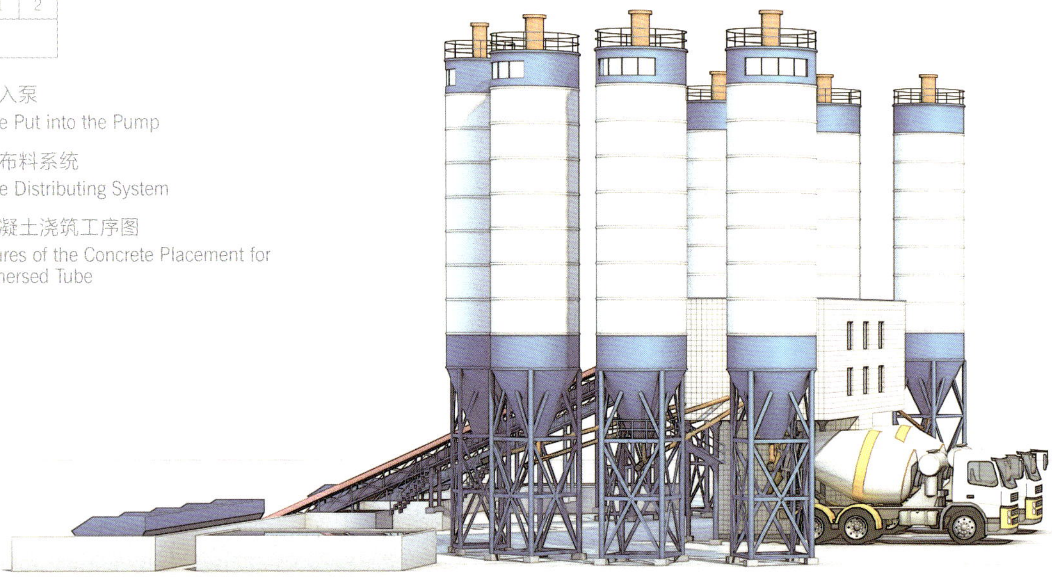

1 搅拌站生产混凝土
Concrete Production by the Mix Plant

2 混凝土搅拌车接料
Concrete Mixer Truck Taking the Material

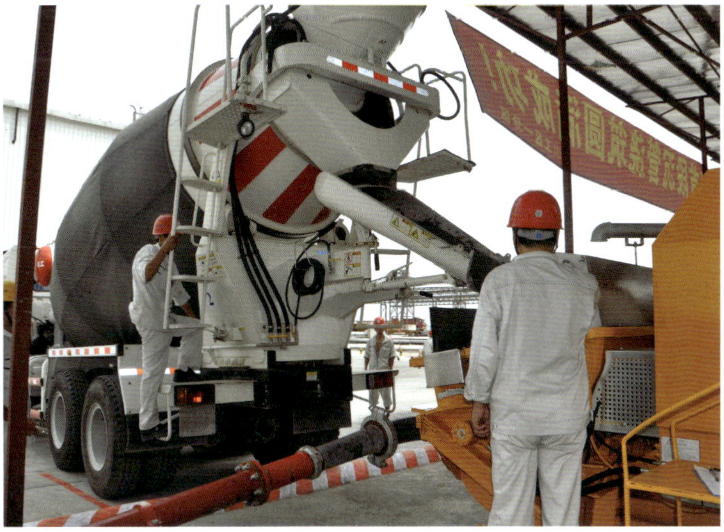

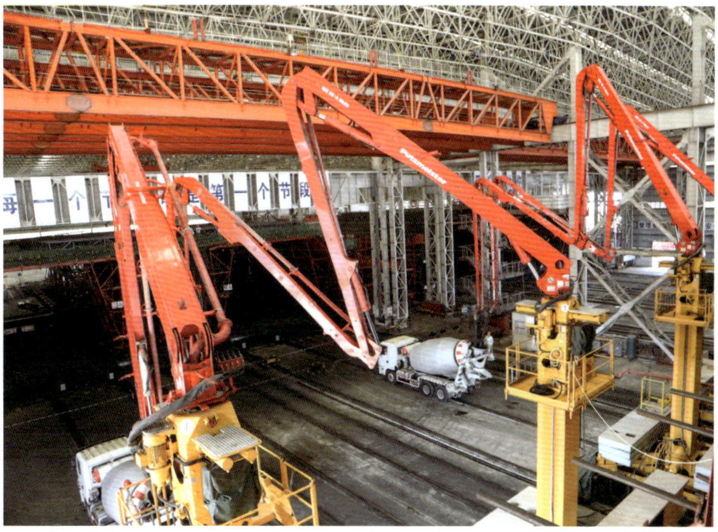

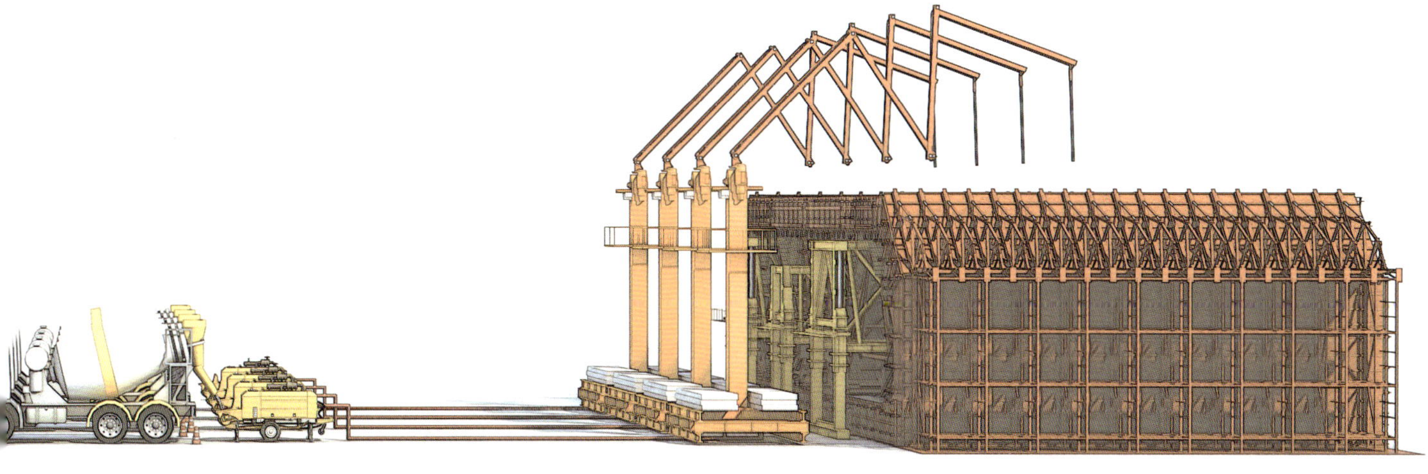

3
混凝土入泵
Concrete Put into the Pump

4
管道输送
Pipeline Transportation

5
布料机布料
Concrete Material Distribution

6
混凝土浇筑
Concrete Placement

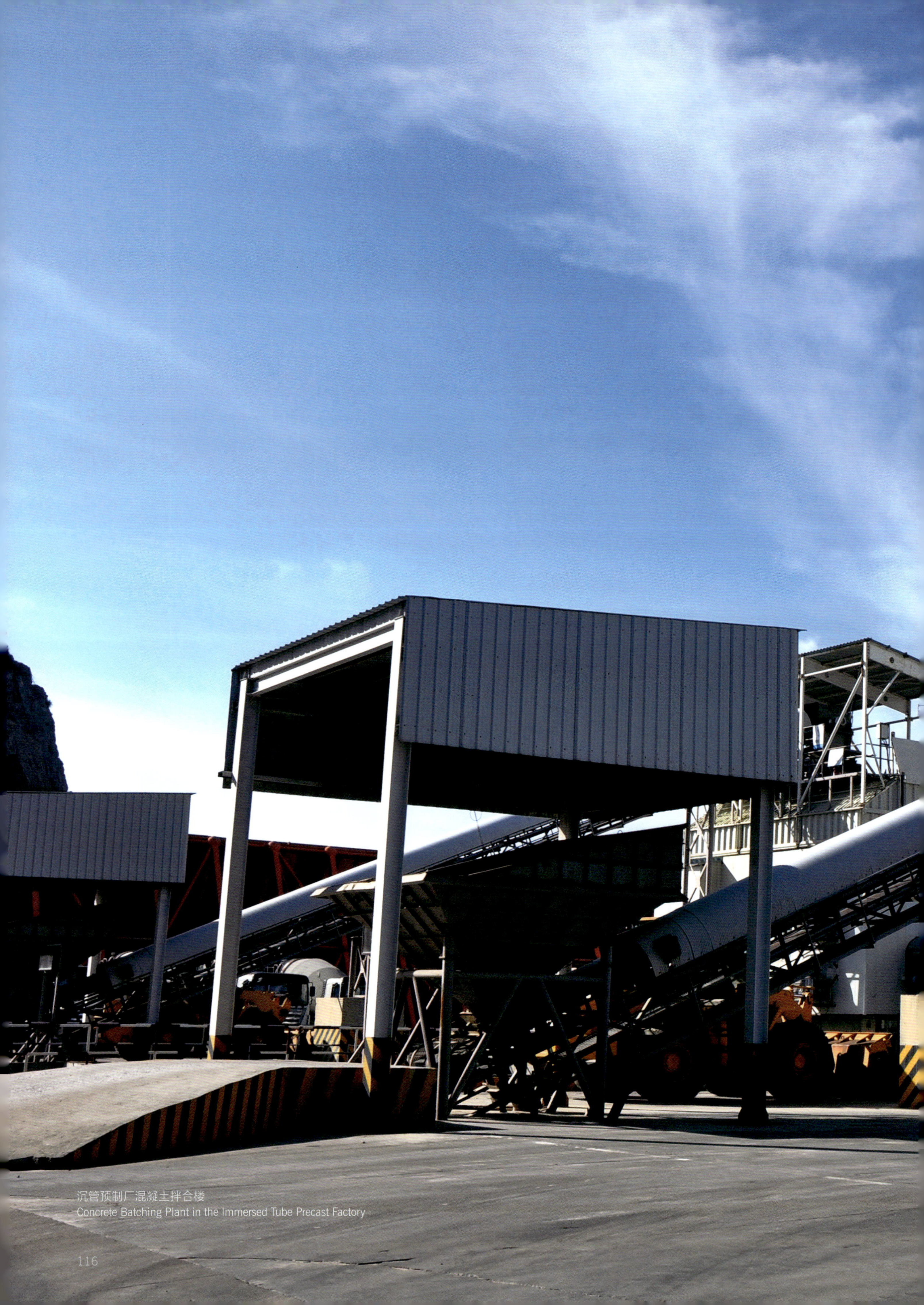

沉管预制厂混凝土拌合楼
Concrete Batching Plant in the Immersed Tube Precast Factory

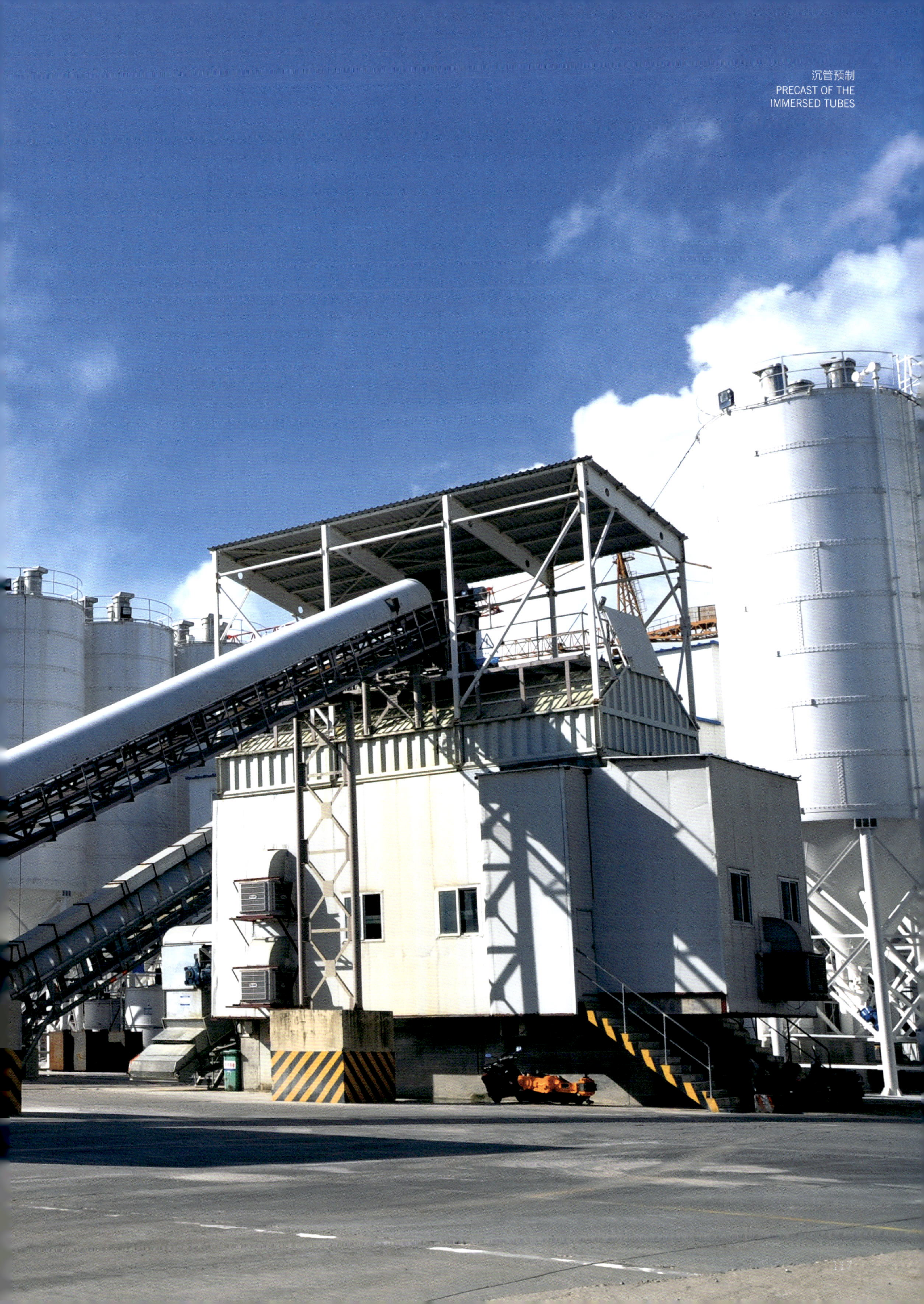

混凝土浇筑

CONCRETE PLACEMENT

根据沉管断面形式，混凝土浇筑总体划分为底板、侧墙和中隔墙、顶板三大区域。

根据各区域构造特点和作业难度，划分为普通区域、钢筋密集区域、下倒角、止水带周边等几种混凝土振捣区域，分别采取不同的振捣设备和振捣要求。

浇筑顺序总体按底板→墙体→顶板的顺序进行。

According to the shape of the cross section of the immersed tube, concrete placement is generally divided into three areas: the bottom plate, the side wall and the partition wall, and the top plate.

According to the structural characteristics and difficulty in the operation in each area, the concrete vibratory mixing areas can be divided into the ordinary area, the rebar intense area, the lower chamfer area and the water-stop area. Different vibrating mixing equipment and different vibratory mixing requirements are used in different areas.

The casting procedure is often arranged in the order of bottom plate, partition wall, top plate.

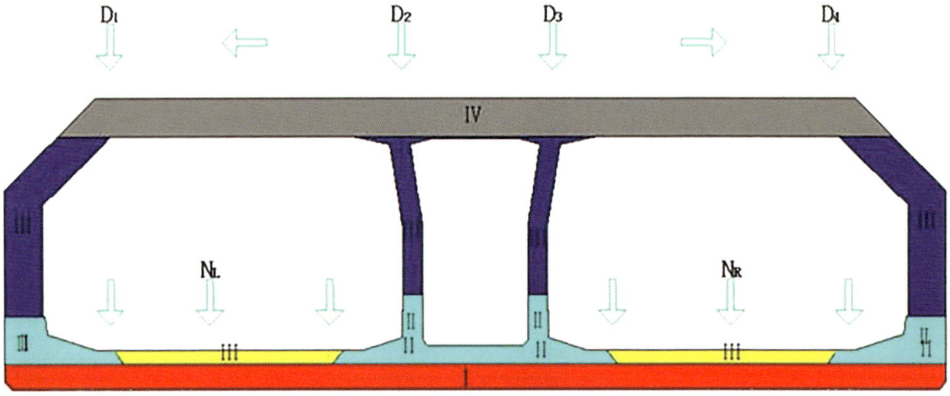

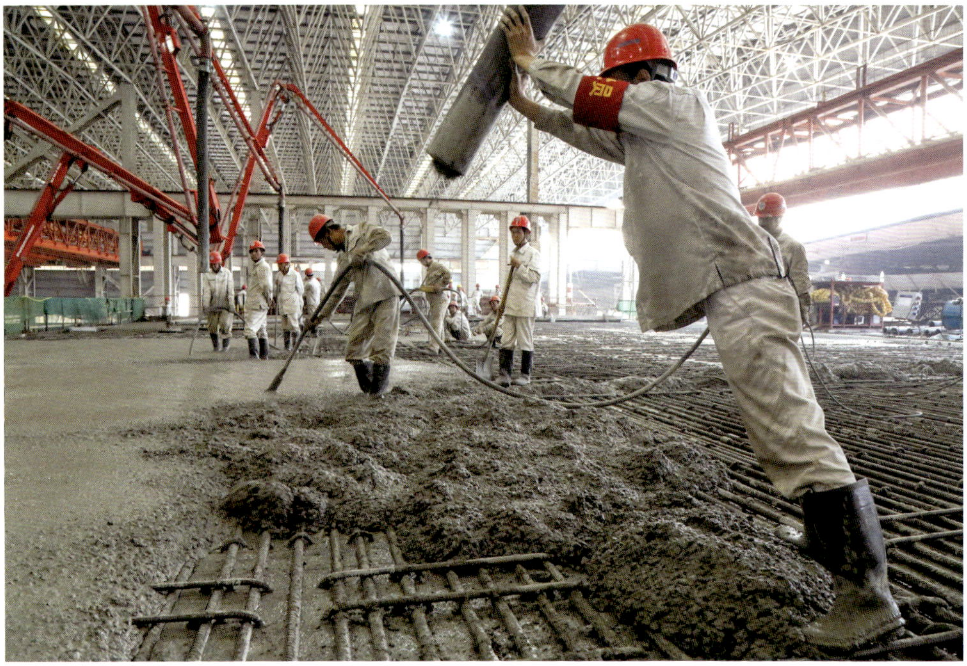

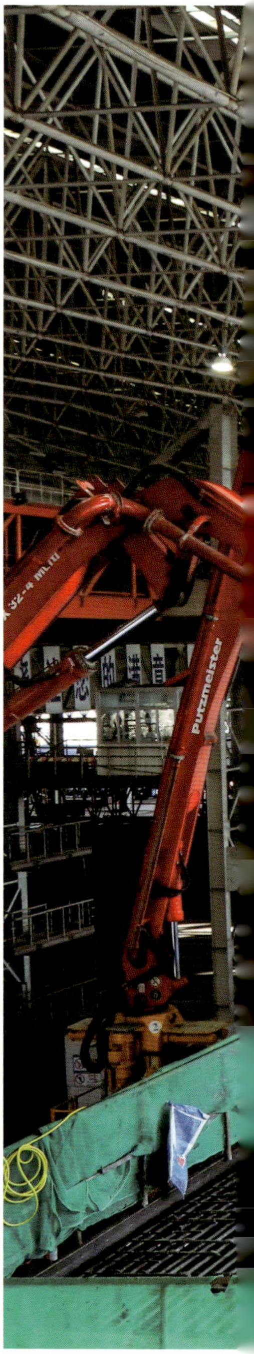

1. 沉管混凝土浇筑顺序图
Sequence Diagram of the Concrete Placement of the Immersed Tube

2. 混凝土布料
Concrete Distribution

3. 混凝土振捣
Concrete Vibrating

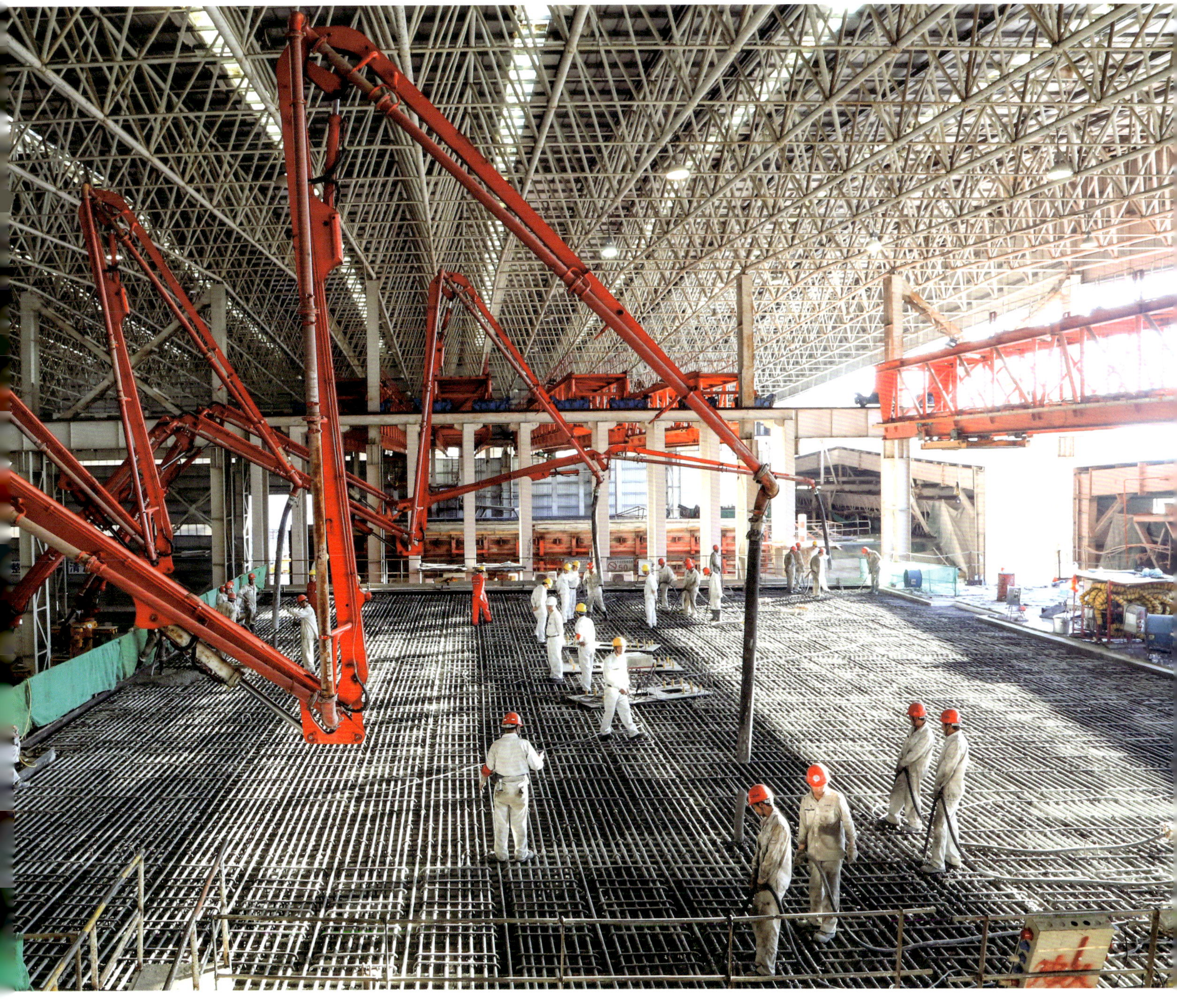

为明确振捣人员岗位责任，实现振捣质量可追溯性，在各区域按布料、振捣作业区域又划分为多个分区，实行定人、定岗、定区域作业。

普通区域指无特殊构造、施工方便的区域，每个振捣人员按划定的作业区域作业；采用 70 型振捣棒，振捣间距 50 厘米，每个振捣点振捣时间为 40~50 秒，上层混凝土振捣时插入下层 5~10 厘米。

侧墙和中隔墙混凝土振捣作业人员需进入钢筋笼内部，在钢筋笼内设置纵向振捣通道提供作业空间。中隔墙安全门、排烟道等大型预留洞室下方，混凝土振捣通过开设振捣孔进行。

下倒角区域受内模遮挡，振捣棒无法直接到达，采用角钢辅助导向将振捣棒送入需振捣的部位，振捣要求与普通区域相同。下倒角与墙体振捣要密切配合，倒角部位要适度翻浆，保证混凝土饱满、密实；翻浆的混凝土经人工平仓至底板。

剪力键、外侧牛腿预埋件、节段端部等钢筋密集区域，采用 50 型振捣棒，振捣间距 30 厘米，振捣时间 40~50 秒。为保证振捣棒顺利到达预定位置，在钢筋笼内预埋振捣棒导向钢笼。

止水带周边混凝土密实度对防水至关重要。受止水带影响，该部位气泡排出困难，混凝土浇筑时先用 70 型振捣棒按要求进行振捣，然后采用进口高频振捣棒进行复振。复振振捣间距 50 厘米，每点振捣时间 50 秒左右。

混凝土浇筑前，在钢筋笼上临时焊接高程控制桩，由测量在控制桩上放样控制高程，收面时按照放样标记控制混凝土高度。

底板和顶板表层混凝土振捣完成后，先用铁锹进行粗平，然后参照高程控制点用铝合金刮尺刮平，进行第一次抹面。待混凝土接近初凝时，用抹面机配合人工进行二次抹面。

In order to clarify the duties of the different vibratory mixing workers and realize the traceability of concrete vibratory mixing quality, all the above areas are further divided into subsectors with regard to the material distribution and vibratory mixing operation, so that fixed person is given fixed work at fixed post in fixed location.

The ordinary area refers to the area that has no special structure and is thus convenient for construction. Every person works in the designated working area. Type 70 vibrating rods are used with a vibrating spacing of 50 centimeters. The vibrating time at each vibrating point is 40–50 seconds. During vibratory mixing, the upper layer of concrete penetrates into the lower layer by 5 to 10 centimeters.

The workers who conduct vibratory mixing operation for the side wall and the partition wall have to enter the interior of steel reinforcement cage. The longitudinal vibrating channel is set in the steel reinforcement cage to provide working space. The vibratory placement of the concrete is done throughout the vibrating holes in the reserved large cavities under the safety entrance and smoke outlet of the middle partition wall.

The lower chamfer area is blocked by the internal module, so the vibratory mixing rod cannot reach inside. The auxiliary angle steel guide is used to send the vibrating rod to this part for vibratory mixing. The requirements for the vibrating operation here are the same as those in the ordinary area. The vibratory mixing at the lower chamfer part should coordinate well with the vibratory mixing for the wall. The chamfer part needs proper mixing to ensure the concrete is well mixed and compacted. The well-mixed concrete needs to be leveled manually on the bottom plate.

For the casting of the steel intensive areas such as shear keys, embedded items of external corbel and the end parts of the segments, Type 50 vibratory mixing rod is used with a mix spacing of 30 centimeters for the duration of 40 to 50 seconds. To make sure that the vibratory mixing rod easily reaches the prescribed location, the guiding steel cage is embedded in the steel reinforcement cage to

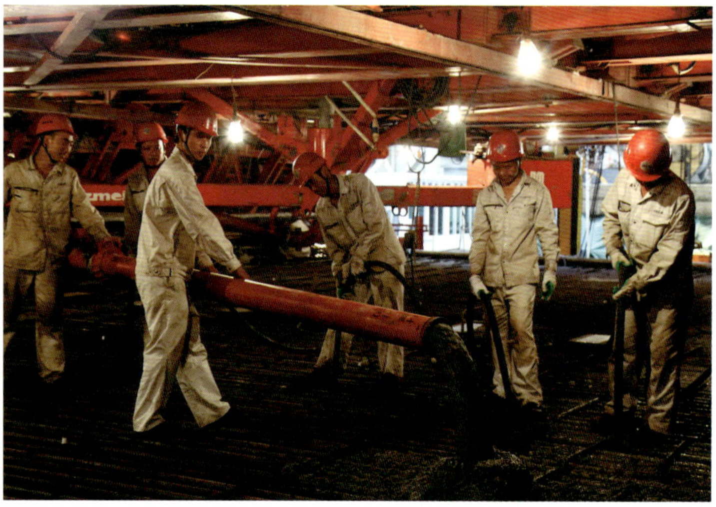

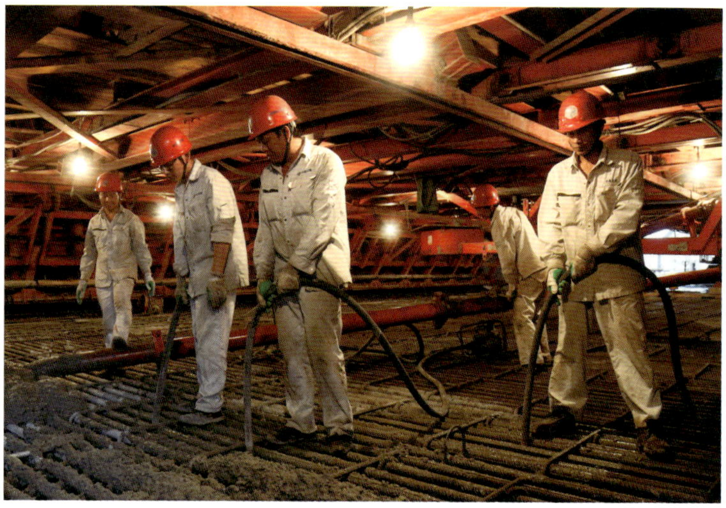

guide vibratory mixing rod.

The density of the concrete surrounding the water-stop is vital to waterproofing. Subject to the impact of the water-stop, it is difficult to discharge the air bubbles at this location. In the process of concrete placement, Type 70 vibratory mixing rod is first used for the vibratory mixing as required, and then an imported high-frequency vibratory mixing rod is used for the second round of mixing at the spacing of 50 centimeters for the duration of 50 seconds at each point.

Before concrete placement, an elevation control pile is temporarily welded onto the steel reinforcement cage for the control of the elevation by sampling measurements, and then for the control of the height of the concrete according to the sampling marks when the surface is closed.

After the concrete vibratory mixing at the bottom and top plates is completed, for the first finishing operation on the concrete surface, rough leveling is done with a spade first, and then aluminum alloy scraper is used for leveling according to the elevation control point. When the concrete is close to initial hardening, the plastering machine, together with manual operation, is used for the second finishing operation on the concrete surface.

1. 沉管底板区混凝土布料
Concrete Distributing in Bottom Plate Area of the Immersed Tube

2. 沉管底板倒角区混凝土振捣
Concrete Vibratory Mixing at the Lower Chamfer on the Bottom Plate of the Immersed Tube

3. 沉管混凝土浇筑
Concrete Placement for the Immersed Tube

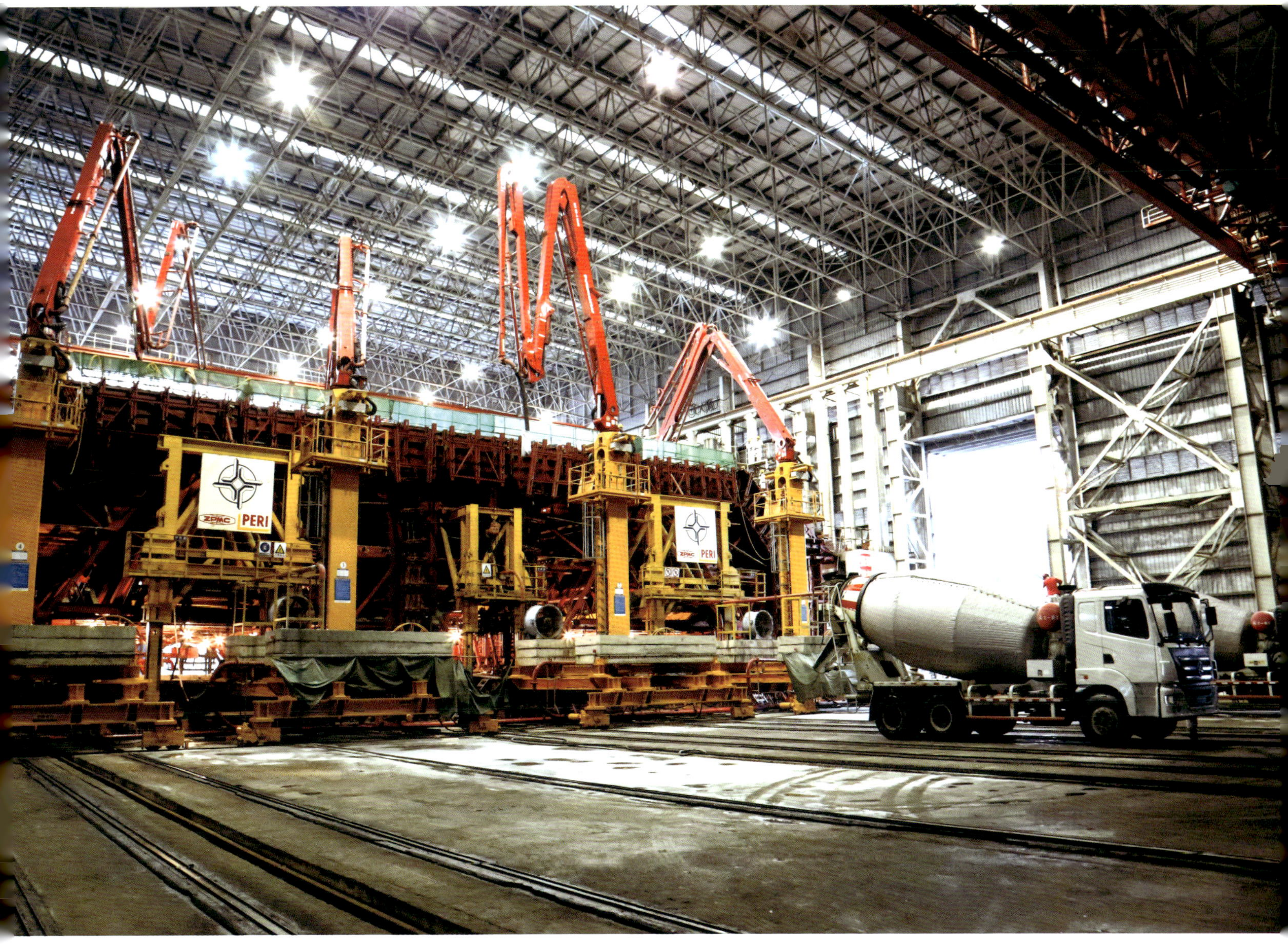

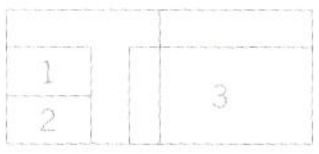

1. 沉管侧墙混凝土振捣
Concrete Vibratory Mixing for the Side Wall of the Immersed Tube
2. 沉管顶板收面
Surface Finishing of the Top Plate of the Immersed Tube
3. 浇筑成型的沉管节段
Immersed Tube Segment Well-Cast

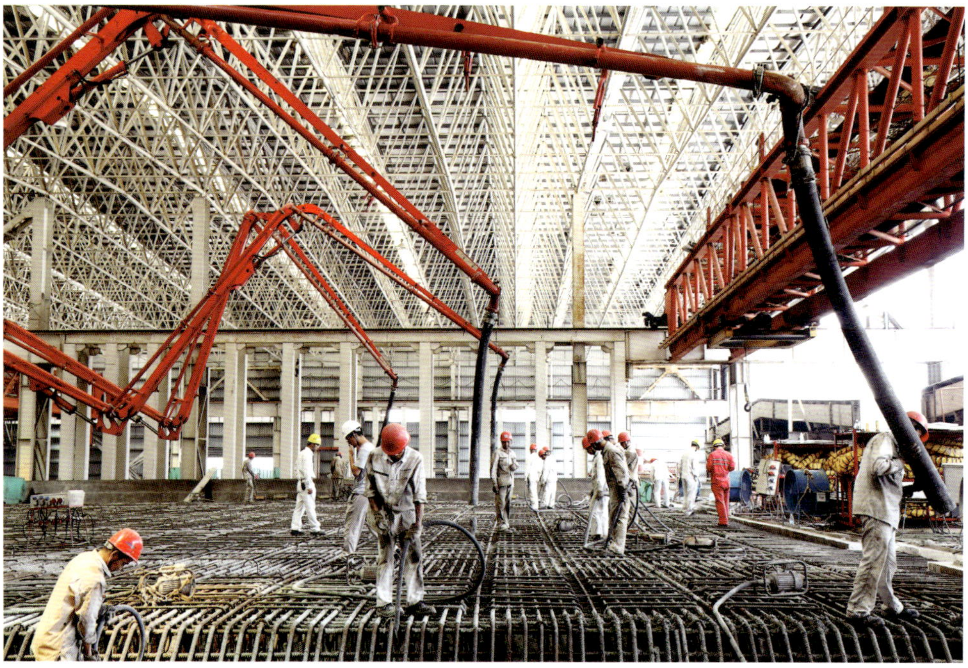

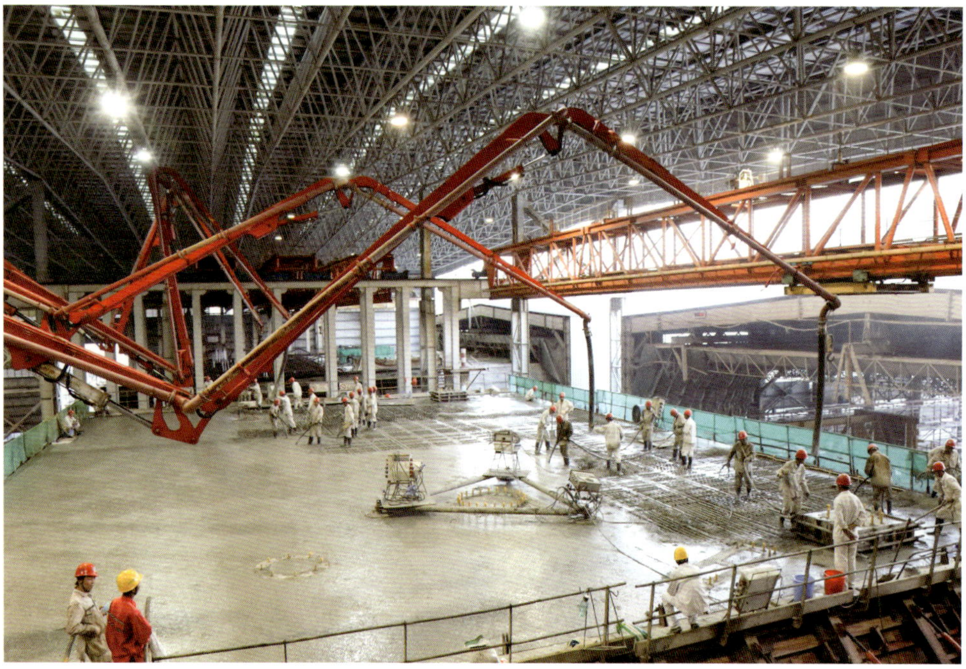

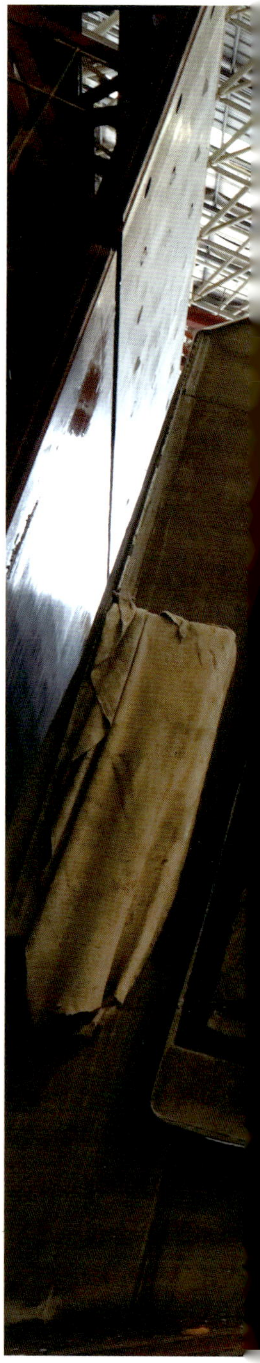

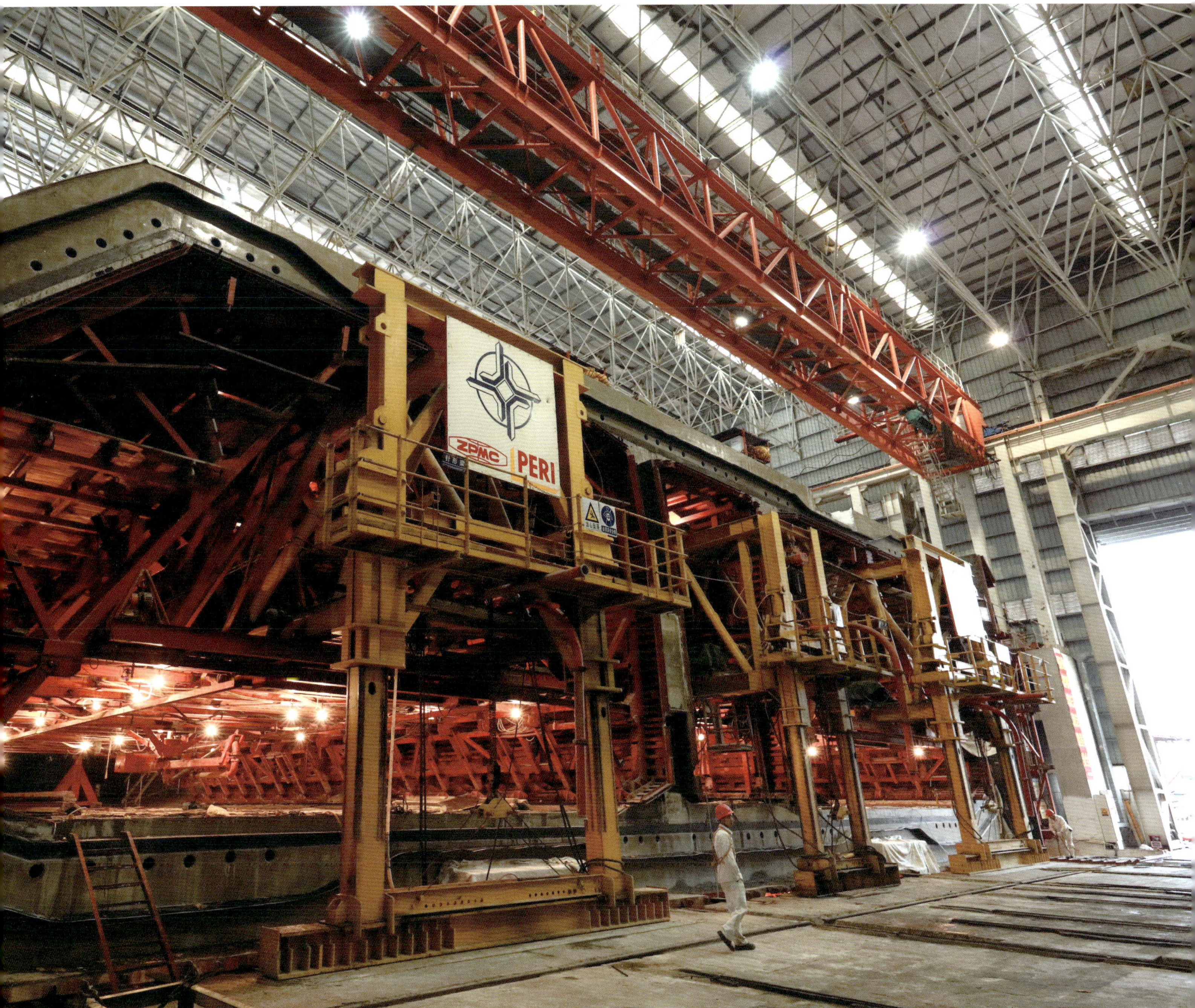
ZPMC
PERI

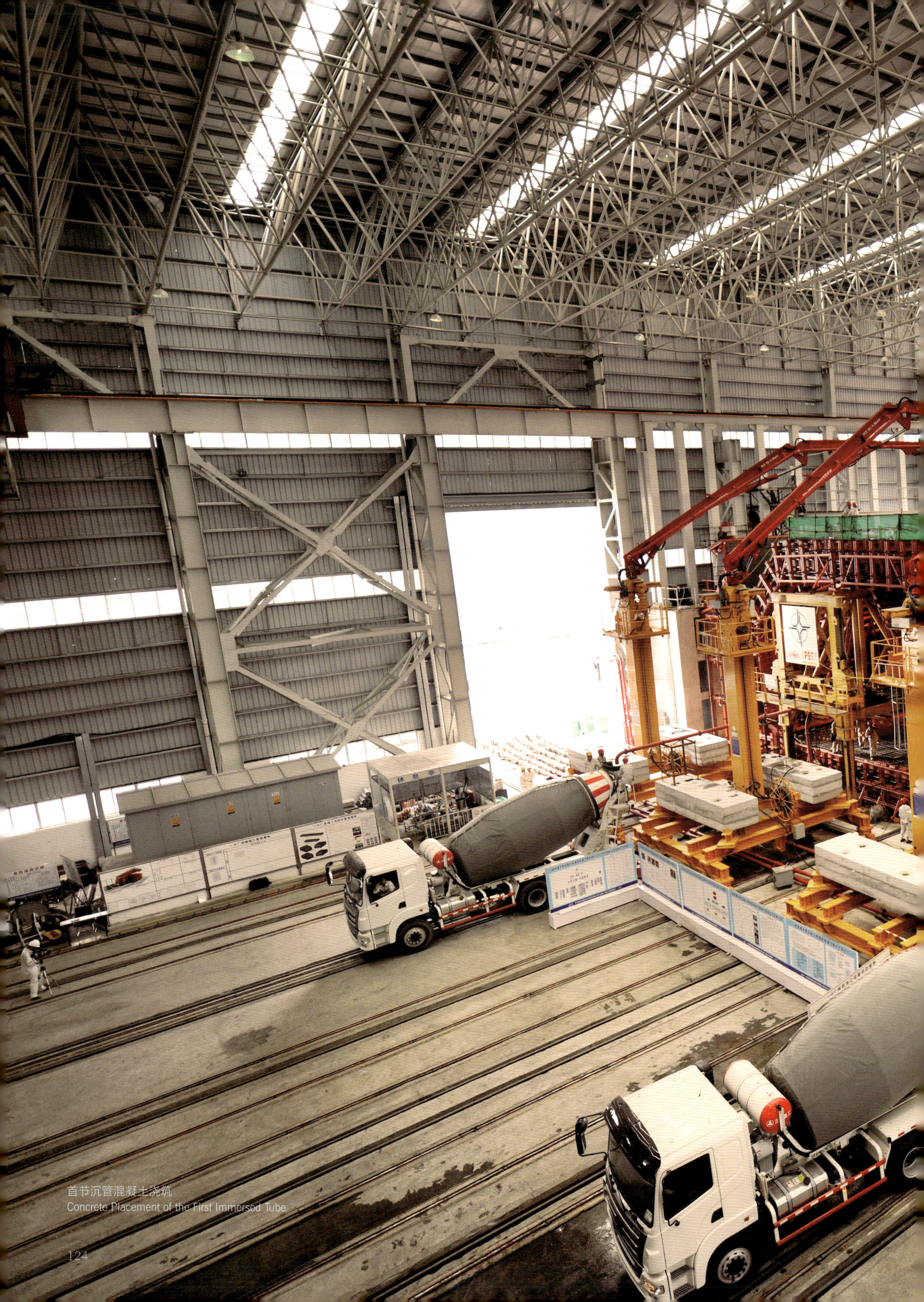

首节沉管混凝土浇筑
Concrete Placement of the First Immersed Tube

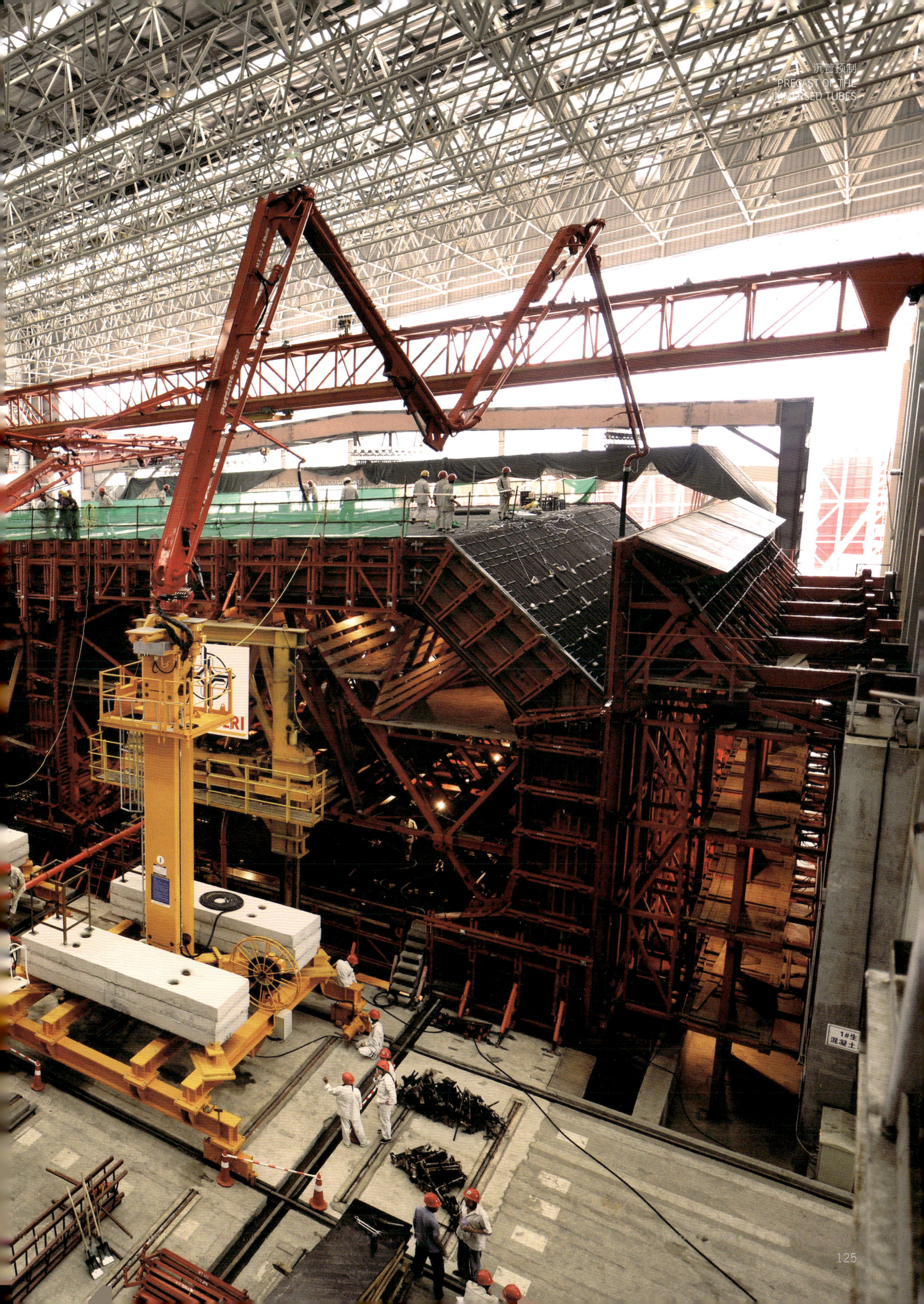

养护
MAINTENANCE

沉管养护系统覆盖分别位于浇筑台座区、厂房与养护棚过渡区、养护棚区的三节节段。在厂房、养护棚以及节段内部特定位置布设传感器，采用无线方式进行节段内部以及养护环境的温度、湿度监测。

按照预设的温度、湿度预警临界值，中控系统对温度、湿度监测值进行处理与判断，通过预设在厂房、养护棚以及针形梁等部位的水管，进行喷淋养护。

由于养护系统覆盖分别位于不同区段的三节节段，各节段的养护要求不完全相同，特别是正在浇筑混凝土的区域，需要喷淋低温冷水降低浇筑环境的温度。因此，养护系统设计时，需要配备可同时提供不同温度养护水的水箱及水路系统。

The maintenance system of the immersed tubes covers three sections located respectively in the casting pedestal area, the transitional area between the factory building and the maintenance shed, and the maintenance shed area. Sensors are deployed at specific positions inside the workshop, maintenance shed and the inside of the tube segments, and the temperature and humidity inside the tube segments and that of the maintenance environment are conducted wirelessly.

According to the preset alarming value of temperature and humidity, the central control system processes and makes judgement on the monitored value of the temperature and humidity, and switches on the water faucets preset in the factory, the maintenance shed and the pointed beam for shower maintenance.

Since the maintenance system covers the three segments located in different areas, the requirements for the maintenance of each segment are not exactly the same. Especially in the area where the concrete placement is being operated, cold water needs to be sprayed to reduce the temperature of the concrete placement environment. Therefore, when designing the maintenance system, it is necessary to supply water tanks and waterway systems that can provide at the same time maintenance water of different temperatures.

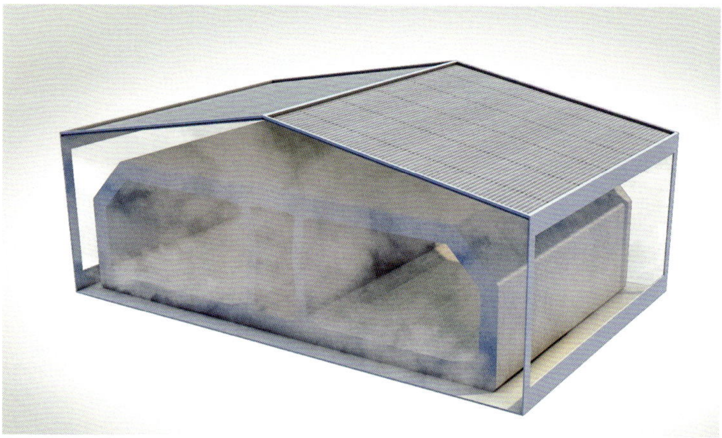

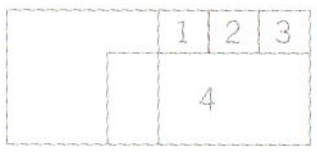

1. 沉管混凝土覆盖养护
   Maintenance of the Immersed Tube by Concrete Covering
2. 沉管养护喷淋系统
   Water Spray System for the Maintenance of the Immersed Tube
3. 沉管养护棚
   Maintenance Shed of the Immersed Tube
4. 沉管温控养护示意图
   Schematic Diagram of the Temperature Control for the Maintenance of the Immersed Tube

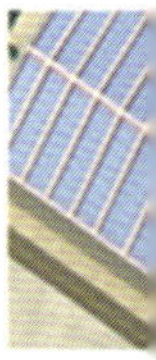

原材
Material

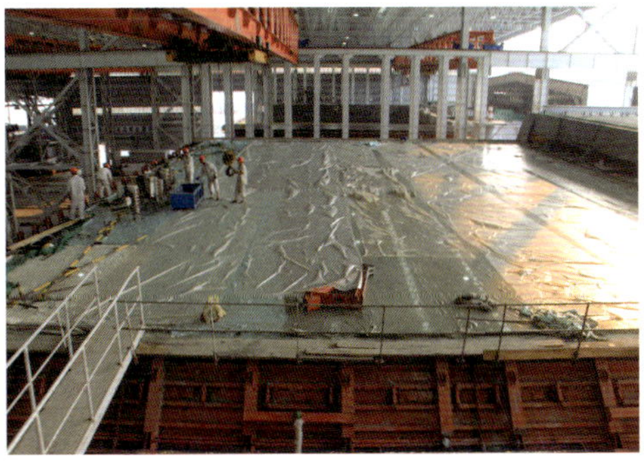

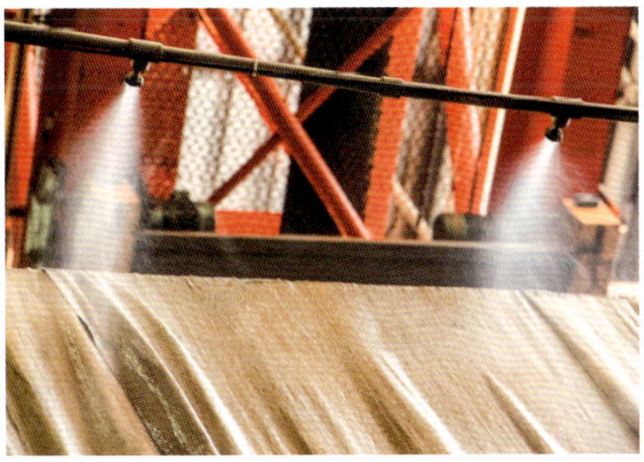

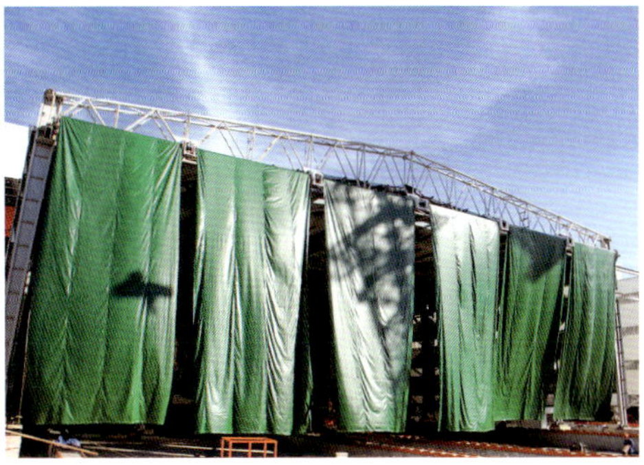

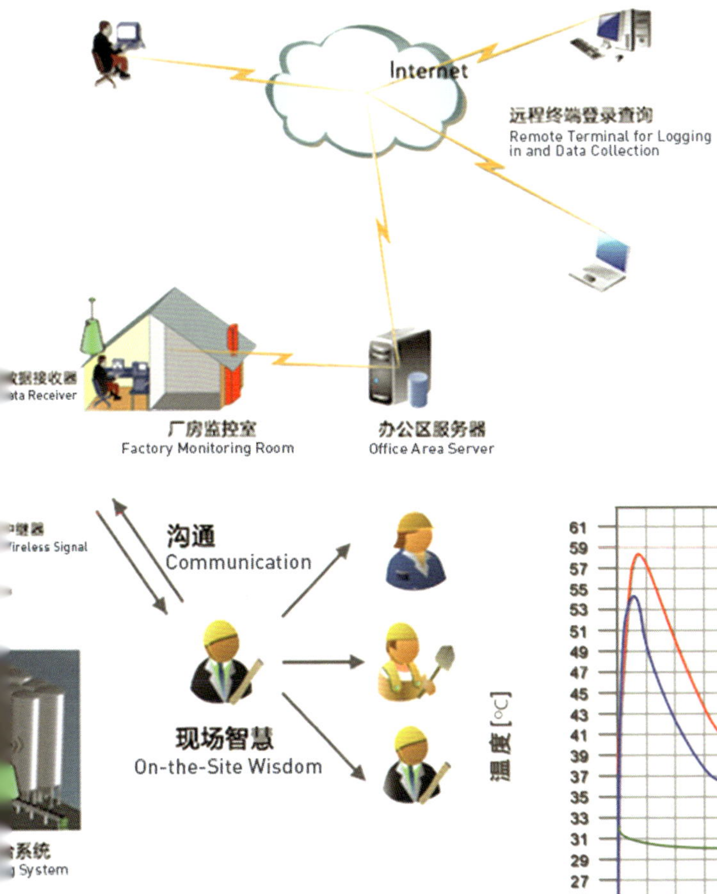

47天温度应力分布
Distribution of Temperature Stress in 47 Days

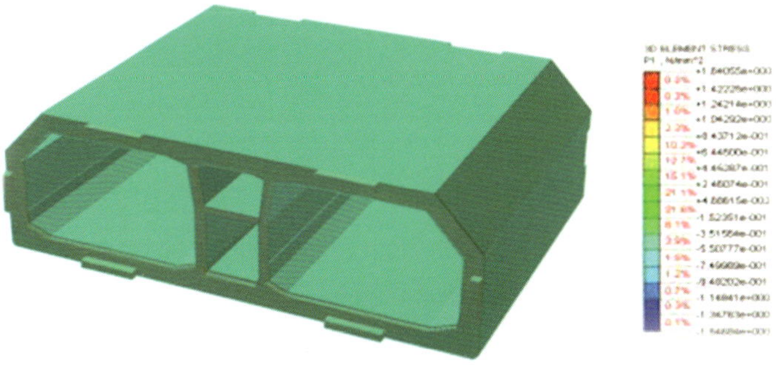

中心、浅层、表层温度发展曲线图
Curves of the Temperature Changes in the Center at the Shallow and Deep Layer

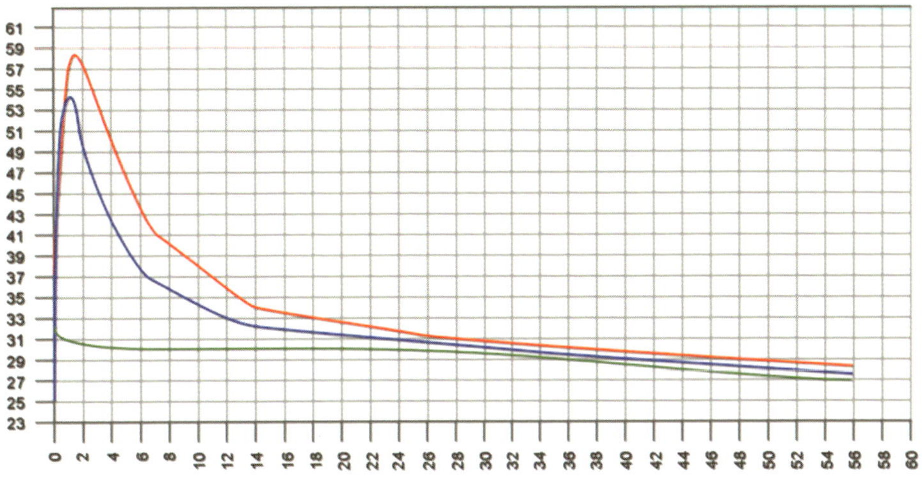

控裂技术

CRACK CONTROL TECHNIQUE

沉管采用全断面浇筑，环境温度高，混凝土标号高、结构断面大、体积大，开裂风险较大，因此沉管混凝土的配制和控裂是确保预制沉管质量的关键。

通过温控仿真分析，确定安全工况和不同施工季节的温控标准，设计温控措施和控制参数。同时，建立温湿度监控系统，保证温控措施的执行和精确控制。

综合温度应力仿真分析和国内外沉管控裂技术资料，制定不同施工季节沉管温控标准，包括浇筑温度、最高温度、内表温差和降温速率 4 项主要技术指标。

根据预制沉管的温控标准，制定水泥、粉煤灰、矿粉、骨料等原材料的温度控制指标和措施。

控制混凝土入模温度≤ 25℃。混凝土温度控制的措施主要有：骨料仓、粉料仓安装喷雾，喷淋系统降低原材料温度；采用制冷水代替常温水拌和混凝土；采用碎冰片代替部分拌和水；运输罐车的罐体包裹吸水帆布并淋水降温；混凝土输送拖泵集中布置，在顶部设置遮雨遮阳棚，棚顶洒水降温；室外泵管采用定型加工吸水海绵包裹，防止阳光暴晒；施工过程中向泵管包裹材料淋水，降低混凝土输送摩擦升温。

The immersed tube is cast by gross section, which features high ambient temperature, high concrete grade, large sectional surface, large tube volume and high risks of cracking. Therefore, the concrete mixing and crack control are the key factors that may influence the quality of the immersed tubes precast.

Through the simulation analysis of temperature control, the temperature control standards for safe working conditions and for construction in different seasons are determined, and the temperature control measures and parameters are designed. At the same time, a temperature and humidity monitoring system is established to ensure the implementation and accurate control of temperature control measures.

Based on the data from the simulation analysis of temperature stress and on the technical data about the immersed tube crack control at home and abroad, the temperature control standards for immersed tube construction in different seasons are formed, including four main technical indexes: casting temperature, maximum temperature, temperature difference between the center and the surface of the concrete, and cooling rate.

The temperature control indexes and measures for cement, fly ash, mineral powder, aggregates and other raw materials are decided according to the temperature control criteria for the immersed tubes.

The temperature of the concrete entering the mold is controlled within the limit of≤ 25℃. Concrete temperature control measures mainly include: the warehouses for the aggregate and powder are equipped with spraying or sprinkling systems to reduce the temperature of the raw materials; cold water instead of room-temperature water is used for concrete mixing; crushed ice is used in place of certain mixing water; the tank of the transport tanker is wrapped up with absorbent canvas drenched with cooling water; the concrete delivery pumps are stationed together and covered with the rain shelter or sunshade that can be used to cool down the pump with water spray; the outdoor pumping lines are covered with water-absorbing sponge specially made to block the sun heat; in the process of construction, cold water is sprinkled onto the material wrapping up the pumping lines to avoid the temperature rise induced by friction during pump delivery.

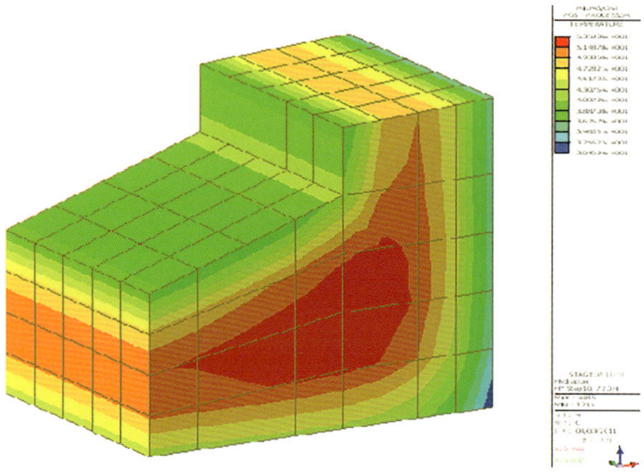

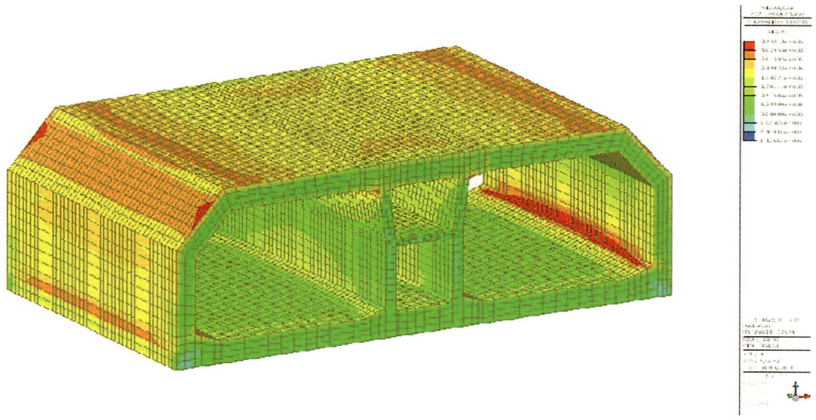

1—2. 沉管部位混凝土水化热温度示意图
Schematic Diagram of the Temperature of the Concrete by Hydration Heat in the Immersed Tube

3. 混凝土运输车包裹降温
Package Cooling of the Concrete Transport Vehicle

4. 制冰机
Ice Producing Machine

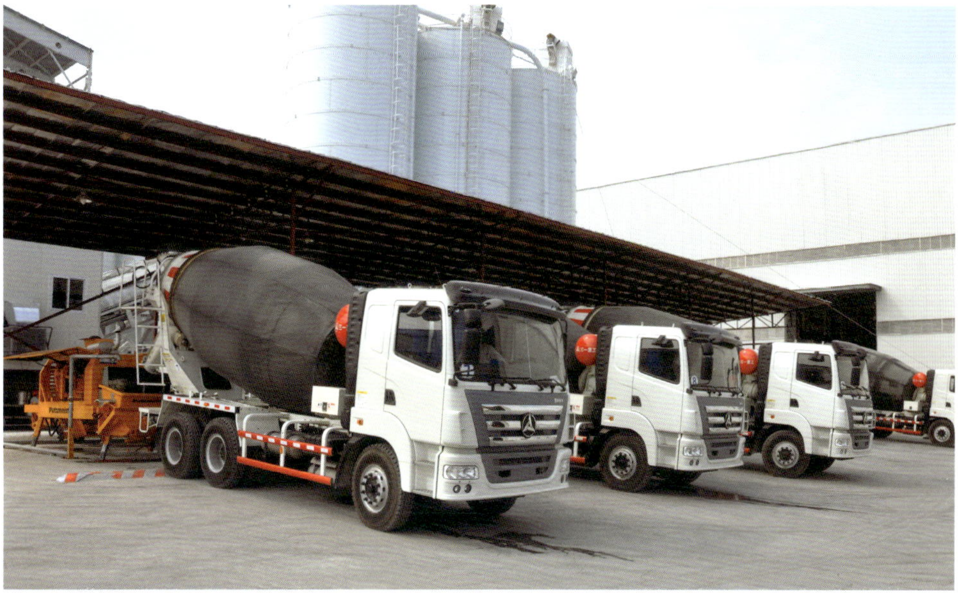

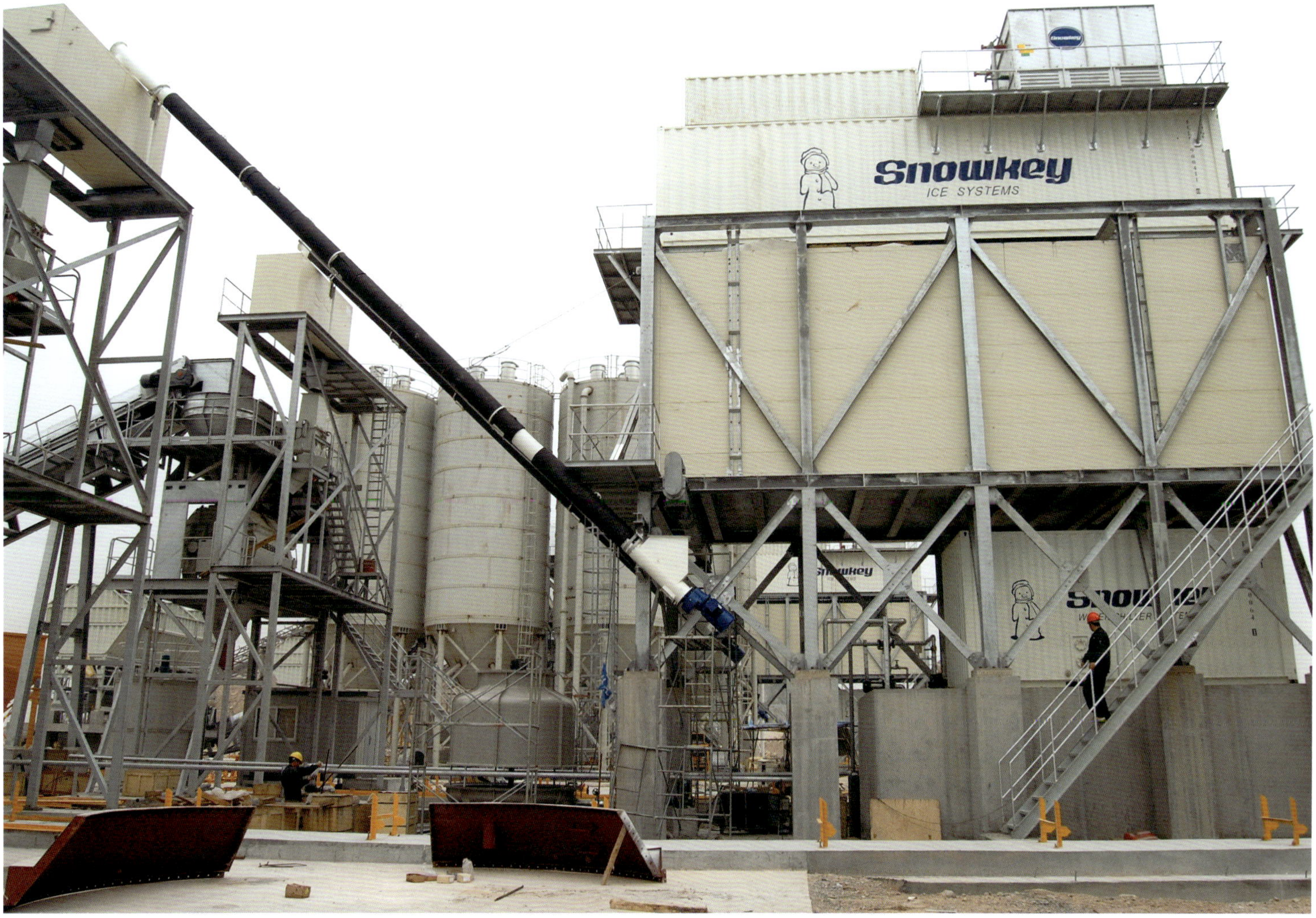

	2
1	

1. 混凝土泵送管道包裹
Wrapping up the Concrete Pumping Lines
2. 粉料仓喷淋控温
Temperature Control by Water Spray in the Powder Warehouse

采用全覆盖模式，埋设固定测点，对原材料、混凝土生产和浇筑、养护的温度、湿度情况进行 24 小时监控。

在原材料仓库、搅拌站、预制厂房和自动养护区安装监测系统实施实时动态监控。

为监测混凝土的温度变化情况，首个节段布设 20 个测点，之后的每节段布设 5 个校验测点。峰值以前每两小时监测一次，峰值出现后每 4 小时监测一次，持续 5 天，然后转入每天测两次，直到温度变化基本稳定。

33 节沉管共 252 个节段，总计布设 2205 个测点。

The temperature and humidity of the raw materials and the concrete during production, placement and maintenance are monitored in the whole process for 24 hours a day at the fixed measuring points.

Monitoring systems are installed in the raw material warehouse, mixing plant, precast workshop and automatic maintenance area for dynamic real-time monitoring.

In order to monitor the temperature changes of the concrete, 20 measuring points are arranged in the first segment, and 5 calibrating points in each of the subsequent segments. One inspection is done every 2 hours before the peak value is reached, and every 2 hours after the peak value, and this goes on for 5 days on end. Then inspections are done twice a day till the temperature is basically stable.

In all, there are 2205 measuring points for the 252 segments of the 33 immersed tubes.

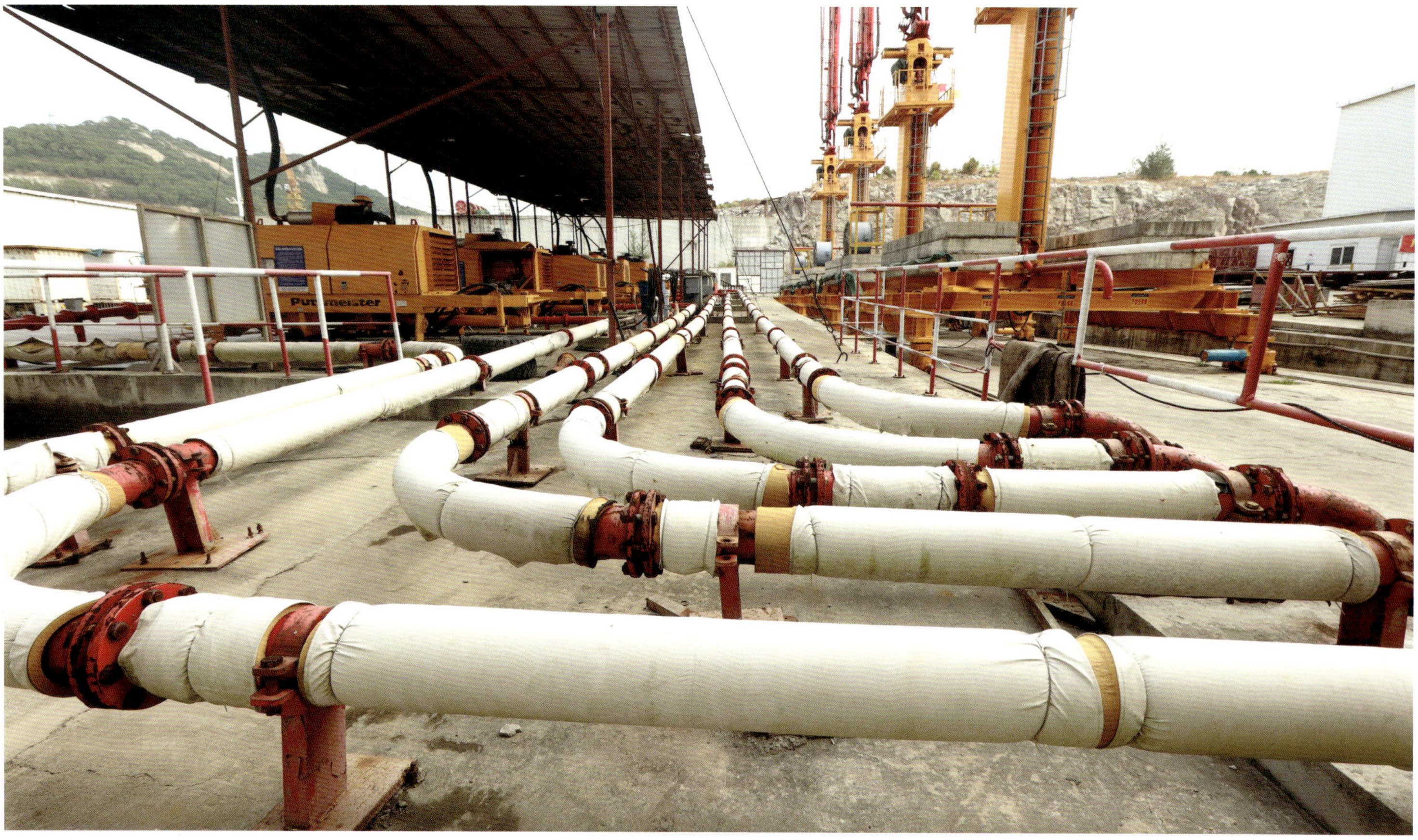

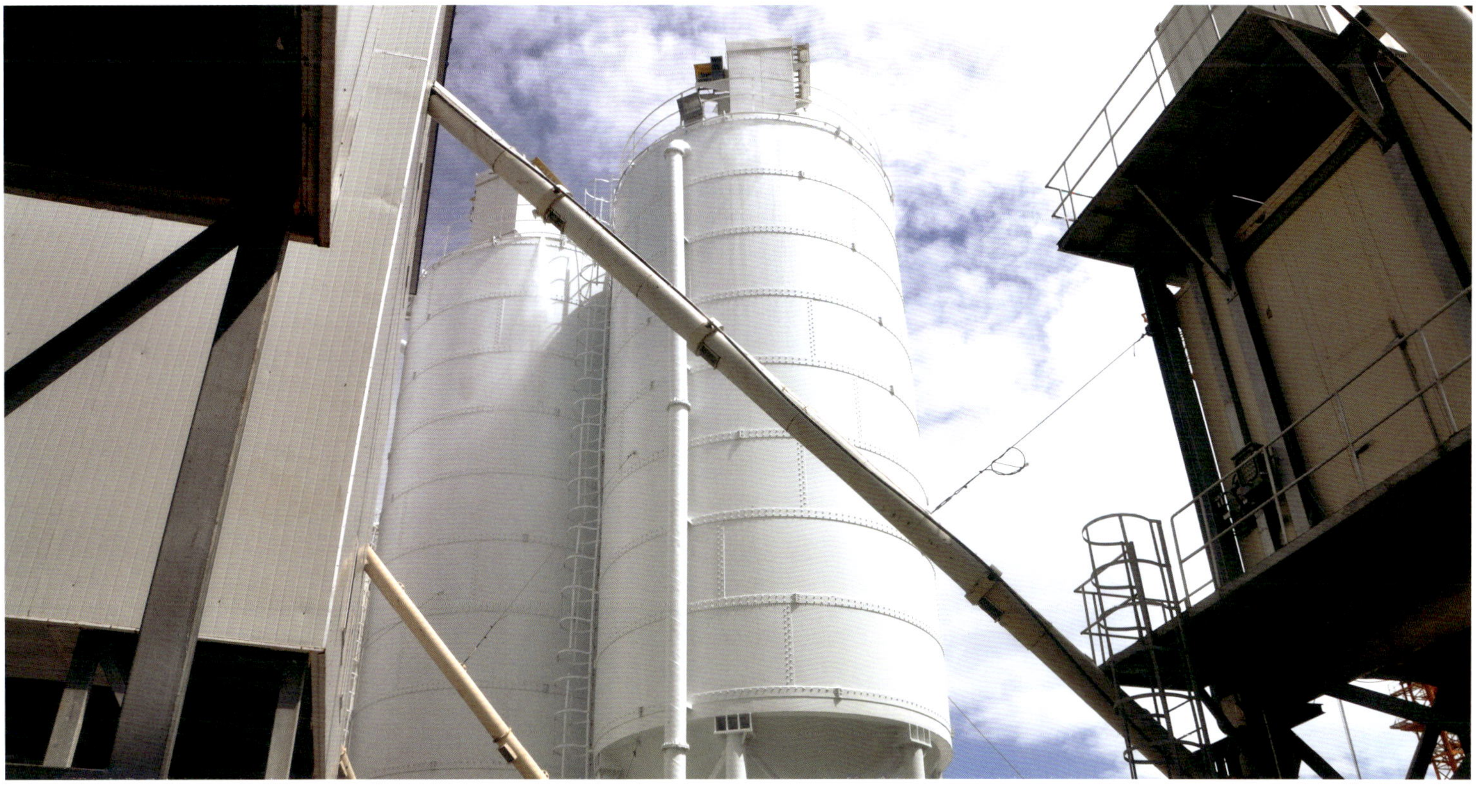

季节 Season	浇筑温度（℃） Casting Temperature	最高温度（℃） Maximum Temperature	内表温差（℃） Differences between Internal Temperature and Surface Temperature	降温速率（℃/d） Cooling Rate
高温季节（月平均气温≥25℃） High-Temperature Season (Average Monthly Temperature ≥25℃)	≤28	≤70	≤25	≤3
常温季节（月平均气温 18 ~ 25℃） Normal-Temperature Season (Average Monthly Temperature between 18℃ and 25℃)	≤23	≤65		
低温季节（月平均气温≤18℃） Low-Temperature Season (Average Monthly Temperature ≤18℃)	≤20			

温控标准
Temperature Control Standard

材料 Material	温度控制指标 Temperature Control Index	温度控制措施 Measures for Temperature Control
水泥 Concrete	≤55℃	水泥出厂≤70℃，船运上岛转入中间仓，使用温度≤55℃ ≤70℃ (when leaving the factory); ≤55℃ (for shipping, embarking on the island and intermediate storage)
矿粉 Mineral Powder	≤45℃	出厂温度≤50℃，中间仓储存倒运，使用温度≤45℃ ≤50℃ (when leaving the factory); ≤45℃ (for intermediate storage and transportation)
粉煤灰 Fly Ash	≤45℃	出厂温度≤50℃，中间仓储存倒运，使用温度≤45℃ ≤50℃ (when leaving the factory); ≤45℃ (for intermediate storage and transportation)
砂 Sand	≤30℃	材料提前进场、入库储存，料场搭棚遮阳，上料通冷却风 Delivery to the factory and storage in advance; cooling with sunshade in the stock yard; cooling air ventilation when loading
石 Rock	≤30℃	材料提前进场、入库储存，料场搭棚遮阳，上料通冷却风 Delivery to the factory and storage in advance; cooling with sunshade in the stock yard; cooling air ventilation when loading
水 Water	≤10℃	2 台 5t/h 的制冷机组制取冷水 2 refrigerating units of 5t/h making cold water
外加剂 Admixture	≤30℃	材料入库储存，现场储罐刷白 Storage in the storage tank painted white in-situ

原材料推荐温度控制标准和措施
Recommended Raw Material Temperature Control Standards and Measures

沉管顶推
INCREMENTAL LAUNCHING
OF THE IMMERSED TUBES

单节沉管重约76,000吨，从预制台座顶推至浅坞，移动距离超过200米，顶推过程中要求轴线偏差控制精度≤5毫米。顶推过程中需解决轨道不平整、顶推力大、沉管混凝土表面拉应力可能出现超标引起开裂的风险。为此，项目总经理研发了多点主动支撑分散顶推系统，通过主动支撑系统、分散顶推系统，解决大质量沉管长距离顶推难题。

顶推系统由滑移系统、支撑系统及顶推系统、导向系统和控制系统组成。

Every single immersed tube weighs about 76,000 tons, and it is pushed forward from the precast pedestal to the shallow dock over a distance of more than 200 meters. In the process of incremental launching, the axial deviation is required to be controlled within the limit of≤5 millimeters, and it is necessary to avoid the possible cracking caused by uneven sliding trolleys, strong pushing force and excessive pulling stress on the concrete surface of the immersed tube. Therefore, the general manager of the project developed a decentralizing launching system with multi-point active supporting points to solve the problems involved in the long-distance pushing of the large-sized immersed tubes via of the active supporting system and the decentralizing launching system.

The incremental launching system consists of the sliding system, the supporting and pushing system, the guiding system, and the control system.

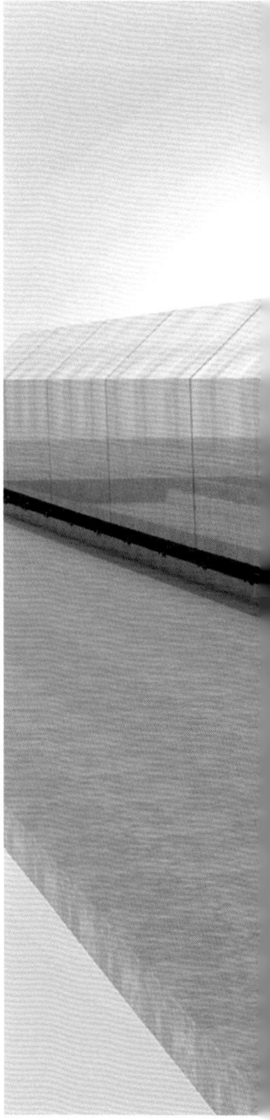

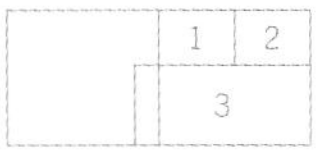

1. 沉管与模板系统分离三维图
3D Diagram of the Separation of the Immersed Tube from the Formwork System
2. 沉管支撑千斤顶三维图
3D Diagram of the Supporting Jack for the Immersed Tube
3. 沉管顶推三维图
3D Diagram of Pushing the Immersed Tube

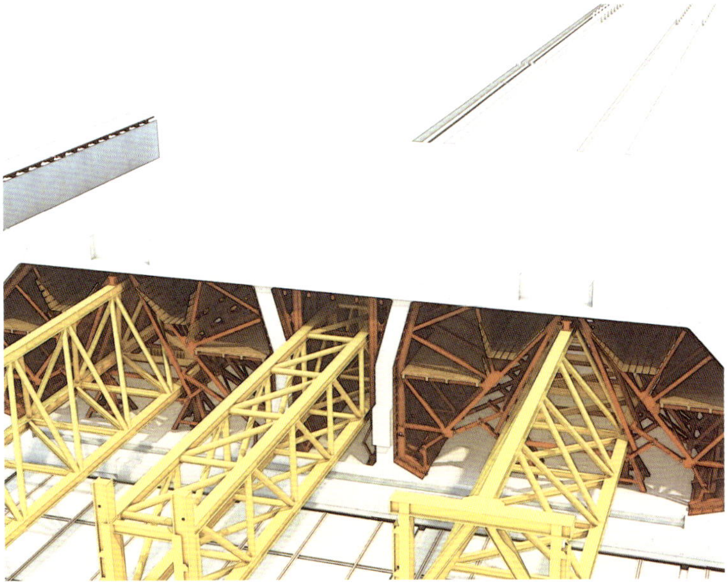

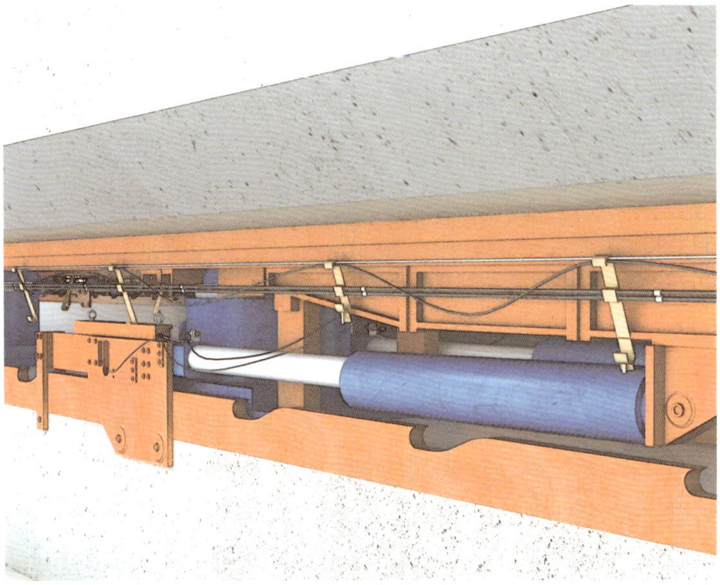

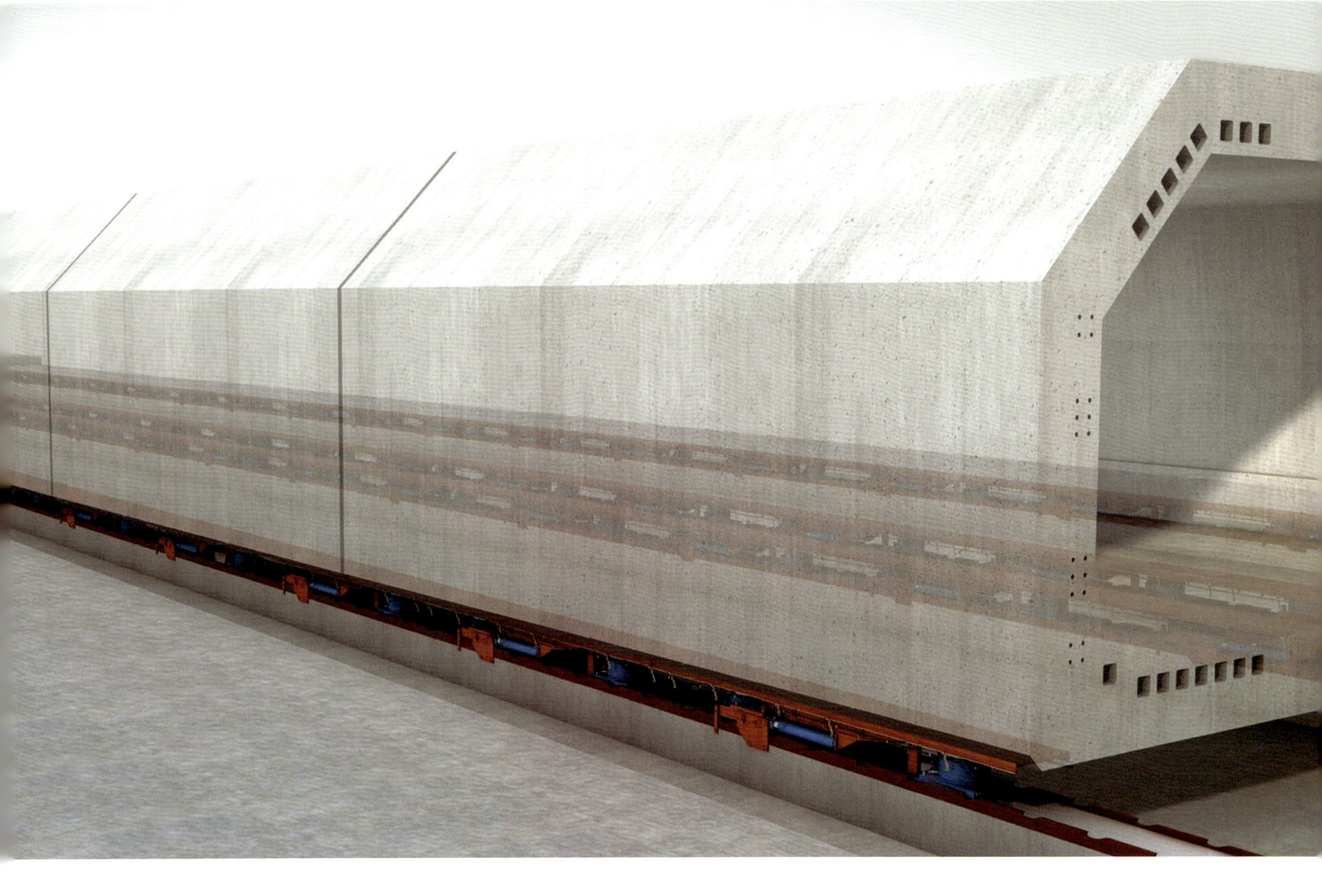

沉管下方设置 4 条顶推滑移轨道梁，在滑移钢轨顶部设置 3 条通长的不锈钢板，其上放置 PETG 板，两者的接触面作为沉管顶推的滑移面。

支撑系统采用三点平衡主动支撑方案，标准沉管 8 个节段共由 192 个支撑千斤顶组成。顶推操作时，始终由 3 台液压泵提供压力支撑预制沉管节段。

4 sliding track beams are set under the immersed tubes, 3 full-length stainless plates are set on top of the steel sliding tracks, and on top of the plates are PETG plates. The contact surfaces of the stainless plates and the PETG plates are the sliding surface to push the immersed tube.

The supporting system adopts the three-point balanced active supporting solution, and the eight segments of the standard immersed tube are supported by 192 supporting jacks. Throughout the pushing operation, three hydraulic pumps provide constant pressure support for the precast immersed tube segments.

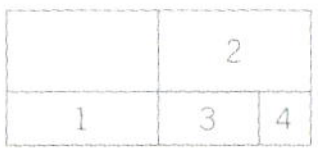

1. 沉管支撑千斤顶分布图
Layout of the Supporting Jacks for the Immersed Tube
2. 沉管支撑千斤顶
Supporting Jack for the Immersed Tube
3. 沉管支撑系统、顶推系统结构图
Structural Diagram of the Supporting System and the Jacking System of the Immersed Tube
4. 沉管支撑千斤顶结构图
Structural Diagram of the Supporting Jack for the Immersed Tube

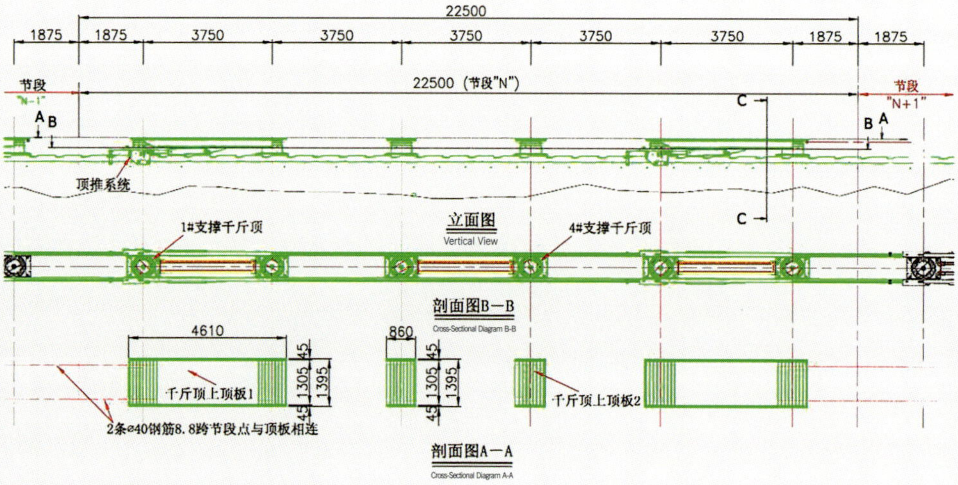

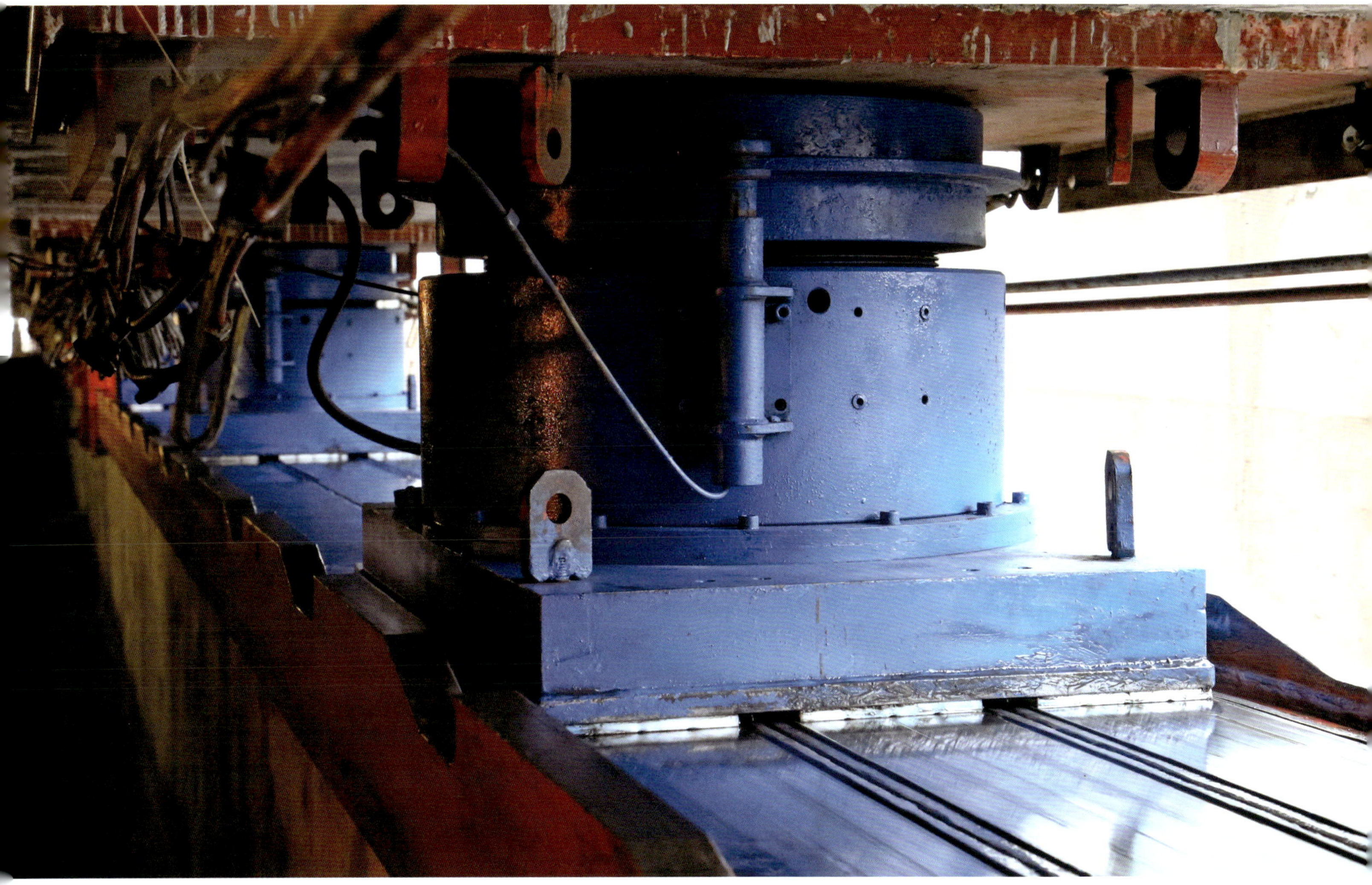

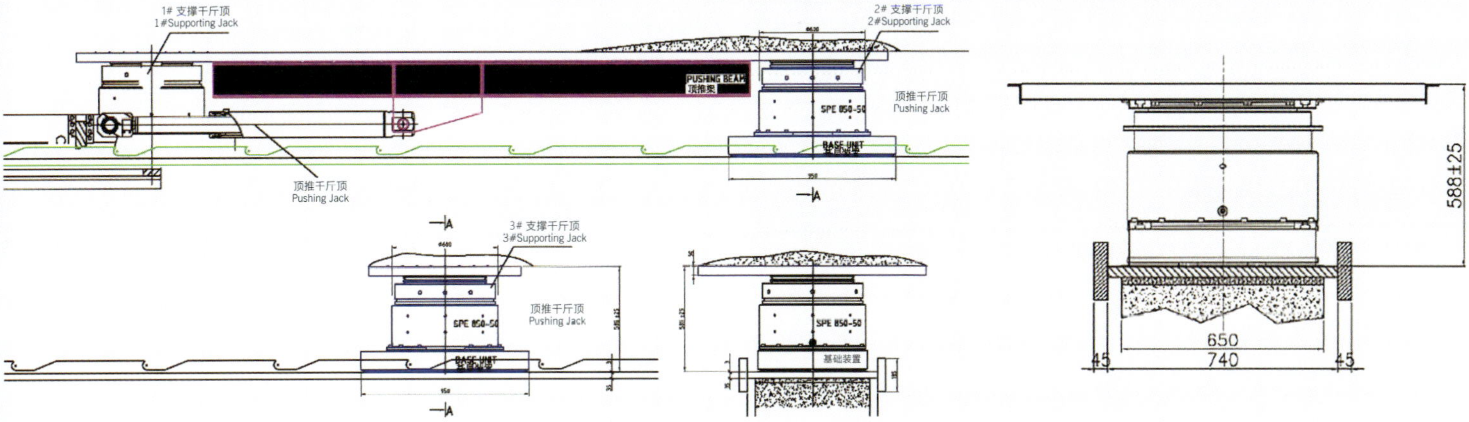
1# 支撑千斤顶
1#Supporting Jack
2# 支撑千斤顶
2#Supporting Jack
PUSHING BEAM
顶推梁
顶推千斤顶
Pushing Jack
SPE 850-50
BASE UNIT
950
A
3# 支撑千斤顶
3#Supporting Jack
基础装置
588±25
650
740
45

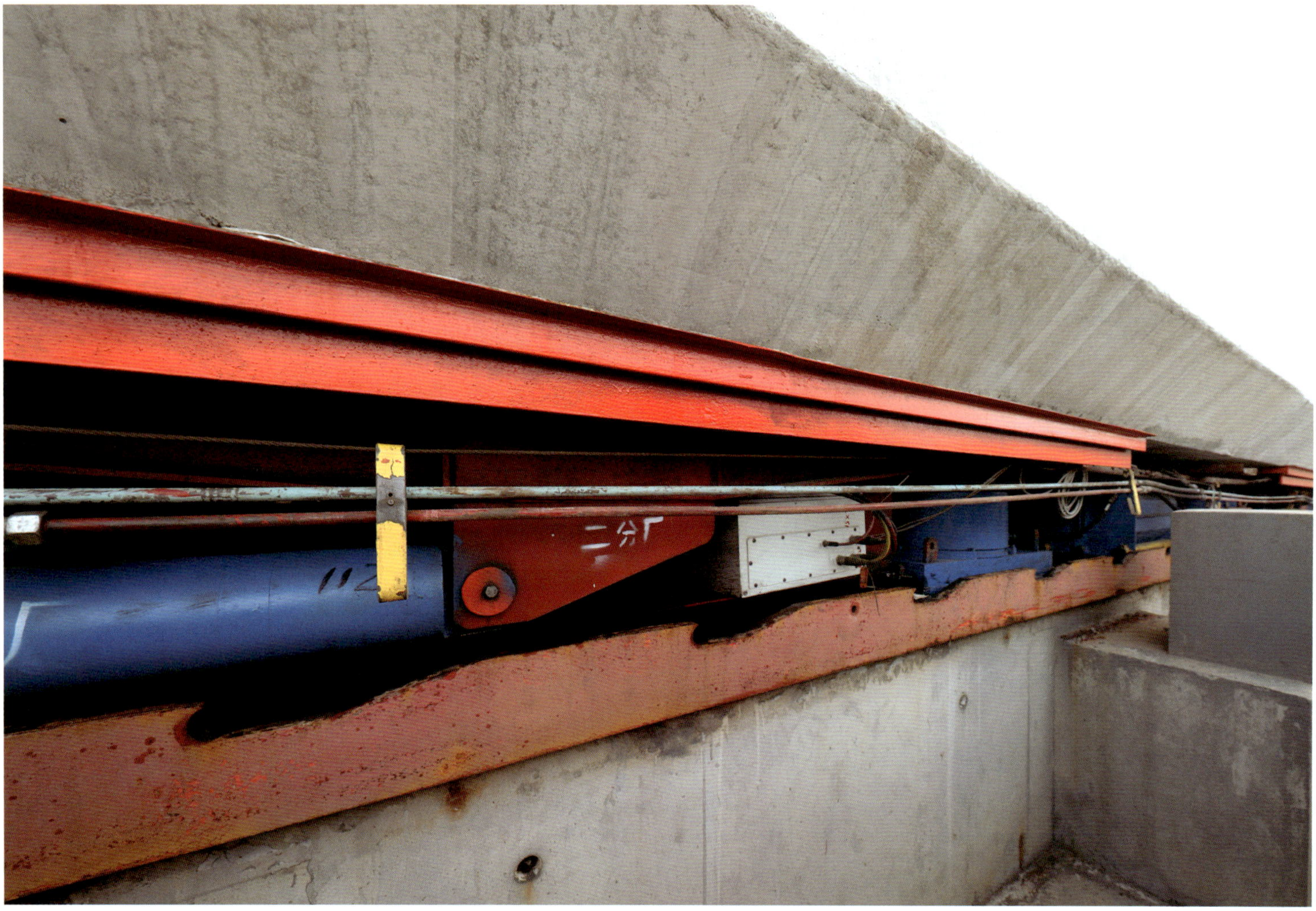
二分厂

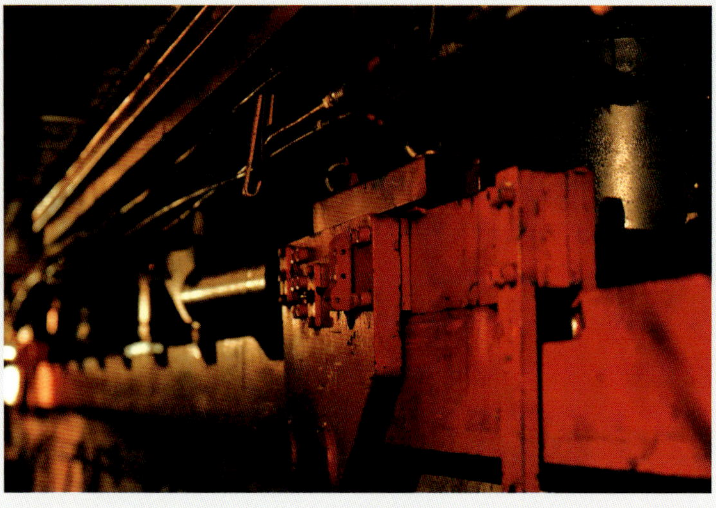

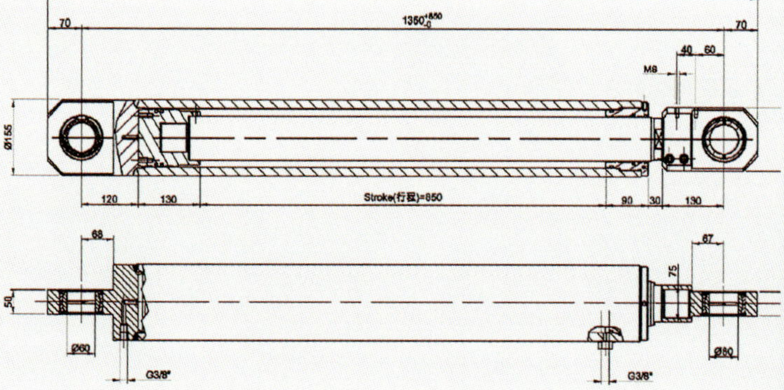
1490
1350
70
70
40
60
M8
Ø155
120
130
Stroke(行程)=850
90
30
130
68
67
75
50
Ø60
Ø80
G3/8"
G3/8"

顶推系统由 168 个顶推千斤顶组成。顶推千斤顶前端支撑在两个支撑千斤顶的连接梁上，另一端销接到带反力销系统的顶推支架上。该系统可将顶推力转移到滑移钢轨上。每台顶推装置由一对长冲程顶推千斤顶组成，型号为 HZP40-850，即能够提供的最大顶推力约为 40 吨，千斤顶最大行程为 850 毫米。

The incremental launching system consists of 168 pushing jacks. The front end of the pushing jack is supported by the connecting beams of the two supporting jacks, and the other end is connected with bolt pins onto the pushing bracket with the counterforce bolt pin system. This system can transfer the jacking force to the sliding tracks. Each pushing device consists of a pair of long-stroke pushing jacks of the model HZP40-850, and it can provide the maximum pushing force of 40 tons over the maximum travelling distance of 850 millimeters.

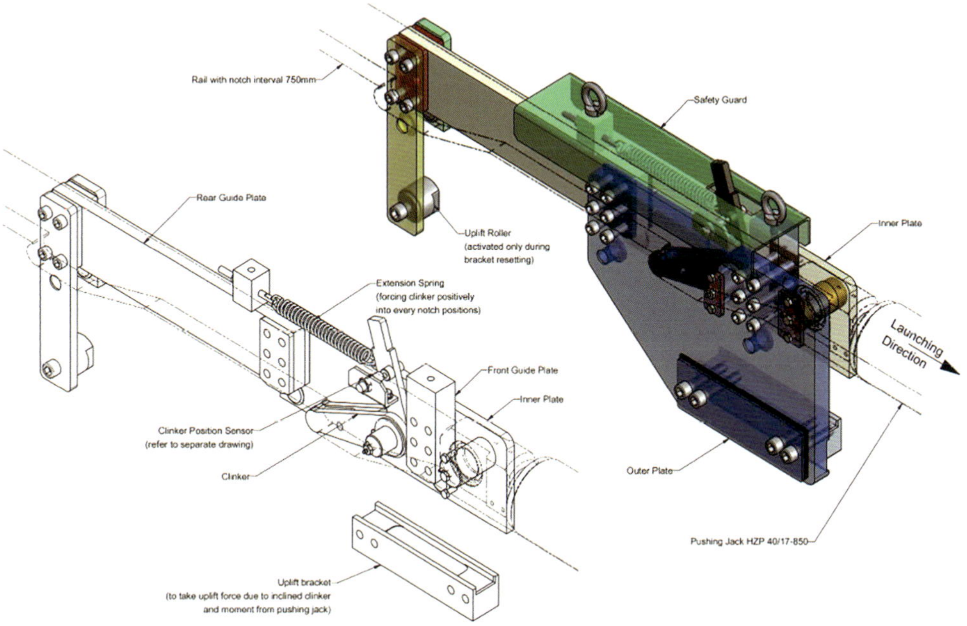

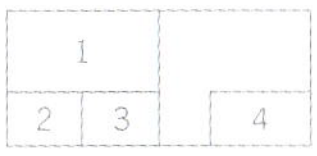

1. 沉管顶推千斤顶
   Pushing Jack for the Immersed Tube
2. 沉管顶推
   Pushing of the Immersed Tube
3. 沉管顶推千斤顶剖面图
   Profile of the Pushing Jack for the Immersed Tube
4. 沉管顶推千斤顶结构图
   Structural Diagram of the Pushing Jack for the Immersed Tube

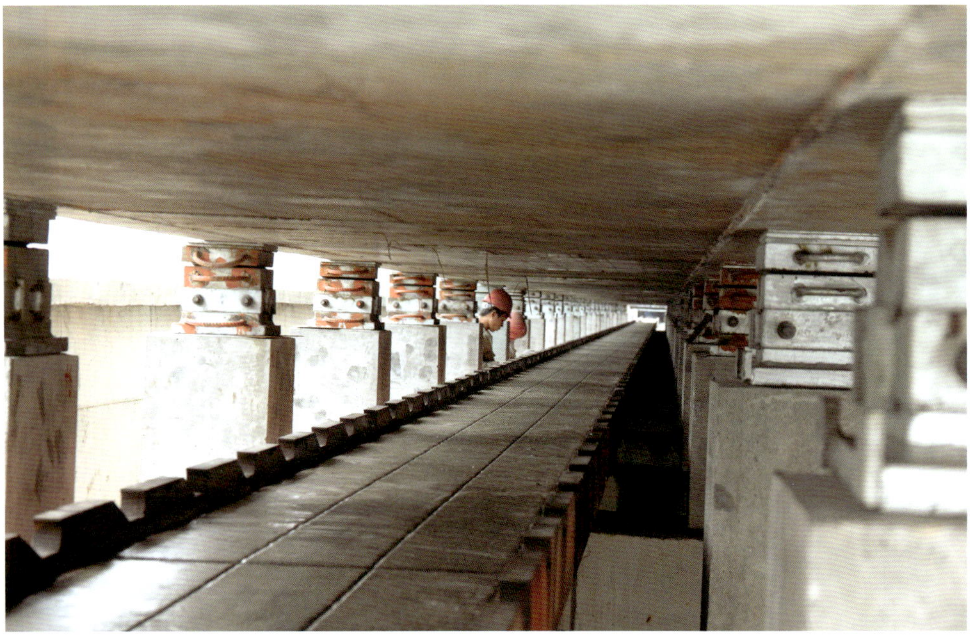

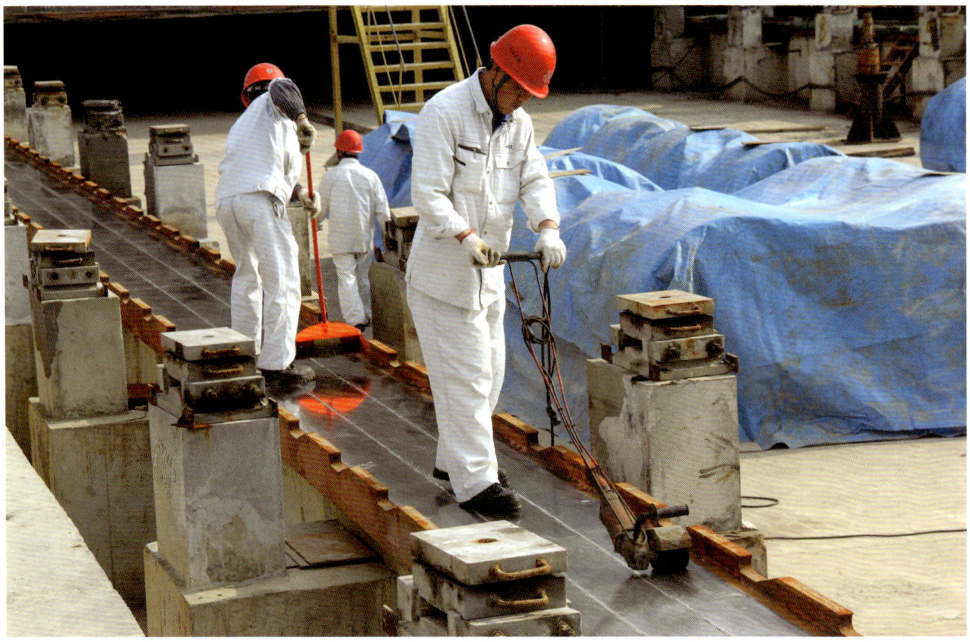

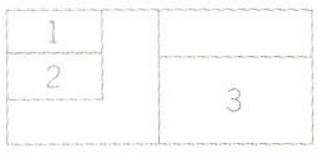

1. 无缘支撑
   Edgeless Support
2. 滑移轨道梁清理
   Cleaning of the Slide Track
3. 沉管顶推
   Pushing of the Immersed Tube

为了实现超大型沉管长距离顶推和毫米级定位，开发了侧导向动态纠偏系统。侧导向装置主要由56吨侧导向千斤顶、穿心式拉杆、两侧导向臂及液压部件组成。安装在沉管下侧，前后端各一套，每套包括两个侧导向千斤顶，对称布置在滑移轨道上。沉管顶推时，轴线偏差超过5毫米自动纠偏。

In order to realize long-distance pushing and accurate positioning of the super-sized immersed tube by millimeters, a dynamic deviation correction system with side guidance was developed. The side guiding device is mainly composed of 56-ton side guiding jacks, piercing pulling rods, guiding arms on the two sides and hydraulic components. These devices are installed on the lower side of the immersed tube, one set at the front end and one set at the back end, and each set includes two side guiding jacks symmetrically arranged on the sliding track. When the immersed tube is pushed forward, any deviation exceeding 5 millimeters is corrected automatically.

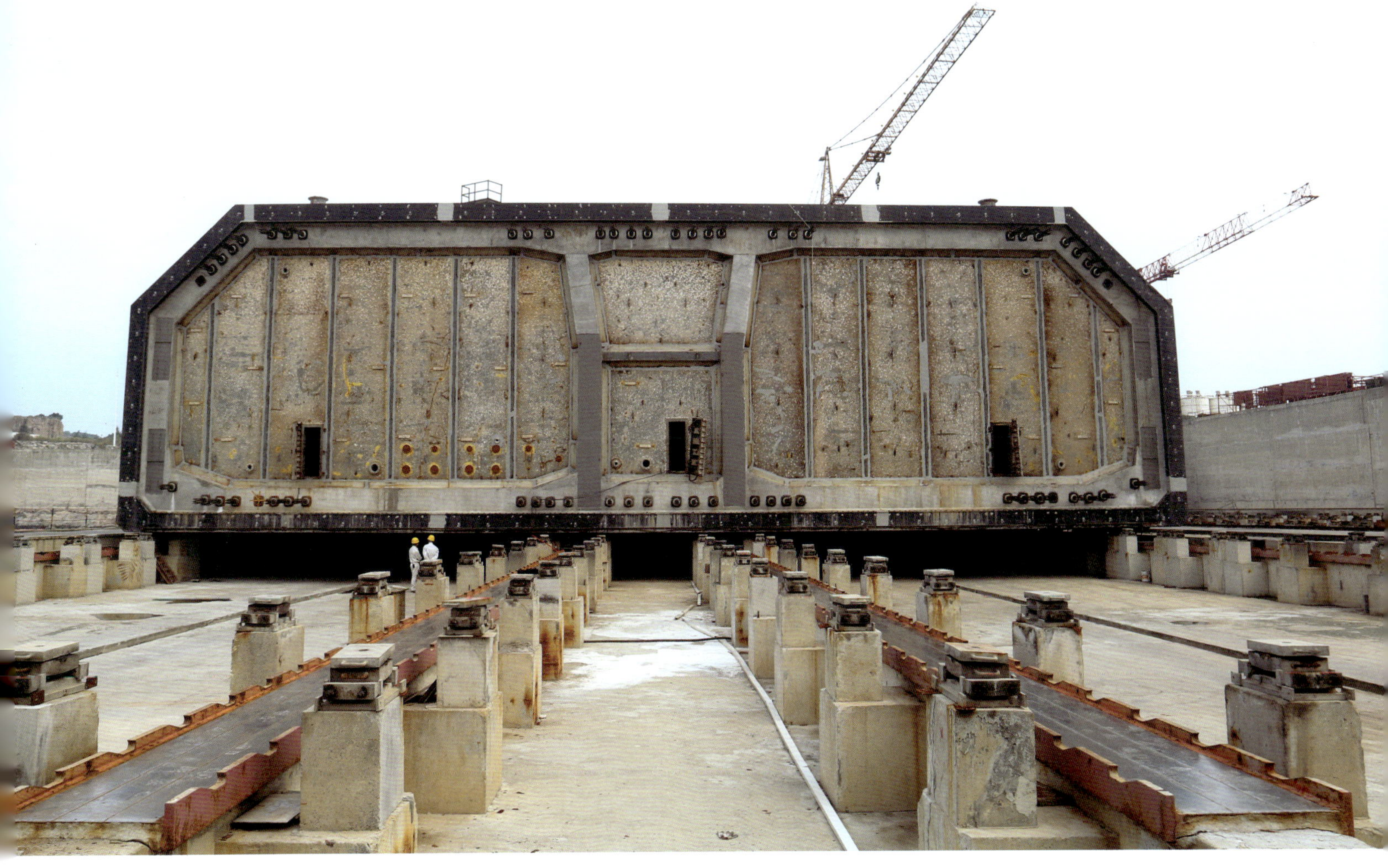

沉管预制厂顺利完成33个沉管顶推横移施工，顶推全过程未造成沉管的结构损伤。随着工艺的成熟，顶推第15批沉管时，仅用时3天，效率较高。

为防止节段接头拉开，从第7批沉管开始，先进行8束预应力钢绞索预张拉后再进行顶推，张拉力为50%设计终应力；等沉管顶推至浅坞后，再进行所有预应力的张拉工作。

The immersed tube precast factory successfully completed the pushing and horizontal moving of 33 immersed tubes, and no structural damage was done to any immersed tube in the whole process. As this technique matured, it took only 3 days to push the 15th batch of immersed tubes to the designed position, known for its high efficiency.

In order to prevent the segment joints from being pulled apart, starting from the 7th batch of immersed tubes, 8 pre-stressing steel stranded wires were pre-tensioned before pushing, and the tension was 50% of the designed ultimate stress. After the immersed tube was pushed to the shallow dock, all pre-stressing tensioning were performed.

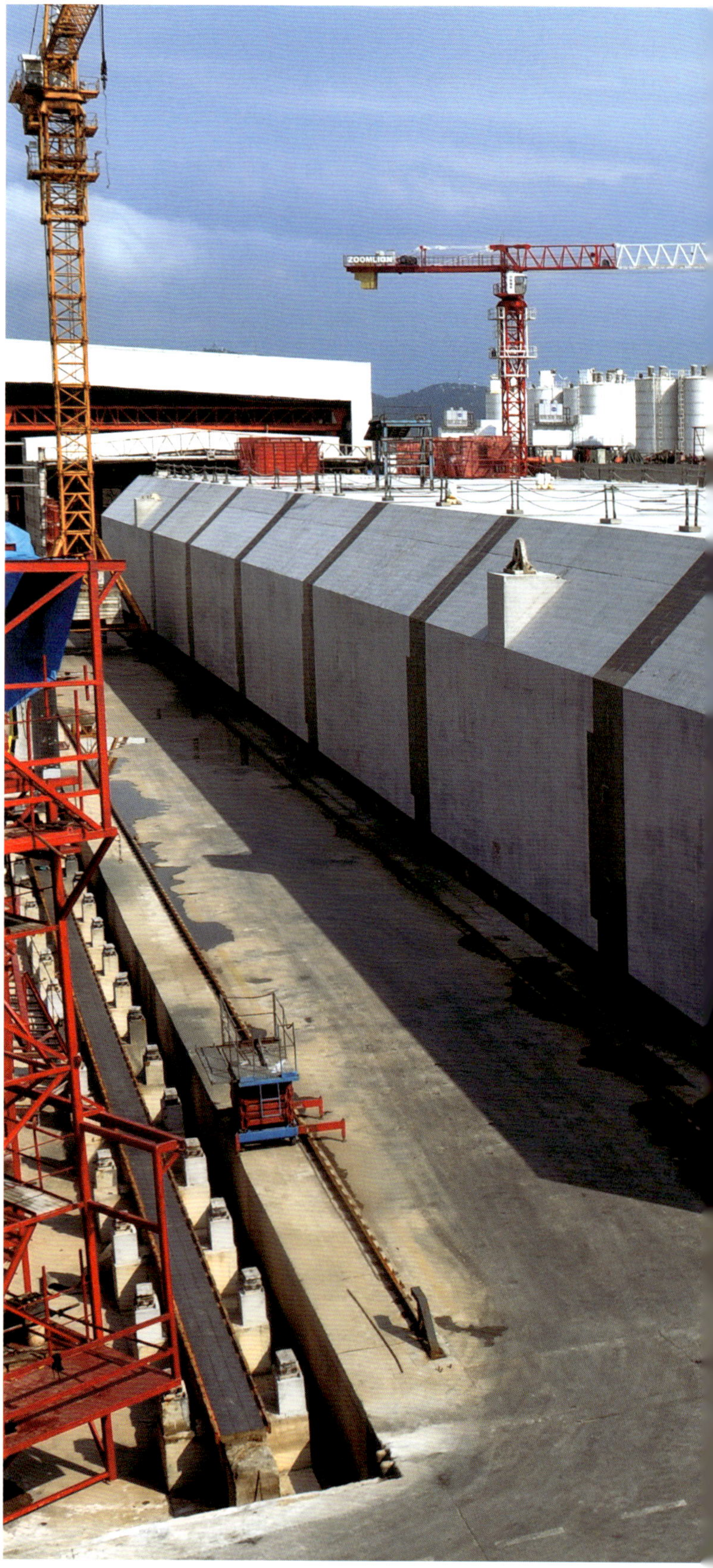

沉管顶推到位
Immersed Tube Pushed to the Designed Position

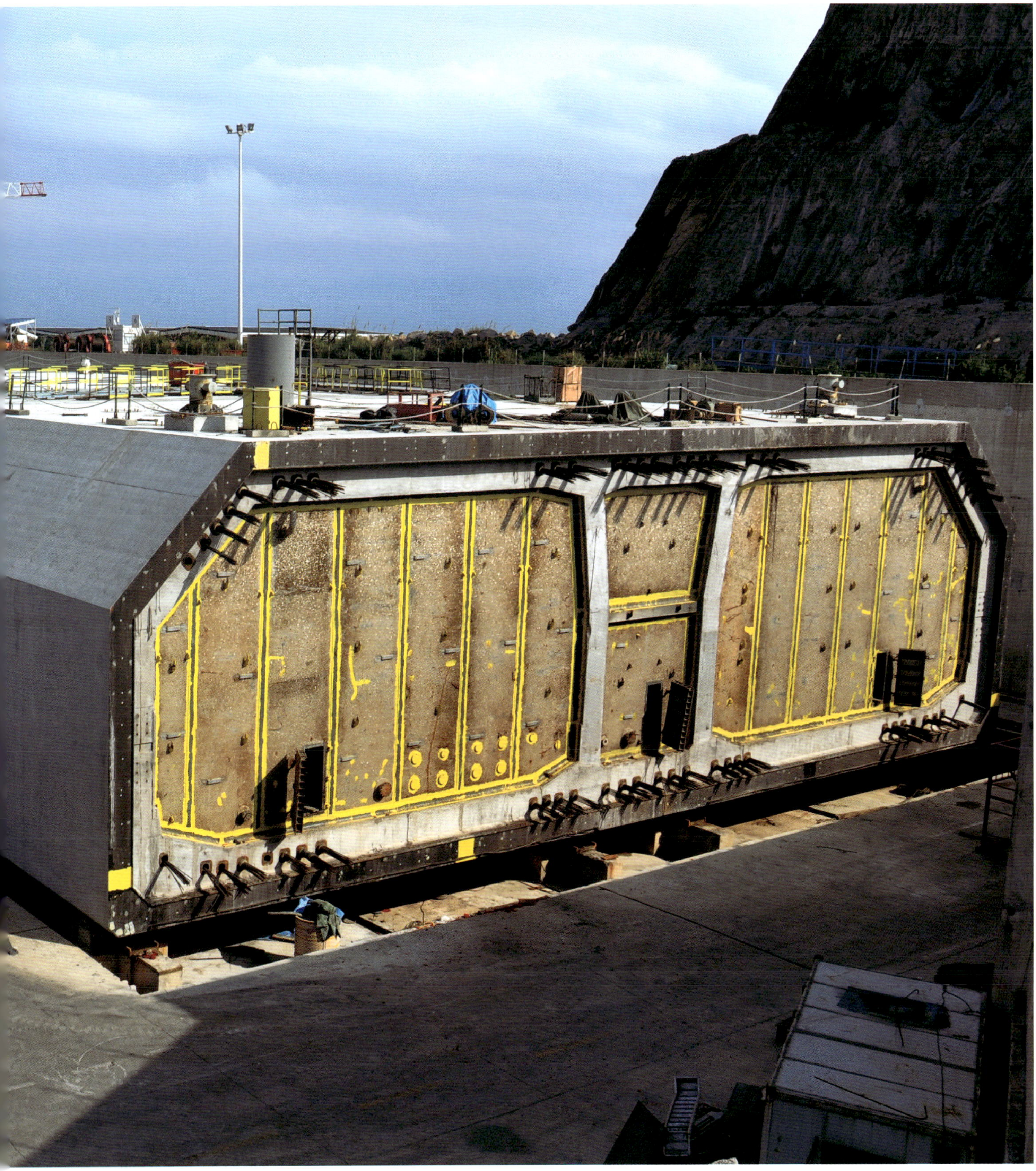

曲线段

CURVE SECTION OF THE TUNNEL

沉管隧道曲线段总长度为 793.4 米，包括 5 节（E29~E33）钢筋混凝土沉管和 1 个钢壳混凝土最终接头，曲率半径 5500 米。

曲线沉管预制通过“以折代曲”的方式进行曲线拟合，节段之间设夹角。单个节段为直线，轴线长 22.5 米，横断面尺寸及混凝土性能要求与直线段沉管相同。

与直线沉管相比，曲线沉管施工具有以下主要差异：曲线沉管每个节段轴线与生产线轴线的夹角均不相同，每个节段施工前均要进行钢筋位置、钢筋安装台架、模板放样和调整，施工控制精度高，工作量大幅增加；由于节段尺寸各异，钢筋变尺型号大量增加，绑扎时对于半成品分类工作须要更加细致；顶板钢筋安装台架底座支撑杆无法与顶推滑轨对齐，存在左右偏位，需增加型钢分载梁；顶推移动过程中钢筋笼重心偏移，对于同步顶推的控制须更加严格；内模支腿、端模角度和支撑位置有变化，模板系统须进行针对性改造；由于沉管重量存在偏心，为加强顶推轴向控制，需增加侧导向液压千斤顶；由于沉管驻停位置左右有偏移，浅坞区沉管驻停位置需增加无源支墩；曲线沉管预应力穿束，张拉变形控制难度增大。

The total length of the curved section of the immersed tube tunnel is 793.4 meters, including 5 sections (E29~E33) of steel reinforced concrete immersed tube and 1 steel-shelled concrete closure joint, with a curvature radius of 5,500 meters.

The precast of the curved tubes adopts the new technique of curve fitting by bending instead of curving. Included angles are kept between two segments. Any individual segment is straight with an axial line 22.5 meters long. The cross-sectional dimensions and concrete performance requirements are the same as those of the straight immersed tubes.

Compared with the straight immersed tubes, construction of the curved immersed tube differs in the following aspects: The included angle between the axis of each segments of the curved immersed tube and the axis of the production line is never the same, so before the construction of each segment, lofting and adjustment must be done concerning the position of the reinforcing steel bars, the jig frames for steel reinforcement installation and the formworks. It need a lot of work to ensure high accuracy in construction control; because of the different sizes of the different segments, the sizes and types of the steel bars change greatly, and the classification of semi-finished products needs more care during the steel reinforcement binding; the supporting rod of jig frame base for top steel plate cannot be aligned with the pushing slide track, resulting in deviation on the horizontal direction, so a load-sharing section steel beam needs to be added; the gravity center of the steel reinforcement cage deviates during the pushing, so the stricter control on the synchronous pushing is necessary; the changes of the supporting rods of the internal formwork, the angles of the end formwork and the supporting positions need the reformation of the formwork system; because the gravity center of the immersed tube may be eccentric, a side guiding hydraulic jack should be added to strengthen the control over the pushing axis; due to the horizontal deviation of the landing position of the immersed tube, passive piers should be added in the landing position of the immersed tube in the shallow dock area; in the process of pre-stressing threading of the curved tube, it is more difficult to control the deformation caused by the tensioning operation.

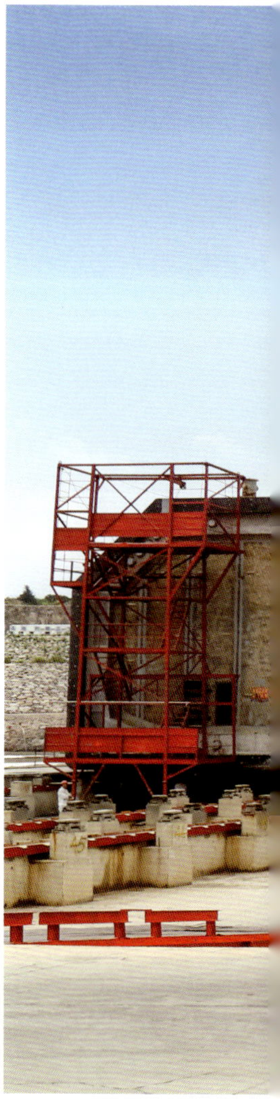

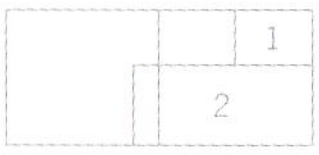

1. 曲线段沉管三维图
   3D Diagram of the Immersed Tube at the Curved Section of the Tunnel
2. 曲线段沉管
   Immersed Tube at the Curved Section of the Tunnel

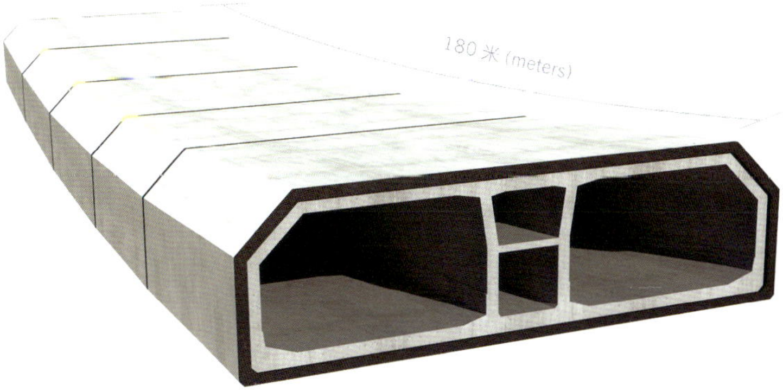
180 米 (meters)

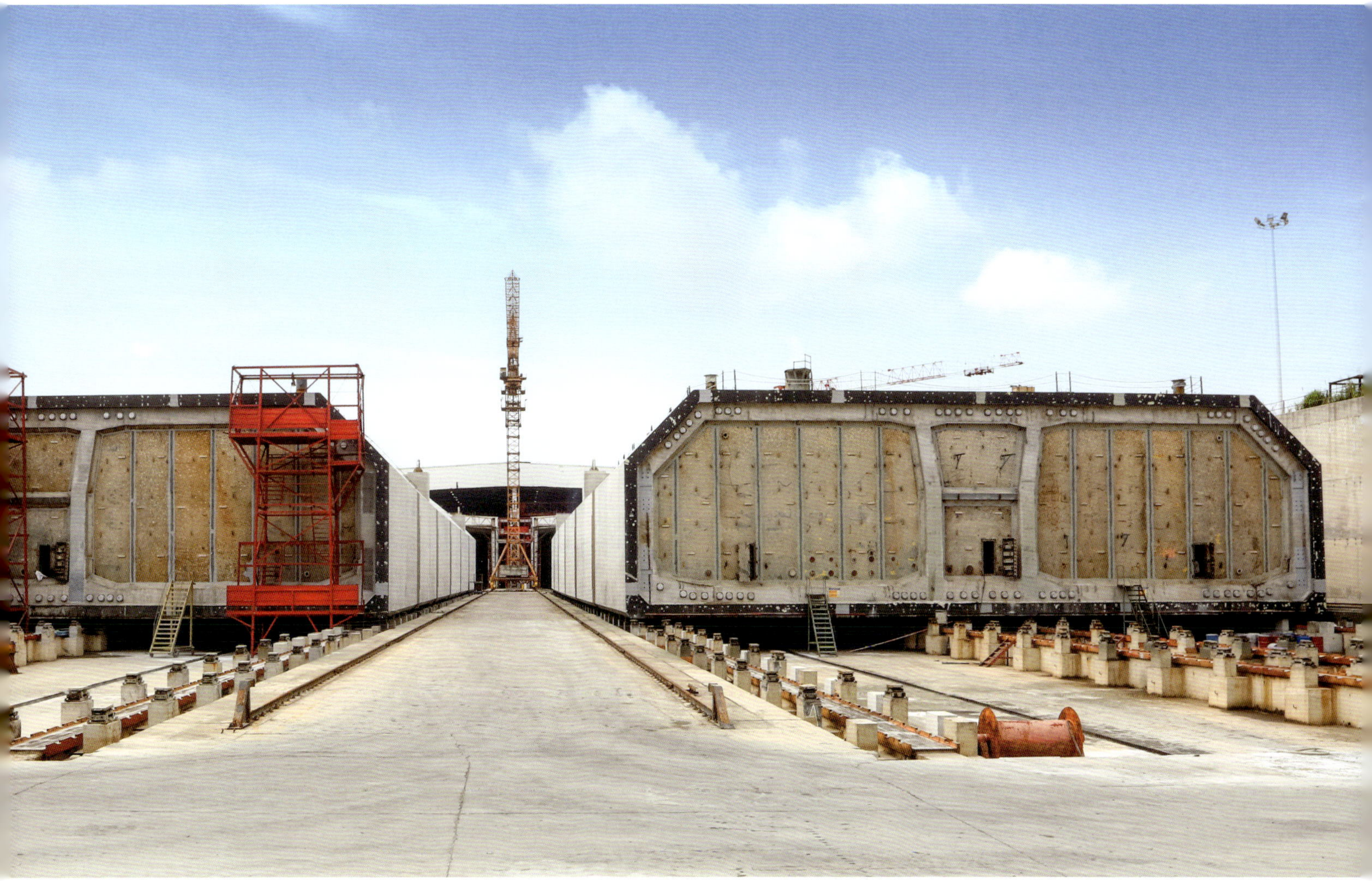

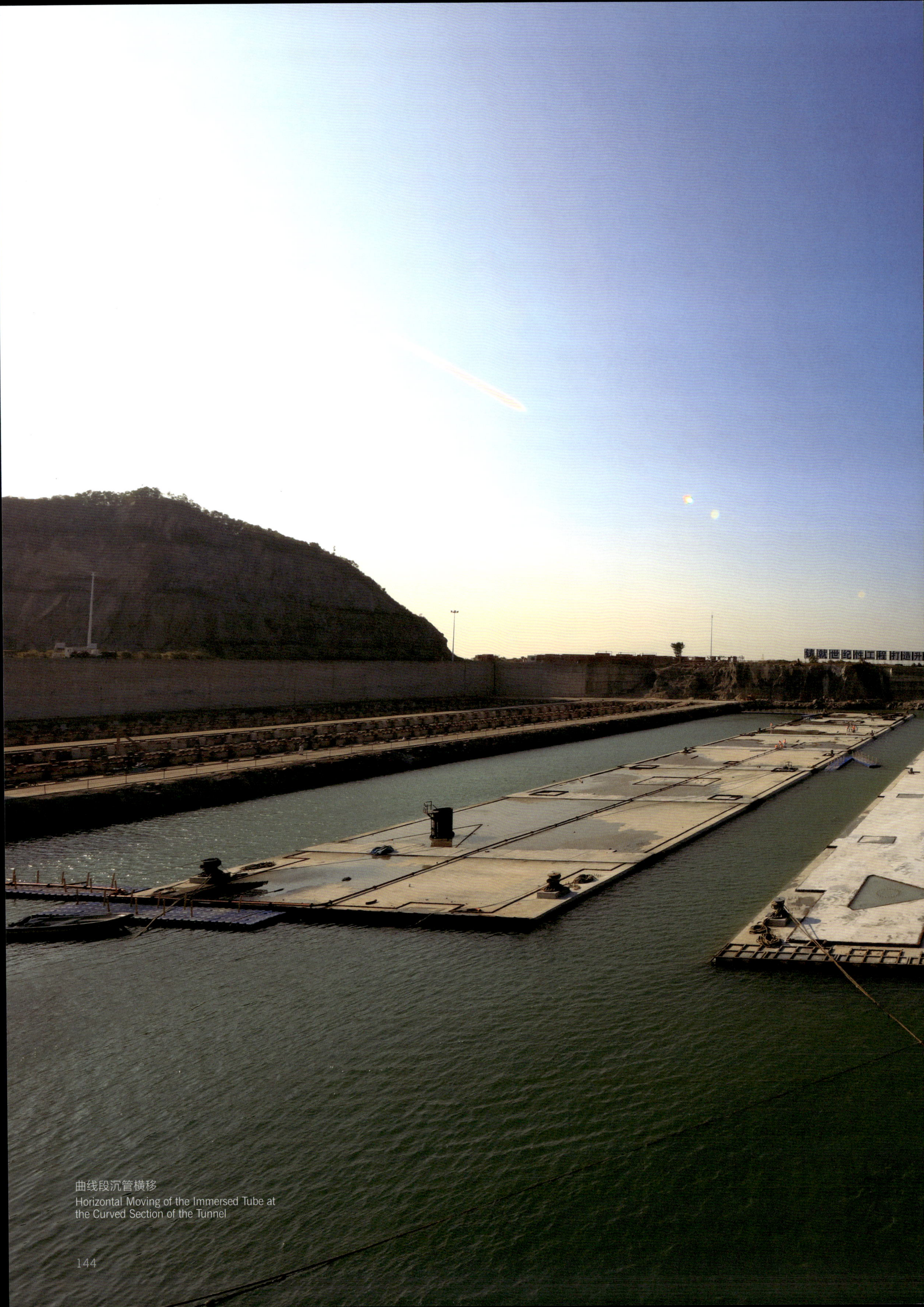

曲线段沉管横移
Horizontal Moving of the Immersed Tube at the Curved Section of the Tunnel

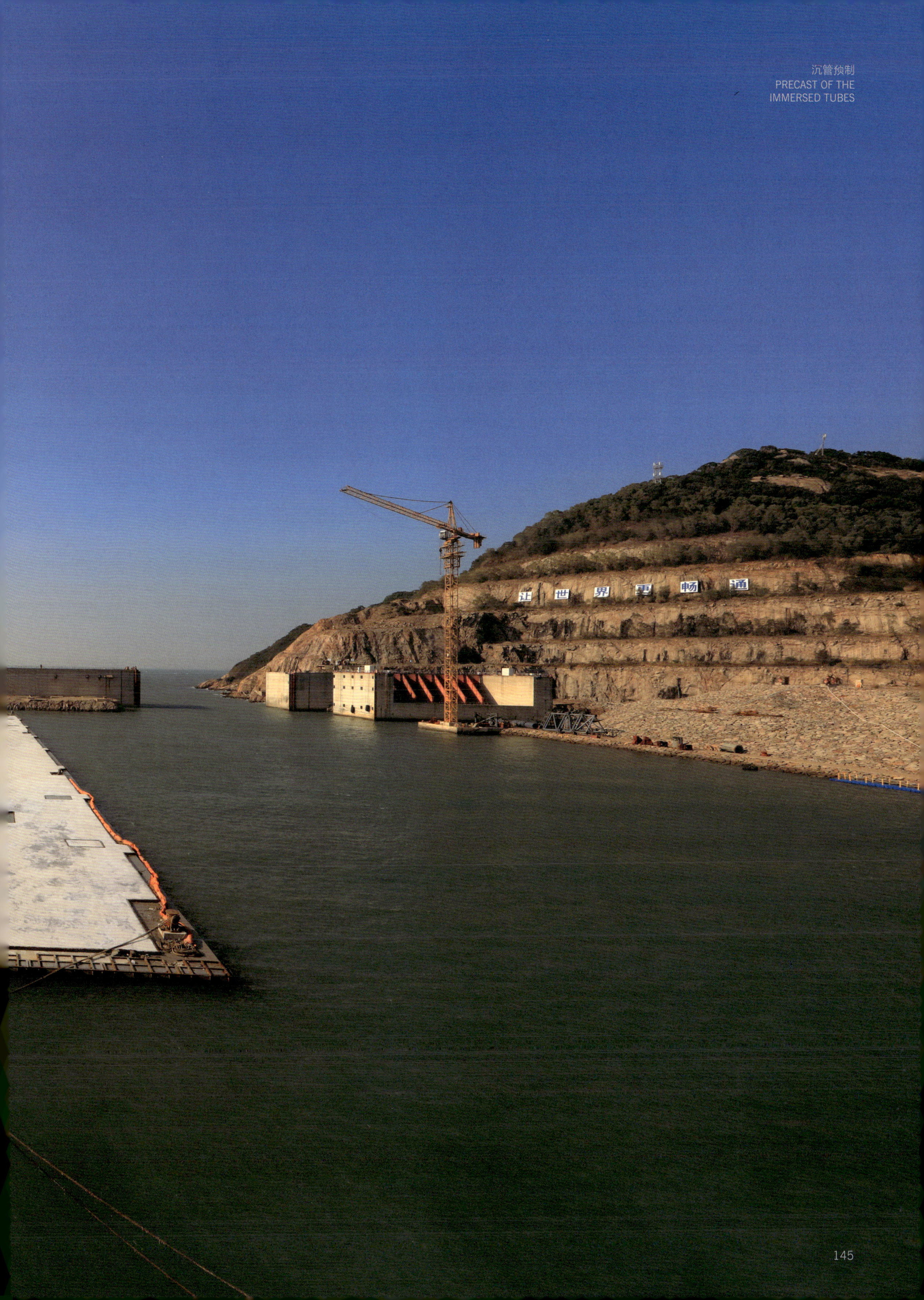
让 世 界 更 畅 通

舾装及横移

OUTFITTING AND HORIZONTAL MOVING

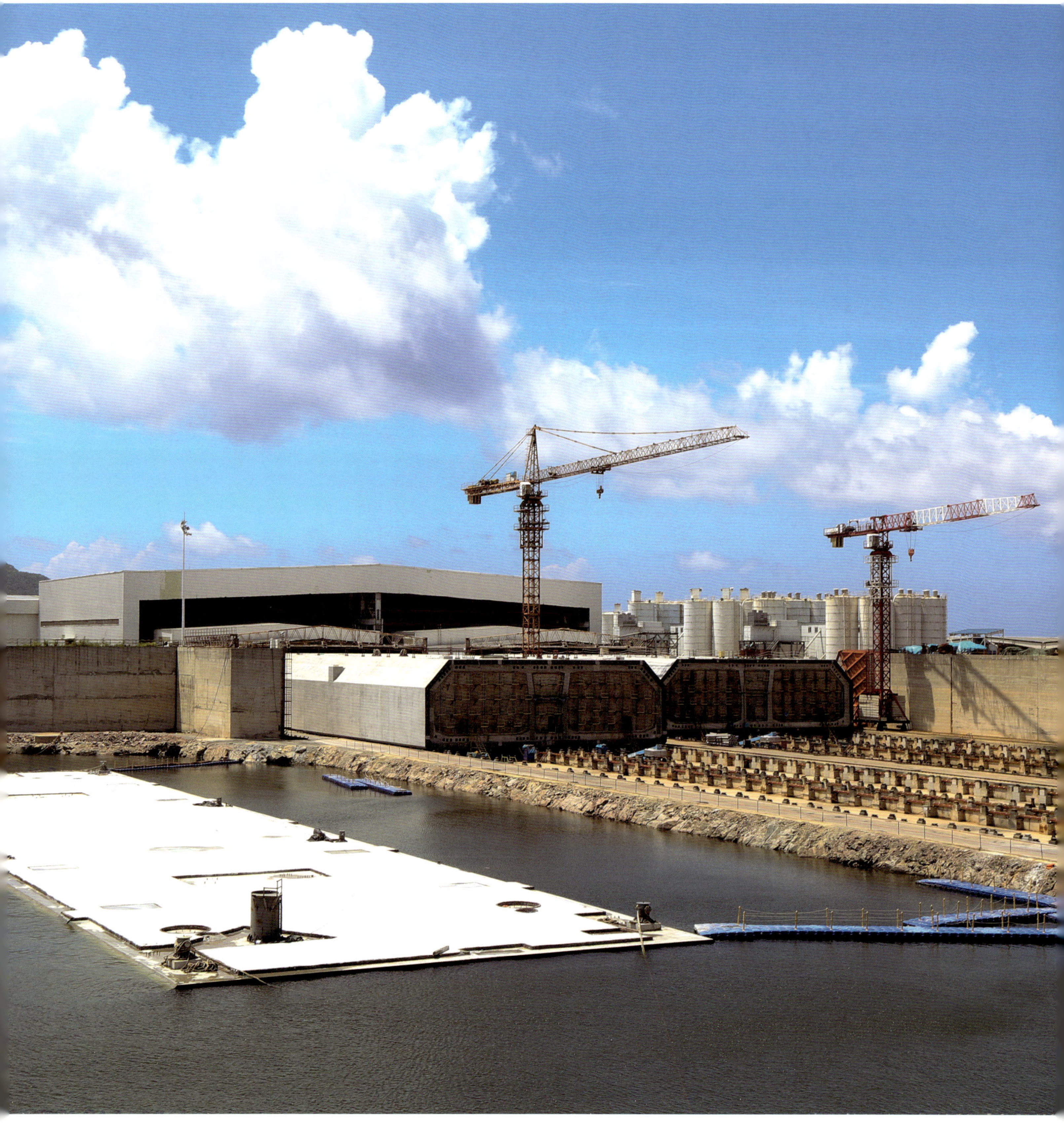

沉管一次舾装施工是沉管浮运安装系统中的重要组成部分，为沉管在浮运安装过程中的水密性、稳定性提供可靠保障。

起浮横移是指沉管从浅坞一次舾装区移往深坞区的施工过程。深浅坞蓄水完成后，对浅坞区已完成一次舾装的沉管水箱灌水压载，使沉管坐底并进行水密性检验；然后排水起浮，横移到深坞系泊。

The initial outfitting is an important part of the float conveyance and installation system of the immersed tube, providing reliable guarantee for the water-proof function and stability of the immersed tube during float conveyance and installation.

Floating and horizontal moving involve the process of moving the immersed tube out of the first outfitting area in the shallow dock to the deep dock. After the impoundment in the deep and shallow docks is completed, water is filled into the water tank of the immersed tube that has been outfitted in the shallow dock, so the immersed tube outfitted sits at the bottom for waterproof test. Then the water tank is drained, so the immersed tube floats up and is moved to the deep dock and anchored there.

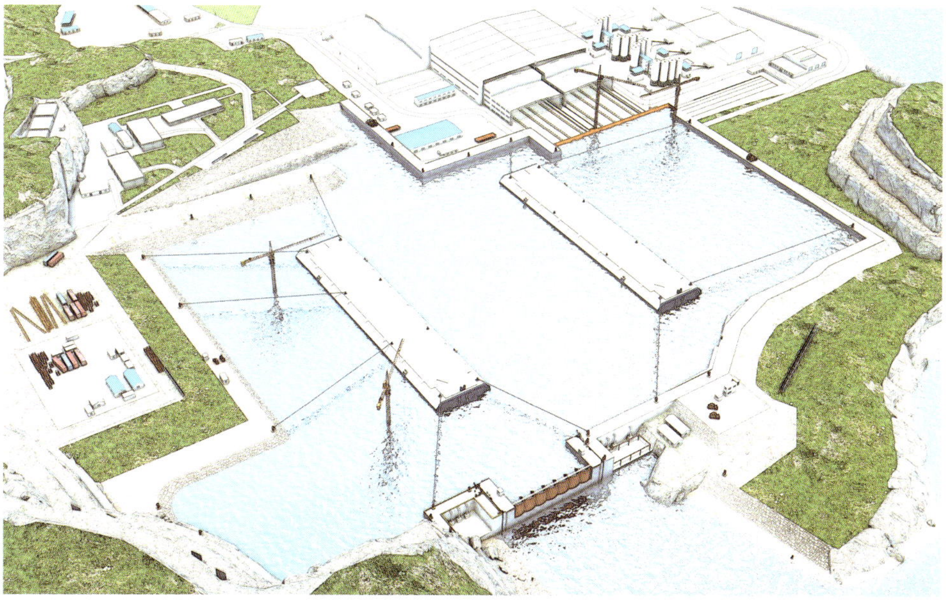

1. 沉管一次舾装
   Initial Outfitting of the Immersed Tube
2. 沉管横移示意图
   Schematic Diagram of the Horizontal Moving of the Immersed Tube

分项工程 Sub-divisional Work	工作量 Work Load
端封门施工 End Sealing	钢封门单侧共 16 件，最大尺寸 2.2 米 ×8.36 米，最大重量 4.2 吨 There are altogether 16 components on one side, with the largest one being 2.2 meters×8.36 meters and the biggest one weighing 4.2 tons
	外侧牛腿单侧共 24 节 There 24 external corbels on one side
	钢梁单侧共 30 根，最大长度 8.525 米，最大重量 5.58 吨 There are 30 steel beams on one side, with the longest one being 8.525 meters and the biggest one weighing 5.58 tons
	钢梁牛腿单侧共 33 个 There are 33 steel beam corbels on one side
压载系统 Ballast System	管系主管采用 φ273 钢管，支管采用 φ219 钢管 The main pipe is the φ273 steel pipe, while the branch pipe is the φ219 steel pipe
	压载水箱单管节 6 个，尺寸为 14.55 米 ×20 米，单个水箱包含 26 根钢立柱 The ballast water tank consists of 6 segments, the dimension is 14.55 meters×20 meters, and each water tank has 26 steel columns
管顶舾装件 Components for Tube Top Outfitting	120 吨系船柱 4 个，65 吨系船柱 4 个，450 千牛吊点 4 个，短人孔 1 个，GINA 保护罩 1 个 4 bollards of 120 tons, 4 bollards of 65 tons, 4 hoisting points of 450 KN, 1 short manhole, 1 GINA protective hood
二次舾装 Secondary Outfitting	管顶测控系统，管内系统调试，船管连接系统 Tube top monitoring system, in-tube adjustment, and barge-tube connecting system

管节舾装主要施工内容
Major Operations for Tube Segment Outfitting

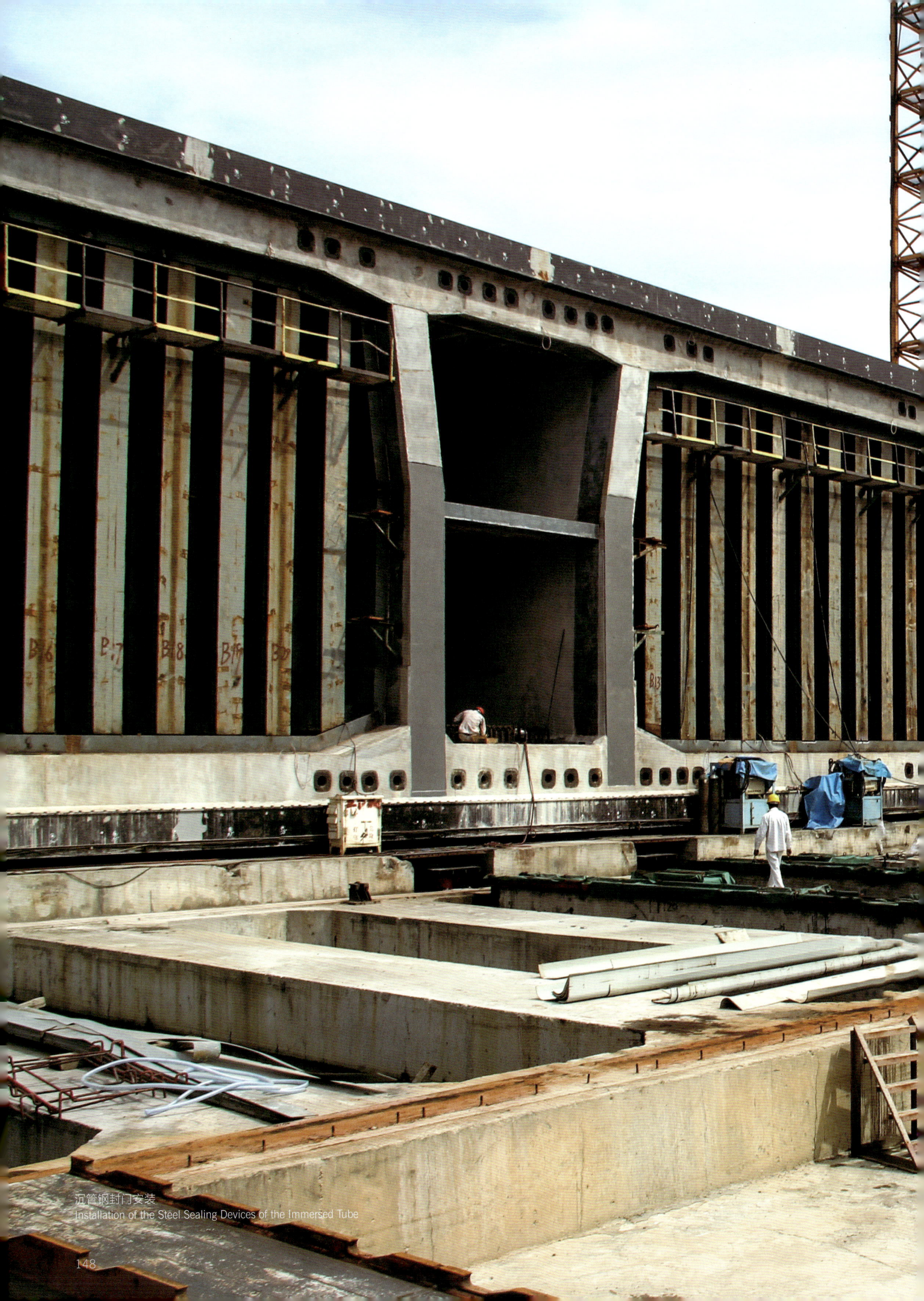

沉管钢封门安装
Installation of the Steel Sealing Devices of the Immersed Tube

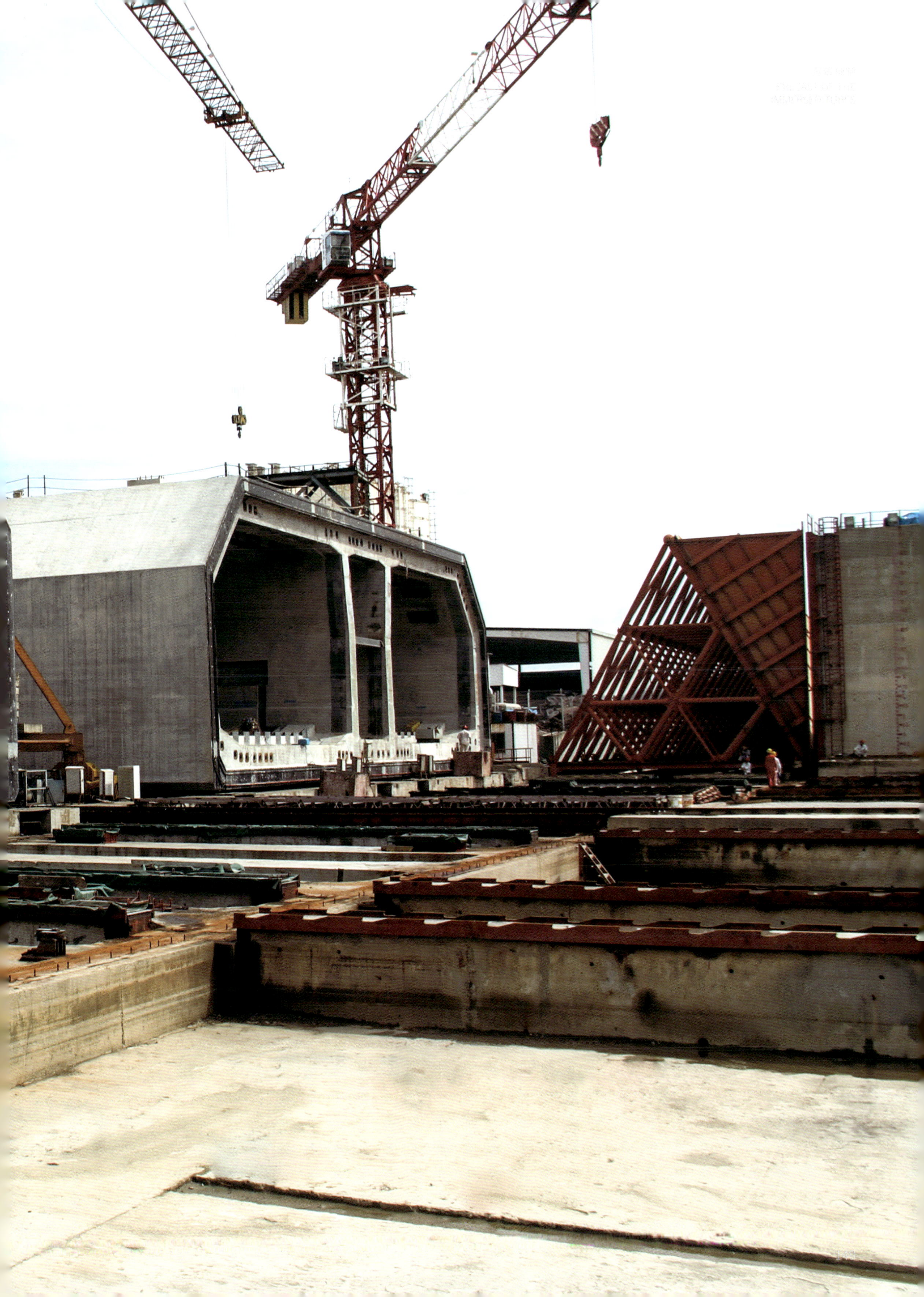

钢封门安装：端封门位于沉管两端，是封闭沉管两端的临时挡水结构，采用梁板结构，可周转使用，主要由钢封门、外侧牛腿、钢梁、钢梁牛腿等部件构成。每侧钢封门共分 16 片，最大重量约 4 吨，并设有 3 处人孔门。

端封门的安装流程为：钢梁牛腿安装→钢梁安装→外侧牛腿安装→钢封门安装→钢封门密封板安装→水密性检验。

Installation of Steel Sealing Devices: The steel sealing devices are installed at the two ends of the immersed tube, and are used as the temporary water-stop structures. The sealing devices adopt the beam-plate structure, and can be recycled. They are composed mainly of sealing devices, external corbels, steel beams and corbels of the steel beam and other components. The steel sealing devices at either end consist of 16 pieces, the maximum weight is around 4 tons, and three manholes are reserved.

The installation procedure of the end sealing devices is as follows: installation of the steel beam corbel, installation of the steel beam installation of the external corbel, installation of the steel sealing devices, installation of the sealing plates and waterproof test.

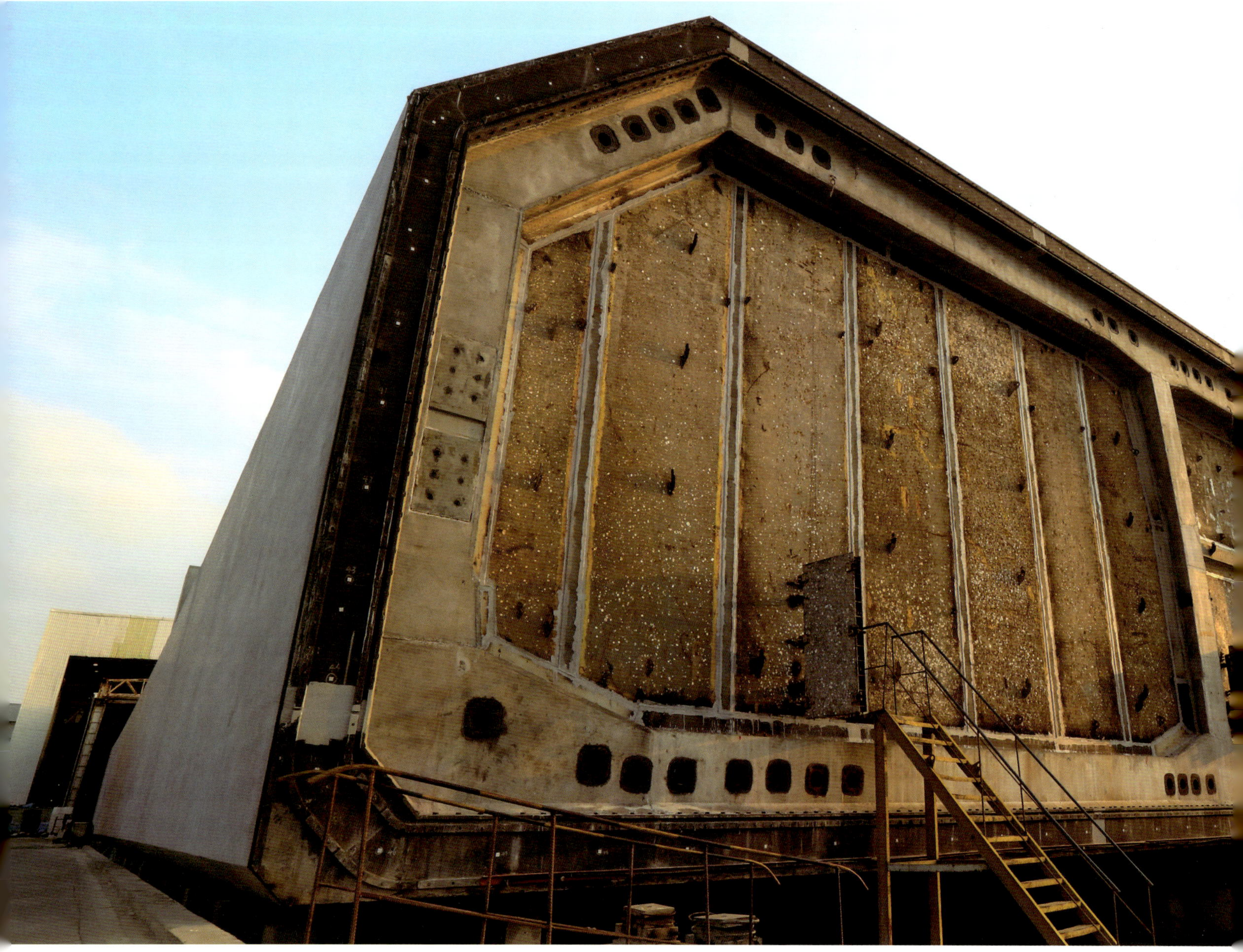

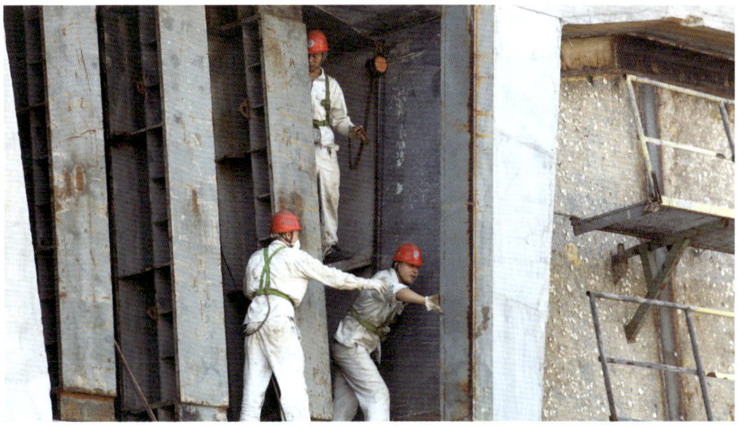

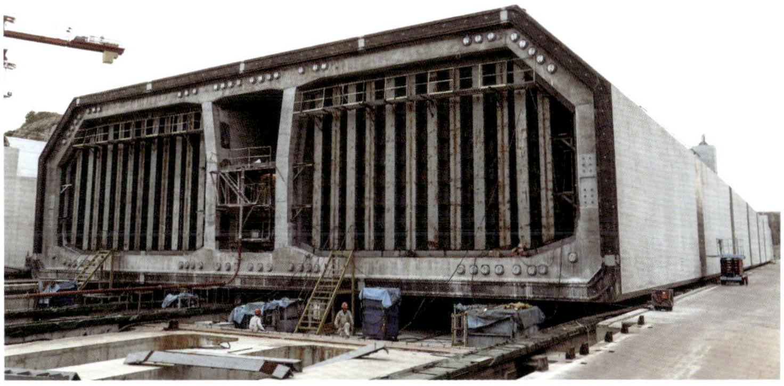

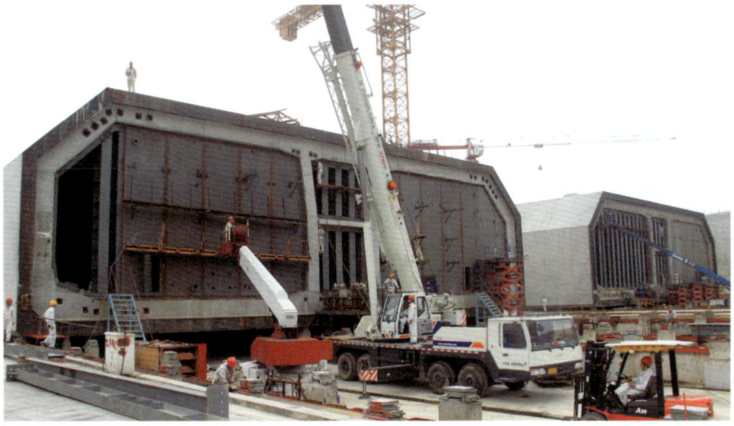

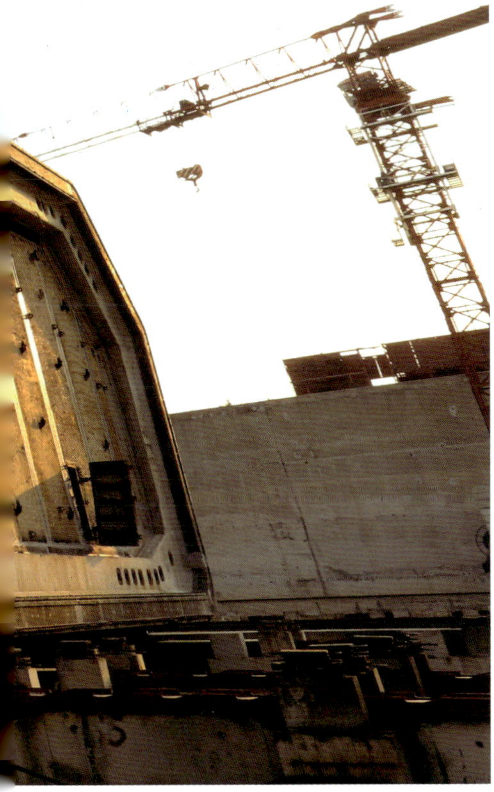

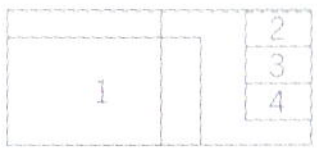

1. 钢封门安装完成
Steel Sealing Devices Installation Completed

2—4. 钢封门安装过程
Steel Sealing Devices Installation

压载水箱安装

Ballast Water Tank Installation

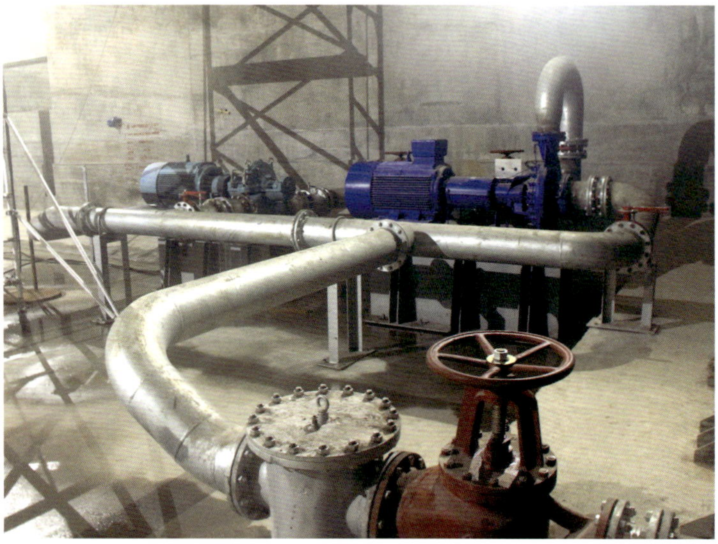

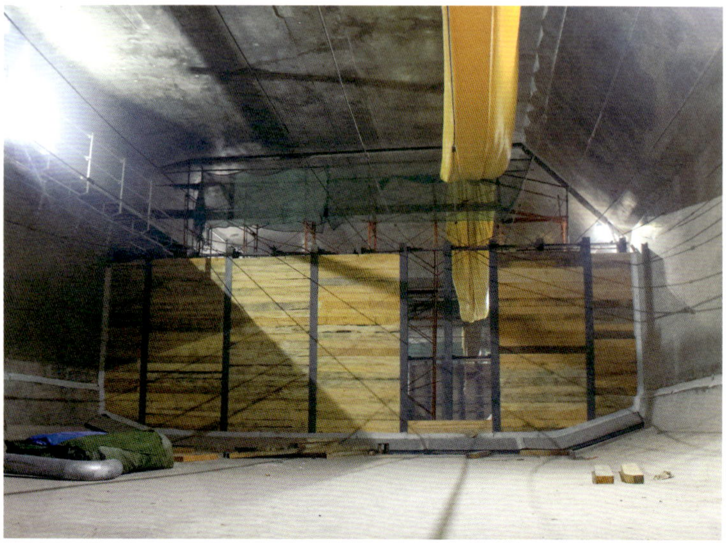

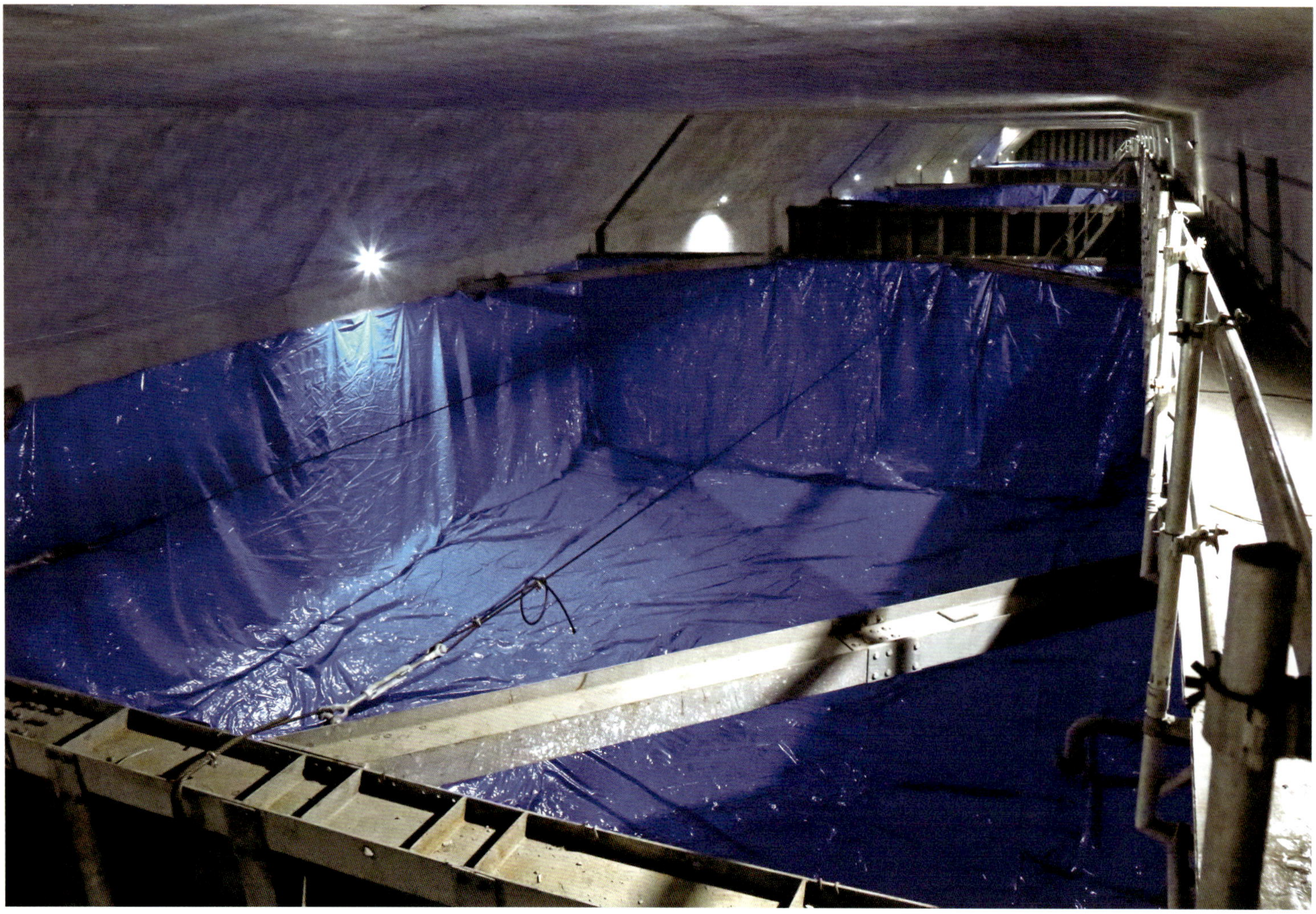

小 OMG 止水带安装

Installation of the Small OMEGA Water-Stop

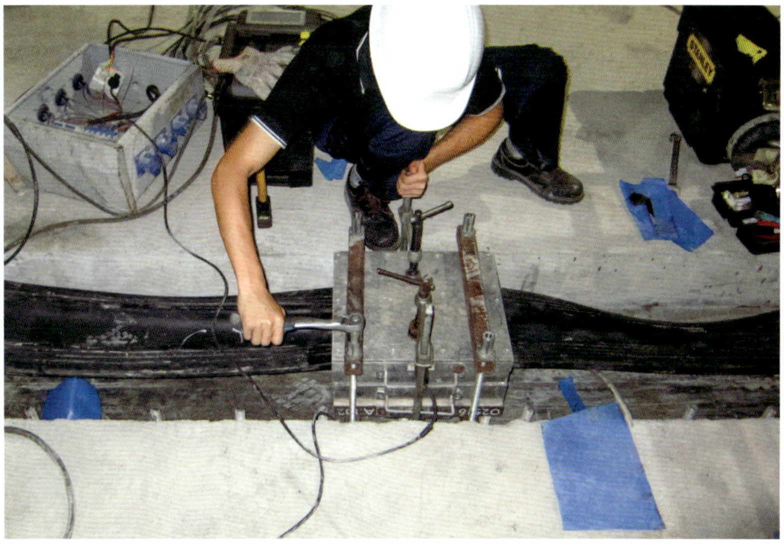

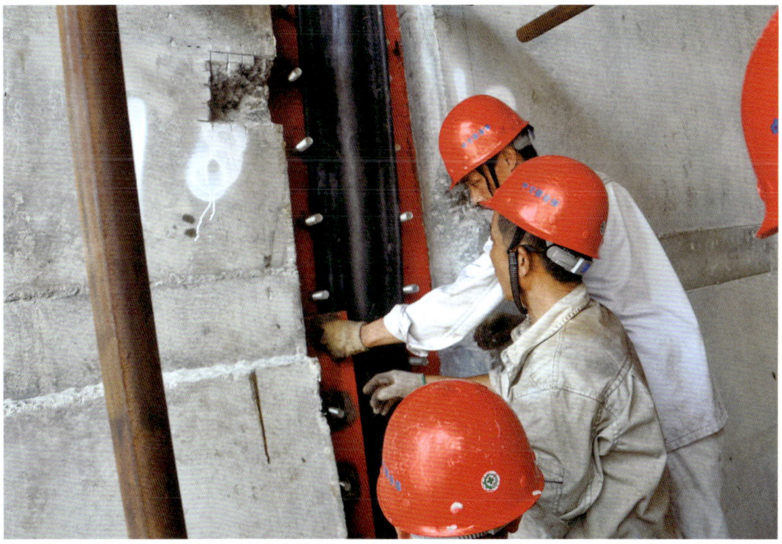

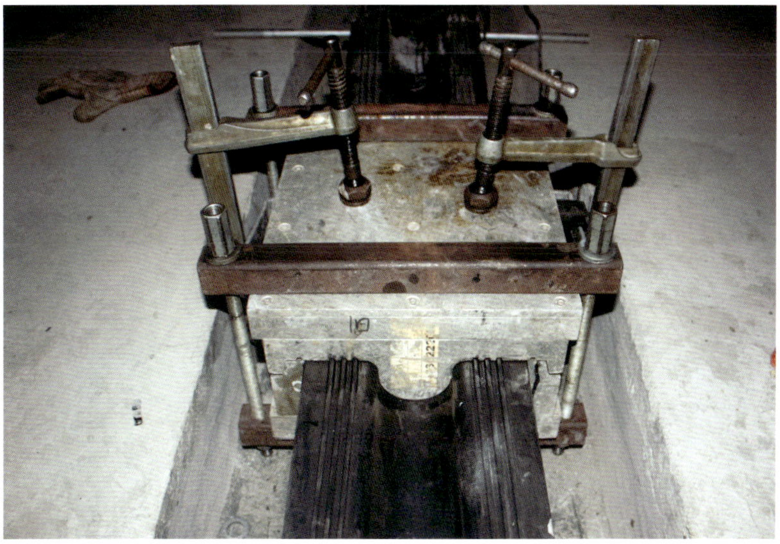

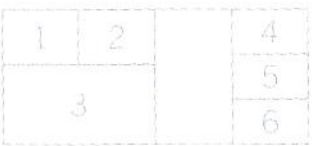

1. 沉管压载水系统
   Ballast Water System of the Immersed Tube
2. 压载水箱安装
   Installation of the Ballast Water Tank
3. 安装完成的压载水箱
   Ballast Water Tank Installed
4. 小 OMEGA 止水带接驳
   Small OMEGA Water-Stop Connection
5. 小 OMEGA 止水带安装
   Installation of the Small OMEGA Water-Stop
6. 小 OMEGA 止水带接驳
   Small OMEGA Water-Stop Connection

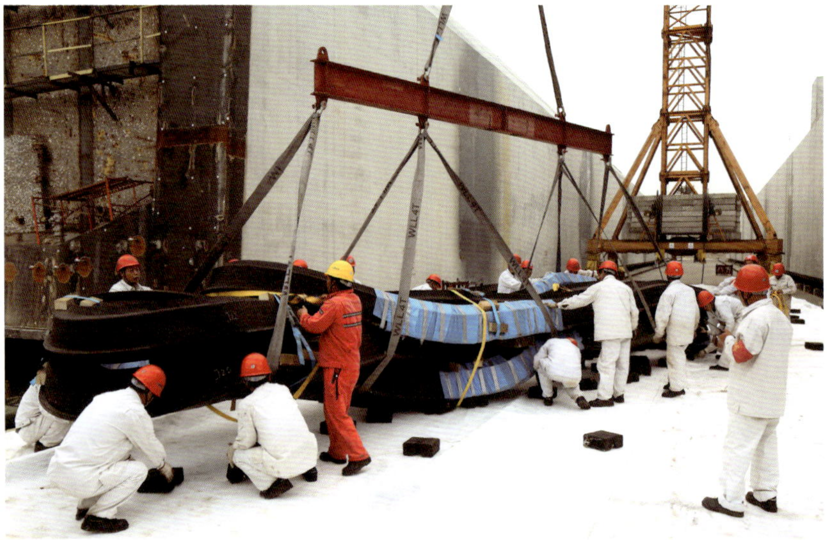

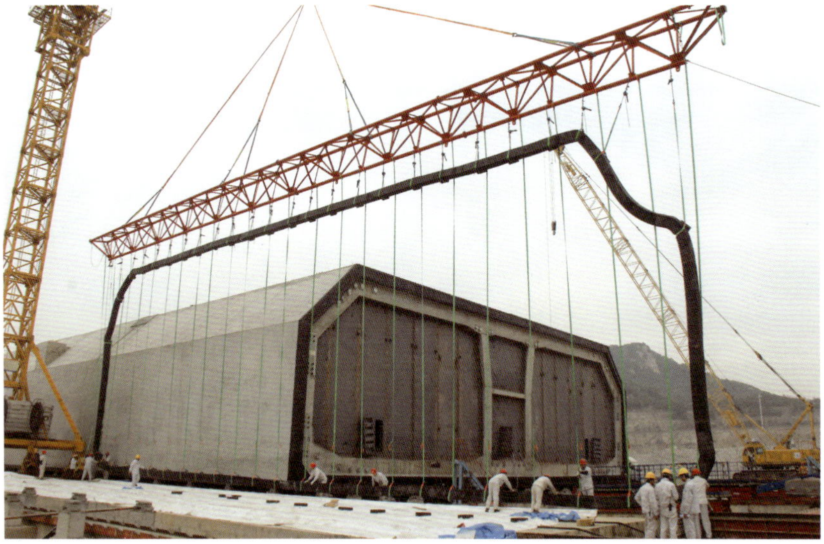

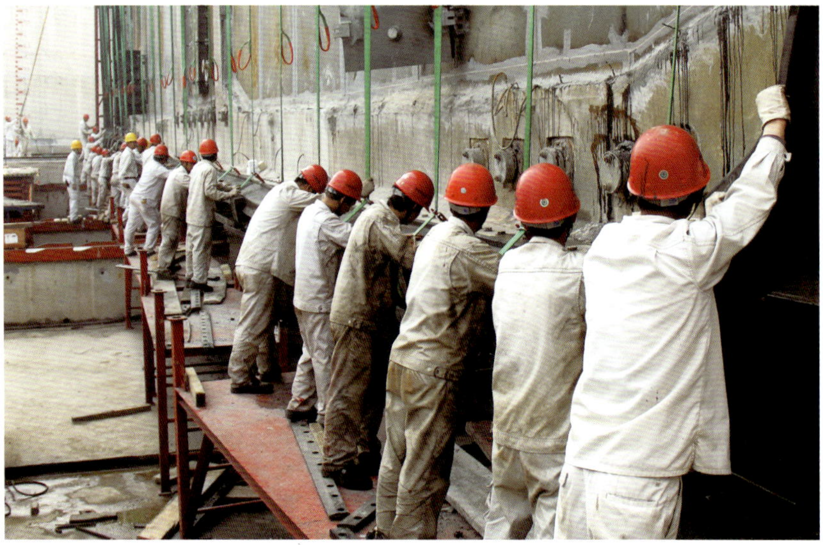

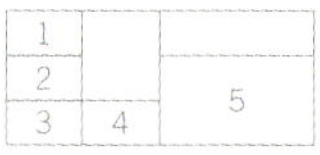

1—3. GINA 止水带安装
GINA Water-Stop Installation

4. GINA 止水带横向剖面图
View of the Horizontal Cross Section of GINA Water-Stop

5. 安装完成的 GINA 止水带
GINA Water-Stop Installed

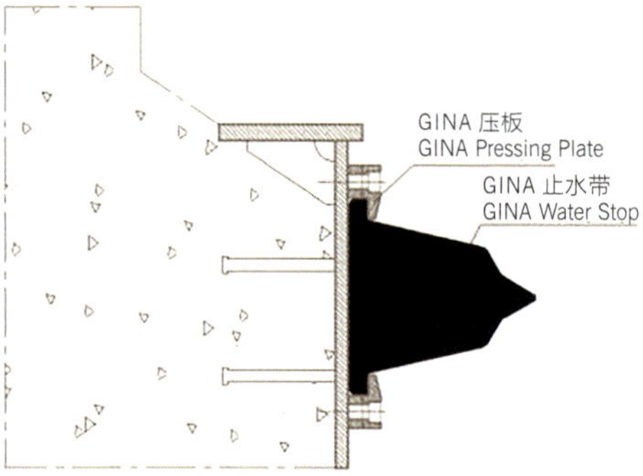

大GINA止水带安装：GINA止水带是沉管隧道沉管接头的重要止水结构，安装在沉管端面的端钢壳上，采用螺栓压板夹紧其两侧翼缘部分。

GINA止水带按每个接头的尺寸在厂家定制，整体环状运输至现场。为方便整体吊装，采用专用吊具多点起吊安装。

安装时，先把GINA止水带固定到吊架上，加装专用橡胶垫，避免因受力过于集中而造成鼻尖位置受损。

安装完成后，需在止水带顶部加装伸出管体前端的一个简易保护罩进行临时保护。

GINA Water-Stop Installation: GINA water-stop is an important water-stop structure at the butt joint of the immersed tube tunnel, and is installed in the steel end shell of the sectional face of the immersed tube. Its two side flanges are clamped by bolt pressing plates.

GINA water-stop is manufactured in the factories according to the size of each butt joint, and then the integral ring-shaped water-stop is transported to the construction site. To facilitate global installation, special hoisting appliances are used for multi-point lifting and installation.

For installation, GINA water-stop is first fixed onto the lifting frame and a special rubber cushion pad is added to avoid damage to the nose tip due to excessively concentrated stress.

After the installation is completed, a simple protective cover stretching out of the front part of the pipe is installed on the top of the water-stop for temporary protection.

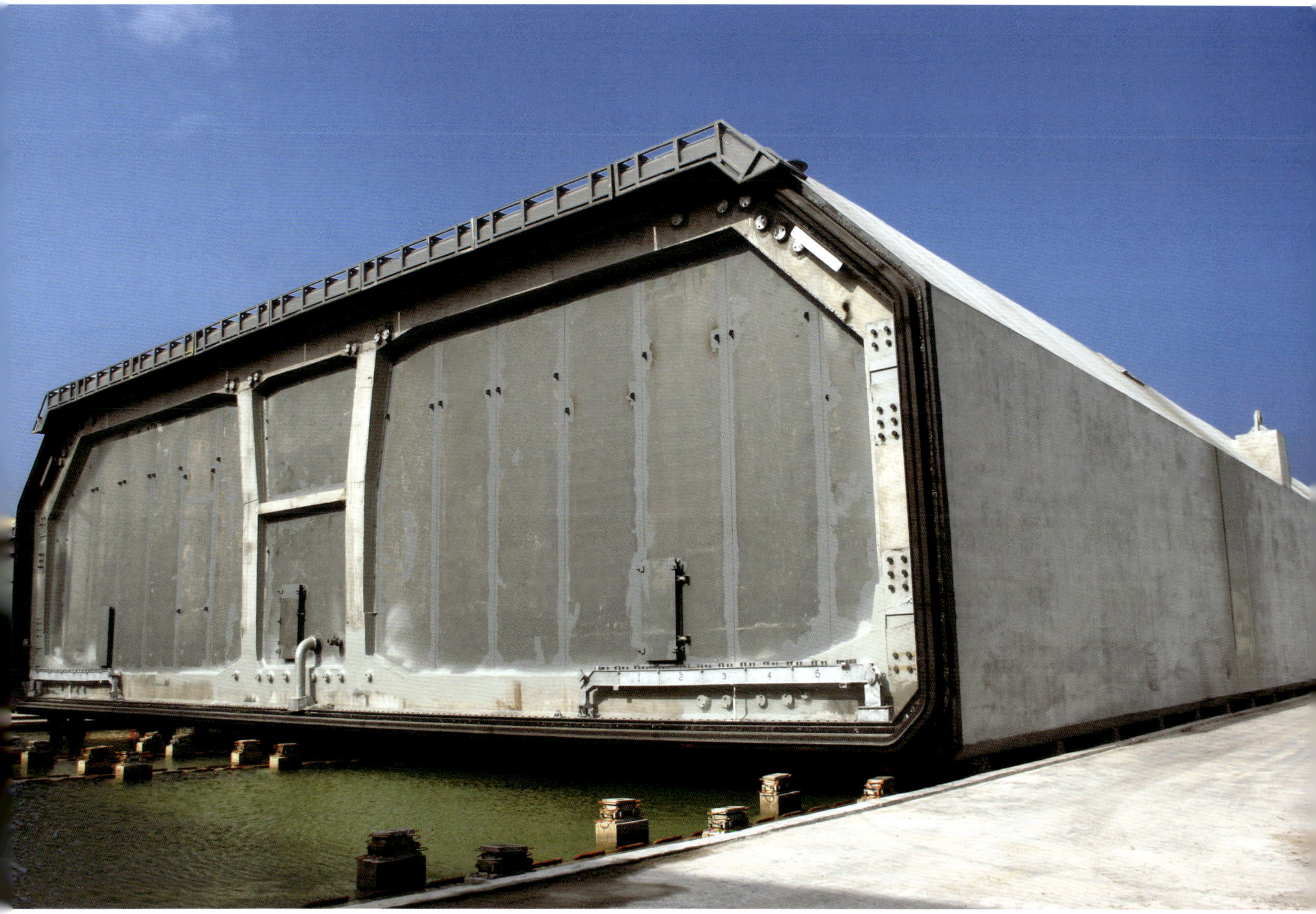

蓄水横移

Impoundment and Horizontal Moving

1. 深坞蓄水
   Deep Dock Impoundment
2. 沉管起浮
   Floating of the Immersed Tube
3. 沉管横移
   Horizontal Moving of the Immersed Tube
4. 安装船与沉管就位连接
   Installation Barge and the Immersed Tube Ready for Connection

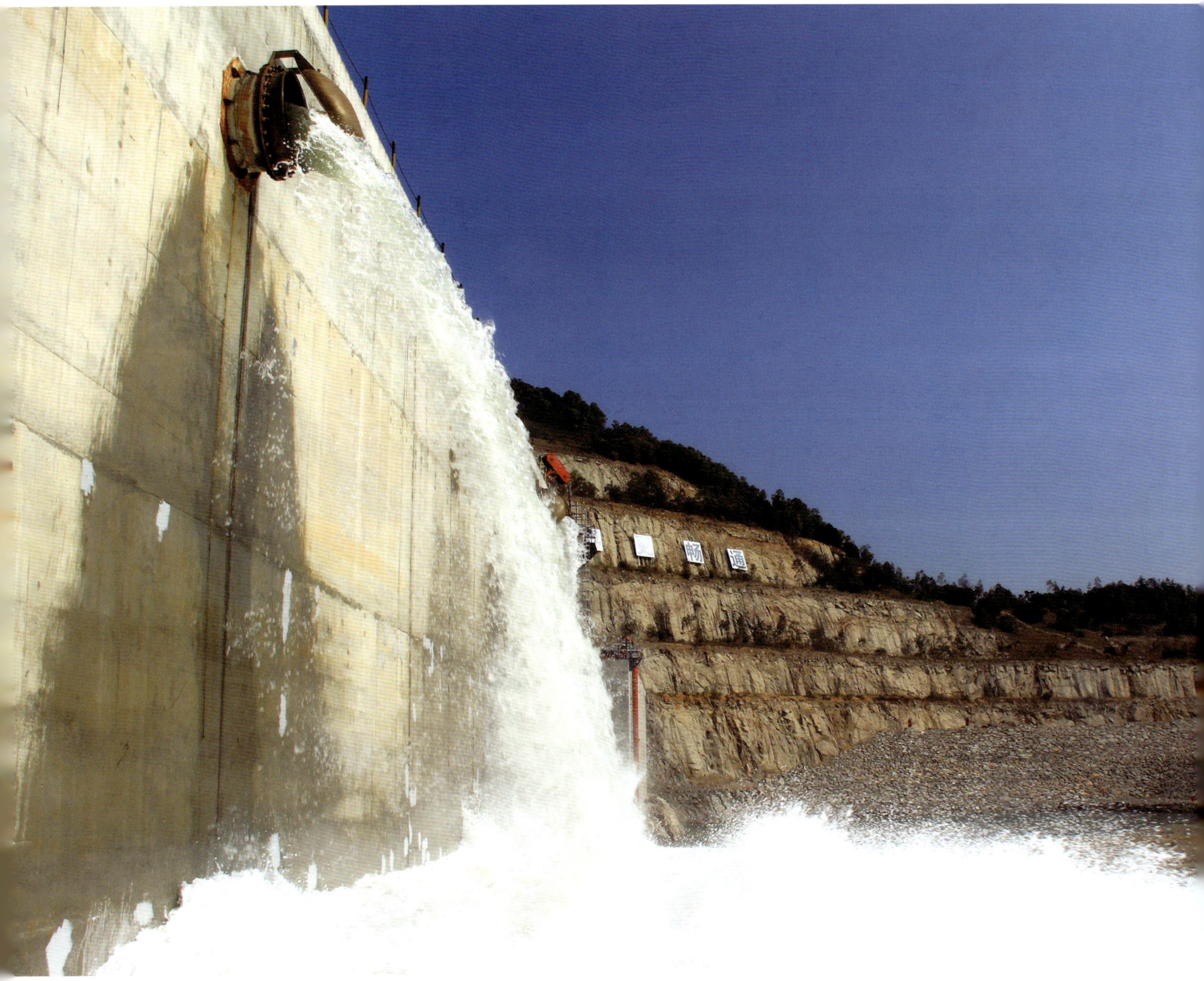

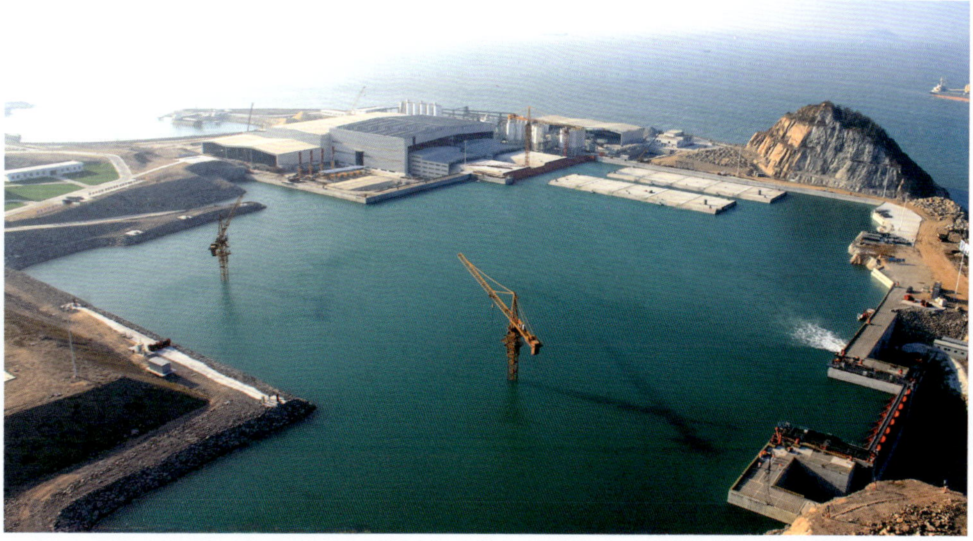

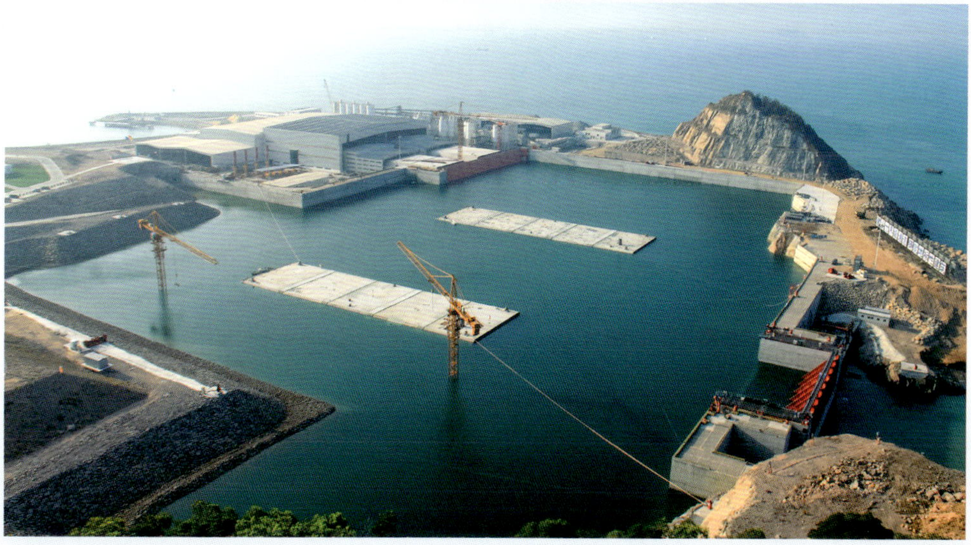

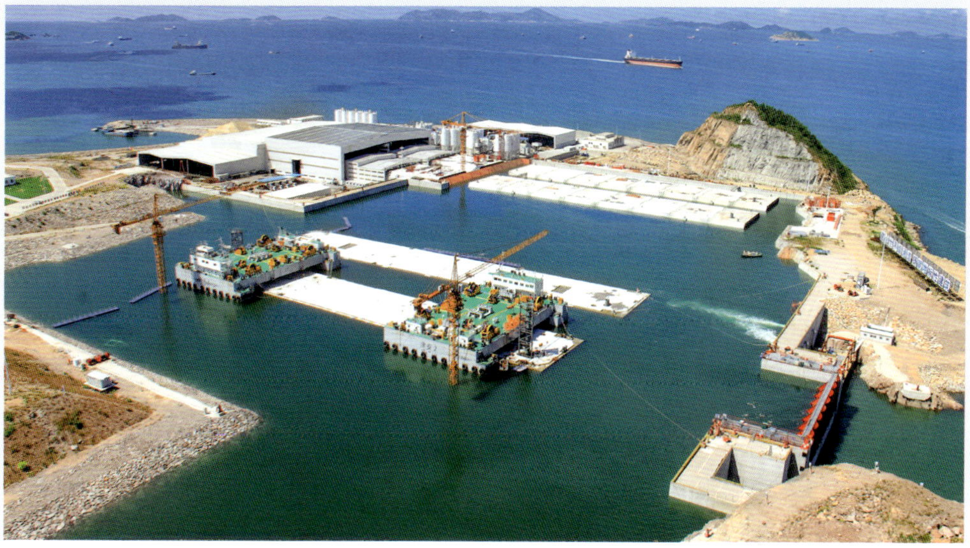

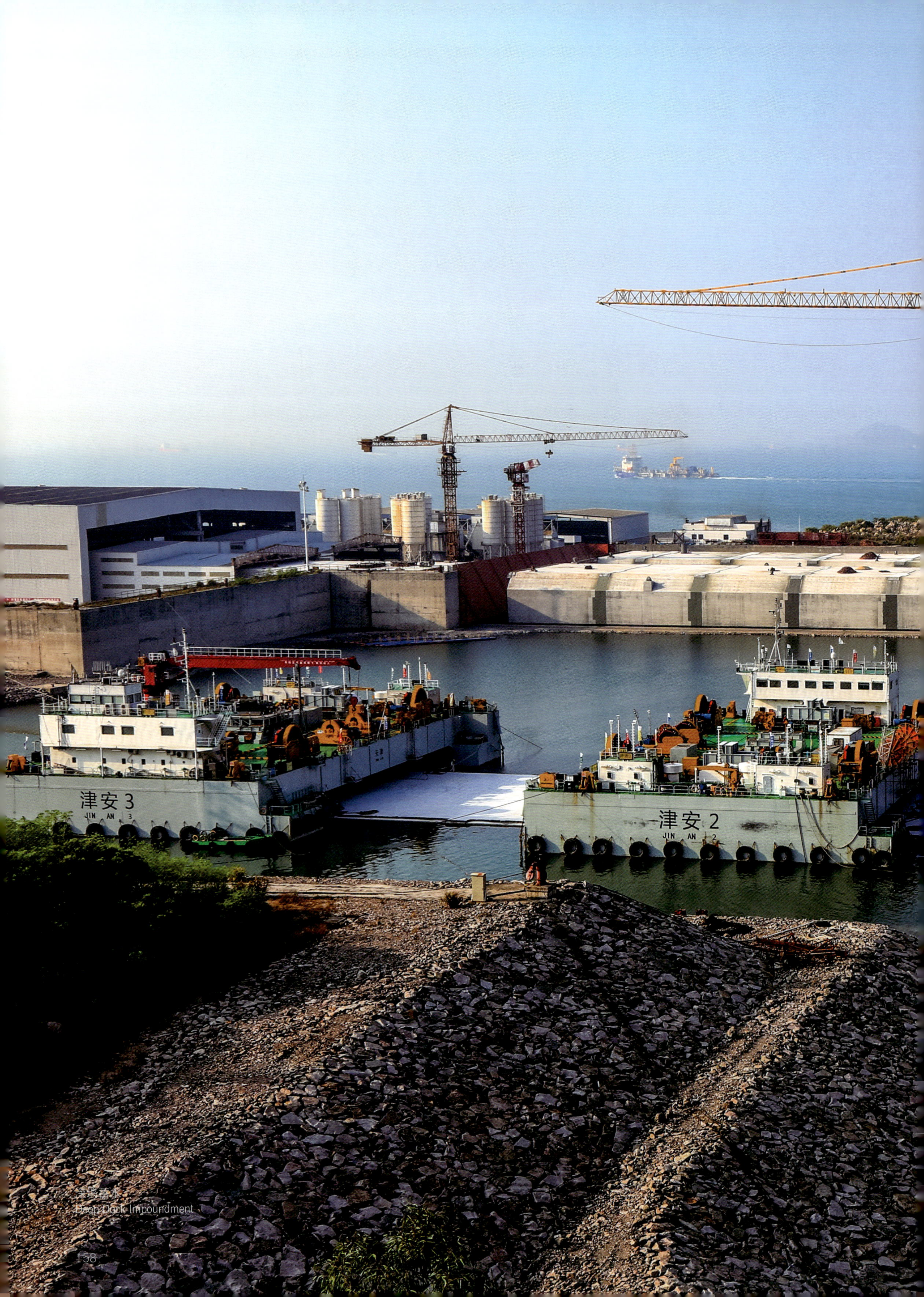

深坞蓄水
Deep Dock Impoundment

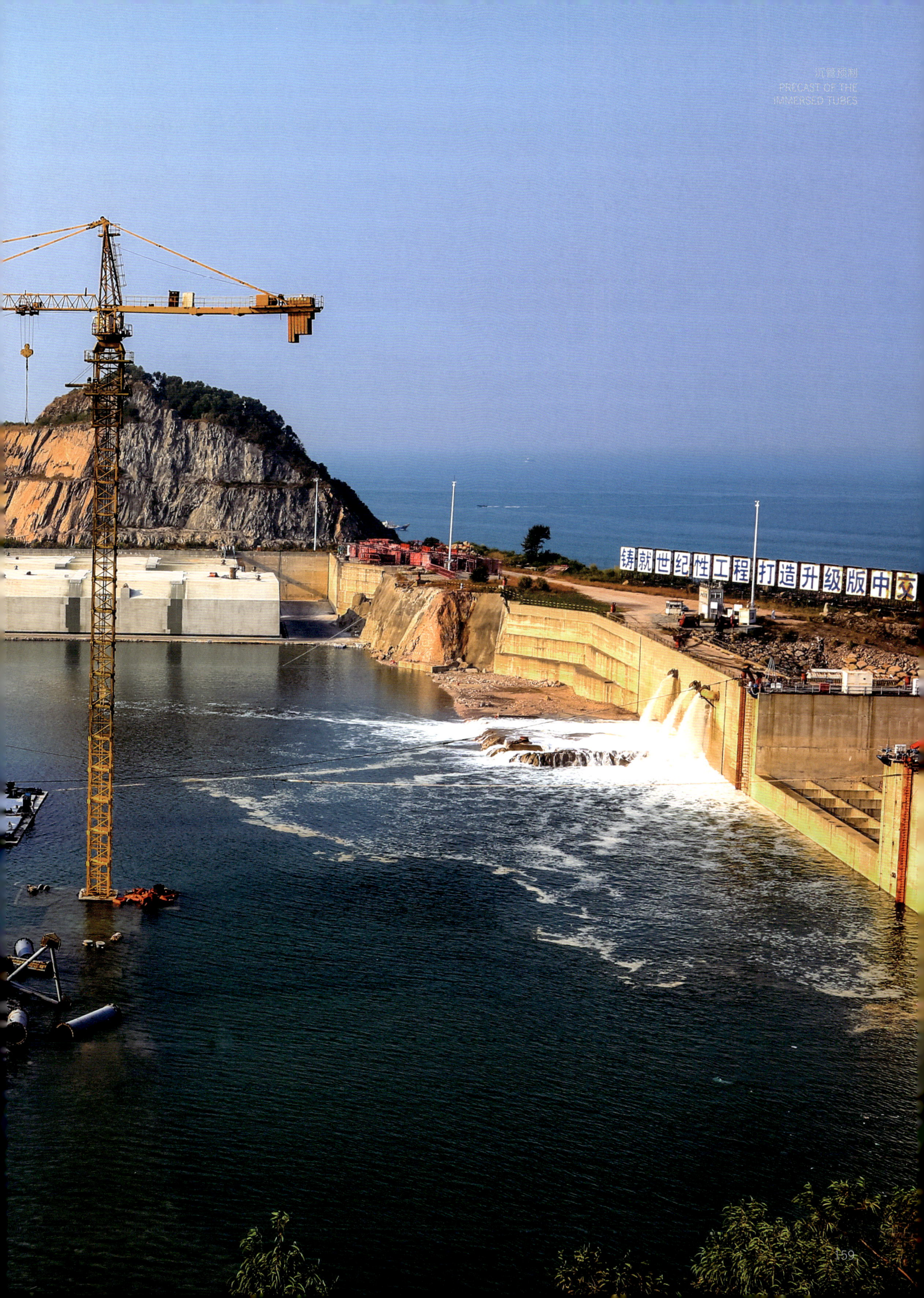
铸就世纪性工程打造升级版中交

二次舾装
SECONDARY OUTFITTING

二次舾装在深坞内进行，主要内容有：浮态标定、测量塔安装、钢端壳清理、水下接头连接、管内压载水系统调试、沉管安装系统联调联试、姿态检测系统安装调试等。

受限于施工场地及交叉工序的影响，同时考虑减少舾装件周转数量，沉管横移到深坞进行系泊寄放，在沉管出坞前进行二次舾装作业。

二次舾装对沉管浮运安装质量与安全具有重要影响，直接影响沉管对接精度，故完成各类舾装件的组装后，进行多次系统联调联试。

导向装置作为沉管对接重要装置，配备 7 套；其余舾装件按照两套进行配置。

管顶舾装：沉管移至二次舾装区后，首先进行绞缆盘台座及四个滚柱导缆器的安装；安装船进坞后，剩余管顶舾装依次展开。压载水系统调试完毕后，调平沉管，进行导向装置安装、标定等管顶二次舾装工作。

测量塔、长人孔：根据不同沉管安装水深，各沉管配置测量塔及长人孔高度不同。测量塔最高达 38.2 米，采取节段式拼接，单节最大高度 4.5 米，重量达 5 吨，完成后必须进行标定。

人孔井作为沉管安装过程中进入沉管内部的应急通道，位于测量塔立柱中间。安装时，需在测量塔立柱节段间铺设橡胶止水板，并涂抹遇水膨胀胶，以保证其 0.5 兆帕水压下的水密性。

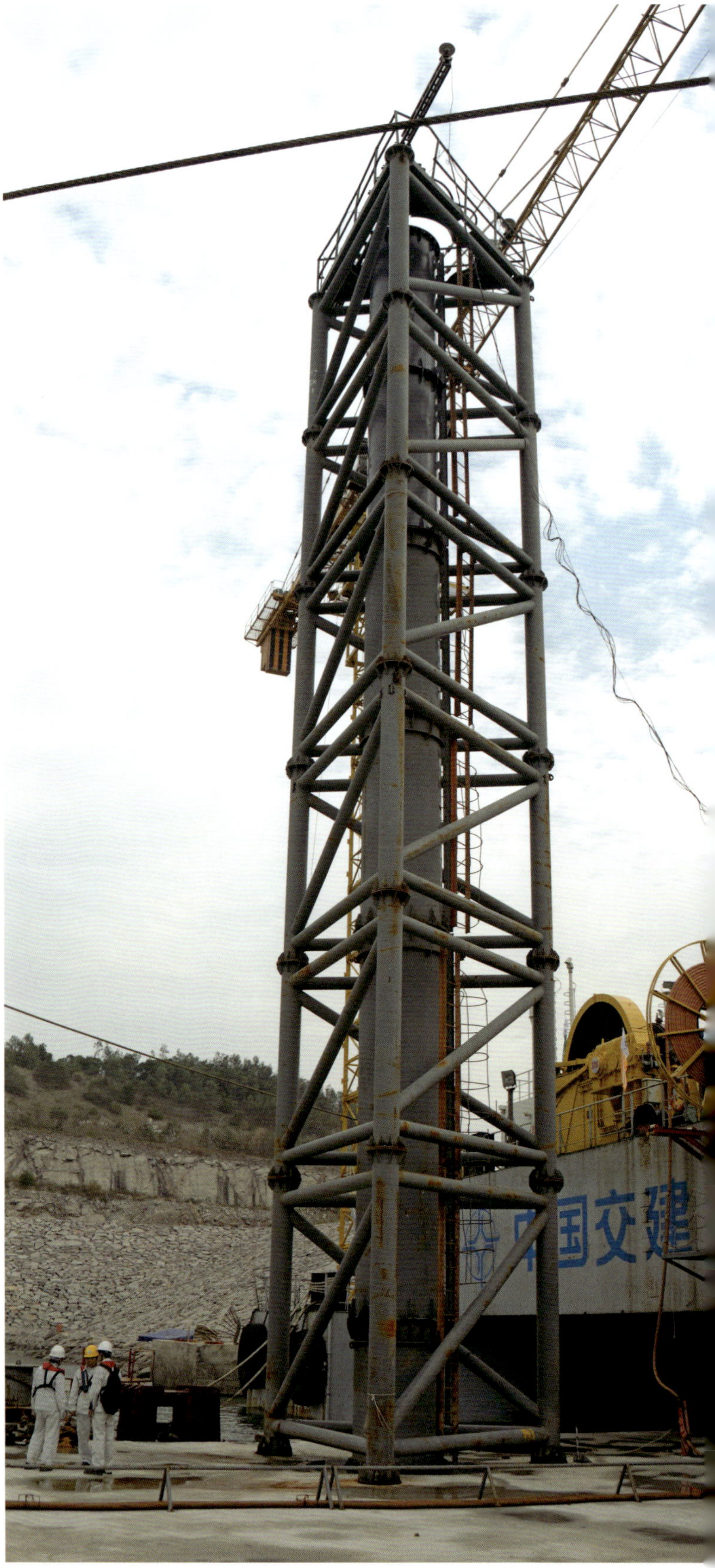

The secondary outfitting is conducted in the deep dock, including mainly floating calibration, installation of the measuring tower, cleaning of the steel end shell, connection of underwater joints, adjusting of the in-tube ballast water system, joint adjusting of immersed pipe installation system, installation and adjusting of the tube position, etc.

Subject to the impact of the construction site and interrelated working procedures, in order to reduce the number of recycled component parts for the outfitting, the immersed tube is moved horizontally to the deep dock and anchored there where the secondary outfitting is done before undocking.

The secondary outfitting has an important influence on the quality and safety of the immersed tube's float conveyance and installation, and it directly affects the accuracy of connecting the immersed tubes. Therefore, after the outfitting is completed, many tests and adjustments are conducted.

As the important device for the butt joint of the immersed tubes, seven sets of guiding devices are equipped. The other outfitting parts need to be prepared in two copies.

Tube Top Outfitting: After the immersed tube is moved to the secondary outfitting area, a cable winch pedestal and four roller fairleads are installed first. After the installation barge enters the deep dock, the rest of the outfitting on the top of the immersed tube begin one by one. After the ballast water system test is completed, horizontally leveling is conducted for the tube, followed by guiding devices installation, calibrating and other outfitting operations.

Measuring Tower and Long Manhole: the heights of the measuring towers and long manholes for different tubes vary according to their different installation water depths. The measuring tower can be as high as 38.2 meters, formed by connecting several segments. The maximum height of these segments of the measuring tower is 4.5 meters, and the maximum weight is 5 tons. The measuring tower must be calibrated after its installation is completed.

The manhole is the emergency passage leading to the interior of the tube to cope with the problems that occur during the installation of the immersed tube, and is located in middle part of the supporting column of the measuring tower. To install the manhole, rubber water-stop plates shall be placed between the different segments of the measuring tower's supporting column, and water-expandable glue is painted on the rubber plates to ensure their water-proof function under the 0.5MPa water pressure.

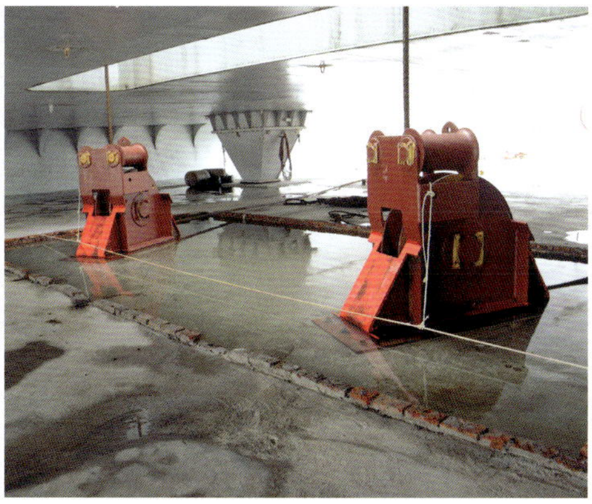

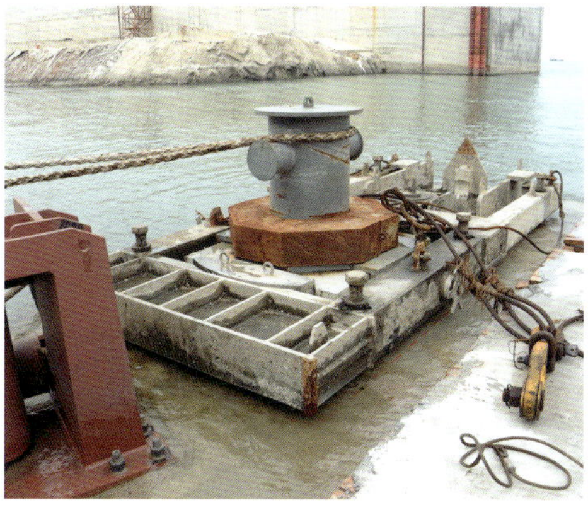

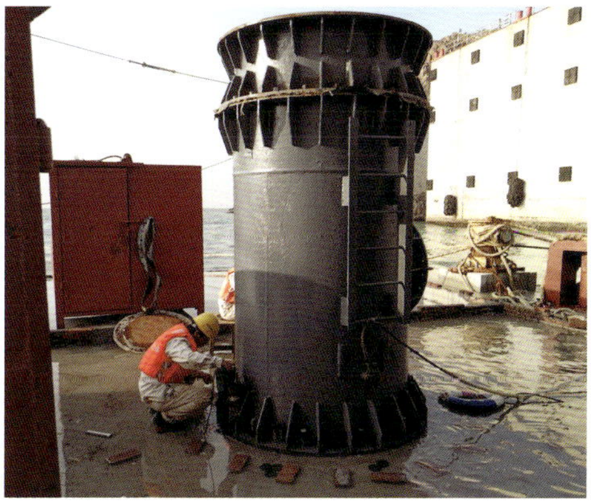

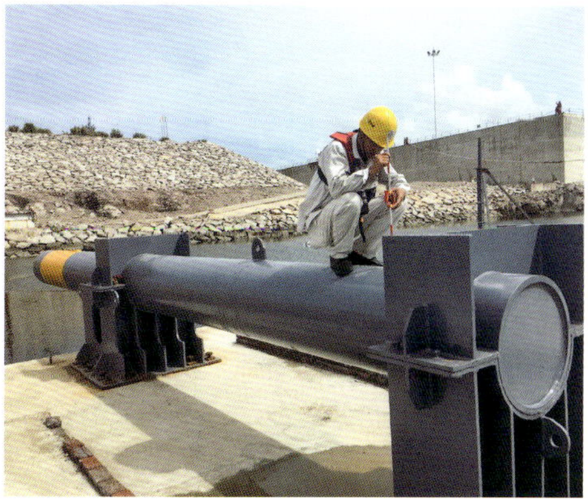

1. 沉管测量塔安装
Installation of the Measuring Tower of the Immersed Tube
2. 沉管滚柱导缆器安装
Installation of the Roller Fairleads for the Immersed Tube
3. 沉管系缆柱安装
Installation of the Immersed Tube Bollard
4. 沉管人孔安装
Installation of the Manhole in the Immersed Tube
5. 沉管对接导向杆安装
Installation of the Guiding Rod for the Butt Joint of the Immersed Tube

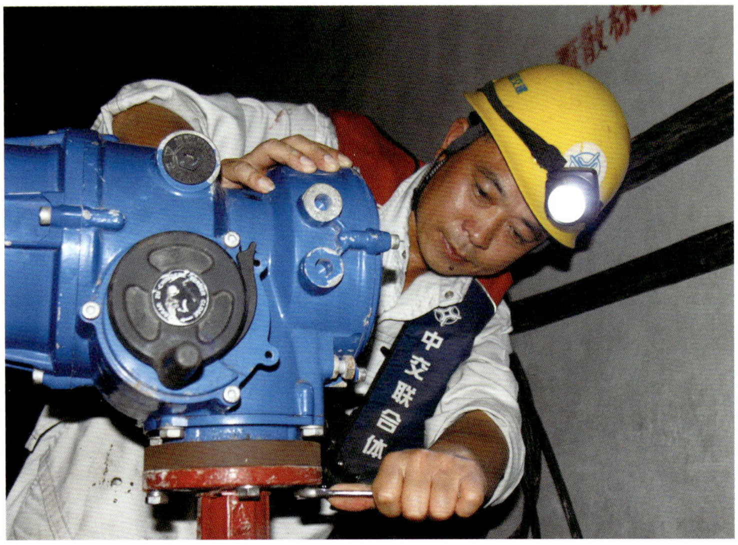
中交联合体

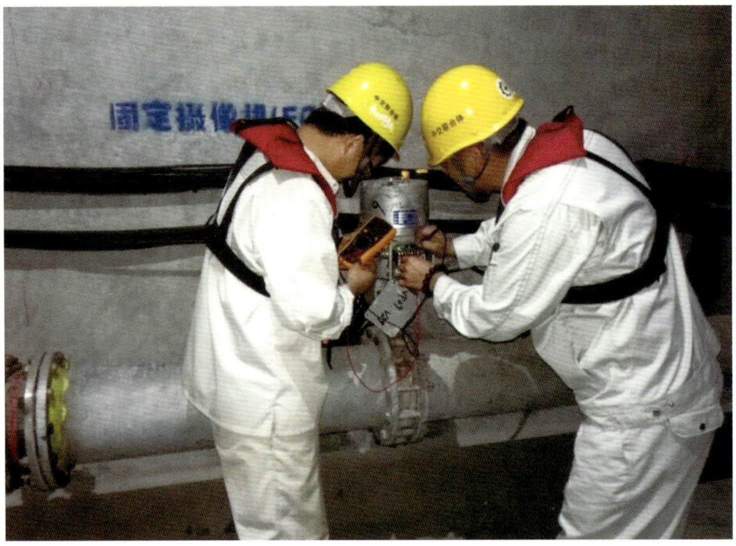

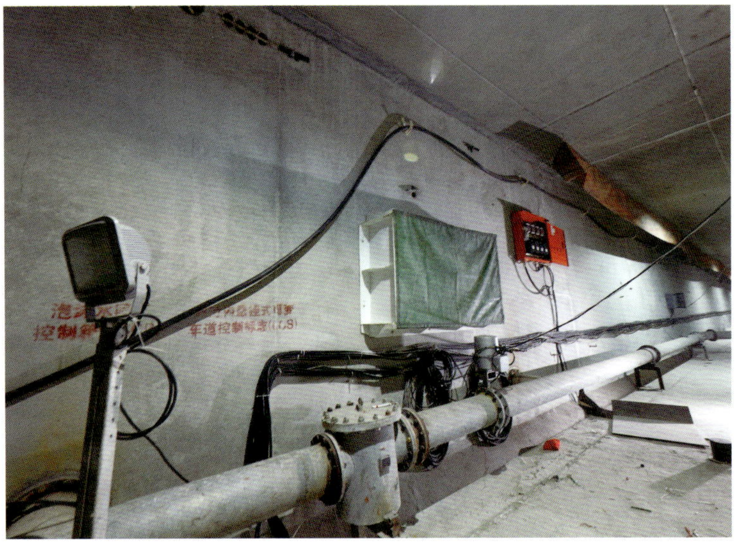

1. 压载水水泵安装
Installation of the Ballast Water Pump

2. 压载水系统阀门驱动头安装
Installation of the Valve Driving Head in the Ballast Water System

3. 管内临时照明系统安装
Installation of the Temporary Illumination System Inside the Immersed Tube

4. 完成二次舾装的沉管
Immersed Tube after the Secondary Outfitting

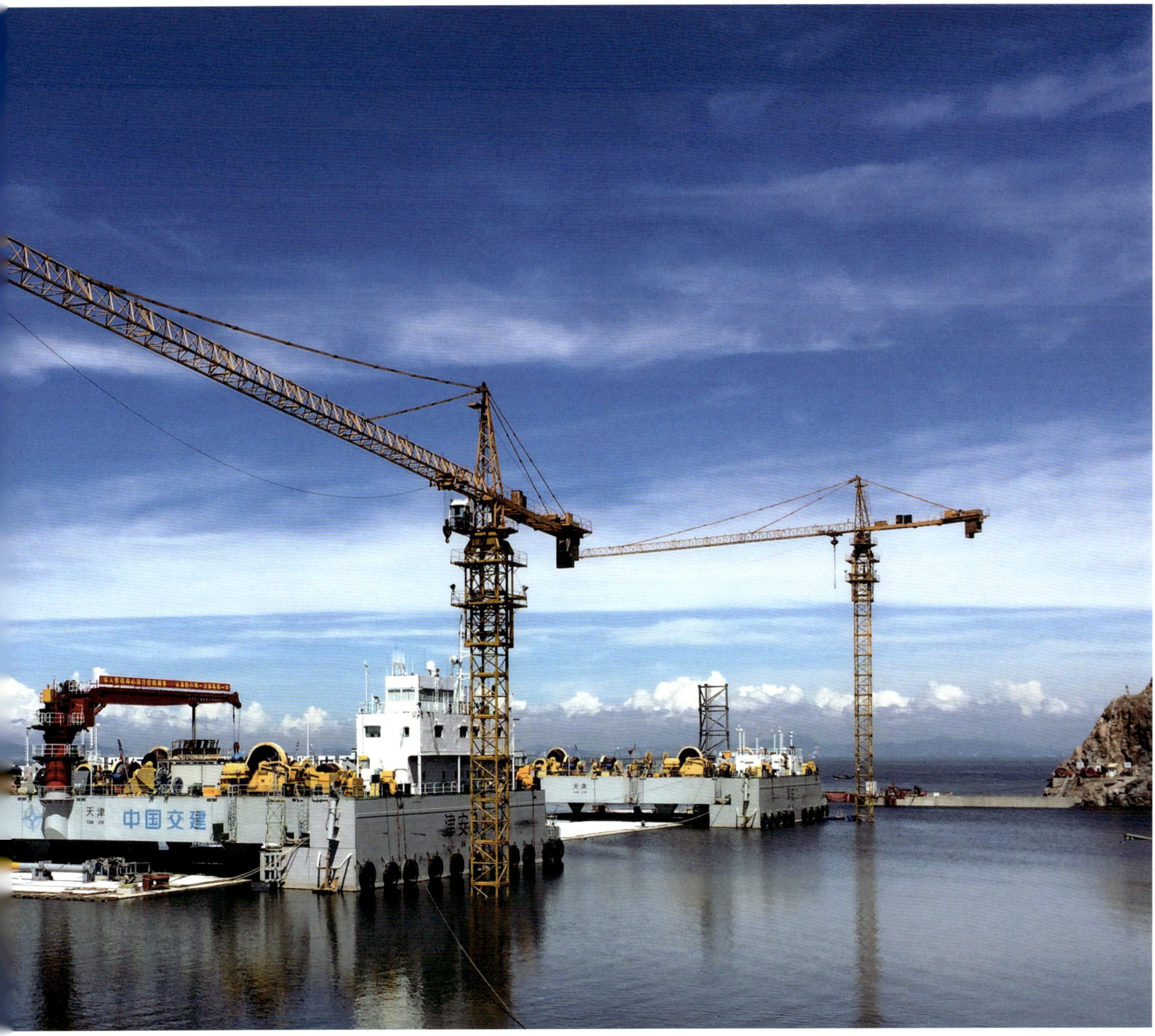

沉管预制完工总结大会建设者合影
Picture of the Honorary Constructors of Hong Kong-Zhuhai-Macau Bridge

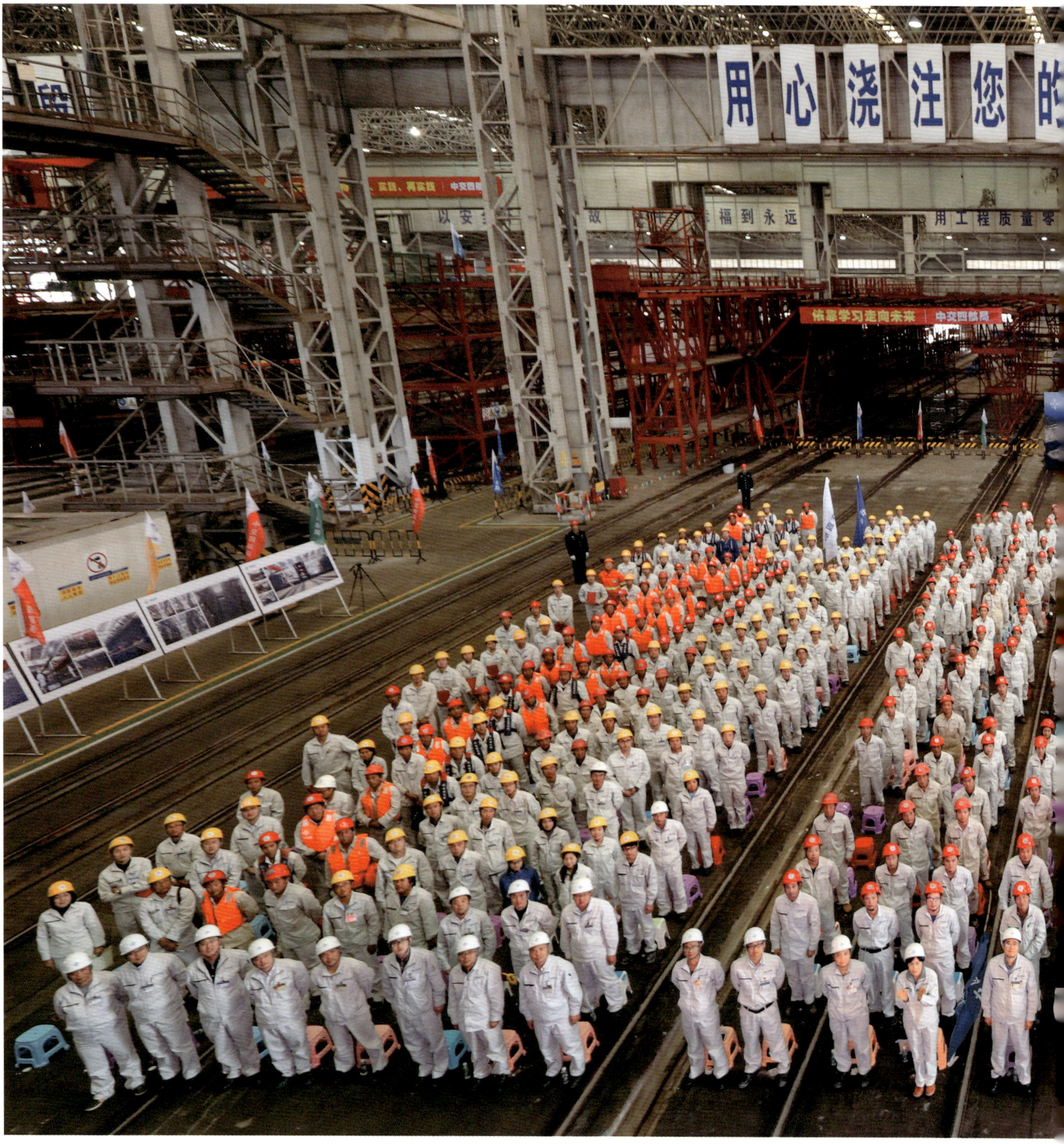

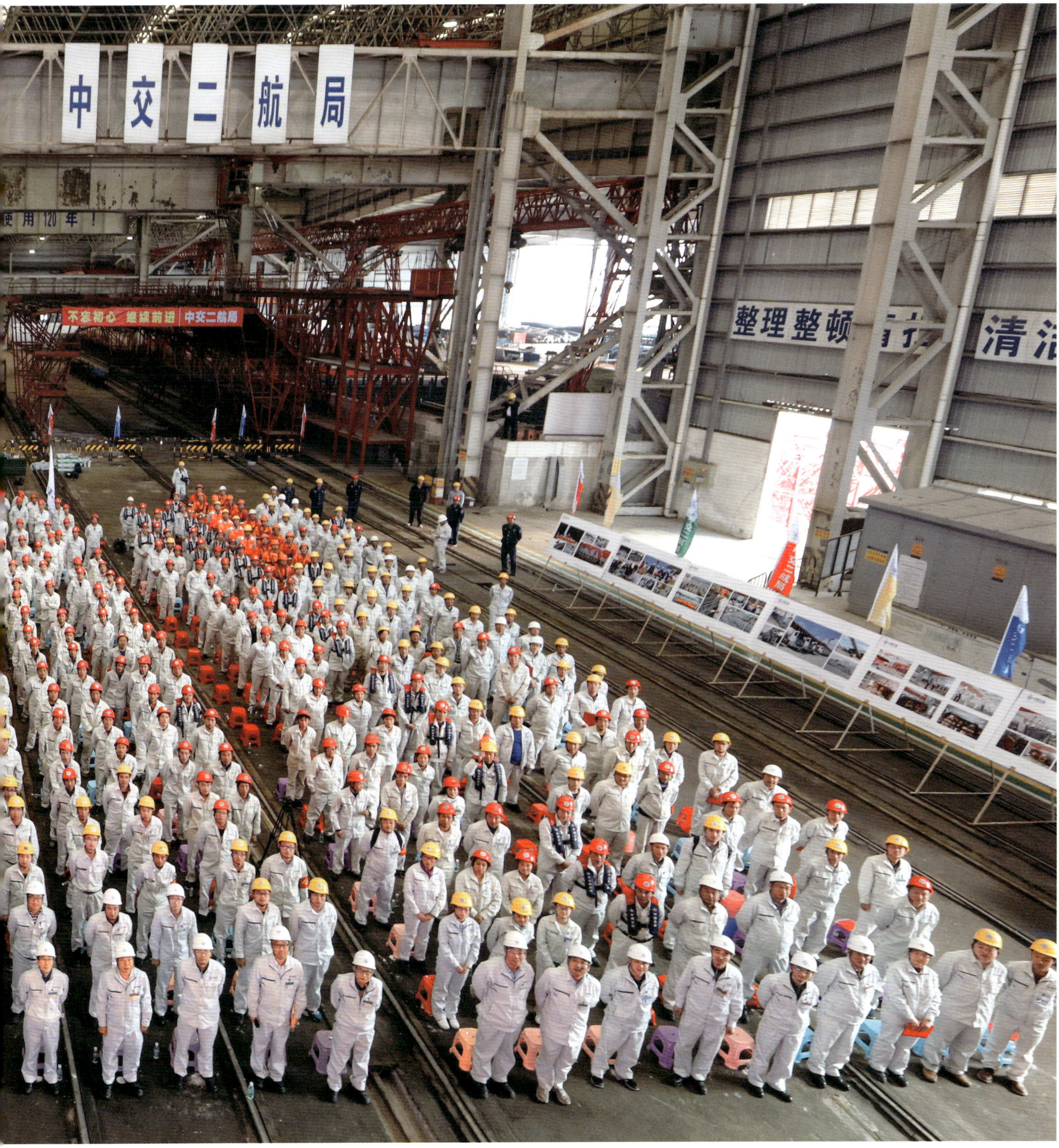
中交二航局
使用120年！
不忘初心 继续前进 中交二航局
整理整顿

画册索引
ALBUM INDEX

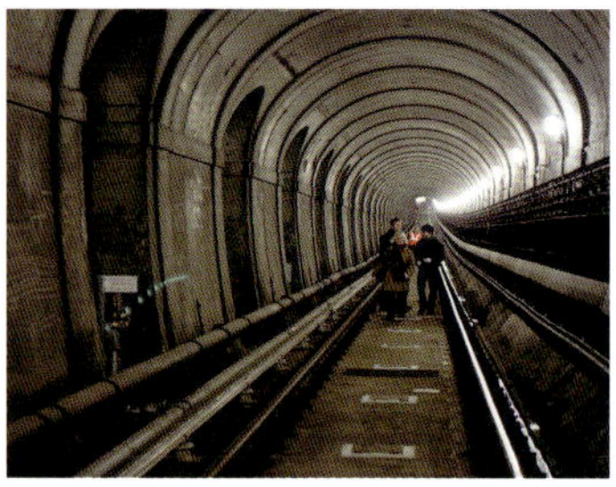

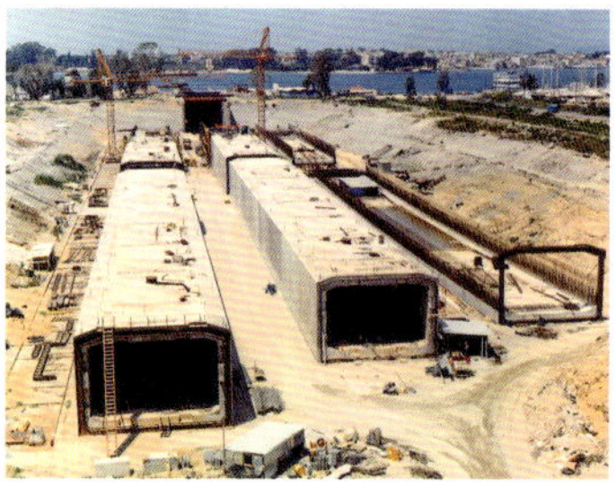

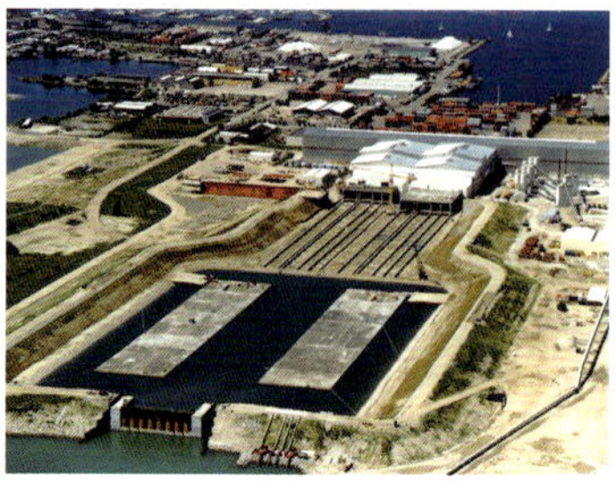

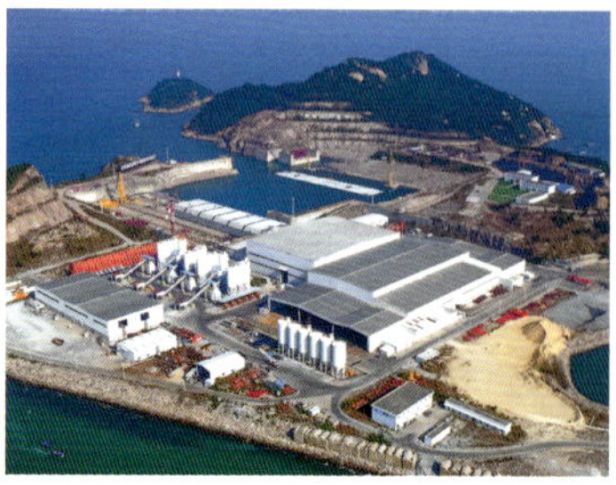

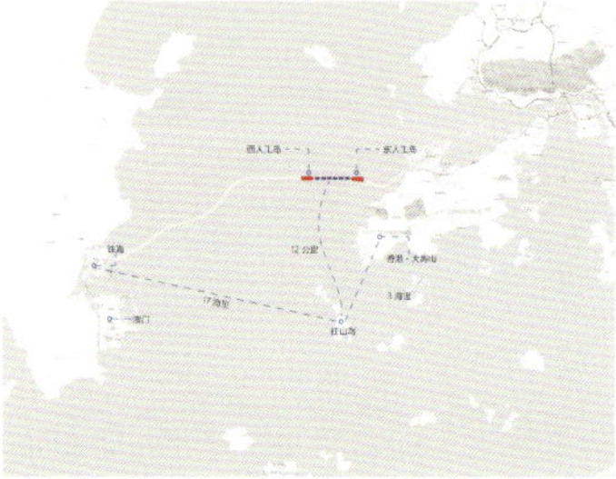

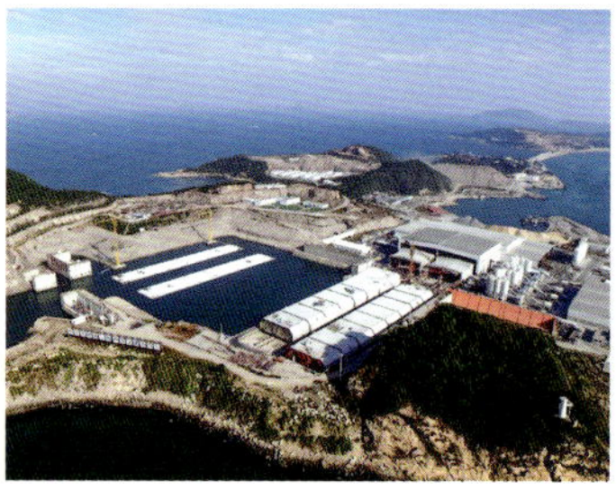

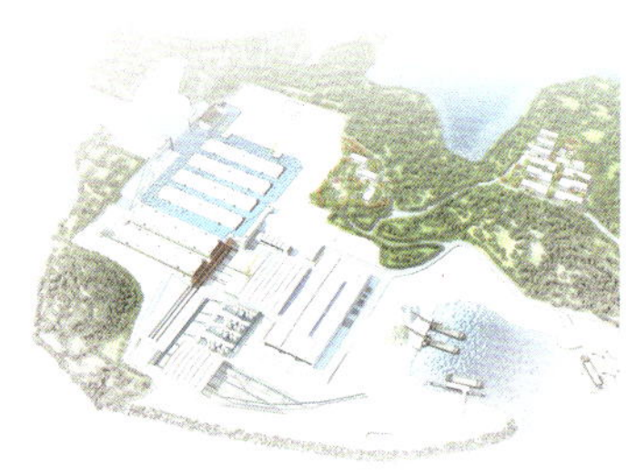

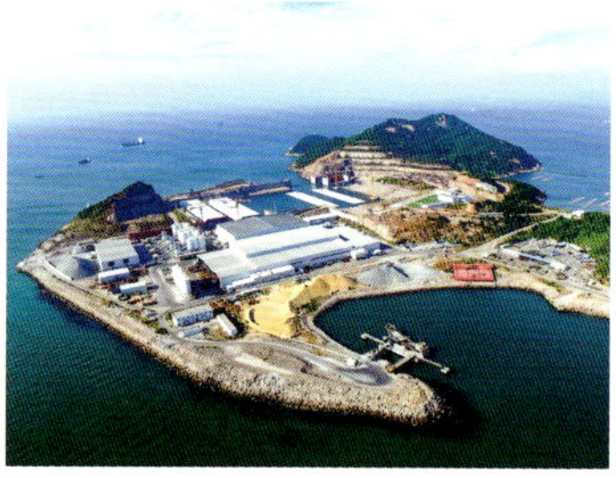

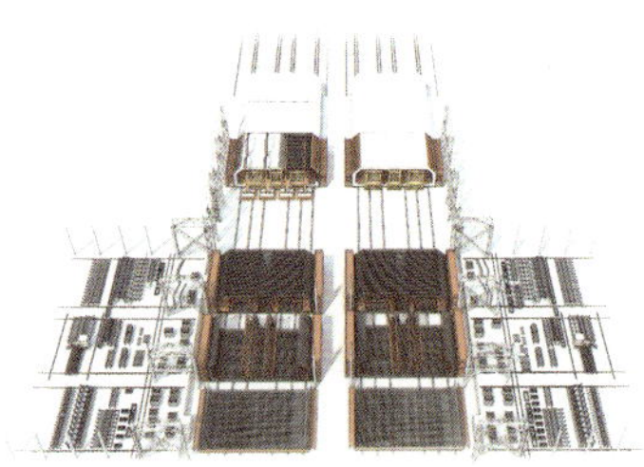

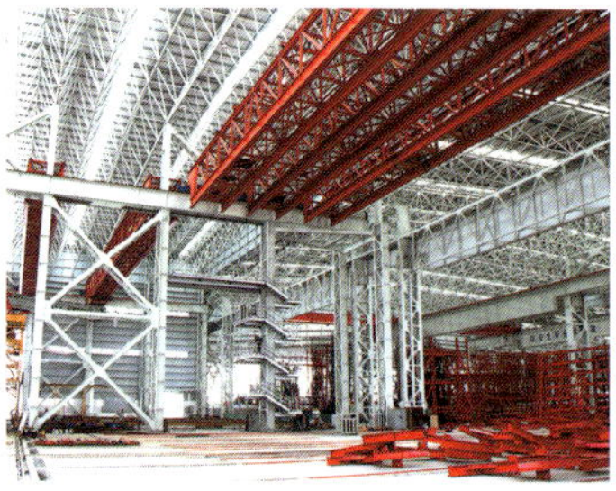

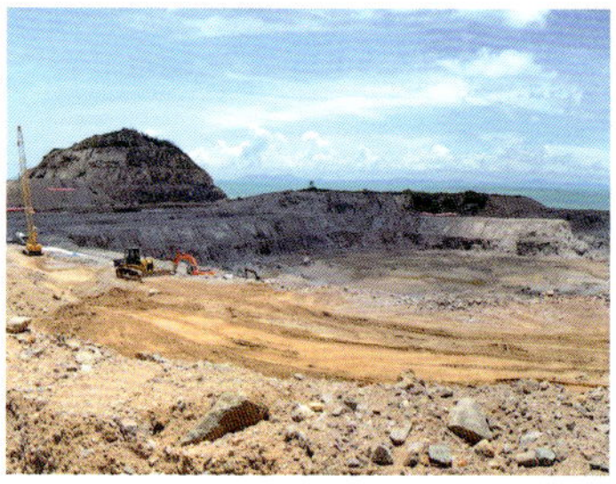

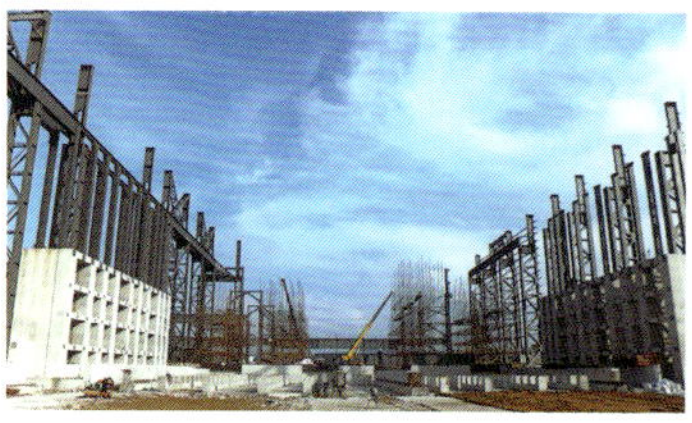

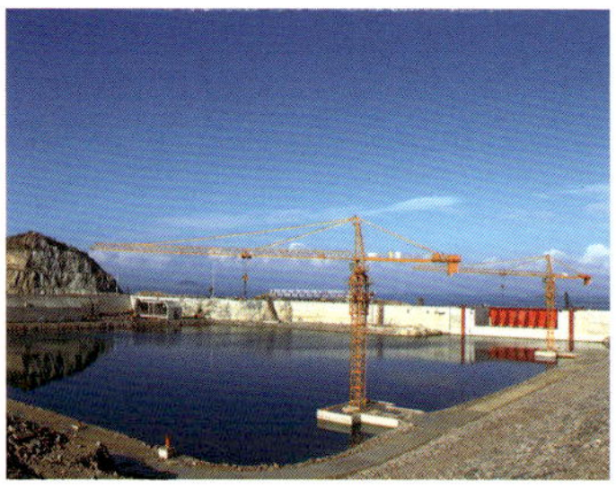

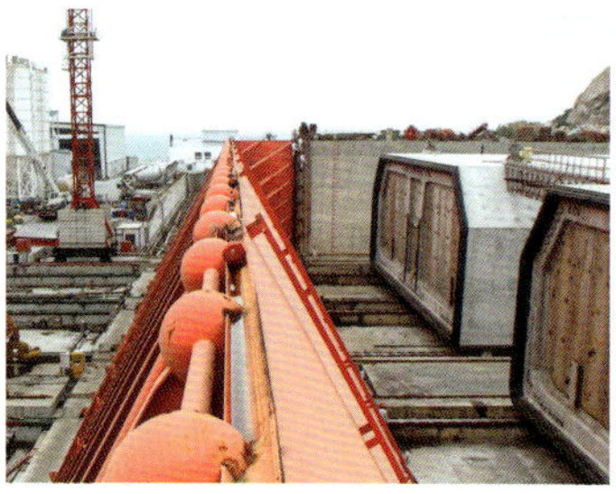

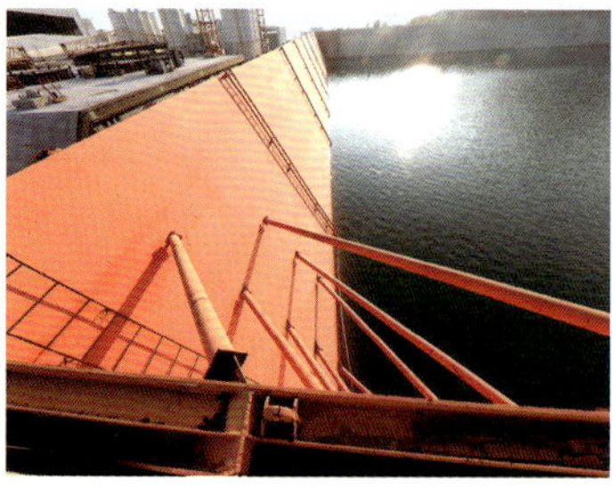

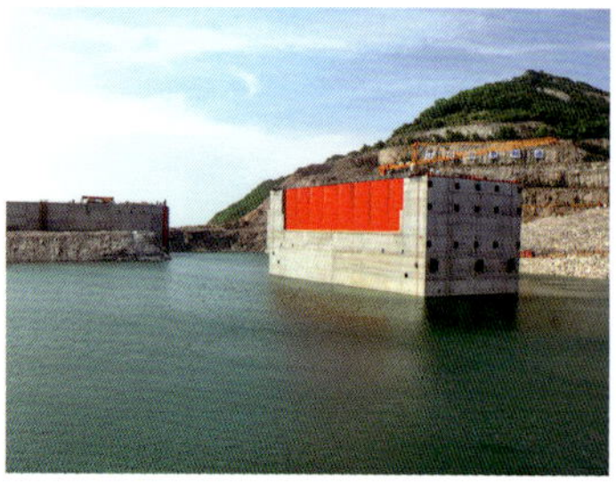

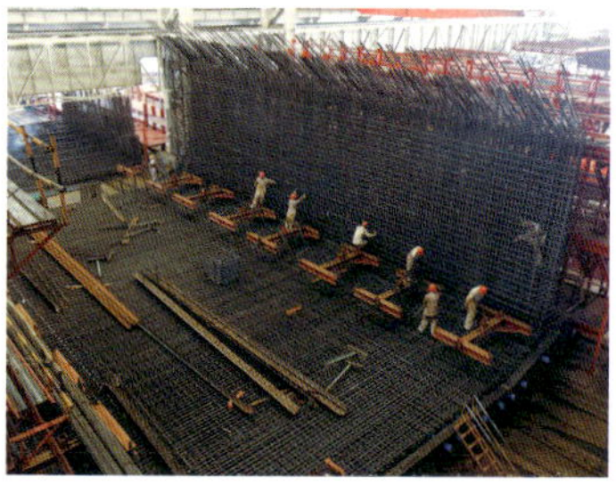

侧墙钢筋绑扎
Side Wall Steel Binding
072

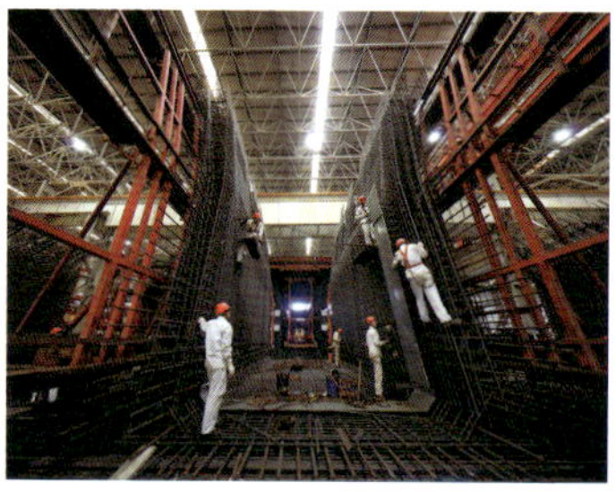

中墙钢筋绑扎
Partition Wall Steel Binding
074

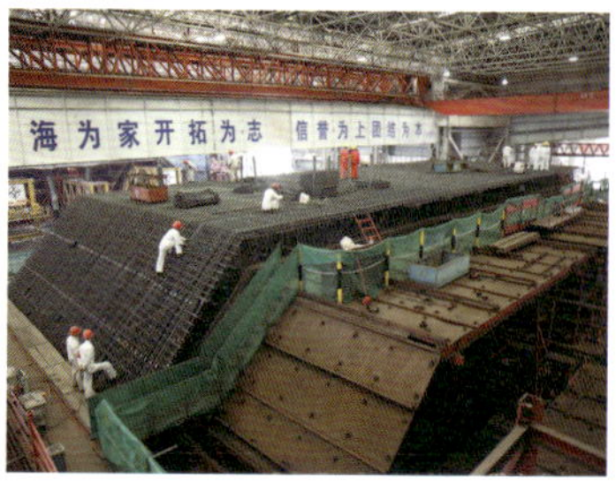

顶板钢筋绑扎
Top Plate Steel Binding
076

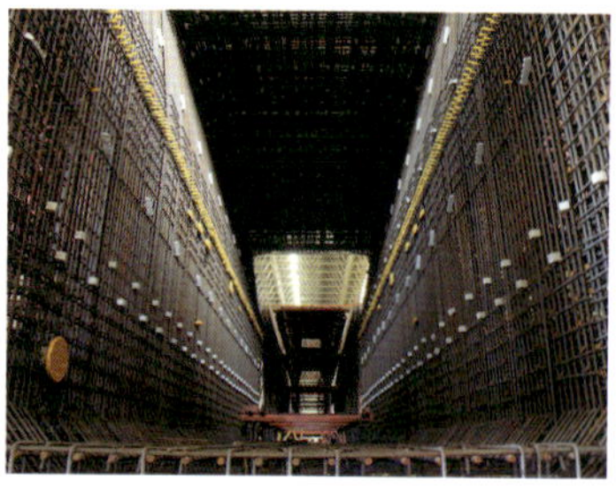

绑扎成型的钢筋笼（中墙）
Steel Reinforcement Cage (for the Partition Wall) Completed
078

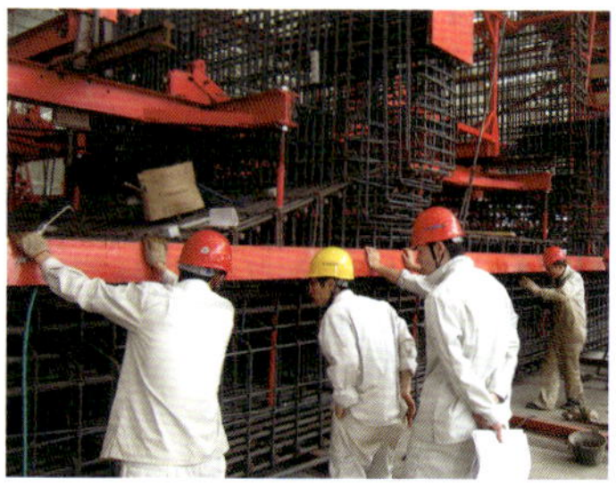

钢端壳安装
Installation of the Steel End Shell
080

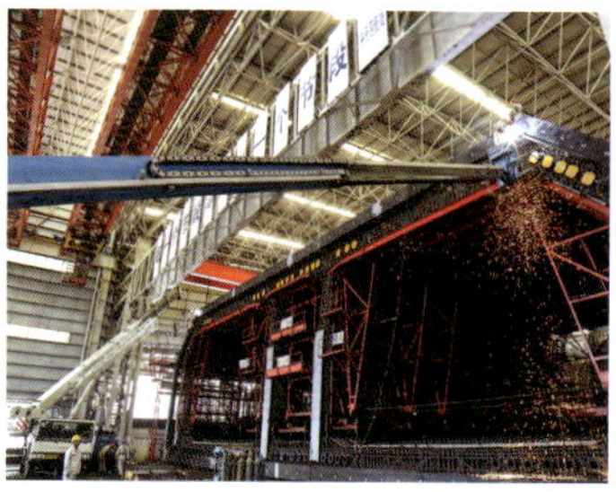

钢端壳焊接
Steel End Shell Welding
083

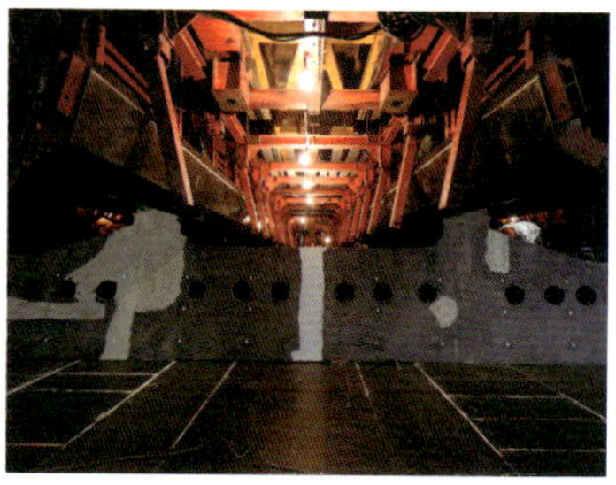

钢帽防腐处理
Steel Cap Anti-corrosion
085

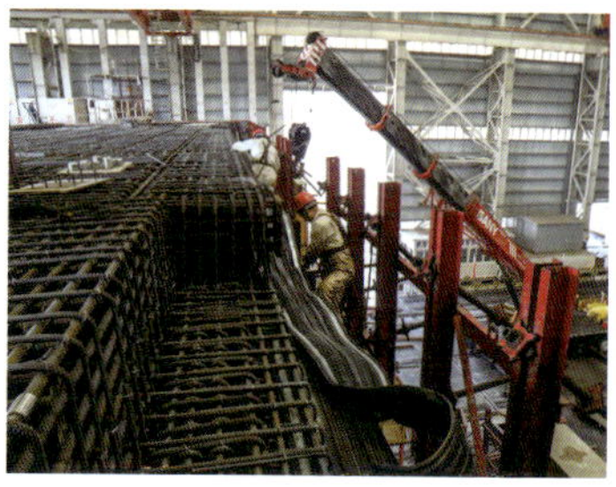

中埋式止水带安装
Embedded Water-Stop Installation
087

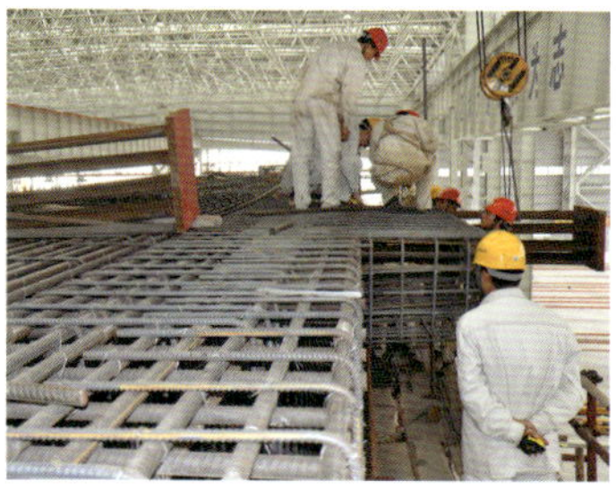

钢剪力键预埋件安装
Installation of the Embedded Items of the Steel Shear Key
088

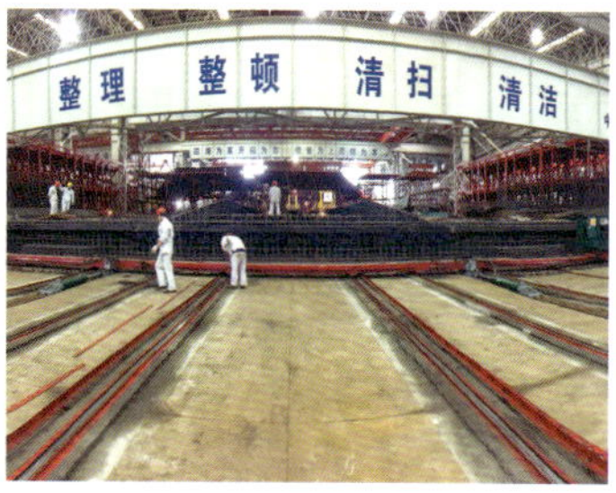

钢筋笼顶推系统
Reinforcement Cage Pushing System
090

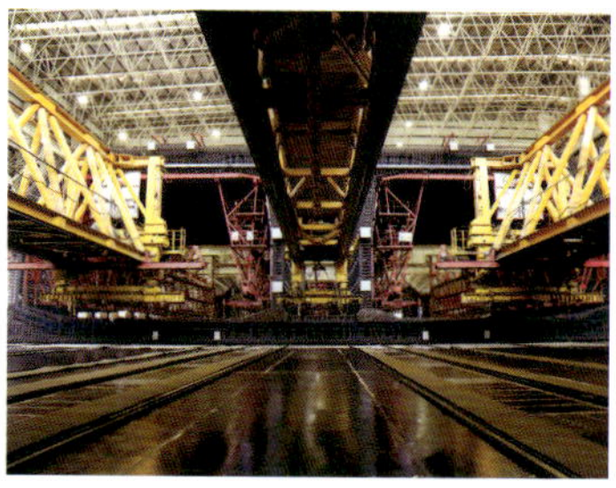

钢筋笼顶推入模
Steel Reinforcement Cage Pushed into the Formwork
092

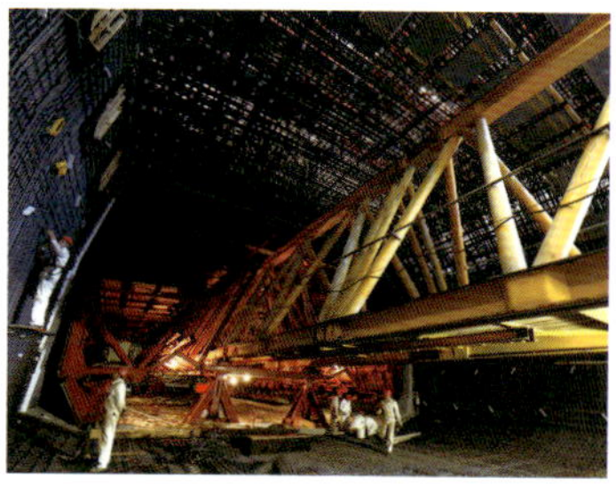

钢筋笼体系转换
System Transition of the Steel Reinforcement Cage
094

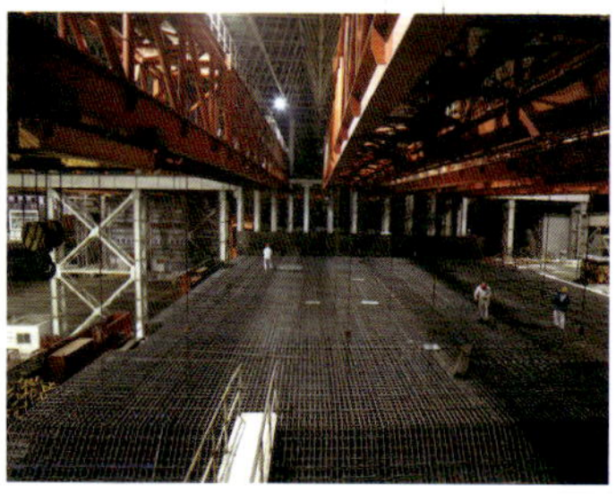

钢筋笼顶部吊架
Hanger on Top of the Steel Reinforcement Cage
097

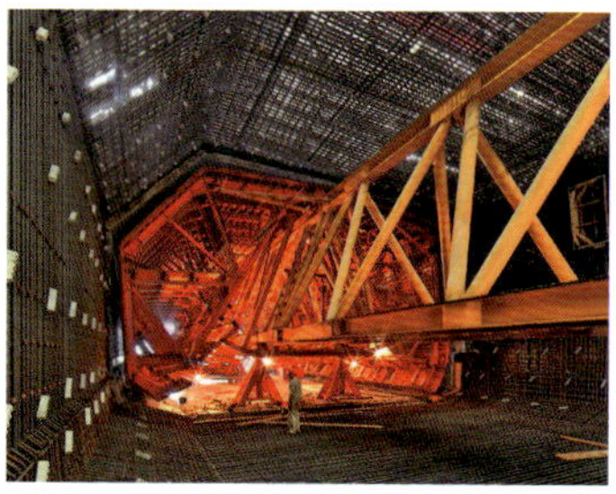

钢筋笼体系转换——内模复位
System Transition of the Steel Reinforcement Cage—Restoration of the Internal Formwork
098

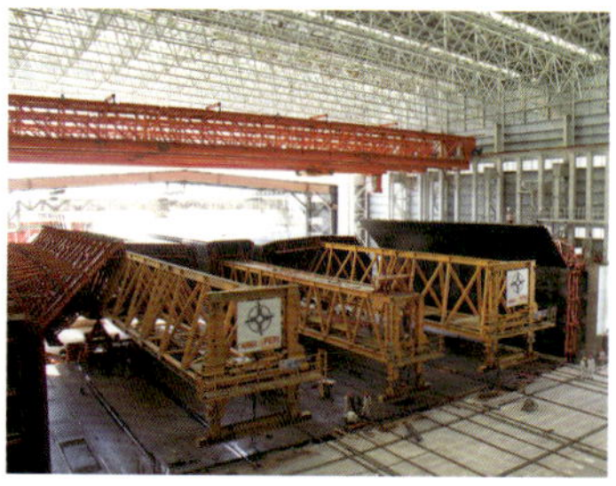

沉管模板系统
Formwork System of the Immersed Tube
101

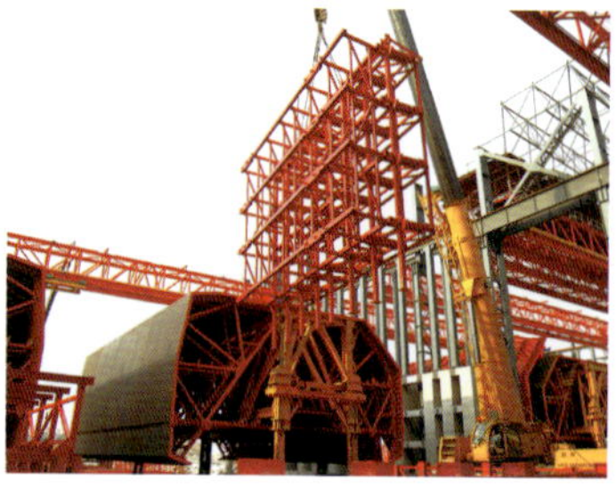

侧模框架安装
Installation of the Side Formwork Frame
102

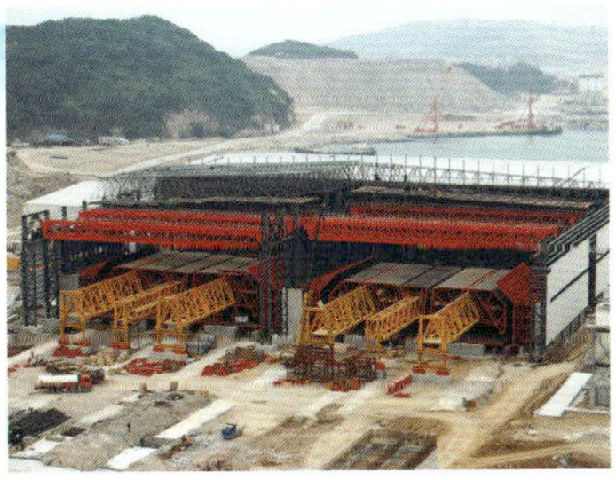

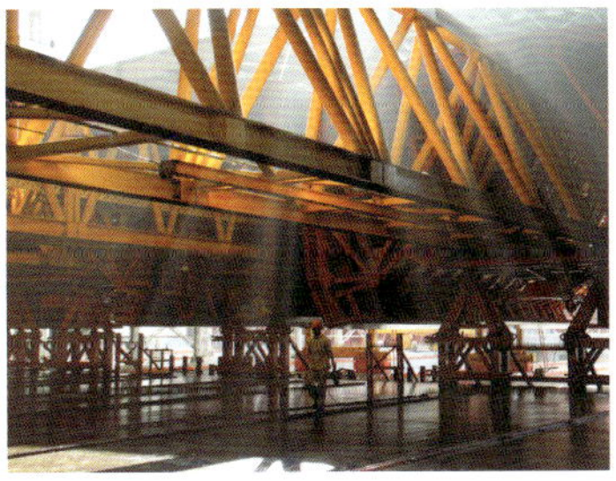

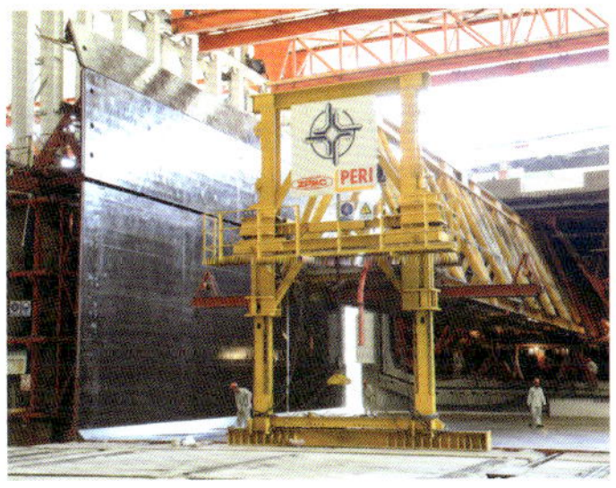

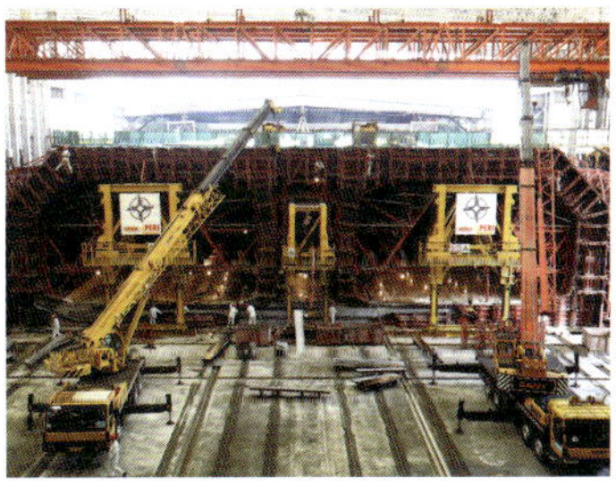

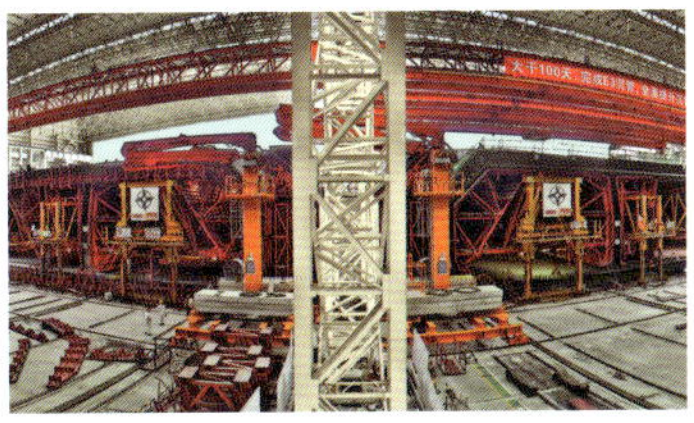

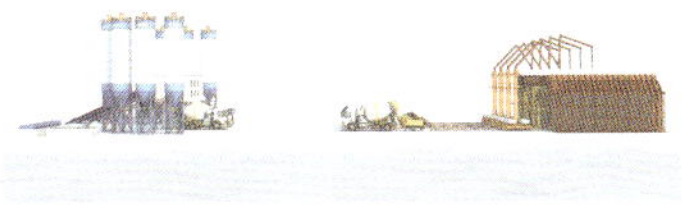

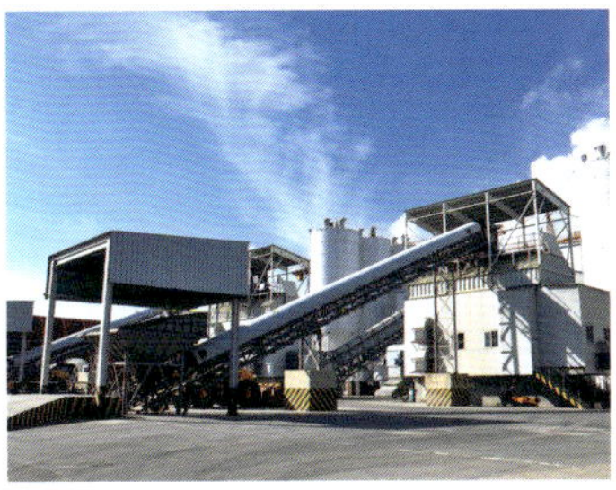

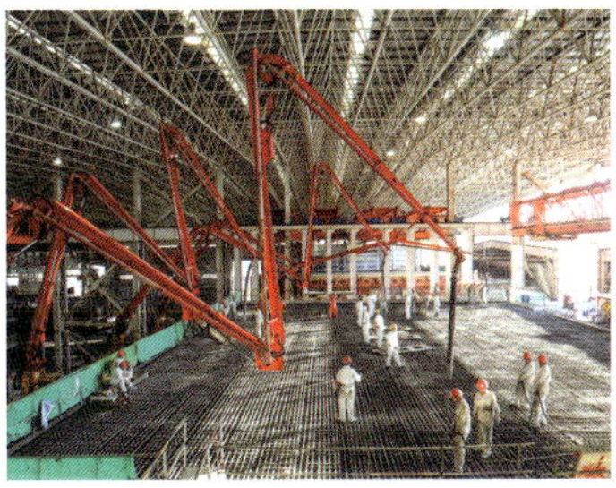

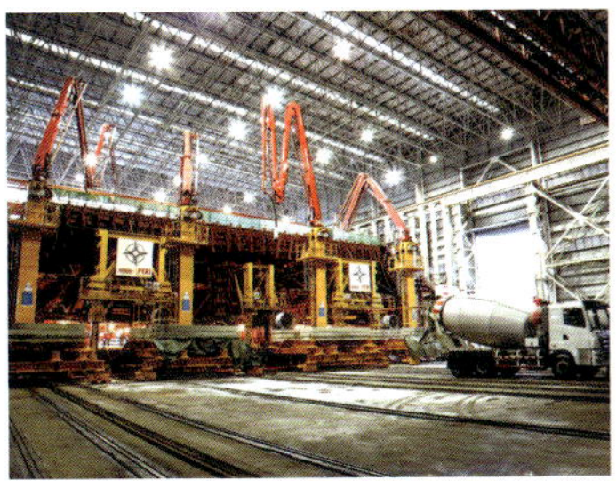

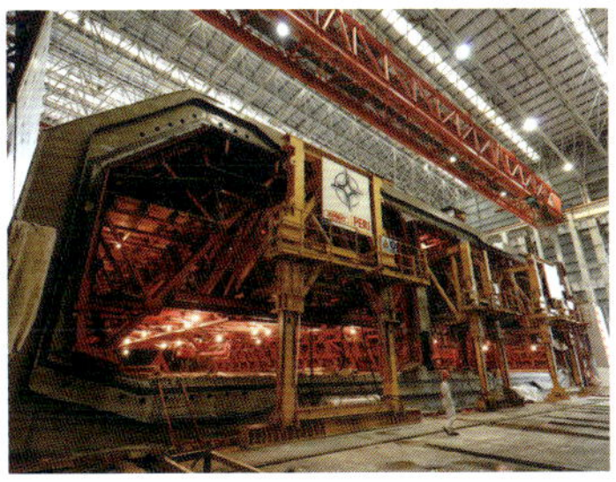

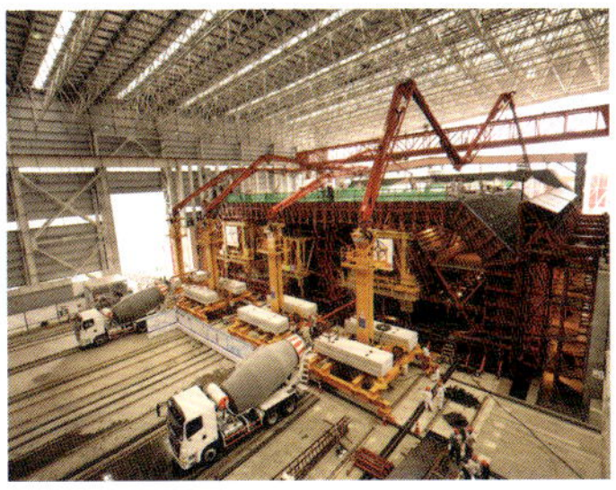

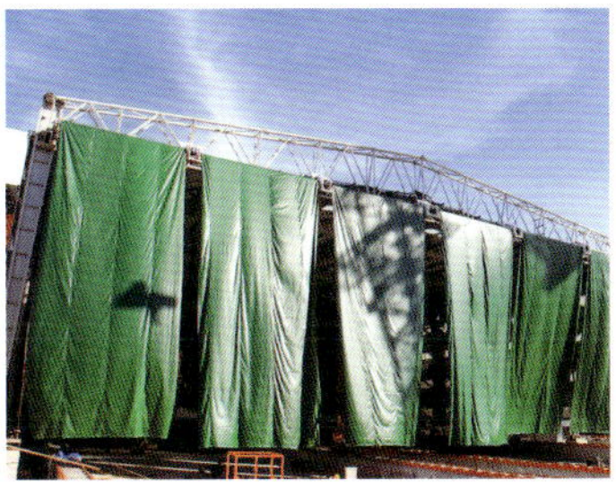

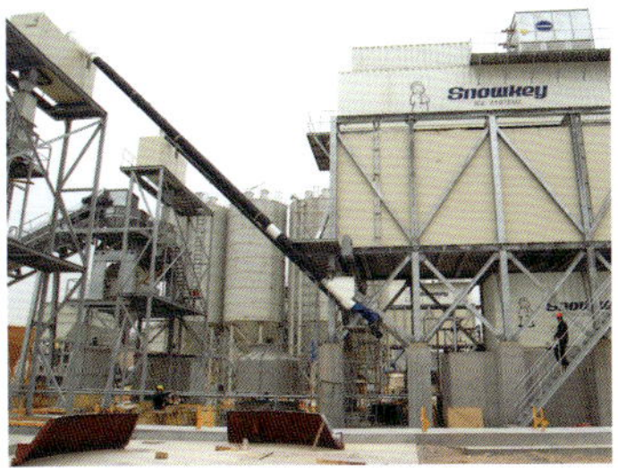

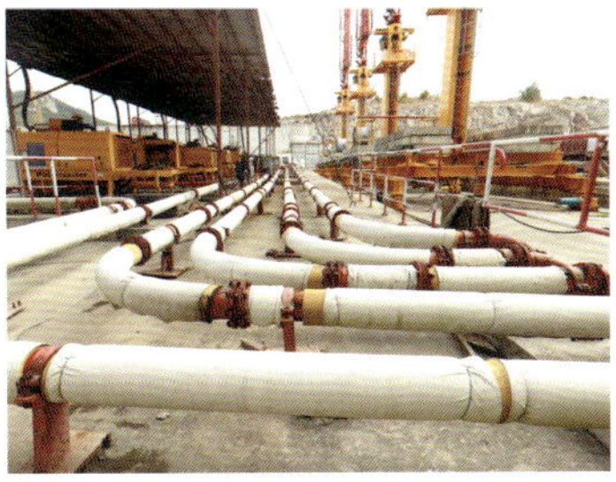

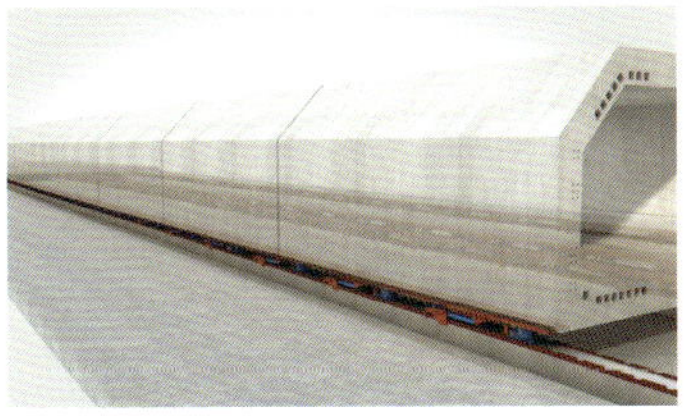

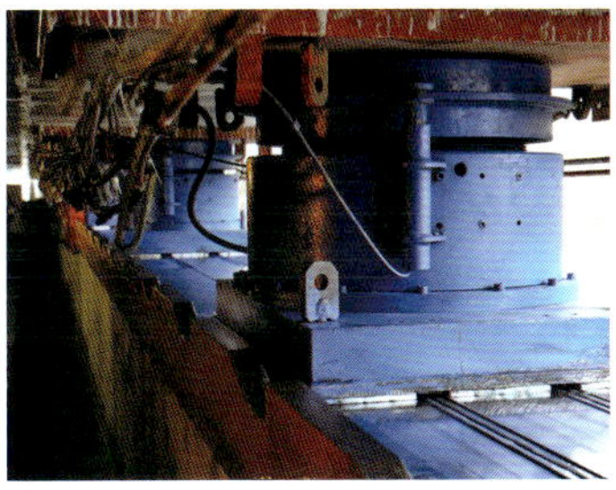

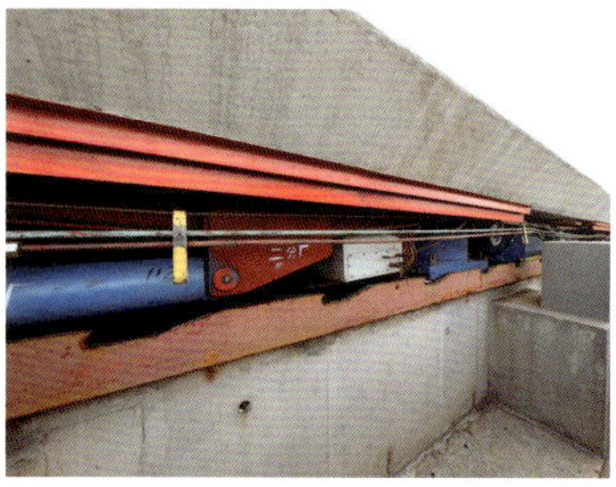
沉管顶推千斤顶
Pushing Jack for the Immersed Tube
136

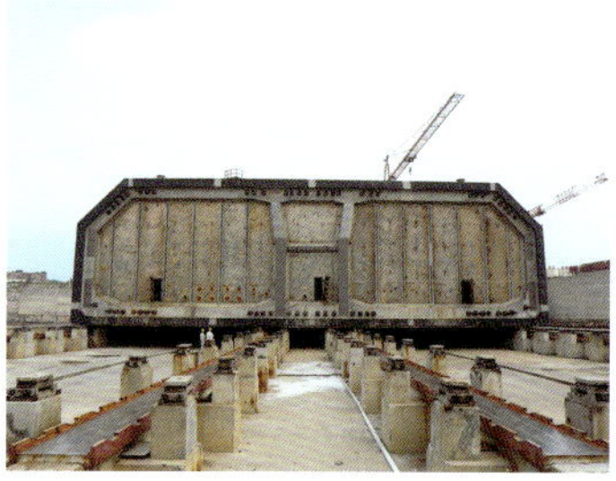
沉管顶推
Pushing of the Immersed Tube
139

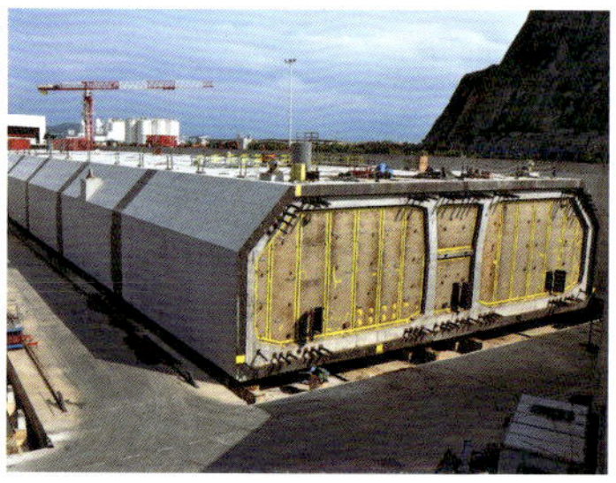
沉管顶推到位
Immersed Tube Pushed to the Designed Position
141

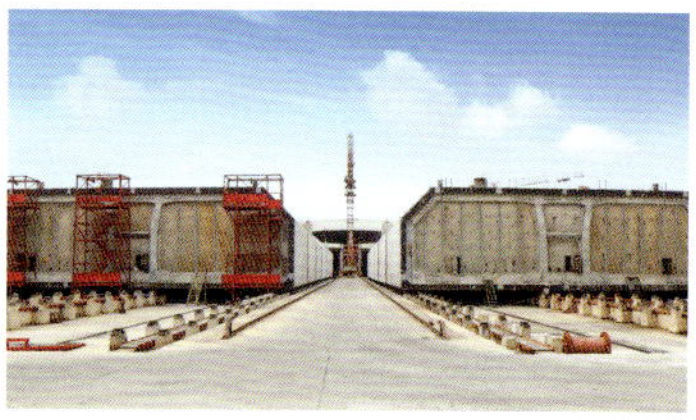
曲线段沉管
Immersed Tube at the Curved Section of the Tunnel
143

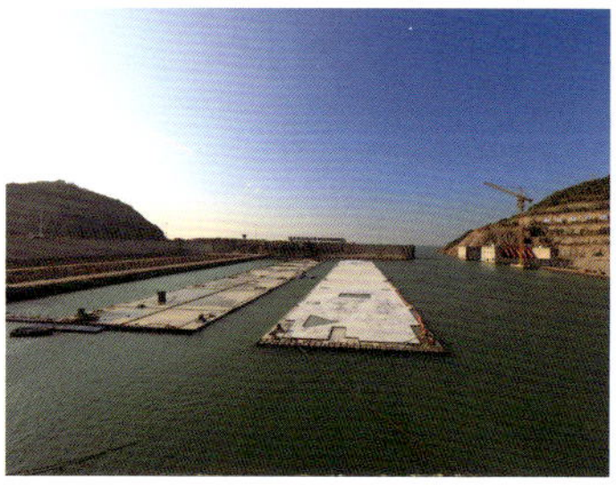
曲线段沉管横移
Horizontal Moving of the Immersed Tube at the Curved Section of the Tunnel
144

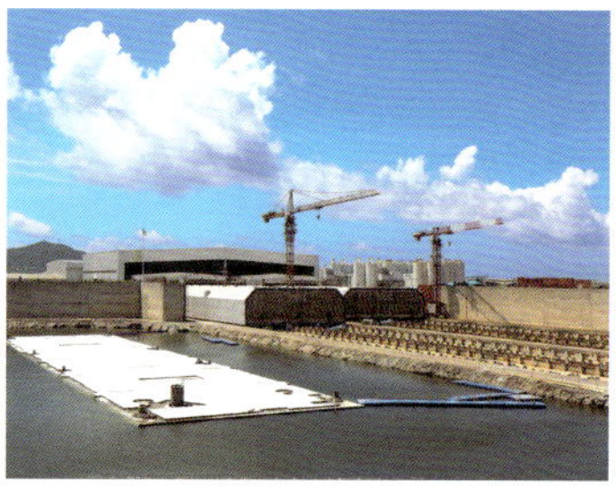
沉管一次舾装
Initial Outfitting of the Immersed Tube
146

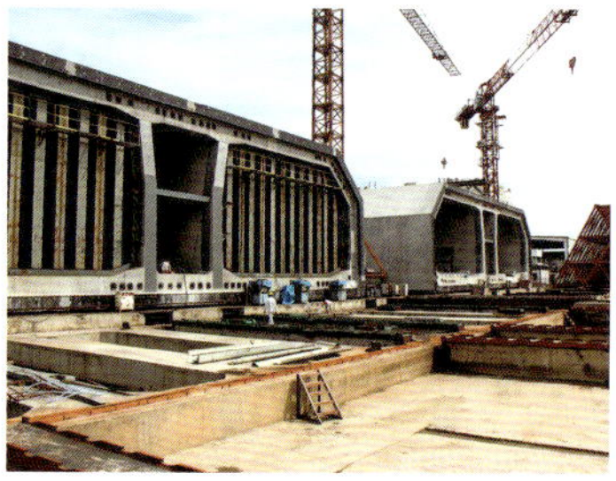
沉管钢封门安装
Installation of the Steel Sealing Devices of the Immersed Tube
148

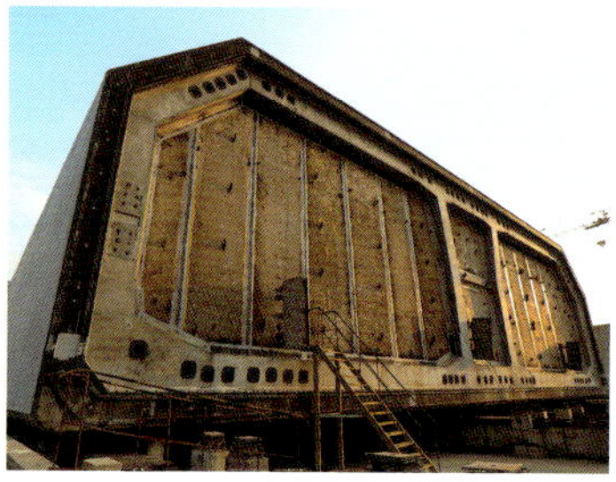
钢封门安装完成
Steel Sealing Devices Installation Completed
150

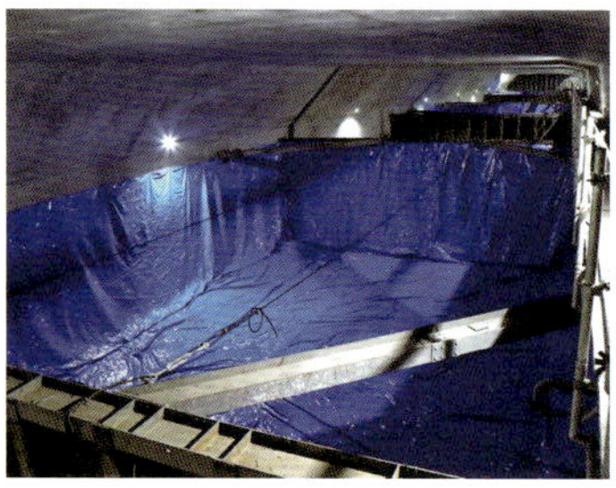
安装完成的压载水箱
Ballast Water Tank Installed
152

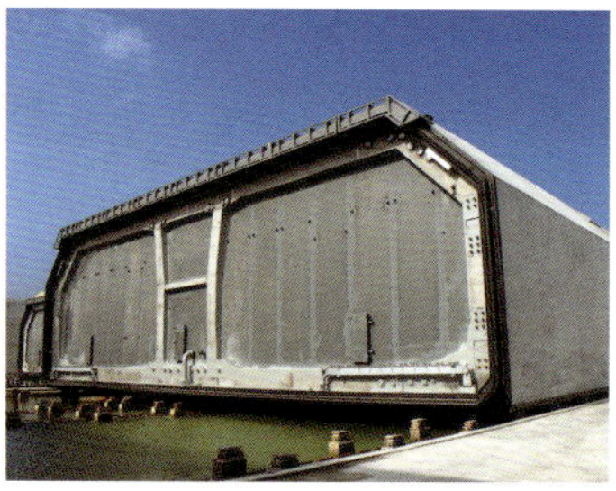
安装完成的 GINA 止水带
GINA Water-Stop Installed
155

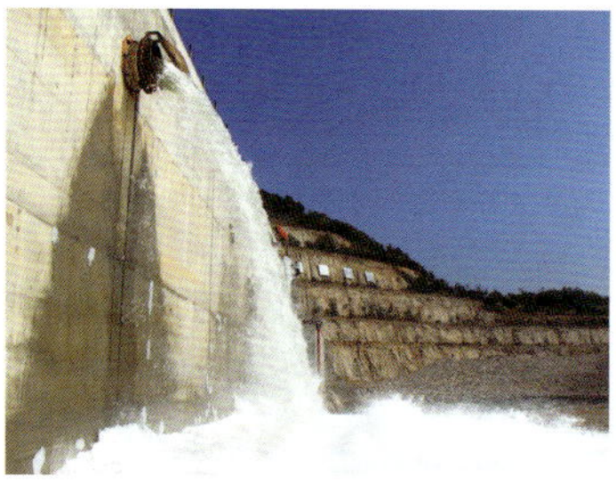
深坞蓄水
Deep Dock Impoundment
156

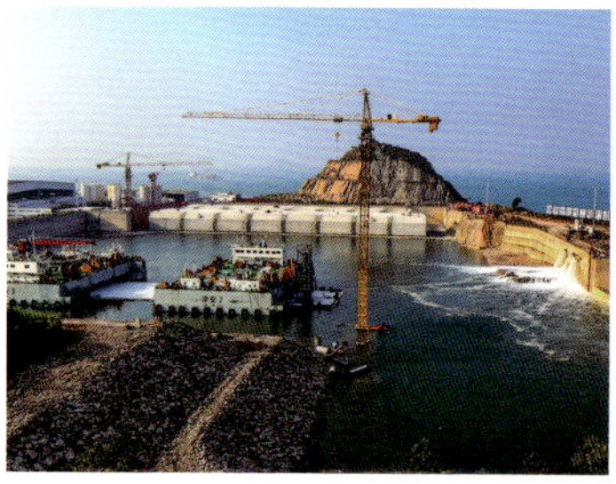
深坞蓄水
Deep Dock Impoundment
158

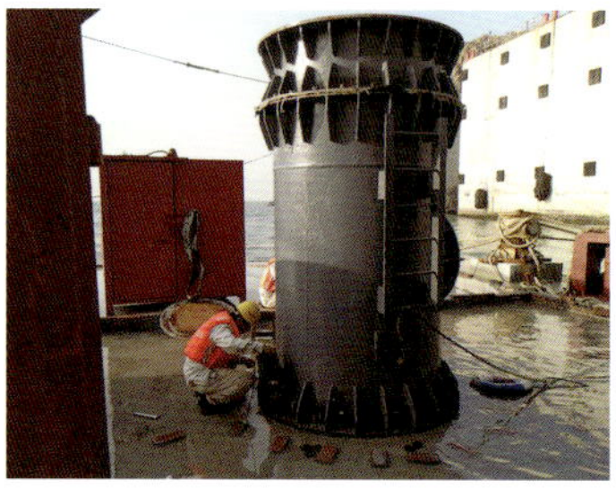
沉管人孔安装
Installation of the Manhole in the Immersed Tube
161

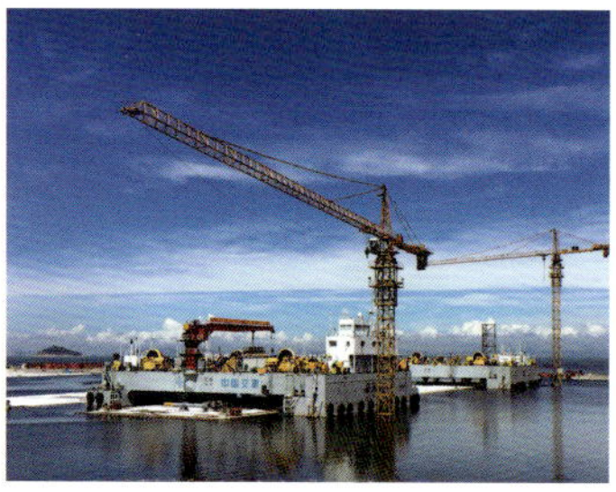
完成二次舾装的沉管
Immersed Tube after the Secondary Outfitting
163

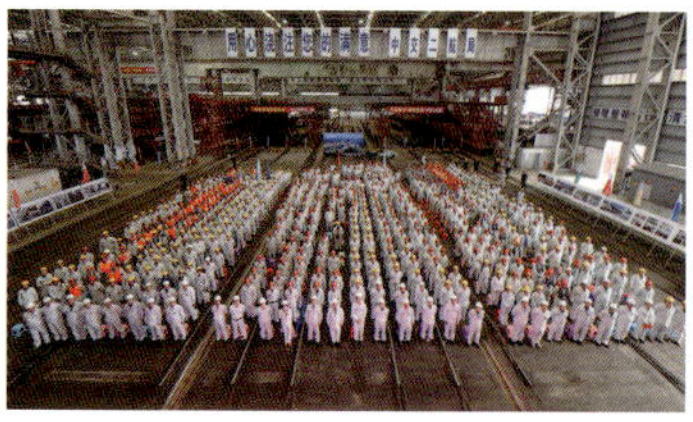
沉管预制完工总结大会建设者合影
Picture of the Honorary Constructors of Hong Kong-Zhuhai-Macau Bridge
164

蛟龙出海

METAMORPHOSIS

港珠澳大桥岛隧工程画册

Album of the Island-Tunnel Project of Hong Kong-Zhuhai-Macau Bridge

中国交通建设股份有限公司 编
CHINA COMMUNICATIONS CONSTRUCTION COMPANY LIMITED

南方日报出版社
NANFANG DAILY PRESS
中国·广州

图书在版编目（CIP）数据

蛟龙出海 / 中国交通建设股份有限公司编. — 广州：南方日报出版社，2019.3
（港珠澳大桥岛隧工程画册）
ISBN 978-7-5491-1987-5

Ⅰ. ①蛟… Ⅱ. ①中… Ⅲ. ①跨海峡桥－桥梁工程－中国－图集
②水下隧道－隧道工程－中国－图集 Ⅳ. ①U4-64

中国版本图书馆 CIP 数据核字（2019）第 045125 号

GANG ZHU AO DAQIAO DAOSUI GONGCHENG HUACE · JIAOLONG CHUHAI
港珠澳大桥岛隧工程画册·蛟龙出海

编　　者：中国交通建设股份有限公司
设计排版：廣角品牌机构
出版发行：南方日报出版社
地　　址：广州市广州大道中 289 号
出 版 人：周山丹
责任编辑：杨柳青　曹　星
责任技编：王　兰
责任校对：裴晓倩
装帧设计：李文俊　田　红　吴　凯
翻　　译：刘风山　郭敬谊
经　　销：全国新华书店
印　　刷：雅昌文化（集团）有限公司
开　　本：635 mm×965 mm　1/8
印　　张：25.25
字　　数：474 千字
版　　次：2019 年 3 月第 1 版
印　　次：2019 年 3 月第 1 次印刷
定　　价：980.00 元（全套 4 册）

目录
CONTENTS

最终接头创新技术
INNOVATIVE CLOSURE JOINT TECHNOLOGY

管内施工
IN-TUBE OPERATION

画册索引
ALBUM INDEX

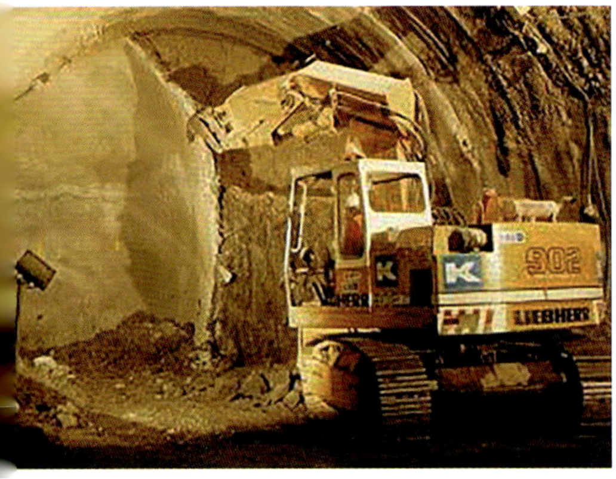

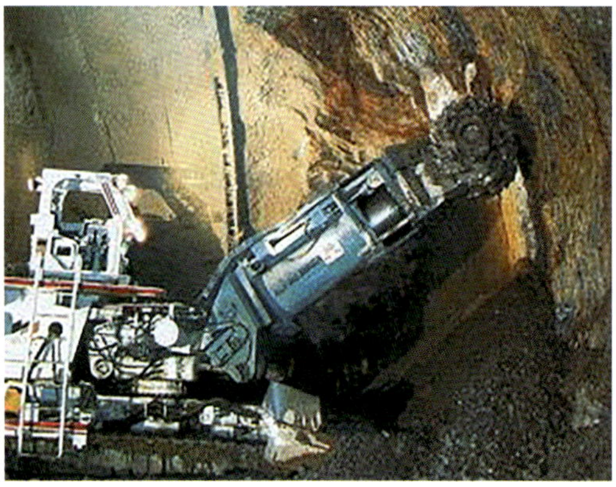

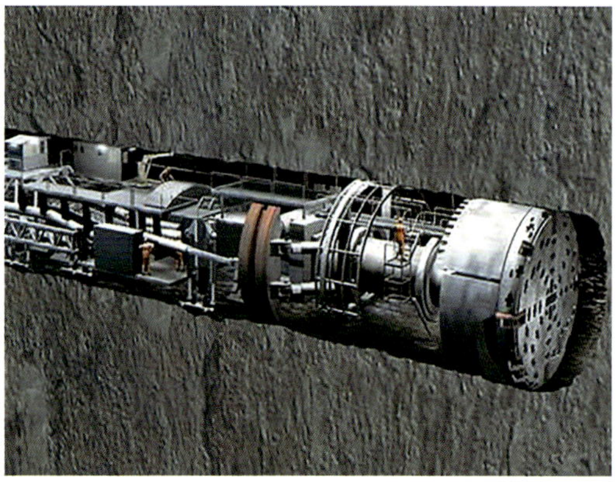

水下隧道背景综述

PROFILE OF UNDERWATER TUNNELING

水下隧道简述
OVERVIEW OF UNDERWATER TUNNELING

沉管法是在20世纪初发展起来的一种修建水下隧道的新工法。

根据国际隧道协会沉管隧道和悬浮隧道工作组1993年报告，所谓沉管隧道，就是在拟修建隧道的江河、海湾或海峡的水底下预先开挖一条基槽，把若干预制的沉管分别浮运至现场，一个接一个地沉放安装，在水下将其相互连接并正确定位在基槽内，其后辅以相关工程施工，使这些沉管组合体成为连接水道两岸陆上交通的隧道型运输载体。

Immersed Tube Tunneling first appeared in the early years of the 20th century as a new form of technology for the construction of underwater tunnels.

According to the 1993 Report issued by the International Tunneling and Underground Space Association, immersed Tunneling was to excavate a foundation trench underneath the rivers, bays or straits in advance, move the pre-made immersed tubes to the working site by float conveyance, immerse and connect the adjacent tubes underneath the water, and position them in the foundation trench, followed by relevant operation, so as to assemble these connected tubes into a transportation carrier connecting the road transportation on the the two ends of the tunnel.

1. 阿根廷佩拉纳河隧道
Paraná Tunnel, Argentina

2. 底特律温莎隧道
Detroit–Windsor Tunnel

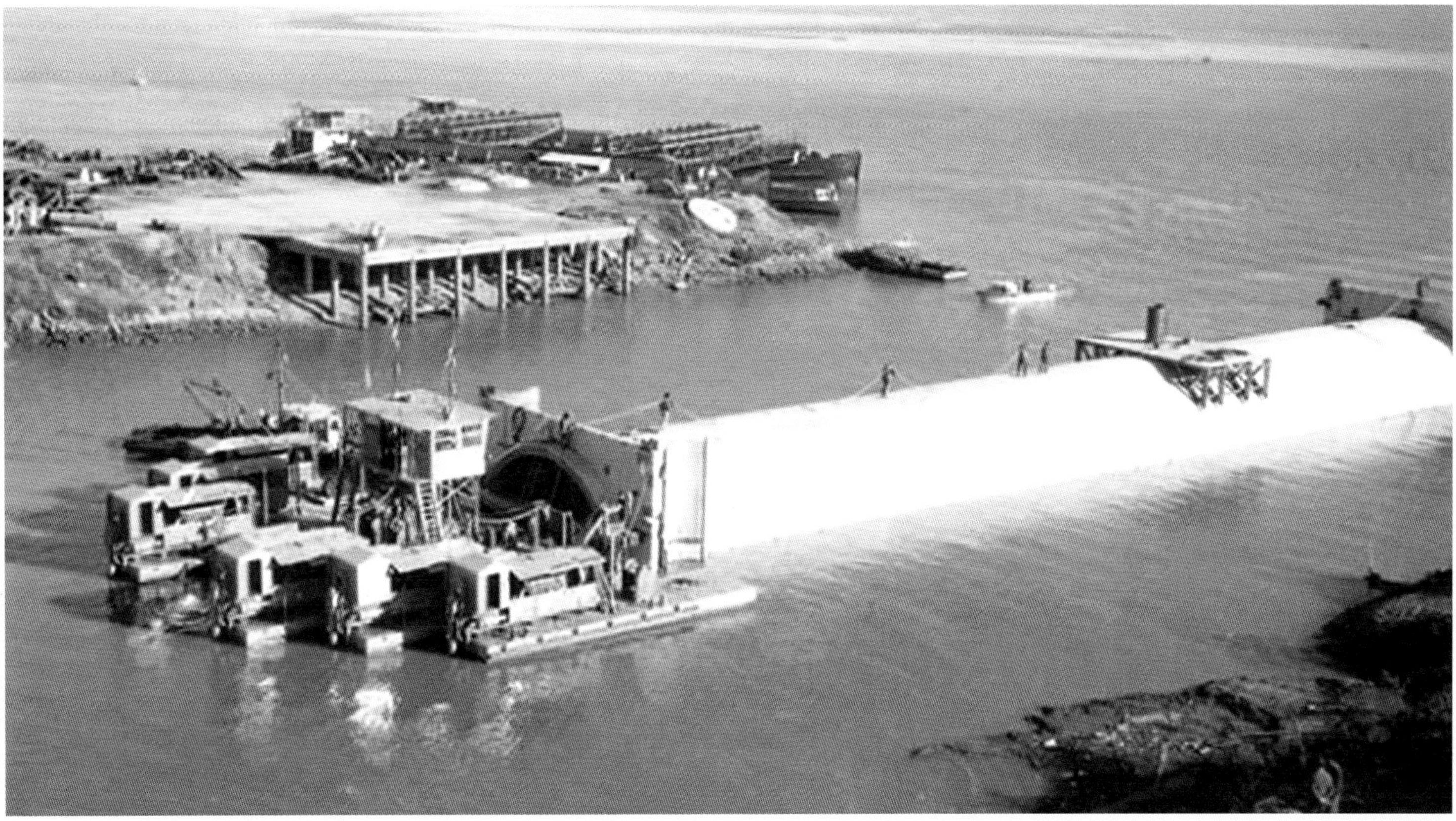

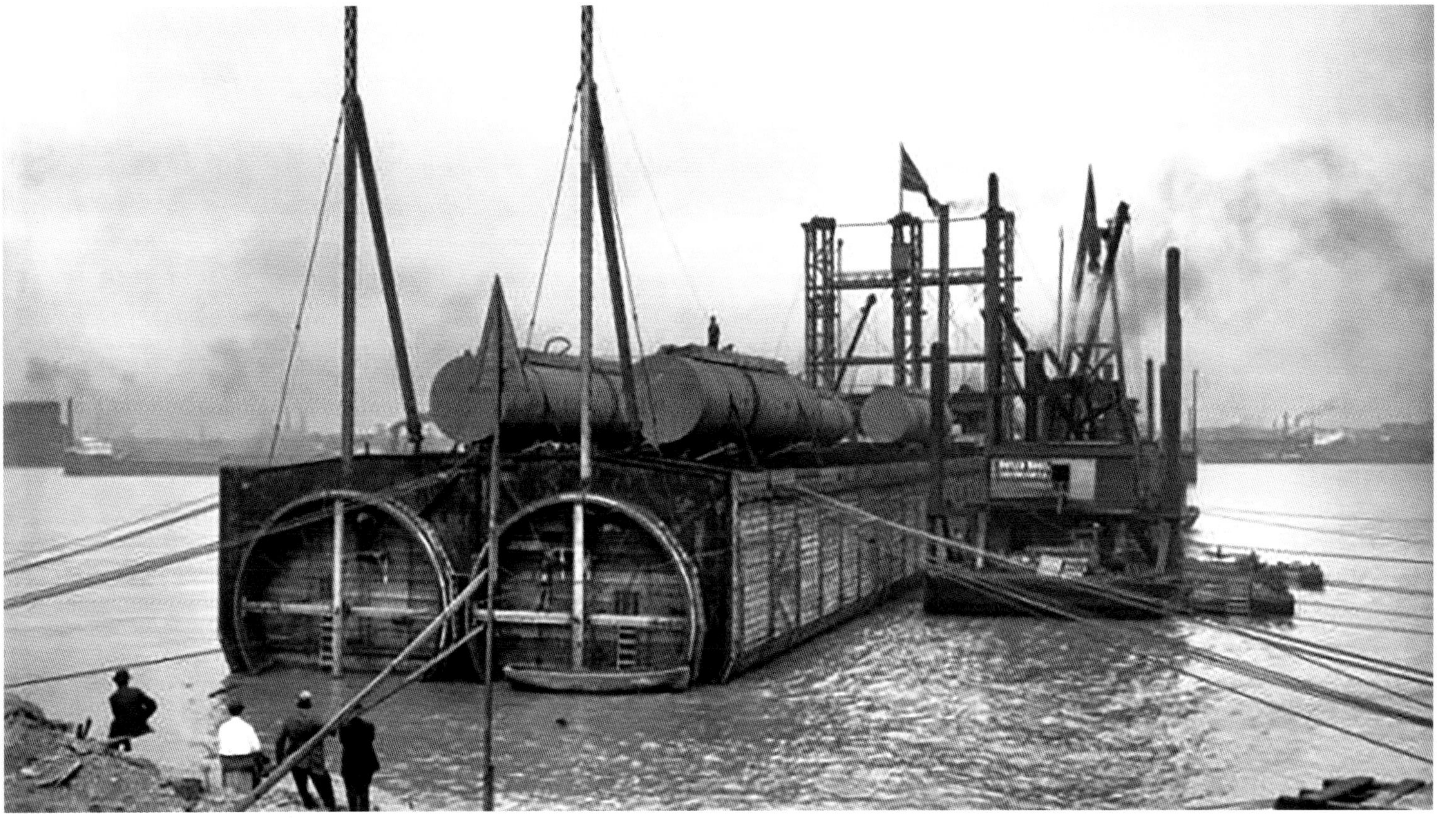

外海沉管隧道介绍

OVERVIEW OF OFFSHORE IMMERSED TUBE TUNNELING

据统计，目前全世界已建成或在建沉管隧道（含各类公共服务隧道）约150多座，属于或接近外海施工环境的沉管隧道包括：美国旧金山海湾快速交通隧道、丹麦—瑞典间的厄勒海峡沉管隧道、土耳其博斯普鲁斯海峡沉管隧道和韩国釜山—巨济沉管隧道等。

这些工程项目的实践及应用成果，推动了外海沉管隧道技术的不断进步和成熟。

近年来，随着我国基础建设水平的不断发展，拟建的水下隧道数量众多，正成为世界上拟建沉管隧道数量最多的国家。

外海沉管隧道大多处于离岸深水环境。

深水大压力条件对沉管结构设计和水密性提出很高要求。开敞水域气象条件多变，水文条件复杂，对选择沉管浮运安装方案带来很大影响。受径流影响，河口区咸淡水交汇，造成水密度垂向变化大，回淤强度大，流速加大，也将对沉管沉放对接带来很大困难。

因此，外海沉管隧道面临水深、流大、波高、回淤和气象复杂等难题，总体施工环境较一般内河沉管隧道更加困难，代表了当前沉管隧道建设的最高水平。

It is estimated that there are about 150 tunnels all over the world, including various tunnels for public service. The immersed tube tunnels that can be regarded as or roughly as offshore tunnels include the Transbay Tube under San Francisco Bay in the U. S., the Oresund Strait Tunnel connecting Denmark and Sweden, the Eurasia Tunnel underneath Bosphorus Strait of Turkey, the Busan-Geoje Tunnel of South Korea, and some others.

The construction and application of these tunnels pushed the technology of offshore immersed tube tunneling to its maturity.

Recently, with the development of China's infrastructure construction, more and more underwater tunnels were planned for construction. China has become one of the countries in the world with the biggest number of underwater tunnels waiting to be constructed.

Most of the offshore immersed tube tunnels are built in the deep water off the land.

Great water pressure under the deep water poses great challenges for the structural design and water-proof quality control of the immersed tubes. Climate changes on the open waters are often drastic; the complicated hydrographical conditions on these waters have great influence on the float conveyance and installation of the immersed tubes. Influenced by the stream flow, salty water and fresh water converge in the river estuary, which may result in the drastic vertical changes in the water density, high back silting intensity, and strong current, which makes it very difficult to land the tubes underneath the water.

Offshore immersed tube tunneling is always faced with such difficult situations as deep water, strong flow, big waves, back silting and complicated weather changes, more difficult than those faced by the immersed tube tunneling in inland rivers, but it suggests the highest level of the immersed tube tunneling in the world today.

序号 No.	隧道名称 Tunnel Name	隧道总长 / 米 Length (m)	管节尺寸 / 米 Tube Size (m)	环境条件 Environment	备注 Remarks
1	旧金山海湾快速交通隧道（1970 年） Transbay Tube under San Francisco Bay (1970)	5825	111*14.6*6.5	横跨海湾 Crossing the Bay	总长最长 Longest
2	纽约 63 号街隧道（1973 年） No. 63 Street Tunnel in New York (1973)	229	114.3*11.7*11.2	海水流速达 2.7m/s Flow speed of the Sea Water at 2.7 Meters Per Second	流速很大 Highest Flow Speed
3	比利时斯海尔德隧道（1980 年） Belgian Scheldt Tunnel (1980)	510	115*47.8*10.1	河水流速达 3.0m/s，最大潮位差 8.86m Flow Speed of the River at 3.0 Meters Per Second, and the Maximum Tidal Range by 8.86 Meters	流速及潮位差很大 High Flow Speed and Large Tide Range
4	荷兰海姆斯普尔隧道（1980 年） Hemspoor Tunnel in the Netherlands (1980)	1475	268*21.5*8.7	运河 Canal	管节最长 Longest Tubes
5	荷兰德雷赫特隧道（1977 年） Dordrecht Tunnel in the Netherlands (1977)	347	115*49.04*8.08		管节最宽 Widest Tubes
6	香港东港跨港隧道（1990 年） Donggang Cross-Harbour Tunnel in Hong Kong (1990)	1859	128*35*9.5	繁忙海港 Busy Port	

典型沉管隧道相关信息表

Information of Typical Immersed Tube Tunnels

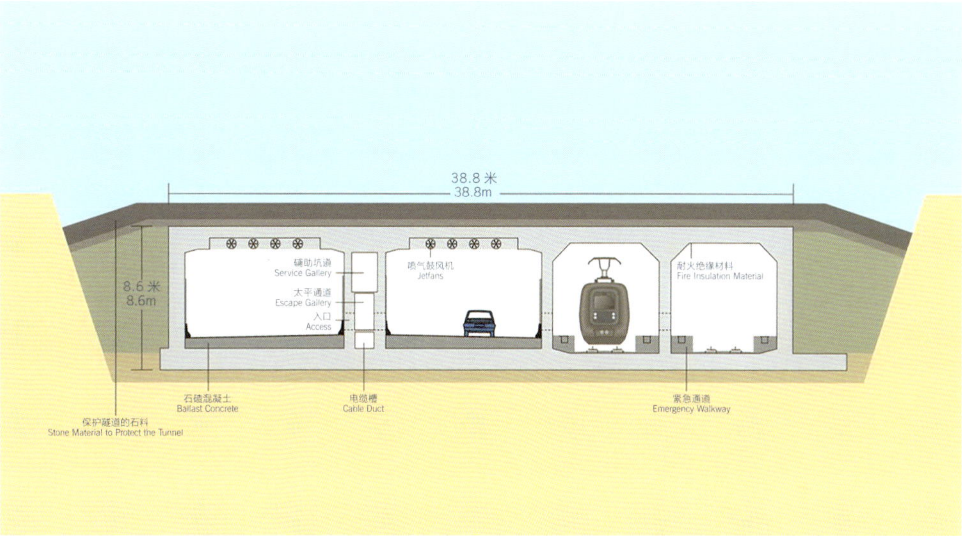

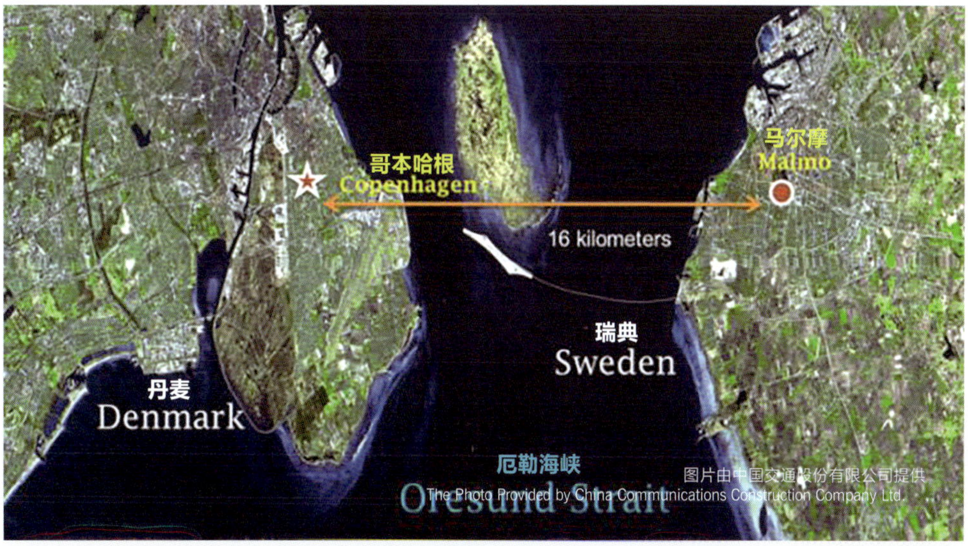

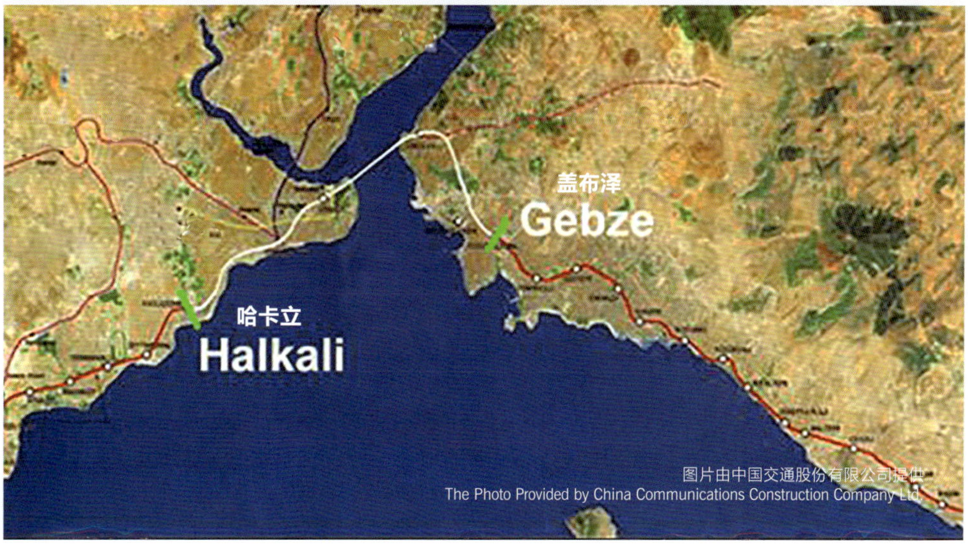

1. 厄勒海峡沉管隧道剖面图
Sectional View of the Immersed Tube Tunnel underneath Oresund Strait
2. 厄勒海峡沉管隧道平面图
Plan View of the Immersed Tube Tunnel underneath Oresund Strait
3. 马尔马雷沉管隧道平面图
Plan View of Marmary Immersed Tube Tunnel

水下隧道的发展简述
DEVELOPMENT OF UNDERWATER TUNNELING

世界沉管技术的研究始于1810年伦敦的沉管隧道试验。

1910年，穿越底特律河，连接起美国和加拿大的双线铁路沉管隧道，宣告"沉管法"隧道正式诞生；1942年，荷兰建成的鹿特丹Mass隧道，是世界上首条钢筋混凝土沉管隧道；1959年，加拿大迪西隧道成功采用了水力压接法进行沉管对接，标志着沉管隧道关键技术的突破。

20世纪60年代后，"沉管法"隧道在世界各国得到普遍应用，进入了一个快速发展阶段。

我国沉管隧道建设起步较晚。

20世纪之前，内地建成的只有浙江甬江公路沉管隧道和广东珠江公铁两用沉管隧道。

虽迄今已先后在广州、宁波、上海、天津、舟山、南昌等地建成十多座内河沉管隧道，但大多长度较短，规模较小，整体施工水平与国际相比尚有较大差距。

随着装备水平的提升和最终接头技术的进步，国内一批跨江河、河口、海湾和海峡的重大交通工程纷纷酝酿采用沉管隧道方式，为我国沉管隧道施工技术赶超国际先进水平提供了平台。

2010年开工的港珠澳大桥沉管隧道即是这新一轮大规模水上交通基础建设的标志性工程。

Studies of immersed tube tunneling technology in the world began with the experiments on the immersed tube tunneling in London in 1810.

The construction of the double-railed immersed tube tunnel in 1910 that ran underneath the Detroit River and connected the United States and Canada marked the birth of the immersed tube tunneling. Rotterdam's Maas Tunnel built in the Netherlands in 1942 was the first immersed tube tunnel made of steel and concrete in the world. The Deas Island Tunnel of Canada built in 1959 adopted hydraulic crimp connection technology for the butt welding of the immersed tubes, which was regarded as a great breakthrough in the critical technology of immersed tube tunneling.

Since the 1960s, the immersed tube tunneling was widely adopted in many countries of the world and it had come to the stage of this technology's rapid development.

The immersed tube tunneling started quite late in China.

Before the 20th century, there were only two immersed tube tunnels in China: one was Yongjiang Tunnel in Zhejiang Province, and the other is Pearl River Tunnel for both road and rail transportation.

There are by now over ten inland river tunnels in such places as Guangzhou, Ningbo, Shanghai, Tianjin, Zhoushan and Nanchang, but these tunnels are usually very short, and the technology involved in their construction lags far behind the international standard.

With the development in equipment and the technology of closure joint, more and more great transportation projects running across rivers, estuaries, bays and straits make use of this technology of immersed tube tunneling, which provides a platform for Chinese immersed tube tunneling technology to catch up with and surpass the other countries in the world.

The construction of the immersed tube tunnel of Hong Kong-Zhuhai-Macau Bridge in 2010 was the cornerstone project of the large-scaled transportation project over the vast seas.

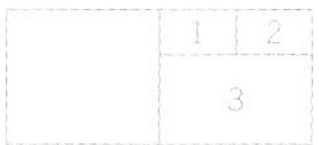

1. 厄勒海峡沉管隧道
   Oresund Strait Immersed Tube Tunnel
2. 伦敦泰晤士河沉管隧道
   River Thames Immersed Tube Tunnel, London
3. 世界著名沉管隧道参数对比示意图
   Comparative Schematic Diagram of the World-Known Immersed Tube Tunnels

隧道名称 Tunnel Name	建成时间 Time of Completion	长度 / 米 Length (m)	管节尺寸 / 米 Tube Size (m)	外包尺寸 / 米 Outsource Size (m)	基础处理 Basic Operation
广州珠江隧道 Pearl River Tunnel in Guangzhou	1994 年	457	105+2×120+90+22	33.00*8.05	压砂法 Sand-Flow Method
宁波甬江隧道 Yongjiang Tunnel in Ningbo	1995 年	420	85+80+3×85	11.90*7.65	压浆基础 Grouting Base
宁波常洪隧道 Changhong Tunnel in Ningbo	2002 年	395	95+3×100	22.80*8.45	桩基囊袋法 Bag Grouting at Pile Foundation
上海外环隧道 Outring Tunnel in Shanghai	2003 年	736	108+104+2×100+3×108	43.00*9.55	压砂法 Sand-Flow Method
广州仑头隧道 Luntou Tunnel in Guangzhou	2010 年	277	55+67+78+77	23.00*8.70	压砂法 Sand-Flow Method

国内部分沉管隧道相关信息表
Information of Some Domestic Immersed Tube Tunnels

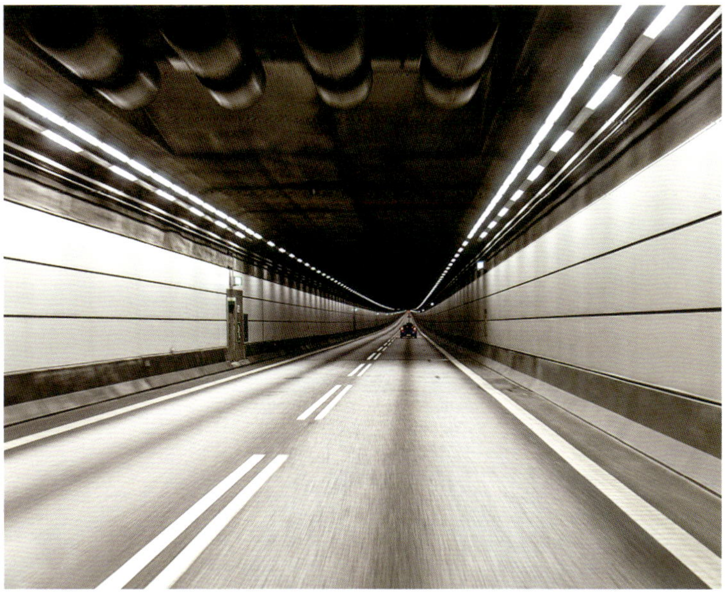

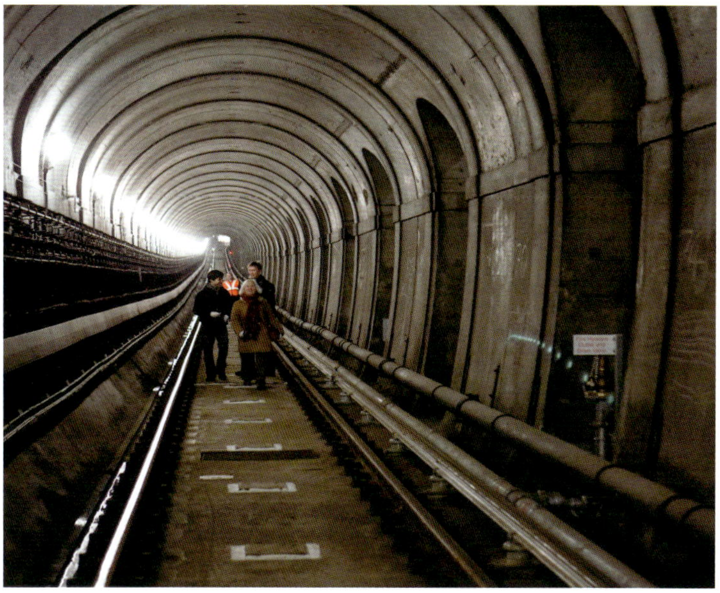

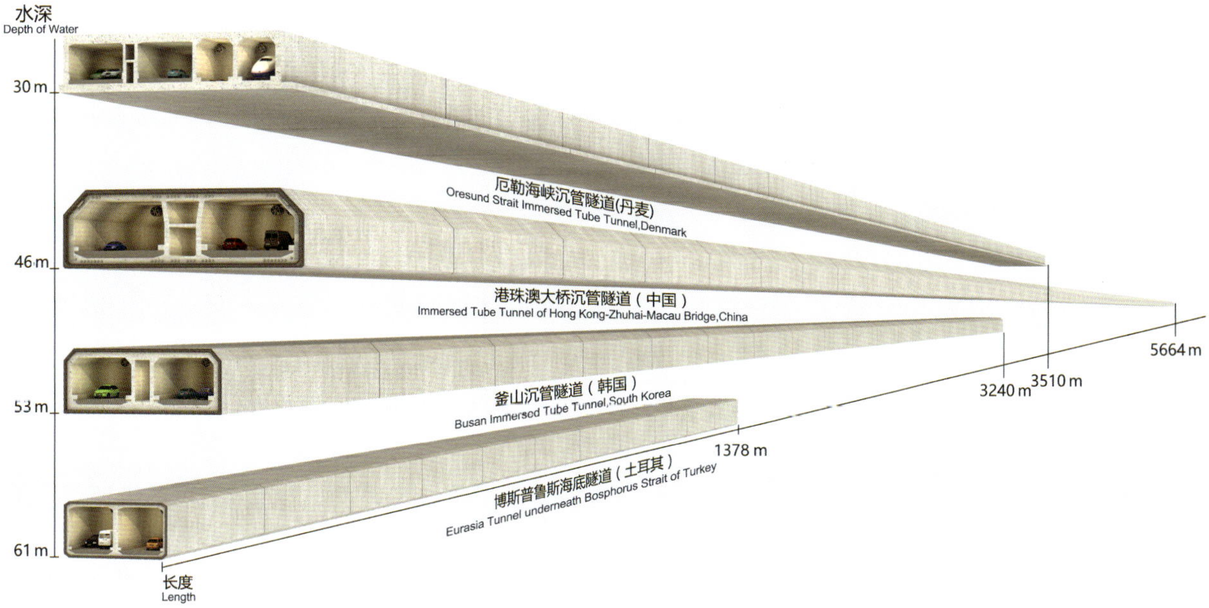

水深
Depth of Water
30 m
46 m
53 m
61 m
长度
Length
厄勒海峡沉管隧道(丹麦)
Oresund Strait Immersed Tube Tunnel,Denmark
港珠澳大桥沉管隧道（中国）
Immersed Tube Tunnel of Hong Kong-Zhuhai-Macau Bridge,China
釜山沉管隧道（韩国）
Busan Immersed Tube Tunnel,South Korea
博斯普鲁斯海底隧道（土耳其）
Eurasia Tunnel underneath Bosphorus Strait of Turkey
1378 m
3240 m
3510 m
5664 m

港珠澳大桥沉管隧道工程概况

PROFILE OF THE IMMERSED TUBE TUNNEL PROJECT OF HONG KONG-ZHUHAI-MACAU BRIDGE

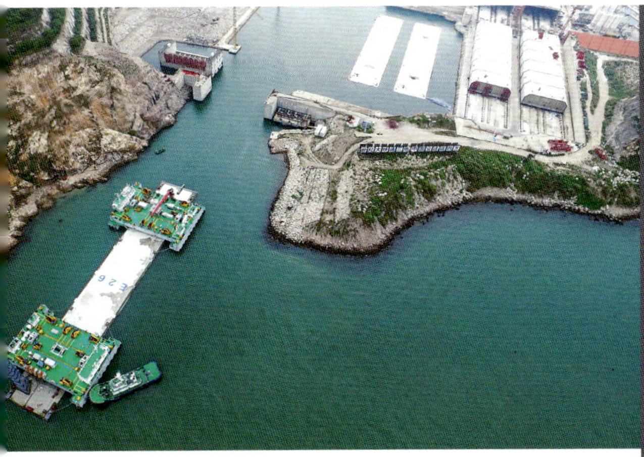

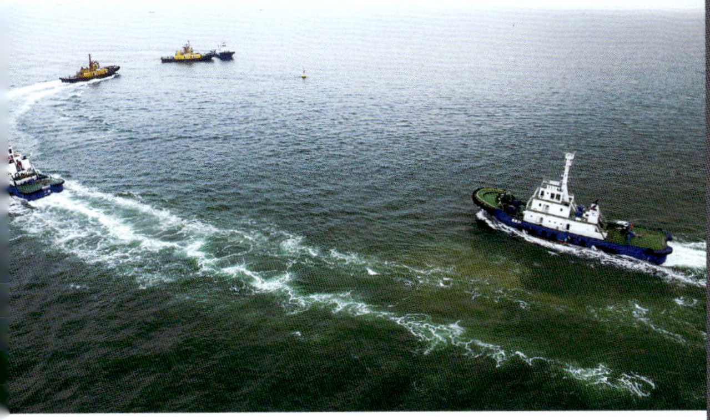

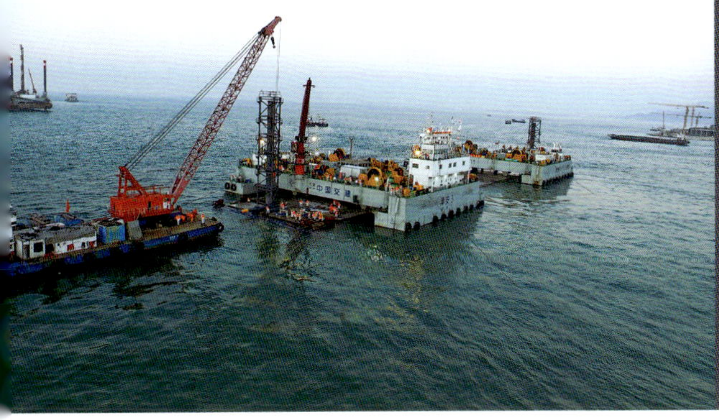

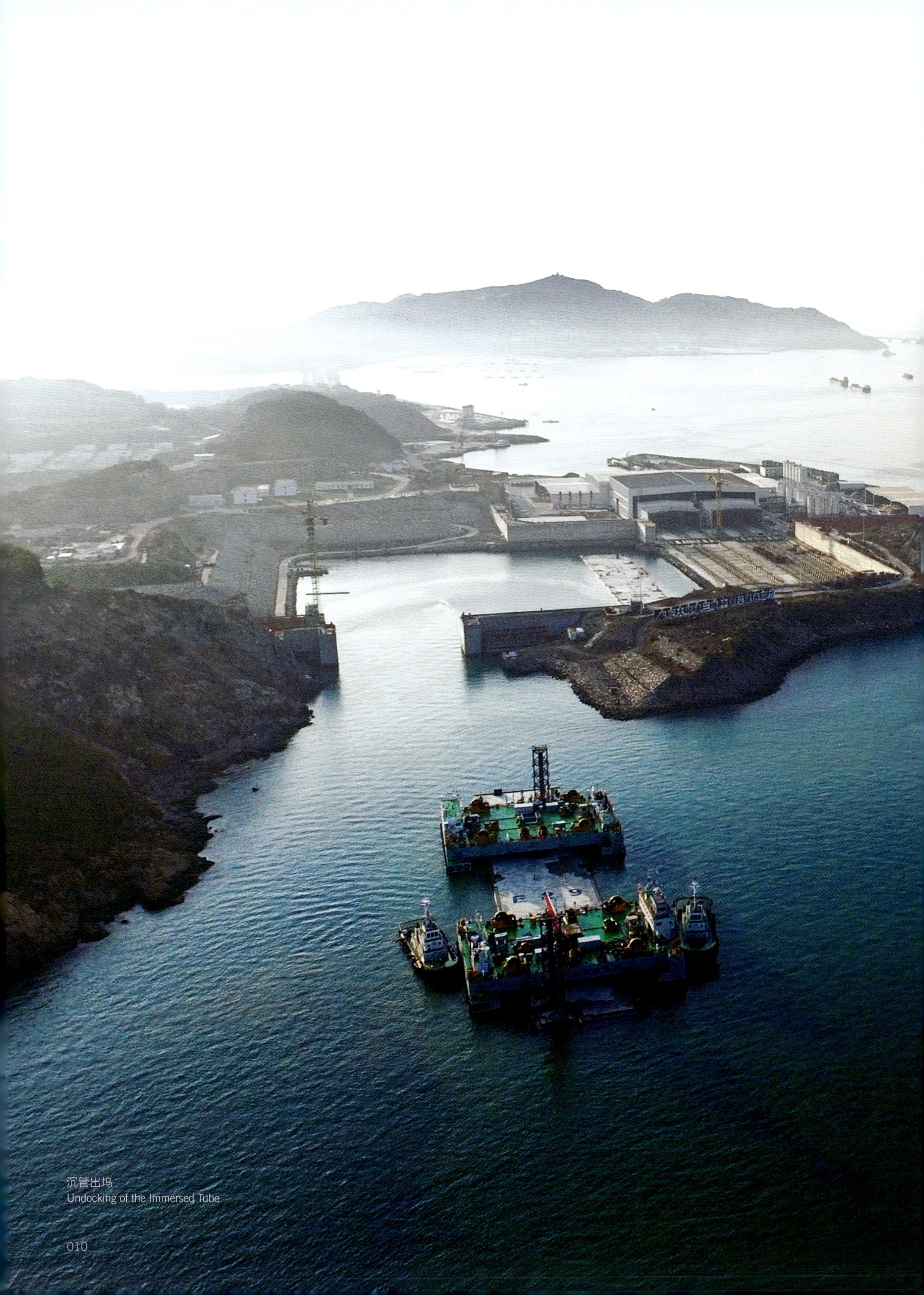

沉管出坞
Undocking of the Immersed Tube

岛隧工程沉管隧道概述

OVERVIEW OF THE IMMERSED TUBE TUNNEL IN THE ISLAND-TUNNEL PROJECT

港珠澳大桥沉管隧道是世界最长的公路沉管隧道、中国第一条外海沉管隧道和世界唯一的深埋沉管隧道，长 6.7 公里，由 33 节沉管组成，标准沉管长 180 米，重约 7.6 万吨。

为了预留 30 万吨级航道，沉管沉放水深近 50 米，第一次被埋入海床下超过 20 米深处。

沉管浮运安装是港珠澳大桥建设最核心的技术。

沉管安装前进行隧道基础施工，主要工序包括基槽开挖、基槽清淤、基床抛石夯平、碎石基床整平。

西人工岛筑岛成陆后，首先在小岛区域进行基坑开挖，完成现浇段隧道施工，提供首节沉管沉放对接条件。

沉管安装自西向东进行，先依次完成 E1~E28 直线段沉管的安装，再由东往西进行 E33~E29 曲线段沉管安装，最后安装位于 E29~E30 之间的最终接头，实现隧道合龙。

The immersed tube tunnel of Hong Kong-Zhuhai-Macau Bridge is the longest immersed tube tunnel in the world, the first offshore immersed tube tunnel in China, and the only deep-buried immersed tube tunnel in the world. It is 6.7 kilometers long, composed of 33 immersed tubes. The standard length of each immersed tube is 180 meters, weighing 76,000 tons.

To form a waterway for vessels of 300,000 tons, the immersed tubes are positioned in the water of about 50 meters deep, and for the first time in human history, the tubes are buried 20 meters deep in the sea bed.

The float conveyance and installation of the immersed tubes was the core technology of Hong Kong-Zhuhai-Macau Bridge construction.

Tunnel base construction is needed before the immersed tube installation, mainly including foundation trench excavation, foundation trench desilting, bedding rock filling, compacting and leveling, and rubble bed leveling.

After West Man-Made Island was finished, the foundation trench was first excavated on the island and a tunnel was constructed, providing convenience for the landing and butt welding of the first immersed tube.

The immersed tube installation moved from the west to the east, wherein the installation of straight immersed tubes from E1 to E28, then the installation of the curved tubes from E33 to E29 from the east to west. The final step of the tube installation was the closure joint between E29 and E30 when the tunnel was finally closed.

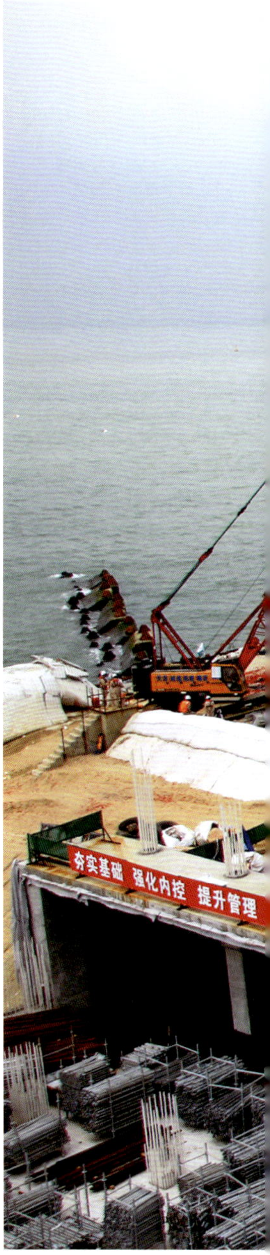

1. E1 沉管与西人工岛暗埋段对接
Butt Welding of Tube E1 with the Buried Tube on West Man-Made Island

2. 港珠澳大桥沉管隧道基础示意图
Schematic Diagram of the Immersed Tube Tunnel Base of Hong Kong-Zhuhai-Macau Bridge

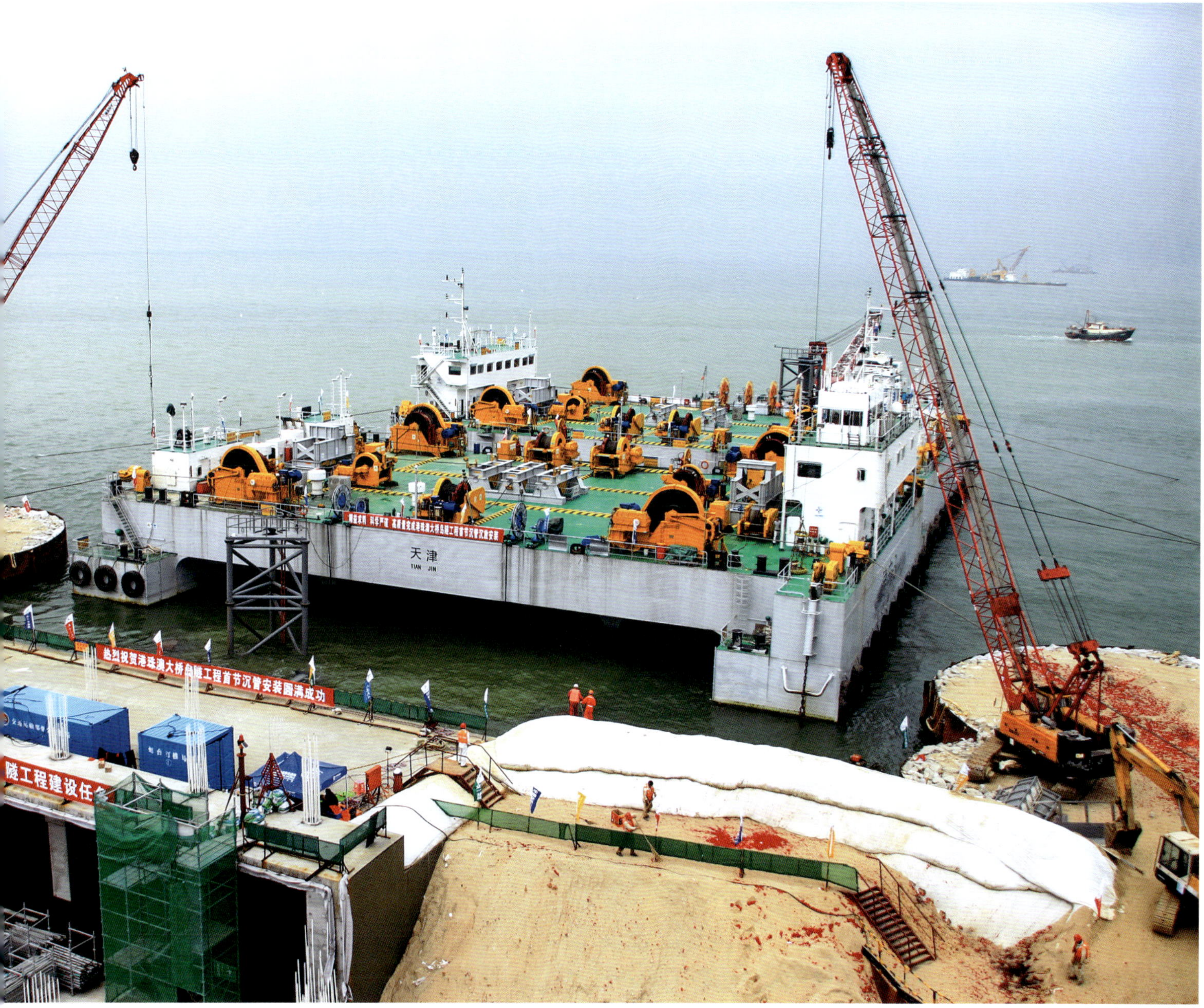
天津
TIAN JIN

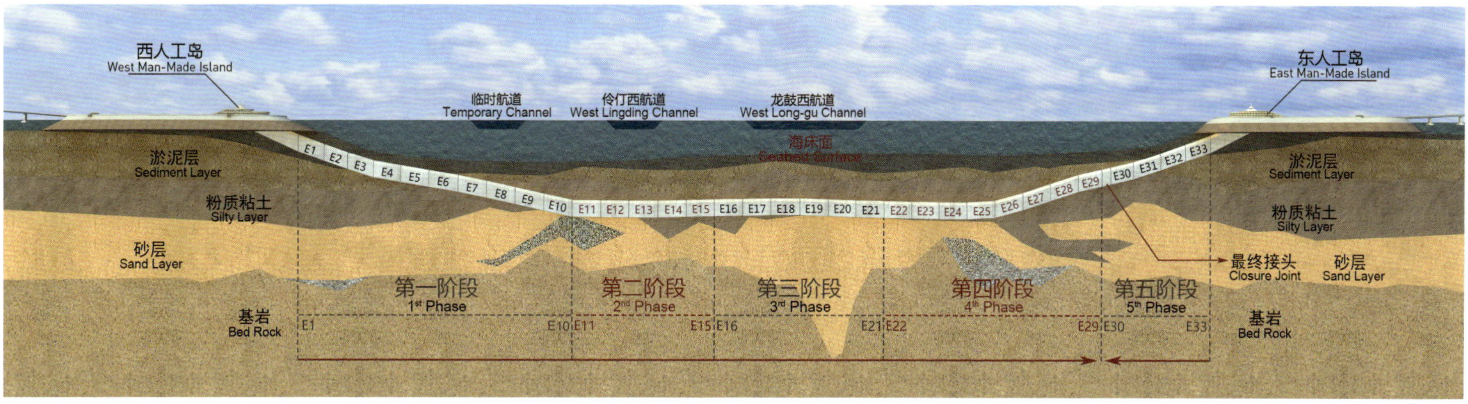
西人工岛
West Man-Made Island
临时航道
Temporary Channel
伶仃西航道
West Lingding Channel
龙鼓西航道
West Long-gu Channel
东人工岛
East Man-Made Island
海床面
Seabed Surface
淤泥层
Sediment Layer
粉质粘土
Silty Layer
砂层
Sand Layer
基岩
Bed Rock
E1 E2 E3 E4 E5 E6 E7 E8 E9 E10 E11 E12 E13 E14 E15 E16 E17 E18 E19 E20 E21 E22 E23 E24 E25 E26 E27 E28 E29 E30 E31 E32 E33
淤泥层
Sediment Layer
粉质粘土
Silty Layer
最终接头
Closure Joint
砂层
Sand Layer
第一阶段
1st Phase
第二阶段
2nd Phase
第三阶段
3rd Phase
第四阶段
4th Phase
第五阶段
5th Phase
基岩
Bed Rock
E1
E10 E11
E15 E16
E21 E22
E29 E30
E33

工程特点和难点
FEATURES AND KEY TECHNICAL POINTS OF THE PROJECT

序号 No.	工程特点 Project Features	特点分析 Characteristics Analysis
1	工程规模大 Large Scale	管节体量大（7.6 万吨级）、数量多（33 节），世界最大规模沉管隧道之一 Composed of 33 tubes, each with a dimension of 76,000 tons, it is one of the large-scaled immersed tube tunnels in the world
2	作业条件差 Poor Working Condition	安装现场远离大陆，外海无掩护施工 The installation was conducted on the sea without special offshore protective facilities
		现场受台风、热带气旋、短时雷暴等恶劣天气影响大 The installation was easy to be affected by such extreme climates as typhoons, tropical cyclones and thunderstorms
		位于珠江口航道运输最繁忙水域，属水上交通安全事故频发敏感区 The construction was conducted over one of the busiest oversea area at the mouth of Pearl river where traffic accidents are common
		外海作业，物资材料、机械设备、施工人员等的组织运输难度大 Oversea operation poses challenges for the transportation of raw materials, equipment, workers and technicians
		岛头区沉管安装作业面狭窄、水流条件复杂 The head part of the island features limited working space and complicated sea currents
3	技术难点多 Diverse Technical Challenges	复杂水流和航运条件下的管节浮运难度大 Complicated currents and traffic are great challenges for the float conveyance of the tubes
		水文与气象作业窗口分析、精细化预报和保障难度大 It is difficult for Hydrological and meteorological window analysis, elaborate forecast and support
		跨海控制测量和高程传递难度大 It is difficult to conduct cross-sea monitoring and elevation transmission
		深水（45 米）长距离（5.6 千米）条件的沉管水下高精度定位测控难度大 It is difficult to exquisitely position and monitor the tubes under water of 45 meters deep over a distance of 5.6 kilometers
		岛头效应产生的挑流严重影响岛隧结合部位置管节的沉放 The deflecting flow at the head part of the island greatly affects the landing of the immersed tubes at the junction part of the island and the tunnel
4	安装工期紧 Short Installation Duration	沉管安装施工作业条件严格，可作业天数有限 Severe conditions leave a limited number of days for the installation of the immersed tubes
		36 个月完成 33 节沉管的安装，与国内外类似工程比较，工期挑战性大 33 immersed tubes are installed within 36 months, which proves to be a greater challenge compared with similar projects at home and abroad
5	环保要求严 Strict Environmental Requirements	施工区域处于白海豚核心保护区，环境保护要求严格 The construction site locates in the central area of the white dolphin reserve, so environmental protection is an urgent issue
6	施工风险大 High Engineering Risks	深水压力条件下的端封门使用安全风险大 Operation of the end sealing devices faces great risks under deep water
		深水条件的潜水作业安全风险大 Divers working underwater faces great risks in deep water
		突发灾害天气条件下现场作业安全风险大 Unexpected extreme weather poses great danger for the oversea operation
		沉管浮运通航安全风险大 The float conveyance of the immersed tubes faces great risks during transportation

沉管浮运、安装施工特点分析表
Features of Immersed Tube Float Conveyance and Installation

	1
	2
	3

1. 中华白海豚
Chinese White Dolphin
2. 珠江口航运
Pearl River Estuary Shipping
3. 伶仃洋海域
Lingding Bay

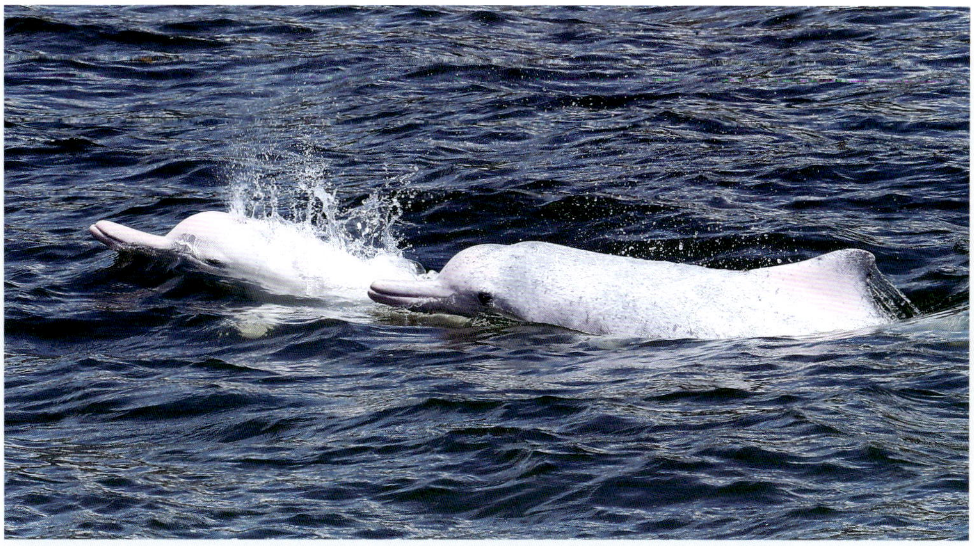

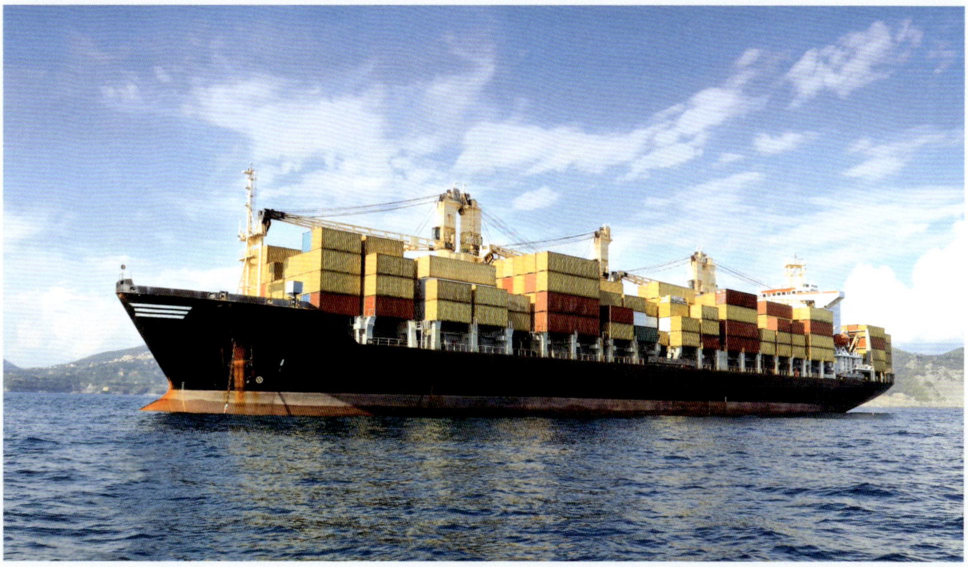

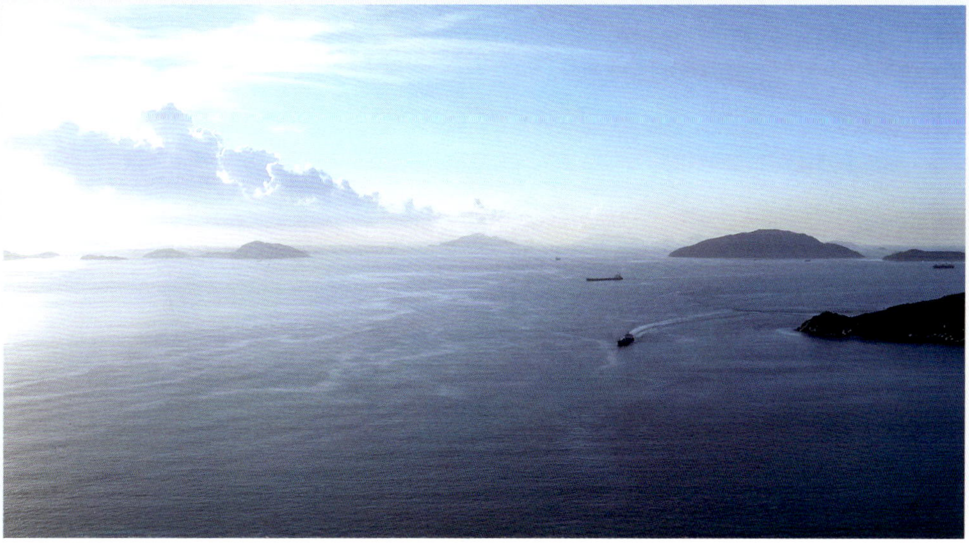

隧道基础施工

TUNNEL BASE CONSTRUCTION

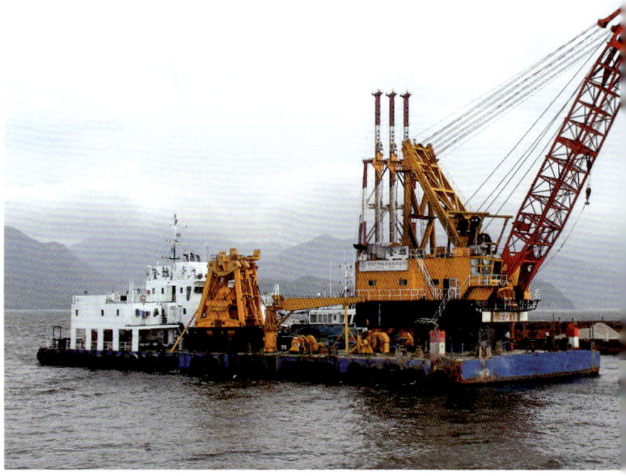

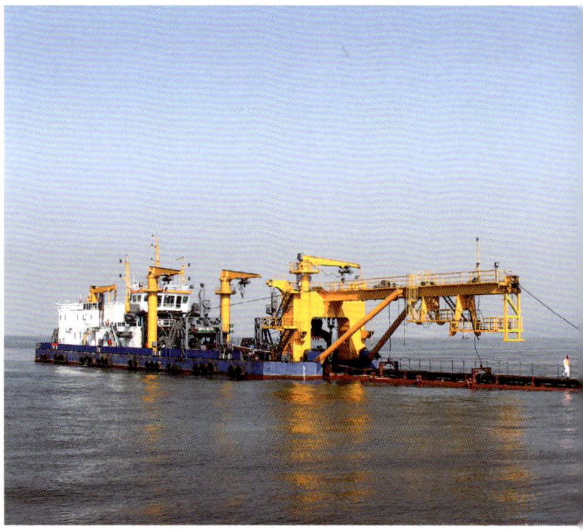

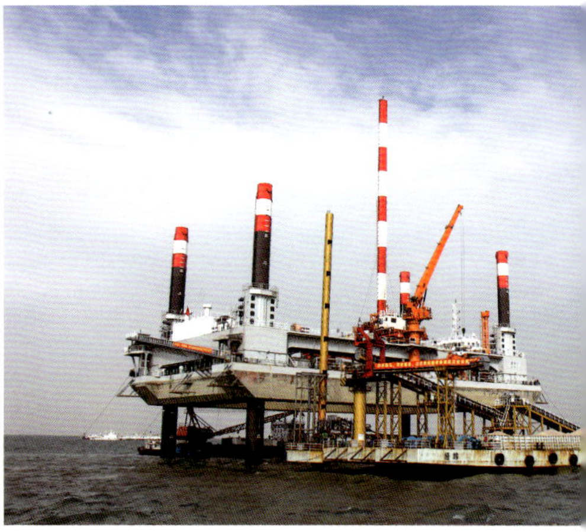

基础施工流程
PROCESS OF TUNNEL BASE CONSTRUCTION

港珠澳沉管隧道基础施工流程图
Flow Chart of the Immersed Tube Tunnel Base Construction
of Hong Kong-Zhuhai-Macau Bridge

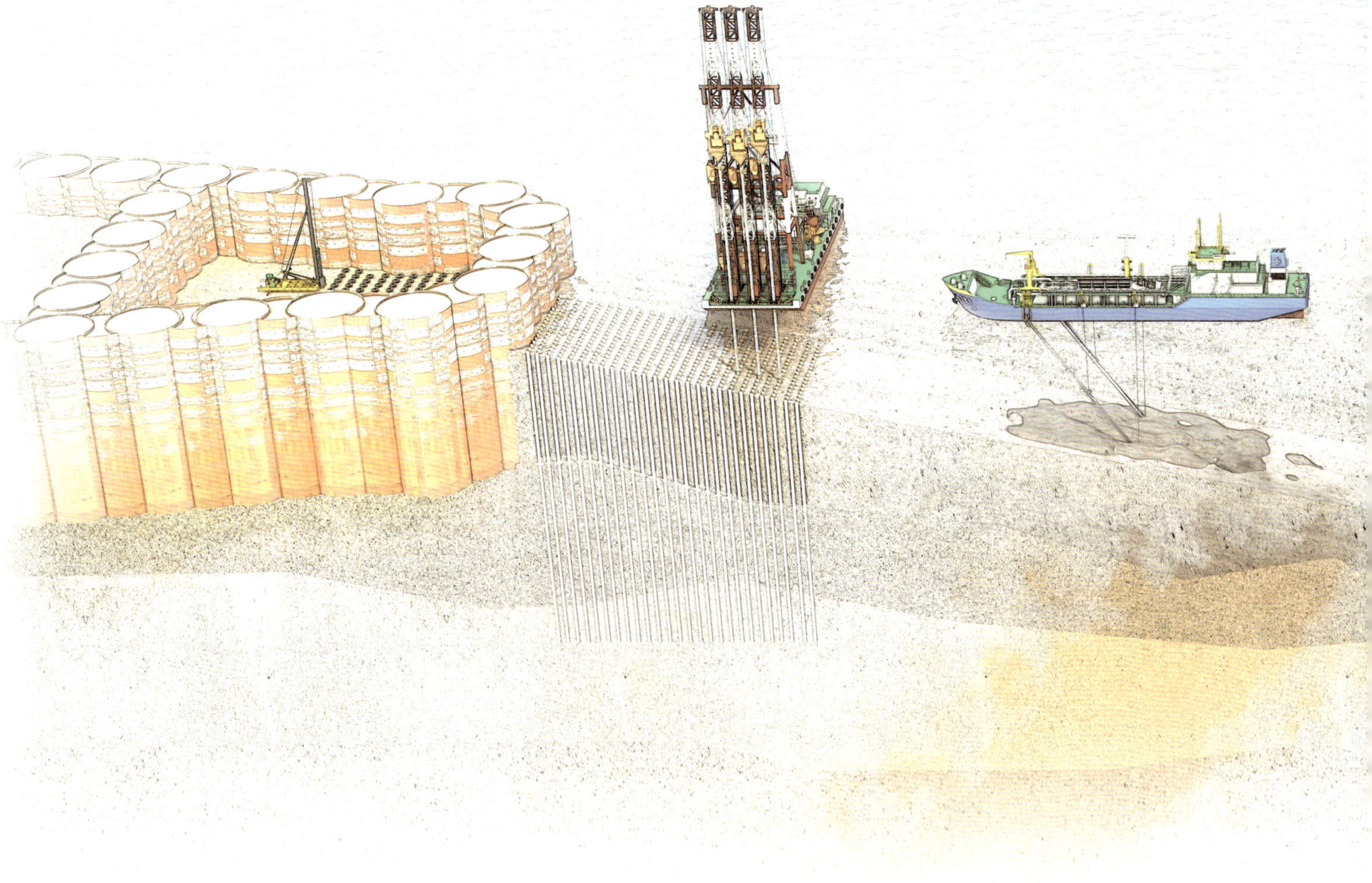

沉管隧道基槽最深处标高约 -48.5 米，最大开挖厚度约 35 米，挖泥总量约 2900 万立方米。

基槽的纵向、横向设计采用多重坡率组合，槽底高程误差控制在 +40~-60 厘米以内。

按照以往工程经验，建设在软土地基的沉管隧道，沉降一般为 20~30 厘米。

港珠澳大桥沉管隧道软土地基最深 30~50 米，回淤厚度超过 20 米，沉降控制难度极大。

The deepest place of the foundation trench for the immersed tube tunnel is about -48.5 meters, its biggest width is 35 meters, and the total volume of excavated sediment is 29,000,000 cubic meters.

The vertical and horizontal design of the foundation trench employed the technique of multiple slope rate combination, and the elevation deviation was controlled between +40 and -60 centimeters.

By former constructional experiences, the immersed tube tunnel built in the soft ground was usually immersed by 20 to 30 centimeters.

The deepest place of the soft ground base for the immersed tube tunnel of Hong Kong-Zhuhai-Macau Bridge lied about 30 to 50 meters under the water, and the back silting was usually over 20 meters thick, so it was quite difficult to control the tubes' landing.

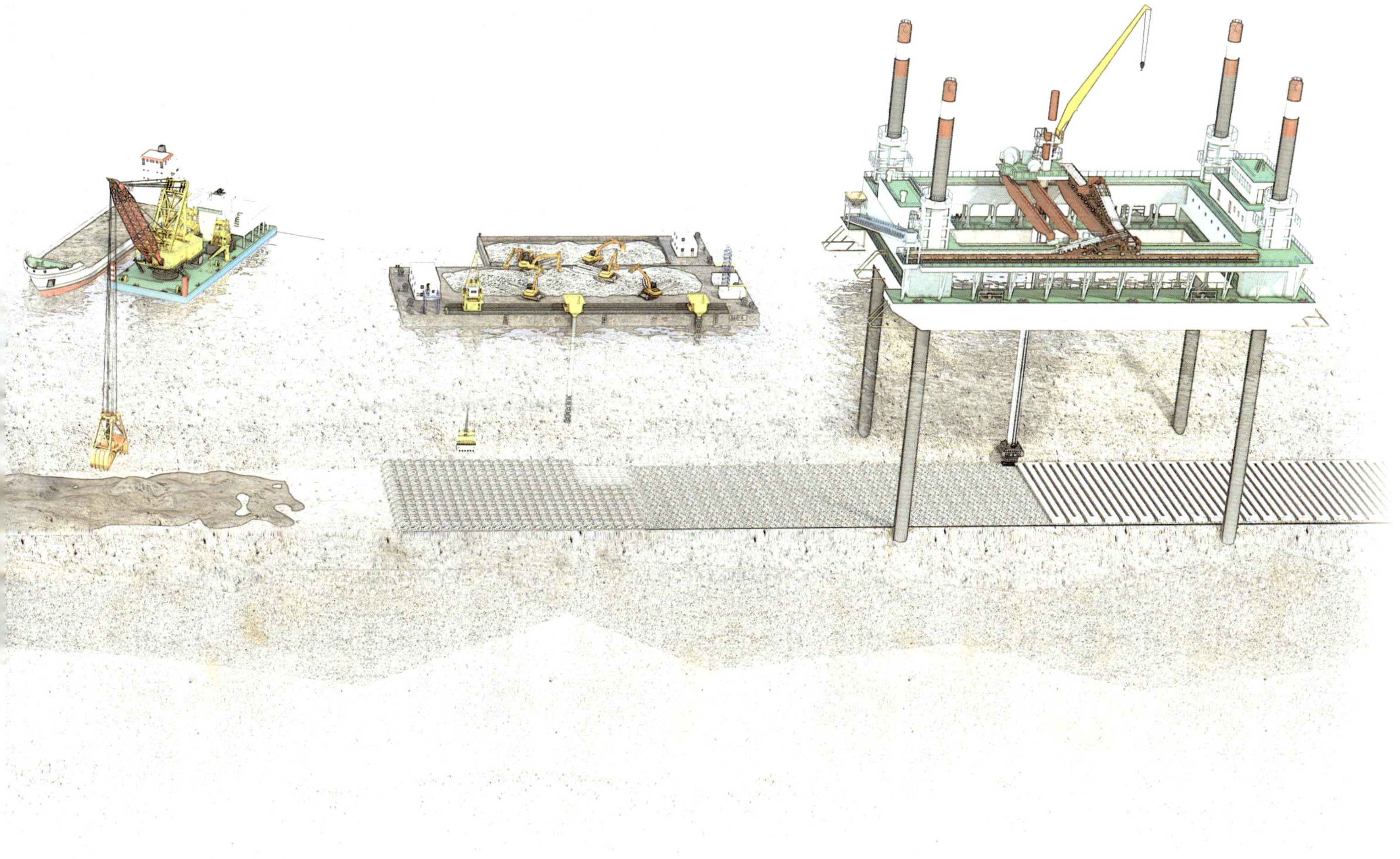

基槽粗挖
DEEP EXCAVATION OF THE FOUNDATION TRENCH

基槽粗挖是指自然泥面至距设计断面线（含边坡设计线及槽底）垂直标高约 3 米间的泥层开挖。

港珠澳大桥海底隧道选用了舱容 10,000 立方米，具有高精度施工能力和特定功能的大型自航耙吸挖泥船进行基槽粗挖施工。

基槽粗挖采用分层、分段开挖工艺，利用超深报警系统预防超深开挖，保证开挖精度。

Deep excavation of the foundation trench means that the excavation begins with the silt that is about 3 meters deep by vertical elevation from the silt surface under the water to the designed fracture surface (including the designed slope surface and the trench bottom).

For the construction of the underwater tunnel of Hong Kong-Zhuhai-Macau Bridge, large-scaled, self-propelled cutter suction dredgers of a volume of 10,000 cubic meters, equipped with high-accuracy construction capacity and other special capacities, were used for the excavation of the foundation trench.

The foundation trench excavation employed such techniques of stratified and segmented excavation. Super-deep alarming system was used to avoid super-deep excavation and guarantee excavation accuracy.

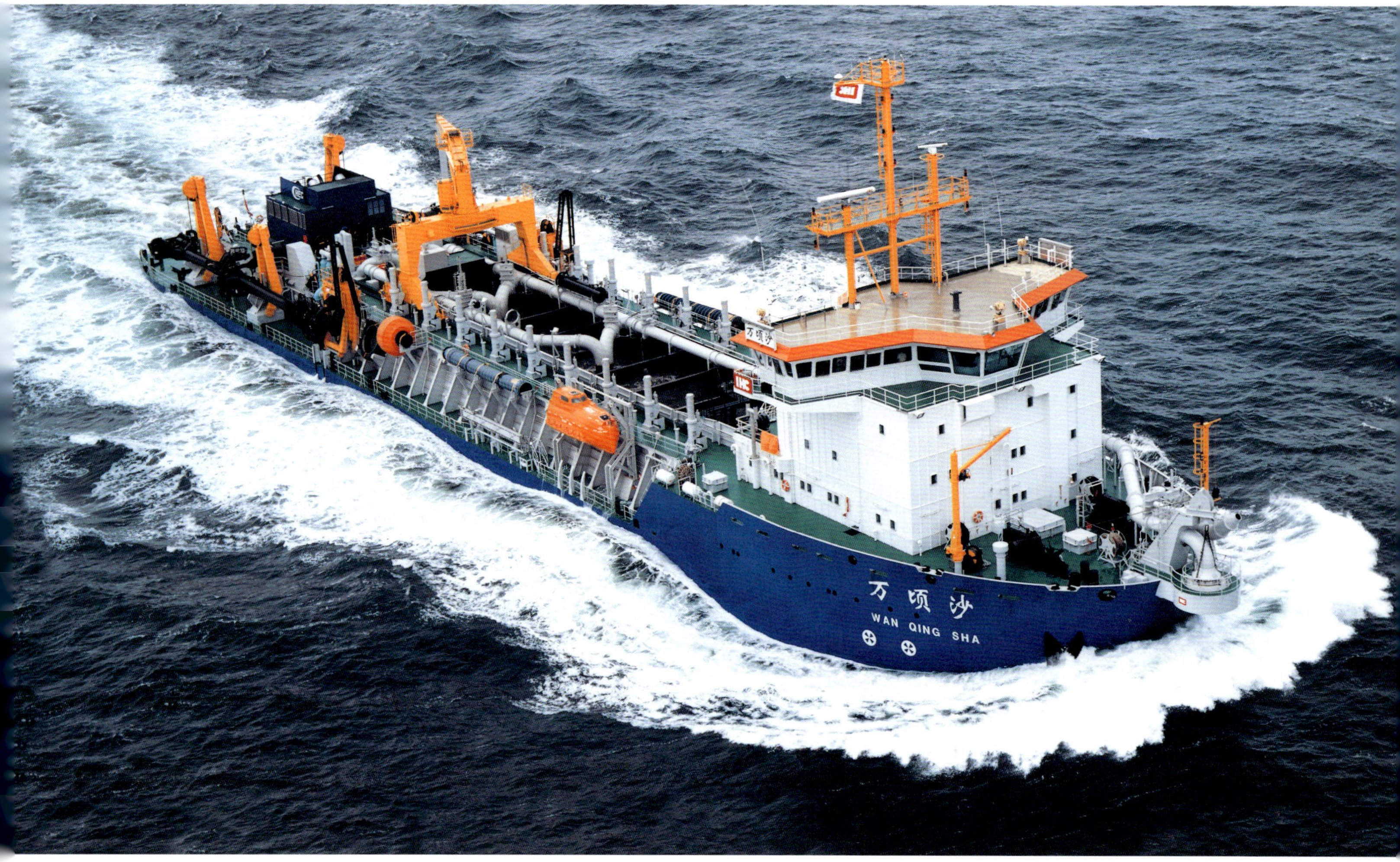

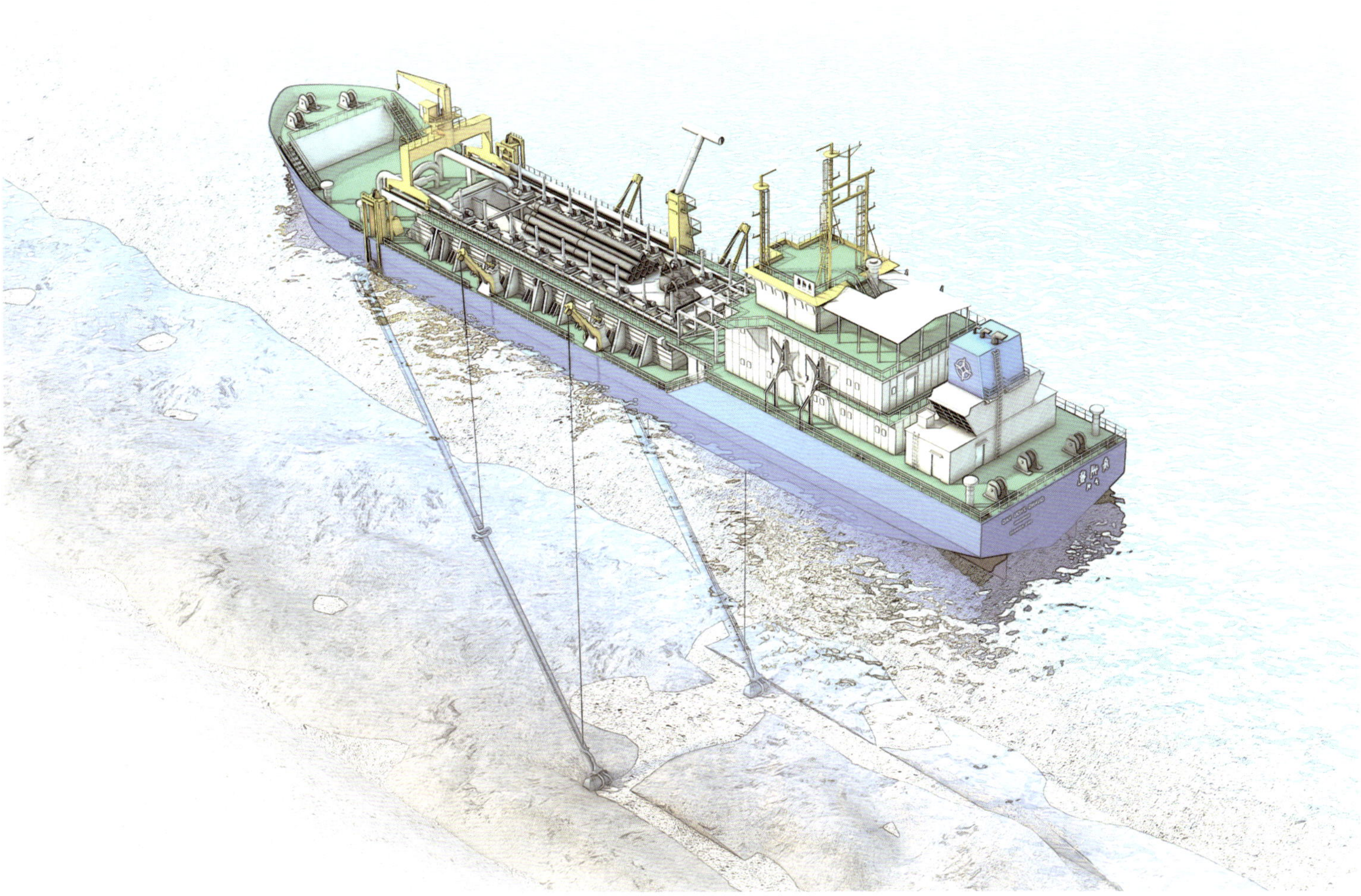

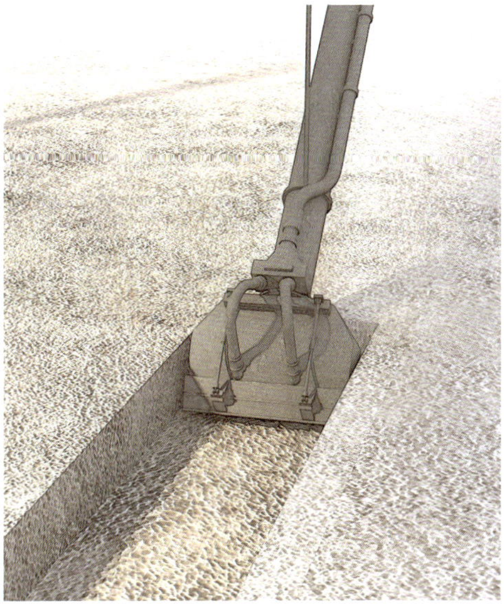

1. "万顷沙"耙吸船
Cutter Suction Dredger "Wanqingsha"

2. 隧道基础粗挖三维图
3-D Diagram of Deep Excavation

3. 耙吸船耙头水下施工三维图
3-D Diagram of Underwater Operation of the Cutter Suction Dredger

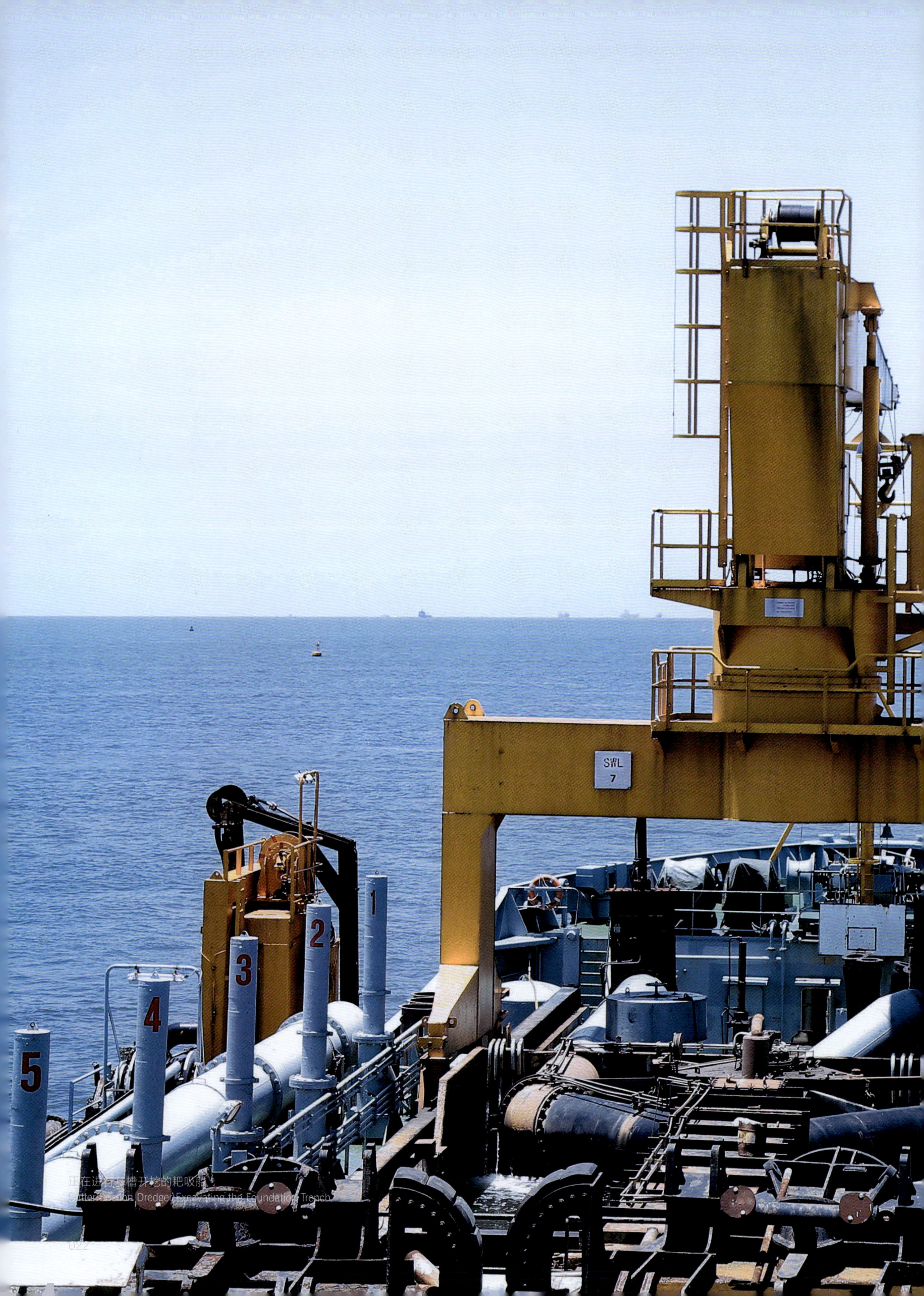

正在进行基槽开挖的耙吸船
Cutter Suction Dredger Excavating the Foundation Trench

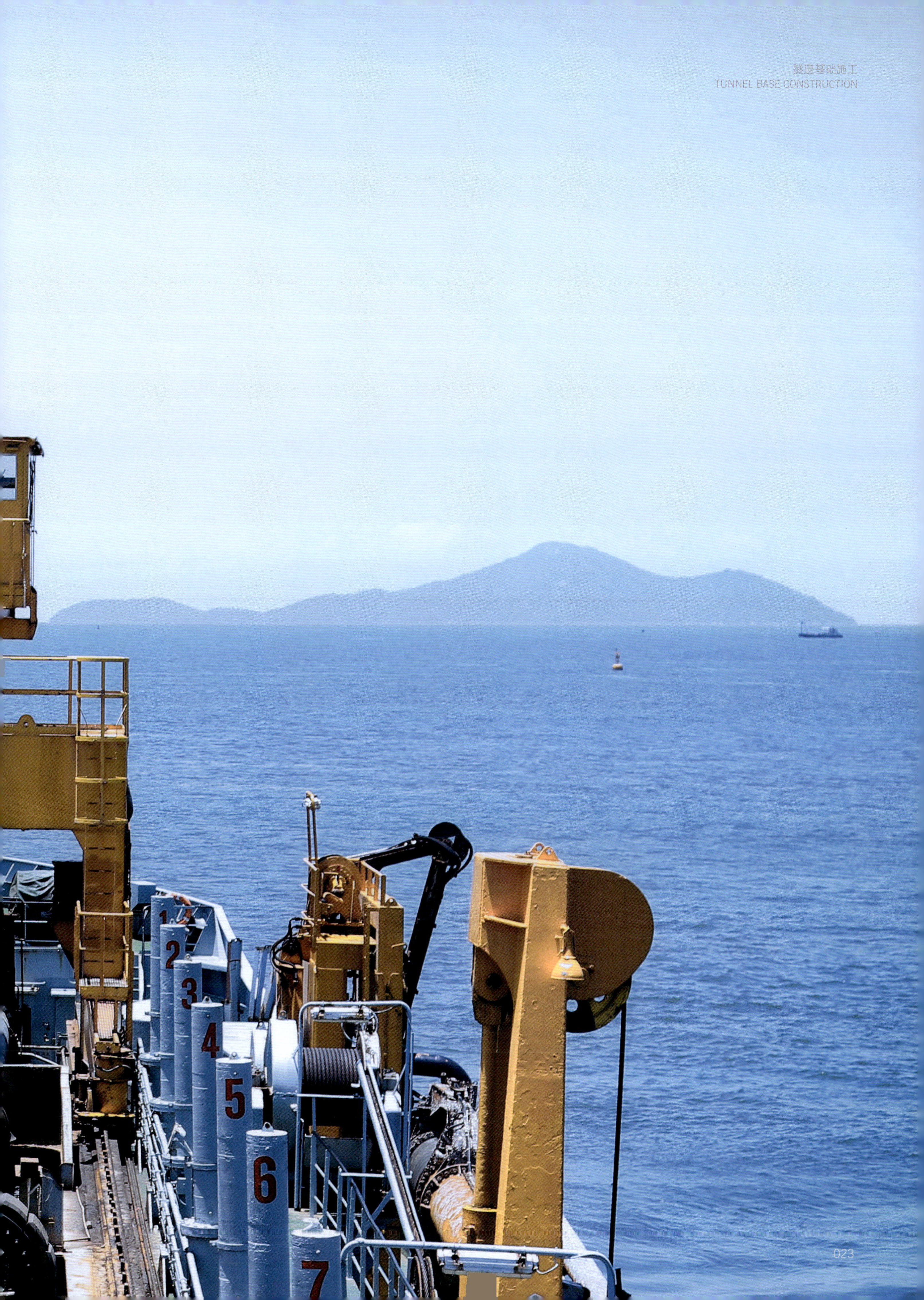
1
2
3
4
5
6
7

基槽精挖

FINE EXCAVATION OF THE FOUNDATION TRENCH

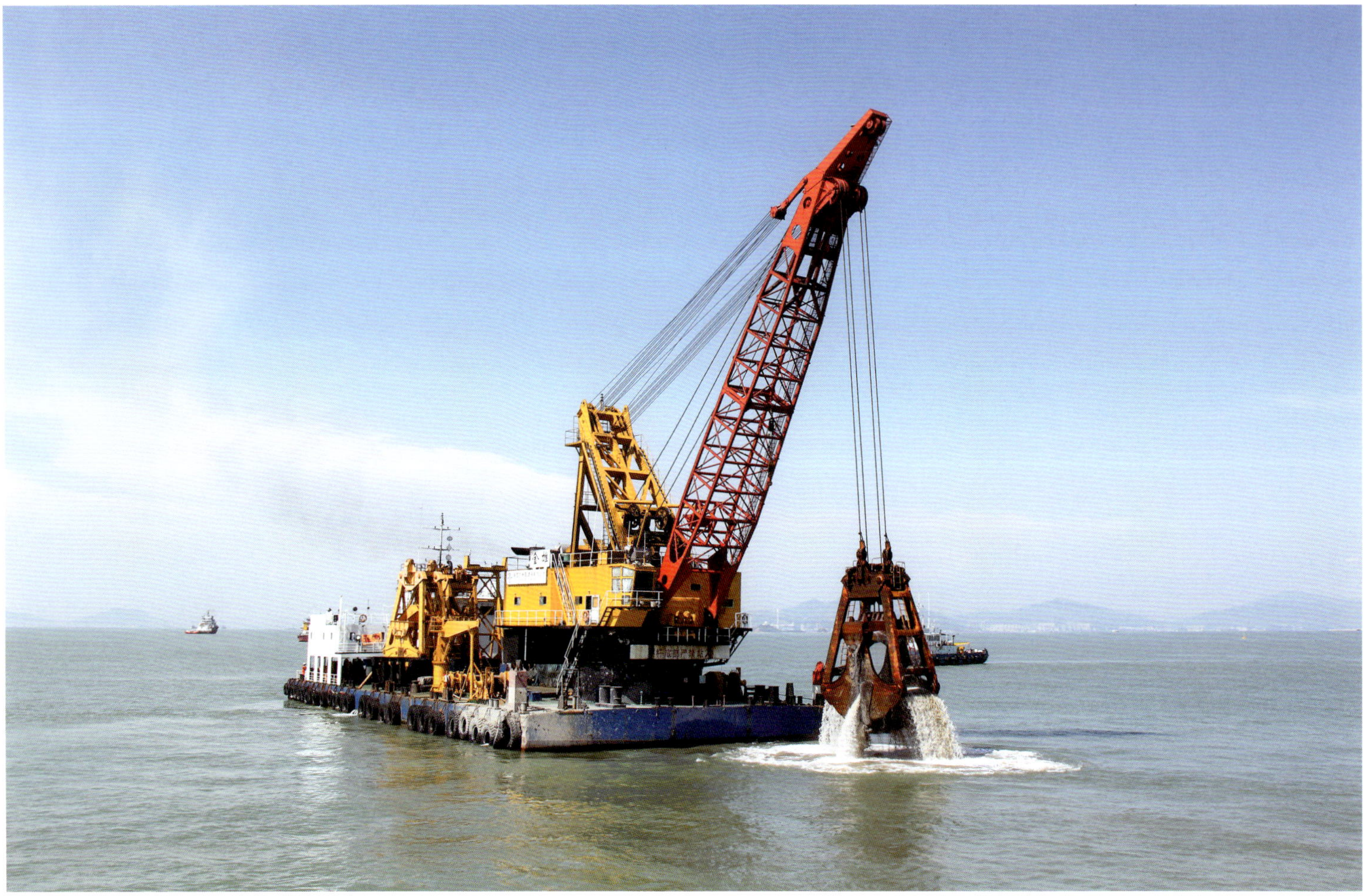

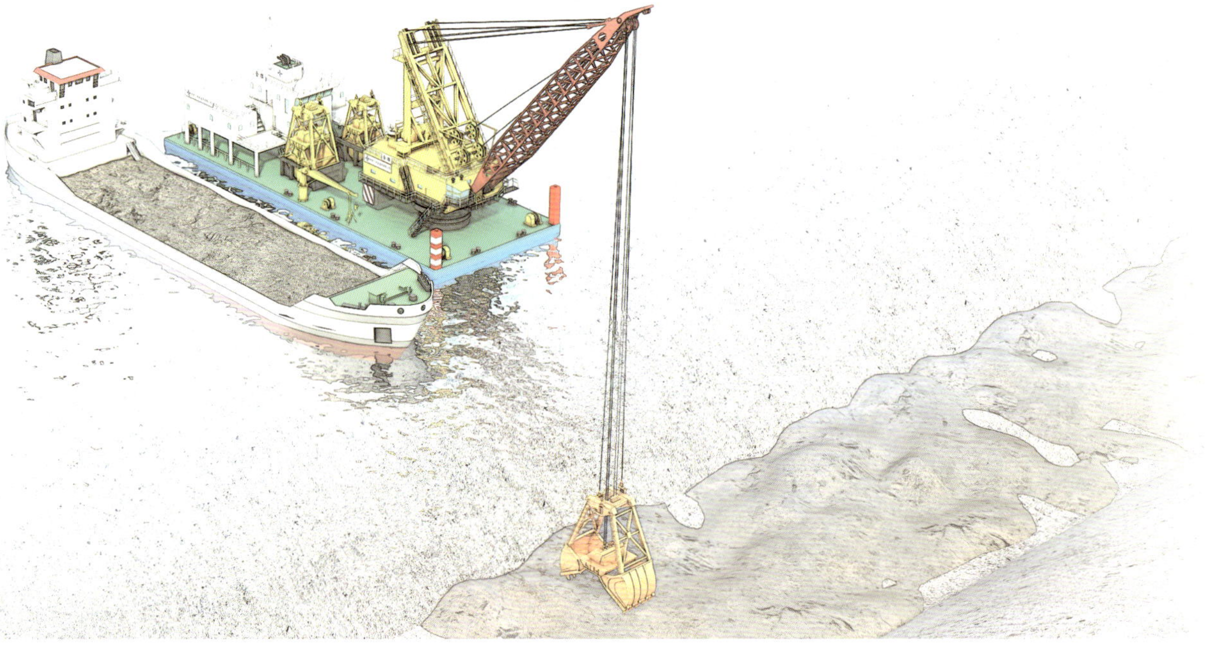

基槽精挖是指隧道基槽粗挖完成后至设计边线垂直厚度约3米的泥层开挖，范围包括基槽槽底精挖及边坡成型区开挖。

港珠澳大桥海底隧道采用了30立方米大型抓斗船进行基槽精挖施工。

该船具备锚缆定位功能，配备海底地形声呐实时探知系统，实时显示开挖过程中水下地形；新开发了定深、平挖功能，在50米水深条件下基槽开挖精度控制在约+40～-60厘米。

突破传统抓斗挖泥船挖掘控制模式，研发了新的高程控制模式。

该船采用RTK-GPS控制高程基准，通过计算机与设备微调系统，增加超深限制、综合偏差调整等功能，实时控制抓斗吊缆长度、抓斗闭合轨迹，消除船舶施工时受潮位、风浪流、斗重变化、船舶吃水等因素影响，实现自动定深和闭斗过程斗唇轨迹线水平移动的平挖功能。

Fine excavation of the foundation trench is excavating the silt 3 meters by vertical elevation downward from the place where the deep excavation reaches to the designed surface, including fine excavation of the foundation trench bottom and the moulding area of the side slopes.

Large-scaled grab dredgers of a volume of 30 cubic meters were used for the fine excavation in the construction of the underwater tunnel of Hong Kong-Zhuhai-Macau Bridge.

The dredgers were equipped with mooring and positioning system and real-time seabed terrain sonar detecting system which were used to display the underwater terrain during excavation. Its new functions of depth detecting and level excavating helped fine excavation in the water of 50 meters deep with an accuracy limit between +40 and -60 centimeters.

A breakthrough was made in the excavation technology that traditional grab dredgers employed, and a new vertical control mode was developed.

These dredgers adopted the RTK-GPS vertical control standard, and made use of the computer and the equipment fine adjustment system to reinforce its super-deep control and integrated deviation adjustment capabilities for the real-time control of the cable length of the grab and the closing trajectory of the grab, so as to eliminate the negative influences by the tide, winds, bucket weight and the vessel's draft, and to realize automatic depth detecting and exert its level excavating function when the grab lip moved horizontally in the process of its closure.

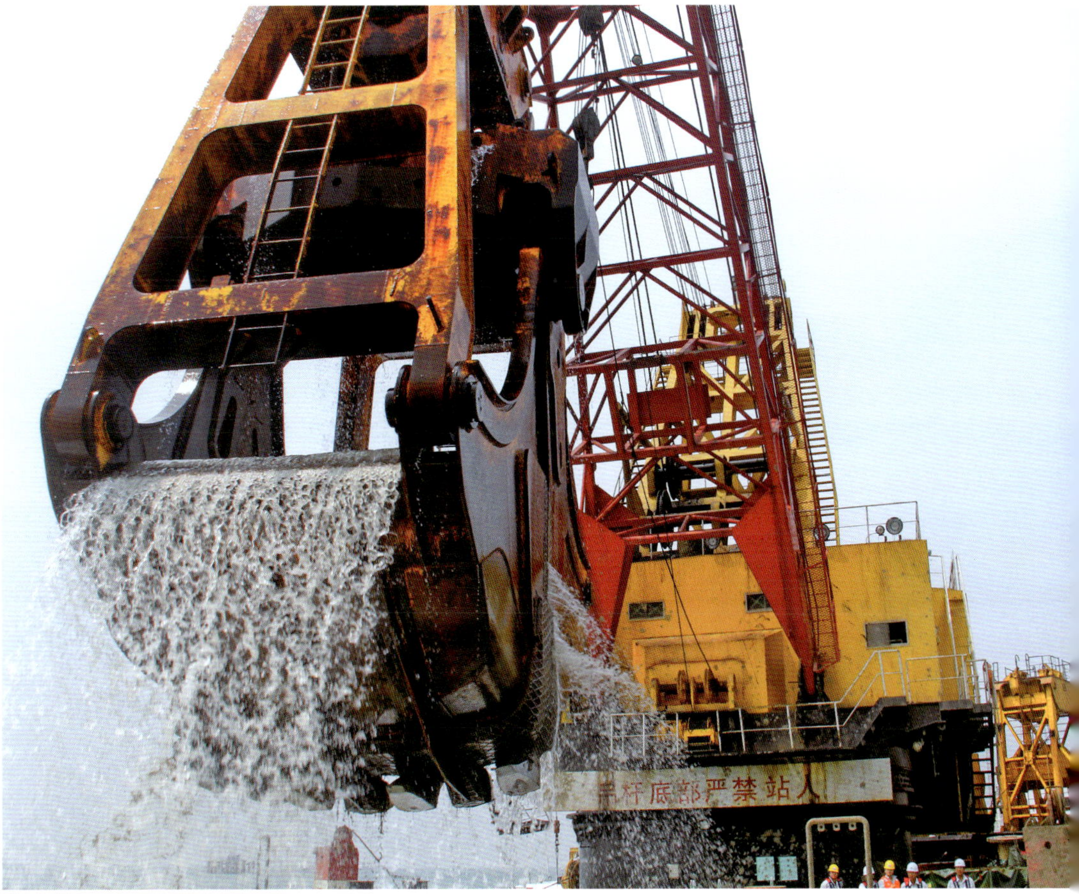

1. 正在进行基槽精挖的抓斗船"金雄"轮
Grab Dredger "Jinxiong" during Fine Excavation of the Foundation Trench

2. 基槽精挖示意图
Schematic Diagram of Fine Excavation of the Foundation Trench

3. 具有平挖功能的"金雄"轮抓斗
Grab of Dredger "Jinxiong" with the Function of Level Excavation

精挖设备技术改造

TECHNICAL ADAPTATION OF FINE EXCAVATION EQUIPMENT

在常规疏浚工程中，抓斗挖泥船一般都采用水深控制模式作业。

该模式需要进行潮位基准面与工程设计高程的转换，受潮位、风浪流、斗重变化等多因素影响，偏差较大。

同时，常规抓斗的闭斗轨迹为“W”型曲线，施工后形成的水下地形高差值较大。

特别是抓斗斗容越大，其在水下形成的高差就越大。

为确保隧道基槽开挖精度，通过对典型施工偏差因素的系统性分析，提出一种新型的抓斗挖泥船开挖控制方法，由计算机控制系统对抓斗挖泥过程的高程进行实时控制，达到有效控制开挖精度的效果。

为避免超挖以及对槽底原状土的扰动，自主研发了抓斗挖泥船智能控制操作系统，替换挖泥船原有的定深控制系统。

应用传感器、网络通讯、计算机、机电一体化、机械配套加工等工业技术，进行船机设备适应性升级和优化，实现挖泥施工过程的可视、可控、可测。

In a normal dredging project, grab dredgers usually employ water-depth control mode.

This mode requires the conversion between the standard tidal front and the designed height by the project, and is easy to be affected by such factors as the tide, winds, bucket weight and others, the result of which is the significant deviation.

Besides, the usual closing trajectory of the grab follows the “W” mode of curve, whereby the underwater terrain's elevation differences are large after the construction.

The bigger the capacity of the grab is, the larger the underwater elevation differences are.

To guarantee the high degree of precision for the foundation trench excavation, a systematic analysis was done about the typical factors in the process of excavation that might cause the deviation. Based on this analysis, a new excavation control method was designed for grab dredgers, whereby a computer was used for the real-time control of the grab's elevation, yet in this way, the excavation precision was guaranteed.

To avoid over-excavation and disturbance of the undisturbed soil at the trench bottom, an intelligence control system for grab dredgers was invented to replace the old depth control system.

Such technologies as sensors, network communication, computers and mechatronics were used for the visualization, monitoring and control of the whole excavation process.

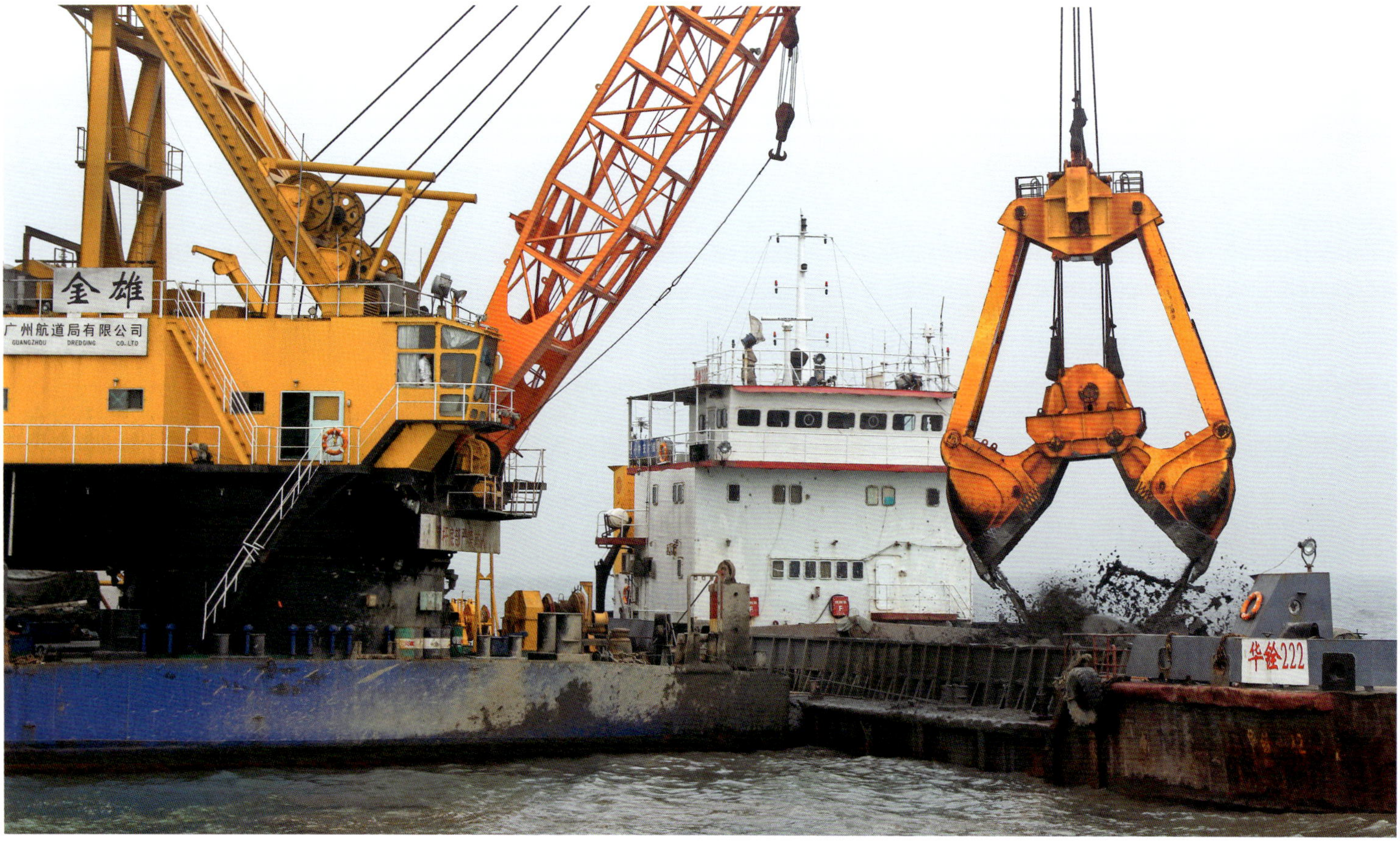

1. 隧道基础开挖装驳作业
   Excavating, Loading and Shipping in Tunnel Base Construction
2. “金雄”轮船位控制
   Anchoring of Dredger “Jinxiong”
3. “金雄”轮精挖轨迹图
   Trajectory Diagram of Fine Excavation of Dredger “Jinxiong”
4. 精挖过程施工质量监测与控制
   Fine Excavation Quality Test and Control
5. 精挖原理图
   Schematic Diagram of Fine Excavation

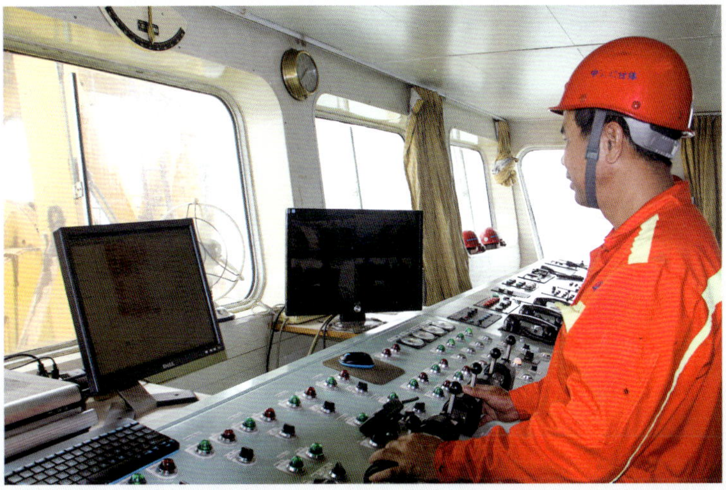

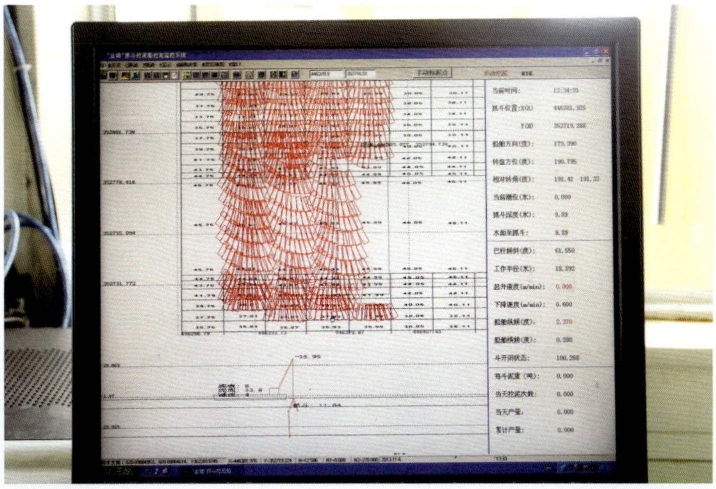

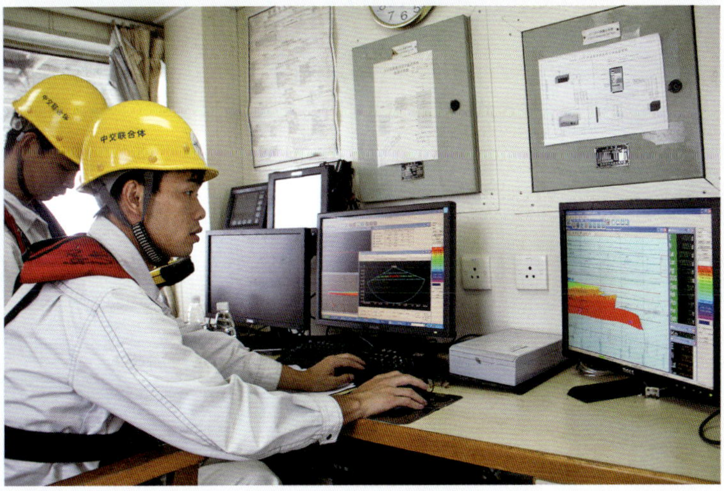

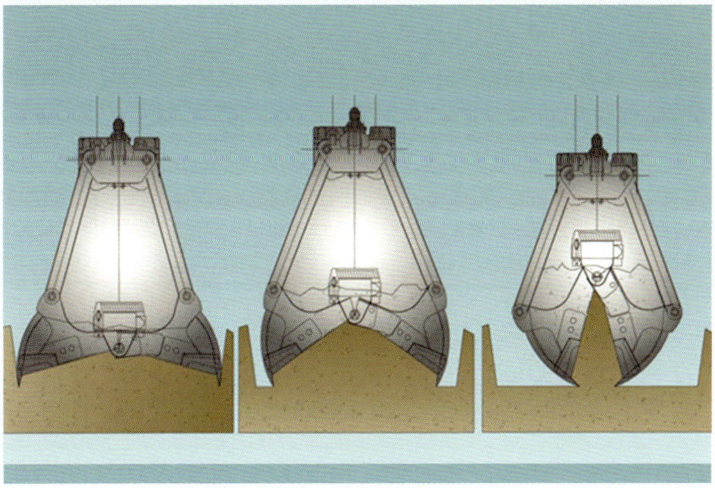

基床抛石夯平
BEDDING ROCK FILLING, COMPACTING AND LEVELING

1. 隧道块石基础溜管式定点抛填施工三维图
   3-D Diagram of Spot Dumped Rockfill through Tipping Pipe in Tunnel Base Construction
2. 水下夯平施工三维图
   3-D Diagram of Underwater Compacting and Leveling

3—4. "振驳 28"进行抛石夯平施工
"Zhenbo 28" during Rockfilling, Compacting and Leveling

研发深水抛石夯平一体化装备，解决外海深水块石基床抛填和夯实技术难题。

采用溜管式定点定量抛填工艺抛填2.0米厚块石，利用APE600液压振动锤进行夯平密实，实现了夯平面平整度±30厘米要求，大幅提升了施工质量和效率。

Integrated equipments for rock filling, compacting and leveling was invented to cope with such technological operations as offshore deep water rock filling and compacting.

The technique of spot filling of fixed volume by tipping pipe was used for big rocks of 2 meters in diameter, and hydraulic vibratory hammers of APE600 type were used for compacting and leveling to meet the requirements for compaction plane flatness within the limit of ±30 centimeters, which considerably improved the project's quality and efficiency.

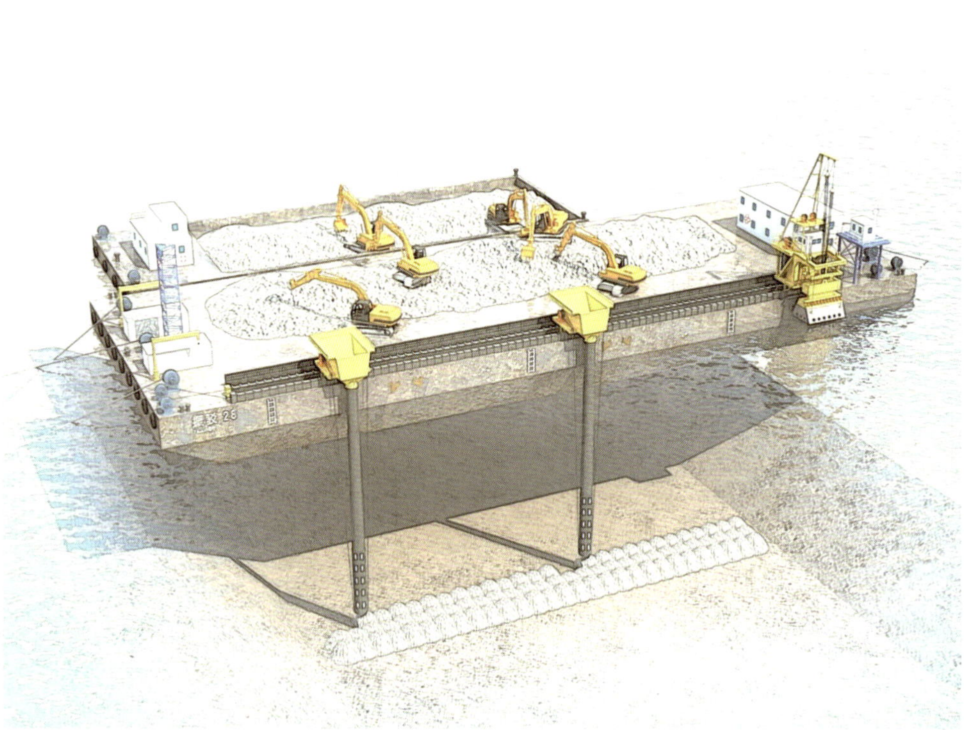

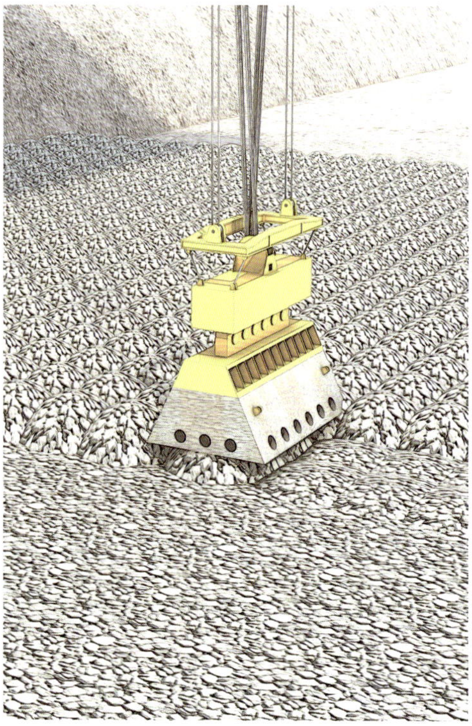

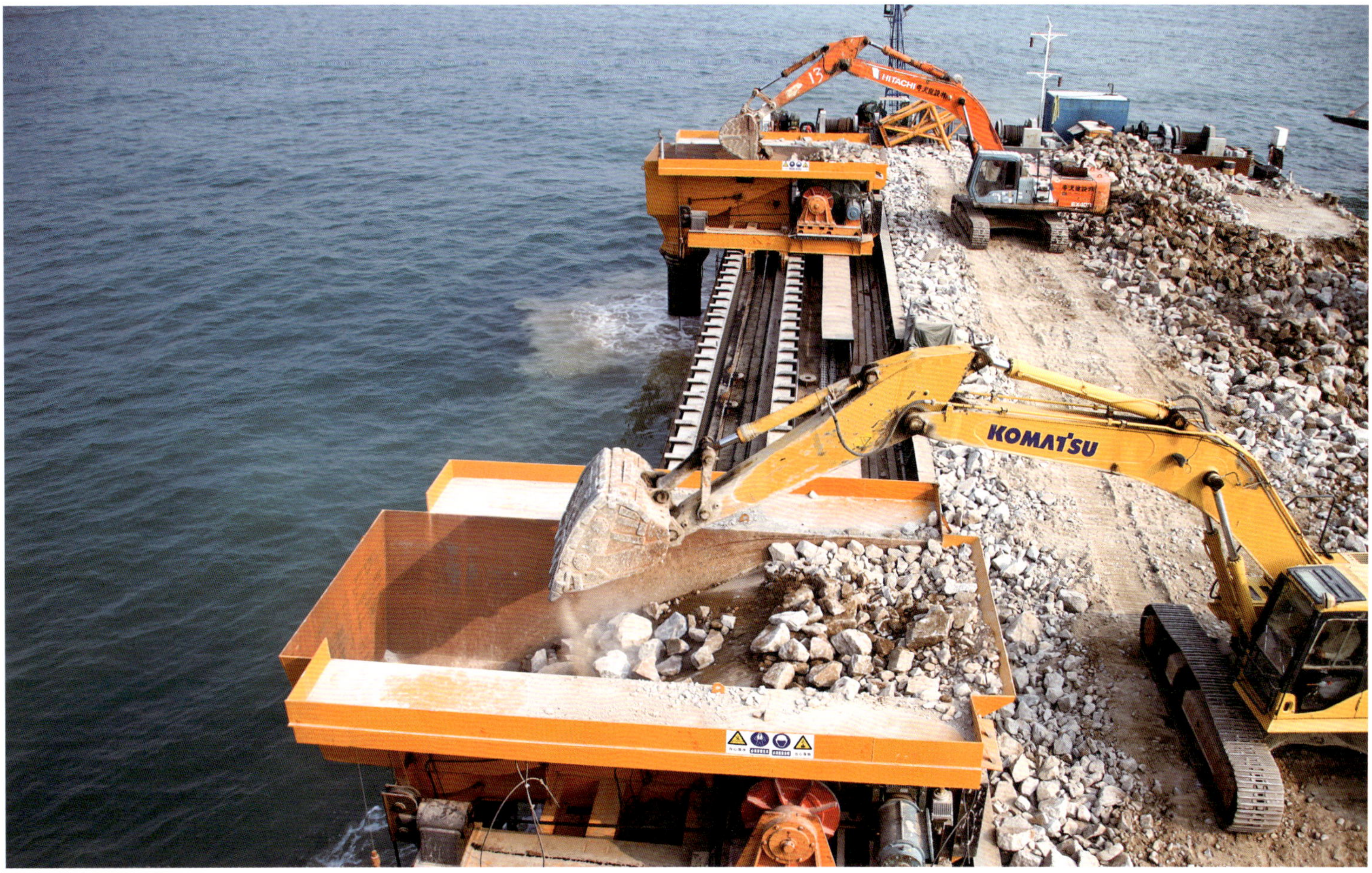
HITACHI
KOMATSU

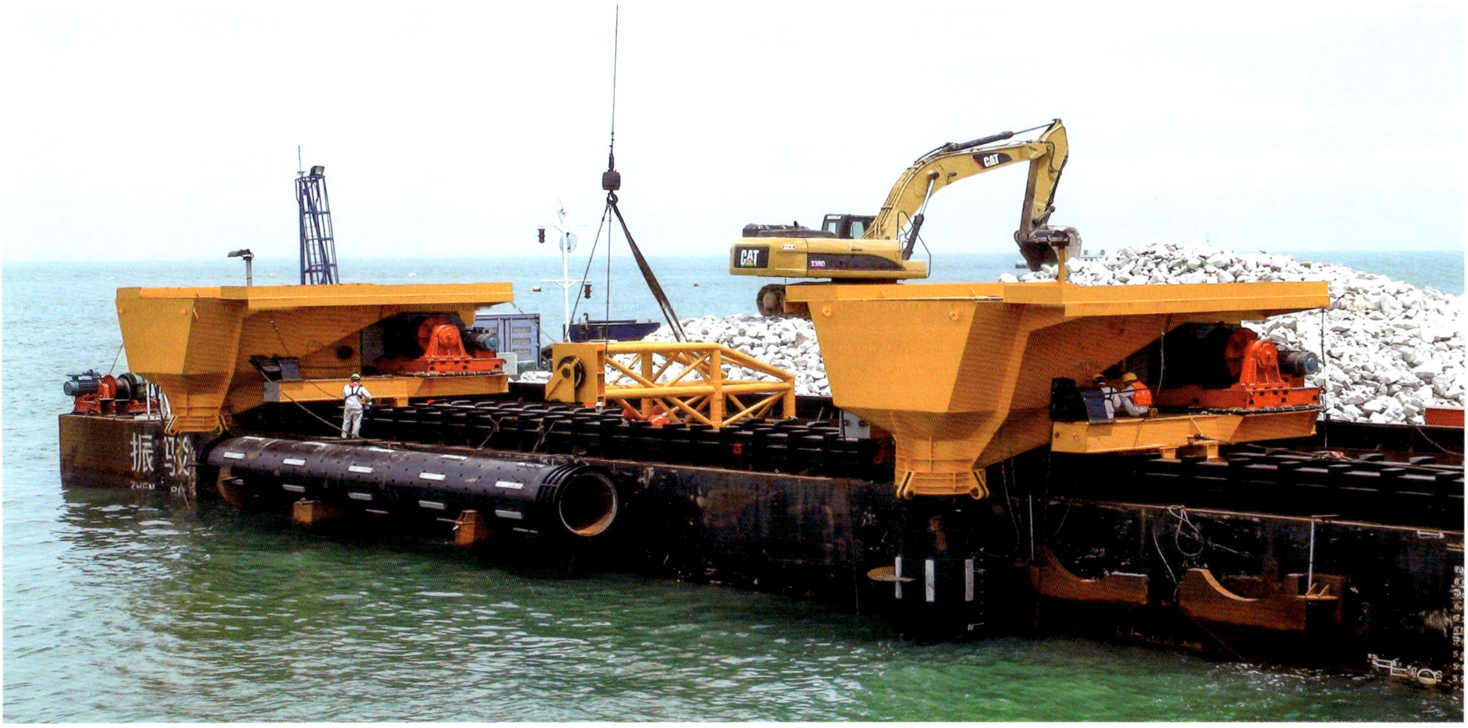
CAT

碎石基床整平
BEDDING RUBBLE LEVELING

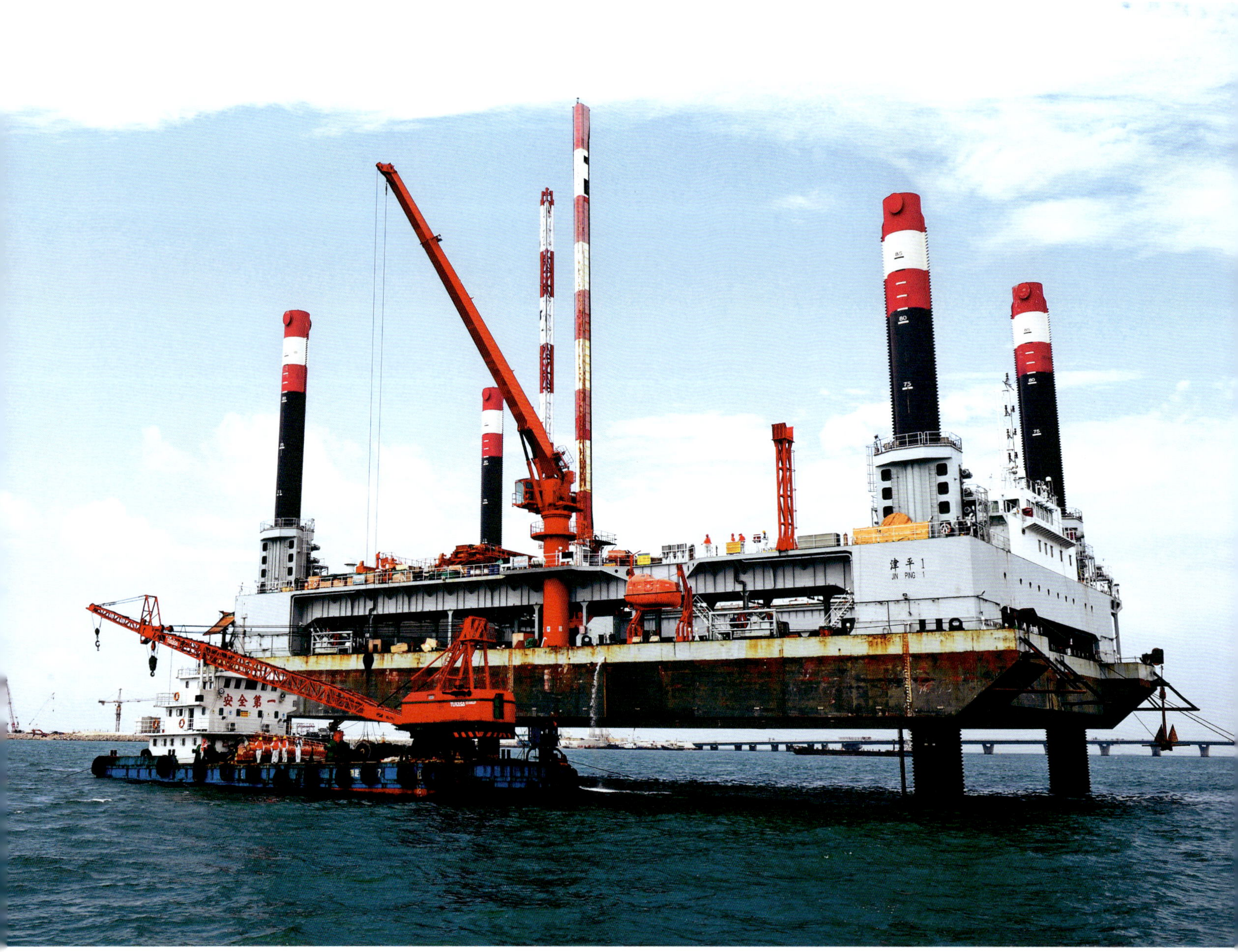

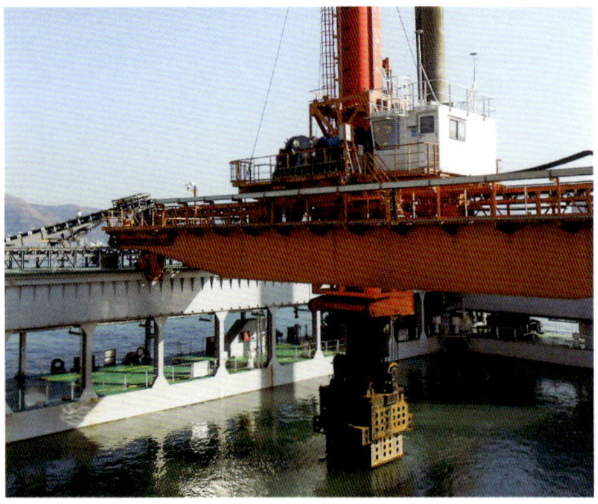

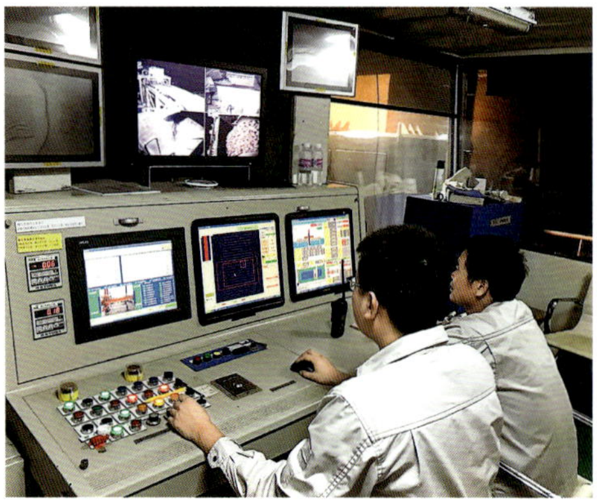

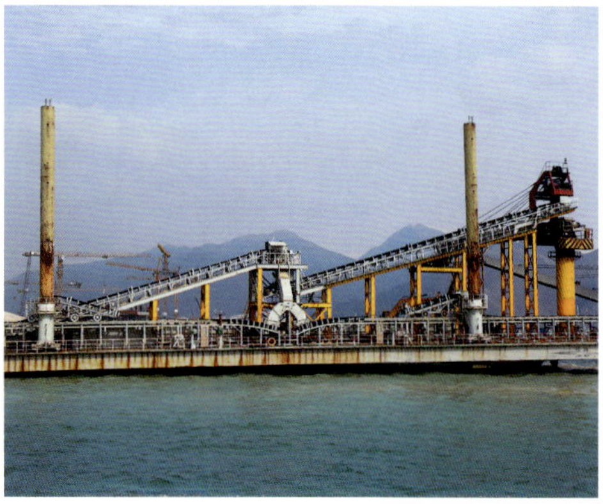

1. "津平 1"碎石整平船
Rubble Leveling Barge "Jinping 1"
2. 碎石整平头
Rubble Leveling Head
3. 可视化监控系统
Visualized Monitoring System
4. "经纬"运料船
Carrier Barge "Jingwei"
5. 碎石基床整平施工三维图
3-D Diagram of Bedding Rubble Leveling

沉管隧道碎石基床整平面积达 24.2 万平方米；整平坡度变化大，纵坡 0.30%~2.98% 不等；标高控制难度大，水深在 15~45 米；整平精度高，误差 ±40 毫米；对整平工艺提出了极高的要求。

为此，集成开发制造平台式高精度碎石基床整平船及测控系统，进行碎石垫层的铺设作业。

平台式整平船集抛石、整平和检测三道工序于一体，有效减少了风、浪、流的影响，保证了质量，提高了工效。

抛石整平管理系统采用实时检测、自动控制等先进技术，保证了 50 米作业水深时施工精度达到 ±40 毫米的要求，实现了 8 个有效工作日内完成单节 180 米沉管碎石基床整平的作业效率。

The total coverage of the tunnel trench bed for rubble leveling was 242,000 square meters; the leveled slope gradients changed drastically and the longitudinal gradients lied between 0.30% and 2.98%; elevation control was difficult and water depth was between 15 and 45 meters; high degree of leveling precision was achieved with an error within the limit of ±40 millimeters. All these required advanced leveling techniques.

Platform-based high-precision rubble bed leveling barge and monitoring system were developed for the placement of the rubble bedding.

Platform-based leveling barges combined rock filling, leveling and testing into one, which effectively counterbalanced the influences of the winds, waves and stream flows. And thus the project quality and efficiency were guaranteed.

The rock filling and leveling system employed such techniques as real-time monitoring and automatic control to meet the demands for the operation precision within the limit of ±40 millimeters underneath the water of 50 meters deep. By this system, the rubble bed leveling operation for one immersed tube of 180 meters long could be finished within 8 working days.

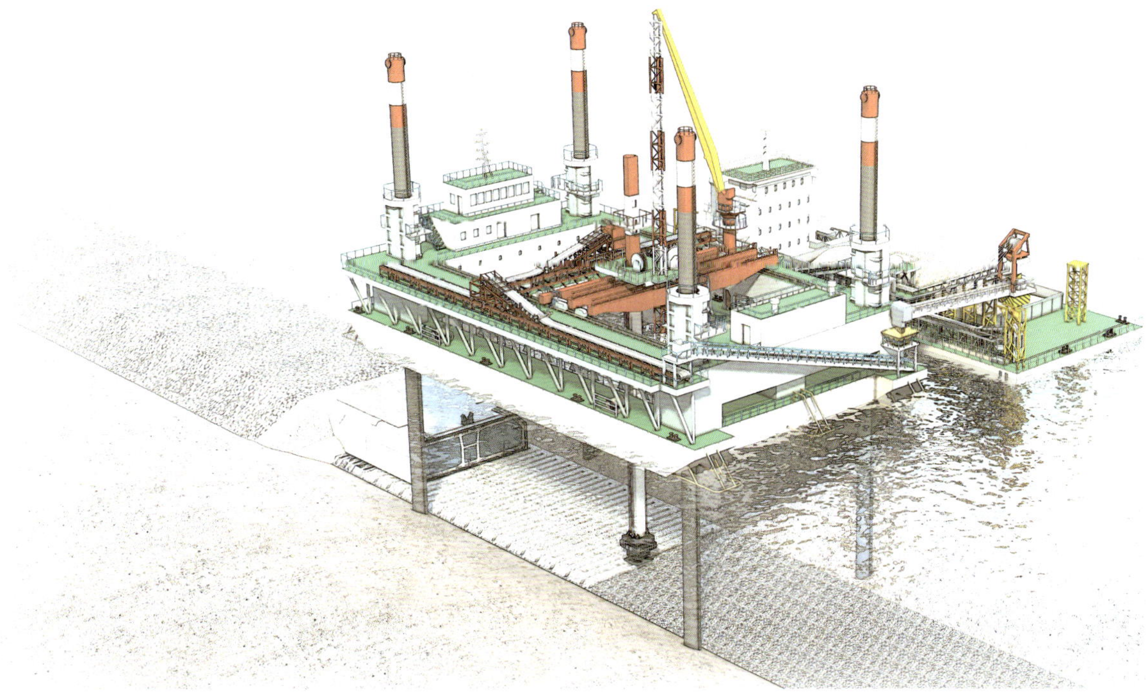

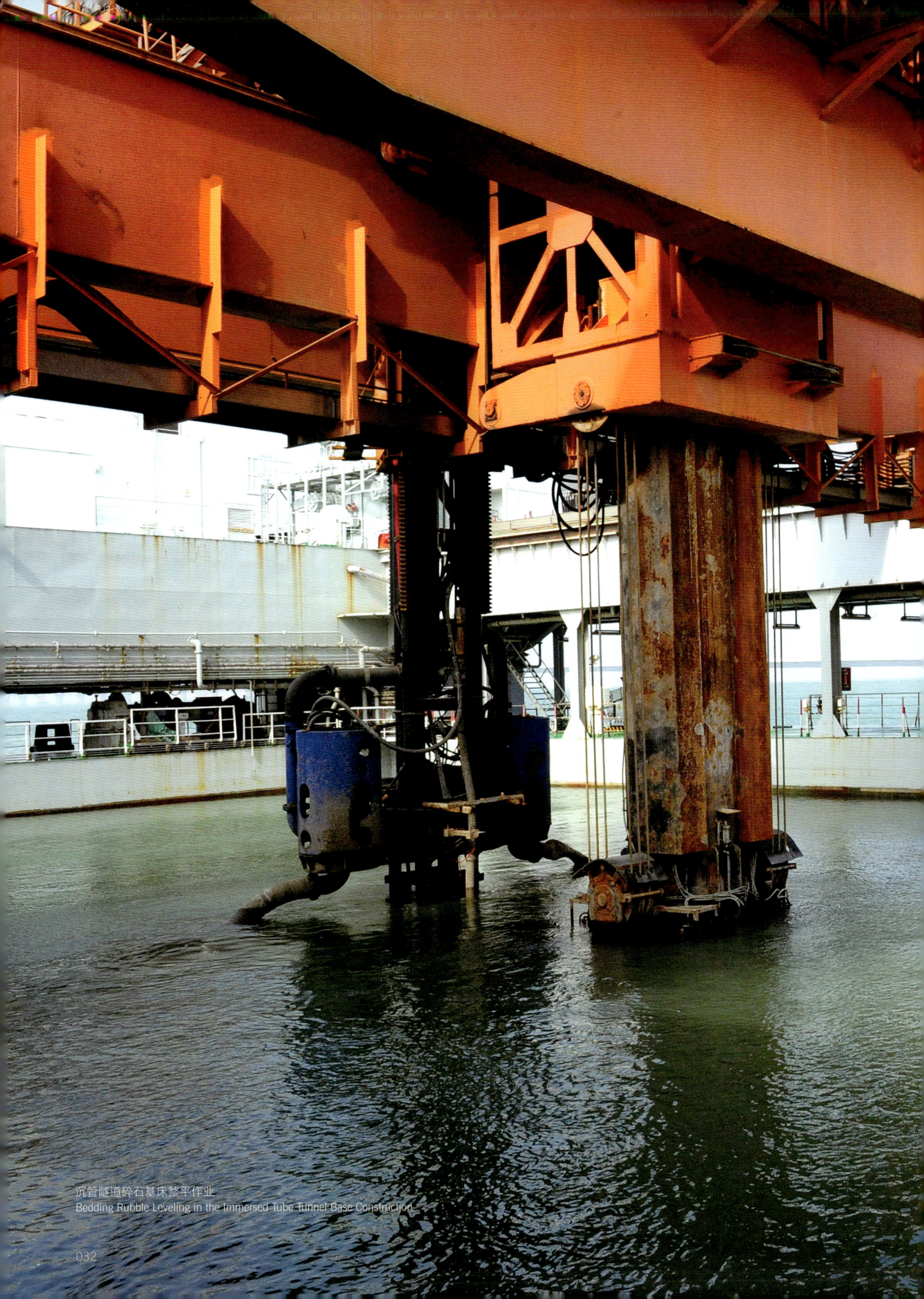

沉管隧道碎石基床整平作业
Bedding Rubble Leveling in the Immersed Tube Tunnel Base Construction

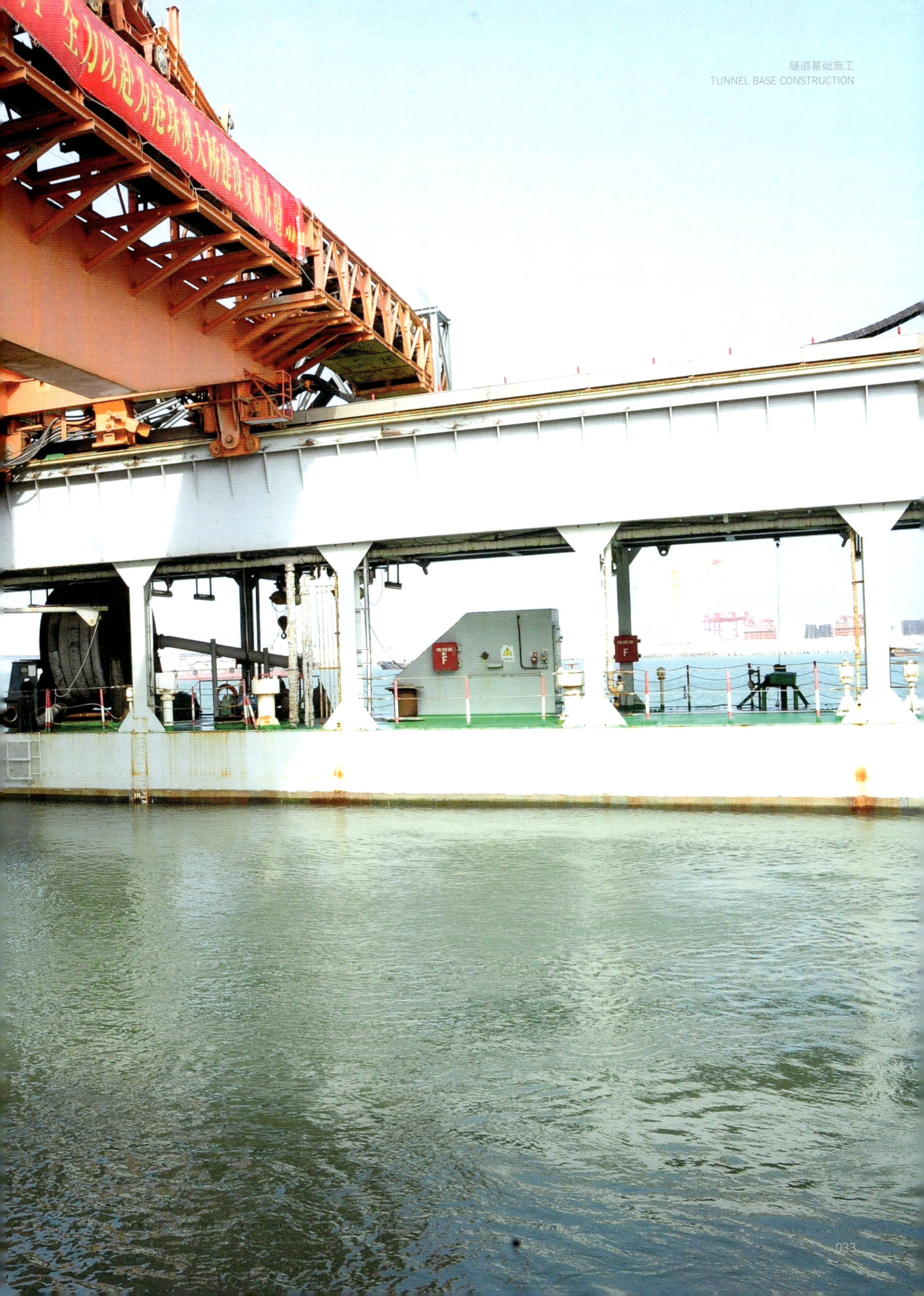
全力以赴为港珠澳大桥建设贡献力量

基槽清淤和防淤

FOUNDATION TRENCH DREDGING AND SILT PREVENTING

基槽清淤是指粗挖结束后至精挖前、抛石夯平前、碎石整平前对基槽、边坡淤积泥沙的清除，以及碎石基床铺设后对基床面回淤浮泥层的清除。

项目总经理部集成开发一系列清淤技术，具备深槽高边坡、块石基床面和碎石基床面的组合式高效清淤能力。

采用专用定点清淤船完成块石基床面上的清淤。

该船充分考虑了对基床面的保护，具备先进的定点吸淤能力和高效的清淤效率，满足50米水深精确清淤要求；通过音叉式高精度密度仪、高清摄像头实现清淤效果的实时监测，能适应基槽清淤和块石基床面清淤，同时有效降低清淤施工对已安沉管钢封门造成破坏的风险。

边坡清淤是指对基槽复合边坡上的淤积物进行精确清除。

2014年底，由于受上游采砂影响，E15沉管安装过程中先后遭遇了基槽突淤和边坡淤积物滑塌，致使近半年时间无法安装沉管。

复合边坡大面积、高精度清淤成为新的难题。

项目总经理部在国内首次成功应用具有动力定位、动态航迹系统及疏浚轨迹导航系统的大型耙吸船，在保证边坡稳定性的前提下，高效率完成了大面积、大方量的复合边坡回淤物清除施工，完美解决了沉管基槽复合边坡淤积物高精度清淤难题，为后续沉管安装提供了坚实保障。

Foundation trench desilting means removing the sediments in the foundation trench and on the side slopes after deep excavation is done but before fine excavation, rock filling, compacting and leveling, and before rubble bedding leveling, as well as removing the back silt on the foundation trench bed after the rubble bedding placement is done.

The project management center developed a series of dredging technologies which were combined to effectively clean the sediments on the side slope of the trench, the rock bed and the rubble bed.

Specially designed spot dredgers were used to clean the sediments on the rock bed.

The dredgers took into consideration the protection of the trench bed, highly effective in spot dredging, and met the demands for the dredging task 50 meters underneath the water. High-precision tuning fork densimeter and HD camera made real-time monitoring possible in the process of dredging, and were used for desilting the foundation trench and the rock bed. The devices could also reduce the risks of damage during the dredging operation to the installed steel sealing devices of the immersed tube.

Side slope dredging means removing the sediments on the composite side slope of the foundation trench.

Towards the end of 2014, as a result of upstream sand mining, the installation of the immersed tube E15 was disrupted by the unexpected sediments in the foundation trench and the collapse of the sediments from the side slope, resulting in a half year's suspension of the installation project.

So the large coverage of the composite side slope and high-precision dredging became new challenges for the project.

The project management center, for the first time in China, made use of the large-scaled cutter suction dredgers with powered positioning system, dynamic flight path system and dredging path navigation system, which, while taking into consideration the stability of the side slope, could effectively accomplish cleaning the immense volume of back-silted sediments on a large area and solved the problems involved in the high-precision dredging on the composite side slope of the foundation trench for the immersed tubes. This proved to be a solid support for later installation of the immersed tubes.

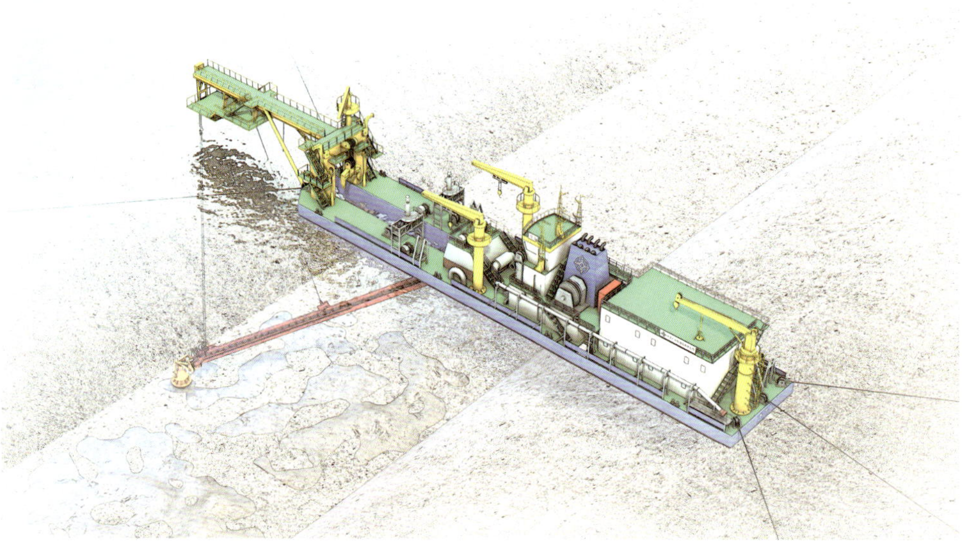

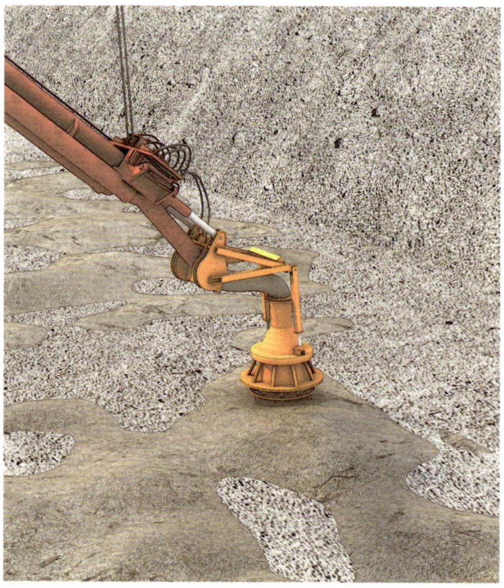

1. 基槽清淤施工三维图
   3-D Diagram of the Foundation Trench Dredging
2. "盖章式"定点清淤三维图
   3-D Diagram of the Sealing-Mode Spot Dredging
3. 清淤头
   Dredging Head
4. 清淤船"捷龙"轮
   Dredger "Jielong"

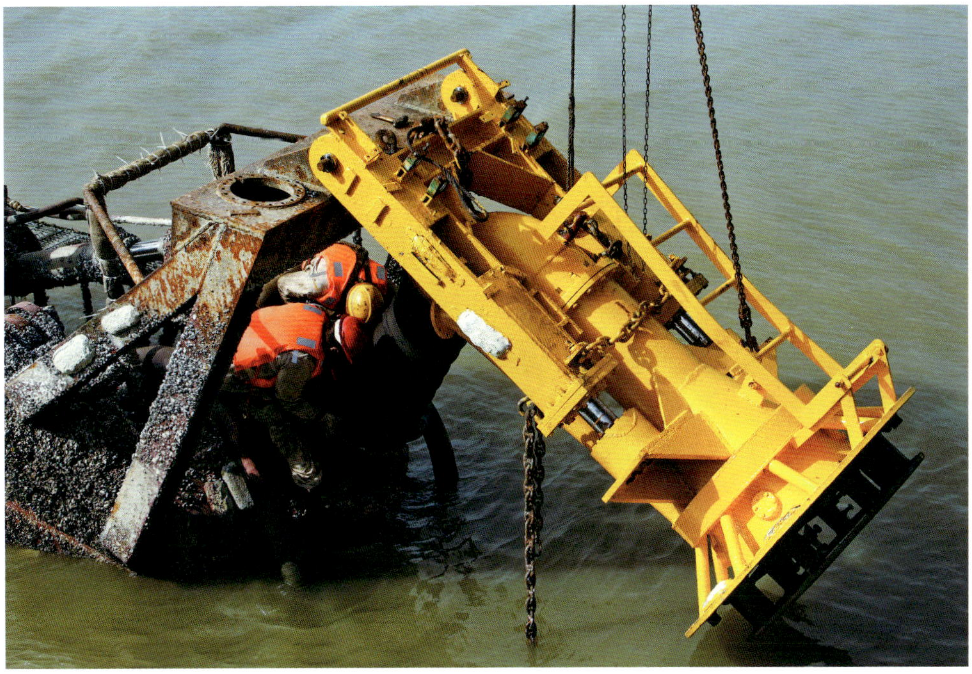

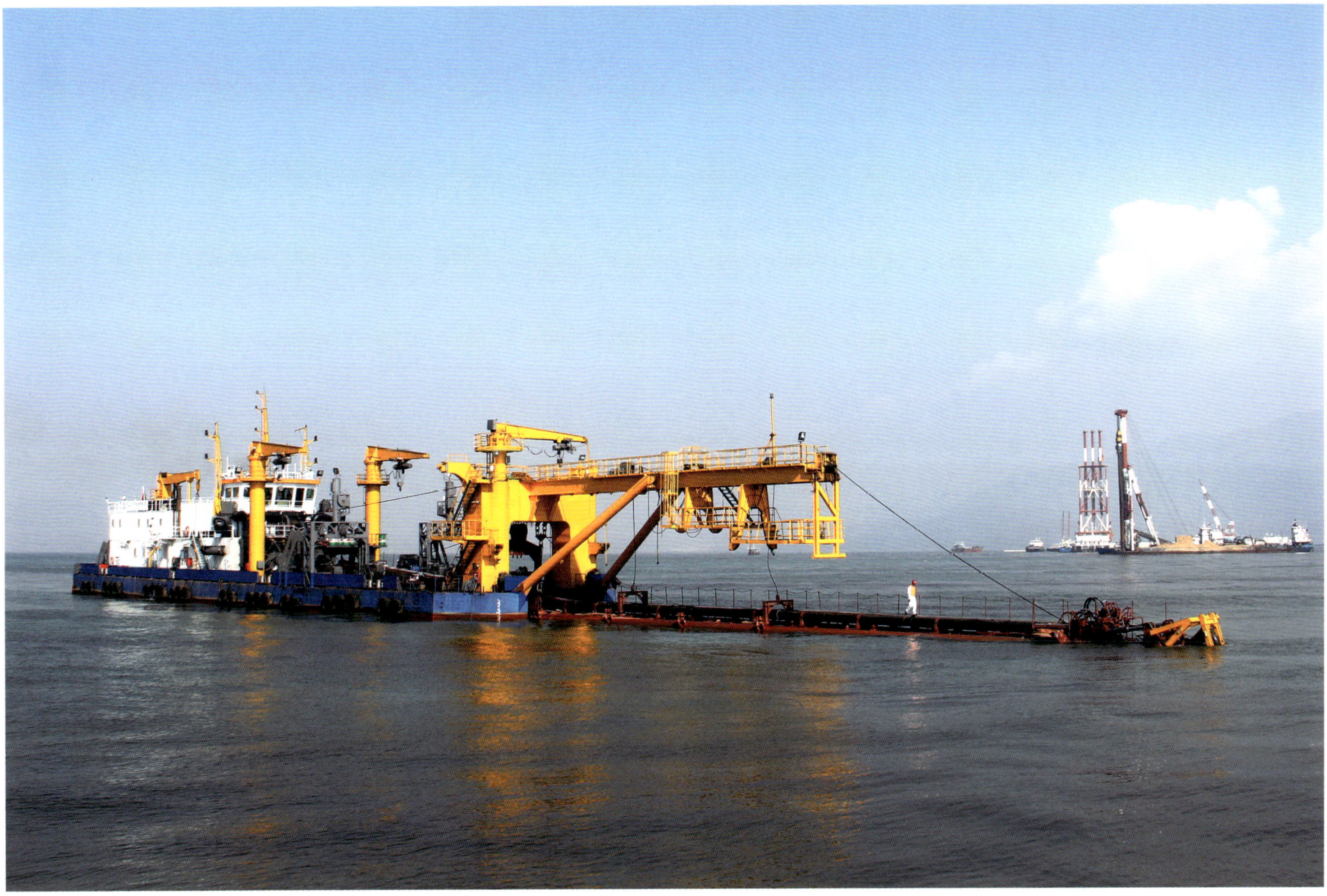

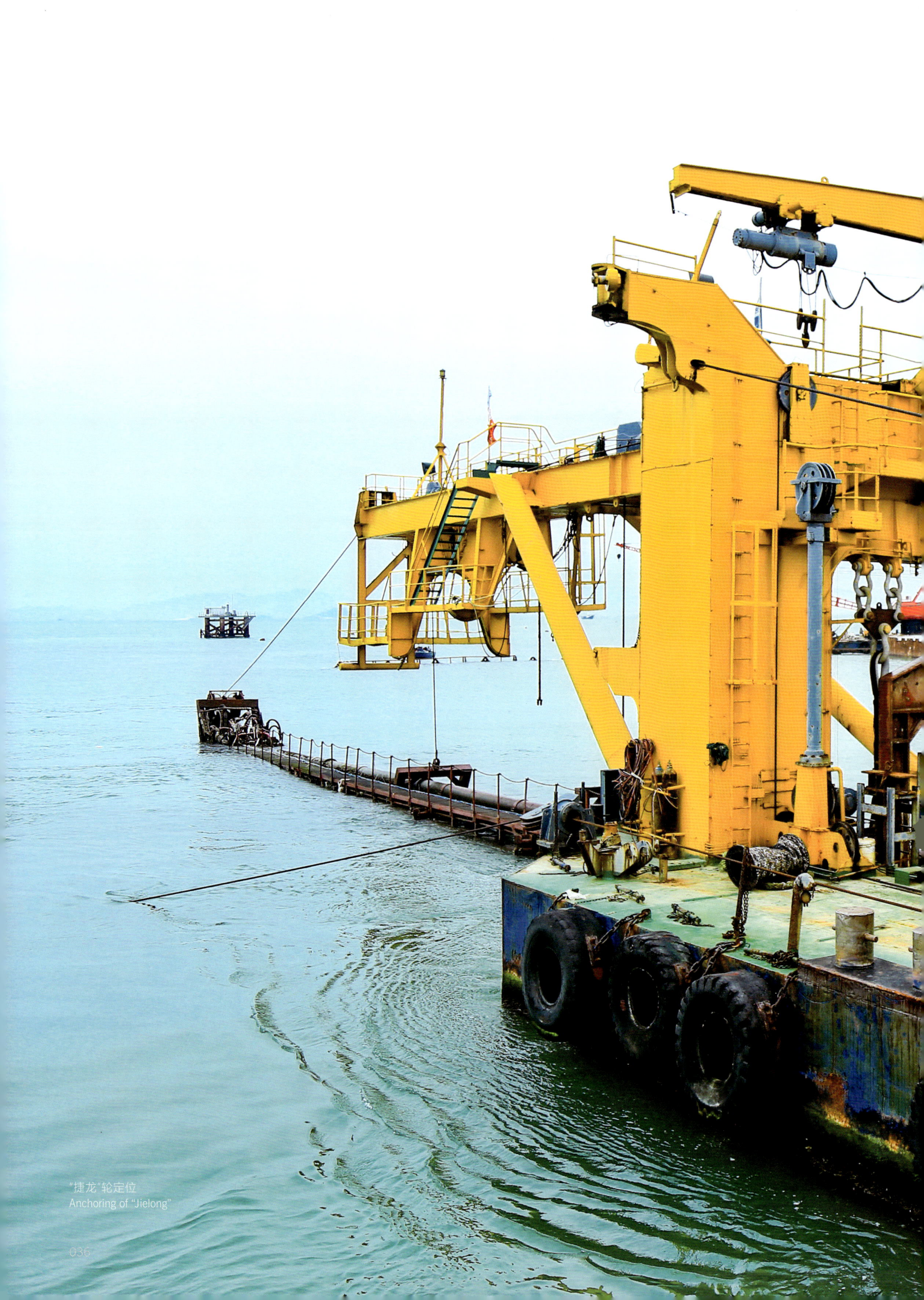

"捷龙"轮定位
Anchoring of "Jielong"

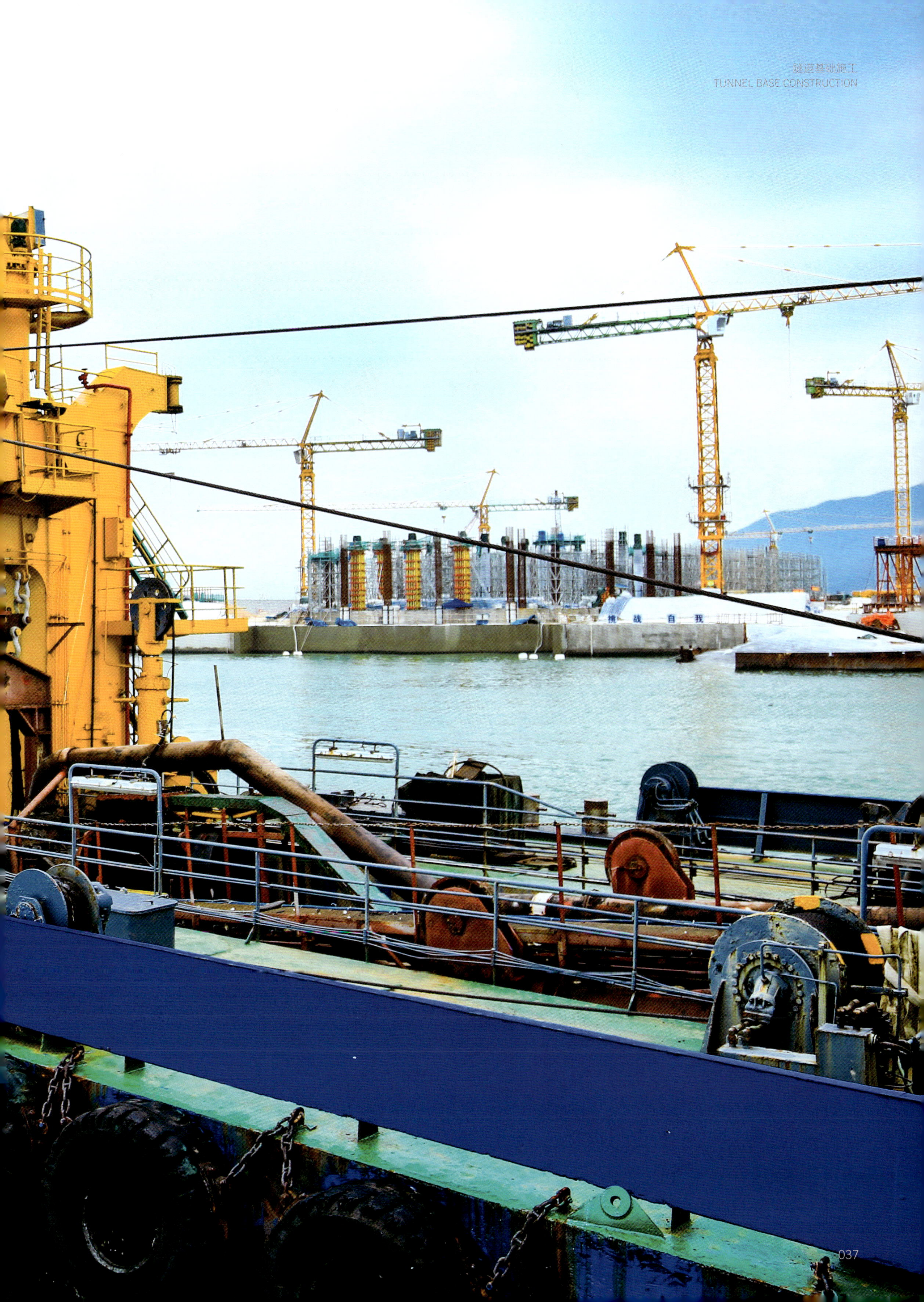
挑 战 自 我

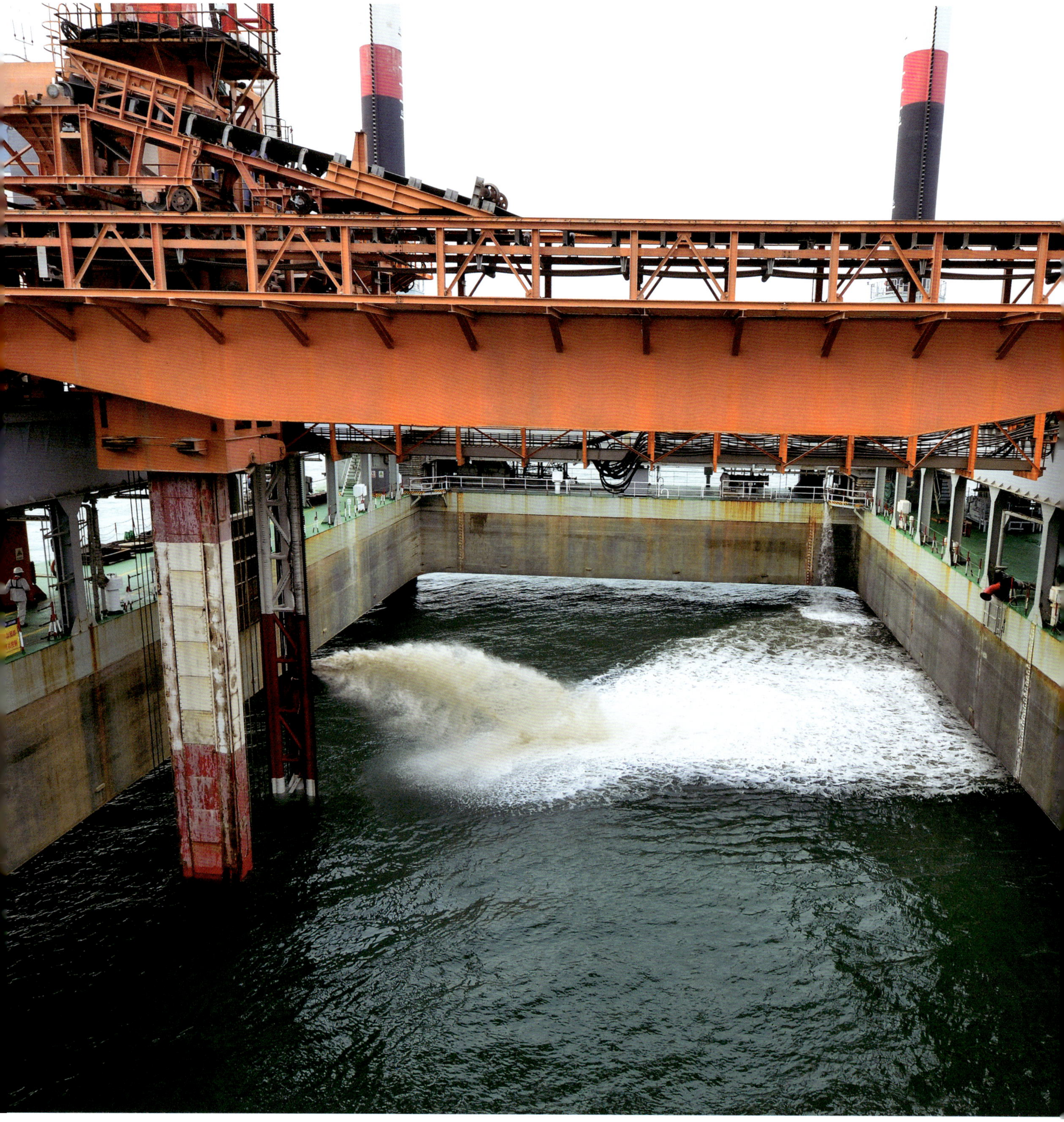

改造整平船，增加平台式碎石基床清淤装备，实现了在水深10~50米范围内，不扰动先铺基床碎石情况下，高效清除基床上的回淤物，具有一天清除一个船位（约1500平方米）碎石垫层上淤泥的能力，解决了碎石基床面上的清淤难题。

Adaptations had been made to the leveling barges. Platform-based rubble bed dredging equipments were added to the barges, which facilitated the effective dredging of the back silt on the trench bed underneath water of 10 to 50 meters deep without disturbing the bedding rubbles that were already placed there. By the adapted dredgers, the sediments of the rubble bed of the coverage of one barge (roughly 1500 square meters) could be cleaned in one day's time. Thus the problem of dredging on the rubble bed was solved.

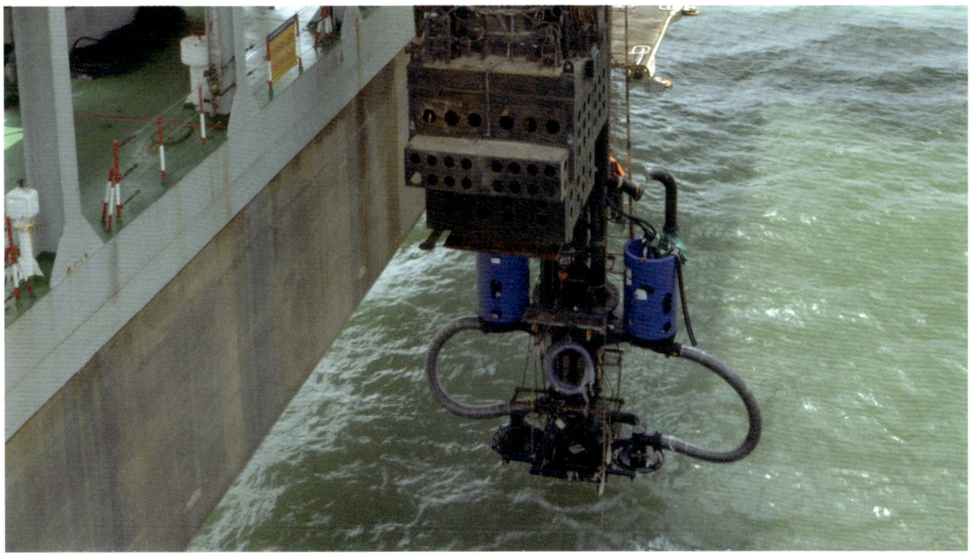

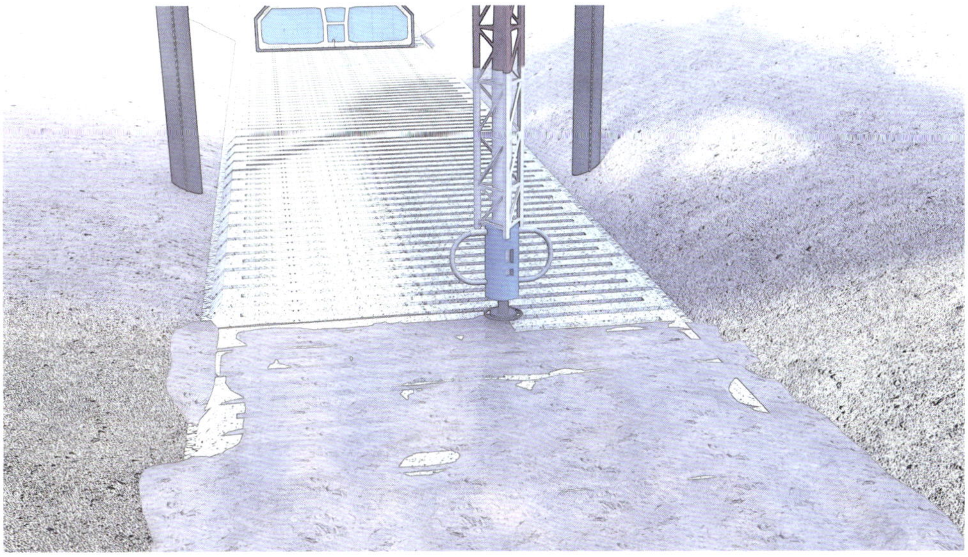

1. "津平 1"进行碎石基床清淤试验
   "Jinping 1" Testing Rubble Bed Dredging
2. 清淤头
   Dredging Head
3. 碎石基床清淤三维图
   3-D Diagram of the Rubble Bed Dredging

开展先铺碎石基床纳淤机理研究，提出了回淤环境下组合基床的纳淤设计流程及方法，在深水基础纳淤和控淤研究方面取得了领先成果。

研发回淤预报系统，解决了深槽中出现的异常回淤问题。

基于现场回淤精细化观测大数据，创新研发了多因素复合型基槽回淤预报模型系统，实现厘米级预报精度，极大地提升了回淤预报的精确度和时效性，为沉管浮运和安装提供了重要保障。

将全断面深水减淤屏创新应用于沉管碎石基床，减少回淤量达50%，成功解决了人工岛岛头段基础防淤控淤难题。

The initiative study of the mechanism of the rubble bedding absorbing sediments concluded by putting forward the flow chart and methods for the composite bedding absorbing sediments in the circumstance of back silting, which was a breakthrough in the study of deep water base absorbing sediments and sediment control.

The study of back silting forecast system provided solution to the problem of abnormal back silting in deep foundation trench.

Based on the data collected by closely observing the real-life back silting, a compound multi-factor foundation trench back silting forecast model was developed to realize precise forecast with an accuracy of centimeters. This technique improved the precision degree and timeliness of back silting forecast, and provided important references for the float conveyance and installation of the immersed tubes in the future.

The innovative use of deep water gross-section silt preventing screen on the rubble bed of the immersed tubes could reduce back silting by 50%, which solved the problems involved in the silt prevention and control at the head part of the man-made island.

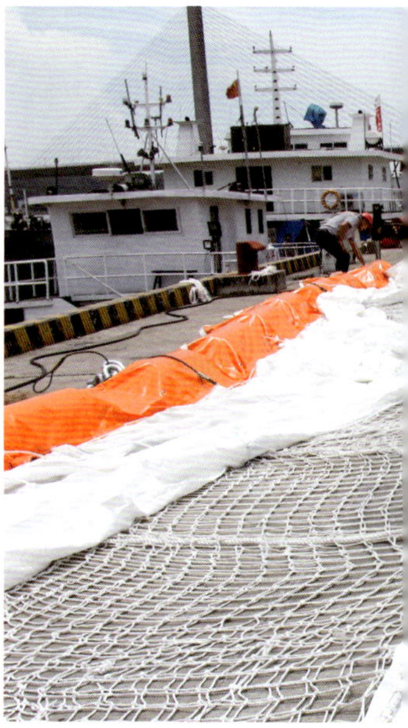

1. 减淤屏
   Silt Preventing Screen
2. 减淤屏安装
   Installation of the Silt Preventing Screen
3. 减淤屏安装完成
   Completion of the Silt Preventing Screen Installation

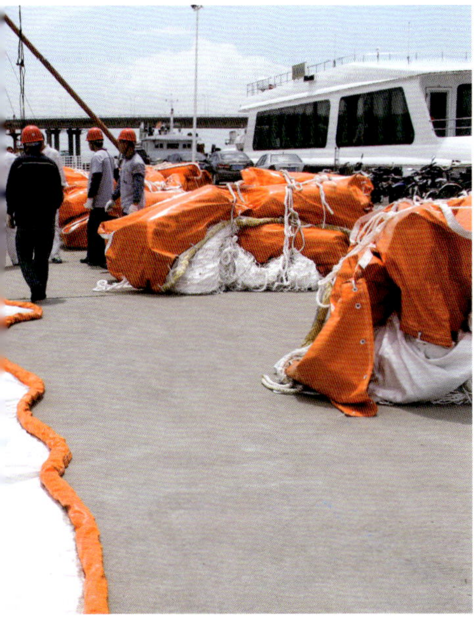

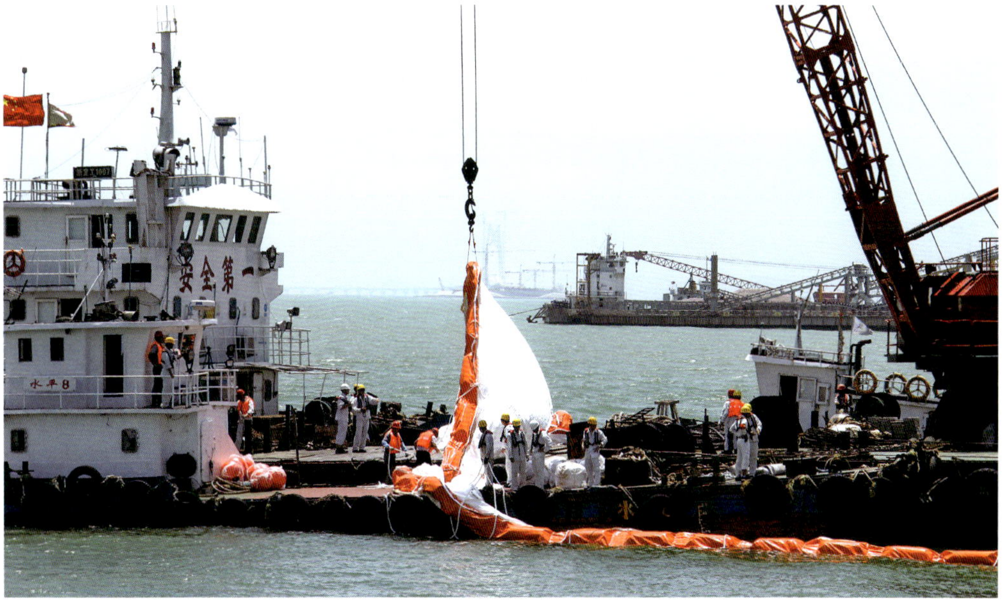
安全第一

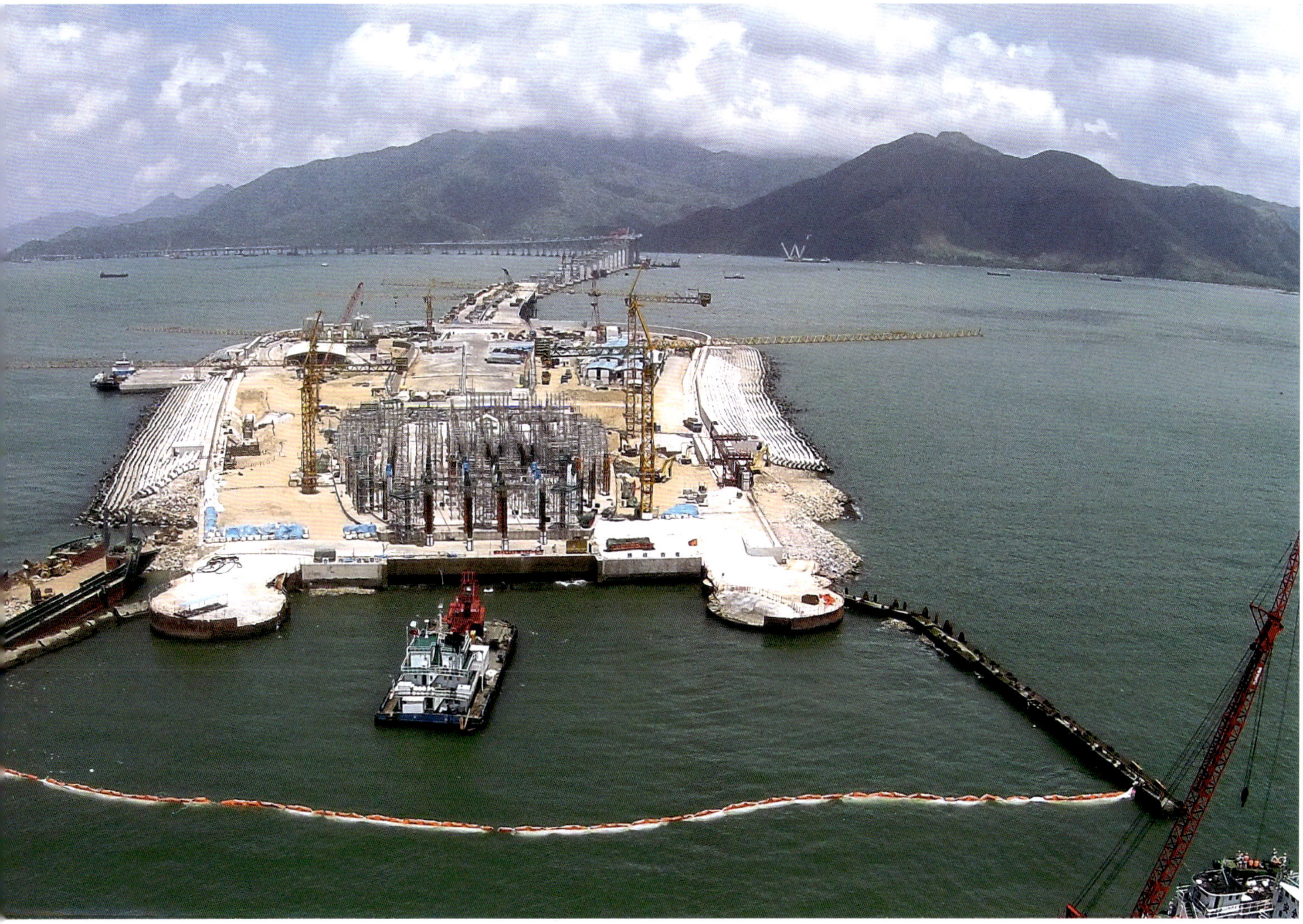

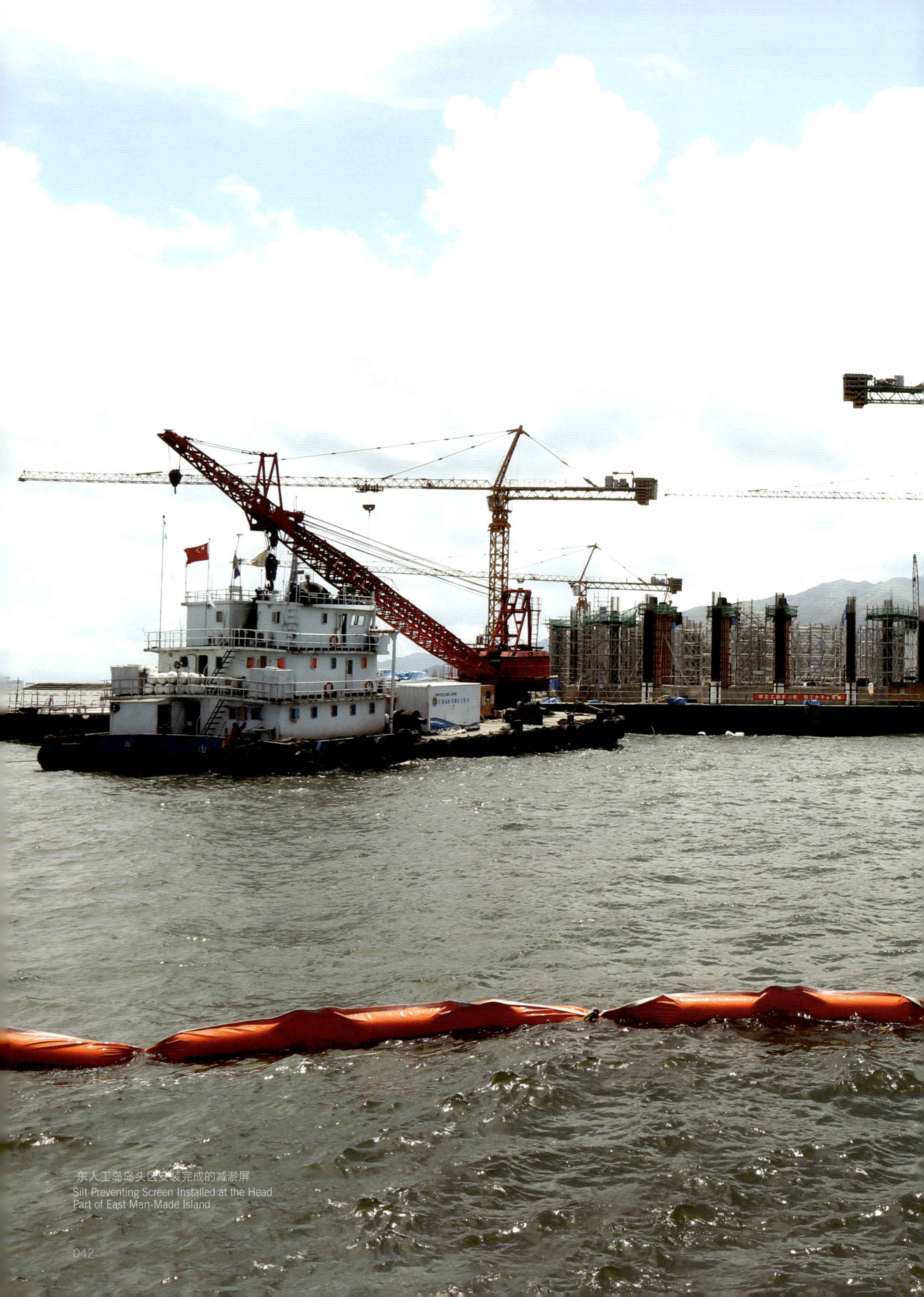

东人工岛岛头区安装完成的减淤屏
Silt Preventing Screen Installed at the Head Part of East Man-Made Island

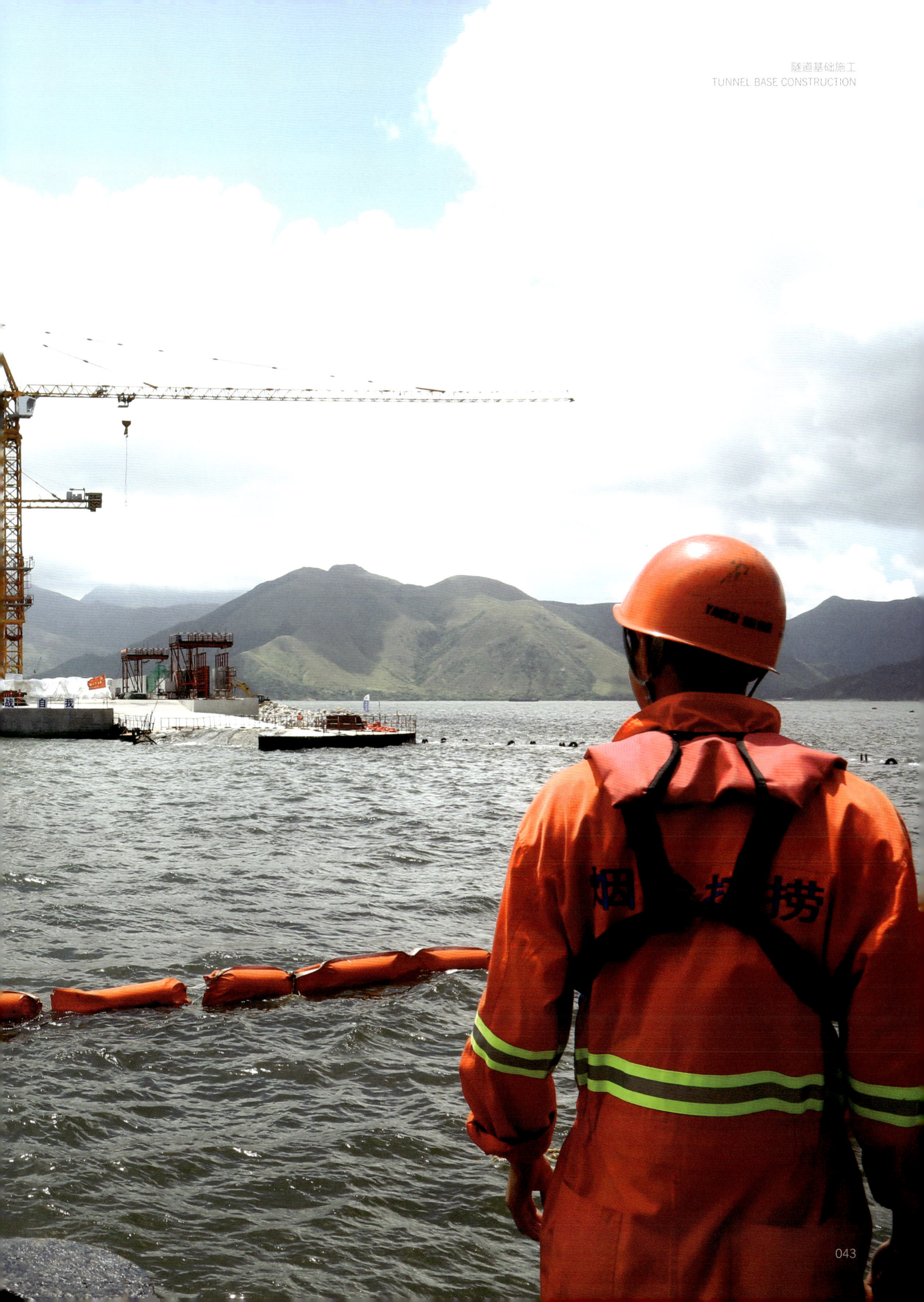

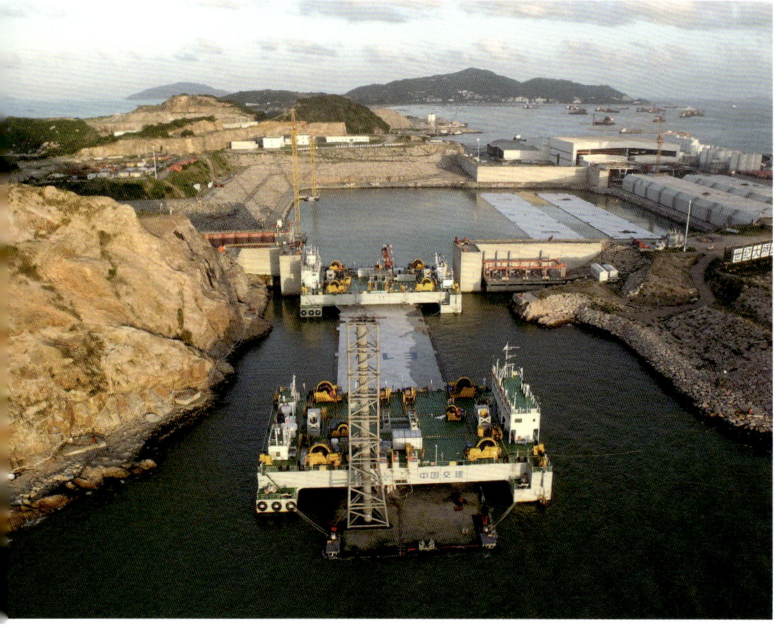

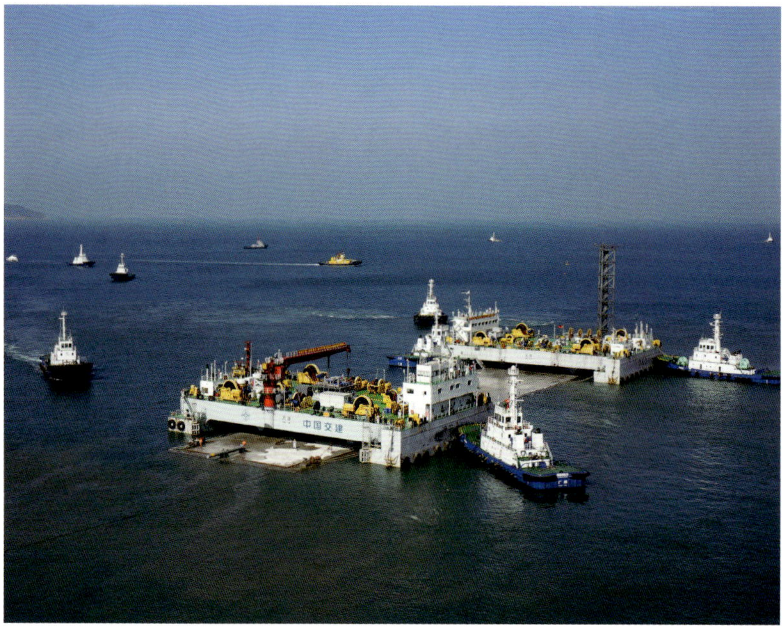

外海沉管浮运安装

FLOAT CONVEYANCE AND INSTALLATION
OF OFFSHORE IMMERSED TUBES

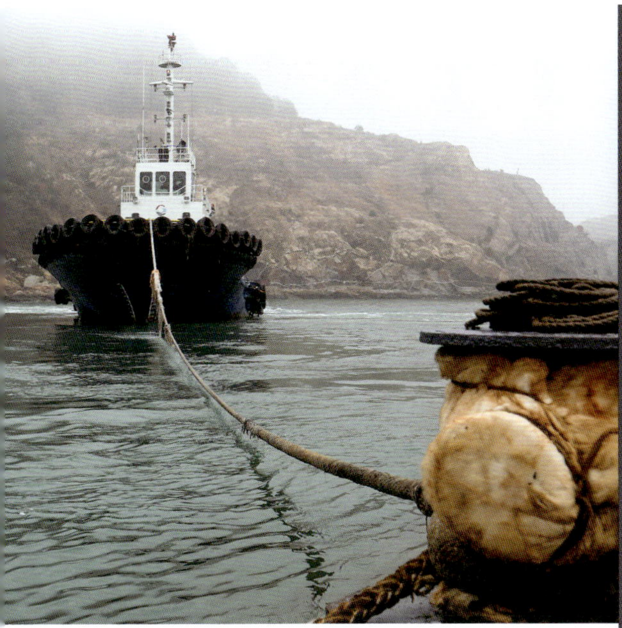

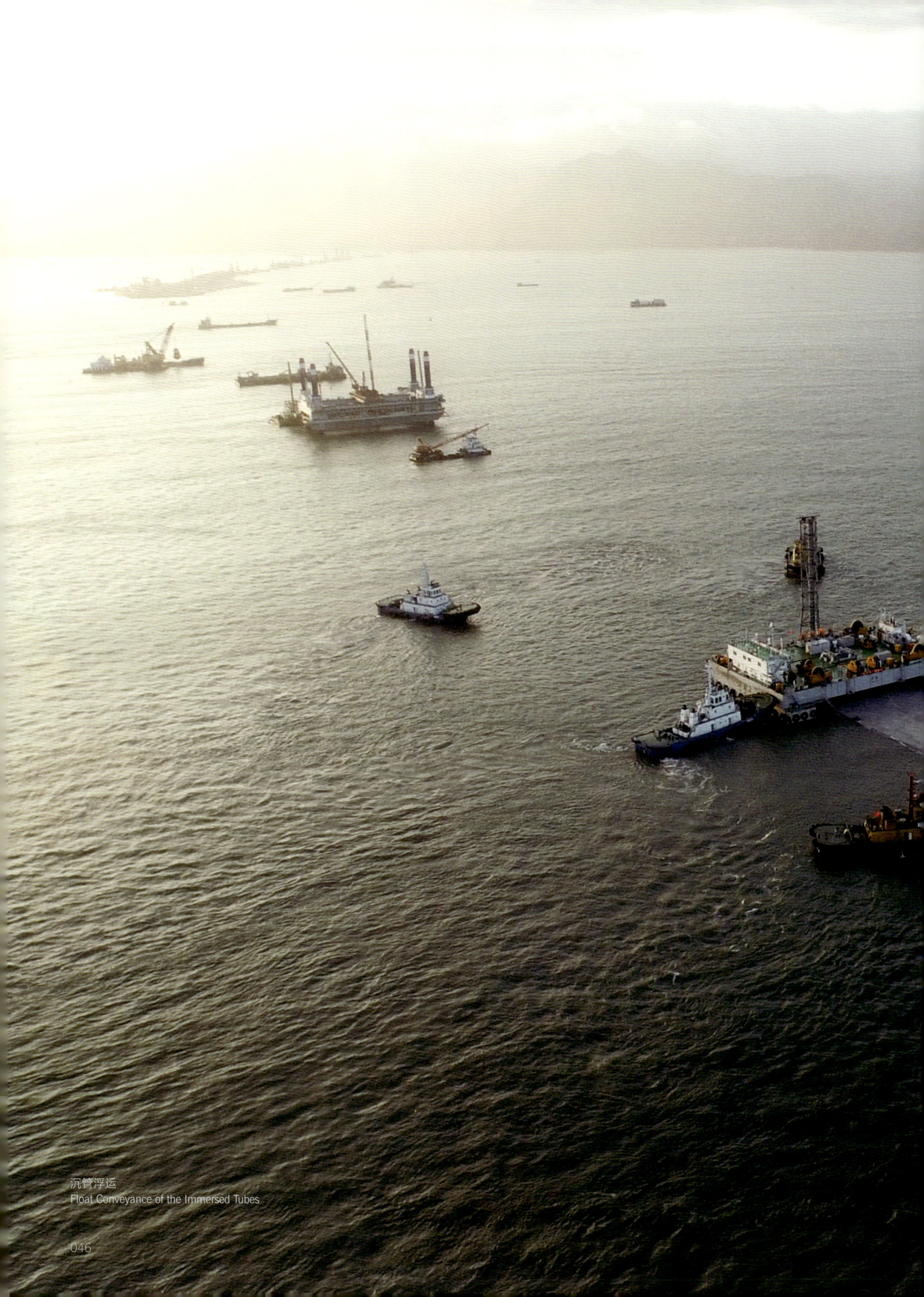

沉管浮运
Float Conveyance of the Immersed Tubes

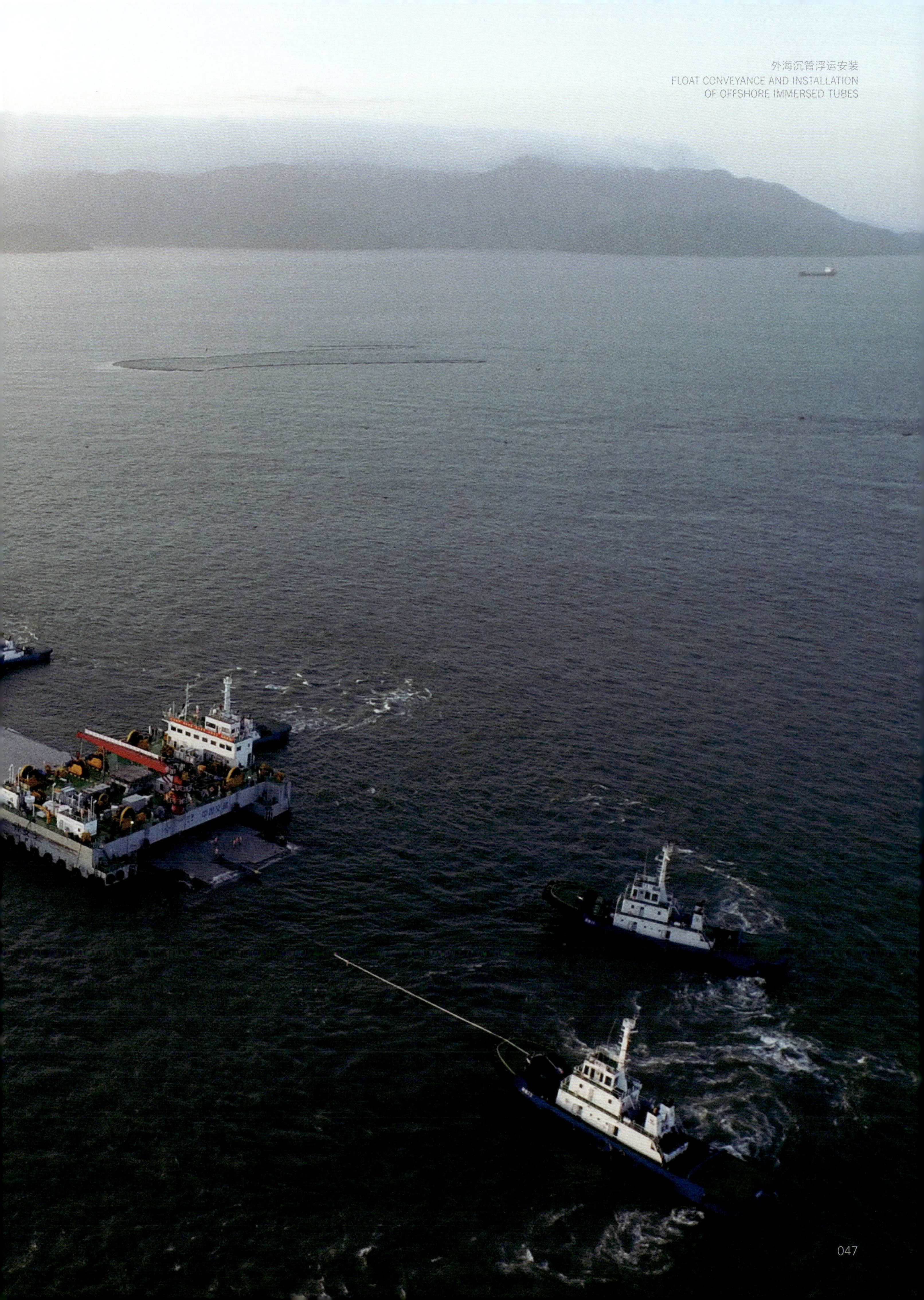

沉管浮运安装介绍

INTRODUCTION TO FLOAT CONVEYANCE AND INSTALLATION OF OFFSHORE IMMERSED TUBES

沉管安装是沉管隧道建设的关键技术。

港珠澳大桥沉管体量世界第一，安装水深近 50 米，须克服大径流、强回淤、深槽等特有的难题，要在复杂海洋工况条件下连续安装 33 节沉管，并达到高精度要求，工程风险和挑战极大。

建设超大型的跨海沉管隧道，此前国内无先例可供参考，面对新课题的技术储备不足、国外技术壁垒森严的困境，要完成工程目标，自力更生进行技术攻关及工法创新是破解外海沉管安装难题的唯一出路。

通过开展自主攻关，项目总经理部研发数字化、信息化和集成化的外海沉管安装专用成套技术装备；自主开发大型沉管外海浮运、系泊、深水无人沉放对接成套施工技术，攻克了巨型沉管在受限海域拖航、锚泊定位、作业窗口管理等诸多难题；自主创新标准化、系统化、流程化的外海沉管安装作业保障管理系统，最终形成了具有中国自主知识产权的外海沉管安装成套技术和装备方案。

The immersed tube installation involved the critical technology of the immersed tube tunneling.

The size of the immersed tubes of Hong Kong-Zhuhai-Macau Bridge was the largest in the world. The tubes were installed under the water of 50 meters deep, during which such special problems as strong streamflow, strong back silting, deep trench had to be solved. Continously installing 33 immersed tubes in severe oceanic environment while meeting the high-precision requirements meant great risks and challenges for the project.

It was an unprecedented project in Chinese construction history to build a super-sized immersed tube tunnel running underneath the deep sea. In the face of lack of necessary technologies and the technological barriers posed by foreign forces and in the face with the great pressure to finish the project as predicted, the only way out for China was to make technological innovations and invent new construction crafts to solve the problems that might occur during the offshore installation of the immersed tubes.

Making full use of the domestic forces, the project management center conducted researches into the development of special digital, information-based and integrated equipments for offshore immersed tube installation. Such technologies concerning the float of conveyance, mooring of large-scaled offshore immersed tube, and unmanned deep water landing and butt joint were developed, which solved the problems involved in towing operation in restricted waters, mooring, positioning, and operation window management. The management system for a standardized, systematized workflow of offshore immersed tube installation was invented, and a series of offshore immersed tube installation technologies and solutions were developed with China's independent intellectual property rights.

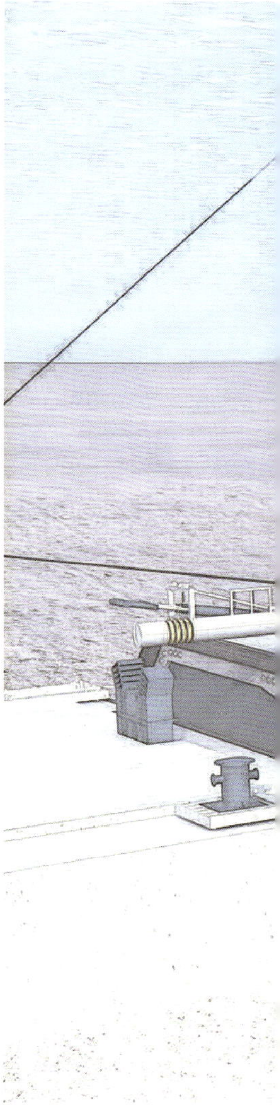

1. 沉管出坞三维图
   3-D Diagram of the Undocking of the Immersed Tubes
2. 沉管浮运三维图
   3-D Diagram of the Float Conveyance of the Immersed Tubes
3. 沉管沉放三维图
   3-D Diagram of the Immersed Tube Landing
4. 沉管对接三维图
   3-D Diagram of the Butt Welding of the Immersed Tubes

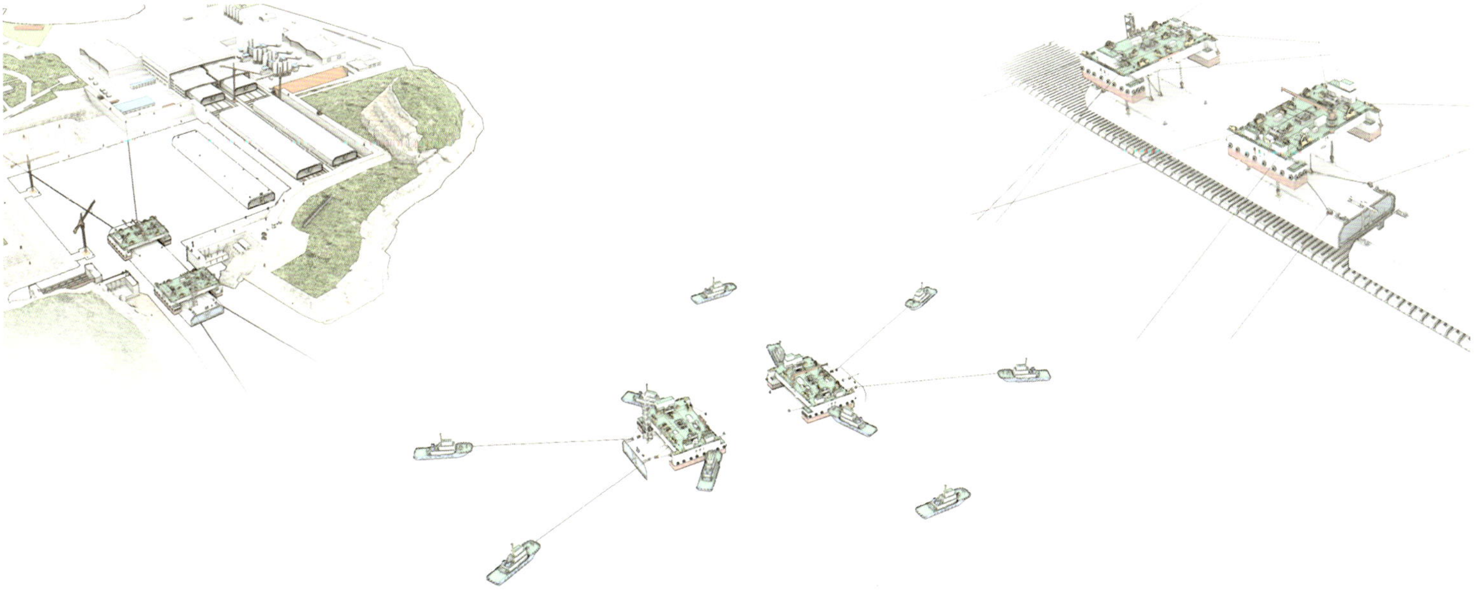

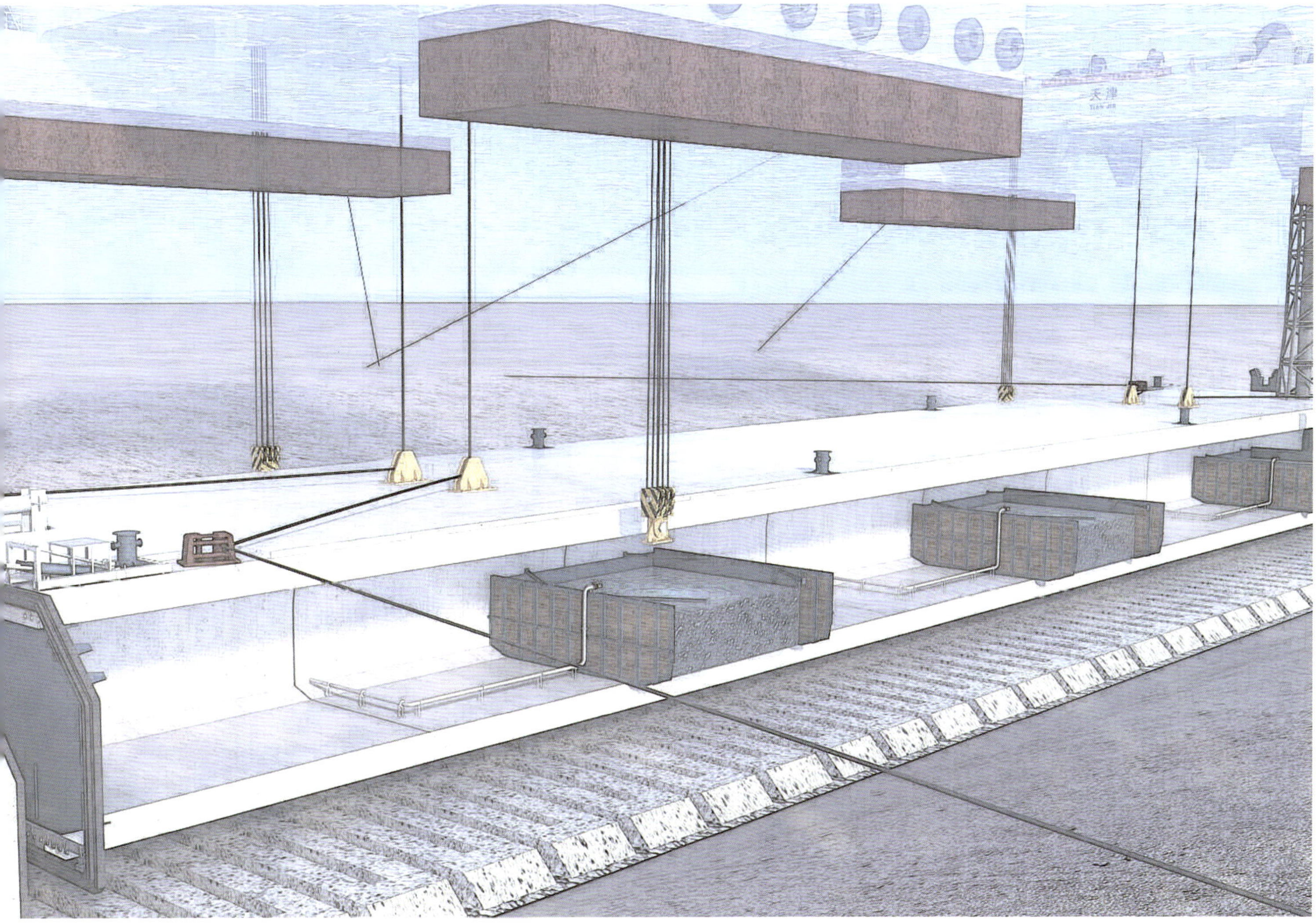
天津

外海沉管安装作业限制条件

REQUIREMENTS FOR THE INSTALLATION OF OFFSHORE IMMERSED TUBES

不利的气象和海况条件几乎影响了基础施工、沉管浮运与安装、最终接头安装等沉管隧道施工的所有工序。

主要影响表现为：

一旦热带风暴或台风来袭，所有施工活动需要立即停止，所有海上施工船舶和设备要进行防台避险；海流流速、波高、波长、风向、海上能见度等因素均会影响沉管浮运沉放作业，导致设定的作业窗口出现频率偏低，可作业天数少，沉放无法按预期完成；流速过大引起局部冲刷，导致基槽不稳定；局部潮流过急给沉放施工、水下作业带来困难；雷雨大风天气影响水上作业并威胁作业安全。

施工海域靠近珠江水系的主要出海口，附近水域港湾、锚地众多，水道纵横交错，船舶航路交叉频繁，通航环境十分复杂，是我国通航密度和通航数量最大的水域之一，也是水上交通事故险情多发水域，被列为全国重点监管水域之一。

The unfavorable weather and oceanic conditions directly influenced nearly all the operation in the immersed tube tunneling like foundational construction, immersed tube float conveyance and installation, and closure joint installation.

The major influences are the followings:

In the face of oncoming tropical storms or typhoons, all construction activities would be stopped, and all the offshore barges and equipments would have to seek protection; such factors as the speed of ocean currents, height and length of the waves, direction of the wind, and the visibility on the sea would influence the float conveyance and landing of the immersed tubes, which might result in the low frequency of visibility of the operation window, reduction of the number of working days, and failure to land the tube; speedy current in the sea might cause washout in certain area, which in turn leed to the instability of the foundation trench; rapid tidal flow in certain area would pose difficulties for tube landing and underwater operation; storms and strong winds would influence the operation over the sea and might endanger the workers' safety.

The major working place was the mouth of Pearl River, which was known for the numerous bays, inlets, anchorages, watercourses, ships and the complicated, busy water transportation there. It is the one of the busiest waters in China troubled by traffic accidents, so it has already been listed among the waters in China needing pivot supervision.

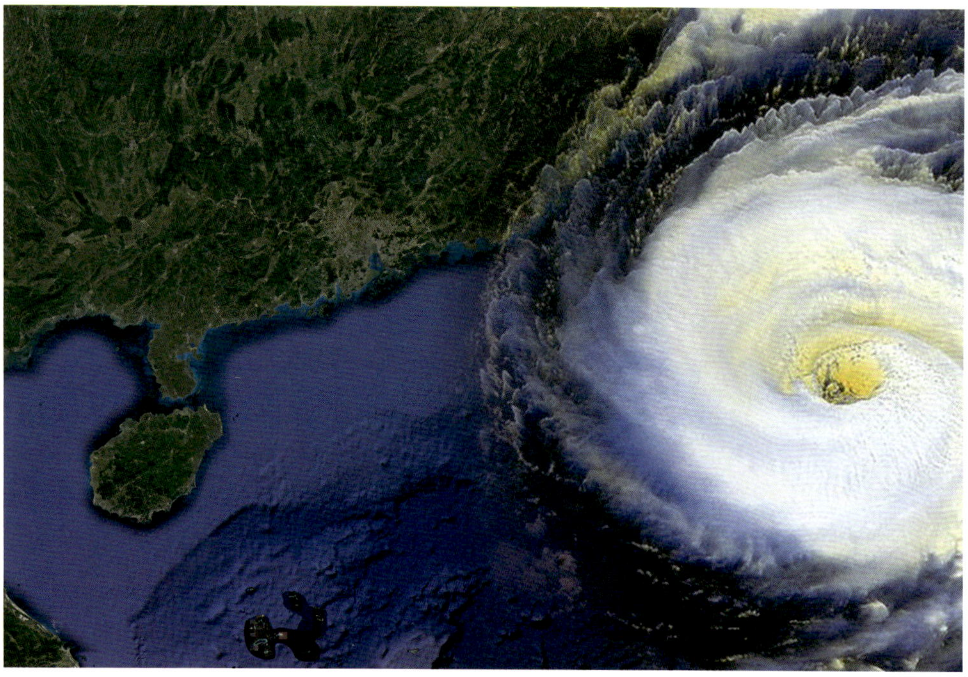

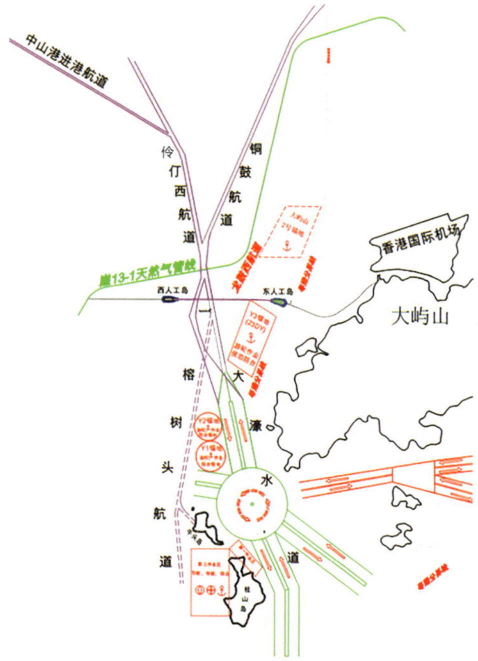

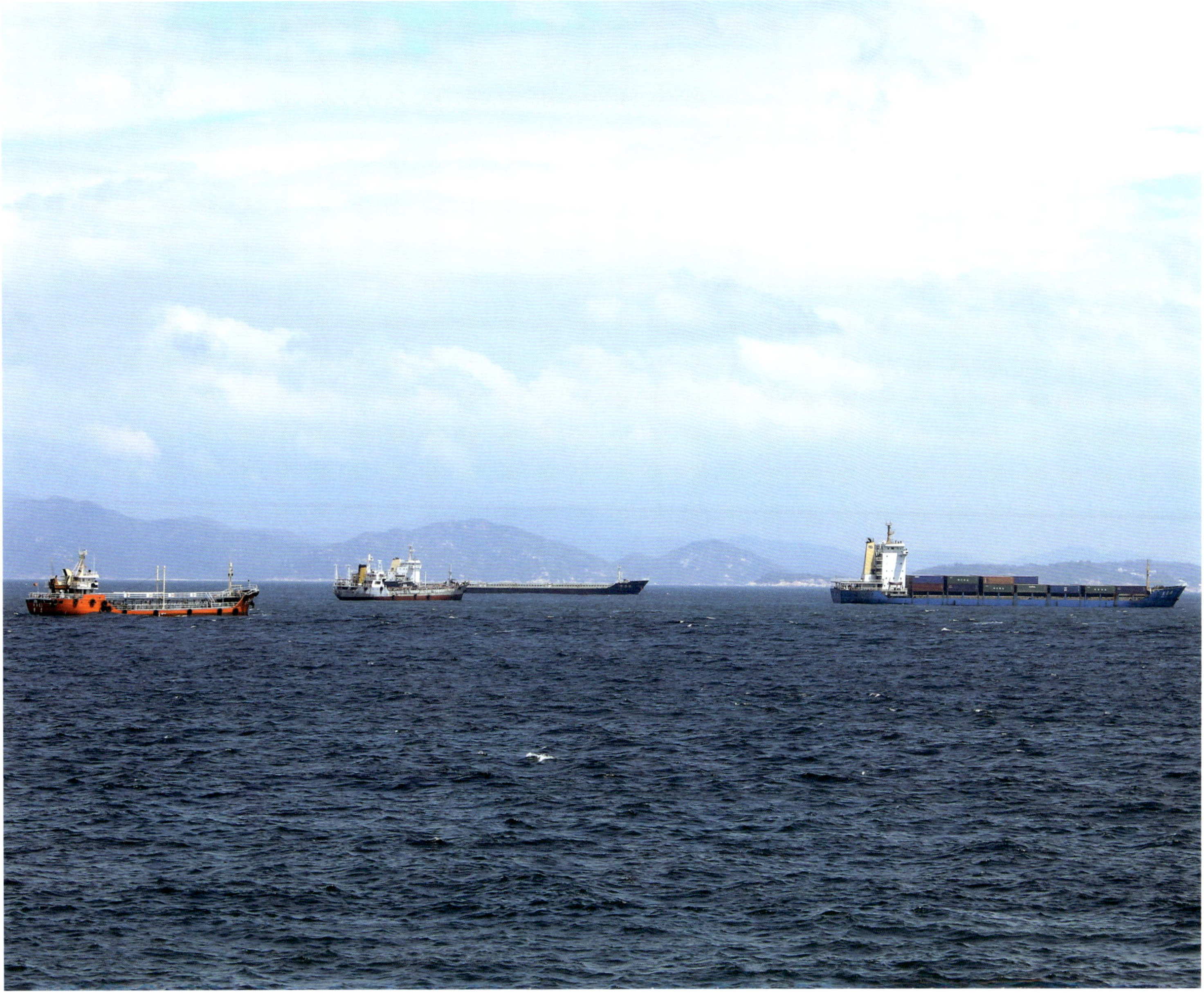

1. 珠江口强台风卫星云图
Satellite Nephogram of Strong Typhoon at the Pearl River Estuary
2. 沉管浮运航道图
Route of the Float Conveyance of the Immersed Tubes
3. 通航船舶密集的浮运航道
Route of the Float Conveyance with Heavy Traffic of Barges

浮运安装作业窗口
OPERATION WINDOW FOR FLOAT CONVEYANCE AND INSTALLATION

作业窗口是指适合沉管安装的时间段，窗口预报是沉管安装决策最重要的依据。

由于工程区域气候复杂多变，灾害性天气频繁，水文条件复杂，符合沉管安装窗口要求的天数甚少，作业窗口分析、精细化预报和保障难度大。

为给沉管安装作业窗口选择和施工决策提供可靠的支持，项目总经理部委托国家海洋环境预报中心进行工程区现场长期水文气象数据观测，建立精细化预报模型和作业窗口预报管理系统。

Operation window refers to the time duration proper for the installation of the immersed tube, and window forecast is the most important evidence to make decision about the installation.

Due to the complicated hydrographical and weather conditions as well as the natural disasters, the working days meeting the window requirements for the immersed tube installation are very few, and operation window analysis as well as precision forecast and support is always faced with great challenges.

To support the operation window choice for the immersed tube installation and provide evidence for decision-making on the operation, the project management center entrusted the National Marine Environmental Forecast Center to conduct long-term hydrographical monitoring and data collection in the project region, trying to construct the precision forecast model and the operation window forecast management system.

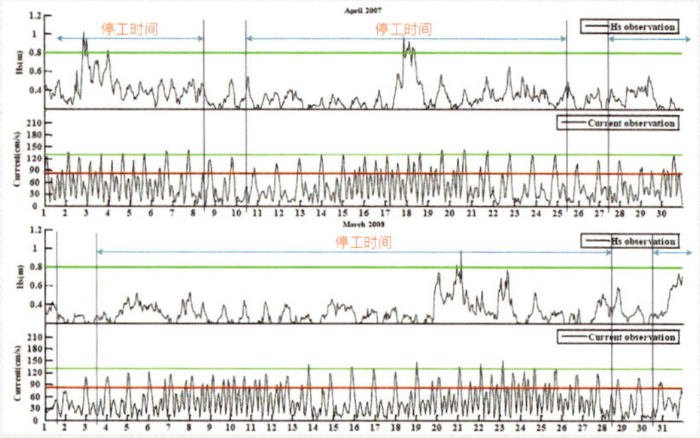

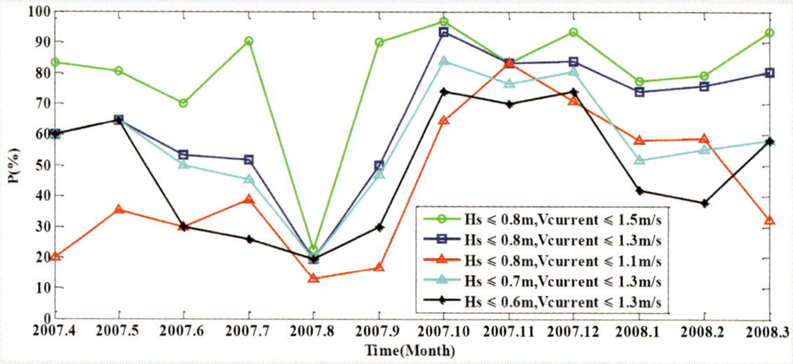

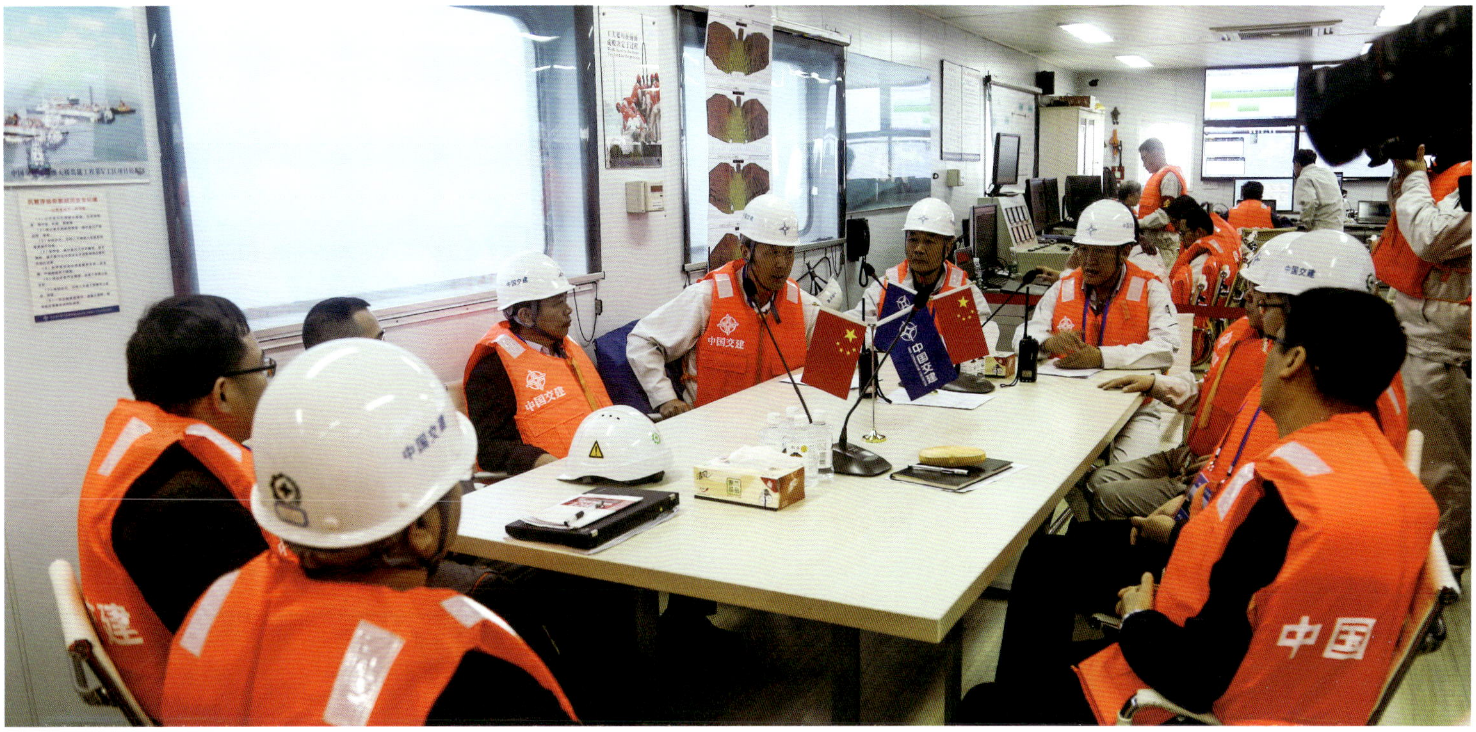

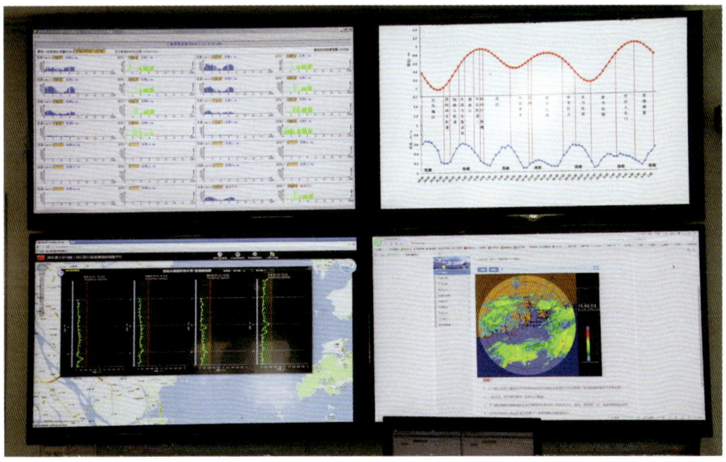

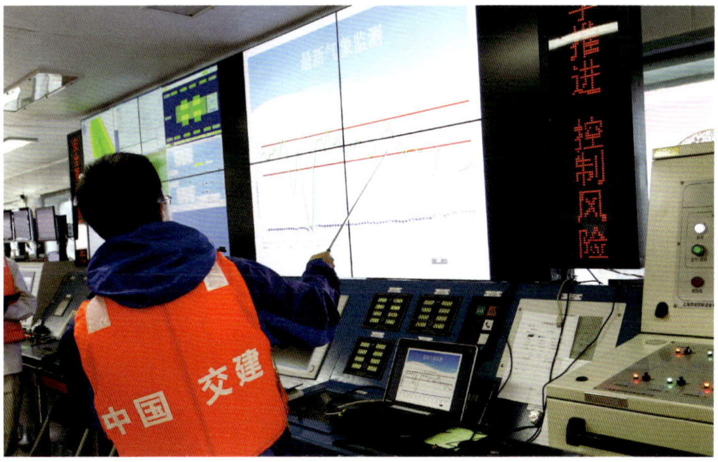

1. 满足作业窗口要求的作业时间图
Operation Time Map Meeting the Requirements of the Operation Window

2. 不同作业窗口的有效作业频率图
Effective Operation Frequency Map of Different Operation Windows

3. 沉管浮运决策会
Decision Making on the Float Conveyance of the Immersed Tubes

4. 沉管浮运安装海洋气象环境
Oceanic Weather Condition for the Float Conveyance and Installation of the Immersed Tubes

5. 通报海洋气象环境
Notification of the Oceanic Weather Condition

沉管安装流程

FLOW CHART OF THE IMMERSED TUBE INSTALLATION

沉管安装是将预制完成的沉管从预制厂浮运至现场，按设计的要求沉放到位并回填覆盖的施工过程，主要工序包括：一次舾装、起浮横移、二次舾装、出坞、浮运、系泊、沉放、对接、回填覆盖等。

沉管在工厂浅坞内进行压载水系统、装配式钢端封门安装等一次舾装；然后关闭深、浅坞门，坞内灌水，沉管起浮试漏；通过坞内绞缆系统横移至深坞内系泊存放；坞内排水，打开深坞门，完成测量塔安装、标定等二次舾装；随后选择沉管施工作业窗口，划定专门的施工水域及沉管浮运航路，沉管绞移出坞；大马力拖轮浮运至沉放现场，沉管系泊；灌水下沉，深水无人沉放定位系统调位，沉放至预先铺设好的碎石基床上，千斤顶拉合，水力压接，GINA 止水带充分压缩形成可靠的沉管柔性水密接头；通过管内的贯通测量复核确认沉管安装偏差，如有超偏，利用精调系统进行隧道轴线精调；满足要求后，进行管外锁定和覆盖回填；最后进行管内舾装件拆除、压载混凝土浇筑和隧道内装工作。

The immersed tube installation means the process of moving the forecast tubes from the manufacturing site to the project region by float conveyance, landing the tubes onto the designed position, and finally covering the tubes by back-filling. The major procedures include the first fitting-out, free-floating and side sway; the second fitting-out, undocking, float conveyance, anchoring, landing, butt welding, and back-filling.

The first fitting-out of the immersed tube will be done in the shallow dock of the ship factory, including installing the ballast water system and assembling the steel sealing devices, followed by closing the deep and shallow dock gates, water filling in the dock, free floating of the tubes and leakage detection. Then the tubes will be moved by side sway into the deep dock and anchored there, followed by dock drainage and the lifting of the deep dock gate. The second fitting-out is done by installing measurement tower and calibration. The third step is the choice of operation window for the immersed tube; the special water area and the watercourse for the float conveyance of the tubes will be decided on, and then the tube is moved out of the dock. After that, a towing barge with high horse power will float the tube to the operation site for landing and get it anchored there; water filling follows to lower the tube underwater and the deep water unmanned landing and positioning system adjusts its position and lands it on the well-placed rubble bed; by jack pulling, hydraulic crimp connection and complete compression by GINA water-stop, a reliable flexible watertight connector for the the immersed tube is formed. The fourth step is the in-tube closure measurement to identify the deviation in the installation the immersed tube ; if a significant deviation, fine adjustment system will be employed to adjust the axis line of the tunnel. When every datum meets the required standard, out-tube locking and back-filling follow. The last step is the removal of the fitting-out parts inside the tube, ballasting concrete grouting and in-tunnel decoration.

作业阶段和内容 Construction Phases and Contents		流速（米／每秒） Flow Speed (m/s)	波高 H,（米） Wave Height (m)	波浪周期（秒） Wave Period (s)	风速（级） Wind Speed (scale)	能见度（米） Visibility (m)
浮运 Float Conveyance	航道浮运 Float Conveyance on The Navigation Channel	0.8	0.8	≤6	≤6	≥1000
	基槽内纵拖 Longitudinal Dragging in the Trench	0.6	0.8	≤6	≤6	≥1000
沉放 Landing	系泊等待 Mooring and Waiting	1.3	0.8	≤6	≤6	≥1000
	沉放实施 Landing	0.6	0.8	≤6	≤6	≥1000
潜水作业 Diving		0.5	0.8	≤6	≤6	≥1000

沉管安装作业窗口限制条件表
Conditions for Immersed Tube Installation Window

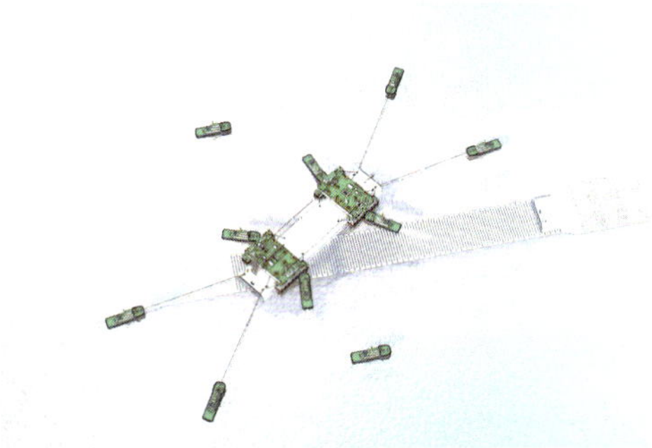
浮运
Float Conveyance

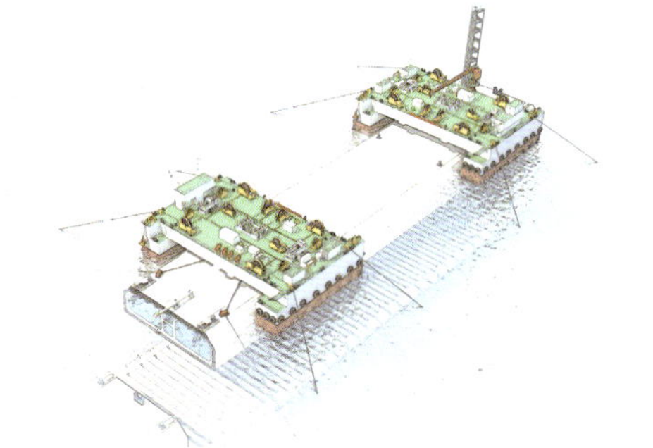
系泊
Mooring

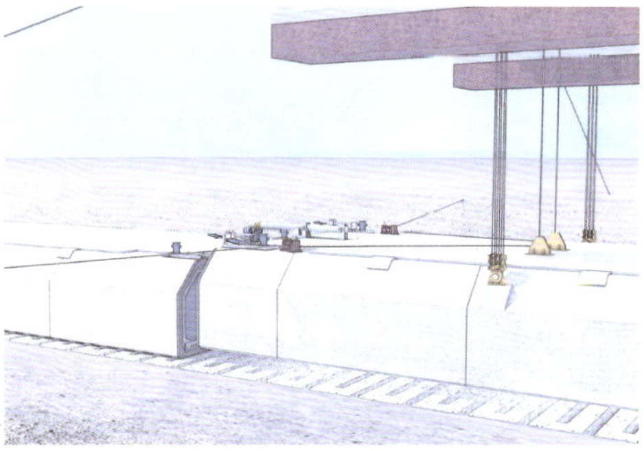
下沉
Sinking

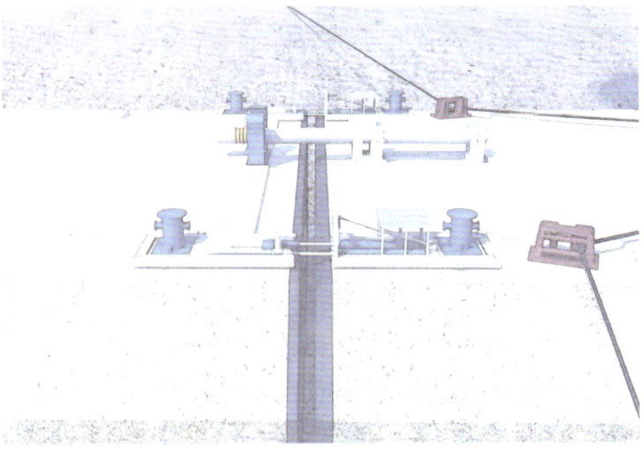
拉合
Closure by Pulling

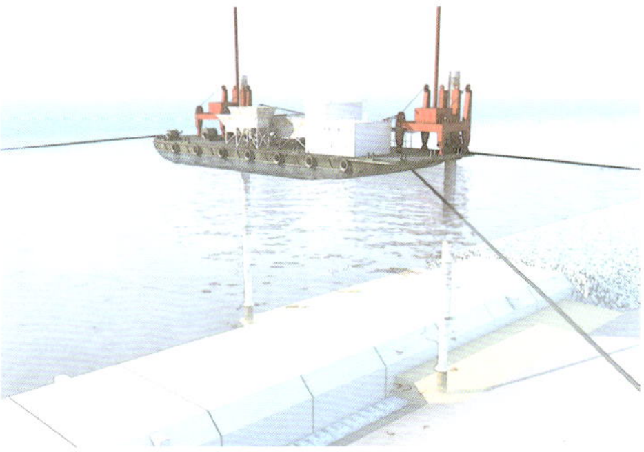
锁定回填
Lock Backfill

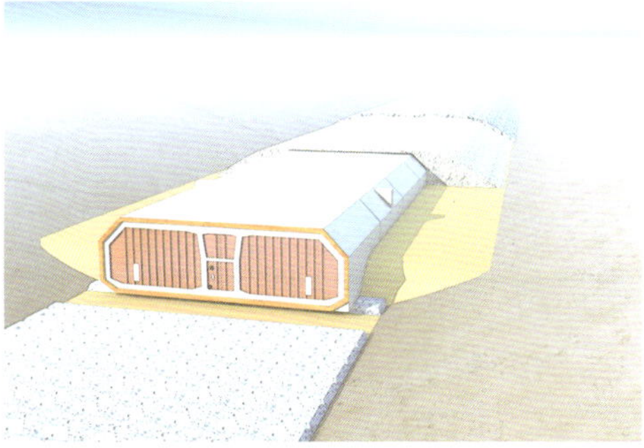
管顶回填及防护
Pipe Top Backfilling and Protection

施工阶段 Construction Phases		作业内容 Construction Contents	作业时间（小时） Construction Time (h)	时间汇总（小时） Total Time (h)	
浮运 Float Conveyance	航道内浮运 Float Conveyance on the Navigation channel	管节西端、东端各检查 1 处 One-Point Examination at Both the West and East End of the Tube	6~10	8~14	26h~48h 气象窗口 26-to-48-Hour Weather Window
	基槽内转向浮运 Swerving and Float Conveyance in the Trench	基槽内管节转向浮运至安装系泊点 In-trench Swerving and Float Conveyance to the Mooring Position for Installation	2~4		
系泊 Mooring	管节系泊 Tube Mooring	系泊缆、安装缆通缆 Threading of the Mooring Cable and the Installation Cable	2~4	18~34	
	等待沉放 Waiting to Be Landed	压载、等待沉放时机 Ballasting and Waiting to Be Landed	6~10		
	管节沉放 Tube Landing	释放吊缆，逐步下沉 Releasing the Hoisting Cable to Lower the Tube	4~6		
	水下拉合 Closure by Pulling Underwater	拉合千斤顶挂钩，进行水下拉合 Connecting the Pulling Jack and the Tube for Underwater Connection	2~3		
	水力压接 Hydraulic Crimp Connection	在已沉管节内进行控制性放水，控制管节的水力压接速度 Controlling the Water Pressure Inside the Landed Tubes to Control the Speed of the Hydraulic Crimp Connection of the Tubes	2~3		
	测量 Measurement	利用测量系统进行管内、外测量，精确测量管节位置，如有必要，可利用精调系统对管节尾端进行适当调整 Measurement Inside and Outside the Tube to Calculate the Position of the Tube, and Tube End Adjustment with Elaborate Adjusting Devices when Necessary	2~4		

管节浮运、沉放施工时间表
Time of Tube Float Conveyance and Landing

浮运演练及相关试验

DRILL AND EXPERIMENT OF FLOAT CONVEYANCE

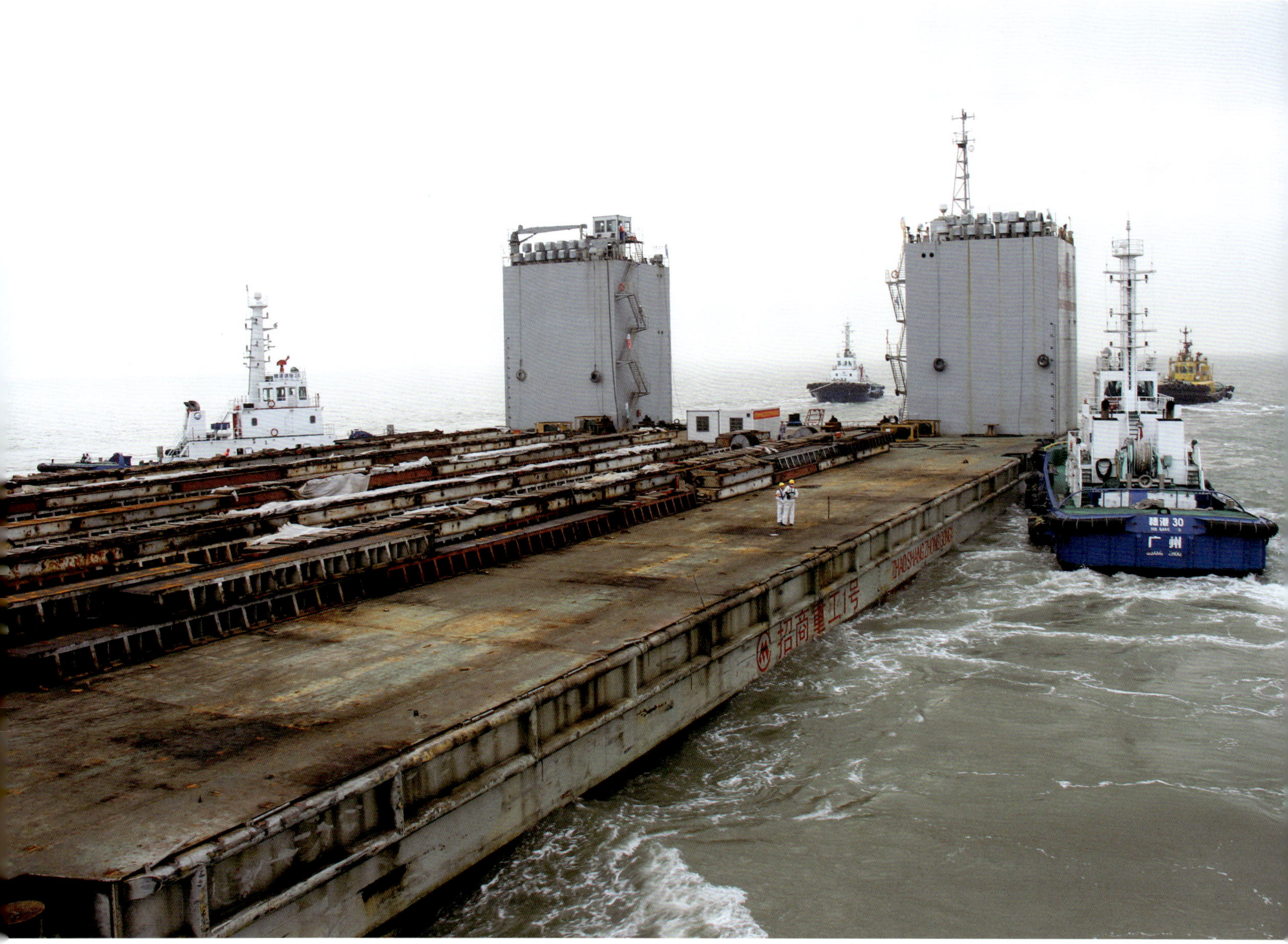

1. 沉管浮运演练
Drill of the Float Conveyance of the Immersed Tubes

2—3. 沉管浮运物模试验
Physical Model Experiment on the Float Conveyance of the Immersed Tubes

项目总经理部联合有关科研单位和院校开展了沉管拖航阻力物模试验、数模计算，对沉管浮运过程中主要控制参数，包括沉管及附属结构所受风阻力、水流阻力和波浪增阻等进行计算、验证，通过分析沉管浮运所需的拖曳阻力，为拖轮配备和拖航方式选择提供数据支持。

为降低首次外海沉管浮运的风险，确保首节沉管浮运安全，分别进行了四次浮运演练，使用大型半潜驳代替沉管模拟出坞和拖航，熟练操作流程，规范指挥口令，熟悉航道和拖轮性能，完善浮运操控方案，大大降低了浮运施工风险，为后期沉管正式浮运做好充分准备。

The project management center worked together with relevant institutions and universities to conduct physical model experiment on and mathematical model calculation of the towing resistance of the immersed tube, and calculate and test the major control parameters in the process of the tube's float conveyance such as the wind resistance of the tube and its accessories, water resistance and wave resistance. Then an analysis of the towing resistance necessary for the float conveyance of the tube was done to provide support for the equipment of the towing barge and ways of towing.

To reduce the risks of offshore tube float conveyance and guarantee the safety of the first section of the tube during its transportation, four drills were done by replacing the immersed tube with large-scaled semi-submersible barge to simulate the undocking and towing of the tube, by which the workers became familiar with the process of the operation, the water route and the capability of the towing barge, the commanding orders were standardized, the plan for the float conveyance was refined, and the risks that might occur during the float conveyance were reduced. All this prepared the ultimate operation of the float conveyance of the tube in the next step.

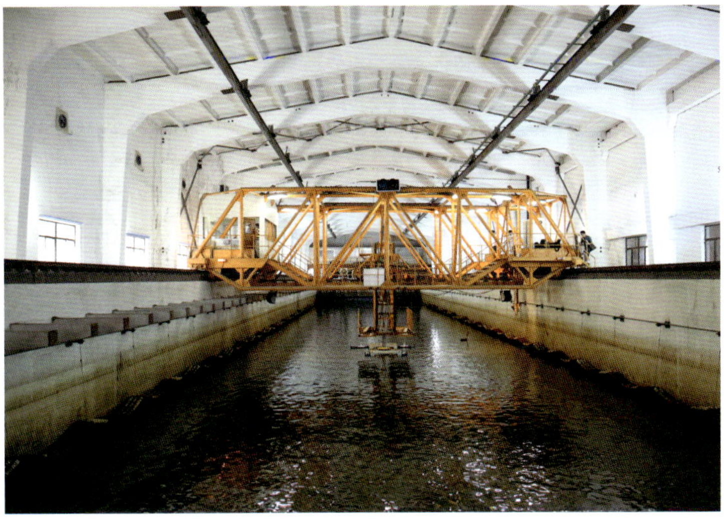

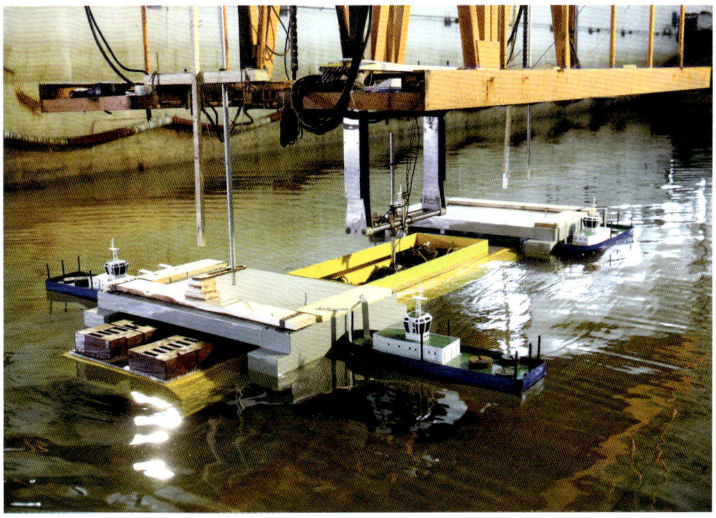

在开敞外海实施沉管安装在我国为首次。

项目总经理部在大连理工大学海岸和近海工程国家重点实验室进行了大规模物模试验，对沉放过程中吊缆、安装缆张力的变化、沉管和安装驳的运动响应和沉管结构设计、沉管结构安全、沉放设备（安装驳吊放系统设计）、沉放工艺制定、施工风险控制等进行验证。

委托上海交通大学海洋工程国家重点实验室进行沉管及安装驳在浮运及沉放过程中的受力情况进行计算研究。

针对干舷消除、管顶与泥面平行和管底距离基槽 4 米的三种沉管沉放典型状态，研究在不同工况下沉管的受力情况。

Offshore installation of the immersed tube in open seas in this project is the first case in China's history of tunnel construction.

The project management center conducted a large-scaled physical experiments in the National Key Laboratory of Coastal and Offshore Engineering, Dalian University of Technology, where such topics as the tension changes of the hoisting cable and installation cable during tube landing, the motion response of the immersed tube and installation barge, the structural design and the structural safety of the tube, landing equipments (the hoisting system of the installation barge), choice of landing crafts as well as construction risks were tested.

The National Key Laboratory of Oceanic Engineering at Shanghai Jiao Tong University was entrusted to conduct a study of the load-carrying capacity of the immersed tube and the installation barge during the tube's float conveyance and landing.

By differentiating the three phases of tube landing like freeboard elimination, parallel between tube top and bedding surface, and the distance of 4 meters from the tube bottom to the foundation trench, the load-carrying capacity of the tube was tested in different working conditions.

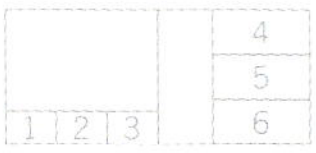

1—3. 沉管浮运数模试验
Mathematical-Model Experiment on the Float Conveyance of the Immersed Tubes

4—5. 沉管数模图
Mathematical Model of the Immersed Tubes

6. 沉管及安装船数模图
Mathematical Model of the Immersed Tubes and Installation Barges

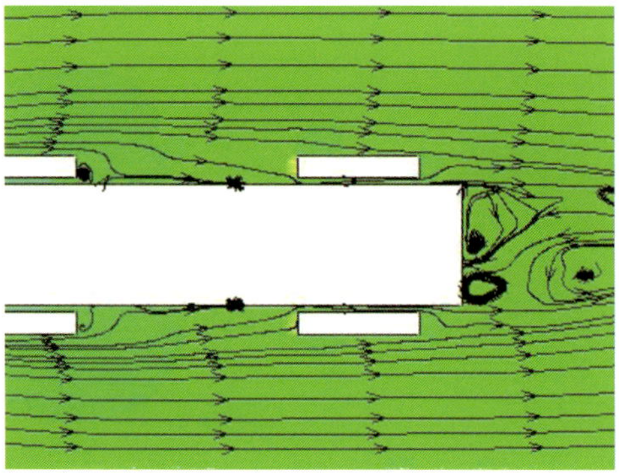

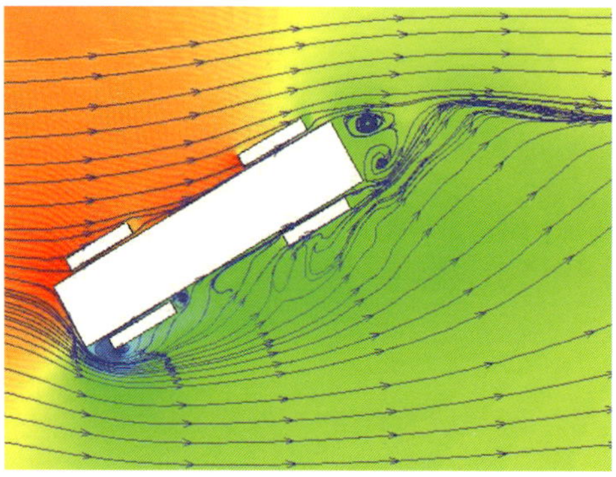

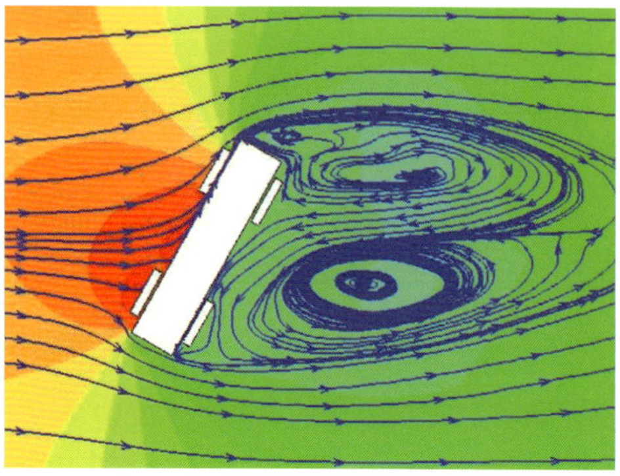

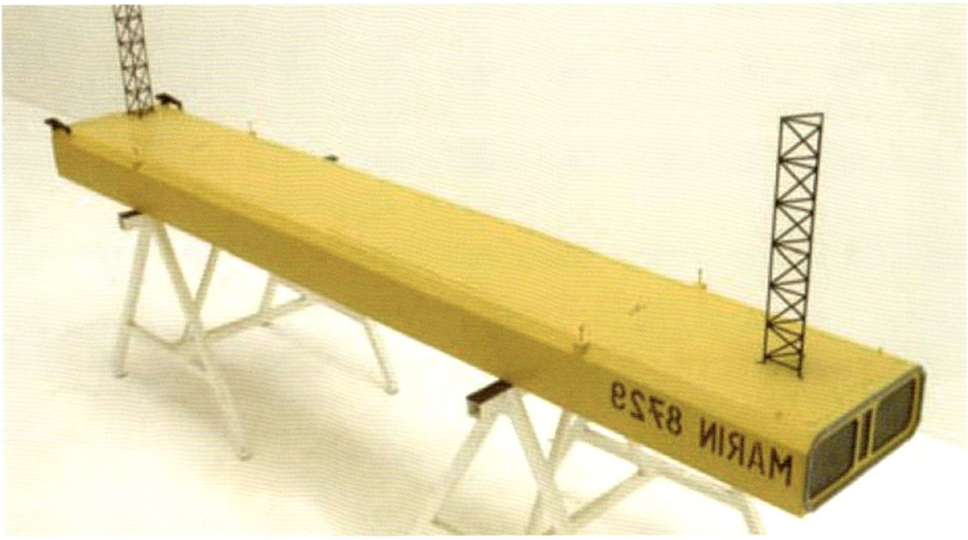
MARIN 8729

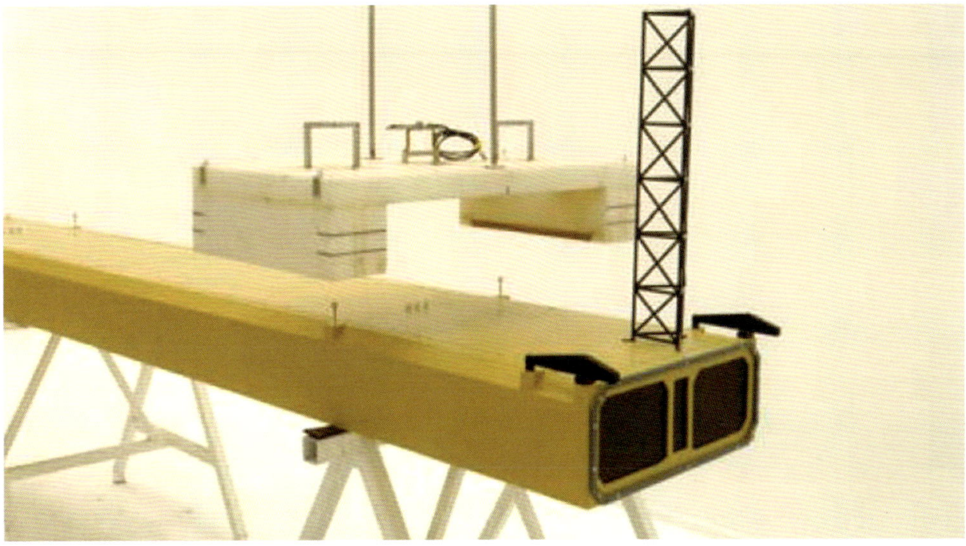

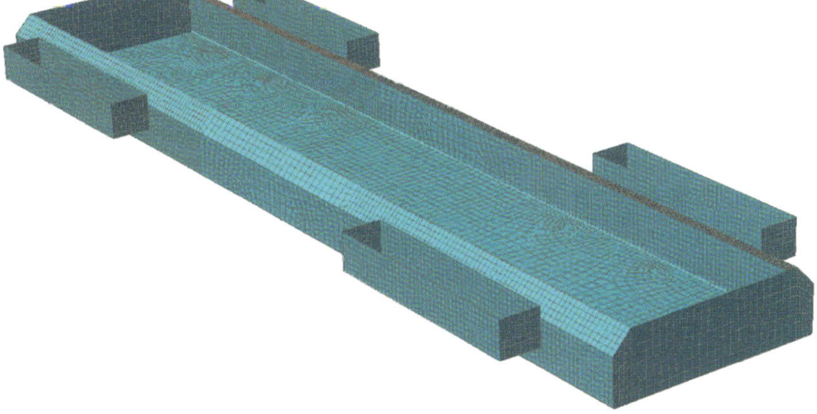

拖轮编队

FORMATION OF TUGBOATS

利用坞口锚点、安装驳上的绞车及岸上的卷扬机共同配合，绞移沉管离开深坞区进入坞口编队区。

出坞和编队在落潮末期或平潮的小流速时段进行，以确保沉管状态由缆系控制转换为拖轮控制平稳可控。

安装驳和沉管出坞门后，根据现场实测海流情况，择机进行浮运拖轮编队，按照既定顺序依次进行拖轮与沉管、安装驳的拖缆连接。

By use of the anchor at entrance of the dock, the winch on the installation barge and the windlass on the banks, the tube was moved out of the deep dock into the area where the tugboats anchored in waiting.

Undocking and tube formation were done towards the end of the tide or when the slack tide slowed down to ensure that when cable control changed into towing barge control, the immersed tube remained controllable.

After the installation barges and the tube moved out of the dock gate, the real-life sea current was estimated to arrange the formation of the towing barges for the float conveyance of the tubes. The towing barges should be connected with the tubes and the towing cables of the installation barges one by one.

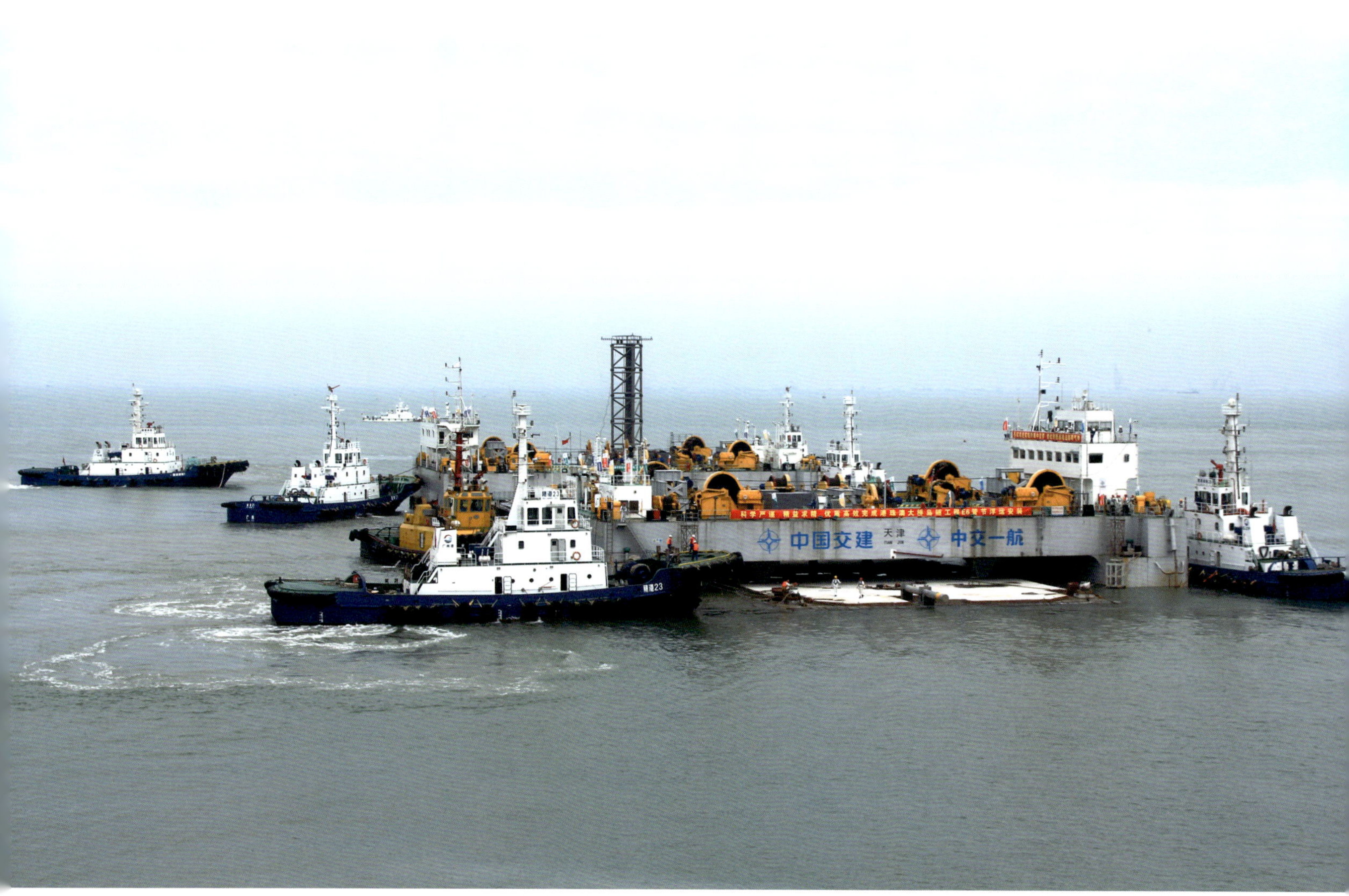

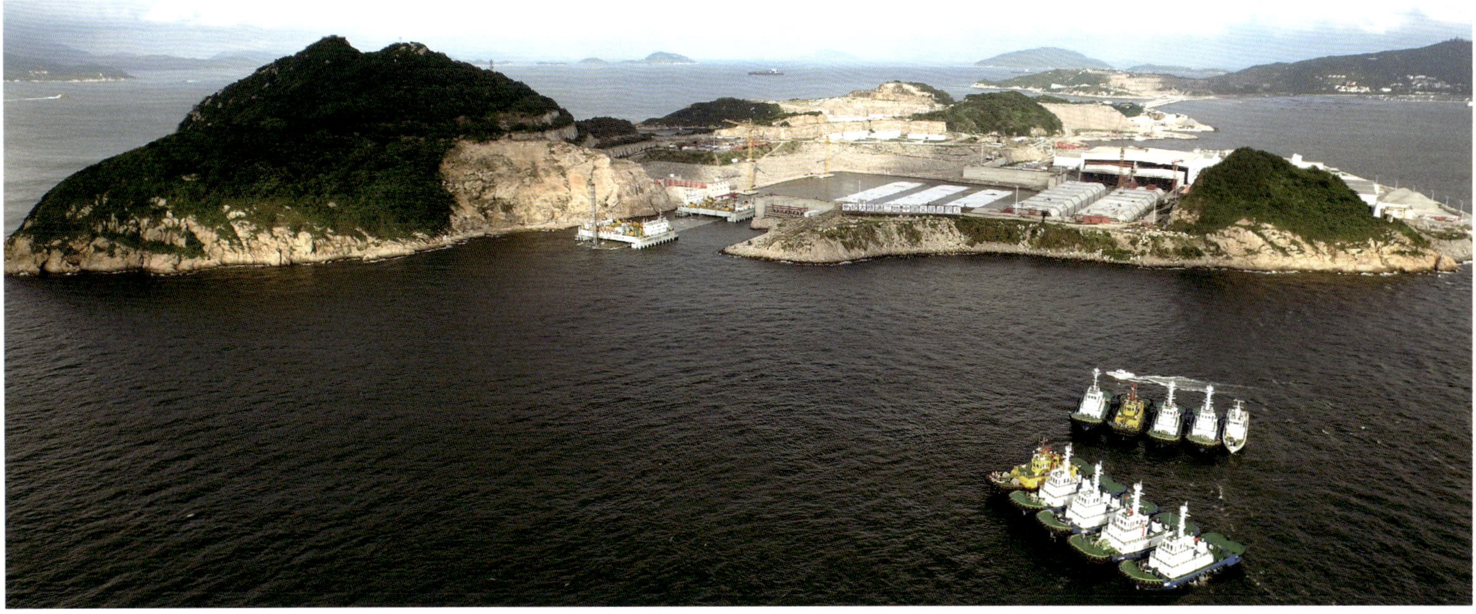

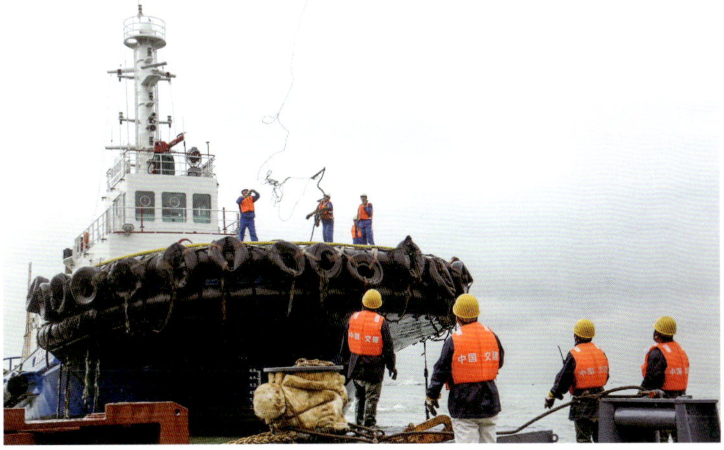

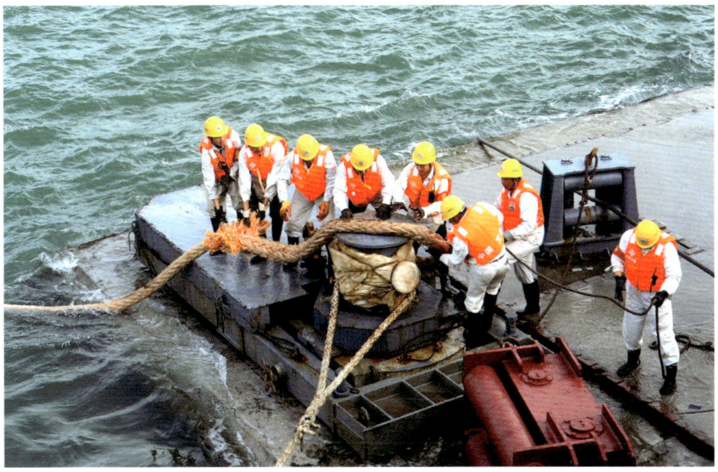

1	2
	3 | 4

1. 沉管拖航编队完成
   Completion of the Immersed Tube Tugboat Formation
2. 拖轮等候拖航编队
   Tugboats Ready for the Formation
3. 拖轮带缆
   Tugboat Heaving Cables
4. 拖轮系缆
   Tugboat Mooring Cables

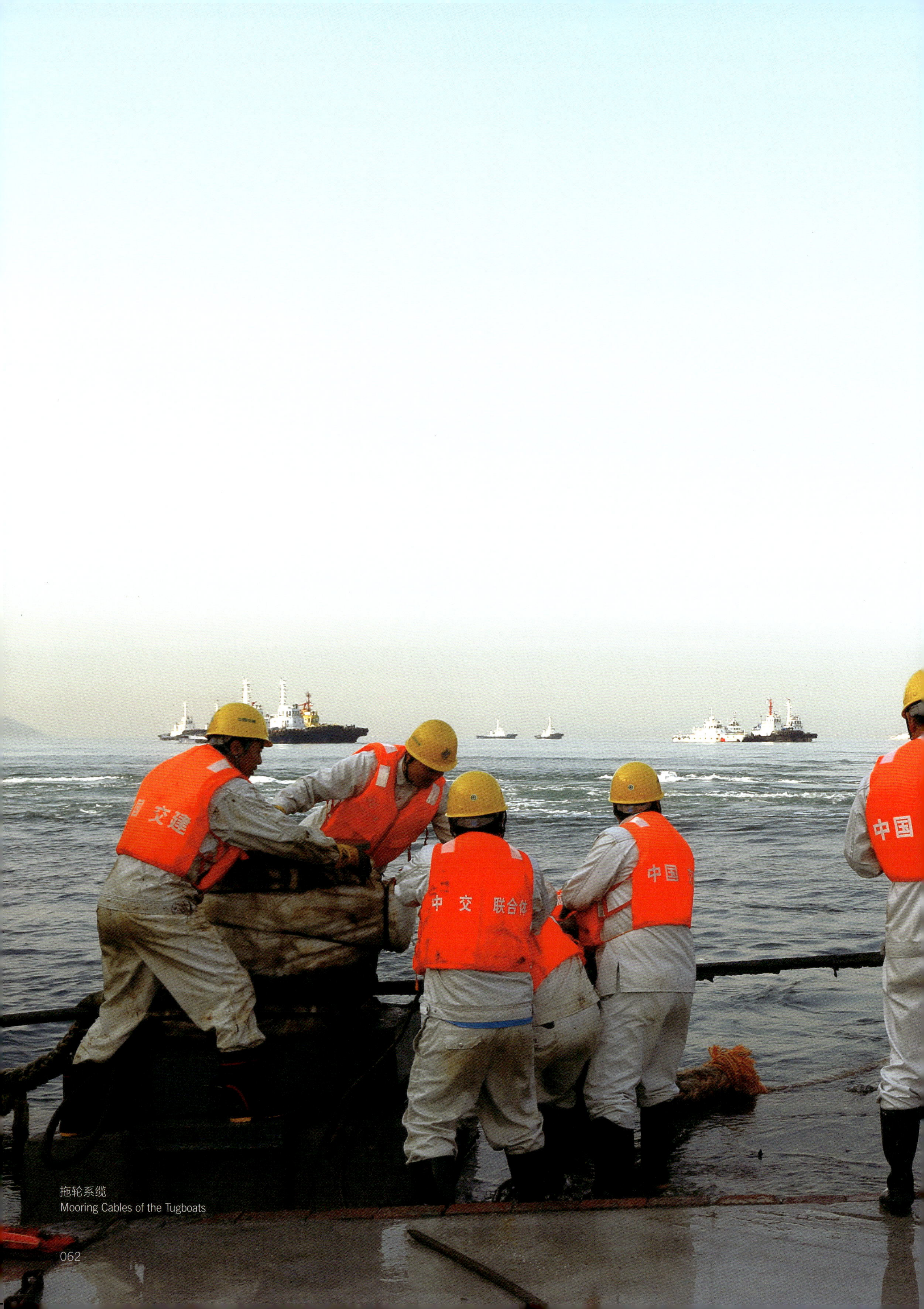

拖轮系缆
Mooring Cables of the Tugboats

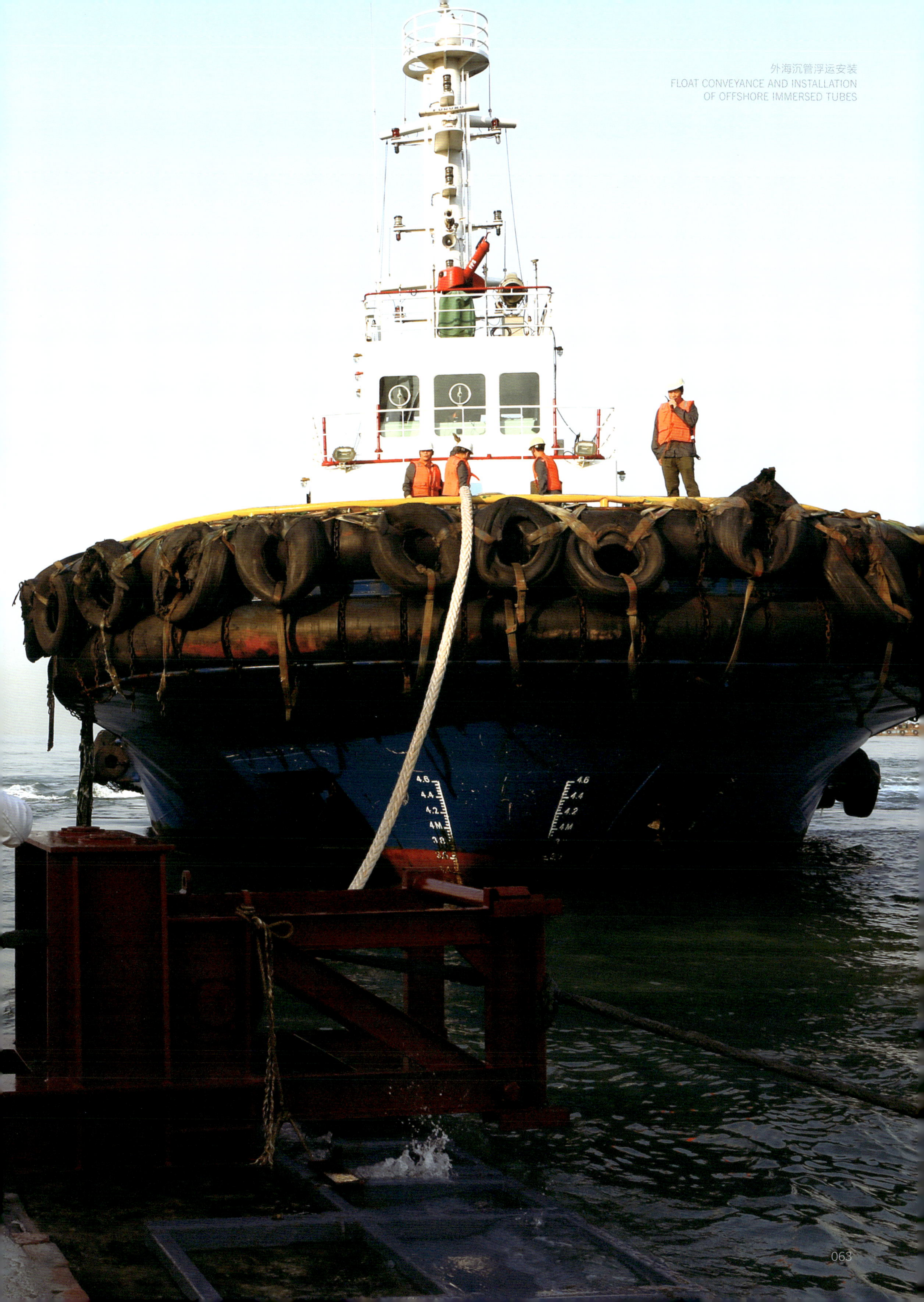
4.6
4.4
4.2
4M
3.8
4.6
4.4
4.2
4M

沉管浮运
FLOAT CONVEYANCE OF THE IMMERSED TUBES

1. 数字化浮运导航系统
   Digital Navigation System of the Float Conveyance
2. 沉管浮运指挥
   Conduction of the Immersed Tube Float Conveyance
3. E33 沉管浮运
   Float Conveyance of the Immersed Tube E33
4. 浮运中的安装船和沉管
   Installation Barges and Immersed Tubes during Float Conveyance

沉管隧道沉管体量超大，外海环境下海流、波浪等水文条件复杂，部分开挖的浮运航道宽度较窄，拖航环境复杂，沉管浮运操控难度非常大，经过大量的模型试验和多次试拖后选择了多拖轮协同拖运方案。

除四角是 4 艘吊拖拖轮加两侧 4 艘绑拖拖轮外，还配备了 2~3 艘辅助和备用拖轮用于沉管横流状态下的基槽浮运，最多时共配置了 13 艘大马力全回转拖轮进行浮运拖航工作。

同时研发数字化导航系统辅助指挥，使沉管浮运过程中位置可视、可控，确保浮运安全。

Because of the super size of the immersed tube, the complicated offshore sea current and wave, the narrow water path for the float conveyance of the tube, the complicated environment for the towing, and the difficulties in controlling the tube transportation, numerous model tests and trial towing were done before the decision on the cooperative towing by several towing barges was made.

Except 4 towing barges performing hoisting and 4 performing towing abreast, 2 or 3 auxiliary and standby towing barges were prepared for the float conveyance of the tubes in case of crossscurrent. In special cases, 13 high horse-power swing-towing barges wre used for the float conveyance of the tube.

A digital navigation system was developed to help make the position of the tube during transportation visible, controllable, and guarantee the safety of the tube transportation.

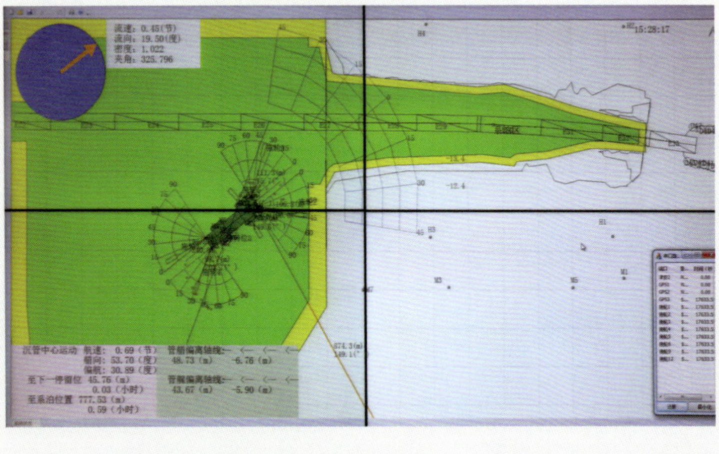

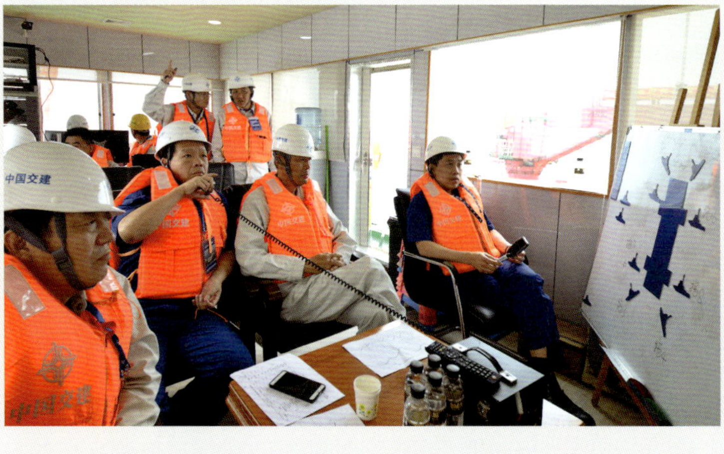

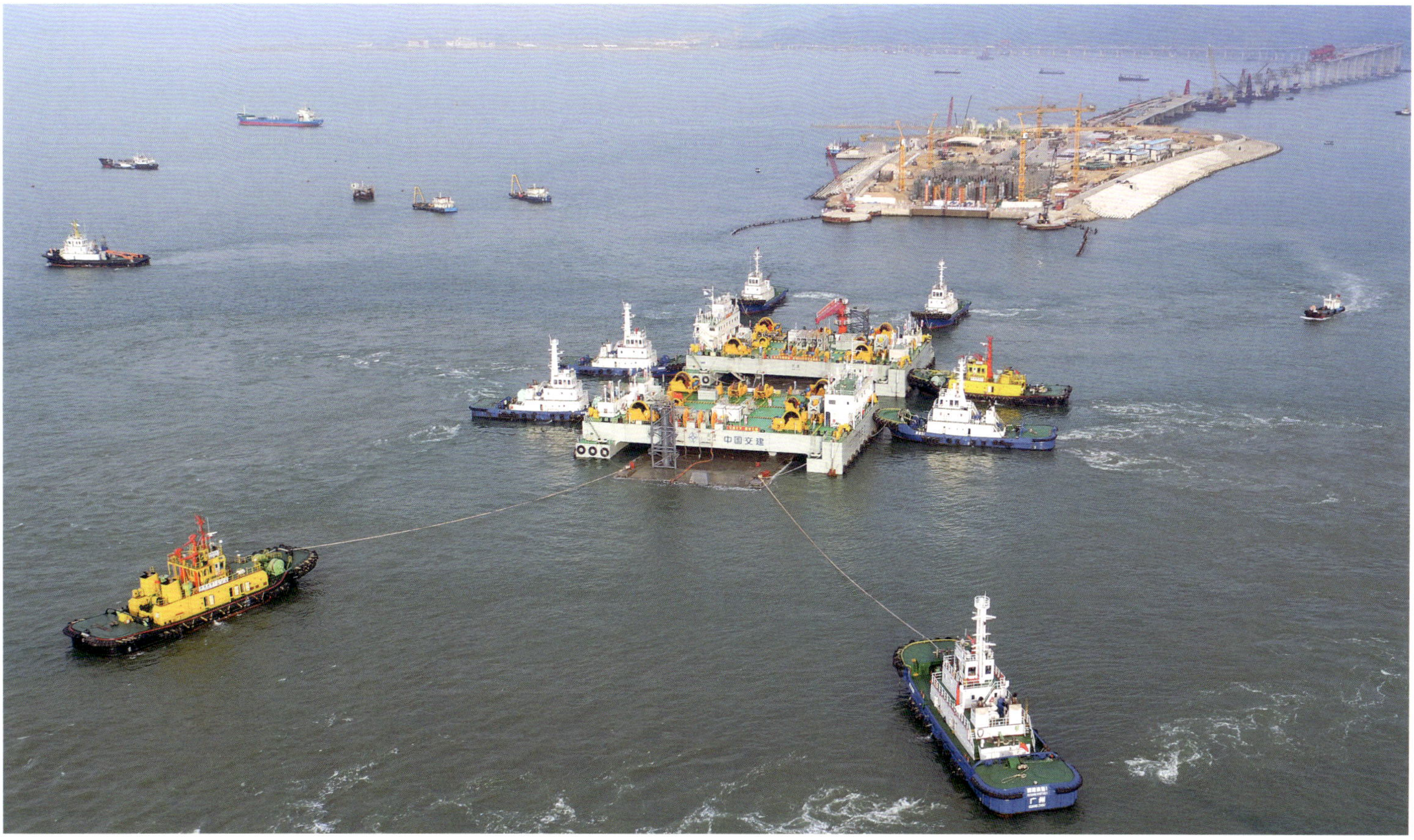

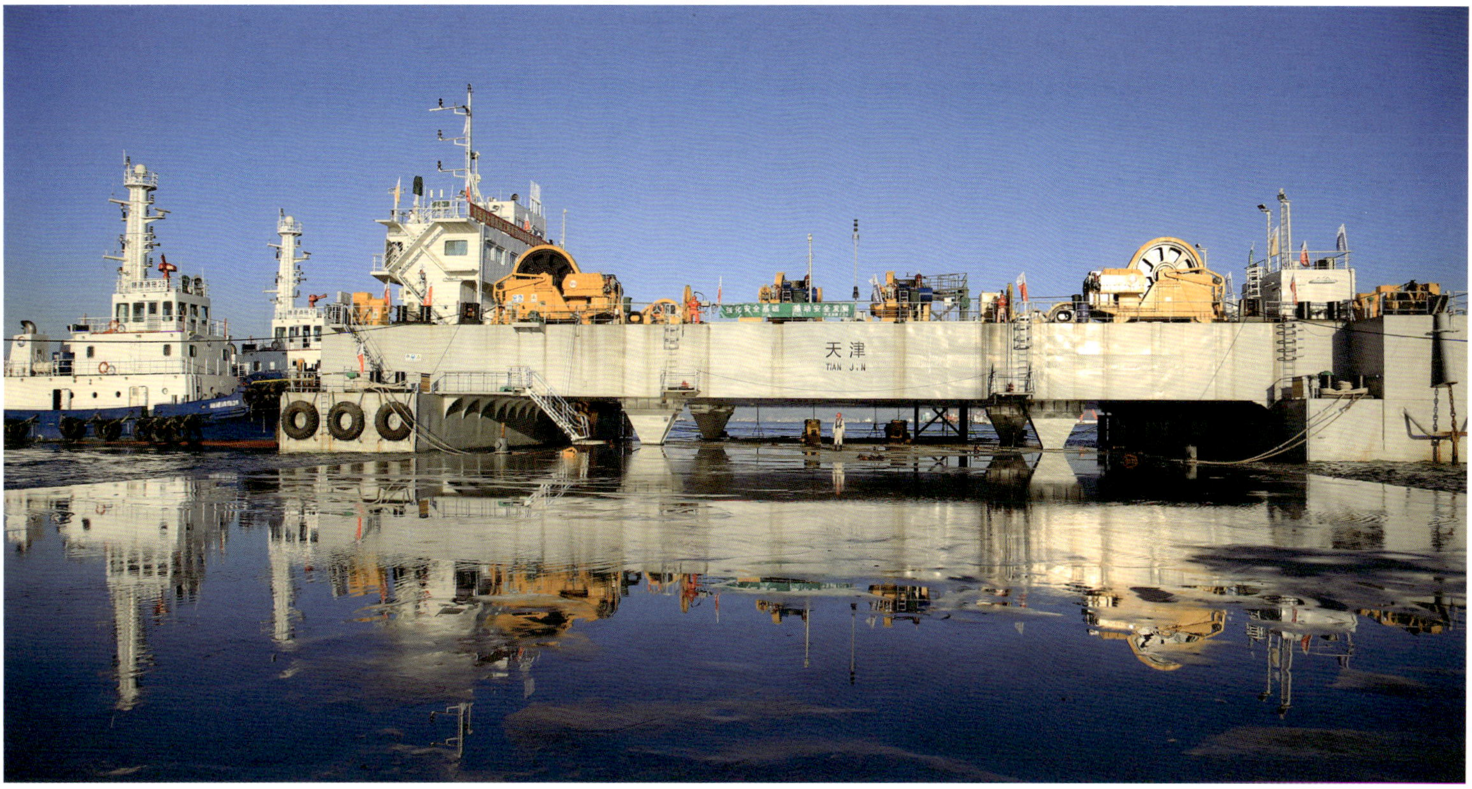
天津
TIAN JIN

E3 沉管浮运

Float Conveyance of the Immersed Tube E33

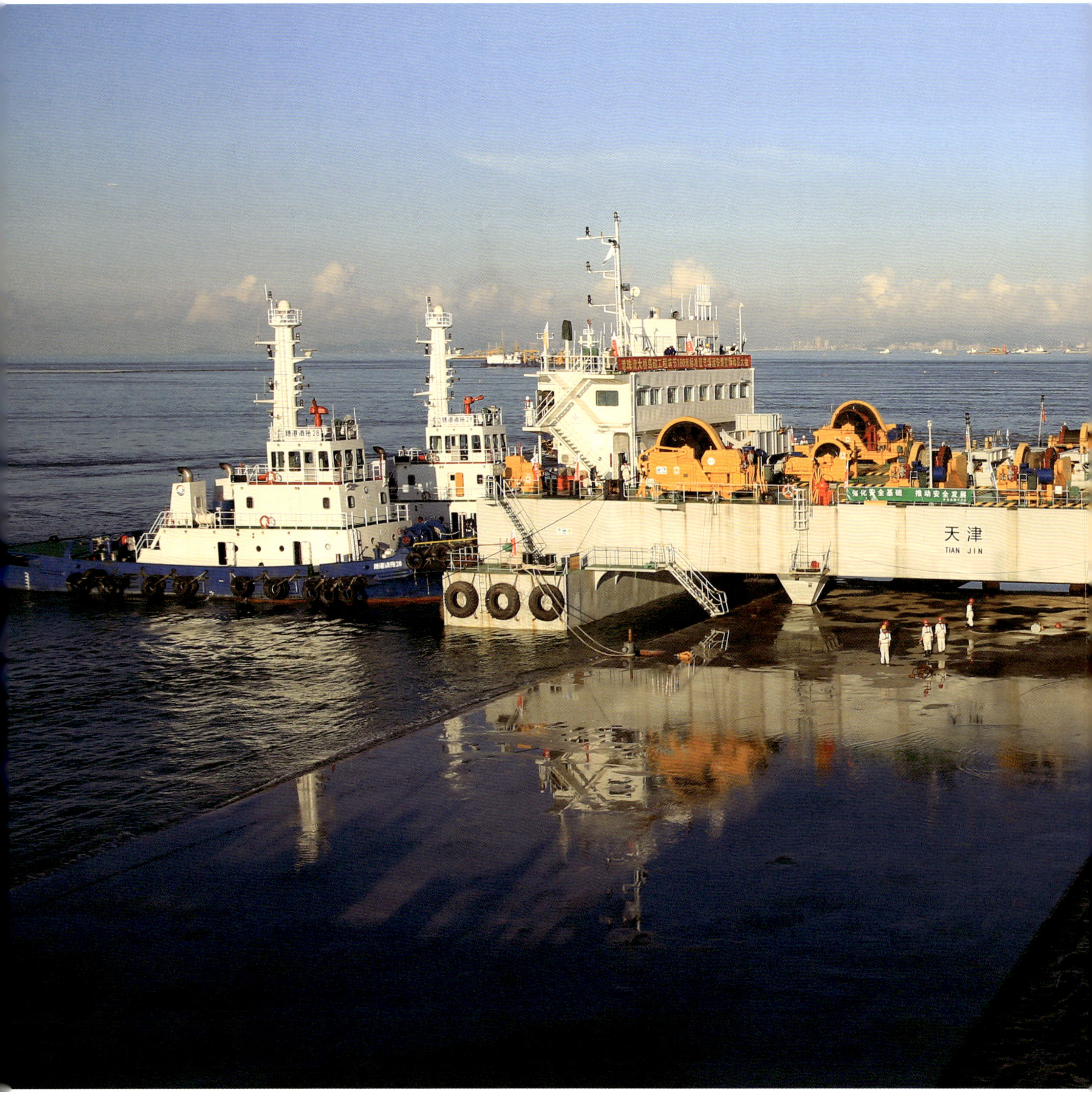

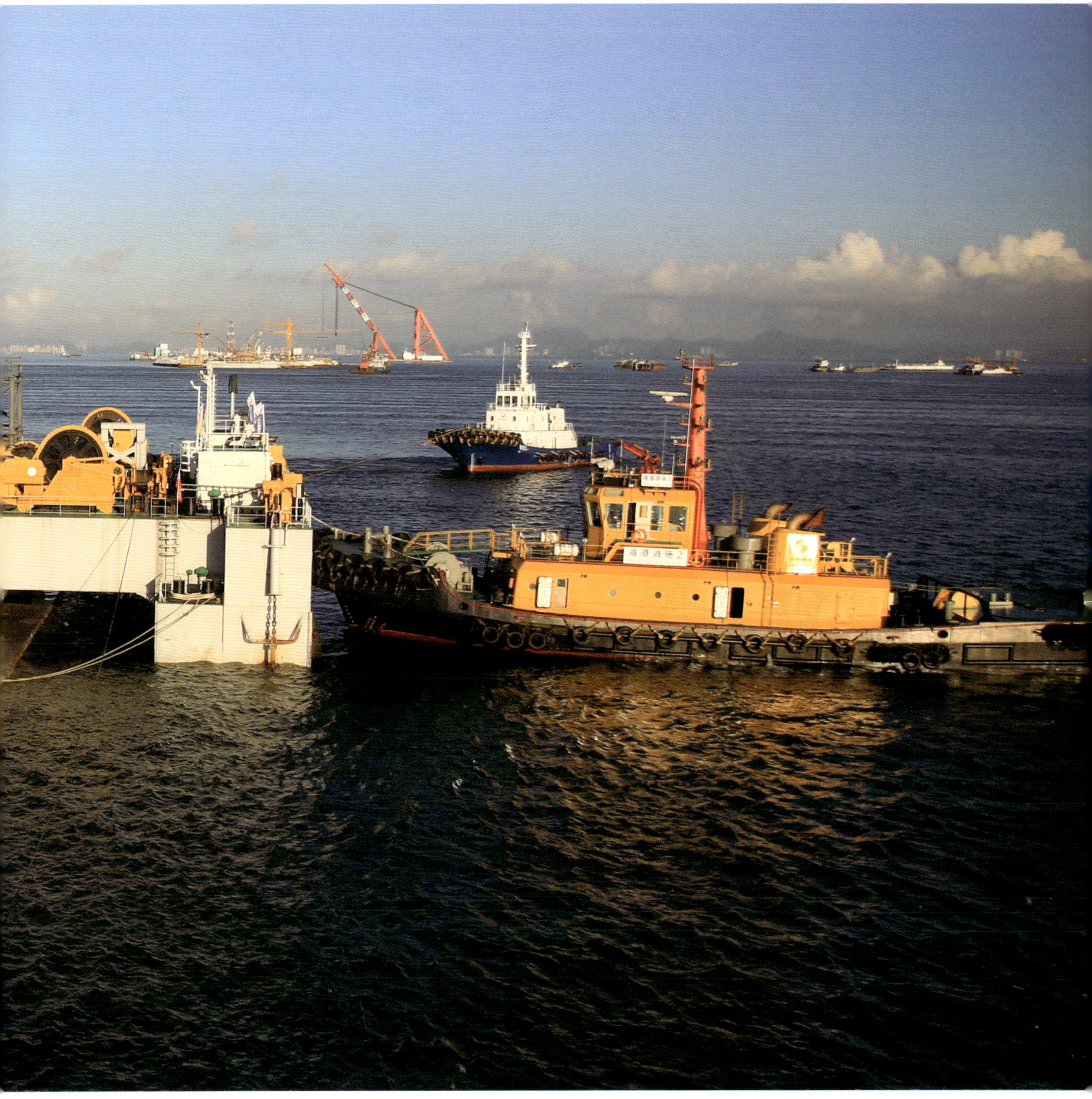

沉管系泊

ANCHORING OF THE IMMERSED TUBES

沉管系泊是指沉管（船、管组合体）浮运至待安装区域后，通过将安装驳上的缆系与预设在海床上的锚碇连接形成多点锚泊系统的过程。

沉管体量巨大，受波浪、水流影响极大，安装驳与沉管组成多浮体柔性受力体系，动力响应复杂，且系泊作业时间受限。

The anchoring of the immersed tube means that when the tube (that is a combination of the barges and the tube) was transported to the installation region, the cables on the installation barge were connected to the anchors on the seabed to form a multi-point mooring system.

Because of its tremendous size, the immersed tube could be easily affected by the wave and current; and the installation barges and the tubes formed a flexible load-carrying capacity system composed of multiple floating equipments that had to deal with the complicated dynamic responses and the limited time for anchoring.

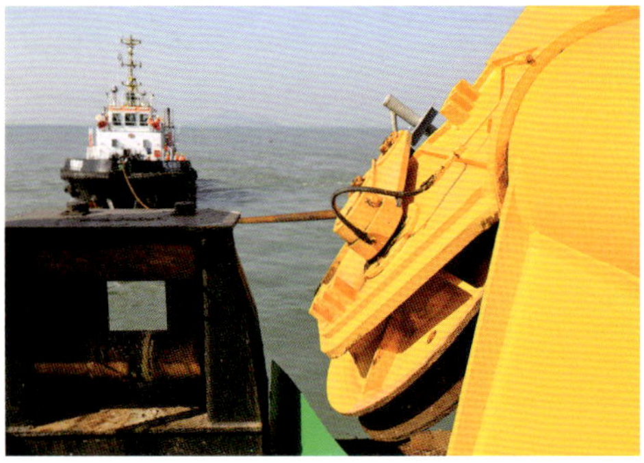

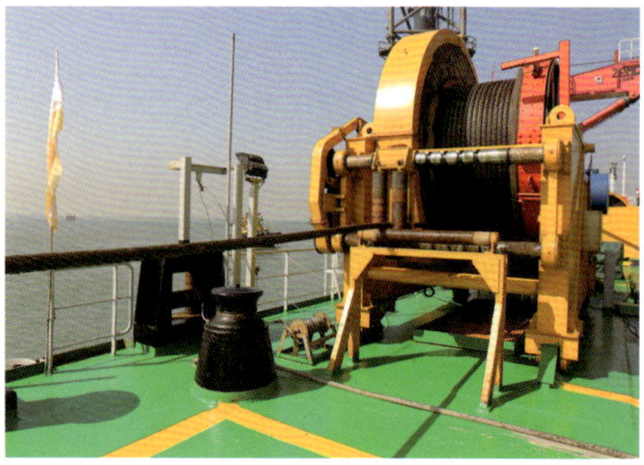

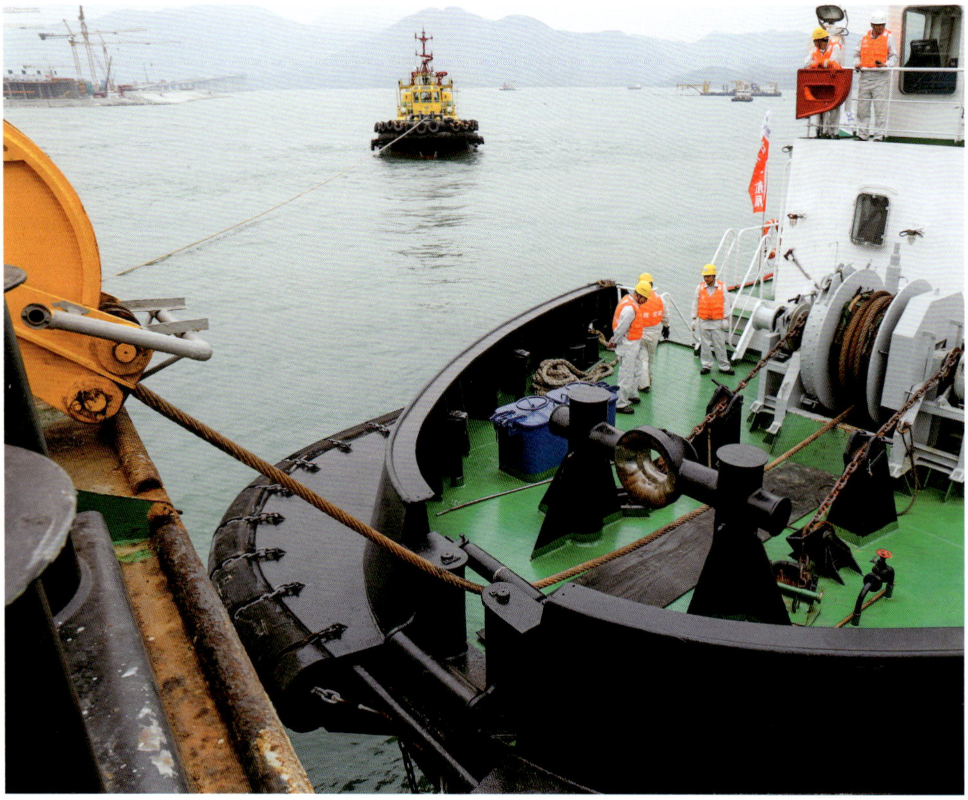

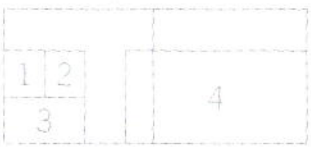

1. M2 缆绳揆缆
   Mooring Cable M2 Uncoiling
2. 系泊锚机
   Mooring Windlass
3. 系泊缆连接
   Mooring Cable Connection
4. 沉管系泊施工
   Anchoring of the Immersed Tubes

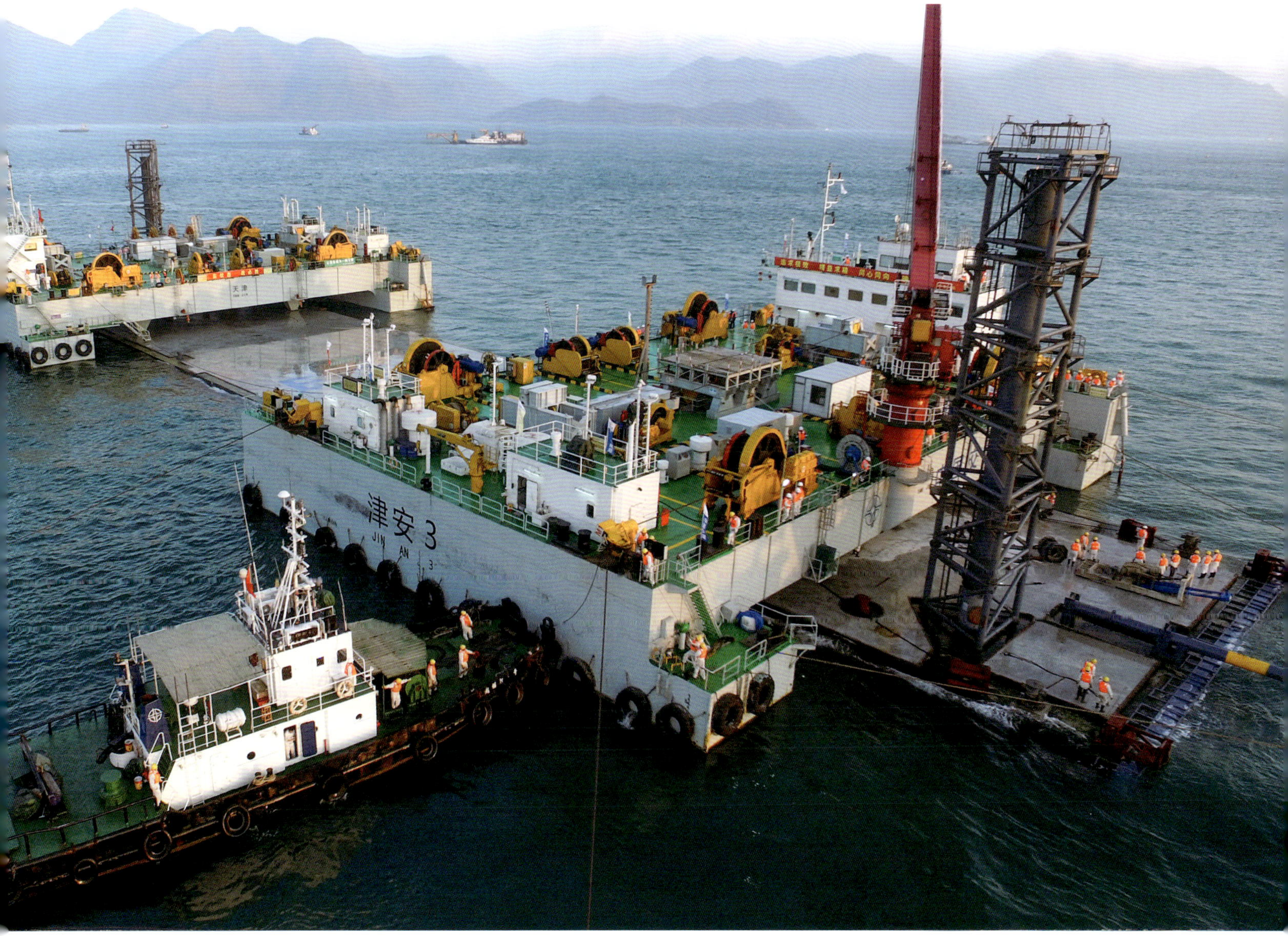

1. 系泊缆系分布图
Distribution of the Mooring Cables

2. 系泊船"起锚艇 15"
Anchor Boat 15 of the Mooring Barge

3. 沉管系泊锚、安装锚布置图
Distribution of the Mooring and Installation Anchors

4. 沉管系泊
Anchoring of the Immersed Tubes

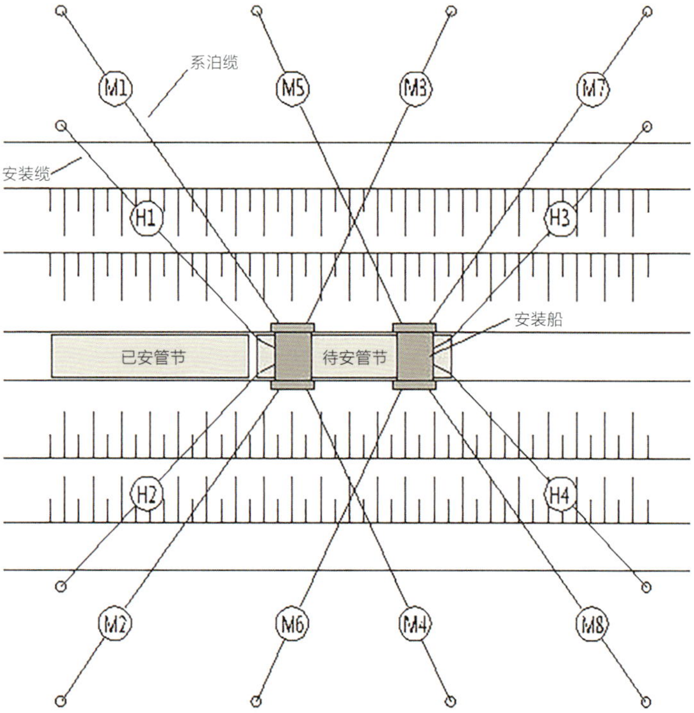

采用 12 点对称锚泊系统，即单个沉管布置 12 口锚，包括 8 口操控沉放驳的系泊锚和 4 口操控沉管的安装锚。

系泊锚和安装锚沿沉管两侧平行于隧道轴线布置，深水区和浅水区相同。

系泊锚距离隧道轴线 300 米布置，安装锚距离隧道轴线 200 米布置，系泊缆和安装缆与隧道轴线的夹角按 45° ~60°控制。

12-point symmetrical mooring system was used, namely a single tube was tied to 12 anchors--8 for the control of the landing barges and 4 for the control of the installation barges.

The mooring anchors and installations anchors were distributed along the two sides of the immersed tube parallel to the axis line of the tunnel. This remained unchanged in both deep water and shallow water regions.

The mooring anchors were positioned in the places 300 meters to the tunnel's axis line, while the installation anchors in the places 200 meters to the axis line of the tunnel. The included angles between the mooring line and installation line with the tunnel's axis line were controlled between 45°~60°.

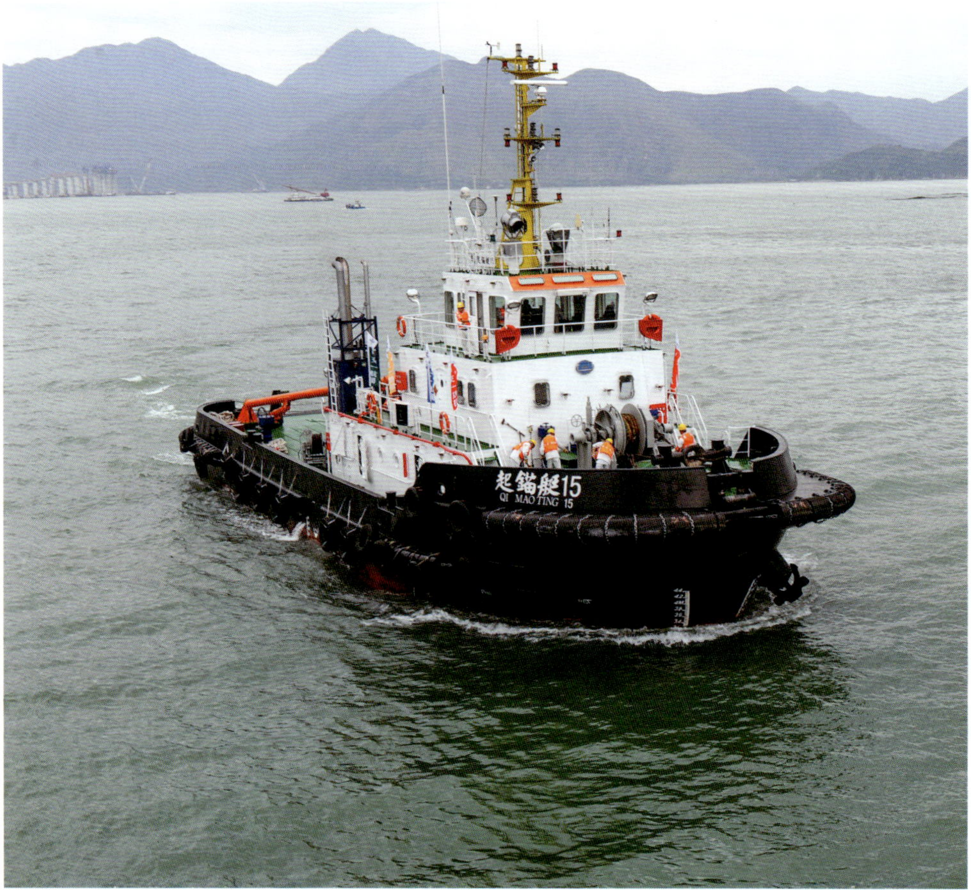

根据对拖曳嵌入式大抓力锚特征和对国内外沉管隧道工程系泊定位锚系的分析研究，结合施工区域淤泥和黏土层较厚的地质特点，项目总经理部开展了多种锚型的锚抓力试验。

通过试验确定了大抓力锚在本工程地质条件下各项性能参数、适用性及具体施工工艺。

综合试验数据，最终选择了 HY-17 型大抓力锚作为沉管定位锚碇。

该锚型实测抓力系数可达 15~20，具有抓重比大的特点，能提供沉管定位抵抗水流所需的稳定锚固力。

Based on the analyses of the features of the high-holding-power draging-embedding anchors and the mooring-positioning anchors used in immersed tube tunneling, as well as the geological features of the thick sediments and clay in the construction region, the project management center conducted various experiments on the holding-power of various anchors.

Experiments were done to decide on various parameters, applicability and application technologies of the high-holding-power anchors in specified geological conditions.

By taking all the experimental data into consideration, HY-17 high-holding-power anchor was chosen as the positioning anchor for the tube installation.

The holding-power parameter of this type of anchor is 15 to 20 by test, featuring by big holding-power-to-weight ratio. It can provide the steady holding power needed to resist the current in tube positioning.

名称 Name	名义抓重比 Nominal Grab Weight Ratio	作业内容 Job Content
AC-14 型锚 AC-14 Anchor	12-14	对淤泥、砂质等地质都有较好的适用性，操控性较好，多用于超大型船、滚装船等 Applicable for sediment and sand ground, easy to handle, and often used on super-large vessels and roll-on-roll-off vessels
HYD-14 型锚 HYD-14 Anchor	9-20	用于硬泥地质，适用于工作船、作业船、浮标定位、海洋平台等 Applicable for hard mud ground, and often used on utility ship, operation ship, oversea platform or for buoy positioning
HY-17 型锚 HY-17 Anchor	10-30	适用于淤泥质及砂质，多用于工程船系泊如起重船、铺管船和石油平台等。制造和结构简单，抓重比系数大，起锚需专用装备 Applicable for sediment and sand ground, and often used on engineering vessels like hoisting barges, tube-landing barges, or oil drilling platform; easy to be manufactured, featured by simple structure, high holding efficiency, and needing special equipment for unmooring

试验用大抓力锚列表
List of Experimental Anchors with High Holding Efficiency

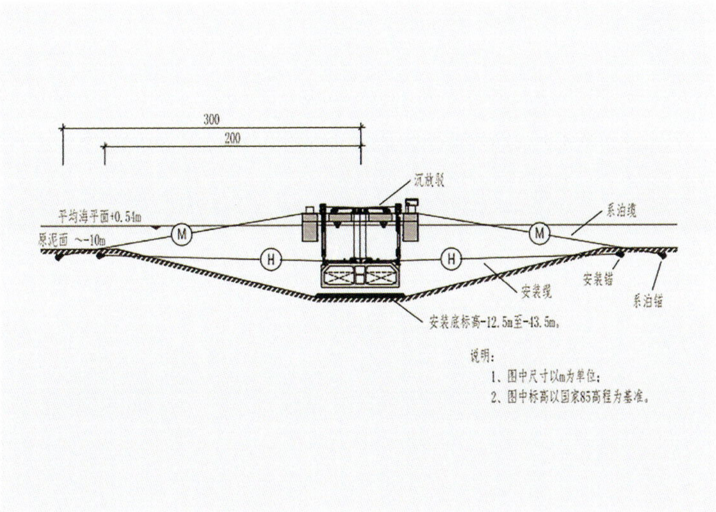

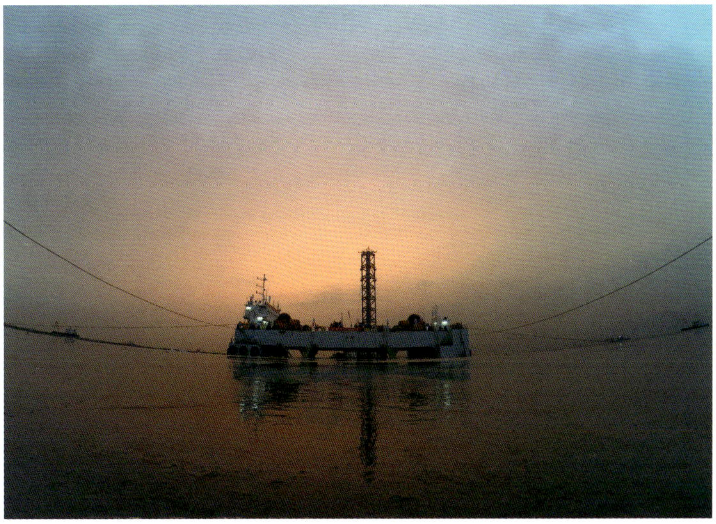

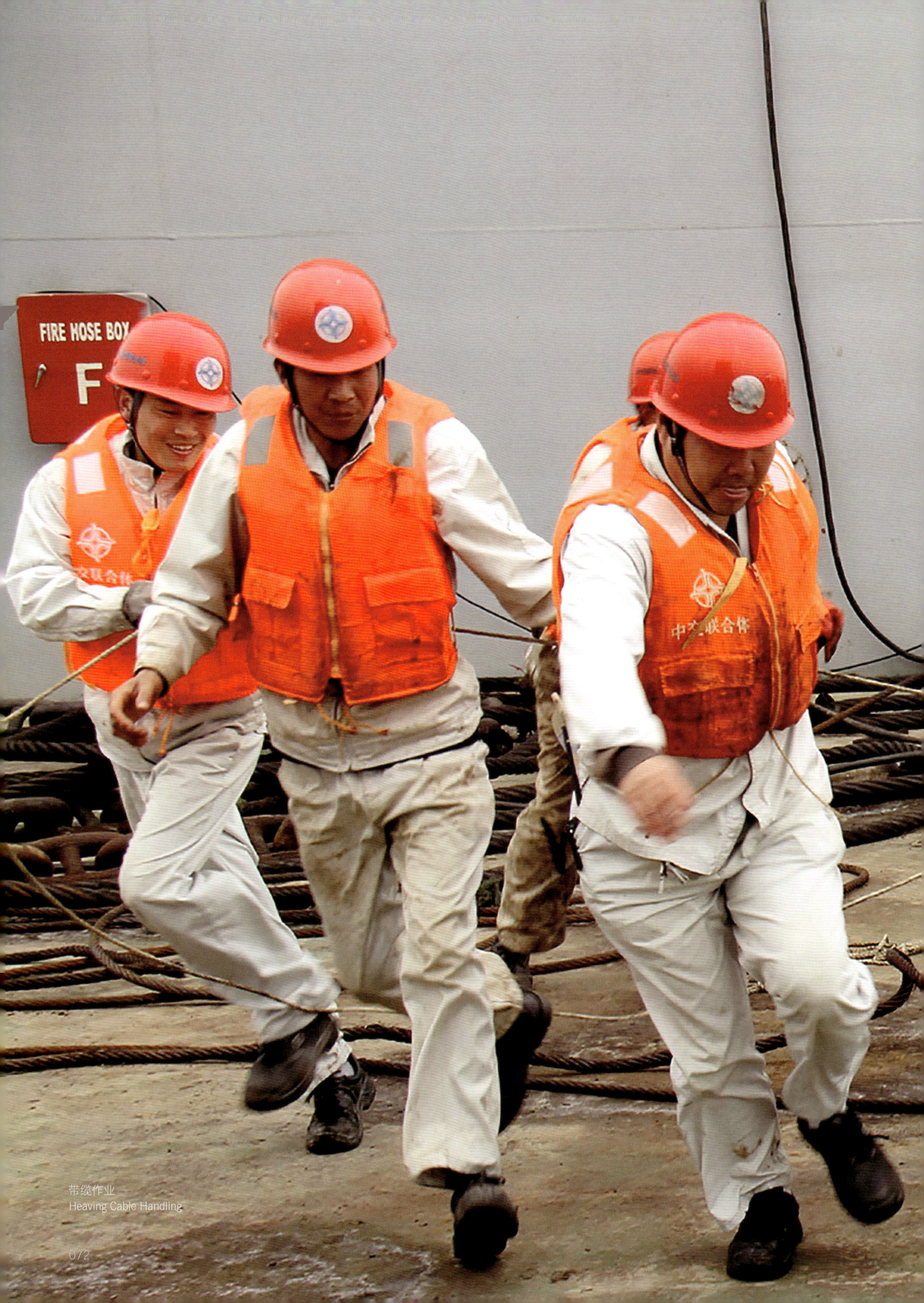

带缆作业
Heaving Cable Handling

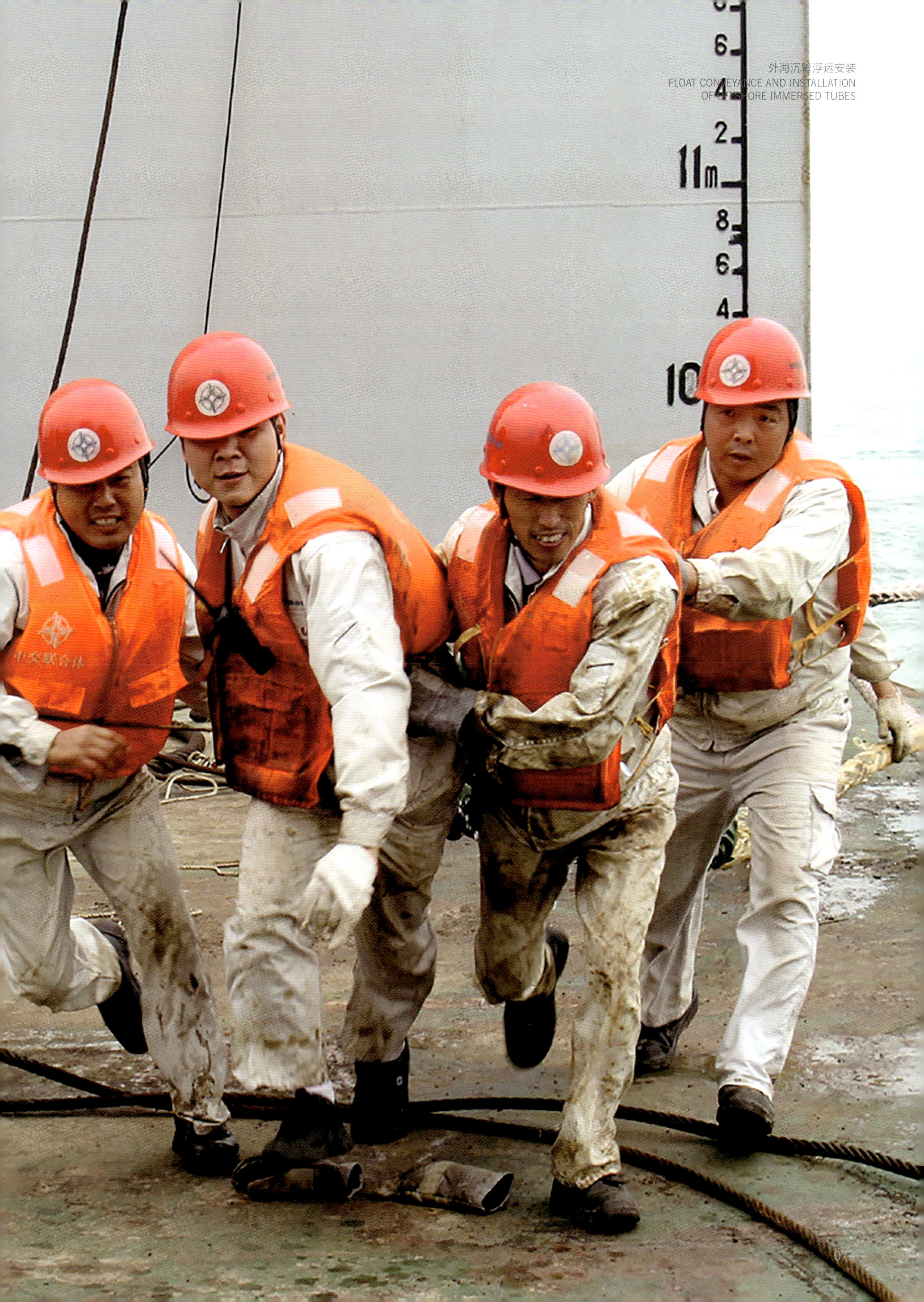
11m
中交联合体

沉管系泊完成后立即开展基床多波束扫测，检测基床、边坡回淤情况。

确认正常后，起重班、舾装班组立即进行 GINA 保护罩、系船柱、羊角滚轮导缆器螺栓等设备拆除作业；安装组、测量队同步开展拉合千斤顶主动单元、深水测控系统收发信器件、水下摄像监控系统等安装施工。

After the anchoring of the immersed tube was finished, multi-beam scanning closely followed to test the conditions of the tunnel bed and back silting on the side slopes.

If everything was normal, hoisting barges and fitting-out barges immediately began to remove the GINA protection shield, barge anchoring pillars, and the bolts of the fairleaders; installation barges and the measurement group would install the active cell of the pulling jack, the information sender and receiver of deep water monitoring system as well as the underwater camera monitoring system.

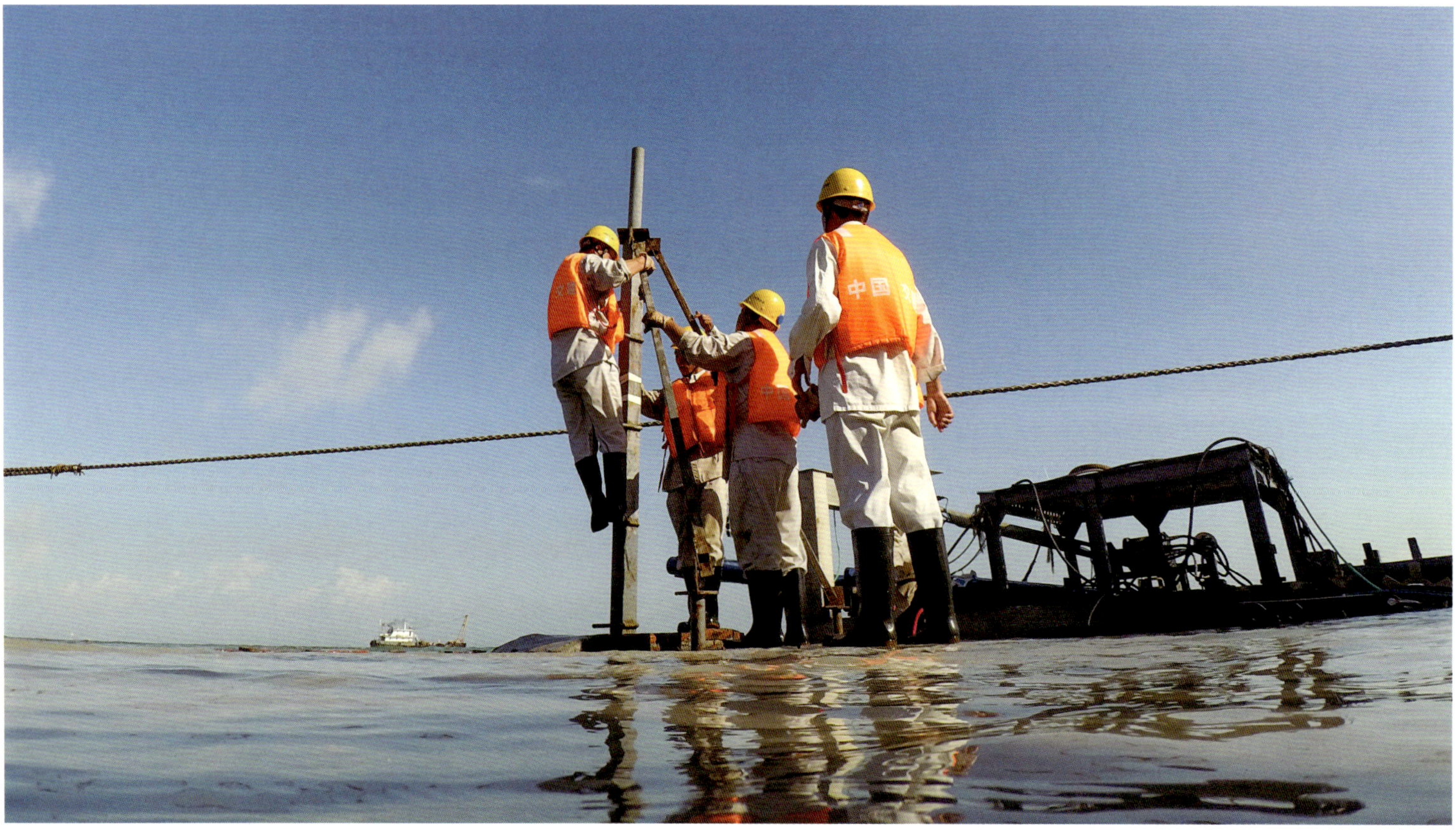

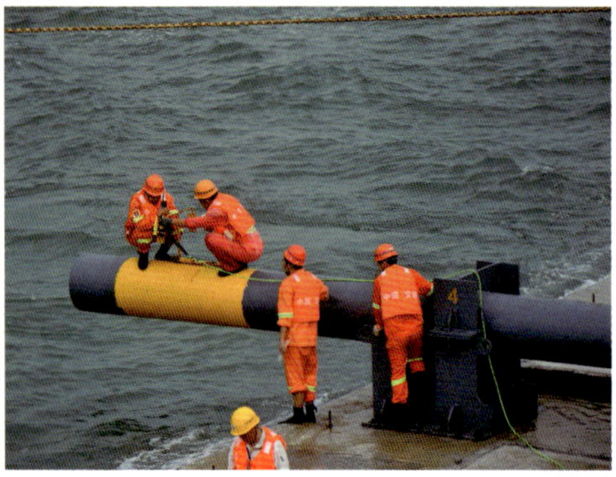

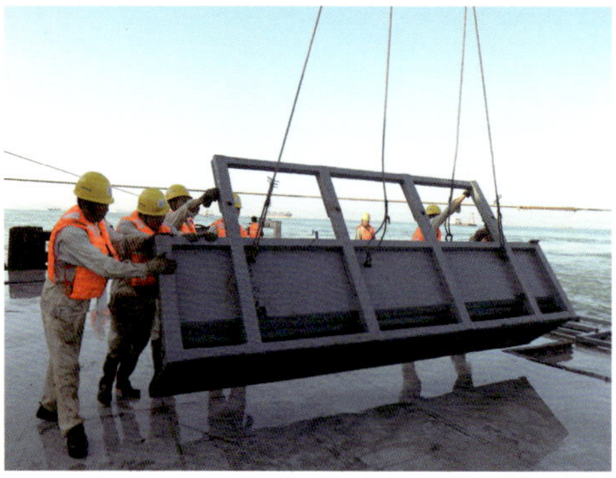

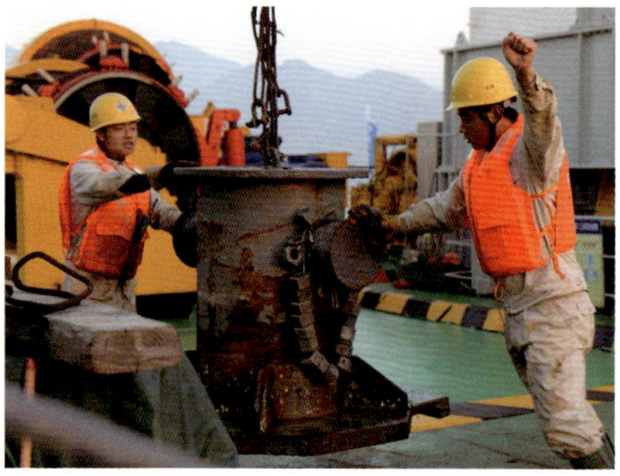

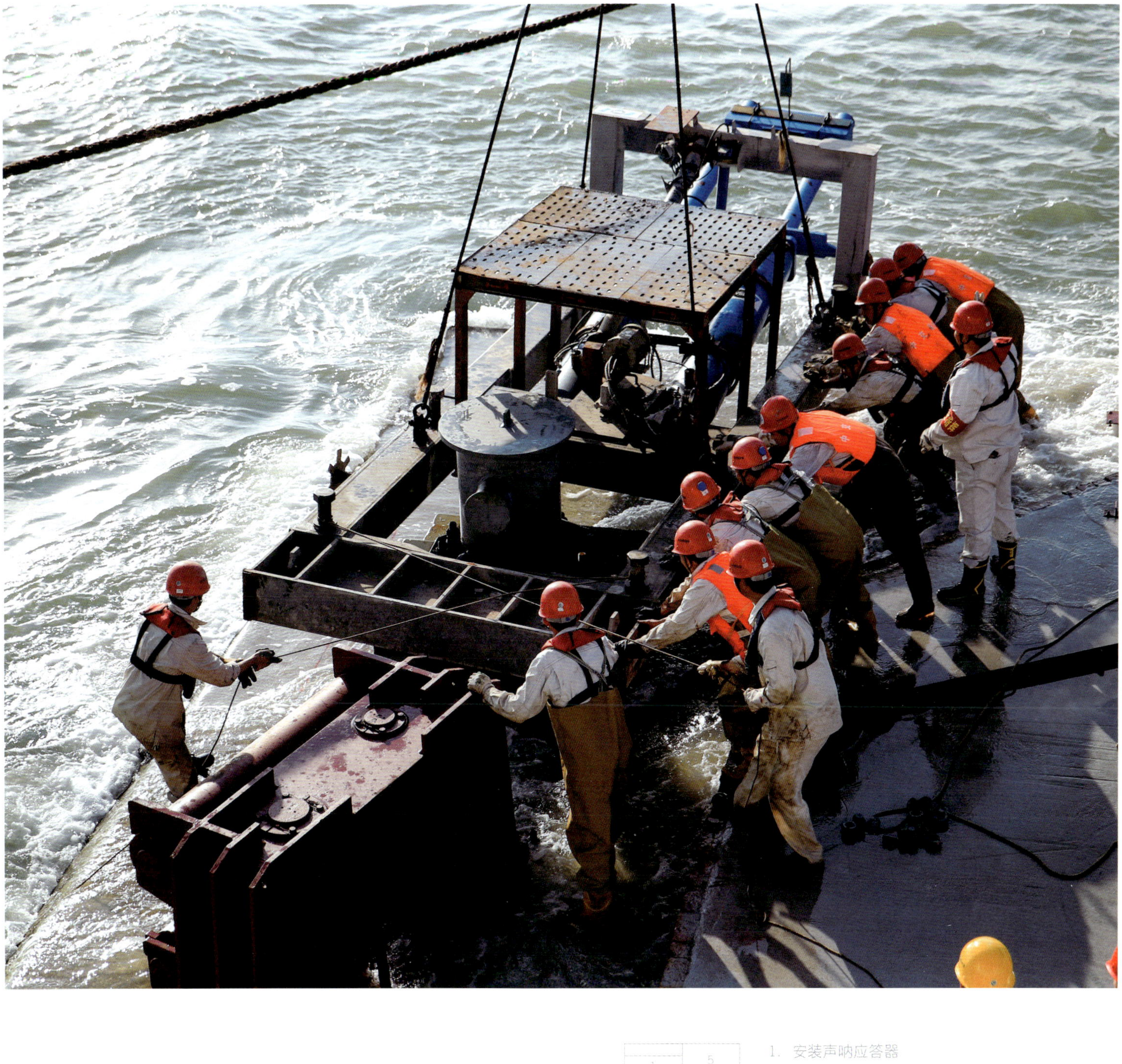

1. 安装声呐应答器
   Installation of the Sonar Transponder
2. 安装水下监控摄像头
   Installation of Underwater Monitoring Cameras
3. 拆卸 GINA 保护罩
   Uninstallation of GINA Protective Hood
4. 拆除系缆桩
   Uninstallation of the Mooring Bollards
5. 安装拉合千斤顶
   Installation of the Pulling Jack

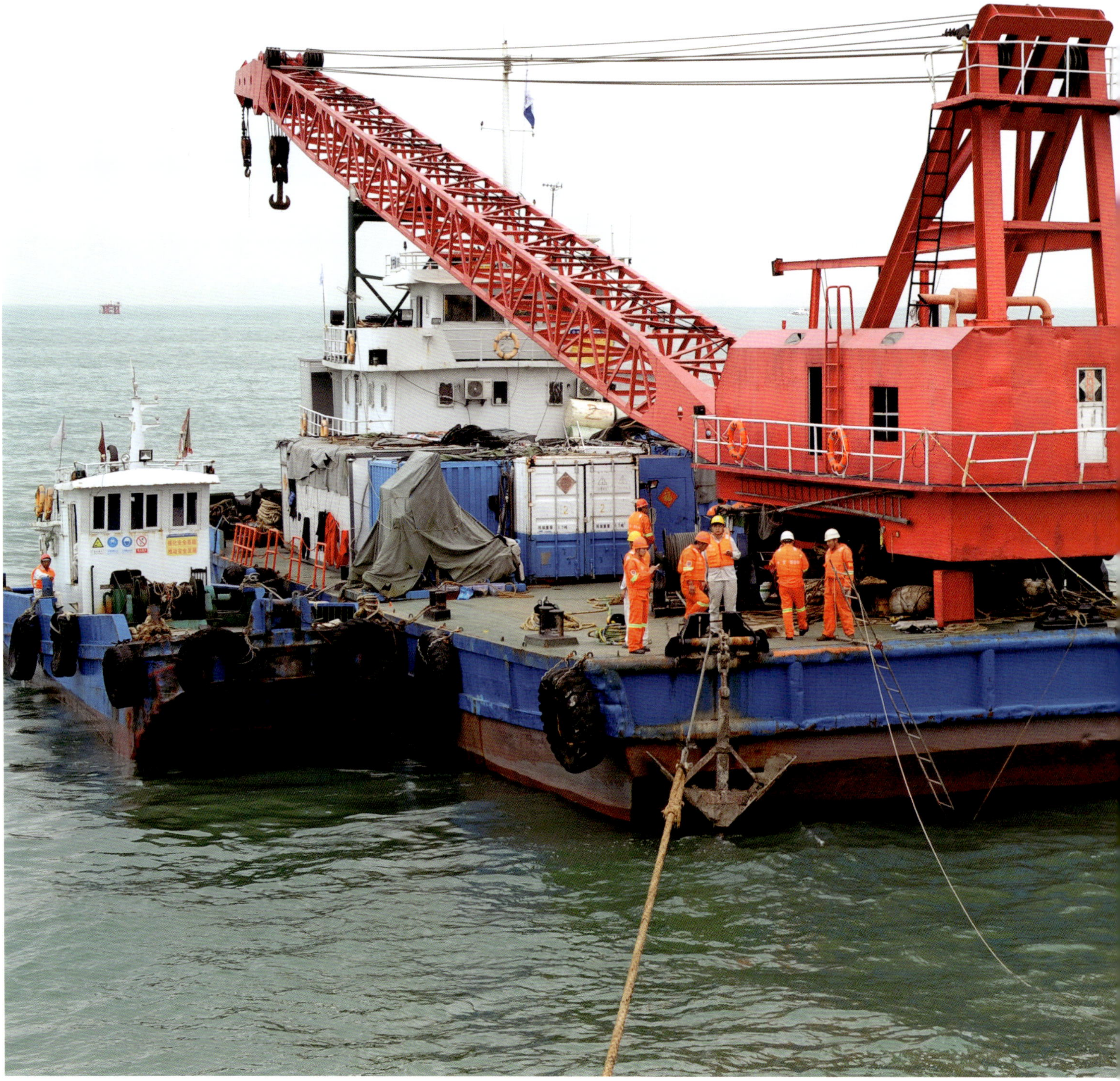

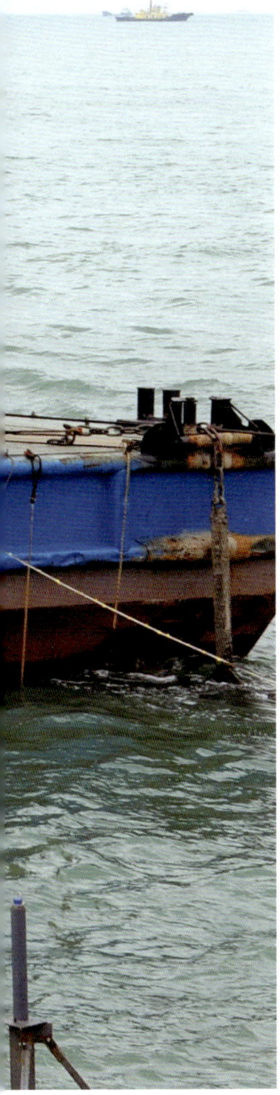

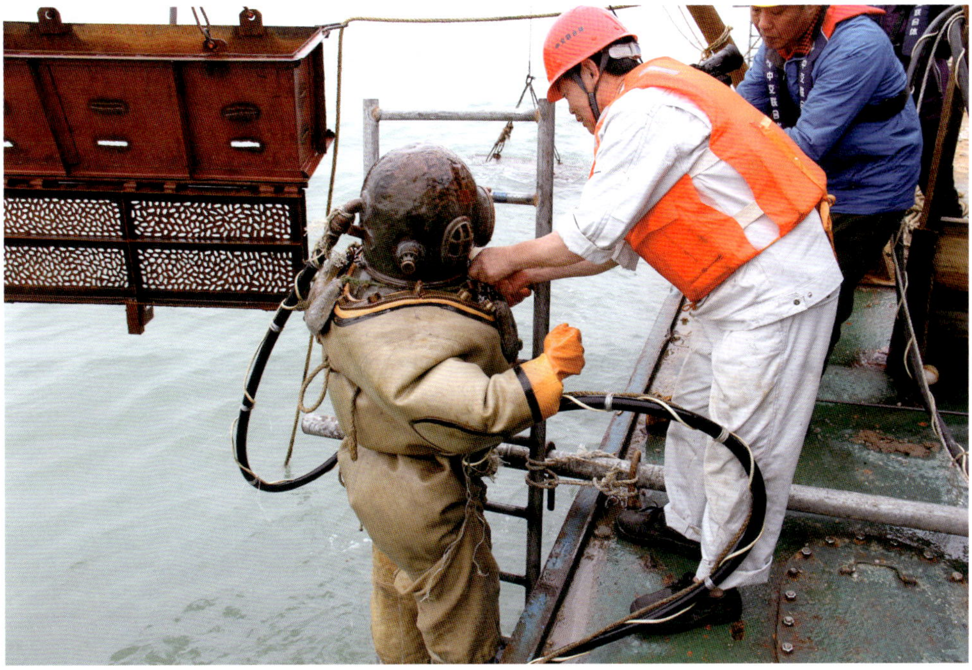

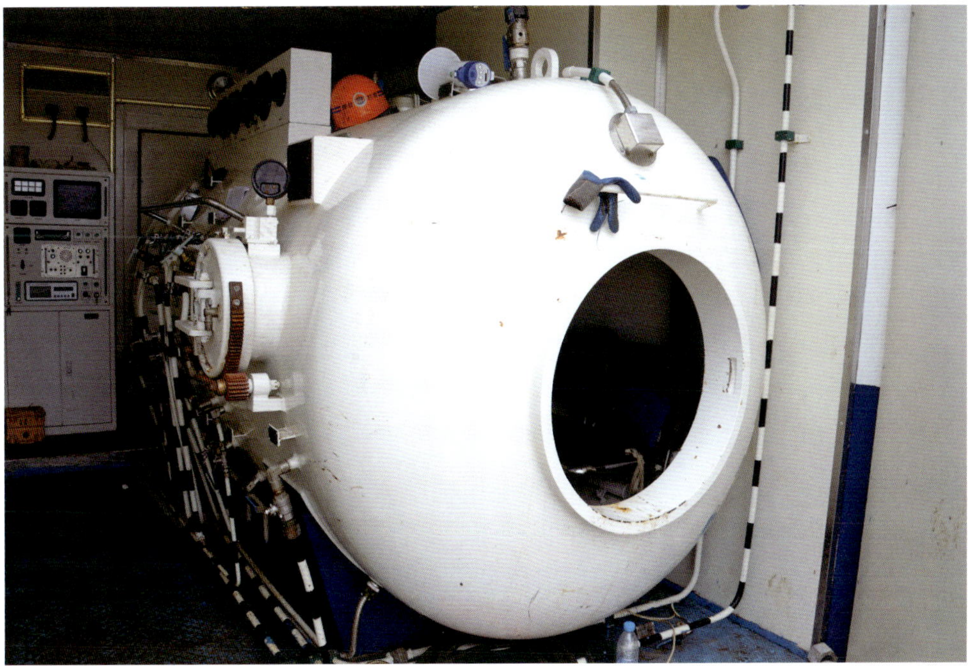

1. 潜水母船"盐中捞 386"
Submarine Parent Barge "Yanzhonglao 386"

2. 潜水员下水探摸作业
Divers' Underwater Exploration

3. 潜水员减压舱
Decompression Chamber for the Divers

沉管沉放和对接

LANDING AND BUTT WELDING OF THE IMMERSED TUBES

沉管沉放是指沉管浮运到安装位置并在水面完成系泊定位后，开始下沉直至坐落于基床顶面的过程，在整个沉管隧道施工过程中占有重要的地位；涉及的关键施工技术包括沉放设备选择和沉放控制方法、沉管压载控制方法、测量定位方法等。

沉管对接是指利用沉放控制系统准确定位下沉至预先铺设好的基床上（先铺法），与已沉放沉管精确对位、连接的过程。

项目总经理部自主研发、设计、制造了集系泊定位、沉放对接、远程操控、监测监控等综合功能于一体的信息化沉管安装装备——双驳杠吊法水下无人沉放定位系统。

该系统包括安装驳和锚泊子系统、管内压载子系统、测量定位子系统、导向子系统、初步拉合子系统、水力压接子系统、水下摄像监控子系统等。

双驳杠吊法水下无人沉放定位系统数字化集成度高，沉管沉放深度控制精确；同步应用遥控遥测技术，沉放和对接过程中管内无人值守和操作，所有操作均在安装驳控制室内完成。

最大沉放水深约 50 米，沉管水下定位精度可达 5 厘米。

The tube landing means that when the immersed tube is moved to the installation site by float conveyance, and the mooring and positioning over the sea surface are done, the tube will be lowered onto the top surface of the foundation trench. This is a very important step in the whole process of the immersed tube tunnel construction. The critical technologies involved here include the choice of immersing equipments, landing control, ballasting control of the tube as well as measurement positioning, etc.

The butt welding of the immersed tubes means that the tube is first lowered onto the precast bed of the foundation trench by the landing control system, and then precisely positioned and connected with the tube already landed there.

The project management center designed and developed the information-based immersed tube installation equipment which combined mooring and positioning, landing and butt welding, remote control, monitoring and testing into one, namely the unmanned underwater double-barge beam-hoisting landing and positioning system.

This system included such subsidiary systems as installation barges and mooring, in-tube ballasting, measurement positioning, navigation, initiative pulling, hydraulic crimp connection, underwather camera monitoring.

This unmanned underwater double-barge beam-hoisting landing and positioning system was highly digitalized, which ensured the precision of depth control of the tube landing; the synchronized application of remote control and remote testing technology guaranteed that no human beings were needed to work inside the tube to monitor and handle problems in the process of tuber landing and butt welding. All operations were finished in the control chambers of the installation barges.

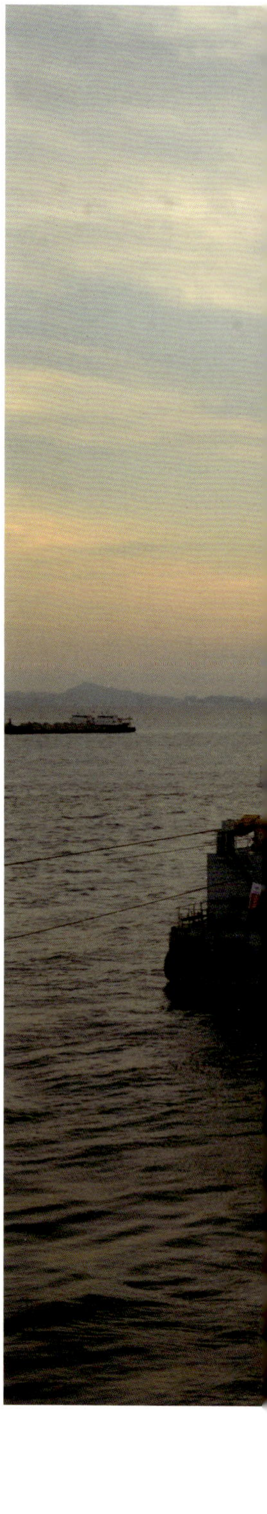

沉管沉放安装

Landing and Installation of the Immersed Tubes

The deepest place was 50 meters under the water, and the underwater positioning accuracy for the immersed tube was within the limit of 5 centimeters.

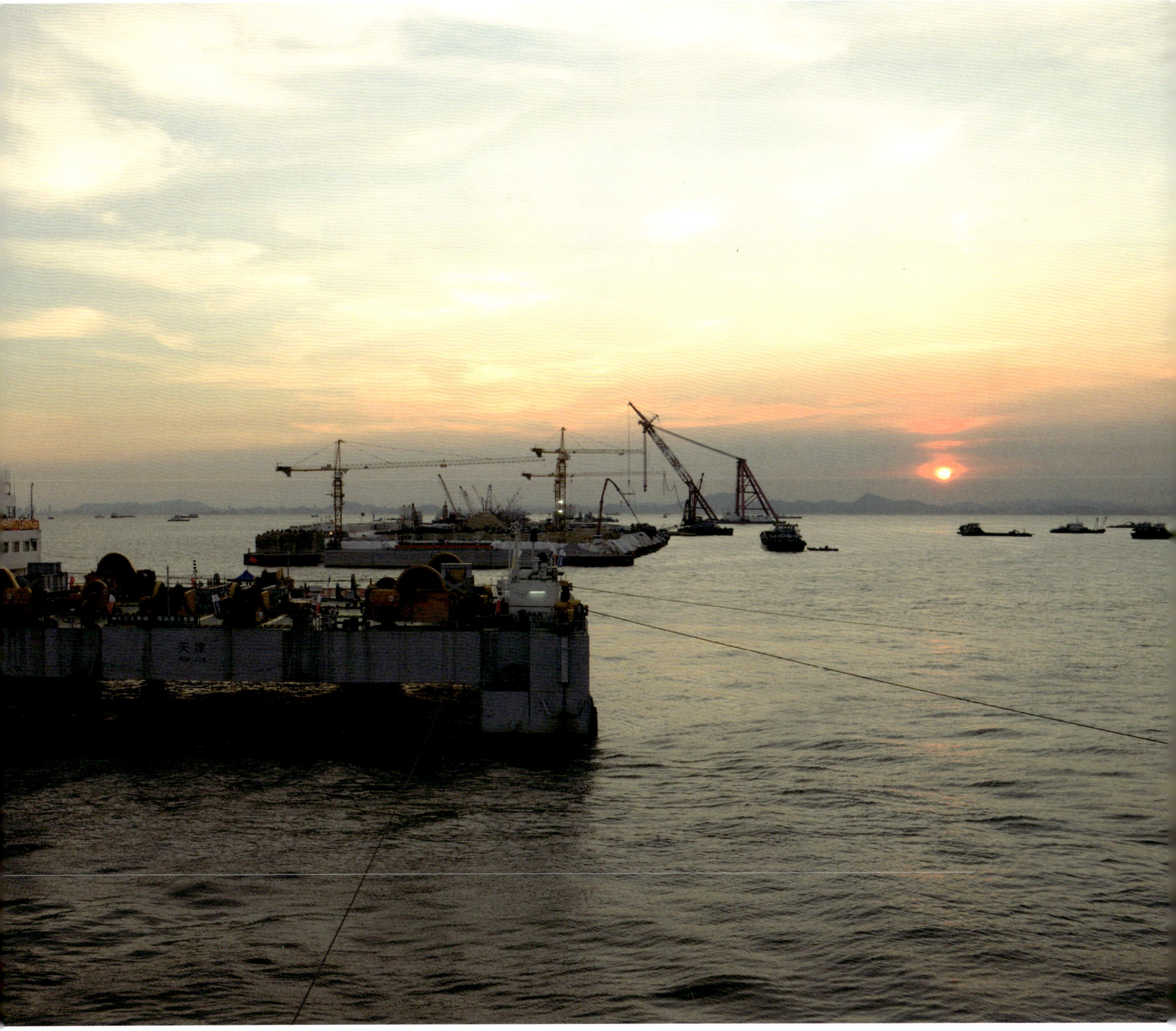

1—2. 沉管下沉
Landing of the Immersed Tubes

3. 沉管沉放安装控制系统
Control System for the Immersed Tube Landing and Installation

4. 沉管沉放安装三维图
3-D Diagram of the Immersed Tube Landing and Installation

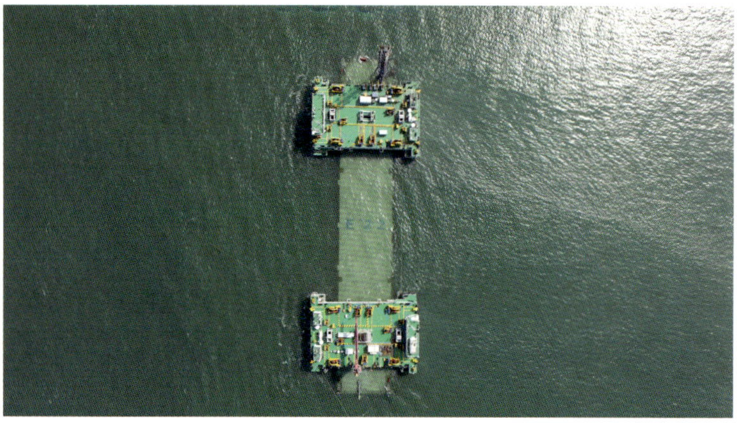

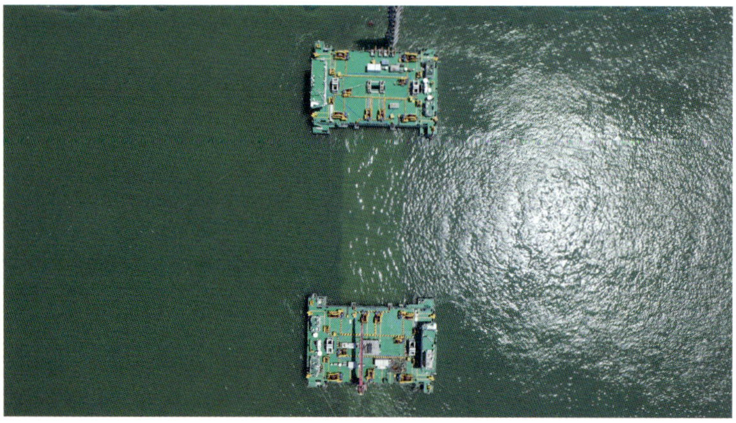

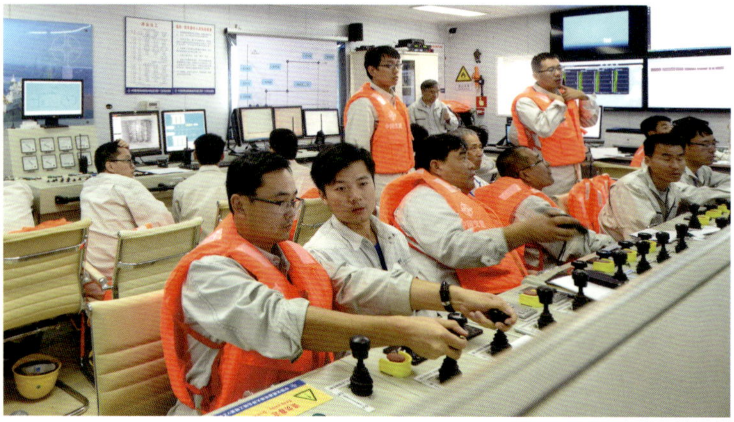

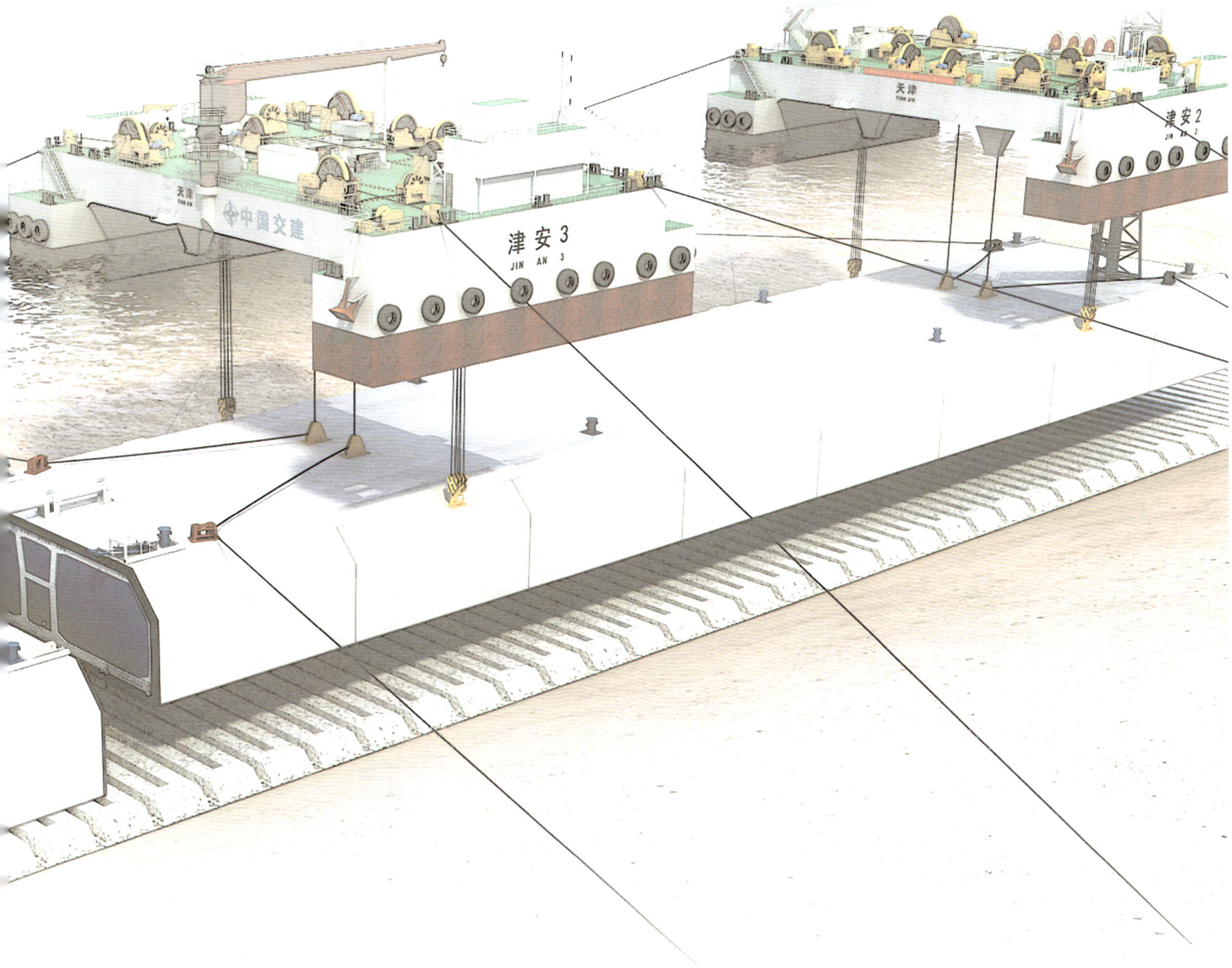
天津
中国交建
津安3
JIN AN 3
津安2

安装驳和控制系统
INSTALLATION BARGES AND CONTROLLING SYSTEM

安装驳共两艘，分为主船、副船，沉管沉放的所有操作在主船控制室内完成。

沉放施工时，通过锚绞车和缆索系统控制沉管在下沉过程中的运动姿态。

每艘安装船上的缆索系统包括系泊缆索（M 缆）、吊索缆索（L 缆）、安装缆索（H 缆），每条缆索与其操作绞车对应，所有的缆索卷筒和绞车均布置在安装船甲板上。

锚绞车选用特大型海工锚机，采取变频驱动方式，能够根据需要灵活更改同步方式以及操作速度、恒张力等各方面需求。

每船锚机配置 4 台 120 吨定位绞车、2 台 65 吨定位绞车、2 台 40 吨提升绞车和 4 台 25 吨辅助绞车，其中定位绞车具有恒张力功能，提升绞车具有同步功能，可以单船两台同步或两船四台同步。

为确保操作准确，每台绞车配有本地操作控制台，并可以在操作室集控。

副船绞车可以在主船上控制。

移船绞车、沉管水平绞车和提升绞车均具备拉力监测、行程监测功能。

主要设备全部采用交流变频电机驱动，各绞车有恒张力和"寸动"功能，绳长、绳速、绳张力均具备无级调整功能，满足沉管的精确定位要求，"寸动"一次定位调整的量值小于 2.5 厘米。

There were two installation barges-the principal barge and the auxiliary barge. All the operation for the tube landing was done on the principal barge.

In the process of landing the tube, the anchoring winch and cables were used to control the moving trajectory of the tube.

The cables on each installation barge included mooring cable (M cable), lifting cable (L cable), and Installation cable (H cable). Each cable had its special winch, and all the cable reels and winches were placed on the deck of the installation barge.

Anchoring winch were equipped with the super-sized marine windlass and employed variable-frequency drives, so they could easily change their ways of synchronization, speed and constant tension.

Each windlass worked with 4 positioning winches of 120 tons, 2 positioning winches of 65 tons, 2 lifting winches of 40 tons and 4 auxiliary winches of 25 tons. The positioning winches could keep constant tension, and the lifting winches helped with synchronization. Two winches synchronized on one barge or four synchronized on two barges.

For accuracy, each winch was equipped with a local control panel, and all controlling operation could be done in the operation cabin.

The winches on the auxiliary barge could be controlled on the principal barge.

Barge-moving winches, horizontal-landing winches, and lifting winches functioned for pulling-force monitoring and moving-trajectory monitoring

All the equipments were equipped with frequency converting AC motors; each winch had the function of constant tension and the "inching" function, whereby the cable length, cable speed and cable tension could be adjusted freely to meet precision requirements for the tube landing. The positioning adjustment by "inching" could be controlled within the limit of 2.5 centimeters.

	1
	2 | 3

1. "津安 2" "津安 3"安装驳
   Installation Barges "Jinaan 2" and "Jinaan 3"
2. 沉管吊装缆
   Hoisting Cable of the Immersed Tubes
3. 沉管沉放安装操控
   Landing and Installation of the Immersed Tubes

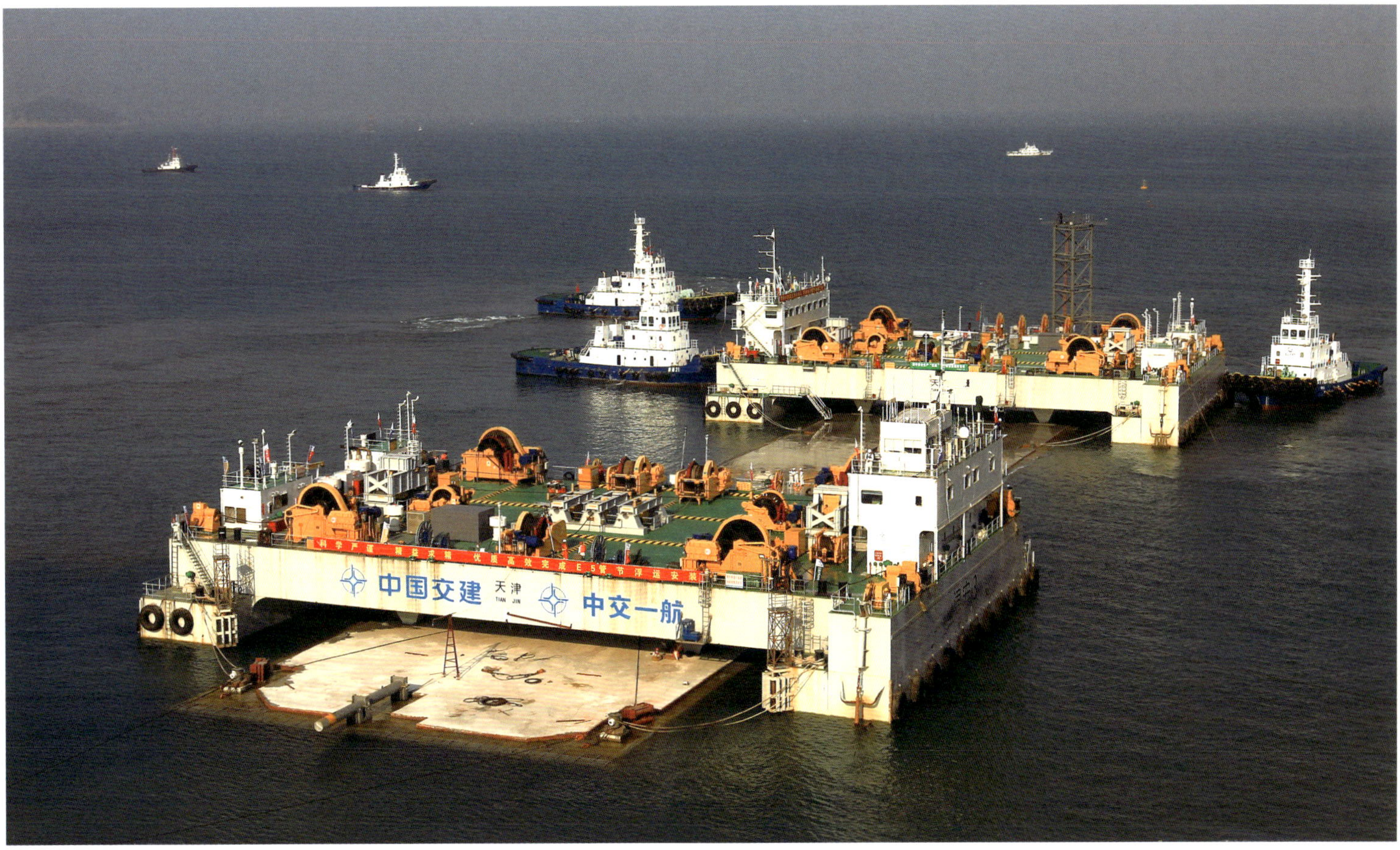
科学严谨 精益求精 优质高效完成E5管节浮运安装
中国交建
天津
TIAN JIN
中交一航

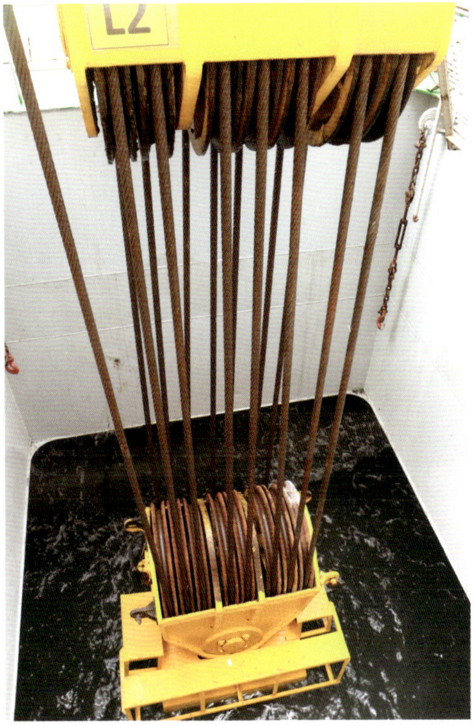
L2

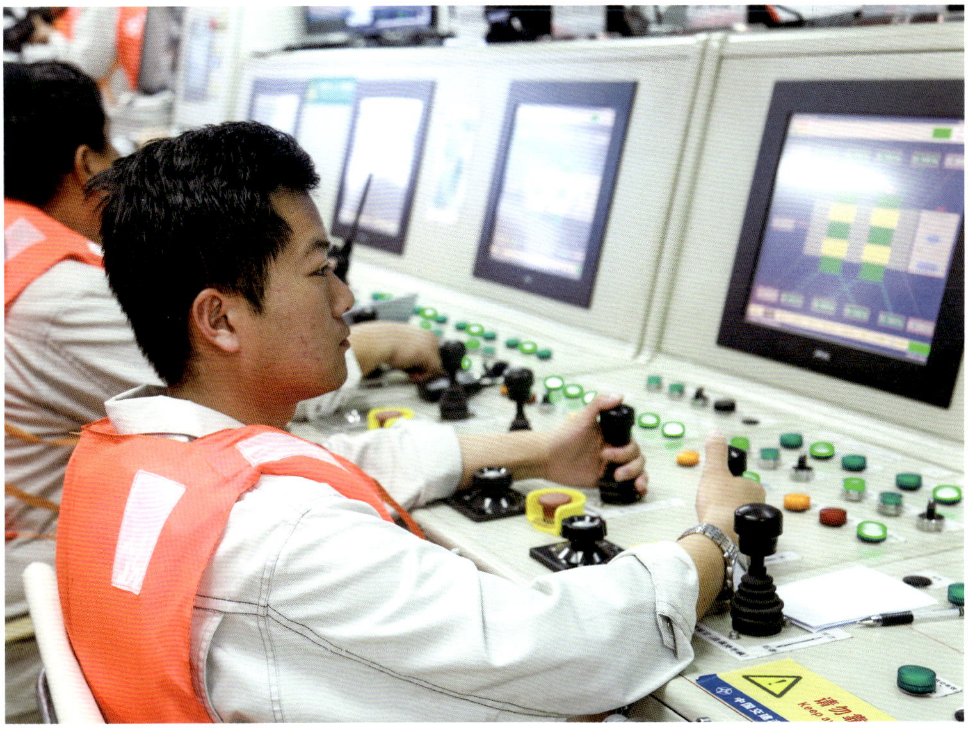

采用体内压载水系统在沉管起浮、系泊、沉放和最终压载时进行压重控制，提供沉放时的负浮力和沉放后抗浮稳定。

压载水系统由压载水箱、压载管路和压载控制系统组成，控制系统的终端设在安装船控制室内，水箱内设置高精度水位传感器，水位实时遥测并显示在控制室的屏幕上，通过实施远程给排水控制，实现精确加排水，及时调整沉管沉放时所需的负浮力等指标。

水箱和管路布置在沉管内部，通过箱内注水或者排水控制沉管的负浮力，其中系统进水通过远程控制和调节阀门利用水压差原理自然进水，系统排水采用压载泵进行排水。

管内控制柜利用水下线缆穿过尾端钢封门并与安装船控制台连接，实现信号的远程传递，其中封门上需要设置水下专用插座供管内和管外水下线缆连通。

Internal ballast water system was used for ballasting control when lifting, mooring, landing the tube and when the final ballasting was done, and provided negative buoyancy when landing the tube and anti-floating stability after the landing.

The ballast water system was composed of ballast water tank, ballast pipe and ballast control system. The terminal of the control system was placed in the operation cabin of the installation barge. In the water tank was a high-precision water level sensor, and the real-time water level was shown on the screen in the operation cabin. Remote control system was used for water supply and drainage with high degree of precision, and for the adjustment of the necessary negative buoyancy during the tube landing and other indexes.

The water tank and the pipes were set inside the immersed tube. The negative buoyancy of the tube was controlled by adding water into the tank or draining the tank. Adding water was realized by remote control or by adjusting the valve, which employed the water pressure difference to push water into the tank. Drainage was done by the ballast pumping.

By the underwater cable running through the steel sealing devices at the end part and connecting the control panel of the installation barge, the in-tube control cabin monitored the remote transmission of signals. Special plug sockets were installed on the sealing devices to facilitate the connection of the cables inside and outside the tube.

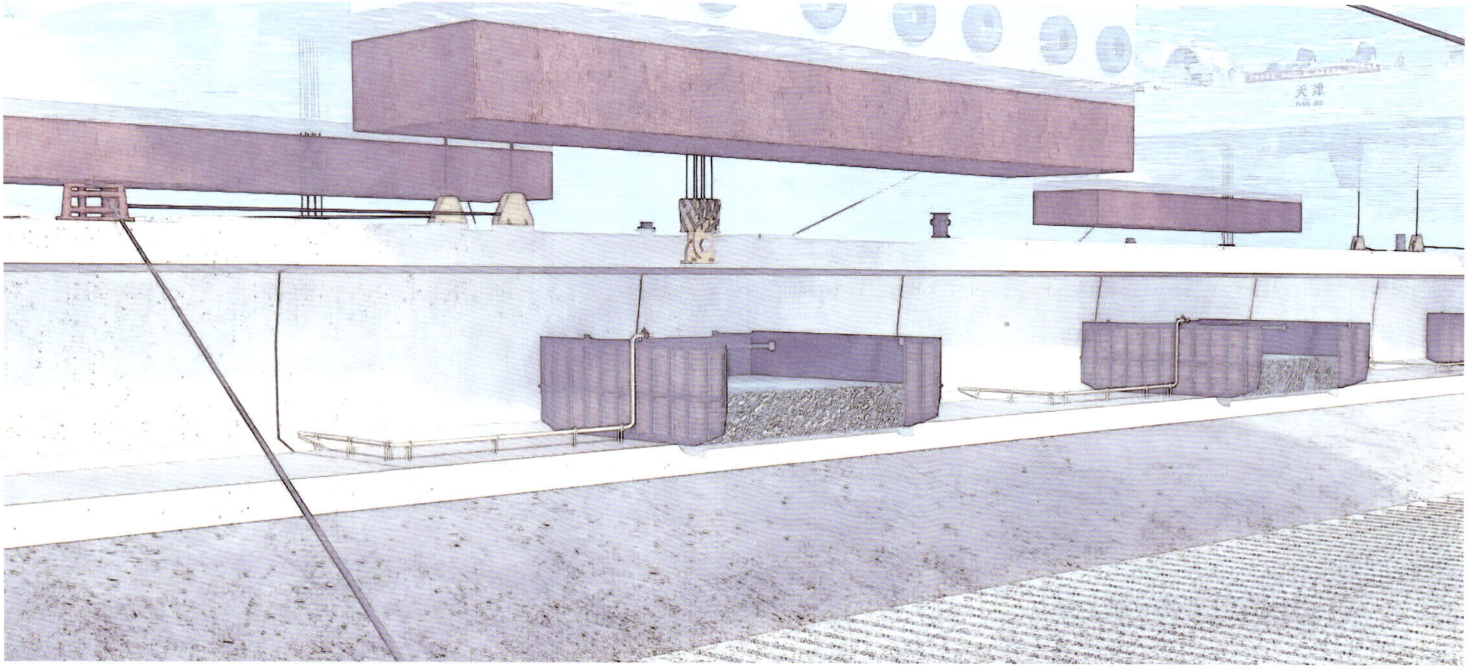

1. 管沉放压载水系统原理图
Schematic Diagram of the Ballast Water System for the Immersed Tube Landing and Installation
2. 压载水控制阀
Control Valve of the Ballast Water System
3. 沉管沉放压载水水箱
Ballast Water Tank for the Immersed Tube Landing

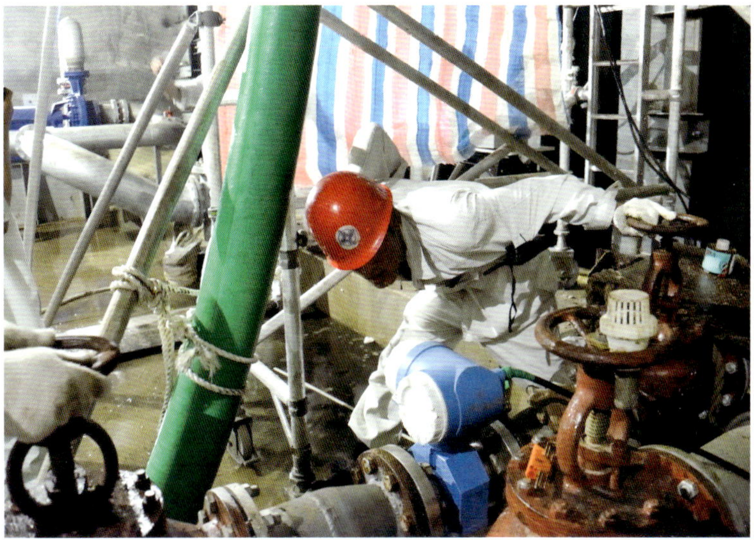

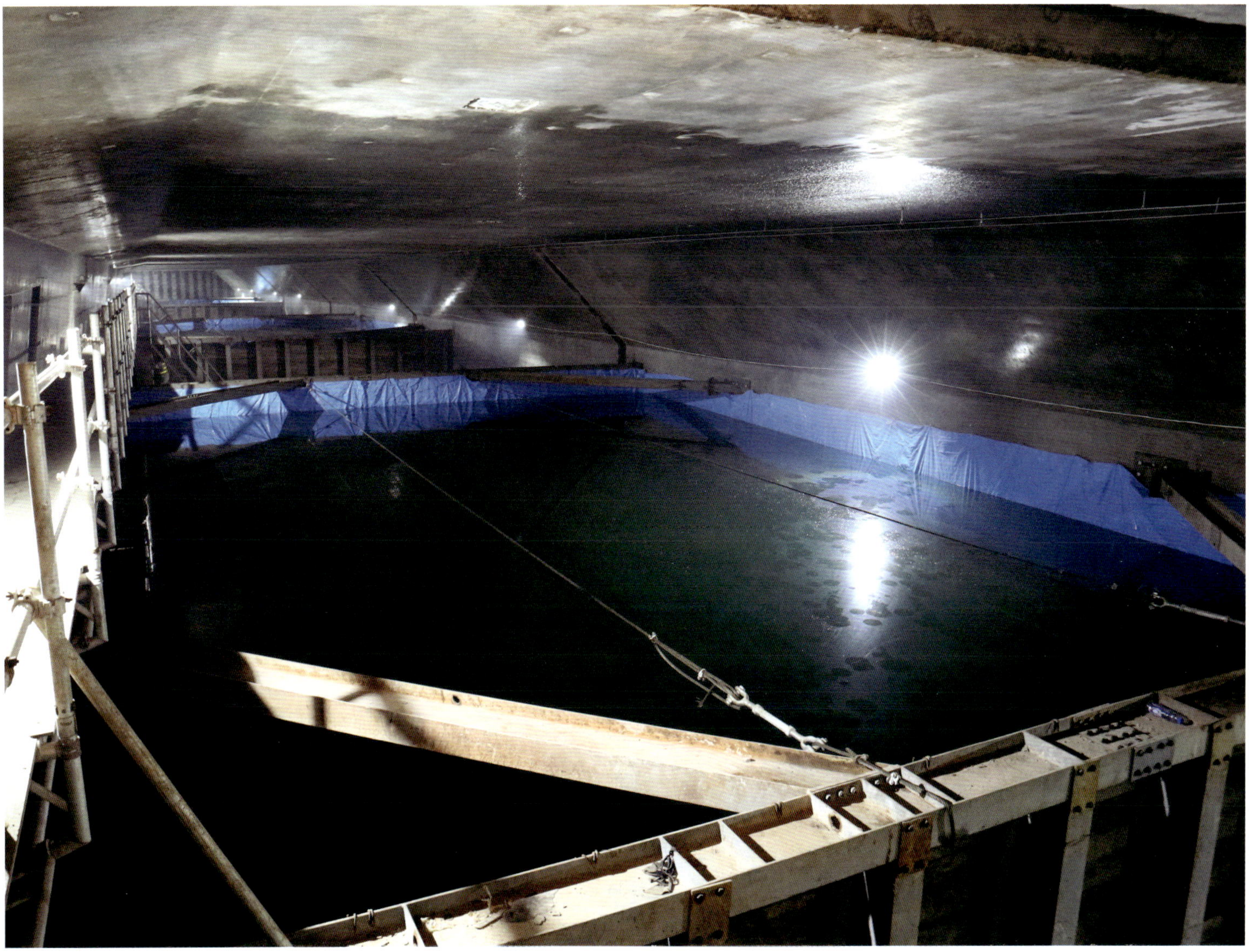

每节沉管设两处拉合点，可以提供800 吨拉合力。

拉合系统采用反钩结构，由安装在已安沉管端部的被动拉合单元和安装在待安装沉管端部的主动拉合单元两部分组成。

控制台设置在安装驳控制室内。

沉管沉放前将主动单元和被动单元安装到位，在待安沉管沉放于碎石基床后，远程操控水下千斤顶，伸出油缸，反钩结构水下自动搭接和拉合，将待安沉管拉向已安沉管，直至待安沉管端部的 GINA 橡胶止水带碰触已安沉管端部的端钢壳，然后千斤顶持续拉合，压缩 GINA 橡胶止水带与已安沉管之间形成密闭结合腔，为后续水力压接创造条件。

千斤顶内置距离传感器可以实时掌控拉合进程，大幅减少潜水员水下工作量，同时也大幅提高了施工效率和质量。

导向定位系统由位于待安沉管首端的导向杆和位于已安沉管尾端的导向托架组成，两者对称布置在沉管轴线上，安装位置需要在陆上进行精确标定。

沉管沉放过程中由锚泊定位系统控制沉管姿态，测控系统引导使导向杆逐渐进入导向托架内，控制沉管对接端的横向定位偏差，直至沉管落于碎石垫层上。

导向托架限位装置采用了钢垫板和螺旋千斤顶两种形式，可以在对接前和对接过程中由潜水员水下进行调整，精确控制沉管对接精度，相对偏差小于 10 毫米。

为了实现沉管的精确安装，沉管隧道尾端采用测量塔绝对定位与对接端水下无线声呐相对定位相结合的测量方案。

较传统方案进行了较大升级，更好地适应了外海深水作业条件，取得了满足施工要求的较高定位精度。

港珠澳大桥沉管安装所用的声呐法采用了无线传输方式，即只在管顶设置声呐传感器，取消所有的水下数据线，水下信号传输全部采用无线传输；安装驳舷侧设置一个送受波器，与控制室通过有线方式连接，大大提高了系统的可操作性和安装工效，降低了施工风险。

Each immersed tube had two pulling points, providing pulling power of 800 tons.

The pulling system employed reversed hooks, composed of the passive pulling unit installed at the end of the immersed tube and the active pulling unit installed at the end part of the tube waiting to be installed.

The control panel was set in the operation cabin of the installation barge.

Before the tube landing, the active unit and passive unit were installed at the designed places. After the immersed tube landed on the rubble bed of the foundation trench, by remote control of the underwater pulling jack, the oil tank stuck out, the reversed hooks automatically got connected and pulled together, pulling the tube waiting to be installed towards the one that was already landed there until the GINA plastic water-stop at the end of the tube waiting to be installed touched the steel shield at the end of the tube already landed there. The pulling jack kept pulling until a binding cavity was formed between the compressed GINA plastic water-stop and the landed tube. All these provided conditions for future hydraulic crimp connection.

The distance sensor inside the pulling jack could monitor the whole process of closure, and saved the divers' trouble of examination underwater. It could also improve the efficiency and quality of the installation.

The guided positioning system was composed of the guide rod at the head part of the tube waiting to be installed and the guide bracket at the end part of the tube already installed. The guide rod and the guide bracket were set on the axis line of the immersed tube, and the installation position needed to be marked precisely while on land.

In the process of tube landing, the mooring and positioning system was used to control the moving trajectory of the tube; the measuring and controlling system directed the guide rod to move into the guide bracket gradually, and monitored the horizontal positioning deviation of the end of the tube until the tube landed on the rubble bed.

The stop block of the guide bracket might be either steel cushion plate or spiral pulling jack, and could be adjusted underwater by the divers before and in the process of butt welding. Thus the butt welding of the tubes could be controlled precisely, and the deviation could be controlled within the limit of no more than 10 millimeters.

For the accurate installation of the immersed tubes, a measuring tower was built at the end part of the immersed tube tunnel for exact positioning, while an underwater wireless sonar system at the position of butt joint was used for necessary positioning.

This upgrading served well the offshore deep water operation, and the high positioning precision met the requirements of the project.

The sonar positioning system used for the immersed tube installation of Hong Kong-Zhuhai-Macau Bridge employed wireless transmission technology. The sonar sensor was set only on the top of the tube while all other underwater data lines were omitted. All the underwater signal transmission took the form of wireless transmission. One transmitter was installed on the broadside of the installation barge, connected by wire with the operation cabin, which guaranteed the operability of the system and the efficiency of the installation, while risks were reduced.

1. 沉管对接拉合千斤顶三维图
3-D Diagram of the Pulling Jack

2. 沉管对接导向定位系统三维图
3-D Diagram of the Guided Positioning System for the Immersed Tube Butt Joint

3. 沉管对接深水测控系统三维图
3-D Diagram of Deep Water Measurement and Control System for the Immersed Tube Butt Joint

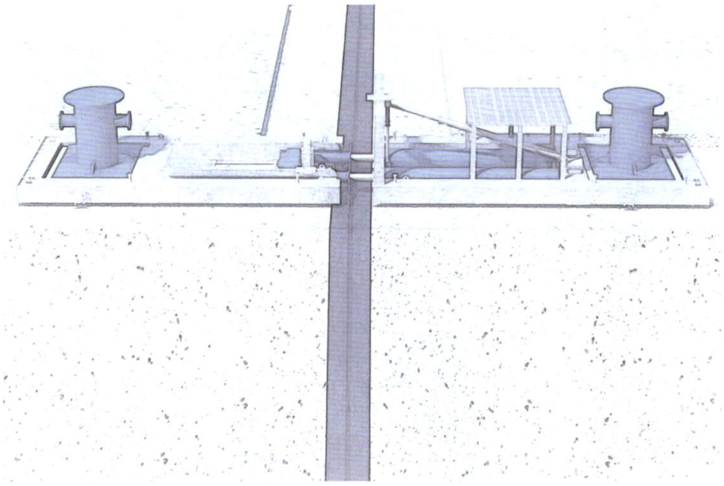

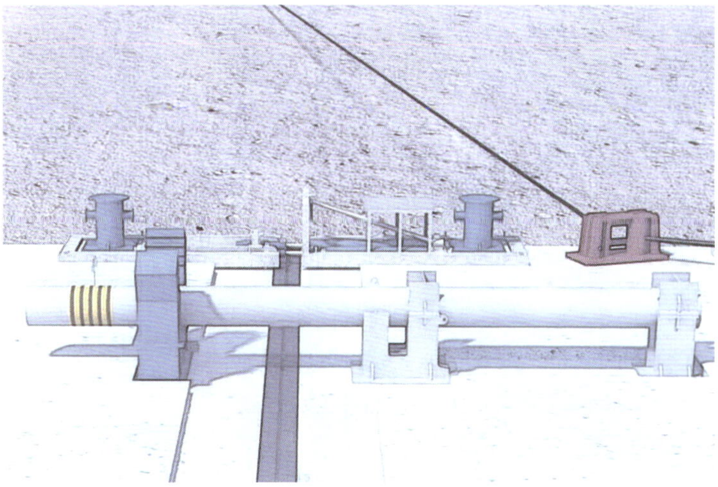

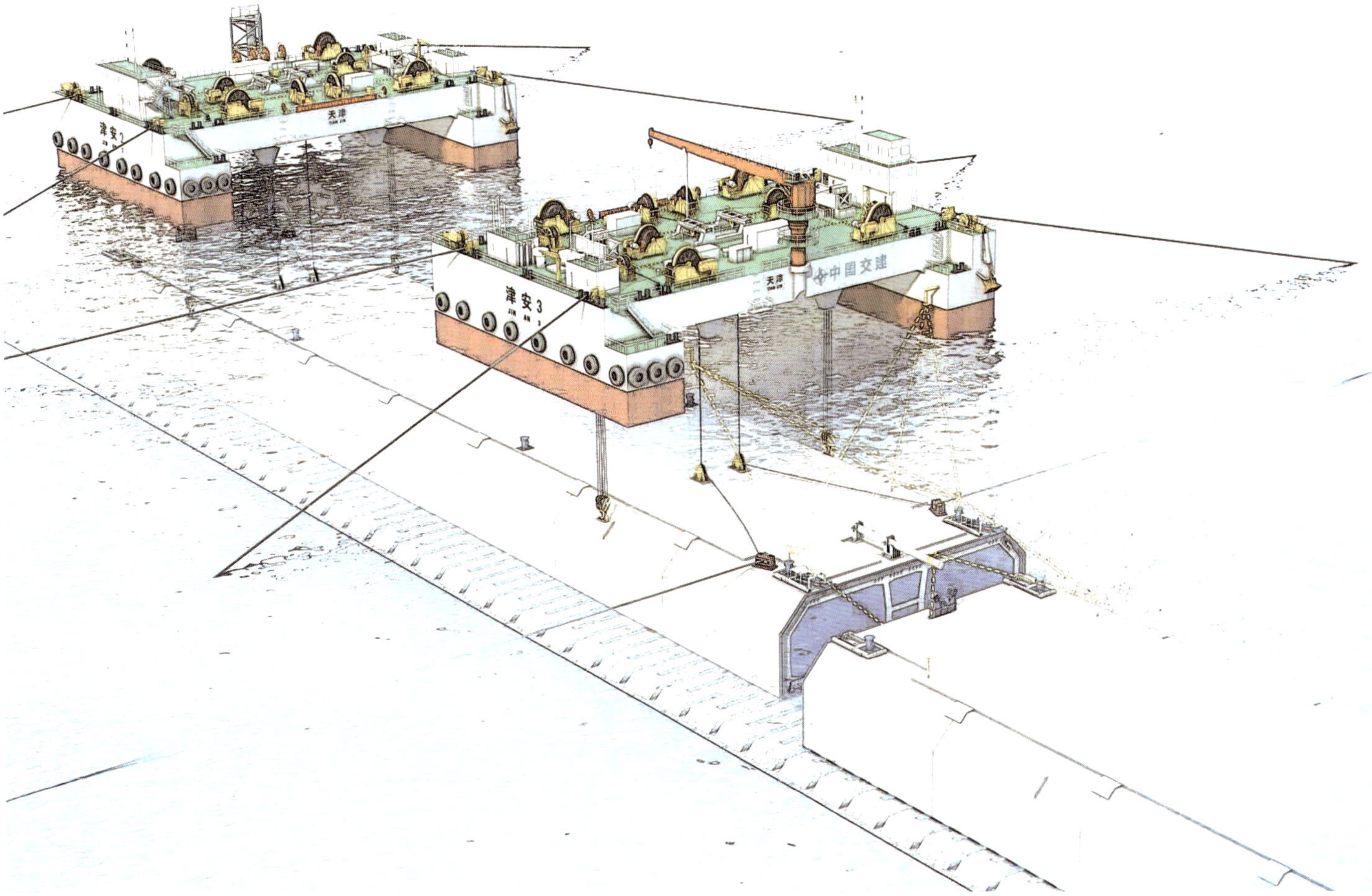
津安3
天津
中国交建

开发水力压接监测和监控系统，完成水力压接。

在沉管拉合完成后，开启水力压接监测系统，打开结合腔进气阀和排水阀进行结合腔排水，通过传感器和流量计实时监测结合腔压力，同步控制排水速度，利用沉管首尾端的水压差将 GINA 止水带压缩至设计值，达到隧道接头完全水密的要求。

A monitoring system was developed to conduct hydraulic crimp connection.

While the tubes were pulling together, the monitoring system for hydraulic crimp connection was started; the inlet valve and the drainage valve of the binding cavity were opened to drain the binding cavity; the sensor and the flow counter were used for real-time monitoring of the pressure inside the binding cavity as well as for the control of the drainage speed; the pressure differences at the two ends of the immersed tube compressed GINA water-stop to the designed point to ensure the requirements for absolute water proof at the butt joint part of the tunnel.

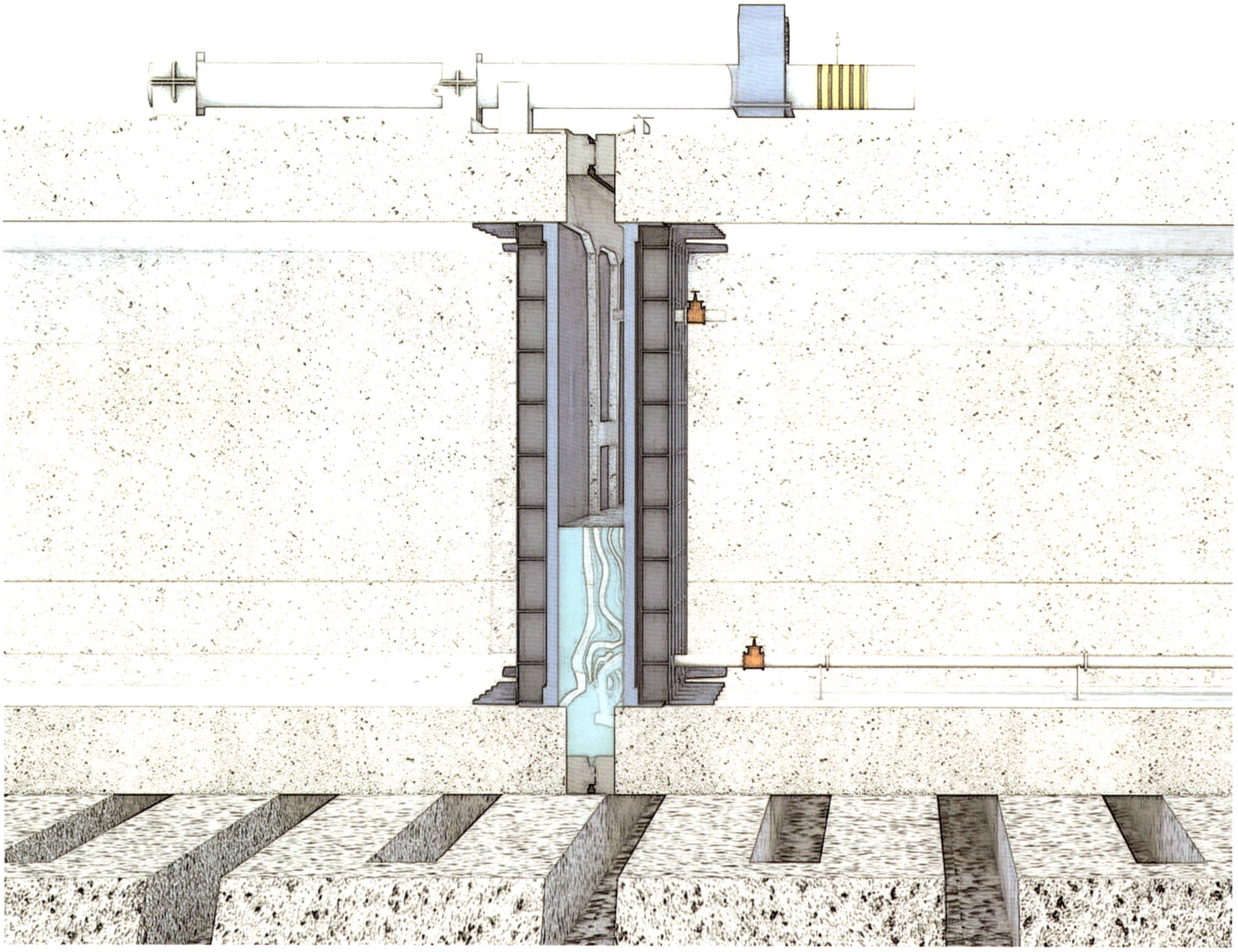

1. 沉管对接水力压接三维图
3-D Diagram of the Hydraulic Crimp Connection for the Immersed Tube Butt Joint

2. 沉管对接水力压接施工
Hydraulic Crimp Connection for the Immersed Tube Butt Joint

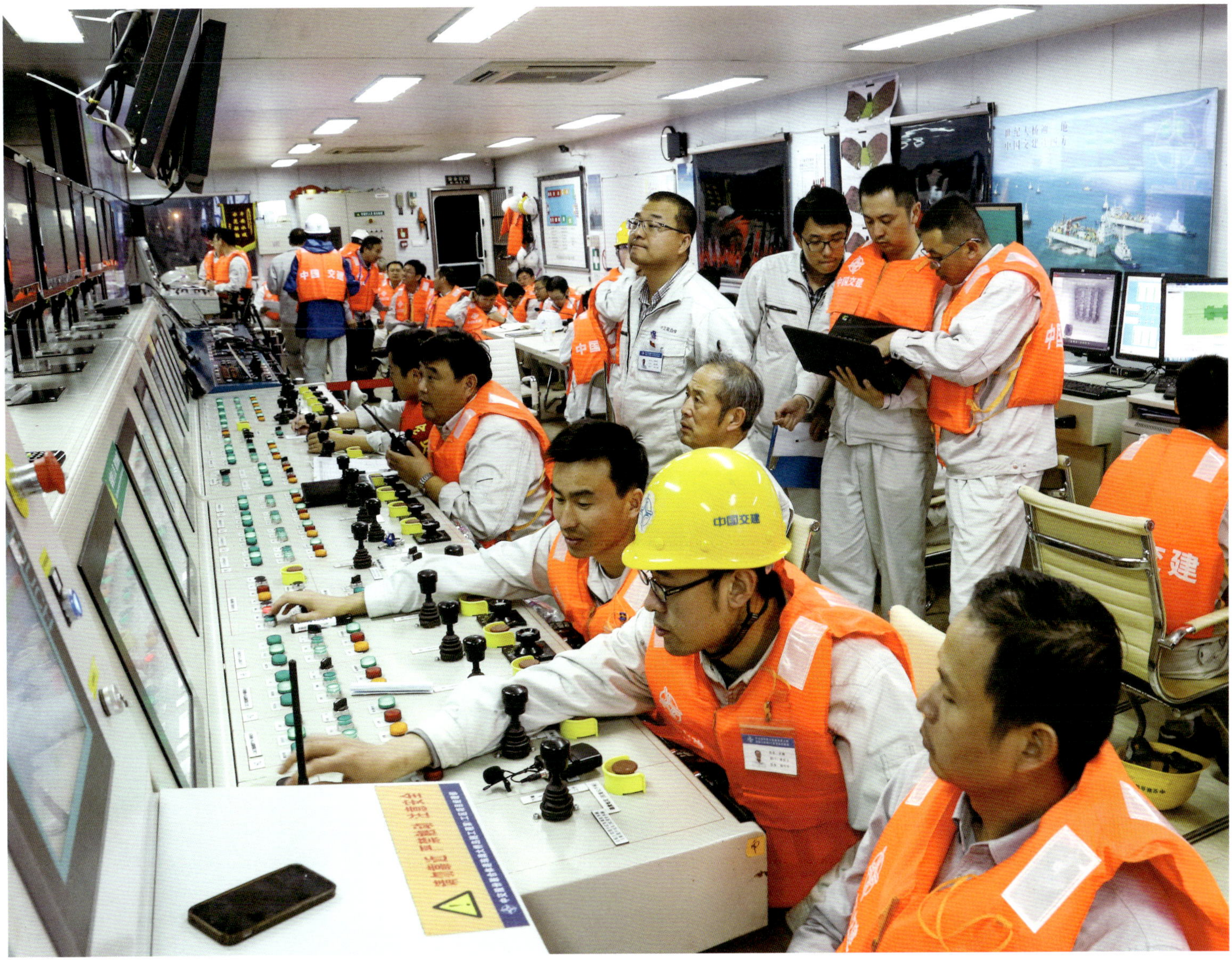

沉管基础密闭结合腔压浆

GROUTING INTO THE ENCLOSED CAVITY FORMED AT THE JUNCTION OF THE IMMERSED TUBES

针对 E31~E32 沉管接头处存在的异常沉降现象，项目总经理部创新性提出了沉管基础密闭腔压浆预压基床、抬升沉管的构想。

利用沉管接头部位的基槽、锁定回填碎石、接头底部自然形成的空腔，通过压浆形成密闭腔，起到了协调差异沉降、预压密实基床、调控沉降形态的目的，创造了一种调控沉管沉降的新方法。

通过注浆填充沉管接头处的管底空间，凝结形成强度后构成的垫层可减少沉管间的差异沉降。

在注浆过程中，浆体渗透填充沉管接头处的管底空间形成压力腔，对碎石基础进行超载预压密实，减少沉管在荷载作用下发生沉降的风险；同时，在密实完碎石基床后，利用压力腔中形成的反作用力对沉管尾部进行抬升，实现对已装沉管的姿态调整。

To cope with the problem of abnormal sedimentation at the butt joint between the immersed tubes E31 and E32, the project management center proposed pre-compressing the trench bed by grouting into the enclosed cavity at the junction of the immersed tubes with an attempt to raise the tube.

An enclosed cavity was formed by grouting into the cavity formed underneath the butt joint between the foundation trench and the rubbles by locking backfill. This functioned to adjust the differential landing of the tube, pre-compress the compact bed, and adjust the landing position. This was a new method to adjust the landing of the immersed tubes.

The bedding formed by grouting into the space beneath the tube at the butt joint of the immersed tubes could reduce the differences of landing between the adjacent immersed tubes.

In the process of grouting, the fluid concrete filled the space beneath the tube at the butt joint of the immersed tubes and formed a pressure cavity. And the supercharge preloading compacted the rubble bed, which reduced the risks involved in the landing of the tubes under heavy load. At the same time, after the rubble bed was compacted, the counterforce in the pressure cavity might raise the end part of the immersed tubes, so as to realize the right positioning of the tube installed.

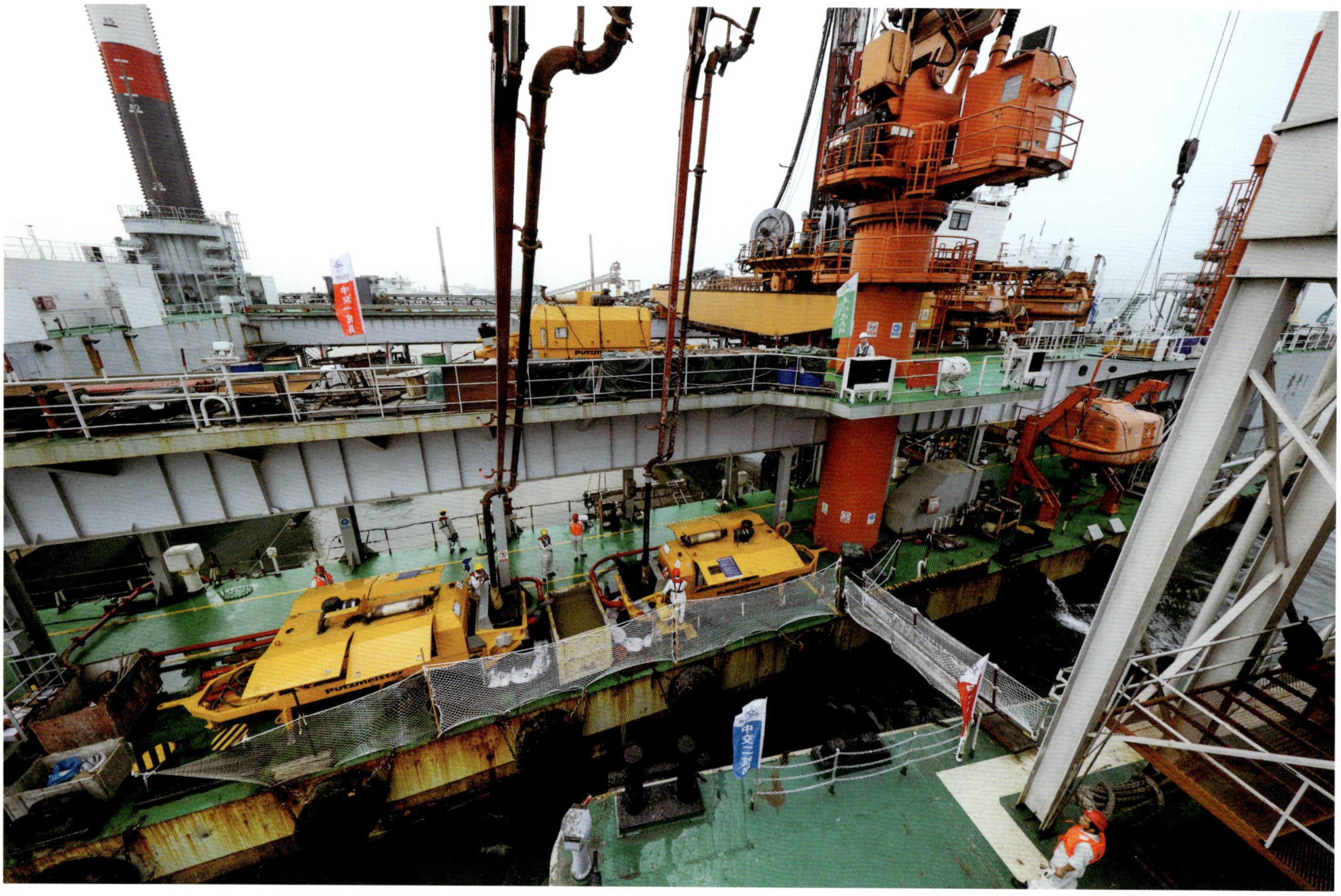

1. 沉管基础密闭腔压浆施工
Grouting into the Enclosed Cavity of the Immersed Tube Base
2. 沉管基础密闭腔压浆原理图
Schematic Diagram of Grouting into the Enclosed Cavity of the Immersed Tube Base
3. 沉管基础密闭腔压浆混凝土泵送管道
Concrete Pumping Line for Grouting into the Enclosed Cavity of the Immersed Tube Base
4. 沉管基础密闭腔压浆混凝土泵送施工
Concrete Pumping for Grouting into the Enclosed Cavity of the Immersed Tube Base

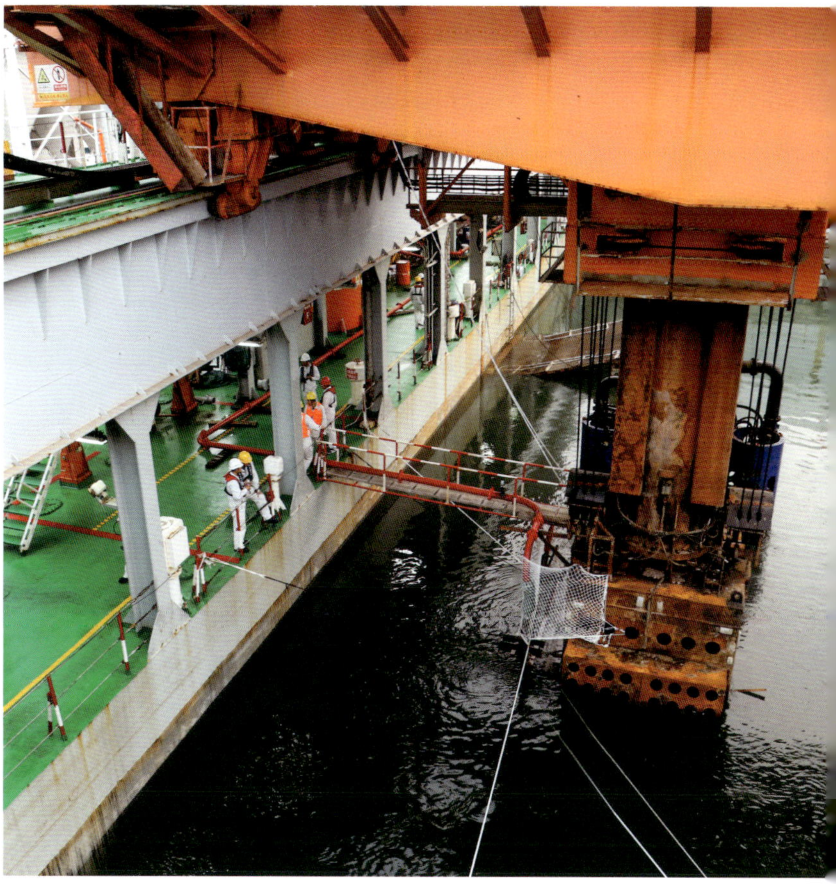

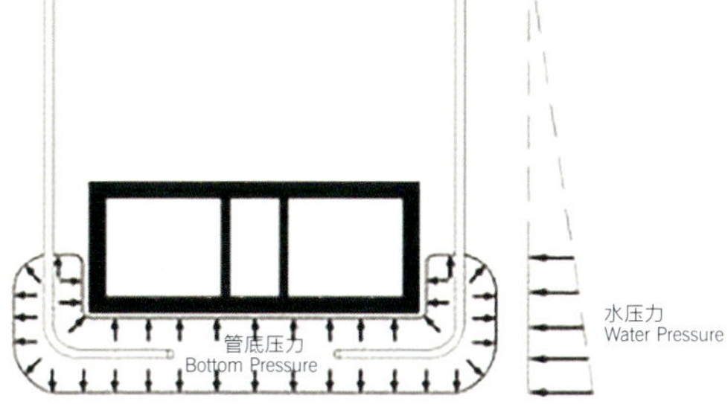

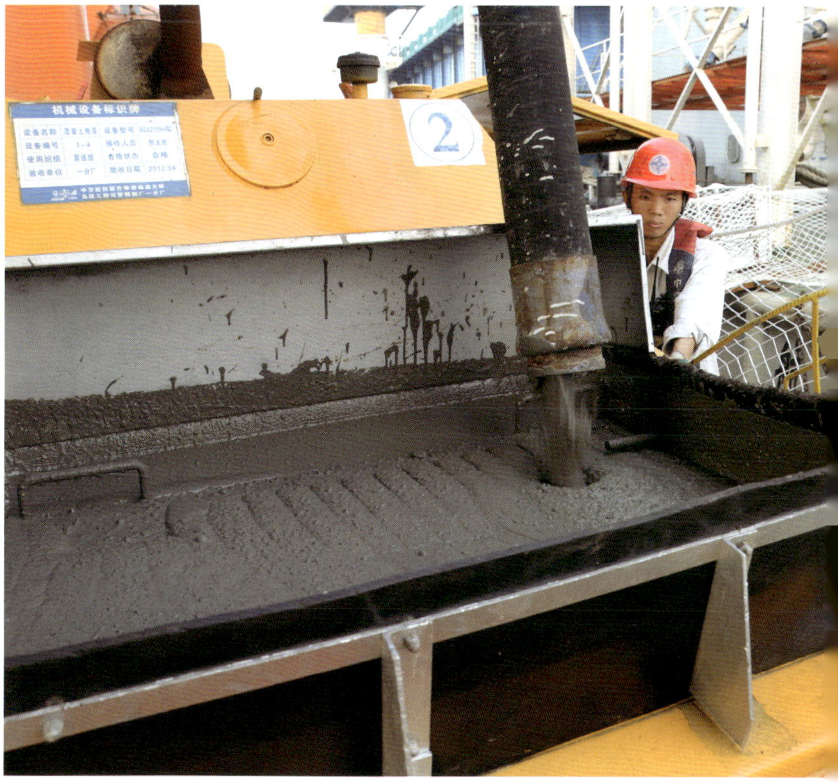

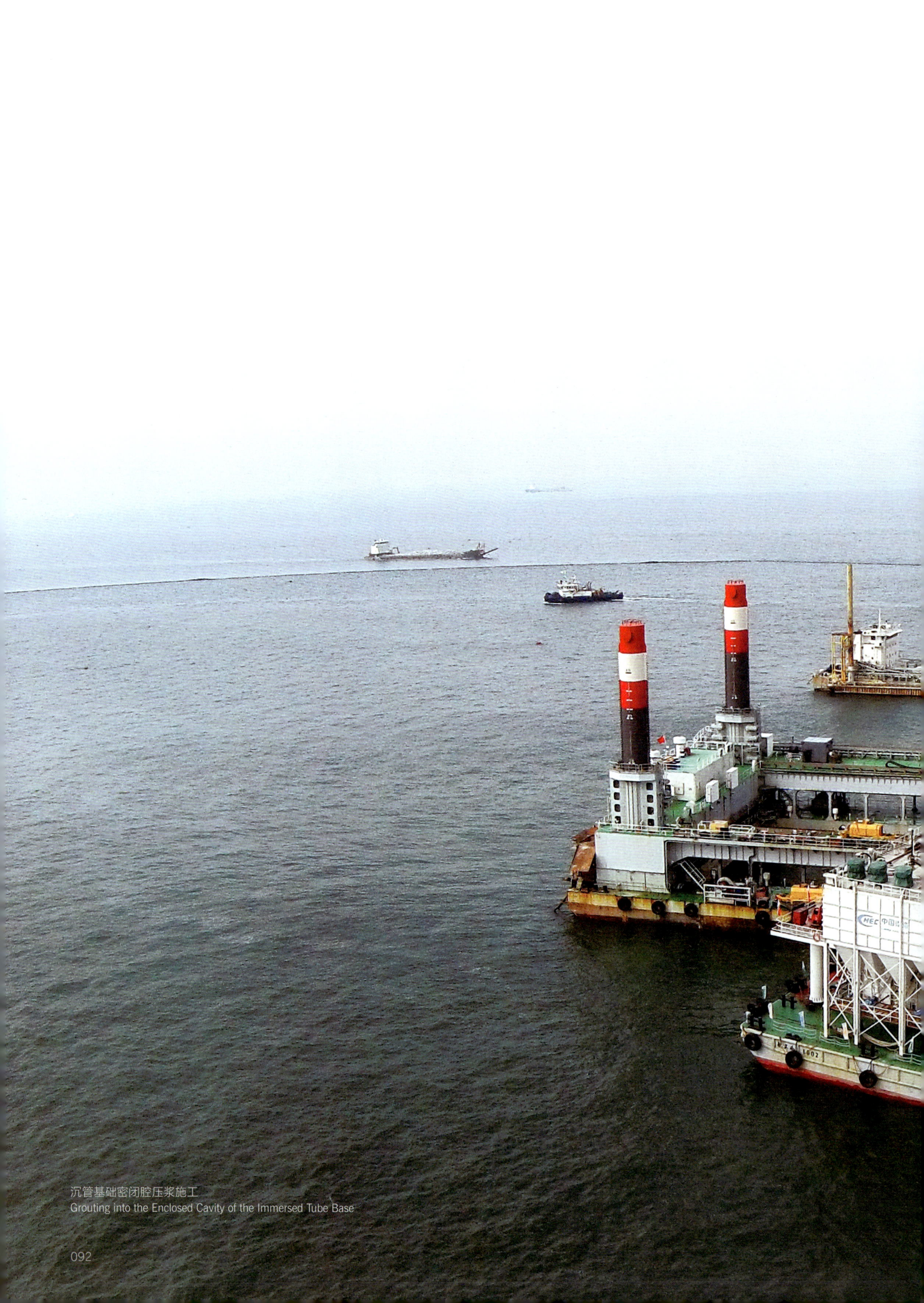

沉管基础密闭腔压浆施工
Grouting into the Enclosed Cavity of the Immersed Tube Base

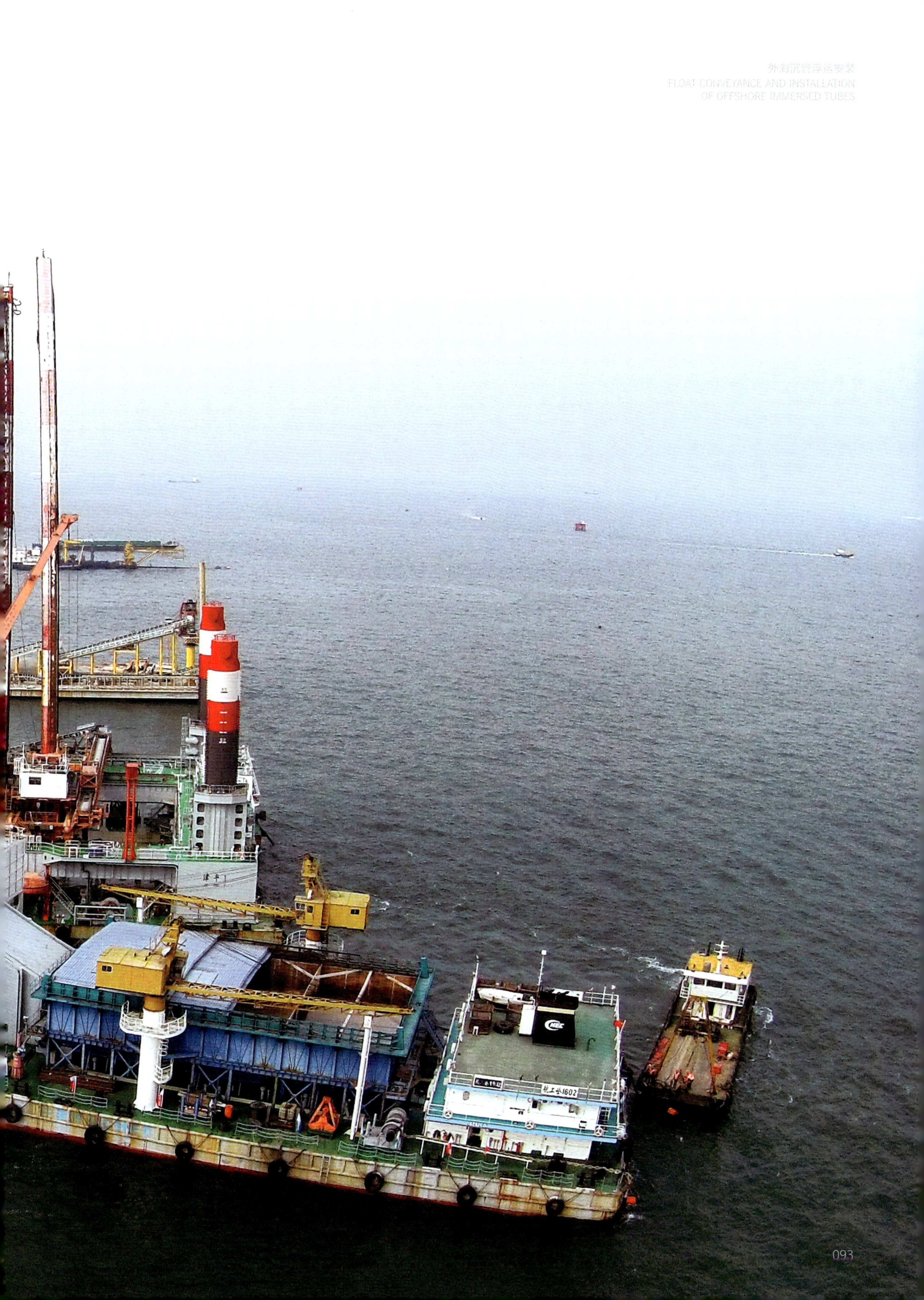

特殊沉管安装

INSTALLATION OF SPECIAL IMMERSED TUBES

港珠澳大桥海底隧道特殊沉管安装包括：隧道两端与人工岛衔接部位的岛头段沉管安装、隧道中段通航航道下方的深水深槽区沉管安装和隧道东段曲线沉管安装。

有别于一般标准段直线沉管，深槽区、岛头段和曲线段沉管安装需要采用特殊的应对措施。

深槽区沉管安装：和其他沉管隧道相比，港珠澳大桥沉管隧道属于深埋式沉管隧道。

隧道区海床原泥面实际标高约为 -7~-12 米，深水区沉管（E9~E27）的基槽开挖底标高约为 -48.5 米，按原泥面平均标高为 -10 米计算，该区段基槽实际最大深度超过 35 米。

深水深槽沉管安装是世界范围内首次尝试，面临巨大挑战。

沉管安装进入深槽以后，受槽内复杂流态及缆系刚度弱化影响，沉管安装面临诸多问题。

沉管重 7.6 万吨，运动动能大，运动响应敏感。

沉管安装系全过程水下作业，槽深最深处达 35 米，沉管运动及姿态监测和控制难度大。

随着基槽深度增加，流态更加复杂，缆系刚度弱化严重，对沉管运动的约束能力迅速下降，对沉管对接精度及安全将造成较大影响。

项目总经理部通过开展大量潮流、密度同步观测，研究深基槽内水流水动力机理，为深基槽水流预报模型建立提供了理论依据。

同时建立沉管对接窗口预报系统，开发了沉管安装水流、运动姿态实时监控系统，保障沉管对接安全。

The installation of the special immersed tube in the underwater tunnel of Hong Kong-Zhuhai-Macau Bridge include the tube installation at the head part of the man-made island and the two ends of the tunnel, the tube installation in the deep trench below the driving lanes of the middle part of the tunnel, and the installation of the curved tubes at the east section of the tunnel.

Different from the common straight tubes at other sections, the tube installation in the deep-trench section, island head section and the curved section of the tunnel needed special techniques.

Tube Installation at Deep Trench Section: Different from other immersed tube tunnel, the tube tunnel of Hong Kong-Zhuhai-Macau Bridge is a deep-buried immersed tube tunnel.

The standard elevation of the original sediment surface on the seabed of the tunnel area was between -7 and -12 meters; the standard elevation for the foundation trench of the immersed tube in deep water region (E9 to E27) was -48.5 meters. If the average standard elevation of the original sediment surface was -10 meters, the real depth of the foundation trench in this section was over 35 meters.

The tube installation in the deep trench in deep water in this project was the first try in the world, and the challenges were great.

When the tube installation came to the deep trench part, due to the complicated current and the weakening cable stiffness, many problems surfaced.

The immersed tube weighed 76,000 tons, its momentum was tremendous, and its motion response was drastic.

The tube installation was completely done underwater. The deepest place of the trench was 35 meters, so it was very difficult to monitor and control the motion and position of the immersed tube.

The deeper the trench was, the more complicated the current became, the more serious the weakening of the cable stiffness became, and the control over the motion of the tube became weaker and weaker. All these would greatly affect the precision degree of the butt welding and the safety of the workers.

The project management center conducted synchronized observation of the tide and its density as well as studies of the mechanism of the hydro-power from the water flow in the foundation trench, which provided evidences for the construction of water-flow forecast model in the foundation trench.

A window forecast system was established to monitor the butt welding of the immersed tubes, and a real-time monitoring system was developed to monitor the water current and the tubes' motion and position during installation. All these guaranteed the safety during the butt welding of the immersed tubes.

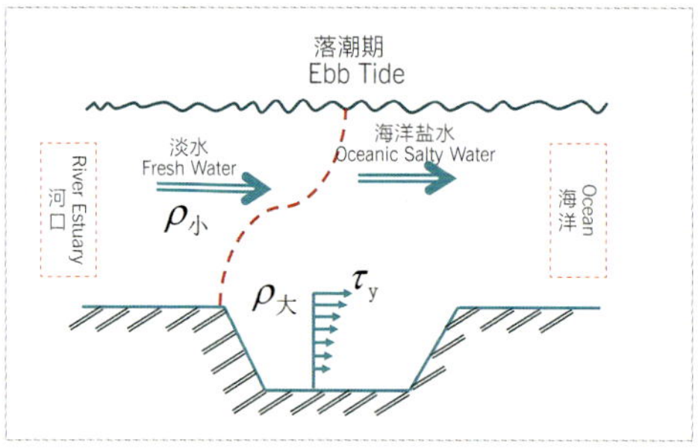

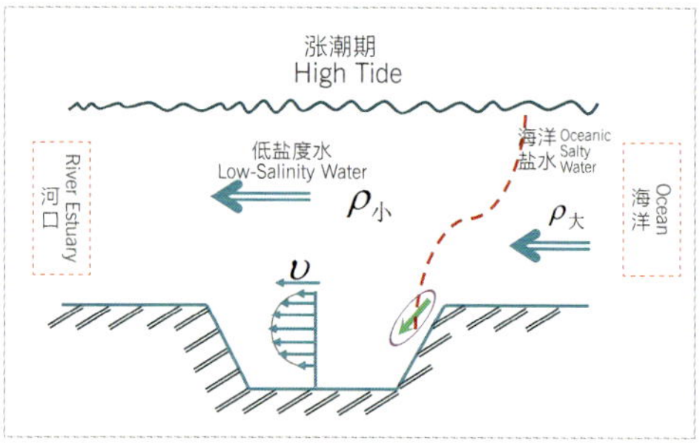

1—2. 深基槽水流水动力机理图
Mechanism Diagram for the Power from Flowing Water in the Deep Foundation Trench

3. 深槽区沉管安装
Immersed Tube Installation in the Deep Trench

4. 深槽区沉管安装三维图
3-D Diagram of the Immersed Tube Installation in the Deep Trench

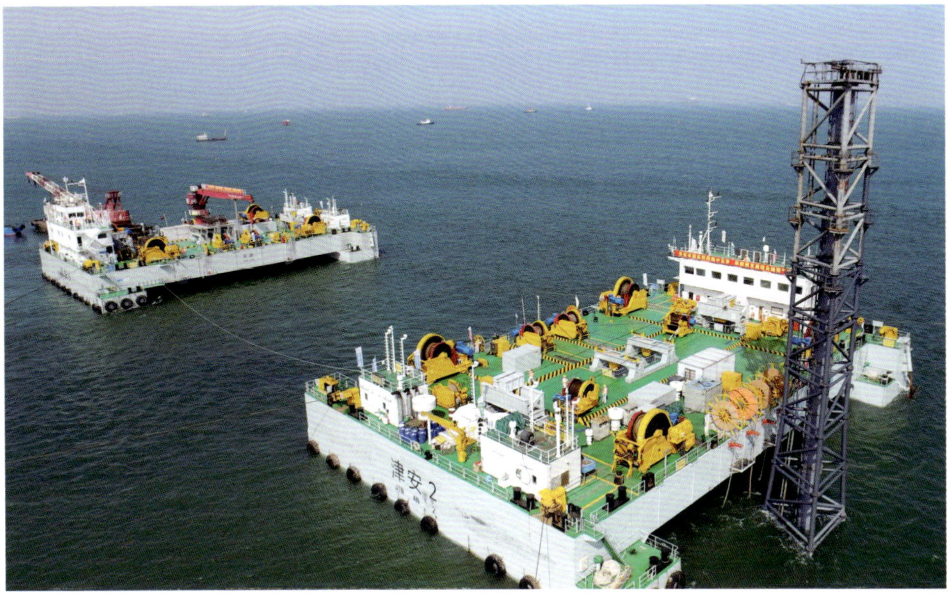

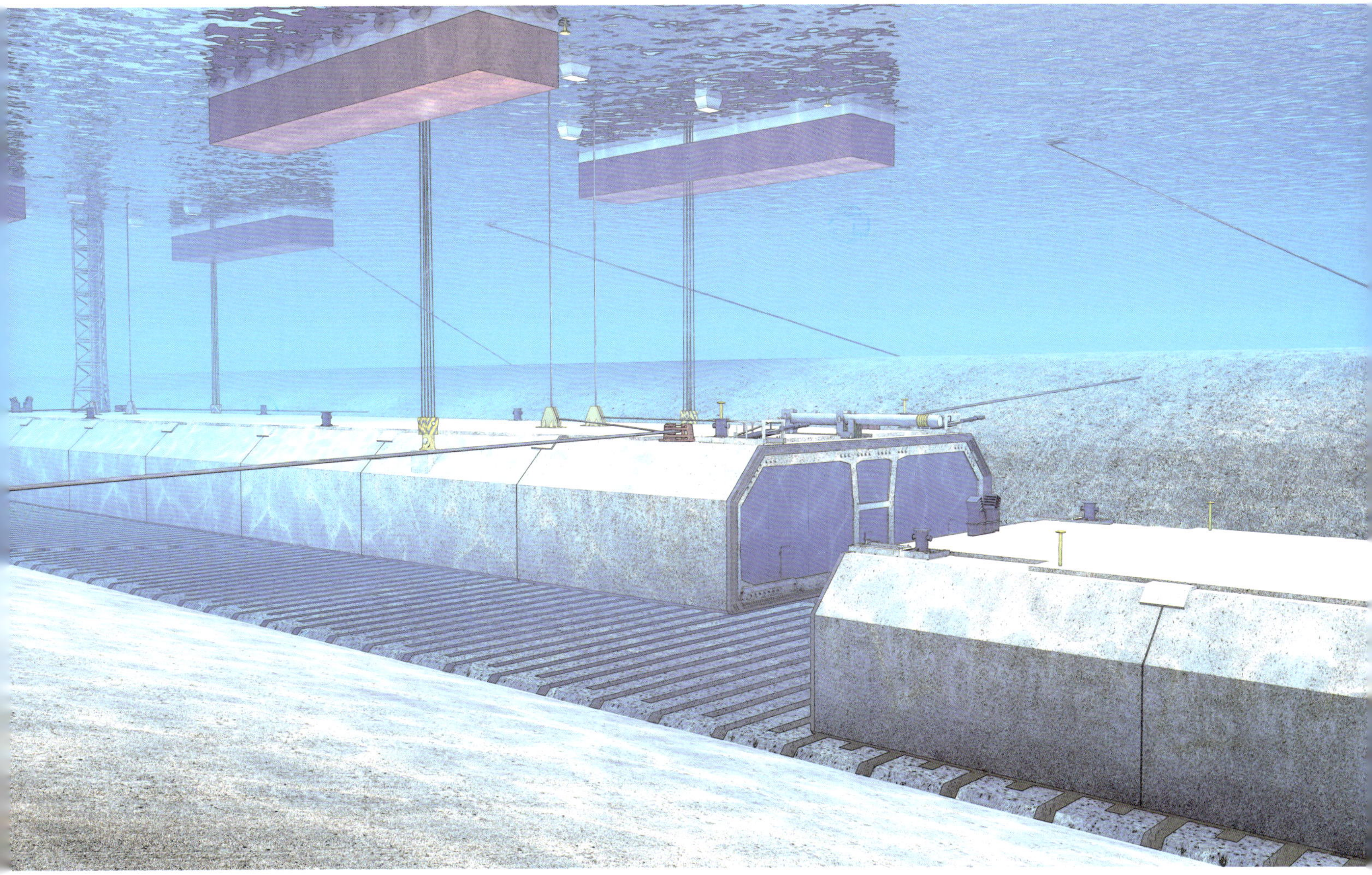

岛头段沉管安装：岛头区受人工岛挑流影响，流态复杂，水深较浅，作业面狭窄，基础施工、沉管移位和沉放时缆系操控难度大，施工船舶进出困难，锚泊定位系统须特殊布置。

为有效减少和控制施工风险，项目总经理部以专题研究和工艺研究相结合的思路，组织开展了一系列数模和物模试验：东、西人工岛岛隧结合部沉放区掩护方案数模试验，东人工岛岛隧结合部掩护方案三维潮流泥沙数学模型试验，东人工岛岛隧结合部施工临时措施波浪局部整体物理模型试验和东人工岛岛头减淤屏试验等；制定实施东人工岛岛头综合防护治理方案，对已完成的东人工岛岛头掩护区内的流场、回淤、浊度、密度等进行观测，为制定防淤和清淤措施提供依据。

Immersed Tube Installation at the Head Part of the Island: The water current at the head part of the man-made island was complicated, the water was shallow, the working space was limited, so all these made it difficult to conduct the base construction, to move the tubes and to handle the cables when landing the tube. And it was also difficult for the barges to move around, and the mooring and positioning system needed to be arranged with great care.

In order to control and reduce the risks during the operation, the project management center conducted studies about the operation techniques and a series of mathematical-model and physical-model experiments: the mathematical model for safety protection at the section where West and East Man-Made Islands met the tunnel, the 3-D mathematical tide and silt model for safety protection at the section where East Man-Made Island met the tunnel, the local-global physical tide model for temporary measures at the section where East Man-Made Island met the tunnel, and the silt preventing screen experiment at the head part of East Man-Made Island. Comprehensive protection and management plan at the head part of East Man-Made Island was made to monitor the water current, back silting, turbidity, density in the protective area at the head part of East Man-Made Island, which provided evidences for making silt preventing and desilting plans.

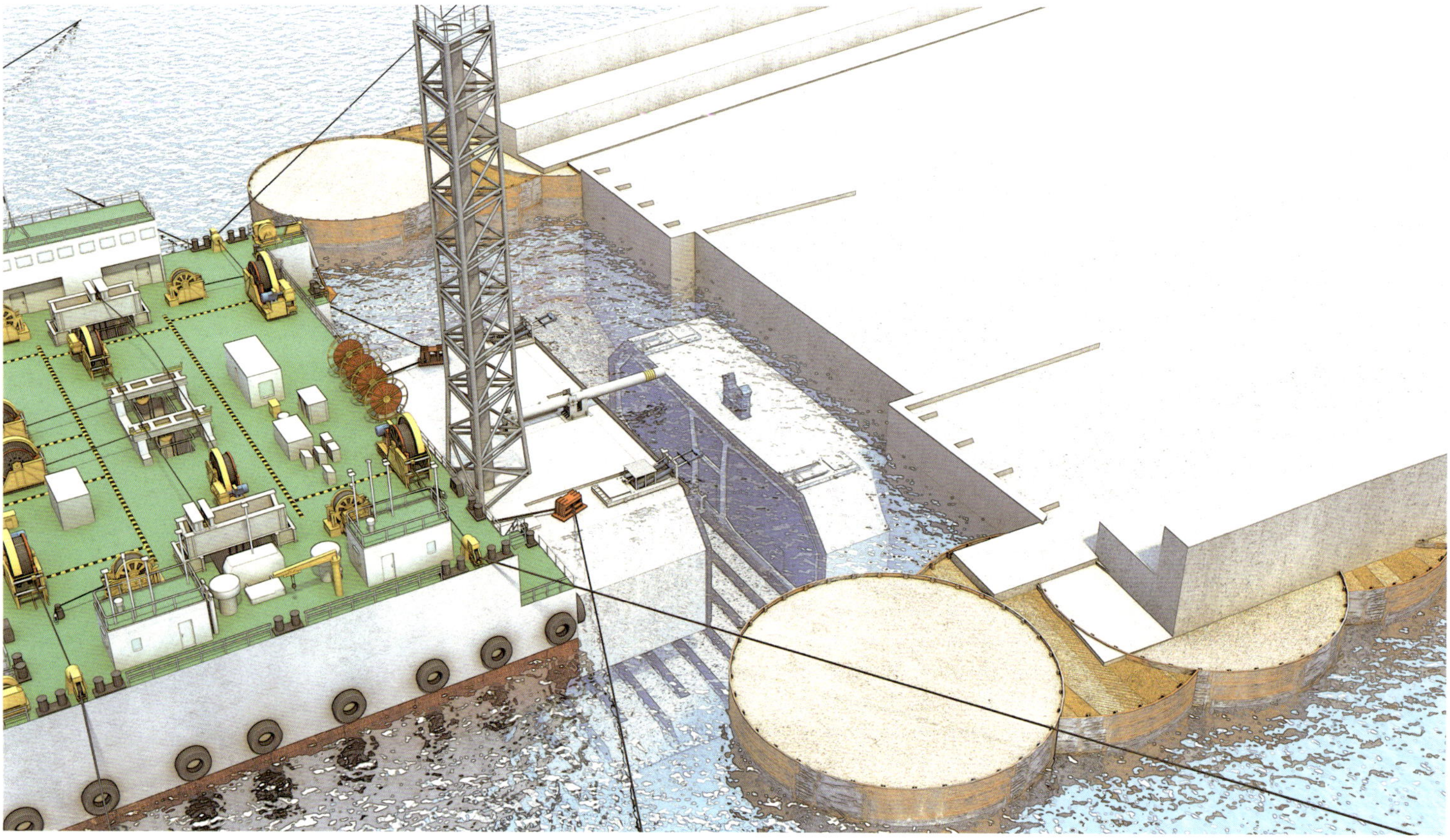

曲线段沉管安装：隧道E29~E33沉管为曲线段沉管，曲率半径5500米，是最后安装的5节沉管。

曲线沉管标准横断面与直线段相同，预制时采用"以折代曲"的方式进行平曲线拟合，即180米长曲线沉管由8节中心线长度为22.5米的直线楔形节段组成，形成一个外长、内短的折线沉管。

曲线沉管碎石基床以沉管首尾两端中点连线为轴线，所有碎石垄垂直于轴线布置，碎石垫层纵坡为首尾两端中点高差与轴线长度比值。

曲线段碎石垫层顶宽42.95米，较直线段宽1.0米，其他参数与直线段相同。

曲线段沉管端部舾装件包括首端导向杆、拉合台座、尾端导向托架、拉合台座，均按轴线垂直于端钢壳布置。

综合考虑沉管形状和曲率的影响布置压载水箱，尽量保证压载的重心与沉管的重心重合。

与直线段标准沉管相比，曲线沉管预制尺寸控制、标定、安装测控等难度高，施工环境和作业条件更加复杂，安装精度和质量标准要求更高，沉放对接姿态和安装轴线控制难度更大，施工风险更高。

Immersed Tube Installation at the Curved Sectionof the Tunnel: The immersed tubcs E29 to E33 in the tunnel were made for the curved section of the tunnel. The curve radius of these tubes was 5500 meters, and they were the last five tubes to be installed.

The standard cross section of the curved tubes was similar to that of the straight tubes. When these tubes were manufactured, the horizontal curve fitting was done by bending instead of curving. That is, the curved tube of 180 meters long was made up of 8 straight wedges whose axis was 22.5 meters.

The rubble bed for the curved tubes took the straight line connecting the middle point of the two ends of the tube as its axis line. All the rubble ridges were perpendicular to the axis line, and the vertical slope rating for the rubble bedding was the ratio of elevation difference of the middle points of the two ends to thc length of the axis line.

The width of the top part of the rubble bedding for the curved section was 42.95 meters, 1.0 meters wider than that of the straight tubes, while the other parameters were identical.

The fitting-out of the end part of the curved tubes involved guide rod at the head part, closure pedestal, guide bracket at the ending part, and closure pedestal. They were arranged while keeping the axis line in a perpendicular position to the steel shell.

When the ballast water tank was arranged, the shape of the tubes and their curvity were taken into consideration to ensure that the ballast gravity center overlaped with that of the tube.

Compared with standard tubes in the straight section of the tunnel, it was more difficult to control, mark and test the precast size of the curved tube, the working conditions were more complicated, and the requirements for installation precision and quality were morc difficult to meet. It was also more difficult to control the position of tubcs during butt welding and were difficult to adjust the installation axis line, and the operation was more risky.

1. 岛头段沉管安装三维图
3-D Diagram of the Immersed Tube Installation at the Head Part of the Island

2—3. 曲线段沉管安装线性控制示意图
Schematic Diagram of the Linear Control for the Immersed Tube Installation at the Curved Part

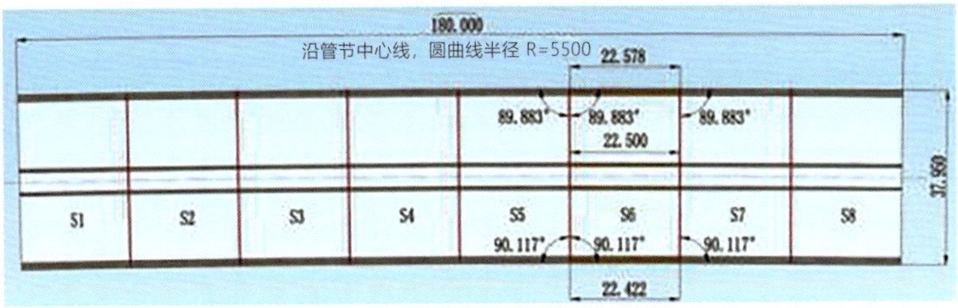

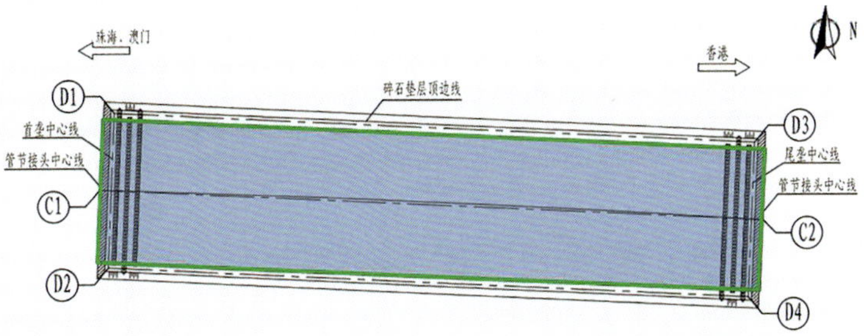

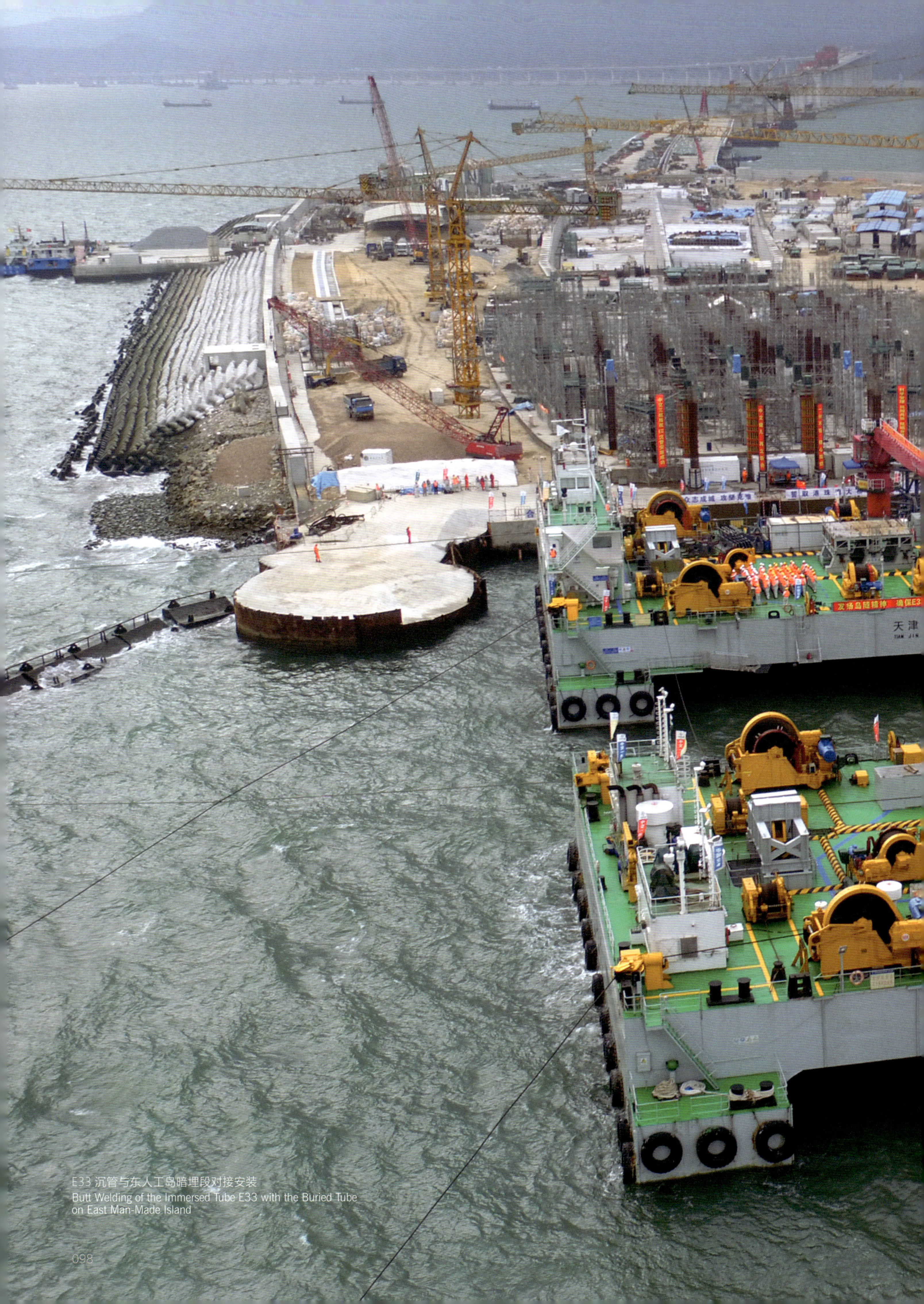

E33 沉管与东人工岛暗埋段对接安装
Butt Welding of the Immersed Tube E33 with the Buried Tube on East Man-Made Island

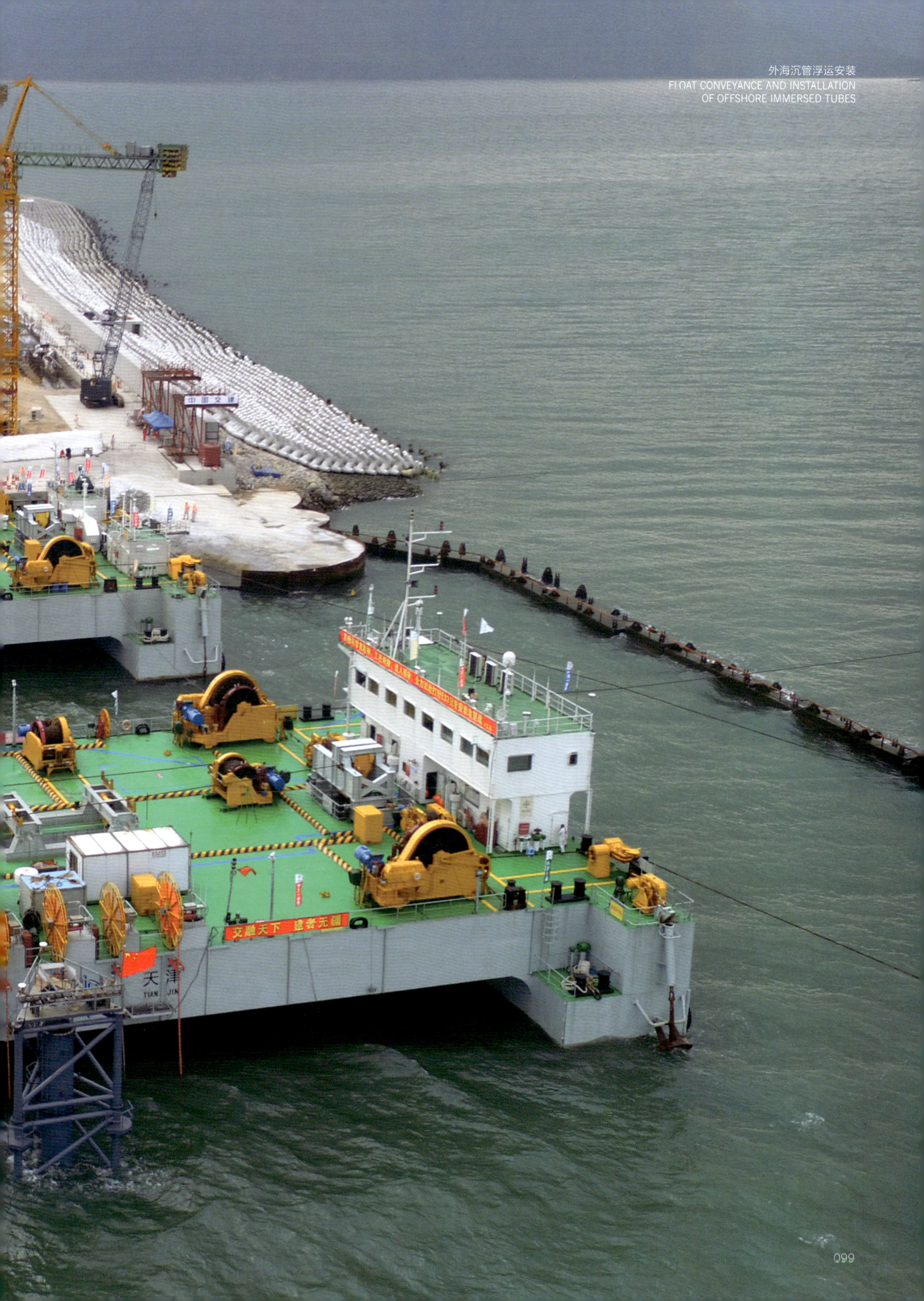

外海沉管浮运安装
FLOAT CONVEYANCE AND INSTALLATION
OF OFFSHORE IMMERSED TUBES

贯通测量
CLOSURE SURVEY

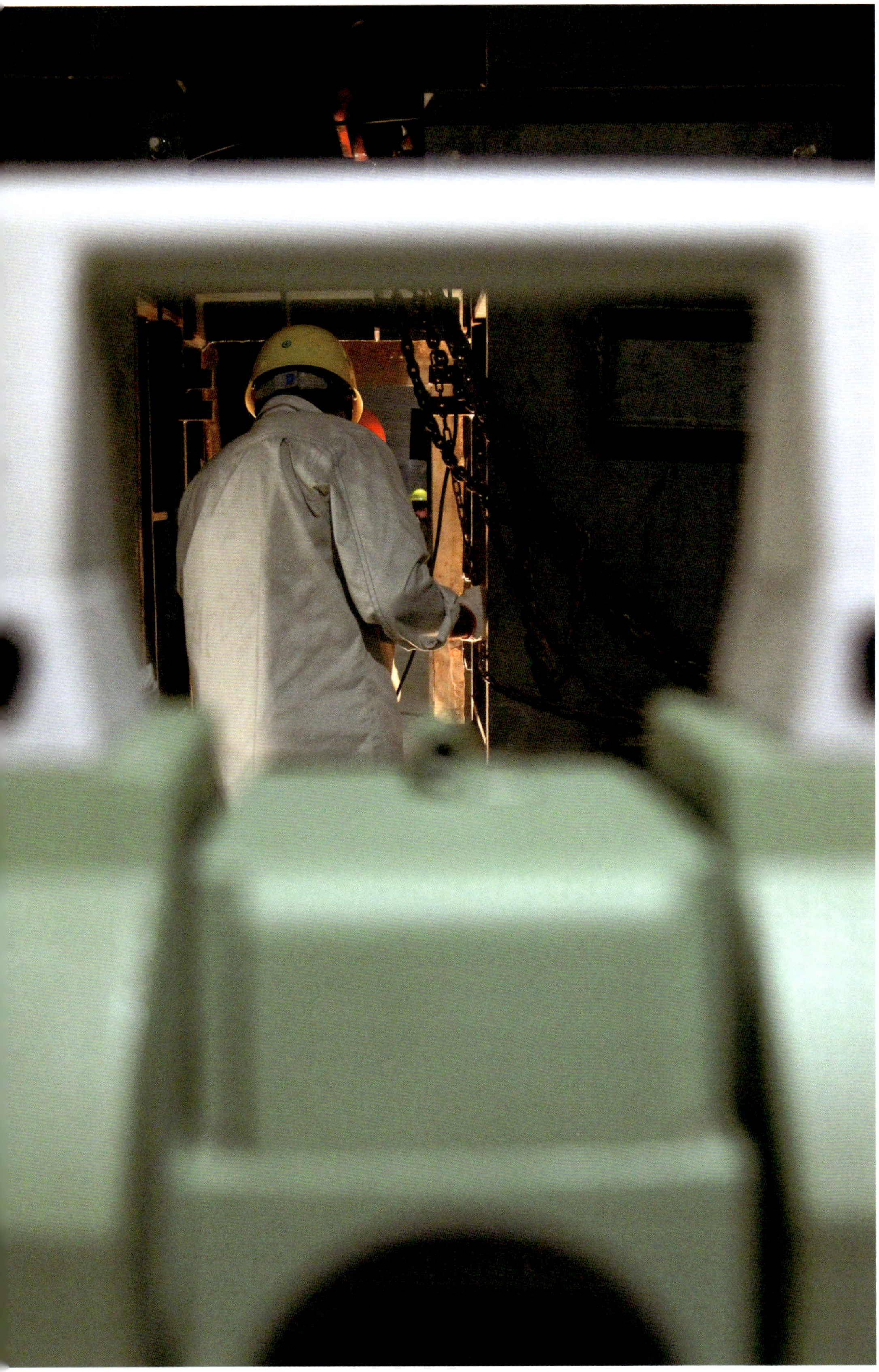

沉管水力压接完成后，打开中管廊人孔门，检查管内情况，进行贯通测量，确认沉管安装轴线和高程偏差是否满足设计要求。

After the hydraulic crimp connection in the immersed tube was finished, the entrance to the internal pipe gallery was open for in-tube examination and closure survey to ensure that the deviation between the axis line for the tube installation and the elevation satisfied the designed requirements.

1. 沉管对接贯通测量
Hole-through Survey for the Immersed Tube Butt Joint

2. 沉管锁定回填
Backfill for Locking the Immersed Tubes

3. 沉管锁定回填三维图
3-D Diagram of Backfill for the Locking of the Immersed Tubes

回填覆盖
BACK-FILL COVERING

沉管安装后，采用专用船舶抛填碎石进行点锁固定，之后进行一般回填，最后采用块石进行覆盖防护。

After the tube installation was completed, special barges were used for rubble backfill to lock the tubes, followed by ordinary backfill. The final step was that big rocks were filled to cover the tubes for protection.

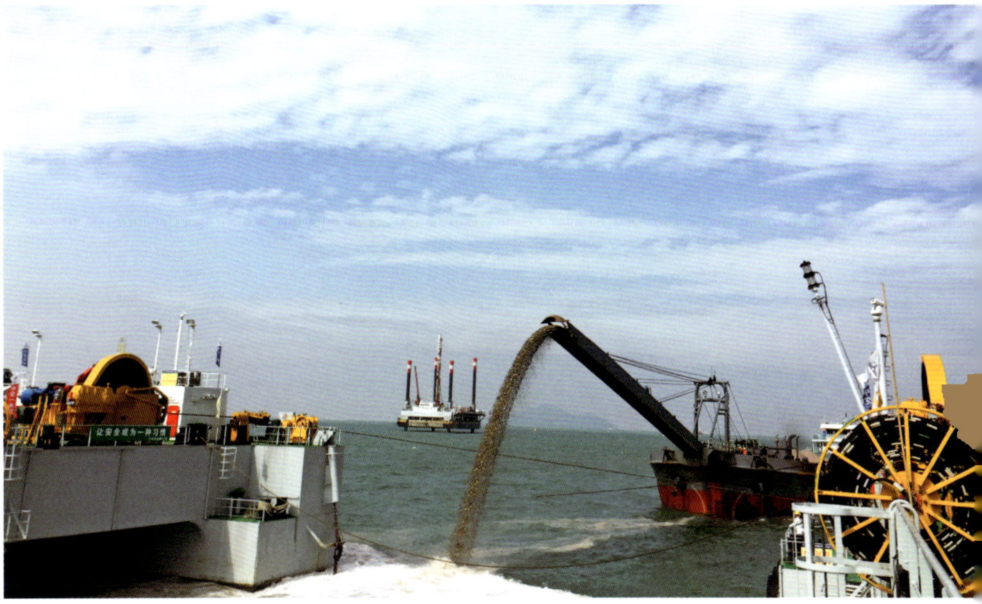

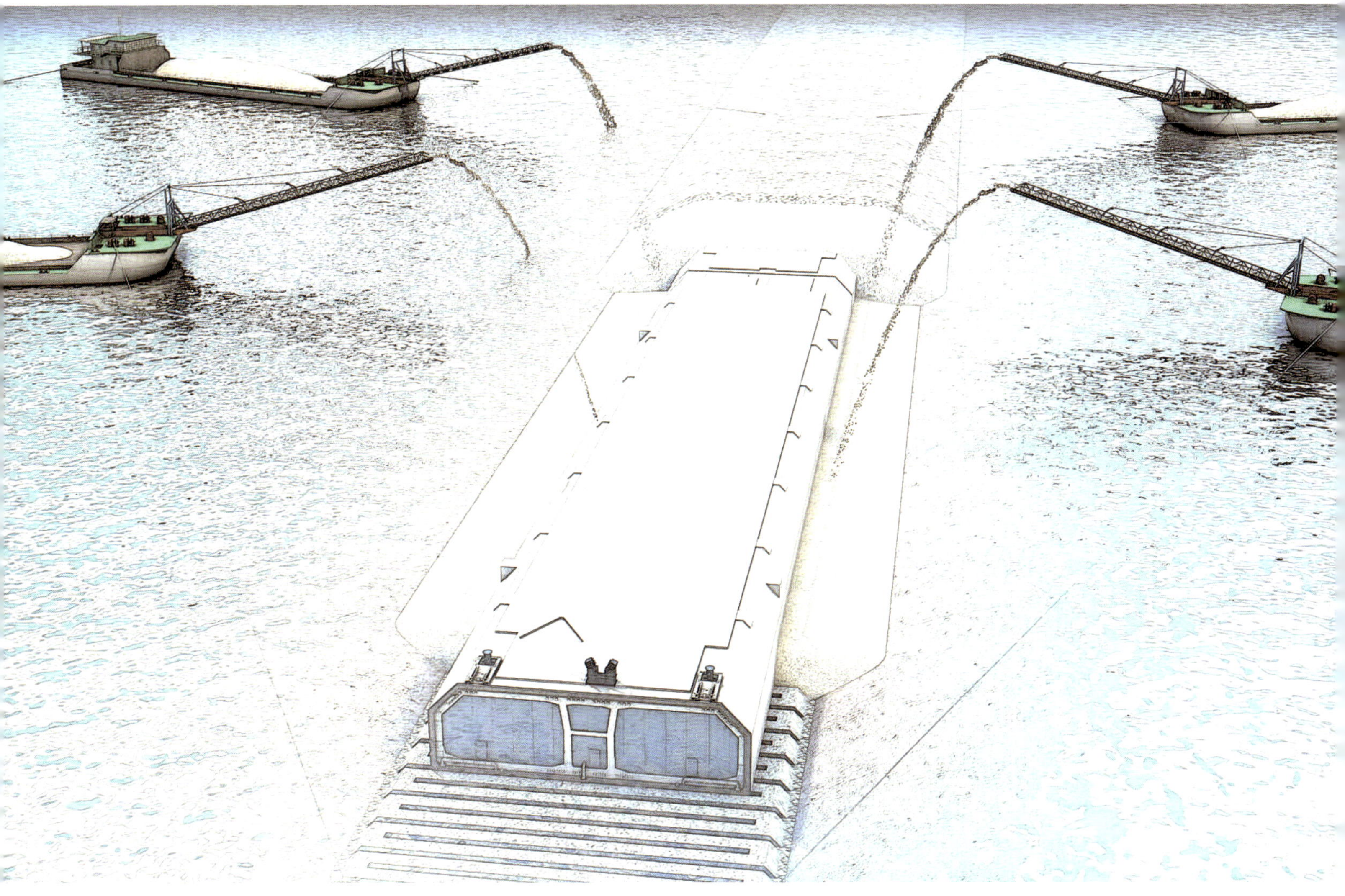

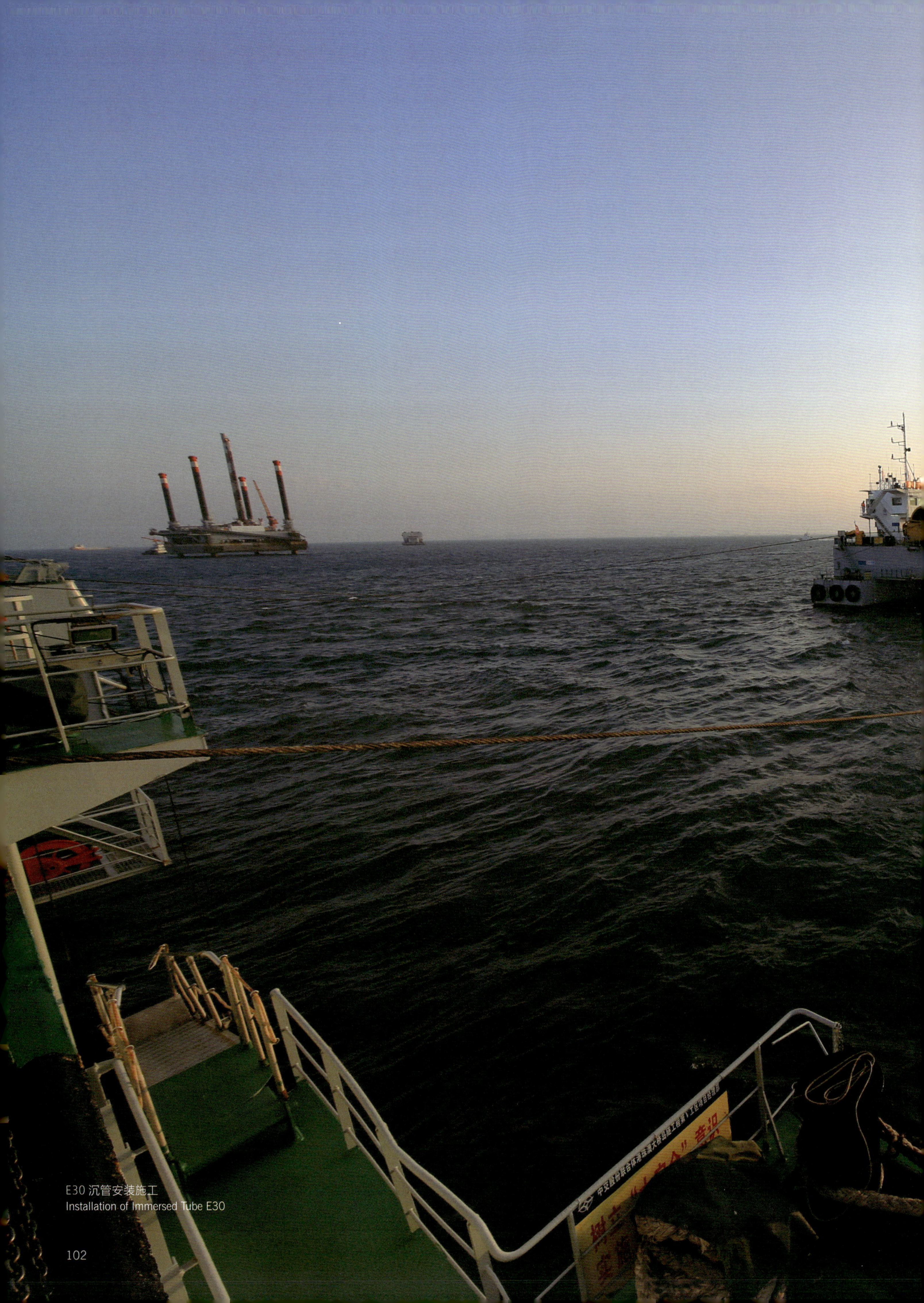
E30 沉管安装施工
Installation of Immersed Tube E30

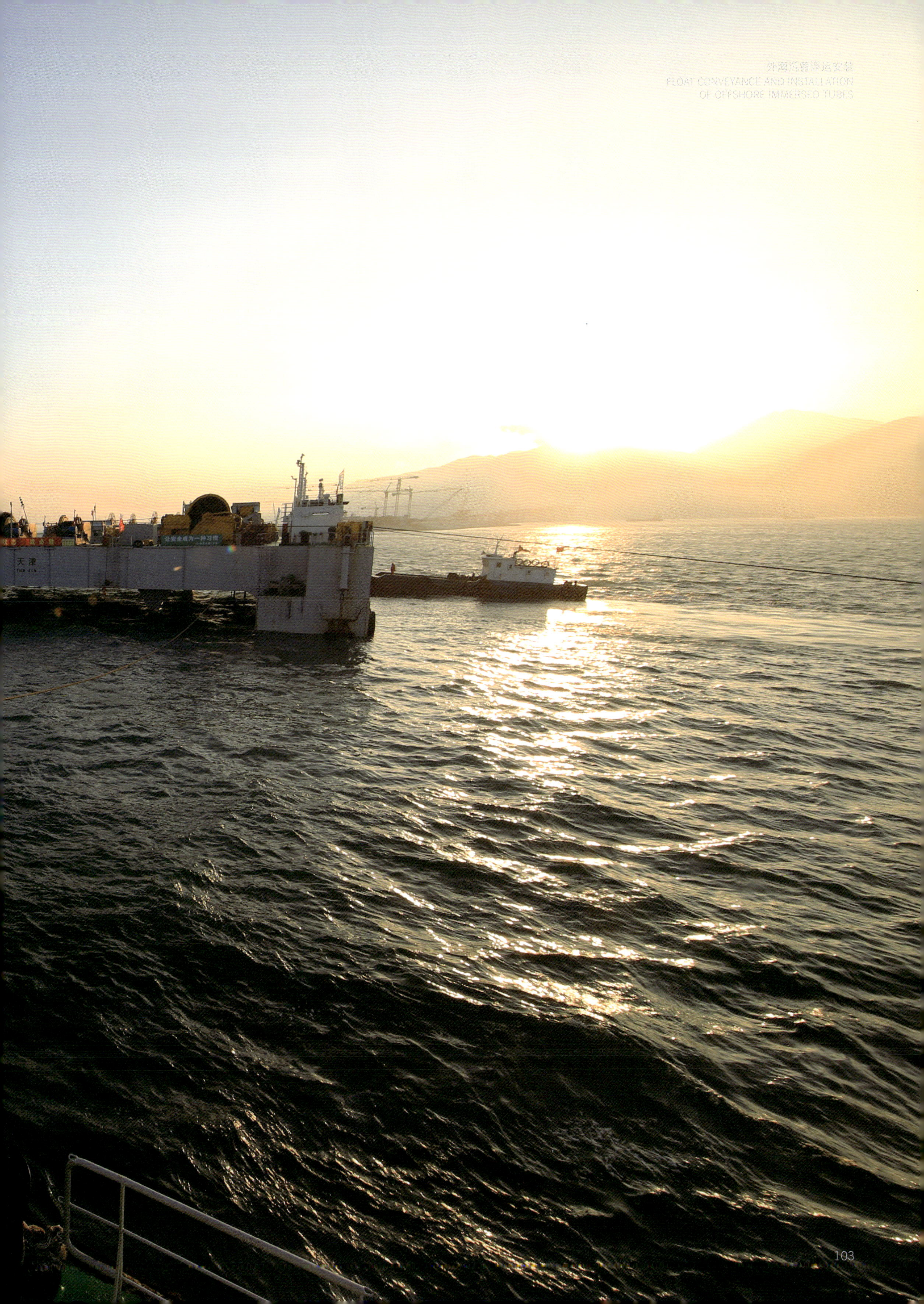
让安全成为一种习惯
天津
TIAN JIN

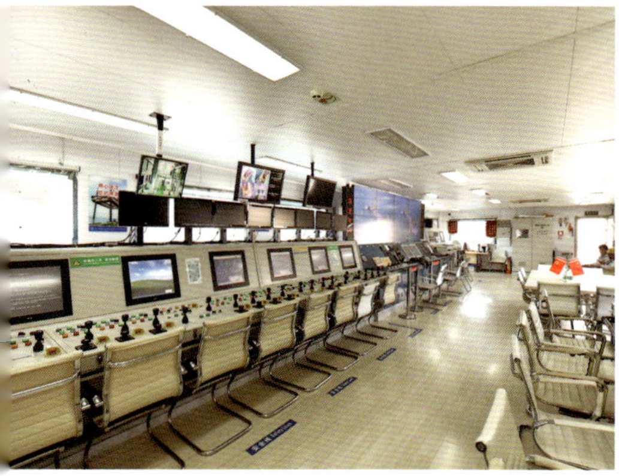

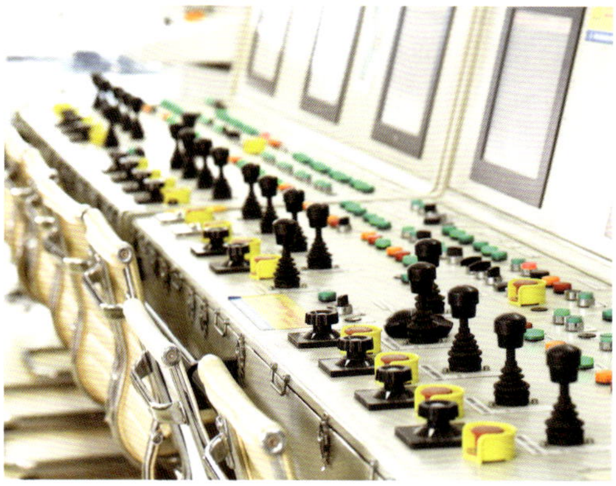

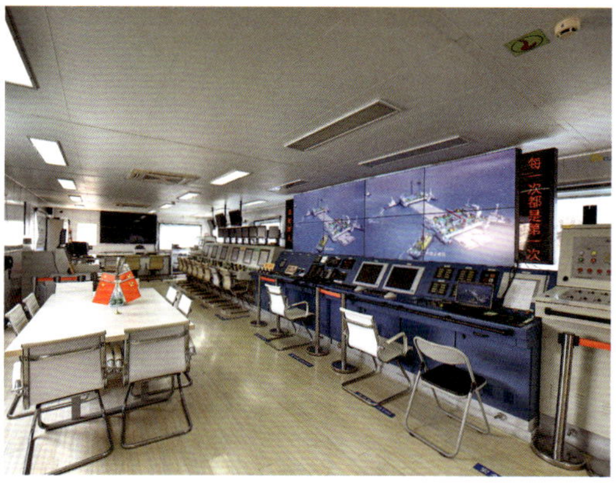

外海沉管安装成套技术、装备和保障体系

TECHNOLOGY, EQUIPMENT AND SUPPORT SYSTEM FOR OFFSHORE IMMERSED TUBE INSTALLATION

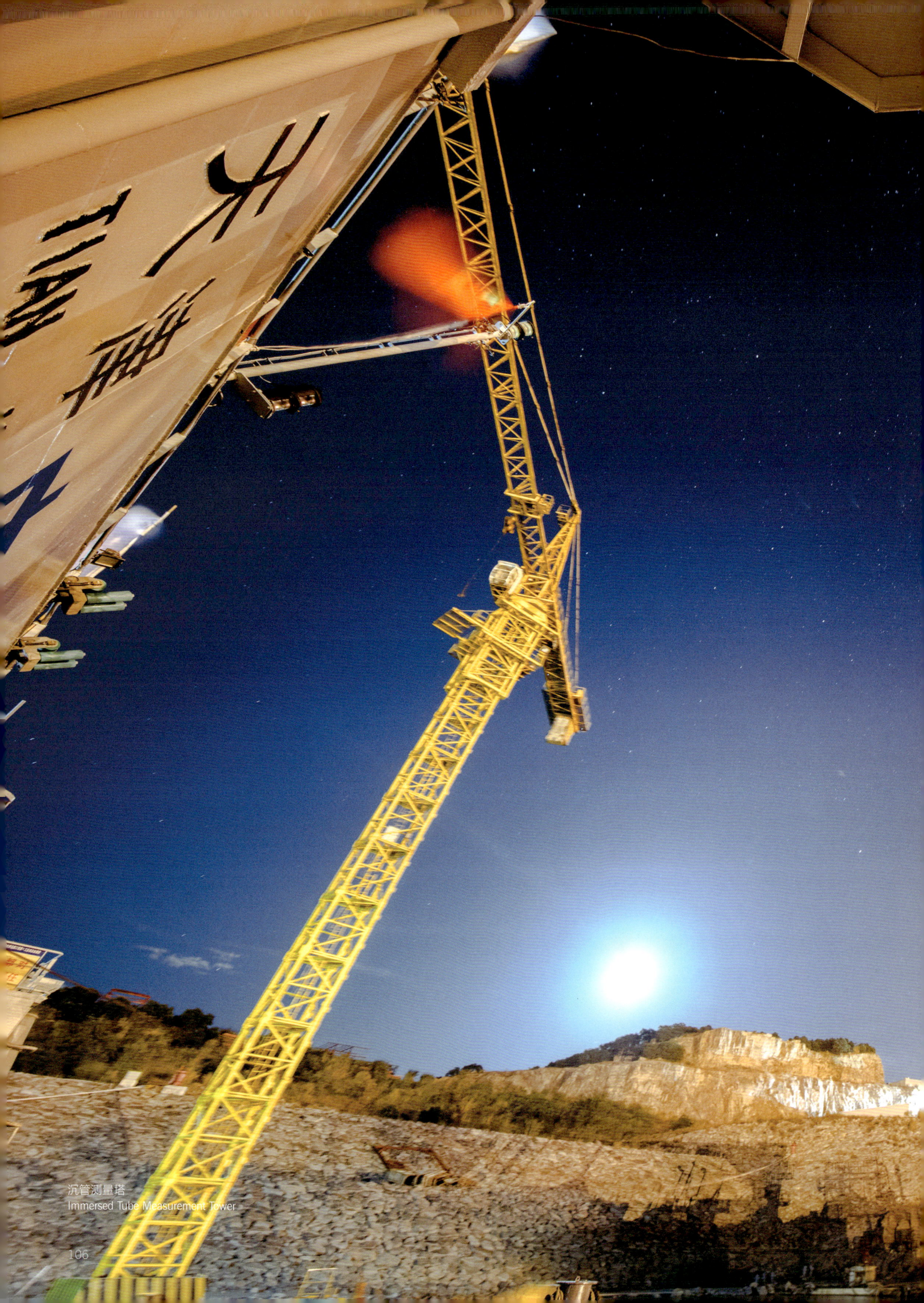

沉管测量塔
Immersed Tube Measurement Tower

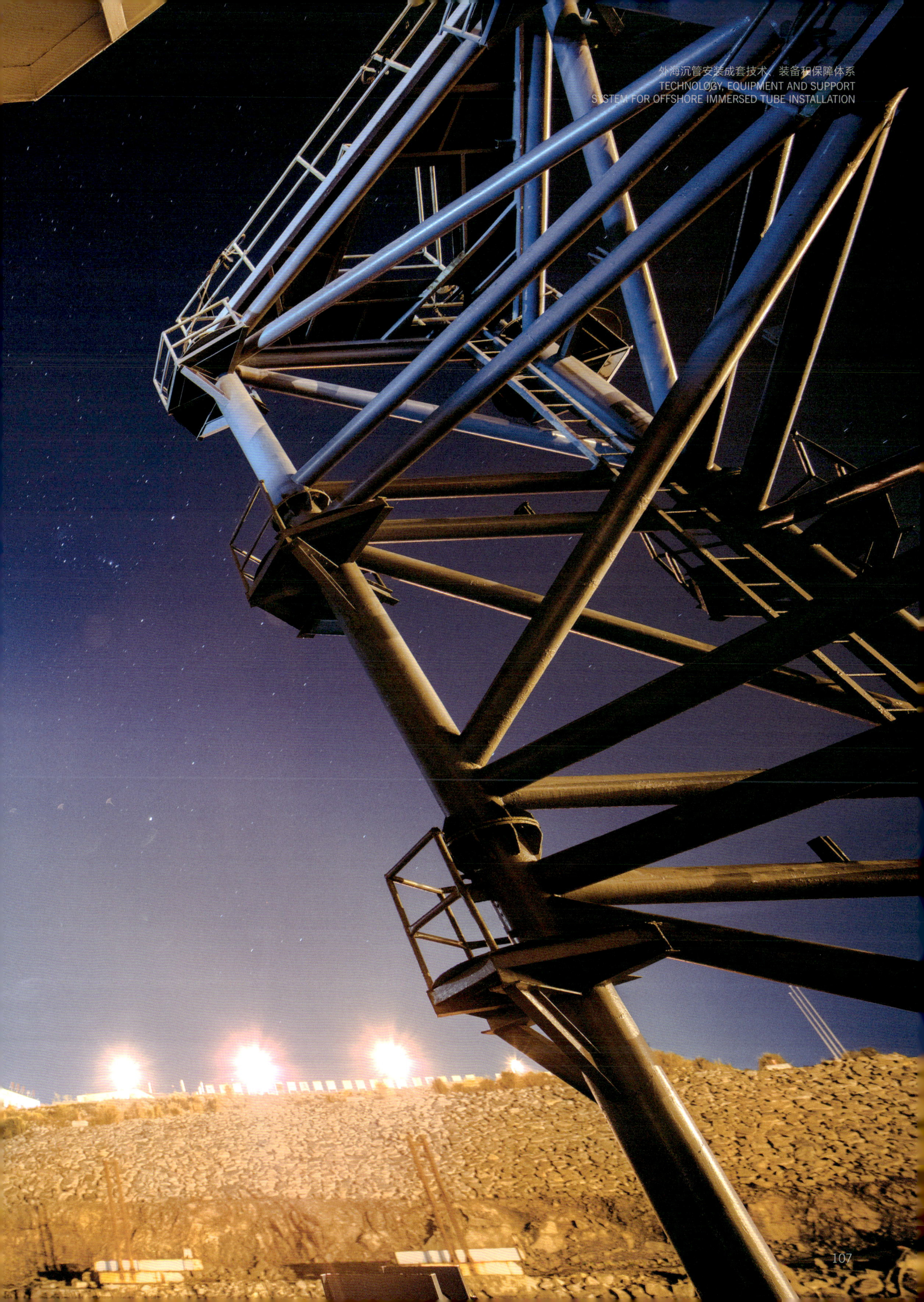

数字化导航系统

DIGITAL NAVIGATION SYSTEM

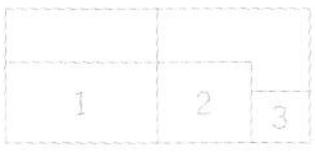

1. 沉管浮运数字化导航系统
   Digital Navigation System for the Float Conveyance of the Immersed Tubes
2. 沉管无人沉放定位
   Positioning System for the Unmanned Immersed Tube Landing
3. 数字化沉管无人沉放定位系统
   Digital Positioning System for the Unmanned Immersed Tube Landing

浮运编队最多时使用 13 艘拖轮同时配合拖运，在国内外均没有先例，单纯依靠指挥人员现场观测拖轮位置无法满足要求。

项目总经理部研发浮运数字化导航辅助指挥系统，实时显示编队浮运过程中的各项技术参数，为浮运指挥、拖轮控制及相关作业提供可视的参考信息，保障了受限航区内沉管长距离拖航安全。

The maximal number of towing barges working together for the float conveyance of the tubes in a formation included 13 barges, which was unprecedented in the world. It was impossible for human beings to command the working of these barges at the working site.

The project management center developed the auxiliary digital navigation system to guide the float conveyance of the tubes. By this system, all the technological parameters during the float conveyance could be mastered, which provided visualized references for commanding the float conveyance, controlling the towing barges or other relevant operation, and guaranteed the safety of long-distance towing of the tubes on limited watercourses.

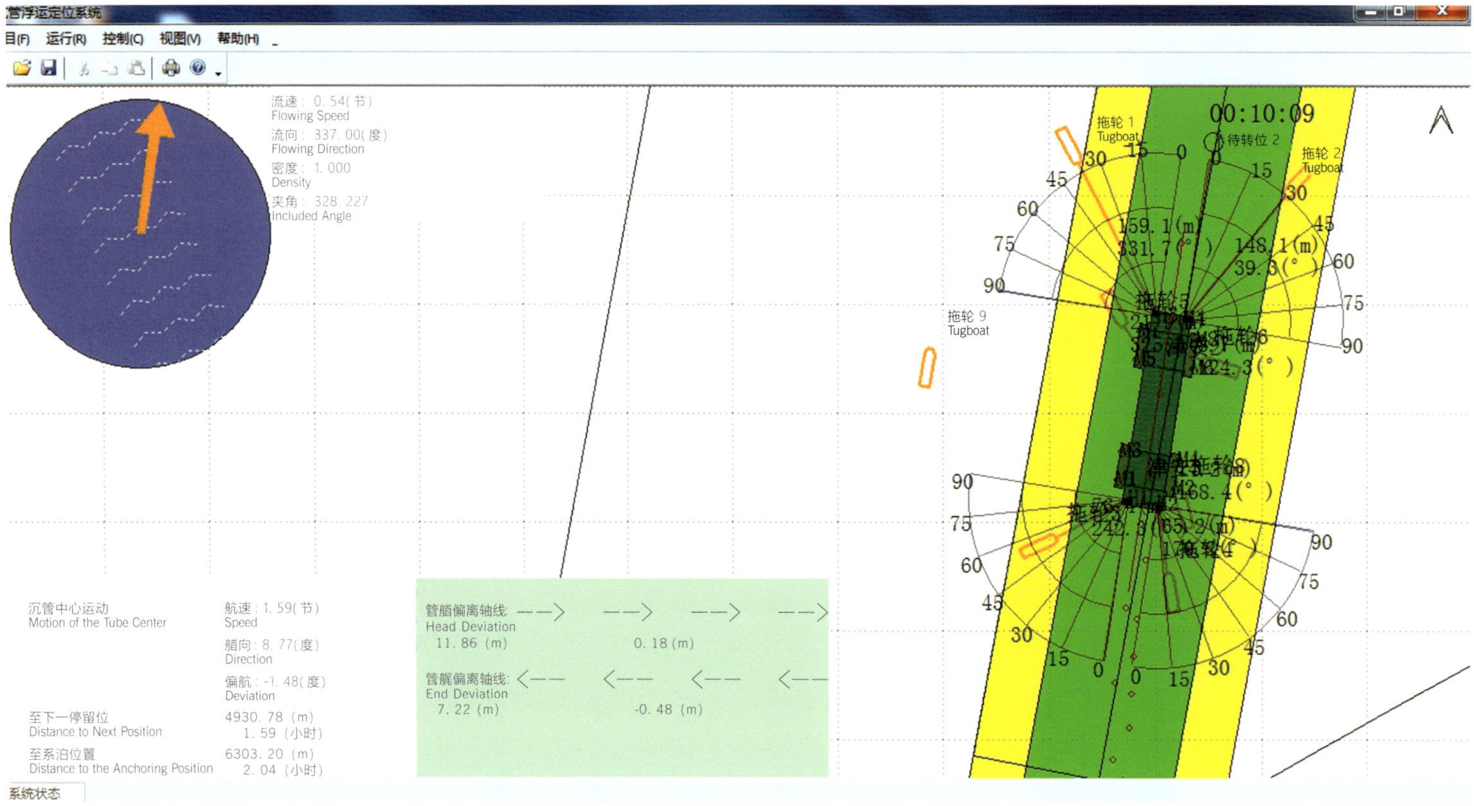

双驳杠吊无人沉放定位系统

POSITIONING SYSTEM FOR UNMANNED DOUBLE-BARGE BEAM-LIFTING LANDING

双驳杠吊法沉放定位系统包括安装驳系统、锚泊定位系统、压载水系统、测控系统、导向定位系统、拉合系统、水力压接系统和体内精调系统等子系统。

沉放时利用横跨在沉管两侧的安装船及配套的锚缆系统控制沉管的空间位置，利用测控系统对沉管进行高精度精确定位，由压载水系统提供沉管下沉时的负浮力。

主、副安装船各配置电力、控制、通讯系统，其中主安装船能远程遥控副安装船。

安装船由两侧浮箱和顶部跨梁三大部分组成，浮箱用来提供整个沉放驳的浮力，顶部跨梁设置工作平台、绞车和滑轮模组、电力装置及控制等系统，控制沉管安装的缆索作业。

The positioning system for unmanned double-barge beam-lifting landing involved installation barge system, mooring and positioning system, ballast water system, monitoring system, guided positioning system, closure system, hydraulic crimp connection system and internal fine adjusting system.

The position of the immersed tube during landing was controlled by the installation barges on the two sides of the tube and the auxiliary mooring system. The monitoring system was used for the hihg-precision positioning of the tubes, and the ballast water system provided the negative buoyancy for the landing tubes.

The principal and auxiliary installation barges were equipped with electric power system, control system and communication system. The principal installation barges could conduct remote control of the auxiliary installation barges.

The installation barge was composed of the floating tanks on the two sides of the ship and the supporting beam over the top of the ship. The floating tanks were used to provide the buoyant force of the whole installation barge, And the operation platform, the winches, the pulley sets, the electric devices and the control system on the supporting beam were used to control the cable works for the tube installation.

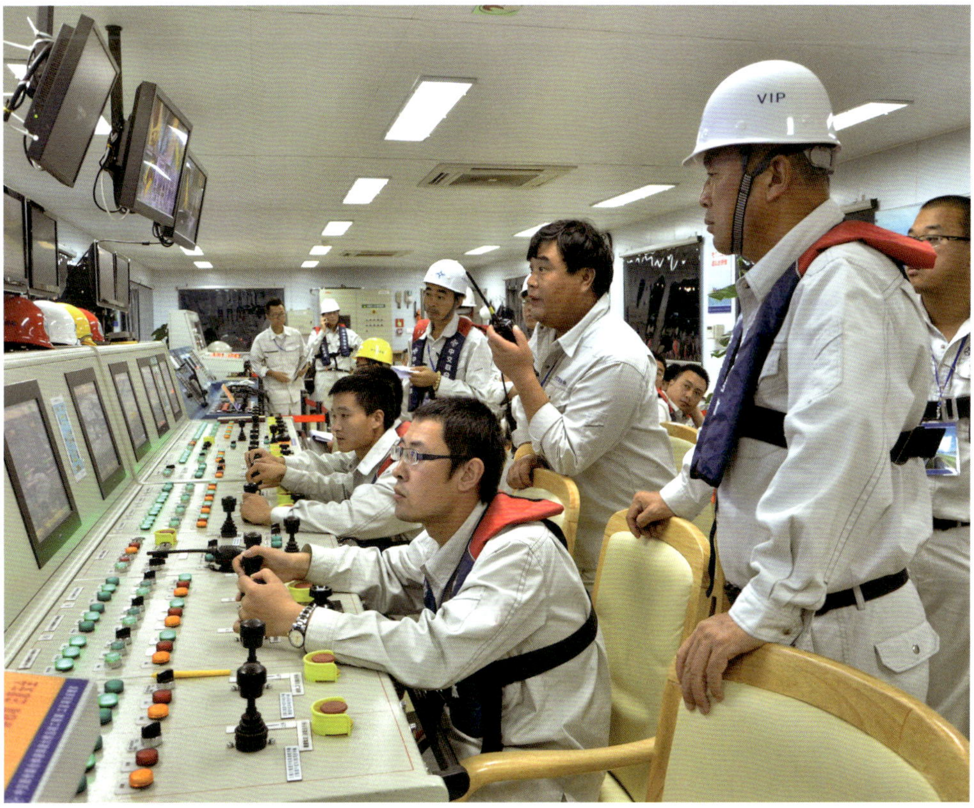

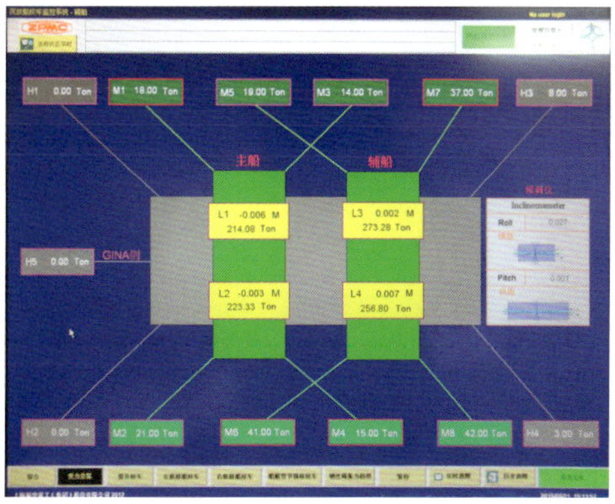

作业窗口预报管理系统

OPERATION WINDOW FORECAST MANAGEMENT SYSTEM

在外海气象、风、浪、流等条件的作用下，要保证沉管作业安全，须提前预报沉管从出坞到对接完成所需几十个小时内的海洋环境条件。

项目总经理部委托国家海洋环境预报中心开展小区域精细化气象、海浪和海流数值预报技术攻关，开发了精细化数值预报系统，实现了施工海域100米空间分辨率、半小时时间分辨率的高精度环境预报；开发了长历时天气预报系统，为基床槽铺设，沉管浮运、沉放等提供精细化“水文气象窗口”，实现了预报时效15天的小区域、长历时、高精度窗口预报。

In the face of the complicated offshore weather changes, winds, waves and currents, to guarantee the safety during the operation, it was necessary to forecast the oceanic environmental conditions in the tens of hours from the undocking of the tube to the moment when the butt welding was completed.

The project management center entrusted the National Marine Environmental forecast Center to develop technologies to forecast detailedly the weather condition, waves and currents in specified region. Precise numerical forecast system was developed to provide high-precision environmental forecast of the spatial resolution within 100 meters and temporal resolution within 30 minutes in the construction marine area. A long-duration weather forecast system was developed to provide precise “hydro-meteorological window” for trench bedding, tube transportation and tube landing for 15 days in specified limited region.

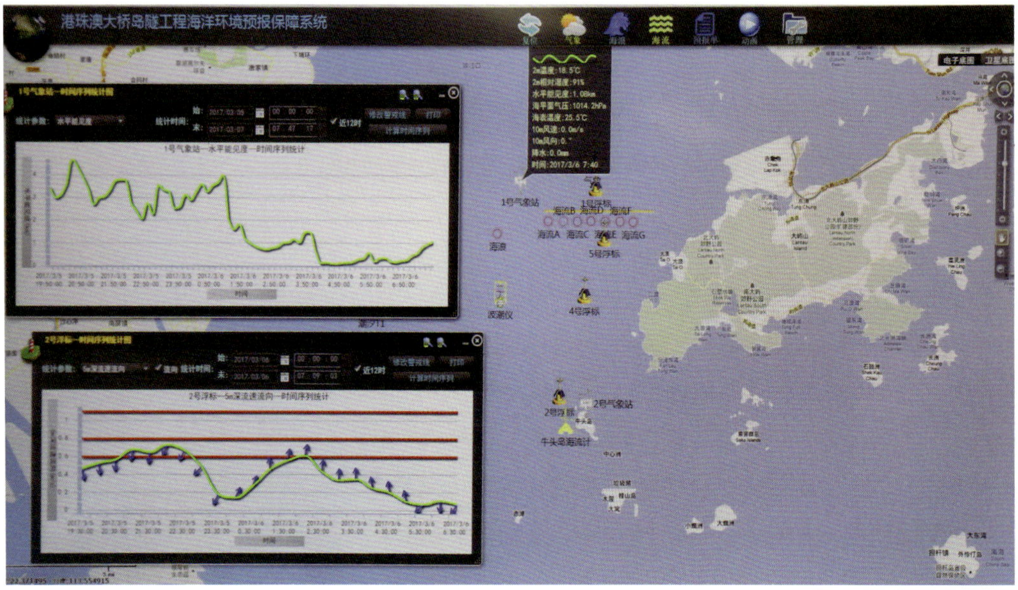

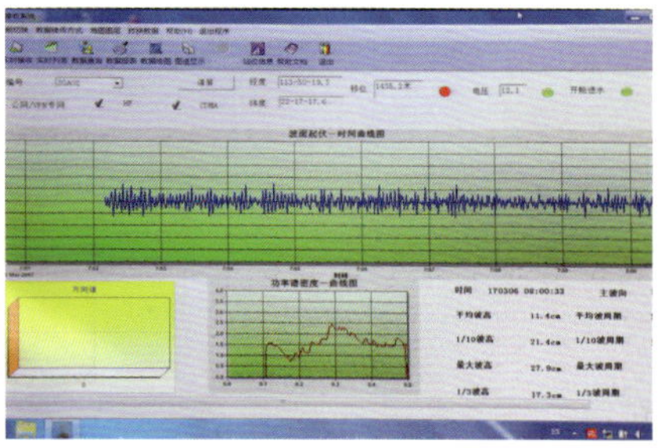

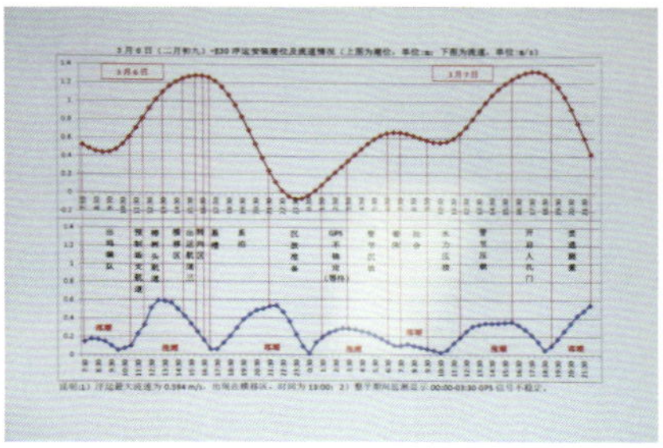

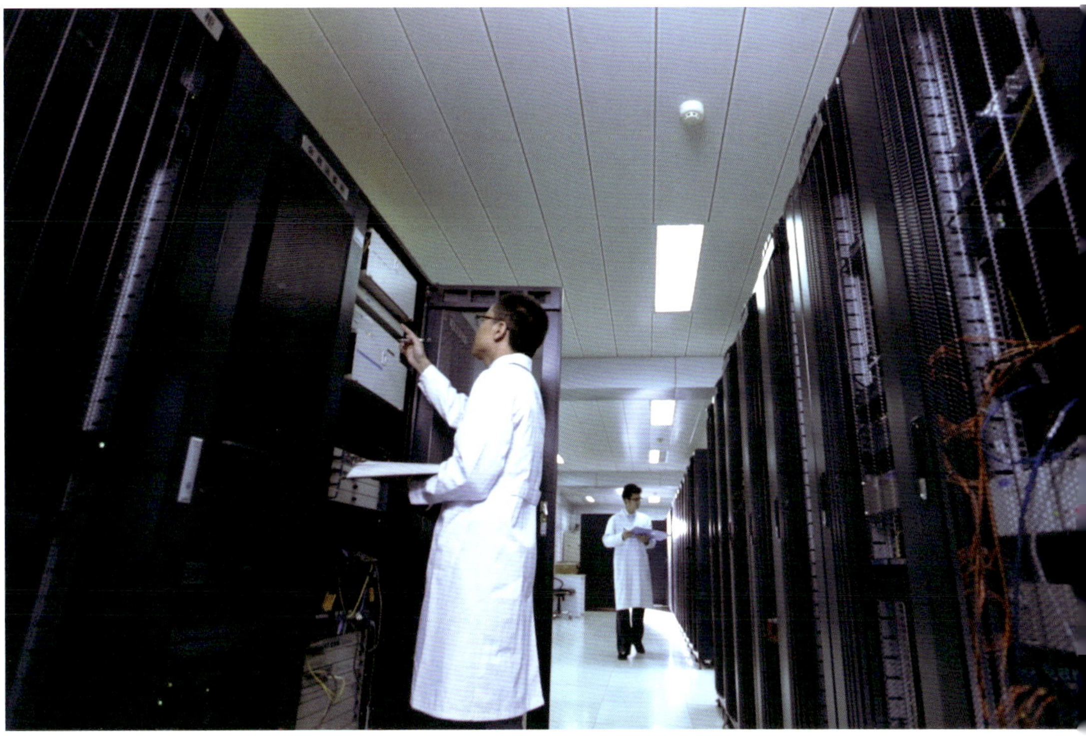

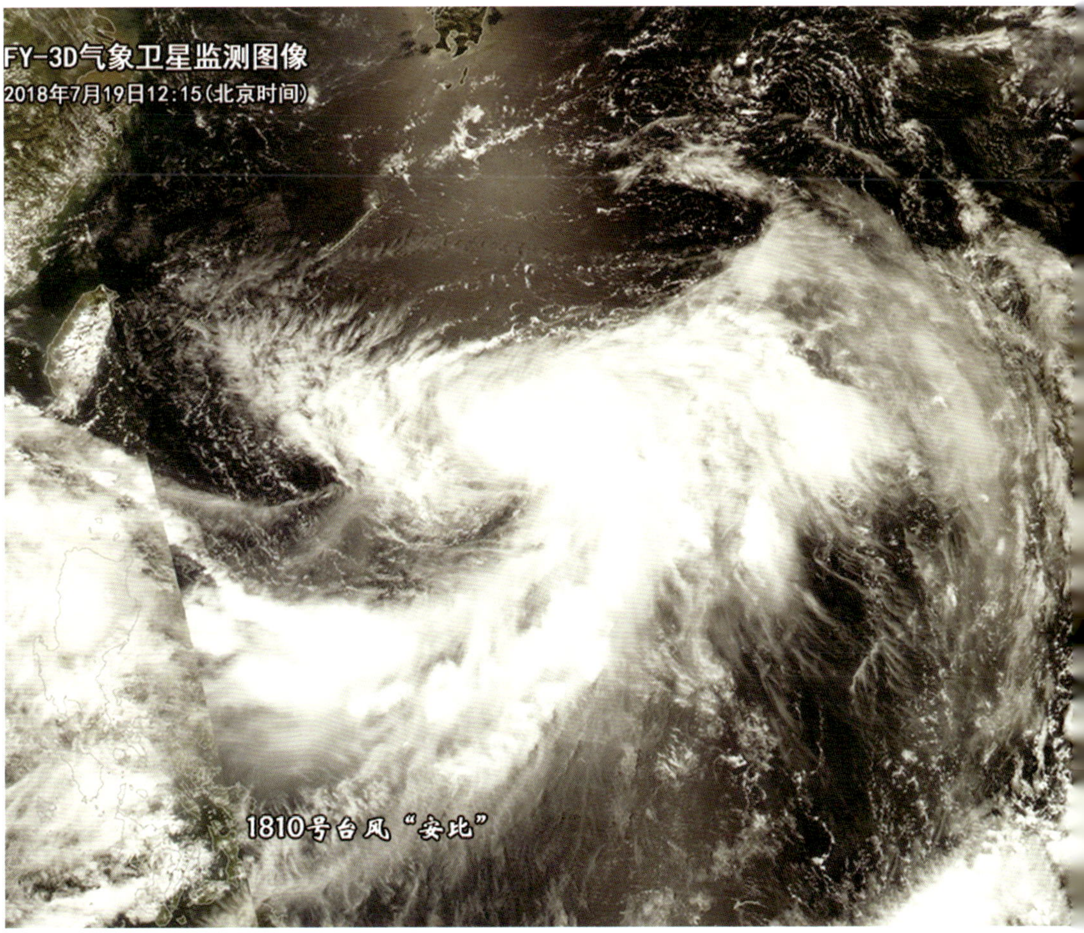

1—3. 沉管浮运安装海洋环境预报保障系统
Oceanic Environment Forecast Supporting System for the Float Conveyance and Installation of the Immersed Tubes

4. 超级计算机分析预报沉管浮运安装海洋环境
Supercomputer Analyzing and Forecasting Oceanic Environment for the Float Conveyance and Installation of the Immersed Tubes

5. 气象卫星监测云图
Meteorological Satellite Monitored Cloud Map

对接窗口预报保障系统
BUTT-WELDING WINDOW FORECAST SYSTEM

沉管施工水域位于盐水楔活动区，在潮汐的作用下，近海深槽海流的水平速度在垂直方向呈"齿轮"结构分布：

涨潮时，底层流速大于表层流速；落潮时，表层流速大于底层流速。

沉管沉放对接需要选择良好的时机，沉管着床、对接操作尽量控制在槽内小流速时段进行，减小水下控制难度和风险。

开发外海深槽沉管安装对接保障系统，解决周边海洋环境对沉管沉放对接影响的难题。

该系统基于外海深槽水动力机理研究结果，利用径流、潮汐、海流耦合技术，实现了深槽全断面实时高精度海流预报，为沉管对接施工决策提供可靠保障。

The construction region of the immersed tubes lay in the salt-water wedge area, where, due to influence of the tidal motion, the horizontal speed of the current in the deep trench near the shore was presented as a vertical "gear" structure.

During the high tide, the current speed at the bottom layer is higher than that on the surface; during the low tide, the current speed on the surface layer is higher than that on the bottom layer.

The landing and butt welding of the immersed tubes needed favorable operation condition. The landing of the tube and the butt welding should be done when the current speed in the foundation trench was low, which could facilitate the underwater control and reduce the risks during opperation.

Thus a support system for offshore deep trench tube installation and butt welding was developed to cope with the complicated oceanic environment unfavorable to the tube landing and butt welding.

Based on the findings from the study of the mechanism of water power in offshore deep trench, this system employed the coupling technology to combine factors of streamflow, tidal wave and sea current for the real-time high-precision sea-current forecast at the gross section of the deep trench, which provided support for decision making as to the butt welding of the immersed tubes.

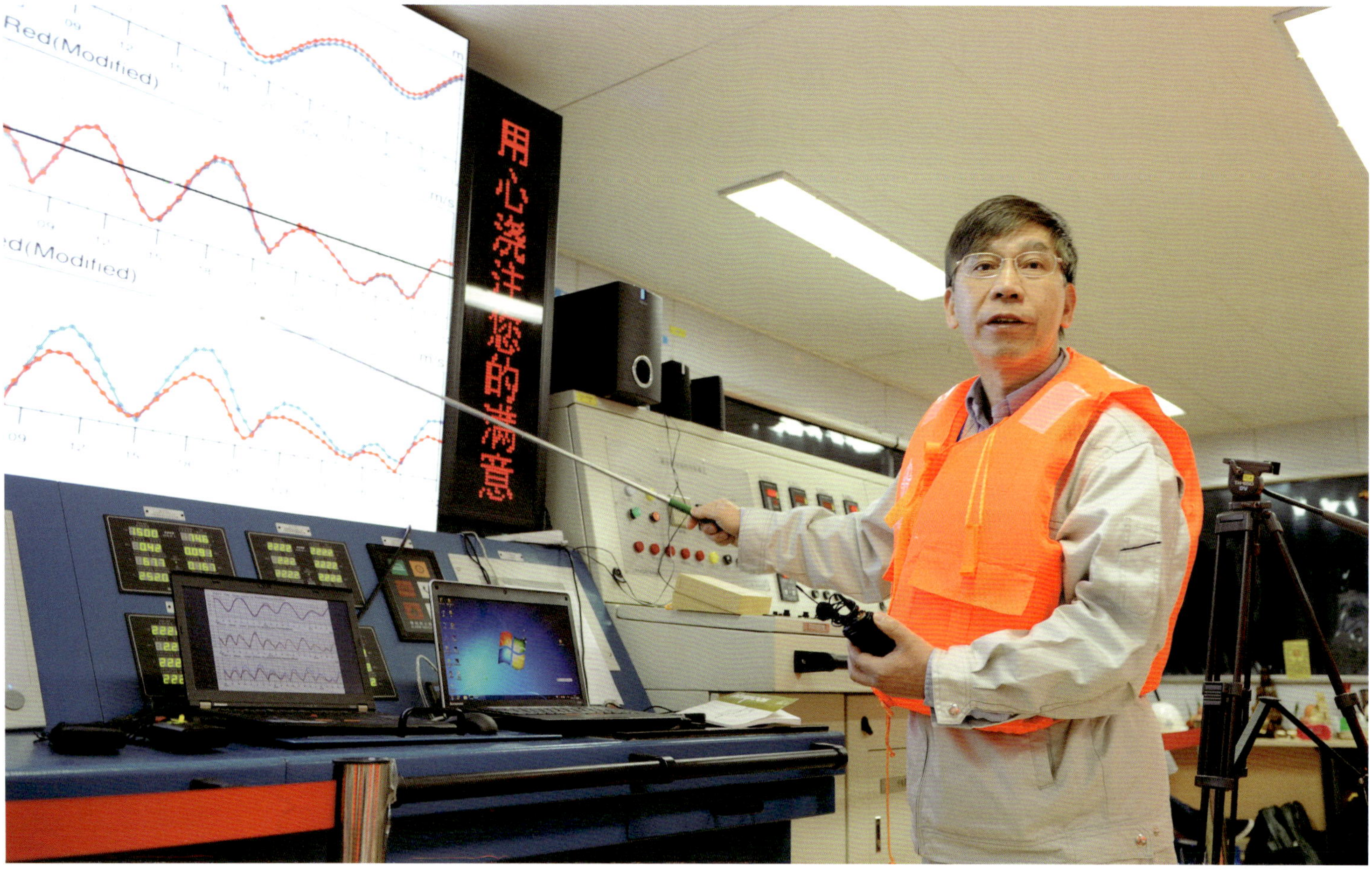

基槽泥沙预警预报系统
FOUNDATION TRENCH SEDIMENT ALARMING SYSTEM

受上游内伶仃岛附近高强度采砂活动影响，基槽内发生异常回淤，导致E15沉管浮运安装两次受阻，造成了极大的工程风险和经济损失。

项目总经理部联合中交第四航务勘察设计院有限公司、交通运输部天津水运工程科学研究院、中山大学、南京水利科学研究院等相关专业单位组成攻关组，开展了大范围的地形地质勘察、泥沙观察、数模分析及回淤观测，获得了大量的实测数据，并据此开发建立了一套数值模拟＋公式预报相联合的多因素复合型基槽回淤预报模型系统，对沉管施工窗口期内基槽淤积情况进行预报，对可能出现的风险进行预警，实现了基槽泥沙淤积预报范围从宏观到局部，预报时效从"年、月"到"逐日"，预报精度由米级到厘米级的精细化提高，极大地提升了回淤预报的精确度和时效性。

Due to the influence of the upstream sand mining around Lingding Island, abnormal back silting happened in the foundation trench, resulting in the interruption of the float conveyance and installation of the immersed tube E15. This accident exposed the construction to great risks and caused tremendous economic loss.

The project management center cooperated with the Fourth Habour Engineering Investigation and Design Institute of the Ministry of Transport, Tianjin Research Institute for Water Transportation Engineering of the Ministry of Transport, Zhongshan University, and Nanjing Hydraulic Research Institute for scientific studies on geological and topographic survey, sand observation, mathematical-model analysis and back silting detection. Based on the data collected, the center established a set of multi-factor composite foundation trench back-silting forecast model system involving numerical simulation and formula forecast, used to forecast the sediments in the foundation trench and the possible risks during the construction window. This system helped realize the local as well as global forecast about the sediments and sand in the foundation trench, from yearly or monthly forecast to daily forecast, and the forecast accuracy improved from meters to centimeters. All this improved the precision and durability of back-silting forecast.

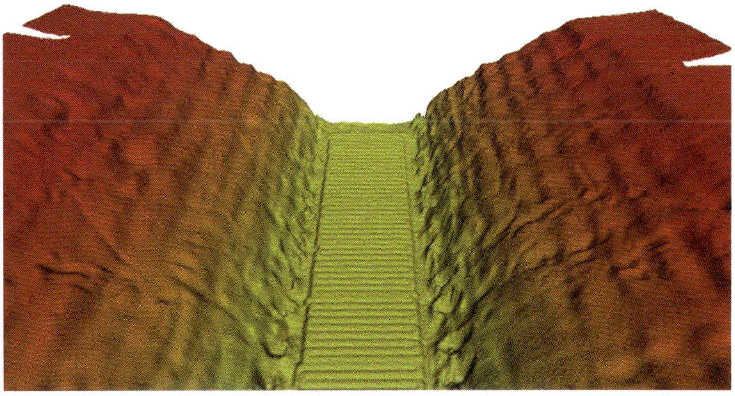

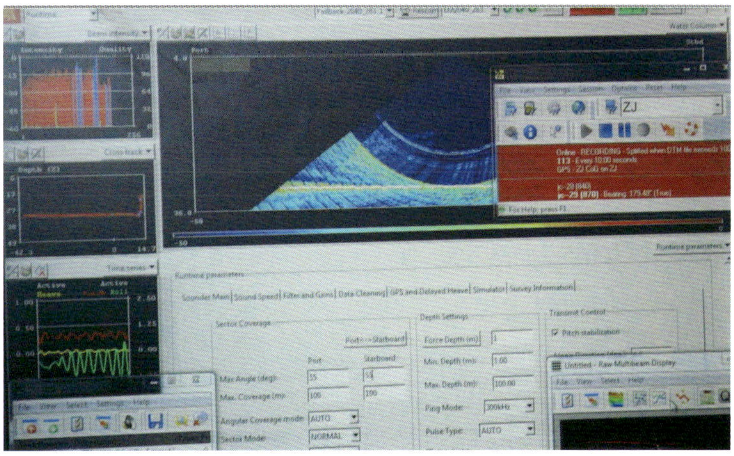

1. 沉管对接窗口海洋气象环境数据分析
Oceanic Weather Data Analysis for the Immersed Tube Butt Joint Window
2. 隧道基床多波束扫测三维图
3-D Diagram of the Multi-Beam Scanning of the Tunnel Base
3. 隧道基床多波束测量系统
Tunnel Base Multi-Beam Scanning System

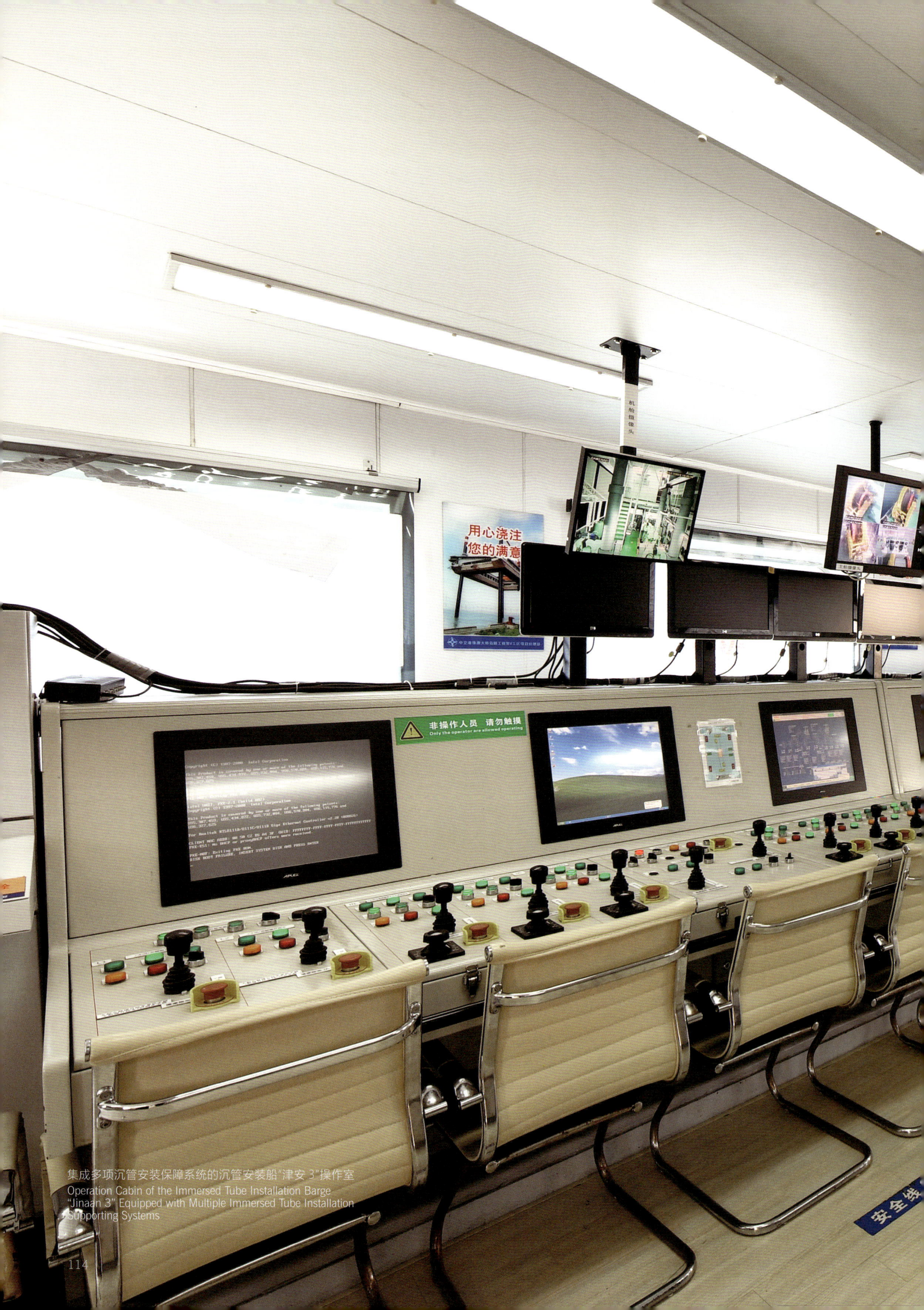

集成多项沉管安装保障系统的沉管安装船"津安 3"操作室
Operation Cabin of the Immersed Tube Installation Barge "Jinaan 3" Equipped with Multiple Immersed Tube Installation Supporting Systems

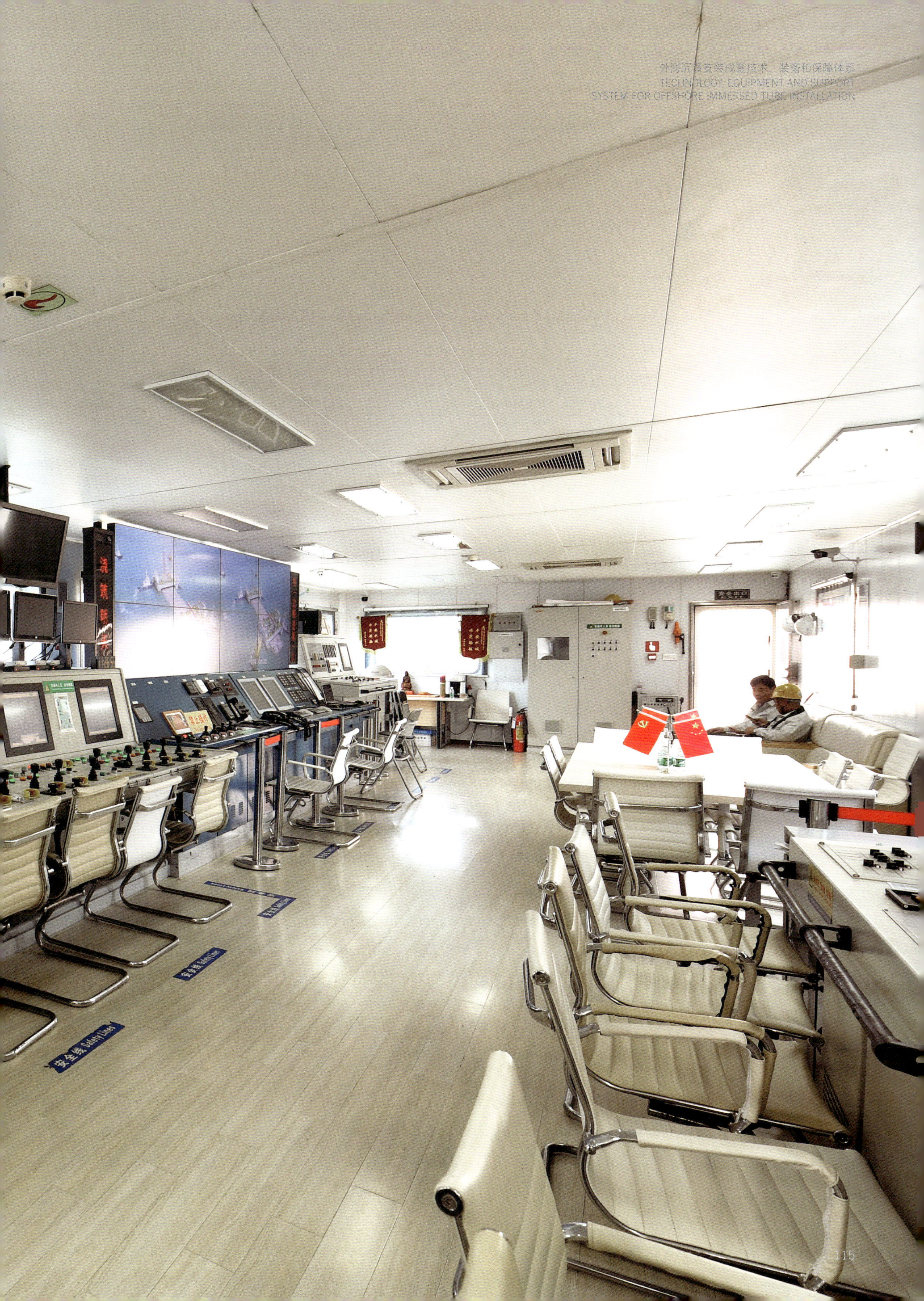
安全线 Safety Lines

异常波监测和报警系统

ABNORMAL WAVE DETECTION AND ALARMING SYSTEM

沉管浮运安装都在海面上进行，当浪高大于一定阈值（窗口限制条件）会导致沉管和沉放驳大幅度晃动，影响沉管稳定性；如果海浪波长尺度与沉管尺度接近，会导致沉管大幅度晃动，难以控制姿态；而且海浪周期与沉管自运动周期紧密相关，当两者周期相近时容易引起共振加大导致沉管大幅晃动，乃至发生断缆和沉管失控等重大风险。

异常波监测和报警系统通过采用波面高频监测、信号快速识别技术，实现了秒级快速识别、波要素自动检测与提前15分钟自动报警的功能，为沉管安装提供了安全保障。

The float conveyance and installation of the immersed tubes were conducted on the sea, so when the wave height surpassed certain threshold value (window limit), the stability of the immersed tube would be affected greatly because the wave might cause the tube and installation barges to sway hard. If the wave length approximated the the length of the tube, the tube would sway violently, which made it difficult to control its position. The moving cycle of the wave was closely relevant to that of the immersed tube, so when their moving cycles were similar, the resonance vibration thereby would result in the violent sway of the tube, even the cables might break and the tube went out of control, or other dangers might result.

Abnormal wave detection and alarming system employed such technologies as wavefront high frequency monitoring, high speed signal detection, so that it could instantly detect abnormal wave, automatically detect the wave parameters,and send alarm 15 minutes in advance, which guaranteed the safety of the tube installation.

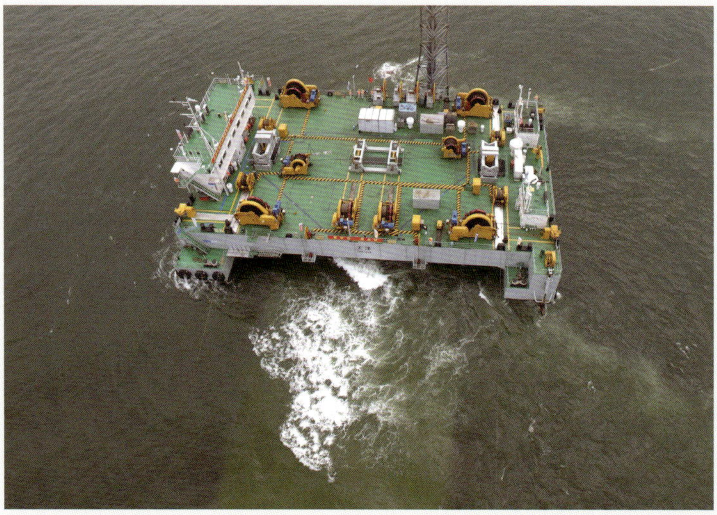

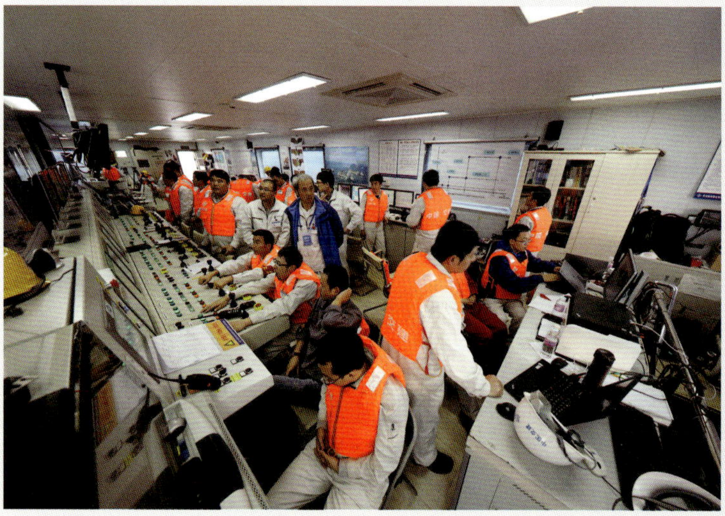

沉管运动姿态监测系统
IMMERSED TUBE'S MOTION TRAJECTORY MONITORING SYSTEM

1. 沉管安装遭遇异常波
   Immersed Tube Installation Troubled by the Extraordinary Wave
2. 异常波监测
   Abnormal Wave Monitoring

3—4. 沉管运动姿态监控系统
   Monitoring System for the Moving Trajectory of the Immersed Tubes

沉管水下运动呈现超低频、微幅的特性，监测难度大；同时由于深槽流态复杂，沉管异常晃动将影响安装质量和安全，需要实时监测反馈信息，为沉管安装决策提供依据。

项目总经理部联合中国航空工业集团304研究所，借鉴航天动态监测技术，研发沉管姿态解算方法，形成了"外海超大沉管深水超低频运动监测系统"。

振动幅值测量精度达到毫米级。

The motion of the immersed tube underwater was characterized by its low frequency and small range, so it was difficult to be detected. Besides, due to the complicate currents in the deep trench, the extraordinary swing of the tube might affect the quality and safety of the installation, so real-time monitoring was necessary for prompt information feedback, and this could provide good support for decision making as to the tube installation.

The project management center cooperated with the 304 Research Institute of China Aerospace Science and Industry Corp and made use of the dynamic monitoring technology of aerospace industry to develop a special method to calculate the position of the immersed tube, resulting in "the super-low-frequency motion monitoring system for offshore super-large immersed tube".

The vibration range value could be calculated by millimeters.

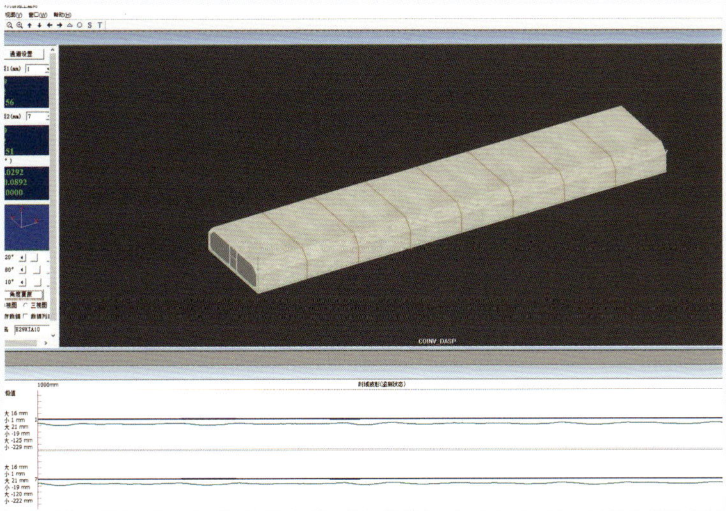

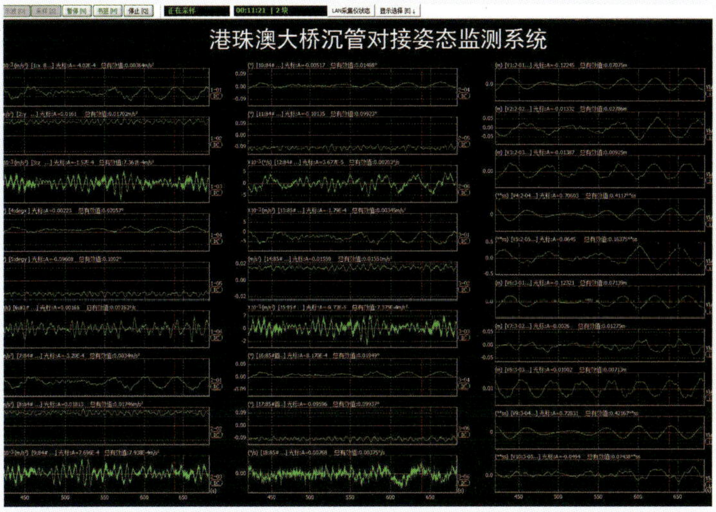

封门结构安全监测系统

SEALING DEVICES SECURITY MONITORING SYSTEM

1—2. 封门结构安全监控系统
Sealing Devices Security Monitoring System

3. 沉管精调施工
Fine Adjustment of the Immersed Tubes

4. 沉管精调千斤顶
Lifting Jack for the Immersed Tube Fine Adjustment

5. 沉管管内精调系统三维图
3-D Diagram of the In-tube Fine Adjustment System for the Immersed Tubes

沉管两端的钢端封门是确保沉管安装作业安全的生命线，通过对端封门施工过程中的变形及渗漏监测，确保端封门的结构安全及防水可靠。

封门结构安全监测系统包括封门变形监测、封门应力监测和封门视频监控等子系统。

The steel sealing devices at the two ends of the tubes are regarded as the life line during tube installation. Monitoring and examining the possible deformation and linkage of the sealing devices during tube installation could help guarantee the structural safety of the sealing devices without leakage.

The sealing devices security monitoring system involved detecting the possible transformation of the sealing devices, monitoring its strain and visualized monitoring of the sealing devices.

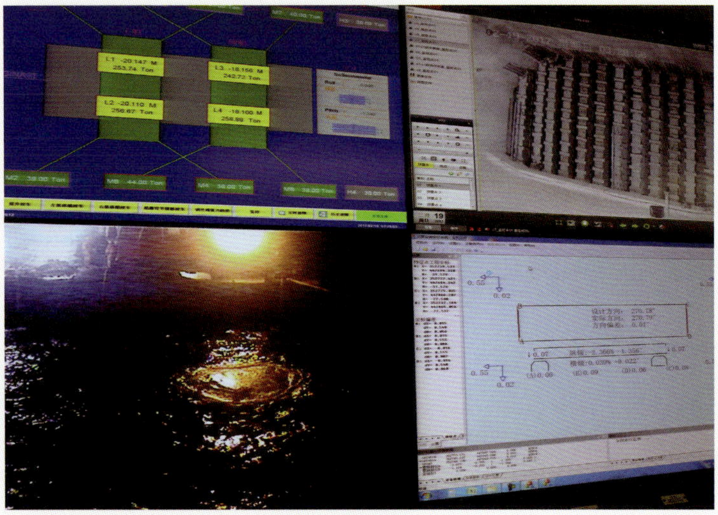

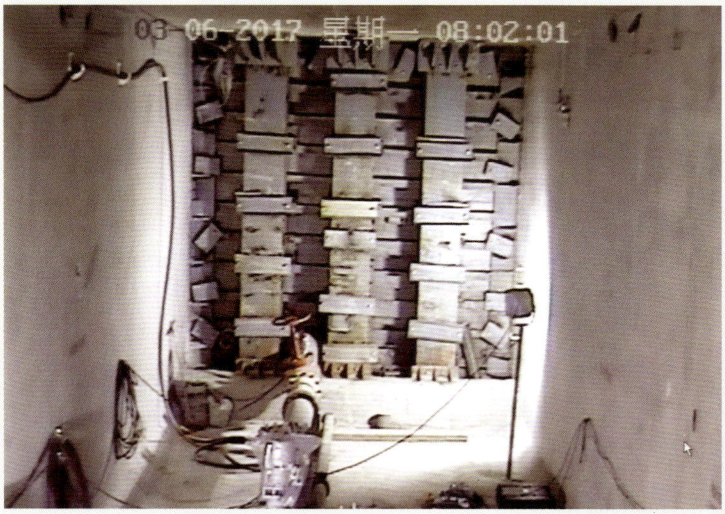

沉管精调系统
IMMERSED TUBE FINE ADJUSTMENT SYSTEM

沉管线形精确调整系统主要用于沉管水力压接后的沉管尾端轴线调整。

水力压接完成后，开启端封门人孔门，对沉管进行贯通测量，根据贯通测量结果确定是否实施精调作业。

该系统利用"顶头摆尾"的原理，千斤顶设置在两节沉管之间的结合腔内，在接头区沉管外墙内侧（GINA 止水带内侧）布置顶推千斤顶和限位千斤顶进行轴线调整。

其中顶推侧布置 10 台 500 吨千斤顶，限位侧布置 2 台 500 吨千斤顶；系统最大顶推力 5000 吨，实现对隧道总体线形的控制。

The linear fine adjustment system for the immersed tube was mainly used to adjust the axis line at ending part of the immersed tube after the hydraulic crimp connection was completed.

After the hydraulic crimp connection was completed, the hole in the end sealing devices was open through which the closure survey was done. The findings of the survey was used to decide whether to conduct fine adjustment.

By referring to the entailed mechanism of this adjustment system, the pulling jack was installed inside the binding cavity between the two sections of tubes, while the pushing jack and the limit jack were installed on the inner side of the tubes' outer walls (the inner side of the GINA water-stop) at the butt joint for axis line adjustment.

On the pushing side were installed 10 pushing jacks of 500 tons; on the limit side were 2 limit jacks of 500 tons. The maximal pushing force of this system was 5,000 tons, which facilitated the control of the overall linear properties of the tunnel.

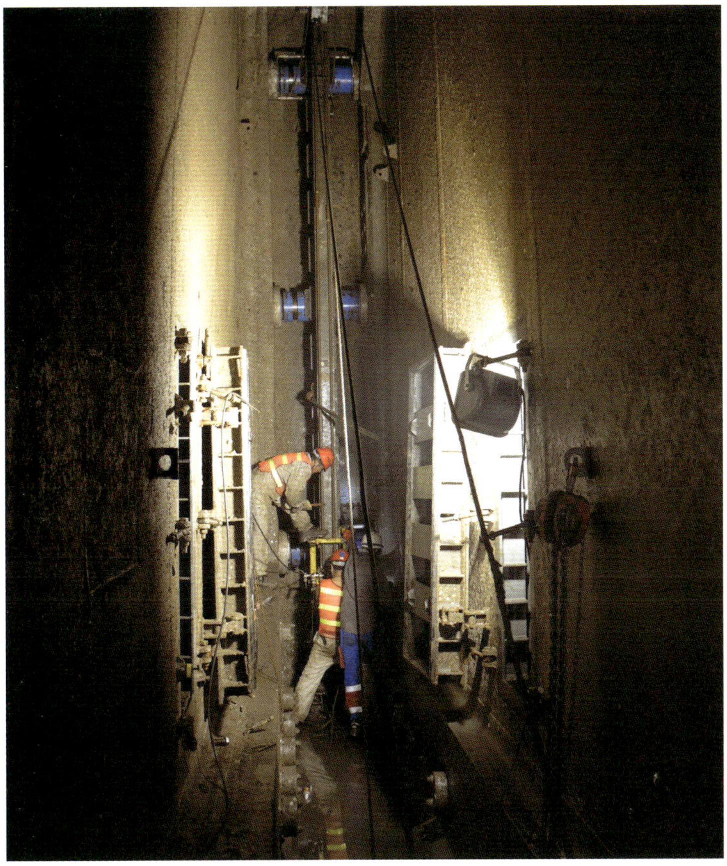

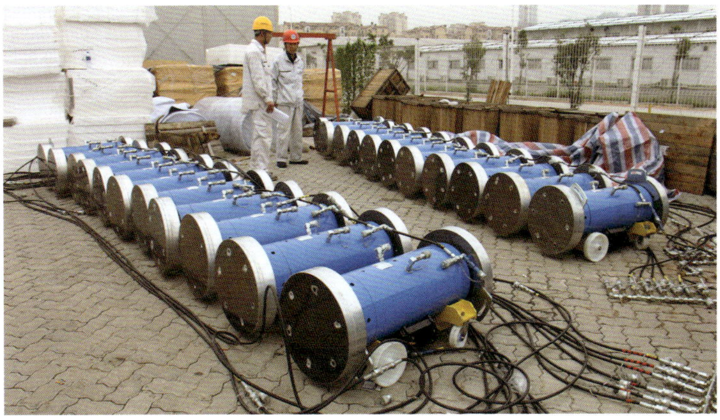

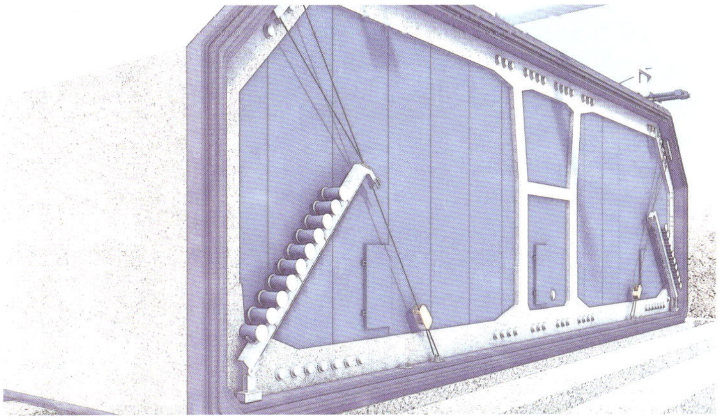

“津安 3”沉管安装船
Immersed Tube Installation Barge “Jinaan 3”

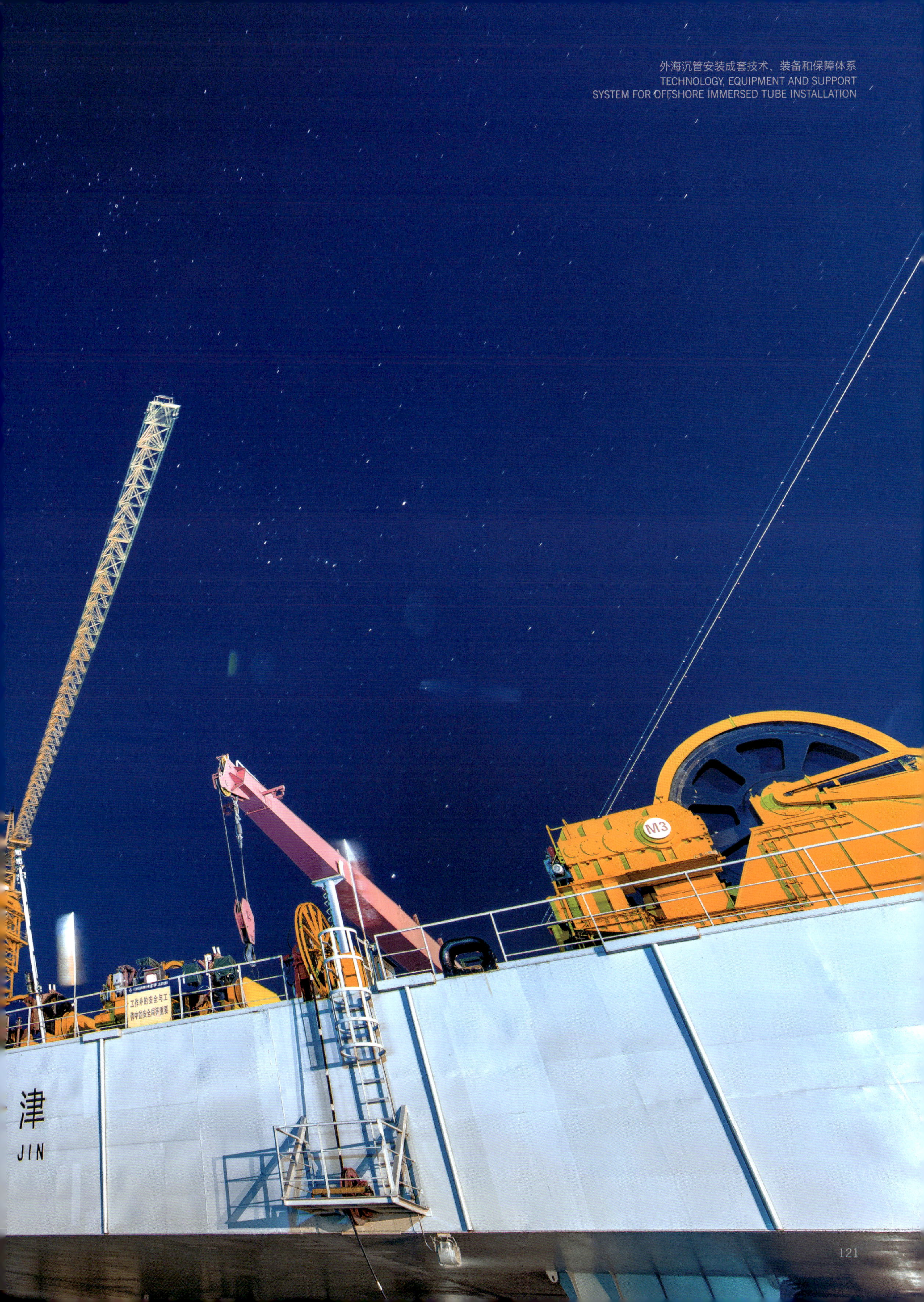
M3
工作外的安全与工
作中的安全同等重要
津
JIN

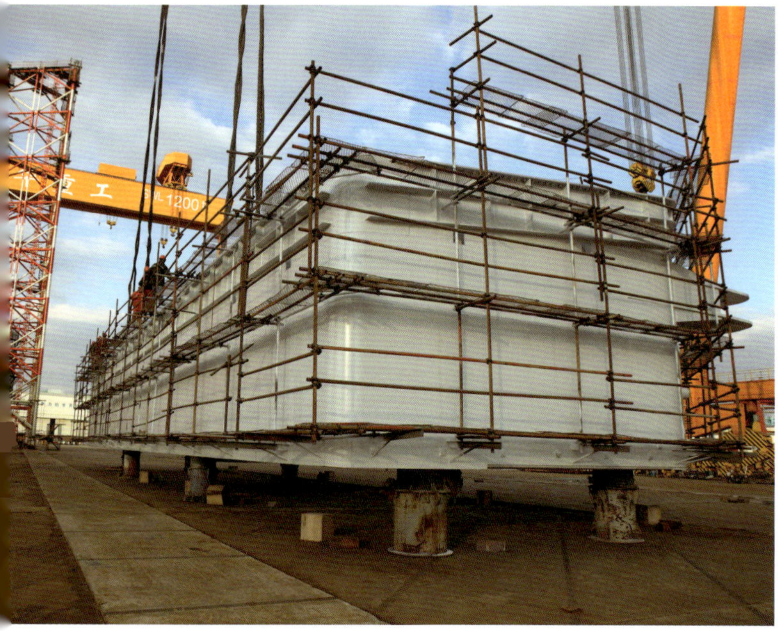

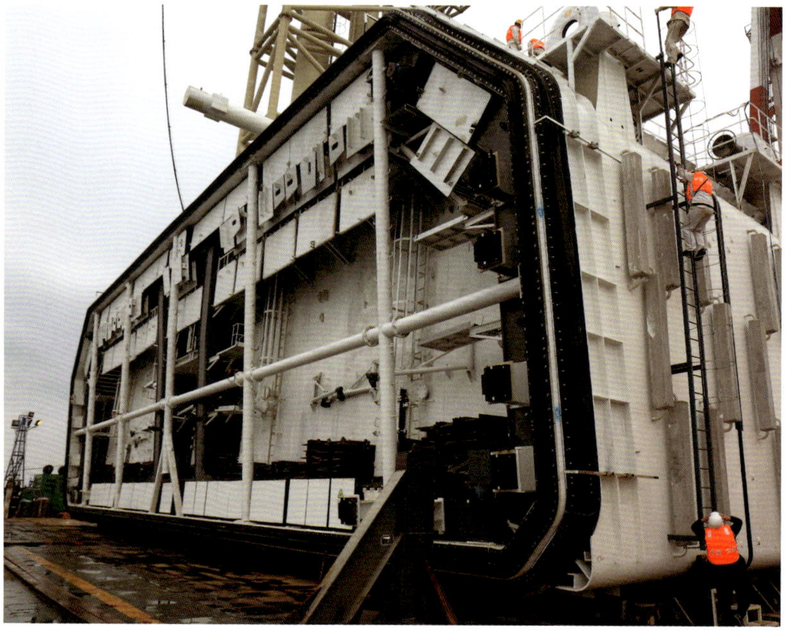

最终接头创新技术

INNOVATIVE CLOSURE JOINT TECHNOLOGY

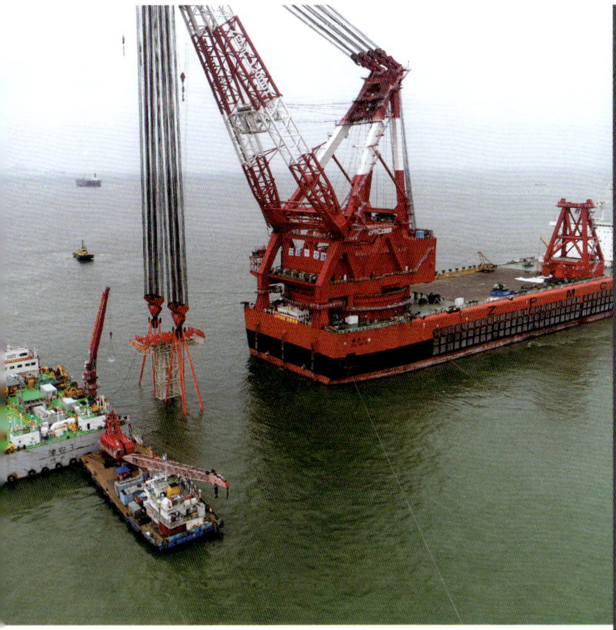

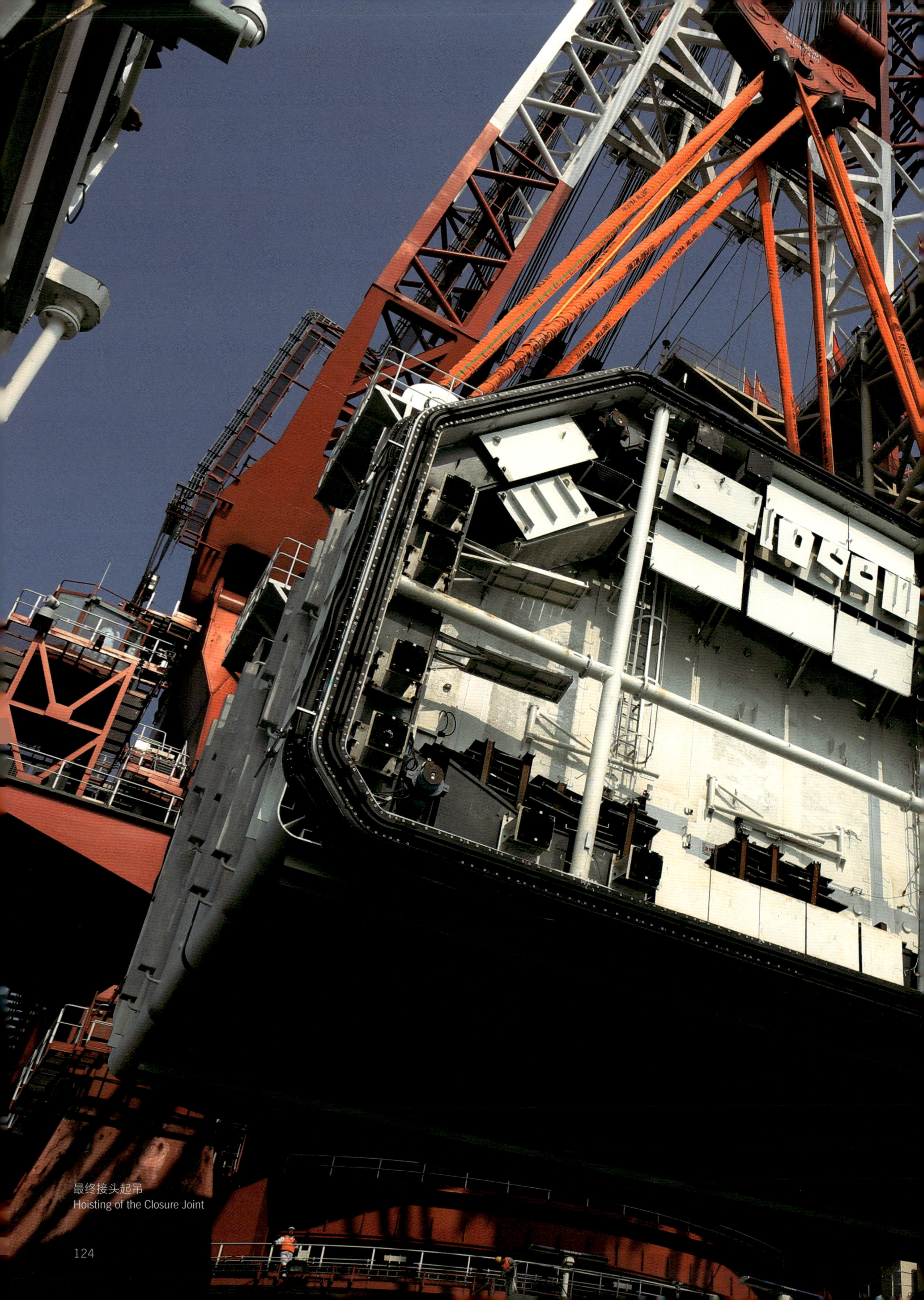

最终接头起吊
Hoisting of the Closure Joint

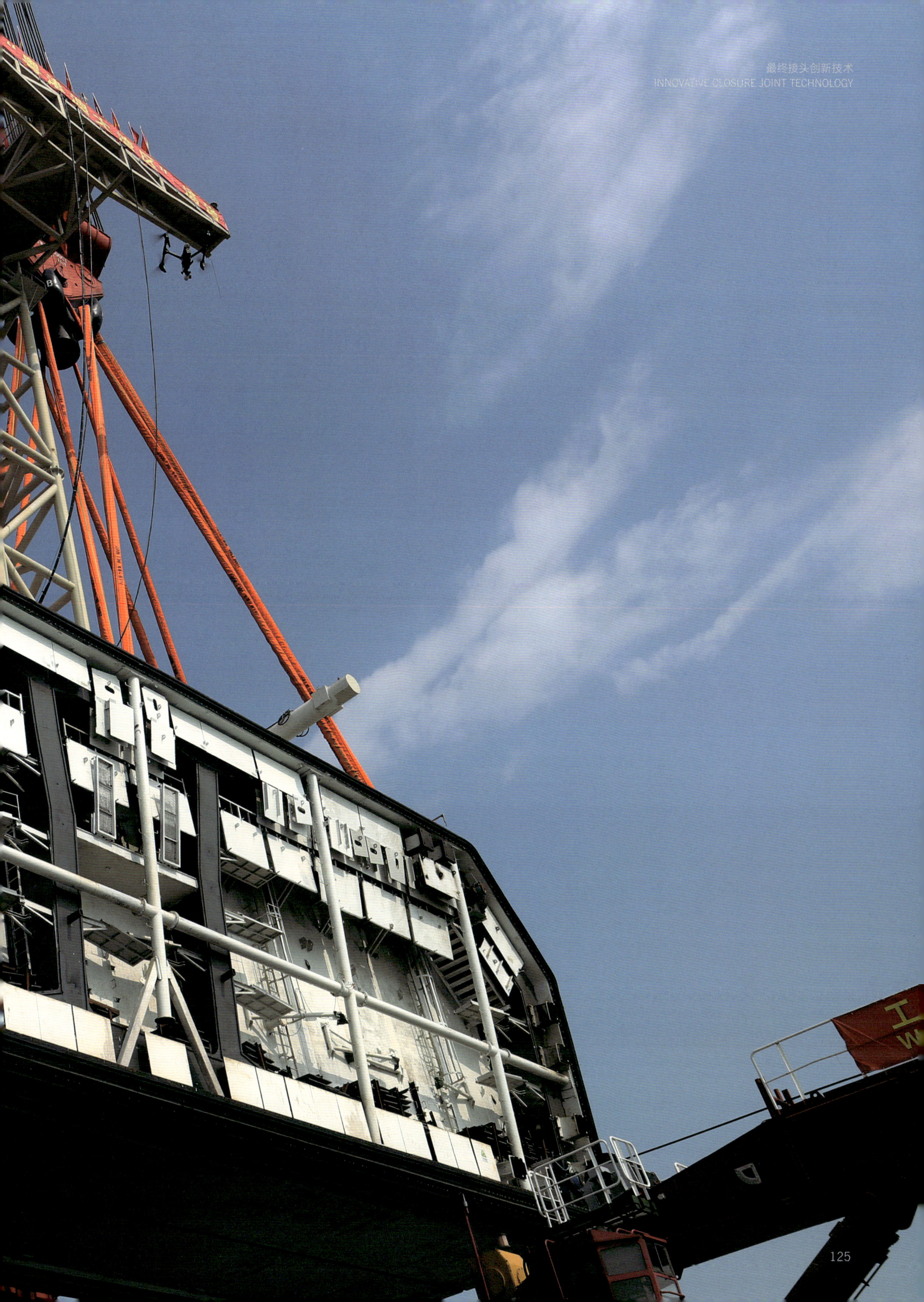

最终接头结构设计

STRUCTURAL DESIGN OF THE CLOSURE JOINT

最终接头是沉管隧道安装的最后一道工序，也是决定整个隧道建设成败的关键。

最终接头位于E29、E30沉管之间，长12米，重量6120吨，由两个对称倒梯形结构组成，整体为钢壳混凝土三明治结构。

中间设置钢壳永久沉管接头，沿周边设置 GINA 止水带及 OMEGA 止水带，采用液压主动顶推系统止水。

该系统包括顶推千斤顶系统、顶推小梁及临时支撑杆系、小梁滑块、小梁前端 GINA 止水带、M 形止水带及 LIP 止水带等。

按原"水下止水板法"设计方案，最终接头工期超过半年，无法满足现场施工的要求。

项目总经理部自 2012 年着手进行最终接头方案的研究，先后赴日本、欧洲进行调研。

通过三年多的研究和攻关，在世界范围内首次提出了可折叠、主动止水的新理念，创新了整体式主动止水最终接头技术，仅用 1 天时间即完成了最终接头浮运、吊装、沉放、顶推止水、结合腔抽水等对接安装工作，实现沉管隧道的快速合龙。

Closure joint was the last procedure of the immersed tube tunneling, but it determined whether or not the tunnel construction was successful.

The closure joint lay between Tube E39 and Tube E30, 12 meters long, weighing 6,120 tons, composed of symmetrical inverted trapezoid structures, and the whole closure joint was a concrete sandwich structure with a steel shell.

In the middle was the permanent butt joint with steel shell, and the outer side were GINA water-stop and OMEGA water-stop which were driven by the active hydraulic pushing system to stop water leakage.

This structure included pushing jacks, pushing trabecular, temporary supporting beam, trabecular slide block, pre-trabecular GINA water-stop, M-shaped water-stop and LIP water-stop.

By the original design of "underwater water-stop," the project duration for closure joint would be over half a year and could not meet the requirements of the project.

Since 2012, the project management center began to study how to perform the closure joint operation and they visited Japan and Europe to find ways to solve the problem.

After 3 years' hard work, for the first time in the world, the center put forward the notion of foldable active water-stop. It innovated the integrated active water-stop technology for the closure joint operation. In only 1 day, all the operations such as the float conveyance of the closure joint, lifting, landing, pushing water-stop, binding cavity drainage were finished, resulting in the quick closure of the immersed tube tunnel.

1. 最终接头主动顶推止水系统剖面图
Sectional View of the Closure Joint Pushing the Waterstop System

2. 最终接头结构剖面图
Sectional View of the Closure Joint

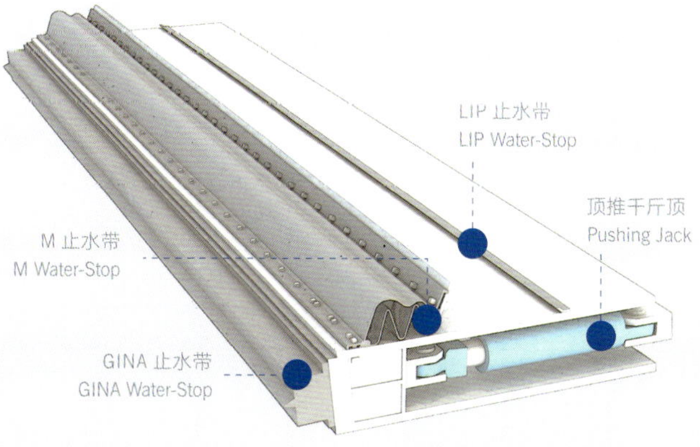
LIP 止水带
LIP Water-Stop
顶推千斤顶
Pushing Jack
M 止水带
M Water-Stop
GINA 止水带
GINA Water-Stop

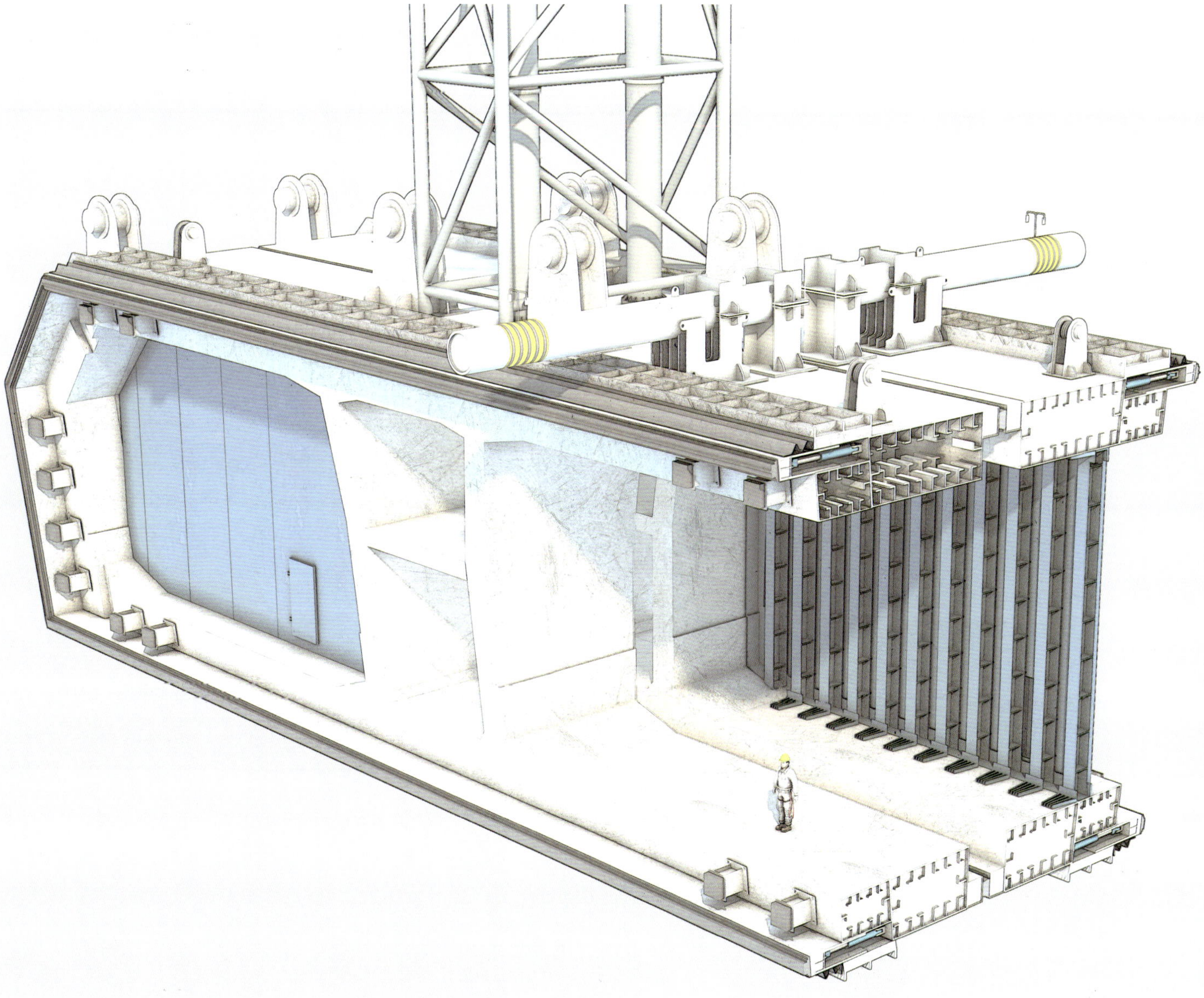

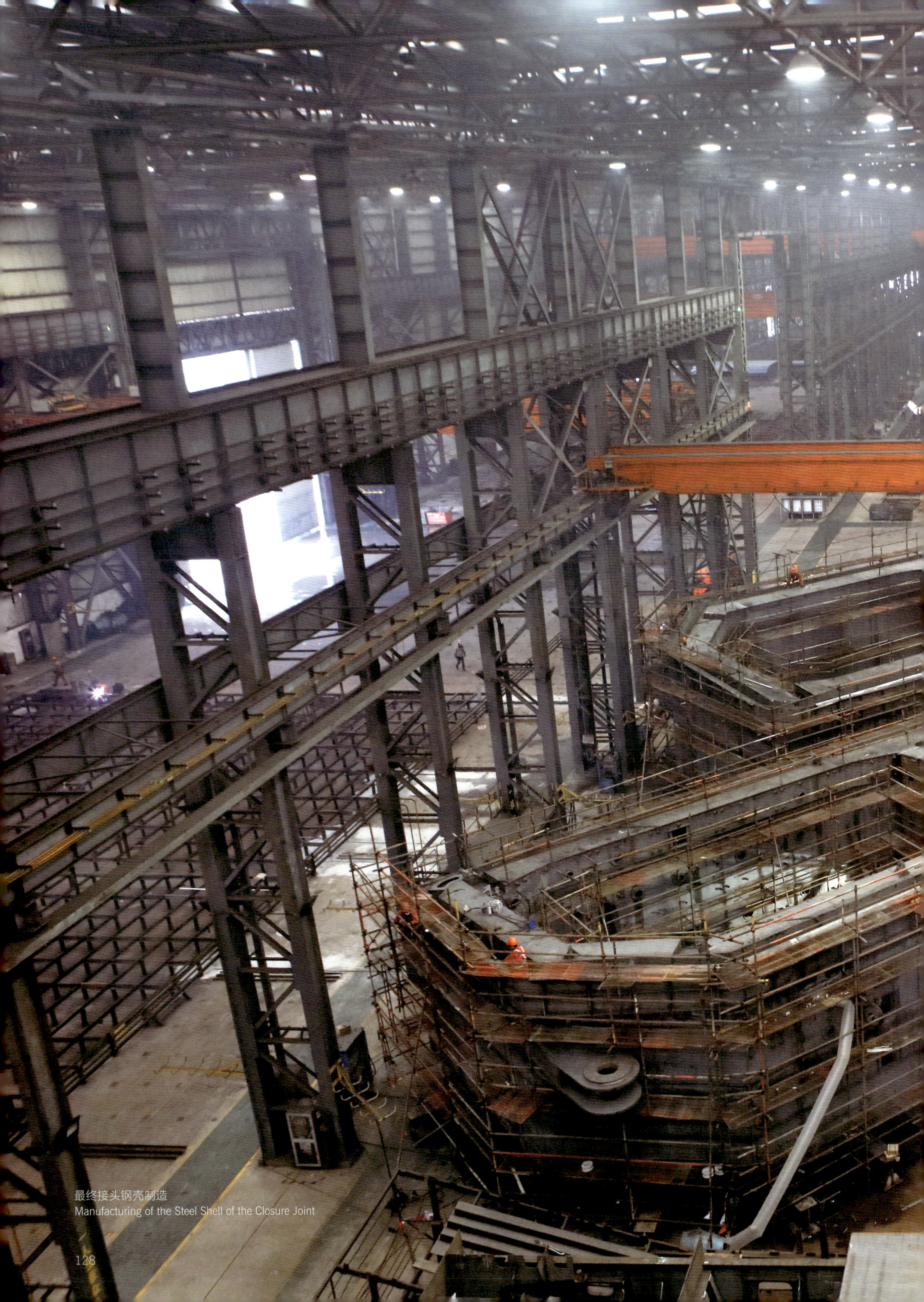

最终接头钢壳制造
Manufacturing of the Steel Shell of the Closure Joint

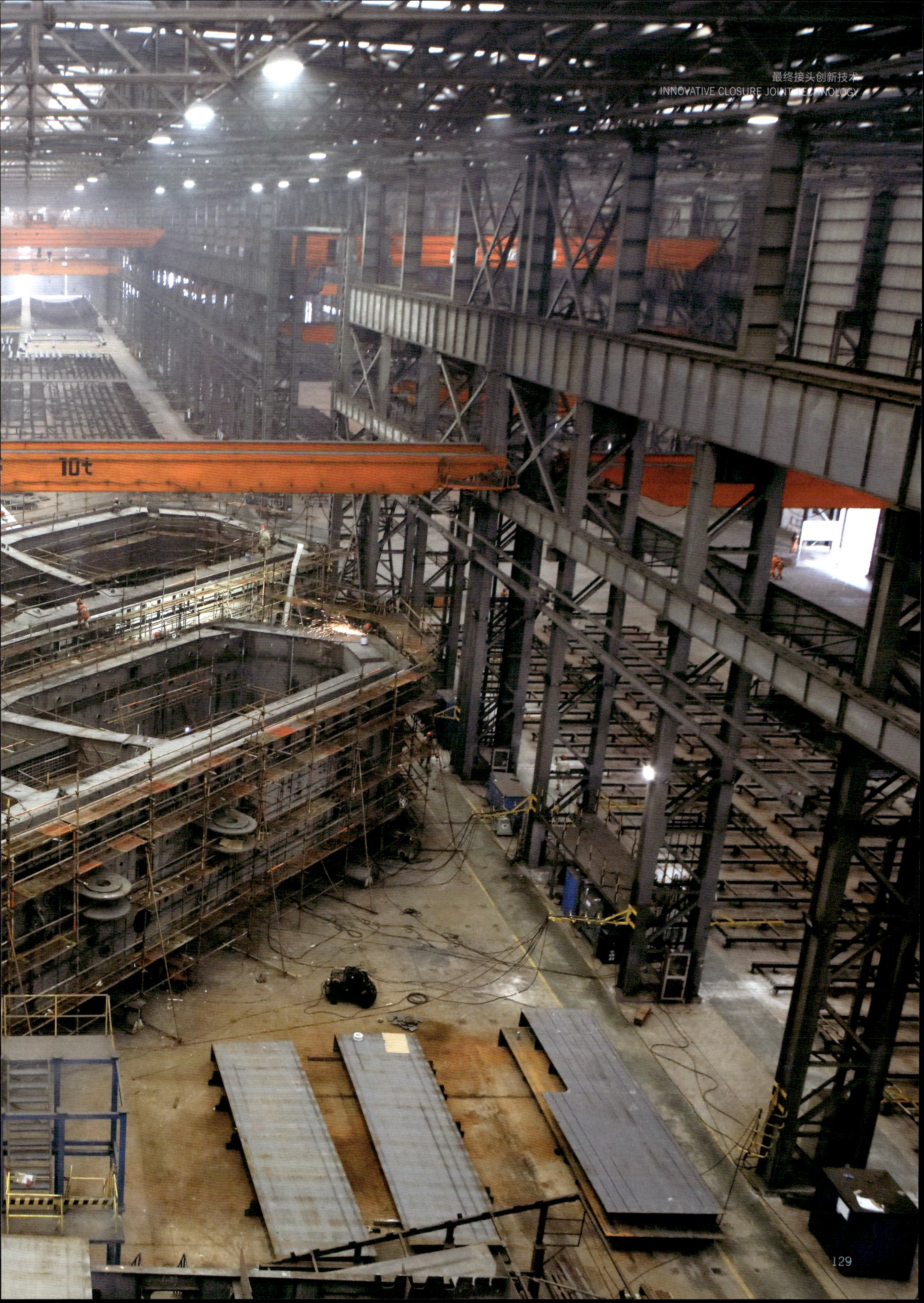
10t

最终接头制造

MANUFACTURING OF THE CLOSURE JOINT

最终接头钢壳结构在振华重工南通基地制造。

钢壳结构由两个对称的倒直角梯形结构经临时预应力张拉组合而成，每个倒直角梯形钢壳结构又分别由本体部分和顶推小梁拼装组合而成。

结构复杂，焊接工作量大，变形不易控制，成形精度要求高，作业空间狭小，工期紧张，制作难度远高于常规钢结构产品。

最终接头先分段制造，再整体拼装焊接。

历经车间内制造、吊装、翻身、组拼、内场转运、冲砂等工序，完成1/2本体结构制造，采用大型液压平板车转运至外场；采用5000吨浮吊和1200吨龙门吊配合，完成1/2本体结构（重约820吨）翻身；设计专用滑移工装，通过临时预应力实现钢壳结构精确合龙。

经过40多天紧张施工，先后完成预应力张拉、GINA止水带压接、钢封门安装、LIP止水带安装、测量塔长人孔安装、吊点安装、三向锁定和无源支撑等附属件安装、M止水带安装、小梁调试等系列工作，2017年2月26日完成最终接头制造。

The steel shell of the closure joint was made at Nantong Base of Zhenhua Port Machinery Company.

The steel-shelled structure was made of two symmetrical inverted right-angled trapezoid structures by combining the temporary prestress pulling forces. Each inverted right-angled trapezoid steel structure was composed of the body structure and the pushing trabecular beam.

The complicated structure, tremendous workload of welding, uncontrollable transformation, high-precision requirements, limited working space, short project duration and manufacturing difficulties together made it a special steel product.

Different segments of the closure joint were made first, and then these segments were welded into one whole structure.

After such procedures as in-dock processing, lifting, turning, piecing together, internal transportation and sand wash, one half the whole body structure was finished before it was moved outside the dock on a large-sized hydraulic conveyance vehicle. Then a floating crane of 5,000 tons and a frame crane of 1,200 tons cooperated to turn over the half-done body structure (about 820 tons). Special sliding devices were designed for the exact closure of the steel-shell structure by using temporary prestress forces.

In 40 days, going through such procedures as prestress expanding and pulling, hydraulic crimp connection by GINA water-stop, steel sealing devices installation, LIP water-stop installation, measuring tower installation, crane installation, 3-directional locking, passive support and other auxiliaries installtion, M water-stop installation, trabecular adjustment, the closure joint was finally done on February 26, 2017.

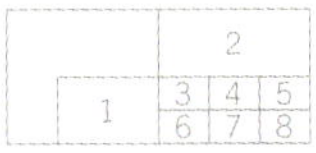

1. 最终接头本体结构拼装
Assembling of the Body Structure of the Closure Joint
2. 最终接头本体结构运输至场外
Body Structure of the Closure Joint Undocking
3. 本体结构起吊
Body Structure Hoisted
4. 本体结构对接
Body Structure Connected
5. 最接接头节段间 GINA 止水带吊装
Installation of GINA Waterstop between the Segments of the Closure Joint
6. 安装 GINA 止水带压板
Installation of the Pressure Plate of GINA Waterstop
7. 安装 GINA 止水带
GINA Waterstop
8. GINA 止水带安装完成
GINA Waterstop Installation Completed

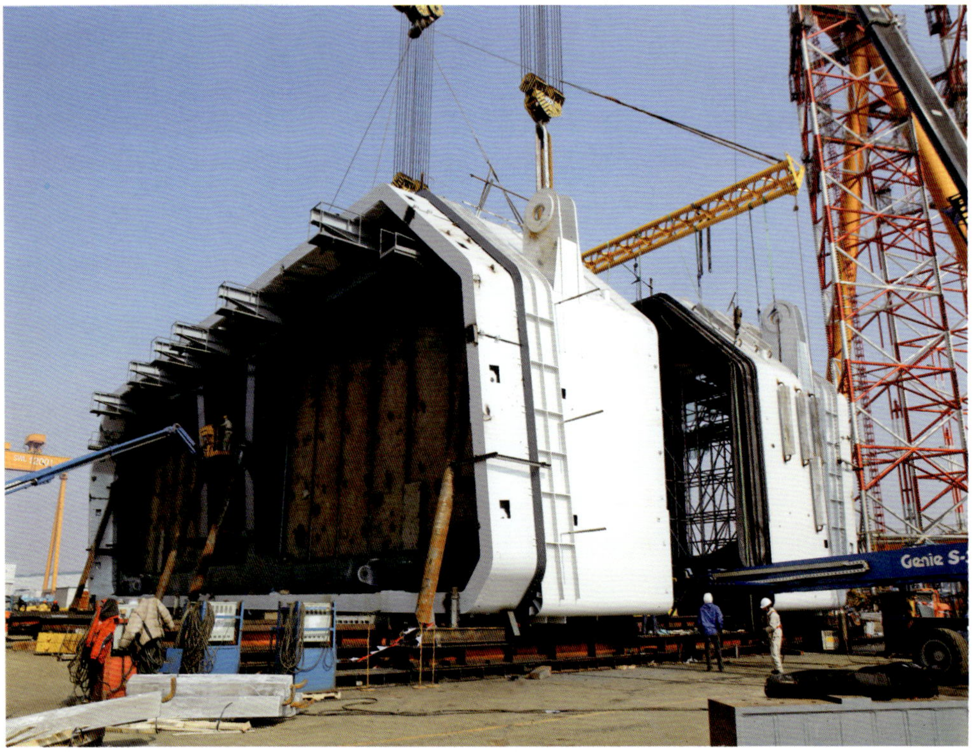

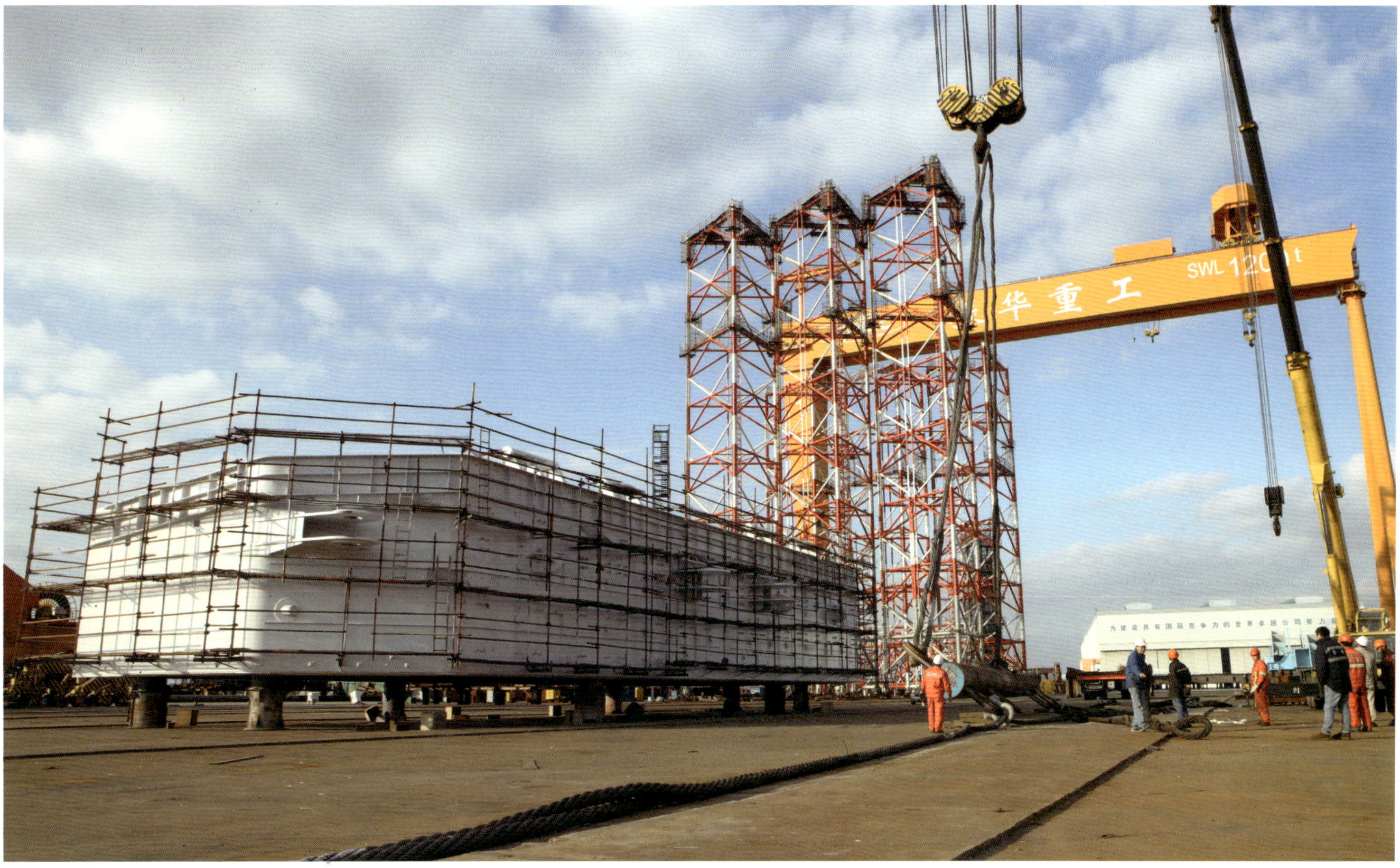
华重工

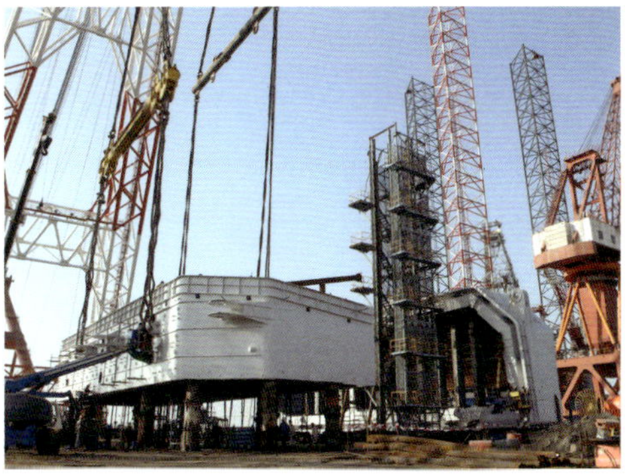

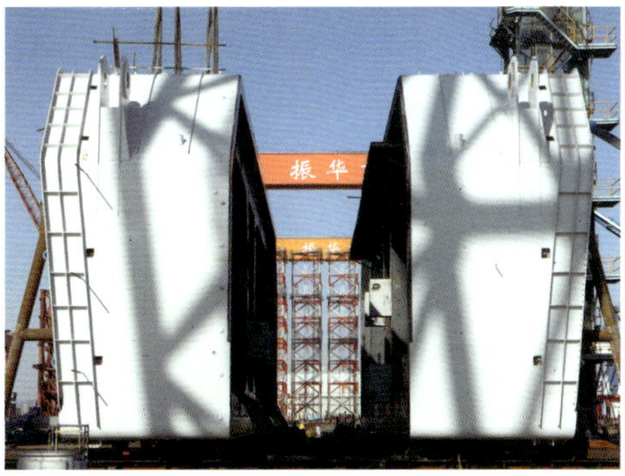
振华

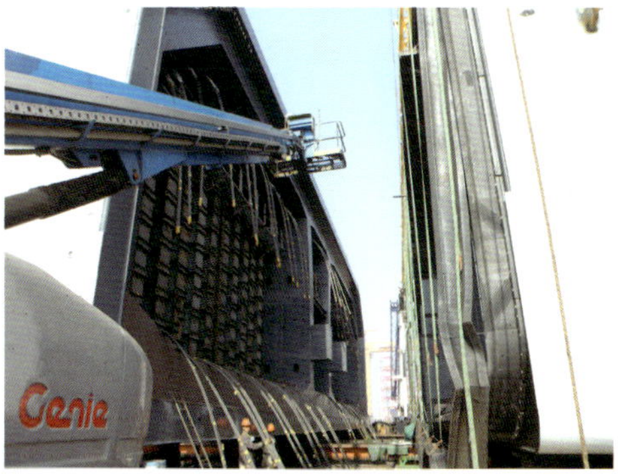
Genie

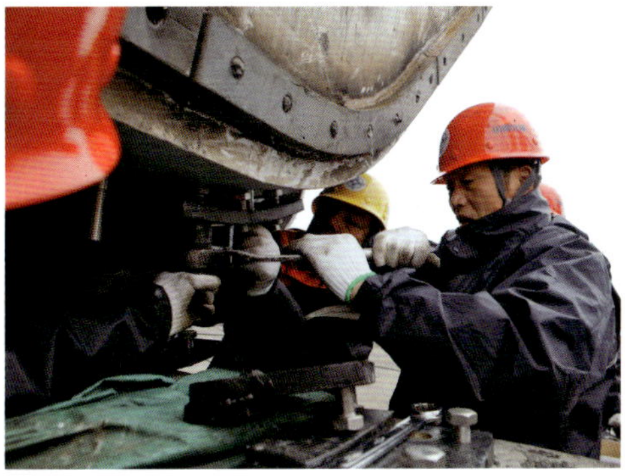

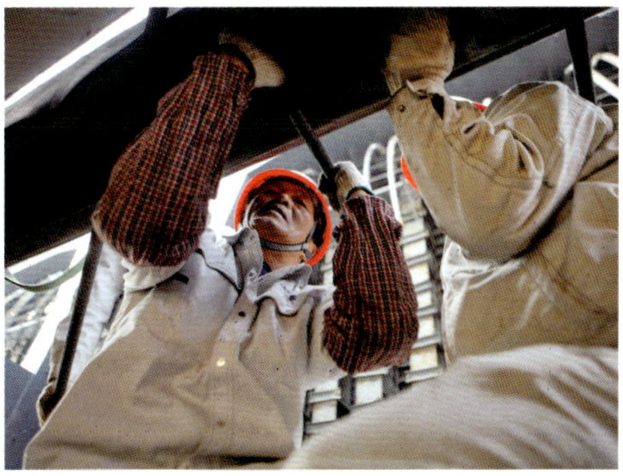

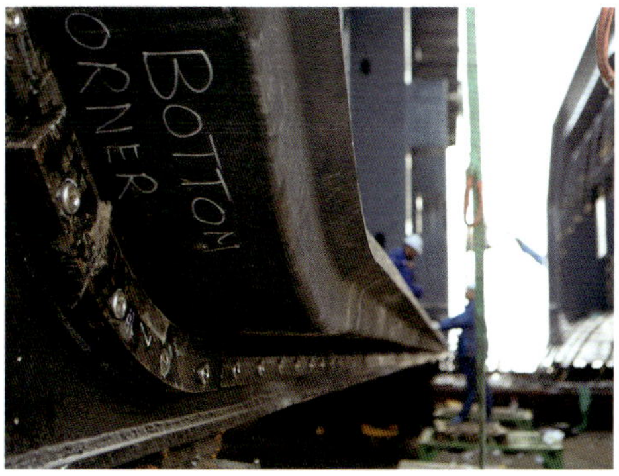
BOTTOM
CORNER

小梁槽口和端钢壳平整度是本体制造的控制重点。

特别是小梁拼装构件柔性大，装配间隙小，油缸安装精度高，小梁焊接变形风险高。

通过采用合理划分块体、整体预制、精密切割下料、精确控制焊缝变形、重要工序模拟、投入大量工艺装备等措施，保证了制造精度，实现了小梁和本体的精密配合拼装。

The trabecular trench mouth and the flatness of the ending steel shell were the critical nodes in the manufacturing of the closure joint.

Especially the great flexibility of the assembling components of the trabecula, the small fitting space, high-accuracy requirements for the oil tank installation and high risk of the trabecular transformation should be treated seriously.

The scientific division, the wholesome precast, precise cutting, precise welding, the simulation of the critical procedures and the use of various manufacturing equipments all guaranteed the precise assemblage of the trabecular structure and the body part.

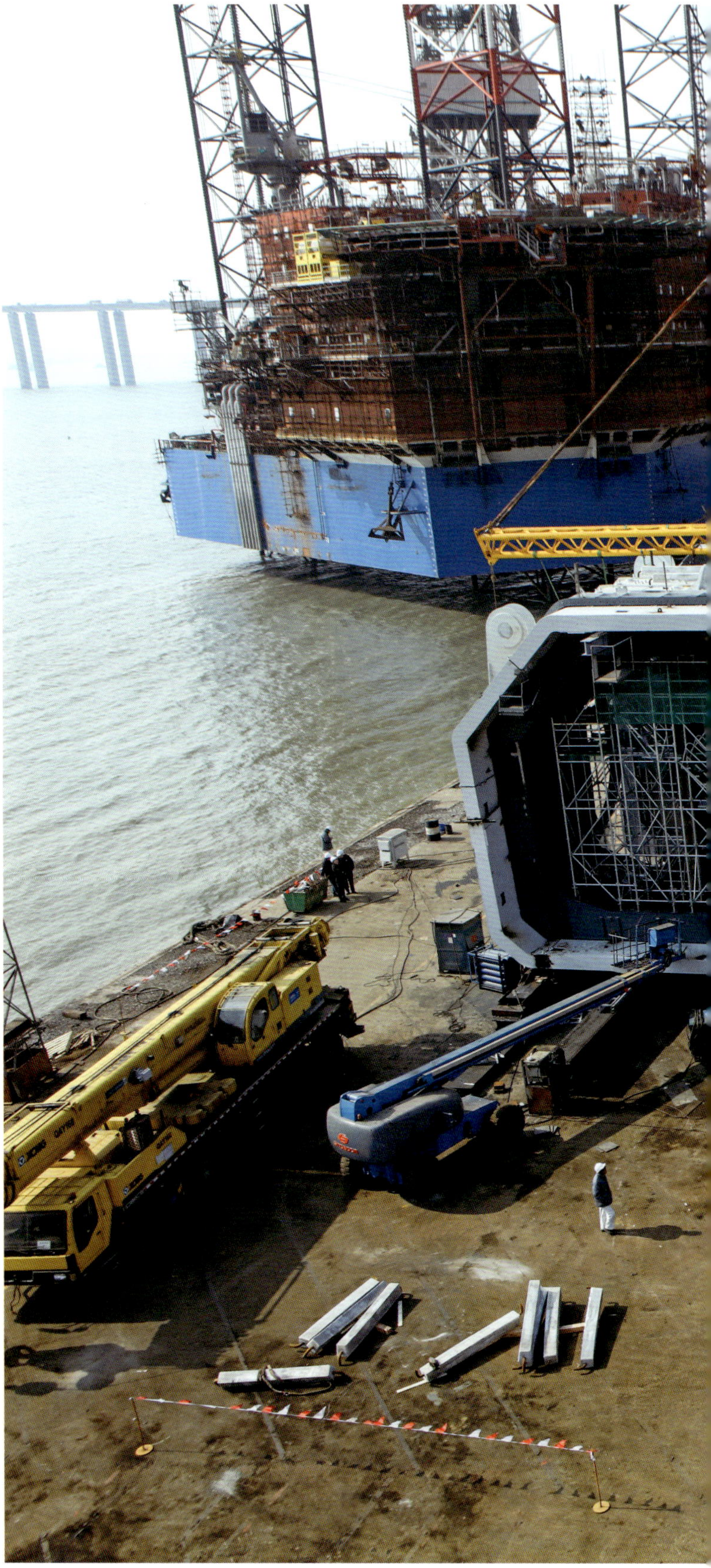

最终接头小梁结构拼装
Assembling the Trabecular Structure of the Closure Joint

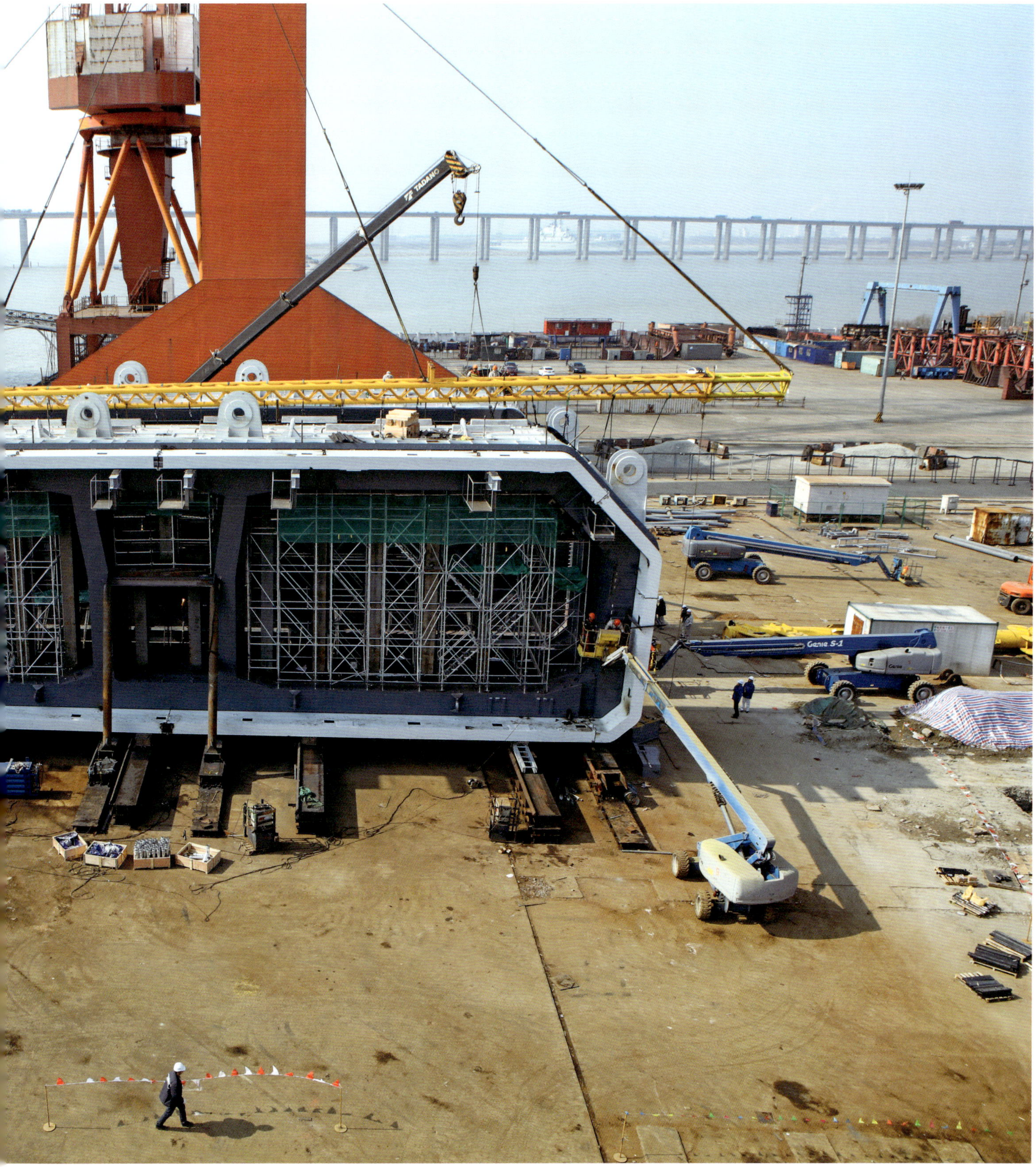
TADANO
Genie S-1

最终接头运输
TRANSPORTATION OF THE CLOSURE JOINT

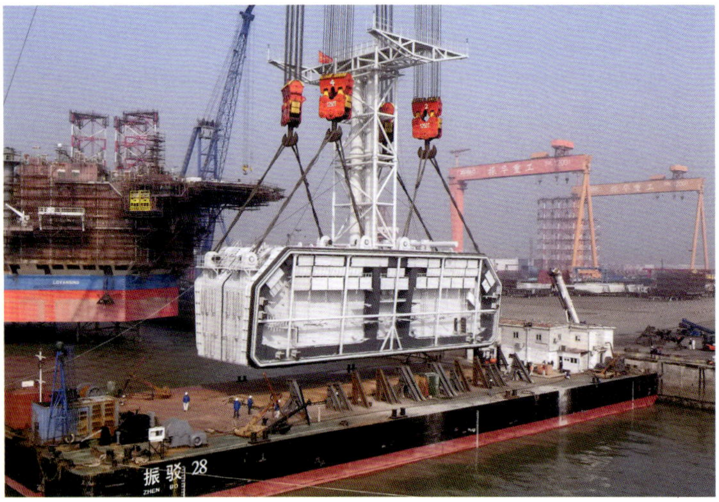

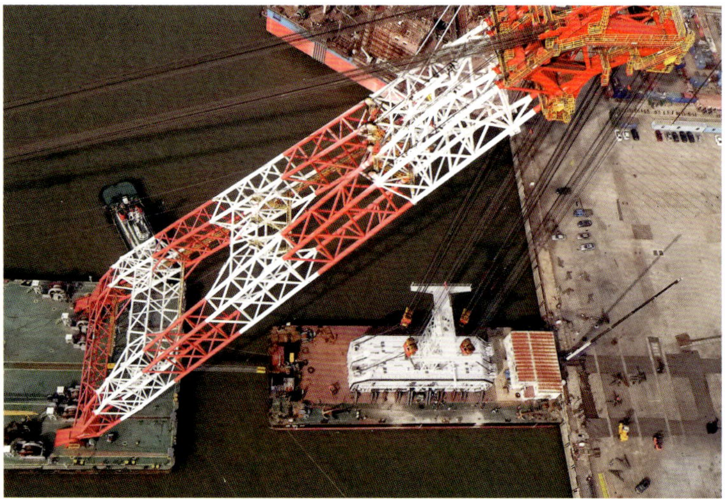

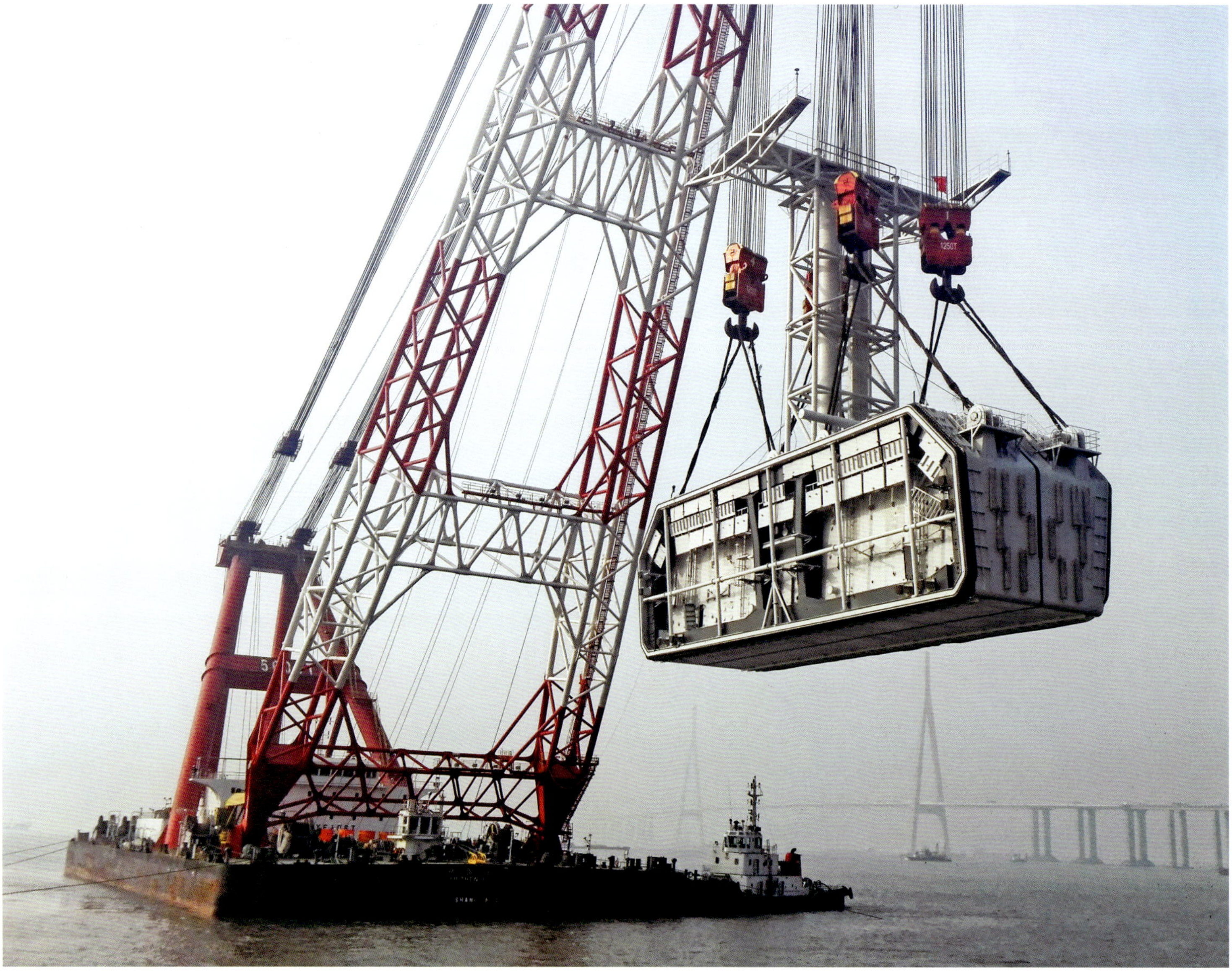

1—3. 最终接头起吊装船
Hoisting and Installation Barge for the Closure Joint

4. 最终接头启运
Shipping the Closure Joint

2017 年 2 月 27 日，最终接头钢壳结构从南通基地启运，经过 1600 公里海上长途运输，于 3 月 7 日顺利抵达沉管预制厂，开始进行高流动性混凝土灌注和舾装调试工作。

On February 27, 2017, the steel structure of the closure joint left Nantong Base, and after 1600 kilometers' travel on the sea, arrived at the immersed tube precast factory on March 7, where the grouting of high-fluidity concrete and fitting-out followed.

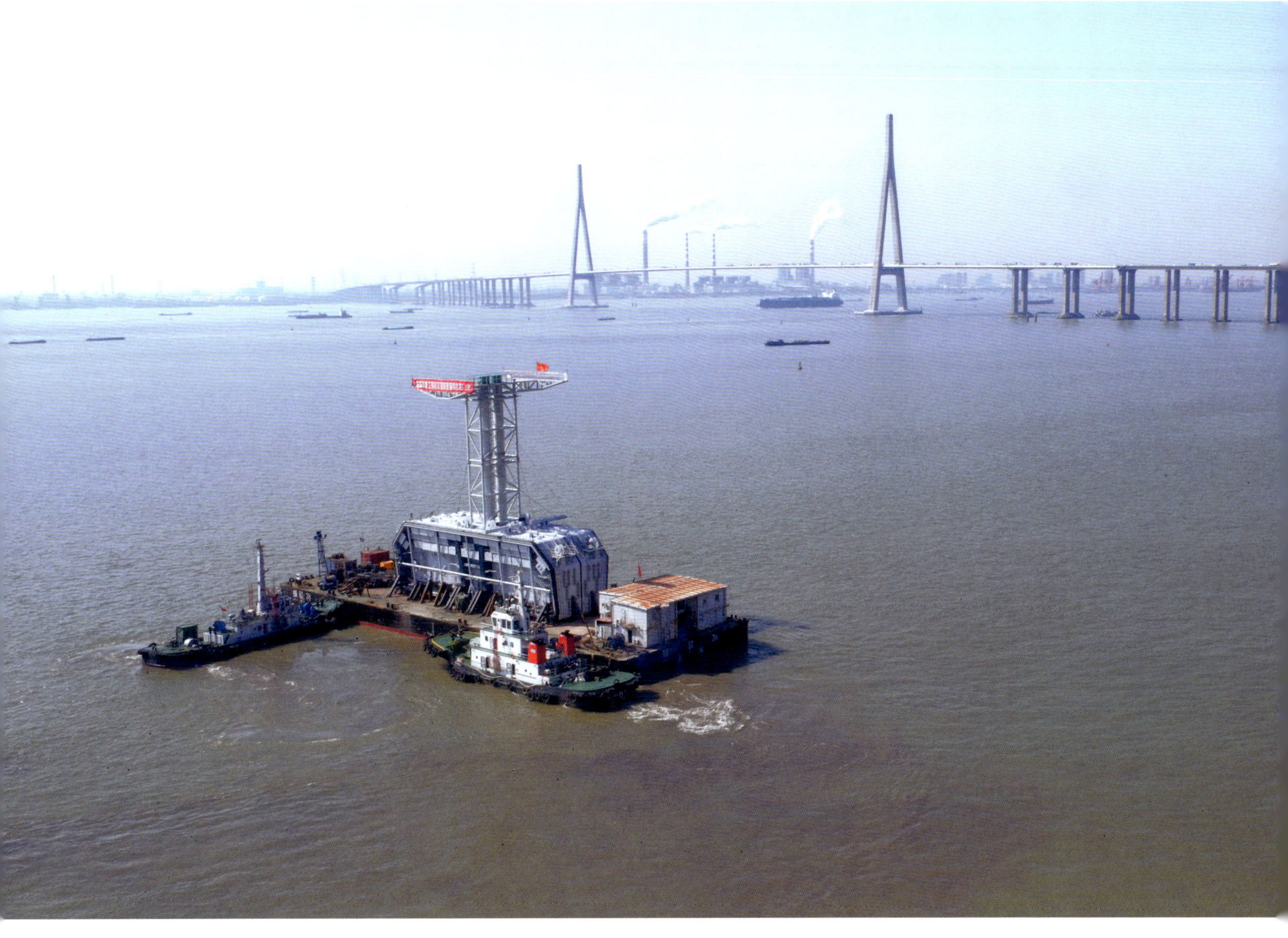

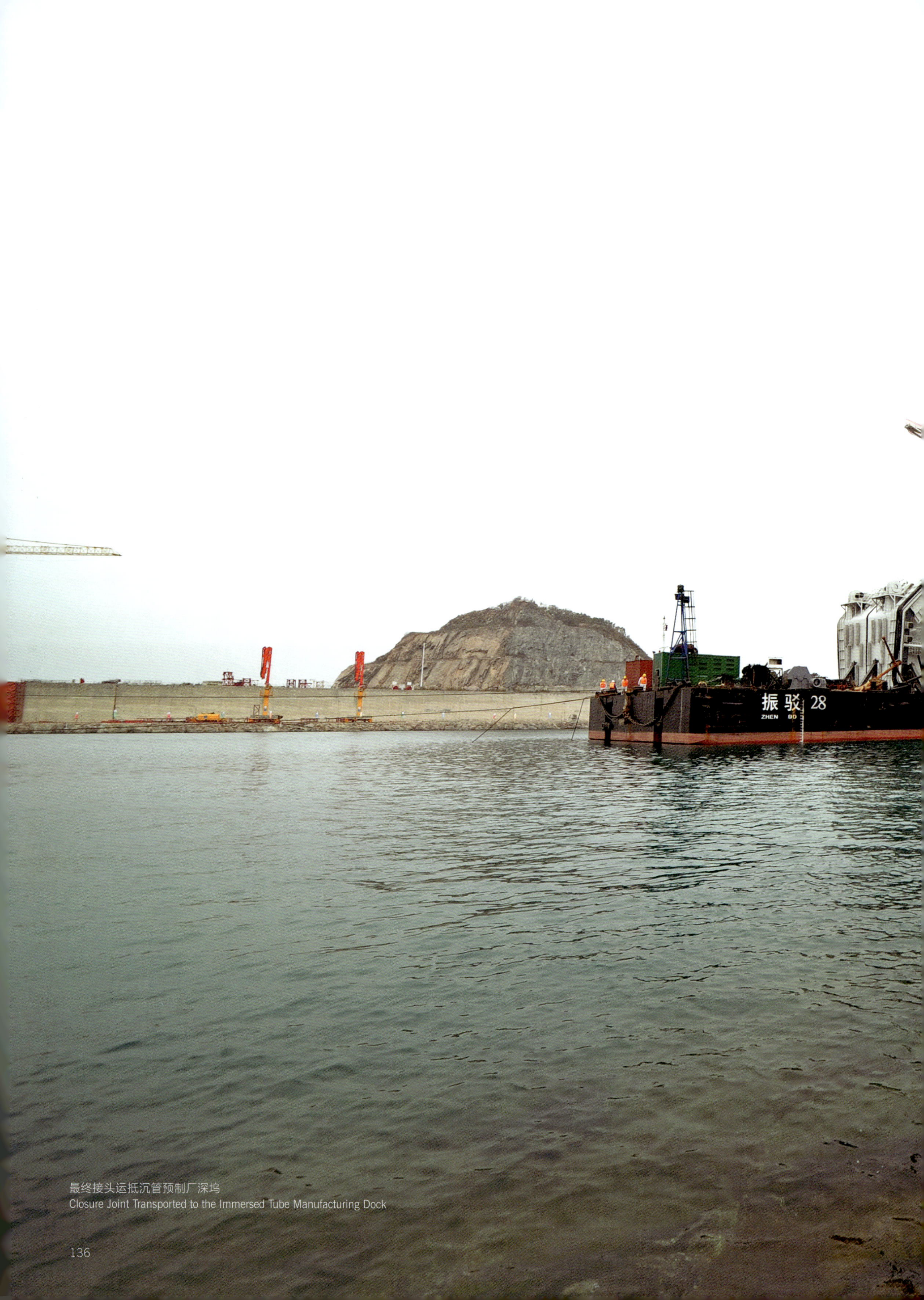

最终接头运抵沉管预制厂深坞
Closure Joint Transported to the Immersed Tube Manufacturing Dock

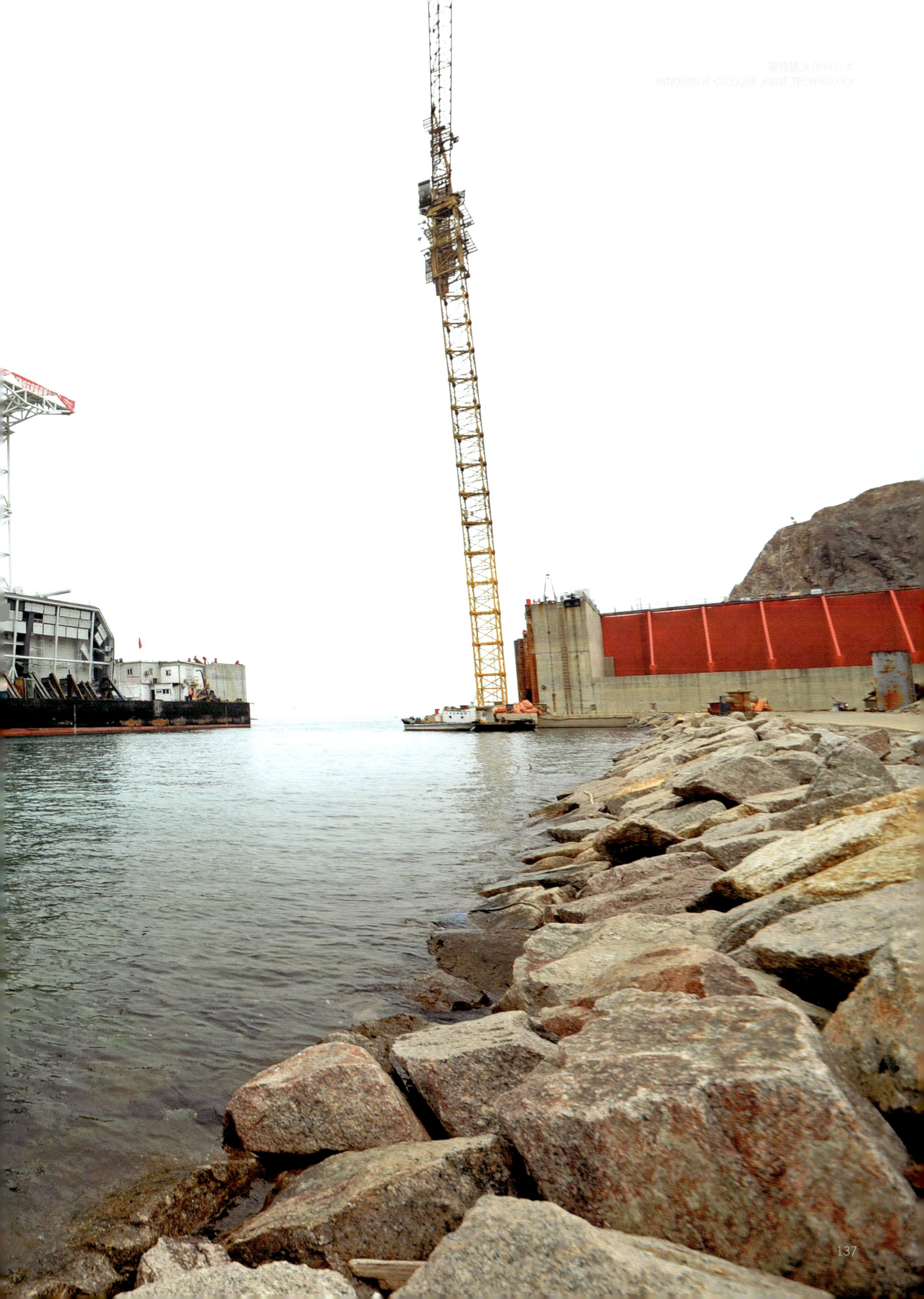

高流动性混凝土配置及浇筑

HIGH-FLUIDITY CONCRETE MIXTURE AND PLACEMENT

高流动性混凝土是在较低水灰比条件下，利用外加剂和掺合料的调节作用，增大新拌混凝土的流动性，同时又具有足够的塑性粘度，使骨料悬浮在水泥浆中，不泌水，不离析，填充钢筋和模板空间，形成均匀致密结构，硬化后具有良好的力学性能及耐久性能。

参照日本施工经验，确定了最终接头高流动性混凝土性能指标。

通过高流动性混凝土的工作性、强度、水化热、收缩变化规律研究，优选出综合性能最优的高流动性混凝土配合比。

先后开展木模型、有机玻璃隔舱小模型、有机玻璃墙模型、有机玻璃顶面+钢隔舱足尺模型等四种不同尺寸模型试验，不断对配合比、浇筑方式、浇筑速度等工艺参数进行验证与调整，在正式施工前固化各种工艺参数，形成贯穿施工全过程的标准化品质管理方法，实现"过程标准化管理"，确保成品质量。

High-fluidity concrete was made by using admixture to enhance the fluidity of the newly compounded concrete with a low water-to-cement ratio. Yet it had enough plastic viscosity, ensuring that the aggregates mixed in the muddy concrete did not suffer weepage and separation and filled the cavity between the steel skeleton and the plate to form well-distributed compact structure with good mechanical properties and good durability.

By referring to the construction experience in Japan, the property index of the high-fluidity concrete for the closure joint was finally decided on.

Based on the studies on the workability, hardness, hydration heat and shrinkage pattern, the optimal mix ratio was chosen to produce the high-fluidity concrete with the best comprehensive performance.

Experiments were conducted on models of four different sizes, including wood model, small organic glass compartment model, organic glass wall model, full-sized organic glass roof plus steel compartment model; adjustments were done about the technological parameters of the mix ratio, concrete placement mode and concrete placement speed before the fixed parameters were decided for the construction. Thus a standard quality management system was formed and used in the whole process of construction to guarantee the quality of the project.

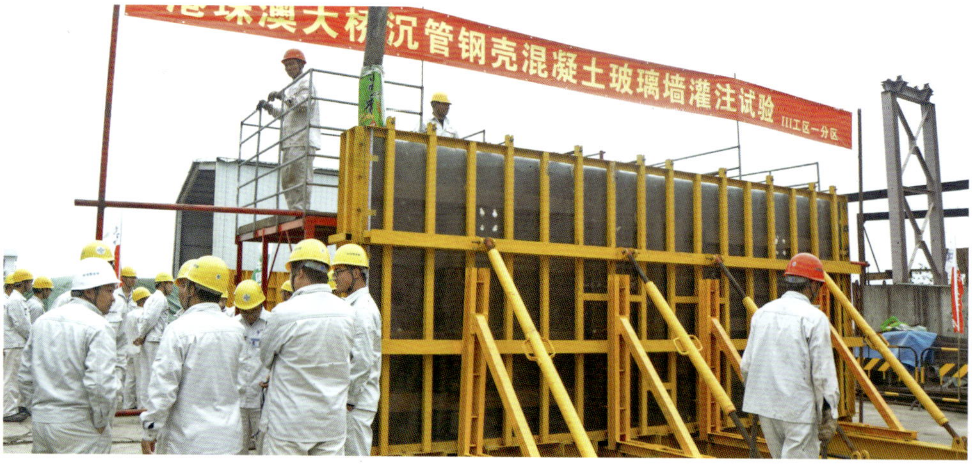

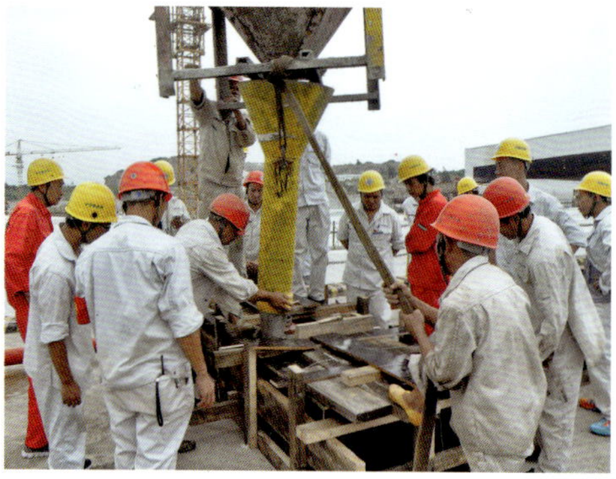

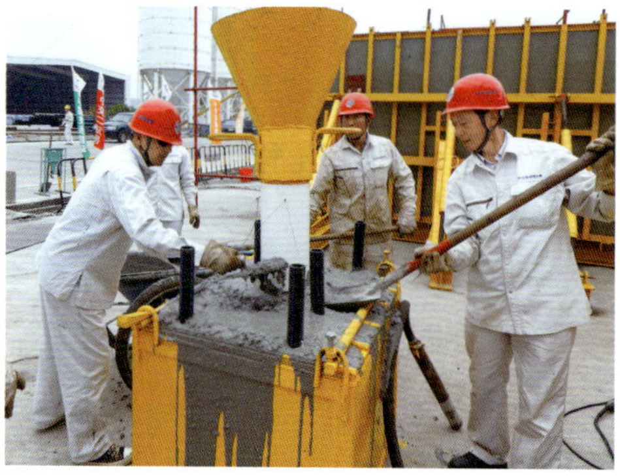

1. 高流动性混凝土玻璃墙灌注试验
   Placement Test of the High-Fluidity Concrete Glass Wall Placement
2. 高流动性混凝土木模试验
   Test of the High-Fluidity Concrete Wood Model
3. 高流动性混凝土隔舱小模型试验
   Test of the Mini High-Fluidity Concrete Compartment Model
4. 高流动性混凝土坍落度检测
   Slump Test of the High-Fluidity Concrete

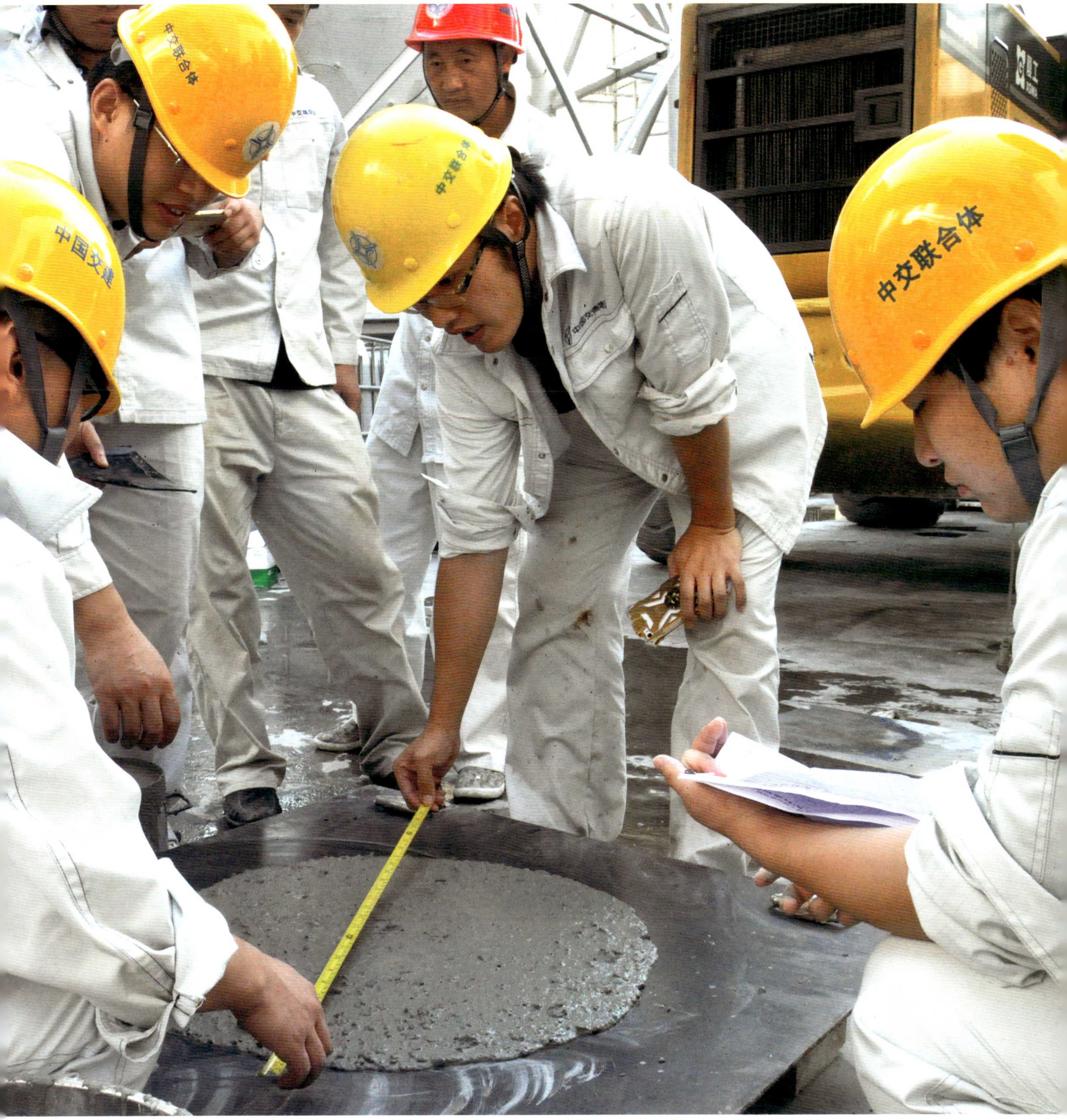
中交联合体
中国交建
中交联合体
中交联合体

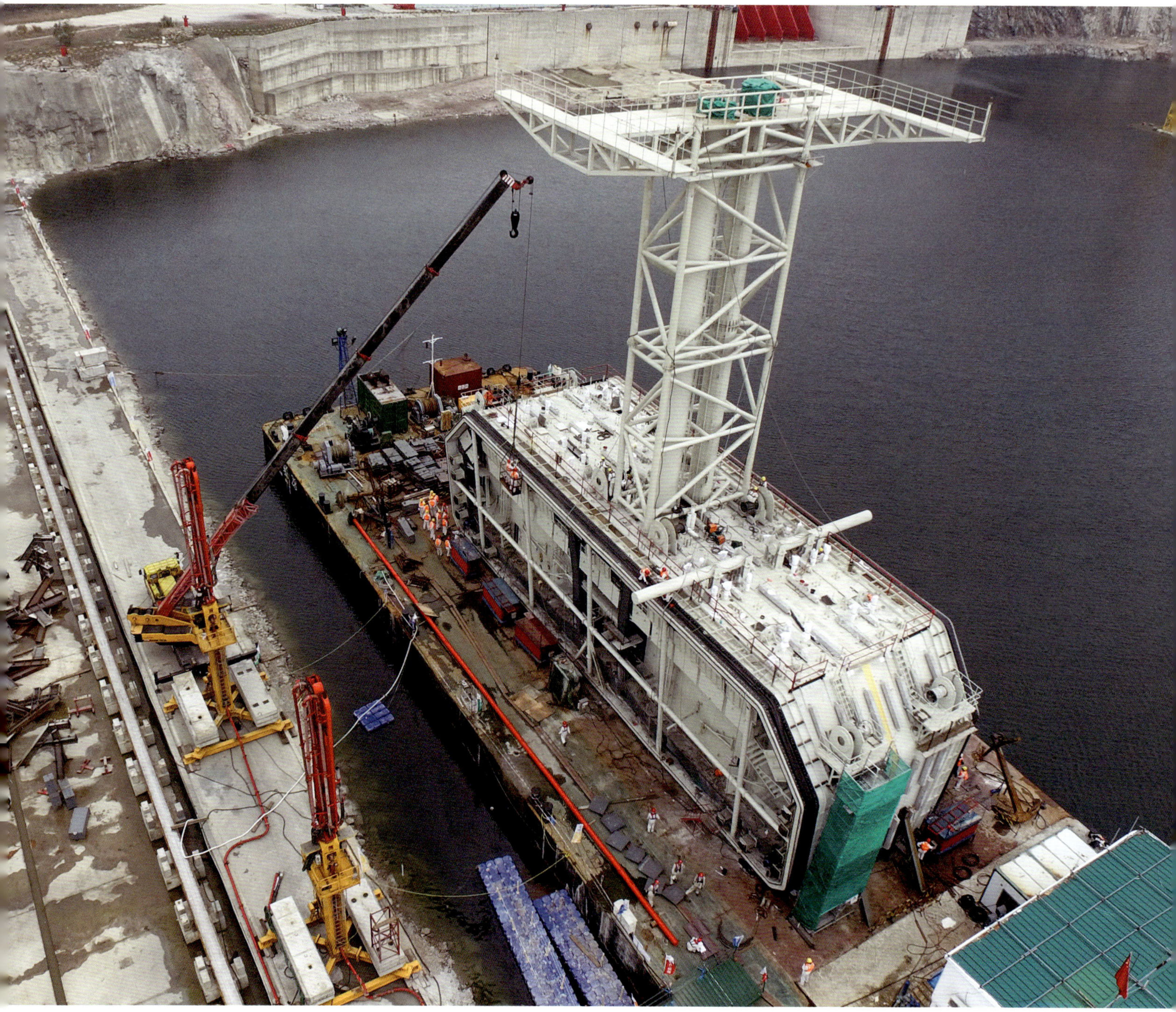

1. 最终接头高流动性混凝土浇筑准备
Preparation for High-Fluidity Concrete Placement at the Closure Joint

2. 最终接头高流动性混凝土浇筑施工
Placement of High-Fluidity Concrete at the Closure Joint

钢隔舱内充分填充混凝土是钢混三明治最终接头施工的关键。

为确保填充密实，需要合理布置纵横隔板分仓、浇筑孔及排气孔位置及细部加劲肋，为混凝土提供便于流动的路径；确保混凝土高流动性，不需振捣就能到达内部结构的远端，在自重作用下流动并均匀填满内部空间。

混凝土硬化过程中不泌水，不分层，收缩量小，钢壳与混凝土之间的间隙不超过 5 毫米。

钢壳混凝土具有高流动性、抗离析性、高填充性、免振捣、自密实和收缩性小等特点，对配合比控制、搅拌时间、运输时间、入模温度、单个隔舱浇筑时间、操作规程及流程、人员培训、应急措施、现场条件等有严格的要求和标准。

为确保浇筑质量，高流动性混凝土自出机至浇筑完成的时间严格控制在 80 分钟内。

历经 14 天，克服接头内部空间异常狭窄、浇筑管路布设复杂、工序转换多等难题，顺利完成 304 个隔舱、约 1280 立方米高流动性混凝土浇筑。

2017 年 3 月 26 日，最终接头浇筑完成。

Full-filling the steel compartment with concrete was the critical step of installing the closure joint.

To ensure compact filling, the vertical and horizontal placement of the dividing plates, the position of the placement hole and air hole and the detailing reinforcing rib needed to be properly arranged to provide the path for the flowing of the concrete. Keep the high fluidity of the concrete, and the concrete could reach the farthest end of the inner structure by its gravity without employing vibration and jolt ramming and fill the whole compartment. It should also been guaranteed that there were no weepage and separation while the concrete hardened.

The objective was minimum shrinkage with a minimum seam of no more than 5 millimeters between the steel shield and the concrete.

Steel-shielded concrete was characterized by its high fluidity, anti-separation, good filling capacity, zero vibration and ramming, self-compaction and minimum shrinkage, and thus posed high demands for mix ratio control, mix time, transportation time, modeling temperature, single compartment placement time, operation flow, workers training, emergency control and the working site.

To guarantee the quality of concrete placement, the time duration should be controlled in the limit of 80 minutes after the high-fluidity concrete came out the mixer and before the replacement was completed.

Within 14 days, various problems such as the extraordinary narrow space inside the closure joint, complicated layout of the replacement pipe and process transformation were solved, and 304 compartments were filled with about 1,280 cubic meters of high-fluidity concrete.

On March 26, 2017, the placement for the closure joint was completed.

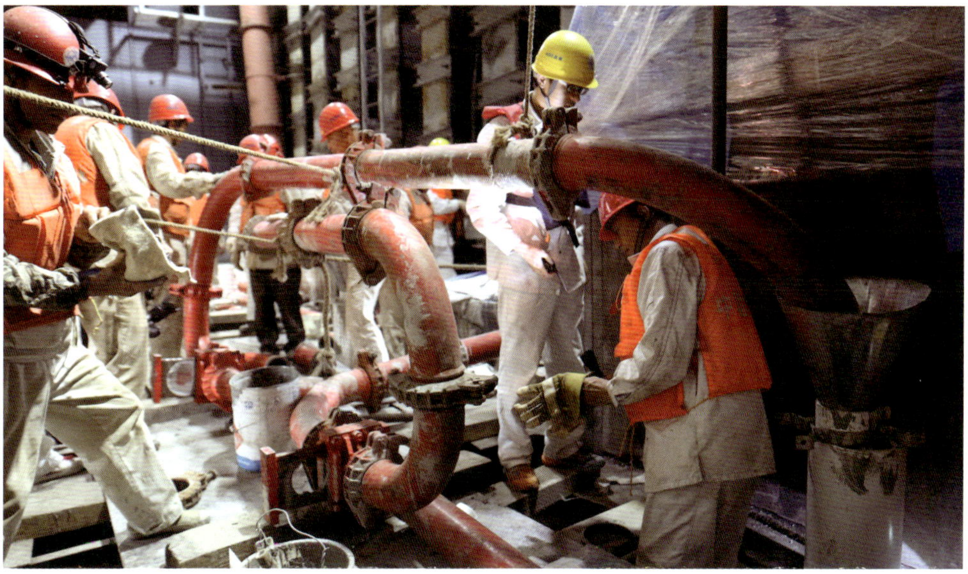

吊带布置方案

ARRANGEMENT OF THE HOISTING CABLES

由于最终接头安装空间狭小（仅12米），吊装下沉时需要将最终接头吊平，倾斜度控制在5厘米以内。

项目总经理部开展大件吊平专题研究，进行了吊带加工长度精度控制攻关、增加销轴护套调整吊带长度攻关、重心和浮心精算等一系列工作，将120米长、900吨吊重、130,000根丝组成的超级环形吊带加工误差控制在5厘米，比规范要求提高了20倍。

"超大型吊带的控制、检测方法"填补了国内外吊索具制造的技术空白。

Because of the very limited space (12 meters only) for the installation of the closure joint, the lowered closure joint should be kept at a horizontal position, and the slope rate should be controlled within the limit of 5 centimeters.

The project management center conducted a specialized research on the horizontal hoisting of large-sized objects, and made many breakthroughs in precise control of the length of hoisting cables, adjustment of the length of the hoisting cables by adding protective sheath to the shaft pin, precise calculation of the gravity center and buoyant center and the other. The deviation when manufacturing the 900-ton super circular hoisting cable of 120 meters composed of 130,000 thin cables was controlled within the limit of 5 centimeters, 20 times that by the common standard.

The control and testing of the super-sized hoisting cable was a breakthrough in the world history of cable manufacturing.

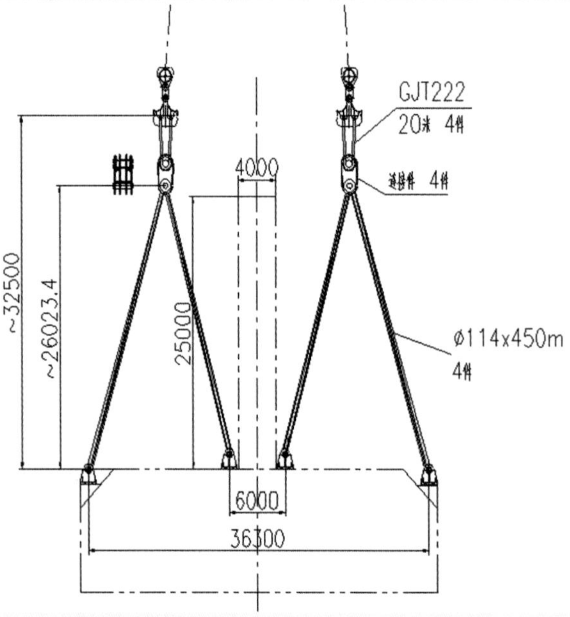

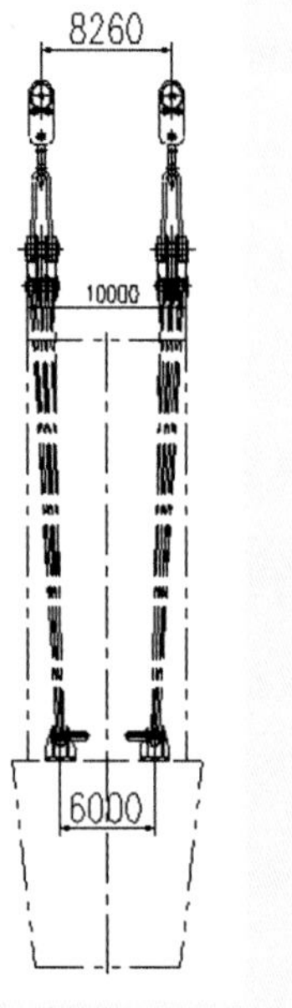

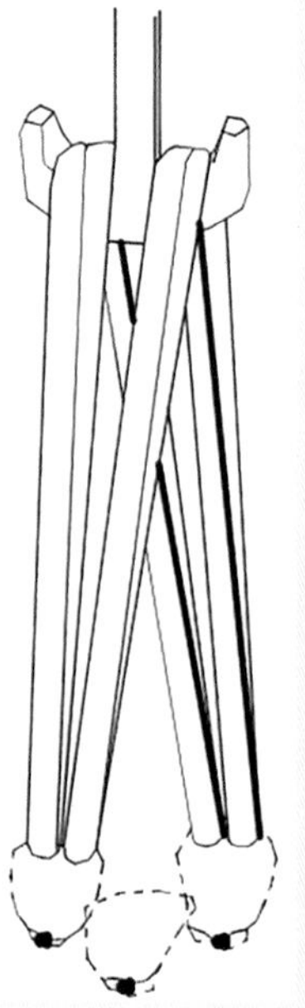

1. 最终接头吊装钢索布置方式图（比选）
Diagram of Distributing the Steel Suspension Cables Hoisting the Closure Joint
2. 最终接头吊索挂钩方案示意图
Schematic Diagram of the Suspension Cable Hook Hoisting the Closure Joint
3. 最终接头吊装布索方式图
Diagram of the Suspension Cable Arrangement for the Hoisting of the Closure Joint

项目 Item	四角最大高差 Maximum Elevation Difference at the Four Angles		
	方案一 Solution 1	方案二 Solution 2	方案三 Solution 3
调平后最大高差 Maximum Elevation Difference after Leveling Adjustment	37mm	6mm	23mm
单根吊带缩短 150mm Shortening a Single Hoisting Cable by 150 Millimeters	65mm	23mm	35mm
单根吊带缩短 300mm Shortening a Single Hoisting Cable by 300 Millimeters		38mm	40mm
吊耳受力均匀性 Evenness of the Load-Carrying Capacity of the Hoisting Hangers	中间吊耳相对外侧受力较大 The central hangers have bigger load-carrying capacity, compared with those on the four sides		
调平难度 Leveling Difficulty	□ 调平时间长，调平难度大 □ 短边方向（东西向）不易调平，高差最大 □ It needs more time and is difficult to even the load-carrying capacity of different hangers □ Those hangers on the short side (east-west direction) are more difficult to even, and suffer the maximum elevation difference	□ 调平时间短，容易调平 □ 短边方向姿态通过吊带长度容易控制 □ It needs less time and is easy to even the load-carrying capacity of different hangers □ The position of those hangers on the short side (east-west direction) are easy to be controlled by adjusting the length of the hoisting cable	□ 调平时间最长，较难调平 □ 短边方向不易调平，（相对方案一高差较小） □ It needs the longest time and is more difficult to even the load-carrying capacity of different hangers □ Those hangers on the short side (east-west direction) are more difficult to even, but enjoy a smaller elevation difference than that for the solution 1

吊带试验总结
Summary of Hoisting Cable Tests

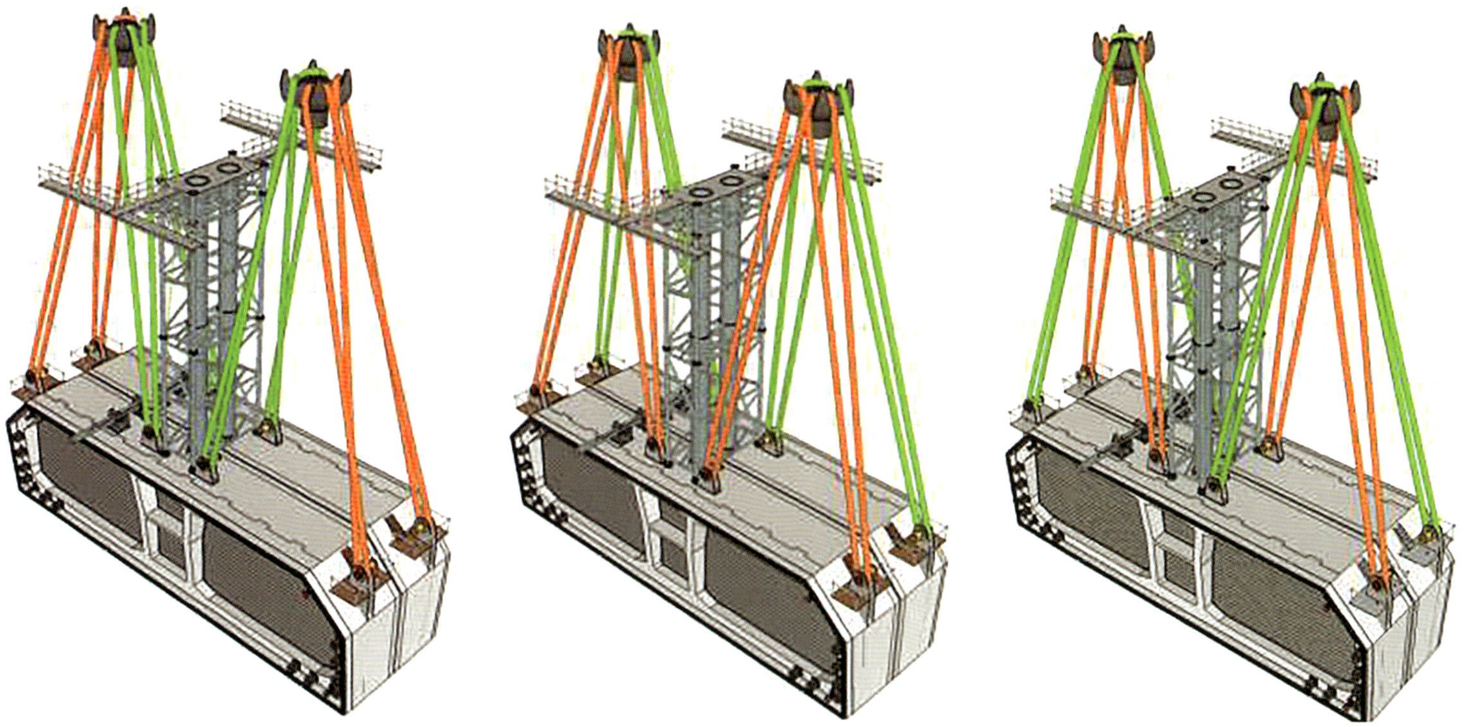

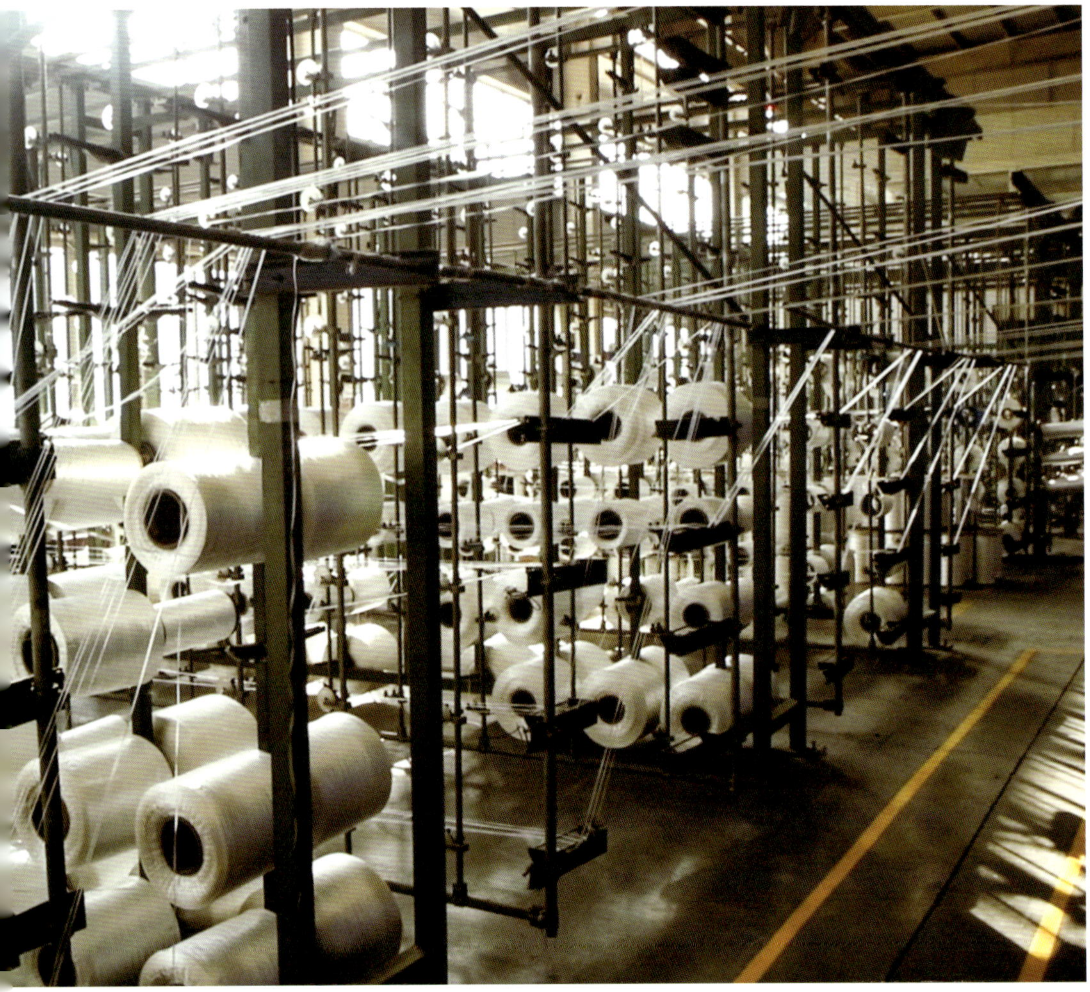

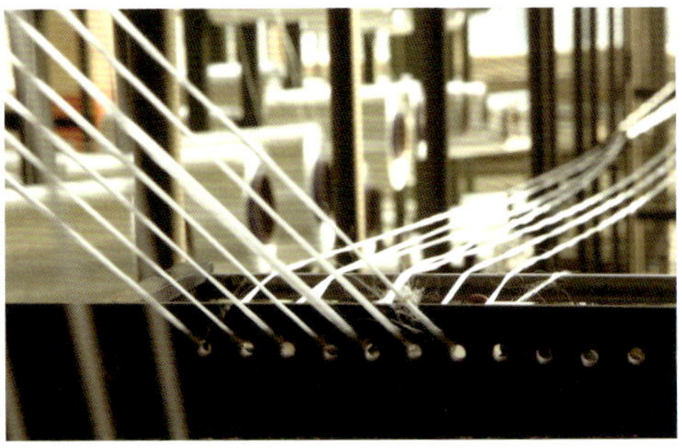

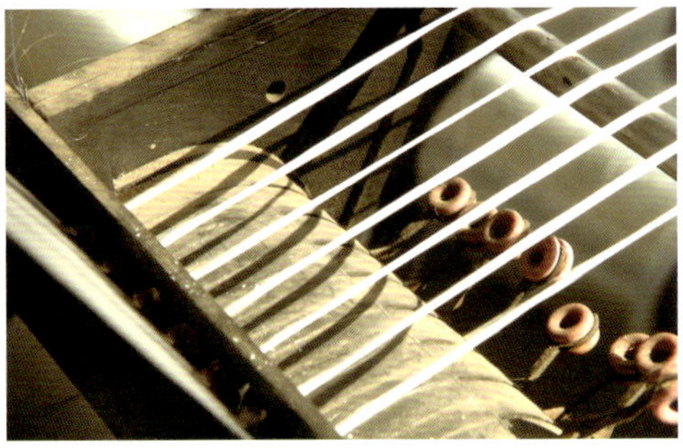

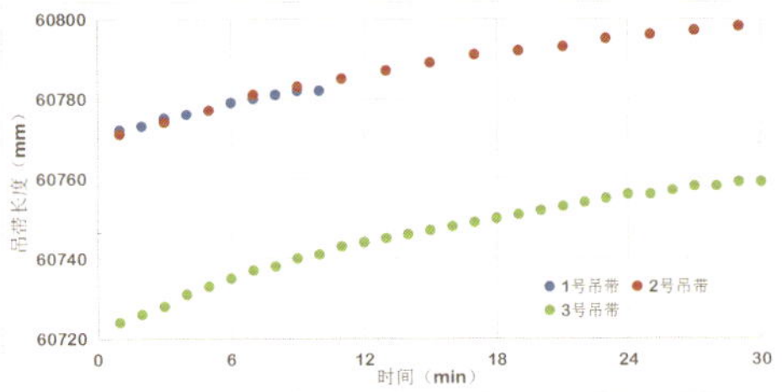

900t / 30min 保载试验最终接头吊索长度变化表

Table for Closure Joint Lifting Cable Changes in Proof Load Test by 900t/30min

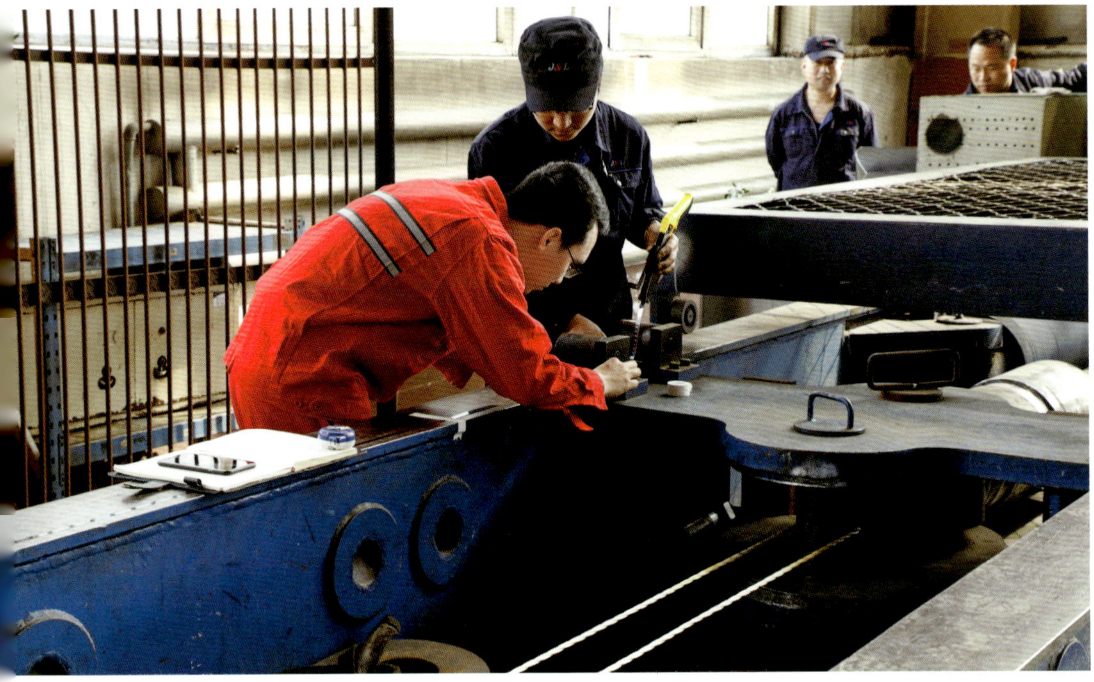

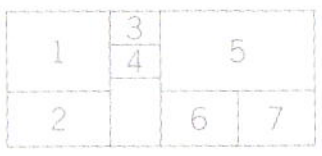

1—4. 最终接头吊索生产

Production of the Suspension Cable Hoisting the Closure Joint

5—6. 吊索吊挂施工

Hoisting of the Suspension Cable

7. 吊索正式应用于最终接头安装

Suspension Cable Used for the Installation of the Closure Joint

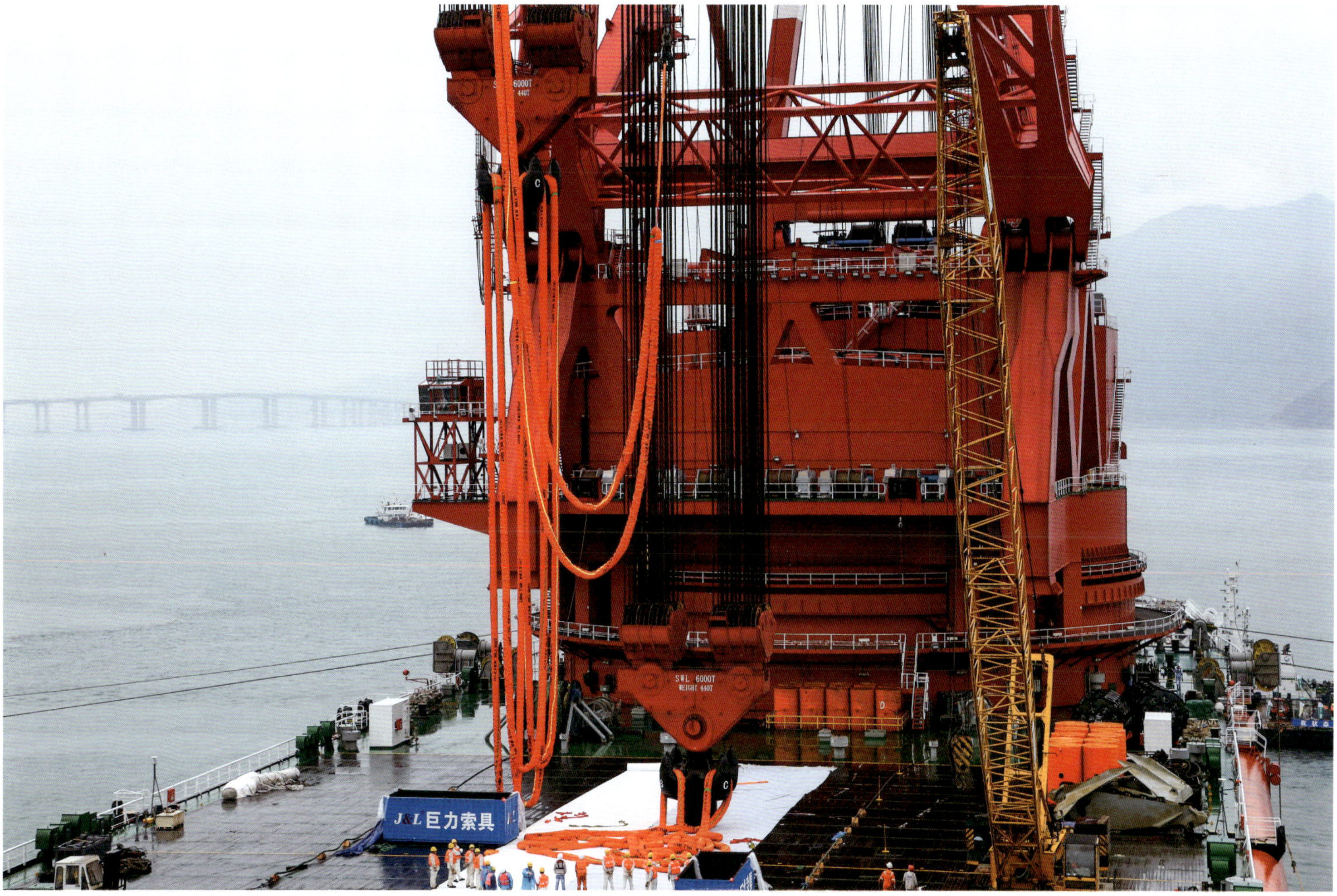
SWL 6000T
WEIGHT 440T
巨力索具

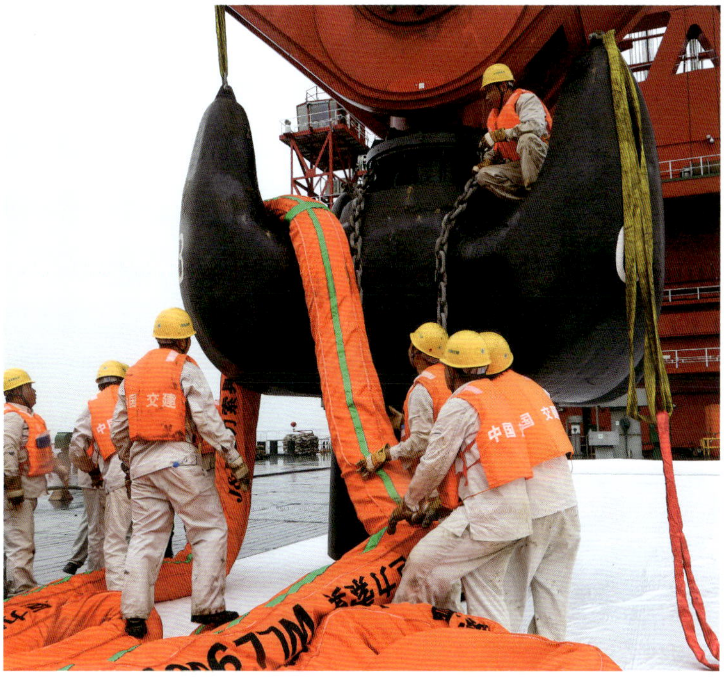

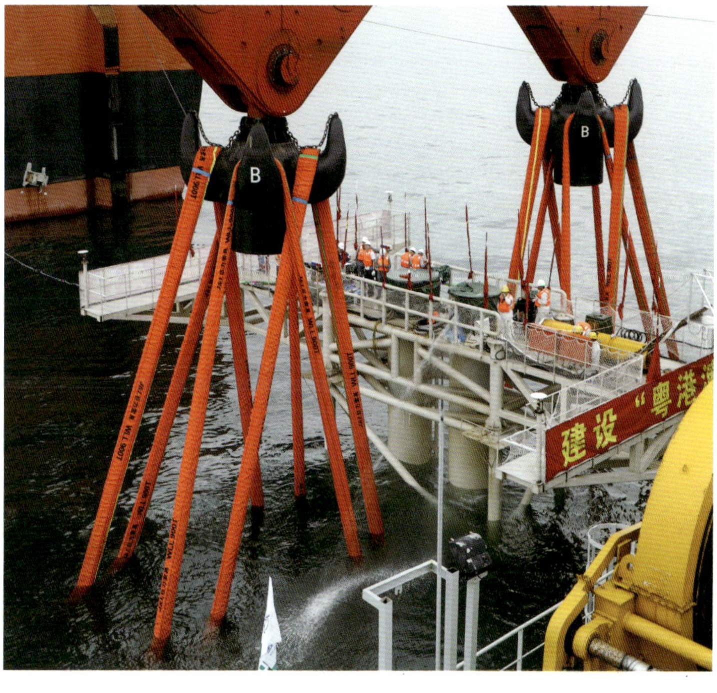
建设

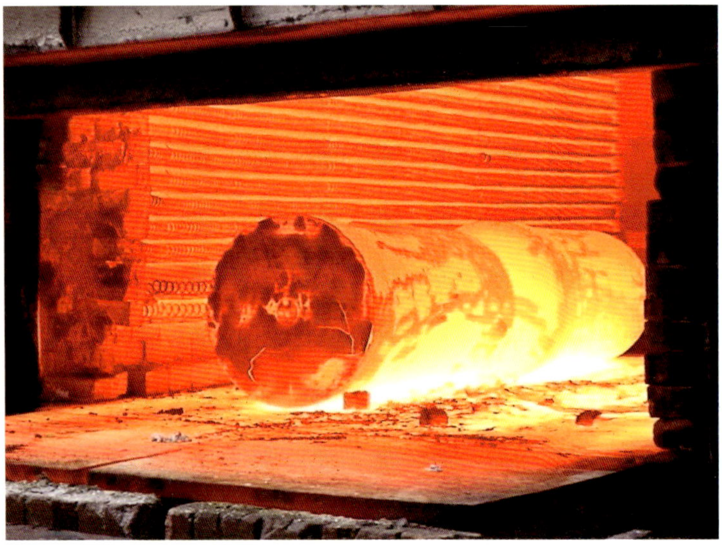

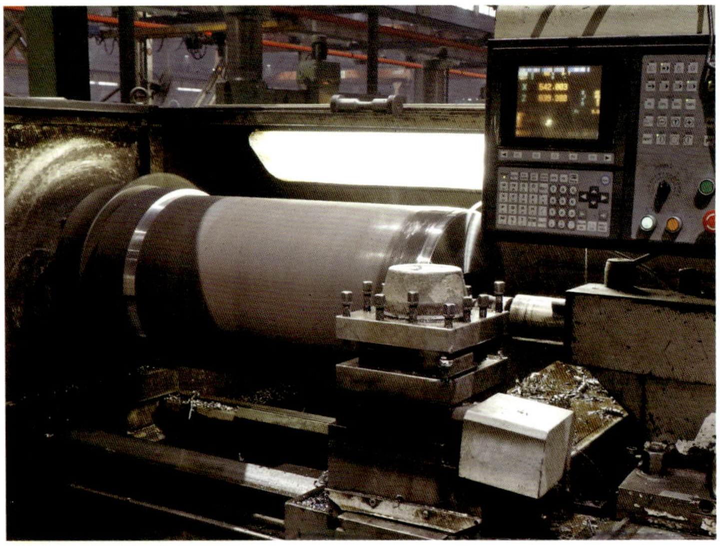

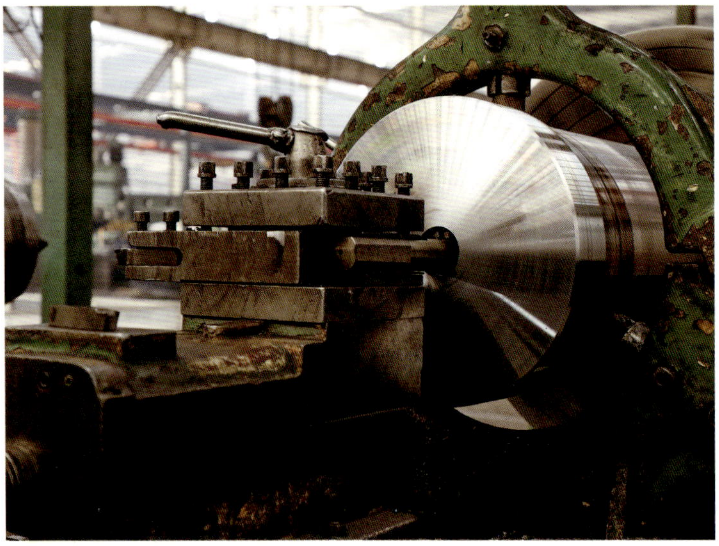

1—3. 最终接头销轴生产过程
Production of Shaft Pins for the Closure Joint

4—5. 最终接头销轴
Shaft Pin for the Closure Joint

6. 安装在最终接头上的销轴
Shaft Pin Installed on the Closure Joint

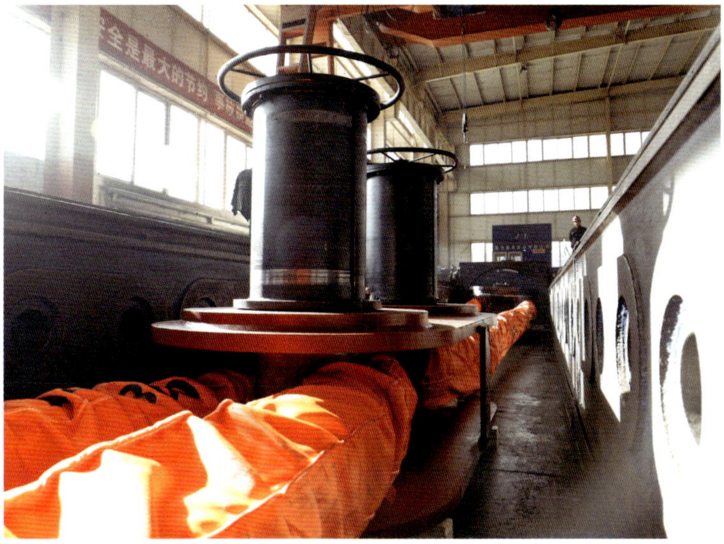

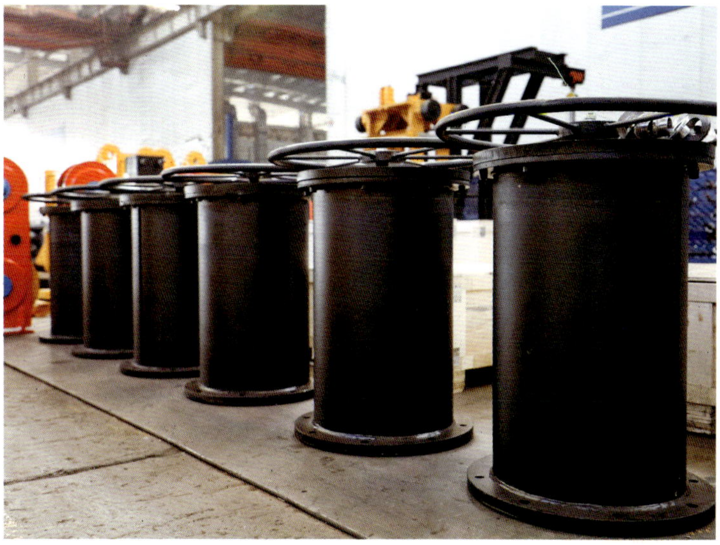

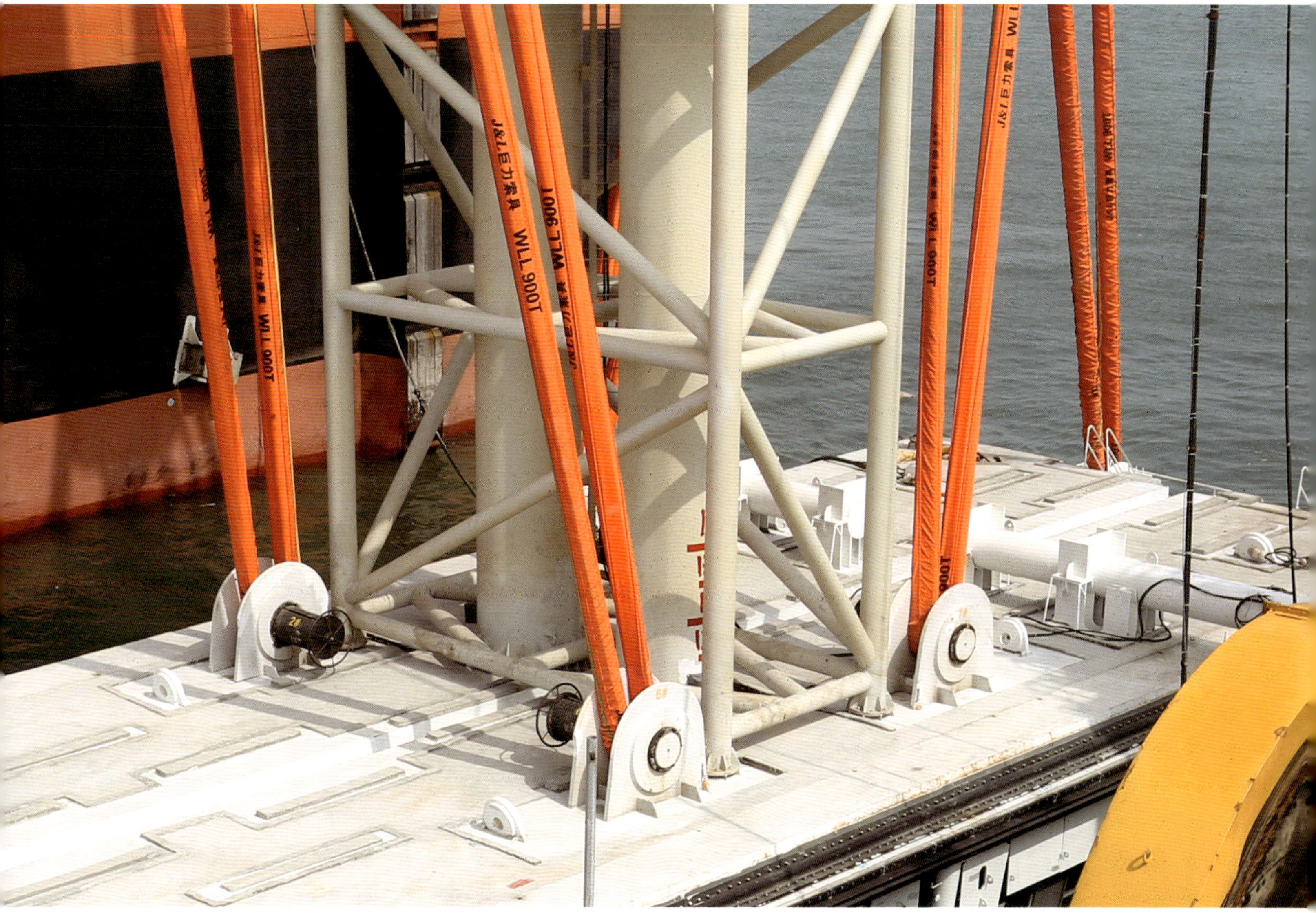
J&I巨力索具
WLL 900T

"振华30"轮是全世界最大的全回转起重船，总长297.55米，型宽58.00米，型深28.80米，最大起重能力达12,000吨。

"Zhenhua 30" was the largest swing crane ship in the world, 297.55 meters long, 58 meters wide, 28.80 meters in depth, with the maximum lifting capacity of 12,000 tons.

1. "振华30"起重船吊钩
   Hook of Crane Barge "Zhenhua30"
2. 全回转起重船"振华30"
   Swing Crane Barge "Zhenhua30"

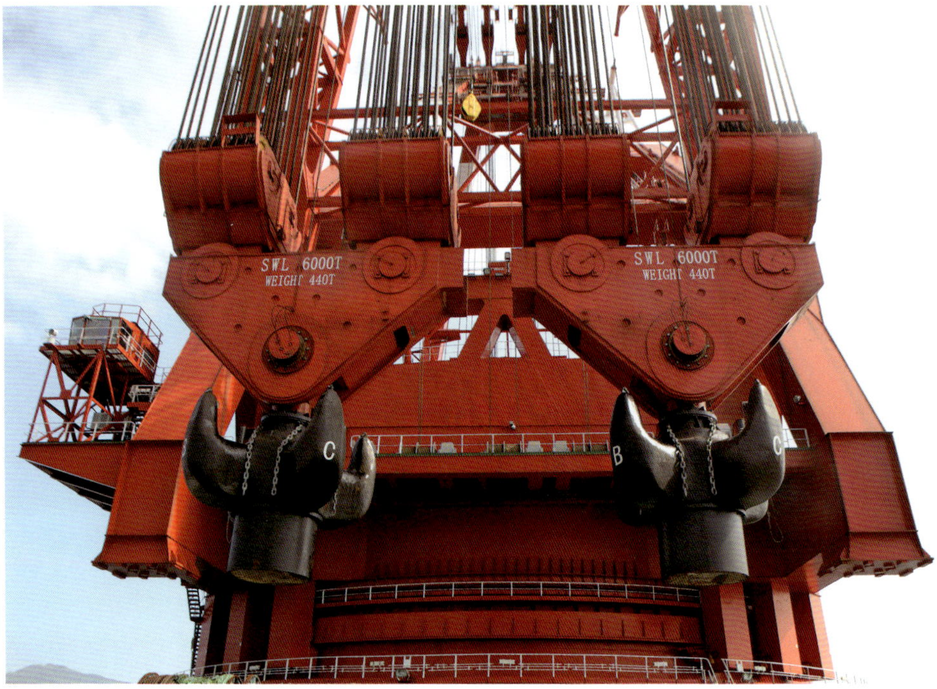

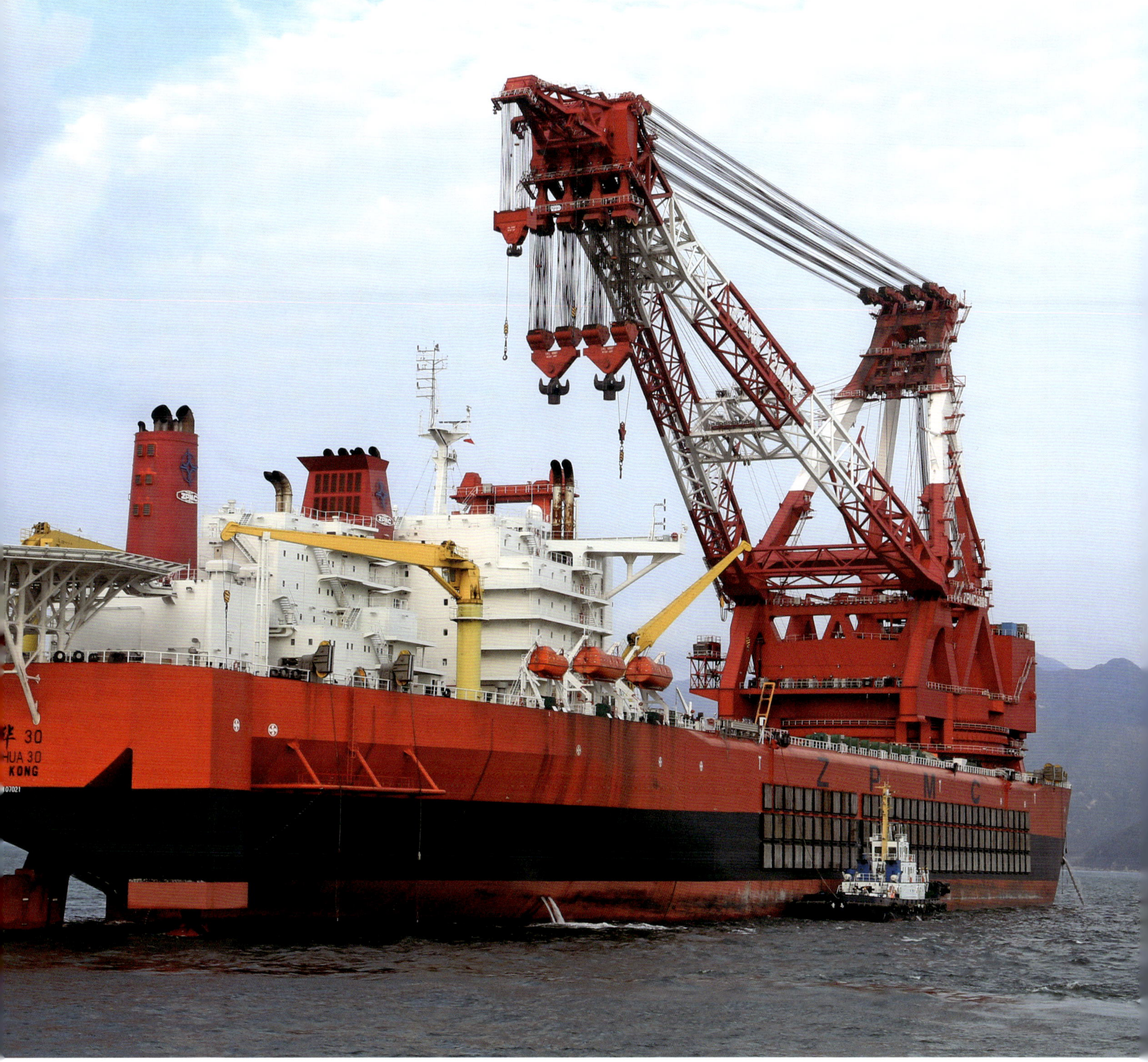
Z P M C

最终接头安装
INSTALLATION OF THE CLOSURE JOINT

选择合适气象窗口，采用12,000吨起重船进行最终接头沉放安装；沉放到位后，启动顶推小梁水平滑动，压缩小梁前端GINA止水带实现止水，形成结合腔后进行管内焊接，与E29、E30沉管实现刚性连接。

其中，大体量楔形块水下龙口受限空间（15厘米）内精确安装、小梁顶推止水、刚接头焊接等均为国内外首次实施。

A proper weather window was chosen and a barge of 12,000 tons was selected for the closure joint landing and installation. When the closure joint was landed on the designed spot, the push system was initiated to push the trabecular beam to move along horizontally, compress GINA water-stop in the front of the trabecular beam to stop water from leaking in. Once the binding cavity was formed, the in-tube welding began for the final connection with the tubes E29 and E30.

Precise installation of large-sized wedges in narrow underwater cofferdam gaps (15 centimeters), trabecular beam pushing to stop water and fixed joint welding were all original operation in the world tunneling.

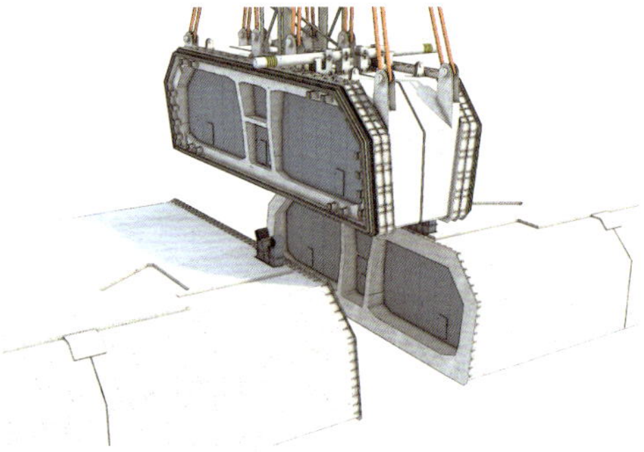
起吊
Lifting

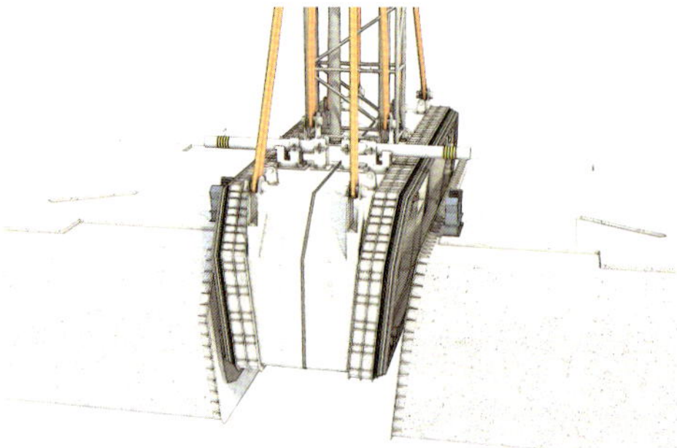
下放
Landing

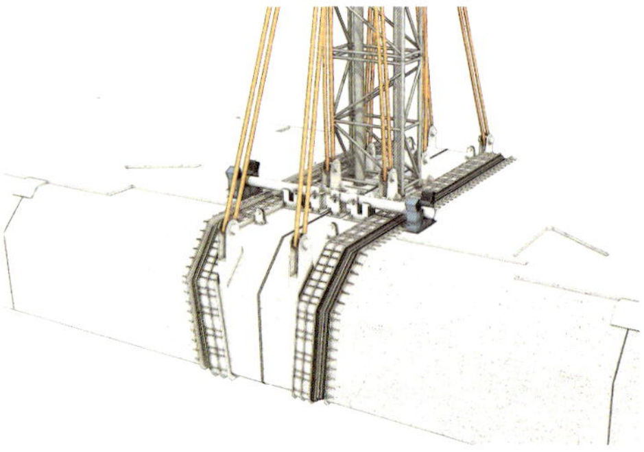
着床
Implantation

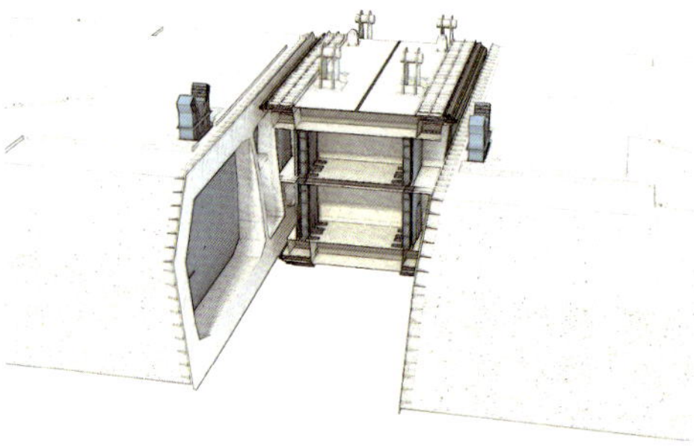
可折叠主动止水结构
Foldable Active Water Stop Structure

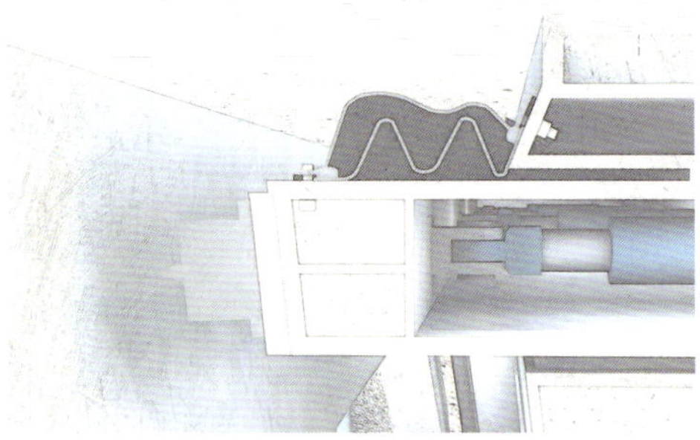
小梁顶推
Trabecular Beam Pushing

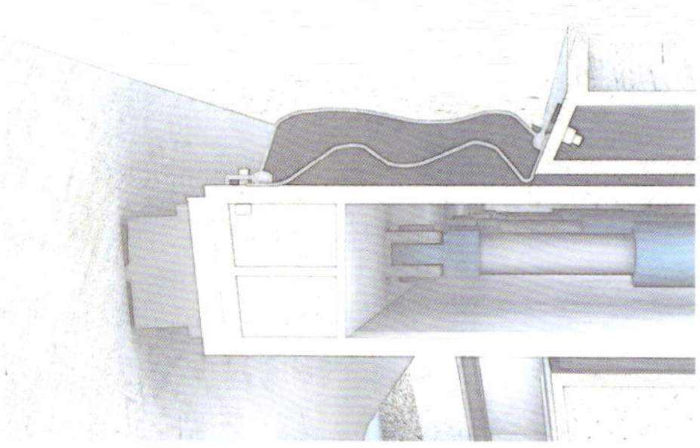
GINA 止水带压缩
Compression of GINA Water Stop

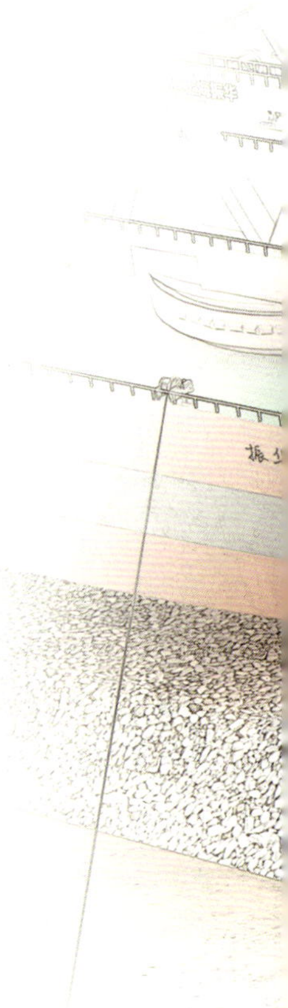

1. 最终接头安装流程图
Flow Chart of the Closure Joint Installation

2. 最终接头安装位置示意图
Schematic Diagram of Closure Joint Installation

3. 最终接头安装三维图
3-D Diagram of the Closure Joint Installation

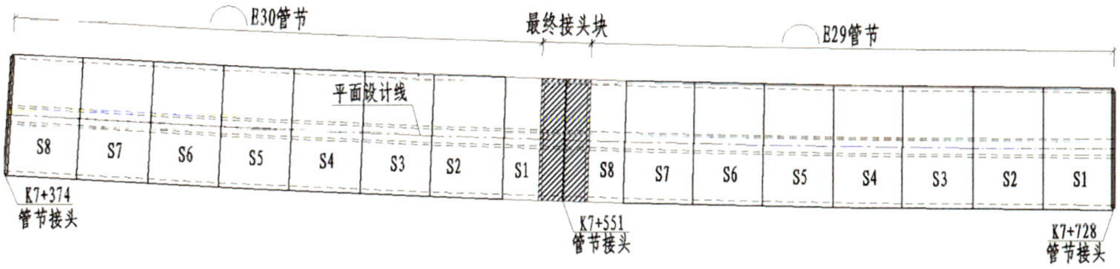

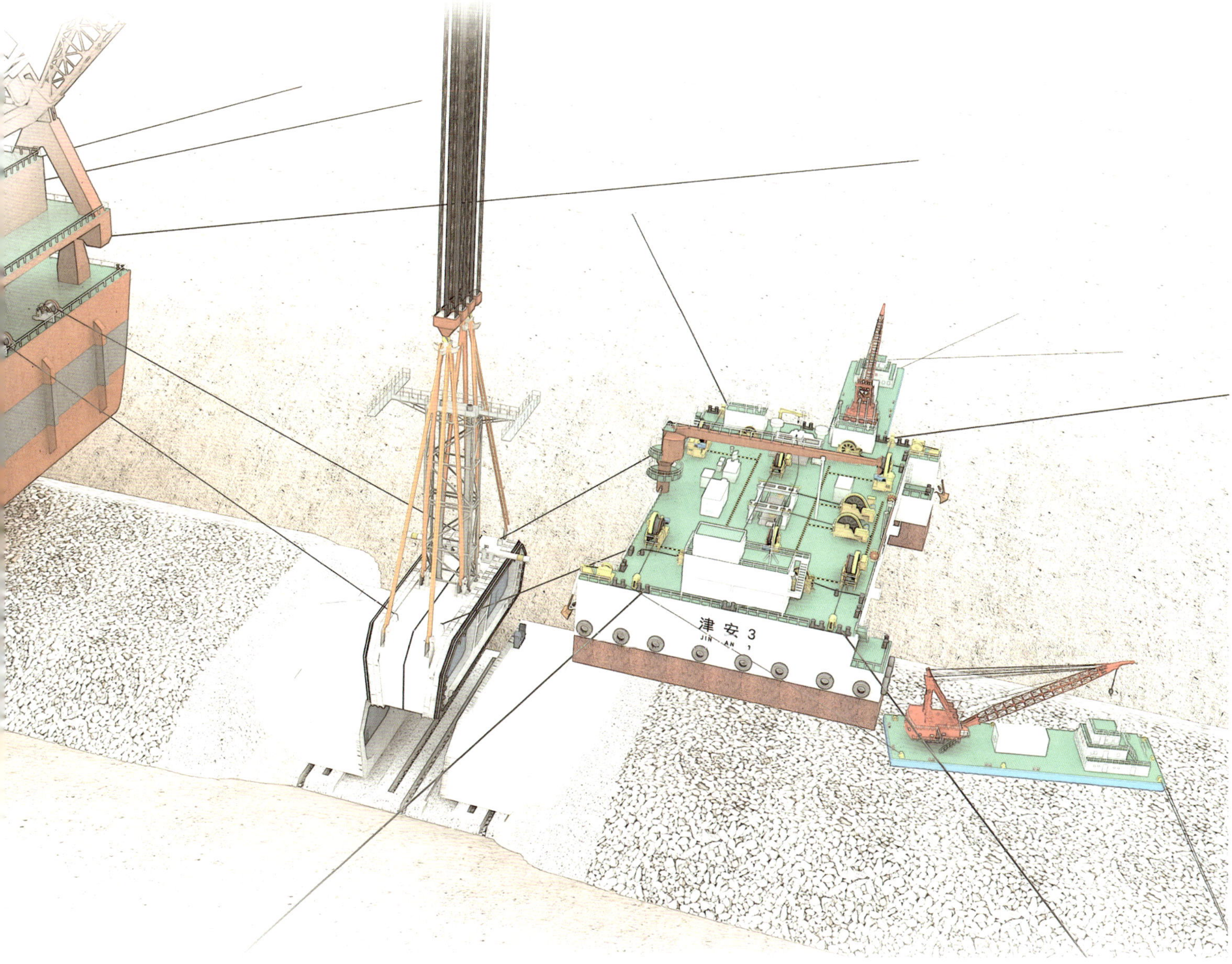

试吊演练

HOISTING PRACTICE

2017年4月2日，项目总经理部开展了最终接头试吊演练，进一步熟悉了吊装流程和现场组织，实测了各关键保障系统与吊索具性能，为最终接头安装积累了宝贵经验。

On April 2, 2017, the project management center performed a series of tests on hoisting of the closure joint to get familiar with the process of hoisting and working site operations. And the efficiency of various critical support system and various hoisting facilities were also tested, which proved to be a precious experience for the installation of the closure joint.

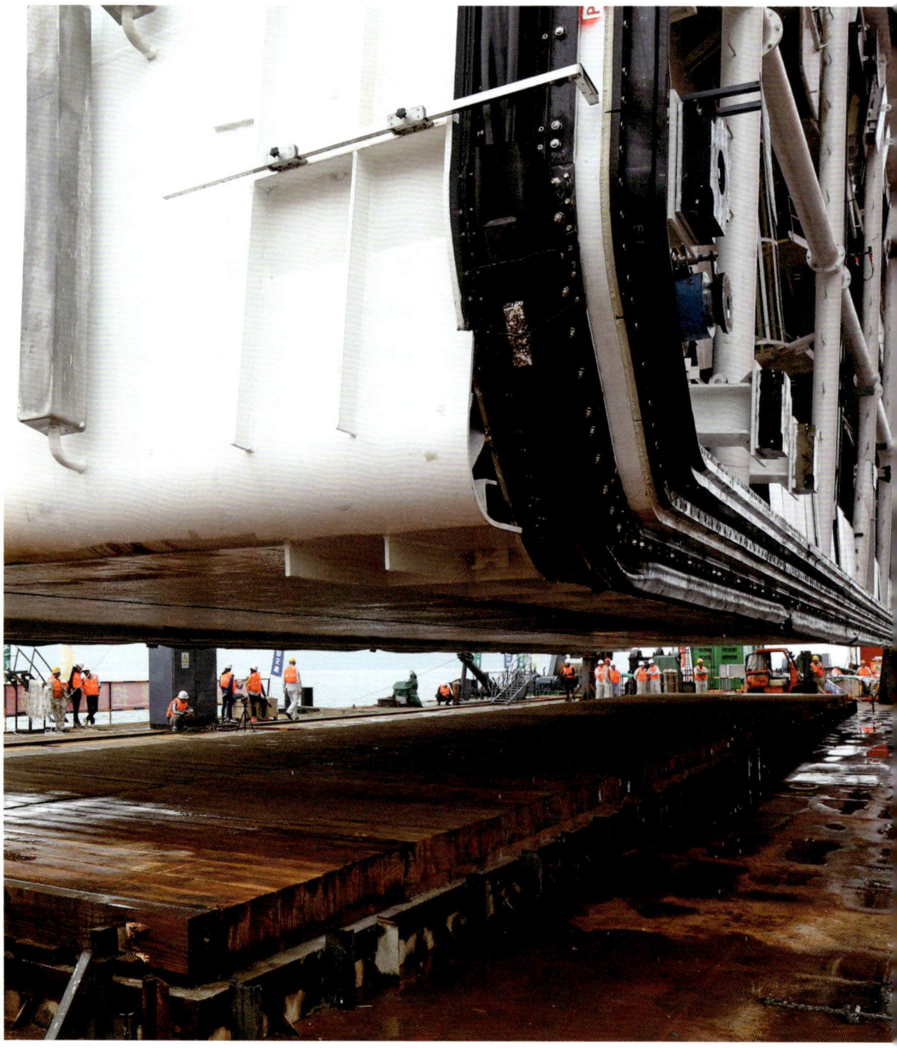

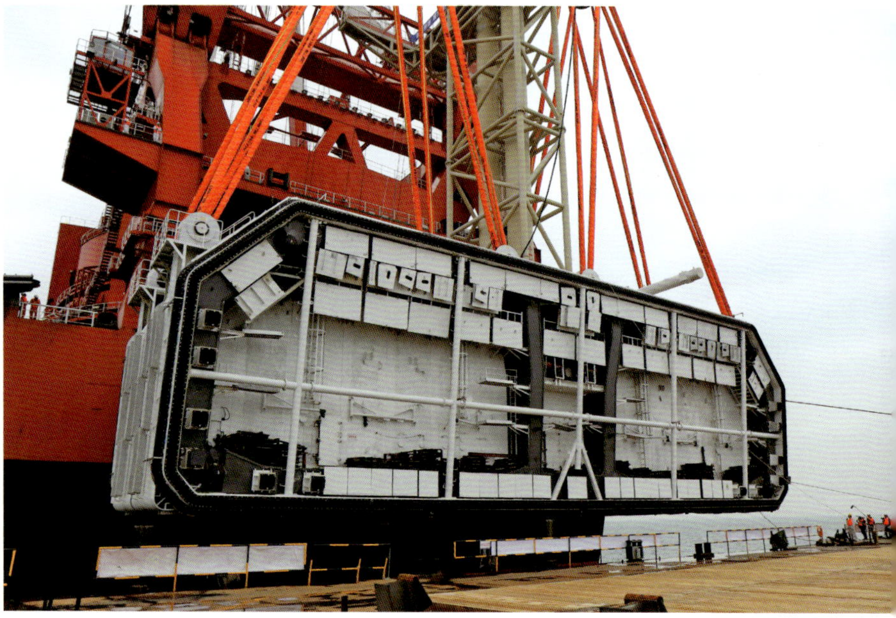

1 3 4 2 5

1. 最终接头试吊
Experimental Hoisting of the Closure Joint
2. 最终接头试吊至预定高度
Closure Joint Hoisted to the Target Height
3. 林鸣指挥最终接头试吊演练
Lin Ming Commanding the Test Hoisting of the Closure Joint
4. 最终接头试吊下沉入水
Landing of the Closure Joint
5. 最终接头入水试漏检查
Leakage Detection of the Closure Joint

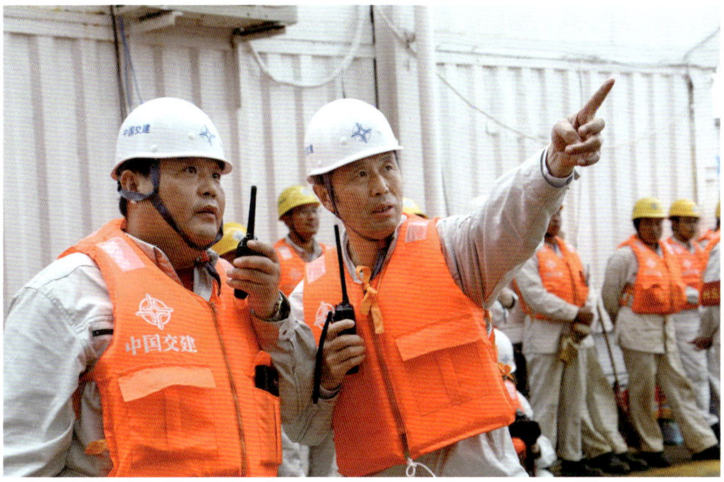
中国交建

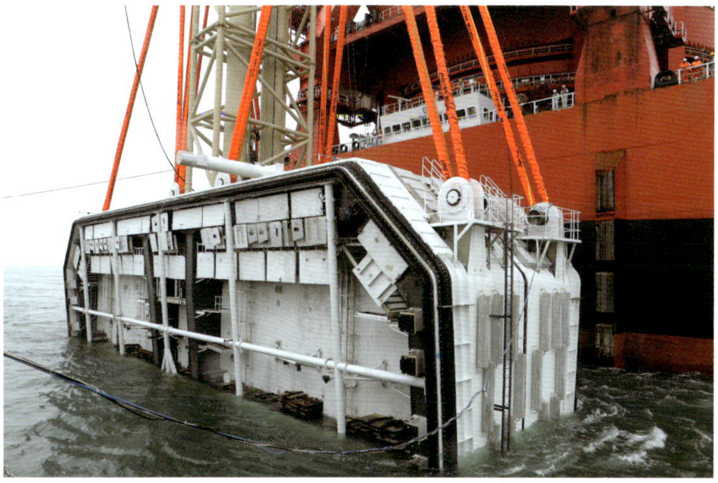

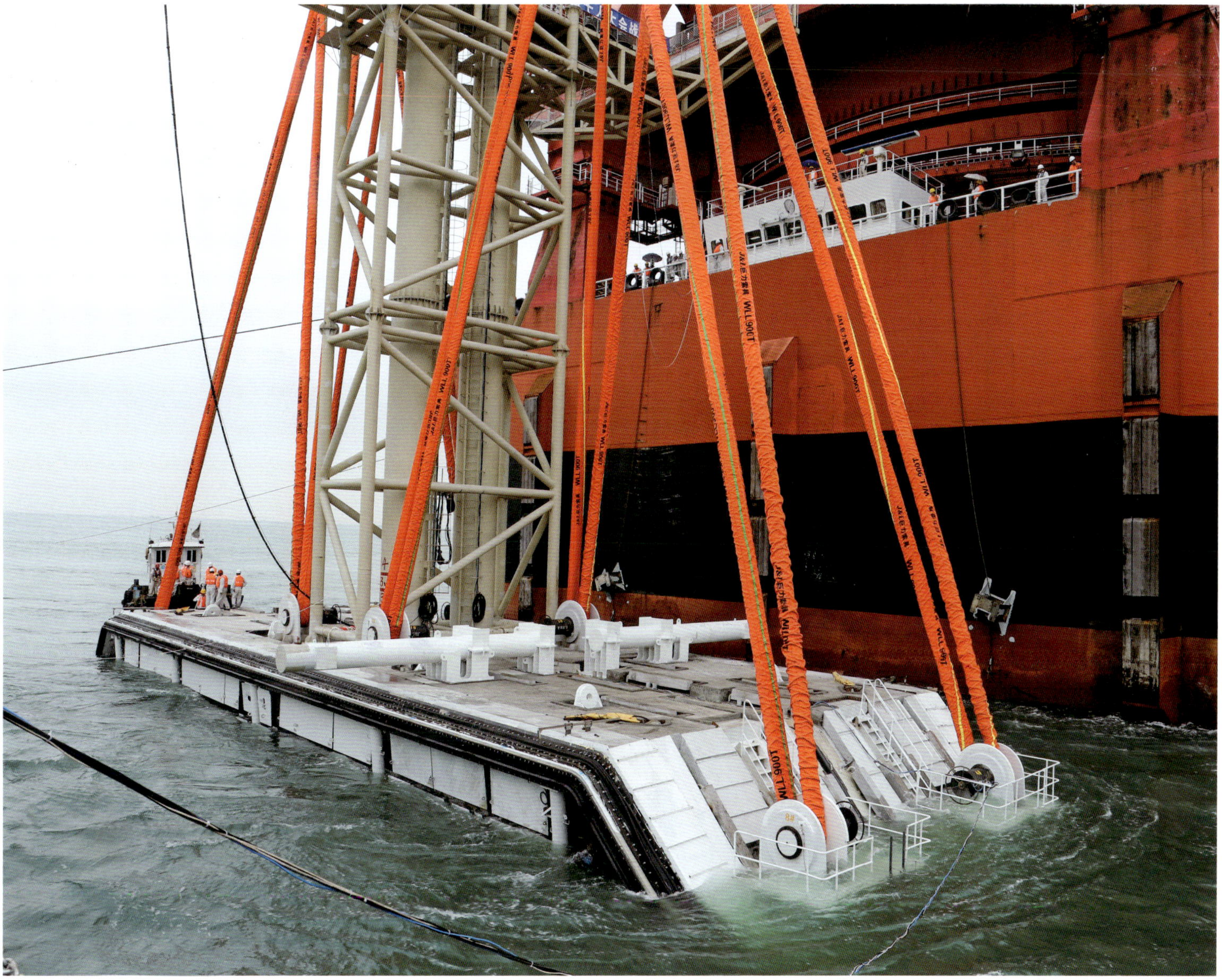
WLL900T

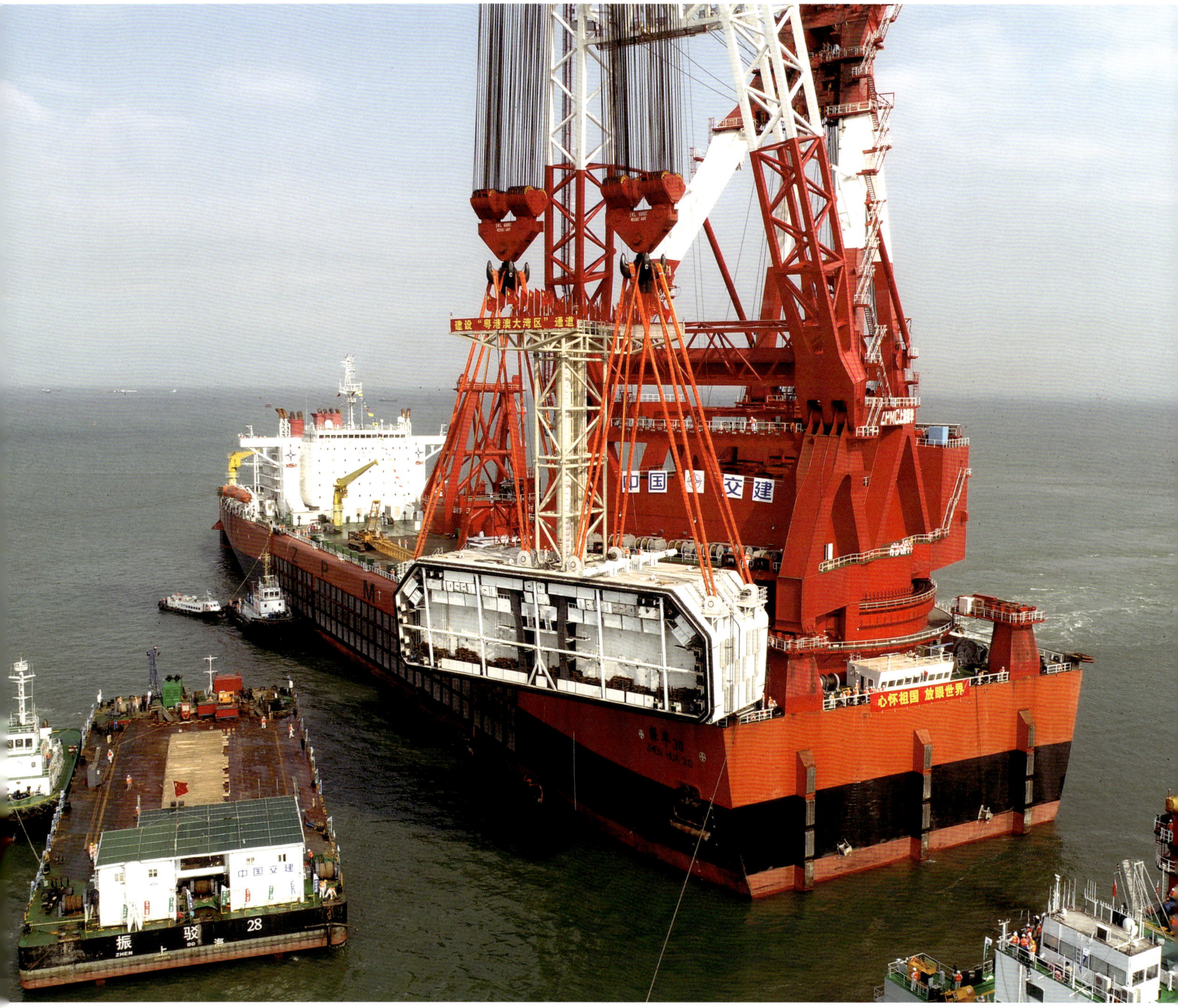

1 2

1. 最终接头起吊、转向
Hoisting and Swerving of the Closure Joint

2. 最终接头旋转 90°，准备沉放
90° Swerve of the Closure Joint before Landing

2017 年 5 月 2 日 5 点 53 分，正值海上日出时刻。

随着林鸣“大臂起、旋转至 90°”的指令，“振华30”轮巨大的吊臂与喷薄而出的红日同时升起。

施工人员精心操控，基础、结构、测量、气象、姿态等监控组密切配合；历经起吊、转动、下沉，11 点 55 分，最终接头即平稳着床，顶推系统同步顶推小梁，GINA 止水带与两侧沉管钢帽紧密贴合压接，世界上第一次做到了深水复杂环境下最终接头滴水不漏。

5 月 3 日，贯通测量结果显示最终接头轴线偏差 15 厘米。

为确保质量，不留遗憾，中国交建建设团队顶住巨大压力，毅然决定进行精调。

经过近 40 个小时的连续施工，顺利解决了临时止水闭合腔压力平衡、顶推系统解压回收、大型浮吊精确定位、6000 吨级最终接头重新起吊等关键难题和最终接头钢封门渗漏等意外情况，圆满完成了最终接头精调施工。

轴线、偏差均达到毫米级，完美再现了深水复杂环境下最终接头滴水不漏，首次在世界沉管隧道建设史上实际验证了最终接头施工方法“工序可逆”，为同类工程建设提供了可复制的施工经验。

At 5:53 on May 2, 2017, it was the moment of sun rising over the sea.

With Lin Ming's command “Crane arm lifted, turn to 90°”, the tremendous crane arm of the barge “Zhenhua30” rose in the morning sunshine.

The mechanics operated the machines carefully, and the workers at different monitoring positions such as tunnel base, structure, measurement, climate, and trailing worked with each other. Lifting, swerving, and lowering were followed by the steady landing of the closure joint at 11:55. The push system pushed the trabecular, and GINA water-stop closely welded with the steel caps on the two sides of the immersed tube. By this, the first case of anti-leakage closure butt welding in complicated situation underneath deep water in the world was perfectly done.

On May 3, the measurement data for the closure suggested the final deviation of the axis line of the closure joint was 15 centimeters.

To guarantee the high quality of the project without any future regret, China Constructions Construction Company decided for fine adjustment under great pressure.

After 40 hours' hard work, the pressure balance in the binding cavity of the temporary water-stop, the decompressed recovery of the push system, the precise positioning of the large floating crane, re-lifting of the closure joint of 6000 tons, as well as the leakage at the steel sealing devices of the closure joint were all adjusted to prepare for the precise operation of the closure joint.

Then the deviation of the axis line was almost negligible and leakage under complicated deep water conditions was perfectly solved. For the first time in the world history of the immersed tube tunneling, this performance proved that the closure joint operation is reversible, and this provided an important construction reference for the same type of construction in the world.

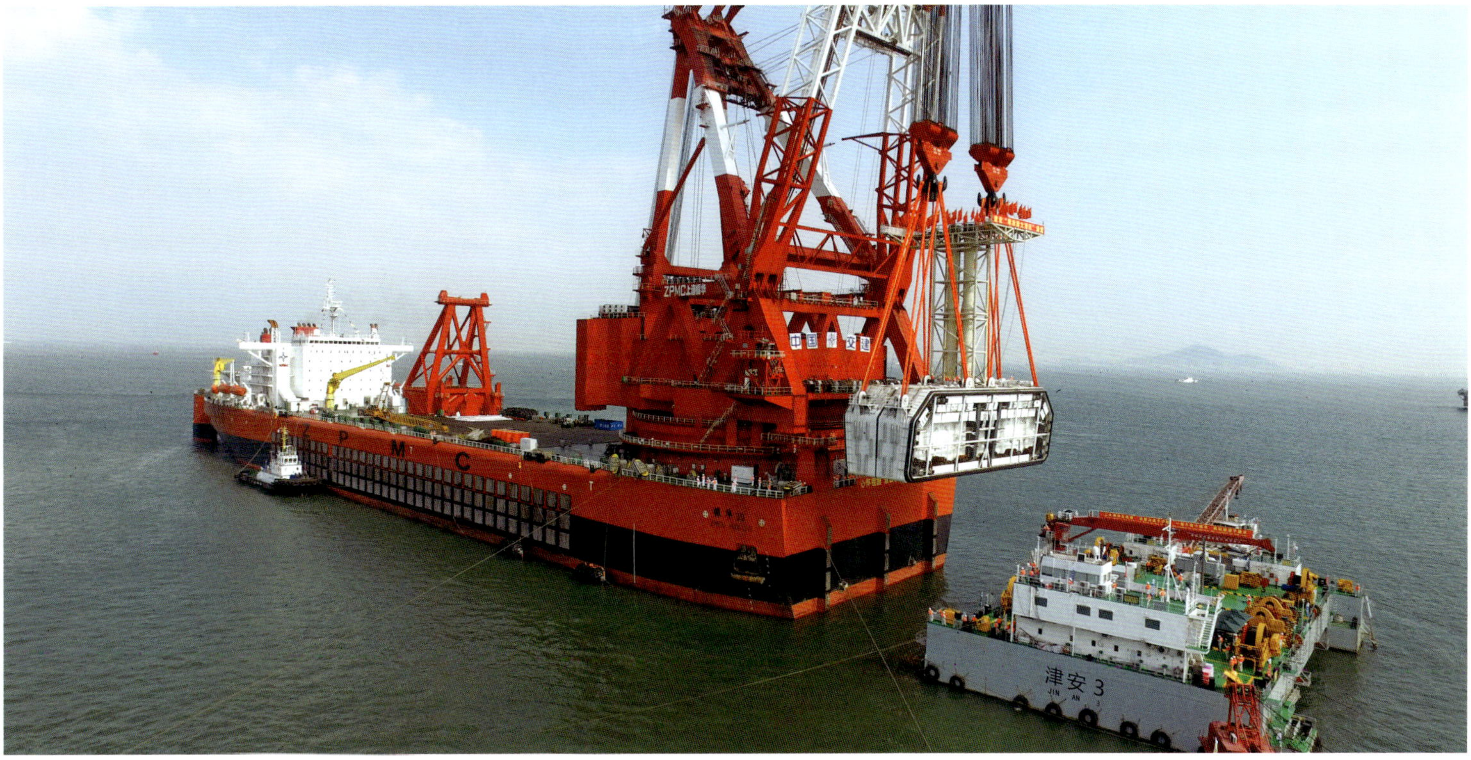

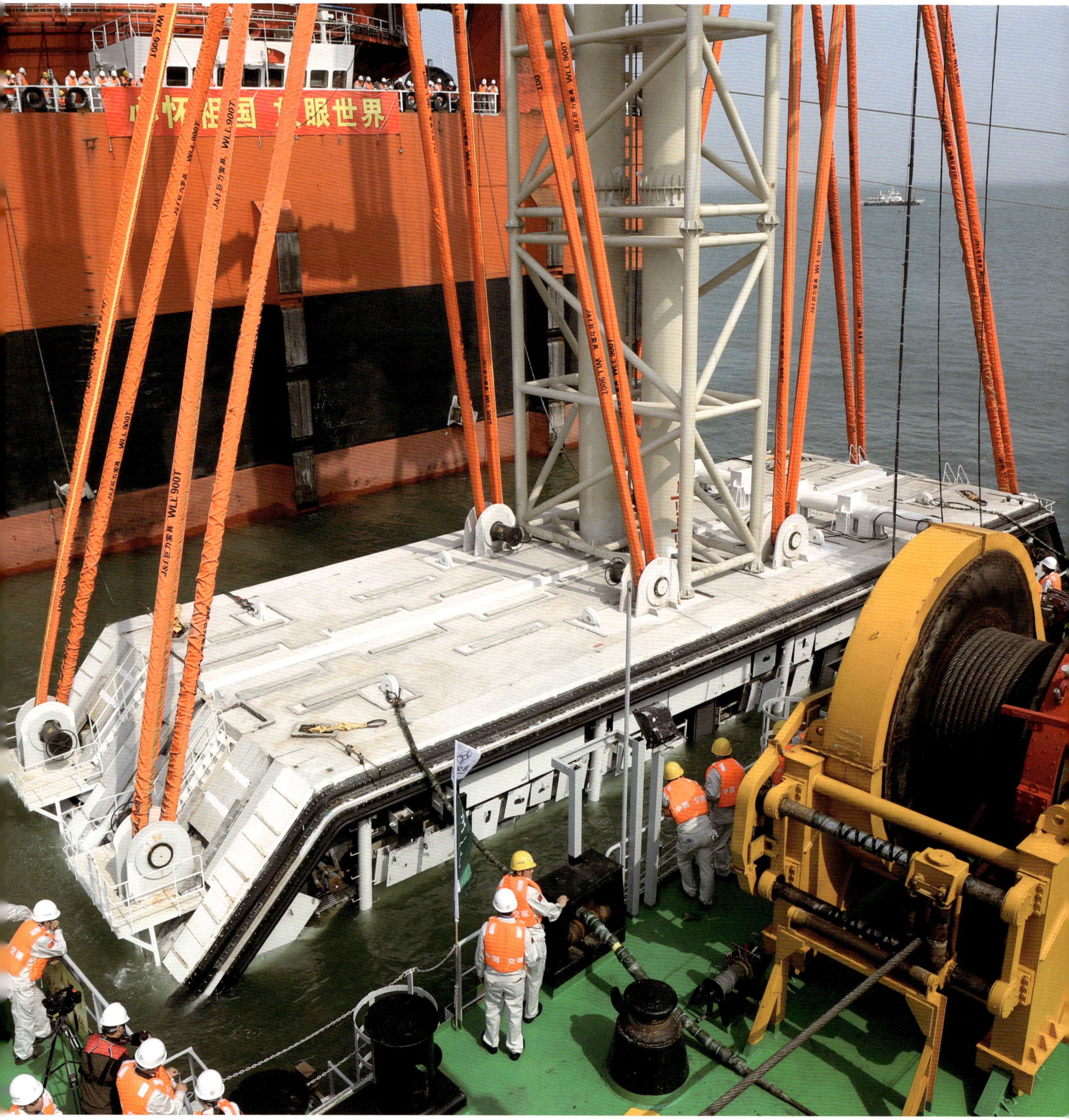
WLL 900T

1. 最终接头沉放施工
   Landing of the Closure Joint
2. 最终接头着床
   Landing of the Closure Joint

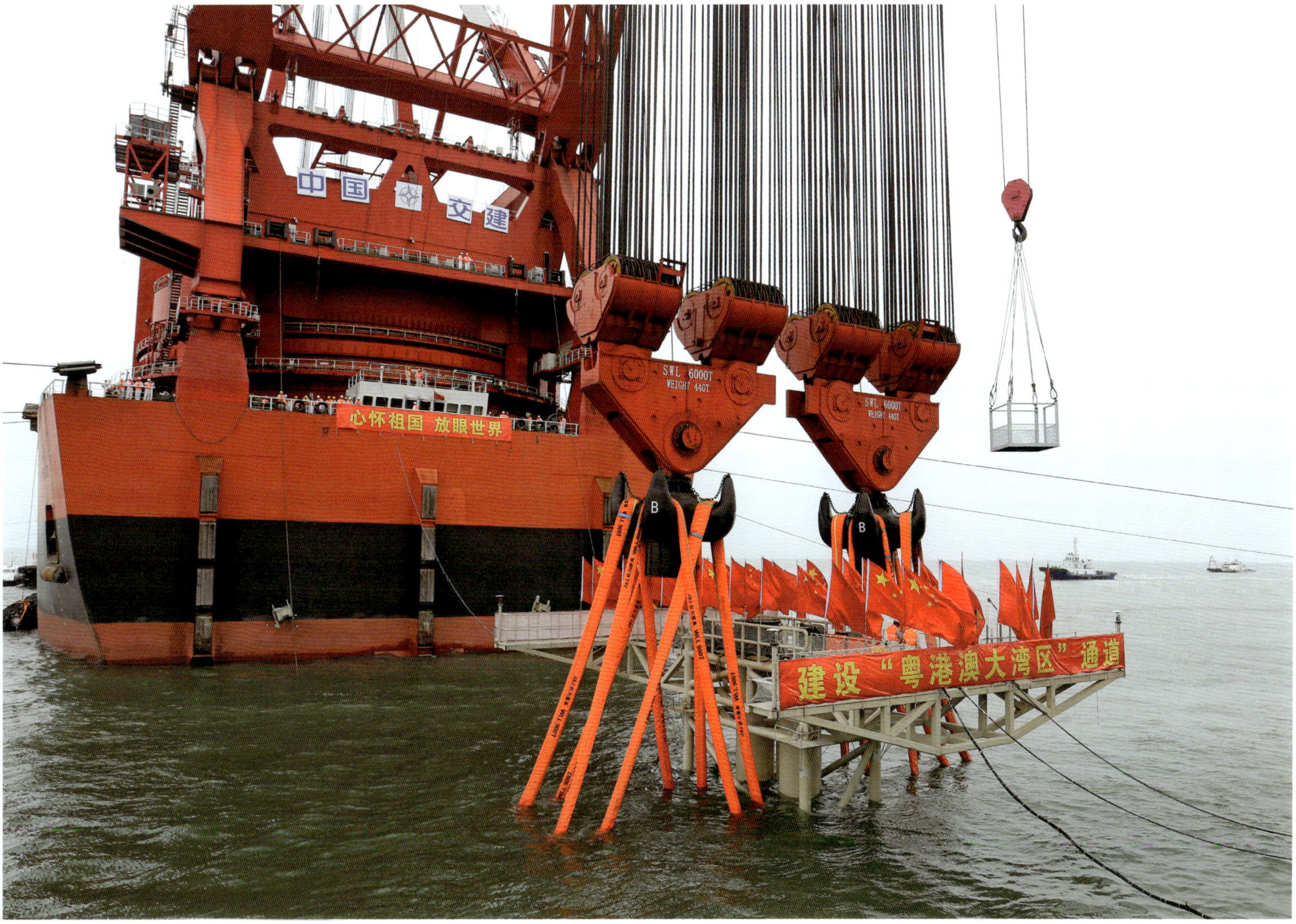

1. 最终接头沉放数据分析
Analysis of the Closure Joint Landing Data

2. 最终接头水力压接施工
Hydraulic Pressure Connection of the Closure Joint

3. 最终接头沉放施工
Enclosure Joint Landing

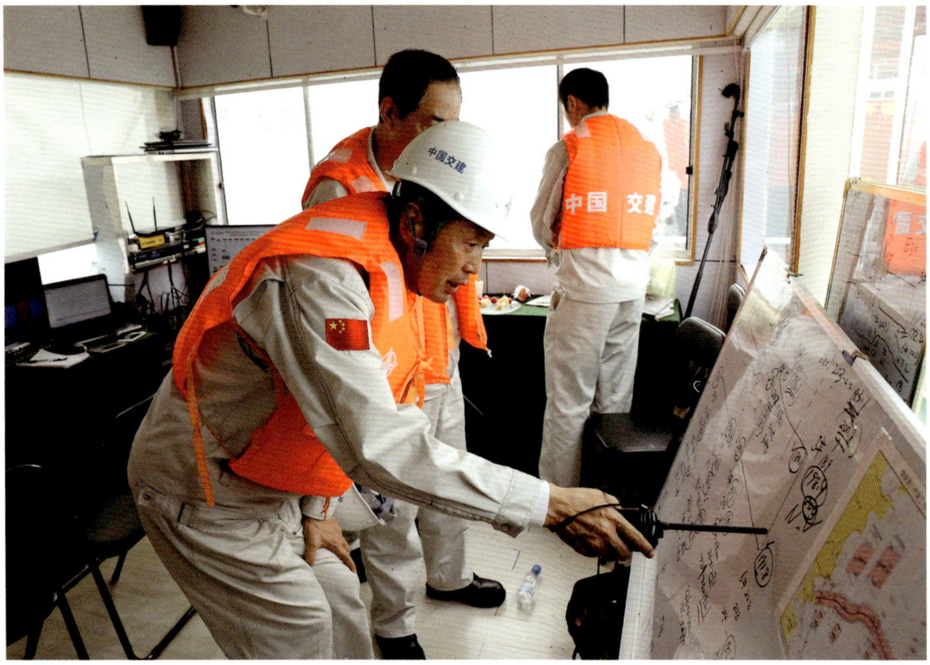

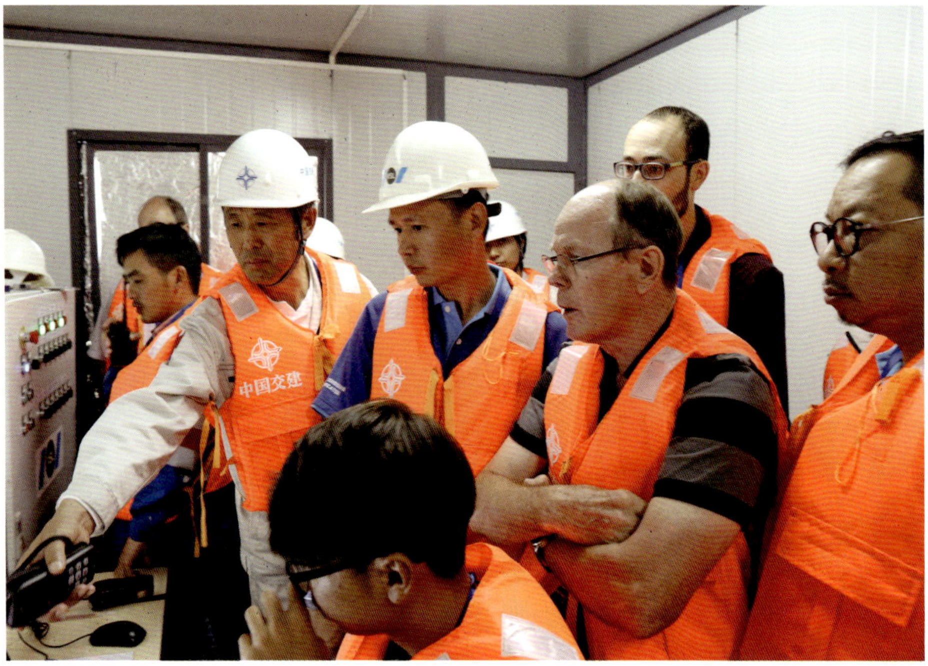

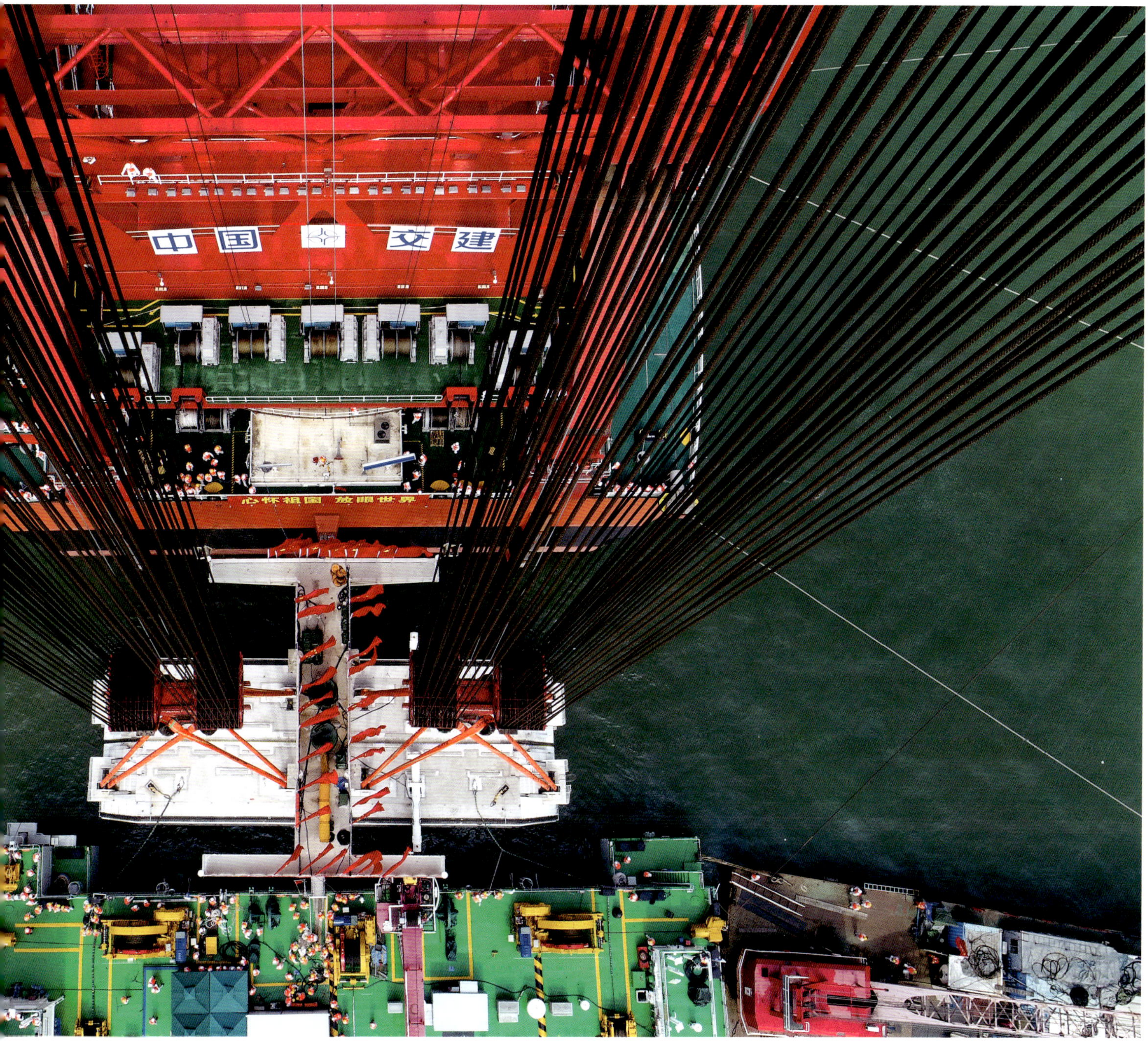
中国交建
心怀祖国 放眼世界

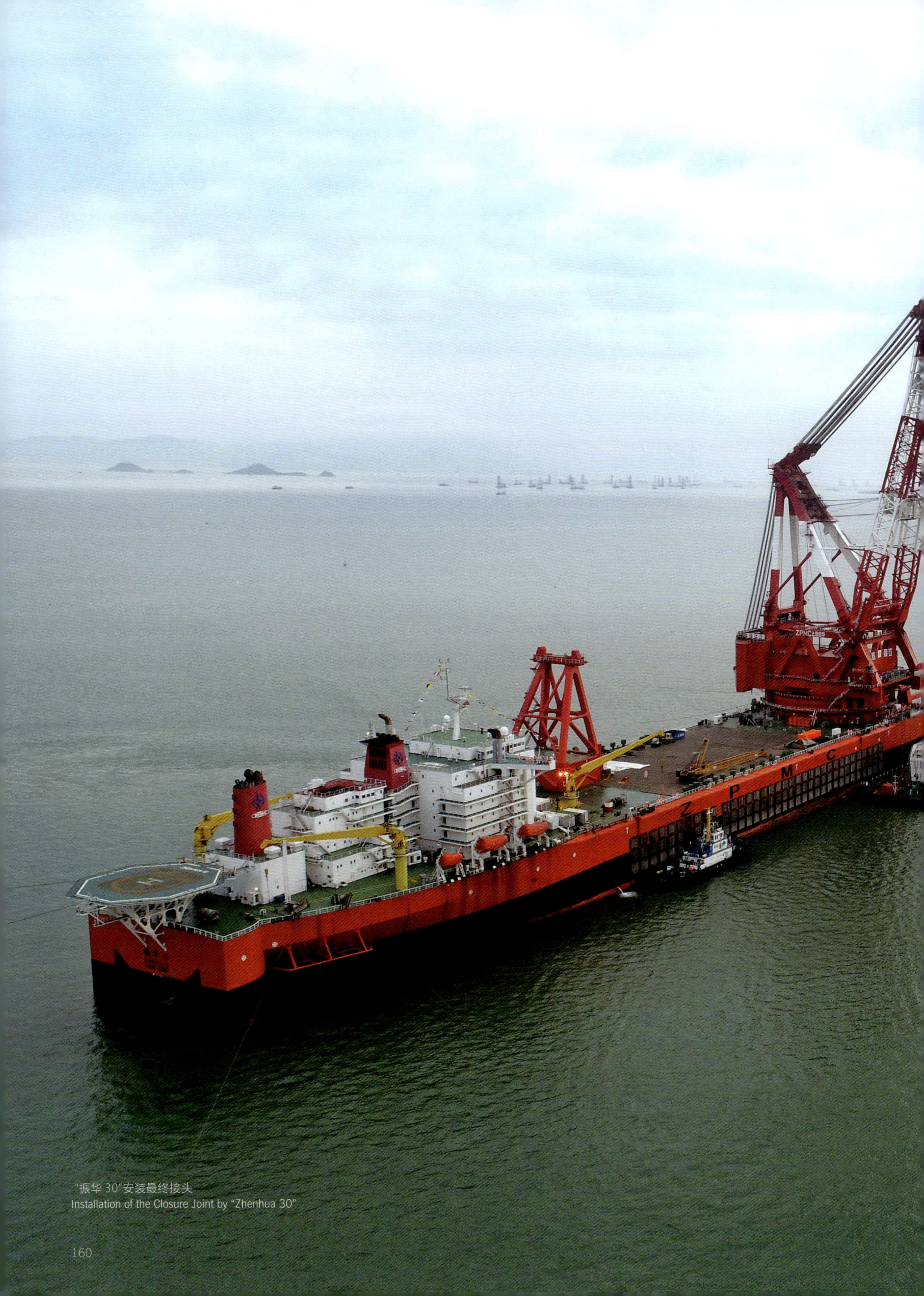

“振华 30”安装最终接头
Installation of the Closure Joint by “Zhenhua 30”

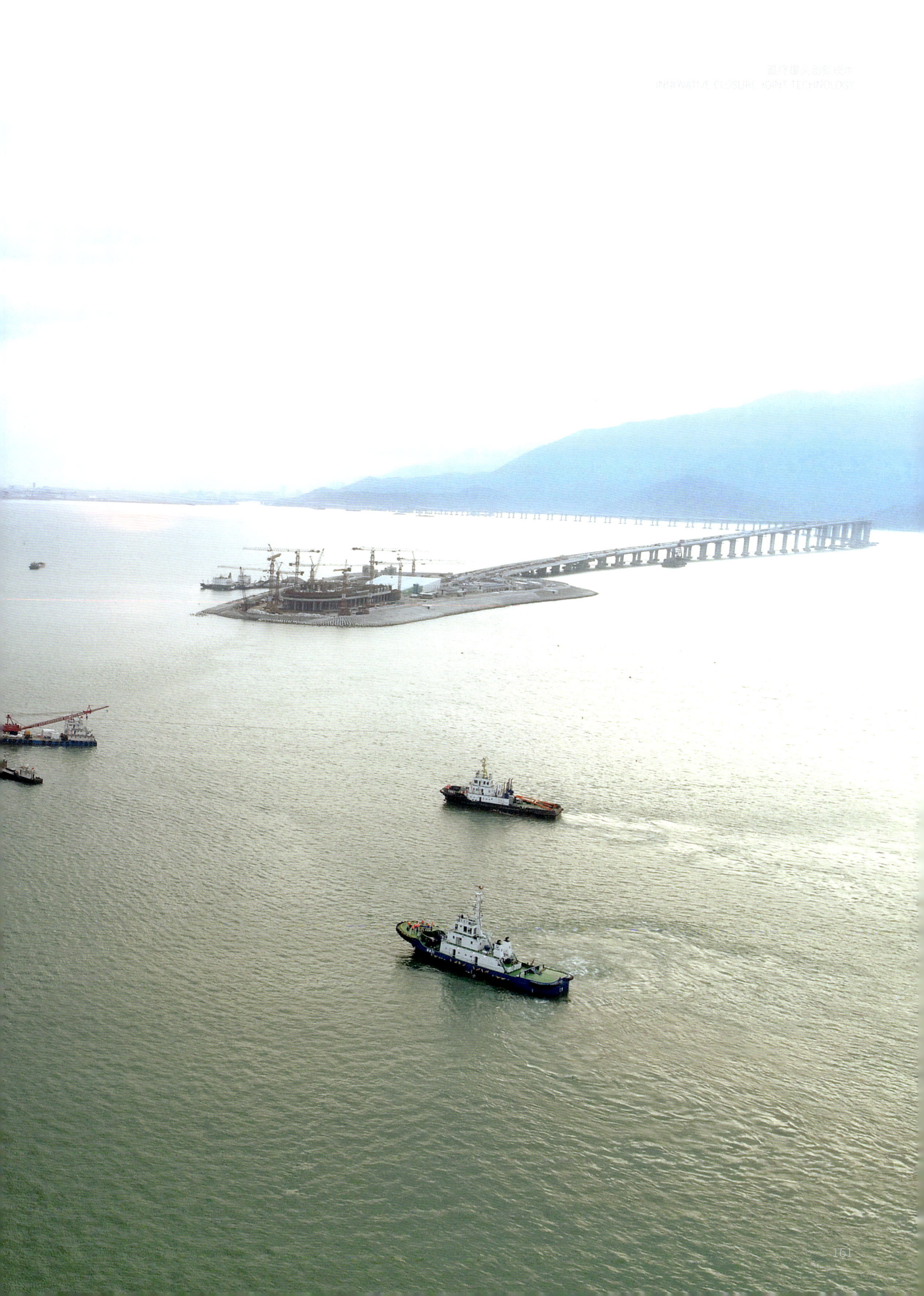

合龙焊接
CLOSURE WELDING

最终接头结合腔排水后需要立即进行刚接头焊接作业。

焊接作业受限在钢封门之间，作业空间狭窄，可使用机械辅助少，大量焊接作业产生的有害烟尘多，作业环境保障难度大。

空间狭窄和有害烟尘排出困难使焊接施工条件更加恶劣，作业难度大，作业效率存在不确定性，施工风险极大。

项目总经理部在上海振华基地，按照1:1比例制作了最终接头结合腔足尺模型，开展了长达一个月的合龙焊接演练，使施工人员熟悉施工环境，掌握施工方法，验证保障措施，提高合龙焊接的保证率。

The steel joint welding followed immediately after the water in the binding cavity of the closure joint was drained.

The welding was done between the steel sealing devices, and the working environment was unwelcome.

The working space was limited, usable mechanical facilitates were few, and the amount of the poisonous gas or smoke was huge. Narrow working space and poisonous smoke made the welding operation risky and the working efficiency indefinite.

The project management center at Shanghai Zhenhua designed a full-size model of the binding cavity of the closure joint by 1:1 ratio, followed by one whole month's closure welding test which familiarized the technicians with the working environment and the operation methods to guarantee the real operation was effective.

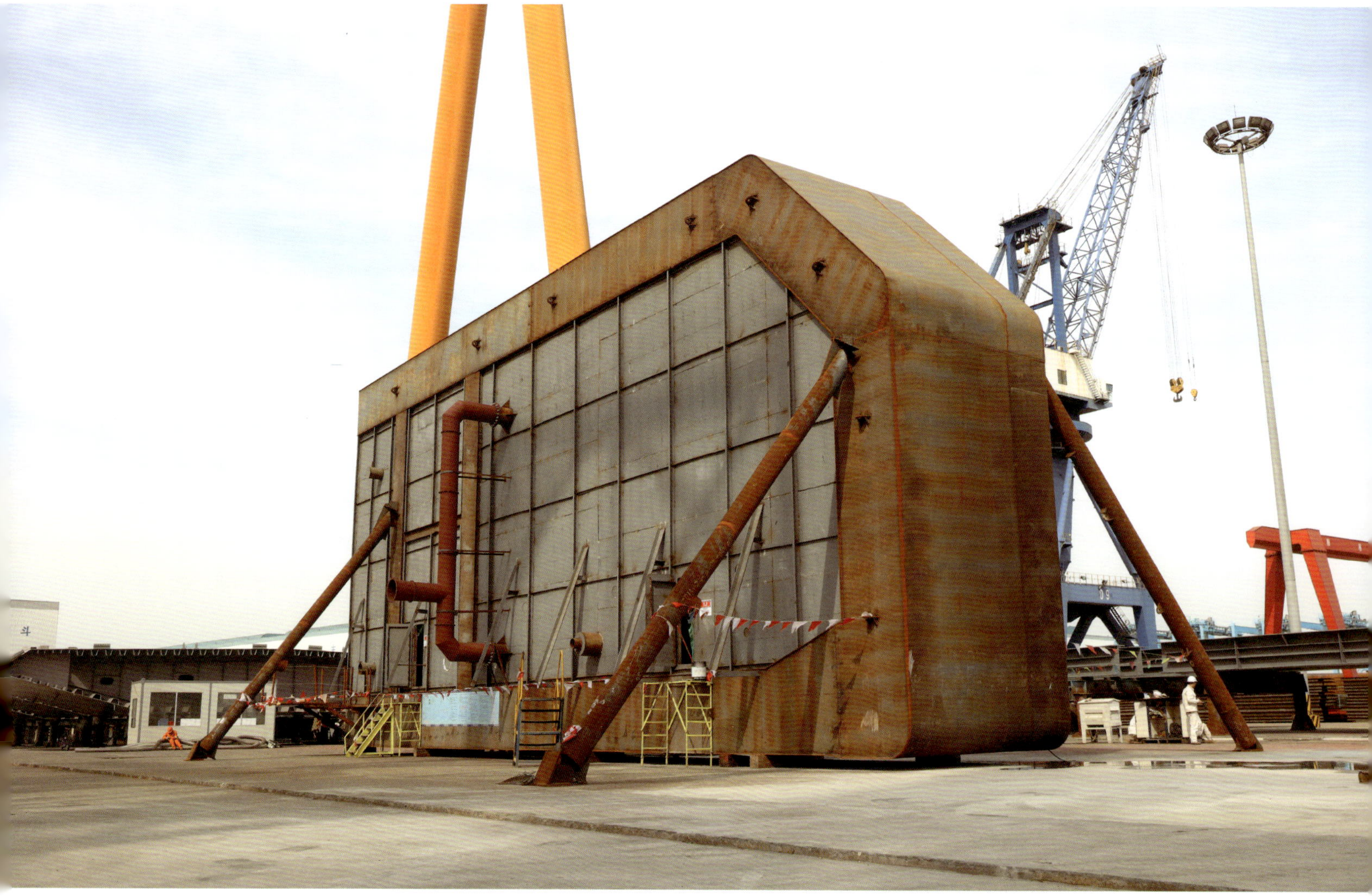

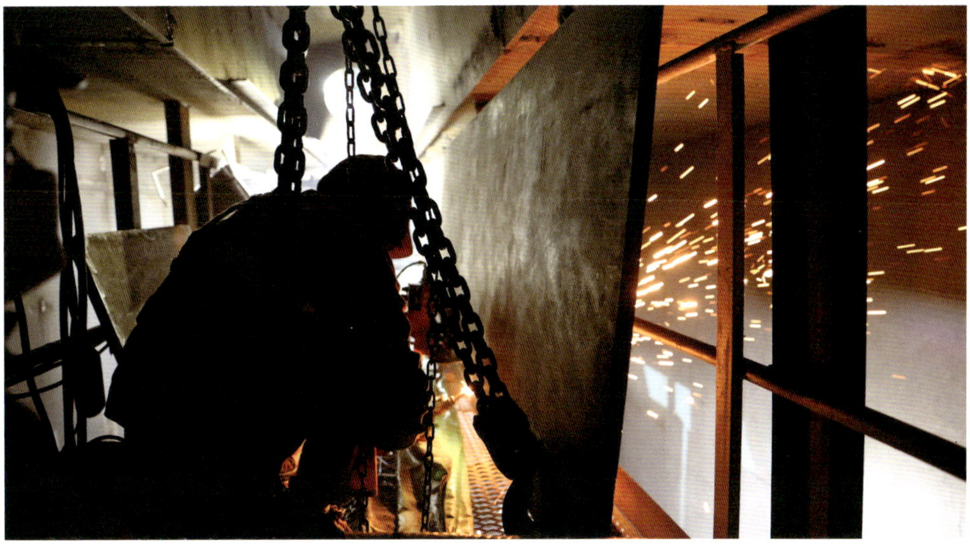

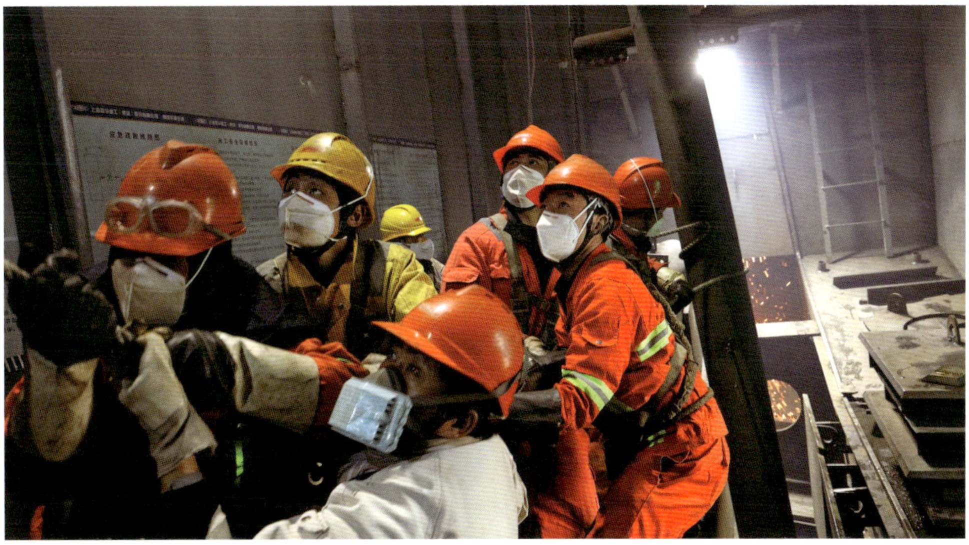

1. 最终接头结合腔足尺模型
   Full-Size Model of the Binding Cavity of the Closure Joint

2—3. 最终接头结合腔焊接演练
   Drill of Welding the Binding Cavity of the Closure Joint

最终接头合龙焊接施工焊接板厚、量大，空间狭窄，空气浑浊，焊接环境恶劣，且要求在最短时间内完成。

为降低安全风险，从5月5日上午7点30分开始，项目总经理部组织250余名高级焊工，采取"三班倒"的方式，历经478小时艰苦奋战，于2017年5月25日15点36分圆满完成合龙焊接。

焊缝总长2280米，一次性探伤合格率98.6%。

合龙焊接完成后，临时止水带的柔性连接变成永久性的刚性连接，标志着海底隧道全线贯通。

The welding plate was very thick and large, yet the working space was very narrow, and the air was stagnant. Such a bad working environment required the welding to be done in the briefest time.

For safety, the welding began at 7:30 on May 5 and the project management center organized more than 250 skilled welders who were divided into 3 shifts. After 478 hours' hard work, the welding was completed at 15:36 on May 25, 2017.

The welding seam was 2280 meters long, and the one-off percentage of pass for the fault detection was 98.6%.

After the closure welding was done, the temporary flexible joint of the water-stop was replaced by the permanent fixed joint, which marked the completion of the underwater tunnel.

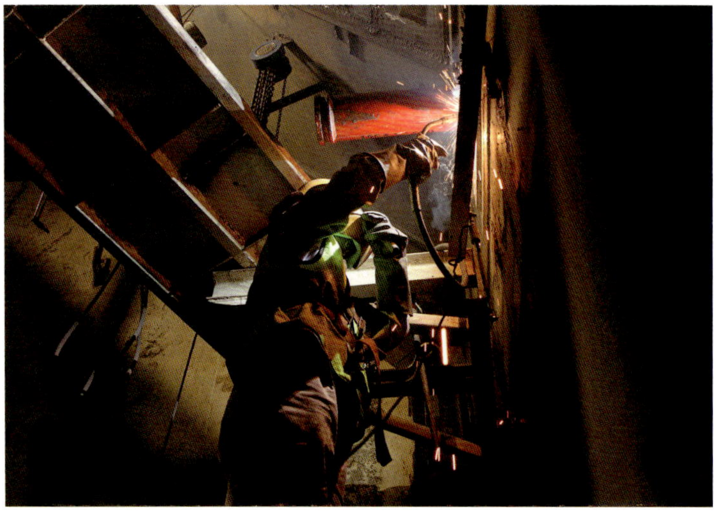

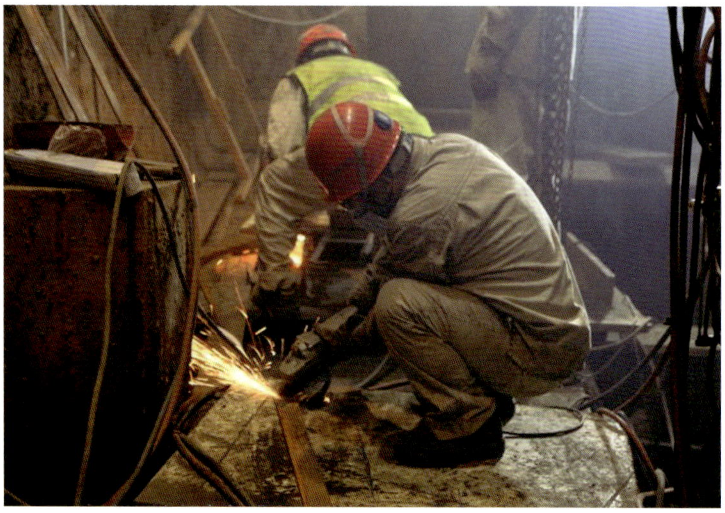

1 3. 最终接头结合腔焊接施工
Welding the Binding Cavity of the Closure Joint

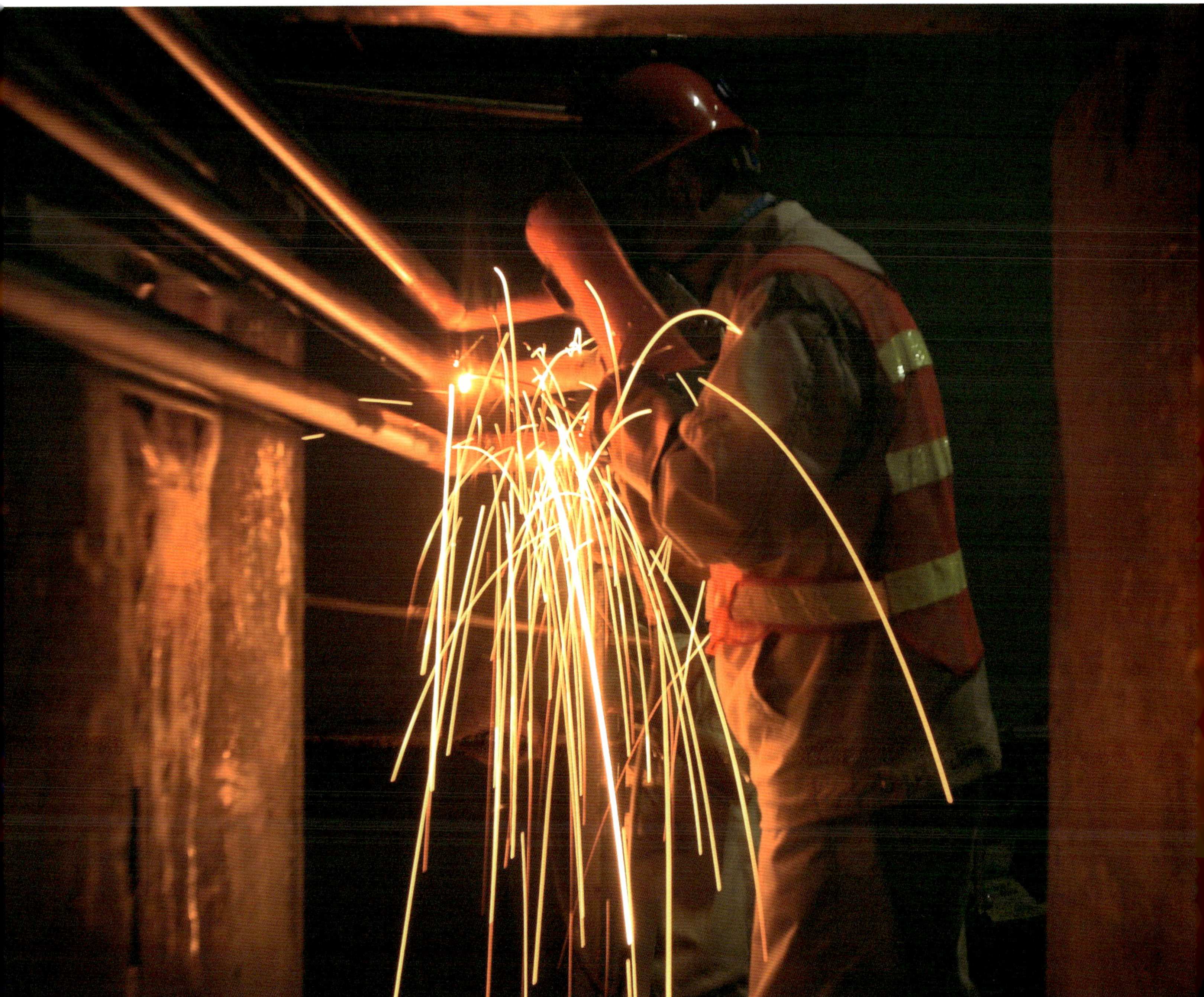

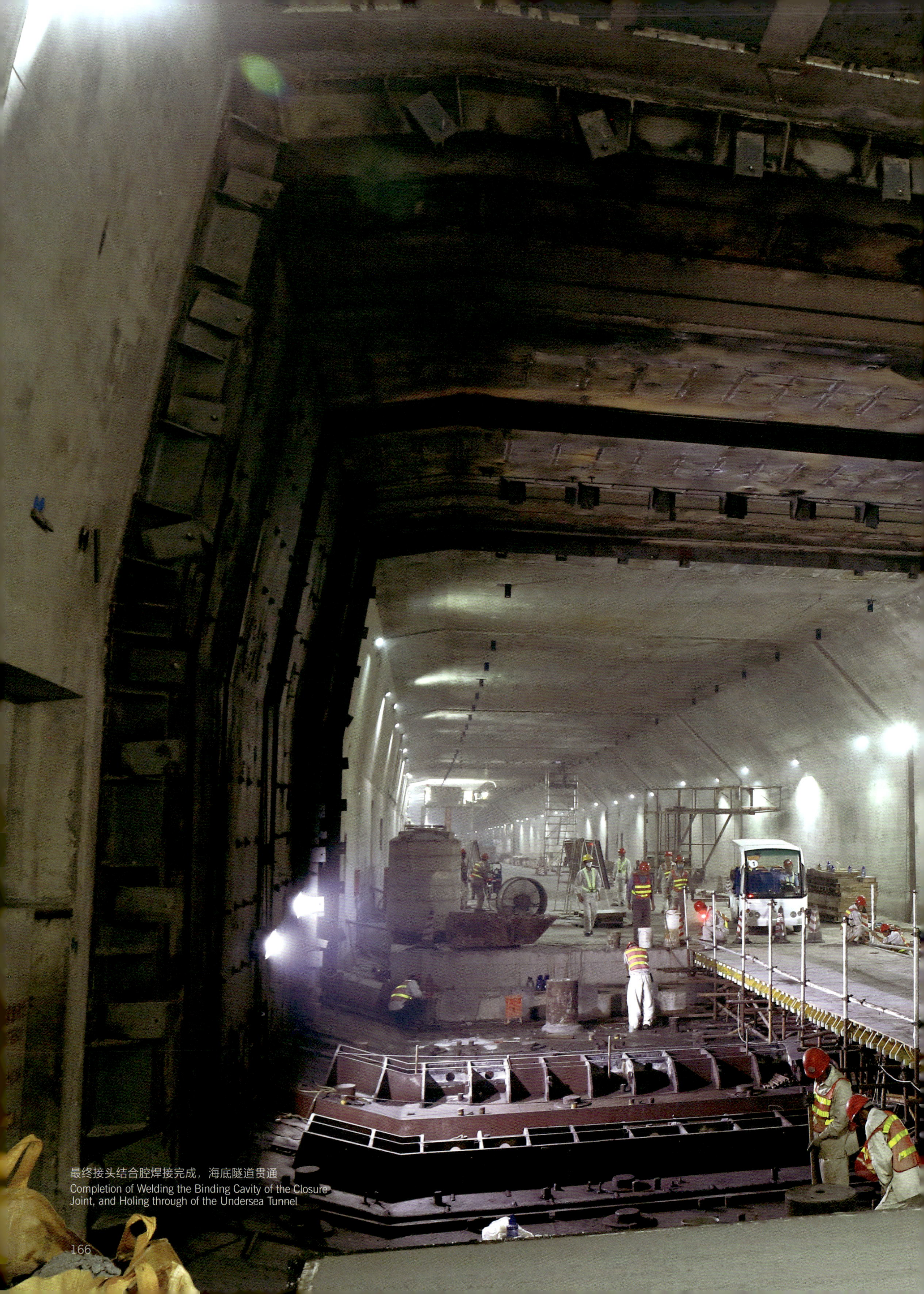

最终接头结合腔焊接完成，海底隧道贯通
Completion of Welding the Binding Cavity of the Closure Joint, and Holing through of the Undersea Tunnel

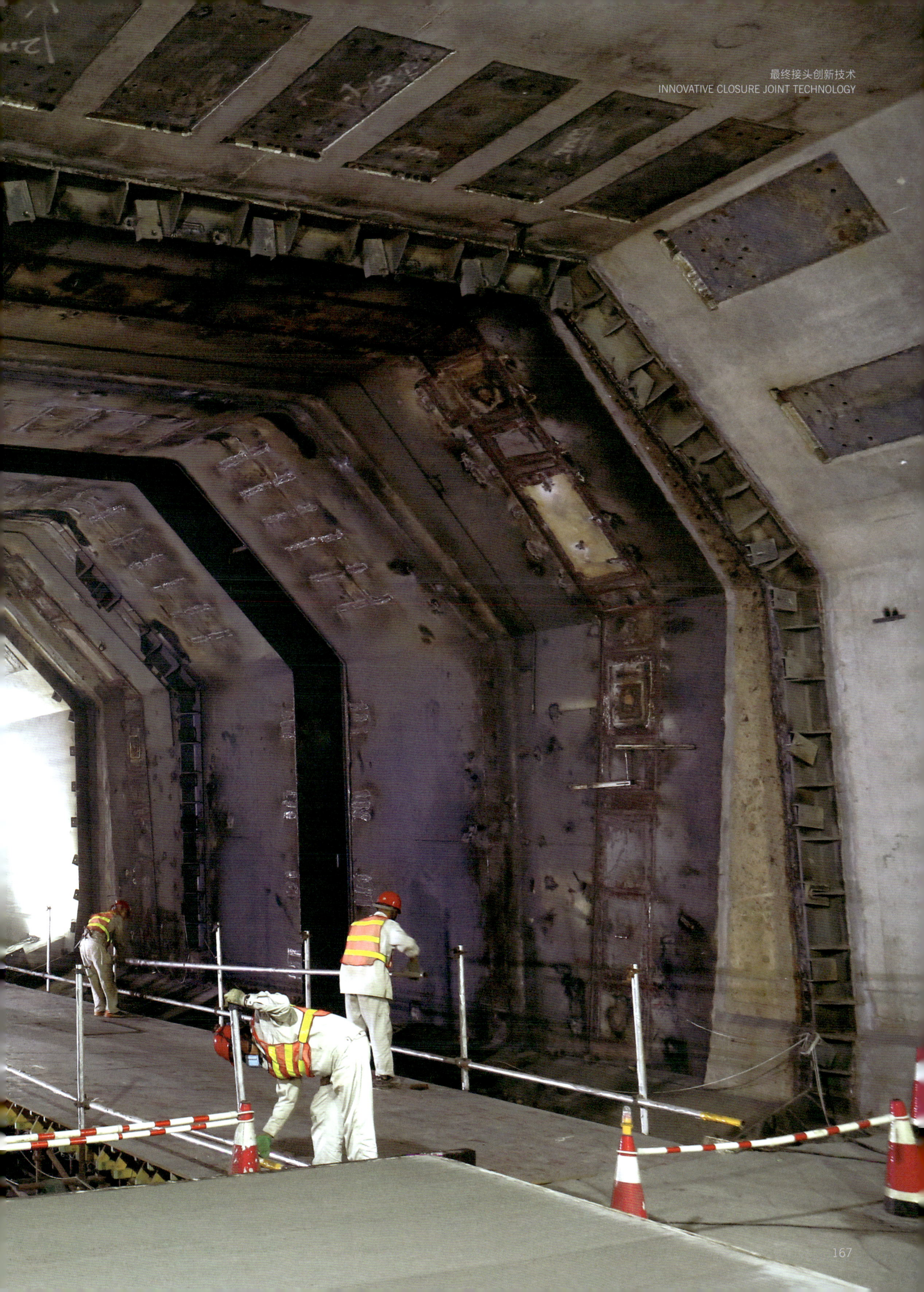

最终接头基础注浆

CLOSURE JOINT BASE GROUTING

为确保 E29、E30 沉管及最终接头的沉降均匀，在最终接头安装完成后，采用超低强度水下不分散混凝土对基础空腔进行注浆填充。

最终接头安装前，在两个刚接头处底部安装注浆管路；最终接头安装及锁定回填后，在隧道两侧安装竖向注浆管路；以整平船为注浆平台，拌合船供料，采用泵送工艺对刚接头部位的基础进行后注浆处理。

To ensure that the landing of the immersed tubes of E29, E30 and the closure joint meet the project requirements, anti-washout concrete of ultra-low intensity applicable for underwater operation was used for the grouting into the base cavity after the closure joint was installed.

Before the installation, grouting pipelines was installed in the bottom part of the two joints. When the closure joint installation and locking backfill were finished, vertical grouting pipeline was installed on the two sides of the tunnel. The leveling barges were used as the grouting platforms where the material provided by the mixing barge was pumped into base part of the closure joint.

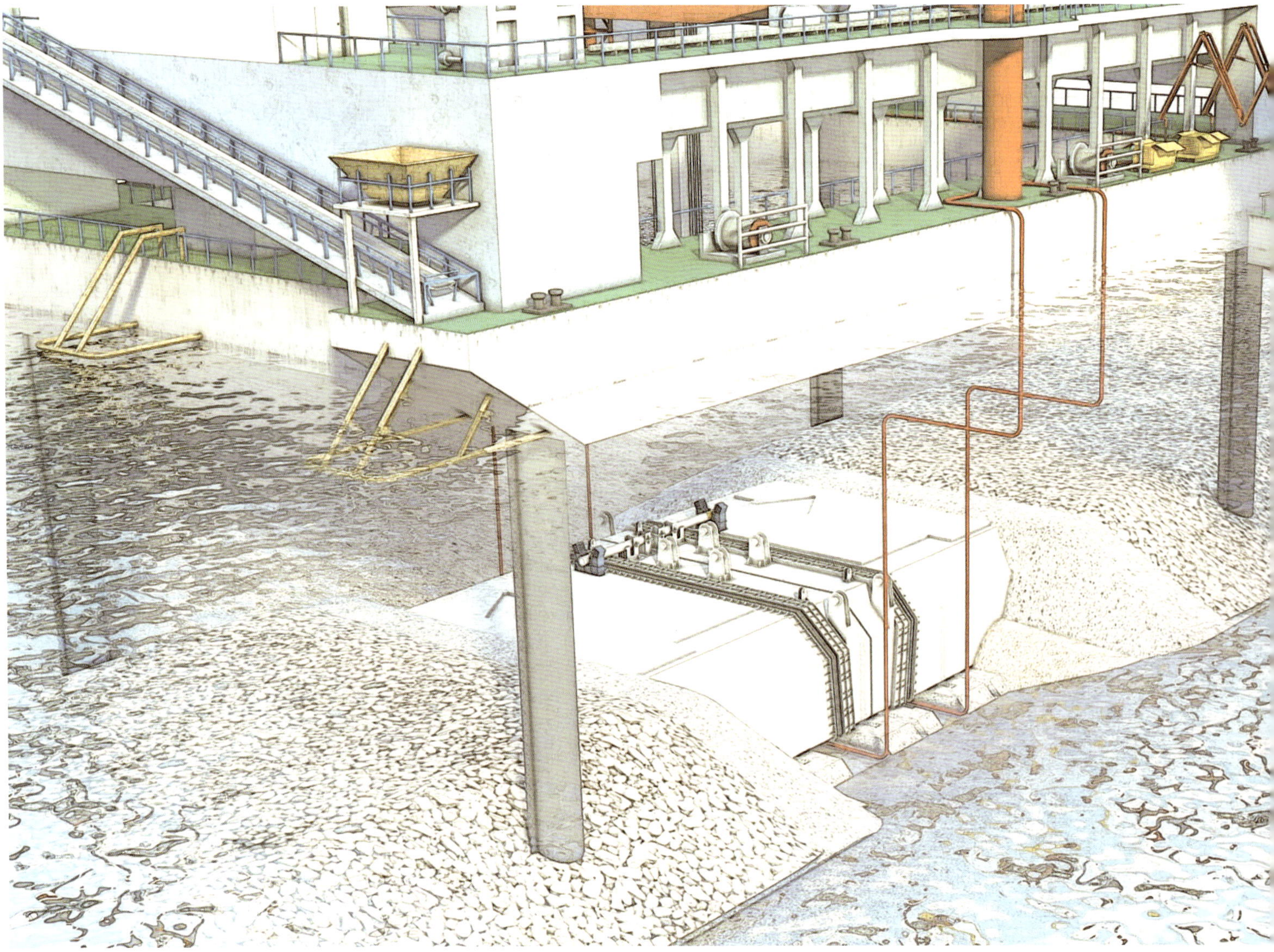

1. 最终接头基础注浆三维图
3-D Diagram of the Closure Joint Base Grouting
2. 最终接头基础注浆管路布设
Pipeline Arrangement of he Closure Joint Base Grouting
3. 最终接头基础注浆施工
Grouting into the Closure Joint Base

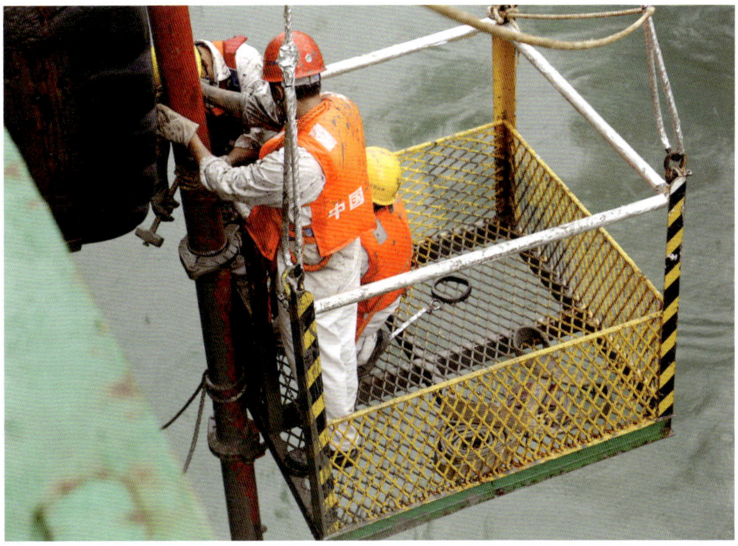

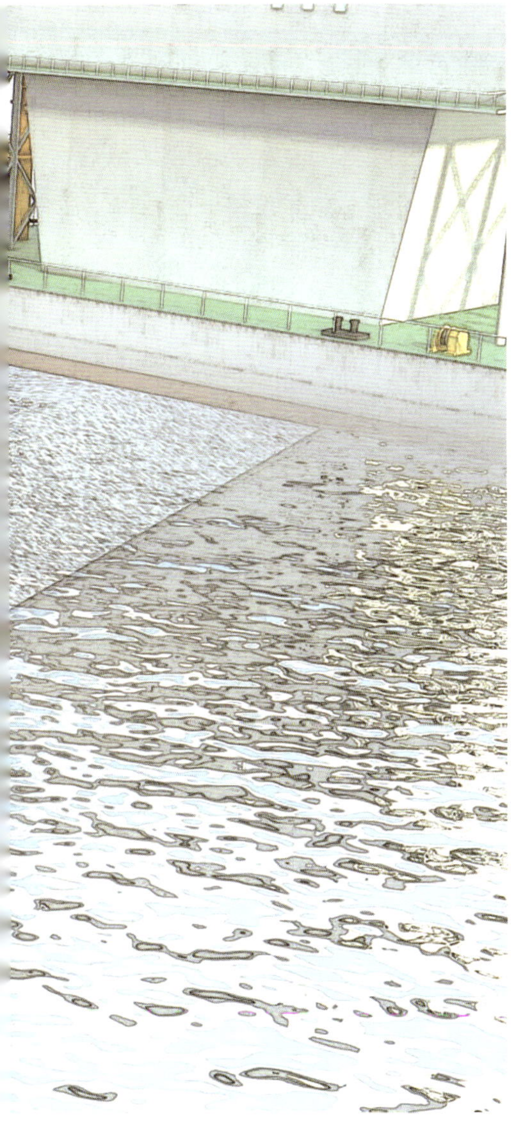

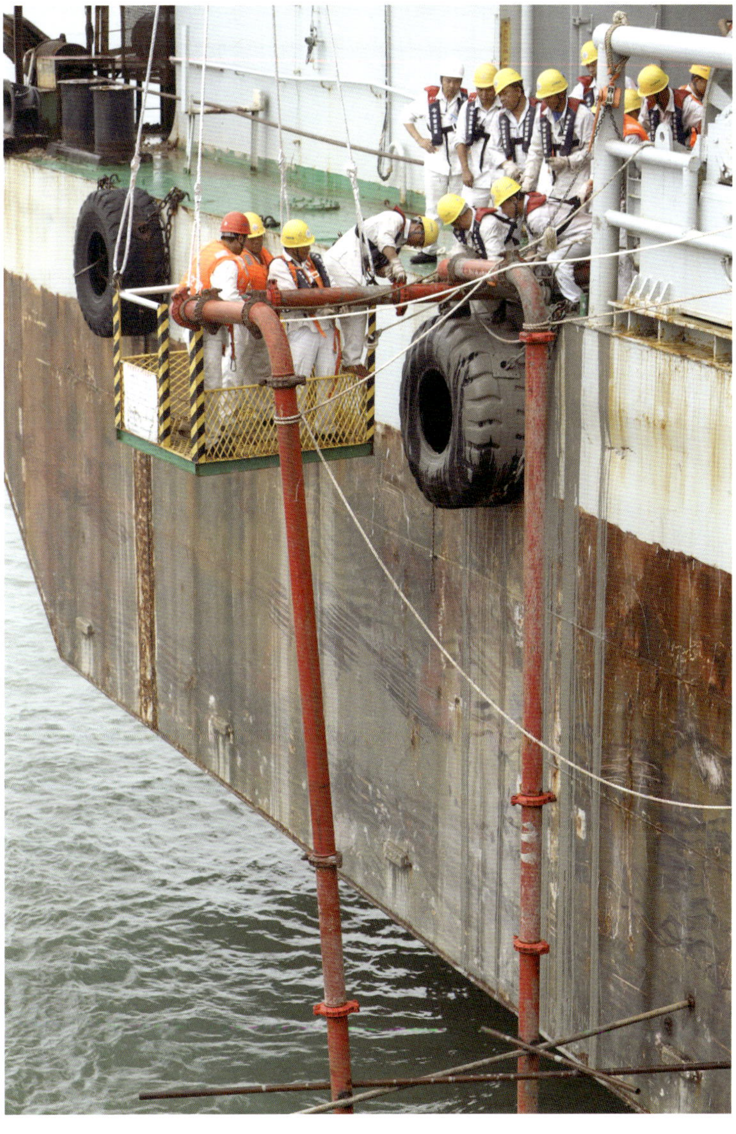

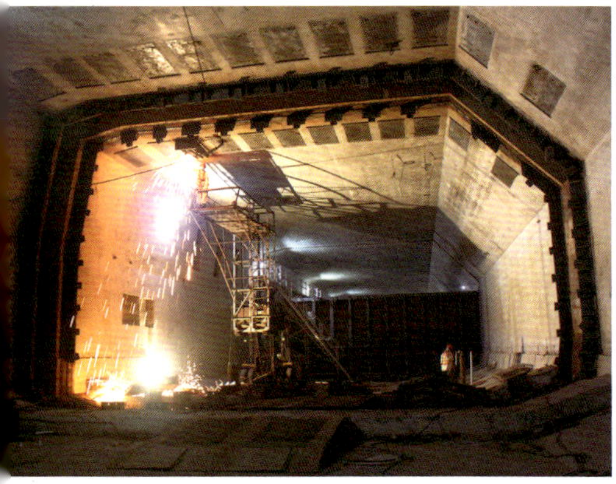

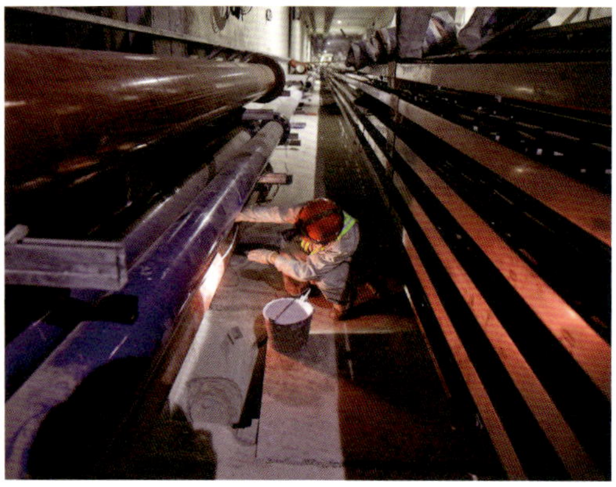

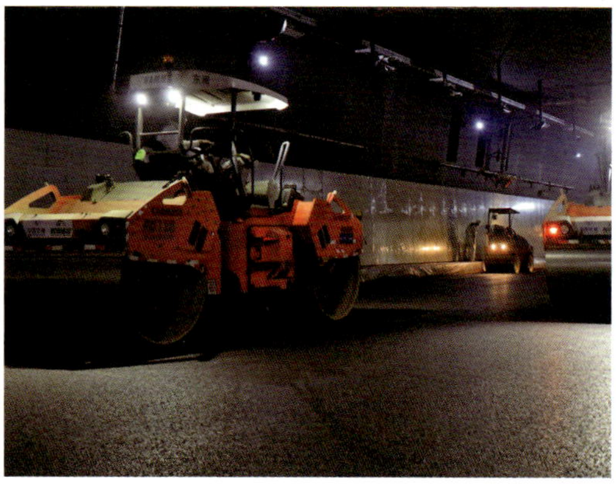

管内施工

IN-TUBE OPERATION

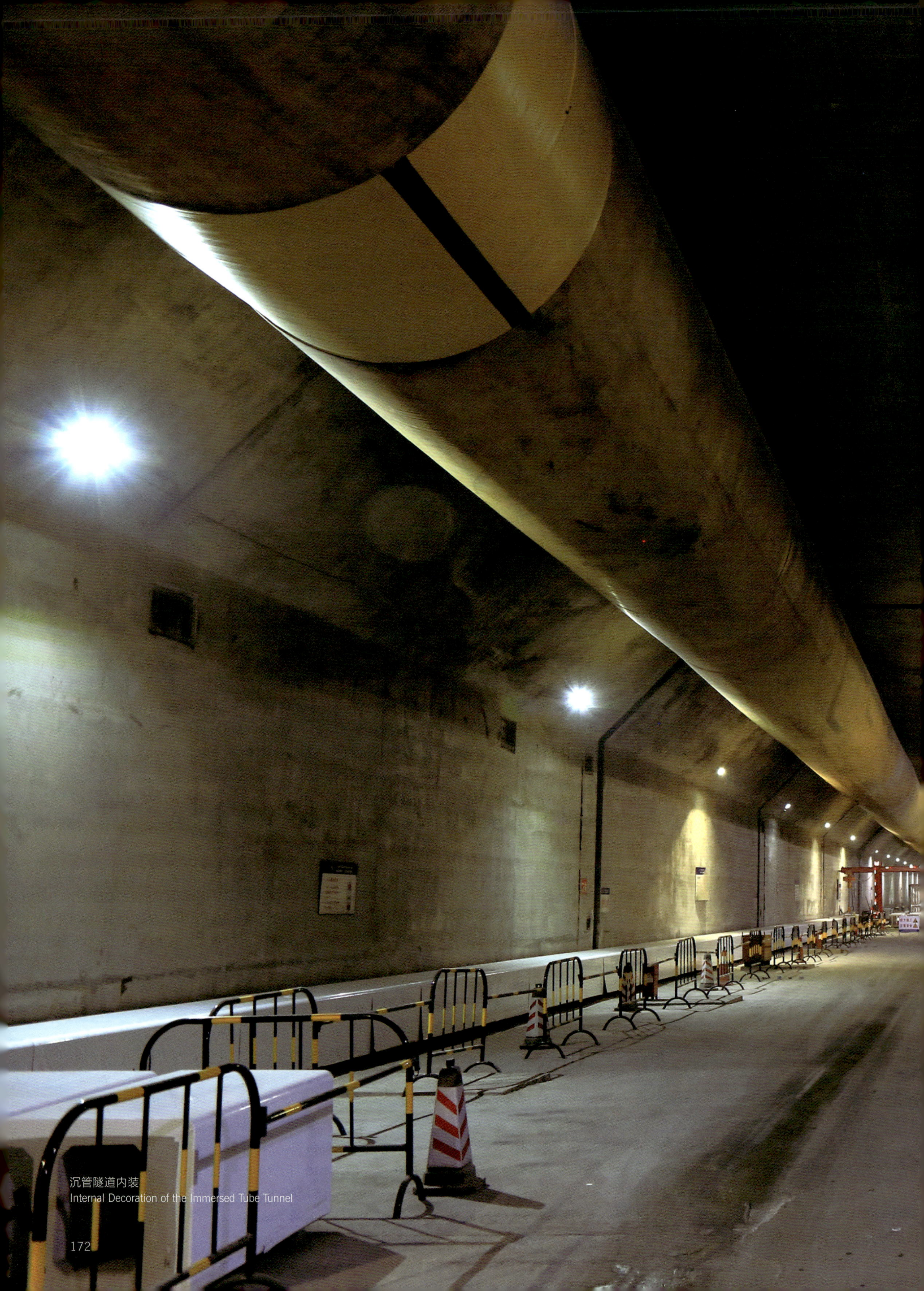

沉管隧道内装
Internal Decoration of the Immersed Tube Tunnel

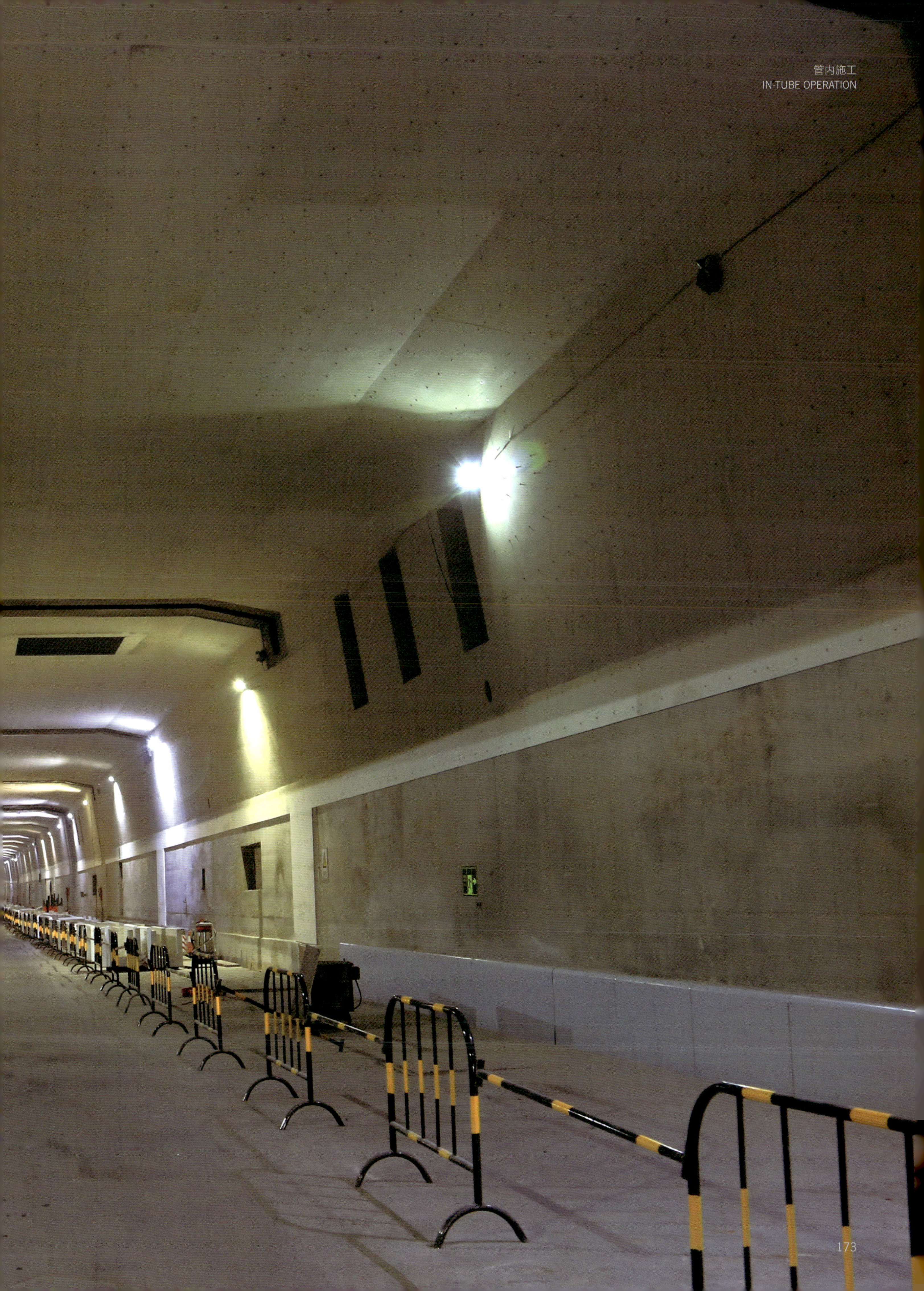

钢封门拆除
REMOVAL OF THE STEEL SEALING DEVICES

沉管钢封门采用循环使用的原则，待沉管安装完成后拆除钢封门运回沉管预制厂用于以后批次沉管舾装；为保证隧道结构安全，建设期间始终保留3道封门以应对突发事件。

The in-tube steel sealing devices could be recycled. After the immersed tube installation was completed, the steel sealing devices were removed and sent back to precast factory for future use. To guarantee the structural safety of the tunnel, three steel sealing devices were kept at hand in the whole process of construction in case any accident might happen.

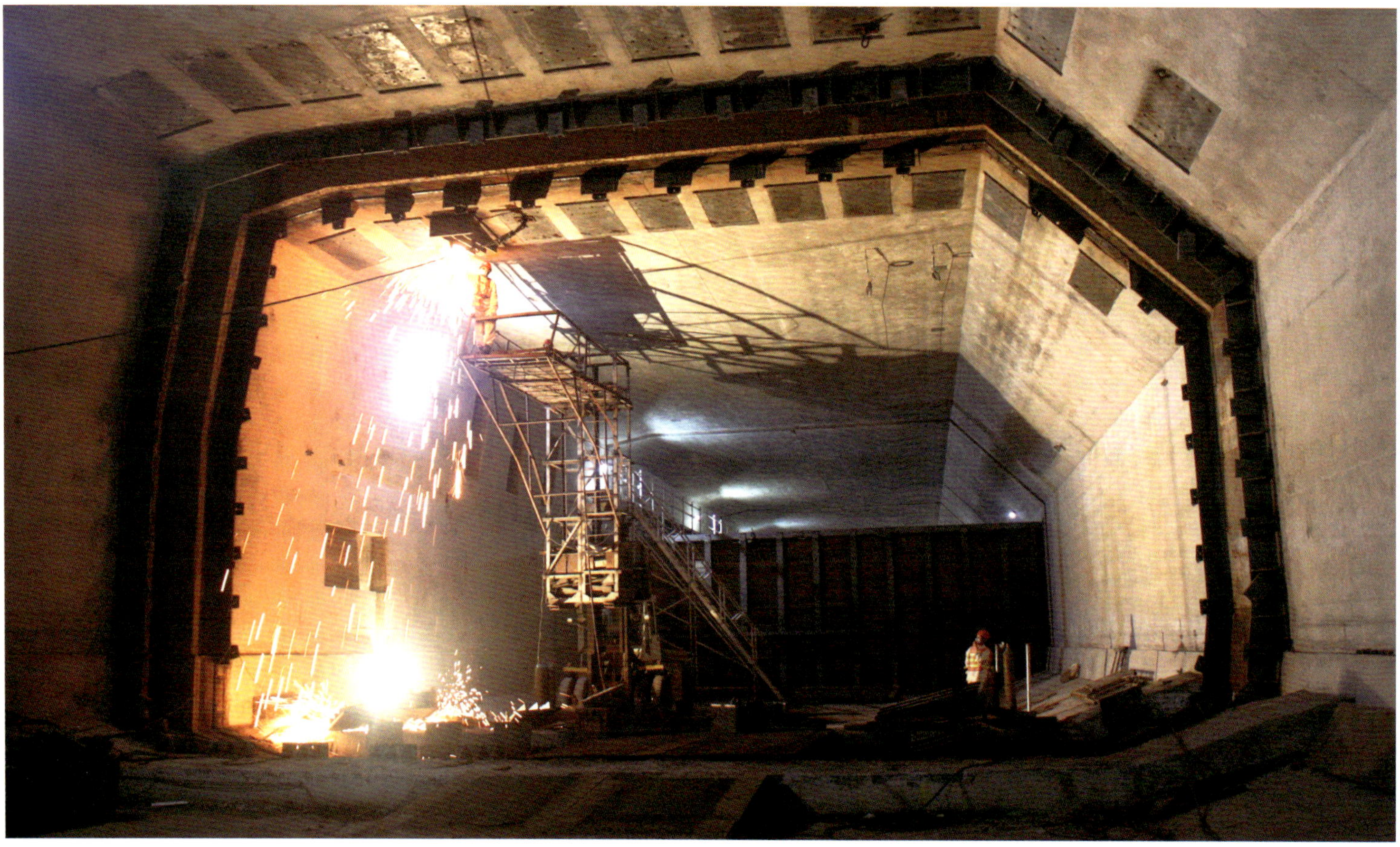

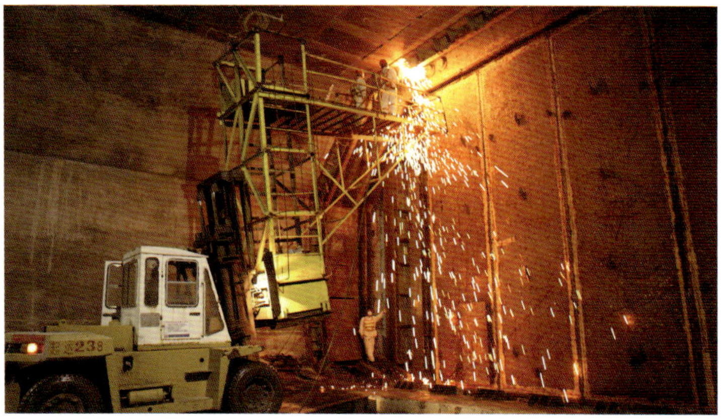

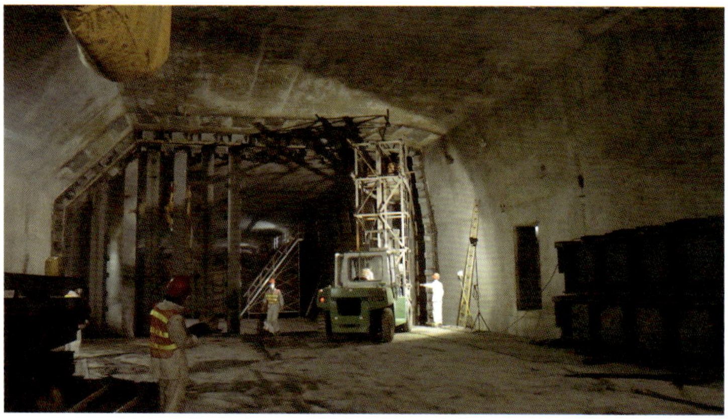

压舱混凝土浇筑

BALLASTING CONCRETE PLACEMENT

为满足抗浮要求，沉管安装完成后，在隧道左右行车道底板浇筑厚约1米的压仓混凝土，实现隧道内压重，并兼做隧道路面路基。

To meet the anti-floating requirements, after tube was landed on the trench bed, ballasting concrete of about 1 meter thick was placed on the bedding under the driving lanes on the two sides of the tunnel. This ballasting concrete placement could also function as the road base in the tunnel.

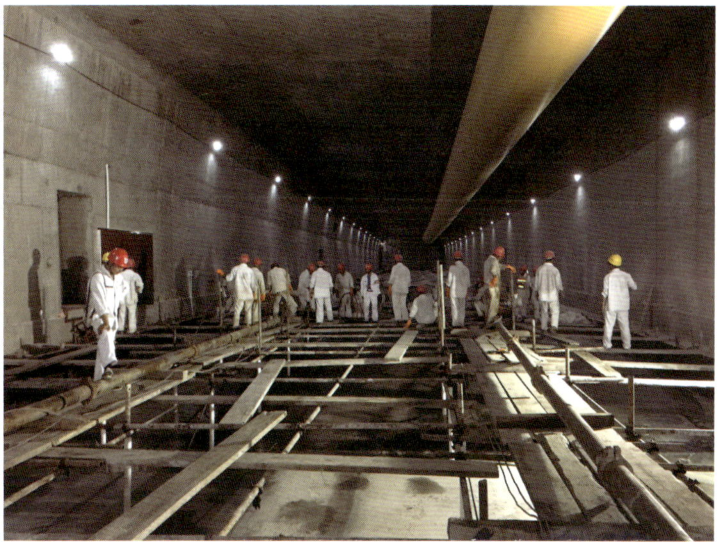

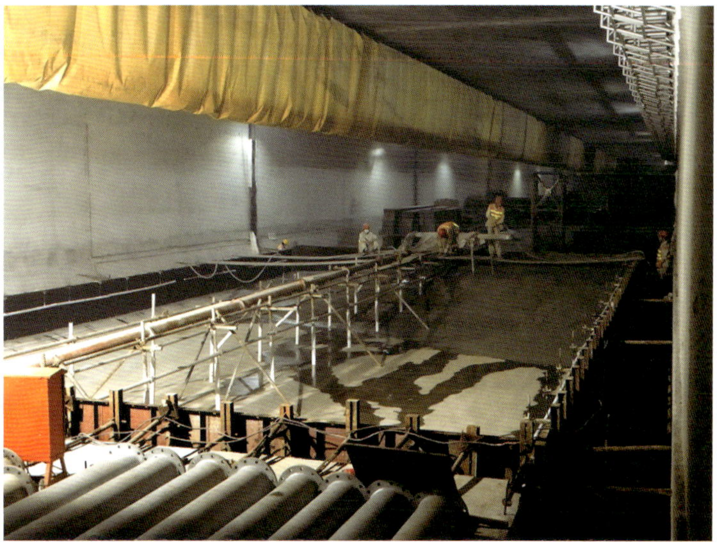

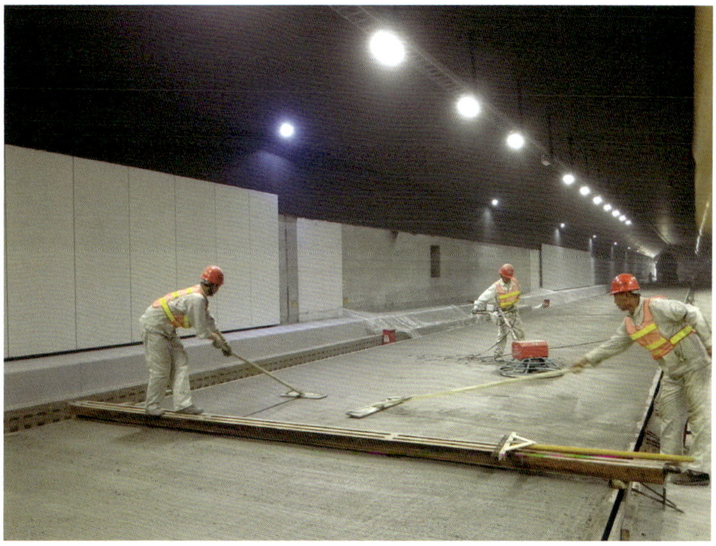

1. 钢封门钢梁拆除
   Removing the Steel Beam of the Steel Sealing Devices
2. 钢封门拆除
   Removal of the Steel Sealing Devices
3. 钢封门牛腿拆除
   Removing the Beam Hangers of the Steel Sealing Devices
4. 压舱混凝土模板搭设
   Construction of the Ballasting Concrete Model
5. 压舱混凝土浇筑
   Ballast Tank Concrete Casting
6. 压舱混凝土浇筑完成并收面
   Ballasting Concrete Placement and Surface Finishing

检修道预制构件
PRECAST UNIT IN THE MAINTENANCE TRAIL

1. 沉管隧道检修道基础浇筑
Grouting into the Maintenance Trail Base in the Immersed Tube Tunnel

2. 沉管隧道检修道安装
Installation of the Maintenance Trail in the Immersed Tube Tunnel

3. 沉管隧道检修道安装质量测量
Quality Measurement of the Maintenance Trail Installation in the Immersed Tube Tunnel

4. 完成安装的沉管隧道检修道
Maintenance Trail Installation Completed in the Immersed Tube Tunnel

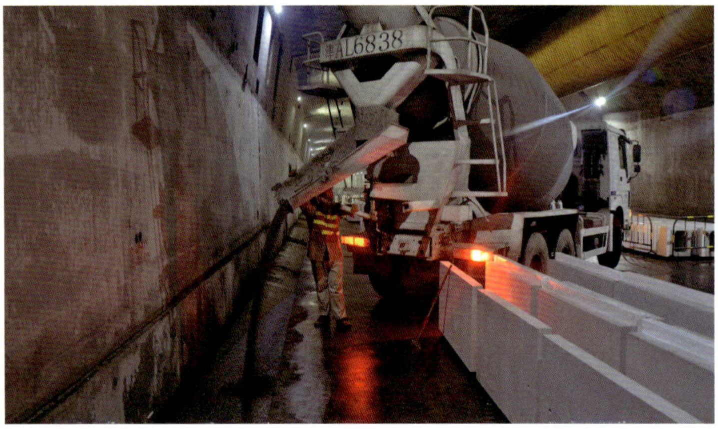

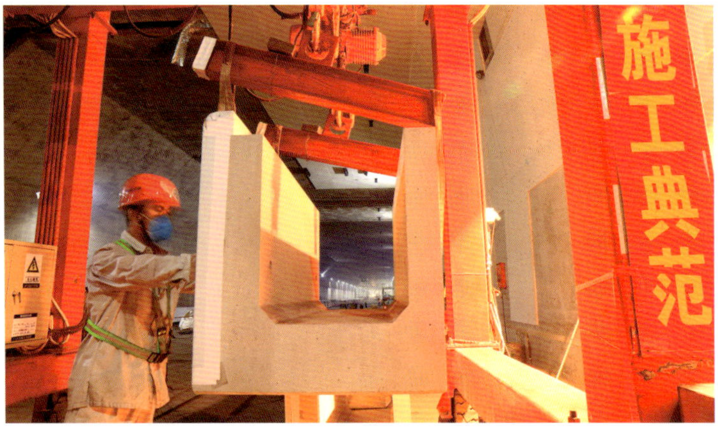

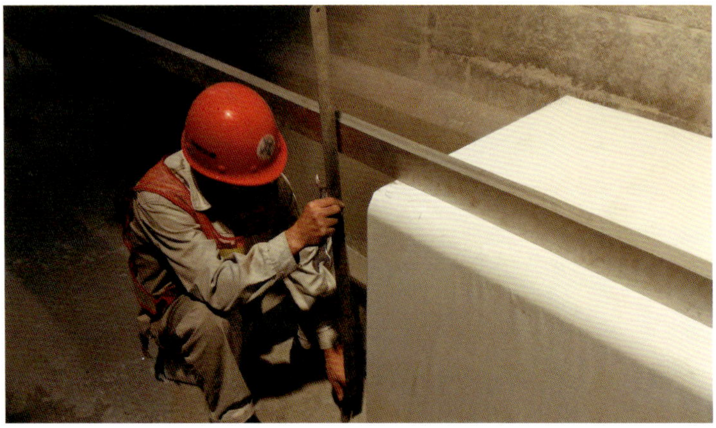

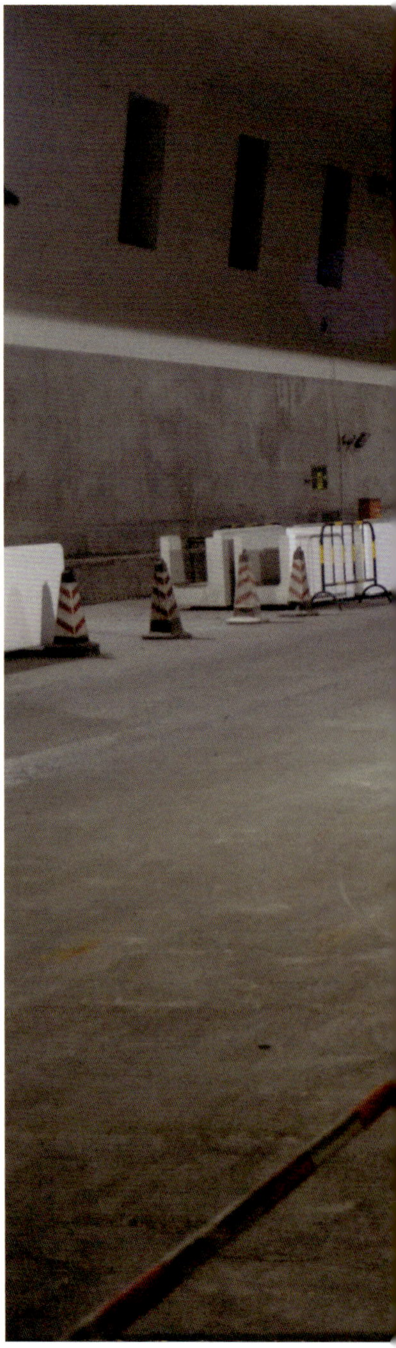

隧道检修道布置在敞开段、减光段外侧和暗埋段、沉管段的内外侧，兼排水沟功能；其中沉管段内侧检修道设有预制盖板，以便后期维护。

检修道采用预制钢筋混凝土结构，强度等级C45，标准长度150厘米，在工厂制造完成后运至现场安装。

The maintenance trail inside the tunnel was positioned in the open section, the outside of the light reduction section, tube burial section, the inside and outside of the tube-landing section, and functioned as drainage ditch. Precast cover plates were positioned in the inside of the tube-landing section for future maintenance.

The maintenance trail employed the precast steel and concrete structures with the C45 strength grading and a length of 150 centimeters which would be moved to the construction site after the precast was finished in the factory.

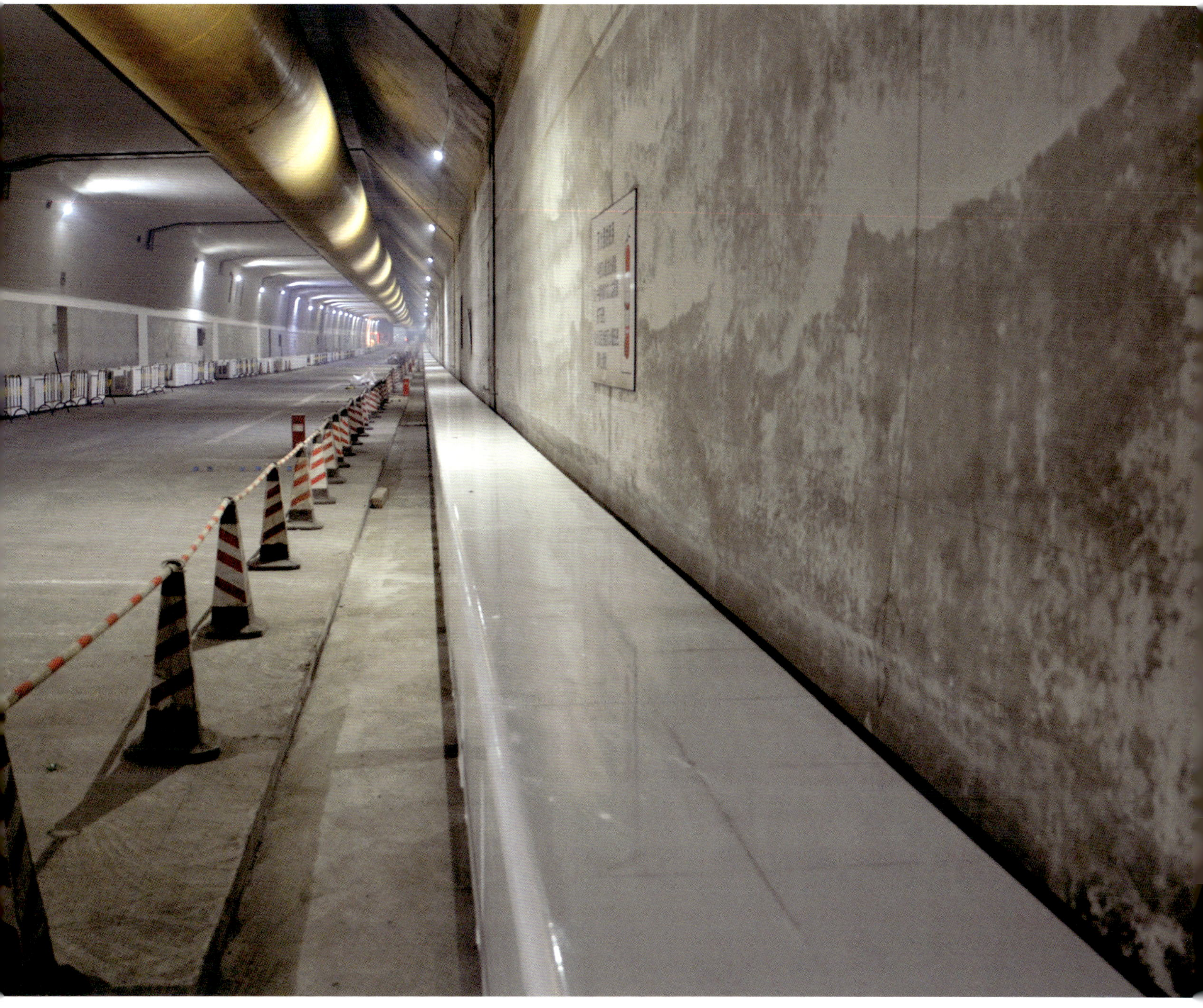

线性排水沟安装

INSTALLATION OF LINEAR DRAINAGE DITCH

暗埋段、沉管段行车道外侧及隧道入口设置排水沟，直径30厘米，底面标高低于检修道底面标高；每隔22.5米设置一沉沙井，以排放路面表层水。

Along the outer sides of the driving lanes in the section of buried tubes and immersed tubes as well as at the entrance of the tunnel, drainage ditches of 30 centimeters in diameter were built. These ditches bottom elevation was lower than that of the maintenance Trail. A sediment well was built every 22.5 meters along the ditch for the drainage of the water on the road surface.

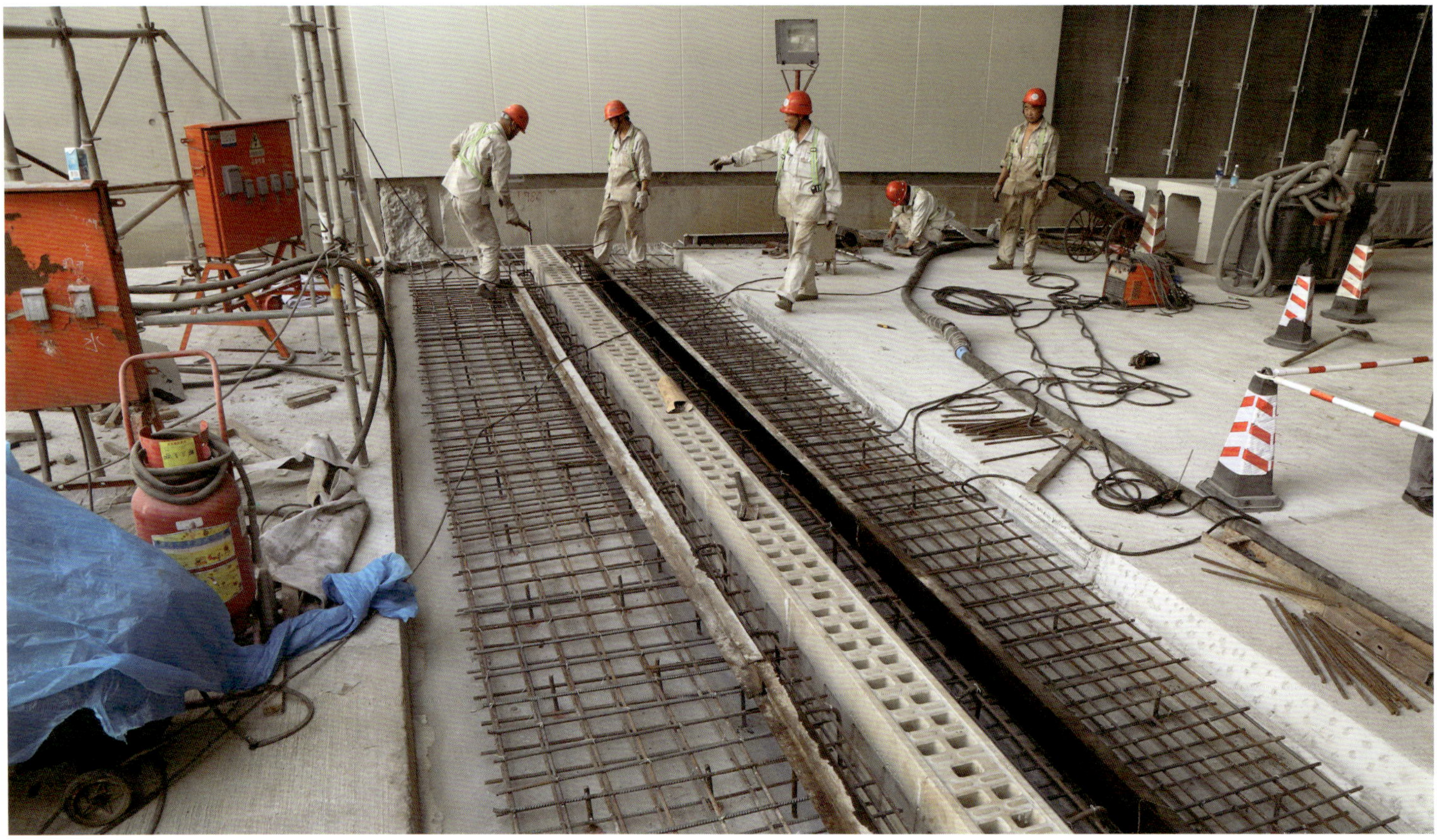

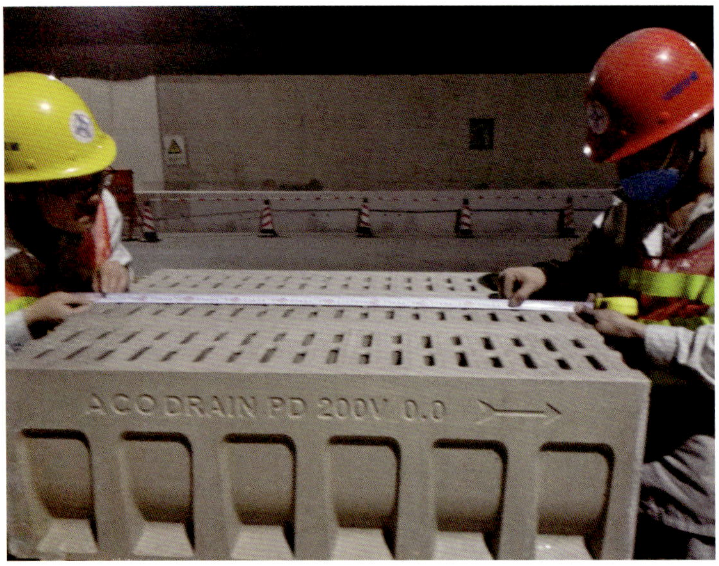

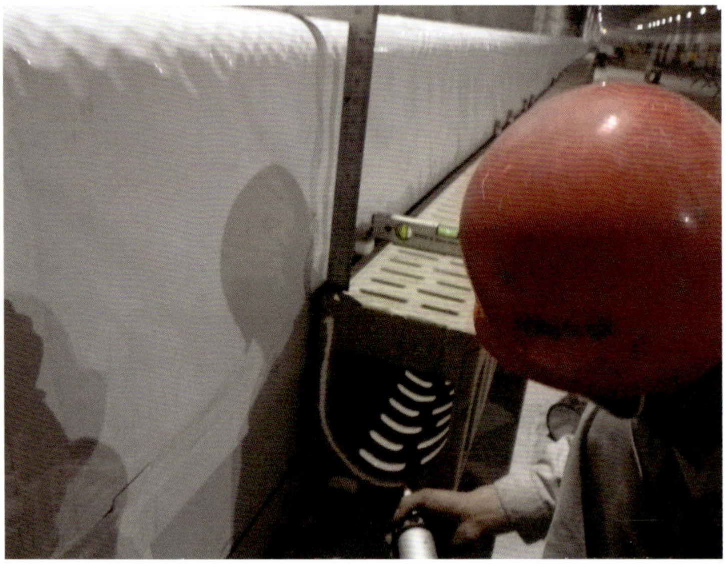

隧道防火板
IN-TUBE FIREPROOF PLATES

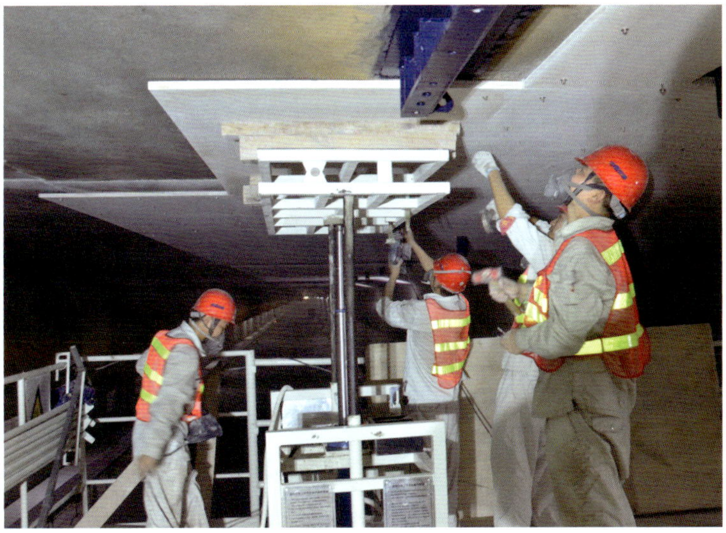

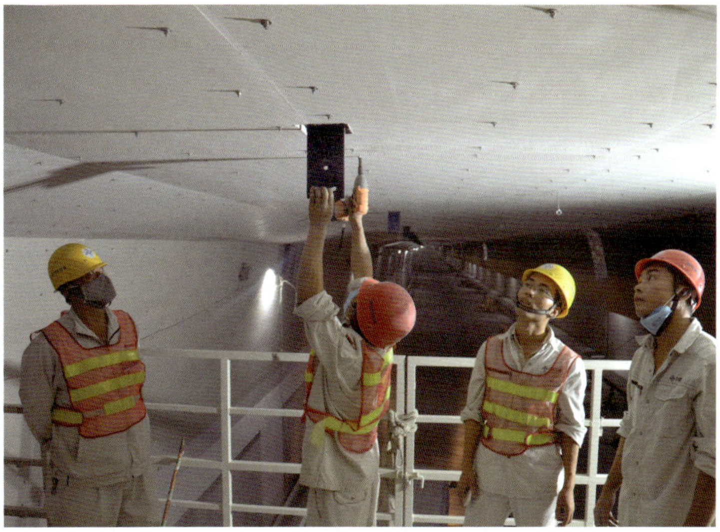

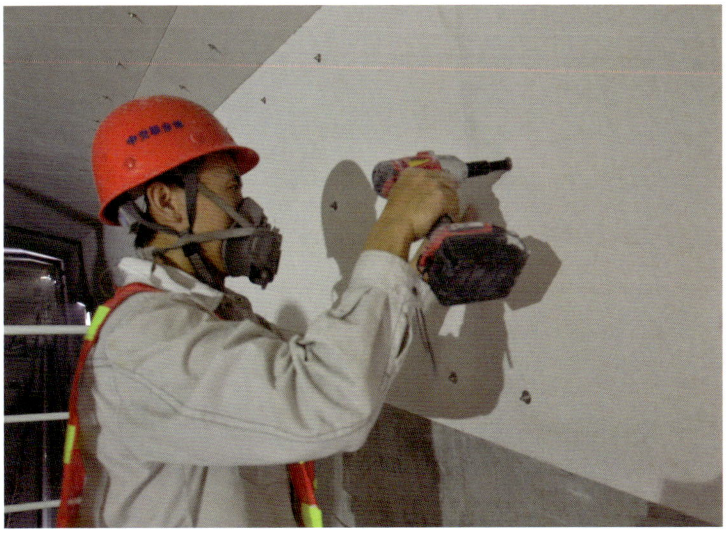

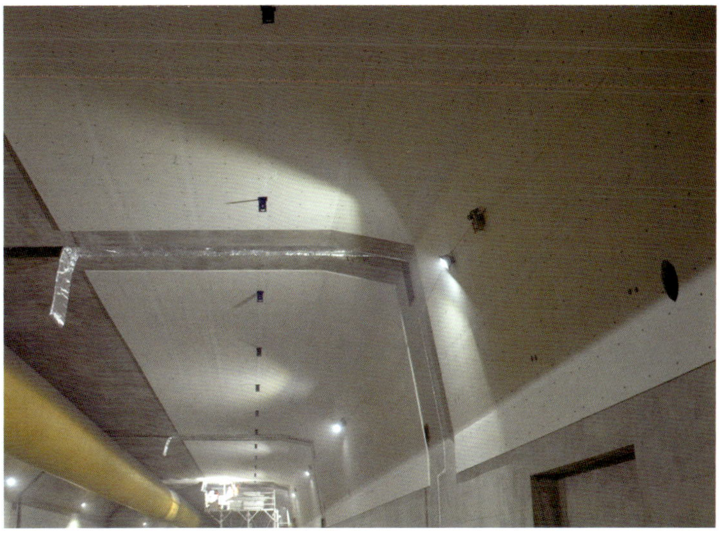

隧道结构防火按一类隧道设计，采用RABT标准升温曲线测试的耐火极限不低于2小时。

采用外敷防火板方式，防火内衬布置在隧道顶部及排烟道内。

The construction of the in-tube fire-proof devices followed the highest standard for tunneling. The fire resisting rating by RABT was 2 hours.

The technique of external application of the fire-proof plates wass adopted, and the internal lining was installed on the ceilings of the tunnel as well as inside the smoke track.

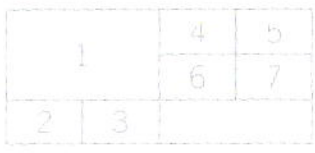

1. 隧道口横截沟安装施工
Installation of Cross-Sectional Trench at the Tunnel Entrance and Exit

2—3. 线形排水沟安装
Installation of the Linear Drainage Ditch

4—7. 隧道防火板安装
Installation of the Fire-Proof Plate inside the Tunnel

管内装修
IN-TUBE DECORATION

隧道装饰采用专用隧道装饰面板（搪瓷钢板），包括行车道两侧检修道顶向上2.75米的范围，通过搭建龙骨安全固定在行车道内壁，实现表面整体平整光滑，色泽一致，边角线形平直顺滑，套割吻合，边缘整齐的效果。

Special decoration plates (porcelain steel plates) were used for the in-tube decoration, including the area within the limit of 2.75 meters on the ceiling of the maintenance trail on the outer sides of the driving lanes. Keels were fixed on the inside walls along the driving lanes. And the walls after the decoration were smooth on surface with soft colors, smooth curves, exact cuttings and neat embeddings.

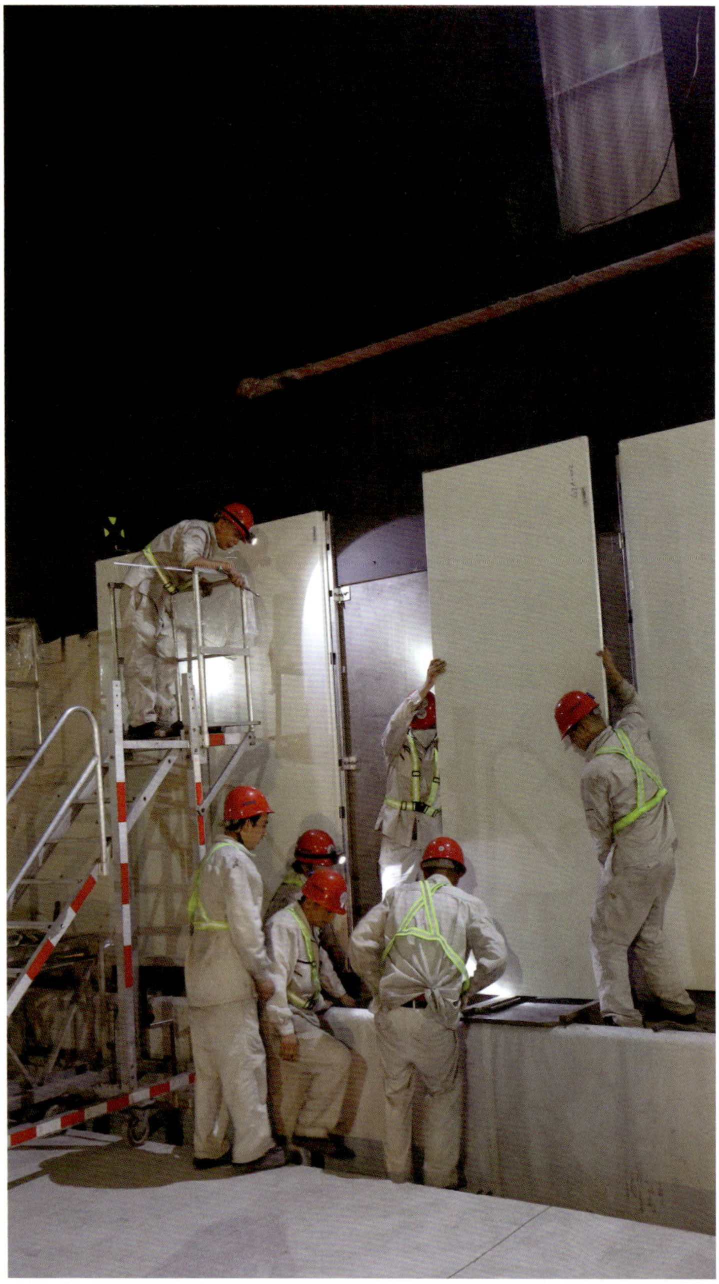

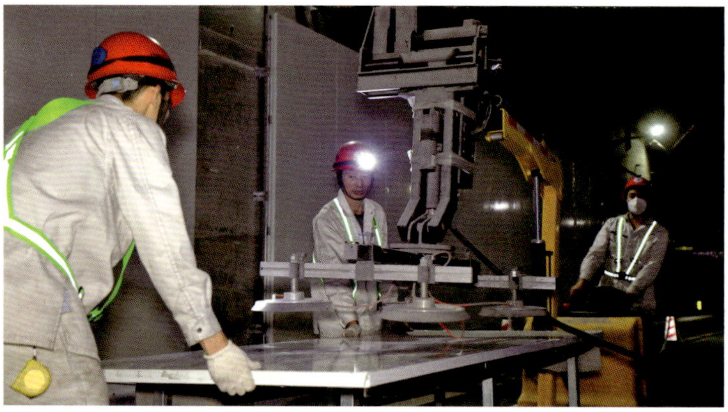

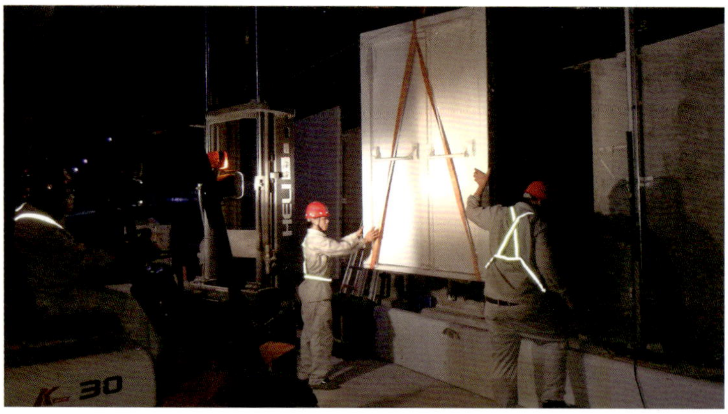

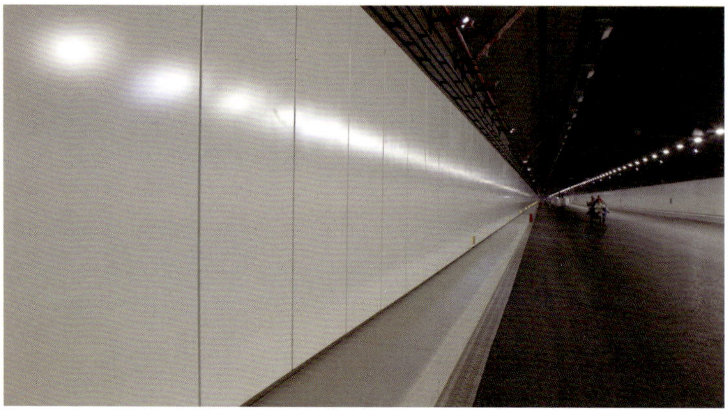

找平层混凝土浇筑

CONCRETE PLACEMENT AT THE LEVELING LAYER

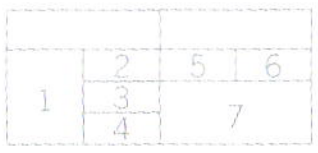

1—2. 搪瓷钢板安装
Installation of the Porcelain Steel Plates

3. 防火门安装
Fire Door Installation

4. 搪瓷钢板安装完成
Porcelain-Steel Plate Installation Completed

5—7. 隧道垫层混凝土浇筑
Bedding Concrete Placement in the Tunnel

在压仓混凝土顶部再次浇筑约24厘米混凝土，对路基进行二次调平，满足路面纵向曲线及横坡要求。

On top of the ballasting concrete, another 24 centimeters of concrete was placed, and a second leveling was done to the road surface to adapt to its vertical curve and transverse slope.

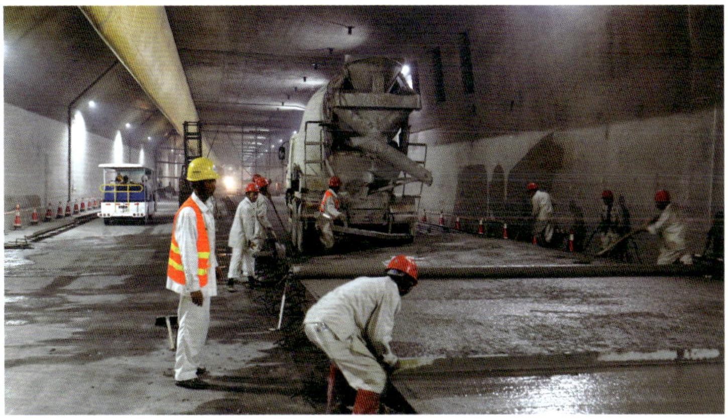

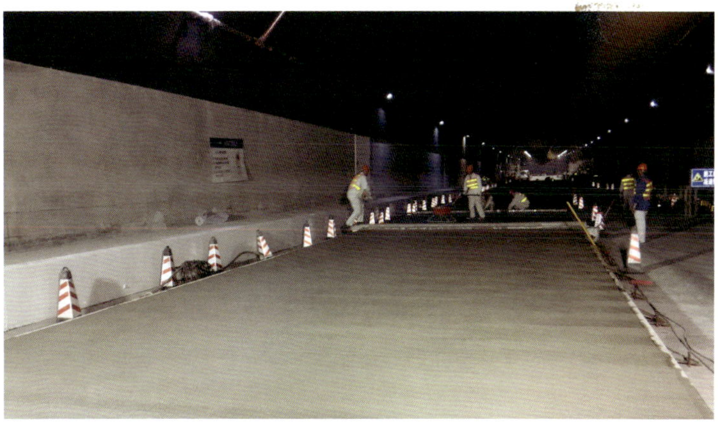

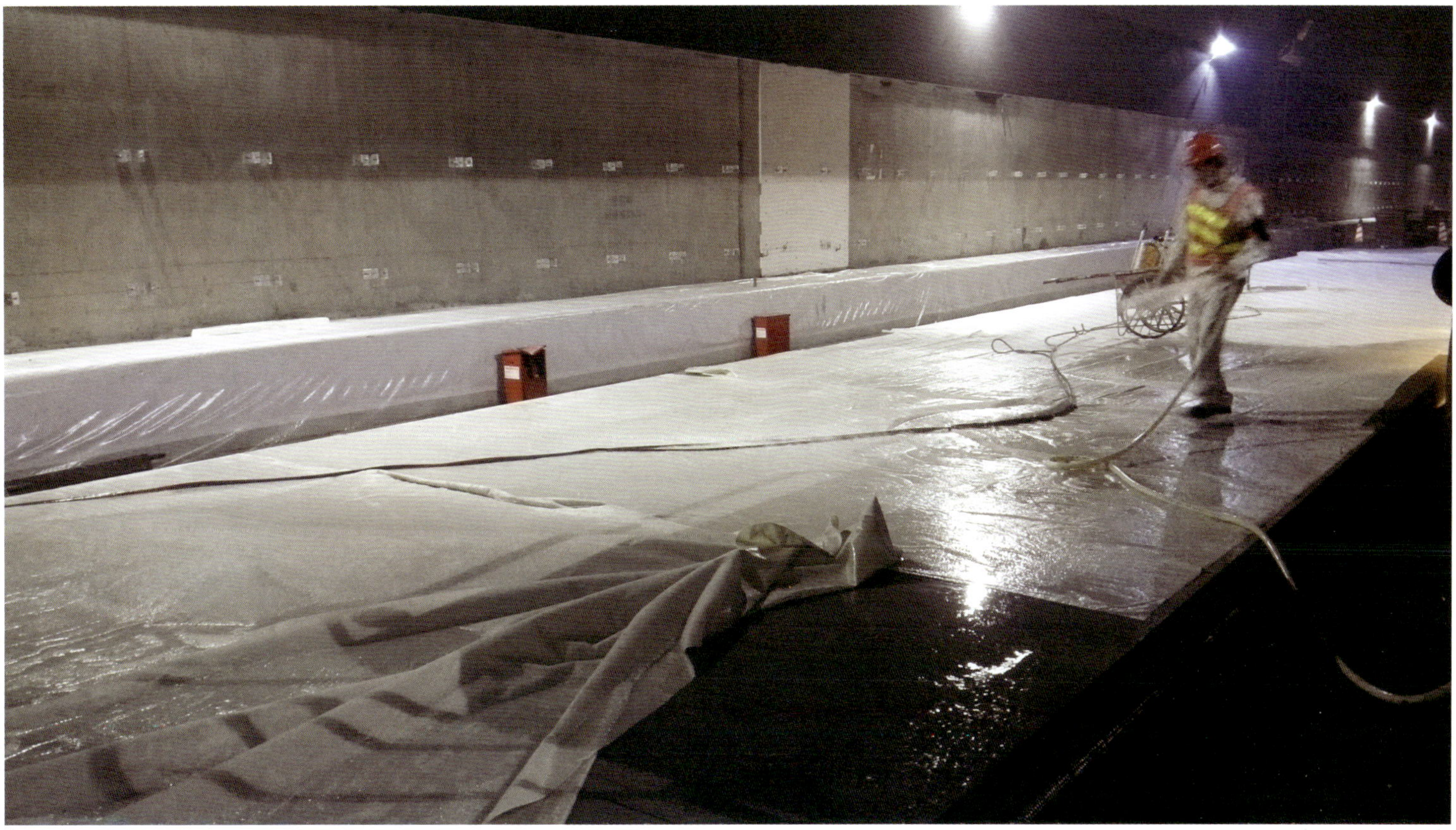

中管廊

INTERNAL PIPE GALLERY

隧道中廊道分为排烟通道、救援通道、综合管廊三层。

其中综合管廊中间设置电缆通道隔断墙，墙身长5982米，设计高度1620毫米，厚160毫米。

The internal pipe gallery of the tunnel was divided into three layers, including smoke track, rescue path and comprehensive-functional gallery.

Inside the comprehensive-functional gallery was the partition wall of the cable track, 5982 meters long, 1620 millimeters high and 160 millimeters thick.

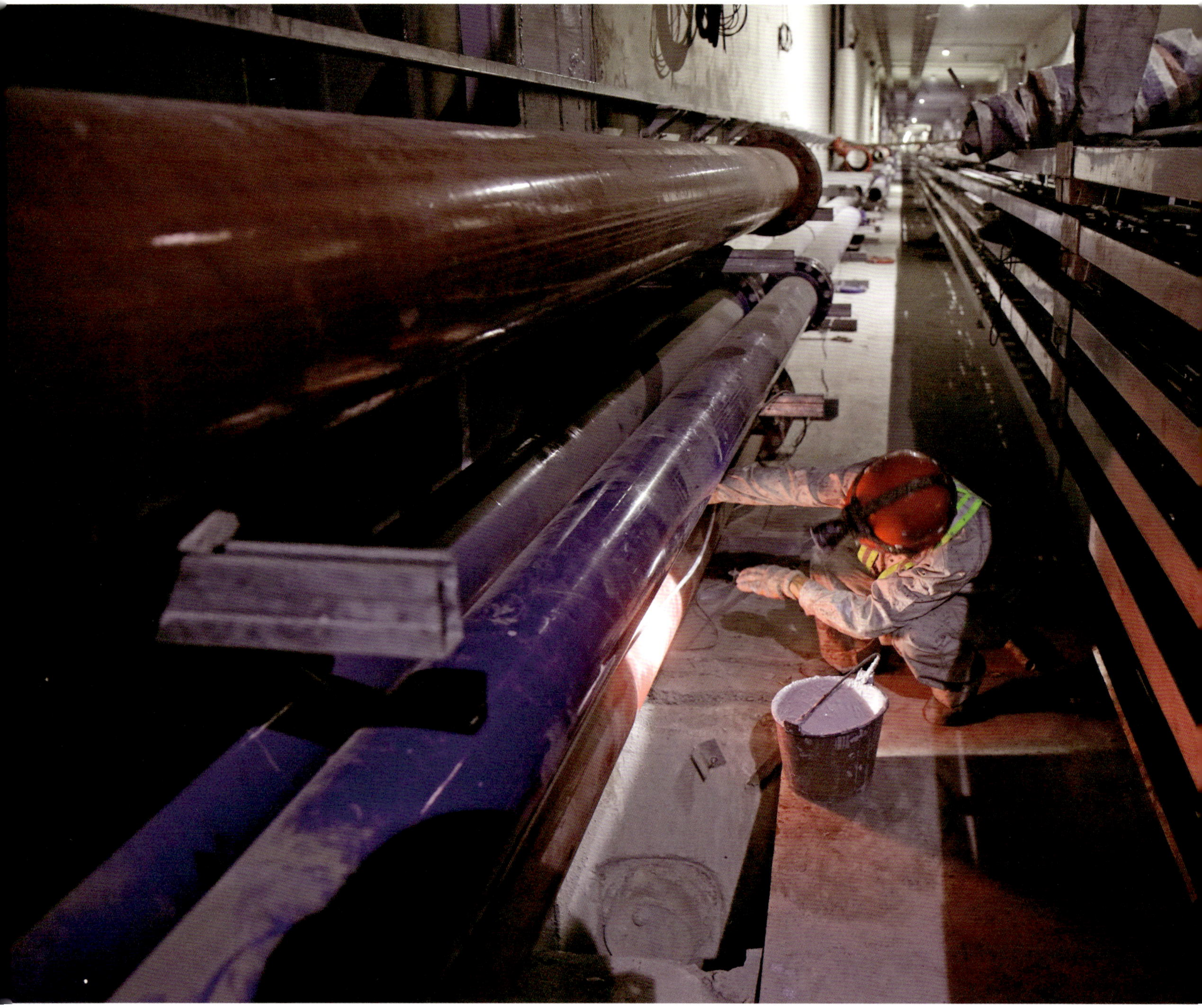

1. 中管廊管线防腐施工
Internal Pipe Gallery and Pipeline Anti-corrosion Operation

2. 中管廊隔墙混凝土浇筑
Concrete Placement of the Partition Wall of the Internal Pipe Gallery

3. 中管廊吊架安装
Installation of the Lifting Frame of the Internal Pipe Gallery

4. 中管廊管线安装
Pipeline Installation in the Internal Pipe Gallery

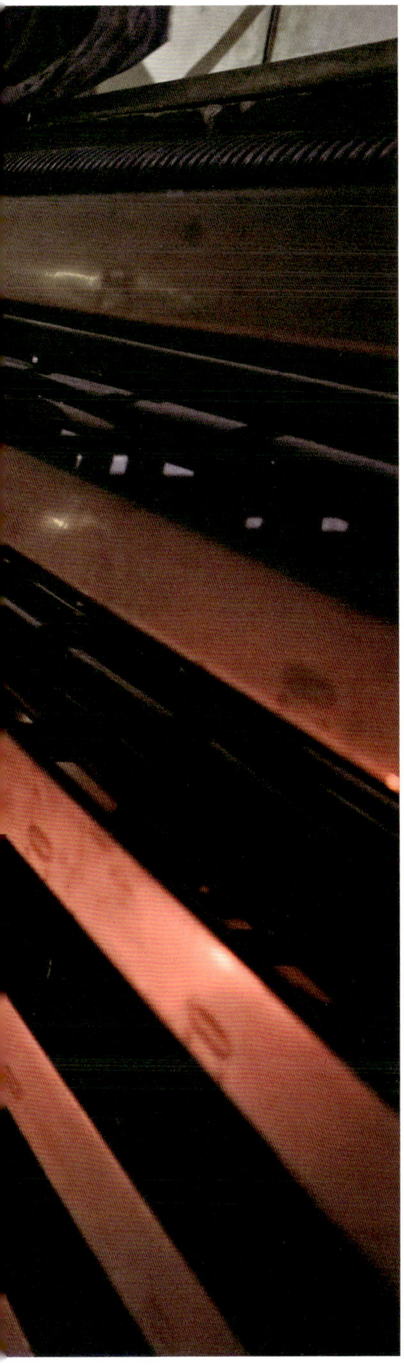

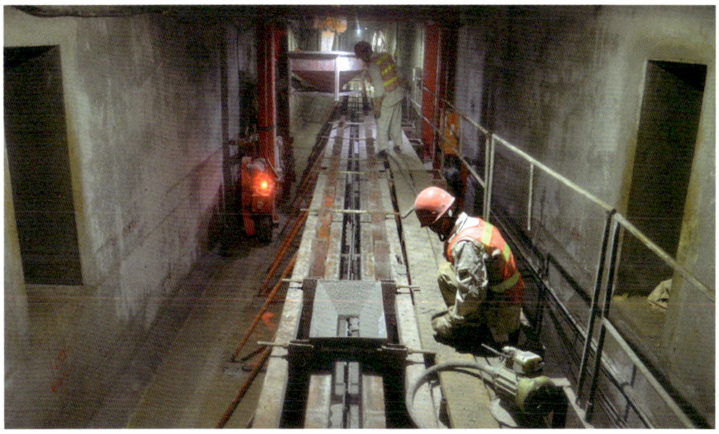

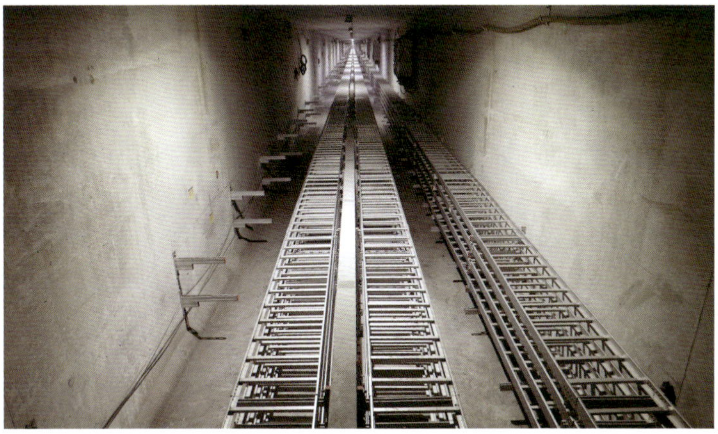

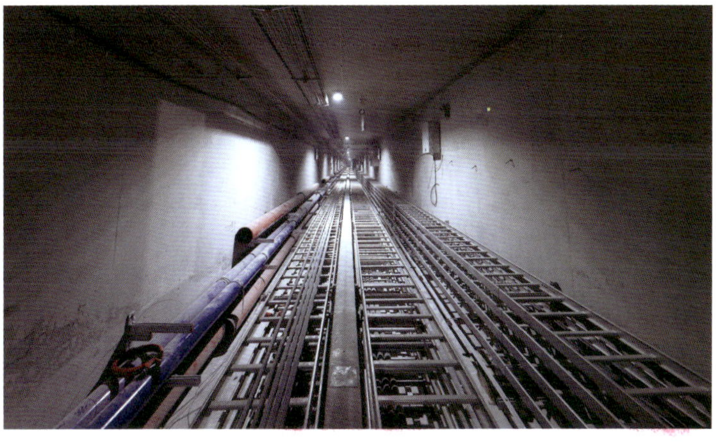

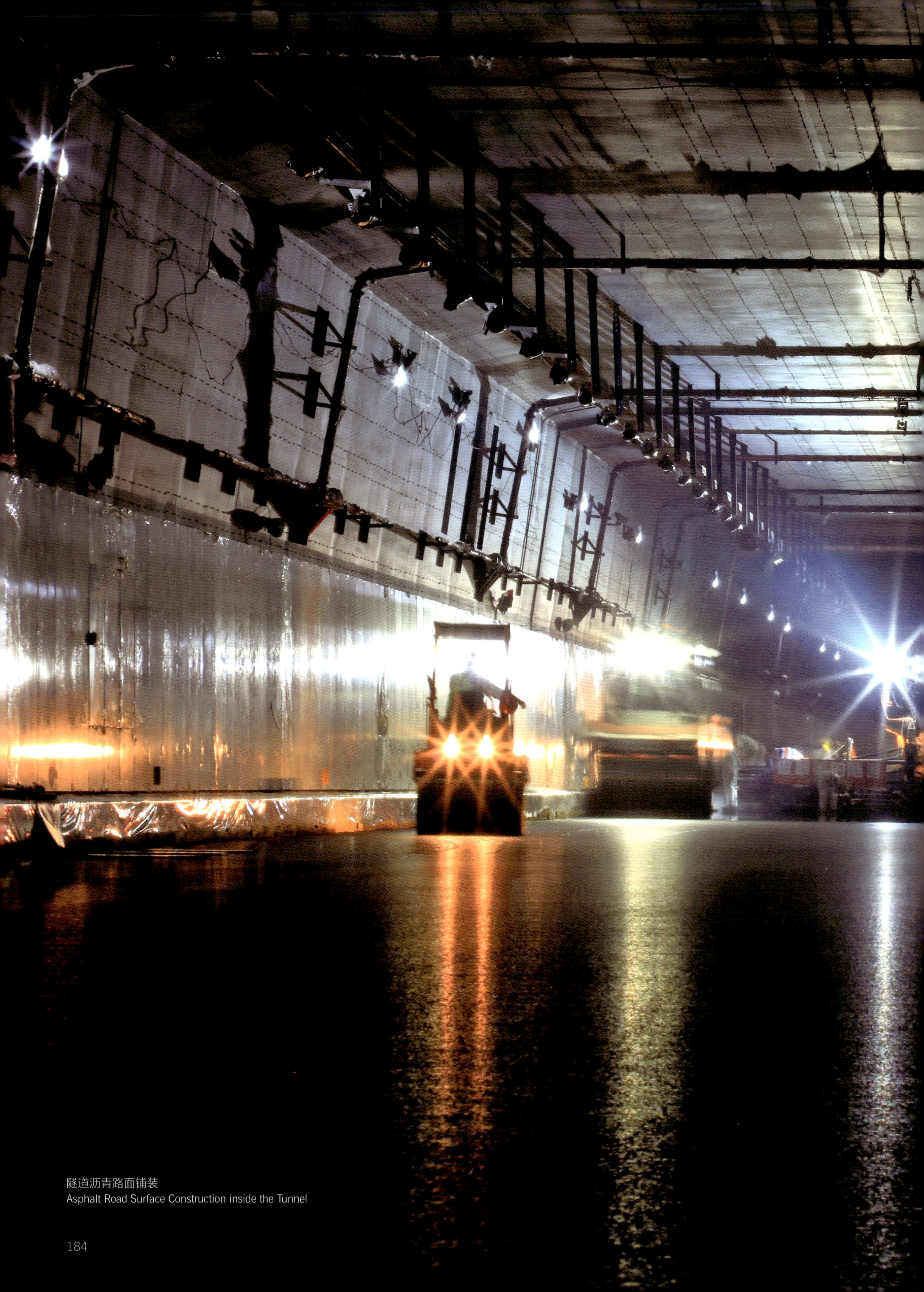

隧道沥青路面铺装
Asphalt Road Surface Construction inside the Tunnel

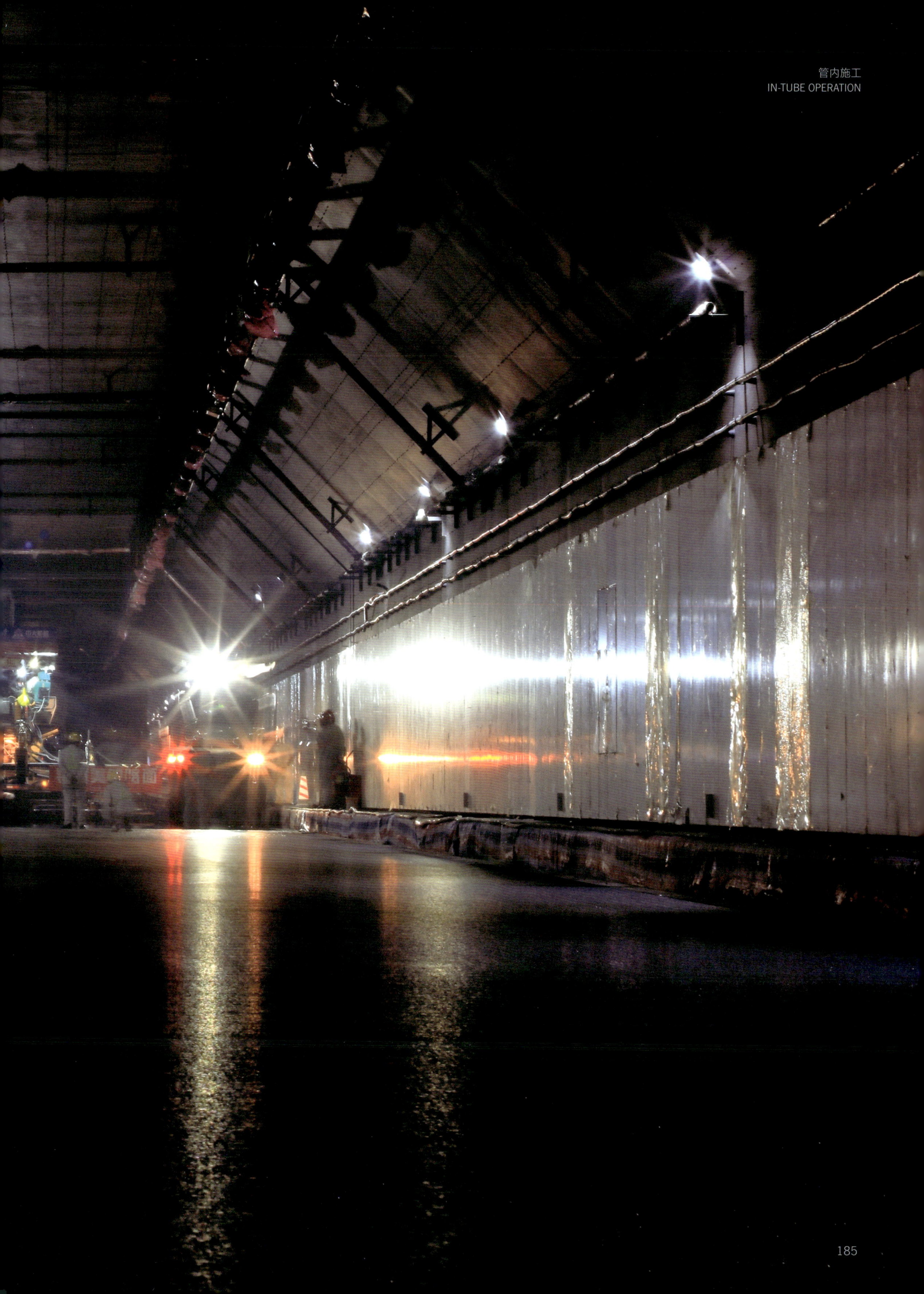

沥青铺装、无缝伸缩缝

ASPHALT ROAD SURFACE CONSTRUCTION
AND THE SEAMLESS EXPANSION JOINT

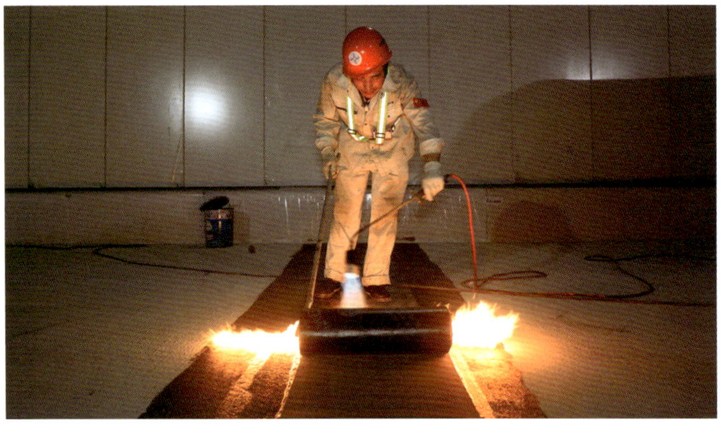

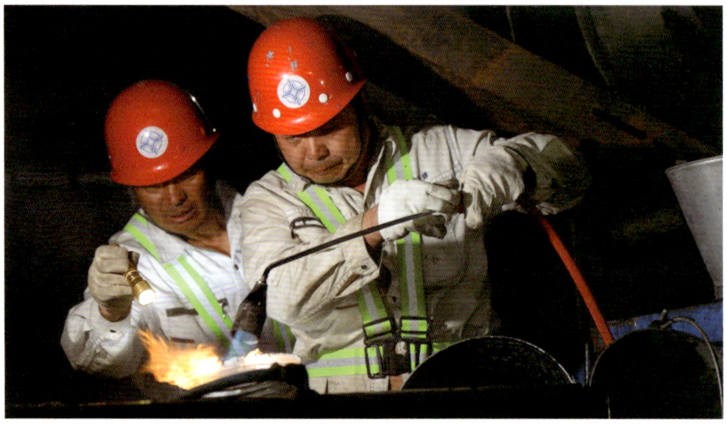

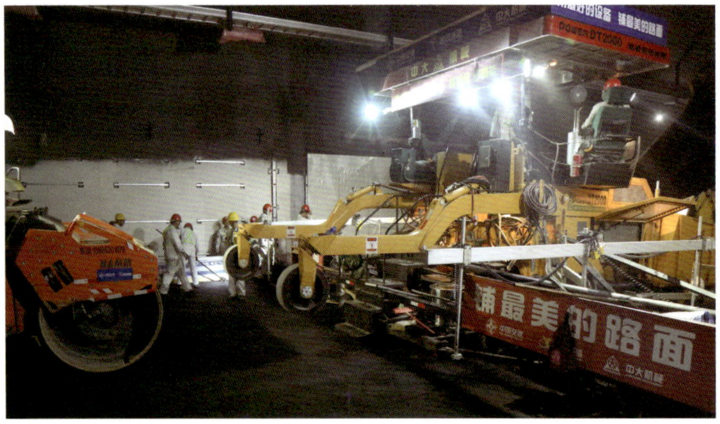

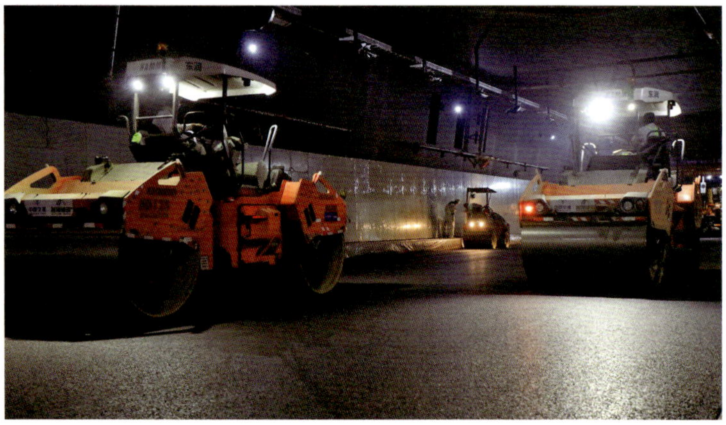

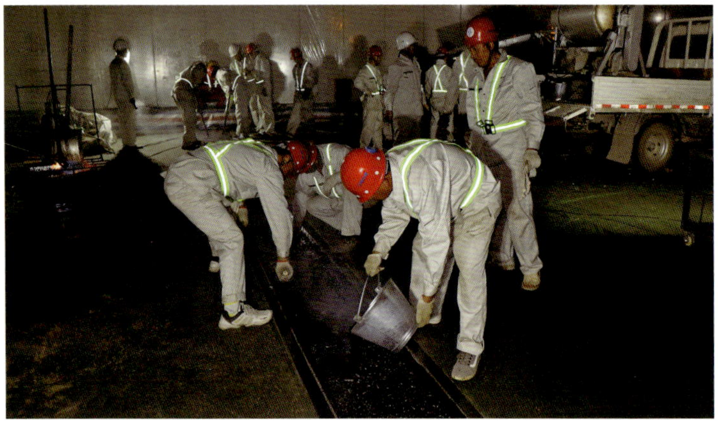

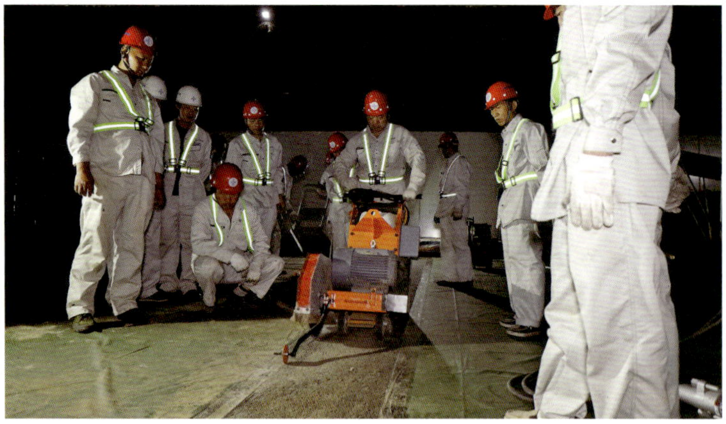

1—2. 防水卷材铺设
Placement of Water Proof Steel Coils

3—4. 隧道沥青路面摊铺
Asphalt Road Surface Pavement in the Tunnel

5—6. 隧道路面无缝伸缩缝施工
Construction of the Seamless Expansion Joint on the Tunnel Road Surface

7. 隧道沥青路面铺设施工
In-tunnel Asphalt Road Surface Construction

沉管隧道路面共15万平方米，荷载采用公路Ⅰ级并提高25%进行计算。

由于隧道内部湿度较大，采用改性沥青碎石分为AC10、SMA16、SMA13 三层逐层进行摊铺。

为适应结构变形，路面结构变形缝处布置无缝伸缩缝，采用高分子聚合体弹性改性沥青混合料填充缝隙，使伸缩接缝处的路面与其它铺装部分形成连续体。

The total coverage of the road surface of the immersed tube tunnel was 150,000 square meters, and Scale I was adopted for the surface load with a 25% raise.

To cope with the immense humidity inside the tunnel, three layers of modified asphalt AC10, SMA16 and SMA13 were used.

To cope with the structural distortion, seamless expansion joints were used in the distortion seams of the road surface, and Elastic modified high polymer asphalt was used to fill the seams, which melted the road surface at the seam part with other parts of the road into a whole.

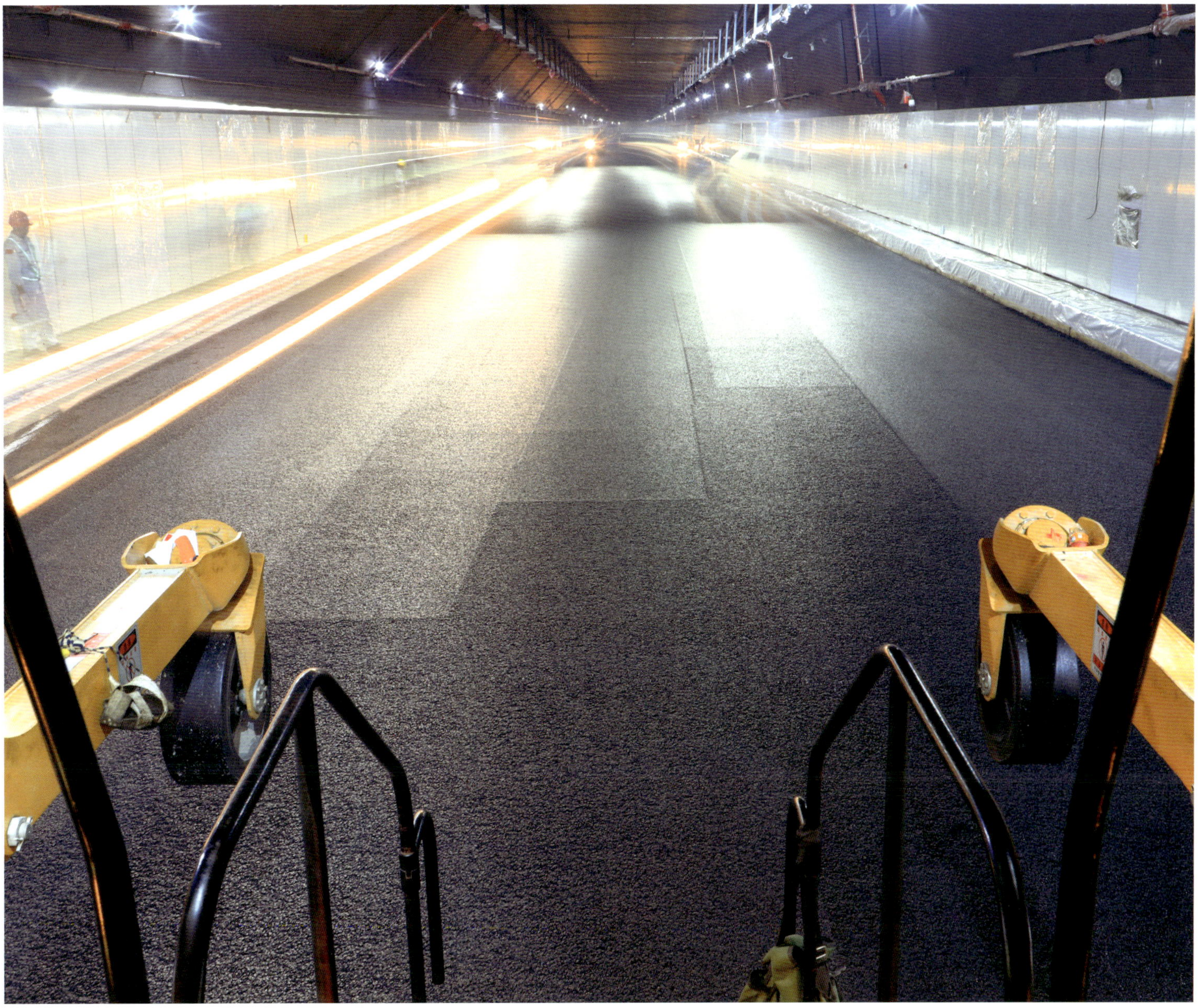

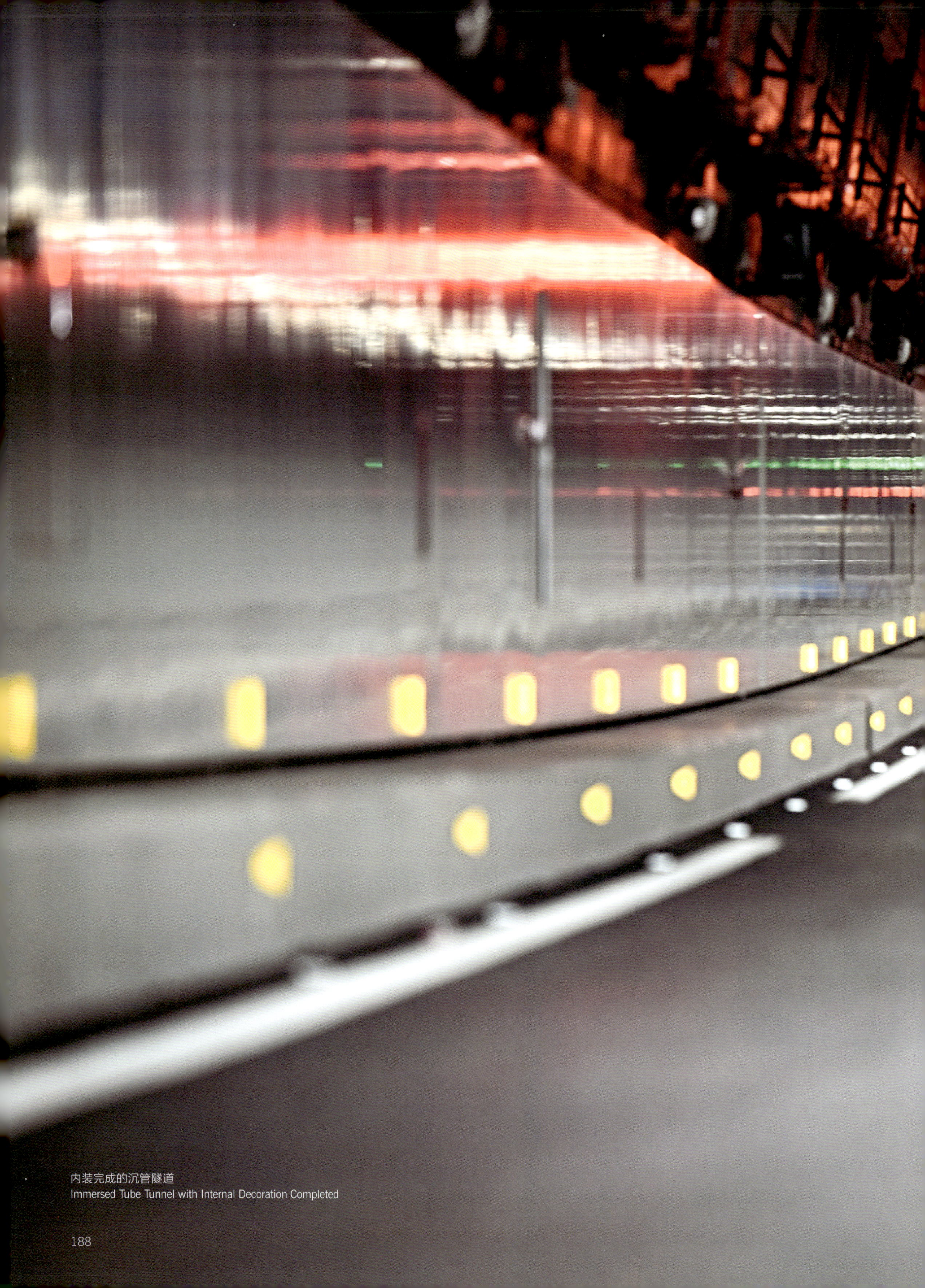

内装完成的沉管隧道
Immersed Tube Tunnel with Internal Decoration Completed

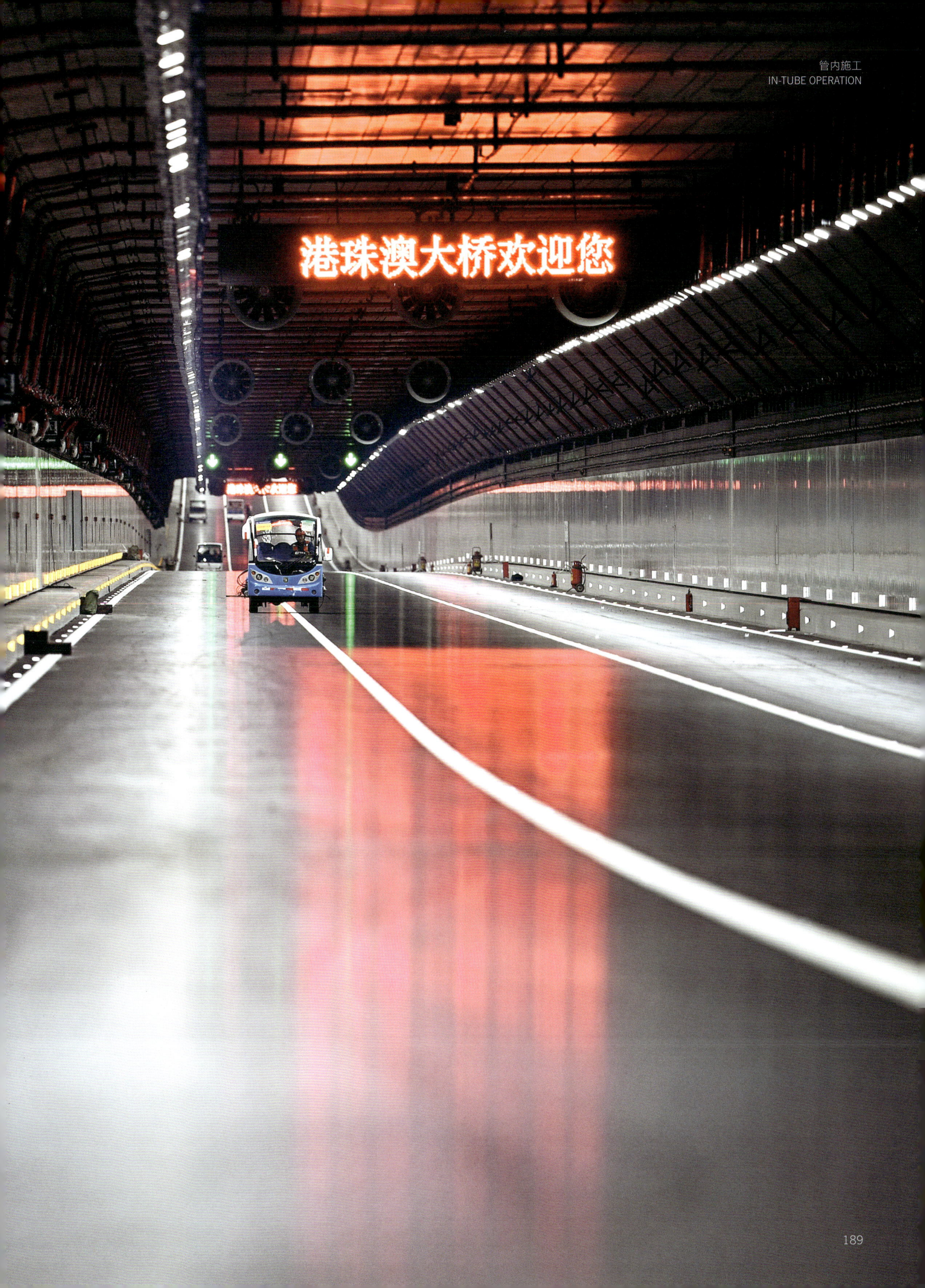
港珠澳大桥欢迎您

画册索引
ALBUM INDEX

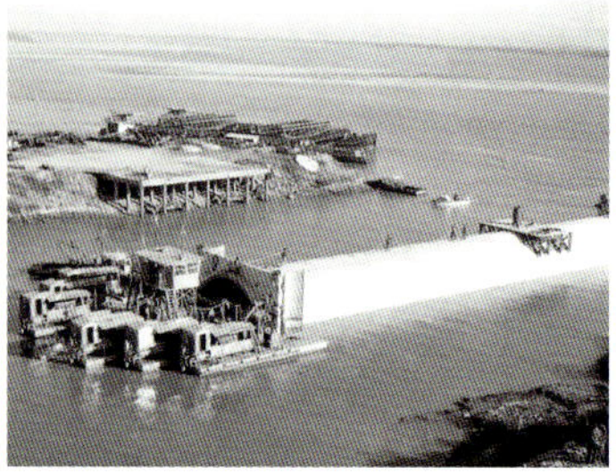

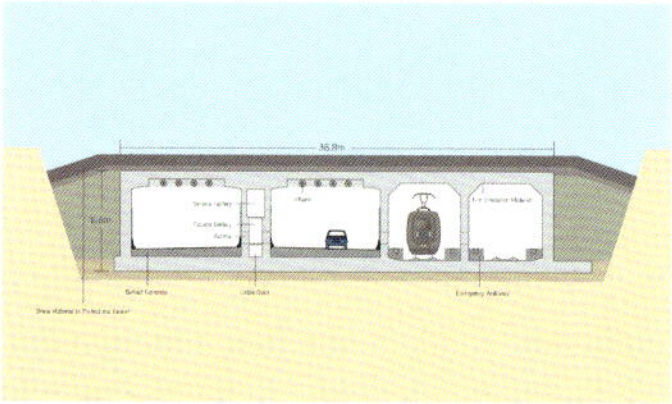

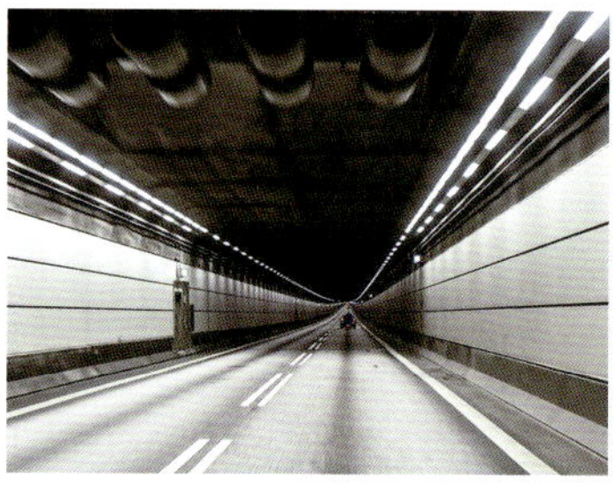

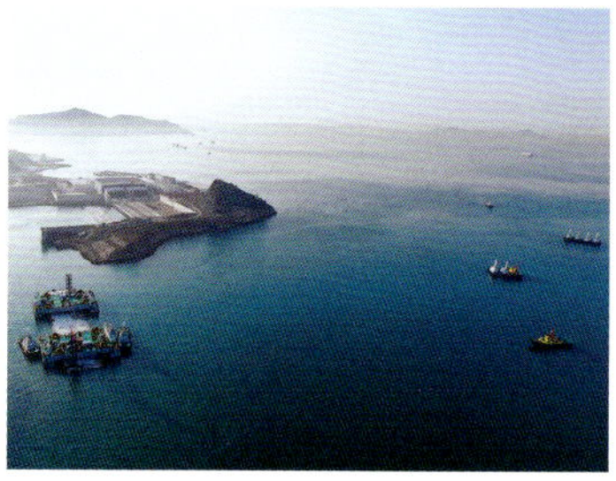

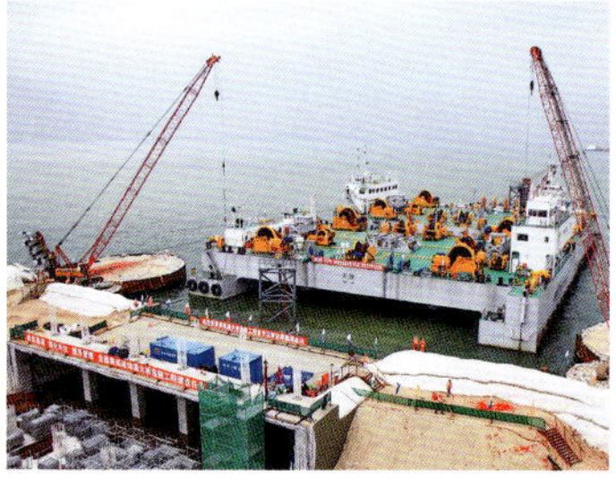

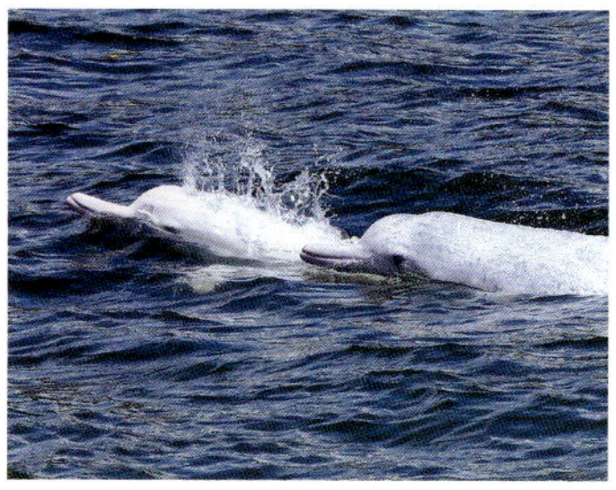

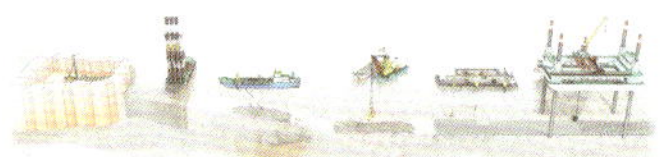

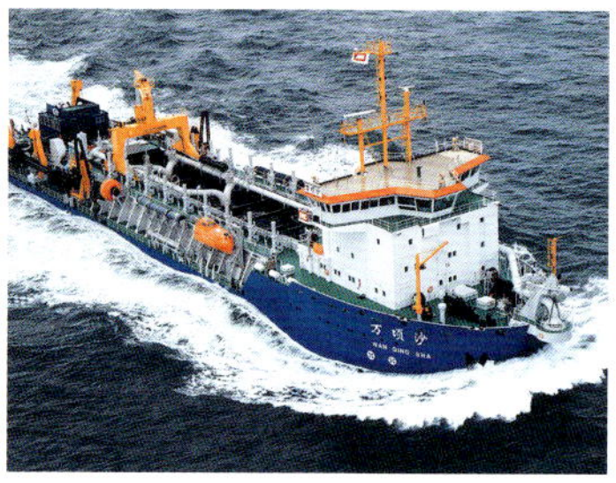

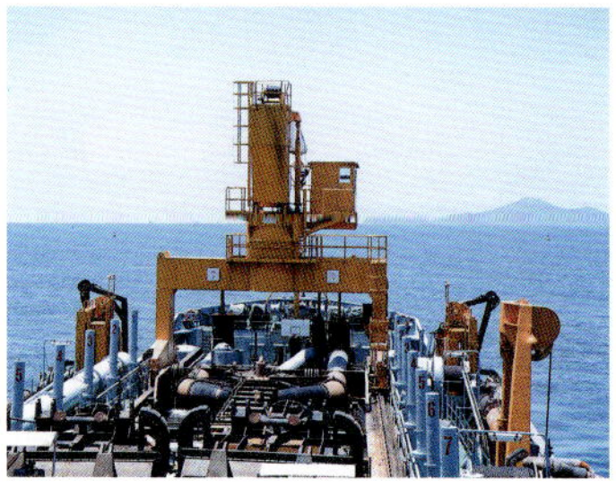

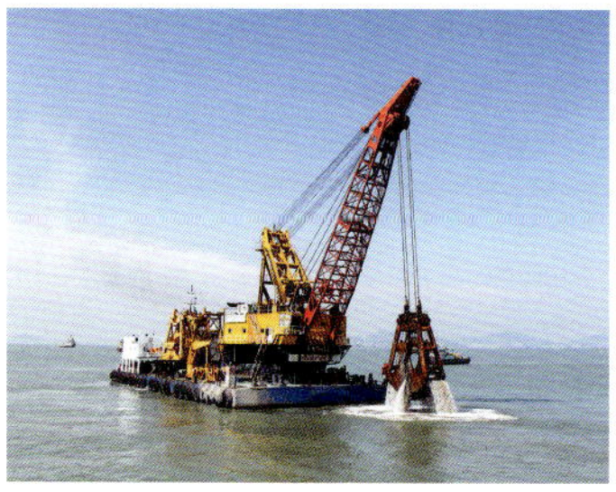

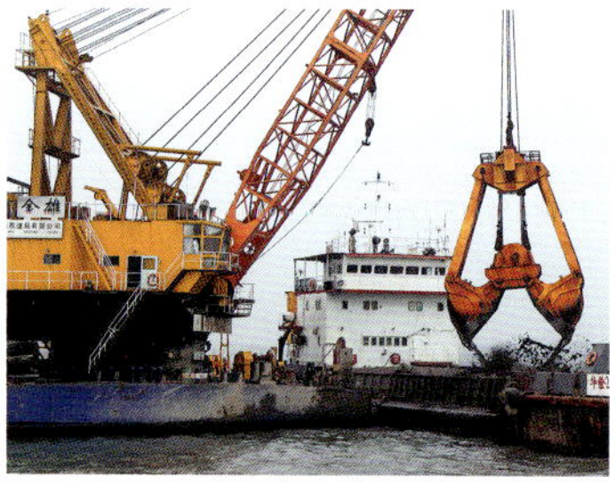

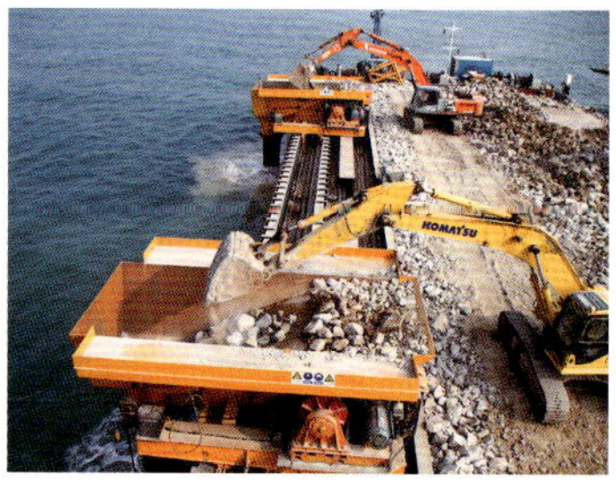

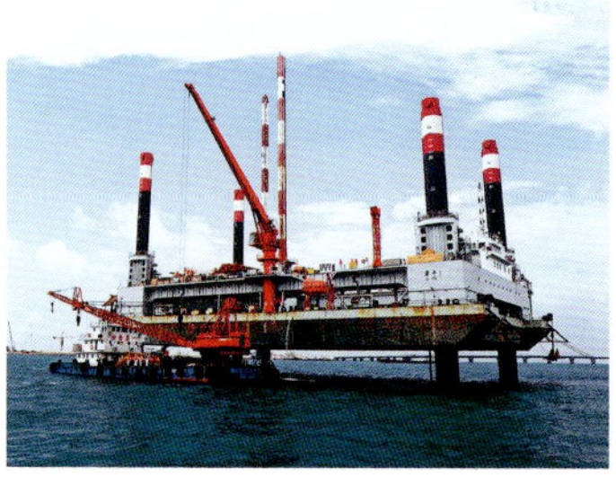

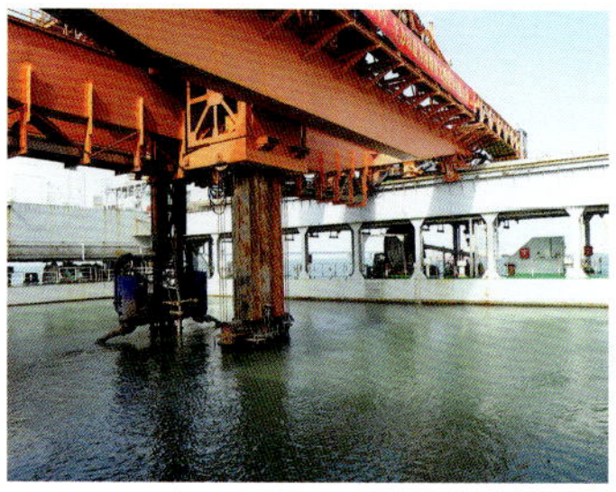

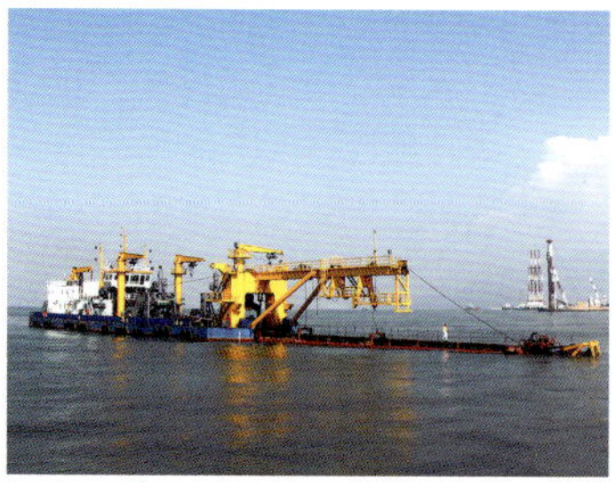

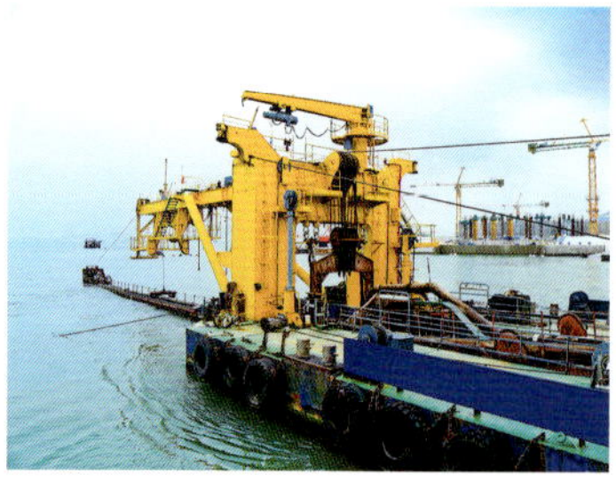

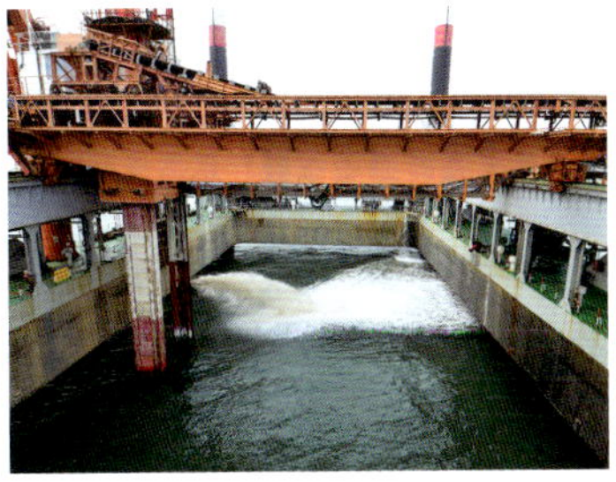

"津平 1"进行碎石基床清淤试验
"Jinping 1" Testing Rubble Bed Dredging
038

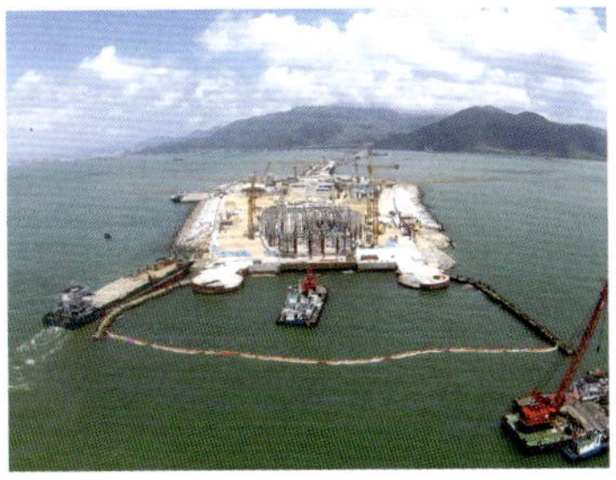

减淤屏安装完成
Completion of the Silt Preventing Screen Installation
041

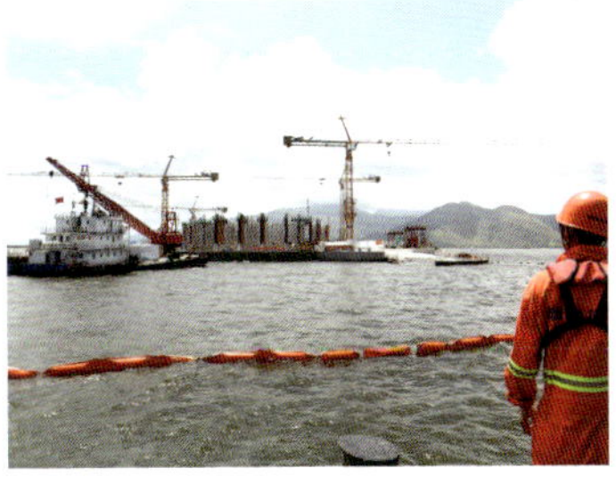

东人工岛岛头区安装完成的减淤屏
Silt Preventing Screen Installed at the Head Part of East Man-Made Island
042

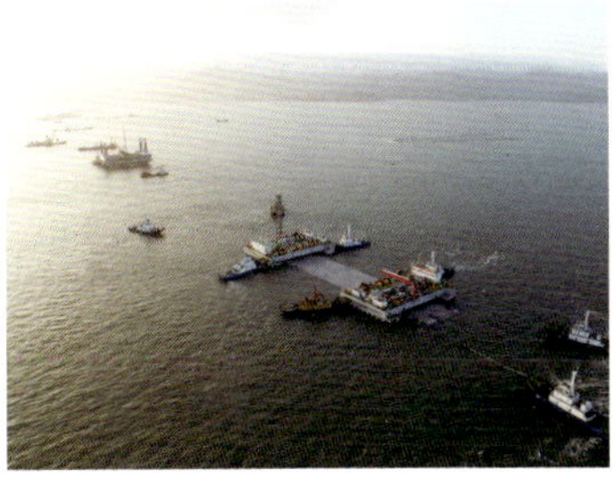

沉管浮运
Float Conveyance of the Immersed Tubes
046

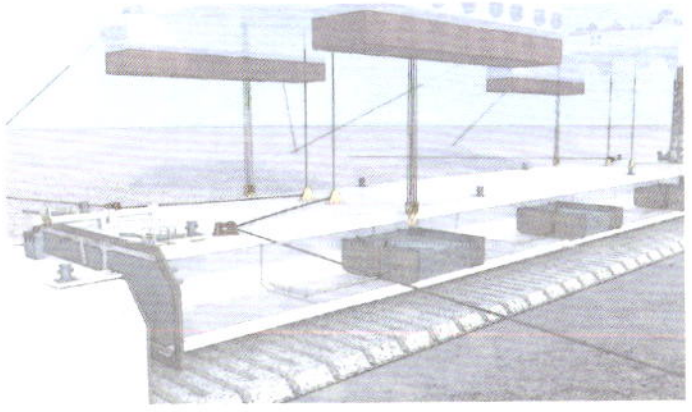

沉管对接三维图
3-D Diagram of the Butt Welding of the Immersed Tubes
049

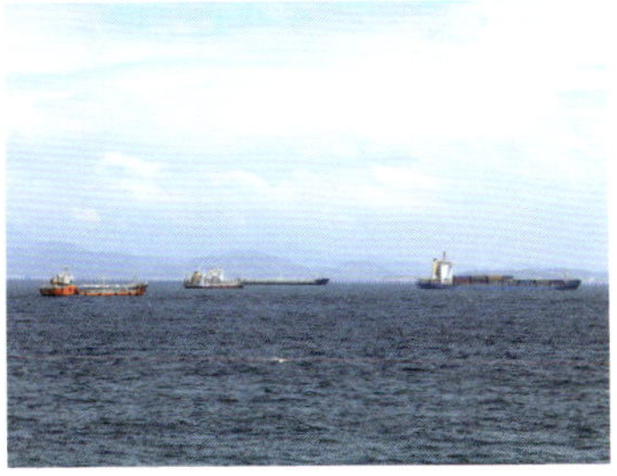

通航船舶密集的浮运航道
Route of the Float Conveyance with Heavy Traffic of Barges
051

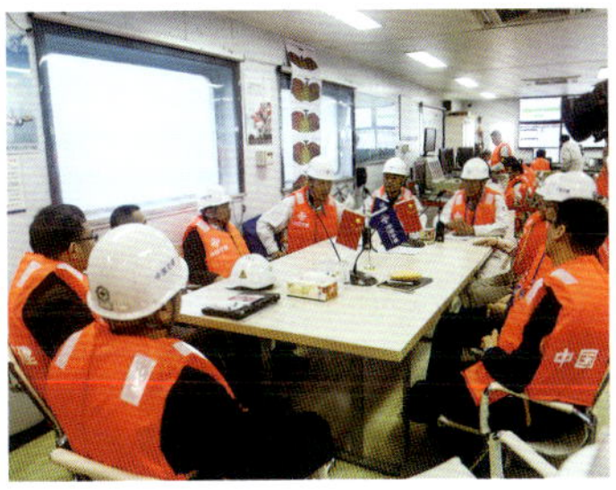

沉管浮运决策会
Decision Making on the Float Conveyance of the Immersed Tubes
053

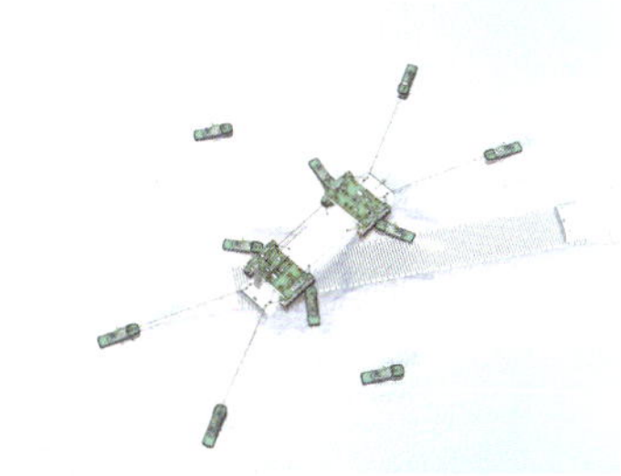

浮运
Float Conveyance
055

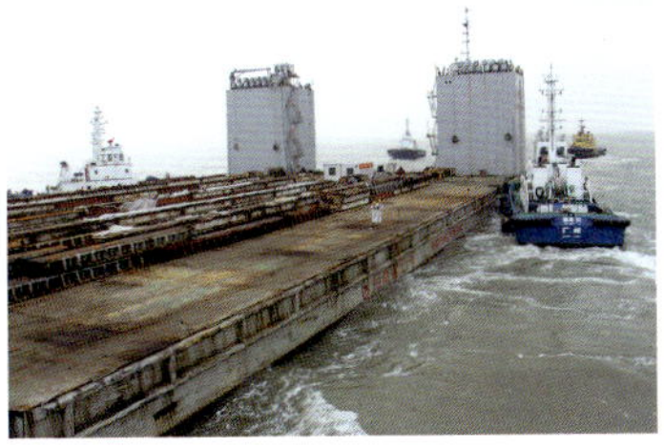

沉管浮运演练
Drill of the Float Conveyance of the Immersed Tubes
056

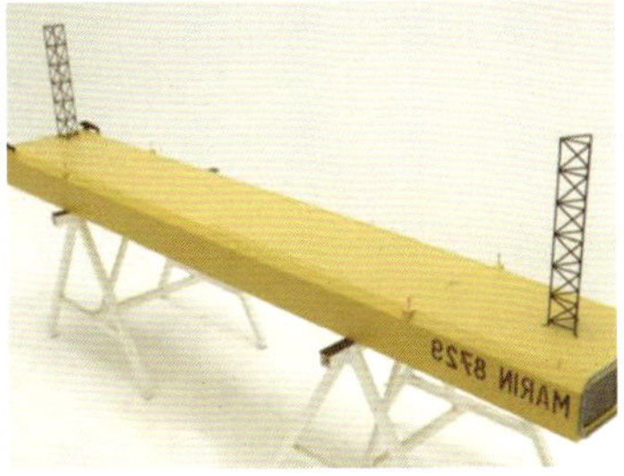

沉管数模图
Mathematical Model of the Immersed Tubes
059

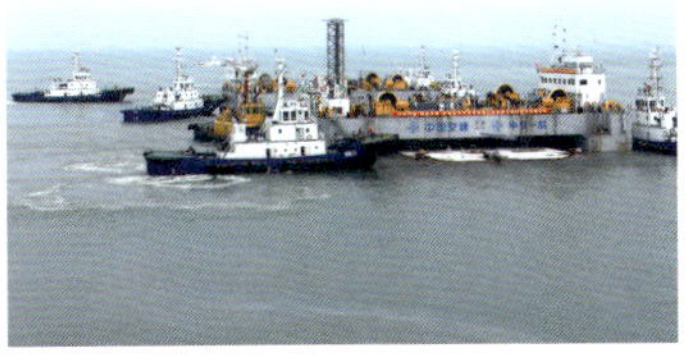

沉管拖航编队完成
Completion of the Immersed Tube Tugboat Formation
060

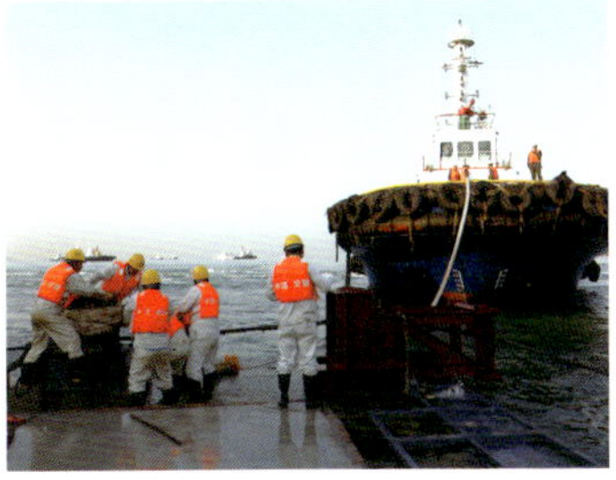

拖轮系缆
Mooring Cables of the Tugboats
062

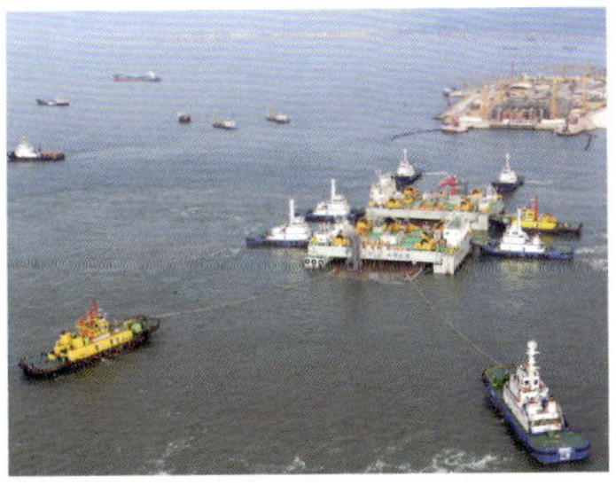

E33 沉管浮运
Float Conveyance of the Immersed Tube E33
065

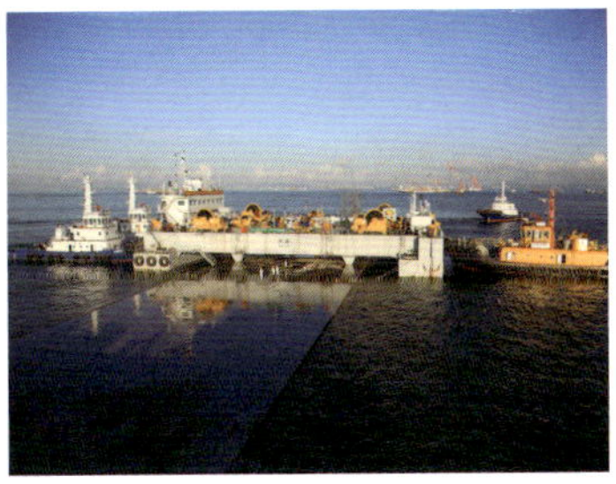

E3 沉管浮运
Float Conveyance of the Immerse Tube E3
066

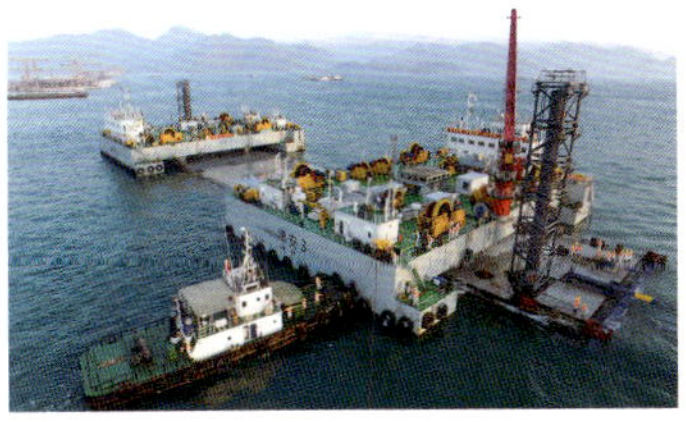

沉管系泊施工
Anchoring of the Immersed Tubes
069

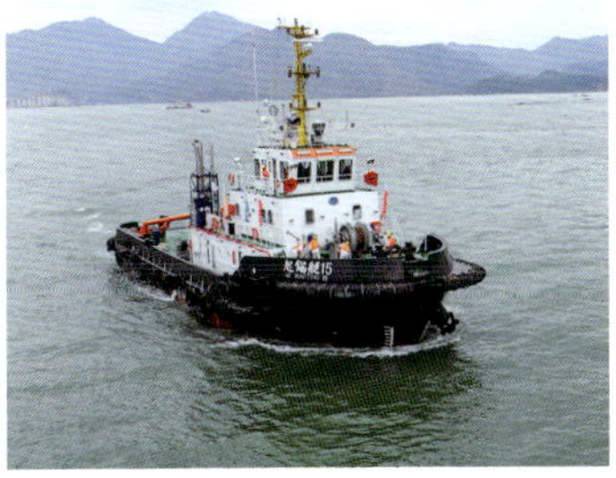

系泊船"起锚艇 15"
Anchor Boat 15 of the Mooring Barge
070

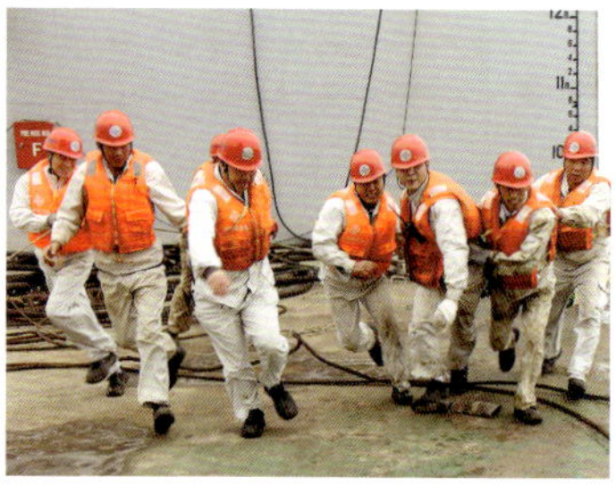

带缆作业
Heaving Cable Handling
072

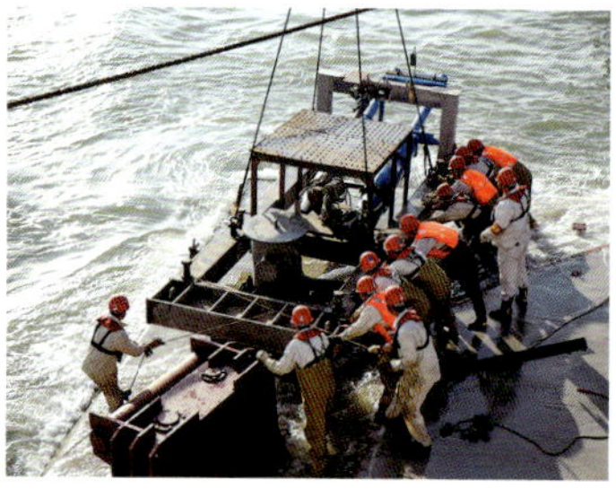

安装拉合千斤顶
Installation of the Pulling Jack
075

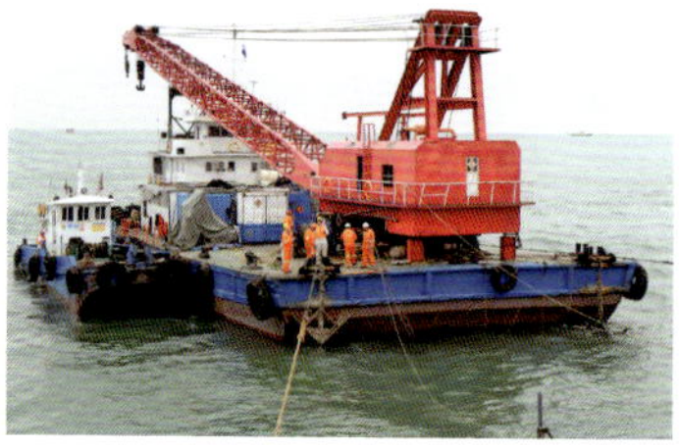

潜水母船"盐中捞 386"
Submarine Parent Barge "Yanzhonglao 386"
076

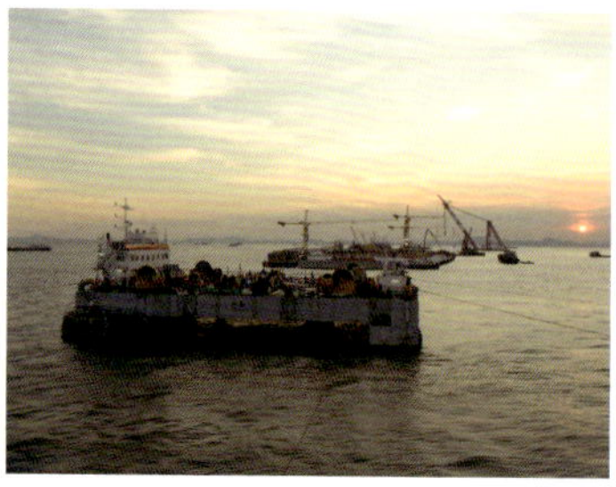

沉管沉放安装
Landing and Installation of the Immersed Tubes
079

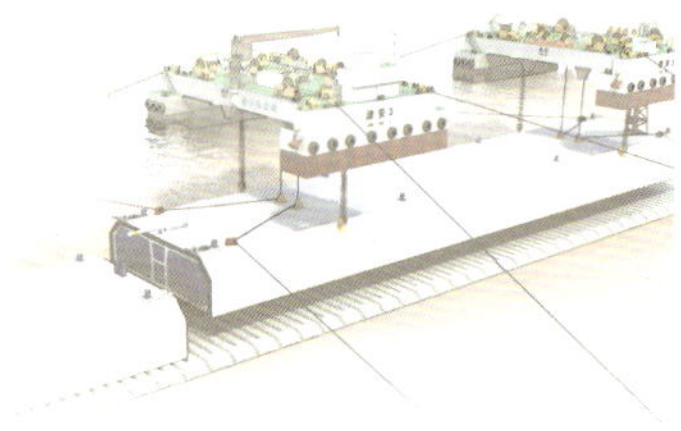

沉管沉放安装三维图
3-D Diagram of the Immersed Tube Landing and Installation
081

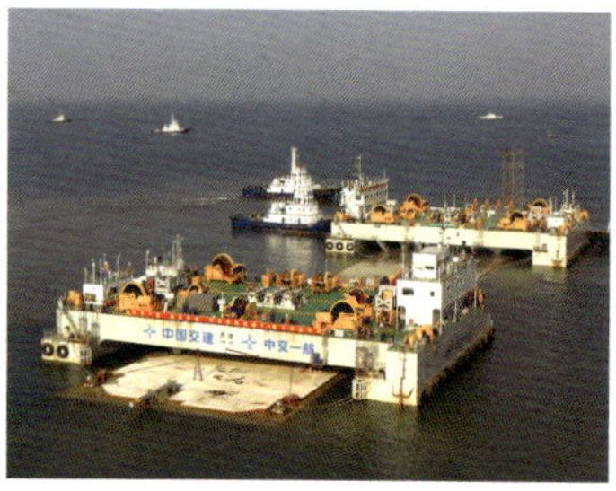

"津安 2" "津安 3"安装驳
Installation Barges "Jinaan 2" and "Jinaan 3"
083

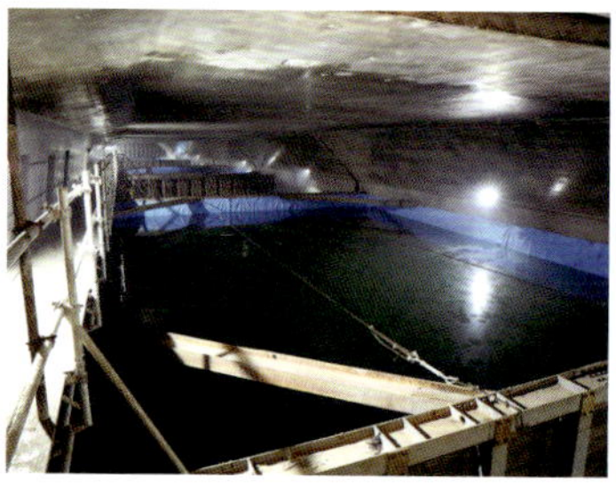

沉管沉放压载水水箱
Ballast Water Tank for the Immersed Tube Landing
085

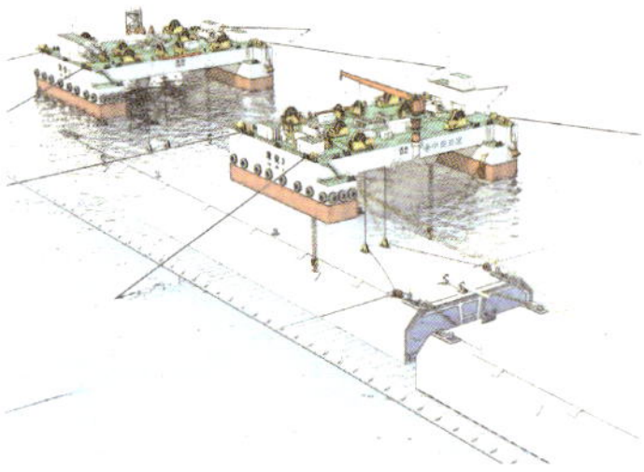

沉管对接深水测控系统三维图
3-D Diagram of Deep Water Measurement and Control System for the Immersed Tube Butt Joint
087

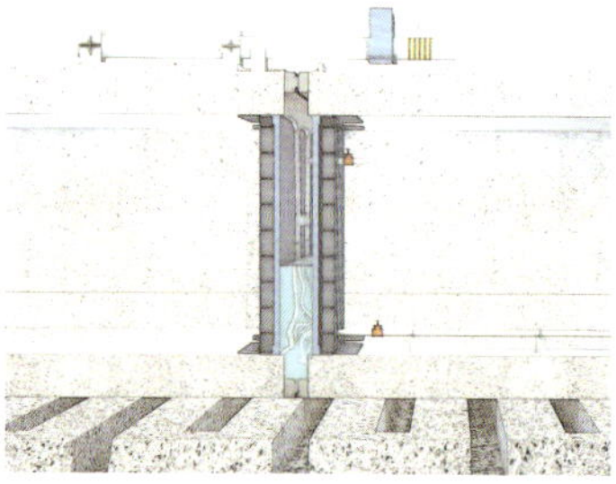

沉管对接水力压接三维图
3-D Diagram of the Hydraulic Crimp Connection for the Immersed Tube Butt Joint
088

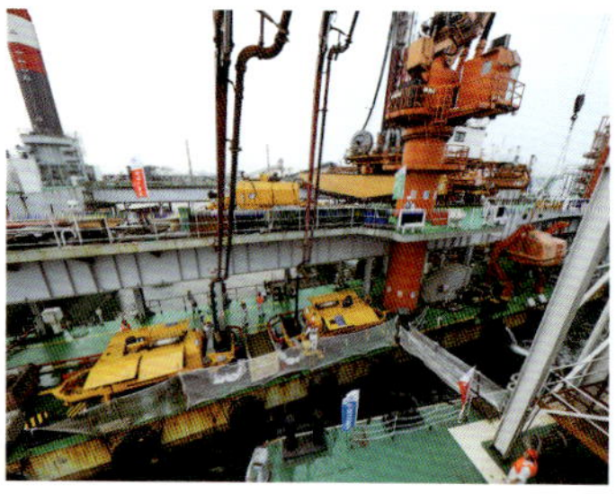

沉管基础密闭腔压浆施工
Grouting into the Enclosed Cavity of the Immersed Tube Base
090

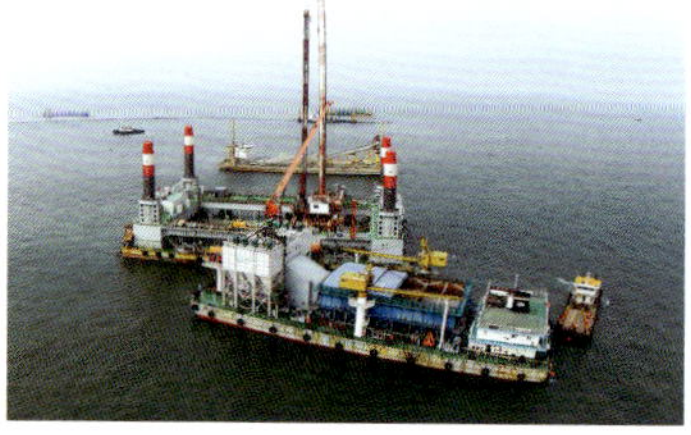

沉管基础密闭腔压浆施工
Grouting into the Enclosed Cavity of the Immersed Tube Base
092

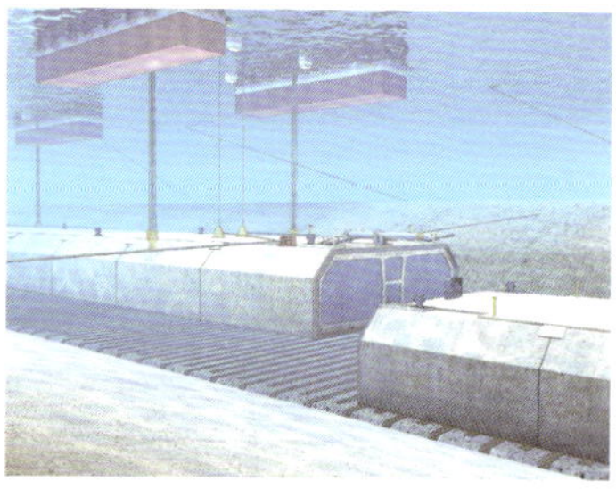

深槽区沉管安装三维图
3-D Diagram of the Immersed Tube Installation in the Deep Trench
095

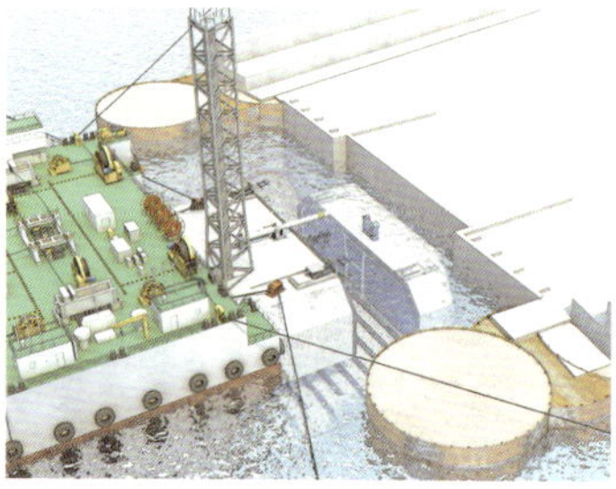

岛头段沉管安装三维图
3-D Diagram of the Immersed Tube Installation at the Head Part of the Island
096

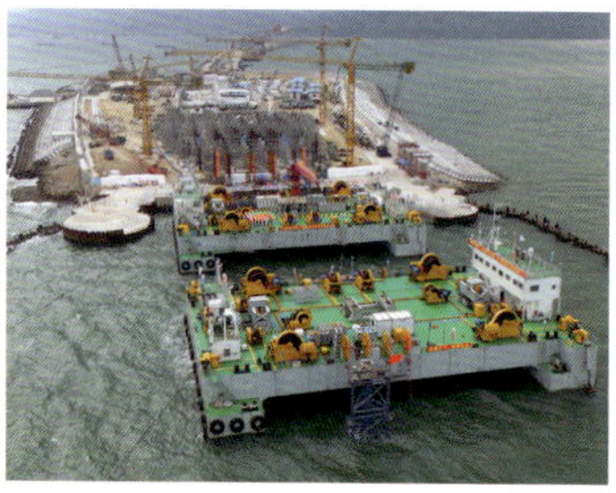

E33沉管与东人工岛暗埋段对接安装
Butt Welding of the Immersed Tube E33 with the Buried Tube on East Man-Made Island
098

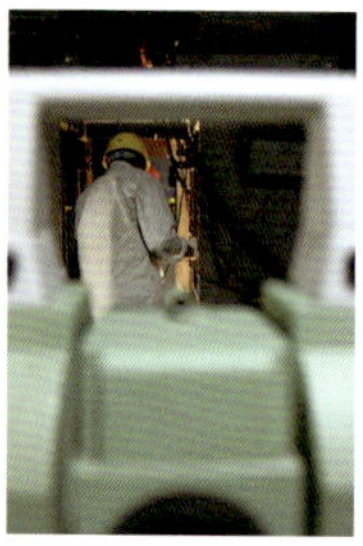

沉管对接贯通测量
Hole-through Survey for the Immersed Tube Butt Joint
100

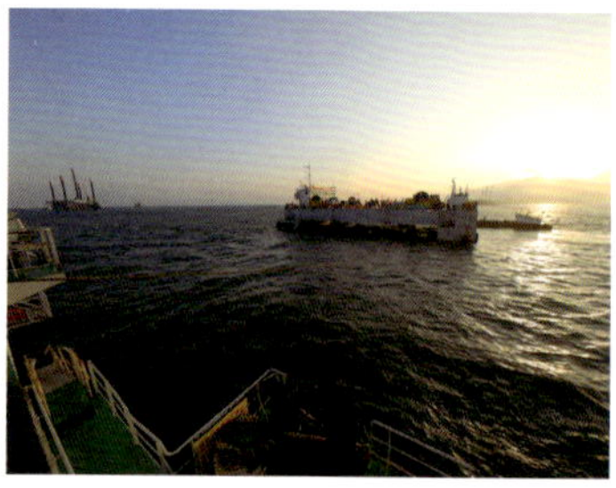

E30 沉管安装施工
Installation of Immersed Tube E30
102

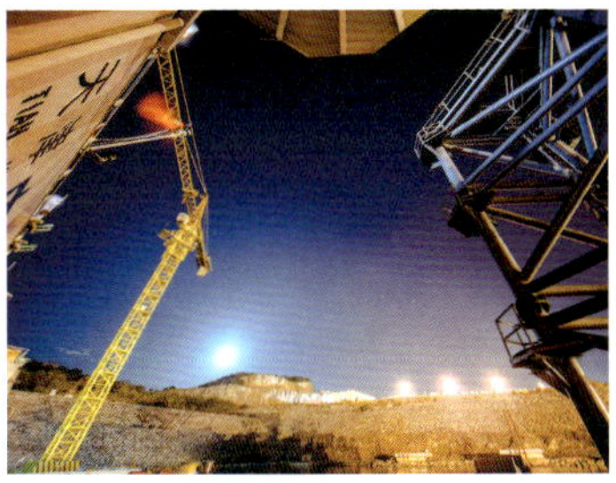

沉管测量塔
Immersed Tube Measurement Tower
106

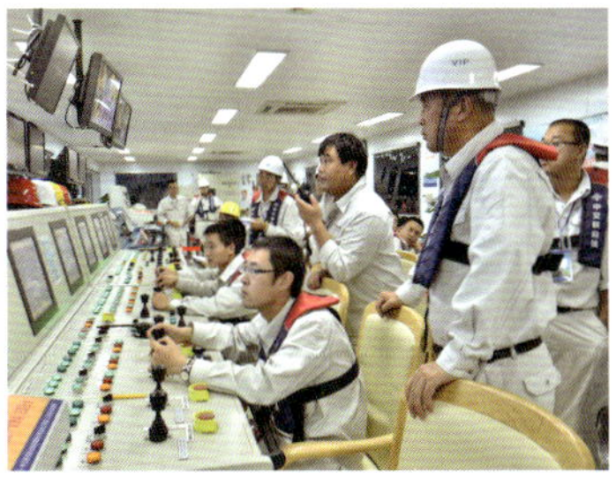

沉管无人沉放定位
Positioning System for the Unmanned Immersed Tube Landing
109

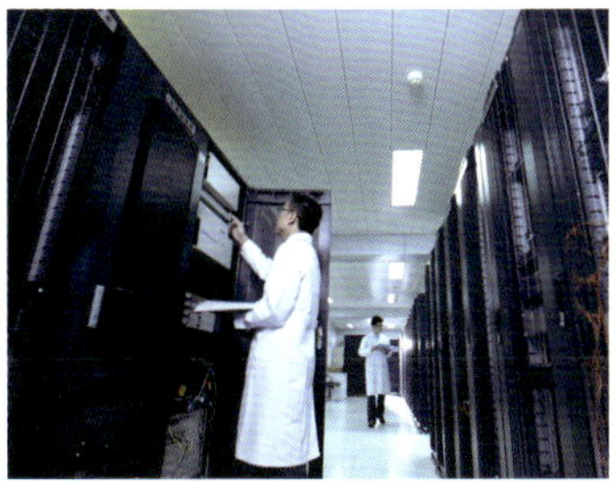

超级计算机分析预报沉管浮运安装海洋环境
Supercomputer Analyzing and Forecasting Oceanic Environment for the Float Conveyance and Installation of the Immersed Tubes
111

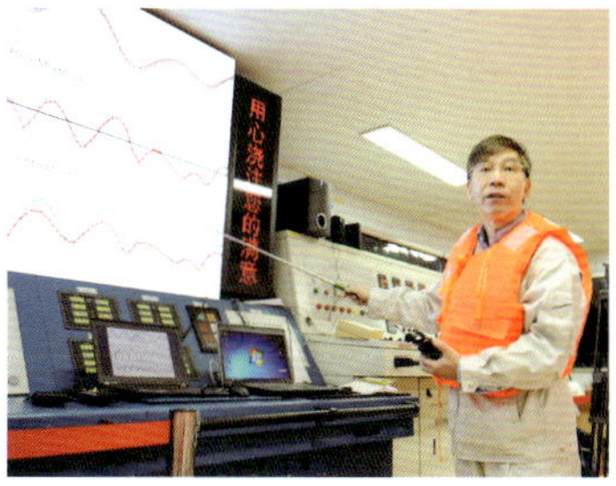

沉管对接窗口海洋气象环境数据分析
Oceanic Weather Data Analysis for the Immersed Tube Butt Joint Window
112

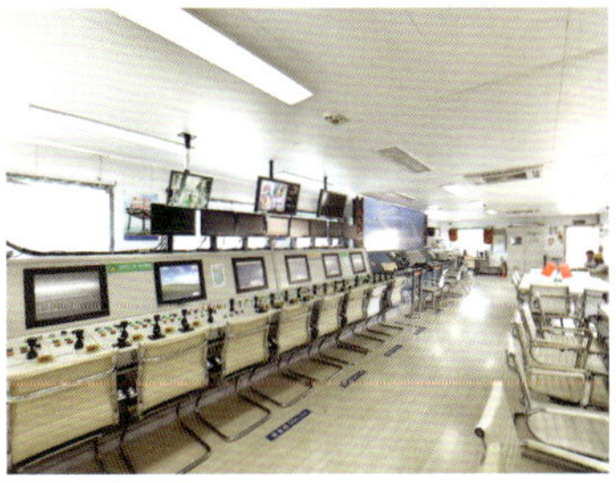

集成多项沉管安装保障系统的沉管安装船“津安3”操作室
Operation Cabin of the Immersed Tube Installation Barge "Jinaan 3" Equipped with Multiple Immersed Tube Installation Supporting Systems
114

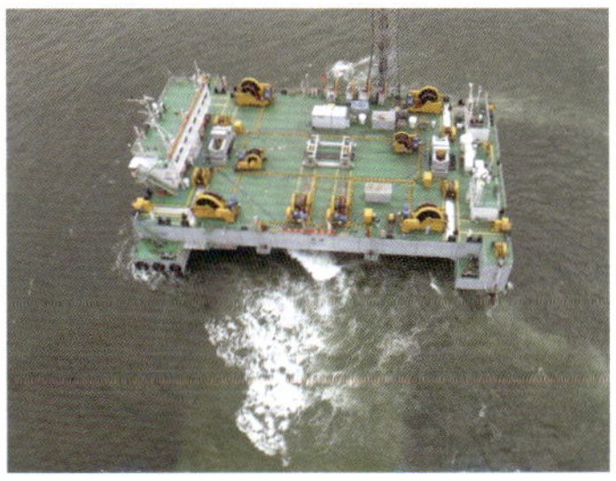

沉管安装遭遇异常波
Immersed Tube Installation Troubled by the Extraordinary Wave
116

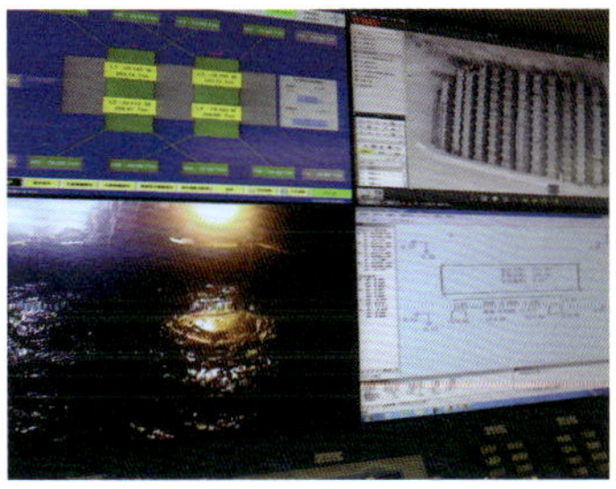

封门结构安全监控系统
Sealing Devices Security Monitoring System
118

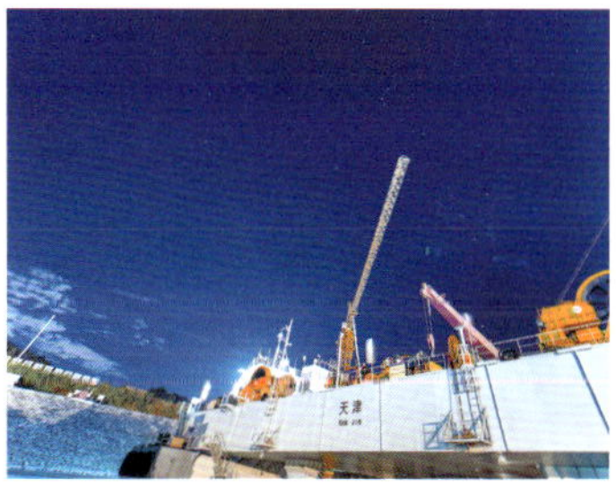

“津安3”沉管安装船
Immersed Tube Installation Barge "Jinaan 3"
120

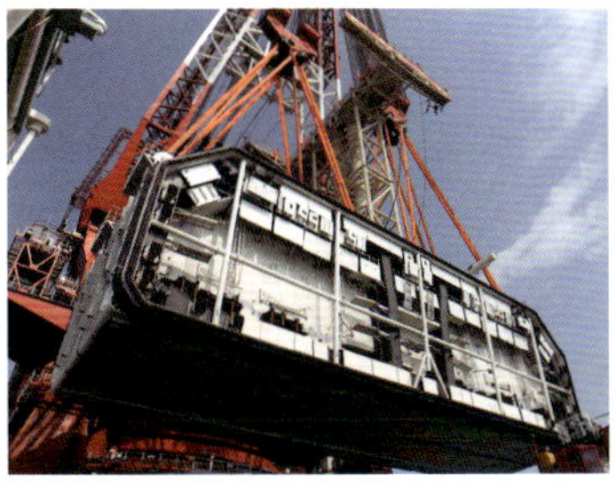

最终接头起吊
Hoisting of the Closure Joint
124

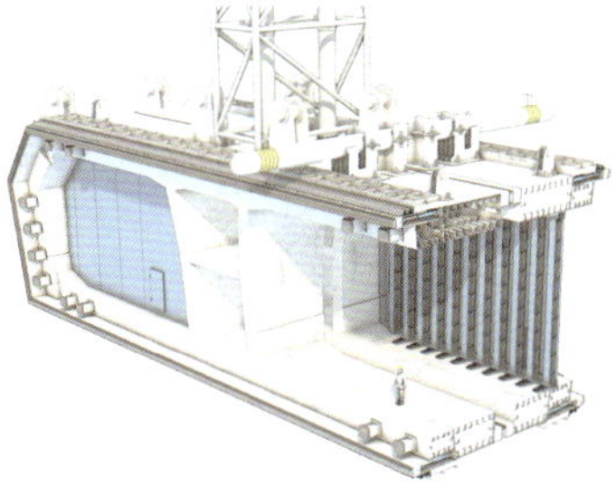

最终接头结构剖面图
Sectional View of the Closure Joint
127

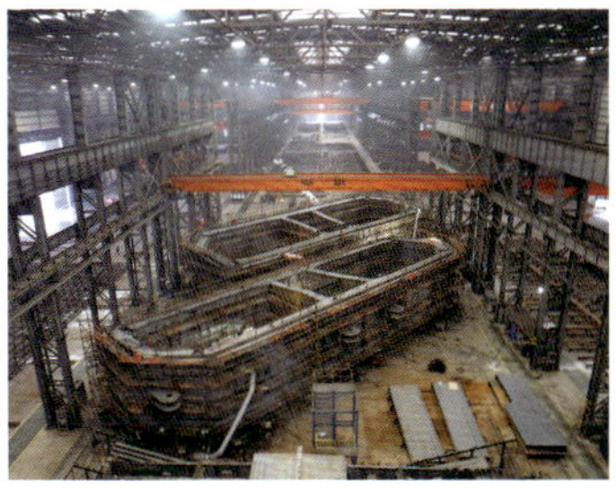

最终接头钢壳制造
Manufacturing of the Steel Shell of the Closure Joint
128

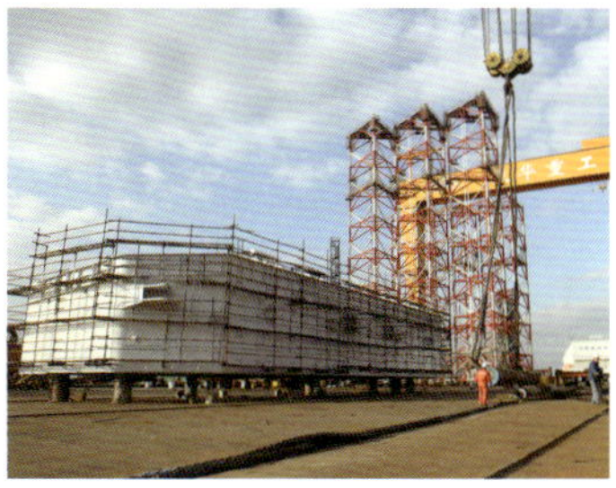

最终接头本体结构运输至场外
Body Structure of the Closure Joint Undocking
131

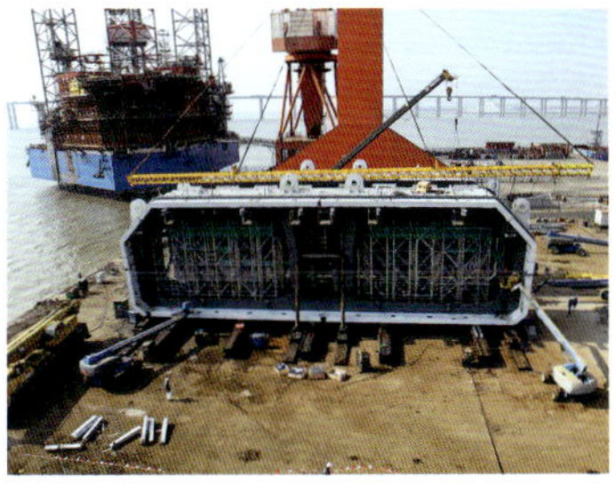

最终接头小梁结构拼装
Assembling the Trabecular Structure of the Closure Joint
133

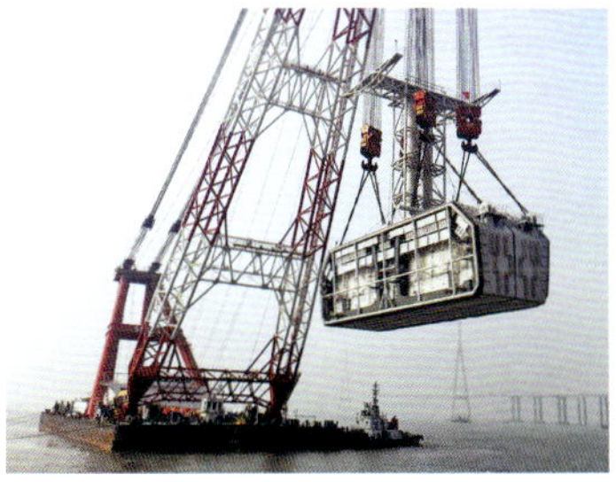

最终接头起吊装船
Hoisting and Installation Barge for the Closure Joint
134

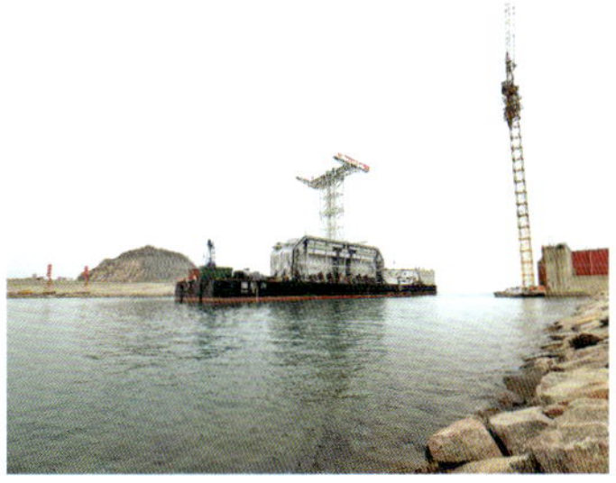

最终接头运抵沉管预制厂深坞
Closure Joint Transported to the Immersed Tube Manufacturing Dock
136

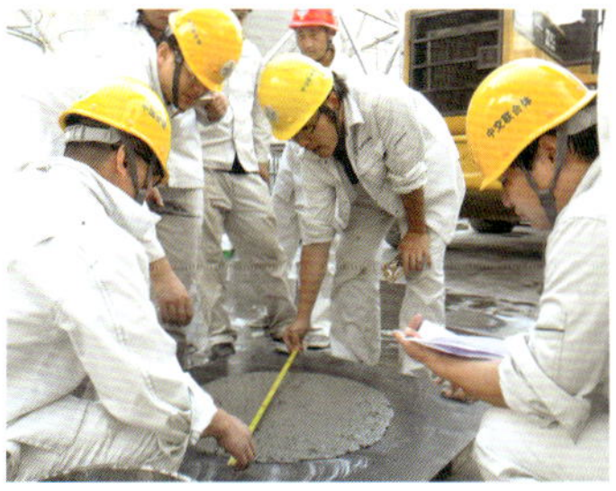

高流动性混凝土坍落度检测
Slump Test of the High-Fluidity Concrete
139

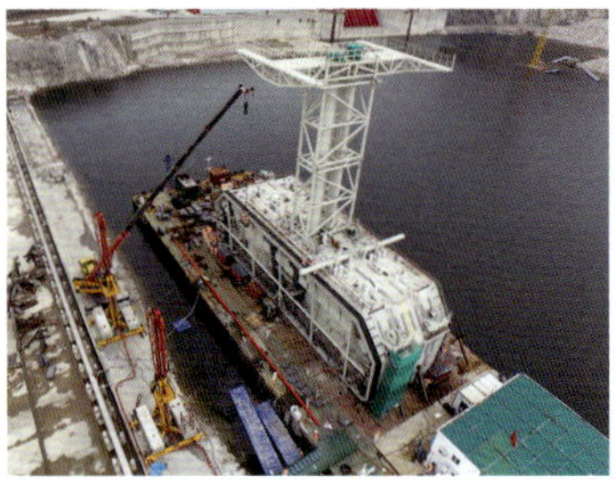

最终接头高流动性混凝土浇筑准备
Preparation for High-Fluidity Concrete Placement at the Closure Joint
140

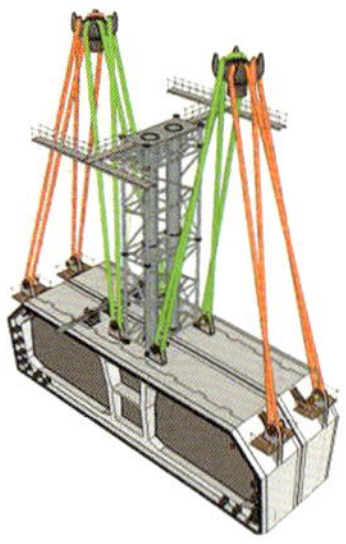

最终接头吊装布索方式图
Diagram of the Suspension Cable Arrangement for the Hoisting of the Closure Joint
143

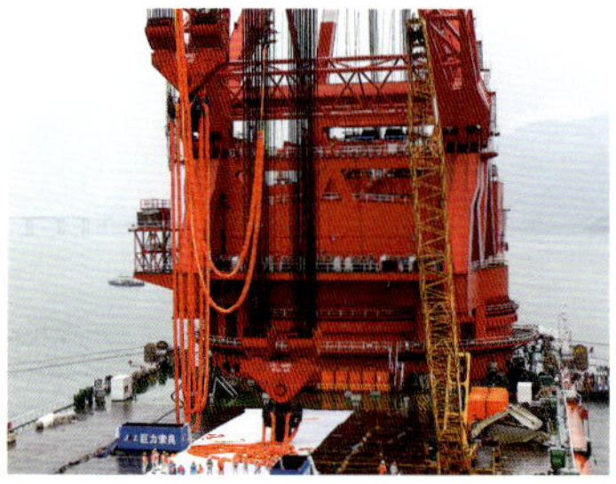

吊索吊挂施工
Hoisting of the Suspension Cable
145

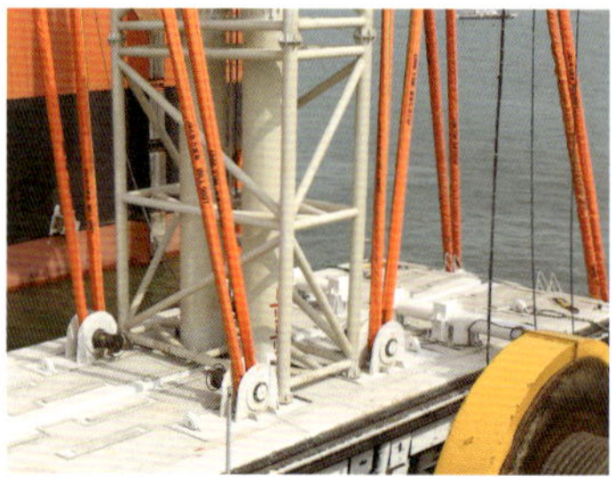

安装在最终接头上的销轴
Shaft Pin Installed on the Closure Joint
147

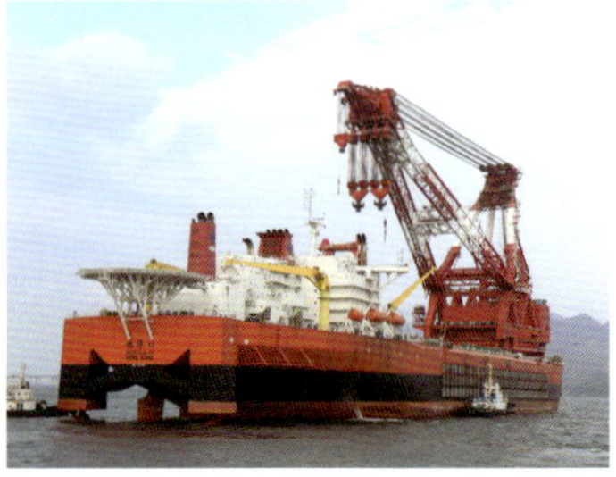

全回转起重船"振华30"
Swing Crane Barge "Zhenhua30"
149

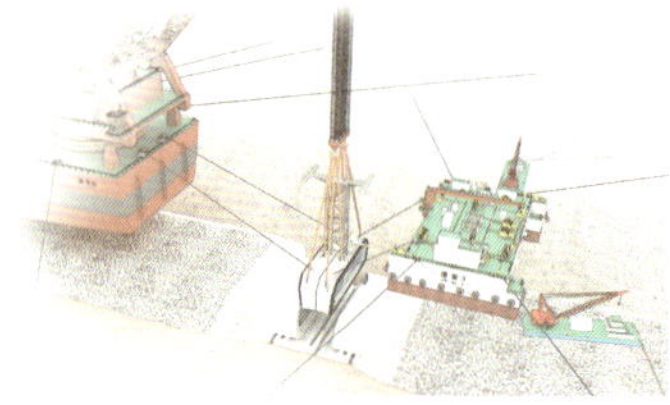

最终接头安装三维图
3-D Diagram of the Closure Joint Installation
151

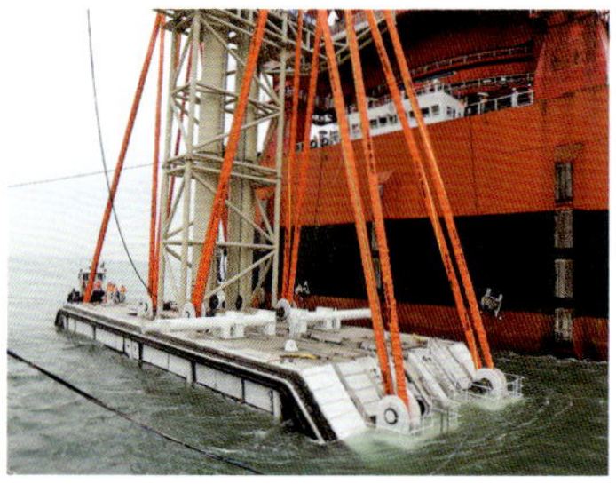

最终接头入水试漏检查
Leakage Detection of the Closure Joint
153

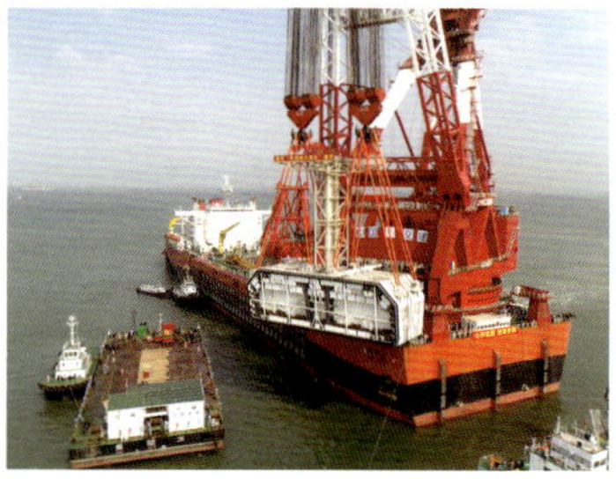

最终接头起吊、转向
Hoisting and Swerving of the Closure Joint
154

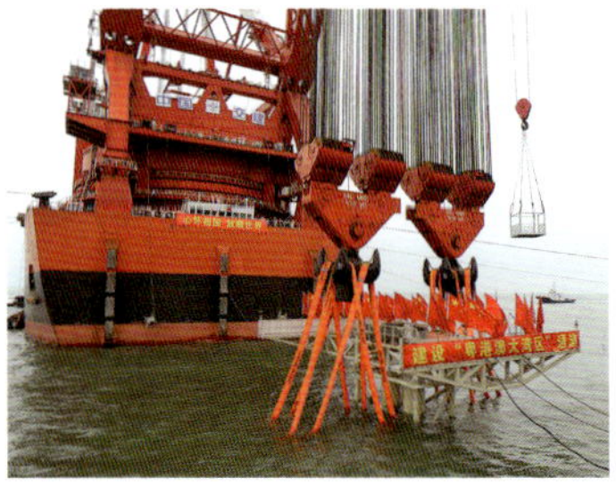

最终接头着床
Landing of the Closure Joint
157

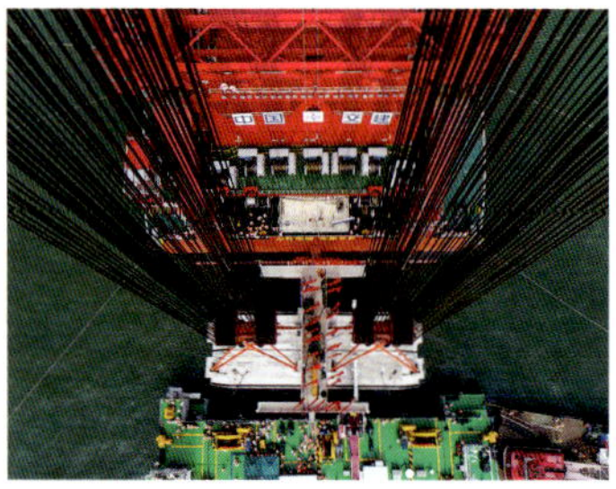

最终接头沉放施工
Enclosure Joint Landing
159

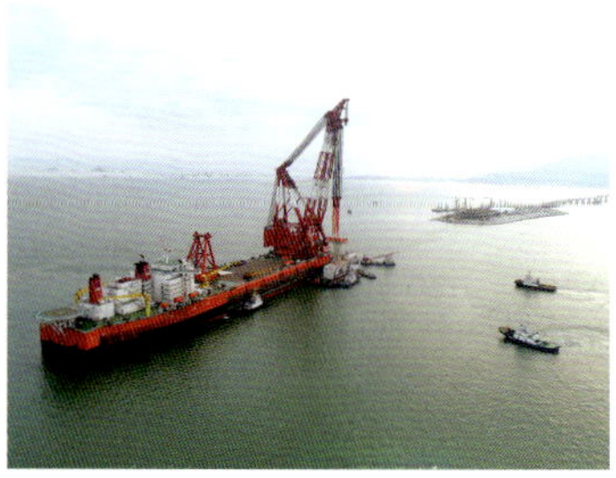

"振华30"安装最终接头
Installation of the Closure Joint by "Zhenhua30"
160

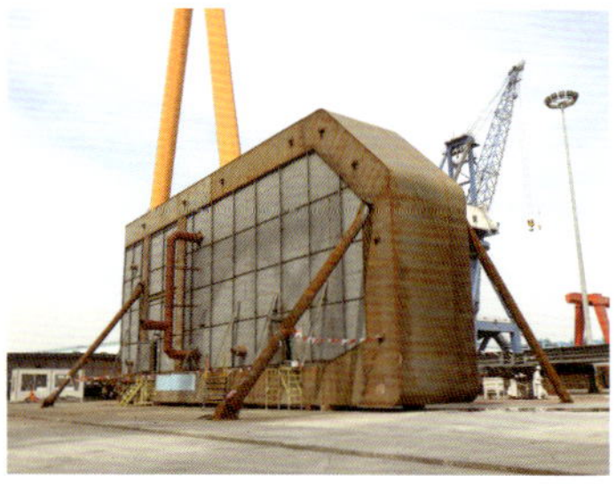

最终接头结合腔足尺模型
Full-Size Model of the Binding Cavity of the Closure Joint
162

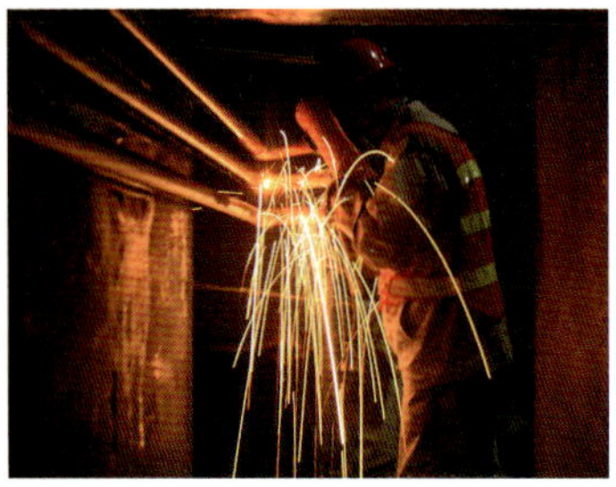

最终接头结合腔焊接施工
Welding the Binding Cavity of the Closure Joint
165

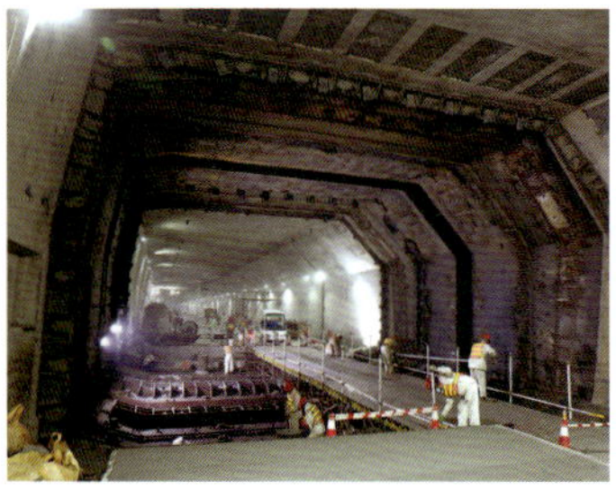

最终接头结合腔焊接完成，海底隧道贯通
Completion of Welding the Binding Cavity of the Closure Joint, and Holing through of the Undersea Tunnel
166

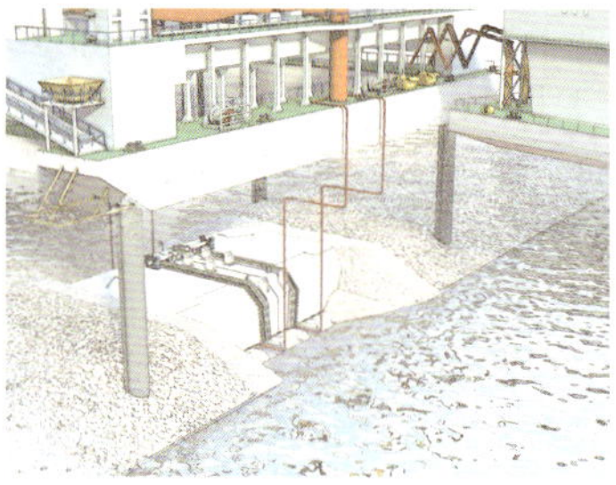

最终接头基础注浆三维图
3-D Diagram of the Closure Joint Base Grouting
168

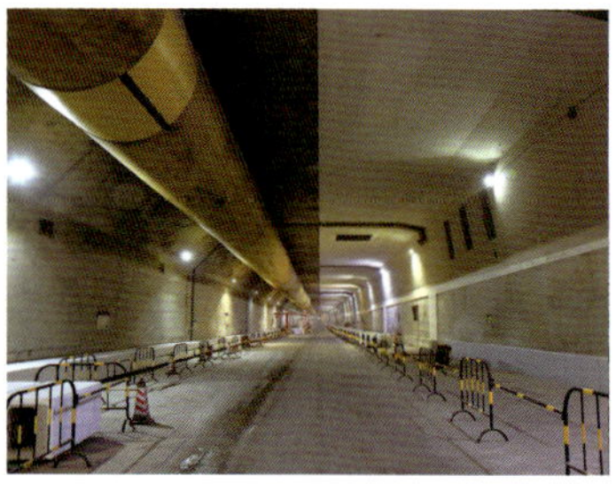

沉管隧道内装
Internal Decoration of the Immersed Tube Tunnel
172

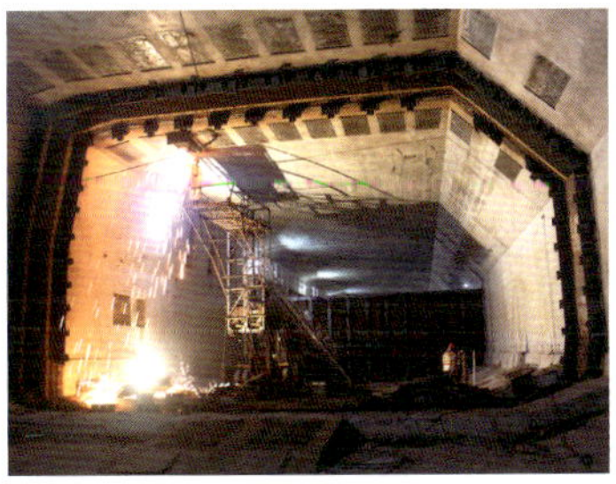

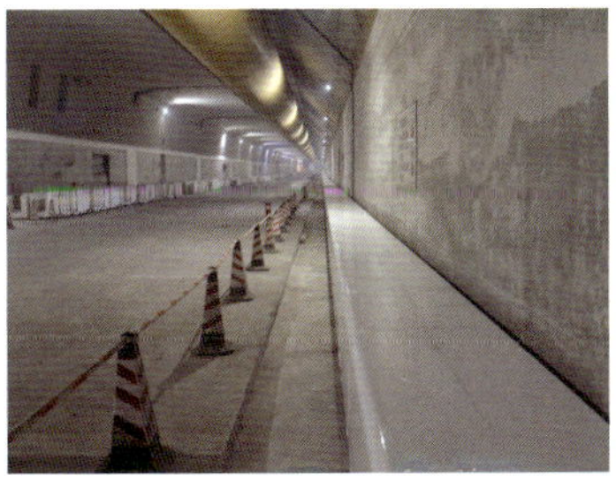

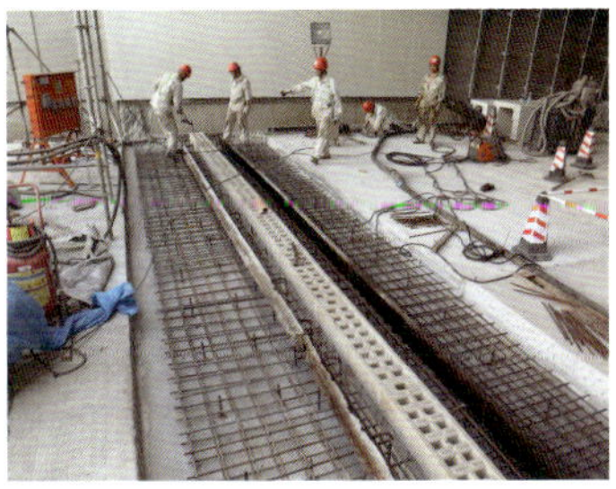

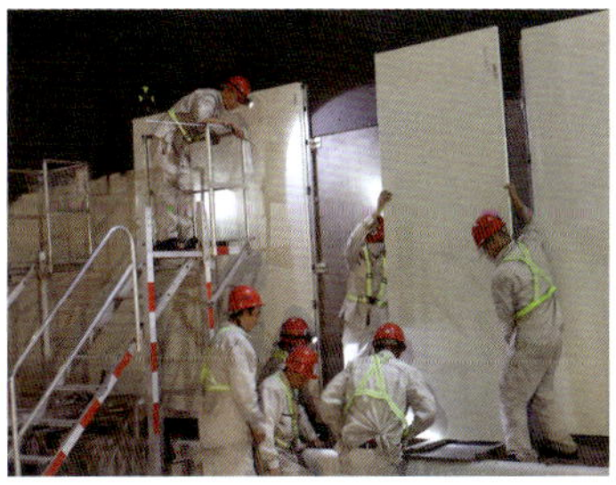

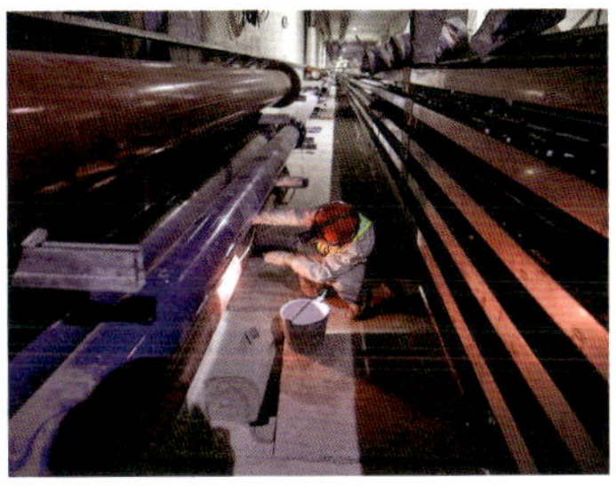

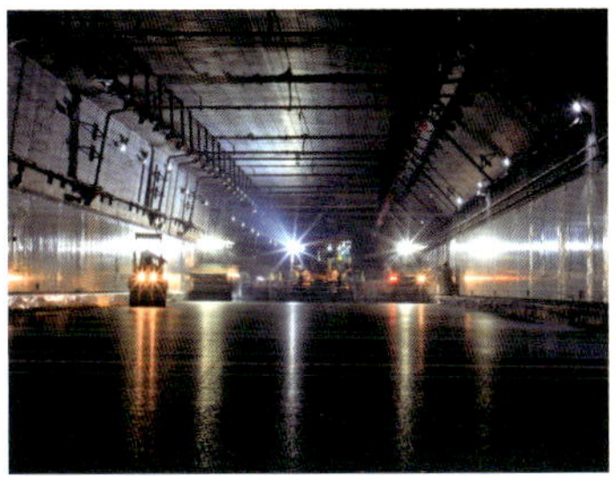

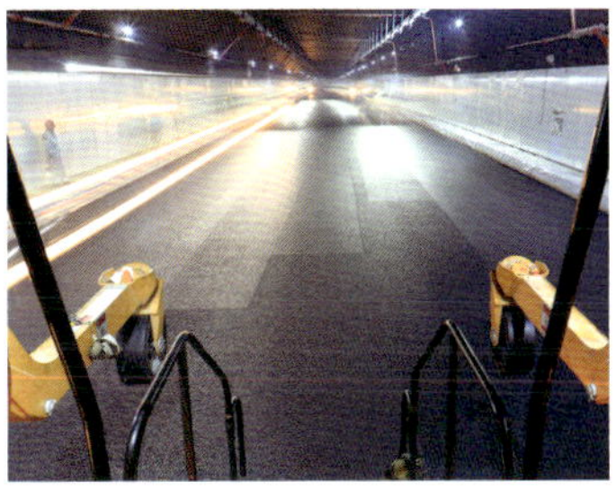

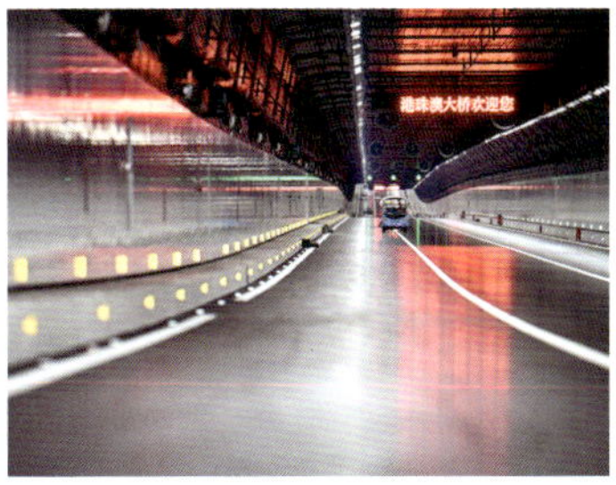

筑岛奇迹

A MIRACLE OF ISLAND RECLAMATION

港珠澳大桥岛隧工程画册

Album of the Island-Tunnel Project of Hong Kong-Zhuhai-Macau Bridge

中国交通建设股份有限公司 编
CHINA COMMUNICATIONS CONSTRUCTION COMPANY LIMITED

南方日报出版社
NANFANG DAILY PRESS
中国·广州

图书在版编目（CIP）数据

筑岛奇迹 / 中国交通建设股份有限公司编. — 广州：南方日报出版社，2019.3

（港珠澳大桥岛隧工程画册）

ISBN 978-7-5491-1987-5

Ⅰ. ①筑… Ⅱ. ①中… Ⅲ. ①跨海峡桥－桥梁工程－中国－图集
②水下隧道－隧道工程－中国－图集 Ⅳ. ①U4-64

中国版本图书馆 CIP 数据核字（2019）第 045126 号

GANG ZHU AO DAQIAO DAOSUI GONGCHENG HUACE · ZHUDAO QIJI

港珠澳大桥岛隧工程画册·筑岛奇迹

编　　者：中国交通建设股份有限公司

设计排版：廣角品牌机构

出版发行：南方日报出版社

地　　址：广州市广州大道中 289 号

出 版 人：周山丹

责任编辑：杨柳青　曹　星

责任技编：王　兰

责任校对：王　燕

装帧设计：李文俊　田　红　吴　凯

翻　　译：刘风山　郭敬谊

经　　销：全国新华书店

印　　刷：雅昌文化（集团）有限公司

开　　本：635 mm×965 mm　1/8

印　　张：22.5

字　　数：418 千字

版　　次：2019 年 3 月第 1 版

印　　次：2019 年 3 月第 1 次印刷

定　　价：980.00 元（全套 4 册）

编委会

Editorial Board

总序
FOREWORD

人类的探索和创新永无止境！

工程建设史上第一次尝试从水下跨越，起始于19世纪中叶英国泰晤士河的一条盾构隧道。之后经历半个多世纪，在1910年，美国建成了世界上第一条沉管隧道。

沉管工法由于其综合了近海工程、水工工程、地下工程、隧道工程的复合性技术，实施难度非常大，因而在隧道建设中应用很少。到目前为止，全世界建成的沉管隧道不到两百条，主要集中在美国、荷兰、日本等发达国家。

中国的沉管隧道建设起步较晚，在20世纪90年代初才建设了第一条规模很小的沉管隧道，而当时国外已经建成沉管隧道近百条。和很多领域一样，中国人需要更多的付出、更深的积淀、更强的意志来追赶和超越。

历史性的时刻总是不期而至。2009年底，港珠澳大桥建设方案横空出世，吹响了中国向世界沉管隧道技术巅峰冲刺的号角。这一跨越伶仃洋，连接香港、珠海和澳门的世纪性工程，吸引了全球目光，注定载入史册。中国交建作为中国工程建设的主力军和国家队，勇挑重担，义无反顾地担负起港珠澳大桥岛隧工程这一关乎全局的控制性工程。深埋海底、长达6.7公里的沉管隧道，放眼全球，都是令人望而生畏的难题。

7年来，岛隧工程建设团队攻坚克难、创新实践，完成了100多项试验研究，创造了500多项技术专利，形成了六大方面创新成果，创造了沉管隧道"最长、最大跨径、最大埋深、最大体量"四项世界纪录，成为令人叹服的工程奇迹。

这一全球瞩目的世纪工程，是中国持续推进改革开放的重要成果，是我们由桥梁建设大国迈向桥梁建设强国的重要标志，也是中国交建开拓创新、追求卓越精神的集中体现。正是凭借这种宝贵精神，中国交建的建设者们不断在更多领域实现突破，持续让中国桥梁、中国港口、中国隧道、中国公路等"靓丽名片"造福全人类。

让我们为可爱可敬的工程建设者们喝彩，为蓬勃发展的中国交建喝彩，为在以习近平同志为核心的党中央带领下蒸蒸日上的伟大祖国喝彩！

Human beings never stopped and will never stop their efforts to explore into the unknown and create the new.

The first effort of underwater project in the history of engineering and construction for underwater construction was the shield tunnel underneath the River Thames of England built in mid-19th century. Over five decades later, the first immersed tube tunnel in the world was built in the United States in 1901.

Immersed tube tunneling involves many complicated technologies such as offshore engineering, hydraulic engineering, underground engineering and tunnel engineering, and is hard to handle, so it is uncommon to use this technique in tunnel construction. By now, there are no more than 200 immersed tube tunnels in the world, and these tunnels can be seen mainly in such developed countries as the United States, the Netherlands and Japan.

It was in recent years that immersed tube tunneling began to be adopted in China. The first small immersed tube tunnel in China was built in the 1990s while there were about 100 immersed tube tunnels in other countries. Like in other fields, China needs to put in more efforts and has to face more challenges to catch up with and finally surpass the others.

The historic moment never hesitates to come. The construction plan of Hong Kong-Zhuhai-Macau Bridge towards the end of 2009 achieved China's breakthrough in immersed tube tunneling. The bridge, spanning across Lingding Bay, connects Hong Kong, Zhuhai and Macau and proves to be an epoch-making project, catching the attention of the whole world. The leading force of China's engineering and construction industry, China Communications Construction Company Ltd.as a state-owned company readily shouldered the responsibility to undertake the island tunnel project, the most critical part of the bridge. An immersed tube tunnel of 6.70 kilometers long buried deep underneath the sea proves to be the most forbidding project all over the world.

In the past seven years, the island tunnel project team has overcome countless difficulties, conducted more than 100 experiments, accomplished more than 500 technical patents and many innovations in six major fields, and created an engineering miracle by breaking four world records with its longest immersed tube tunnel of the largest span, the biggest burial depth and the biggest dimension.

Winning global attention in the new century, this gorgeous project proves to be the result of China promoting reform and opening to the world, initiating the change of China from a big bridge builder to a bridge-building superpower and exhibiting China Constructions Construction Company Ltd.'s innovative spirit and desire for perfection. This precious business spirit enables the engineers of China Communications Construction Company Ltd. to make breakthroughs in more fields and serve the world with "Chinese bridge" "Chinese port" "Chinese tunnel" and "Chinese highway."

Acclaim for the beloved engineers, acclaim for the flourishing China Communications Construction Company Ltd. and acclaim for our thriving motherland led by the Central Committee of the Communist Party headed by President Xi Jinping.

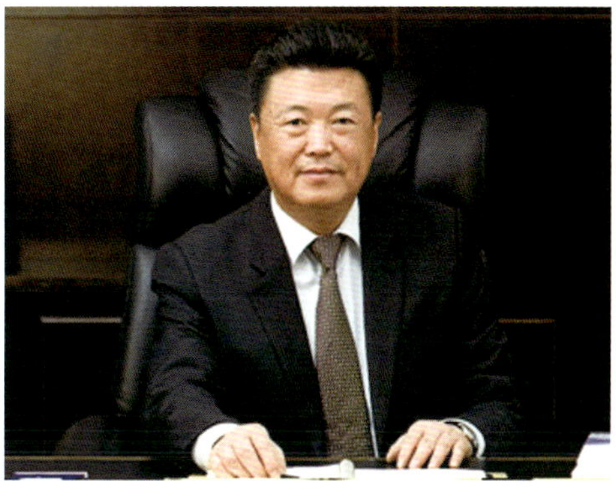

中国交通建设股份有限公司董事长、党委书记

Chief Executive and Secretary of the Party Committee China Communications Construction Company Ltd.

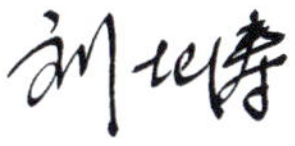

Liu Qitao

目录
CONTENTS

港珠澳大桥总体综述
PROFILE OF HONG KONG-ZHUHAI–MACAU BRIDGE

快速成岛创新技术
INNOVATIVE TECHNOLOGY OF MAN-MADE ISLAND RECLAMATION

海上深基坑工程
OFFSHORE DEEP FOUNDATION TRENCH PROJECT

岛上结构施工
CONSTRUCTION OF THE ISLAND STRUCTURES

画册索引
ALBUM INDEX

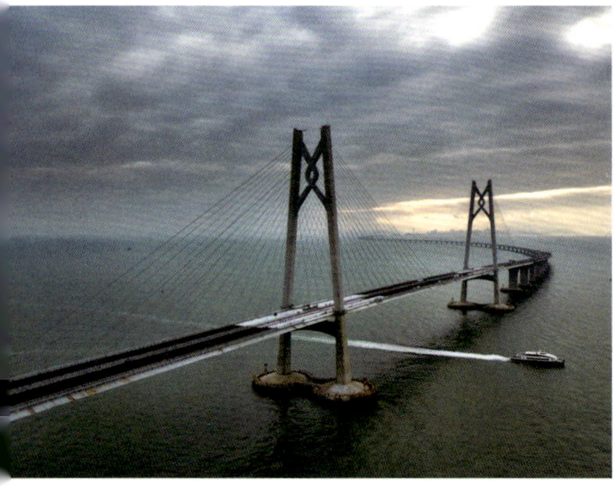

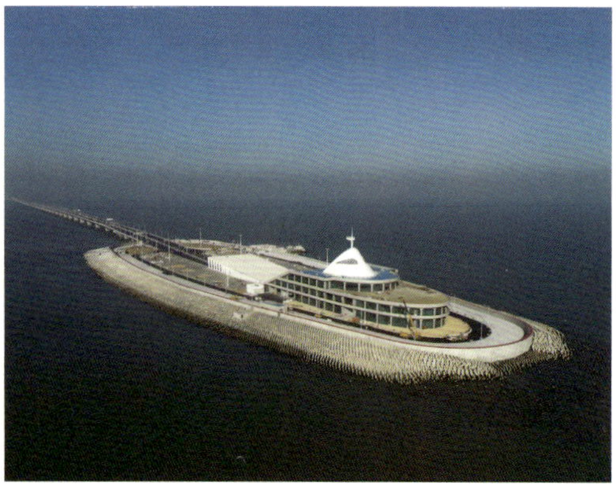

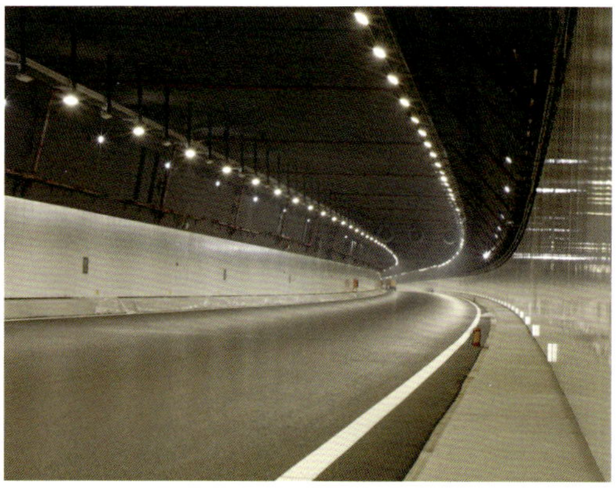

港珠澳大桥总体综述

PROFILE OF HONG KONG-ZHUHAI–MACAU BRIDGE

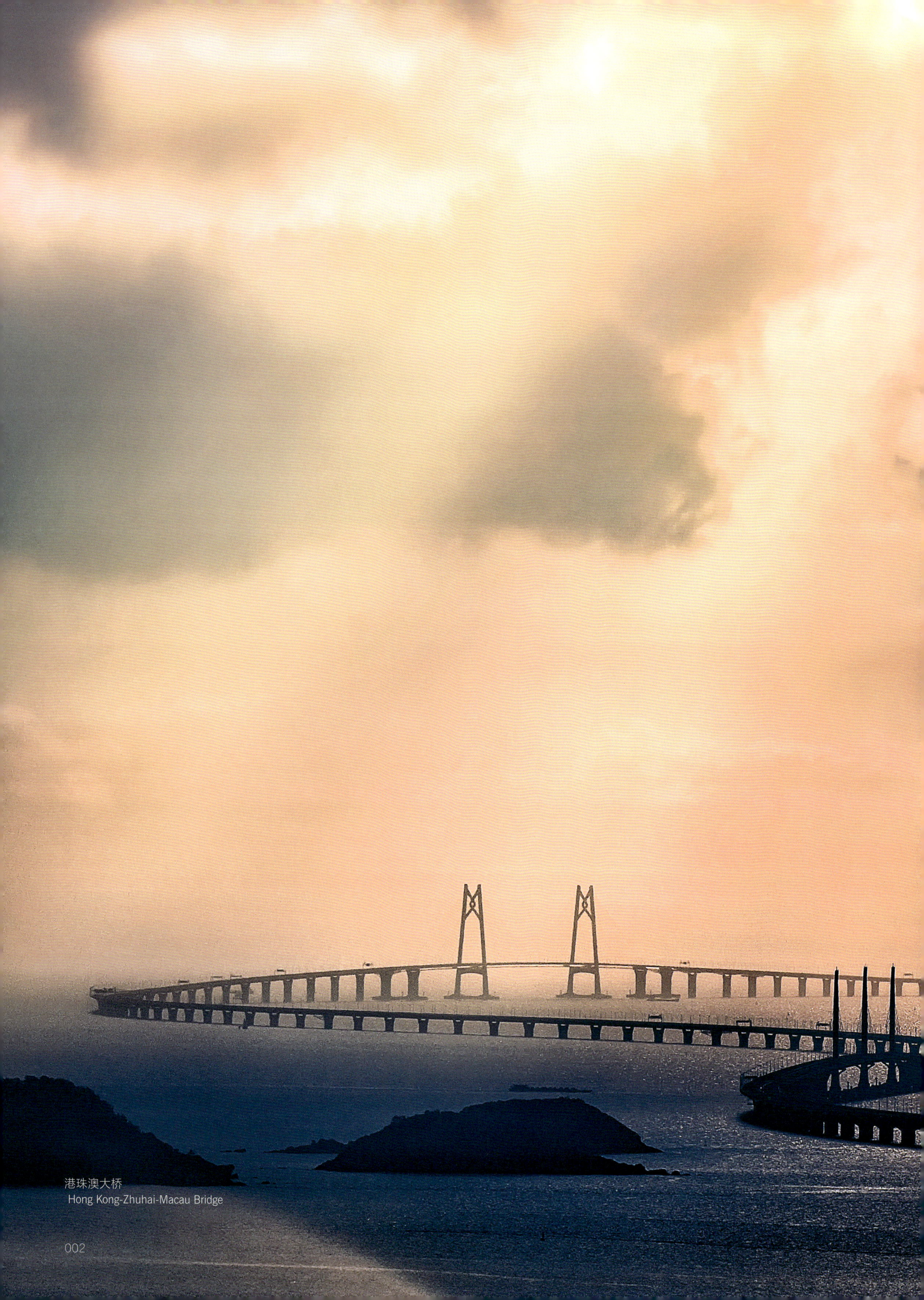

港珠澳大桥
Hong Kong-Zhuhai-Macau Bridge

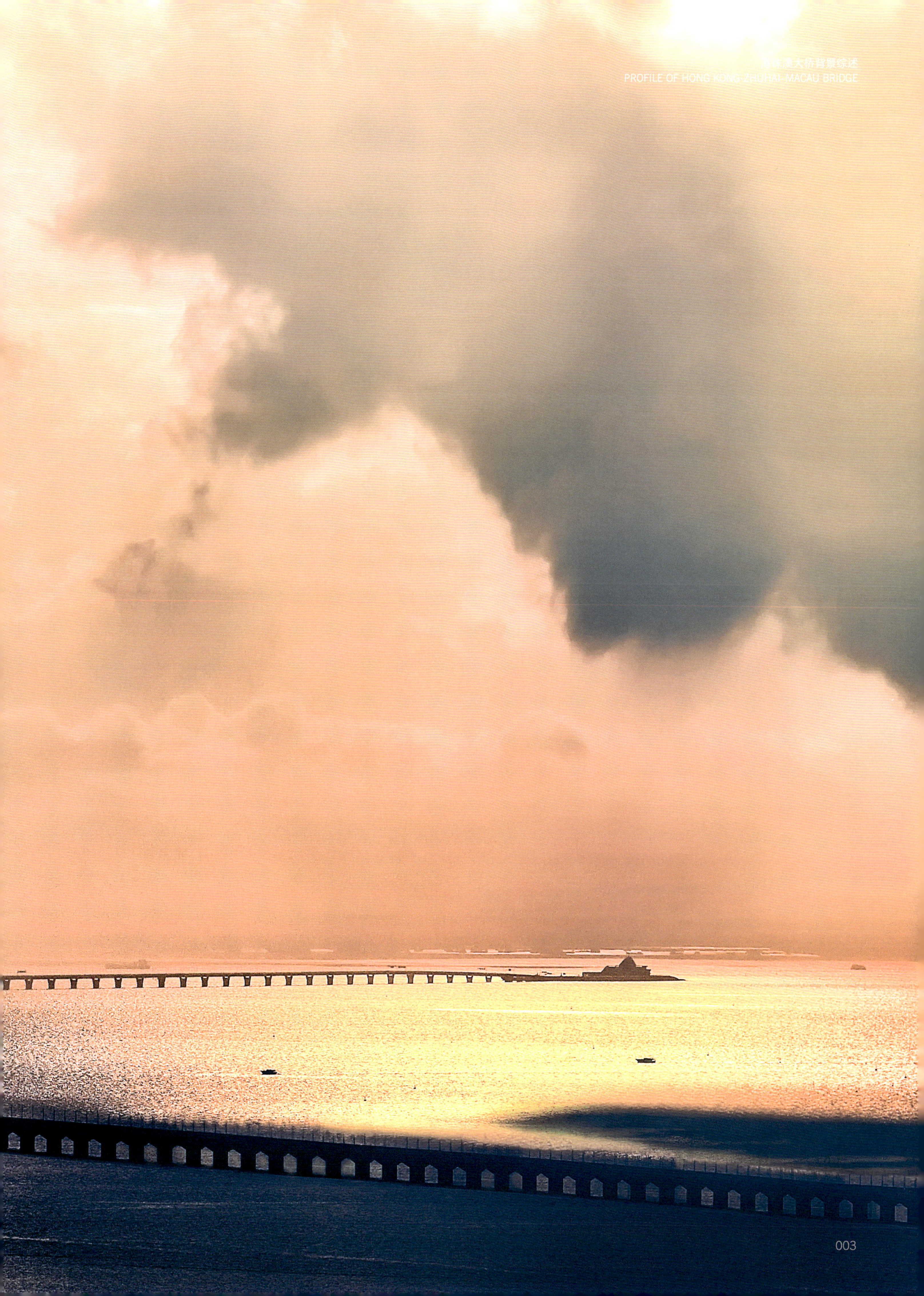

背景概述
BACKGROUND

中国珠江口，一座55公里的港珠澳大桥如巨龙卧波，连接起香港、珠海、澳门三座城市，从此三地成一体，瀚海变通途。

这座由桥、岛、隧组成的交通集群工程，是目前世界上最长的超大型公路跨海通道，设计使用寿命120年。

2009年底动工，2017年7月实现沉管隧道贯通，20,000多名建设者用智慧与汗水把桥隧技术推向了一个崭新的高度。

港珠澳大桥凝结着中国数十年桥梁工程的各项成果，记录了中国在外海沉管隧道技术领域的巨大跨越，展示了中国工程建设实力，是世界桥梁史上公认的巅峰之作。粤港澳大湾区，中国又一个新的经济增长极，正扬帆起航。

Hong Kong-Zhuhai-Macau Bridge, 55 kilometers long, crouching over Pearl River Estuary like an eastern dragon, links Hong Kong, Zhuhai and Macau into a whole, turning the chasm dividing them into a thoroughfare.

A combination of bridges, islands and tunnels, it is the world's longest super-size highway over the sea with a designed life span of 120 years.

Beginning at the end of 2009, the immersed tube tunneling project was completed in July 2017. Over 20,000 constructors pushed the technology of bridge-tunnel construction to its new height with their wisdom and hard work.

Hong Kong-Zhuhai-Macau Bridge combines many technological innovations of China in bridge construction in the past decades, records China's big leap in offshore immersed tube tunneling technology, and exhibits China's strength in construction engineering. It is recognized as the peak in the world history of bridge construction. The Guangdong-Hong Kong-Macau Grand Bay Area, another new economic growth pole of China, has set sail.

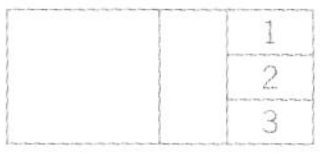

1. 青州航道桥
   Qingzhou Channel Bridge
2. 九洲航道桥
   Jiuzhou Channel Bridge
3. 江海航道桥
   Jianghai Channel Bridge

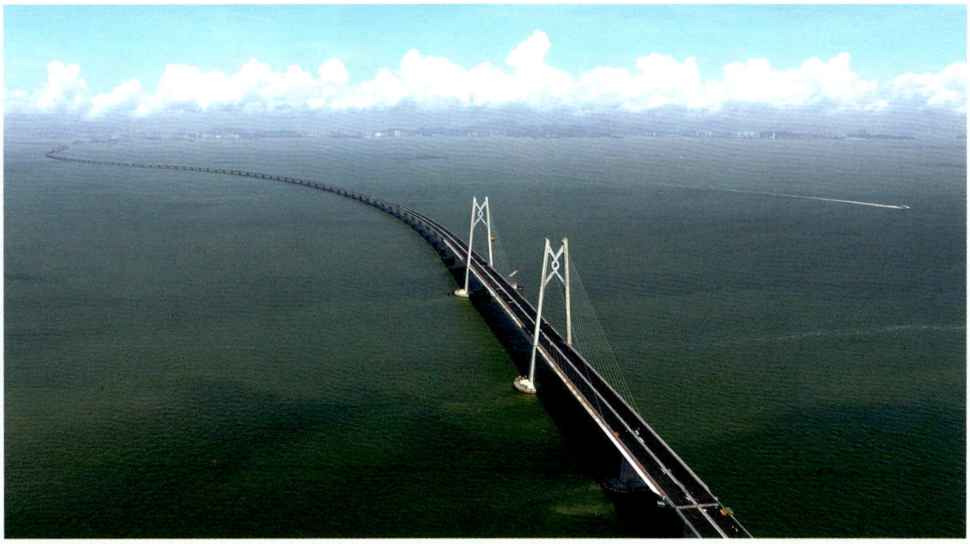

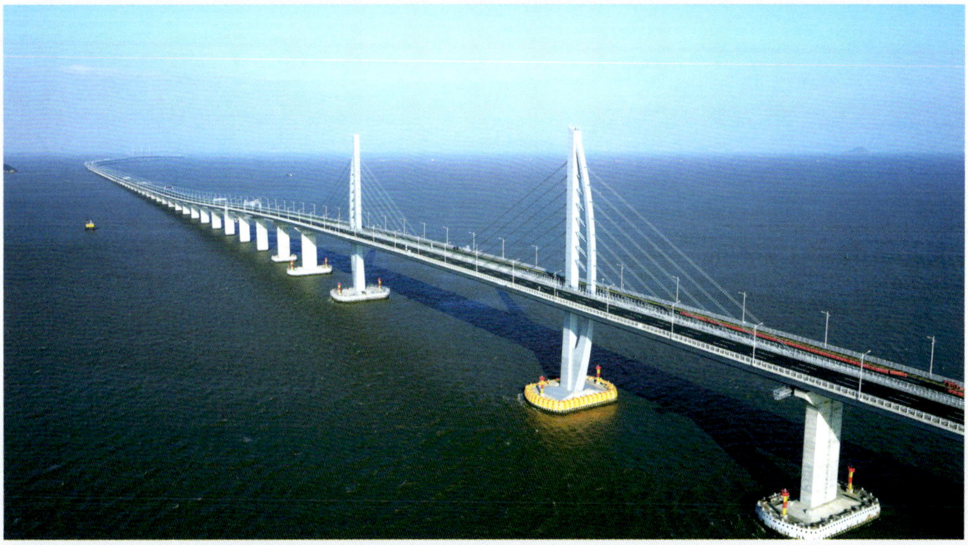

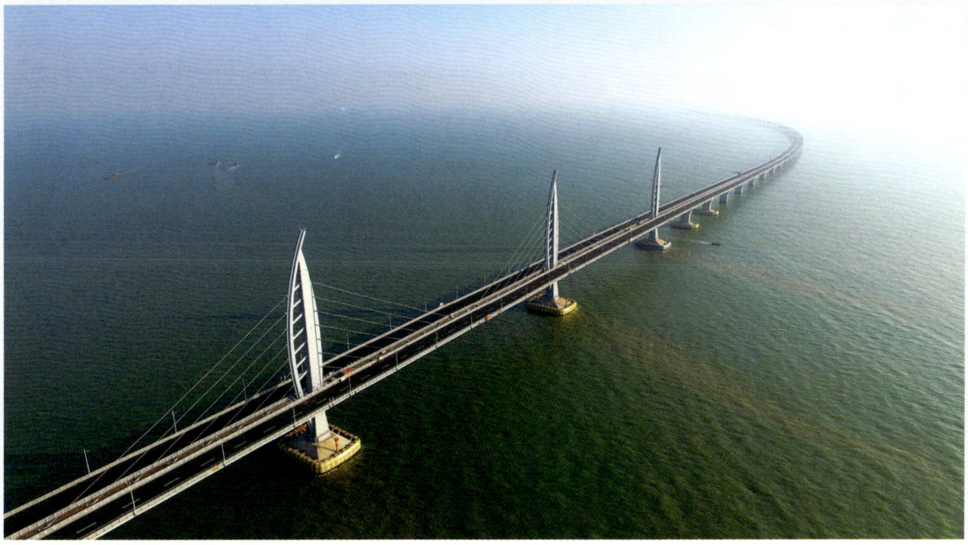

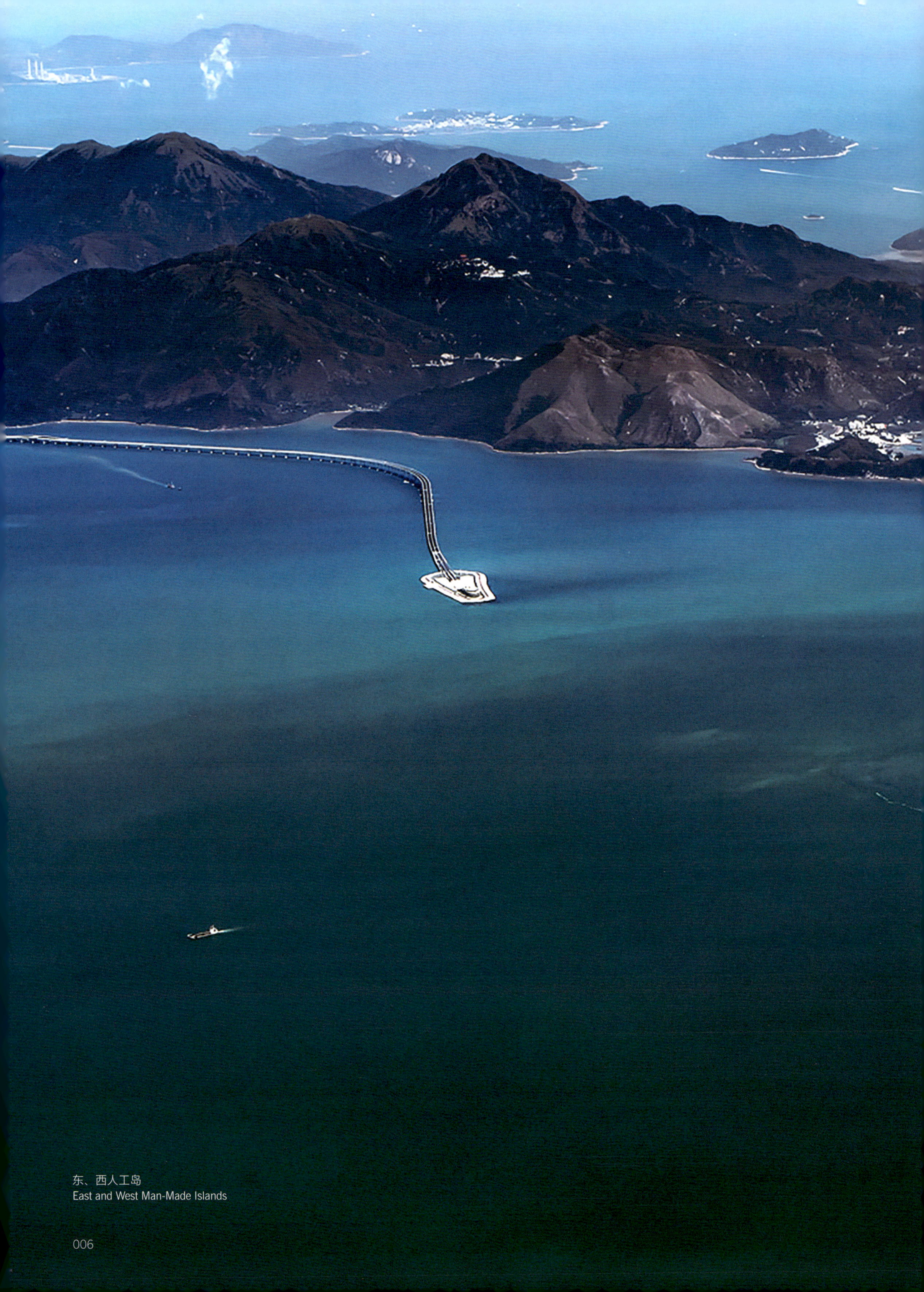

东、西人工岛
East and West Man-Made Islands

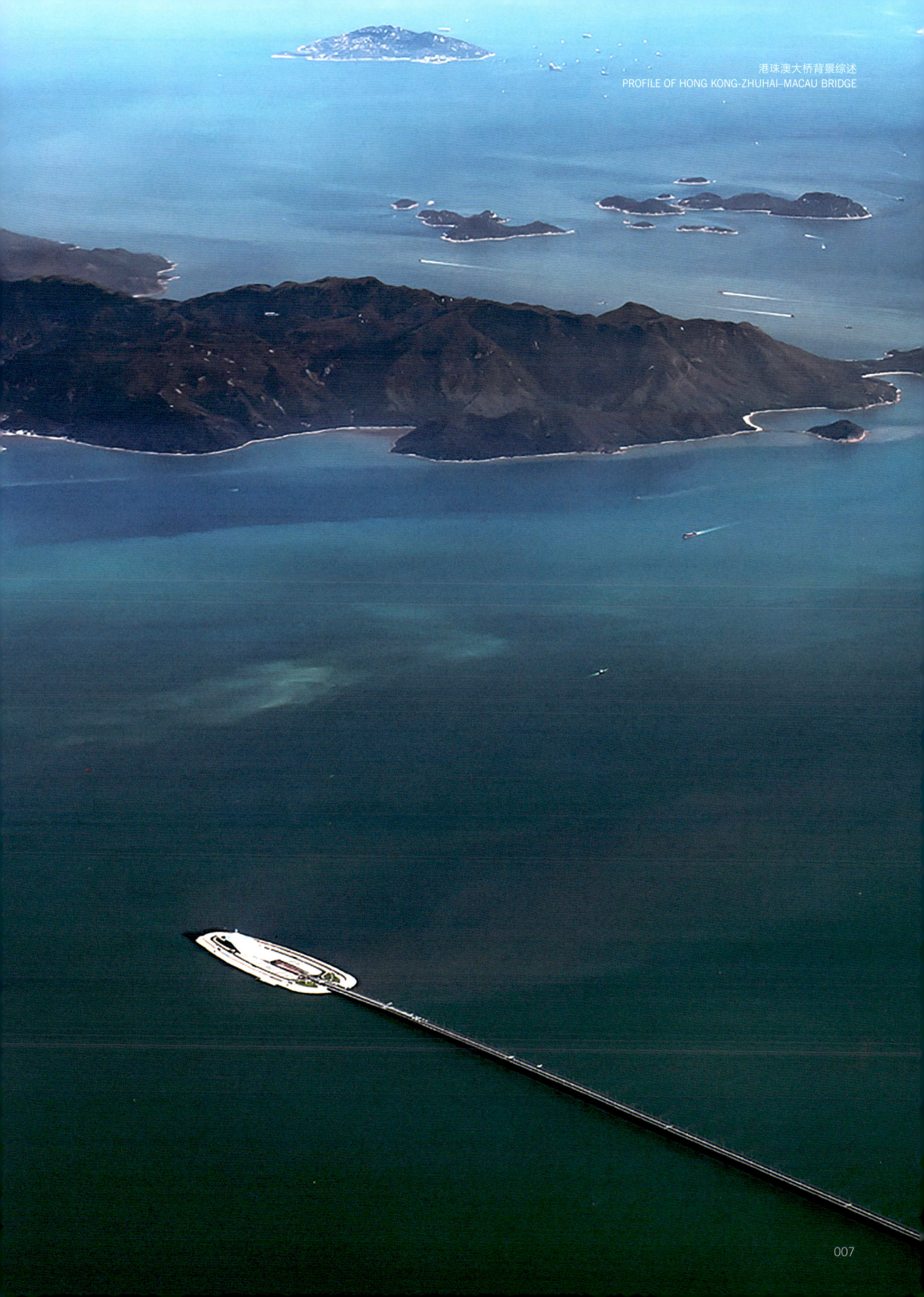

珠江，从中国西部的云贵高原蜿蜒而下，在这里汇入大海。在这个喇叭形入海口的周围，环绕着广州、深圳、东莞、中山、珠海五个港口。

这里大小航道纵横交错，过往船舶每天超过 4000 艘（次），是世界上最繁忙的水域之一。在这样的环境里建造 55 公里长的跨海大桥，既要不影响当地的航运需求，又要让公路与水路相得益彰。

在珠江口航运规划中，要为未来预留 30 万吨级船舶的通航能力，预留航道深度达 29 米；伶仃主航道距离香港大屿山国际机场仅 3 公里左右，航班密集，如在航道区建设桥梁，限高不超过 88 米。

受航空限高和预留航道深度限制，部分桥梁须采用海中隧道方式，并且主航道区域隧道埋深必须超过航道预留深度。

实现桥隧转换需要在海中填筑人工岛。珠江口为弱洋流海域，根据珠江水利委员会要求，大桥阻水率不得超过 10%。港珠澳大桥海底隧道选择了对人工岛的长度需求较小，但实施风险较大的沉管隧道方案。

由此，一条 6.7 公里的海底沉管隧道、全长 55 公里的超级工程在珠江口诞生。

The Pearl River winds down all the way from the Yunnan-Guizhou Plateau in West China and flows into the sea here. Five ports, namely Guangzhou, Shenzhen, Dongguan, Zhongshan and Zhuhai, locate around the trumpet-shaped estuary.

Many navigation channels cross over each other here. With over 4000 vessels sailing through this area every day, it has become one of the busiest places on water in the world. And building a bridge of 55 kilometers long over the sea in such an environment should avoid any negative influences over the local shipping business on the one hand, and harmonize the transportations by road and over the sea.

According to the plan for the water transportation at Pearl River Estuary, the channels here should satisfy the passage of vessels of 300,000 tons in the future with the water depth of over 29 meters. Furthermore, the main channel across Lingding Bay is only about 3 kilometers away from the flight-intensive Hong Kong International Airport at Lantau Island, so the height of the bridge built in this area should be controlled within 88 meters.

Due to these limitations, some parts of the bridge have to be built as tunnels under the sea, and the depth of the buried tunnel below the watercourse must be bigger than that reserved for the watercourse.

The transition between the bridge and the tunnel needs man-made islands built in the sea. Pearl River Estuary is a region with weak oceanic current, and according to the requirements by Pearl River Water Conservancy Committee, the water-blocking rate of the bridge should not exceed 10%. Hence, the underwater tunnel project of Hong Kong-Zhuhai-Macau Bridge employed the technology of the immersed tube tunneling which depended not so much on the length of the man-made islands but enjoyed the high risk.

As a result, a super project with a total length of 55 kilometers and a 6.7-kilometer-long immersed tube tunnel materialized at the Pearl River Estuary.

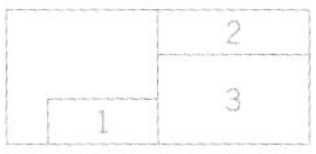

1. 岛隧工程效果图
Design Sketch of the Island-Tunnel Project

2. 东、西人工岛航拍
Aerial Photo of East and West Man-Made Islands

3. 港珠澳大桥卫星图
Satellite Map of Hong Kong-Zhuhai-Macau Bridge

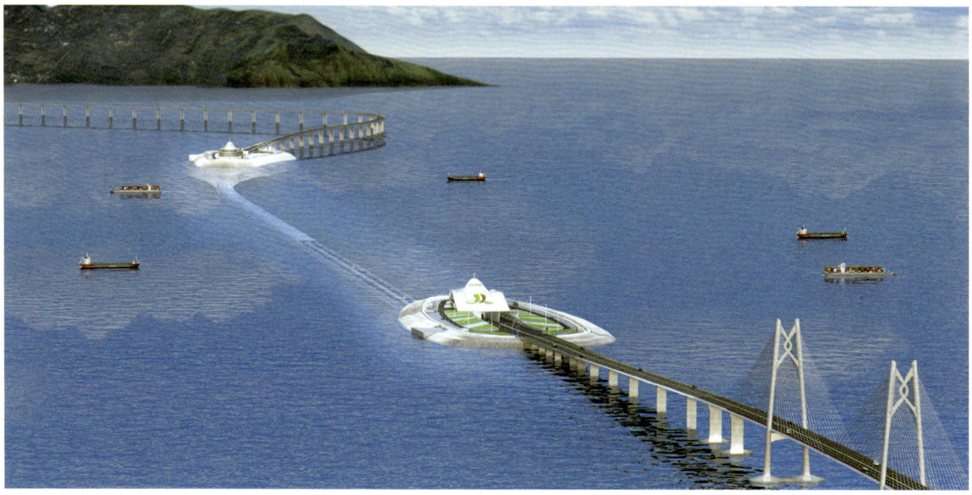

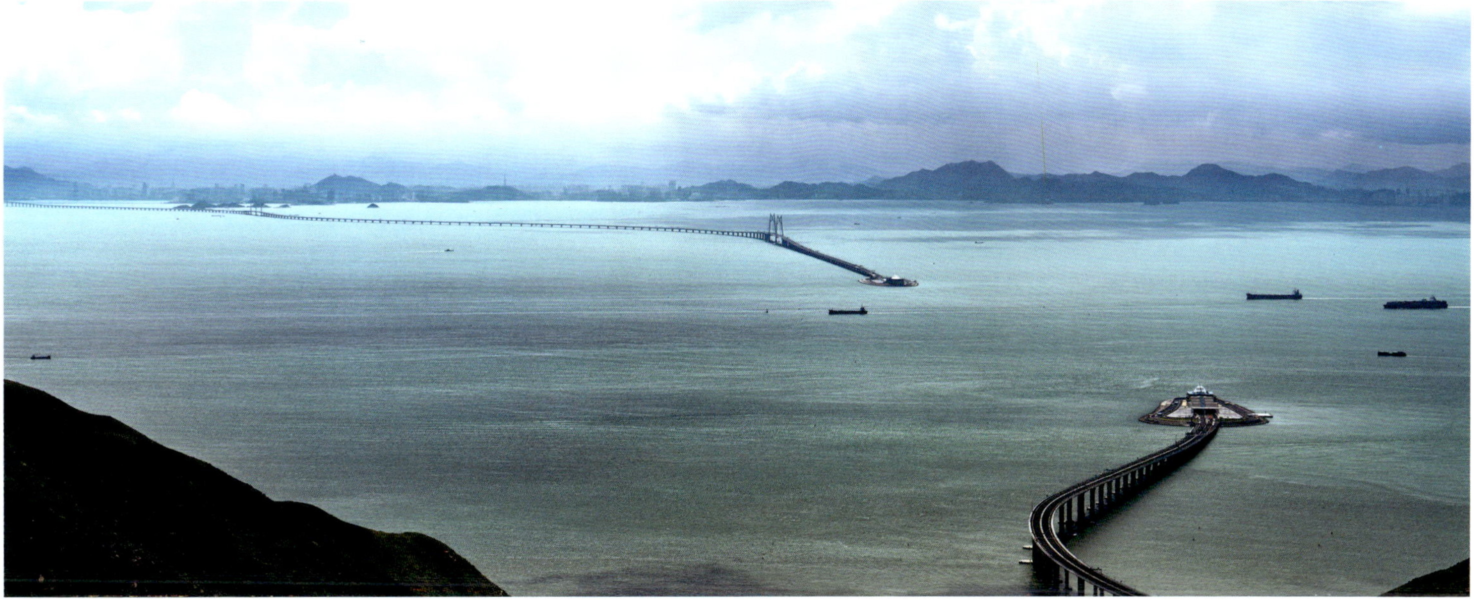

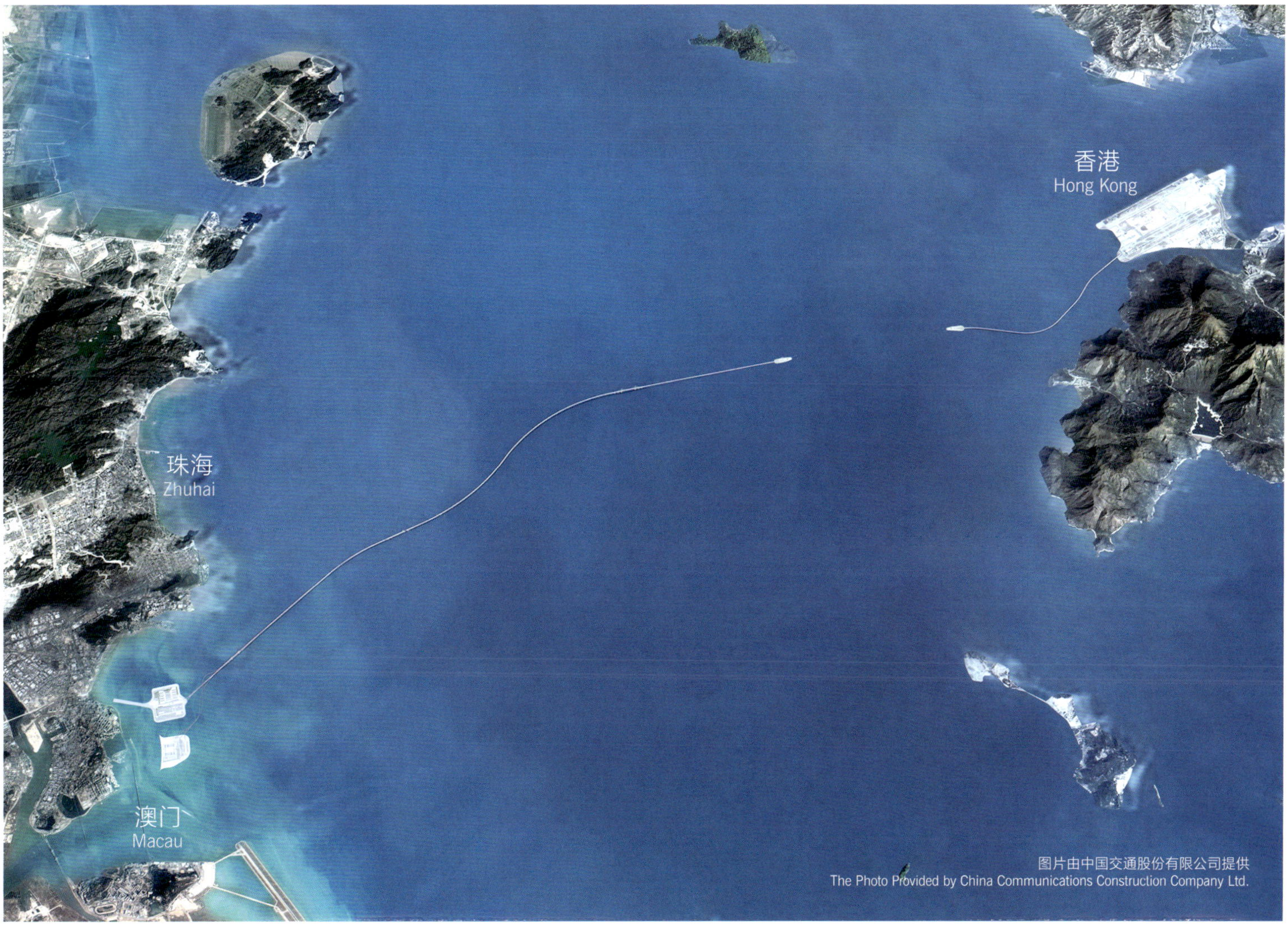

图片由中国交通股份有限公司提供
The Photo Provided by China Communications Construction Company Ltd.

技术挑战
TECHNICAL CHALLENGE

港珠澳大桥沉管隧道是当今世界最长公路沉管隧道，世界唯一深埋沉管隧道，也是中国第一条外海沉管隧道，其工程规模和技术难度位居世界同类工程前列。

岛隧工程是大桥的控制性工程，包括两个外海人工岛和一条沉管隧道。6.7 公里的海底隧道由 33 节沉管和 1 节重达 6000 吨的最终接头连接而成，一节标准沉管长 180 米，宽 37.95 米，高 11.4 米，重 7.6 万吨。

港珠澳大桥工程施工区受台风、冬季季风、强对流、大雾天气等恶劣环境影响，全年可作业时间有限。厚达 30—50 米的软土地基和回淤环境给结构设计和沉降控制带来极大难度；工期紧张、通航密集以及工程实施处于中华白海豚保护区，更增加了工程建设难度。

面对这一世界工程难题，中国交建建设者科学规划，自主创新，从挑战中寻求机遇、从必然中寻求自由，同步推进勘察、设计、科研、装备研发和现场施工，开展了 100 多项试验研究，攻克系列难题，形成了 500 多项专利，仅用 7 年时间，实现了隧道合龙贯通，创造了世界工程史上的奇迹。

The immersed tube tunnel of Hong Kong-Zhuhai-Macau Bridge is the longest highway immersed tube tunnel in the world, the only one deep-buried immersed tube tunnel of the world. As the first offshore immersed tube tunnel in China, it tops the similar projects in the world in terms of the project scale and its technical difficulty.

The island-tunnel project, composed of two man-made islands in the open sea and an immersed tube tunnel, is the key part in the construction of the whole bridge. The 6.7-kilometer-long underwater tunnel is made up of 33 immersed tubes and a closure joint weighing up to 6000 tons. The standard tube is 180 meters long, 37.95 meters wide, 11.4 meters high and 76,000 tons in weight.

The work site of the Hong Kong-Zhuhai-Macau Bridge project was subjected to impacts of such adverse conditions as typhoons, monsoon in winter, strong convection and heavy fog, and the time allowable for the construction throughout the year was limited. In addition, the soft earth foundation with a depth of 30 to 50 meters and back silting posed great difficulty to the structural design and landing control of the tubes. And the limited project time, the heavy traffic on the sea and the need to protect the Chinese White Dolphin in this area made it more difficult to conduct the construction.

To overcome these difficulties in this world-class project, the constructors of China Communications Construction Company Ltd. conducted countless innovative studies, made every effort to find opportunities and free themselves from technical bondage, and used what they found in the engineering survey, design, scientific research, equipment development and site construction. Over 100 experimental studies were conducted, a series of problems were conquered, and over 500 patents were obtained. In just seven years, the tunnel was completed and ready for transportation, which proved to be a miracle in the world history of engineering.

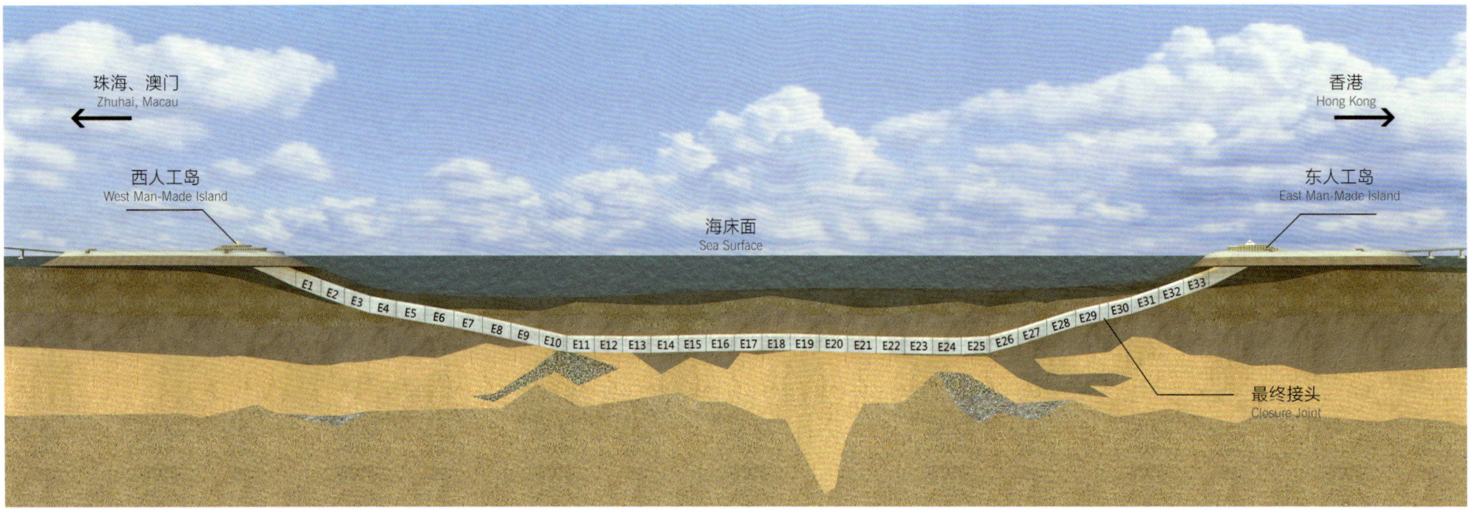

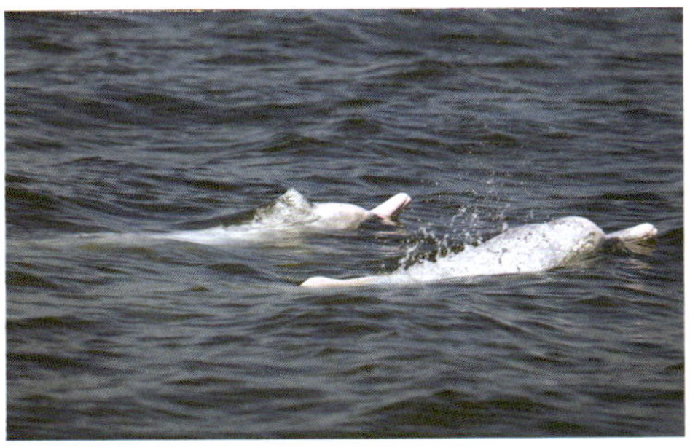

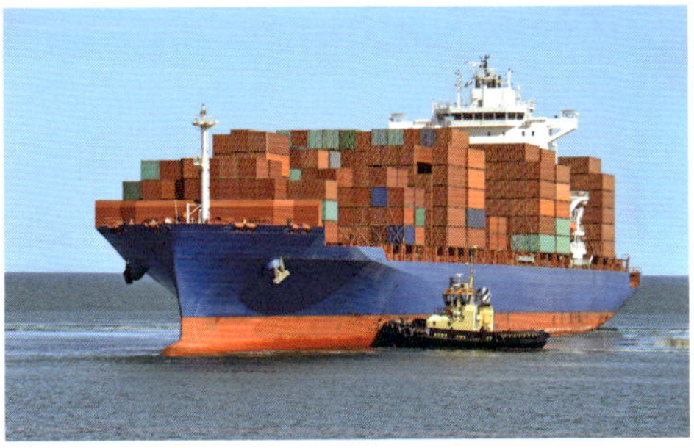

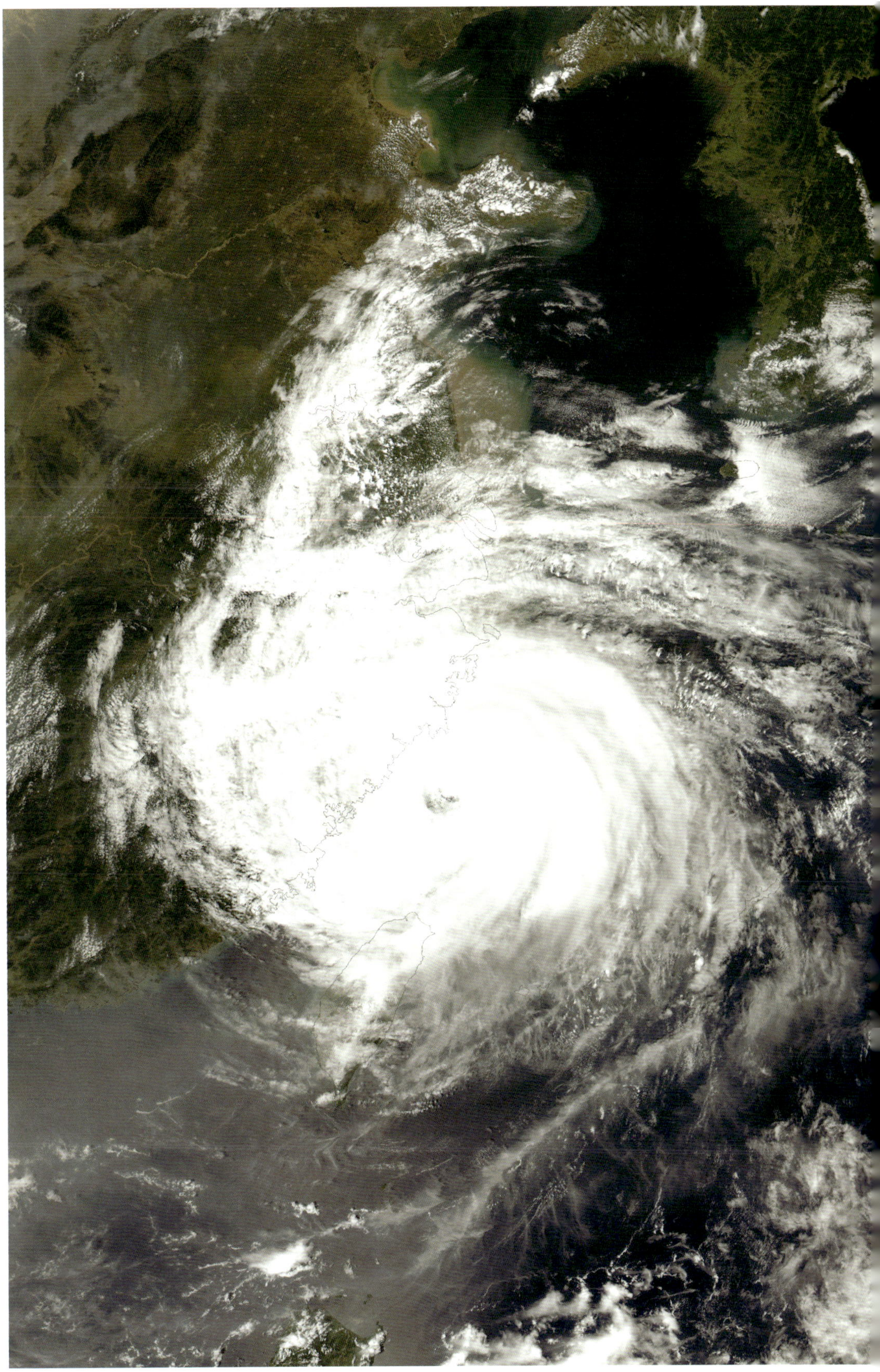

1. 岛隧工程隧道纵剖图
   Longitudinal Sectional View of the Island-Tunnel Project
2. 中华白海豚
   Chinese White Dolphins
3. 伶仃洋海域通航船舶
   Vessels Sailing over Lingding Bay
4. 台风卫星云图
   Satellite Cloud Map of a Typhoon

港珠澳大桥岛隧工程平面图

PLAN VIEW OF THE ISLAND-TUNNEL PROJECT OF HONG KONG-ZHUHAI-MACAU BRIDGE

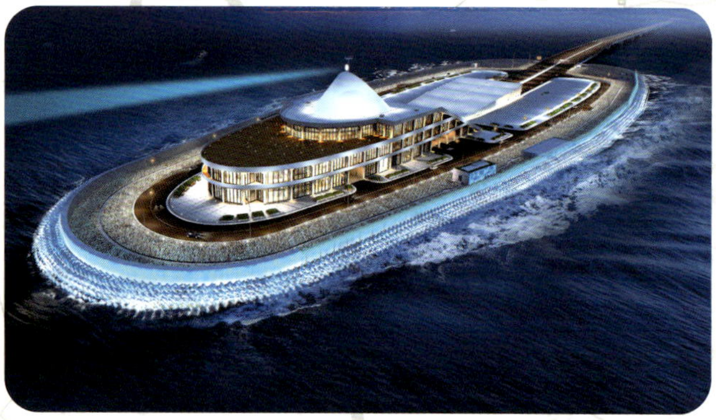

西人工岛
West Man-Made Island

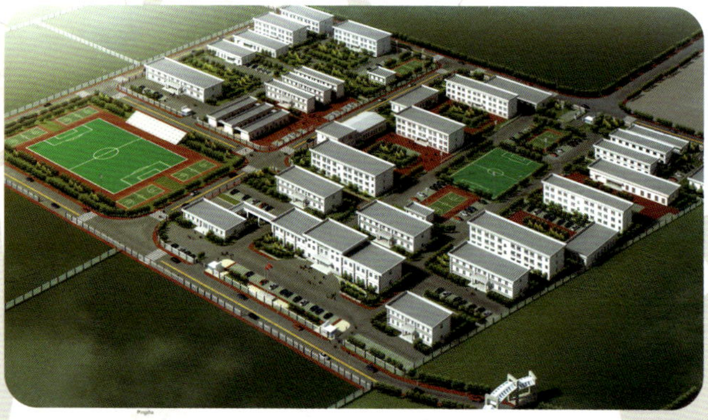

施工总营地
General Construction Camp

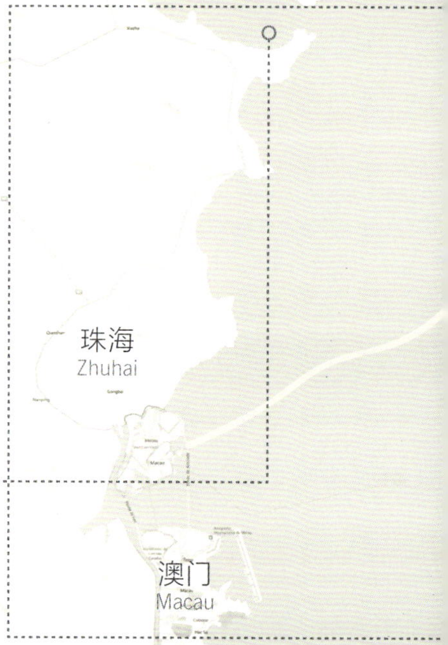

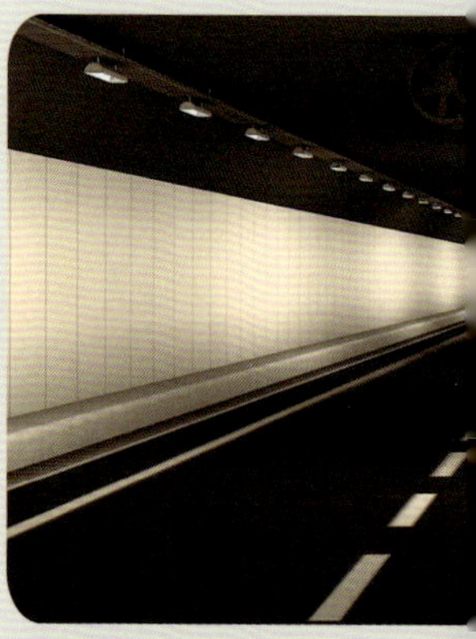

沉管隧道
Immersed Tube Tunnel

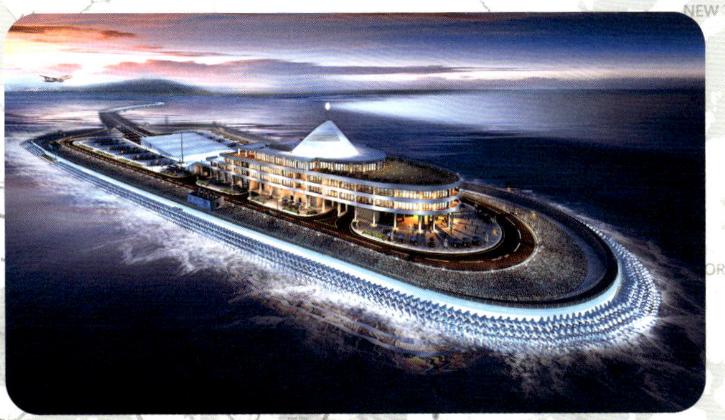

东人工岛
East Man-Made Island

香港
Hong Kong

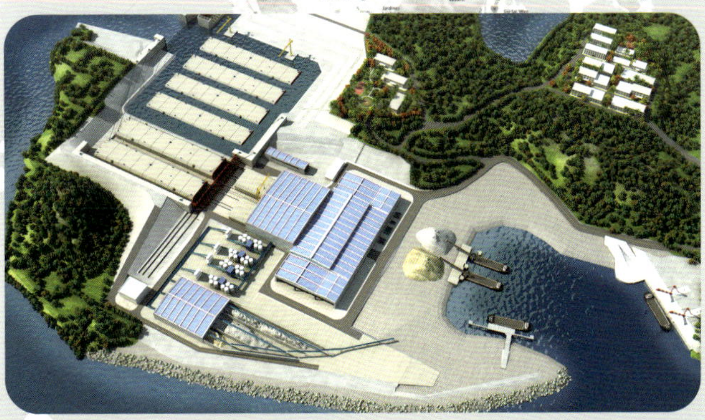

桂山岛
Guishan Island

沉管预制厂
The Immersed Tube Precast Factory

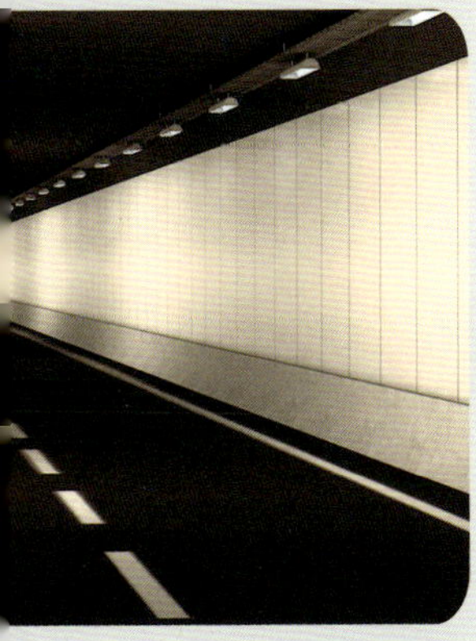

图片由中国交通股份有限公司提供
The Photo Provided by China Communications Construction Company Ltd.

总体施工组织管理

ORGANIZATION AND MANAGEMENT OF THE GENERAL CONSTRUCTION

岛隧工程项目采用了“设计施工总承包”模式，中国交通建设股份有限公司牵头，组建设计施工联合体进行项目实施工作。在充分发挥大型基建集团在项目管理、设计、科研、施工、制造、资金等方面综合能力的同时，按照专业特长进行合理分工，由联合体成员分别担任设计咨询、管理咨询及施工技术支持，推行伙伴关系理念，集众人之志、扬各家专长，有效融合设计及施工优势，共同解决问题，有效地控制了风险，保证了工程质量及工期。

在具体组织机构上，项目采用扁平化的两级管理方式，建立了“总部 + 工区”的管理架构。由项目总经理部统筹协调设计、施工团队，按照“设计施工联动、施工驱动设计”原则进行一体化管理，促进了各项工作有序高效推进。

The island-tunnel project adopted the “Design-Construction General Contracting” mode, with China Communications Construction Company Ltd. taking the lead to form a design and construction group to conduct the project. While giving the large infrastructure group companies freedom in project management, design, scientific research, construction, manufacturing and finance, the members of the design and construction group divided their tasks according to their professional advantages into design consultation, management consultation and constructional technical support. The group stuck to the concept of partnership, and made effective use of the wisdom and their design and construction advantages to solve problems that occurred during the construction, reduce the risks, guarantee the quality of the construction and finish the project on time.

As to the administration, the project adopted a two-layered management system by establishing a “headquarters + work area” management framework. The project management center divided the duties of the design and construction teams, and conducted integrated management by the principle of “design cooperating with construction while construction initiating design”, which promoted the orderly and efficient advancement of all work.

1. 港珠澳大桥施工总营地
General Project Camp of Hong Kong-Zhuhai-Macau Bridge

2. 组织管理机构图
Project Management and Organization Chart

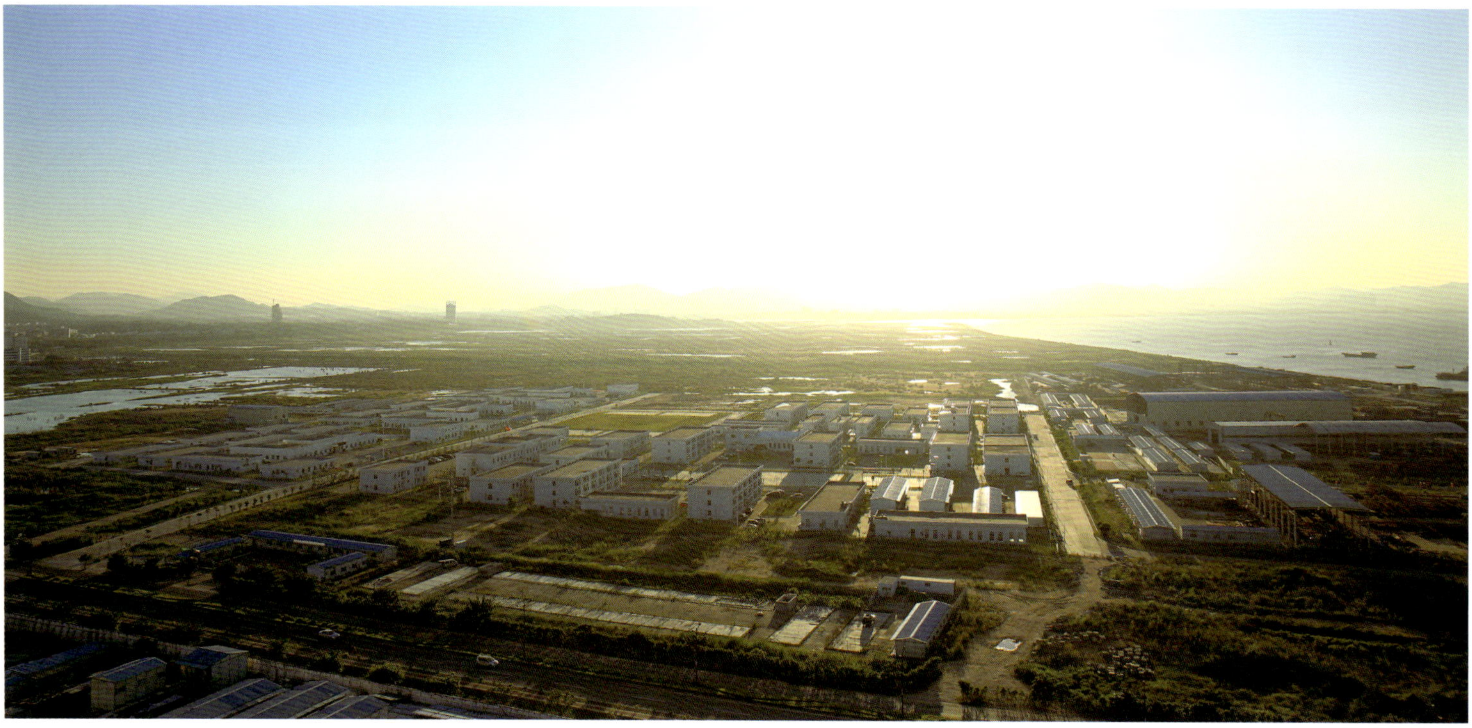

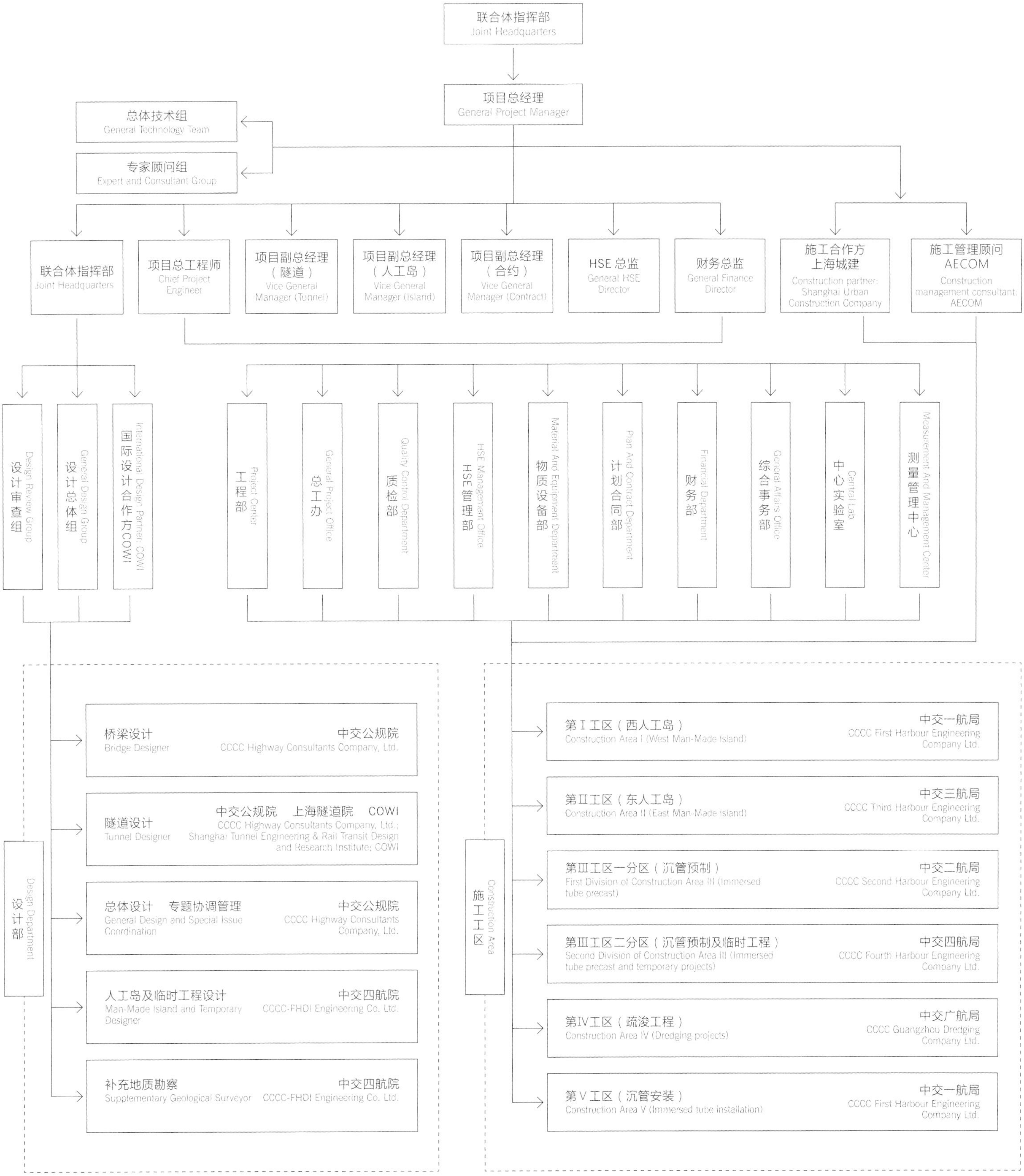
联合体指挥部
Joint Headquarters
项目总经理
General Project Manager
总体技术组
General Technology Team
专家顾问组
Expert and Consultant Group
联合体指挥部
Joint Headquarters
项目总工程师
Chief Project Engineer
项目副总经理（隧道）
Vice General Manager (Tunnel)
项目副总经理（人工岛）
Vice General Manager (Island)
项目副总经理（合约）
Vice General Manager (Contract)
HSE 总监
General HSE Director
财务总监
General Finance Director
施工合作方 上海城建
Construction partner: Shanghai Urban Construction Company
施工管理顾问 AECOM
Construction management consultant: AECOM
设计审查组
Design Review Group
设计总体组
General Design Group
国际设计合作方COWI
International Design Partner: COWI
工程部
Project Center
总工办
General Project Office
质检部
Quality Control Department
HSE管理部
HSE Management Office
物质设备部
Material And Equipment Department
计划合同部
Plan And Contract Department
财务部
Financial Department
综合事务部
General Affairs Office
中心实验室
Central Lab
测量管理中心
Measurement And Management Center
设计部
Design Department
桥梁设计
Bridge Designer
中交公规院
CCCC Highway Consultants Company, Ltd.
隧道设计
Tunnel Designer
中交公规院 上海隧道院 COWI
CCCC Highway Consultants Company, Ltd.; Shanghai Tunnel Engineering & Rail Transit Design and Research Institute; COWI
总体设计 专题协调管理
General Design and Special Issue Coordination
中交公规院
CCCC Highway Consultants Company, Ltd.
人工岛及临时工程设计
Man-Made Island and Temporary Designer
中交四航院
CCCC-FHDI Engineering Co. Ltd.
补充地质勘察
Supplementary Geological Surveyor
中交四航院
CCCC-FHDI Engineering Co. Ltd.
施工工区
Construction Area
第Ⅰ工区（西人工岛）
Construction Area I (West Man-Made Island)
中交一航局
CCCC First Harbour Engineering Company Ltd.
第Ⅱ工区（东人工岛）
Construction Area II (East Man-Made Island)
中交三航局
CCCC Third Harbour Engineering Company Ltd.
第Ⅲ工区一分区（沉管预制）
First Division of Construction Area III (Immersed tube precast)
中交二航局
CCCC Second Harbour Engineering Company Ltd.
第Ⅲ工区二分区（沉管预制及临时工程）
Second Division of Construction Area III (Immersed tube precast and temporary projects)
中交四航局
CCCC Fourth Harbour Engineering Company Ltd.
第Ⅳ工区（疏浚工程）
Construction Area IV (Dredging projects)
中交广航局
CCCC Guangzhou Dredging Company Ltd.
第Ⅴ工区（沉管安装）
Construction Area V (Immersed tube installation)
中交一航局
CCCC First Harbour Engineering Company Ltd.

精细化勘察
ELABORATE SURVEY

2010年12月起，针对岛隧工程区域的地质环境，项目总经理部开展精细化补充勘察,引进国际勘察标准，聘请国际地质工程师现场跟船监理，对勘查设备、采样方法、样品保存运输进行全程管控。

精细化补充勘察设计共用时6—7个月，给沉管隧道设计提供了准确参数，也为人工岛成岛技术创新提供了可靠依据。

布孔：在隧道线路的横断面上每50米布两个孔，中间25米处加一个孔，呈梅花形布置，密集取样。

设备：采用带波浪补偿器的钻机平台，以减少波浪对钻杆的扰动；采用薄壁取土器和带有防震措施、加海绵层保护层、密封运输的样品设备箱，最大限度减少土样变化；采用国际上最先进的孔压静力触探设备开展水下原位试验，在无扰动的情况下准确掌握土质情况。

试验：精细化验证土体在应力释放后再还原的状态。

建模：建立地质数据模型，建成地质资料库。

把关：设计师全程参与勘察，对取样进行现场审查、现场记录。

Starting from December 2010, the project management center conducted elaborate supplementary surveys of the geological environment of the island-tunnel project area by following the international survey standards and hiring the internationally well-known geological engineers to carry out onboard supervision over the surveying equipment, sampling methods, sample storage and transportation.

The elaborate supplementary survey took 6 to 7 months in total and provided accurate parameters for the design of the immersed tube tunnel and data for the technical innovation in the construction of the man-made islands.

Borehole Drilling: Two boreholes were drilled every 50 meters on the cross section of the tunnel and one in the middle point of the two boreholes, thus forming a pattern of quincunx for dense sampling.

Equipment: A rig platform with wave compensator was adopted to lessen the disturbance of waves for drilling pipes. To minimize the changes of soil samples, thin-wall soil samplers and sample boxes with shockproof devices and a protective sponge layer for sealed transportation were adopted. The most advanced static pore pressure sounding equipment in the world was used to carry out in-situ underwater tests to monitor accurately the soil quality without disturbance.

Test: The elaborate verification of the state of the soil restoration after stress release was provided.

Model Building: Geological data models and the geological database were built.

Control: The designers participated in the survey, conducting on-site survey and on-site record of the samples.

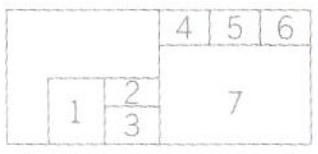

1. 海床式静力触探试验示意图
Schematic Diagram of Static Seabed Sounding Test
2. 静力触探试验探头
Static Sounding Test Detector
3. 波浪补偿海洋钻机
Offshore Wave Compensation Drilling Rig
4. 波浪补偿海洋钻机调试
Adjustment of the Offshore Wave Compensation Drilling Rig
5. 海床式静力触探试验作业
Static Seabed Sounding Test
6. 海床式静力触探试验海床平台
Platform of Static Seabed Sounding Test
7. 液压升降钻探平台
Hydraulic Lifting Drilling Platform

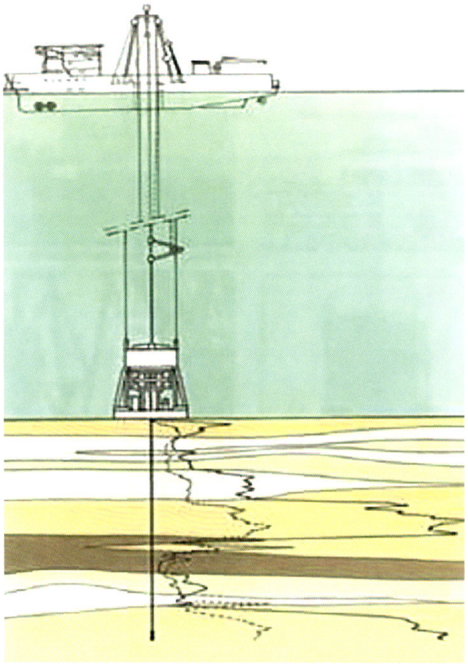

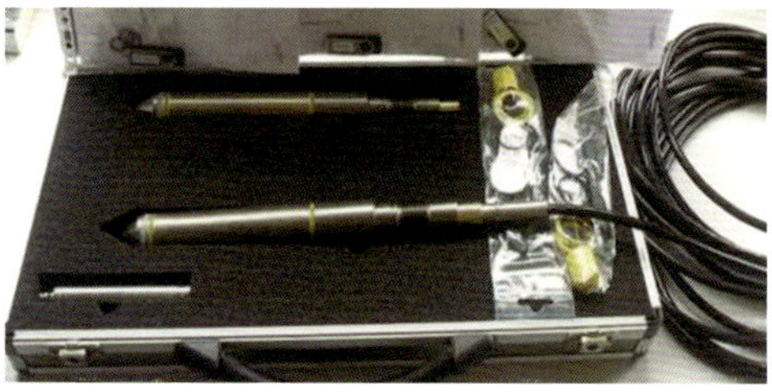

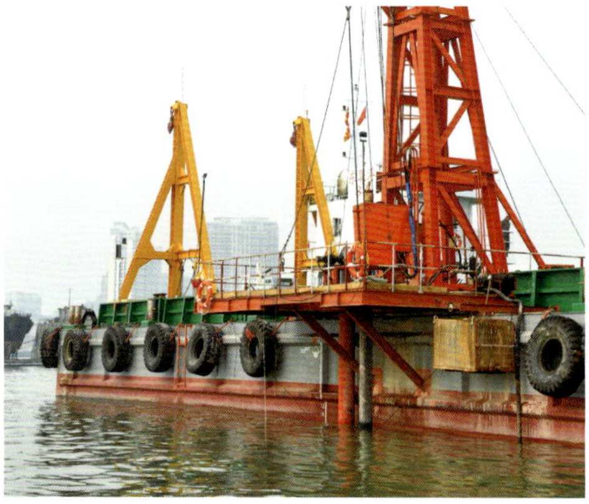

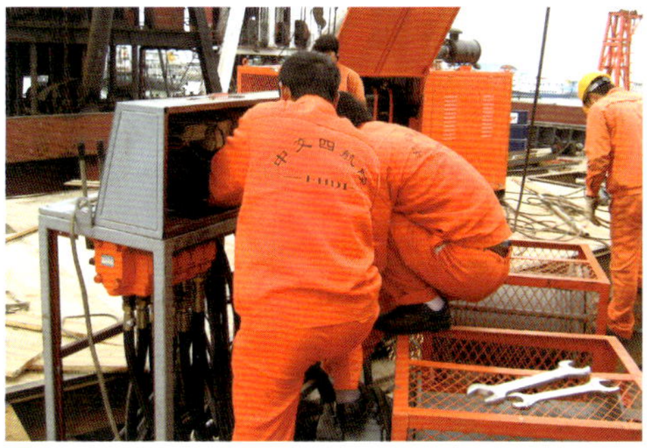

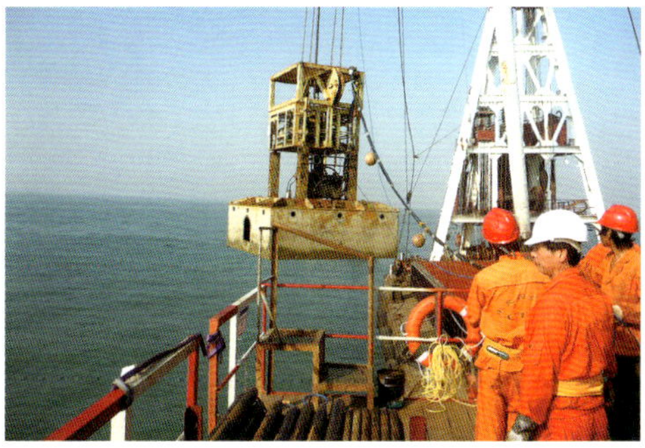

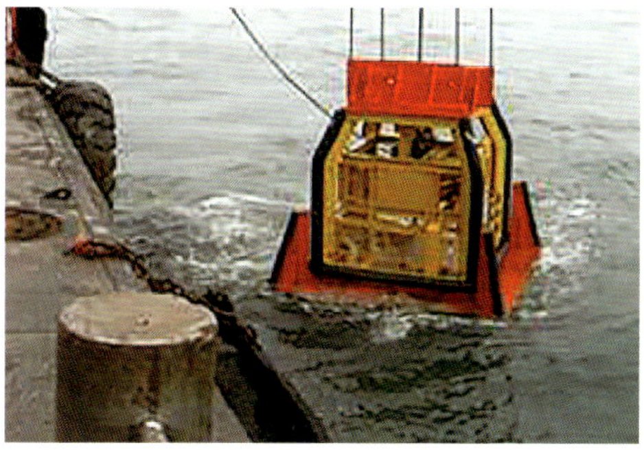

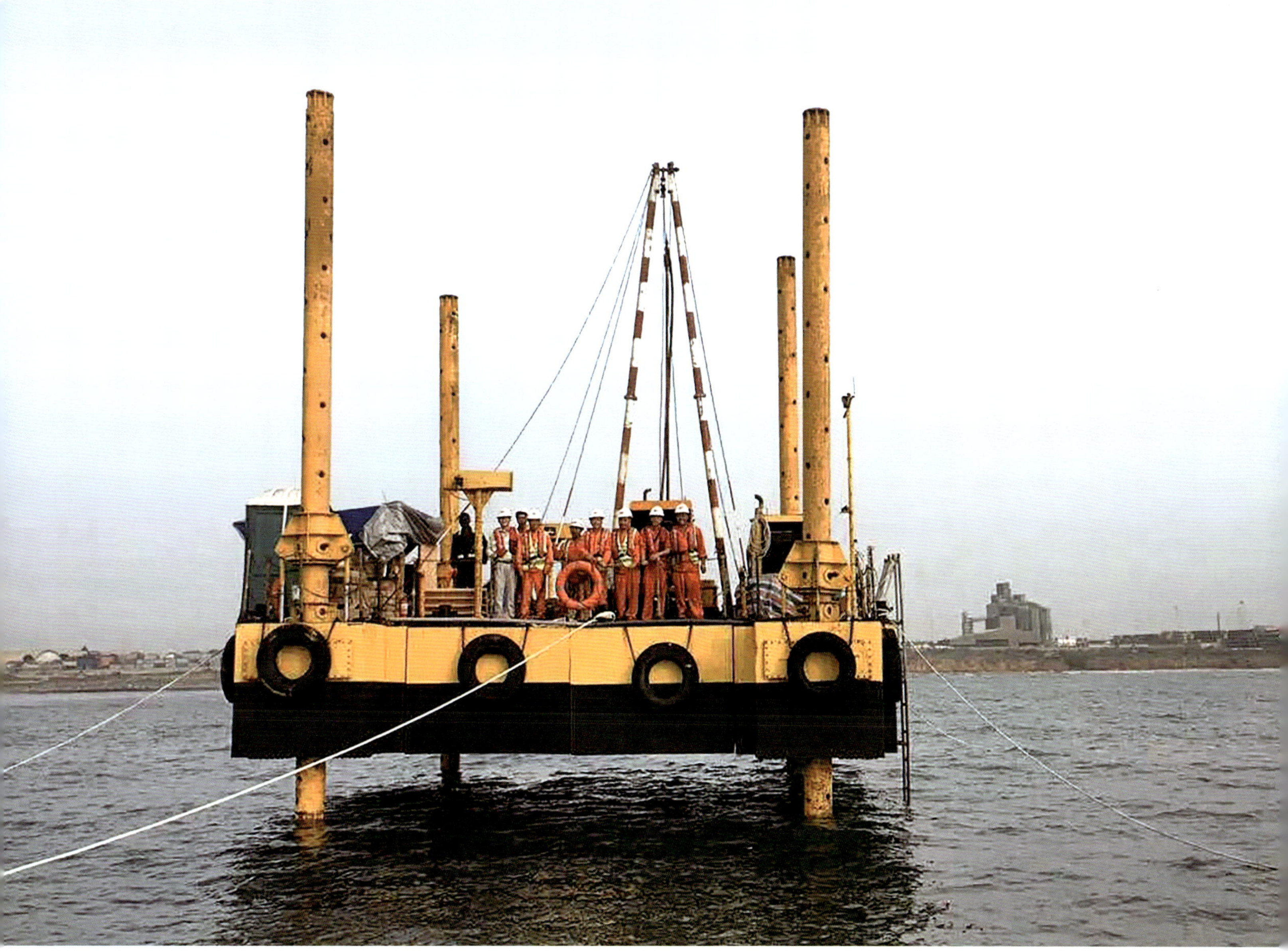

快速成岛创新技术

INNOVATIVE TECHNOLOGY OF MAN-MADE ISLAND RECLAMATION

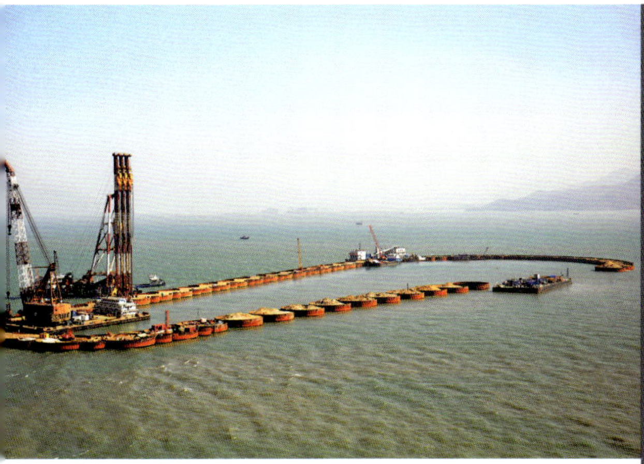

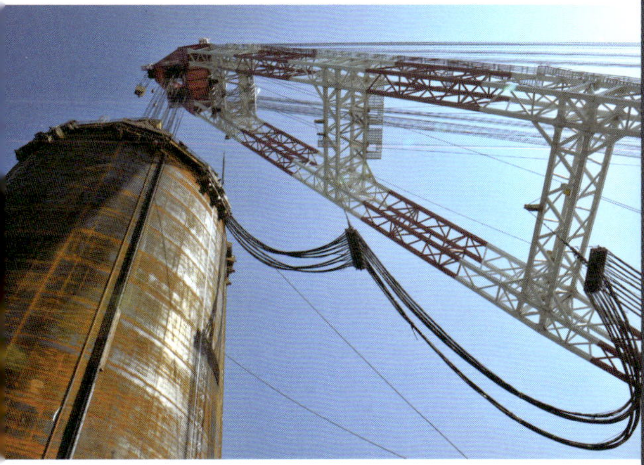

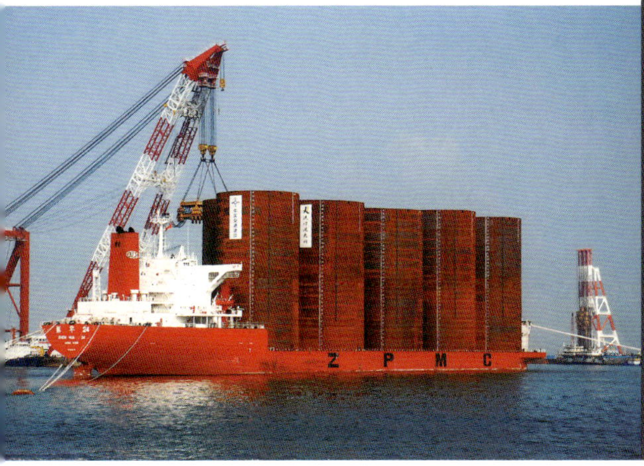
Z P M C

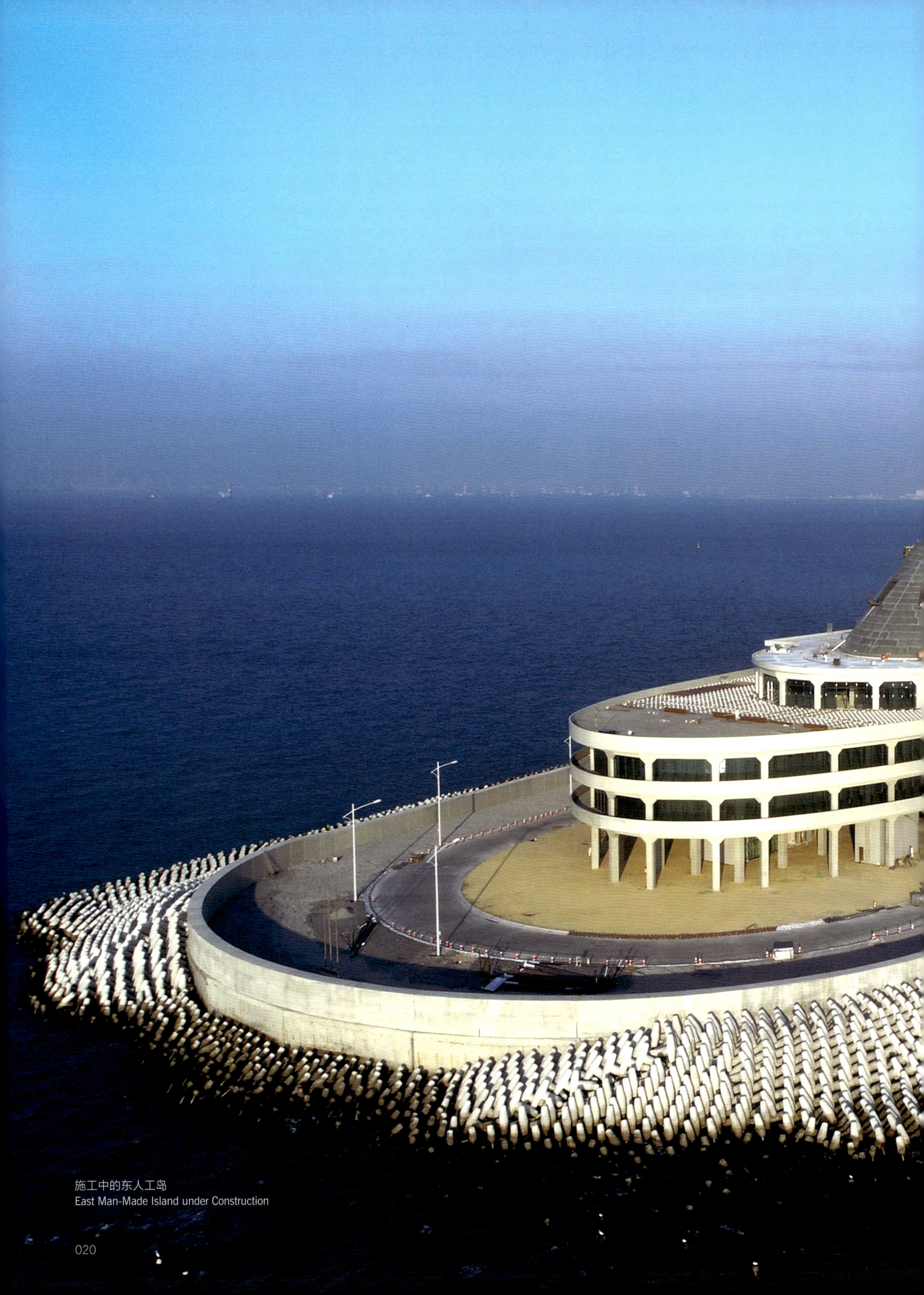

施工中的东人工岛
East Man-Made Island under Construction

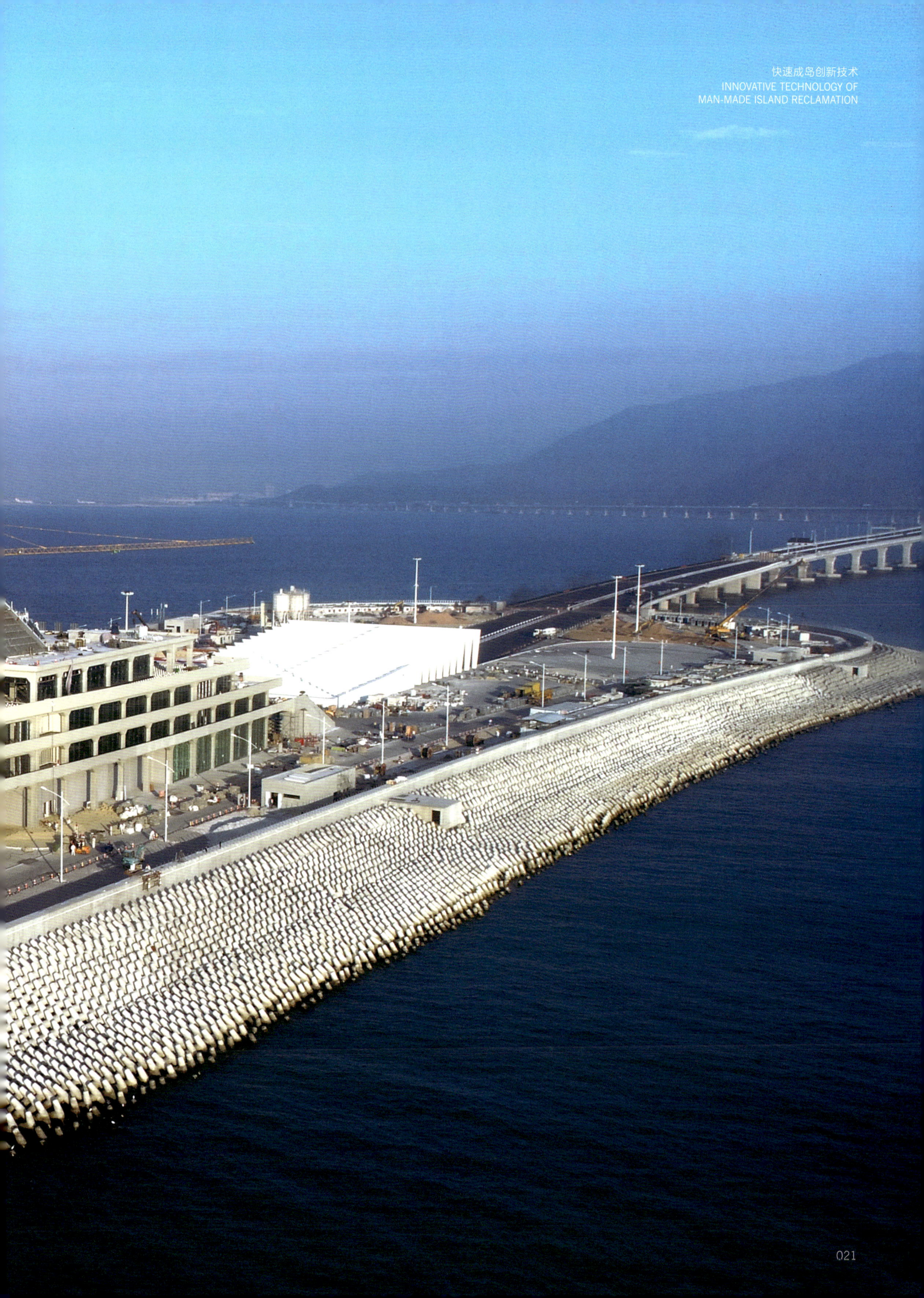

创新技术介绍
INTRODUCTION TO THE INNOVATIVE TECHNOLOGY

1. 东、西人工岛钢圆筒平面布置图
   Layout Plan for the Steel Cylinders on the East and West Man-Made Islands
2. 西人工岛钢圆筒快速成岛效果图
   Design Sketch of Rapid Reclamation of West Man-Made Island with Steel Cylinders
3. 西人工岛钢圆筒快速成岛流程图
   Flow Chart of Rapid Reclamation of West Man-Made Island with Steel Cylinders

为节省工期，控制施工船舶数量，保障施工安全及自然环境，尽量减少开挖量，岛隧工程首次应用了大直径钢圆筒深插快速成岛技术。采用八锤联动液压振动锤组，把120个直径22米，高40.5—50.5米，500余吨重的钢圆筒直接插入海底不透水层，钢圆筒之间插入弧形钢板副格，形成稳定的岛壁围护止水结构。

岛壁围护止水结构形成后，仅用100天，顺利完成了岛内软土地基加固和深基坑开挖作业，为岛上过渡段隧道施工和岛上建筑建设提供了良好条件。

In order to save construction time, limit the number of construction barges, ensure construction safety, protect natural environment and minimize excavation volume, the island-tunnel project for the first time adopted the technology of driving the large-diameter steel cylinders into the sea bed for rapid island formation. 120 steel cylinders of 22 meters in diameter and 40.5 to 50.5 meters in height, weighing over 500 tons, were directly driven into the impermeable stratum below the seabed by the hydraulic vibratory driving equipment consisting of eight hammers. The cylinders were connected with arc-shaped steel plates to form a stable protective waterproof wall of the island.

100 days after the protective water-stop wall of the island was completed, the soft soil foundation reinforcement and deep foundation trench excavation within the island's protective walls were completed, thus providing favorable conditions for the tunnel construction in the transition section of the tunnel and the construction of the buildings on the islands.

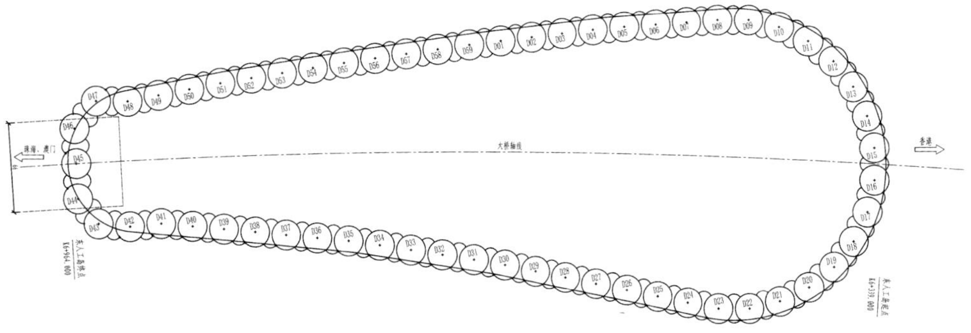

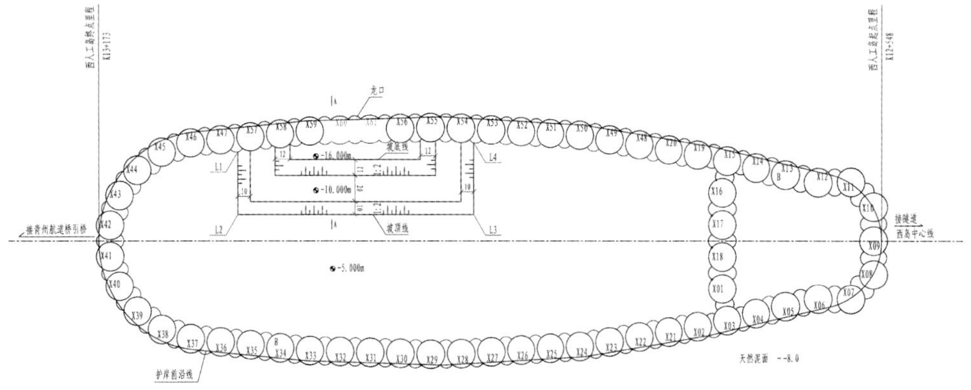

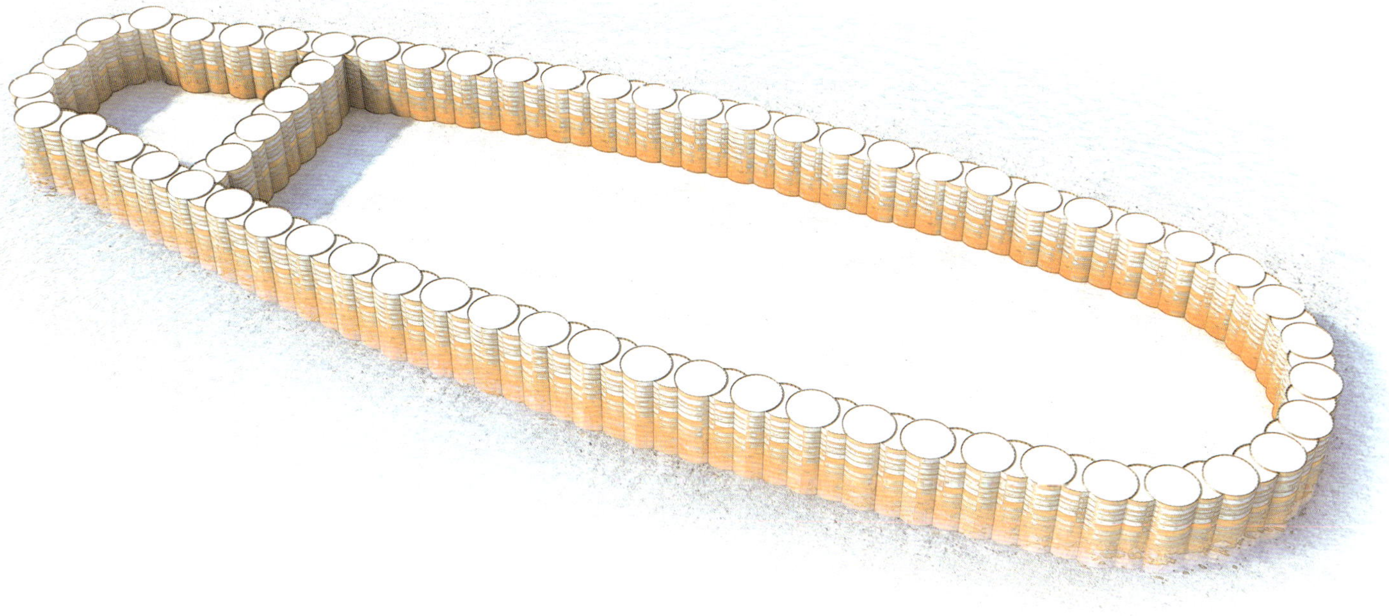

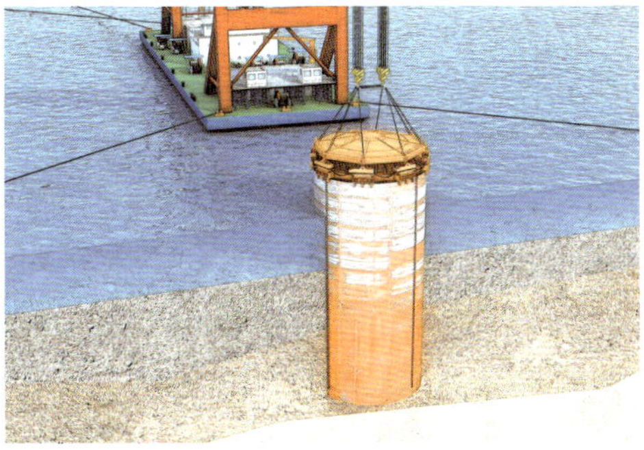

钢圆筒振沉
Vibratory Driving of the Steel Cylinders

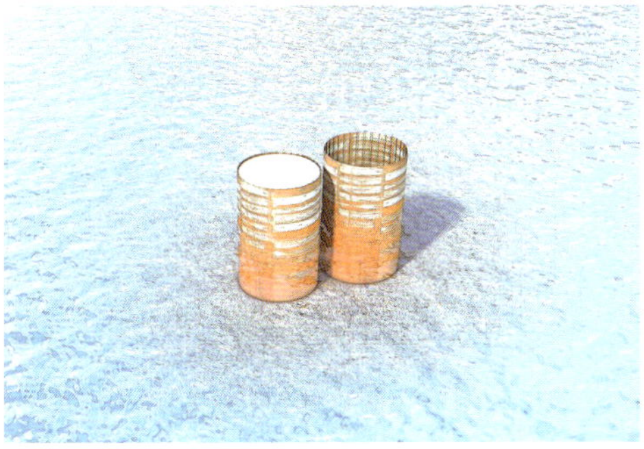

钢圆筒回填砂
Sand Backfill in the Steel Cylinders

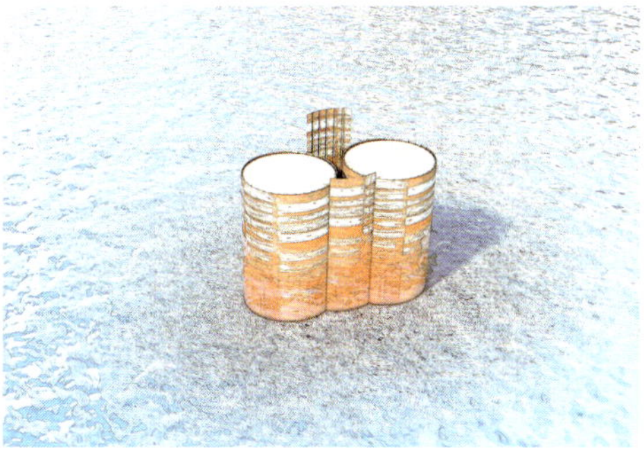

副格振沉
Vibratory Driving of the Connecting Rails

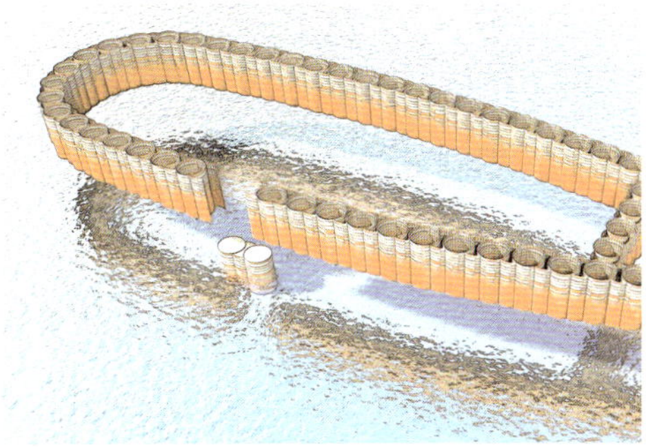

钢圆筒振沉完毕
Vibratory Driving of the Steel Cylinders Completed

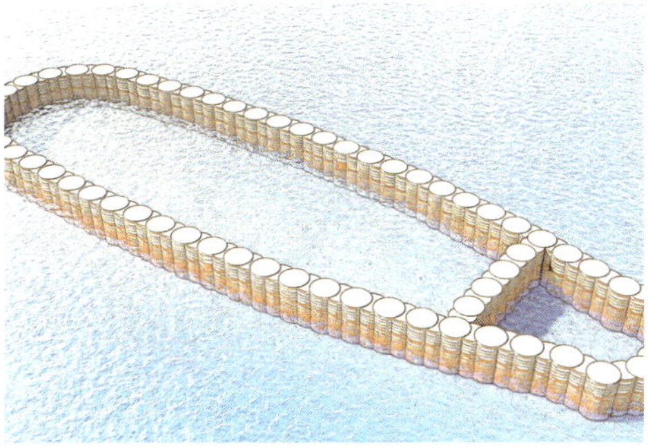

止水围堰结构
Water-Stop Wall

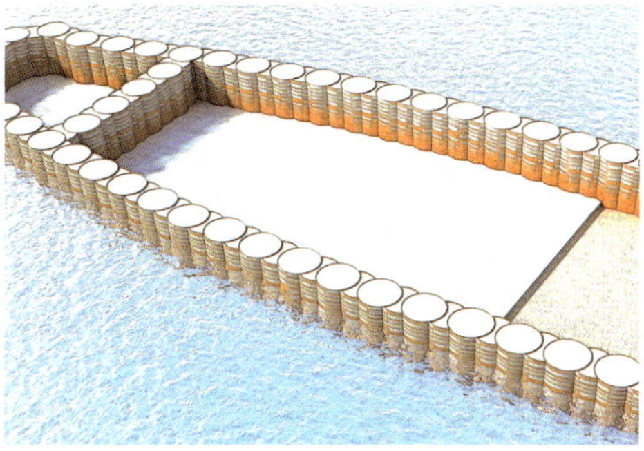

岛内回填砂、超载预压
Sand Backfill and Surcharge Preloading

东人工岛最后一个钢圆筒振沉
Vibratory Driving of the Last Steel Cylinder on East Man-Made Island

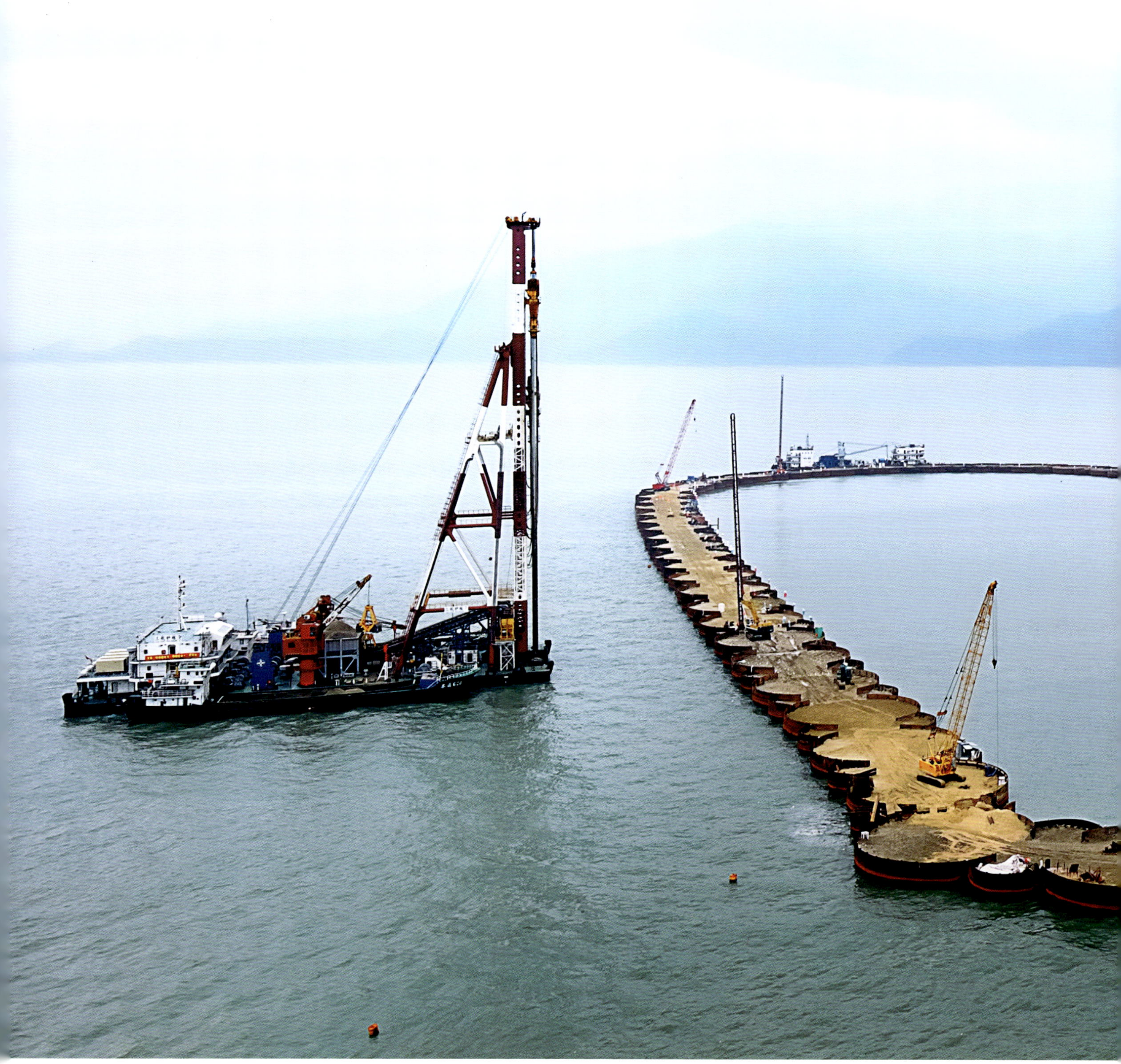

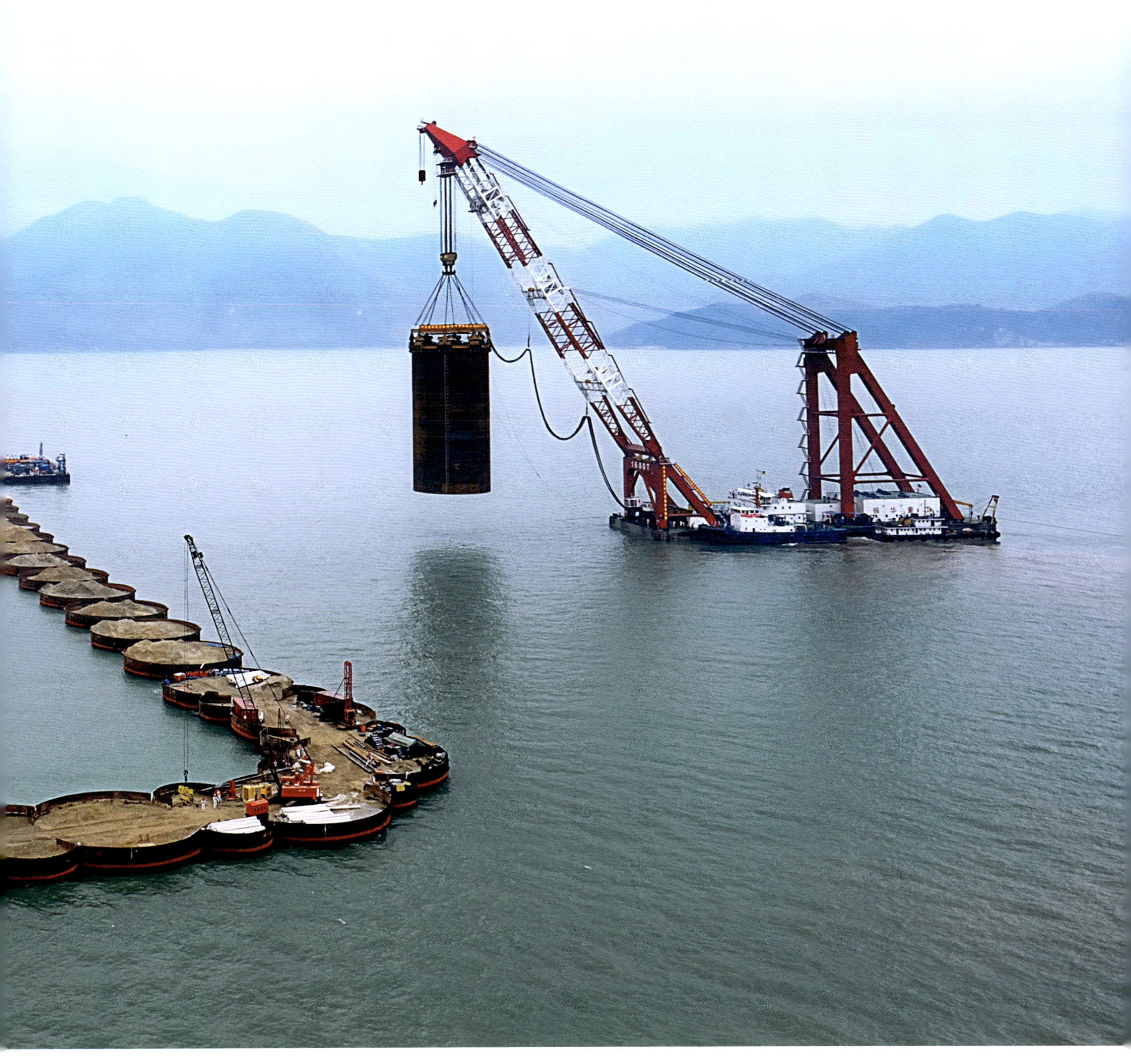

钢圆筒快速成岛方案

RAPID ISLAND RECLAMATION SOLUTION USING STEEL CYLINDERS

人工岛是实现海中桥隧转换的枢纽。采用传统抛石筑岛工艺，现场施工船舶达几百艘，至少须耗时三年，工期、环保、安全都得不到有效保障。

中国交建总工程师，港珠澳大桥岛隧工程项目总经理、总工程师林鸣提出了一个大胆设想：采用大钢圆筒深插入海直接围合成岛。

没有先例，没有标准，也没有装备，这个方案是否可行？林鸣没有贸然抛出这个方案，他决定先研究这个方案有哪些制约因素，从否定中找到肯定。

2009年9月的一天，林鸣交给王汝凯一个任务：用三个月的时间，证明"深插大钢圆筒快速成岛"方案不可行。

王汝凯是全国工程勘察设计大师，中交第四航务工程勘察设计院有限公司的原总工程师，对珠江口的地质、水文十分熟悉。

四航院随即专门组织技术团队，从论证方案不成立的角度对38个专题进行研究。经过三个多月的潜心研究，王汝凯的团队认为，珠江口的深厚软土地基确实给人工岛建设造成了麻烦，但是对钢圆筒深插却是个有利条件，采用大钢圆筒深插入海直接围合成岛具有可行性。

这个方案否定不了，但是有三个需要解决的问题迫在眉睫。

大体积的钢圆筒如何制造运输？有没有设备能打得下去？圆筒筑岛后的止水如何实现？

又经过半年攻关，三个问题也一一找到了应对的办法：上海振华重工有足够的能力解决钢圆筒制造和运输问题；振沉设备研发可以向全球招标，借用国外成熟技术；而止水问题可以用钢圆筒与副格的组合来解决。

钢圆筒快速成岛创新方案从否定开始，到一步步走向可能，又经过层层优化，终于从设想变成了现实。

The man-made islands are the hubs to realize the transition between the bridge and the tunnel under the sea. By the traditional island construction technique of rock filling, hundreds of construction barges would have to work on site for at least three years, yet that couldn't guarantee the construction time, environment protection and engineering safety.

Lin Ming, Chief Engineer of China Communications Construction Company Ltd. and General Manager and Chief Engineer of the island-tunnel project of Hong Kong-Zhuhai-Macau Bridge, proposed that large-sized steel cylinders were to be driven deep into the seabed for rapid reclamation of the man-made islands.

No precedents, no easy standards, no usable equipment! Is this plan feasible? Lin Ming did not put into practice this plan rashly. Instead, he first decided to investigate into the factors that might affect the implement of the place, trying to find what was positive among the unfavorable.

One day in September 2009, Lin Ming gave a task to Wang Rukai, asking him to prove within three months that the plan of "driving large-sized steel cylinders into seabed to form islands" was impossible.

Wang Rukai, the master of engineering survey and design and former Chief Engineer of the Fourth Habour Engineering Investigation and Design Institute of the Ministry of Transport, was very familiar with the geological and hydrological conditions of Pearl River Estuary.

The Fourth Habour Engineering Investigation and Design Institute thereby organized a special technical team to conducted 38 special studies trying to prove the impossibility of the steel cylinder proposal. After more than three months of painstaking research, Wang Rukai's team believed that the deep soft soil seabed in Pearl River Estuary would cause trouble to the construction of the man-made islands, but it was favorable for the deep driving of the steel cylinders into the seabed. It was concluded that it was feasible to build man-made islands by using deep driven steel cylinders.

Lin's proposal could not be denied, but three problems needed immediate solutions.

How were the large-sized steel cylinders manufactured and transported to the working site? Was there any available equipment to drive the cylinders deep into the seabed? How was waterproofing realized after the island was formed?

After another six months of research, the three problems were solved one by one: Shanghai Zhenhua Port Machinery Company (ZPMC) had the capacity to manufacture and transport the cylinders; the vibratory ram-driving equipment can be provided by global bidding and by using foreign technologies; waterproof problem could be solved by combining steel cylinders with auxiliary steel connectors.

The solution of using steel cylinders for rapid island reclamation began with negation, was proved possible step by step, and was finally turned into reality by rounds of optimization.

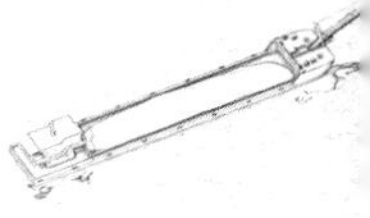

1. 林鸣与王汝凯
   Lin Ming and Wang Rukai
2. 快速成岛效果图
   Sketch of Rapid Island Reclamation

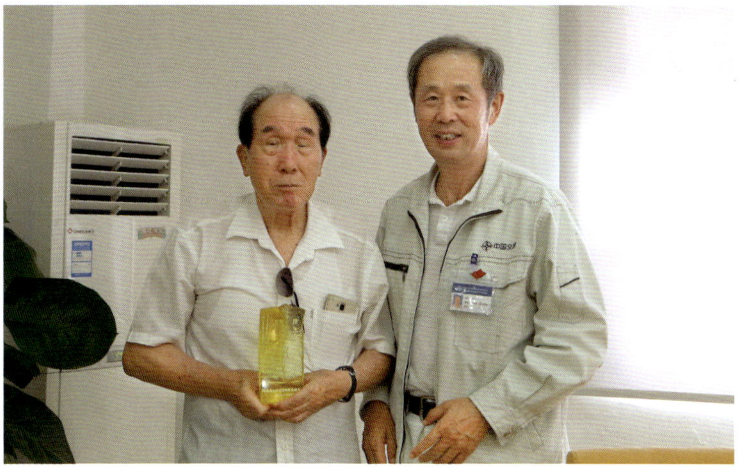

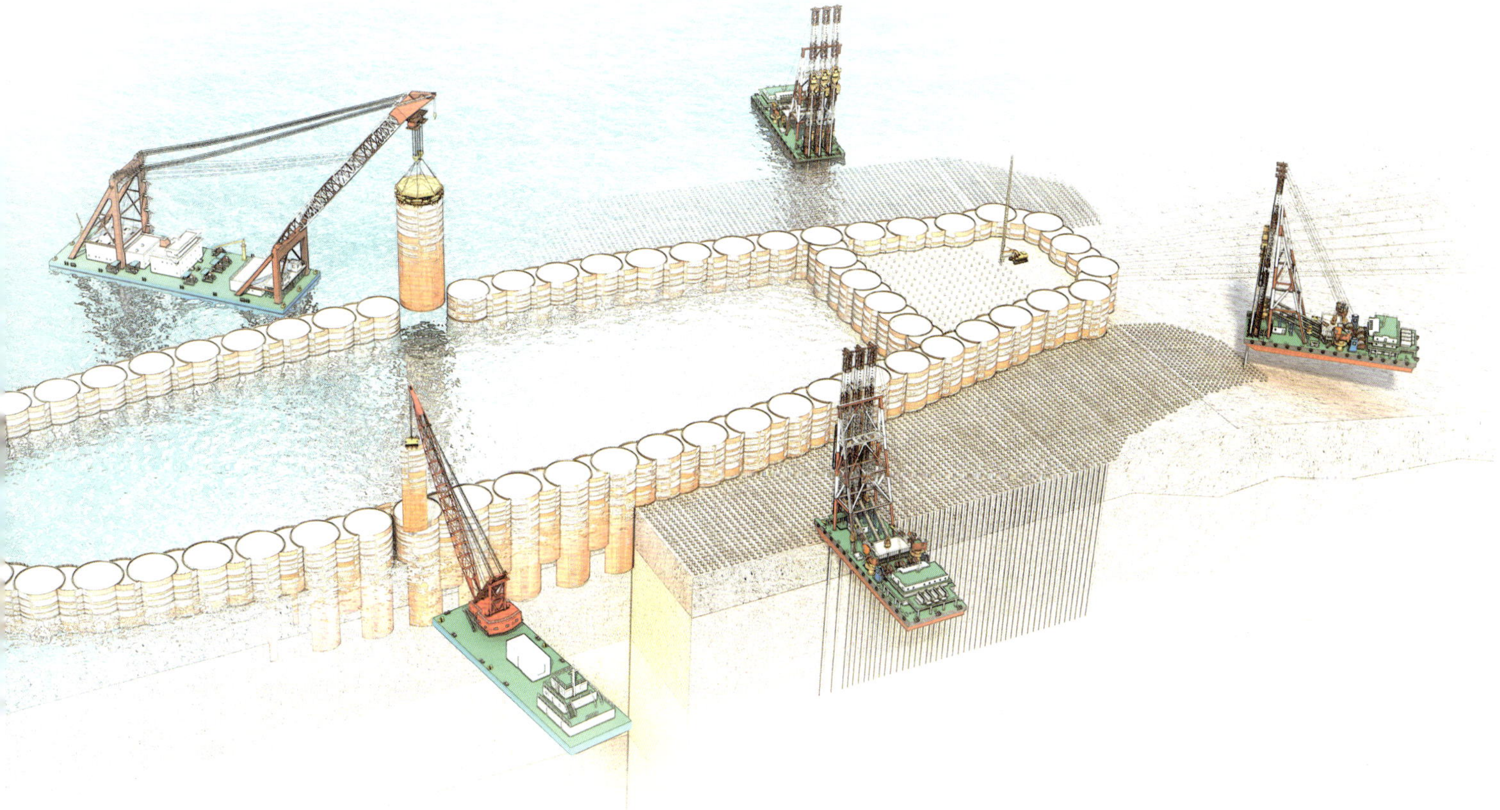

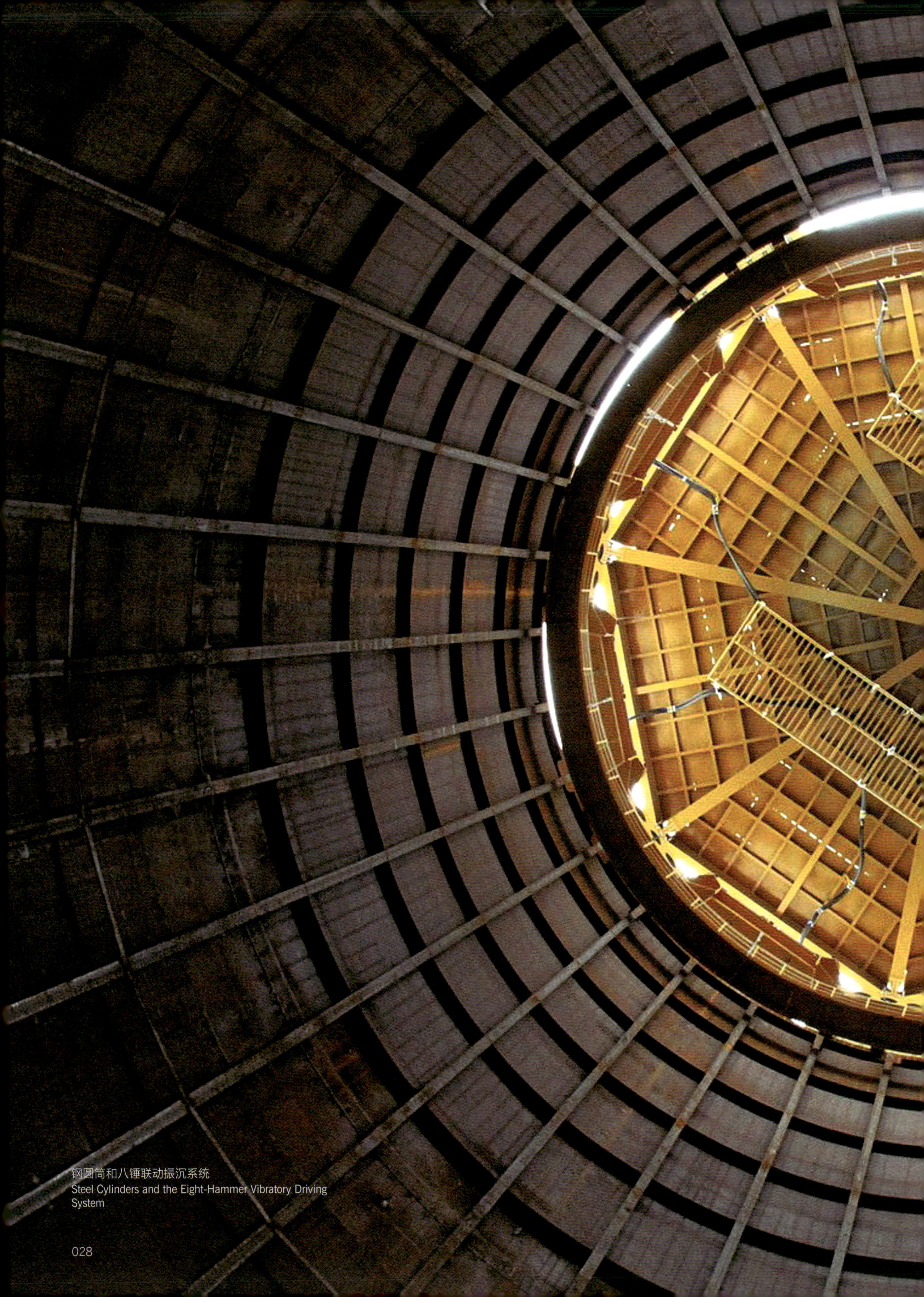

钢圆筒和八锤联动振沉系统
Steel Cylinders and the Eight-Hammer Vibratory Driving System

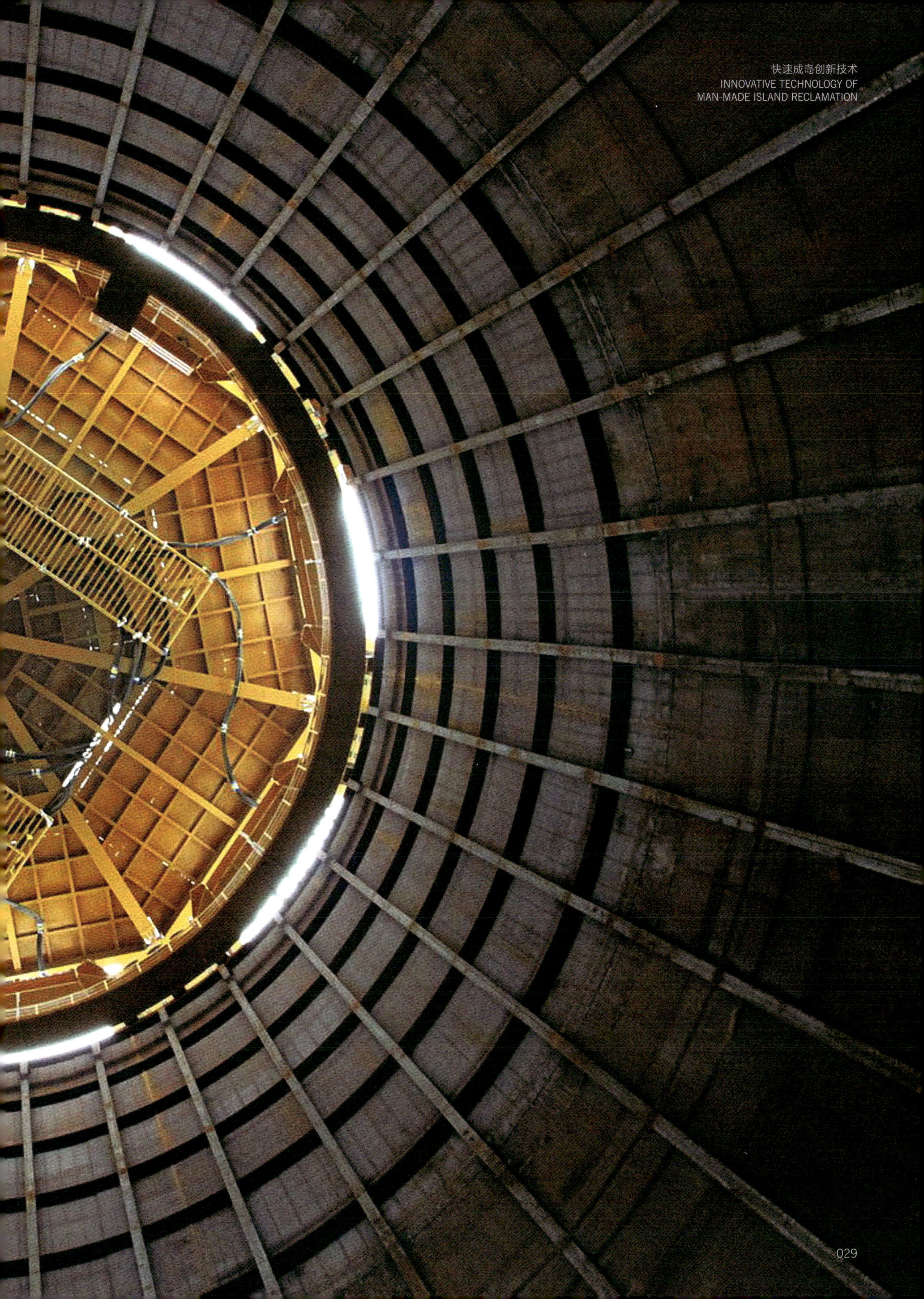

钢圆筒制造

MANUFACTURE OF THE STEEL CYLINDERS

人工岛所需的120个钢圆筒在上海振华重工（集团）有限公司长兴岛基地的工厂内制造，总重约6万吨；采用万吨级远洋运输船运输至珠海施工现场。快速制造120个超大直径钢圆筒，是实现快速成岛的必要条件。

作为中国交建的全资子公司，振华重工是世界知名起重机和大型钢结构制造商，曾为美国旧金山大桥和英国昆斯费里大桥、上海东海大桥等大型桥梁提供数十万吨钢构件，拥有大型门式起重机、大型浮吊和22艘远洋运输船，以强大的机械制造能力和远洋运输能力成为钢圆筒制造厂商的首选。

每月20—25个大钢圆筒在这里制造完成发船起运，120个钢圆筒半年内全部制造完成，为港珠澳大桥东、西人工岛快速成岛提供了坚实的保障。钢圆筒直径22米，壁厚16毫米，高度为40.5—50.5米。单个圆筒重量451—513吨。钢圆筒采用两节对接法，先制作20.9米高的钢圆筒为标准节段，再根据整体高度制作上节筒体与标准节段对接。制作时，每个小节段按圆周方向划分为六个单元板，宽度为筒体周长的1/6，约11.5米。最后将上下两节筒拼接为成品筒。

对接完成后，利用长兴基地450吨和500吨门式起重机进行外场装船。门式起重机轨道两侧有90米×300米场地，可供22组钢圆筒小节段同时拼装。采用4000吨浮吊将钢圆筒吊装至运输船上，绑扎固定后从海上运输至施工现场。

All the 120 steel cylinders needed for island reclamation were manufactured in the factory at Changxing Island Base of ZPMC, with a total weight of approximately 60,000 tons. They were transported to the working site at Zhuhai by an ocean-going vessels of 10,000 tons. Rapid manufacturing of the 120 steel cylinders with super-large diameter was the necessity for rapid island reclamation.

As a wholly-owned subsidiary of China Communications Construction Company Ltd., ZPMC is a world-famous manufacturer of cranes and large-sized steel structures. It has ever provided hundreds of thousands of tons of steel components for the San Francisco Bridge in the United States, the Queensferry Crossing in Britain and the Donghai Bridge in Shanghai. It has large gantry cranes, large floating cranes and 22 ocean-going carriers, and is thus the first choice for steel cylinder manufacturing in China for its strong mechanical manufacturing capacity and offshore maritime transportation capacity.

20 to 25 large steel cylinders were manufactured here every month and shipped 120 steel cylinders were completed in half a year, providing the solid support for the rapid formation of the east and west man-made islands of Hong Kong-Zhuhai-Macau Bridge. Each of the steel cylinders was 22 meters in diameter, 16 millimeters in wall thickness and 40.5 to 50.5 meters in height. The weight of a single cylinder was 451 to 513 tons. The steel cylinder was manufactured by connecting its two sections. First, a steel cylinder of 20.9 meters high was manufactured as the standard section, and then the upper section was connected to the standard section according to its global height. When fabricated, each section was divided into six plates along the circumferential direction, and the width of each plate was 1/6 of the circumference of the cylinder, about 11.5 meters. Finally, the upper and lower sections were assembled into one complete cylinder.

After the two sections of a cylinder were connected, the gantry cranes with a capacity of 450 tons and 500 tons from Changxing Island Base were used to load the cylinders onboard the barges waiting outside the factory. On both sides of the gantry crane track, there were two empty plots of 90 meters × 300 meters used for the assemblage of 22 pairs of steel cylinder sections at the same time. The steel cylinders were hoisted up and put onboard the shipping barges by a 4000-ton floating crane, and then were transported safely to the construction site on the sea after being fixed onto the decks of the shipping barges.

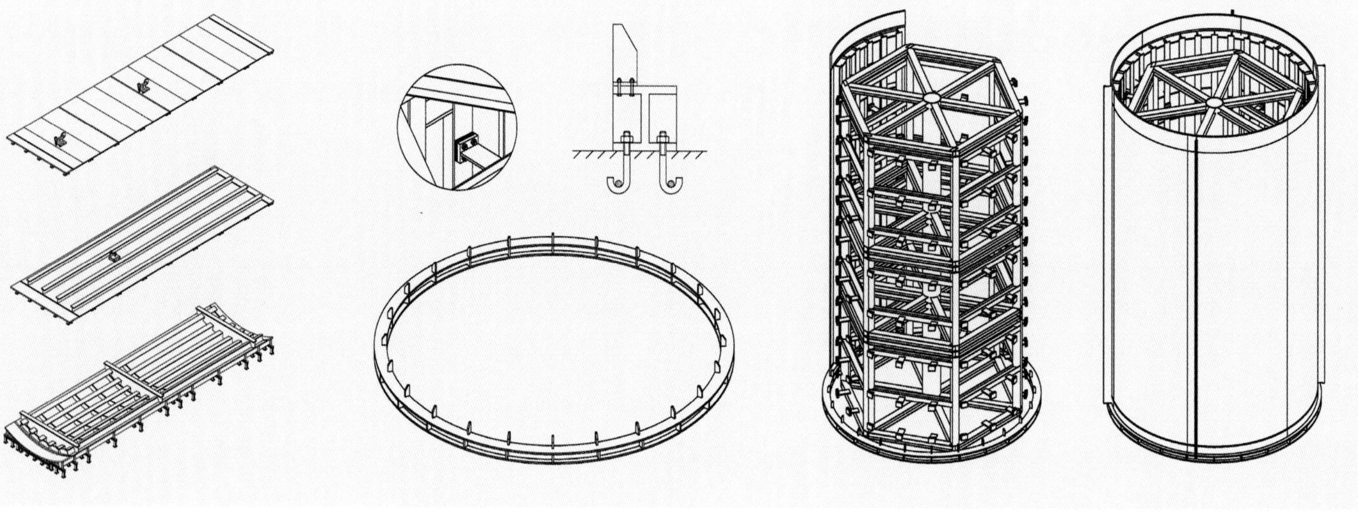

1. 钢圆筒制造流程图
Flow Chart of the Steel Cylinder Manufacturing

2. 板单元制作
Plate Unit Manufacturing

3. 卷板
Coil Plates

4. T 型钢焊接
T-Bar Welding

5. 板单元厂内制作
Manufacturing of the Plate Unit in the Factory

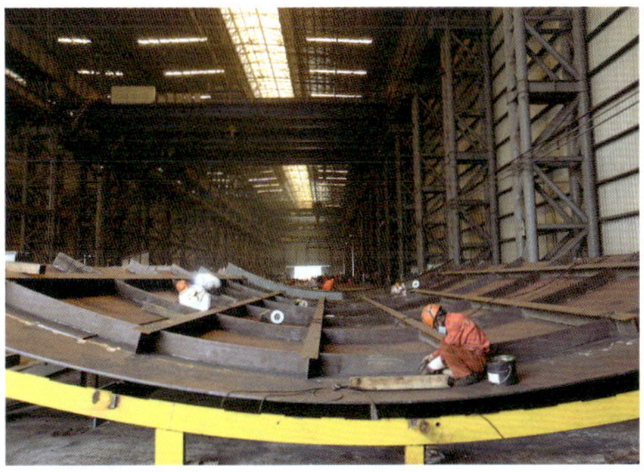

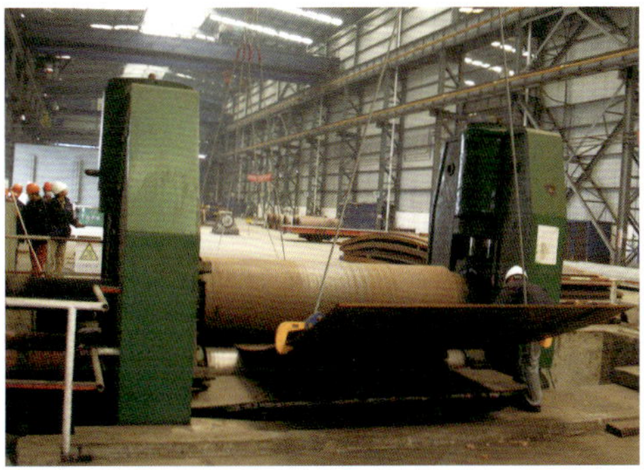

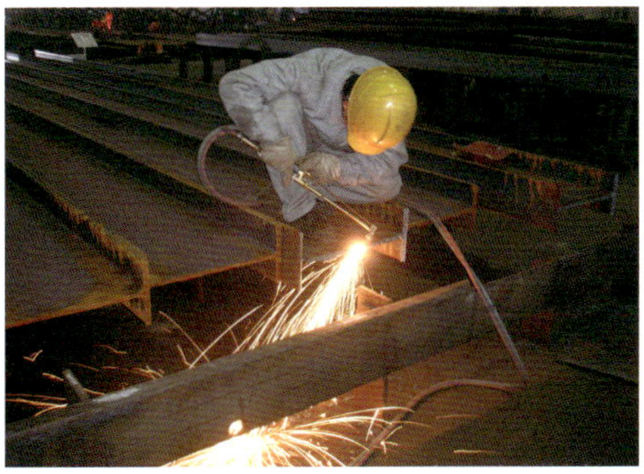

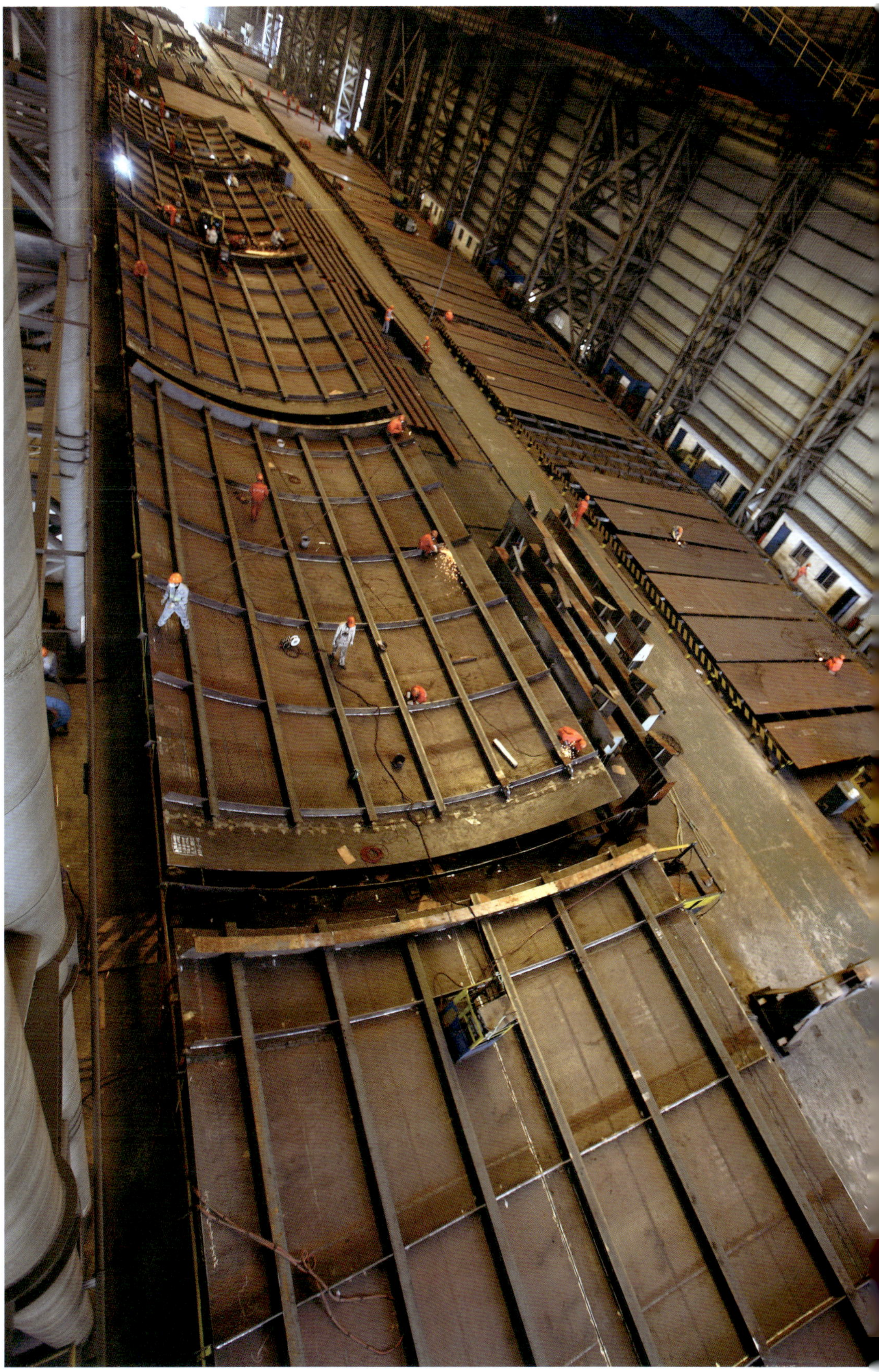

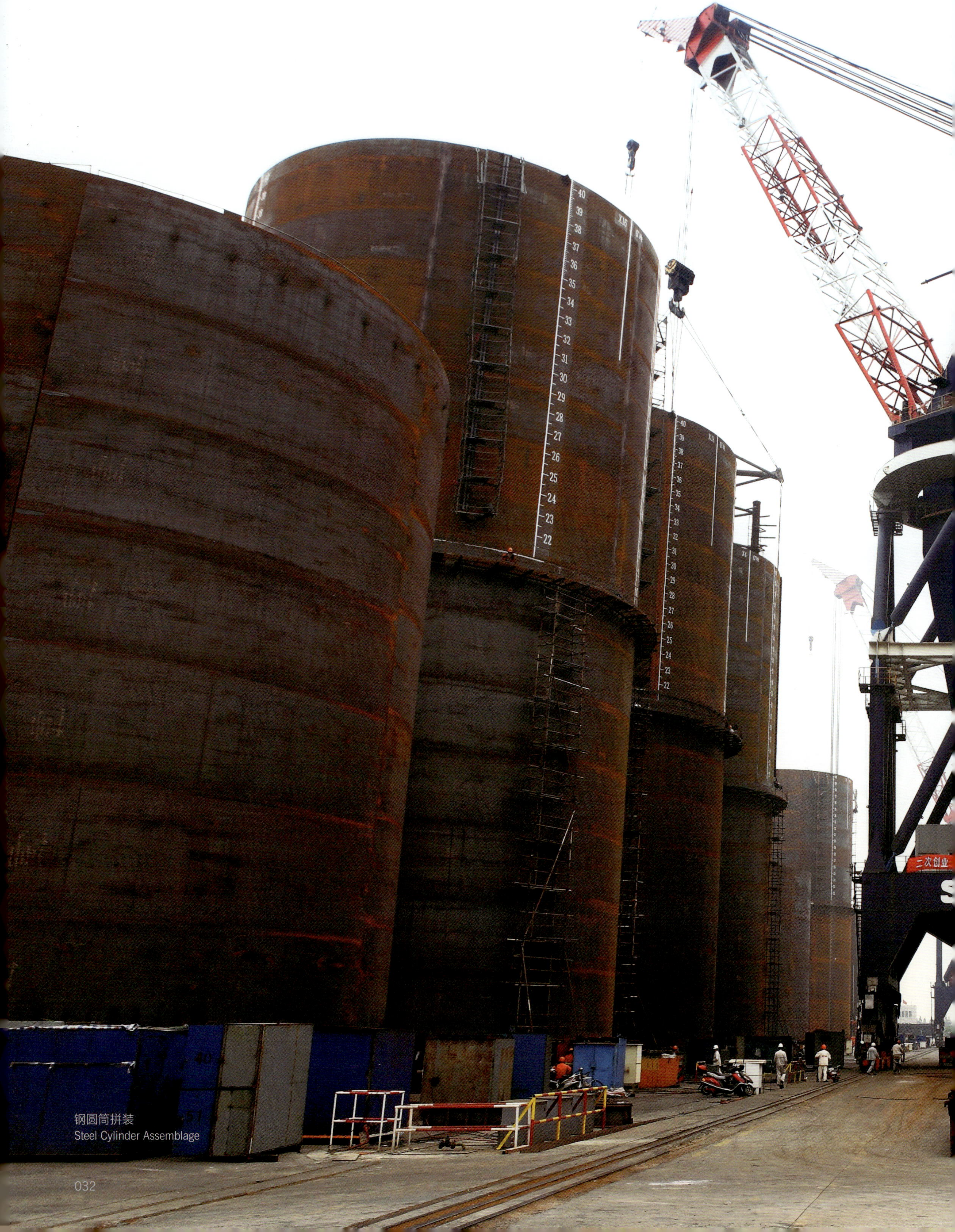

钢圆筒拼装
Steel Cylinder Assemblage

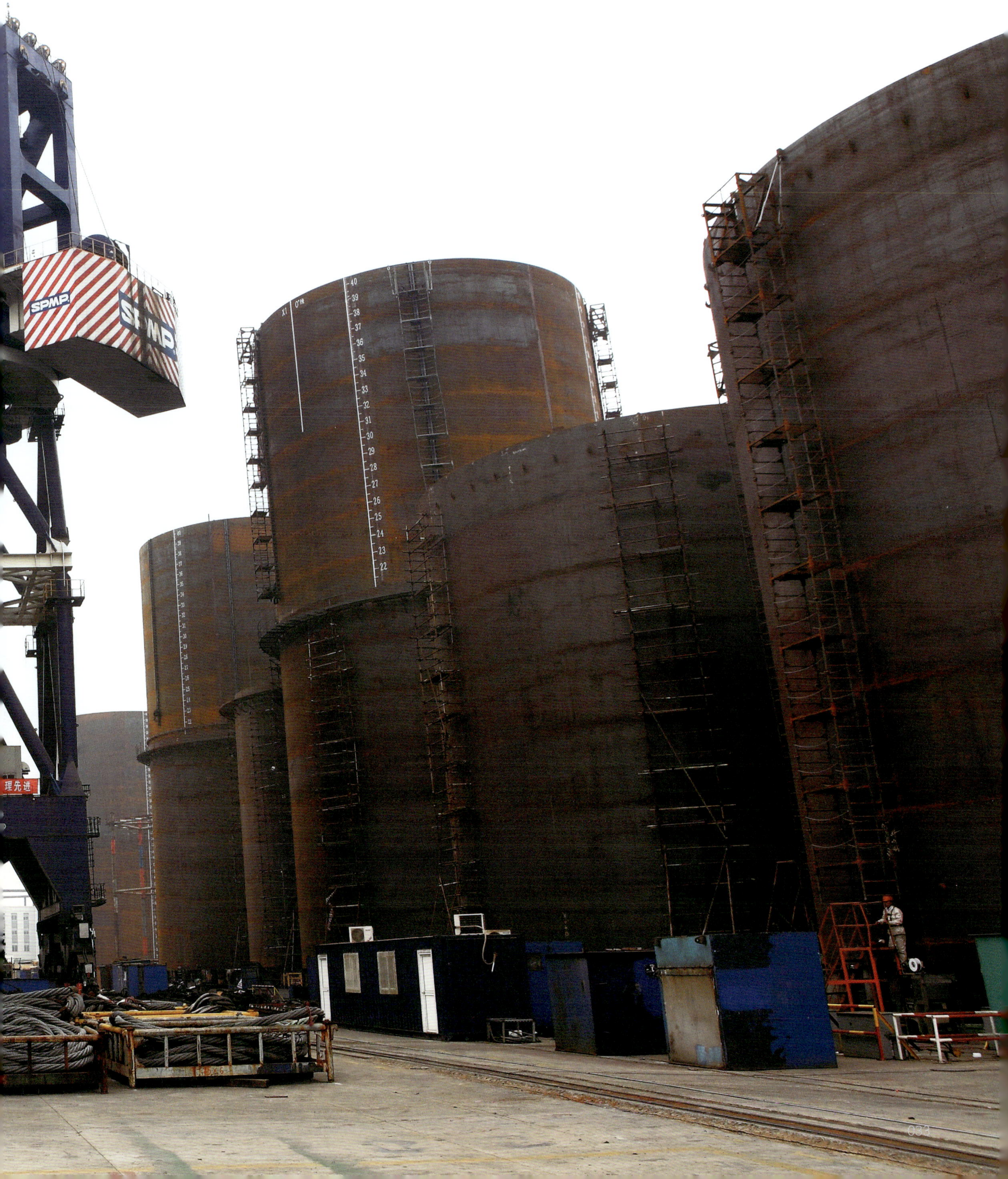
SPMP
理先进

1. 板单元竖立
Erected Plate Units
2. 板单元竖向拼接
Longitudinal Welding of the Plate Units
3. 半筒体纵缝焊接
Longitudinal Seam Welding of Half Cylinders
4. 上下筒体对接
Connection of the Upper Cylinder with the Lower Cylinder
5. 钢圆筒外拼接
External Joint of the Steel Cylinder

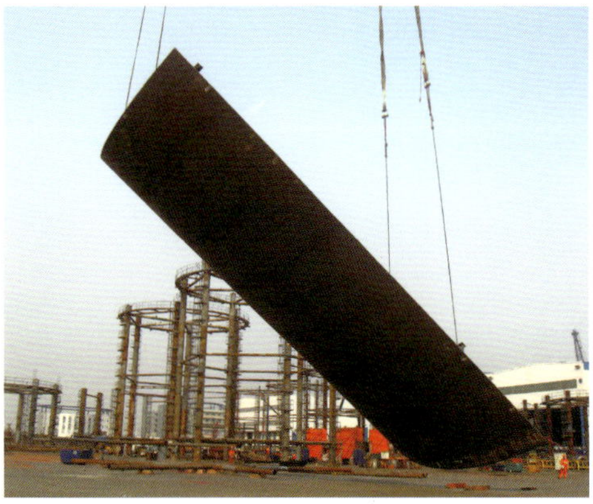

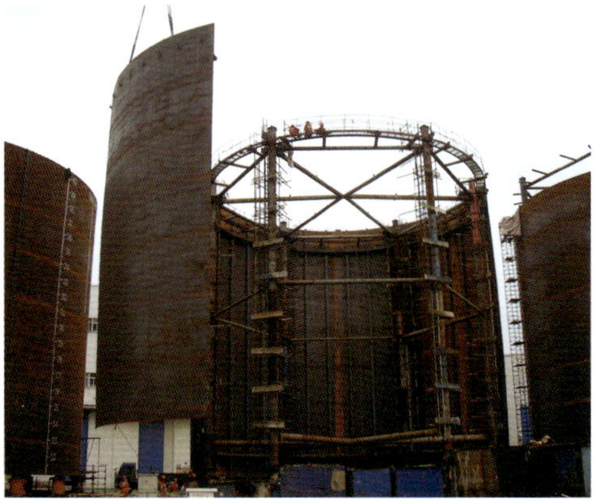

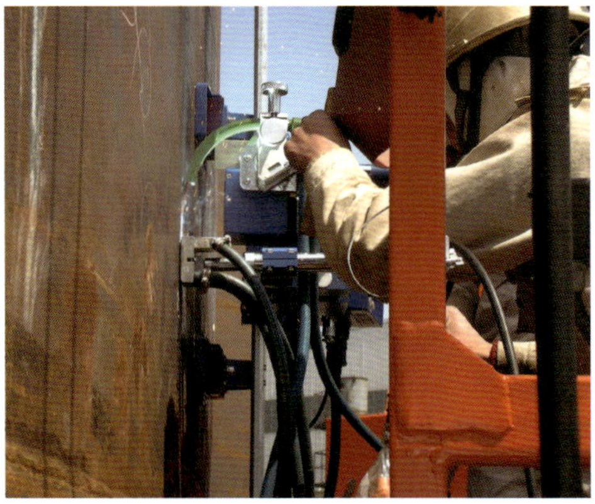

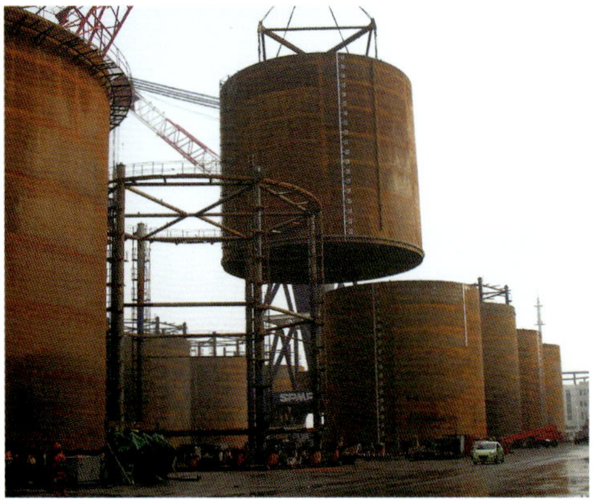

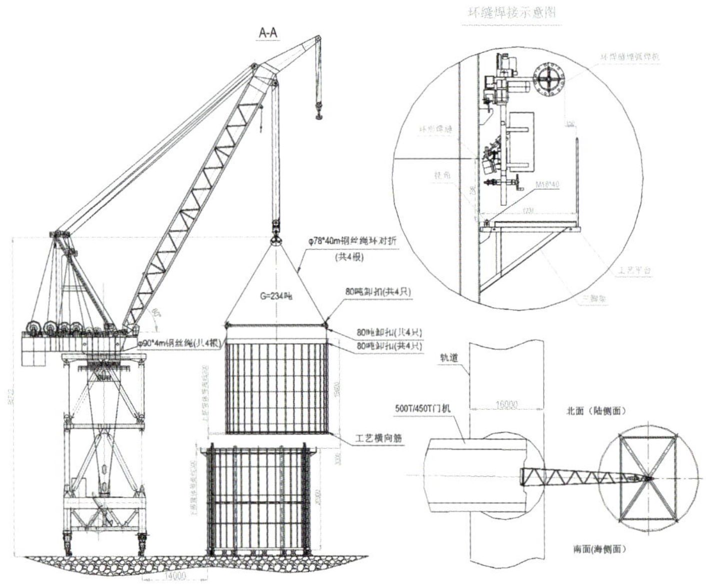

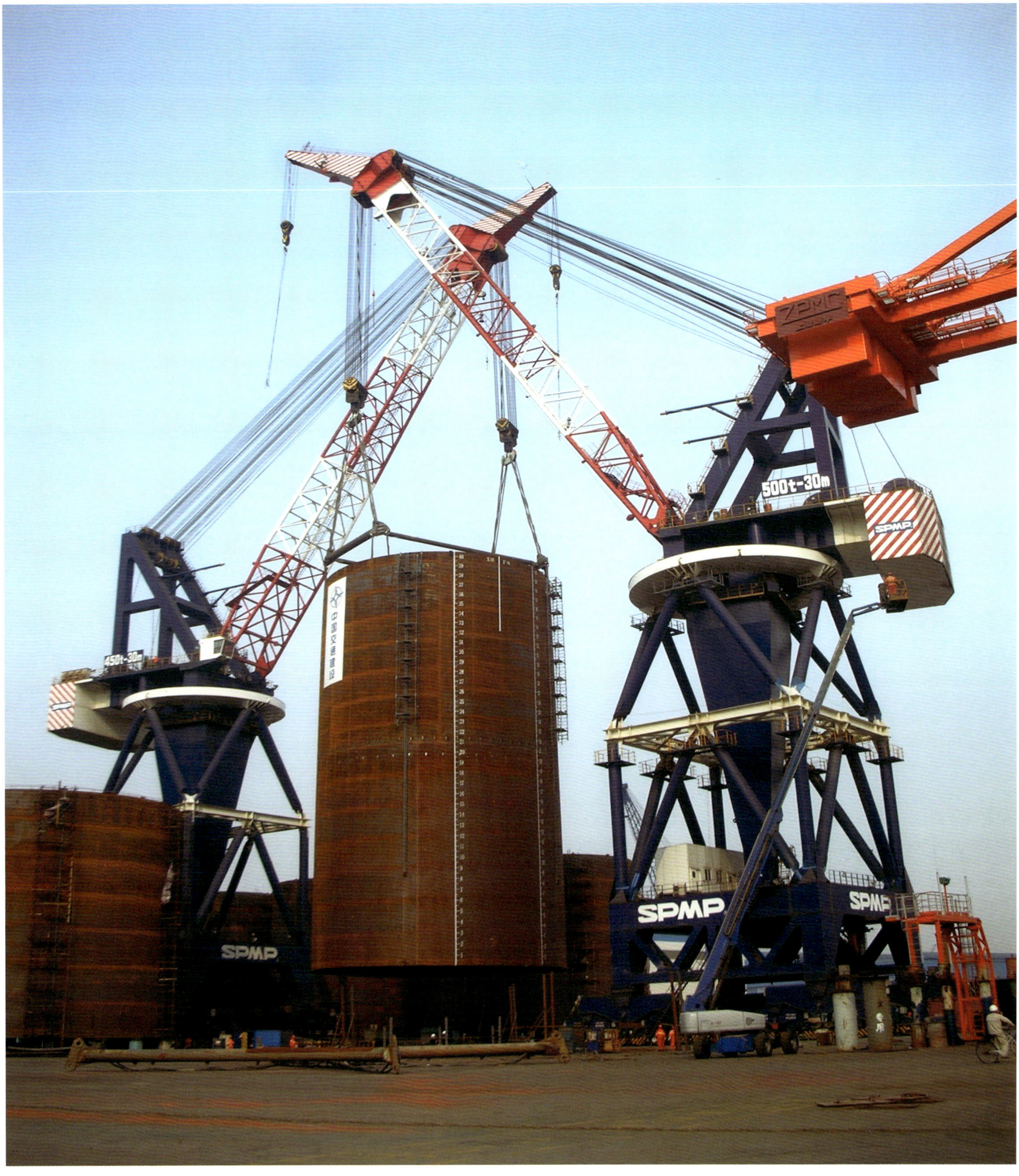
ZPMC
500t-30m
450t-30m
SPMP
中国交通建设

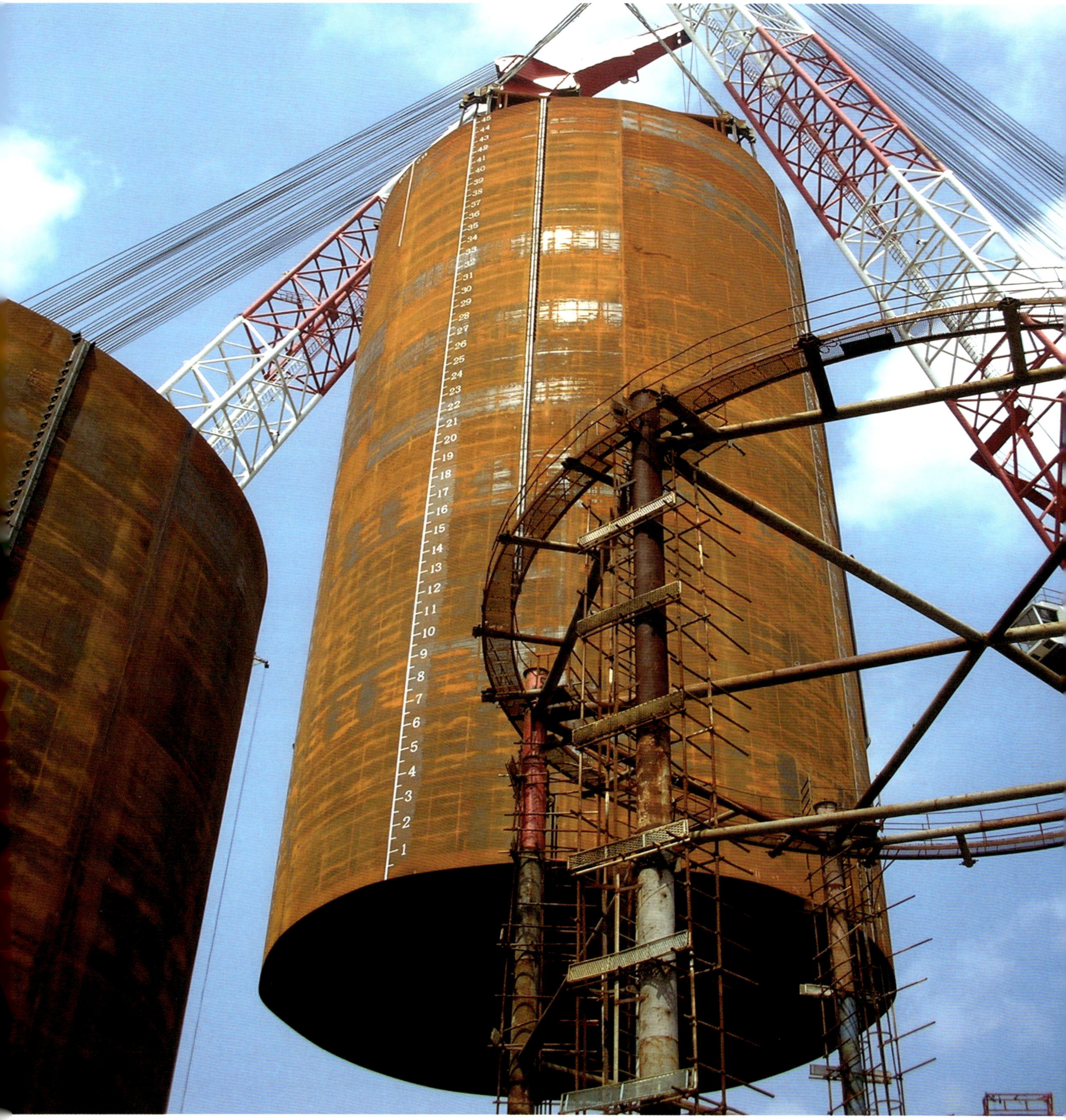
45
44
43
42
41
40
39
38
37
36
35
34
33
32
31
30
29
28
27
26
25
24
23
22
21
20
19
18
17
16
15
14
13
12
11
10
9
8
7
6
5
4
3
2
1

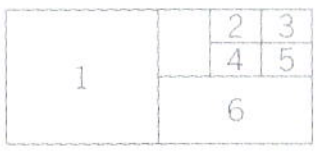

1. 钢圆筒转运
Transportation of the Steel Cylinders
2. 筒体装船
Loading of the Cylinders Onboard the Carrier
3. 筒体船上绑扎
Binding of the Cylinders Onboard
4. 筒体船上加固
Fixation of the Cylinders Onboard
5. 固定完成
Cylinder Binding and Fixation Completed
6. 钢圆筒吊装示意图
Schematic Diagram of the Cylinder Hoisting and Installation

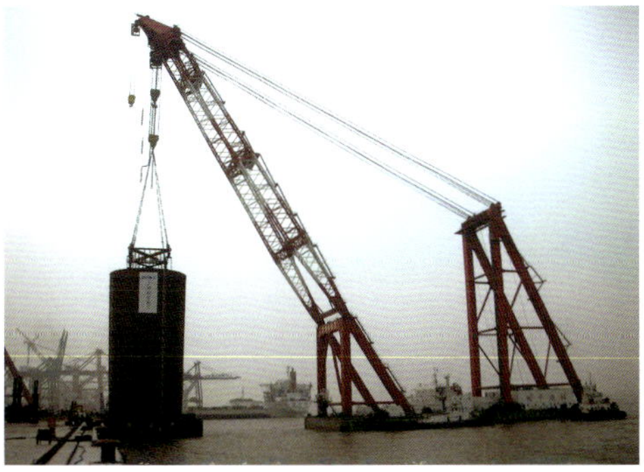

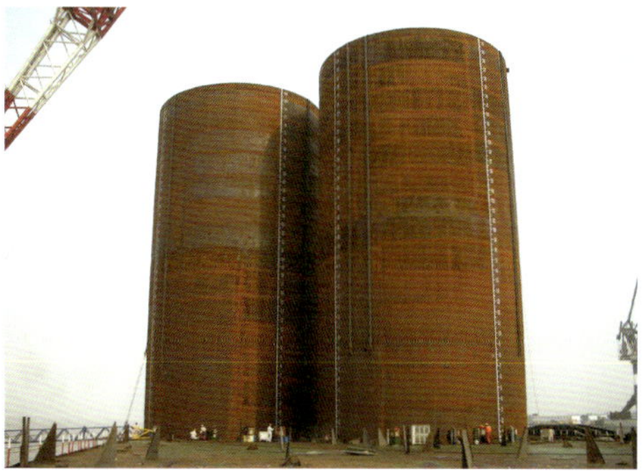

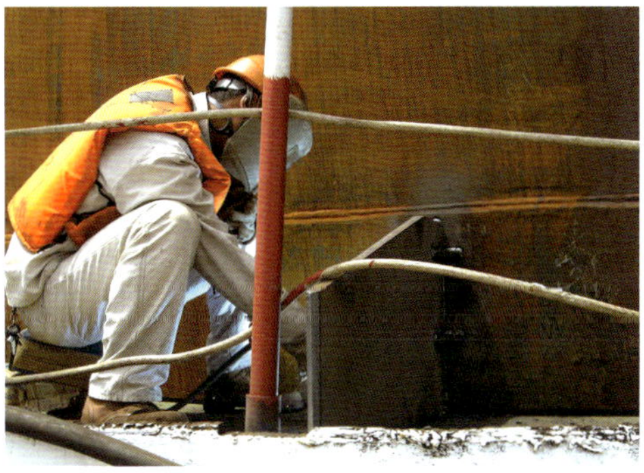

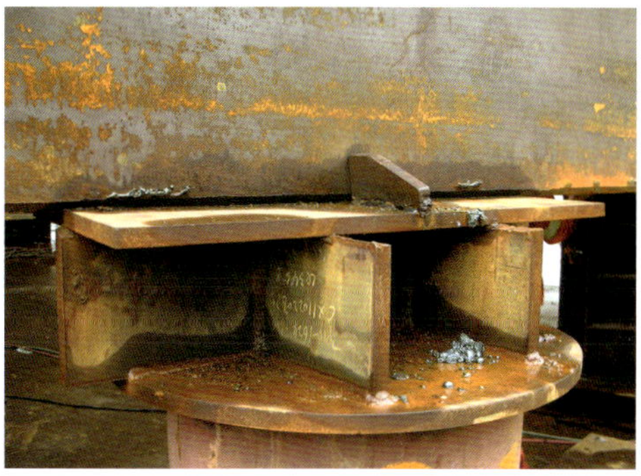

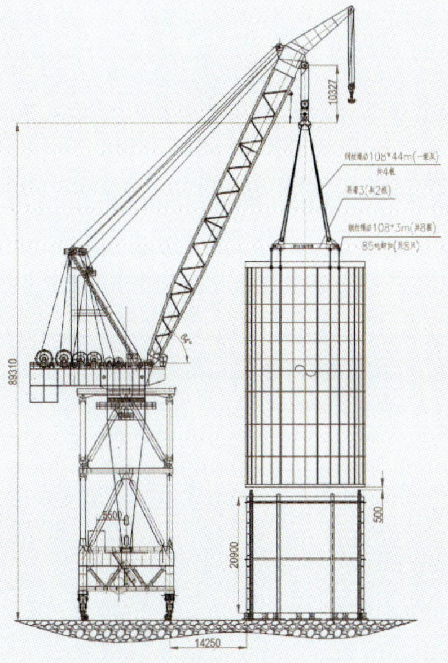

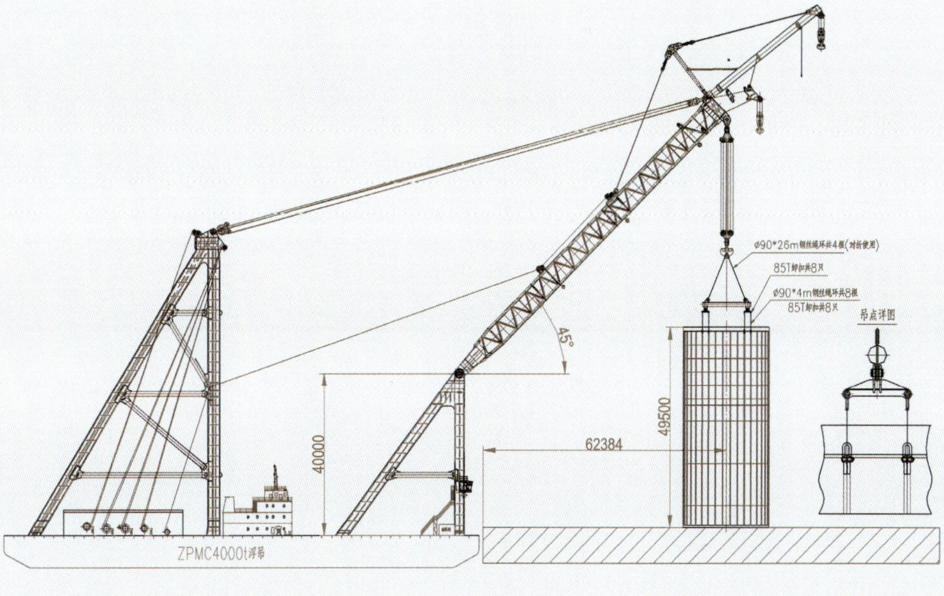

钢圆筒运输
TRANSPORTATION OF THE STEEL CYLINDERS

2011年5月2日，“振驳28号”装载着首个钢圆筒及振动锤组动力系统从上海长兴岛基地出发，历时7天1600公里长途运输，于5月8日抵达珠海。随后，由3艘7万吨远洋轮改装的运输船，每船装载8—9个钢圆筒，陆续运抵珠海。

这些巨型钢圆筒把运输船甲板全部占满，几乎挡住了驾驶员的视线。这些钢圆筒排列起来就像一堵墙，在海上运输时一旦遇到大风，运输船将无法控制。1600公里航程如何安全运输成了一个难题。

以航线上的水文天气等数据为基础，振华重工建立了计算模型，对船舶的稳定性、动力等进行详细计算，就钢圆筒加固及运输制定专项方案；同时，在运输船上安装卫星信号接收系统，由WINI公司专门提供气象水文信息，确保运输船能避开8级以上的风圈，在设计海况条件内航行。

运输船分批次从上海长兴岛基地出发，穿越台湾海峡，跨越三大海域，顺利抵达施工现场，累计航行50,000多公里。

On May 2, 2011, the shipping barge “Zhengbo 28”, loaded with the first steel cylinder and the vibratory hammer driving system, sailed out from Changxing Island Base, Shanghai, and after 7 days' voyage covering 1600 kilometers, arrived at Zhuhai on May 8. Then three shipping barges—three modified 70,000-ton ocean-going vessels—carried 8 to 9 steel cylinders each and shipped them to Zhuhai one after another.

The super-sized steel cylinders loaded on the decks of the carriers almost completely blocked the view of the pilots. These steel cylinders arranged in line looked like a wall. The strong winds on the sea would make it extremely difficult for the shipping barge to handle. How to transport the cylinders safely on the 1,600-kilometer voyage was a great challenge.

Based on the hydrological and weather data along the sailing route, ZPMC established a calculation model to calculate the stability and dynamic power of the barges, and a special plan was made for steel cylinder fixation and transportation. At the same time, a satellite signal receiving system was installed on the shipping barge, and WINI Company was invited to provide meteorological and hydrological information to ensure that the shipping barges could avoid strong wind circles measured 8 on the Beaufort Scale and navigate under the designed marine conditions.

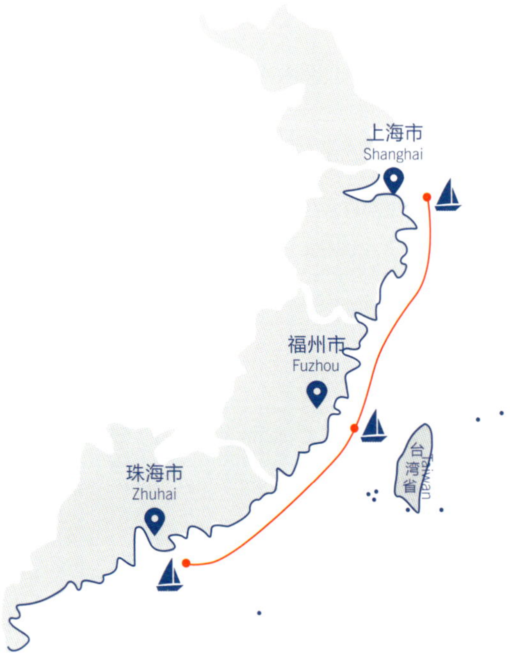

图片由中国交通股份有限公司提供
The Photo Provided by China Communications Construction Company Ltd.

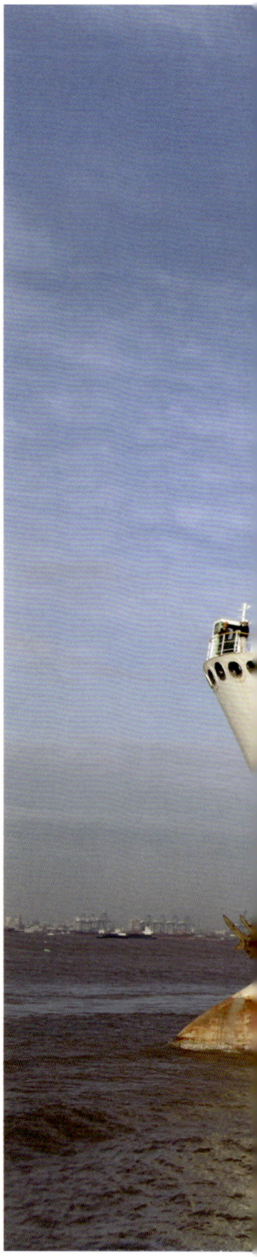

The shipping barges with the steel cylinders onboard set out in batches from Changxing Island Base, Shanghai, crossed the Taiwan Strait and the three sea areas, and finally reached the working site at Zhuhai after sailing over 50,000 kilometers.

1. 钢圆筒运输路线
Transportation Route of the Steel Cylinders

2. 钢圆筒启运
Steel Cylinders Starting Sailing

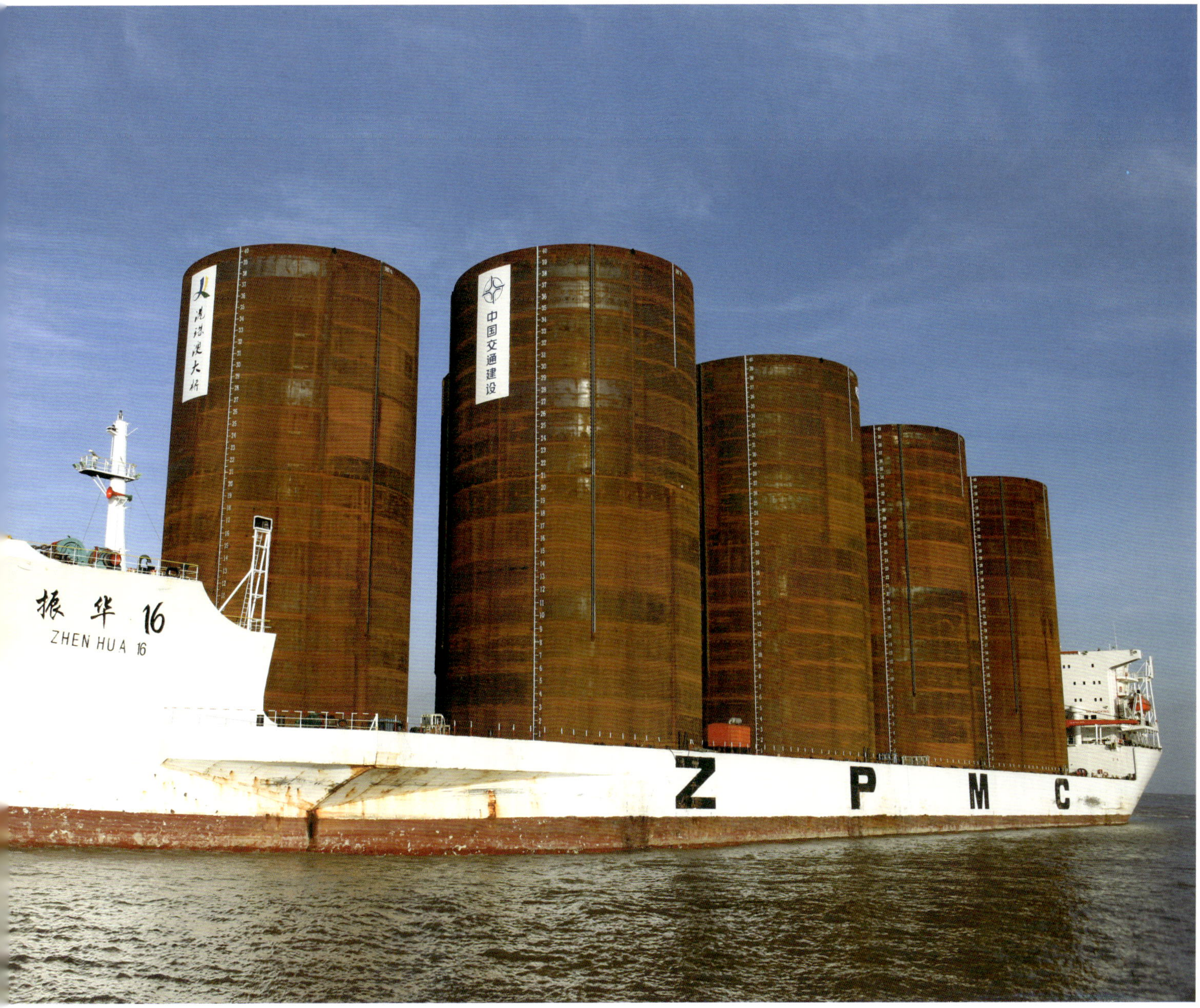

运输船现场停泊定位

ANCHORING AND POSITIONING OF THE SHIPPING BARGES

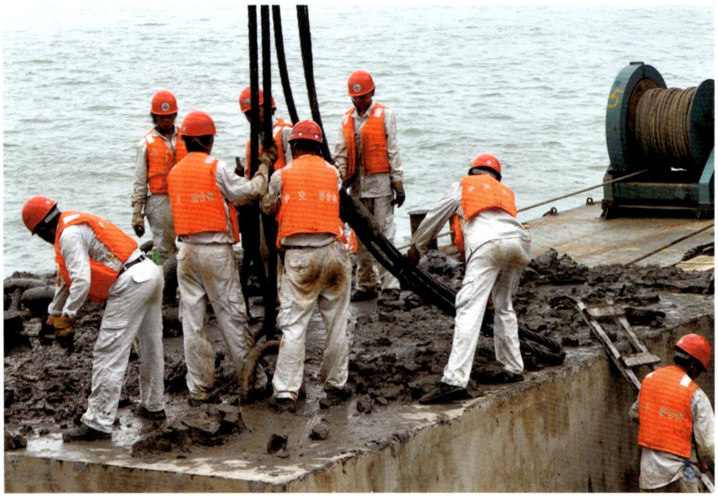

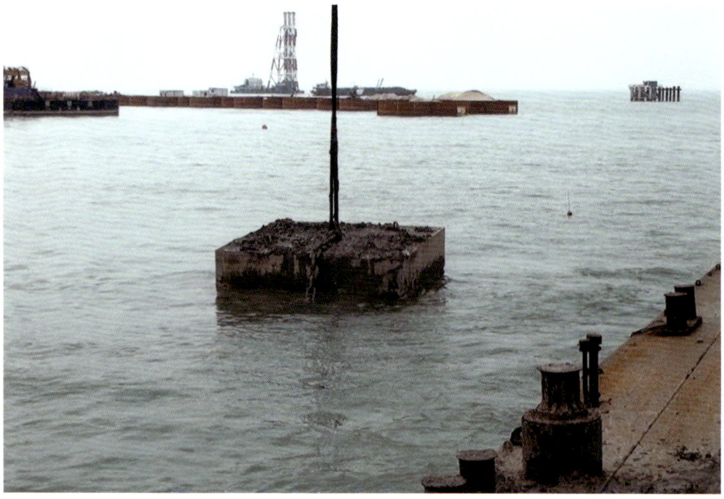

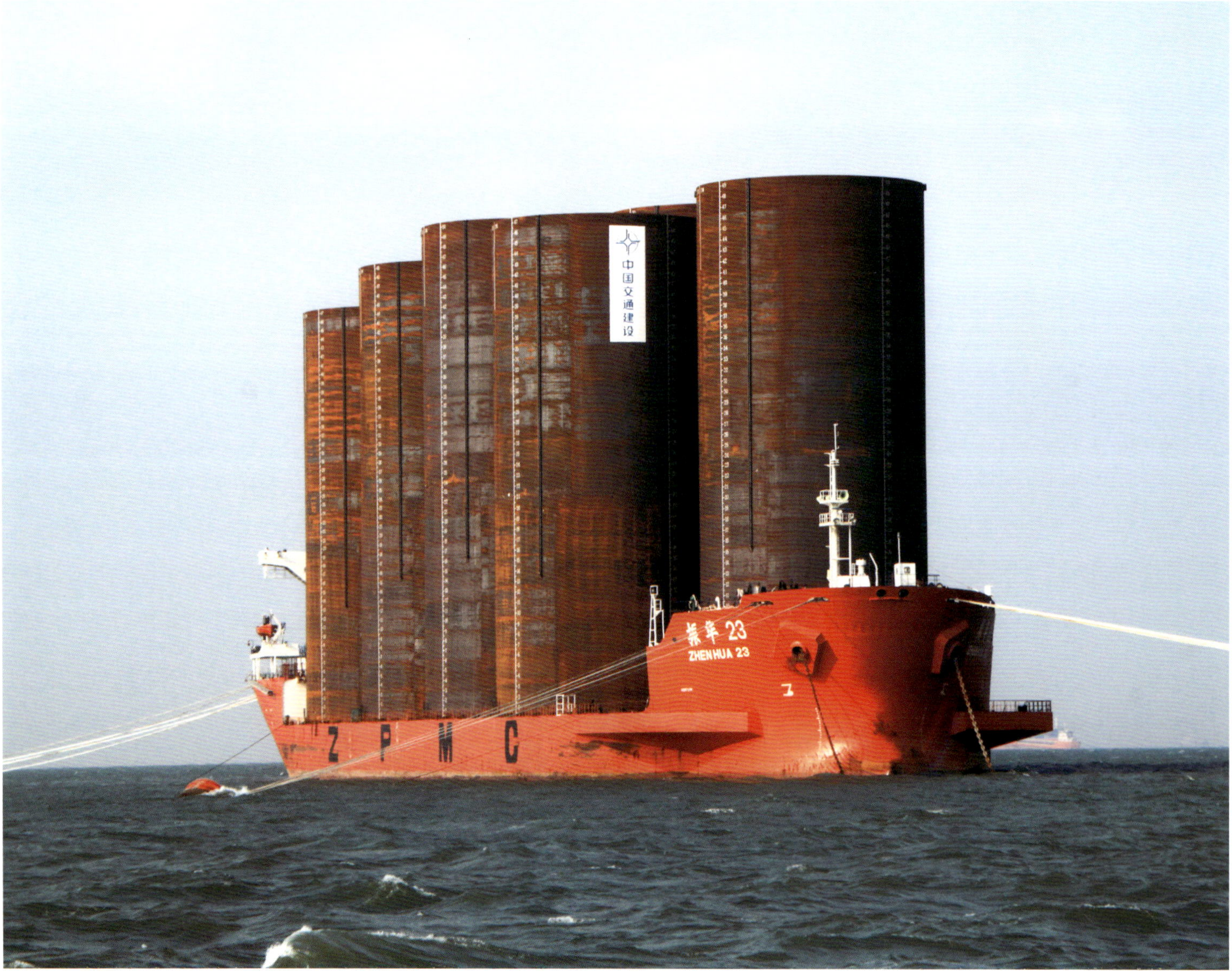

运输船抵达施工海域后完成系泊，由1600吨的起重船依次从运输船上吊起钢圆筒，移动到定位驳船旁，精确定位后再进行打设。

运输船、定位驳船、起重船的准确定位是首先要解决的问题，为解决9级大风导致的走锚现象，采用了400吨锚碇块，再回填10,000方砂石料的锚固方案，解决了运输船系泊难题。

After the shipping barges with the steel cylinders onboard arrived at the working site and the anchoring was done, the cylinders were hoisted up one by one by the crane barge with a capacity of 1600 tons and were moved to the positioning barge where the cylinders, after precise positioning, were driven into the seabed.

The first problem to be solved was the accurate positioning of the shipping barge, the positioning barge and the crane barge. To avoid anchor dragging incurred by the strong winds measured 9 on the Beaufort Scale, anchorage blocks of 400 tons were used together with the backfilling of 10,000 cubic meters of sand and gravel to cope with the problem involved in shipping barge anchoring.

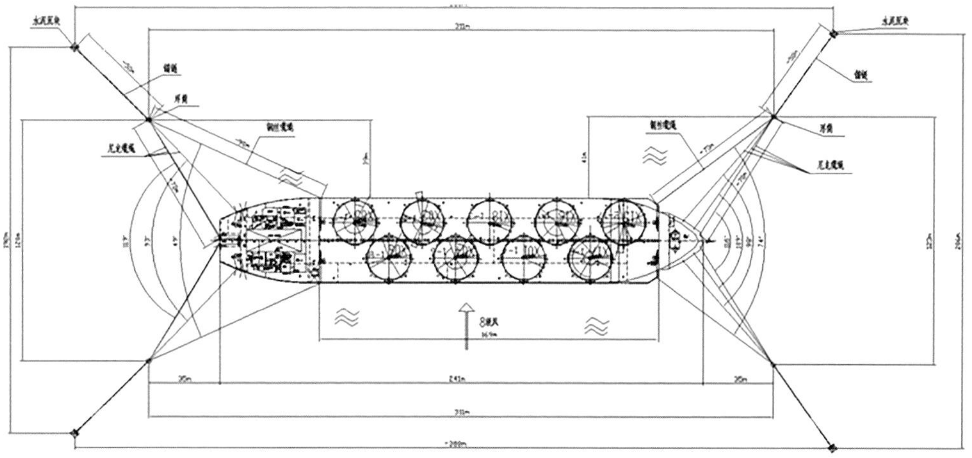

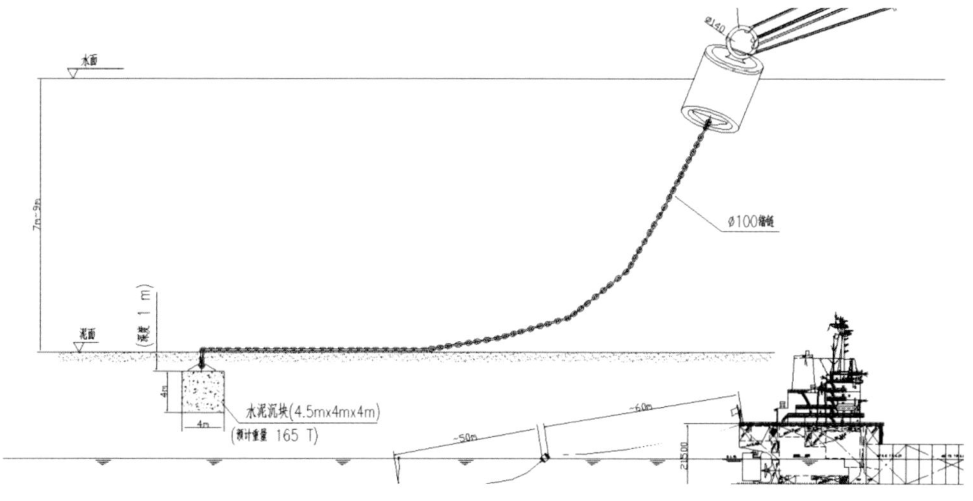

1	2	
3		4

1. 锚碇块
Anchoring Block
2. 锚碇块安放
Placement of the Anchoring Block
3. 钢圆筒运输船系泊
Anchoring of the Steel Cylinder Shipping Barge
4. 钢圆筒运输船系泊示意图
Schematic Diagram of the Anchoring of the Steel Cylinder Shipping Barge

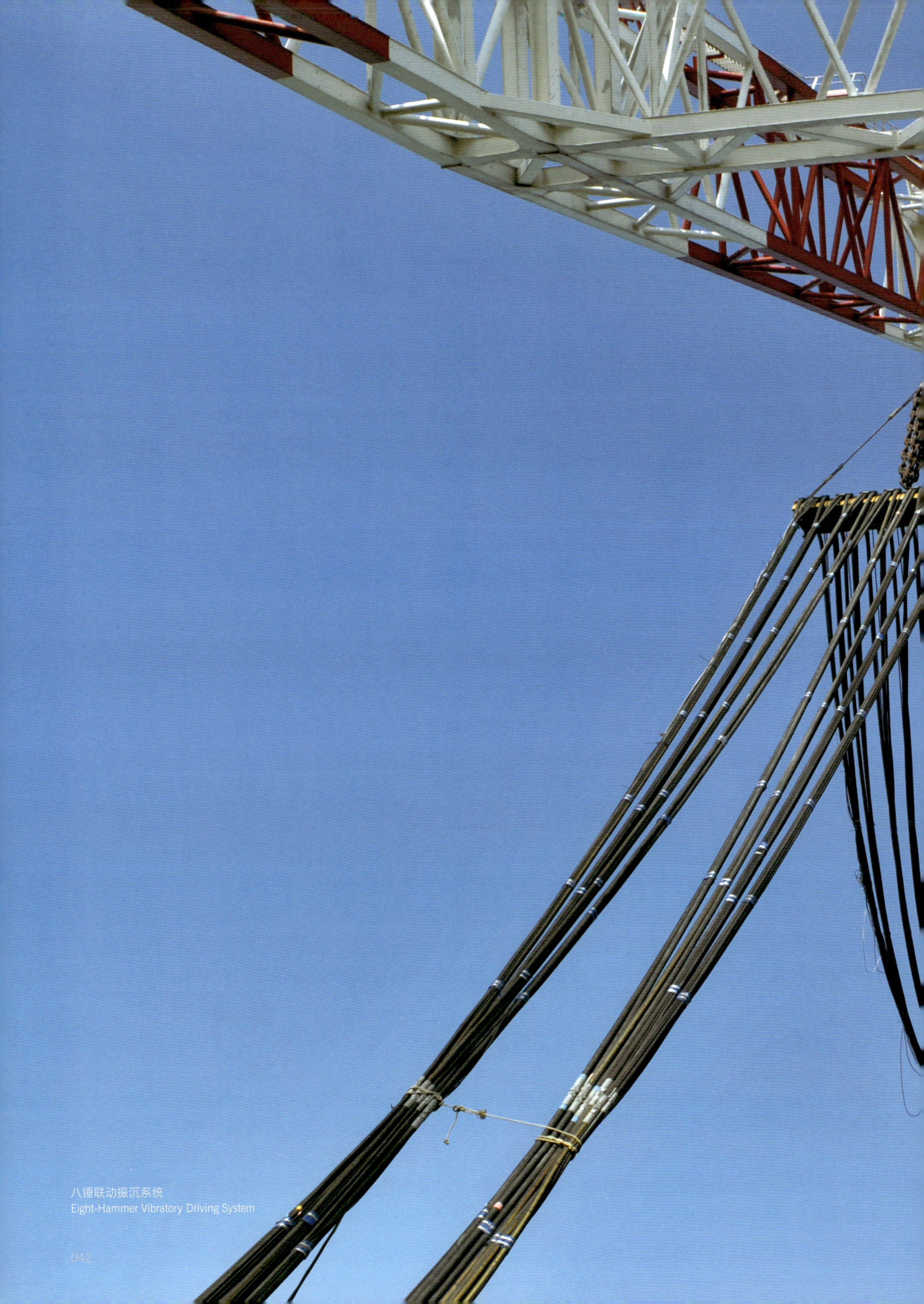

八锤联动振沉系统
Eight-Hammer Vibratory Driving System

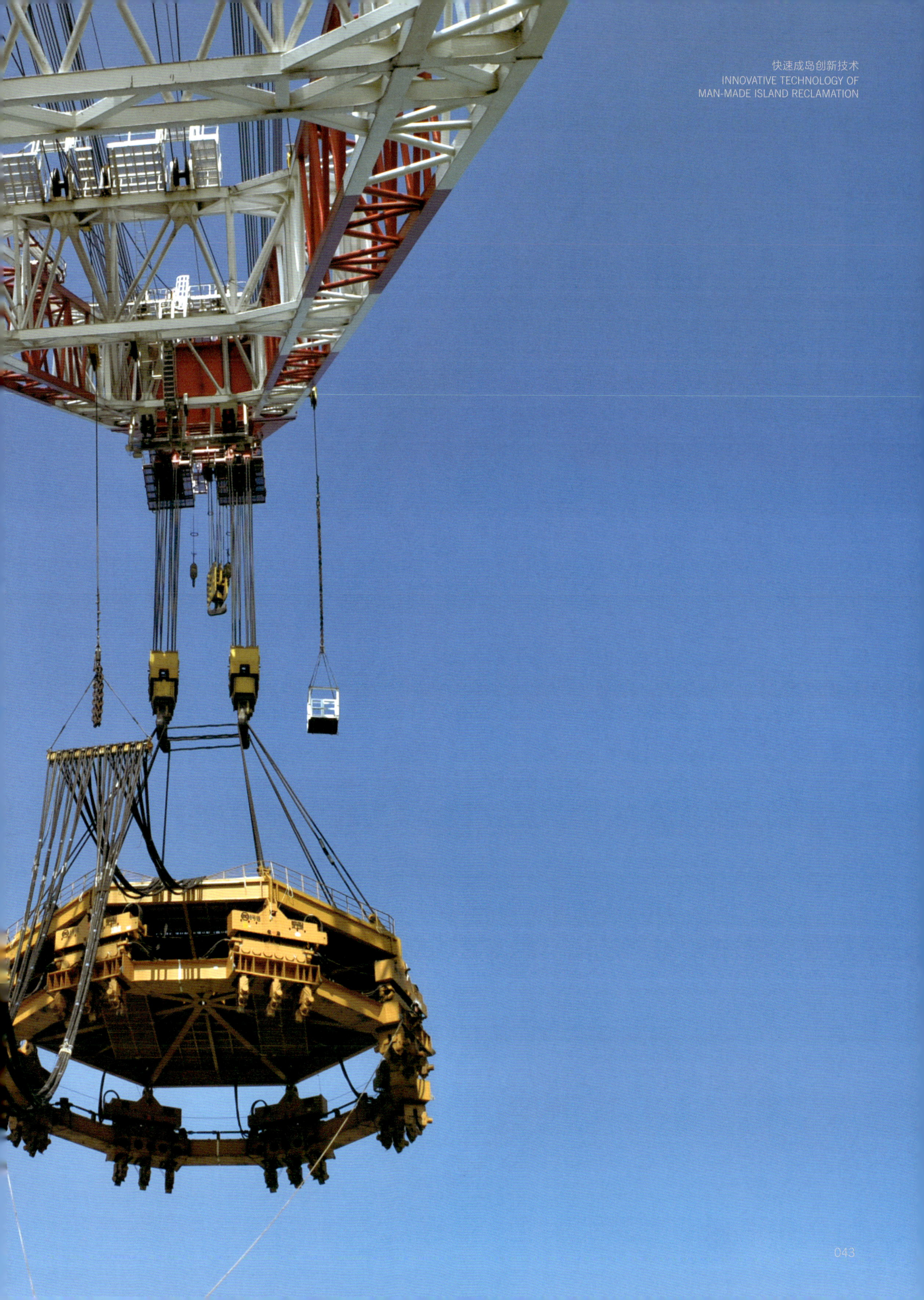

八锤联动振沉系统

EIGHT-HAMMER VIBRATORY DRIVING SYSTEM

深插钢圆筒快速成岛的核心问题是振沉。这就必须找到能提供足够激振力的振动锤，并在90天内完成制造、组装、测试工作，实现多台振动锤同步作业，使激振力能均匀有效地传递到钢圆筒底部。港珠澳大桥人工岛钢圆筒振沉采用8台APE600振动锤联动振沉系统，这在过去的工程中没有先例。

振沉系统由吊架、振动锤、同步装置、共振梁、液压夹具和液压设备等组成。其中共振梁、吊架由振华重工负责制造。这是一个中心直径22米、截面宽2.4米、高1.2米的圆环形箱梁，重达120吨，顶面安装8个振动锤和同步轴，底面安装24个液压夹具。为确保振动锤组巨大的激振力合力居中，并能均匀、有效地传递到钢圆筒底部，共振梁平整度控制在2毫米之内，使振动锤与共振梁达到完美配合。

2011年4月12日，8台振动锤设备陆续运达上海。此时，距离第一个钢圆筒预定振沉的时间仅剩下一个月，组装人员2天完成了拆箱工作，10天完成了振沉系统整体组装。2011年4月23日，振沉系统空载试振一次成功，比预计时间缩短了整整一个月。

The core problem of rapid island formation with deep-driven steel cylinders was the vibratory driving technique. Therefore, it was necessary to find a set of vibratory hammers that could provide enough driving power, and to complete the manufacturing, assembling and testing of the hammers within 90 days in order to realize the synchronized operation of several vibratory hammers to send exciting force evenly and effectively to the bottom of the steel cylinder. The vibratory driving system consisting of 8 APE600 vibratory hammers was adopted to drive the steel cylinders down in the formation of the man-made islands of Hong Kong-Zhuhai-Macau Bridge, which was unprecedented in the history of engineering.

The vibratory driving system consists of a hanging bracket, vibratory hammers, a synchronization device, a resonance beam, a hydraulic clamp and hydraulic equipment. The resonant beam and the hanging bracket were manufactured by ZPMC. It is a 120-ton ring box girder with a center diameter of 22 meters, a sectional width of 2.4 meters and a height of 1.2 meters, and with 8 vibratory hammers and synchronizing shafts installed on the top and 24 hydraulic clamps installed on the bottom. In order to ensure that the huge excitation force of the vibratory hammers is concentrated on the bottom of the steel cylinder evenly and effectively, the levelness of the resonant beam is controlled within the limit 2 millimeters, so that the vibrating hammers and the resonant beam could match perfectly.

On April 12, 2011, the eight vibratory hammers were delivered to Shanghai one after another when only one month was left before the first steel cylinders were driven down into the seabed. The assembling technicians completed unpacking within 2 days followed by the assembling of the vibratory system compartments within 10 days. On April 23, 2011, the trial operation of vibratory driving system was performed successfully, which was a whole month ahead of schedule.

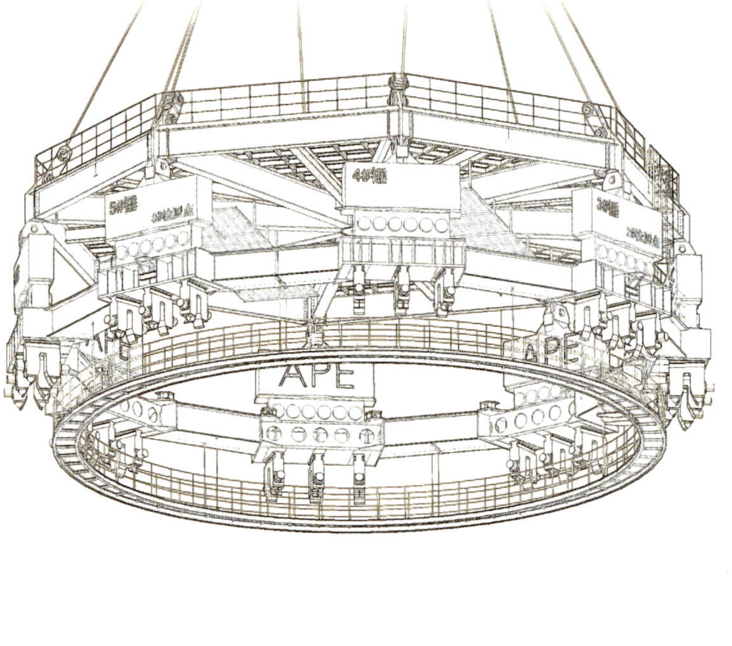

1. 八锤联动振沉系统三维效果图
3-D Design Sketch of the Eight-Hammer Vibratory Driving System
2. 施工中的八锤联动振沉系统
Eight-Hammer Vibratory Driving System in Operation

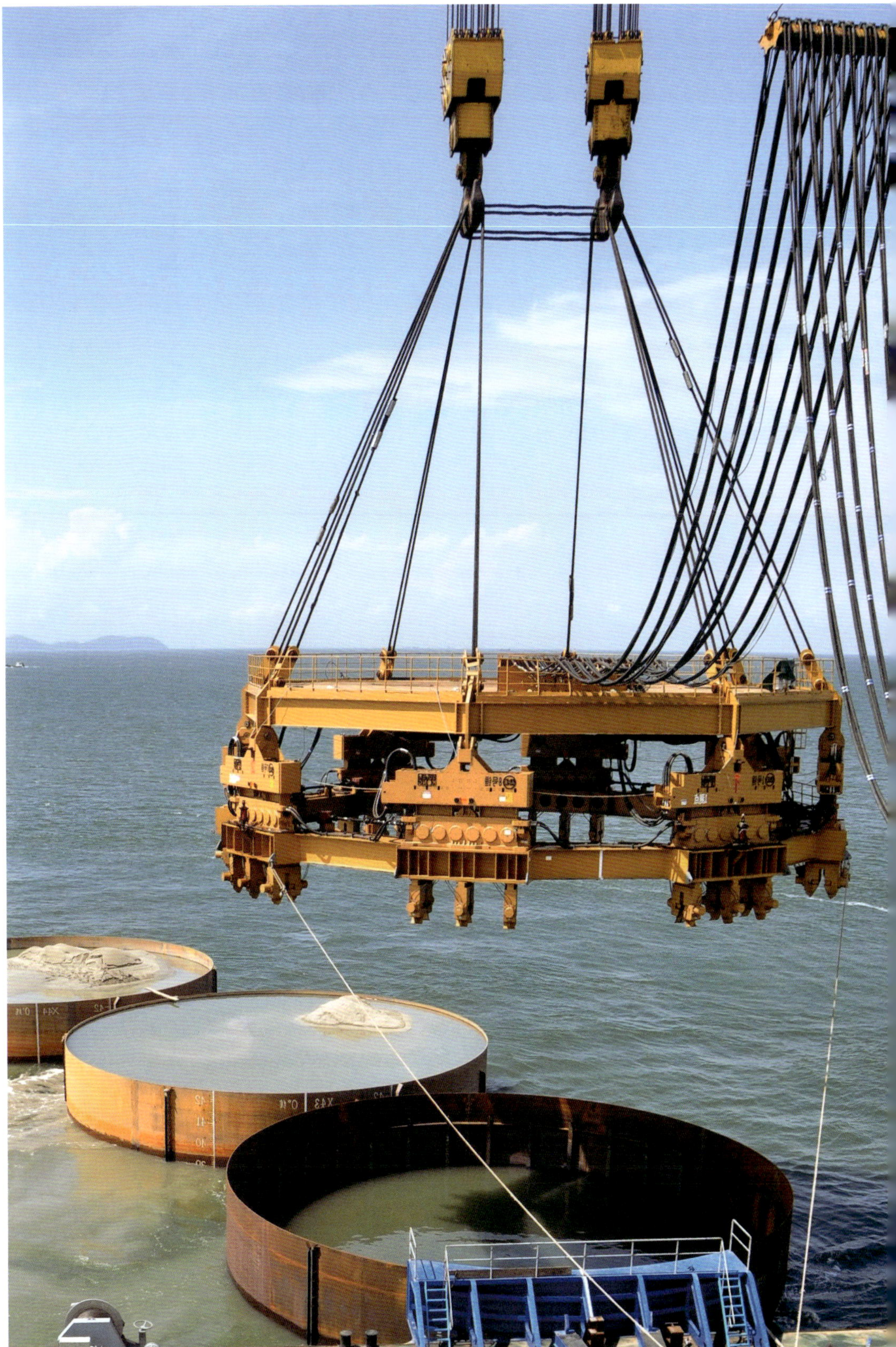

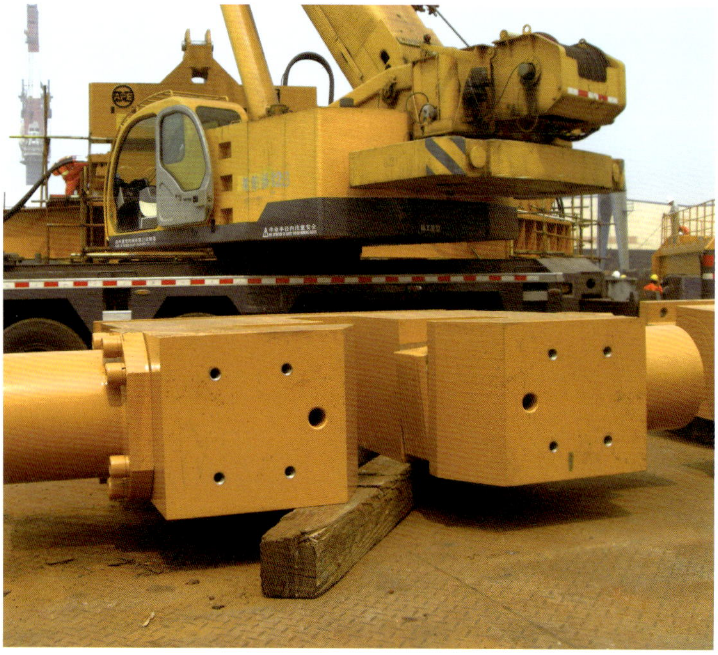

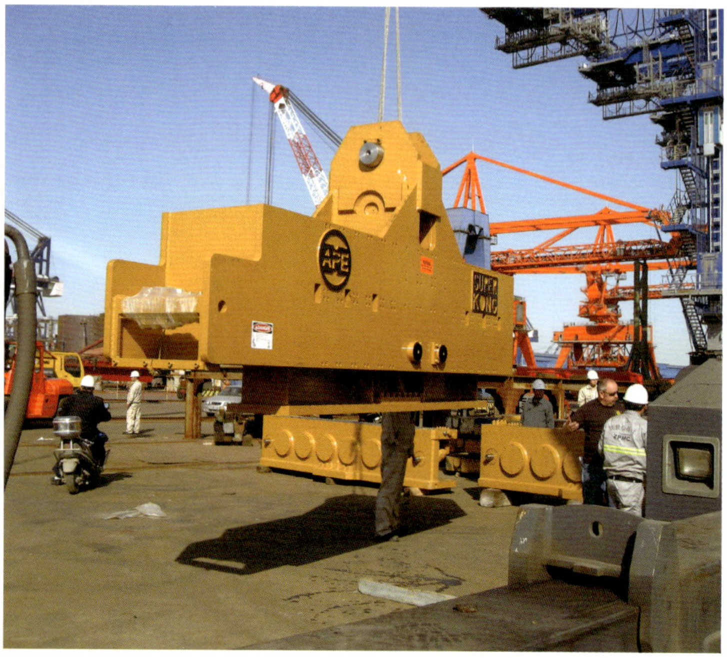
APE
SUPER KONG

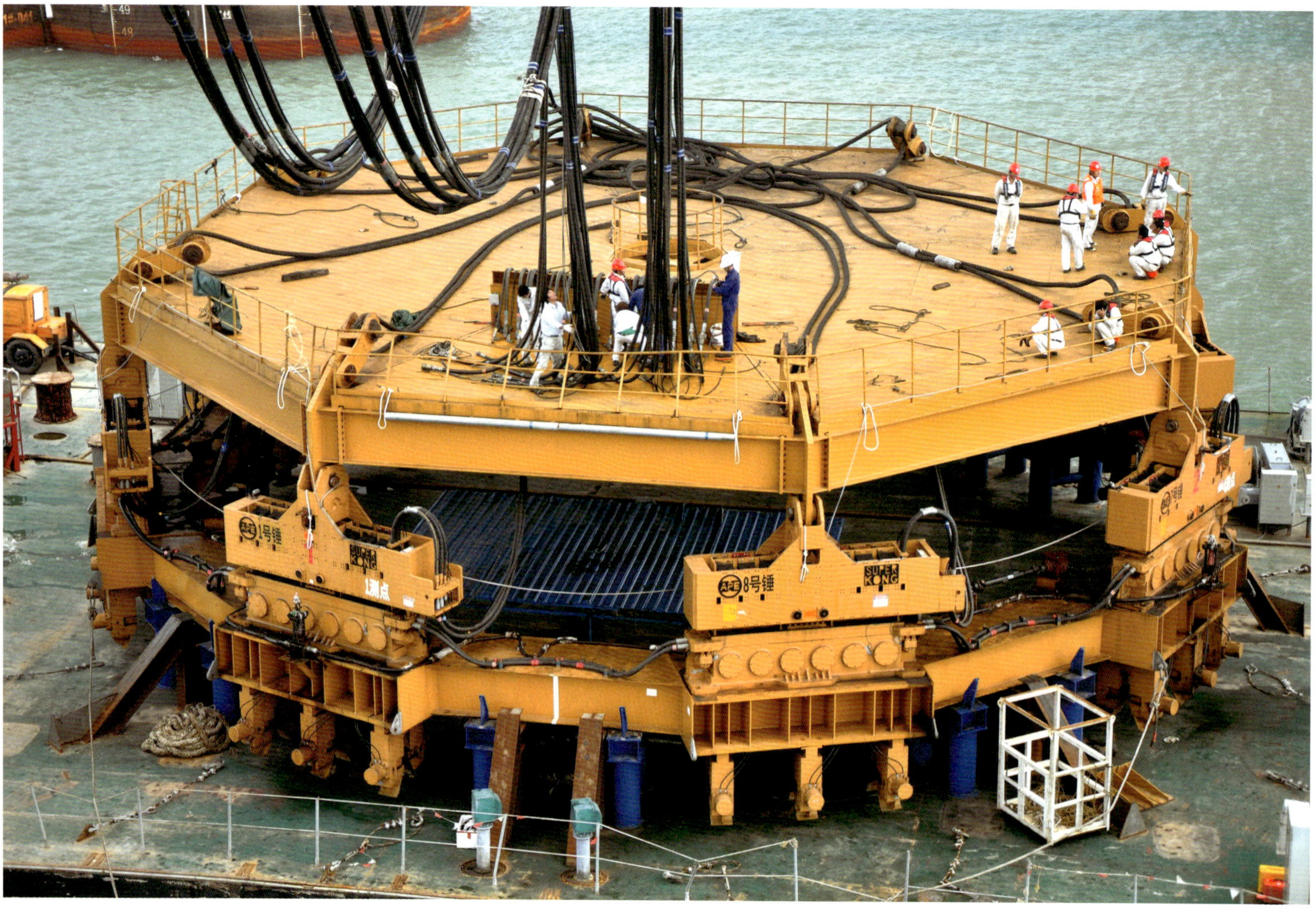
APE 1号锤
SUPER KONG
1测点
APE 8号锤
SUPER KONG

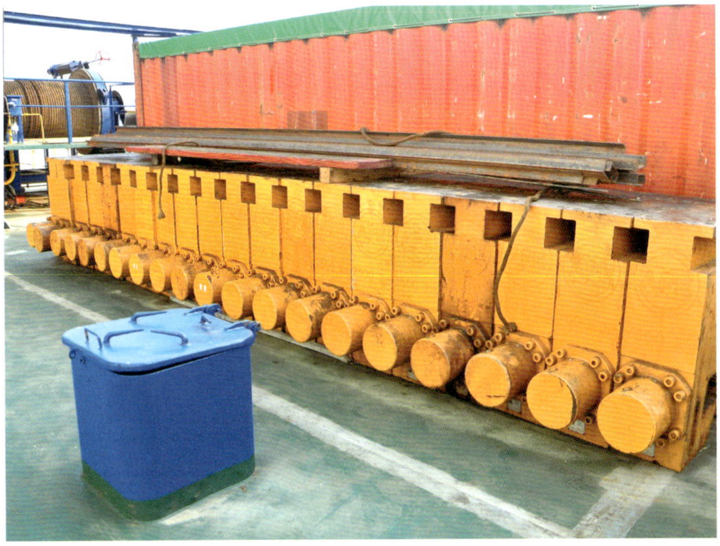

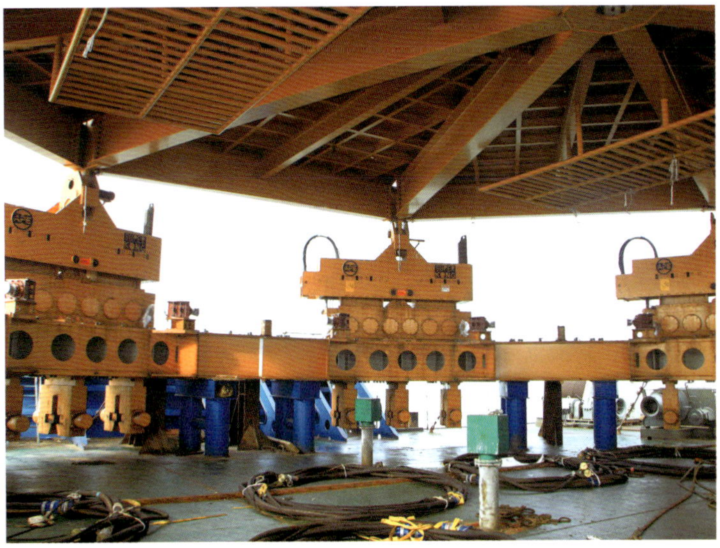

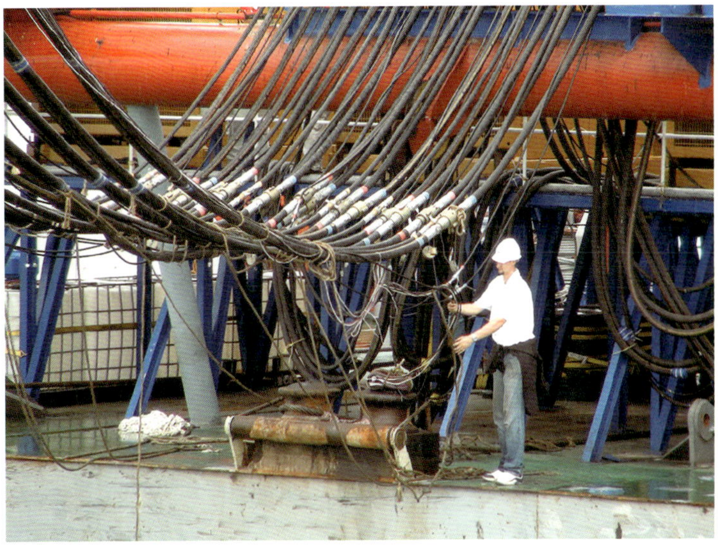

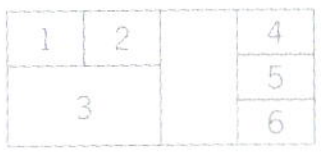

1. 液压夹具
   Hydraulic Clamp
2. 振动锤组装
   Assembling of the Vibratory Hammers
3. 八锤联动系统调试
   Adjustment of the Eight-Hammer Driving System
4. 液压夹具
   Hydraulic Clamp
5. 共振梁
   Resonance Beam
6. 高压油管
   High Pressure Oil Pipe

钢圆筒振沉

VIBRATORY DRIVING OF THE STEEL CYLINDERS

"把功夫用在前面，成败决定于过程，一丝不苟于细节，风险防控于微末"，这是林鸣多年工程实践形成的习惯，是项目贯穿整个工程的管理精髓。

从振沉设备的招标研发，到钢圆筒的制造运输，再到第一个钢圆筒顺利振沉入海，钢圆筒快速筑岛的大胆设想终于变成了现实。

这也催生出岛隧工程项目的核心文化："每一次都是第一次。""每一次都是第一次"成为岛隧工程所有建设者共同遵循的准则，为建设世界最大沉管隧道发挥了巨大作用。

"If efforts lead, success comes in the process; if care prevails, risks lose trails." This is Lin Ming's summary of his years' engineering practice, and it became the essence of the project management throughout the whole project.

From the bidding for the invention of the vibratory driving equipment to the manufacture and transportation of the steel cylinders and then to driving the first steel cylinder into the seabed, the bold assumption of rapid island formation with steel cylinders finally turned into a reality.

This also gave birth to the core culture of the island-tunnel project: "Every try is the first try." It became a general guideline for all the constructors of the island-tunnel project and played a tremendous role in the construction of the world's largest immersed tube tunnel.

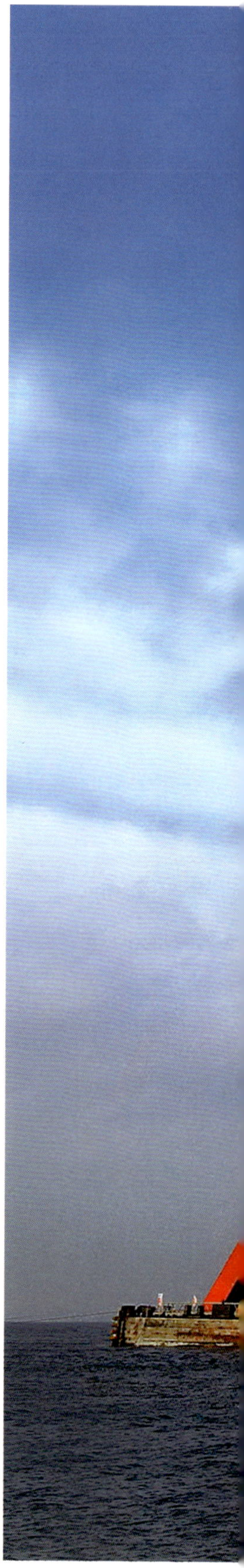

钢圆筒起吊

Steel Cylinder Lifting

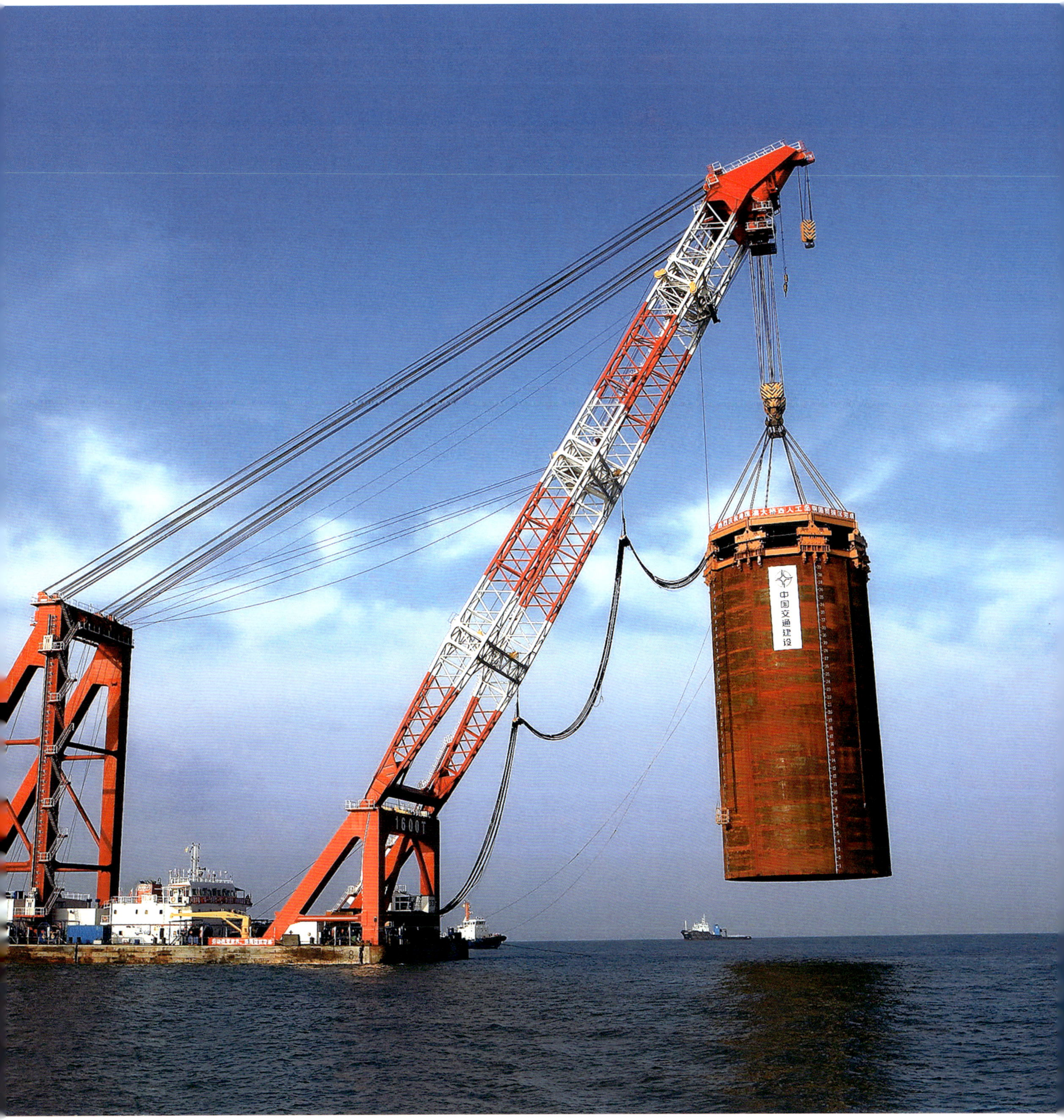
中国交通建设
1600T

1. 钢圆筒取筒
Unloading of the Steel Cylinder

2. 钢圆筒定位
Positioning of the Steel Cylinder

3. 钢圆筒自沉
Automatic Sinking of the Steel Cylinder

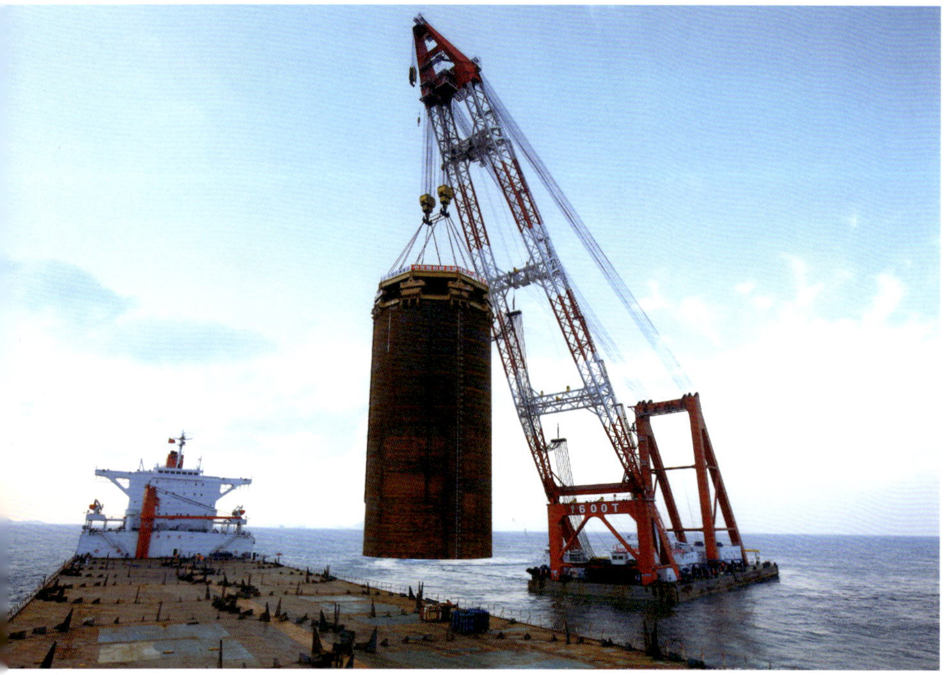

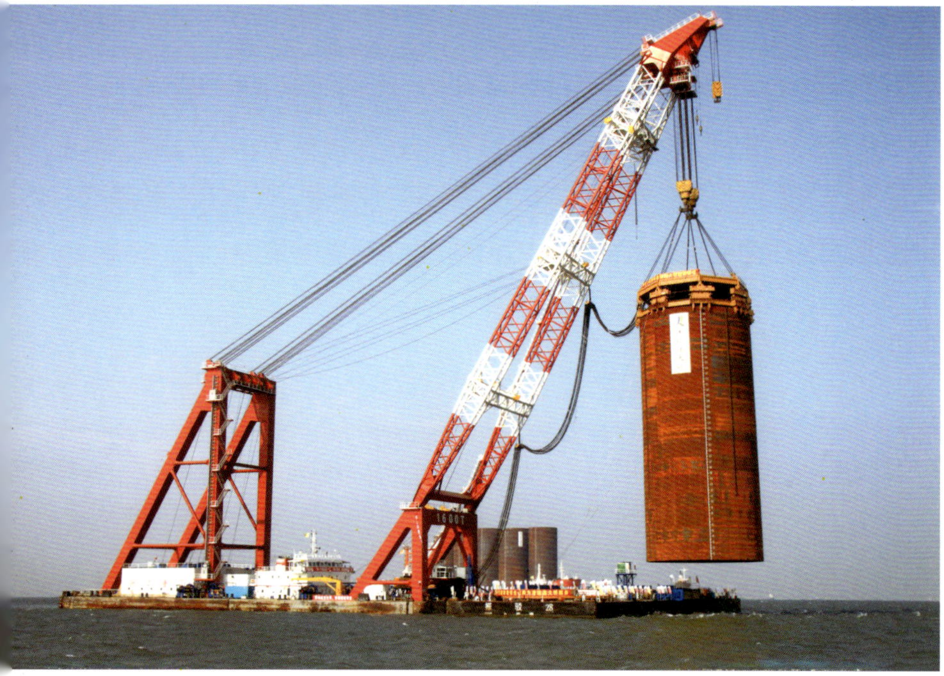

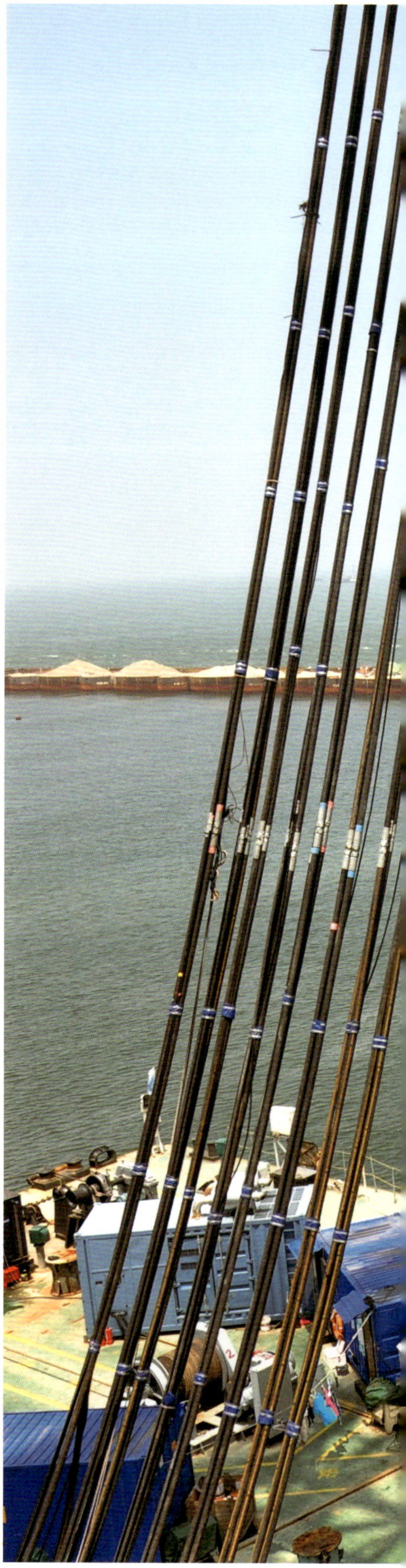

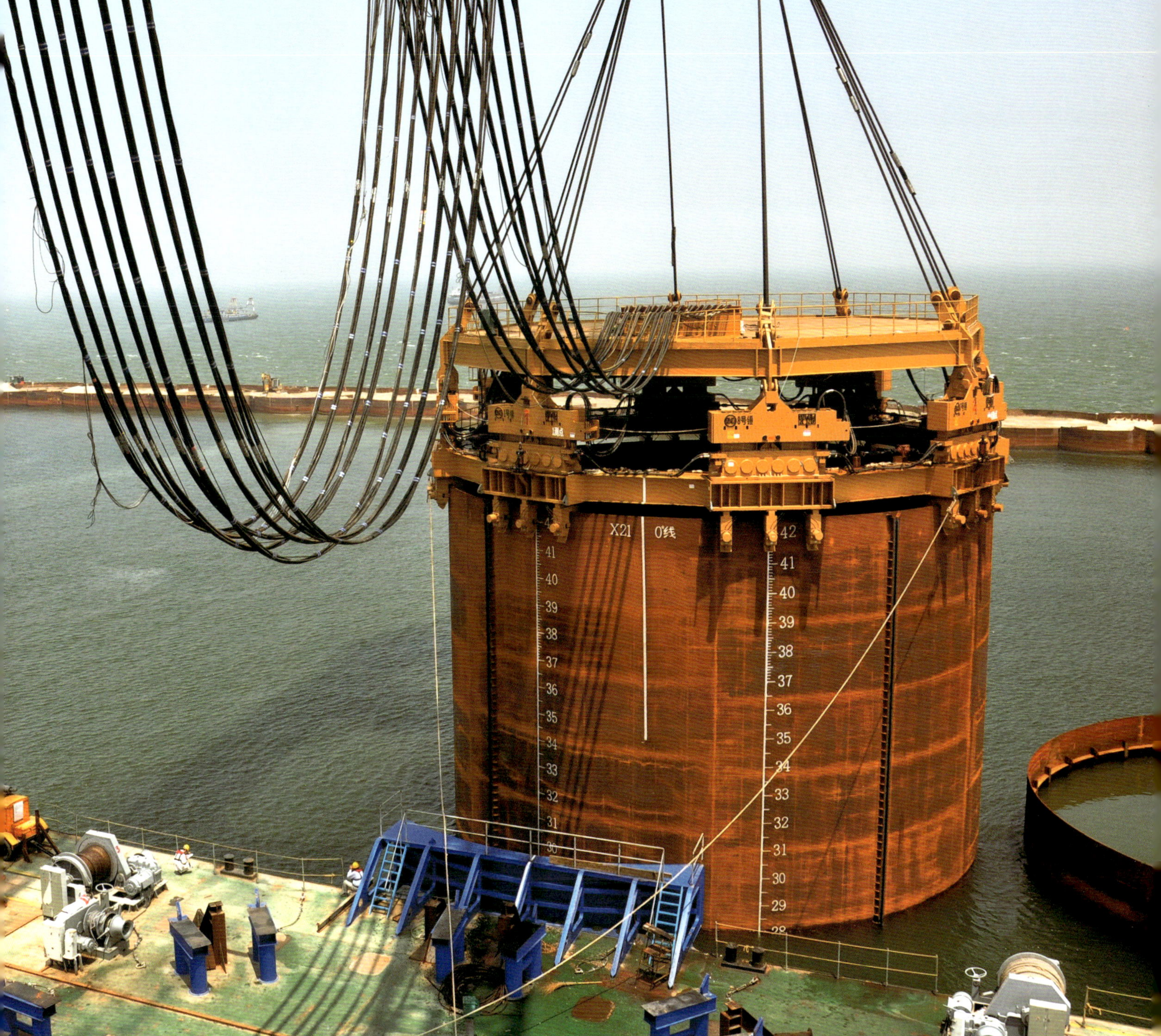
X21
0'线

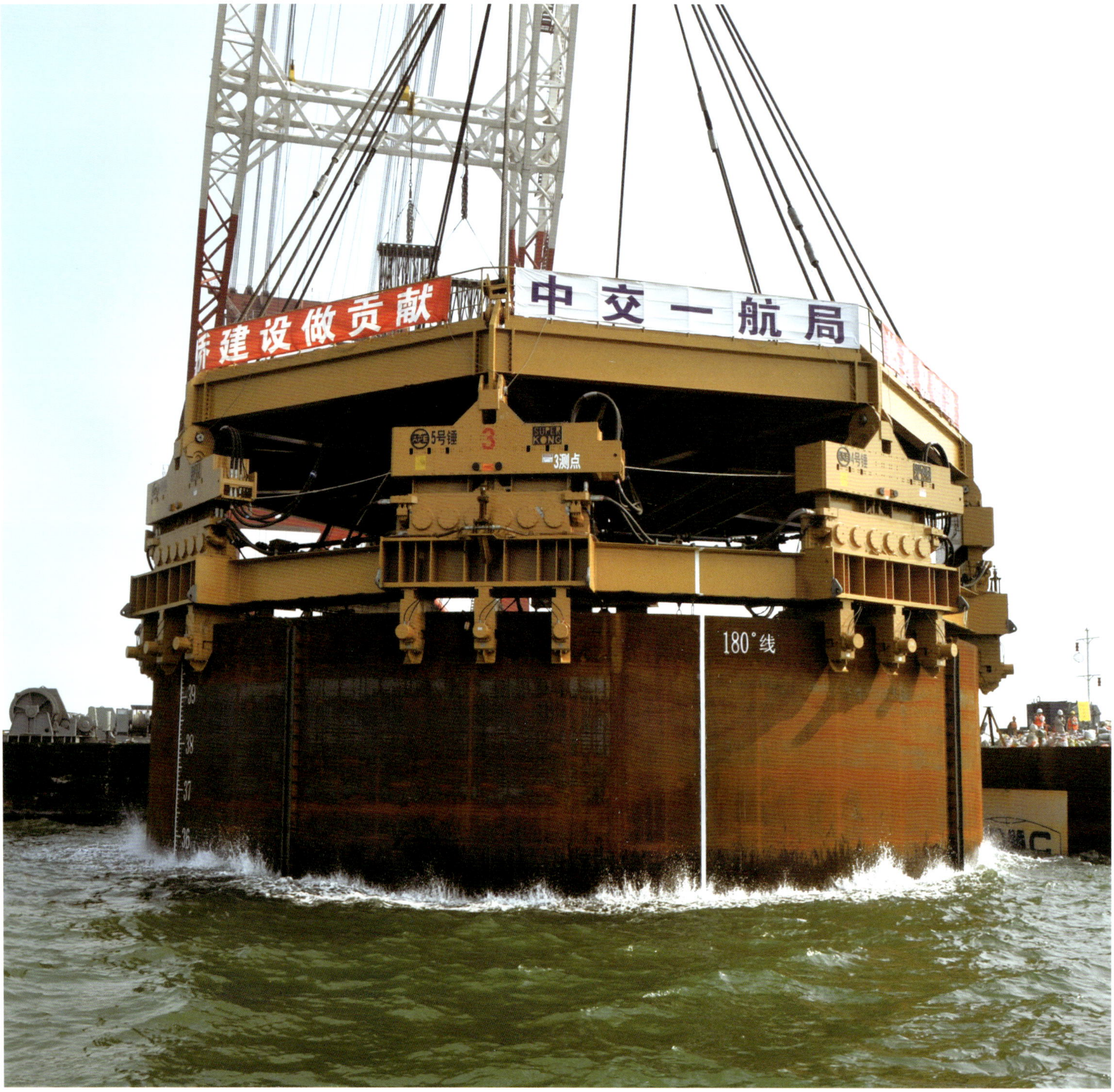

1 2

1. 钢圆筒振沉
Vibratory Driving of the Steel Cylinder

2. 振沉完成的钢圆筒岛壁结构
Steel Cylinder Walls of the Island after the Vibratory Driving Completed

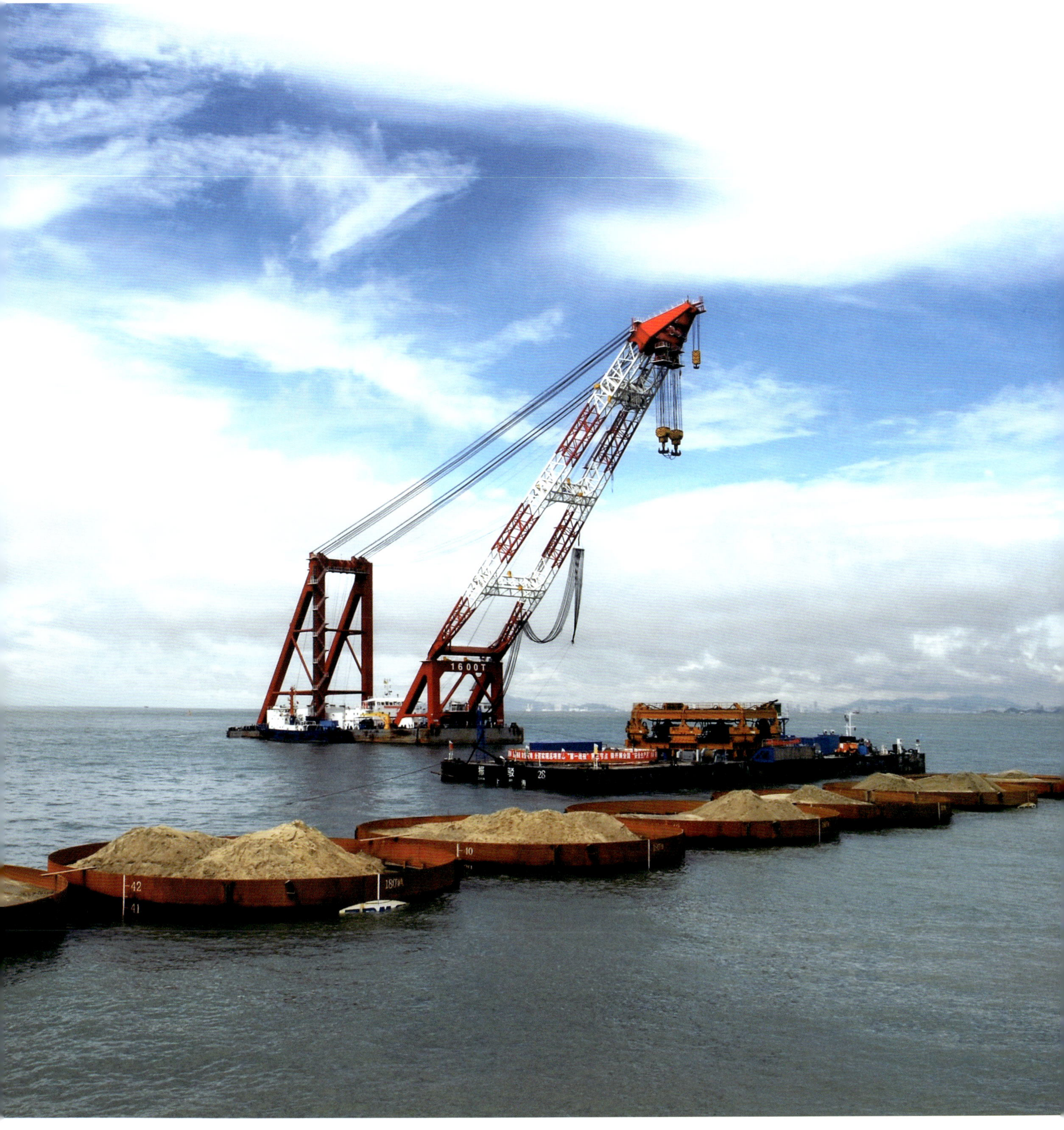
1600T

成岛后的东人工岛
East Man-Made Island Completed

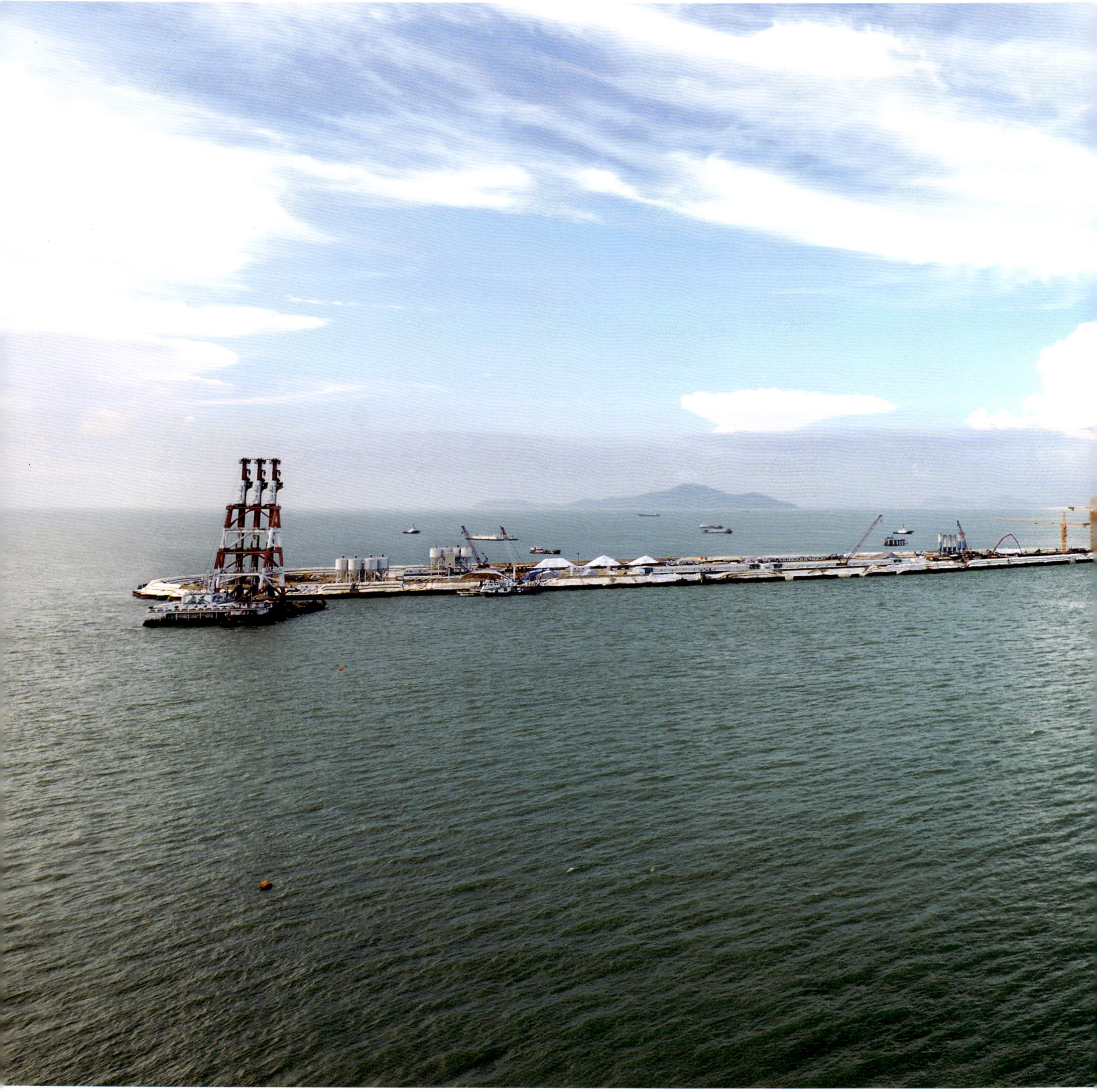

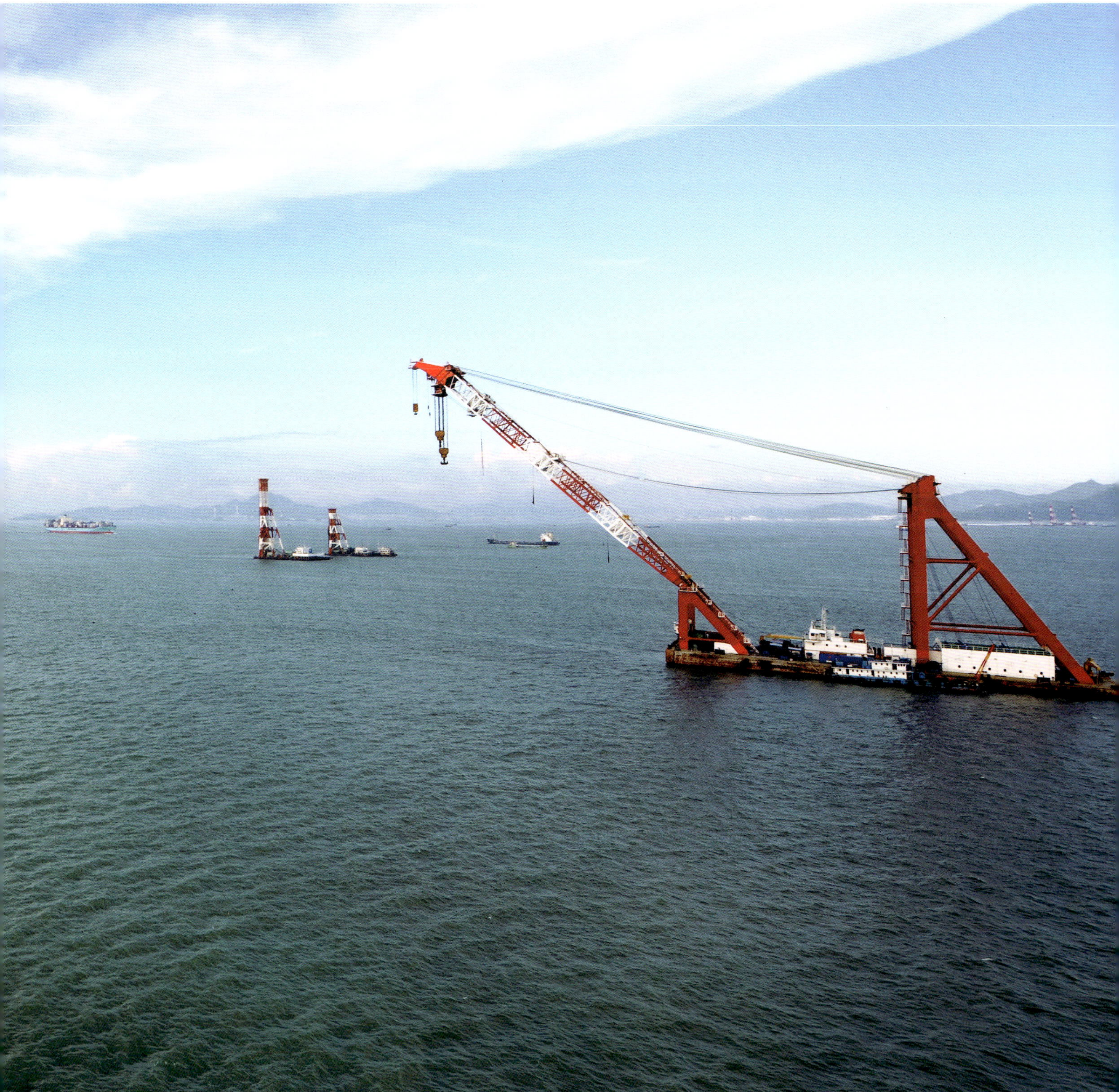

钢圆筒沿人工岛岸壁前沿线布置，西人工岛设置61个钢圆筒，东人工岛设置59个钢圆筒。

西人工岛内设置分隔围堰，把岛体分为西小岛和西大岛两个部分。西小岛用于隧道止推段施工先行建设，是沉管隧道首节沉管对接的关键。

振沉施工按先西小岛，后西大岛的施工整体安排进行。

振沉前，"振驳28号"作为定位船驻位于起重船与待振沉钢圆筒之间，"振华16""振华17"运输船抵达施工海域；"振驳28号"粗定位后，起重船吊起钢圆筒完成精定位及垂直度调整，再进行振沉。

钢圆筒自下沉开始至振沉结束，全程采用"钢圆筒施工定位监测系统"监控钢圆筒振沉过程中的姿态，及时进行调整和纠偏。依次打设，逐步形成围闭结构。

The steel cylinders were arranged along the revetment of the man-made islands, and 61 steel cylinders were installed in West Man-Made Island while 59 in East Man-Made Island.

A partition cofferdam divided the west man-made island into two parts: the major island and the minor island. The minor island was used for the construction of the thrust section of the tunnel, so it was crucial for the butt welding of the first immersed tube of the tunnel.

The vibratory driving operation started on the minor island first and continued on the major island as designed.

Prior to the vibratory driving operation, "Zhenbo 28", as the positioning barge, stationed between the crane barge and the cylinder waiting to be driven into the seabed, while the shipping barges "Zhenhua 16" and "Zhenhua 17" arrived at the sea area of the working site. After "Zhenbo 28" was roughly positioned, the crane barge lifted the steel cylinder for accurate positioning and vertical adjustment before the vibratory driving operation.

The steel cylinder's position was monitored by the "steel cylinder positioning monitoring system" throughout the whole process of driving the cylinder into the seabed. Prompt adjustment and correction were done. The cylinders were driven into the seabed one by one, and a closed structure was formed.

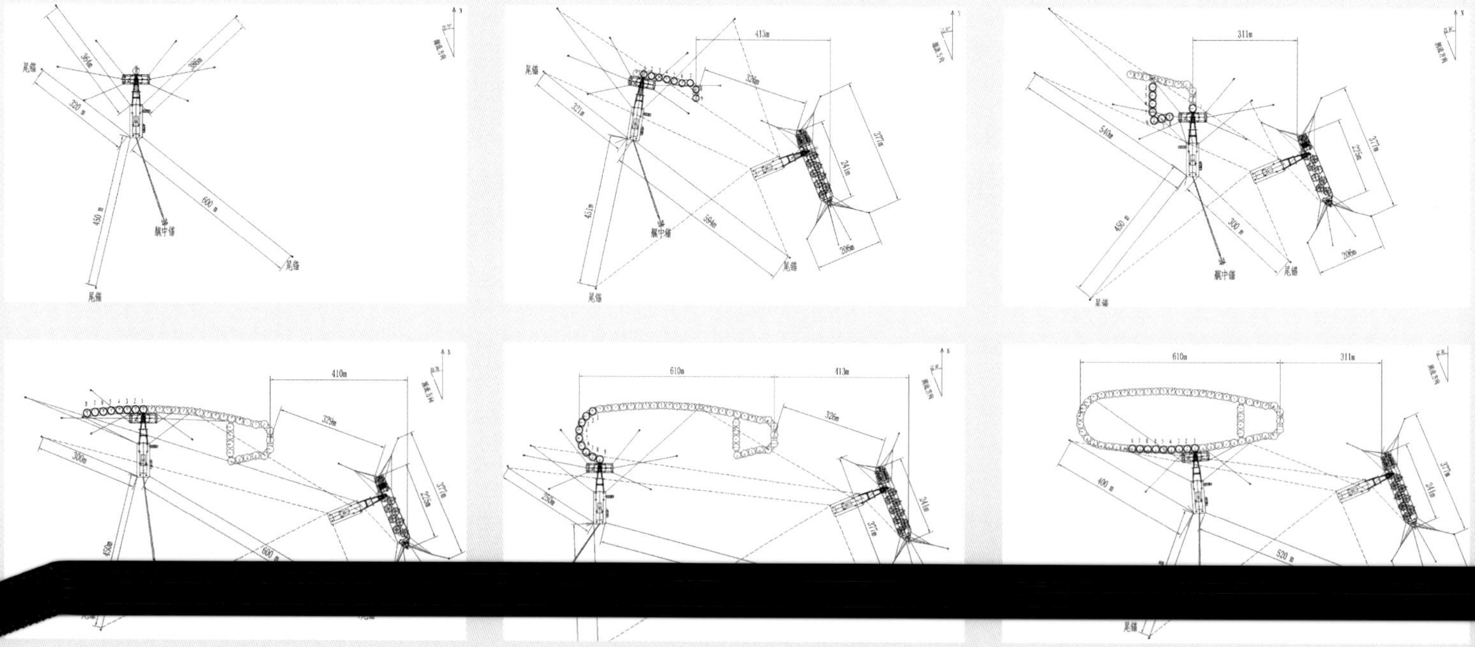

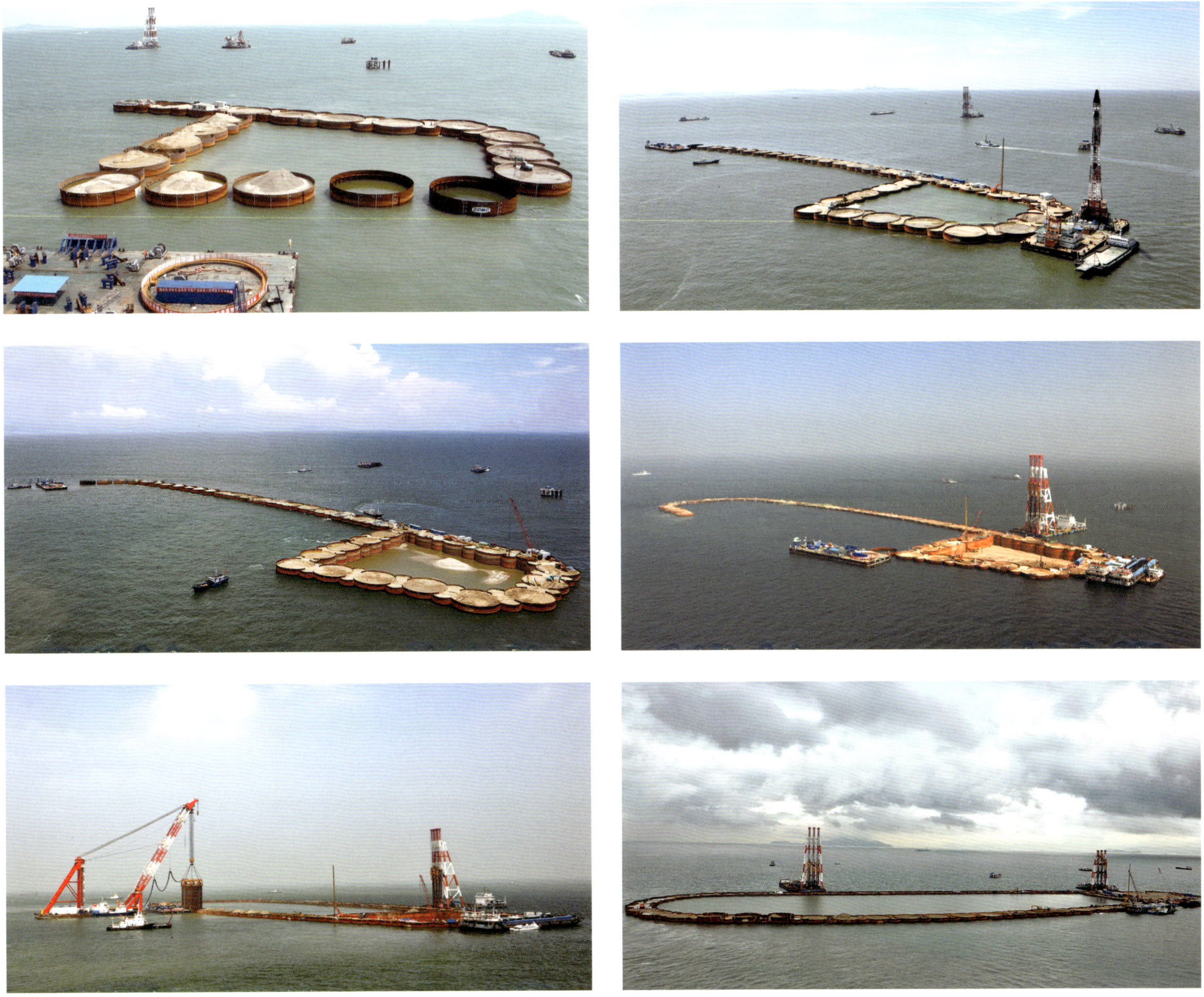

2

[redacted]

1. 钢圆筒取筒定位振沉示意图
Schematic Diagram of the Unloading, Positioning and Vibratory Driving of the Steel Cylinder

2. 西人工岛成岛过程
Process of West Man-Made Island Reclamation

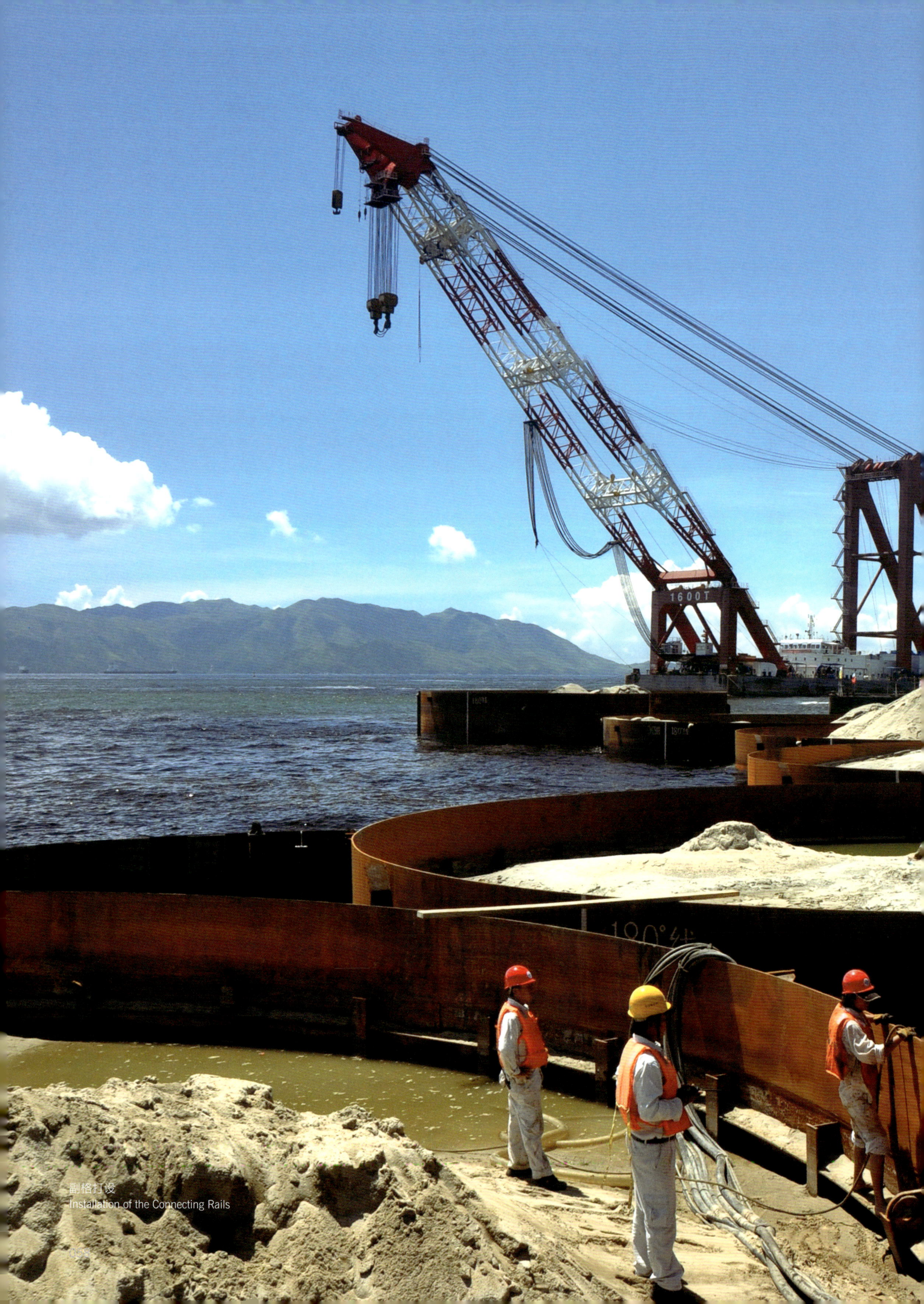

副格打设
Installation of the Connecting Rails

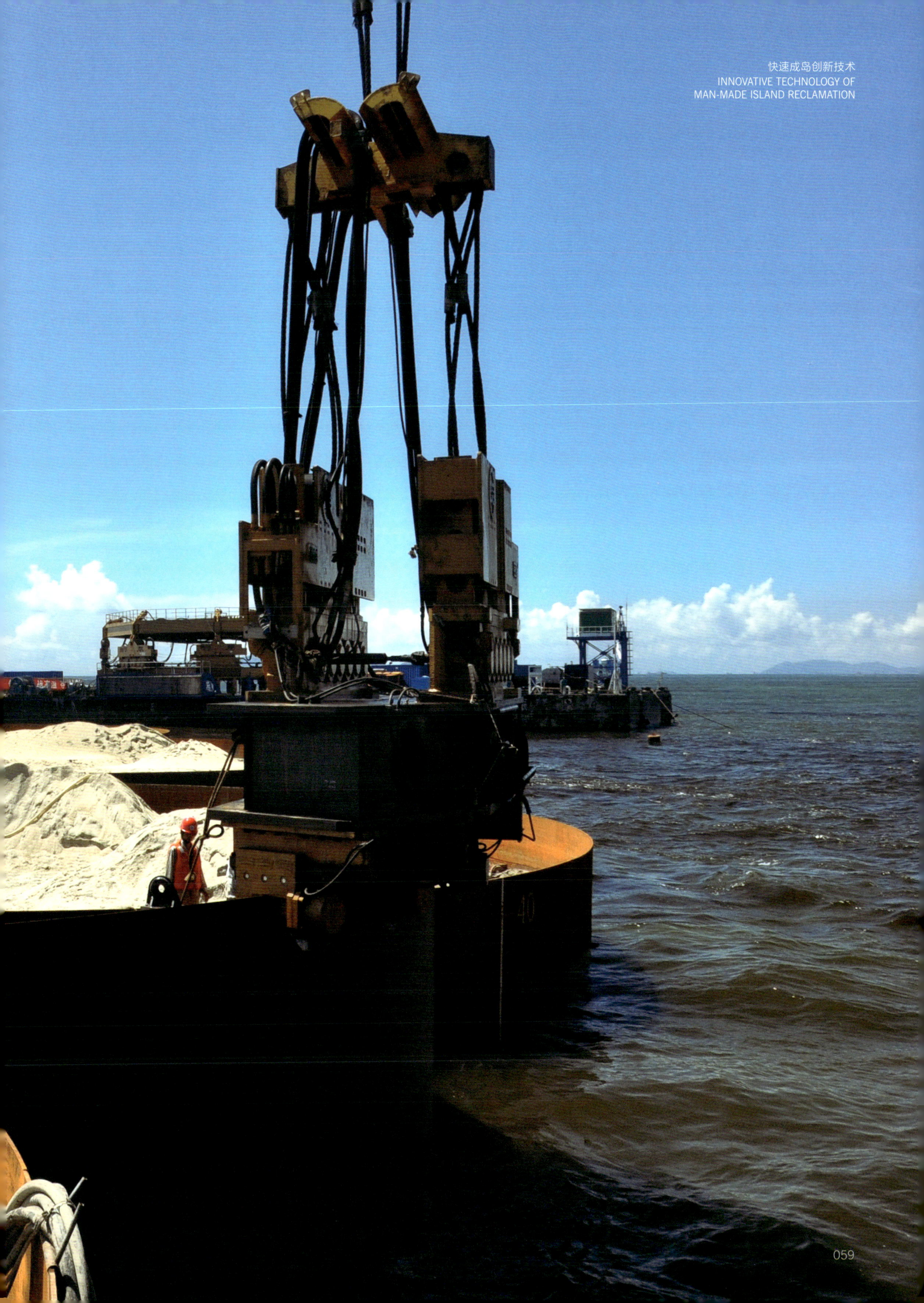

副格试验与制造
TESTING AND FABRICATION OF THE CONNECTING RAILS

1. 天津副格试验
   Connecting Rail Test in Tianjin
2. 副格和钢圆筒连接榫槽
   Connecting Rail and the Connecting Slots on the Steel Cylinder
3. 副格打设试验摩擦起火
   Sparking by Friction in the Connecting Rail Test

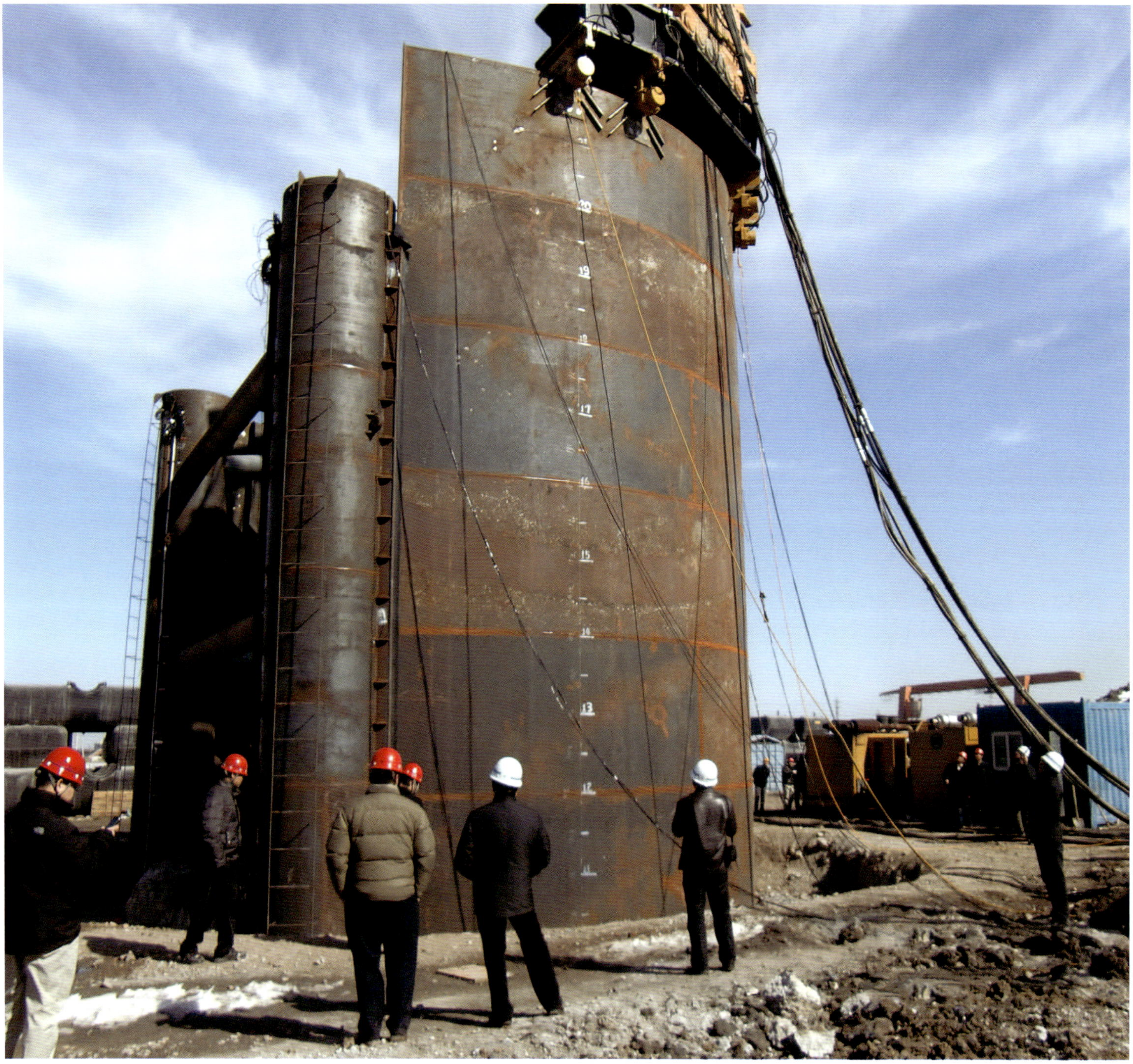

深插入海的钢圆筒相隔两米，钢圆筒上预设宽榫槽，插入副格进行止水。项目总经理部综合比选日本格型钢板和国产弧形钢板，决定采用国产弧形钢板制作副格。

2010年底至2011年4月，副格打设试验在天津进行。采用两台APE400振动锤，分别进行了12、14、16毫米厚的弧形钢板副格试验。但是问题频现，20多米高的弧形钢板不是摩擦起火就是钢板撕裂口。

项目总经理部多方查找原因，反复尝试，经对振动锤拆分检查，发现两个锤在齿轮齿数上有细微差别，造成齿轮转速不一样，导致两个锤在高频率振动时出现不同步现象。在对振动锤进行更换之后，副格试验取得成功。

There were two meters between every two steel cylinders driven deep into the seabed, and the connecting rails to block waters were inserted into the wide slots pre-made on the surface of the steel cylinders. The project management center chose the curved steel plates manufactured by Chinese companies instead of those produced in Japan after thorough comparison.

From the end of 2010 to April, 2011, the connecting rail test was conducted in Tianjin. Two APE 400 vibrating hammers were used to conduct tests on the connecting rails made of steel plates of 12, 14 and 16 millimeters thick. Problems materialized one after another. The curved steel plates of 20 meters high either sparked hard in friction or were tore apart or curved.

The project management center made various investigations into the possible causes. After countless tries and examination of the disassembled hammers, they discovered that two hammers had slight differences from the others in the number of teeth of the gears which led to the different rotation speeds of the gears and the derangement in the process high-frequency vibrations. Once the vibratory hammers were replaced, the problems were solved.

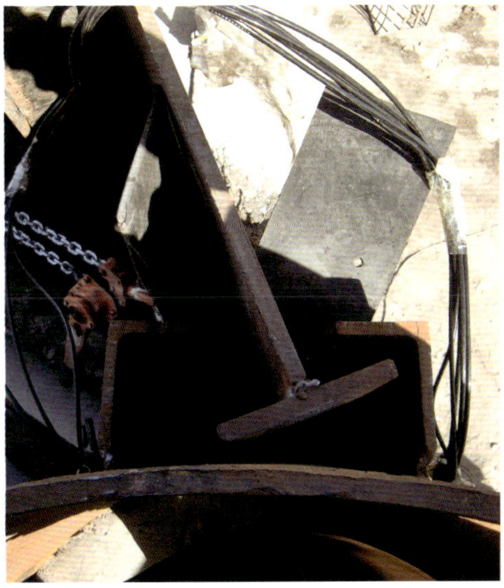

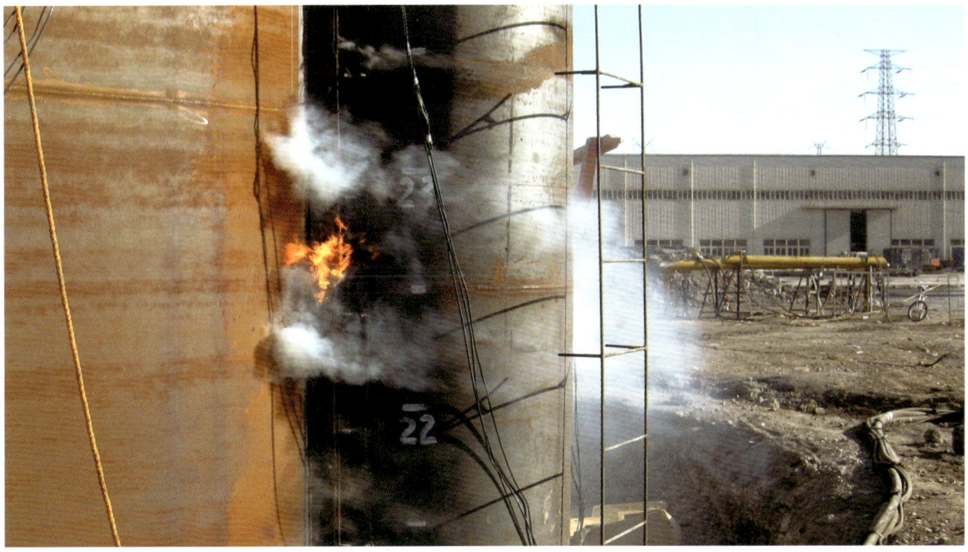

副格在江门新会预制厂制造。

副格仓主体采用弧形钢板连接，共分为 4 种组合。标准副格设计弧长 11,236 毫米，弦长 9540 毫米，副格长 30 米，厚 14 毫米，标准段重量约 57 吨。

钢圆筒与副格仓止水连接：钢圆筒上宽榫槽与副格仓两端焊接钢板形成 T 型锁口连接，在宽榫槽外侧安装防渗角型胶皮，宽榫槽内填充止水材料。

根据现场施工计划，副格施工时需要的起重船、自航驳等各类施工船舶须提前驻位，以提高施工效率。

The connecting rails were manufactured in the precast factory at Xinghui, Jiangmen.

The body part of the connecting rail compartment was formed by connecting arc-shaped steel plates in four combinations. The arc length of the standard connecting rail was 11,236 millimeters, the chord length was 9540 millimeters, and the connecting rail as a whole was 30 meters long, 14 millimeters thick, weighing approximately 57 tons.

Water-stop by connecting the steel cylinders and connecting rails: The wide slots on the steel cylinder formed T-shaped interfaces with the steel plates welded to the two ends of the connecting rails; anti-seepage angular rubber pads were installed on the outside of the wide slots, and the inside of the slots were filled with waterproof materials.

According to the construction plan, all kinds of construction vessels such as crane barges and self-propelled barges needed to be stationed in advance for the installation of the connecting rails to improve the construction efficiency.

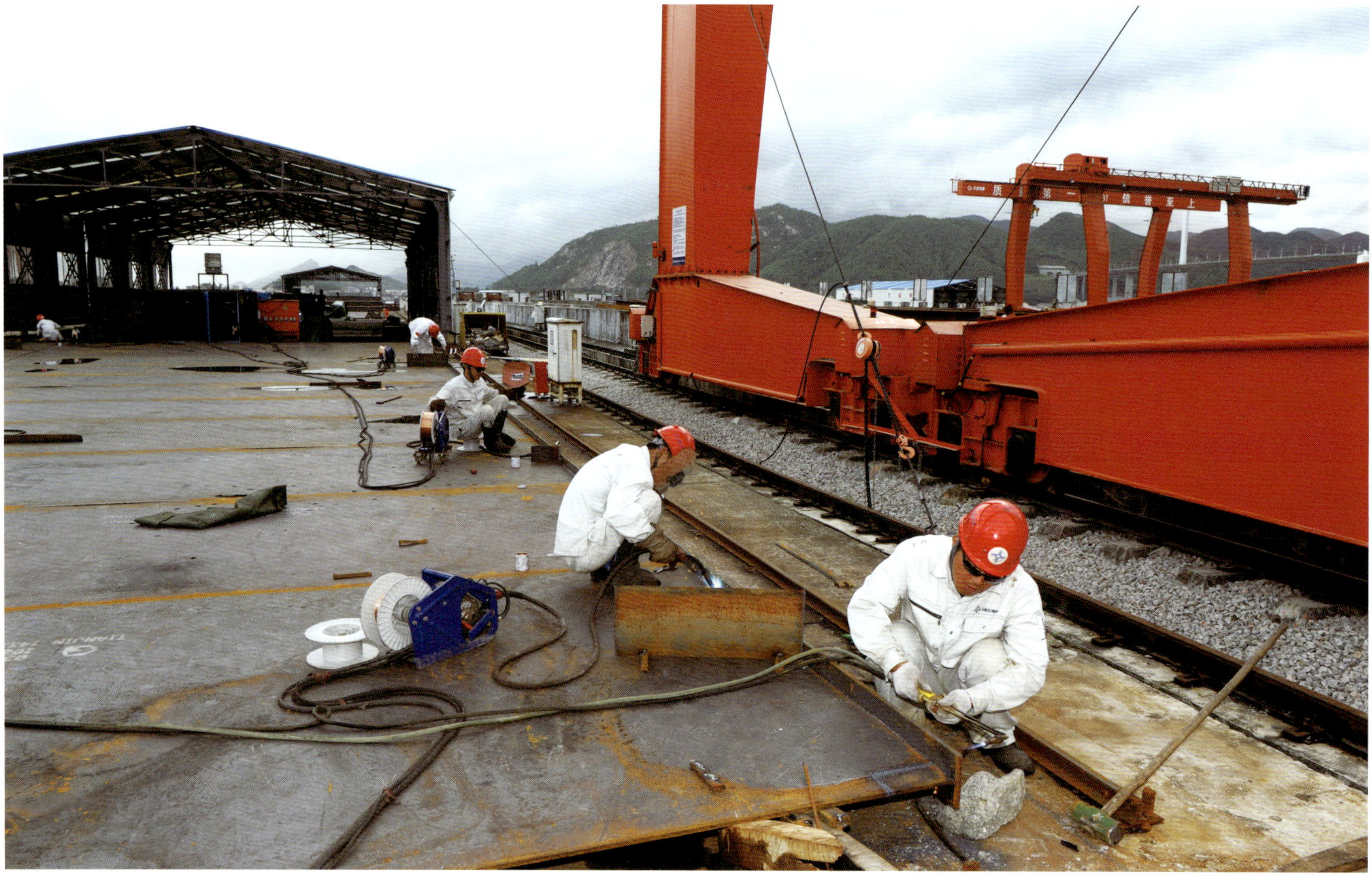

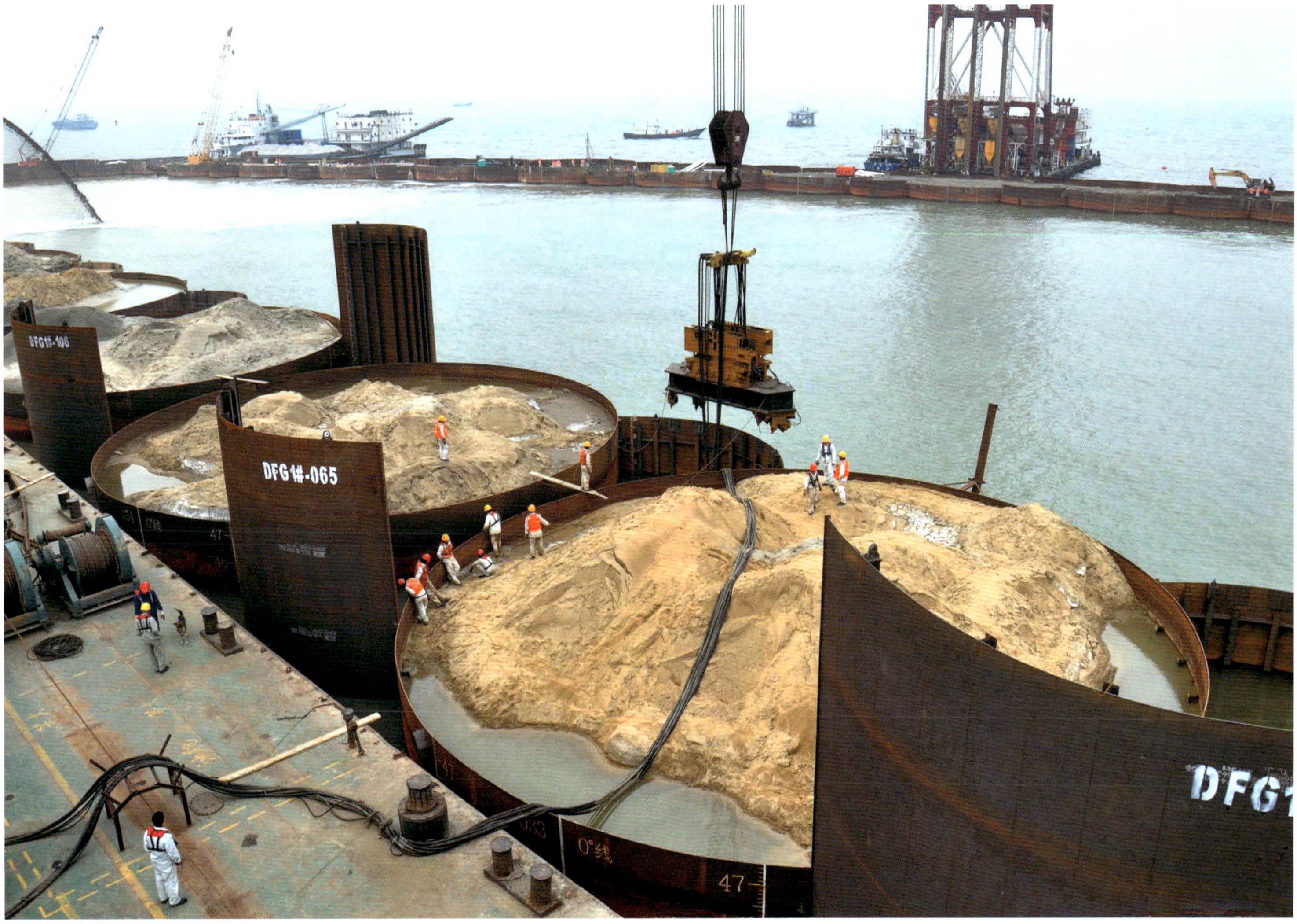

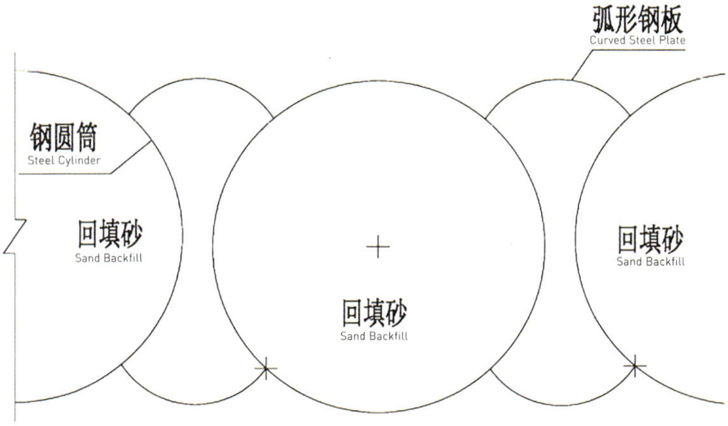

1. 新会副格制造
   Fabrication of the Connecting Rail in Xinhui
2. 东人工岛副格振沉
   Vibratory Driving of the Connecting Rail in East Man-Made Island
3. 副格打设平面图
   Plan View of the Connecting Rail Driving

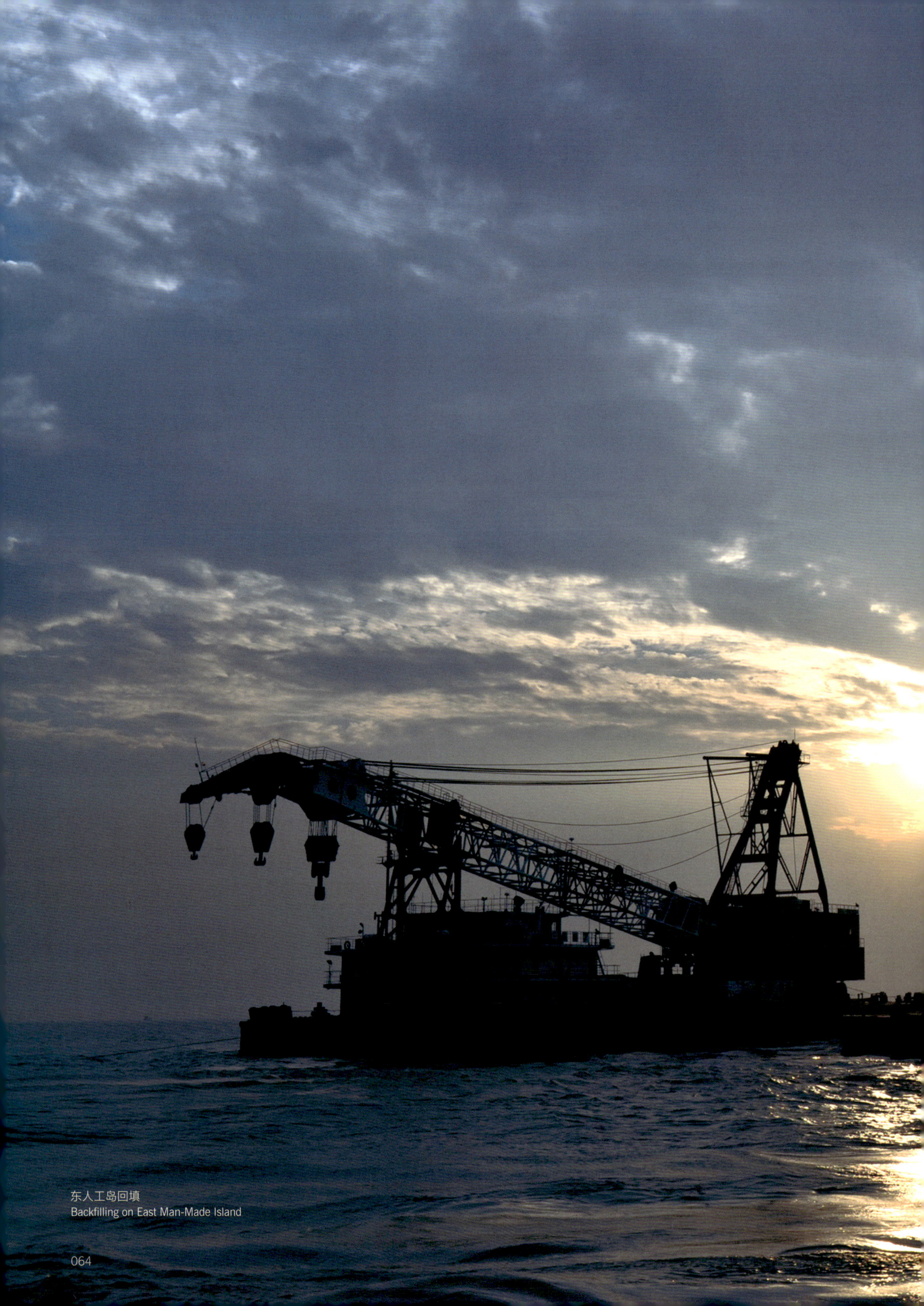

东人工岛回填
Backfilling on East Man-Made Island

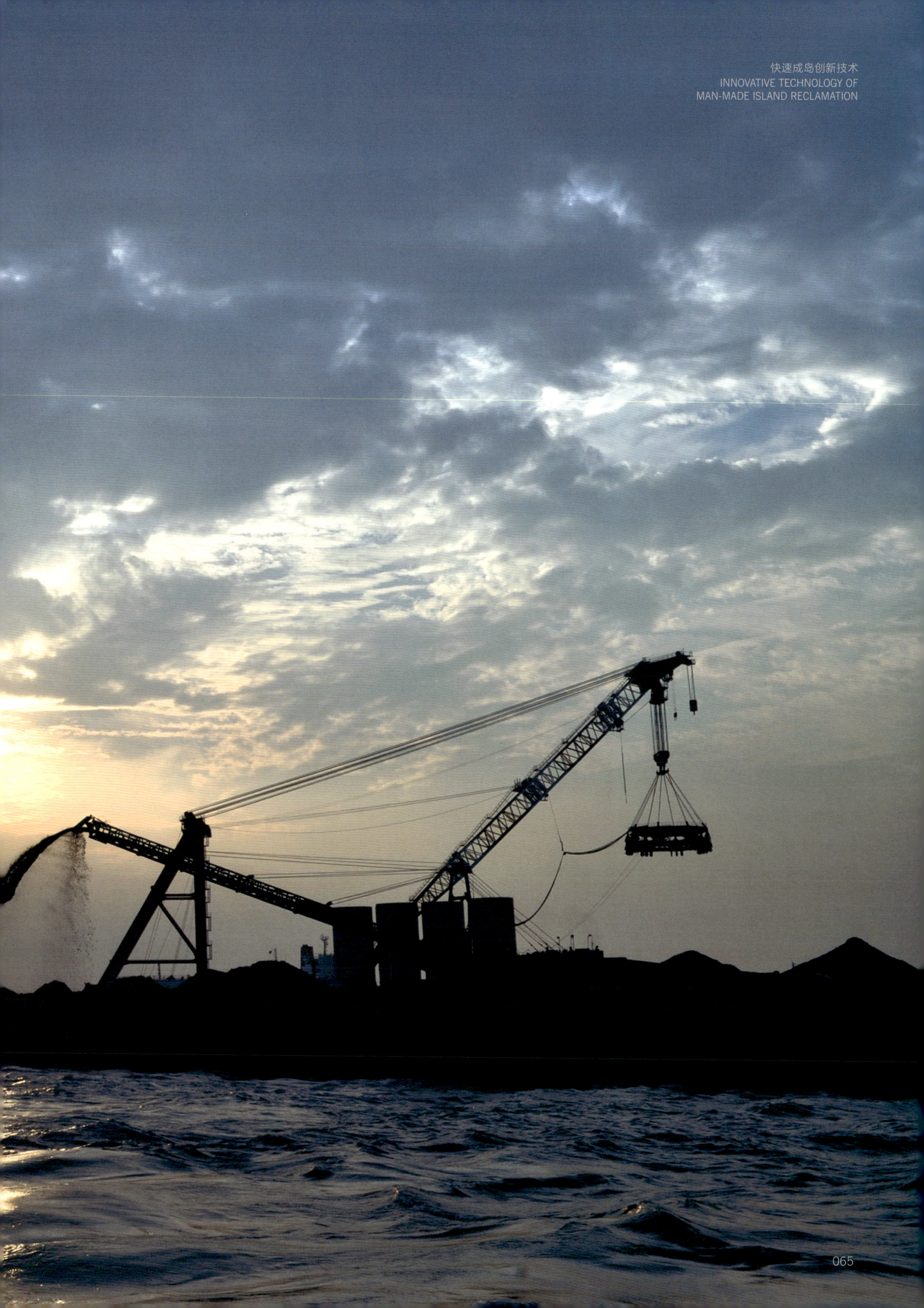

筒内回填

BACKFILL INSIDE THE CYLINDERS

钢圆筒振沉就位后，4条5000吨皮带抛砂船依次进行筒内抛砂，确保钢圆筒稳固。

回填时，抛砂船在钢圆筒前驻位，皮带机输送中粗砂至筒内及副格内，填充料落点应在钢圆筒及副格的中心，以防钢圆筒及副格因填充料压力不均匀造成侧倾和变形。根据皮带船的抛砂效率和人工打水砣实时测定抛砂顶面标高，确保筒内及副格内抛砂标高达到设计要求，且预留一定的沉降量。

在逐步围护成形的岛内海域，同时采用开底驳进行回填砂，迅速形成人工岛结构。

After the steel cylinders were driven to their designed position, sand was dumped into them by four 5000-ton sand-filling belt conveyor vessels to ensure the stability of the steel cylinders.

During backfilling, the sand-filling barges were positioned in front of the steel cylinder, and the belt conveyor delivered medium coarse sand into the central part of the cylinders and the connecting rails to avoid tilting and deformation of the cylinders and the connecting rails. The elevation of the sand filled was measured by the man-handled plummet and by calculating the sand filling efficiency of the belt conveyor barge, to ensure that the elevation of the sand filled reached the designed altitude with certain space reserved for the settlement.

Hopper barges were used simultaneously for the sand backfilling into the area fended for the construction of the island, by which the man-made island structure materialized quickly.

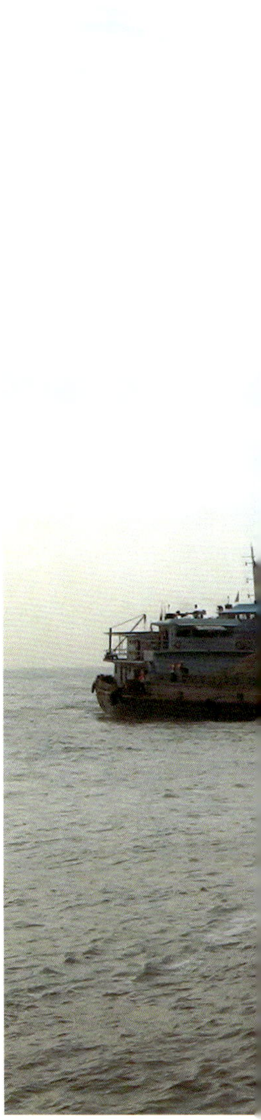

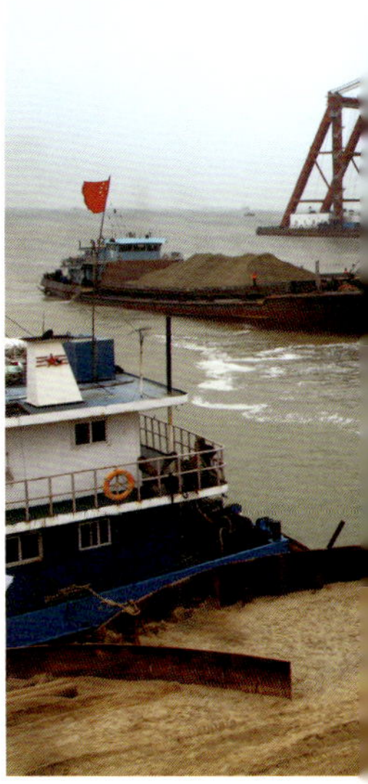

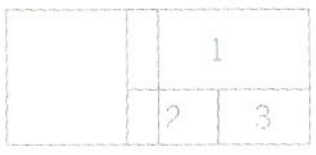

1. 西人工岛首个钢圆筒回填砂
Sand Backfilling of the First Steel Cylinder in West Man-Made Island

2—3. 岛内回填砂施工
Sand Backfilling in the Island

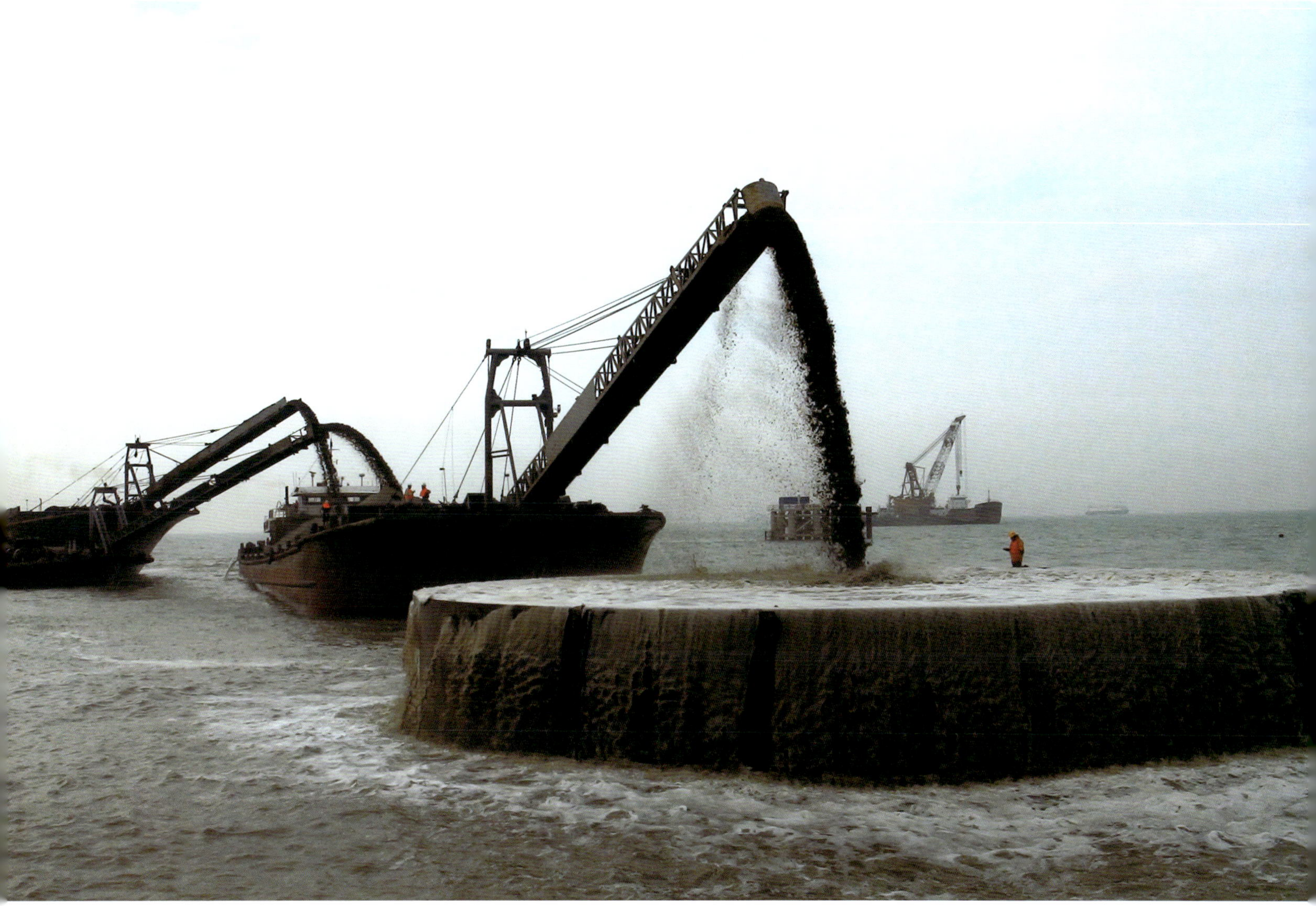

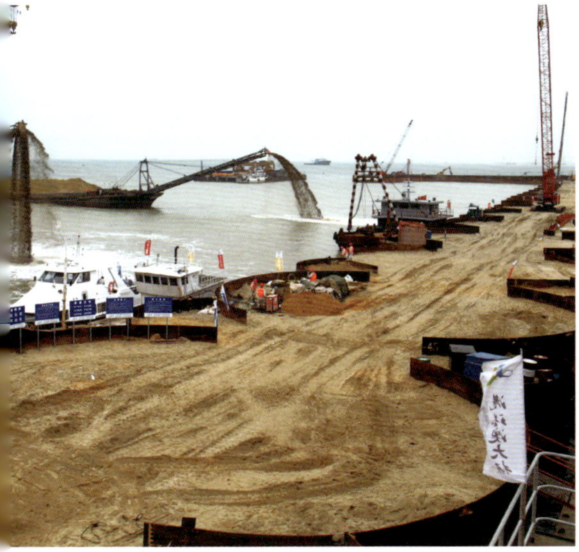

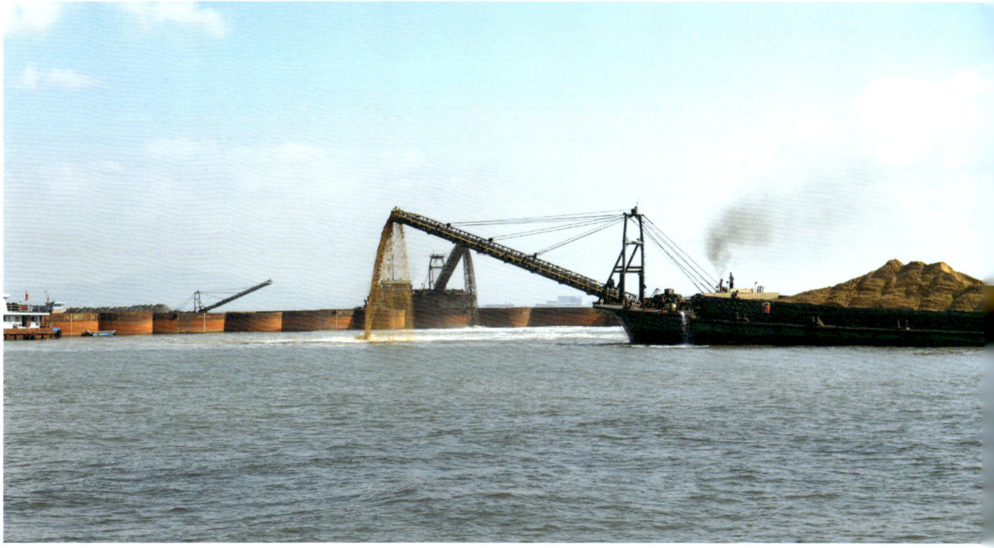

回填完毕的东人工岛
East Man-Made Island with Backfilling Completed

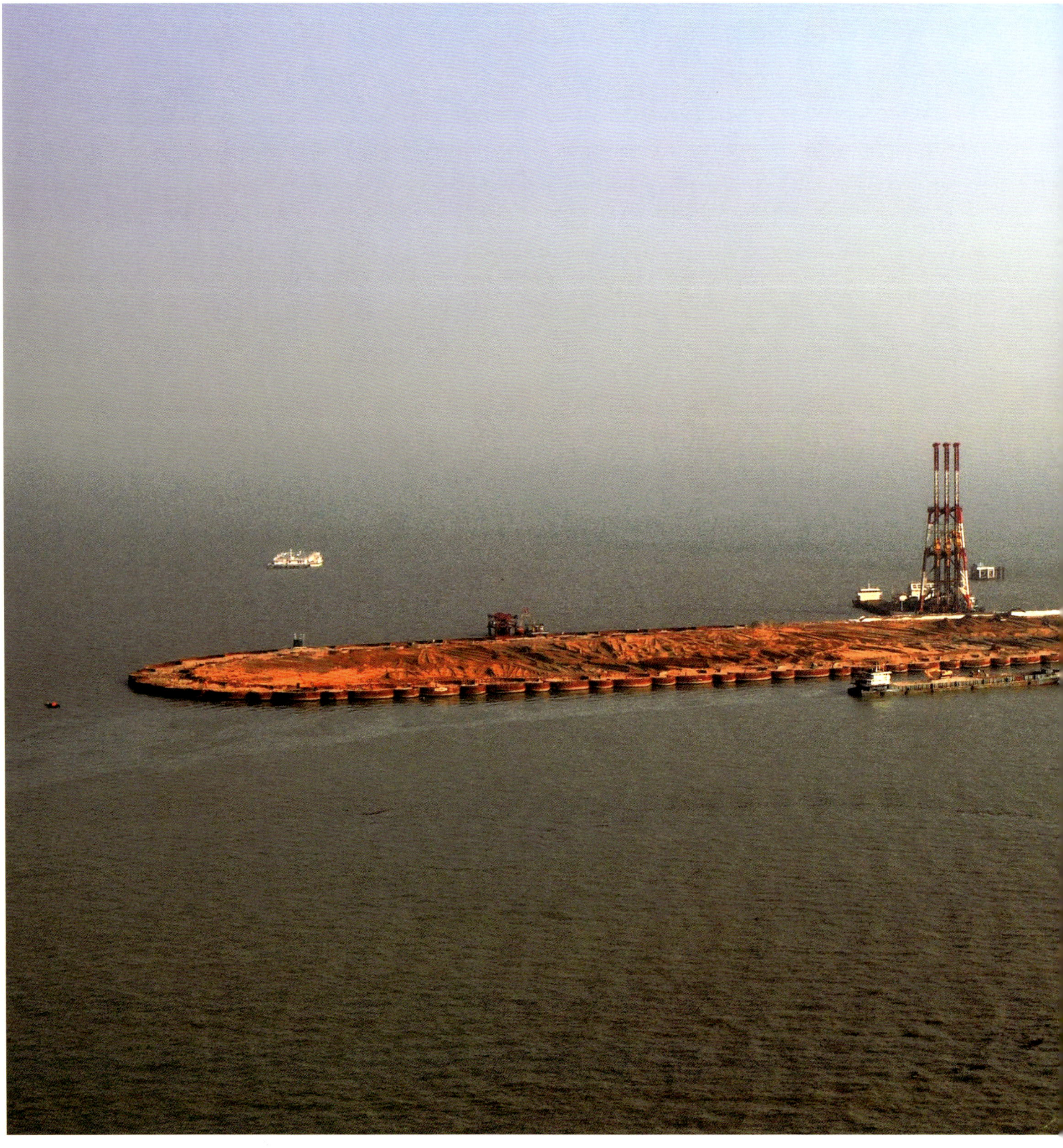

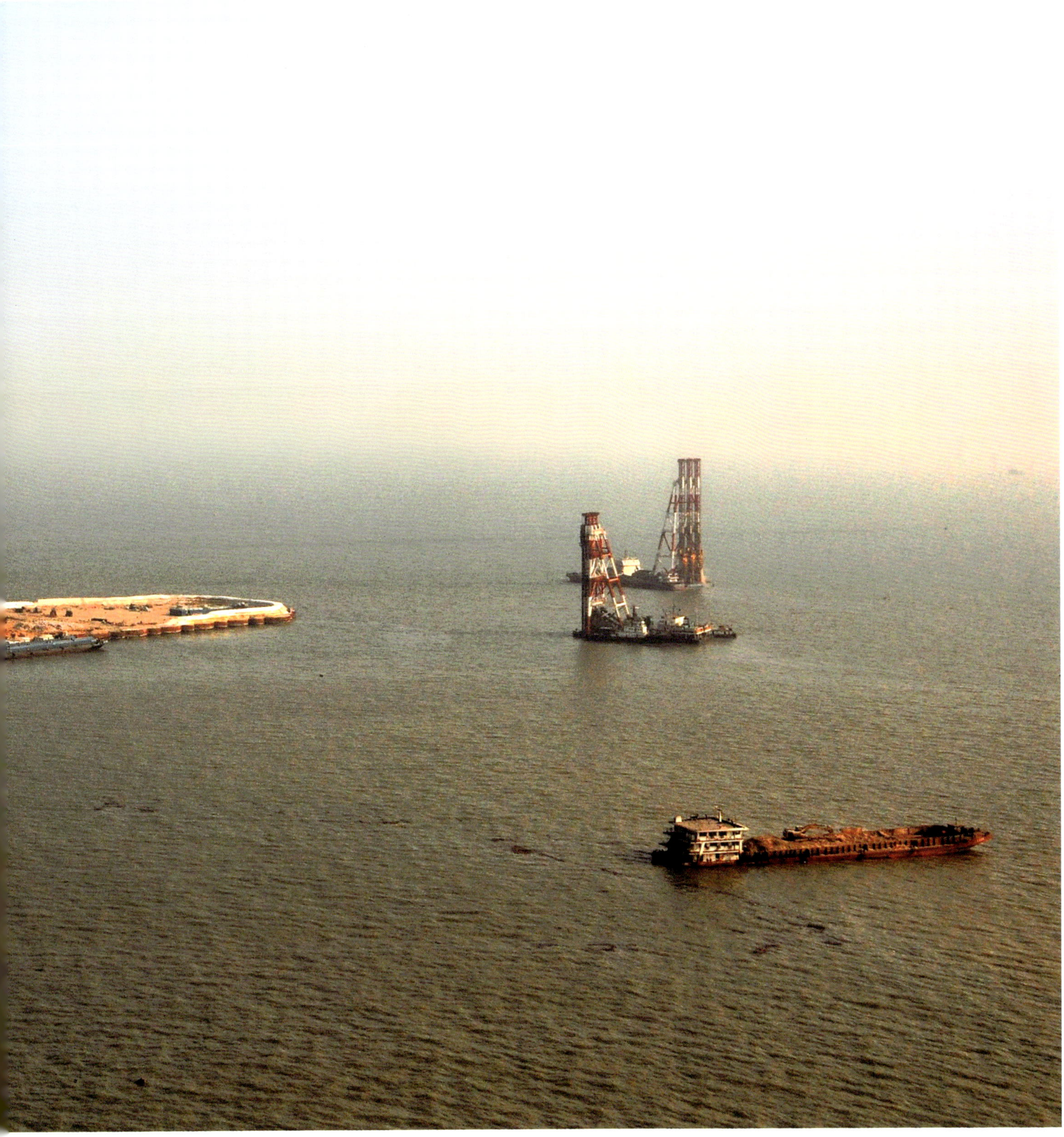

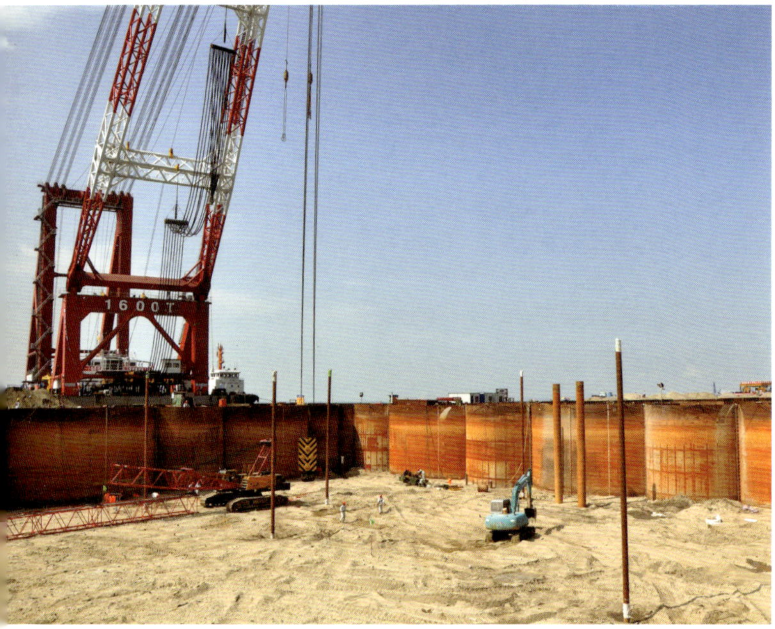

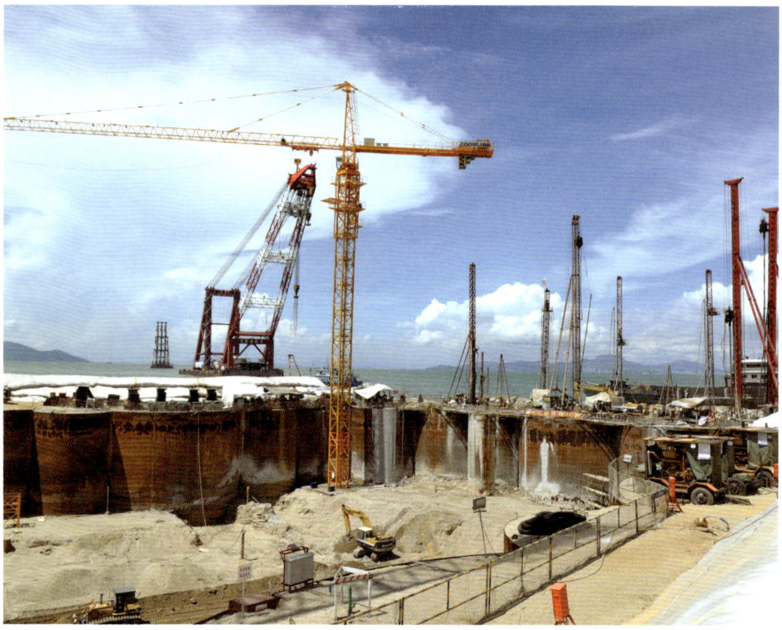

海上深基坑工程

OFFSHORE DEEP FOUNDATION
TRENCH PROJECT

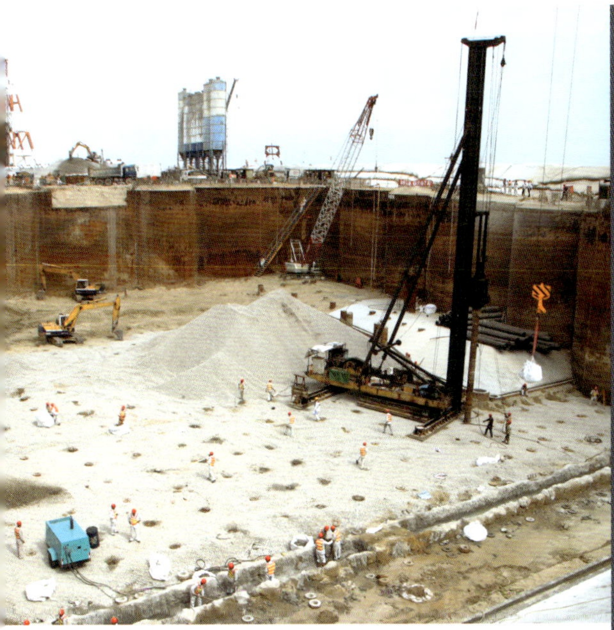

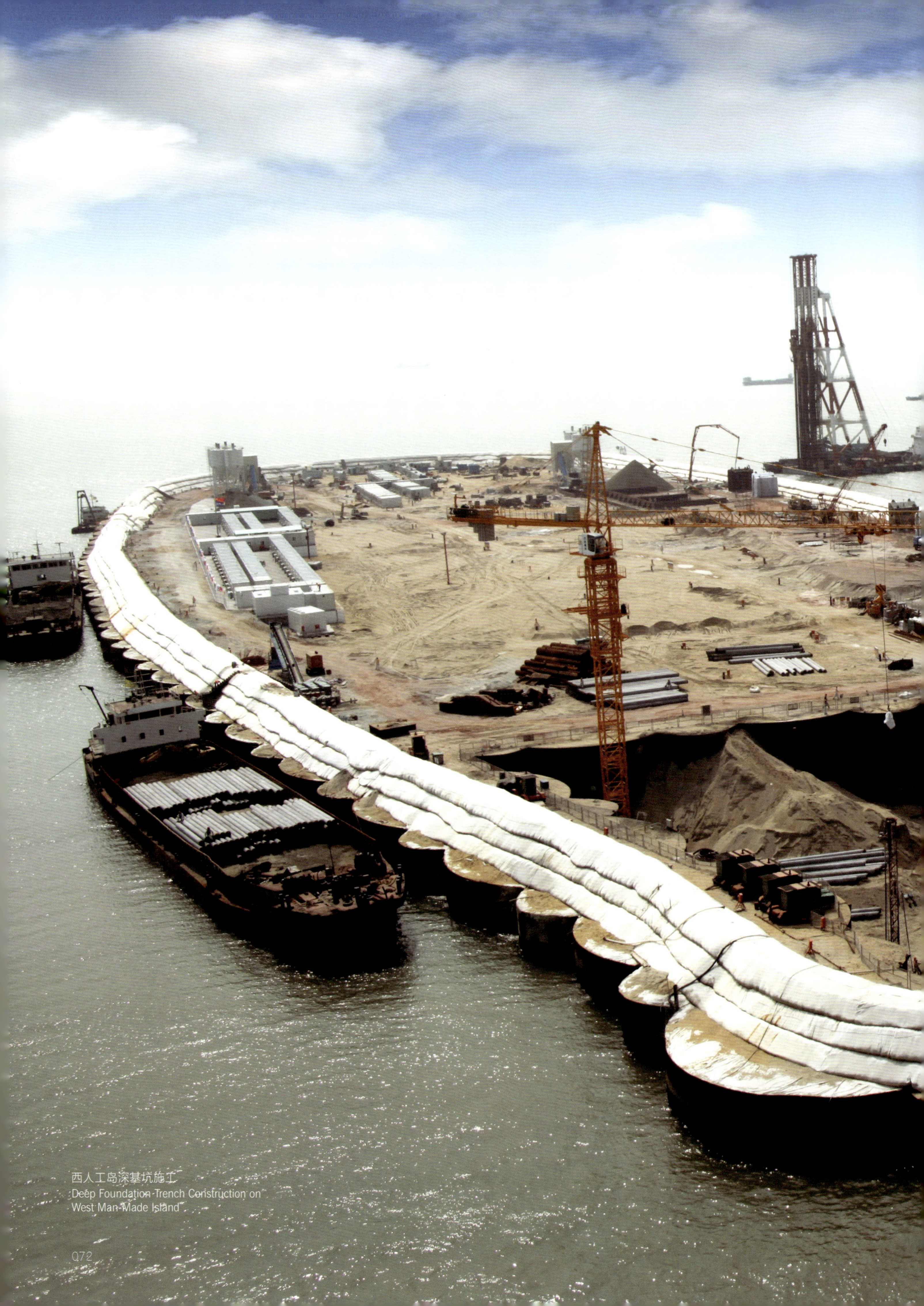

西人工岛深基坑施工
Deep Foundation Trench Construction on West Man-Made Island

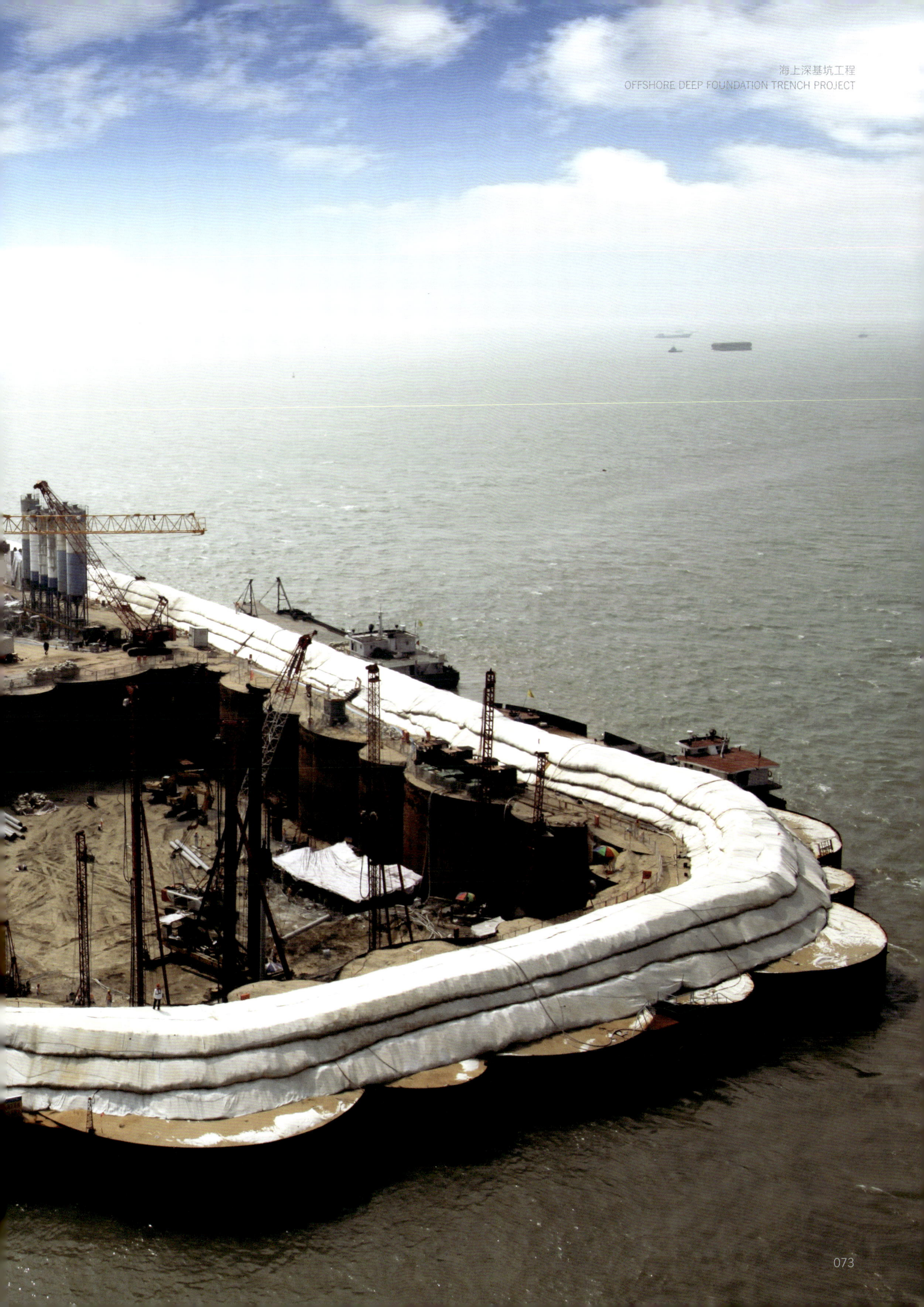

岛内基础工程

ISLAND FOUNDATION PROJECT

从海床淤泥面到不透水层的土质，人工岛基础一共有5个大层，12个亚层。岛体内外的水都是相通的，要做排水加固处理，就必须先对岛体内外进行隔绝。如果采用抛石筑堤成岛的方案，还要建一圈地下连续墙，工期较长；而深插钢圆筒快速成岛方案的巧妙之处就在于，不仅可以实现海上快速成岛，同时钢圆筒加副格还形成了围护止水结构，实现了岛内与岛外的隔绝。

西人工岛施工水域原泥面标高-8.0—-10.0米，顶面交工标高为+5米。通过回填砂形成陆域，在岛内打设塑料排水板，并通过降水井排水，仅用100天就完成了岛内30—50米厚的软土地基加固。"像把豆腐压成豆腐干一样"，使岛内的地基坚实稳定。

The island foundation consisted of 5 major stratums and 12 sub-stratums from the surface of the silt on the seabed to the impermeable layer. The water inside and outside the island was interlinked. Drainage and reinforcement require the inside of island to be insulated from the outside. If traditional technique of riprap were used to build the island, a continuous circle of underground wall needed to be built, which would take a long time. The charm of the craft of rapid island formation with deep-driven steel cylinders was that it could not only guarantee rapid island formation over the sea, but also the steel cylinders and connecting rails were used to form a water-stop structure to insulate the inside of the island from the outside.

The standard elevation of the original mud surface in the construction area of West Man-Made Island underwater is -8.0 to -10.0 meters, and the elevation of the top surface when the project was finished was + 5 meters. While backfilled sand was used to form the land mass, plastic (PVC) drainage boards were installed on the island, together with drainage through the dewatering well. It took only 100 days to solidify the 30-50-meter-thick soft soil foundation of the island. "It's like pressing tofu into dried bean curd", and the foundation of the islands was thus made solid and stable.

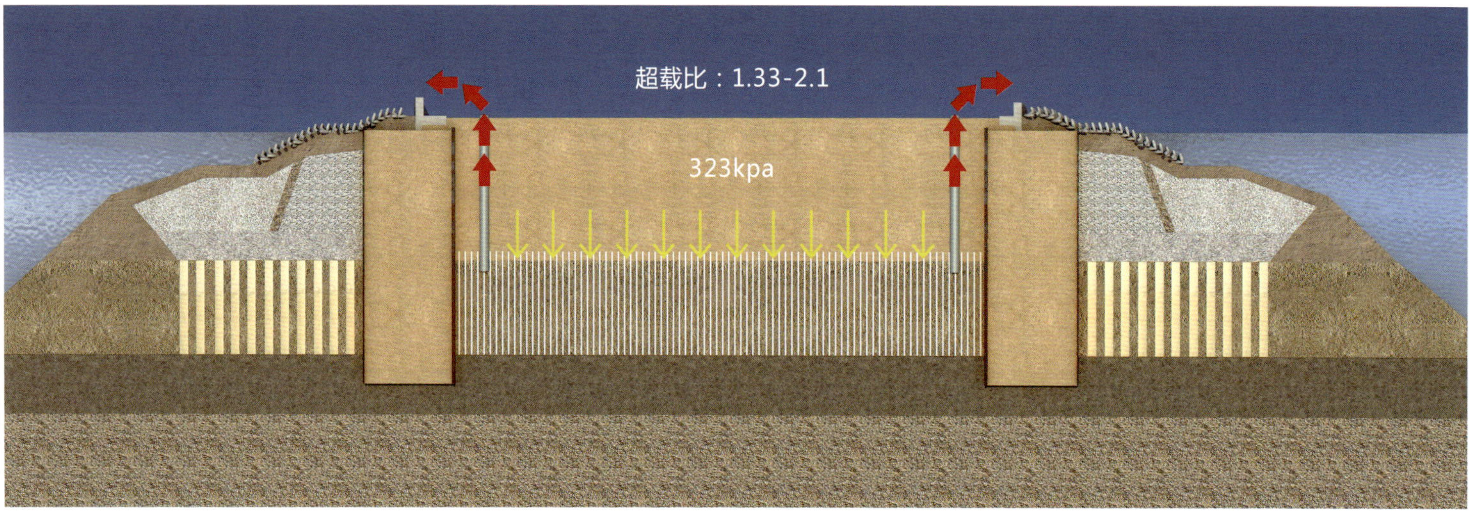

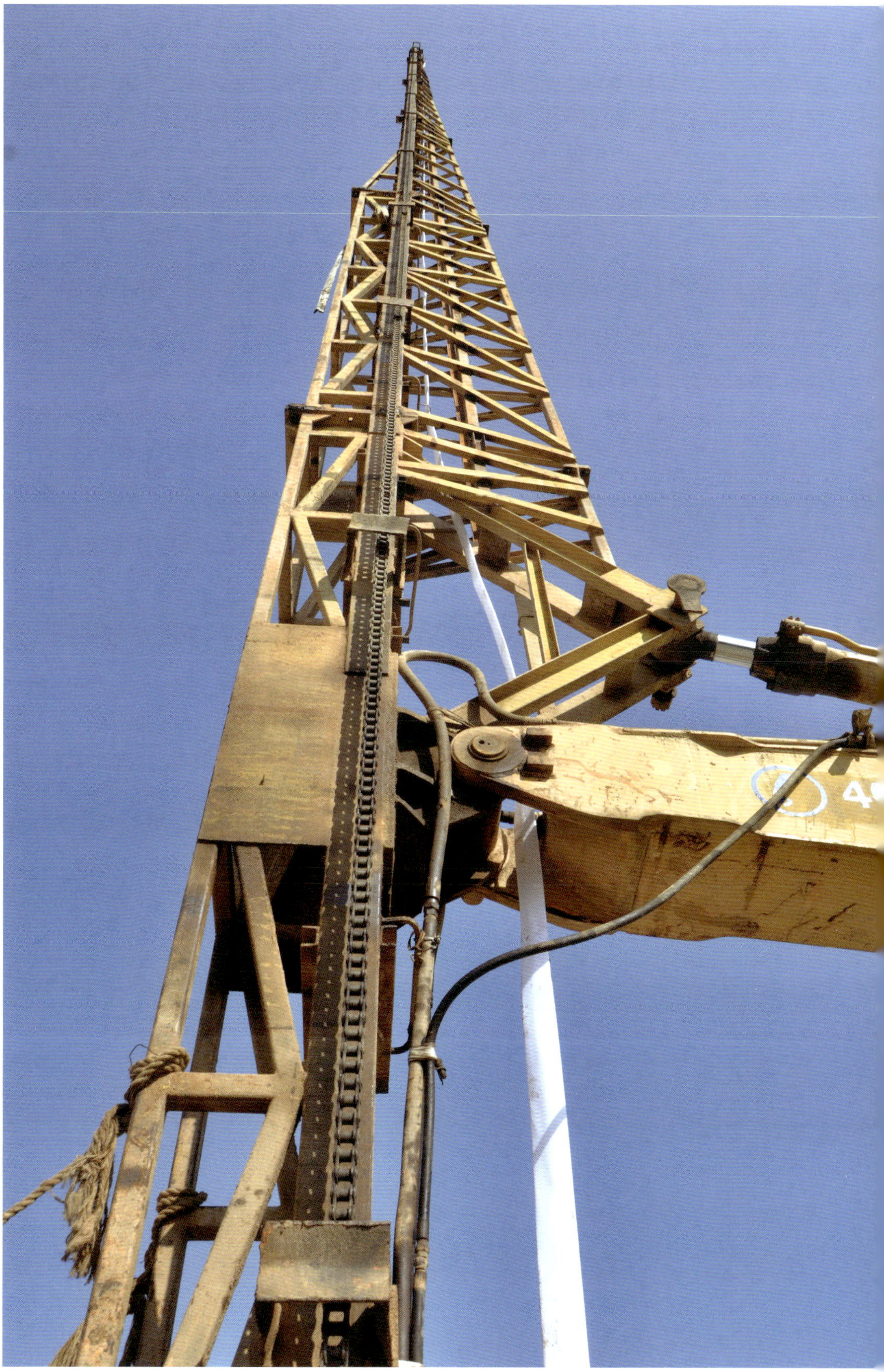

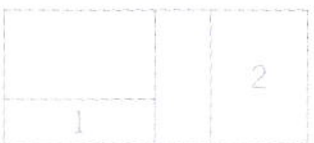

1. 人工岛超载预压示意图
Schematic Map of the Surcharge Preloading on the Man-Made Islands

2. 人工岛塑料排水板打设
Sinking of the Plastic Drainage Board on the Man-Made Islands

1. 人工岛塑料排水板打设施工
Sinking of the Plastic Drainage Boards on the Mad-Made Islands

2. 人工岛塑料排水板、降水井打设
Sinking of the Plastic Drainage Boards and the Construction of Dewatering Well on the Man-Made Islands

3—5. 塑料排水板打设施工
Sinking of the Plastic Drainage Boards

东、西人工岛塑料排水板打设分为岛内区和护岸圆筒区。岛内区施打作业面标高为-5.0米（东岛-6米），排水板板顶标高为-11.5米，底标高为-35米，最大打设深度为-42米，打设时需要穿过20多米的回填砂层。

塑料排水板采用原生料D型板，正方形布置，间距均为1米。东、西人工岛各打设塑料排水板约10.2万根。

The sinking of the plastic drainage boards on East and West Man-Made Islands were done separately in the inside part of the islands and the cylinder area as the fending walls of the islands. The land surface elevation of the island area was - 5.0 meters (-6.0 meters on East Island), the top of the drainage boards was -11.5 meters, the bottom -35 meters, and the maximum depth to drive the boards into was -42 meters. Sinking of the plastic drainage boards needed poling through the backfilled sand stratum over 20 meters thick.

The plastic (PVC) drainage boards, made of the D-type plastic board, were arranged in the square shape with 1 meter between each two boards. About 102,000 plastic drainage boards were installed on the two man-made islands.

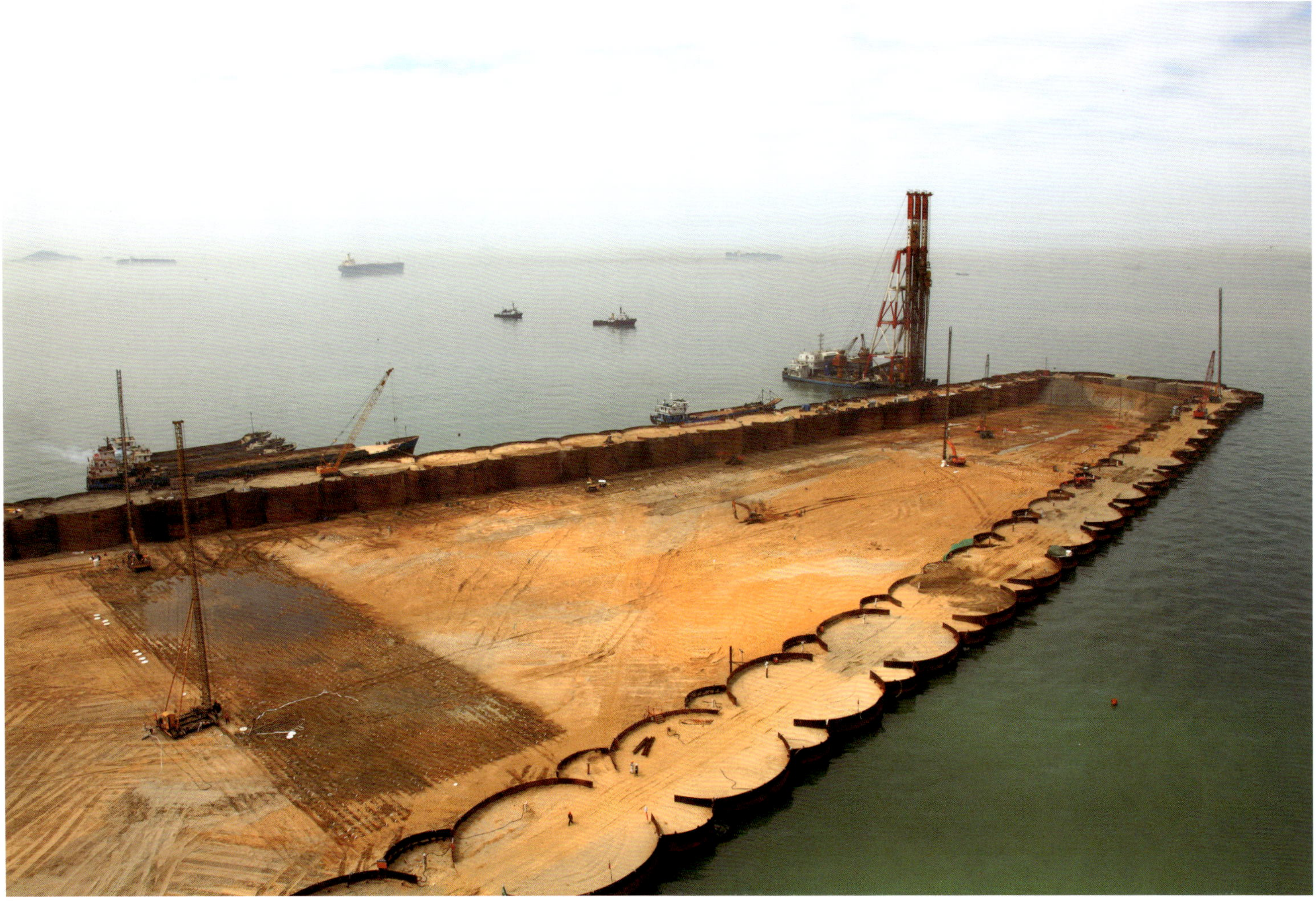

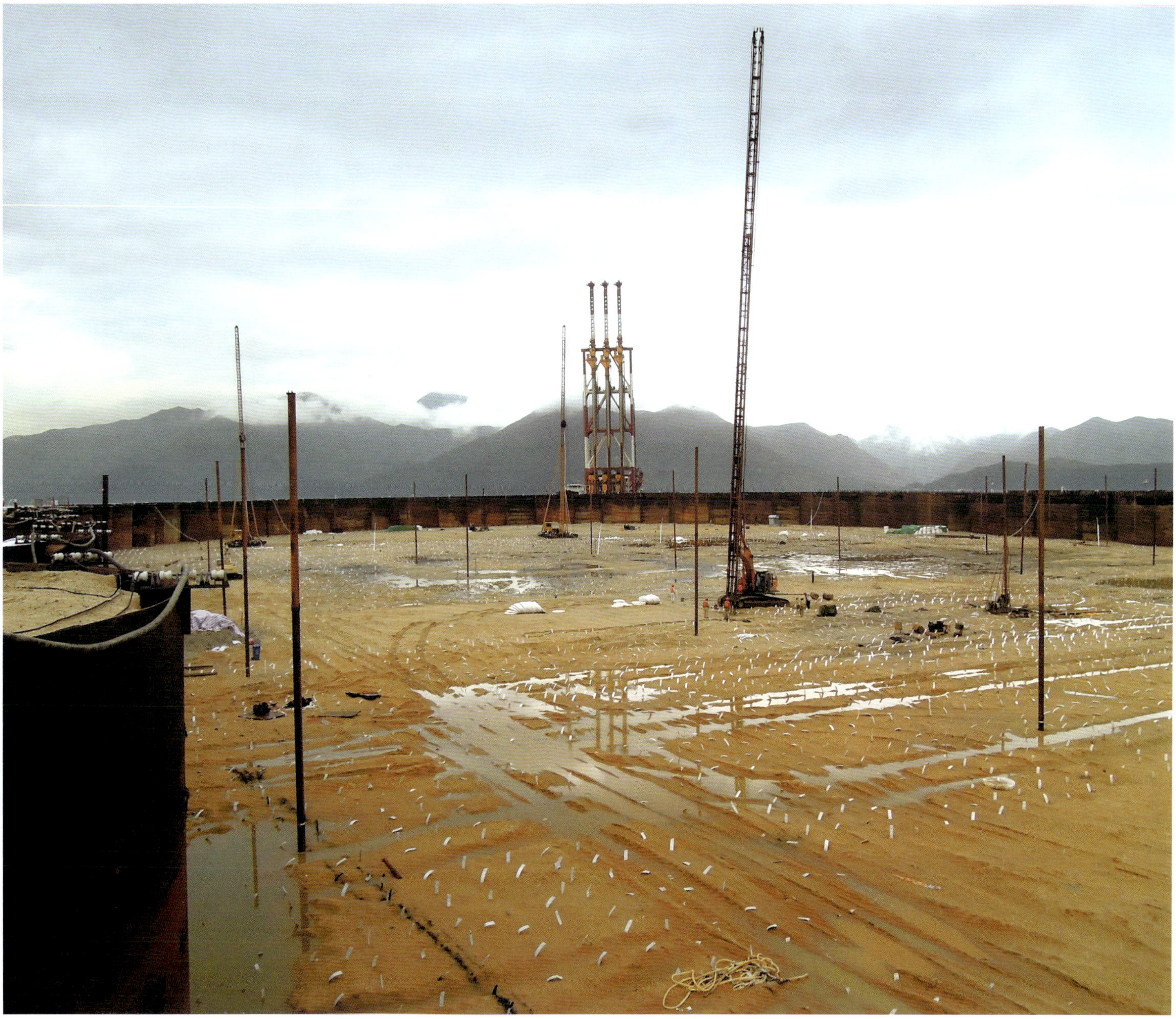

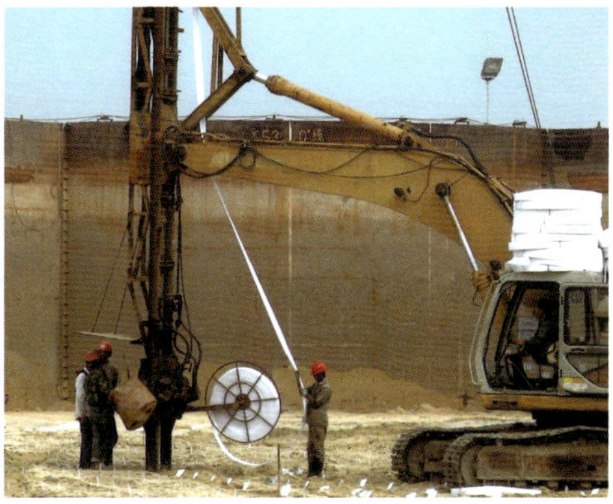

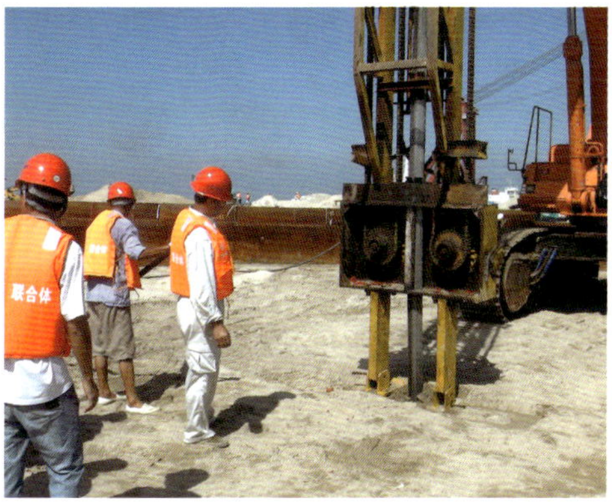
联合体

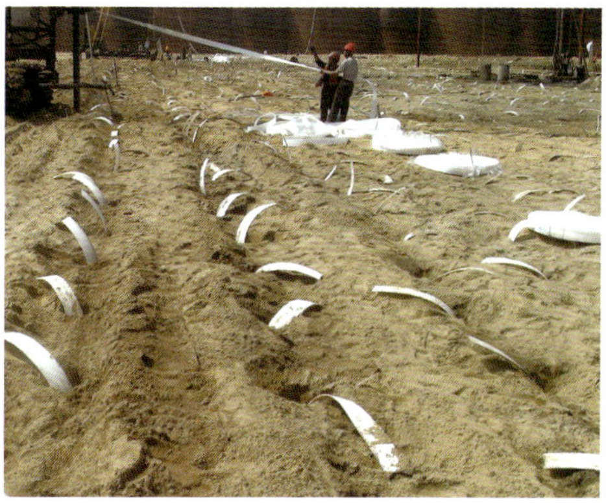

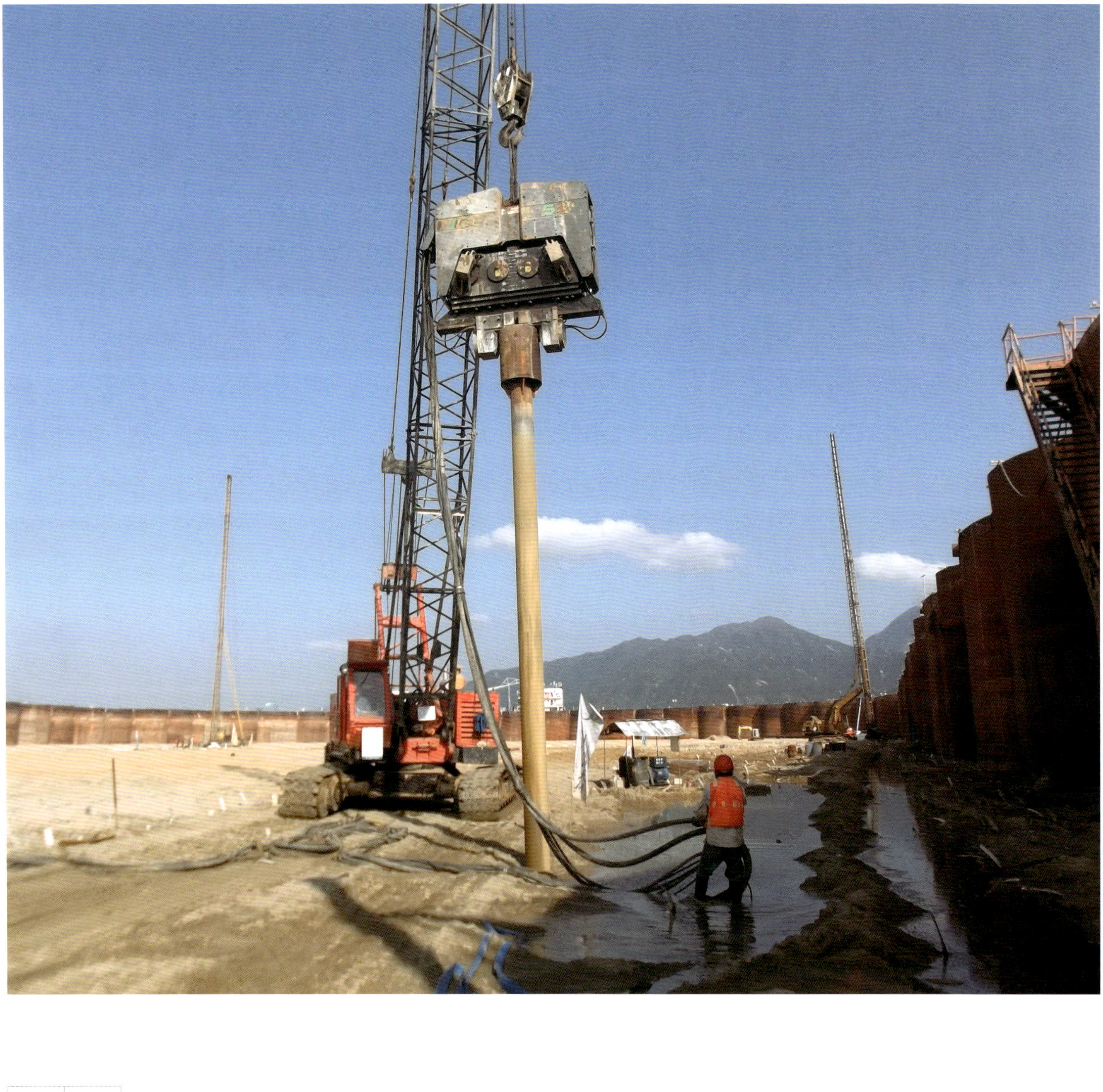

1. 降水井打设
Construction of Dewatering Well

2—4. 人工岛降水施工
Construction of Dewatering Devices on the Man-Made Islands

打设降水井：岛内区及护岸圆筒区塑料排水板施工完成后，整平回填砂至堆载设计标高，在人工岛钢圆筒、副格区及岛内施打200多个降水井。降水井用于降低岛内、筒内回填砂的水位，使中粗砂浮容重变成干容重，为地基加固提供超载。

堆载预压：岛内区塑料排水板及降水井施工完成后，在-5米（东岛为-6米）作业面上开始分级加载回填，加载厚度不超过2—3米；静置10天后，根据检测沉降结果及时调整加载速度和厚度。因岛体封闭，加载时利用皮带自卸驳靠泊在钢圆筒外侧，直接往岛内输送砂土，然后用推土机整平。

Construction of Dewatering Wells: After the construction of the body part of the islands and the installation of the plastic drainage boards in the cylinder area around the islands was completed, sand was backfilled and leveled to the altitude in accordance with the surcharge design. More than 200 dewatering wells were drilled in the steel cylinder area, the connecting rail area and inside the fending structure of the island. Dewatering wells were used to reduce the water level after the sand backfilling inside the island and in the cylinders, so as to change the floating density of medium coarse sand into dry density and to provide overload for foundation solidification.

Surcharge Preloading: After the installation of the plastic drainage boards and the construction of the dewatering wells inside the island, loading and backfilling started on the working surface with the altitude of -5 meters (-6 meters on East Island), and the surcharge was no more than 2 to 3 meters thick. After standing for 10 days, the loading speed and thickness were adjusted in time according to the settlement results calculated. Since the body part of the island was an enclosed structure, a belt conveyor barge would be moored on the outside of the steel cylinder to deliver the sand directly into the island area which was leveled with a bulldozer.

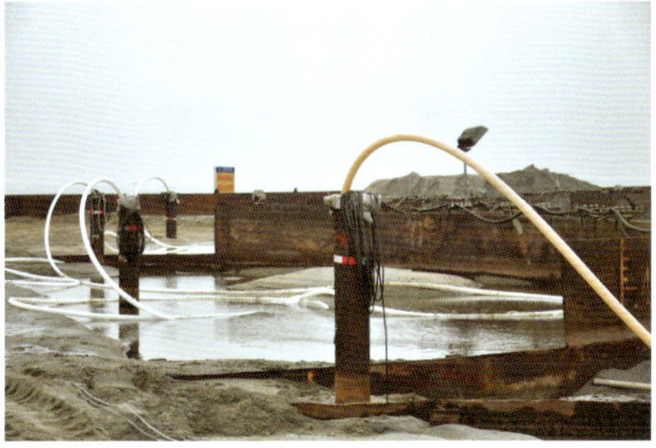

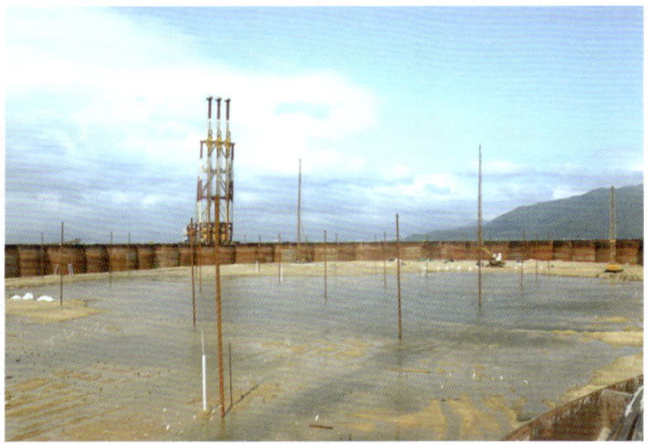

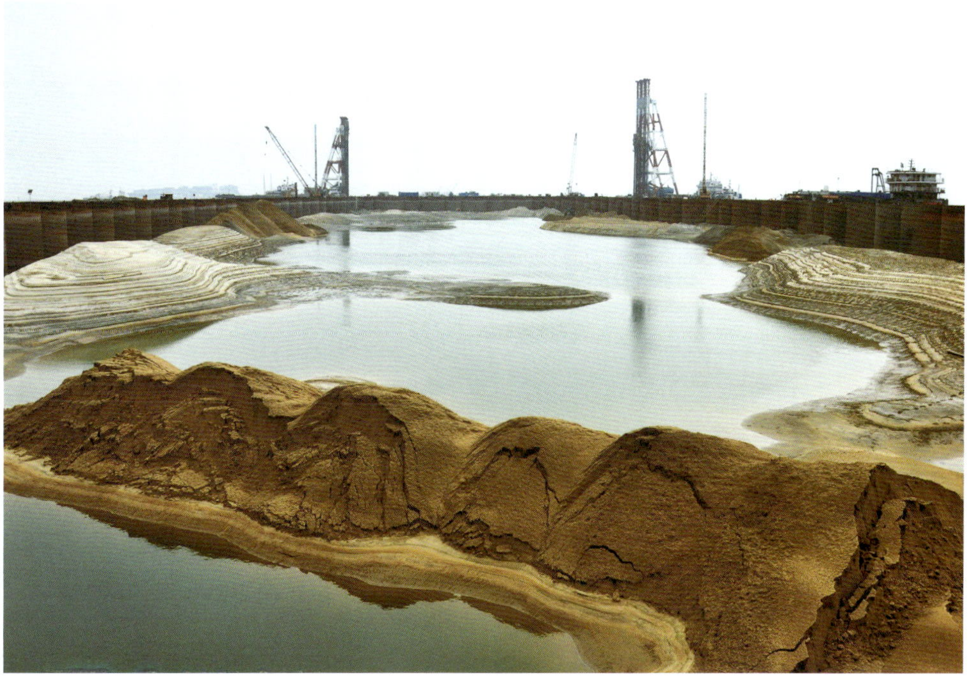

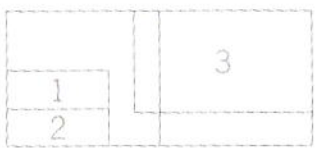

1. 人工岛岛壁围堰结构
Cofferdam on the Man-Made Islands
2. 围堰管袋铺设
Placement of Cofferdam Bags
3. 西人工岛岛壁围堰结构
Cofferdam on West Man-Made Island

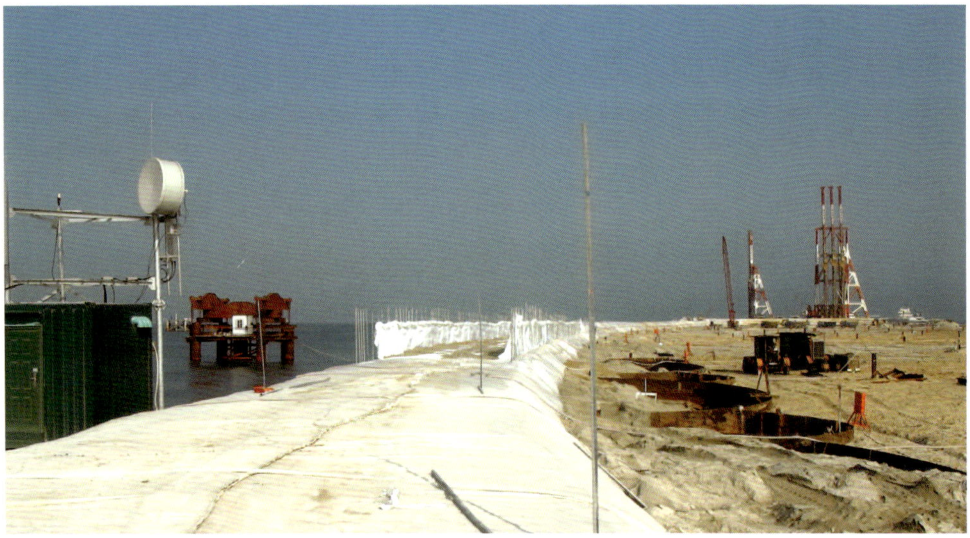

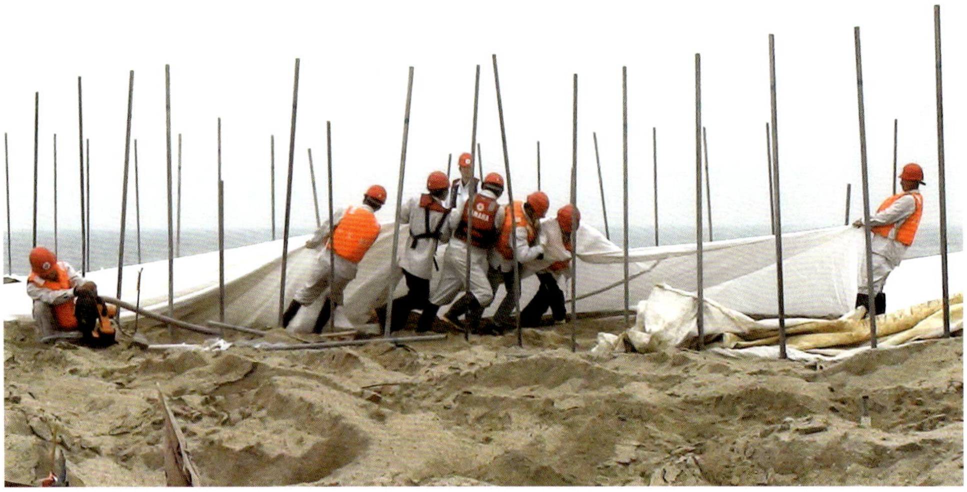

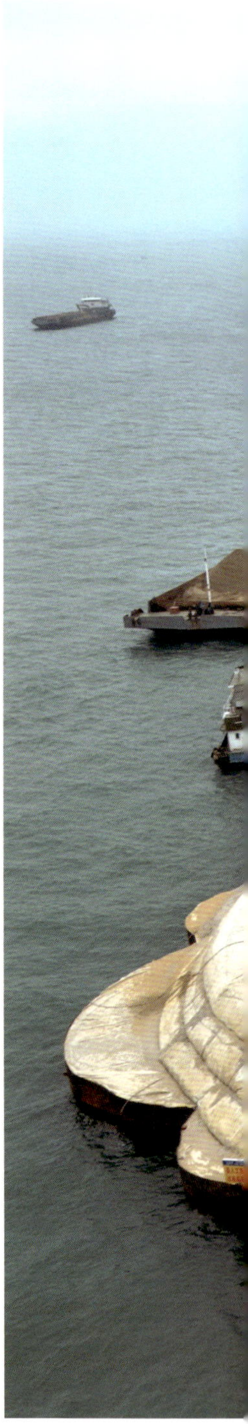

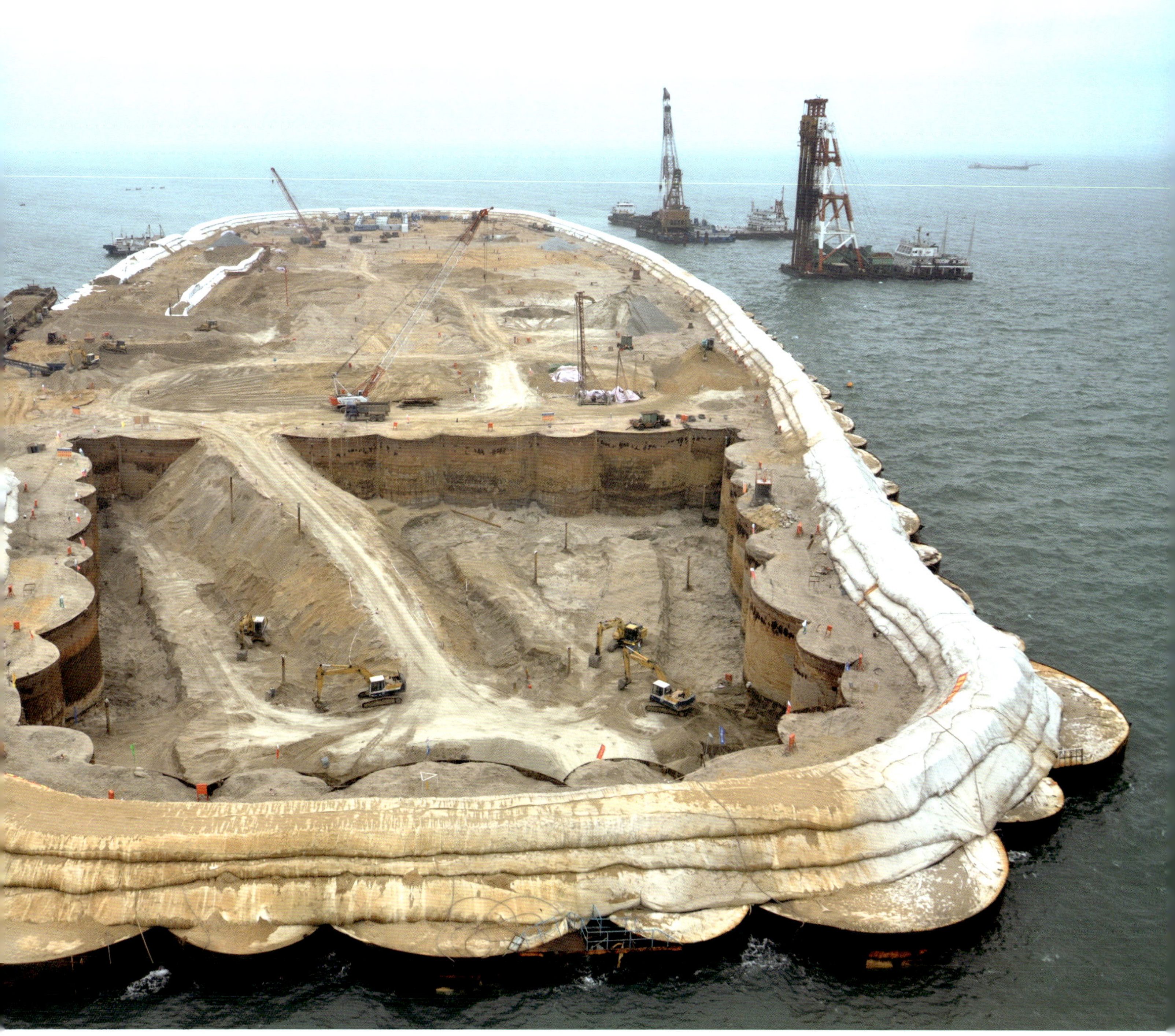

外海基坑施工

CONSTRUCTION OF OFFSHORE FOUNDATION TRENCH

6.7公里的海底隧道由5664米的沉管隧道和1086米的岛上现浇段隧道组成。岛上现浇段隧道包括暗埋段和敞开段。

暗埋段长163米，浇筑完成后覆盖砂土，其上构建建筑物，用于人工岛的运营管理和观光旅游。

在暗埋段建设前须开挖基坑。西人工岛基坑深17米，开挖面积近40,000平方米，如此大规模的外海深基坑开挖极为罕见。在深基坑开挖阶段，钢圆筒是基坑的围护止水结构，独自承受近17米的巨大水压力和相应波压力，极端情况下可能出现位移甚至倾覆转动。因此，其稳定性是保证岛内安全施工的关键。

The 6.7-kilometer undersea tunnel consisted of the 5664-meter-long immersed tube tunnel and the 1086-meter-long cast-in-place tunnel on the island. The cast-in-place section of the island tunnel included the buried section and the open section.

The buried section was 163 meters long and it was covered with sand and soil after the construction was completed. Buildings were constructed over the tunnel for operation management and tourist purpose.

Excavation of the foundation trench was required before the construction of the buried section of the tunnel. The foundation trench on West Man-Made Island was 17 meters deep and the excavation area was nearly 40,000 square meters. Such a large-scale deep foundation trench excavation in the open sea was extremely rare. In the deep foundation trench excavation stage, the steel cylinders, as the water-stopping structure of the foundation trench, withstood the huge water pressure of nearly 17 meters and the corresponding wave pressure, and might end with displacement or even overturning in extreme cases. Therefore, the stability of the steel cylinders was the key to the safety of the island construction.

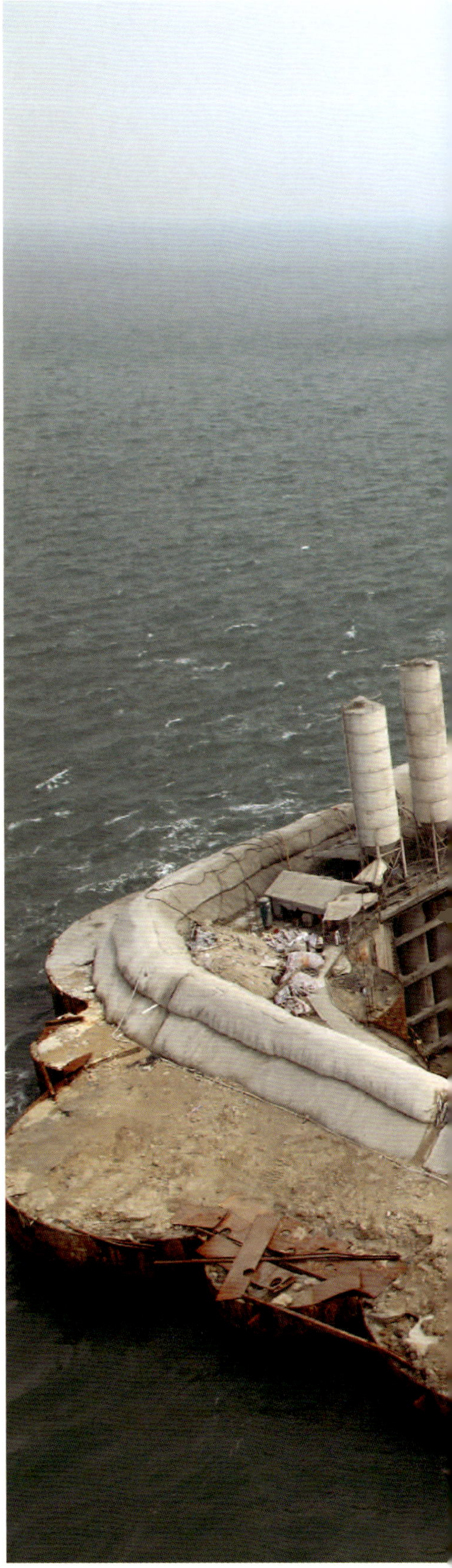

东人工岛深基坑开挖施工

Deep Foundation Trench Dredging on East Man-Made Island

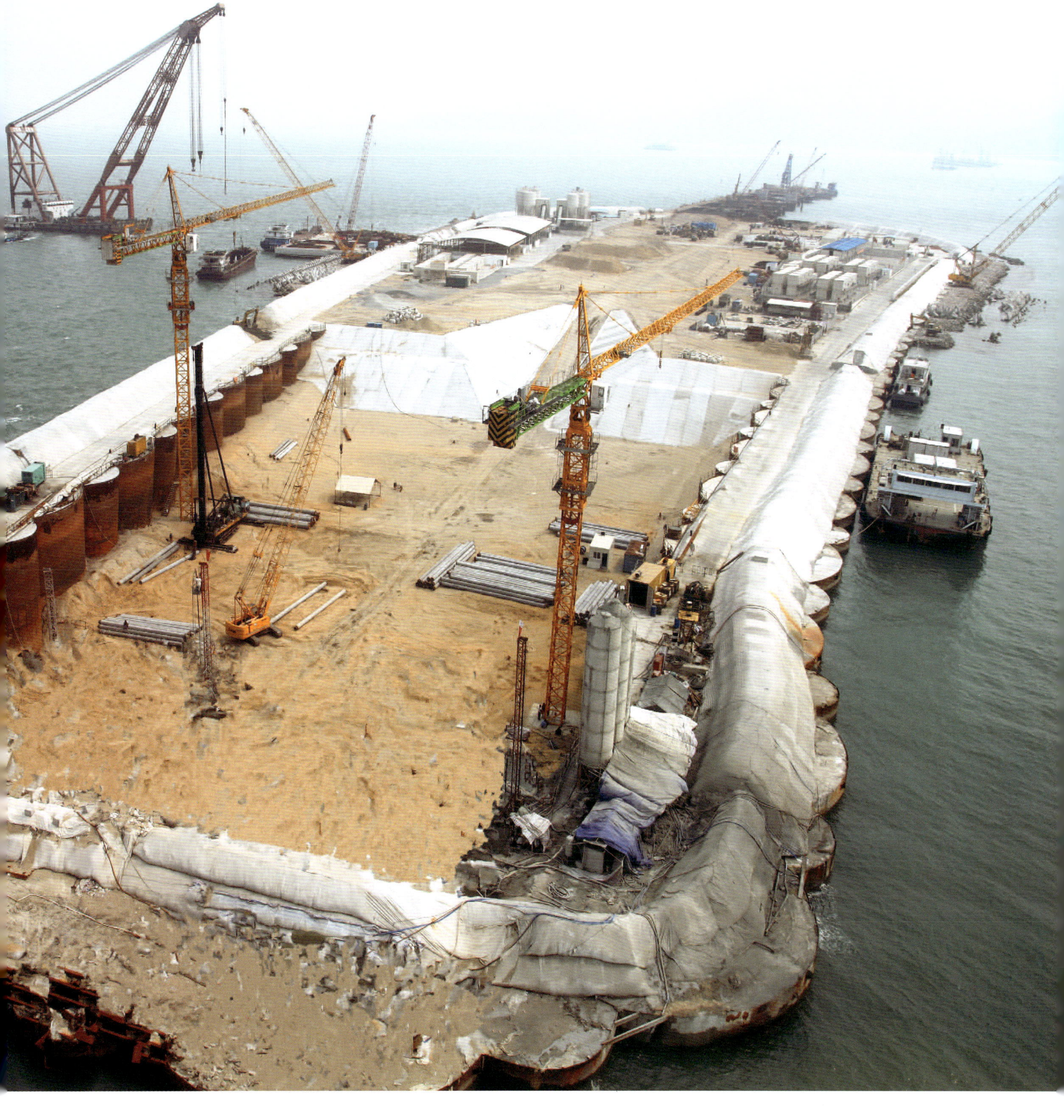

基坑开挖完成后，随即进行现浇段隧道基础施工：打设PHC桩、高压旋喷桩及止水帷幕施工。

After the foundation trench excavation was completed, the construction of the base for the cast-in-place tunnel section began immediately: sinking PHC piles, sinking high-pressure jet grouting piles, and building the water-stop screen.

1. 西人工岛深基坑开挖
   Deep Foundation Trench Dredging on West Man-Made Island
2. 深基坑回填砂开挖转运
   Sand Backfilling and Transportation for Deep Foundation Trench

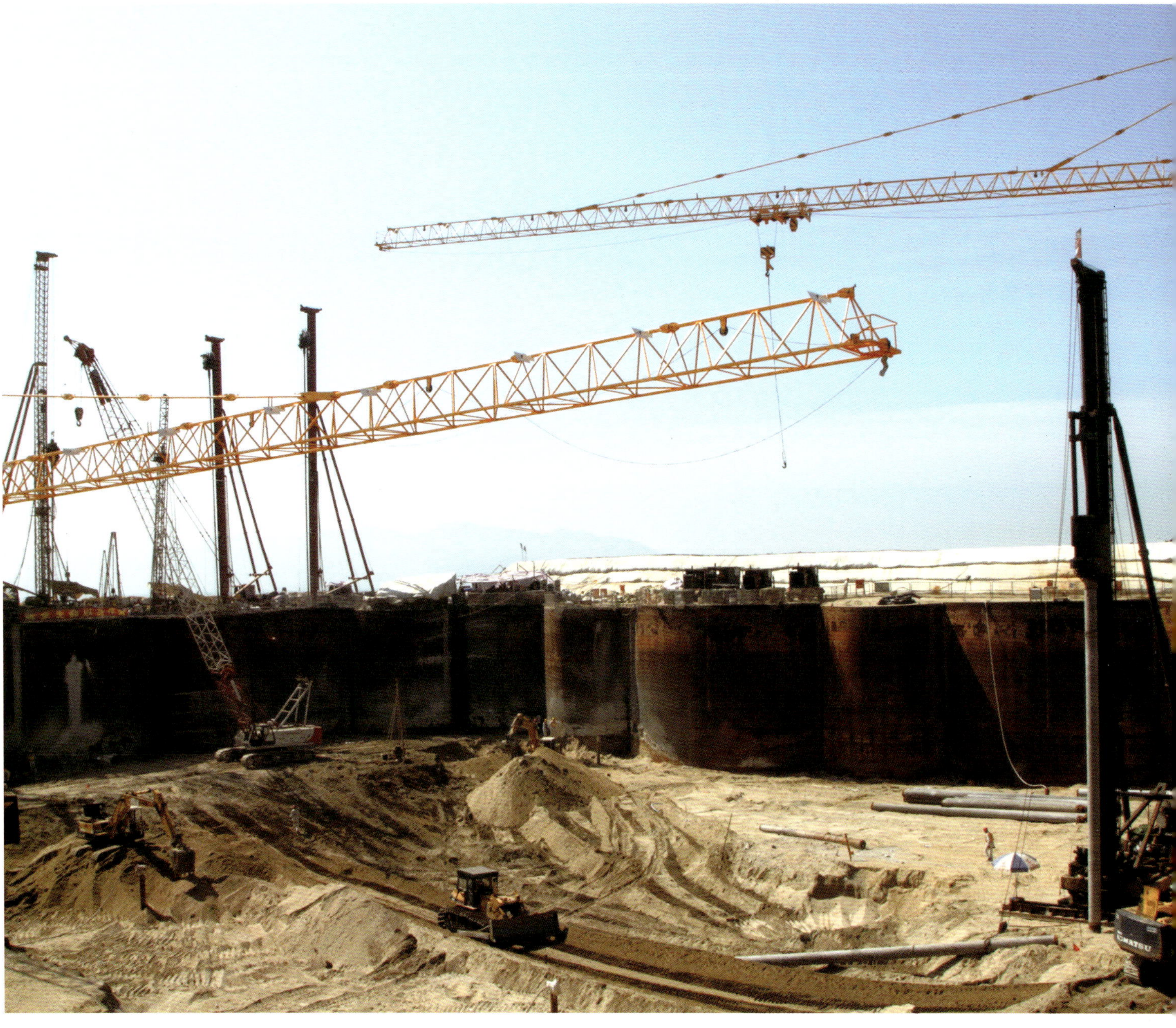

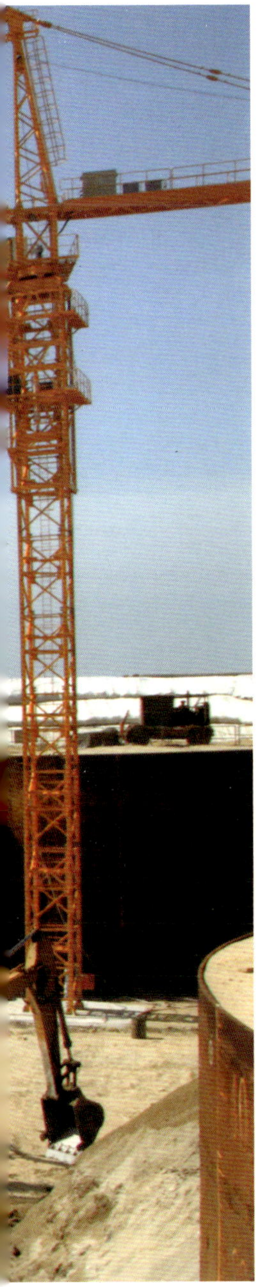

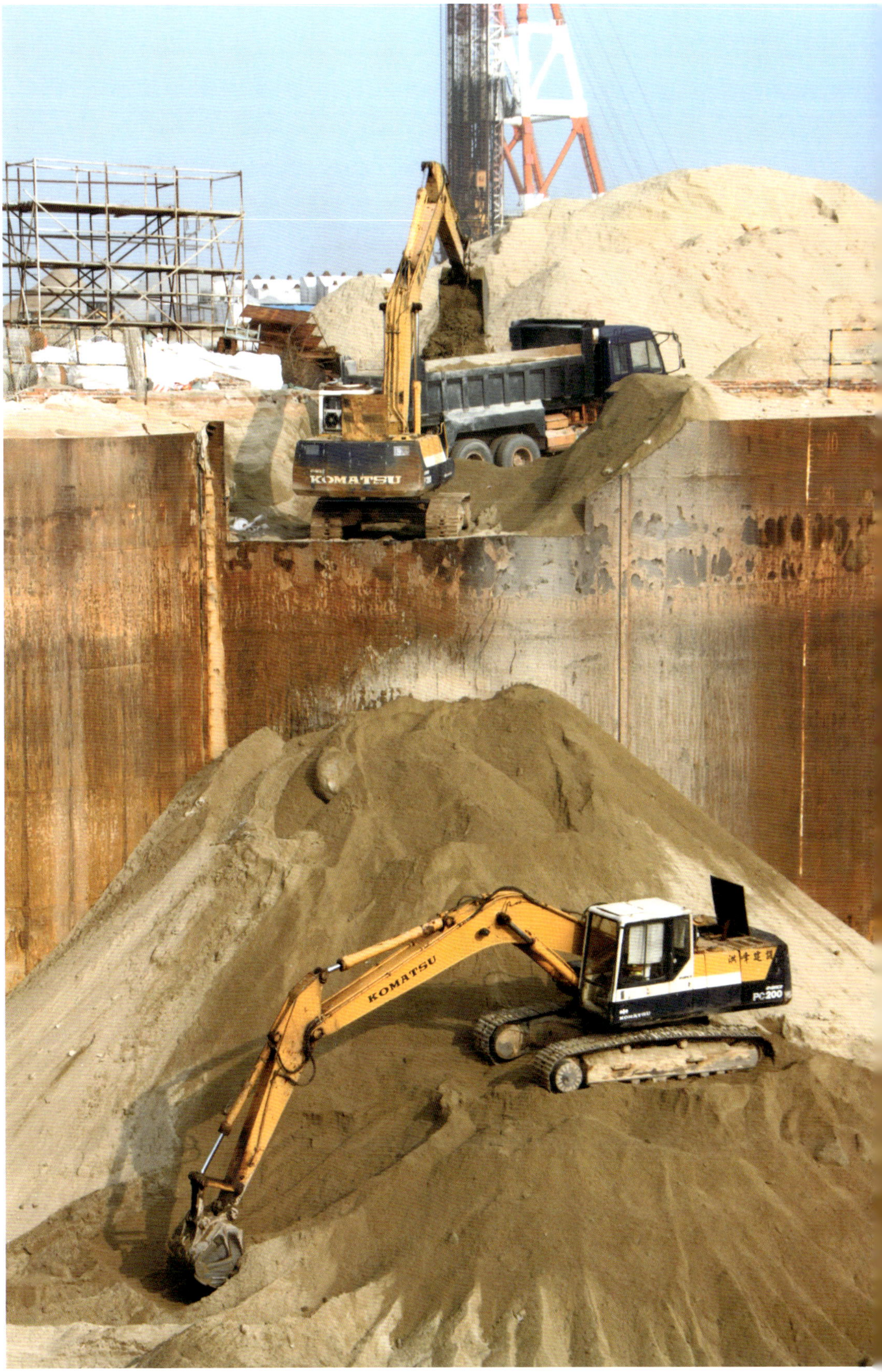
KOMATSU
KOMATSU
PC200

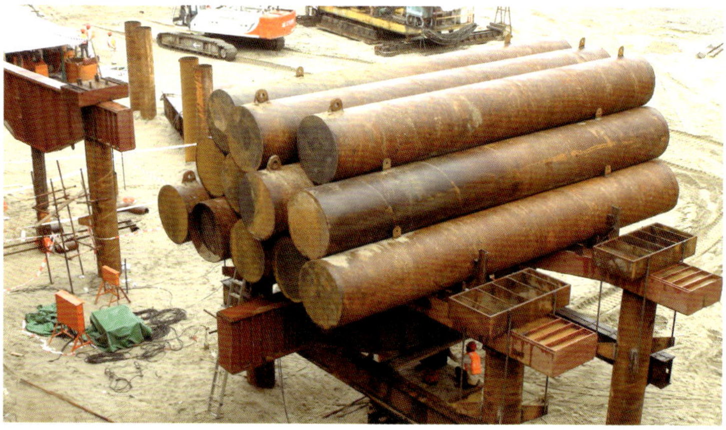

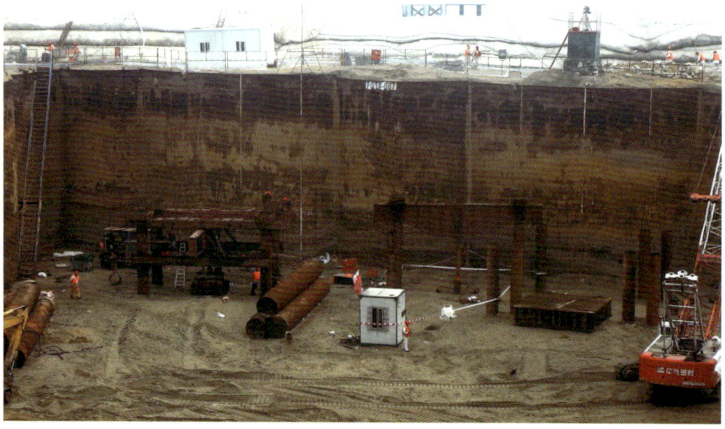

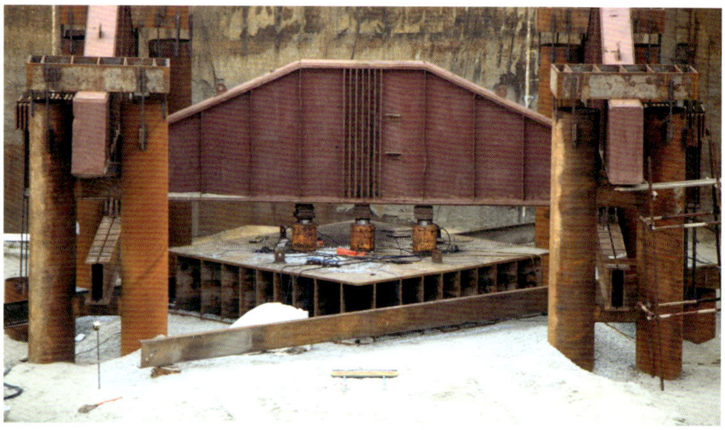

1. 基坑内荷载试验平台
Platform for Loading Test in the Foundation Trench

2. 旋喷加固地基荷载试验
Loading Test of Foundation Consolidated by Jet Grouting

3. PHC 桩静荷载试验多桩复合地基试验完成
Completion of the PHC Pile Static Loading Test and Multi-pile Composite Foundation Test

4. 西小岛 PHC 桩打设
PHC Pile Sinking on the Minor West Island

5. 西小岛 PHC 桩接头焊接施工
Butt Welding of the PHC Piles on the Minor West Island

6. PHC 桩芯混凝土浇筑完成
Completion of Concrete Placement for the PHC Piles

7. PHC 桩打设
Sinking of the PHC Piles

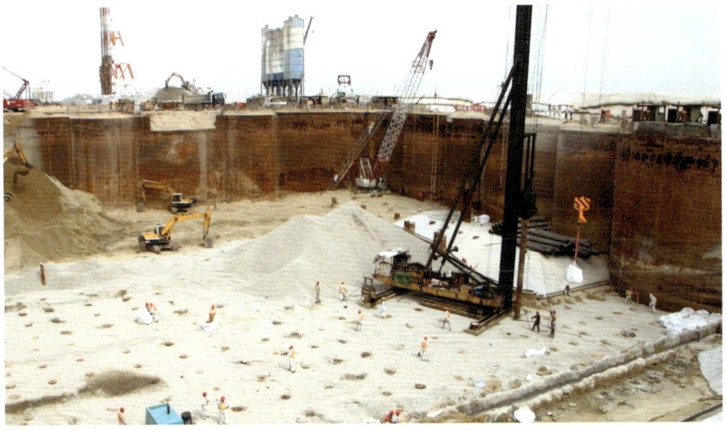

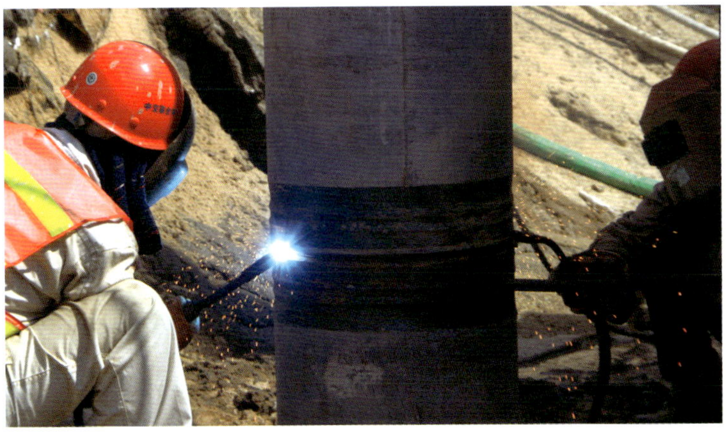

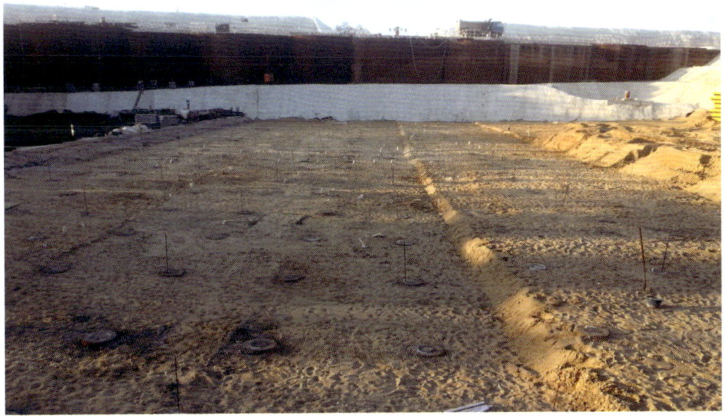

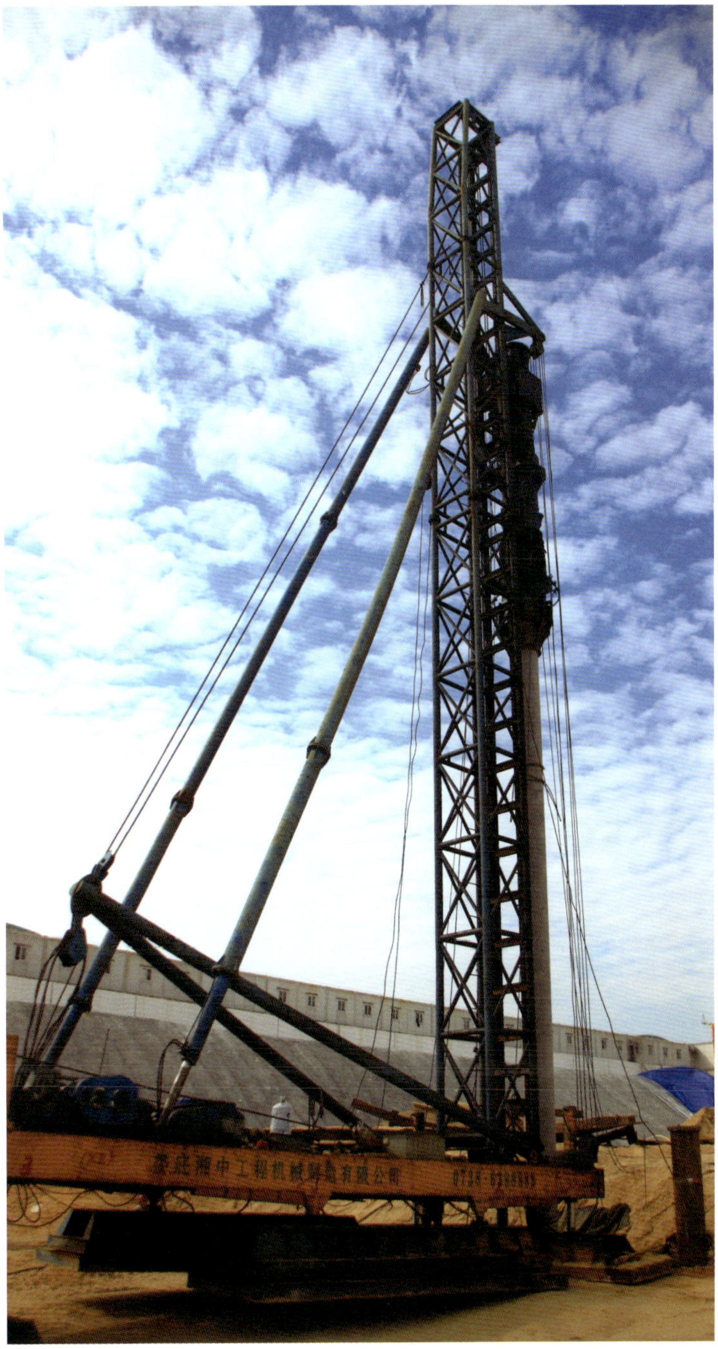

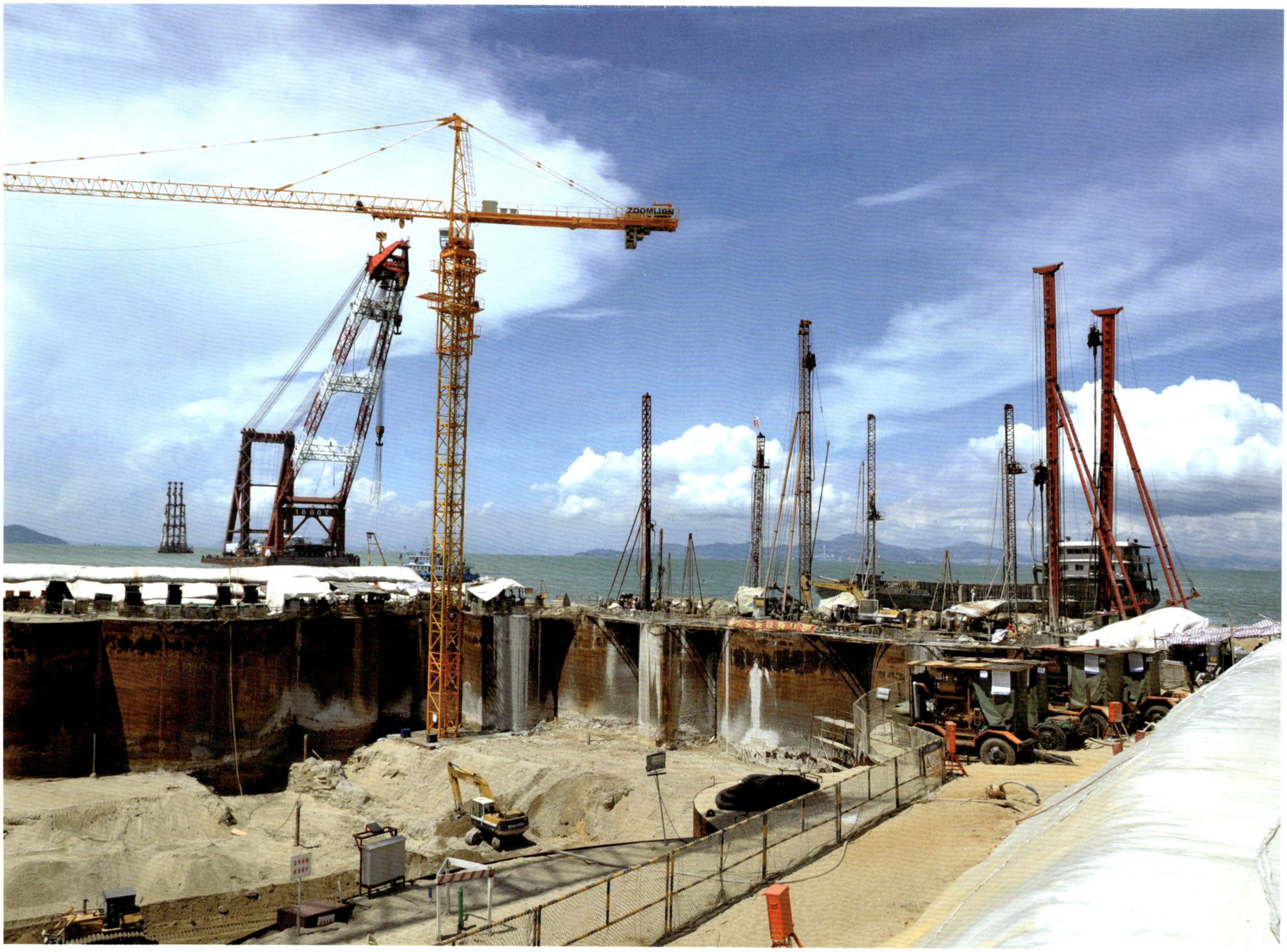
ZOOMLION

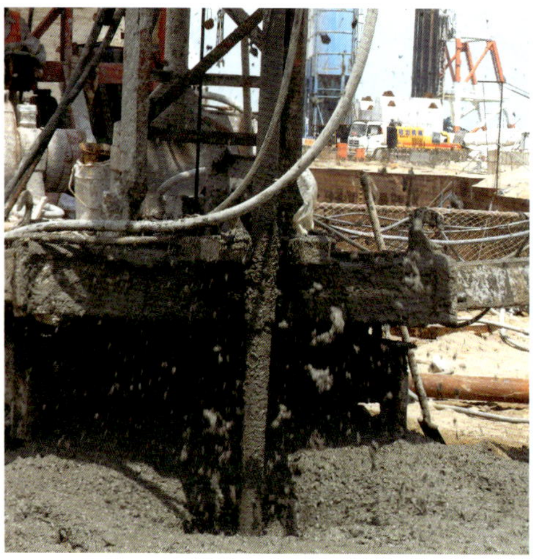

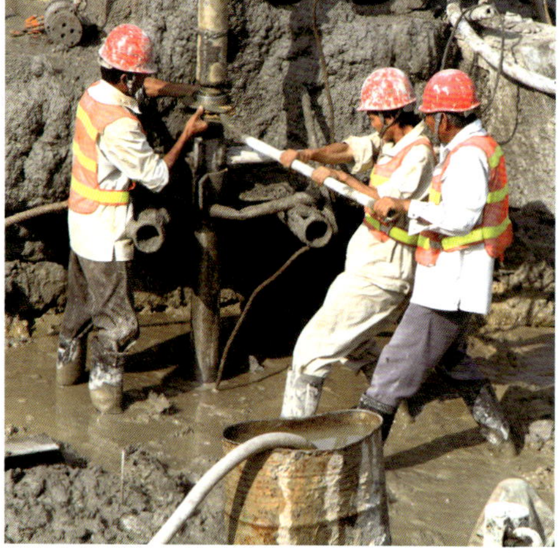

1		4
2	3	5

1. PHC 桩打设及旋喷桩施工
PHC Pile Sinking and Construction of the High Pressure Jet Grouting Piles
2. 西人工岛钢圆筒内高压旋喷桩施工
Construction of the High Pressure Jet Grouting Piles inside the Steel Cylinders in West Man-Made Island
3. 西小岛坑内高压旋喷桩施工
Construction of the High Pressure Jet Grouting Piles inside the Foundation Trench of the Minor West Island
4. 西岛暗埋段碎石垫层铺设
Rubble Bedding for the Buried Section on West Man-Made Island
5. 西小岛内碎石垫层整平
Rubble Bed Leveling on the Minor West Island

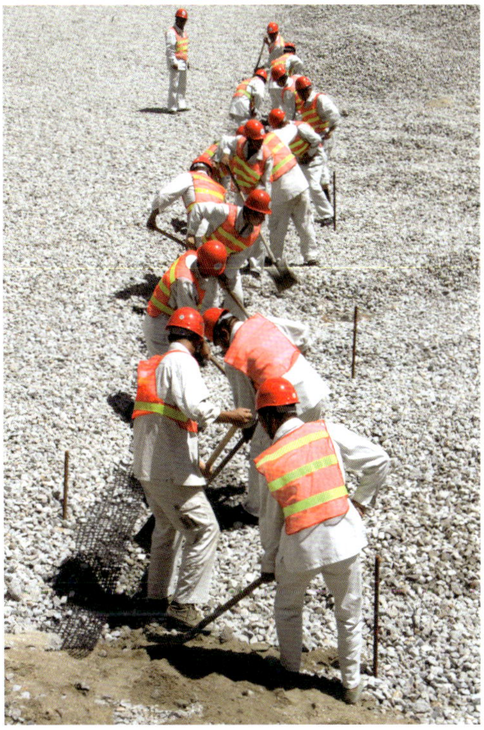

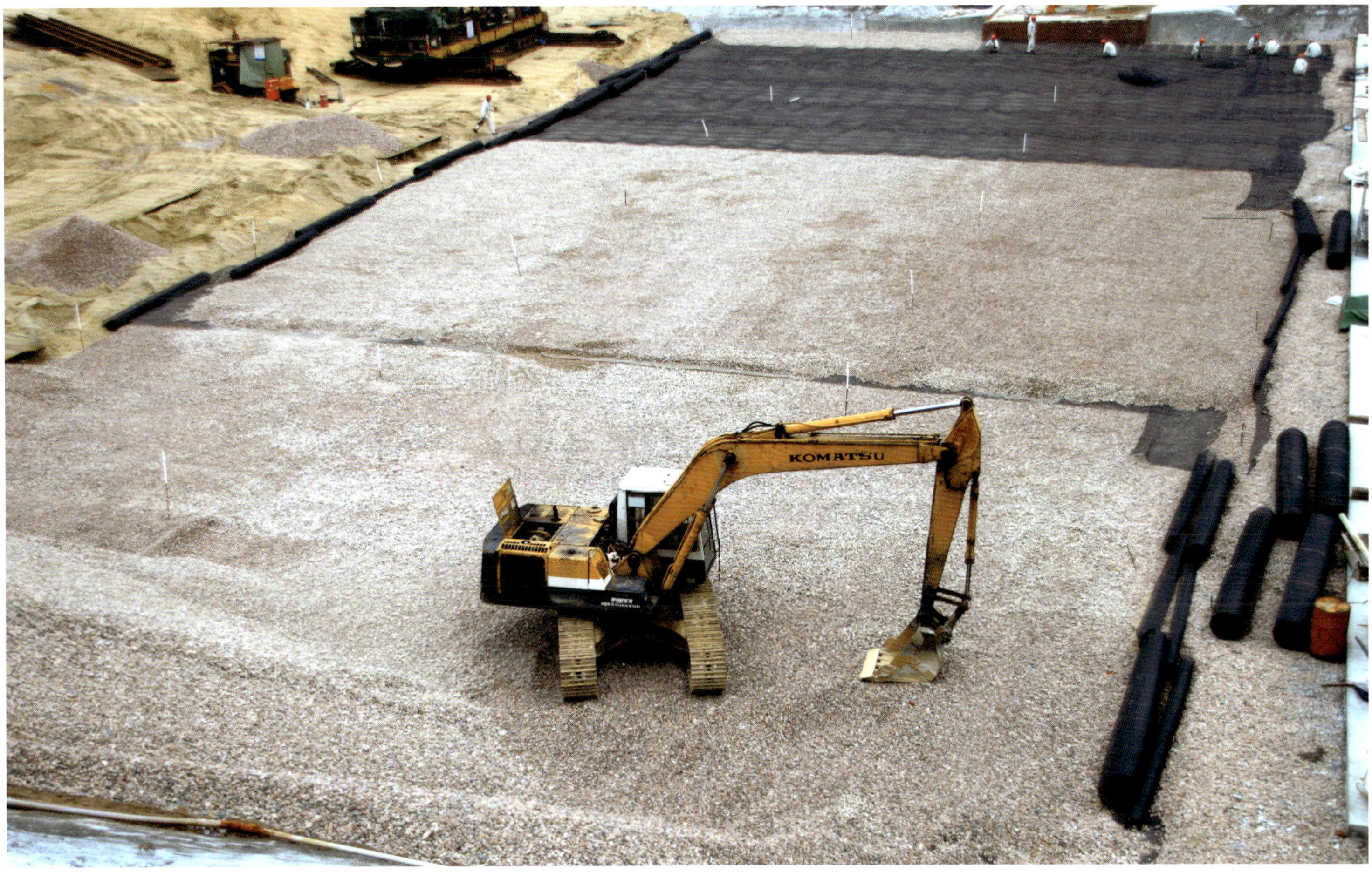

打设挤密砂桩

SINKING OF THE SAND COMPACTION PILE

挤密砂桩技术在人工岛岛壁基础、岛上救援码头基础、岛隧过渡段沉管基础等得到大规模应用，累计打设130万立方米，成为国内第一个大规模成功应用挤密砂桩进行软基处理的工程，在世界工程建设中也属罕见。

岛隧过渡段沉管基础原设计为钢管减沉桩，后优化为综合采用PHC桩、高压旋喷桩、挤密砂桩及天然地基组成的复合地基结构形式。

岛隧过渡段采用40%—50%—70%置换率的挤密砂桩进行逐步过渡，实现地基刚度过渡的协调。然后根据过渡段荷载变化，在需要加固的地基上抛碎石层进行超载预压，开挖后铺设碎石基床，形成碎石垫层+复合地基的隧道基础。

SCP (sand compaction pile) technology was extensively applied to the construction of the island revetment foundation, island rescue dock foundation and the immersed tube foundation of the transitional section of the island-tunnel project. The total volume of SCP amounted to 1,300,000 cubic meters, so it was the first project in China in which SCP had been applied in such large-scale soft ground solidification, and was also rare in the world.

According to original design, the steel tubular piles used to avoid settlement were to be used for the base construction of the immersed tube in the transitional section of the island-tunnel project. The optimized PHC piles, high pressure grouting piles, sand compaction piles and the natural base were used together to form compound foundation structure.

Sand compaction piles with the replacement rates of 40% to 50% to 70% were used for the transition in the transitional section of the island tunnel to coordinate the rigidity transition of the tunnel foundation. Then, according to load variations in the transitional section, a layer of gravel was added to the foundation that needed to be reinforced for surcharge preloading; after the excavation was done, a gravel bed was placed to form the tunnel base by "gravel bedding + compound foundation".

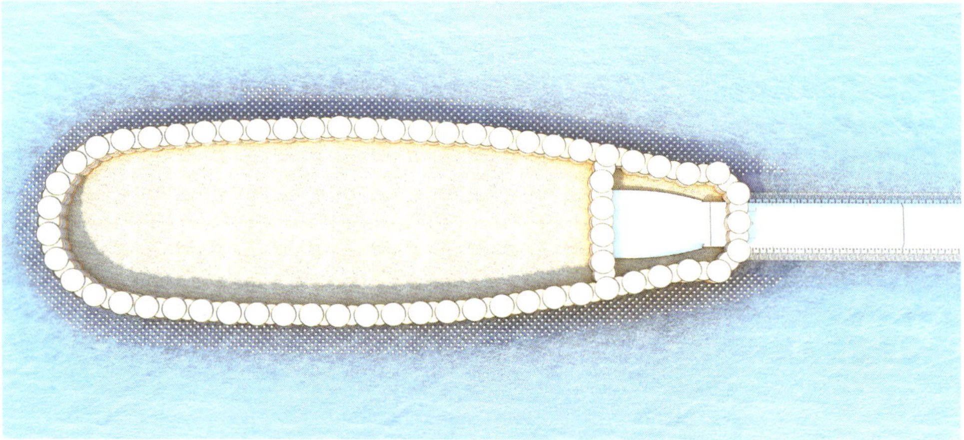

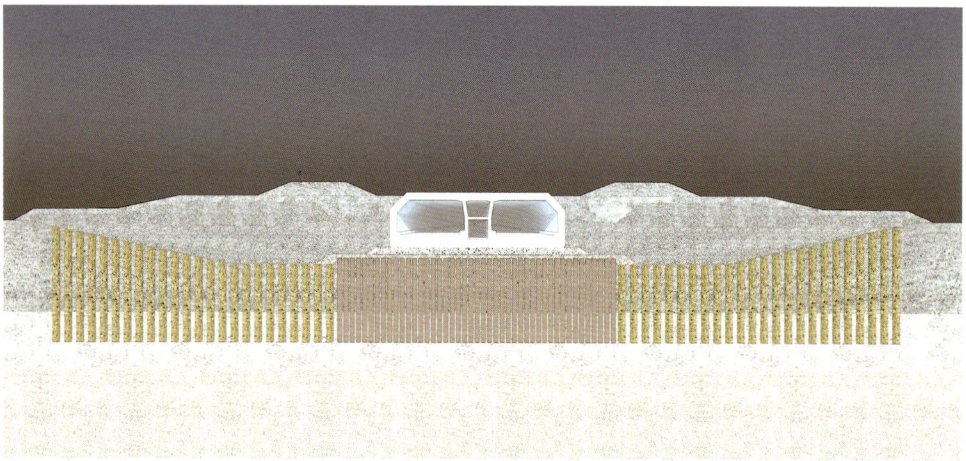

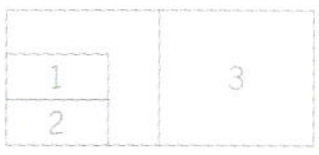

1. 西人工岛挤密砂桩岛壁区示意图
Schematic Diagram of the Sand Compaction Pile Wall of West Man-Made Island

2. 隧道基础横截面示意图
Schematic Diagram of the Cross Section of the Tunnel Foundation

3. 过渡段挤密砂桩打设
Sand Compaction Pile Sinking in the Transitional Section of the Tunnel

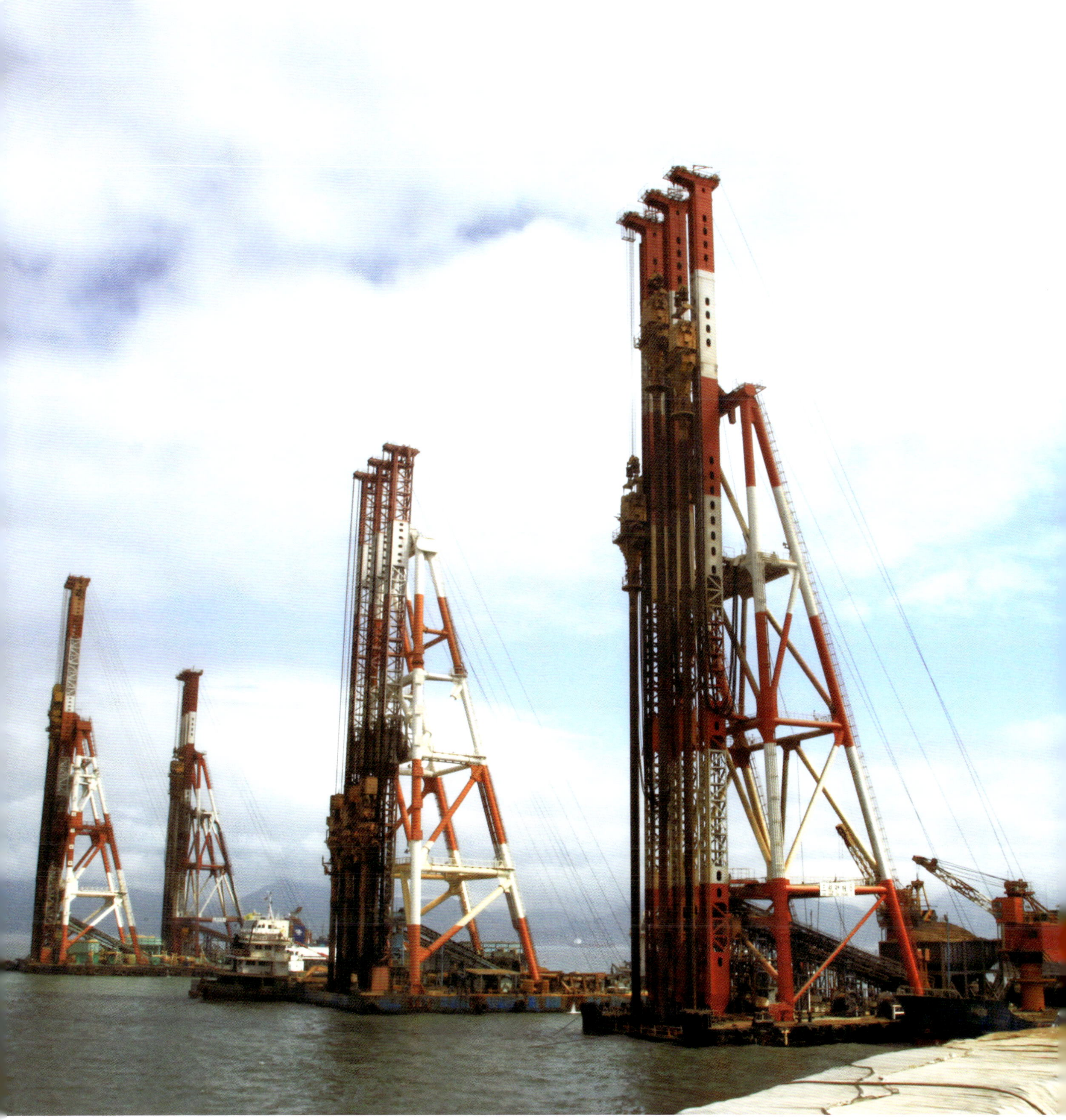

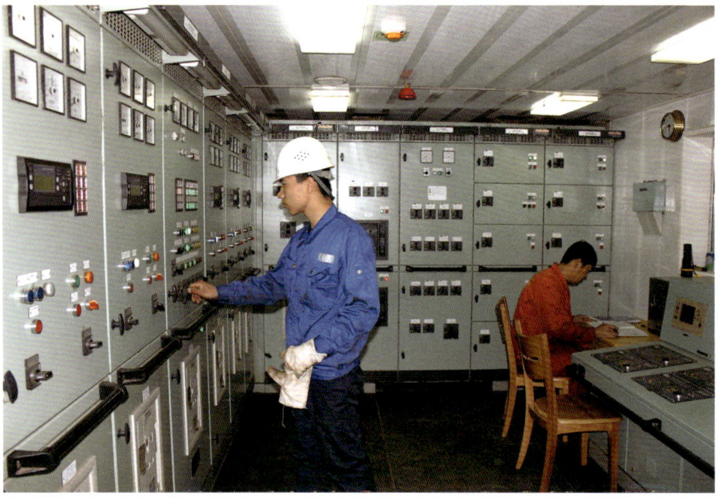

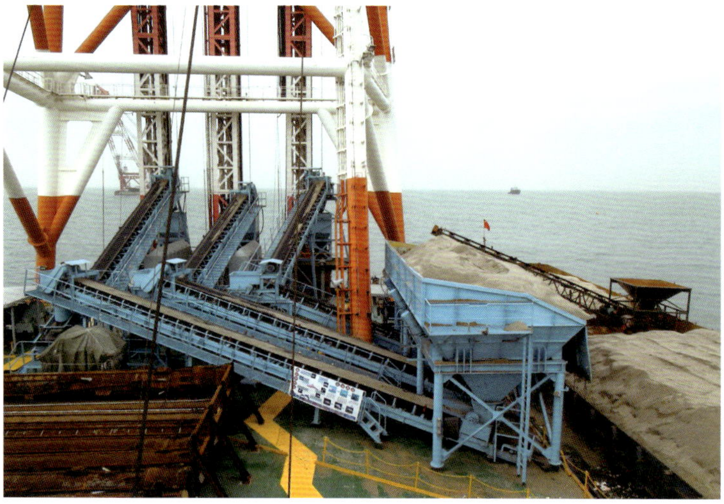

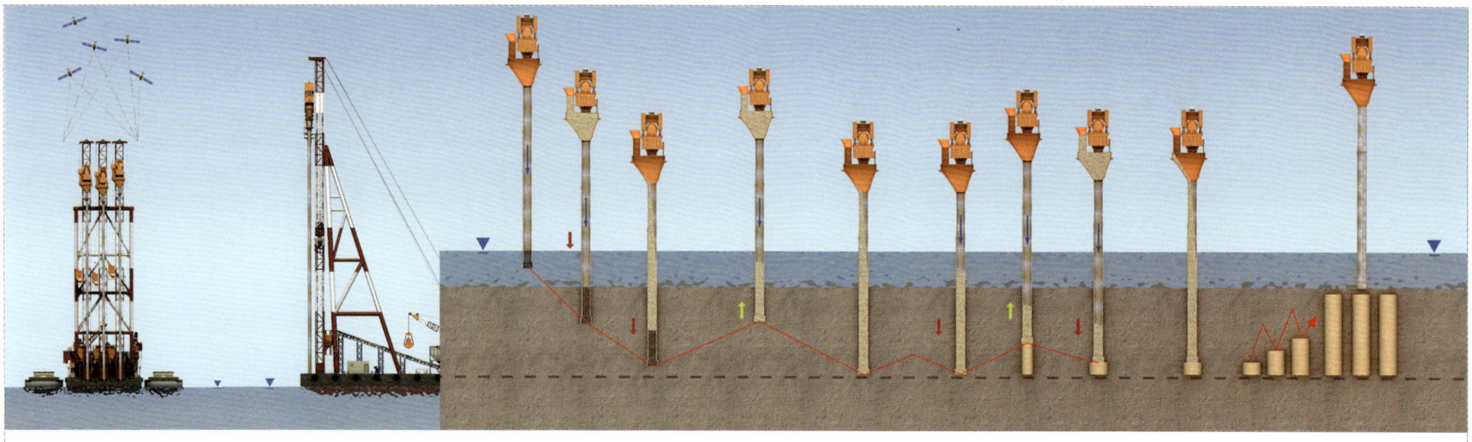

采用陆上参考站及 GPS 测量系统进行船舶定位，测泥面标高及水深
The land-based reference station and GPS measurement system were used to locate the ship and measure the height and depth of the mud

下砂桩套管，入水后加压排水
Sand pile casing, pressurized drainage after entering water

沉设砂桩套管进入土层一定深度，减压灌砂
The sand pile pipe was placed into the soil layer at a certain depth

加压及持压施打砂桩套管接近处理土层底标高
Pressurized and pressurized sand coated pile casing to approach the bottom elevation of soil layer

持压、上拔砂桩套管，排出管内泥柱，端部处理
Holding the pressure, placing the sand pile pipe, discharging the mud column in the pipe, and dealing with the ends

灌砂、加压施打砂桩套管至处理土层底标高
Sand filling, pressurized sand pile casing treatment to the bottom elevation of soil layer

加压上拔砂桩套管，排砂形成一定高度砂桩
The sand pile was installed on the top of the sand and the sand pile was formed at a certain height

持压振动回打扩径，形成一段挤密砂桩
The pressure and vibration were expanded to form a section of compaction sand pile

重复 7—8 进行多次循环，逐段形成整根挤密砂桩，完成后进行泥面测量
Repeated 7-8 is carried out for several times, and the whole compaction sand pile was formed by stages. After completion, mud measurement was completed

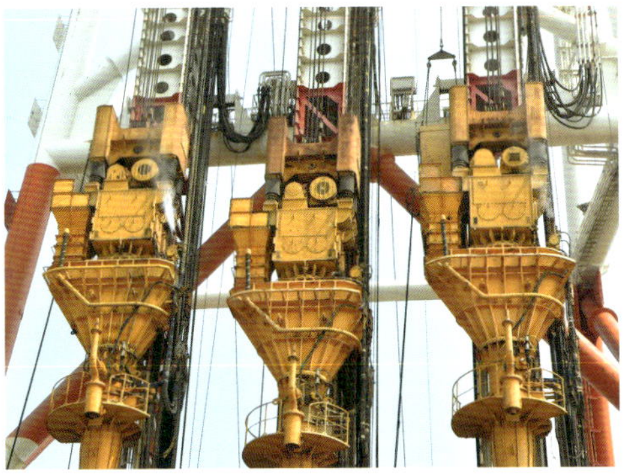

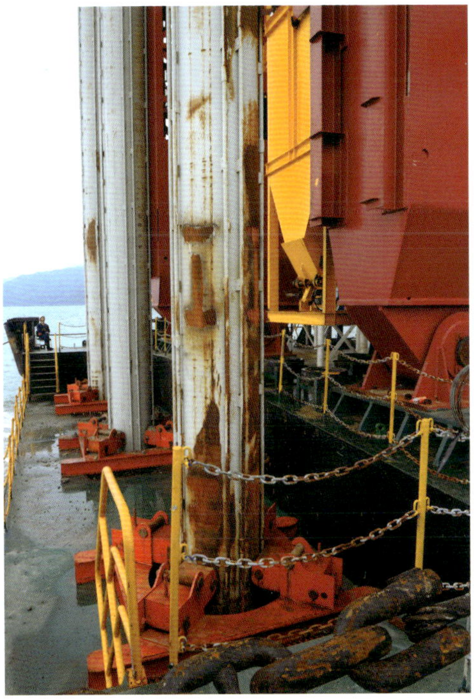

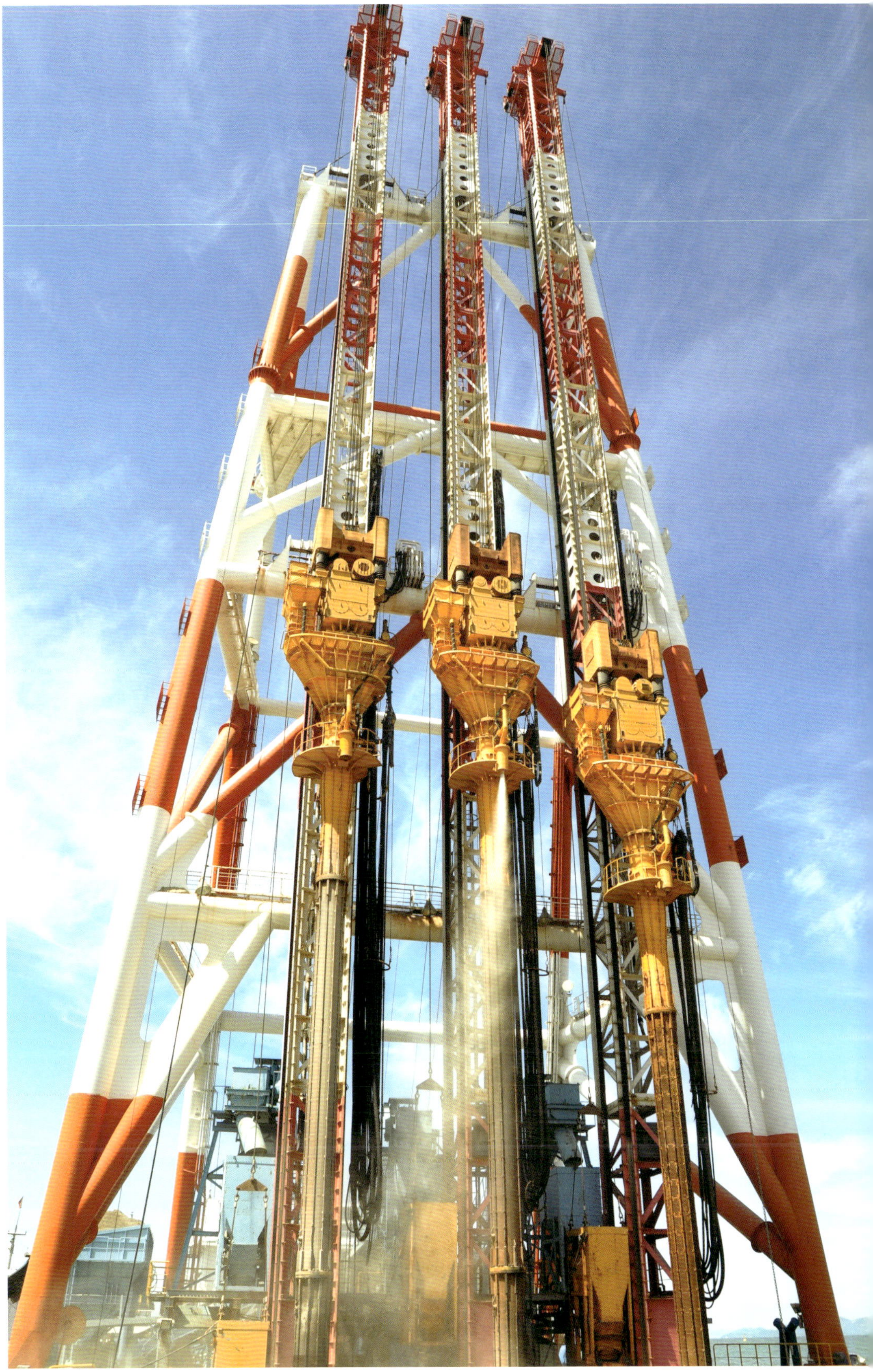

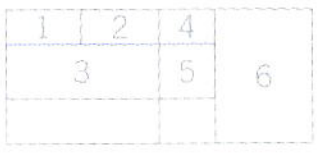

1. 挤密砂桩船操作室
   Operation Room of the Sand Compaction Piling Barge
2. 砂桩船运料
   Sand Pile Barge Shipping Constructional Materials
3. 挤密砂桩打设示意图
   Schematic Diagram of Sand Compaction Piling
4. 挤密砂桩沉管振动锤
   Vibratory Hammer for Sand Compaction Pile Sinking
5. 挤密砂桩桩管
   Sand Compaction Pile Pipe
6. 挤密砂桩打设
   Sand Compaction Pile Sinking

人工岛钢圆筒深插入土与副格围合成岛后，在钢圆筒外围铺设斜坡堤，形成永久岛壁结构。

为避免岛壁块石抛填与码头施工的互相干扰，东、西人工岛救援码头采用了挤密砂桩重力式沉箱码头方案。

这是中国第一个在软土地基上采用挤密砂桩基础建设的重力式码头。经现场荷载试验，采用60%挤密砂桩置换率获得了成功，其承载力满足重力式码头的要求。

After the man-made islands were formed by using the steel cylinders driven deep into the seabed and connected into a whole by the connecting rails fastened onto the cylinders, a slope dyke was built closely outside the steel cylinders to form a permanent island fending structure.

In order to prevent the rock filling that was employed to build the fending wall of the island and the dock construction from disturbing each other, the gravity caisson technique with sand compaction piling was adopted in the construction of the rescue docks of the east and west man-made islands.

This was the first gravity wharf in China using the technique of SCP foundation construction on soft soil foundation. According to the on-the-site load tests, sand compaction piling technique with a replacement rate of 60% was a success and the dock's loading capacity met the requirements of the gravity wharf.

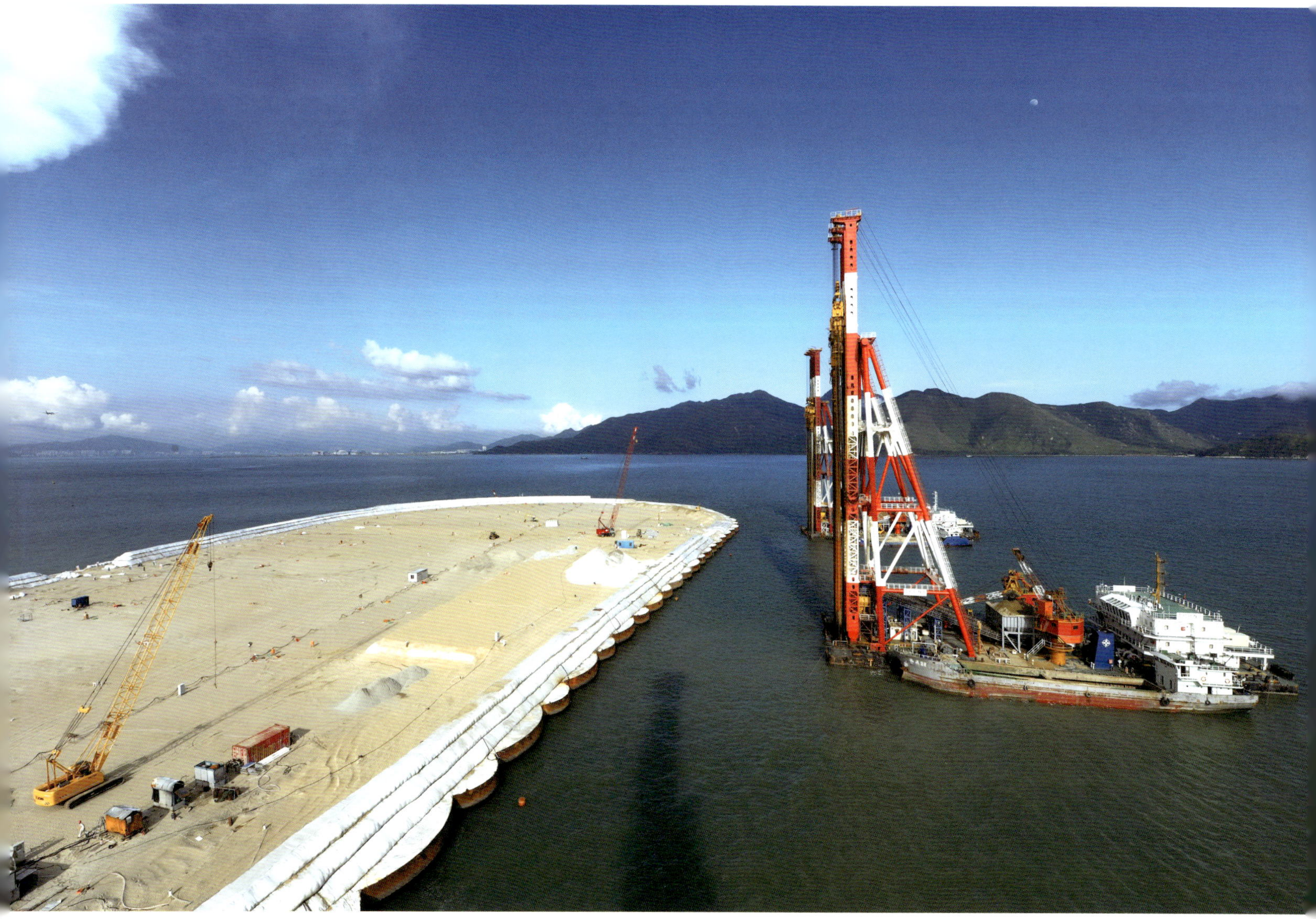

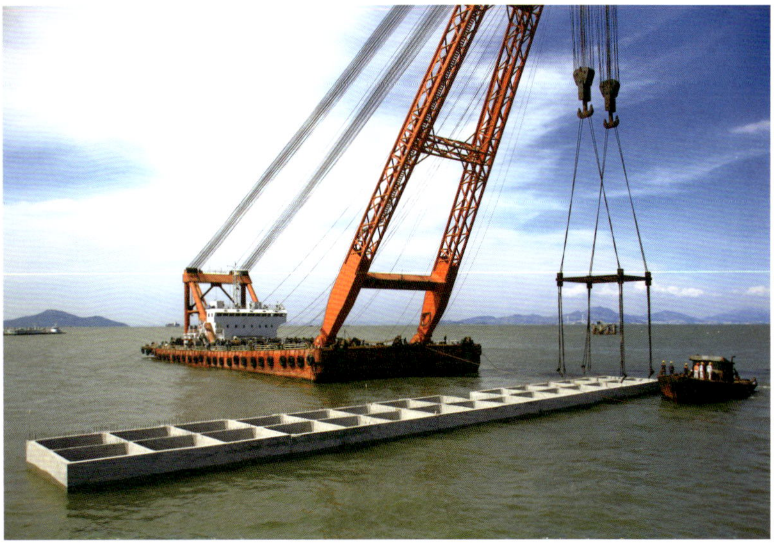

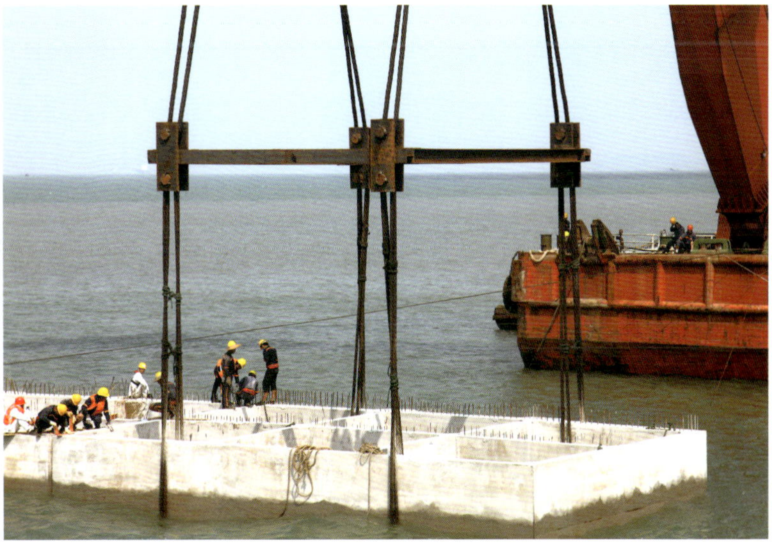

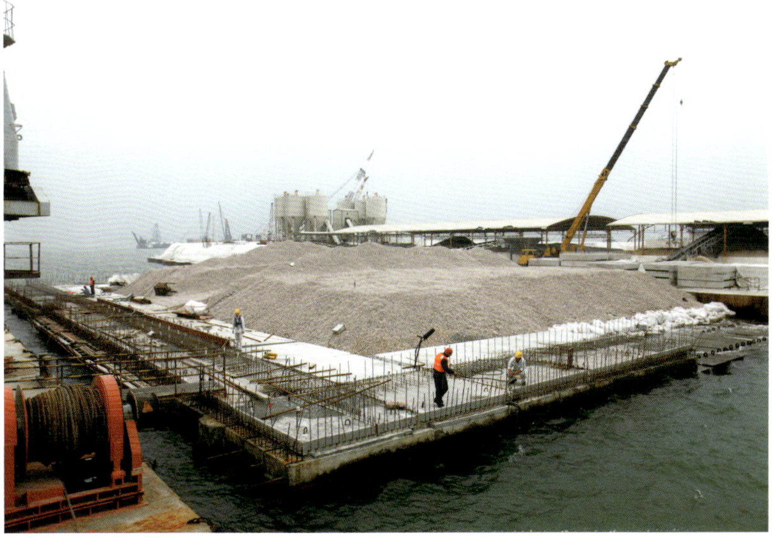

1. 东人工岛岛壁区挤密砂桩打设
Sand Compaction Pile Sinking in the Island Wall Area on East Man-Made Island

2—4. 救援码头沉箱安装
Installation of the Rescue Dock Caisson

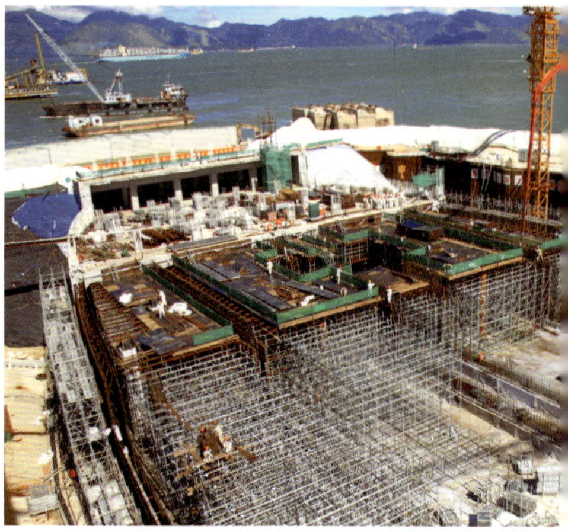

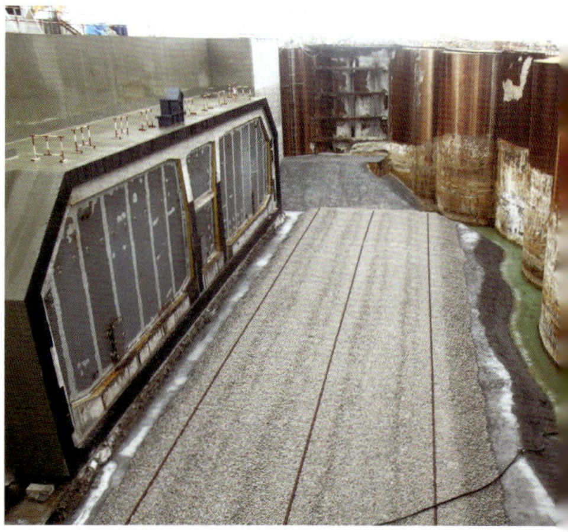

岛上结构施工

CONSTRUCTION OF THE ISLAND STRUCTURES

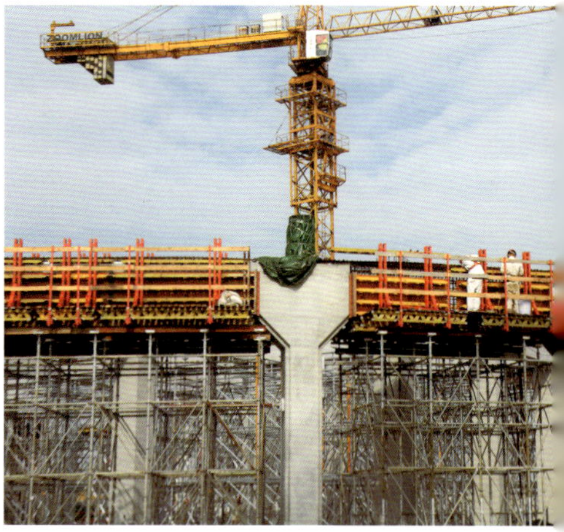

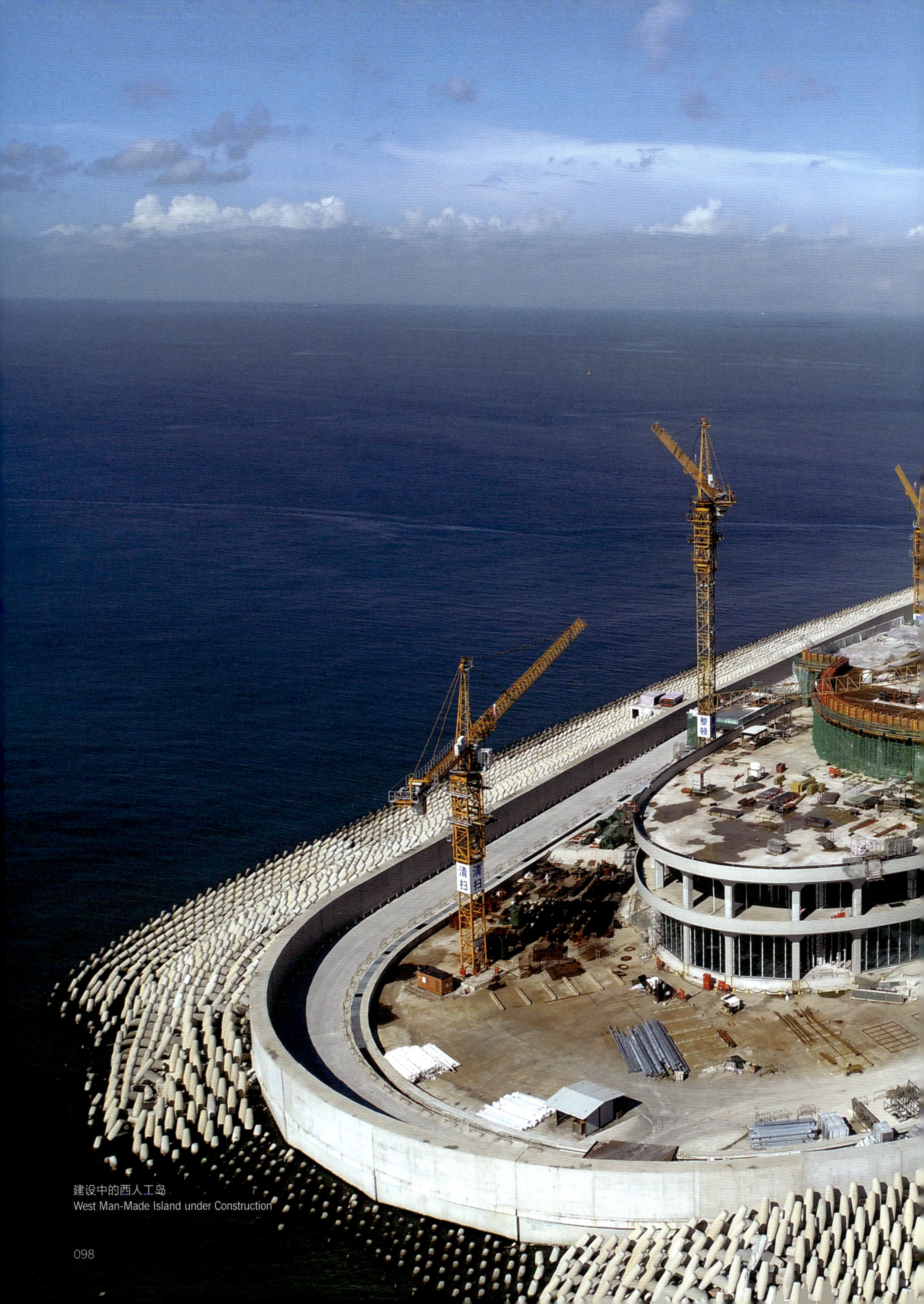

建设中的西人工岛
West Man-Made Island under Construction

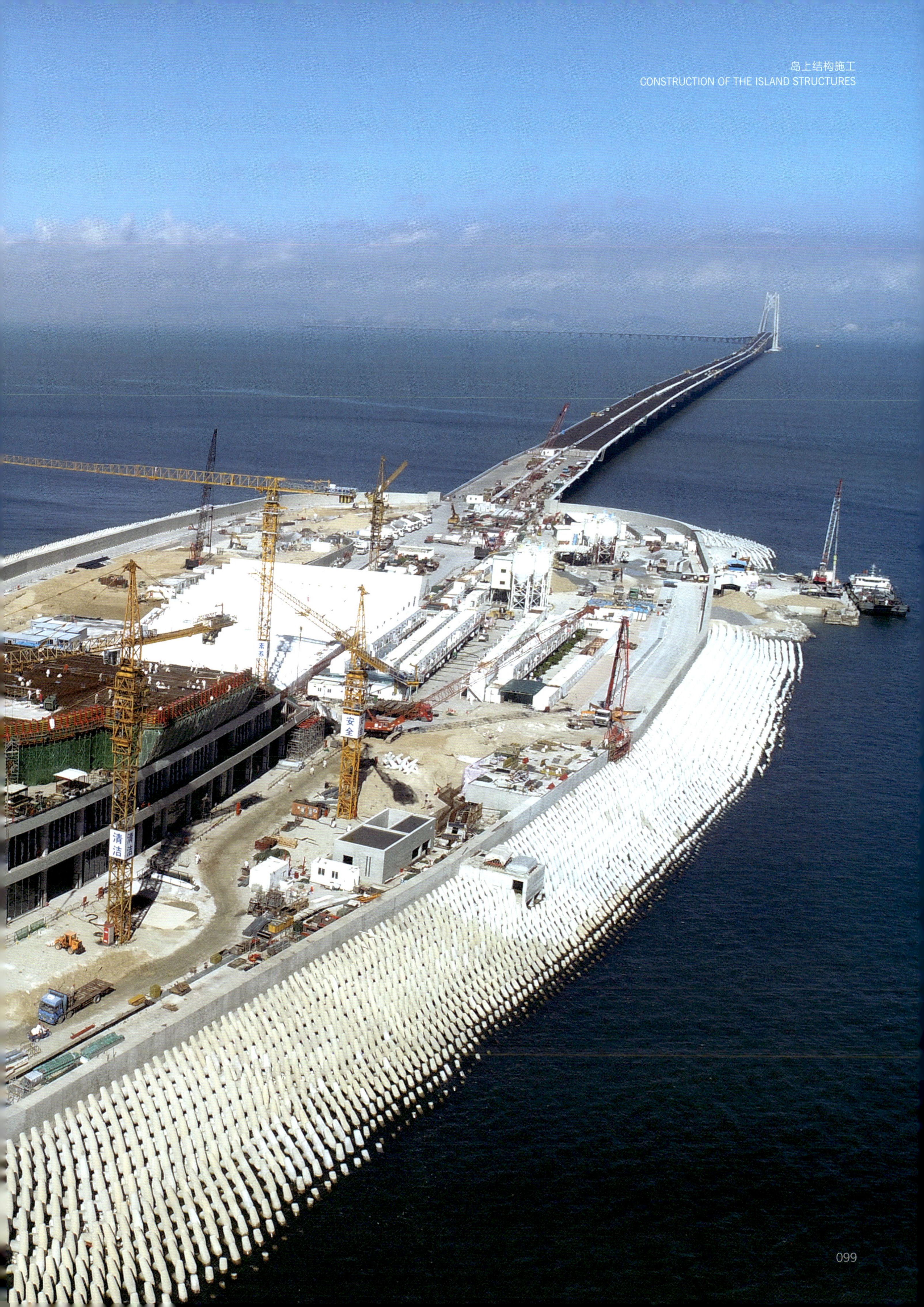
清洁
安全

暗埋段
BURIED SECTION

暗埋段沉管采用两孔一管廊的结构形式。与沉管相接部位采用单箱双室管廊箱型结构，横断面宽37.95米。其主体结构分两层浇筑：第一层包括底板整体、两侧285厘米高侧墙、两道304厘米高中隔墙；第二层浇筑为除顶部空箱结构的剩余部分。

与敞开段相接部分为单箱四室管廊箱型结构。因两侧分别增加了一个结构空箱作为岛上建筑的地下室，横断面宽度由37.95米渐变至53.73米。其主体结构分三层进行浇筑：第一层包括底板整体、两侧285厘米高侧墙、两道304厘米高中隔墙；第二层浇筑中间4道墙体；第三层浇筑侧墙及顶板。为施工方便，其中侧墙与弧形外侧墙的变化区域，也作为第三层浇筑。

The immersed tube in the buried section adopted the structure of two holes with one pipe gallery. The part connected with the immersed tube adopted a pipe gallery box structure of one single box with double chambers with a cross section of 37.95 meters wide. The body structure was cast in two layers: the first layer included the whole bottom plate, the 285-centimeter-high side walls on both sides and two 304-centimeter-high partition walls in the middle; the second layer included the rest parts excluding the hollow box structure on the top.

The part connected with the open section was the pipe gallery box structure of one single box with four chambers. The width of the cross section gradually changed from 37.95 meters to 53.73 meters due to the addition of an empty structural box on each side as the basement of the building on the island. The main structure was cast in three layers: the first layer included the whole bottom plate, the 285-centimeter-high side walls on both sides and two 304-centimeter-high partition walls in the middle; the second layer was the four walls in the middle; the third layer was the side walls and the roof. For the convenience of construction, the transitional area from the side walls to the arc-shaped outside wall also belonged to the third layer.

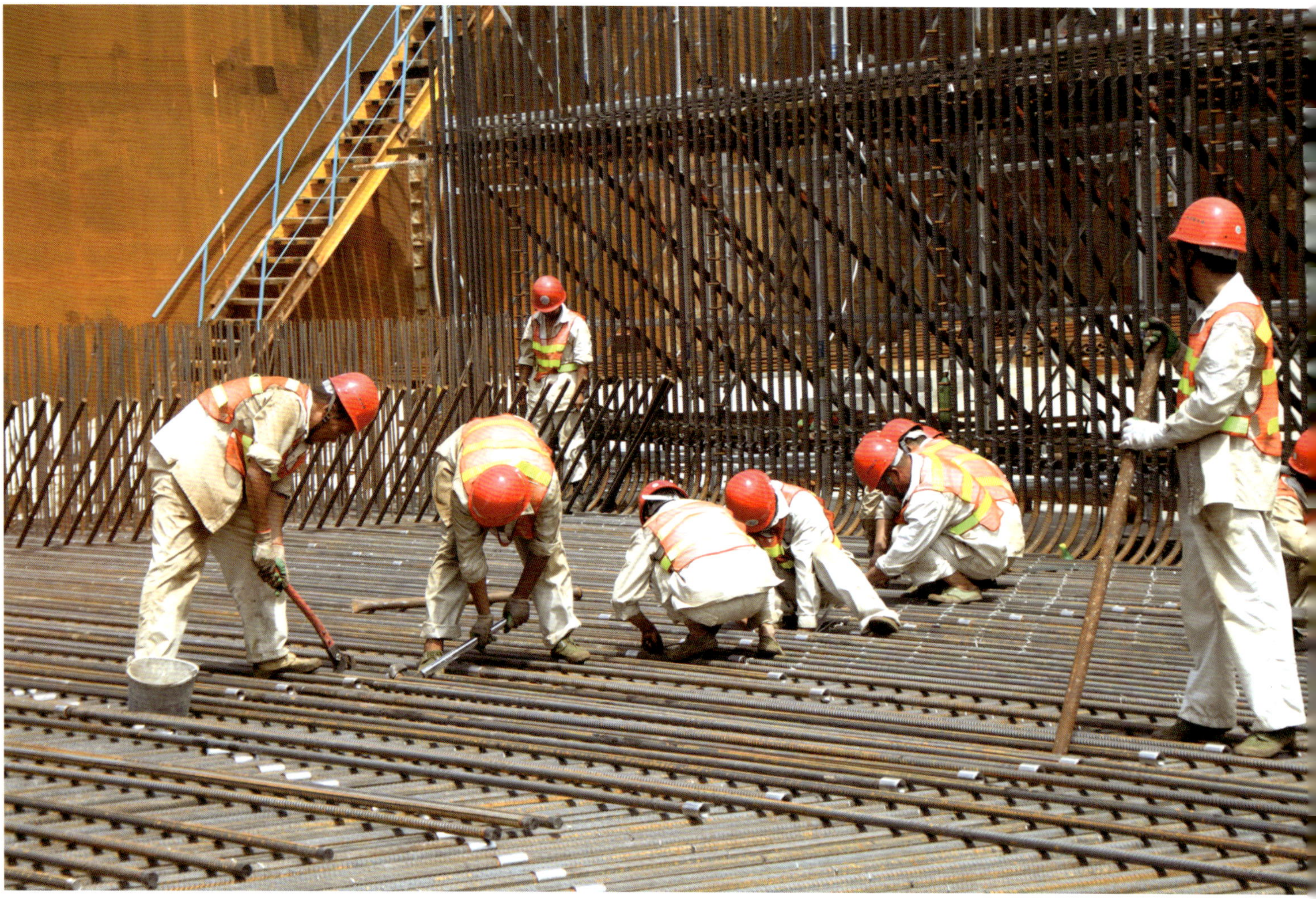

1. 西人工岛暗埋（止推）段结构施工
Construction of the Buried (Thrust) Section on West Man-Made Island

2. 西人工岛现浇段支架搭设
Installation of the Scaffolds in the Cast-on-Site Section on West Man-Made Island

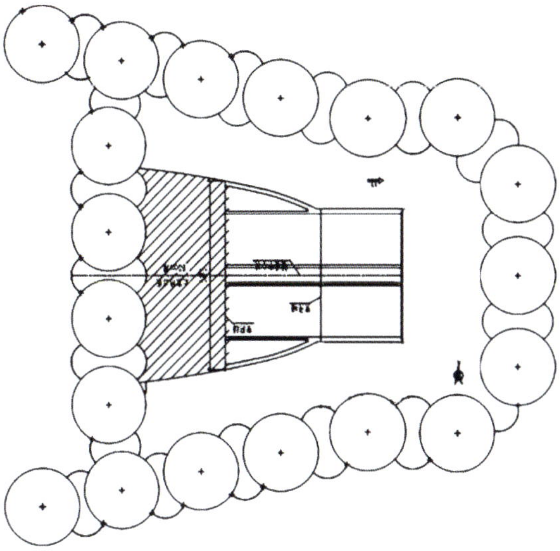

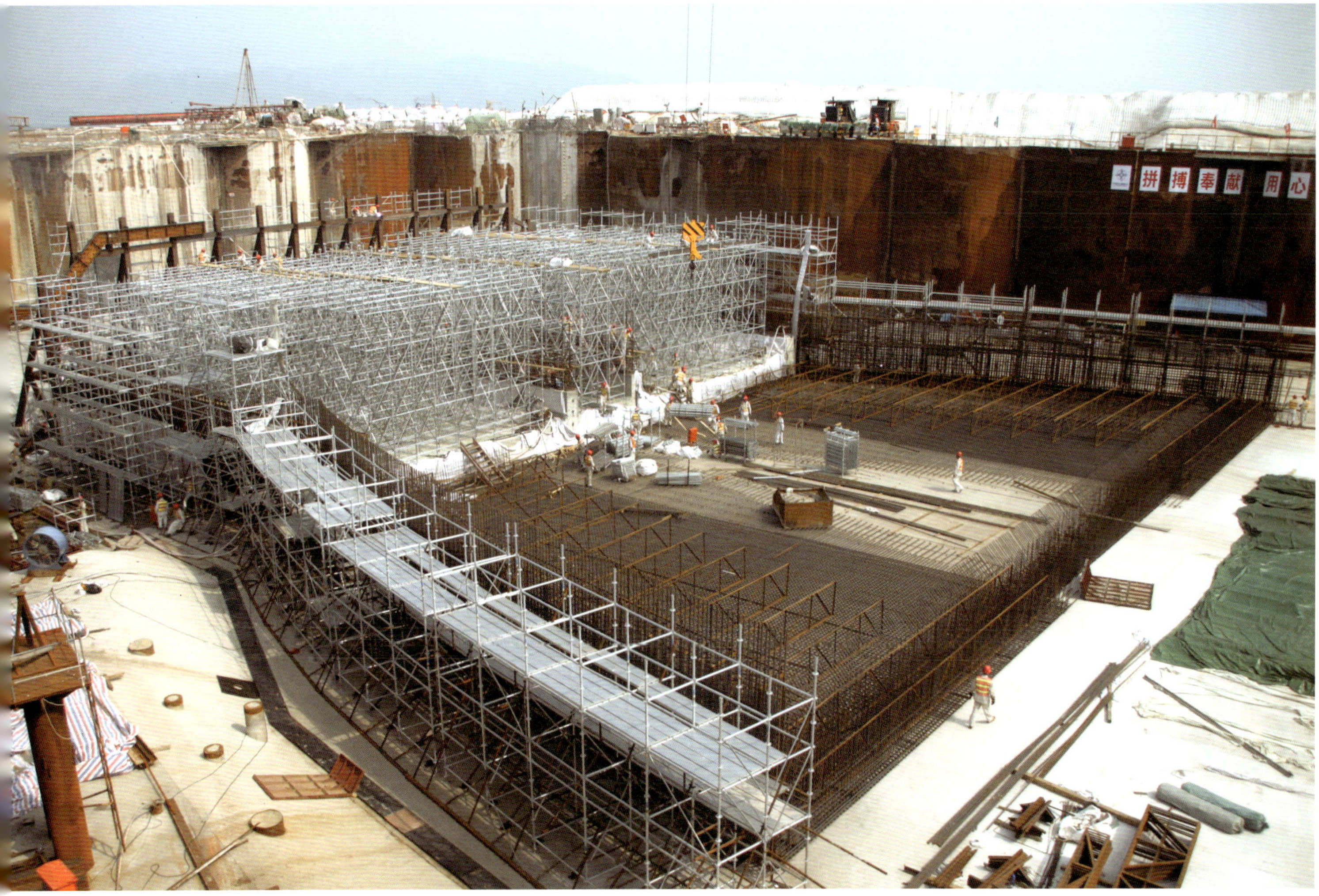

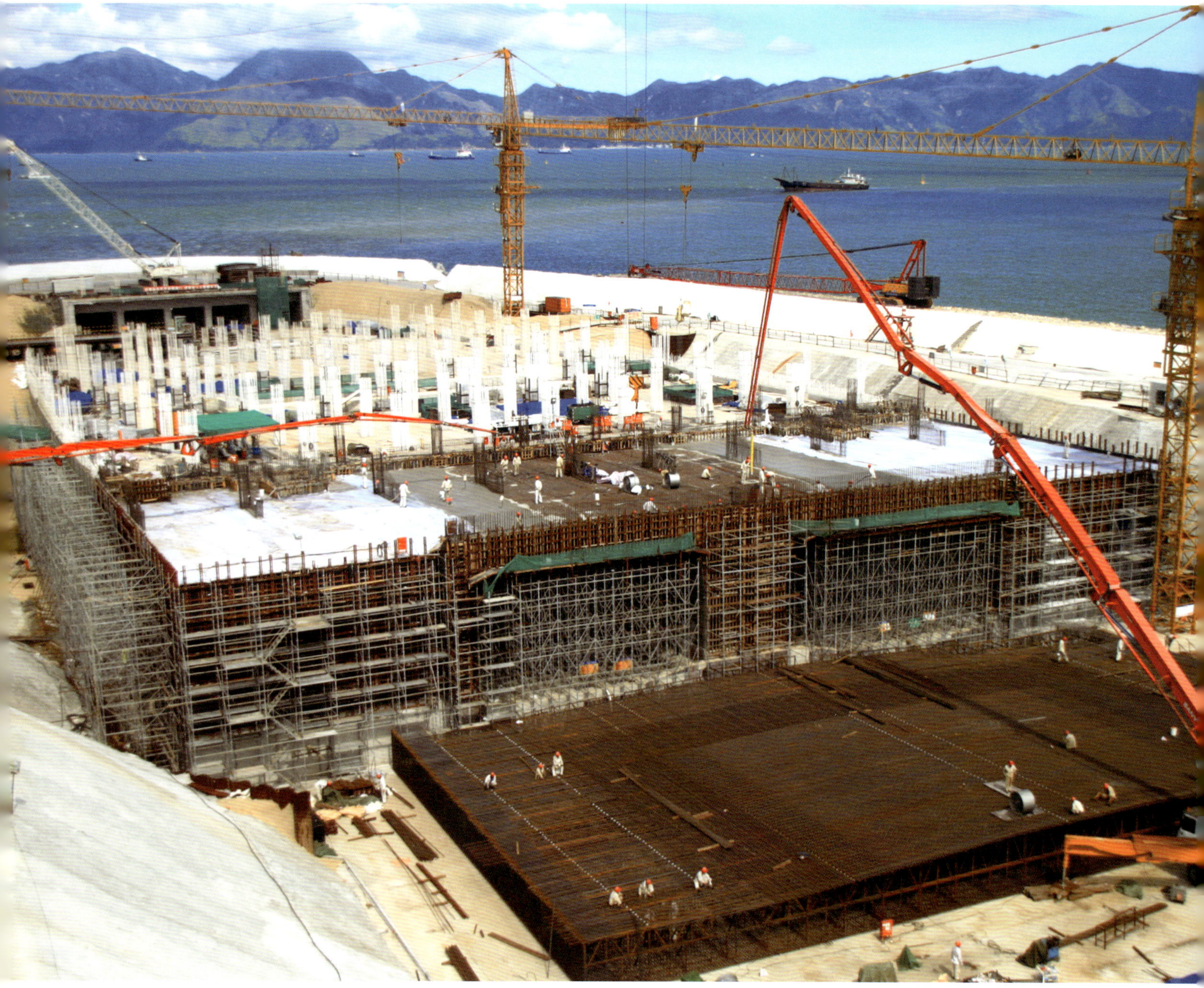

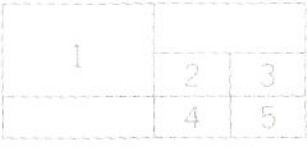

1. 东人工岛暗埋段混凝土浇筑
   Concrete Placement in the Buried Section on East Man-Made Island
2. 暗埋段侧墙钢筋绑扎
   Steel Bar Binding for the Side Wall of the Buried Section
3. 暗埋段端钢壳安装
   Steel Shell Installation in the Buried Section
4. 人工岛暗埋段二次止水墙结构施工
   Construction of the Secondary Water-Stop Wall in the Buried Section of the Man-Made Island
5. 暗埋段外包聚脲防水施工
   External Polyurea Waterproof Construction in the Buried Section

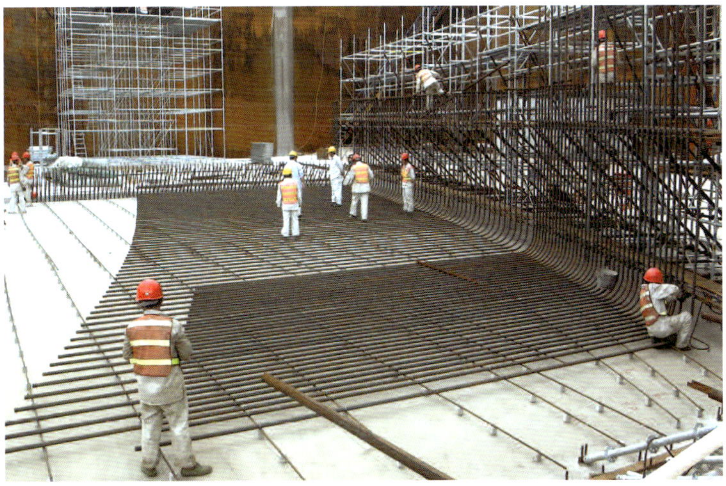

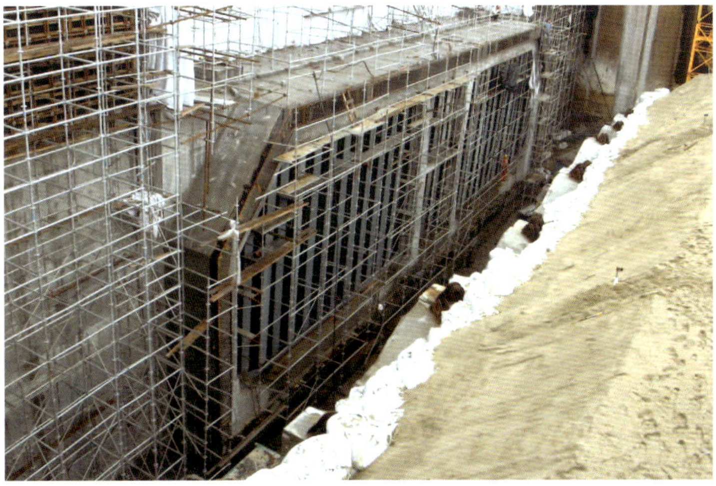

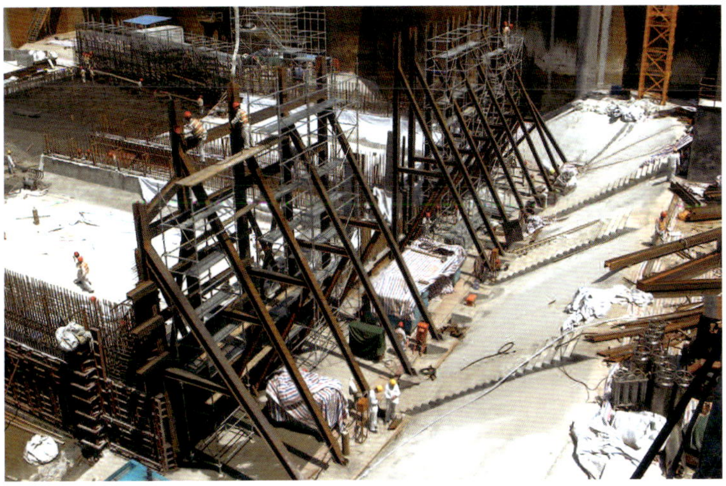

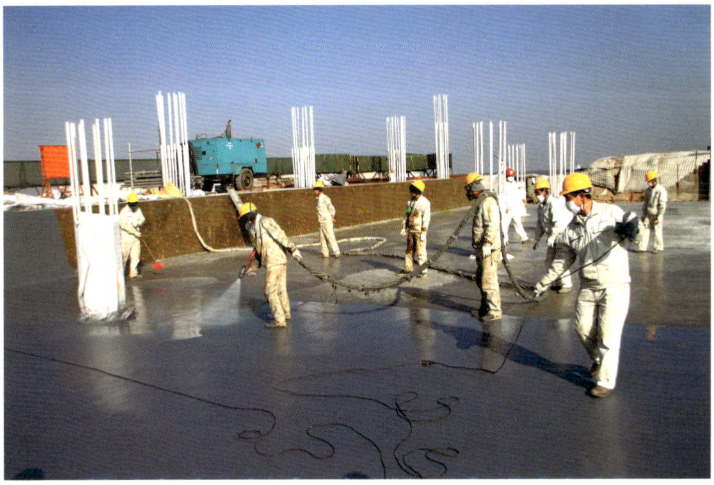

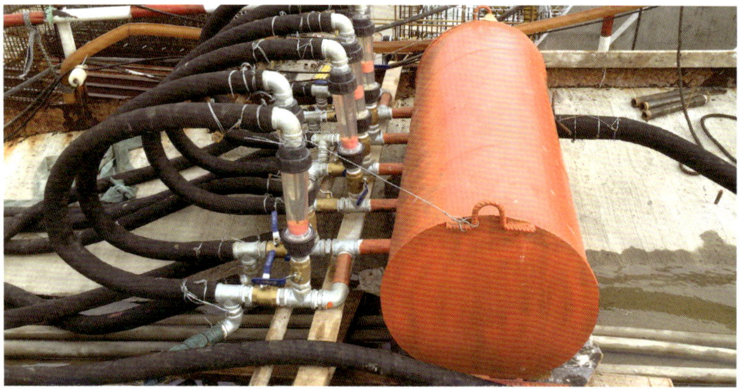

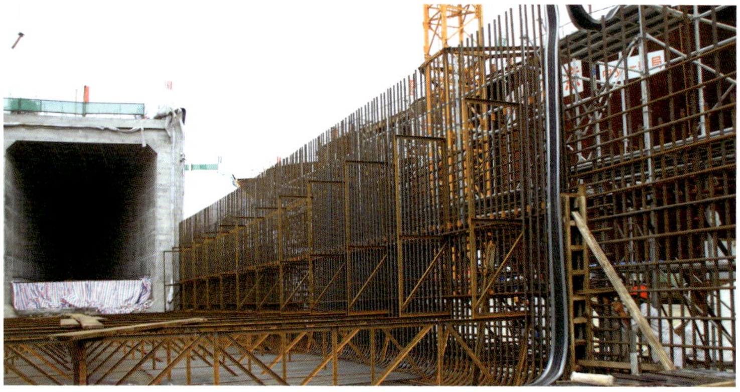

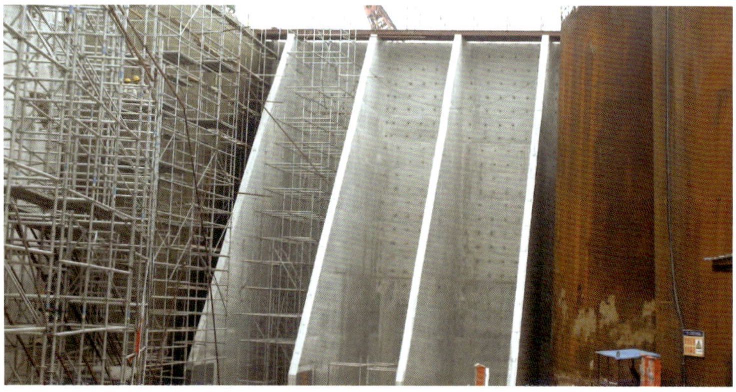

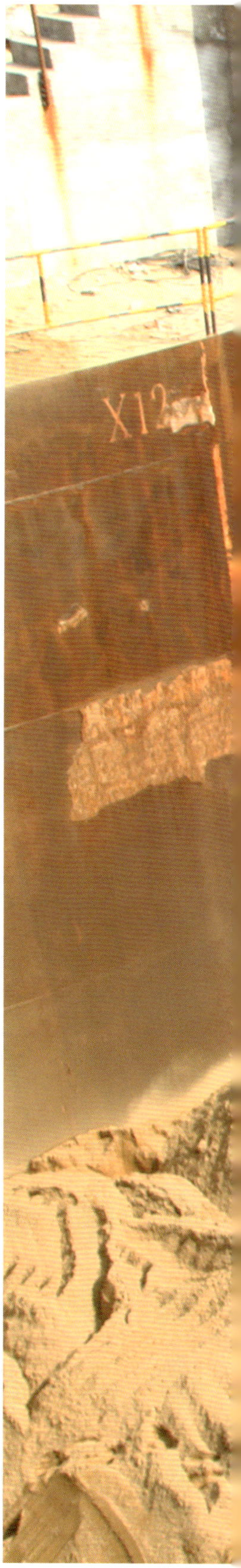

1. 大体积混凝土浇筑冷却水系统
Cooling Water System for Large Volume Concrete Casting

2. 西人工岛暗埋段中埋式止水带安装
Installation of the Embedded Water-Stop in the Buried Section on West Man-Made Island

3. 东人工岛暗埋段二次止水墙
Secondary Water-Stop Wall in the Buried Section of East Man-Made Island

4. 西人工岛暗埋段二次止水墙回填
Secondary Water-Stop Wall Backfilling in the Buried Section of West Man-Made Island

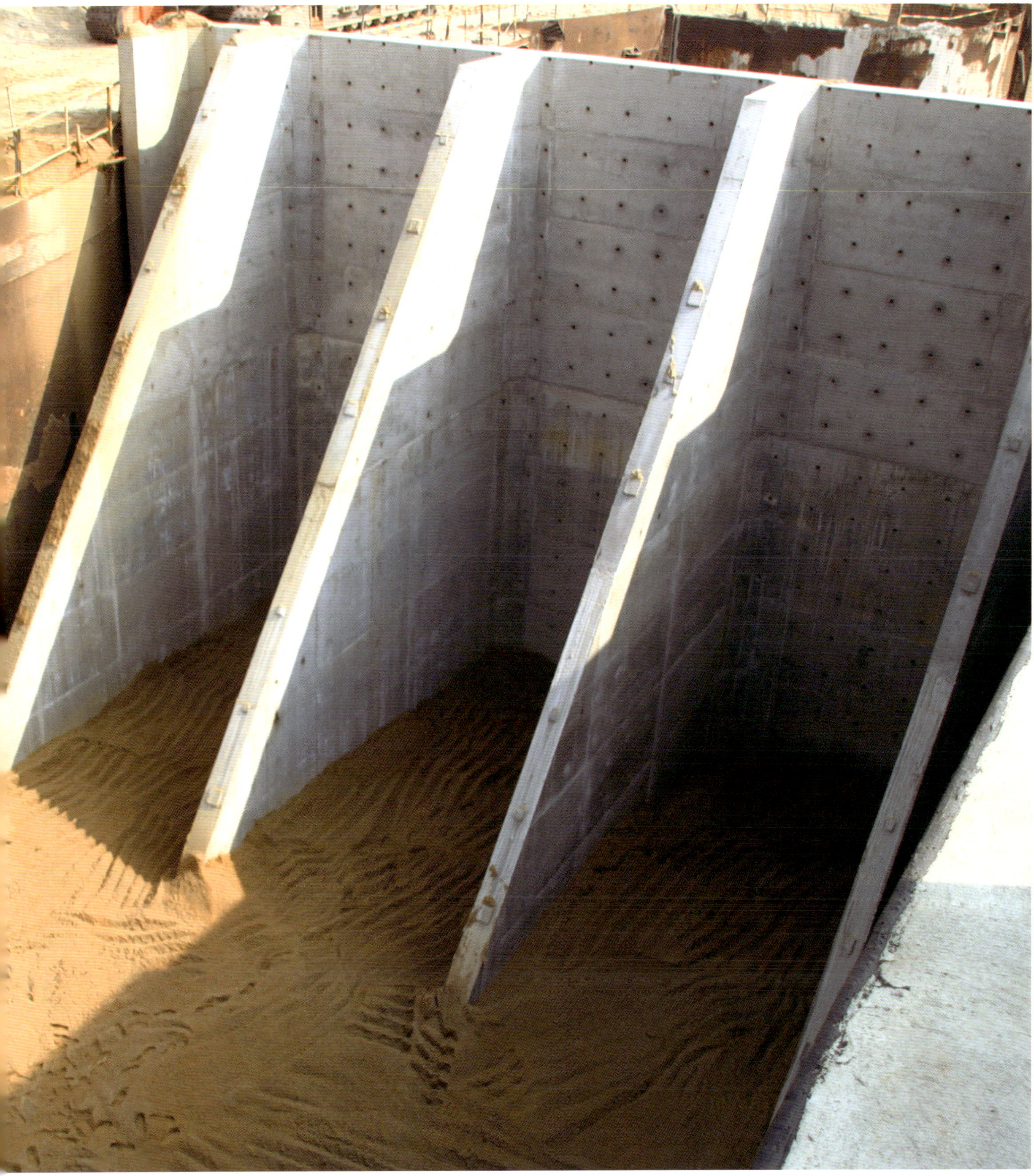

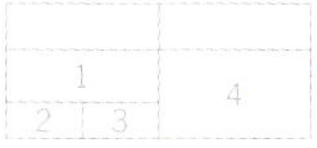

1. 西人工岛暗埋段隧道
Tunnel in the Buried Section of West Man-Made Island
2. 东人工岛岛隧结合部碎石垫层铺设
Rubble Bedding at the Island-Tunnel Junction on East Man-Made Island
3. 东人工岛岛隧结合部防淤盖板安装
Installation of the Silt Prevention Cover at the Island-Tunnel Junction on East Man-Made Island
4. 东人工岛暗埋段钢封门回水试验
Backwater Test on the Steel Sealing Devices in the Buried Section on East Man-Made Island

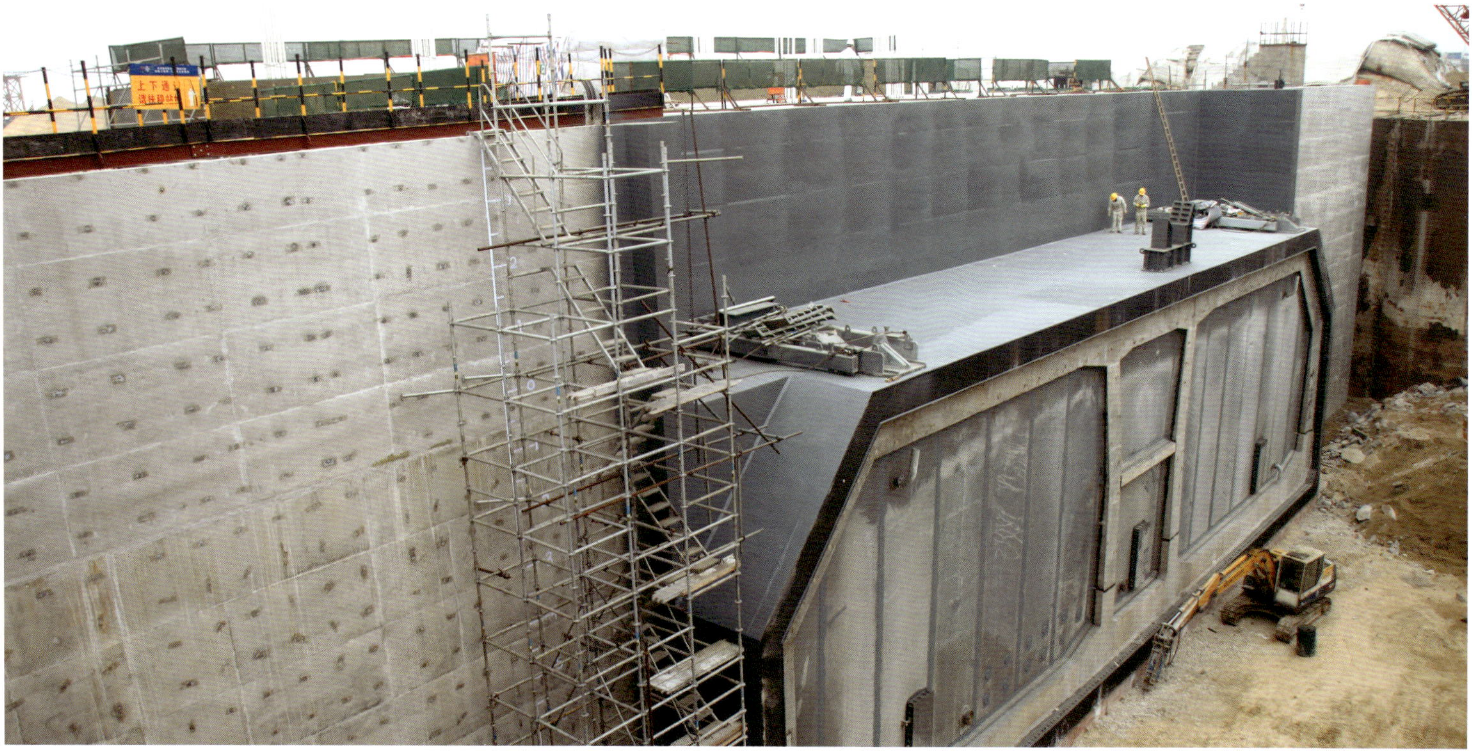

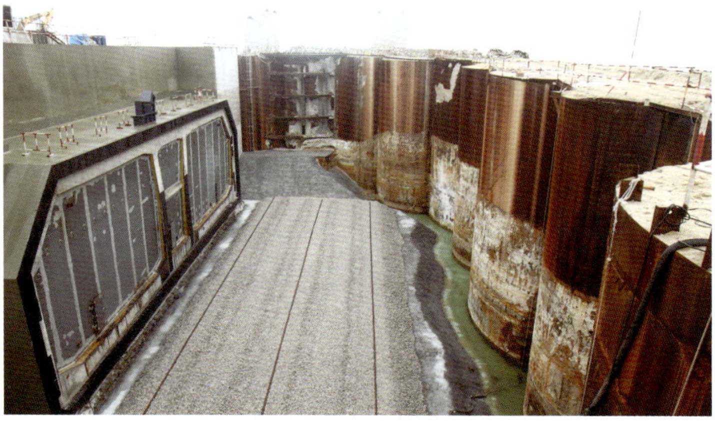

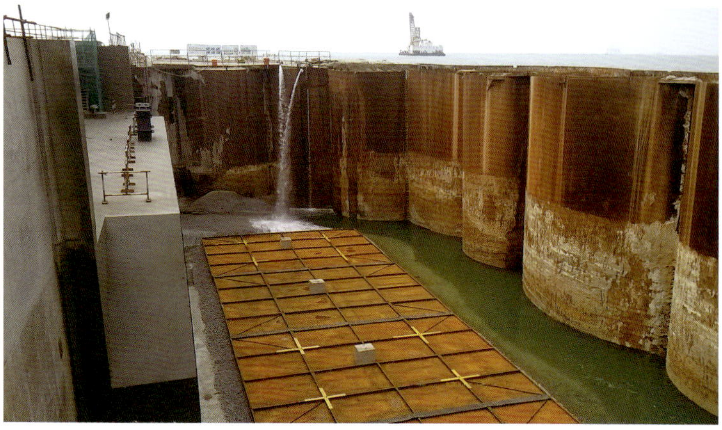

岛隧结合部用于实现沉管与岛上隧道的对接。施工分为基础加固、岛上二次止水挡水结构施工、暗埋段止推段施工、钢封门施工、钢圆筒切除、沉管基础施工等工序。其中，钢圆筒切除为水下-16.5米切割，并进行钢圆筒顶部处理。

The part connecting the island and the tunnel was used for the butt joint between the immersed tube and the island tunnel. The construction was divided into such different stages as foundation reinforcement, construction of secondary water-stop and water-blocking structures, construction of the thrust part of the buried section, steel sealing devices installation, resection of the steel cylinders, base construction for the immersed tubes, etc. By the way, the resection of the steel cylinders was conducted -16.5 meters under the water and the top part of the steel cylinders also underwent relevant operation.

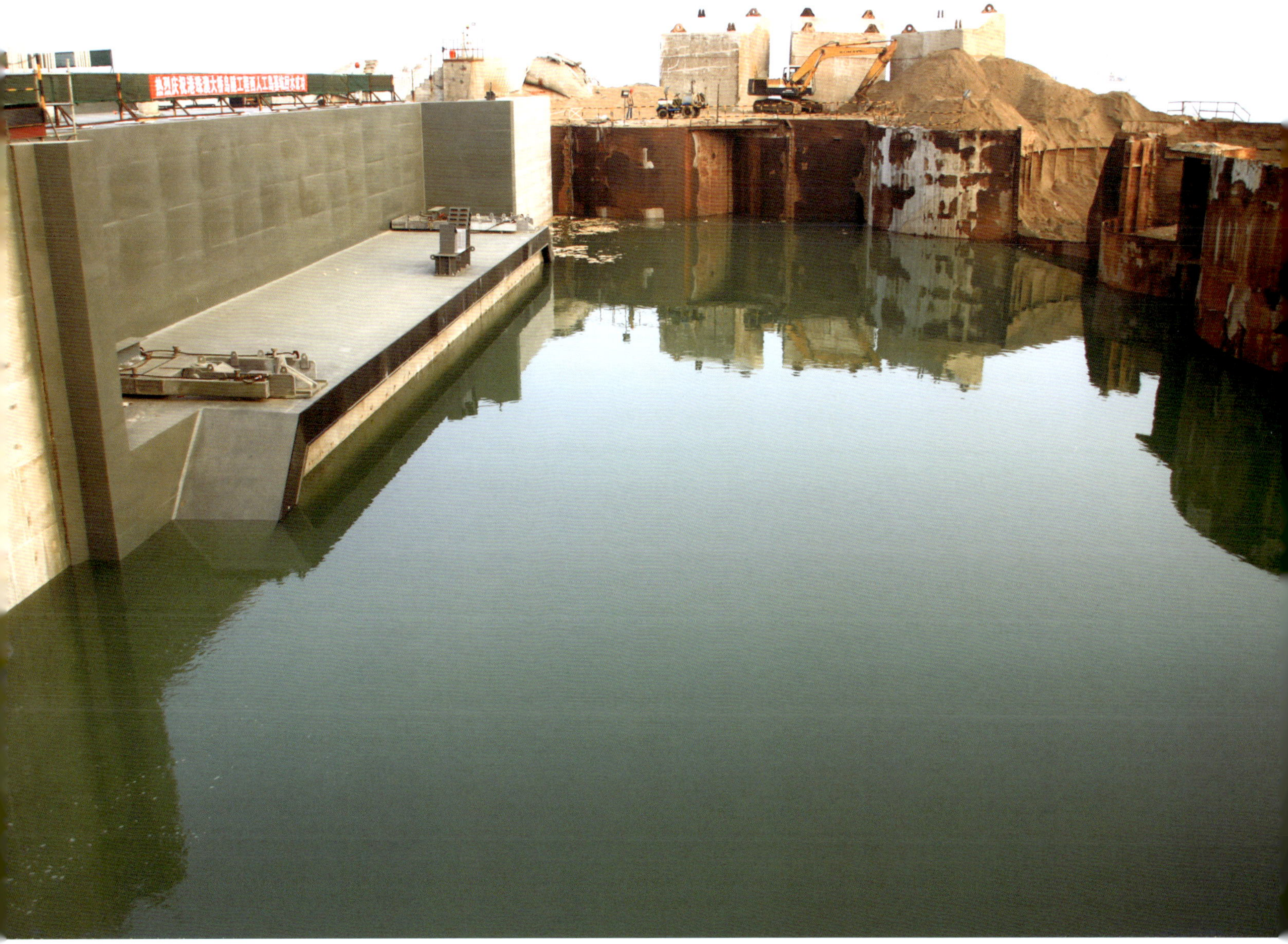

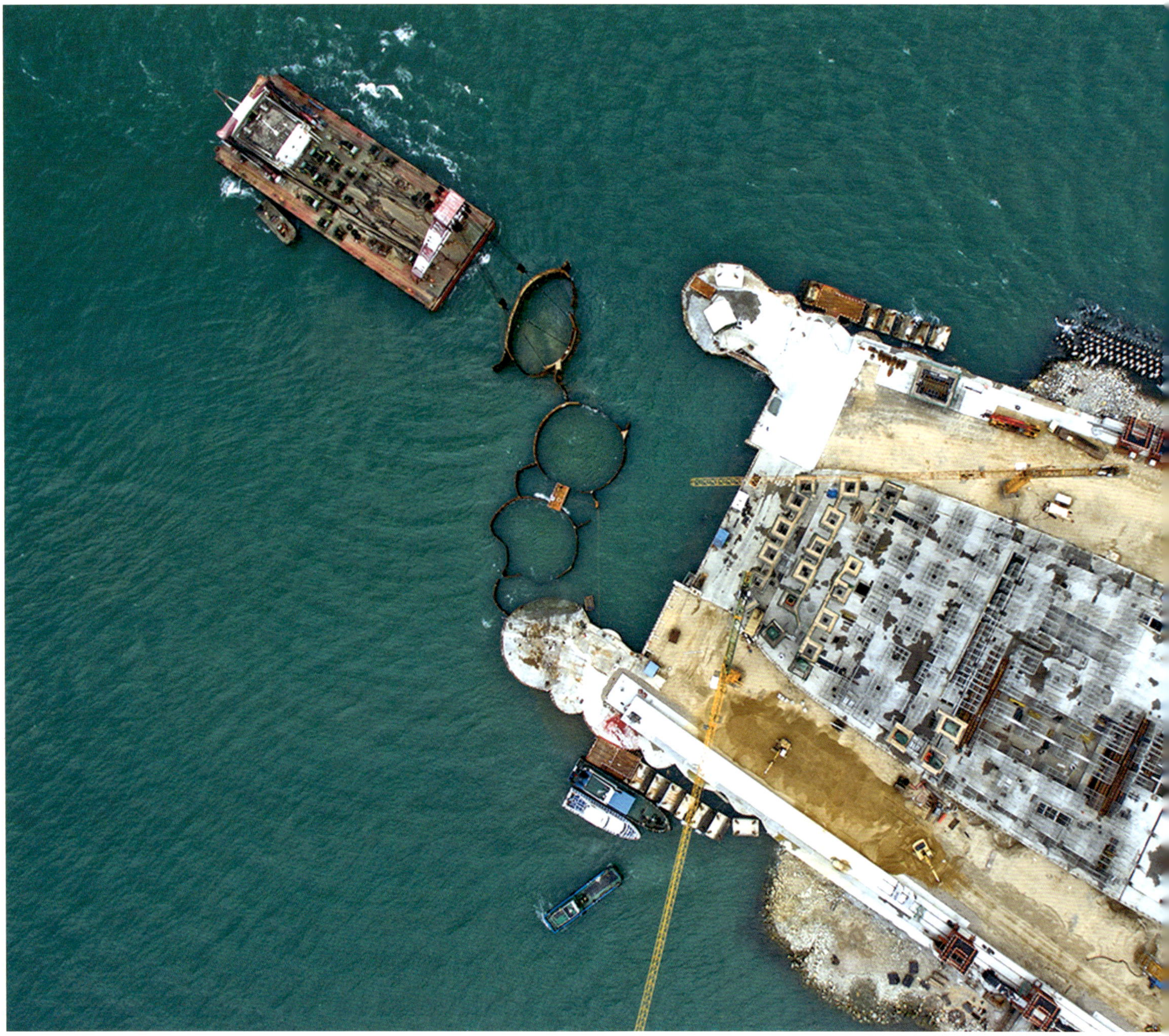

1	2
	3

1. 东人工岛岛头钢圆筒拆除
Removal of the Steel Cylinder at the Head Part of East Man-Made Island
2. 岛头钢圆筒拆除前筒内挖砂
Sand Dredging in the Steel Cylinder before the Cylinder Removal
3. 钢圆筒拆除吊离
Removal of the Steel Cylinder

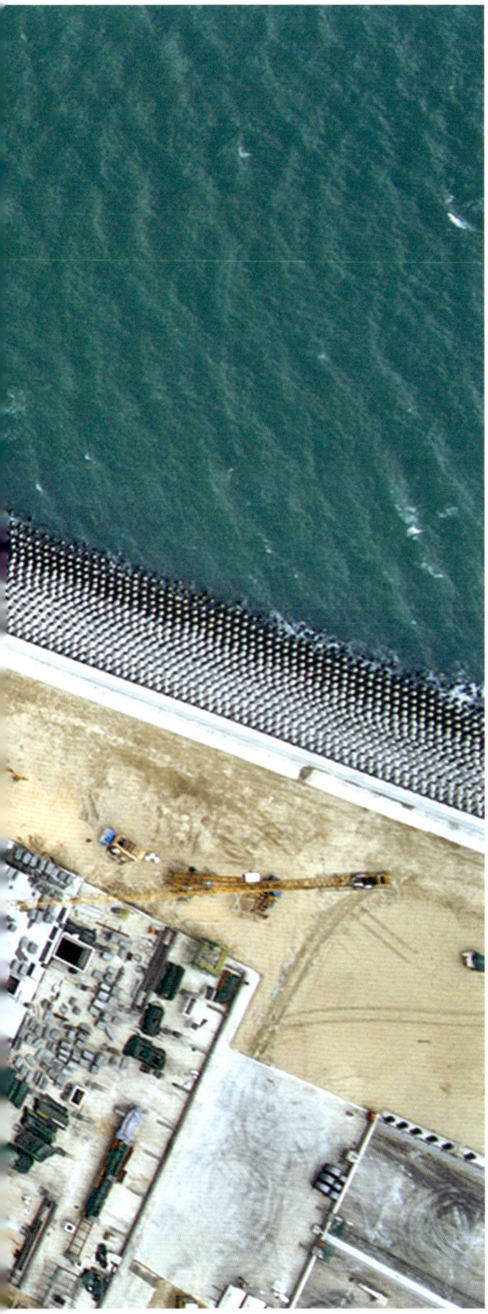

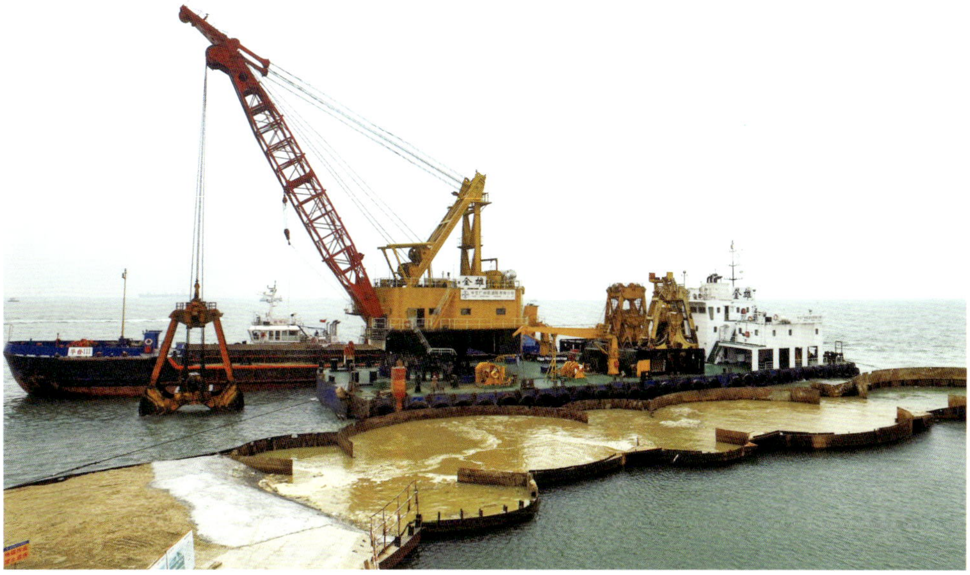

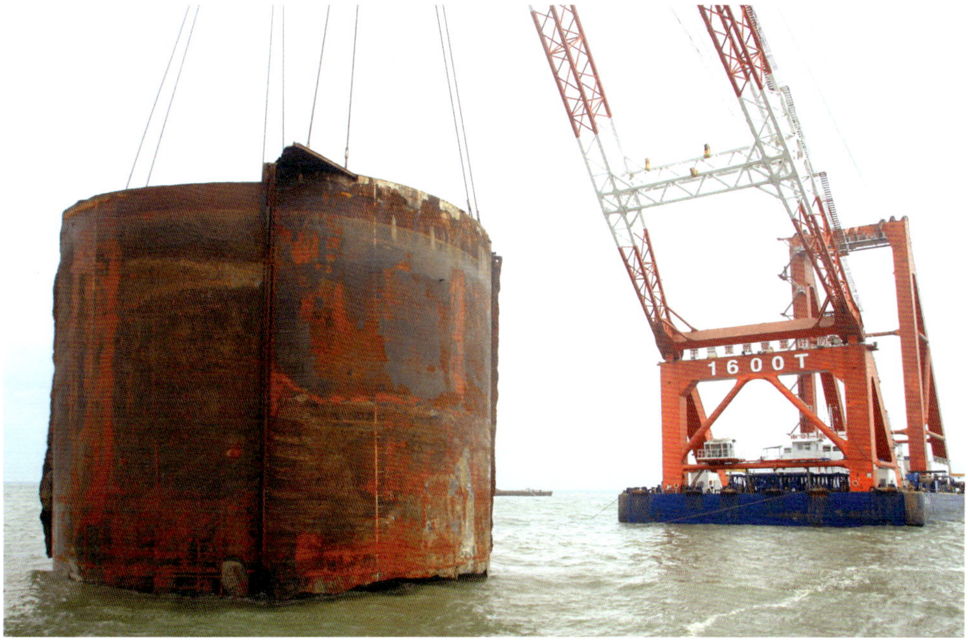
1600T

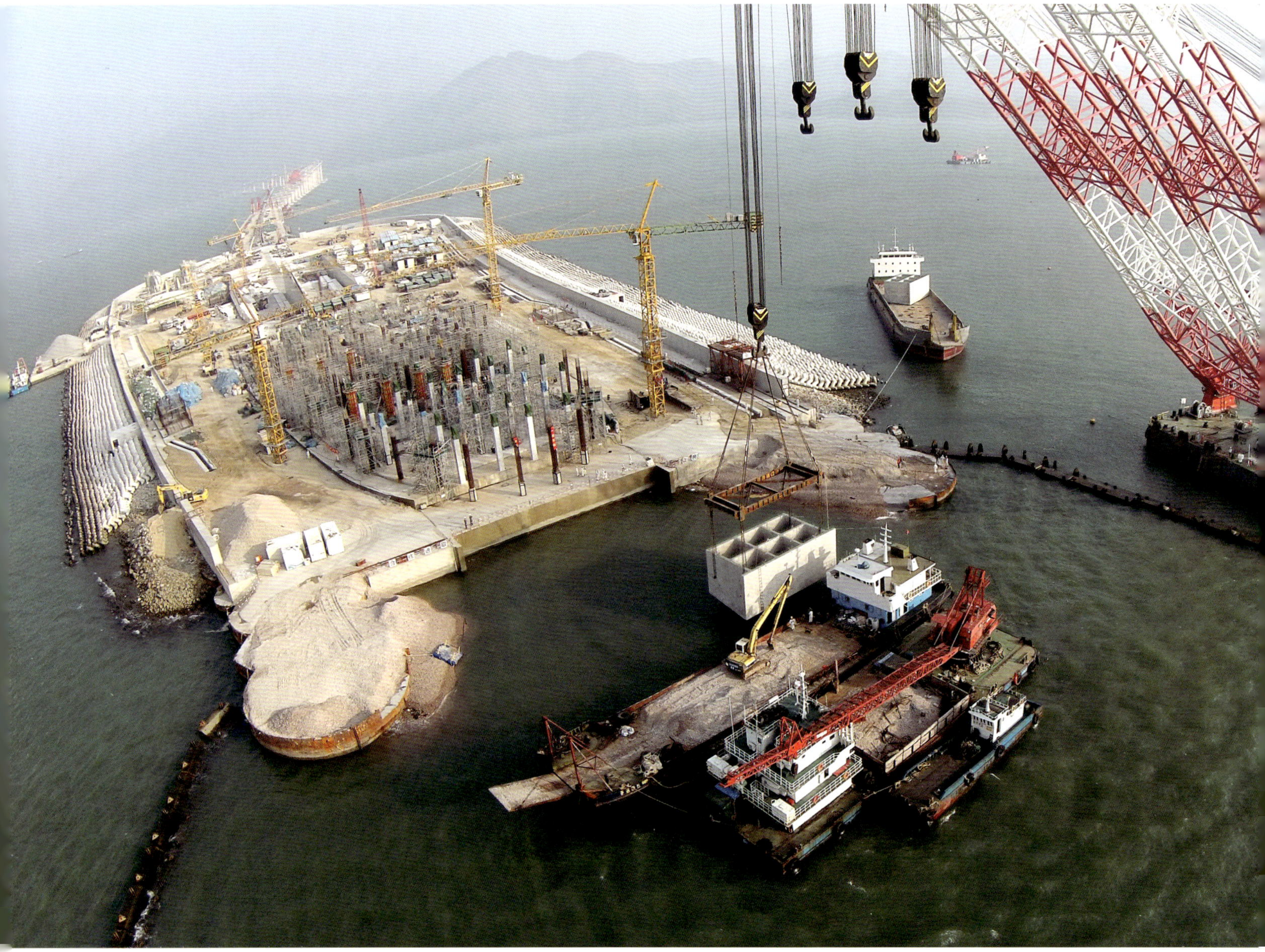

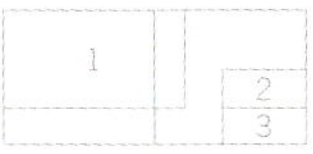

1. 东人工岛减载沉箱安装
Load-Shedding Caisson Installation on East Man-Made Island

2. 轻质材料回填
Backfill of Lightweight Materials

3. 减载沉箱安装完毕
Loading-Shedding Caisson Installation Completed

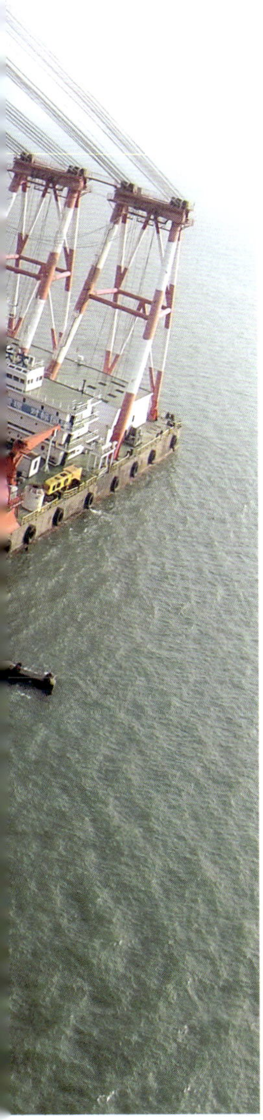

减载沉箱：在岛隧结合段采用减载沉箱结构，回填轻质材料，以减轻沉管上部荷载。沉箱在工厂预制完成后运输至现场吊装。

Load-Shedding Caisson: Load-shedding caisson and backfilling light-weighted materials were applied to the link part between island and the tuunel to reduce the loads on upper tunnel elements. The caissions were fabricated in factory before being transported to the working site for installation.

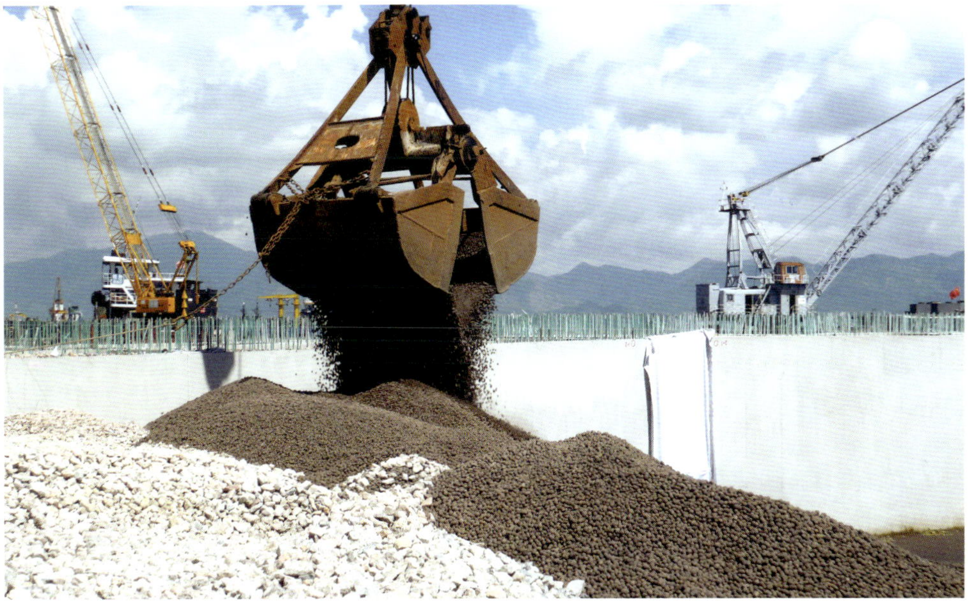

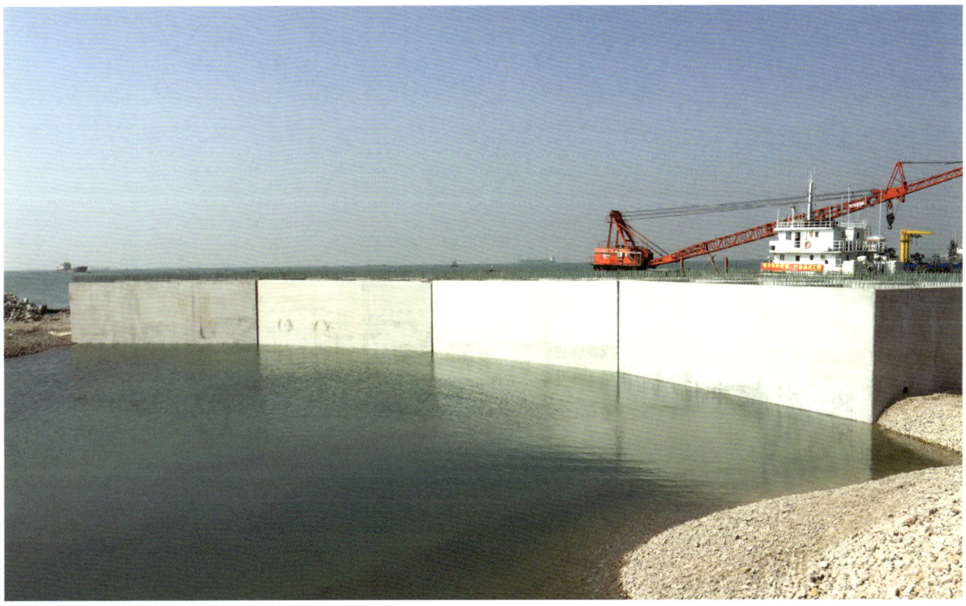

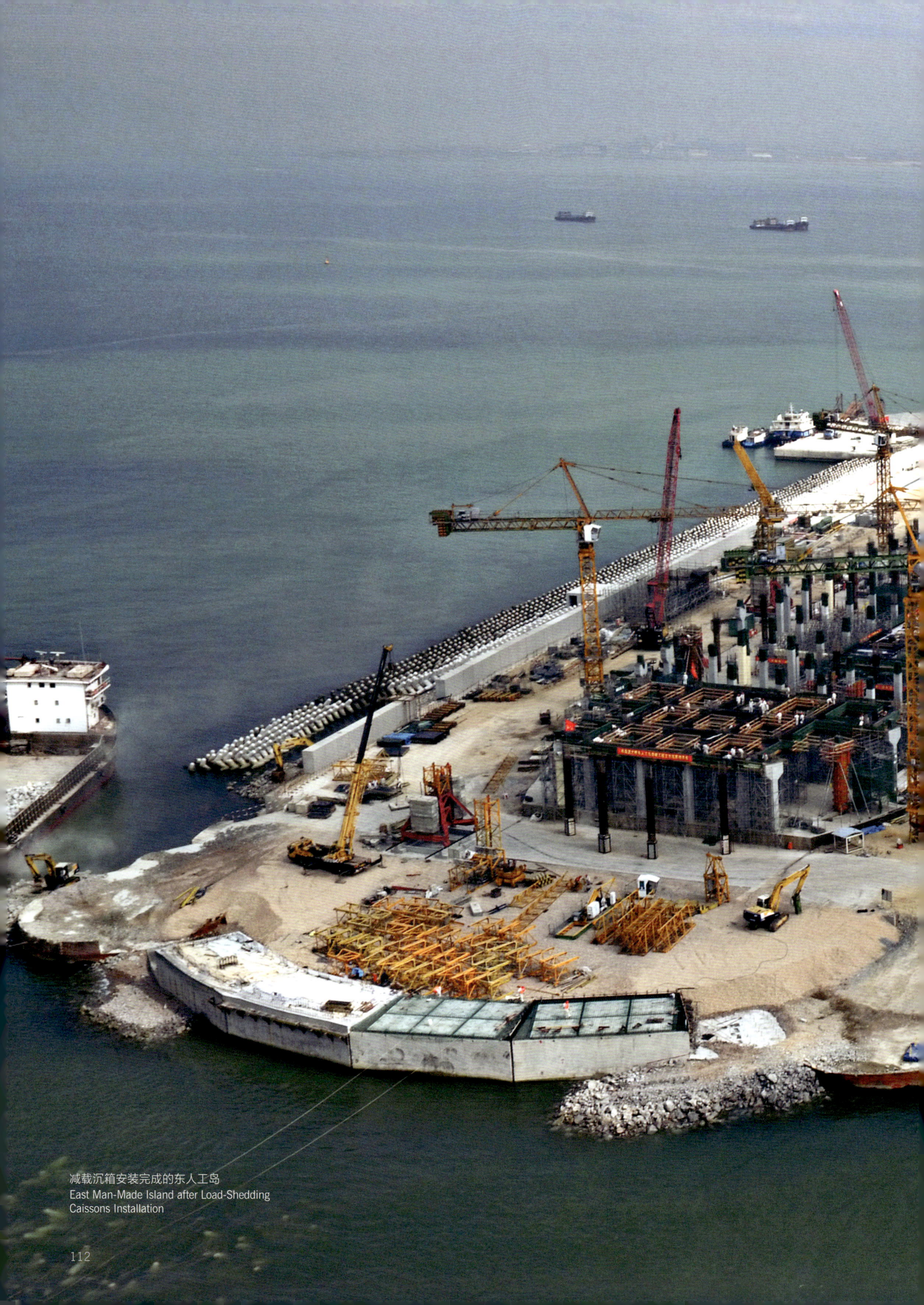

减载沉箱安装完成的东人工岛
East Man-Made Island after Load-Shedding Caissons Installation

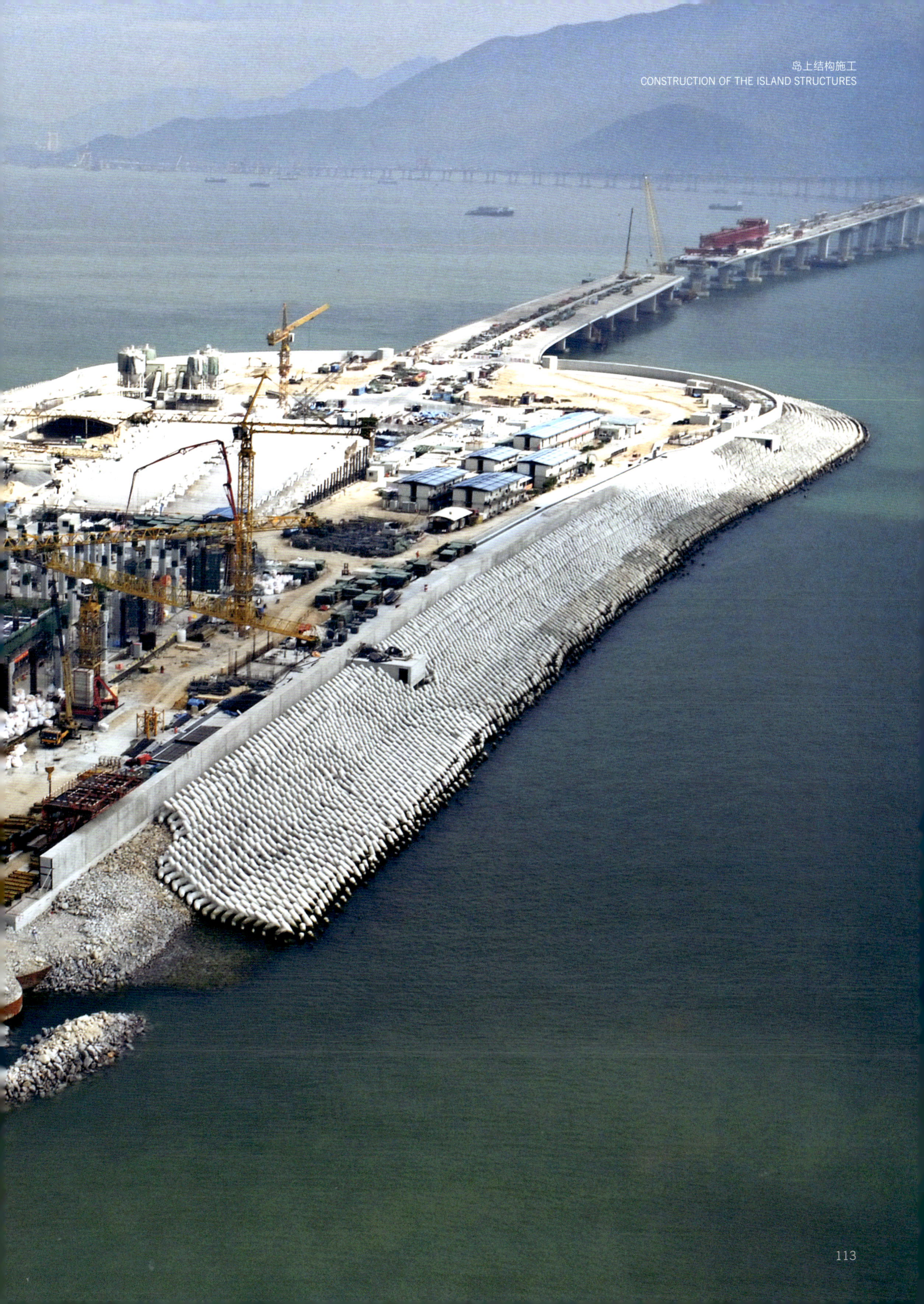

岛上结构施工
CONSTRUCTION OF THE ISLAND STRUCTURES

敞开段

OPEN SECTION

隧道敞开段分为减光段及U形槽段，减光段横断面为山形结构，宽度由41.12米变化至60.37米，双向六车道，设置2.98%纵坡，与隧道主体结构相同，设计使用年限均为120年，结构安全等级及防水等级为一级。U形槽段长217米，两侧设置趾板；减光段部分长110米，顶部设置有光栅结构。

The open section of the tunnel was divided into the light-reducing section and a U-shaped groove section. The light-reducing section was a triangular cross-section with a width changing from 41.12 meters to 60.37 meters and the slope gradient of 2.98%. There were six driving lanes in two directions in this section, similar to that of the major structure of the tunnel. The designed life span of the tunnel was 120 years, and the structural safety and waterproof levels were of Level 1. The U-shaped groove was 217 meters long, with toe boards on both sides. The light-reducing section was 110 meters long with a grating structure on the top.

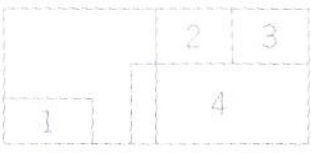

1. 隧道敞开段
   Open Section of the Tunnel
2. 隧道敞开段底板浇筑
   Casting of the Bottom Plate in the Open Section of the Tunnel
3. 隧道敞开段中隔墙模板安装
   Installation of the Partition Wall Frame in the Open Section of the Tunnel
4. 隧道敞开段底板、中隔墙钢筋笼绑扎
   Steel Cage Binding for the Bottom Plate and the Partition Wall in the Open Section of the Tunnel

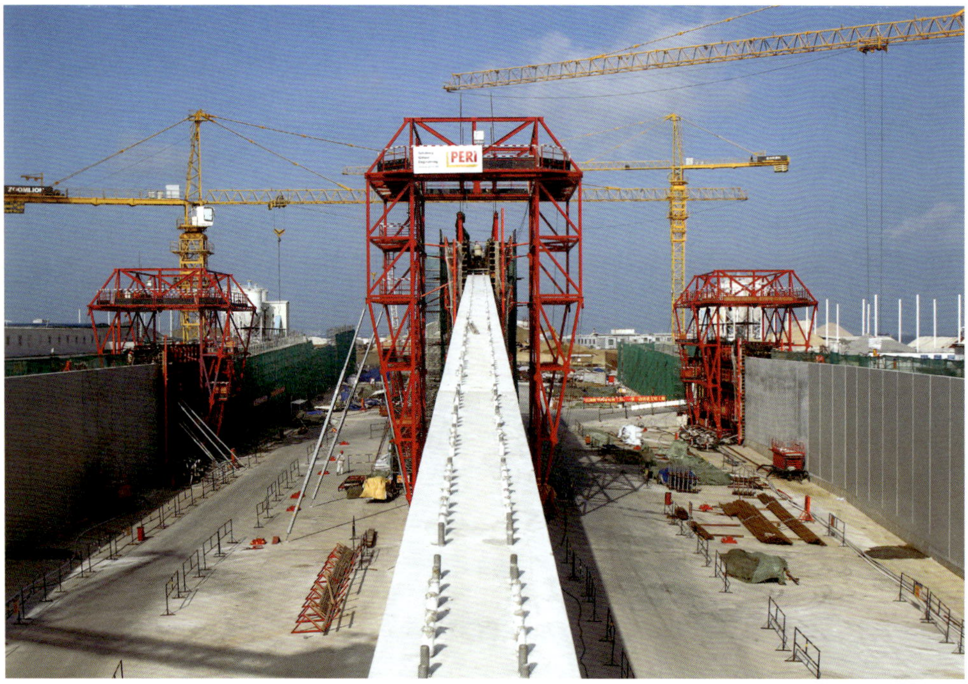

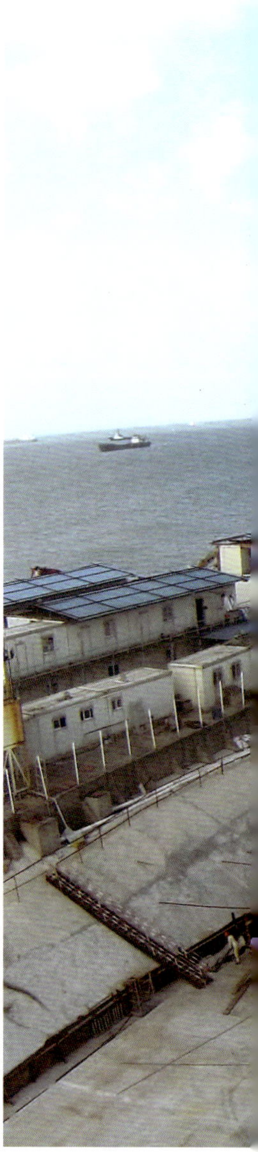

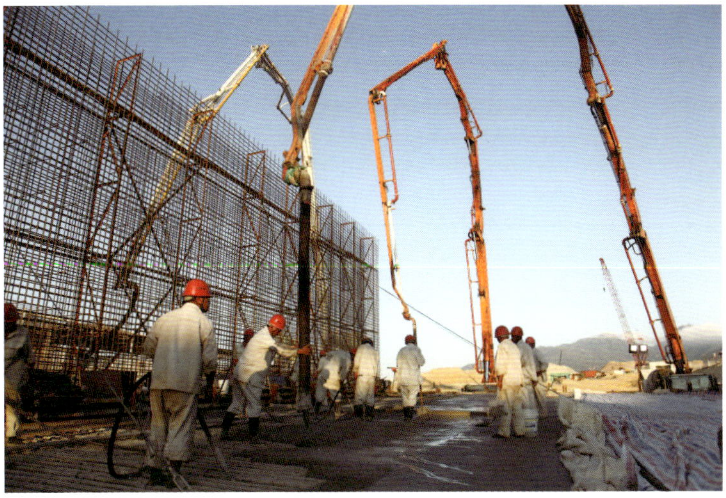

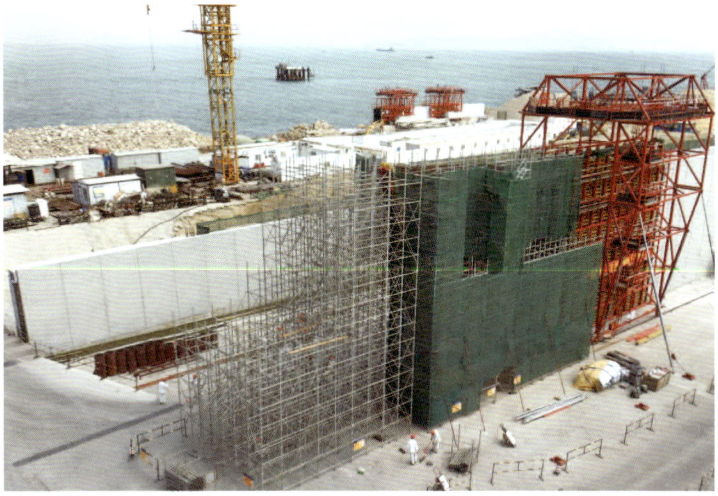

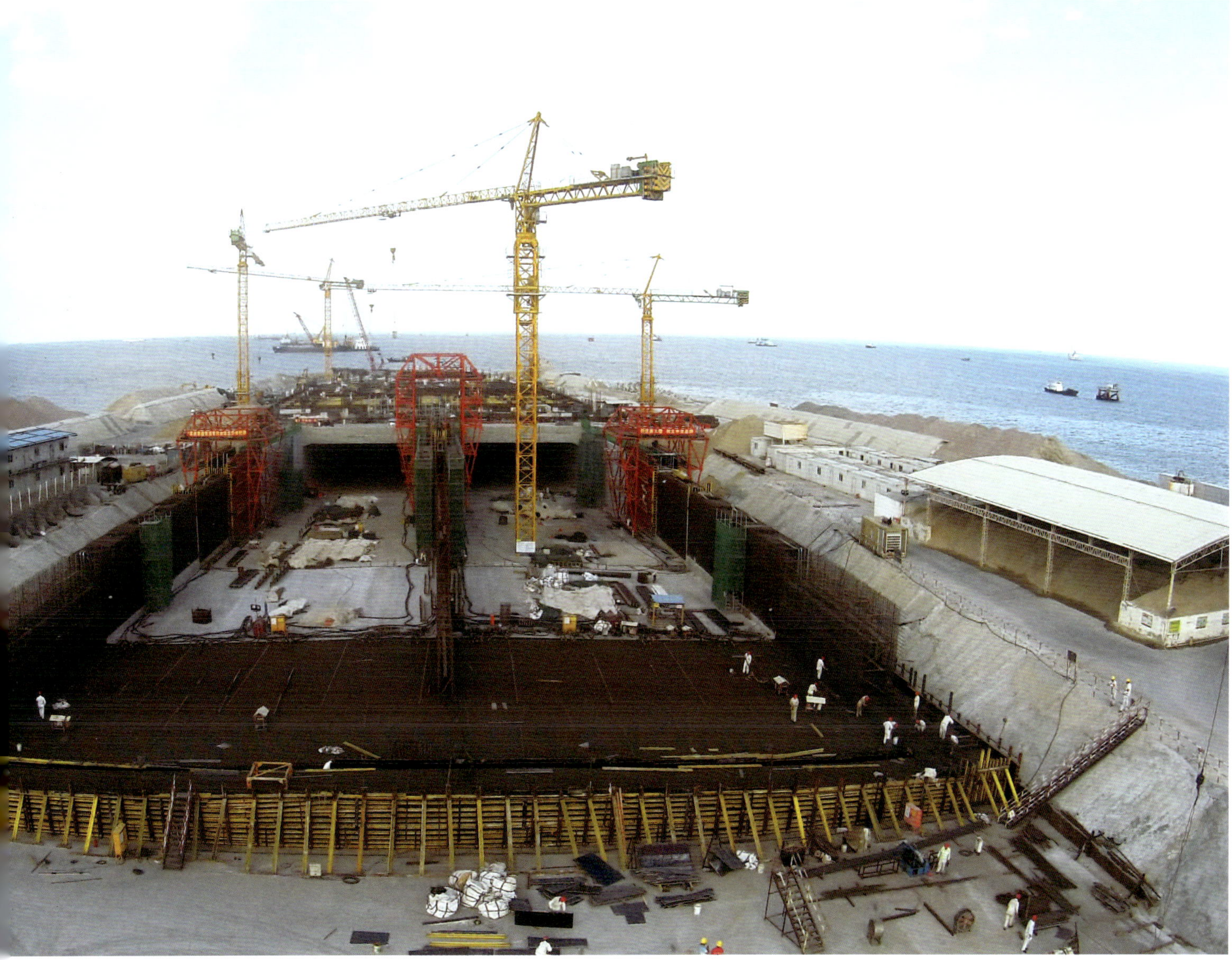

浇筑成型的敞开段
Well-Cast Open Section

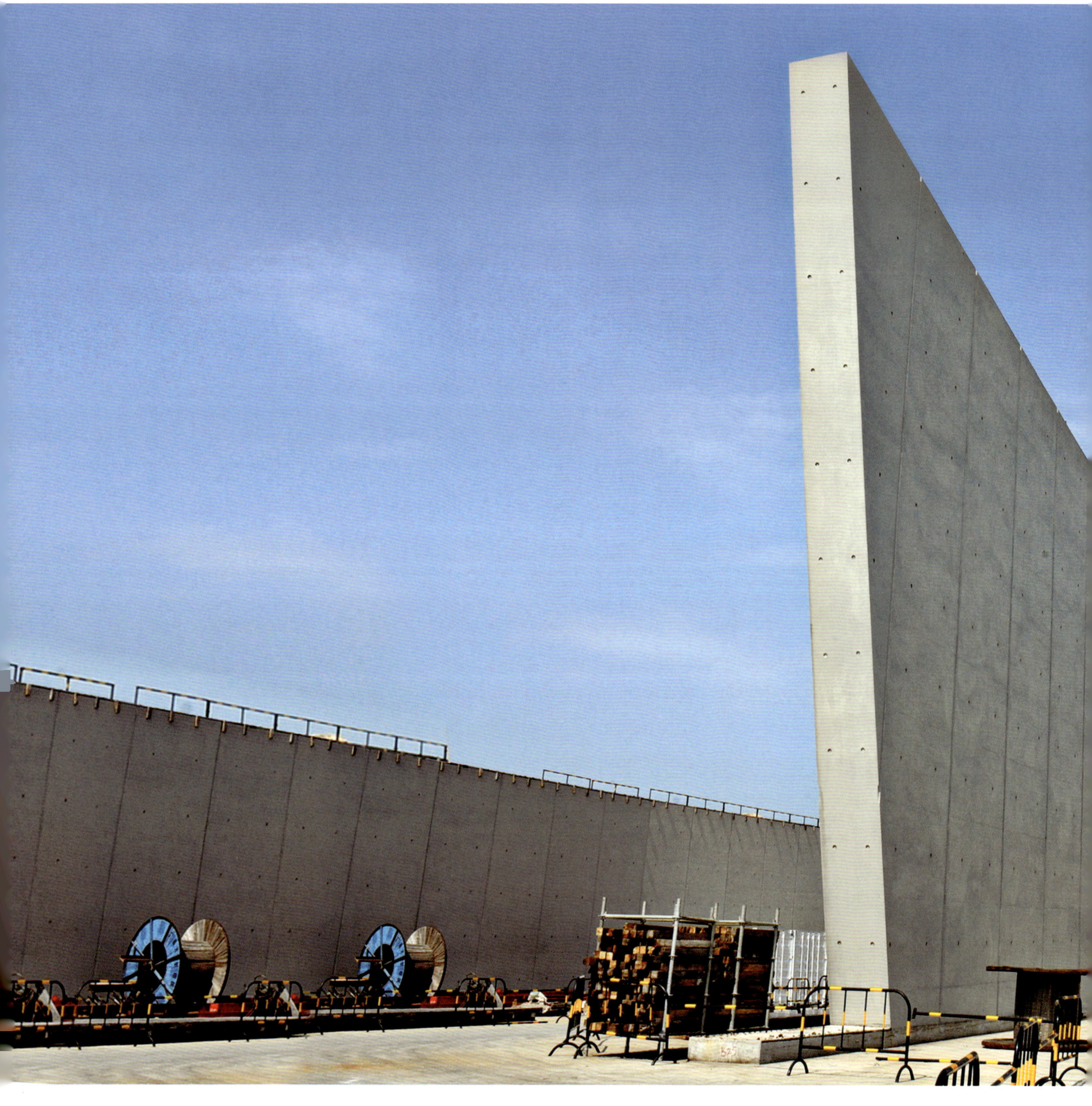

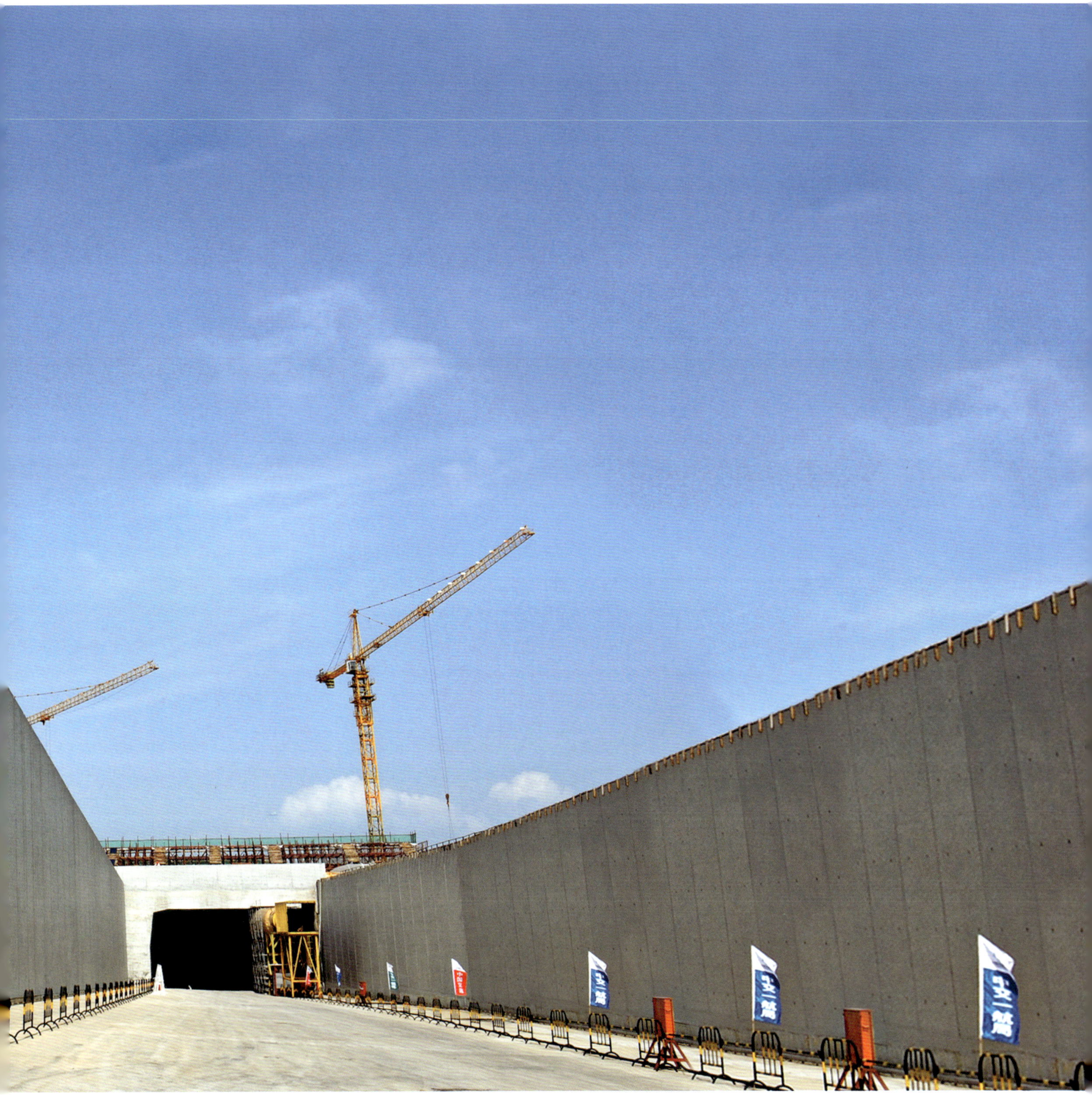

减光罩
LIGHT-REDUCING GRATING

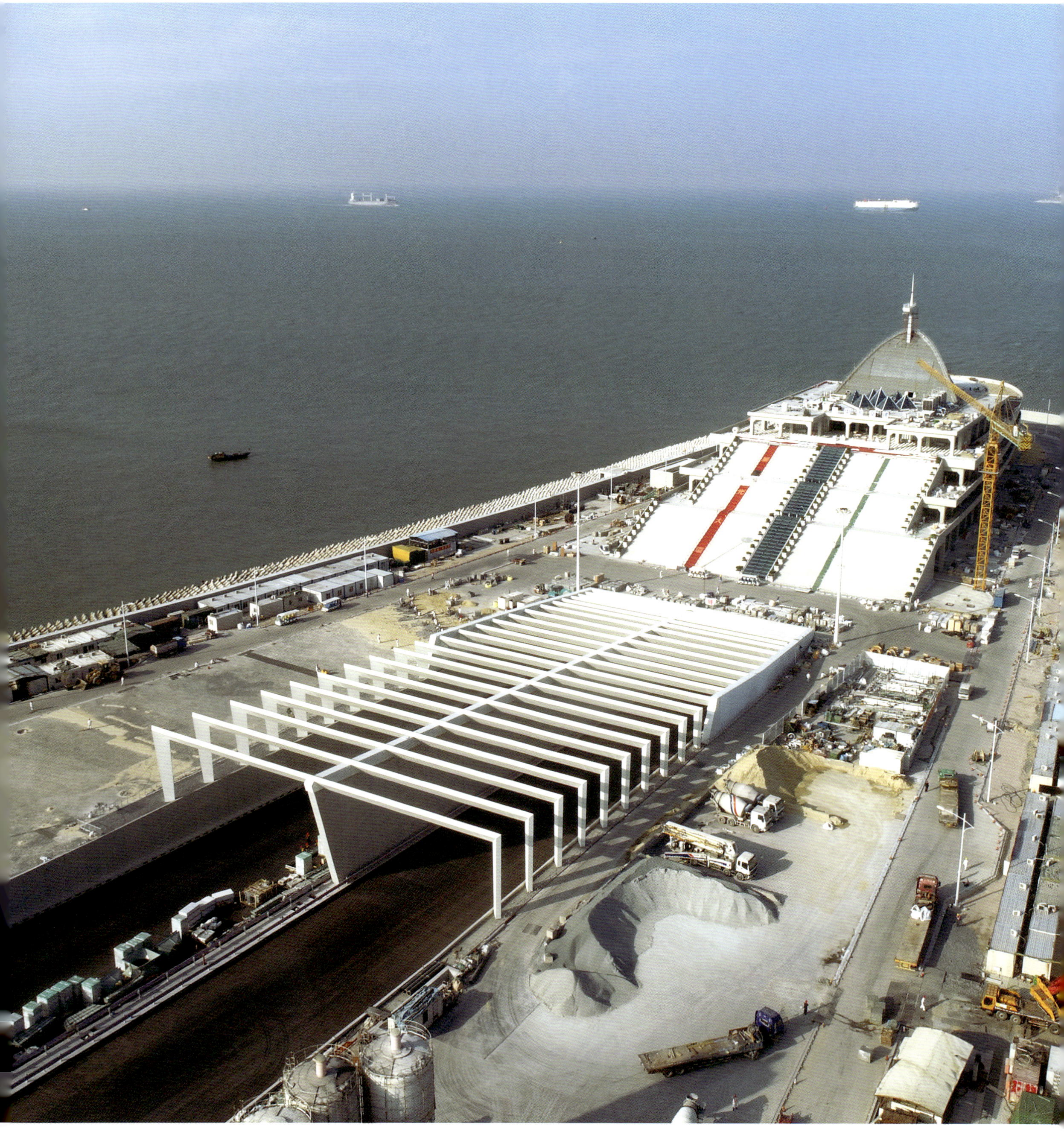

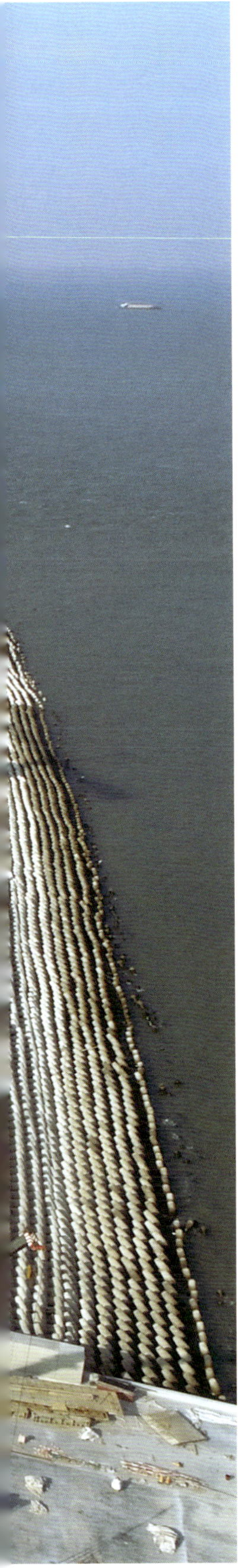

减光罩位于隧道出入口，门式百叶型钢架结构。东、西人工岛减光罩各由22根构架组成，总重量2370吨，采用耐候钢。构架立柱在水平面上旋转45度，横梁在竖直面上倾斜45度，间距、高度依次递减，起到减光效果。

The light-reducing grating, a gate-type shutter-like steel structure, was located at exit and entrance of the tunnel. Each of the light-reducing gratings on the east and west man-made islands was made up of 22 weather-resistant steel beams with a total weight of 2370 tons. The vertical frame could rotate by 45 degrees on the horizontal plane, while the horizontal beam could tilt by 45 degrees on the vertical plane. The space between the gratings and the height of the vertical frames decrease in turn, thus producing the light-reducing effect.

1. 东人工岛减光罩
   Light-Reducing Grating on East Man-Made Island
2. 减光罩钢构件安装
   Installation of the Steel Components Parts of the Light-Reducing Grating

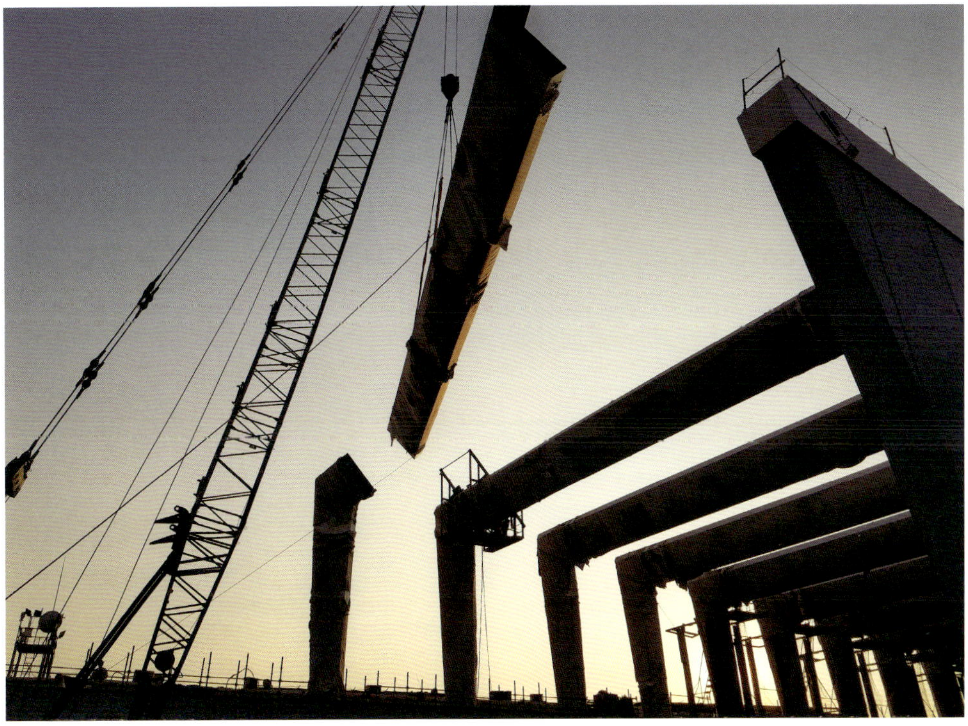

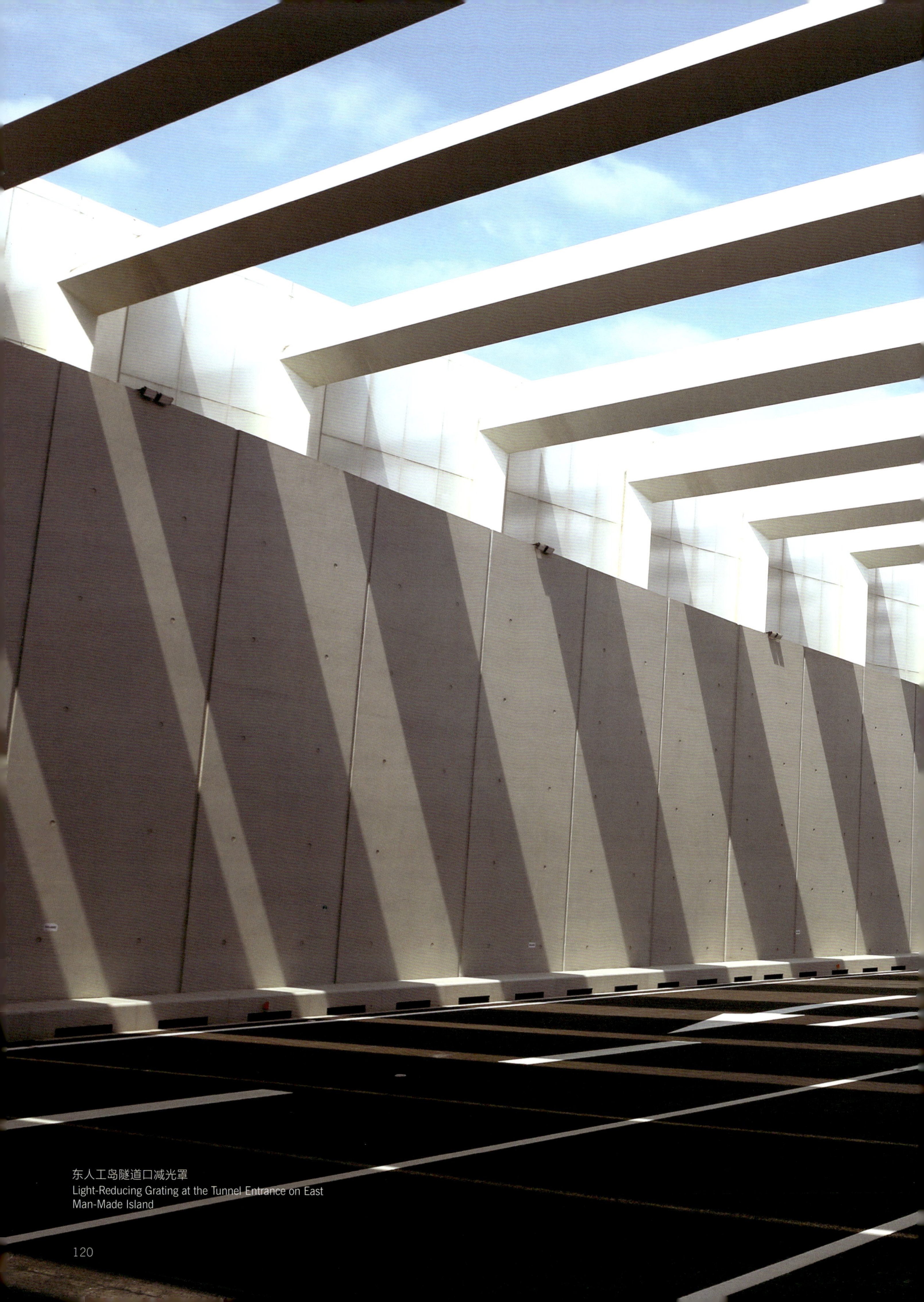

东人工岛隧道口减光罩
Light-Reducing Grating at the Tunnel Entrance on East Man-Made Island

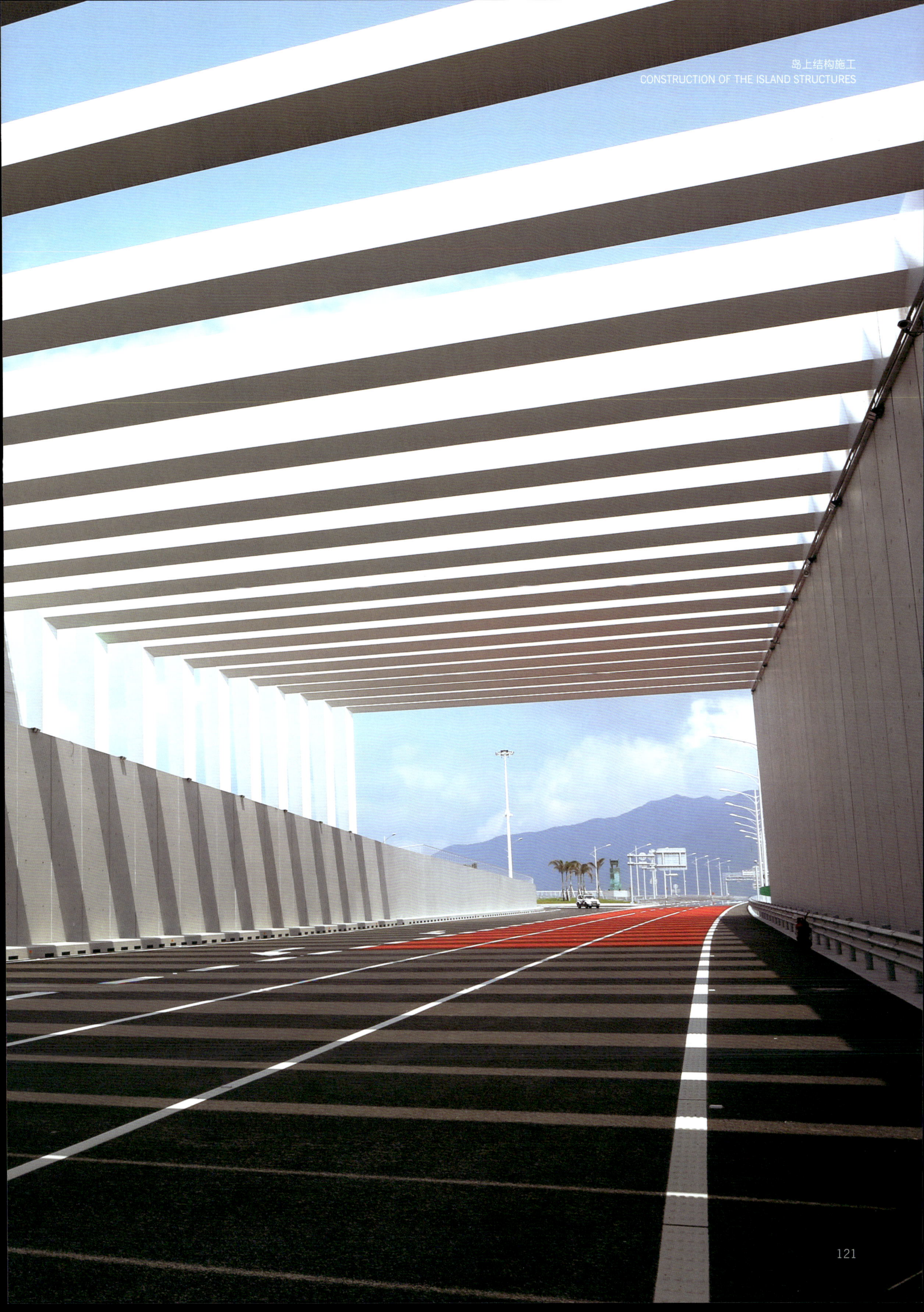

岛壁结构
ISLAND REVETMENT

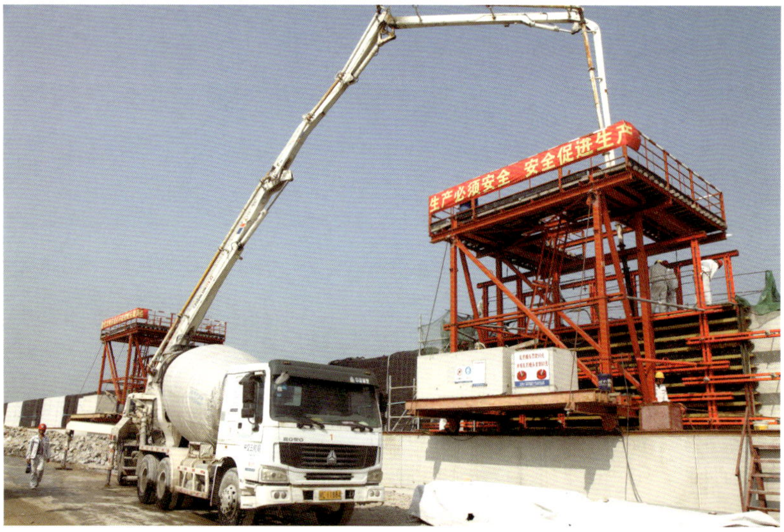

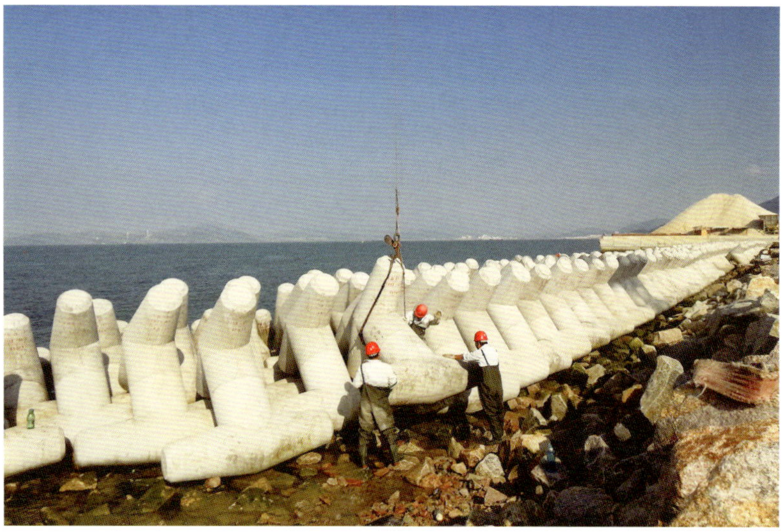

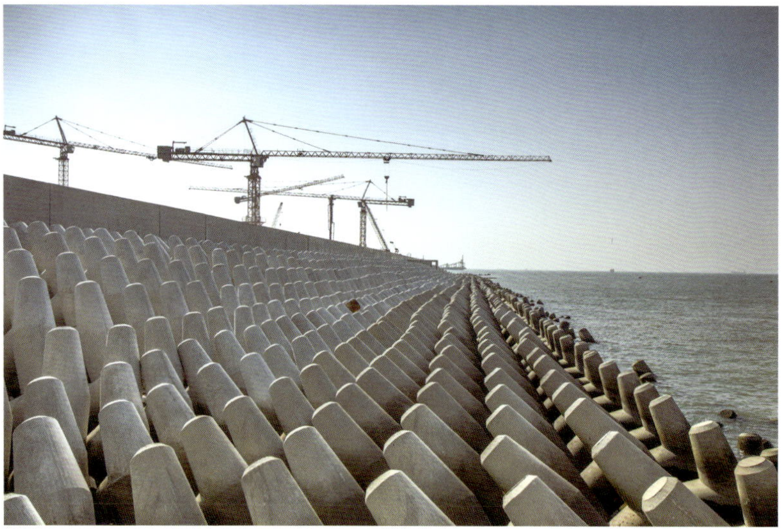

1. 东人工岛挡浪墙墙身混凝土浇筑
Concrete Placement for the Wave-Blocking Wall on East Man-Made Island
2. 人工岛岛壁扭工字块安装
Installation of the Twisted Blocks on the Fending Wall of the Man-Made Island
3. 西人工岛防浪堤
Anti-wave Dyke of West Man-Made Island
4. 东人工岛挡浪墙
Wave-Blocking Wall of East Man-Made Island

人工岛挡浪墙采用重力式素混凝土结构。其主要结构断面形式为"L"形。挡浪墙混凝土强度等级为C30，墙身为清水混凝土，西人工岛挡浪墙顶标高8.0—9.5米，全长1287米；东人工岛挡浪墙顶标高8.0—8.5米，全长为1386米。每两段挡浪墙间的结构缝宽度为10毫米，以纵向每3米设置一道造型缝。

The revetment of the man-made islands adopted the gravity plain concrete structure. The cross section of its main structure took the "L" shape. The concrete strength of the wave-blocking wall, made of fair-faced concrete, was C30, and the elevation of the wall of West Man-Made Island was 8.0 to 9.5 meters, and the total length was 1287 meters. The elevation of the wave-blocking wall of East Man-Made Island was 8.0-8.5 meters, and the total length was 1386 meters. The width of the structural joint between every two sections of the wave-blocking wall was 10 millimeters, and a modeling joint was kept every 3 meters in the longitudinal direction.

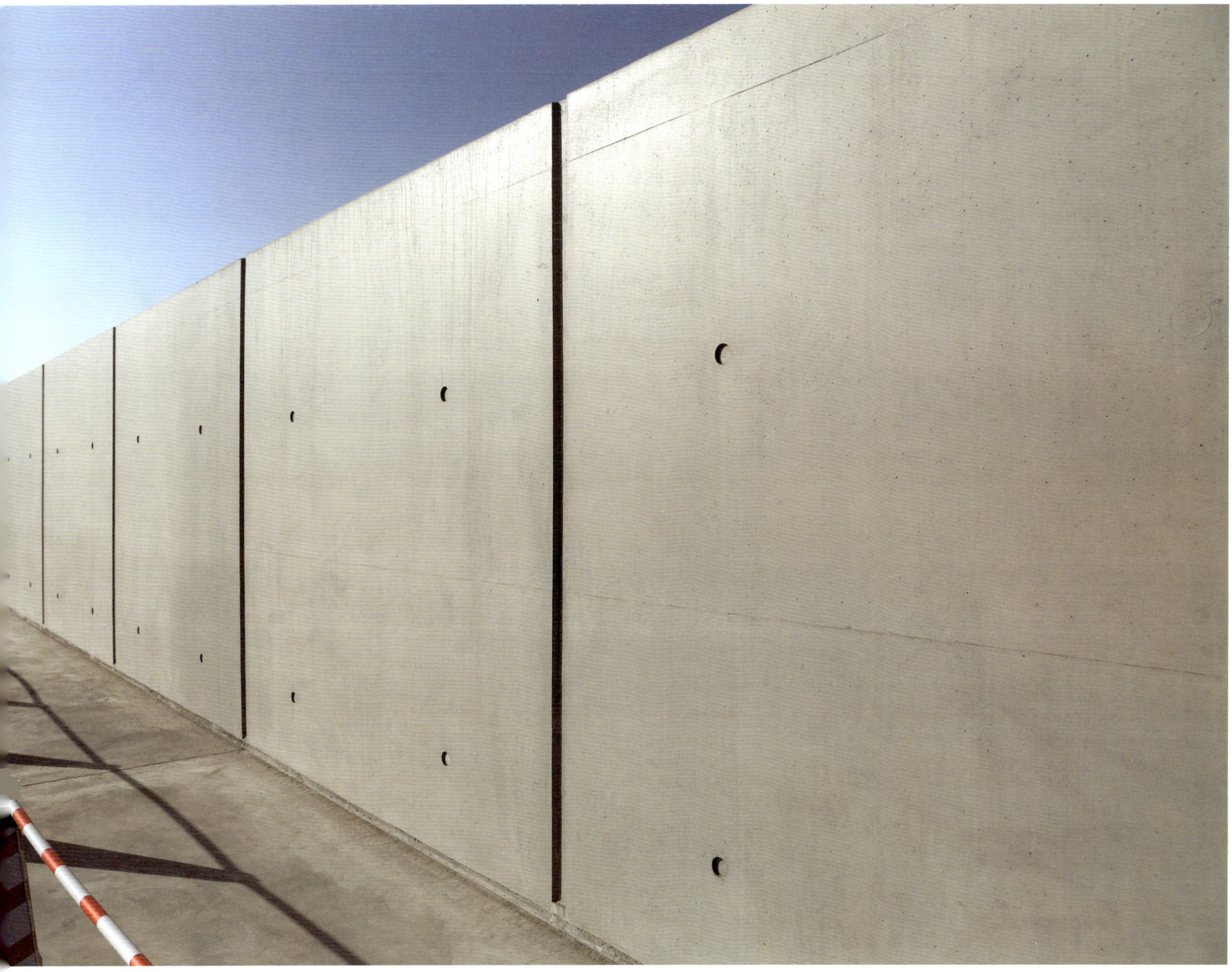

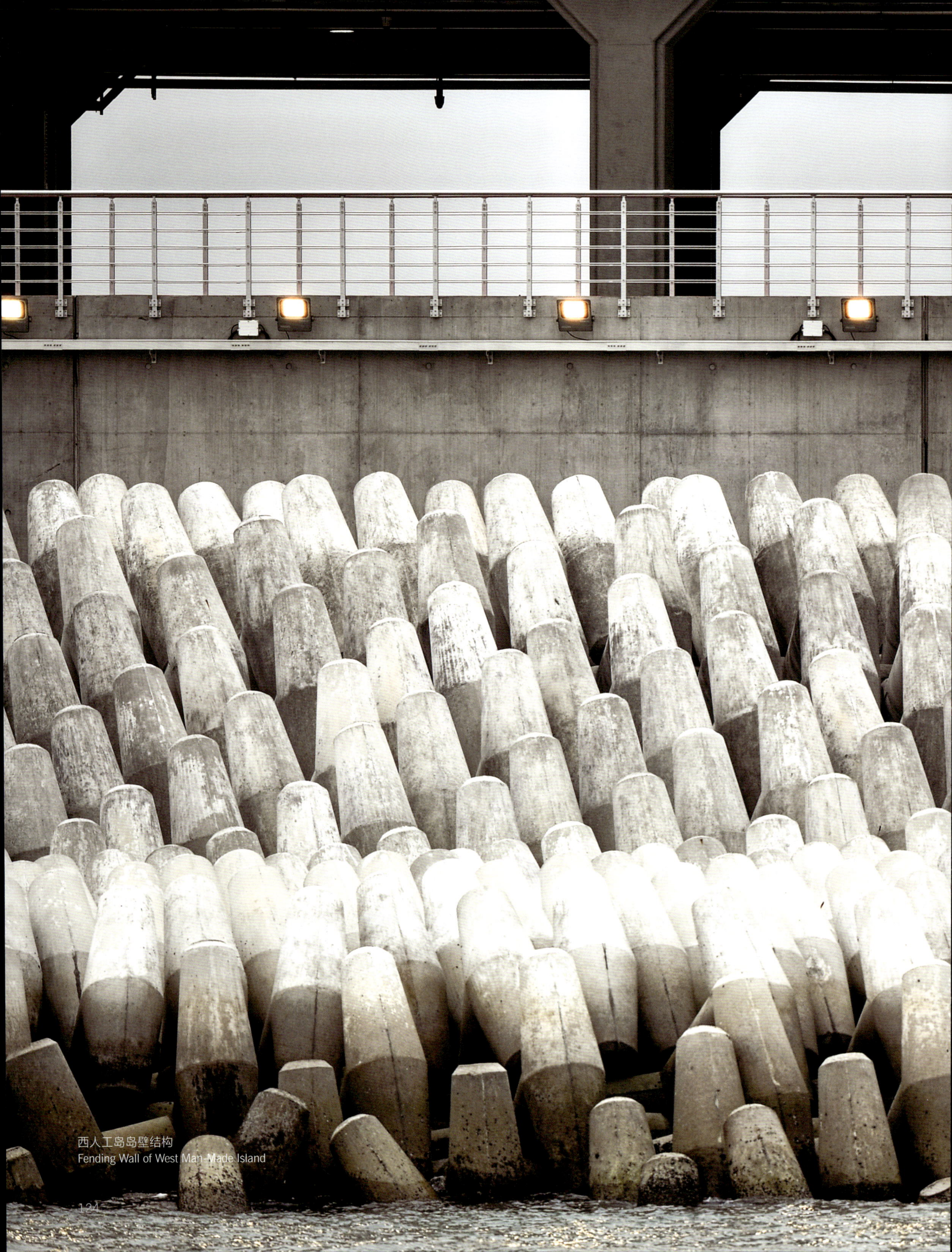

西人工岛岛壁结构
Fending Wall of West Man-Made Island

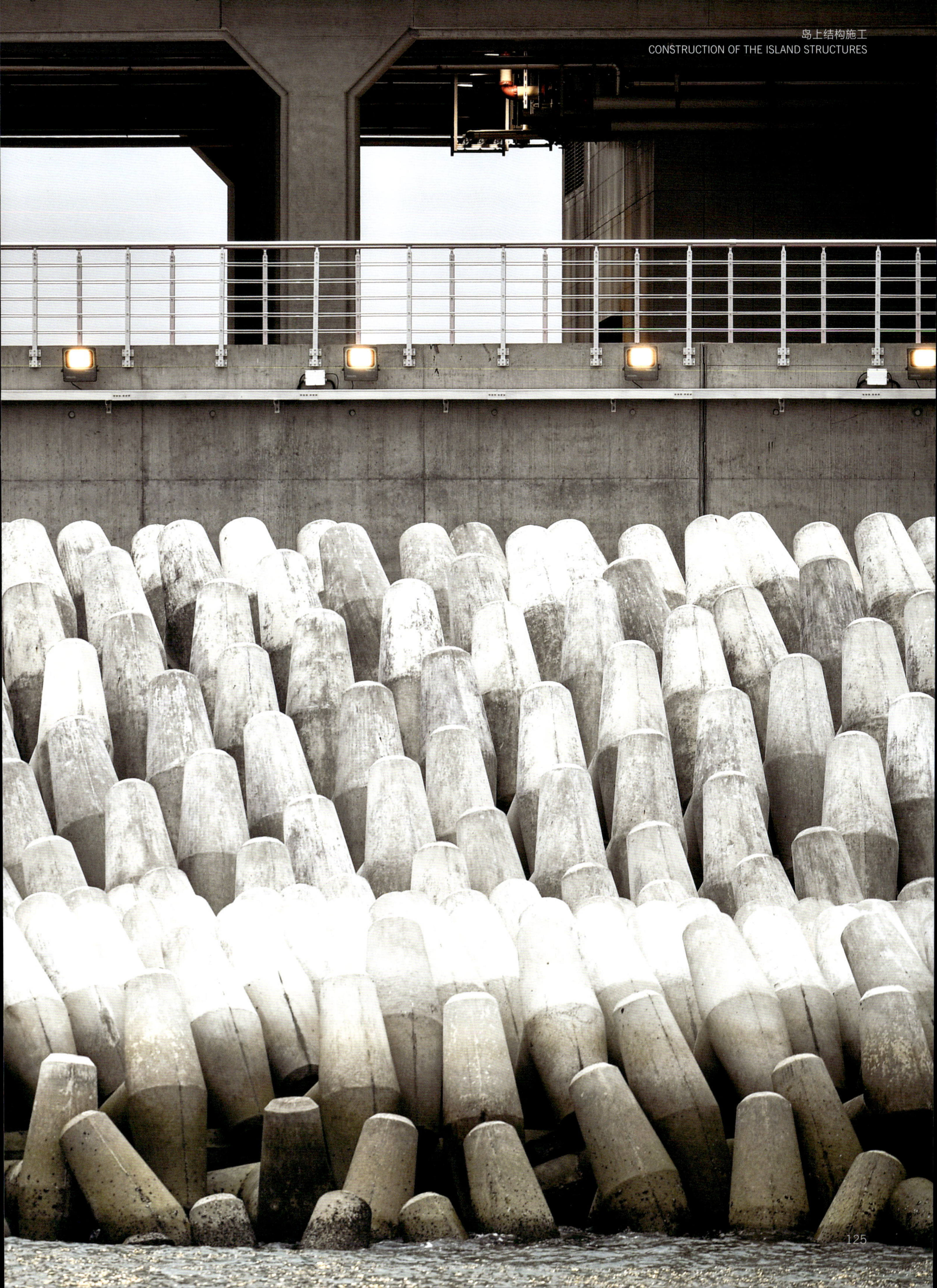

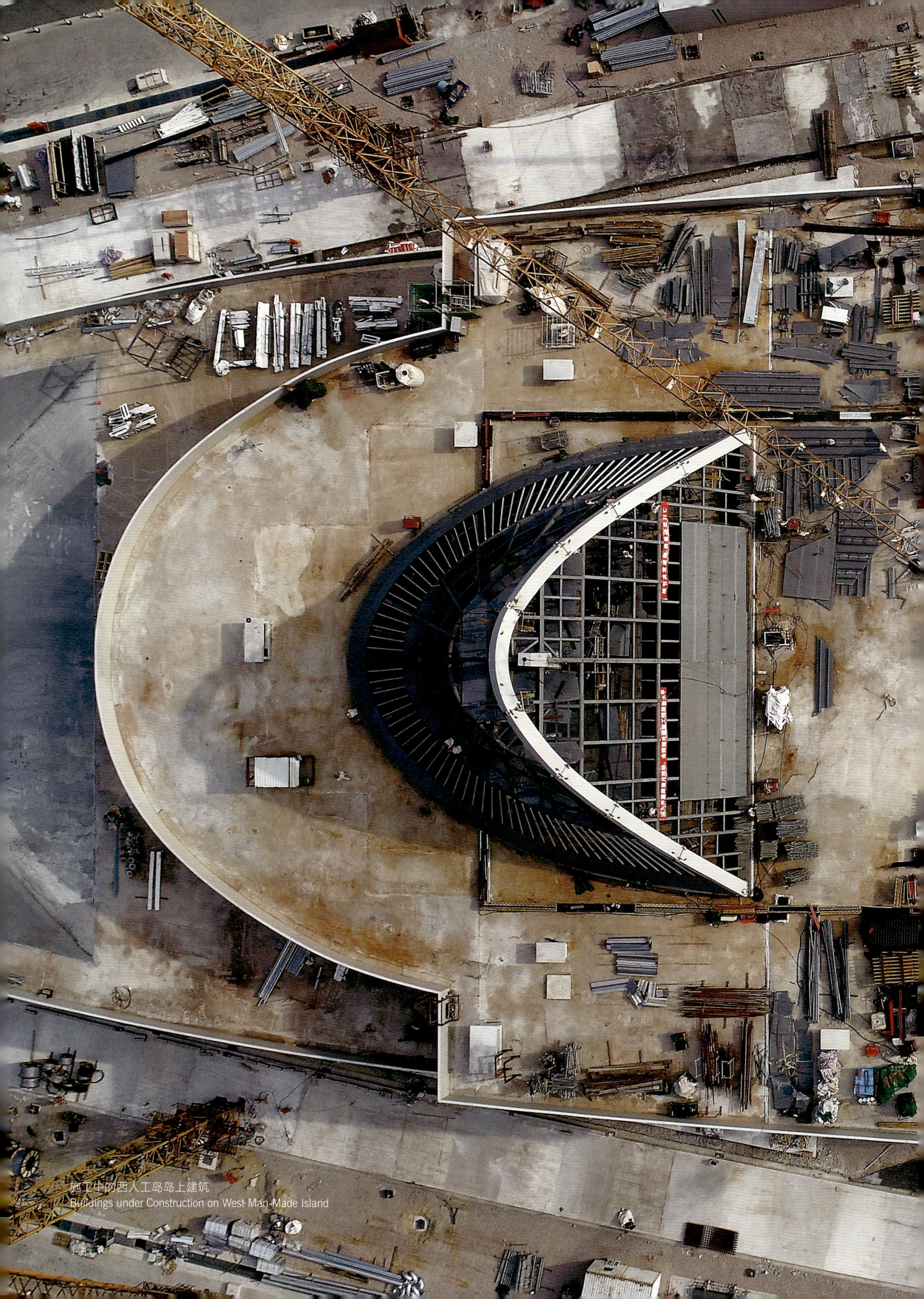

施工中的西人工岛岛上建筑
Buildings under Construction on West Man-Made Island

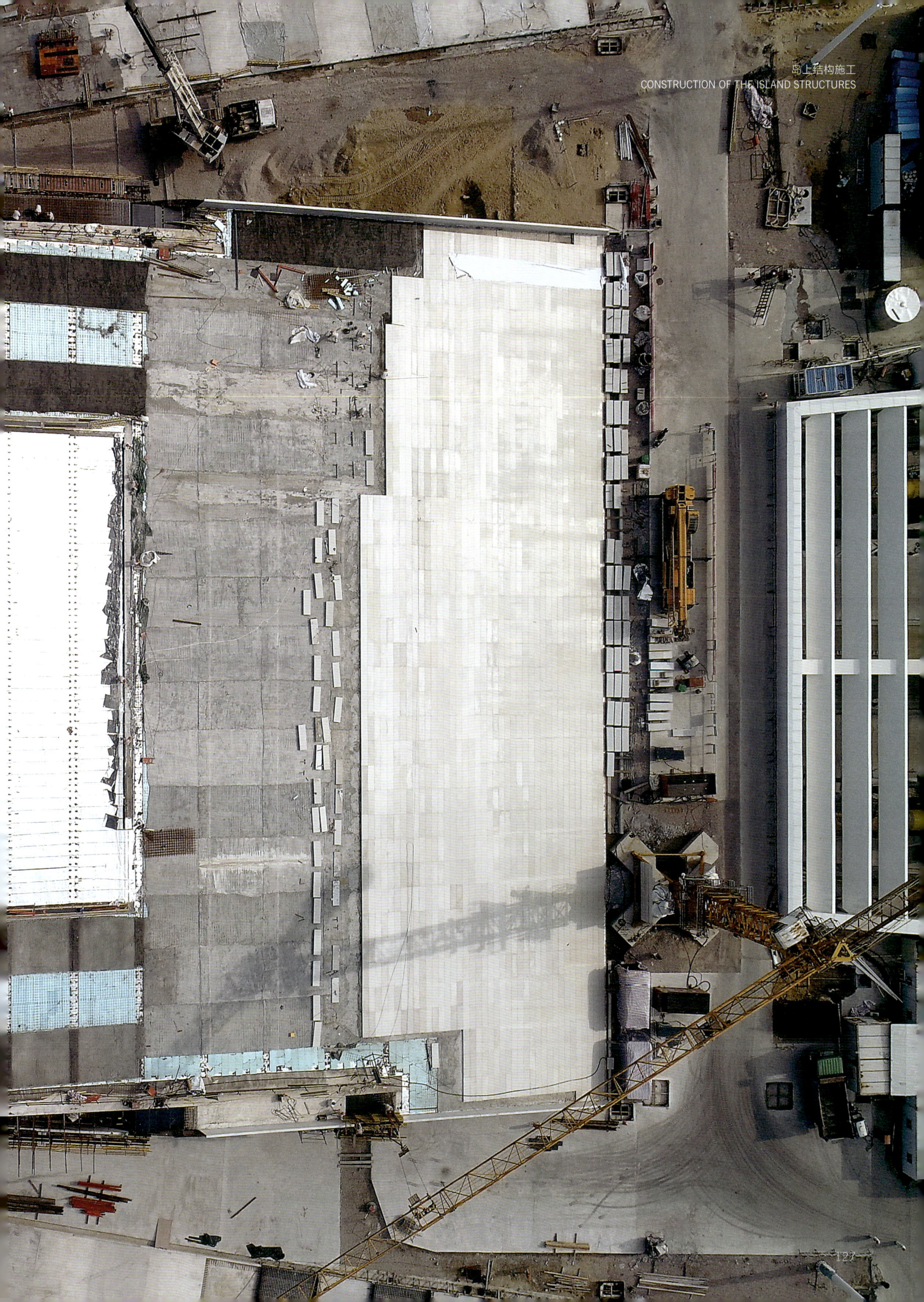

岛上建筑
BUILDINGS ON THE ISLAND

岛隧工程所设计的岛上建筑方案，在业主招标比选的若干设计方案中胜出。无论是整体游轮造型，亦或是主体建筑所采用的骑楼风格，都体现了粤港澳地区文化融合的特征。

从核心功能上来说，桥岛隧结构中的人工岛是用来衔接跨海大桥和海底隧道的道路转换，同时为隧道的通风和事故火警排烟提供通道。但是，仅具有通风作用，对于具备地标性质的港珠澳大桥人工岛来说太过浪费。因此，西人工岛增添了港珠澳大桥行政管养的功能，东人工岛则被规划为旅游观光景区。这样的变化，使得人工岛需要建筑集纳这些功能，而通风口则被融入到两个岛的主体建筑中去。

与所有陆地或者港区建筑不同，岛上的一切基础设施没有市政管网可以连通，都要从零开始规划，跨越 20 多个专业设计领域，涵盖 40 多个单体指向，涉及粤港澳三地行政、法律、建筑等方面的标准和习惯。

仅就西人工岛而言，要入驻三地联合办公的行政、道路监控、养护、消防、边检、公安、海关、排水防涝、海洋和天气监测预警、白海豚保护等十几个部门。每个部门都有自身的需求和必备的设备，需要专门的设计来预留空间和排布管线。另外，所有城市公共基础设施，例如供电、给排水、污水处理、垃圾处理等系统也要在设计之中。每一个设计都要经过无数次的沟通、协调和修改才能完成。

同时，为了适应海上高盐雾的恶劣环境，岛上建筑是中国第一次在外海采用清水混凝土工艺建造，在设计难度之外更增加了施工难度。项目总经理部通过严格管理、改进工法、加强培训、严格监管等措施，仅用了 8 个月的时间，提前完成了原本需要一年完成的施工。

The construction plan for the buildings on the islands of the island-tunnel project defeated other bidding competitors and became the guideline of the construction of the buildings on the islands. Either

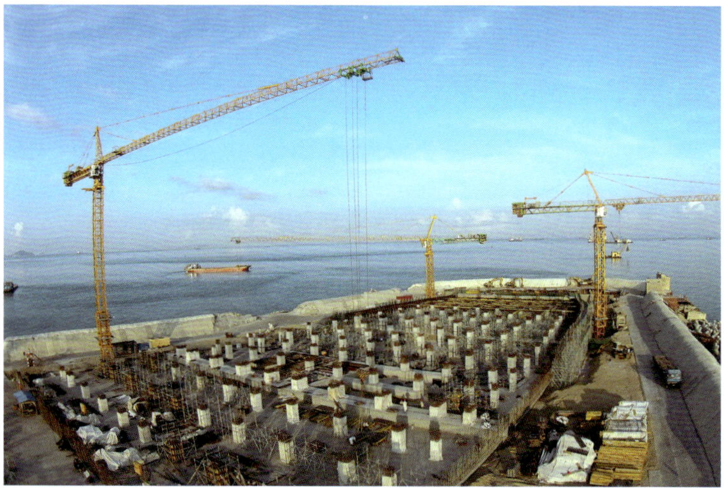

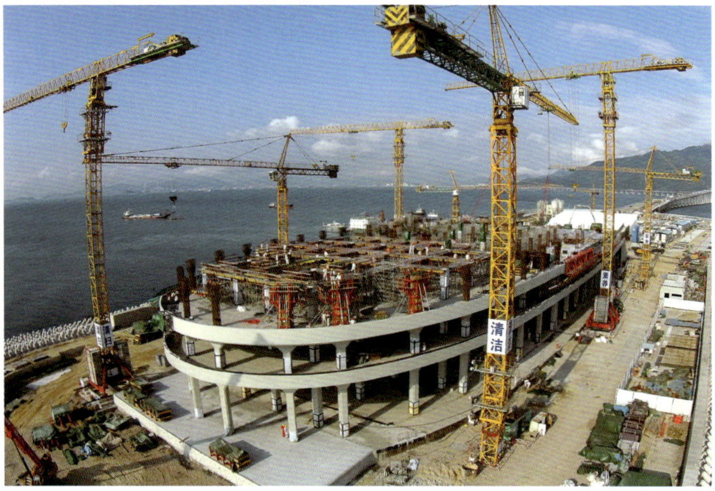

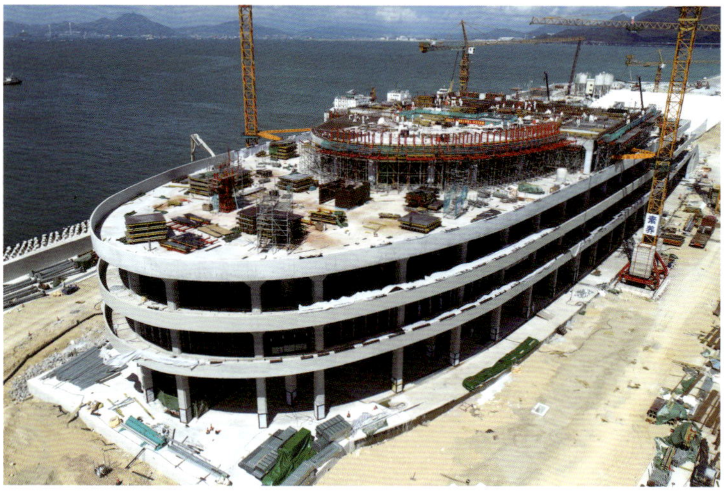

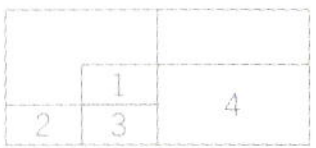

1—3. 人工岛岛上主体建筑施工
Construction of the Main Buildings on the Man-Made Islands

4. 封顶后的东人工岛岛上主体建筑
Topped-out Main Building on East Man-Made Island

the global cruiser shape or the arcade style for the main buildings combined the cultures in Guangdong, Hong Kong and Macau.

As to its core functions, the man-made islands in the bridge-island-tunnel structure were created for the transition between the cross-sea bridge and the undersea tunnel, and were also used to provide a channel for tunnel ventilation and emergency fire smoke exhaust. However, if they were built only for the purpose of ventilation, that would be a waste for the landmark—Hong Kong-Zhuhai-Macau Bridge. Therefore, West Man-Made Island had also the function of administration and maintenance of the Bridge while East Man-Made Island was designed as a tourist sight. Therefore, the main buildings constructed on the two islands needed to combine all these functions and the ventilation structures would be incorporated into the main buildings.

Unlike other land or port buildings, all the infrastructure facilities on the islands were not linked to any urban network, and everything had to be planned from scratch, spanning more than 20 professional fields of designing, involving more than 40 specific functions as well as relevant administrative, legal, architectural standards and customs of Guangdong, Hong Kong and Macau.

As to West Man-Made Island, dozens of municipal departments such as administration, road monitoring, maintenance, fire control, immigration control, public security, customs, drainage, Chinese white dolphin protection, oceanic and weather forecast would be stationed on the island, and each department had its own special needs and necessary equipment, so special designing was necessary to reserve spaces and arrange pipelines. In addition, all the urban public infrastructures, such as power supply, water supply and drainage, sewage treatment and garbage disposal, should also be included in the design. Every design had to go through communication, coordination and modification.

At the same time, in order to adapt to the harsh environment of high-salt fog on the sea, the buildings on the islands for the first time in China made use of fair-faced concrete in the open sea, which added construction difficulty to the design difficulty. Through strict management, improvement of construction methods, reinforced training, strict supervision and other measures, the project management center completed the construction in only eight months which otherwise would need one year.

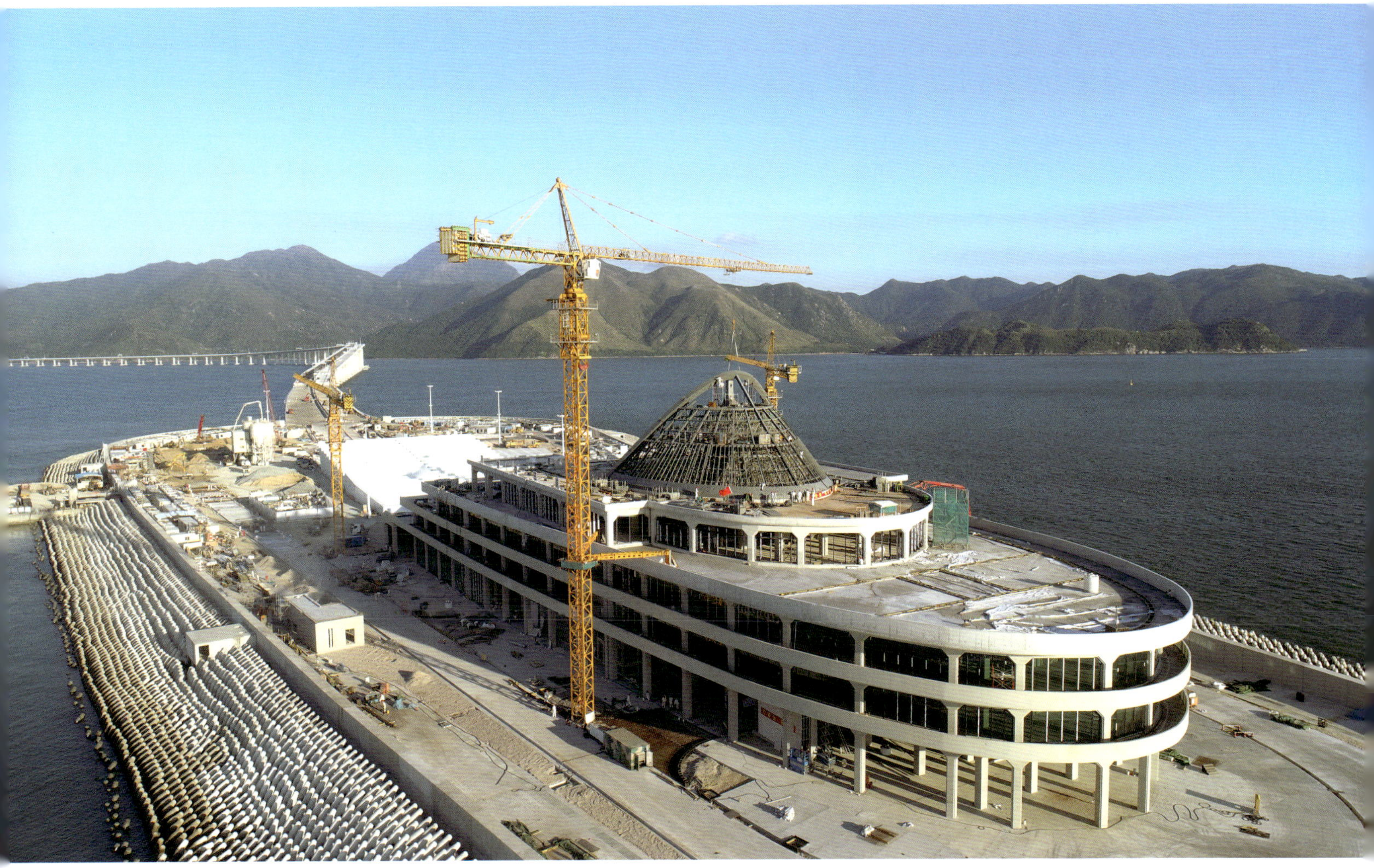

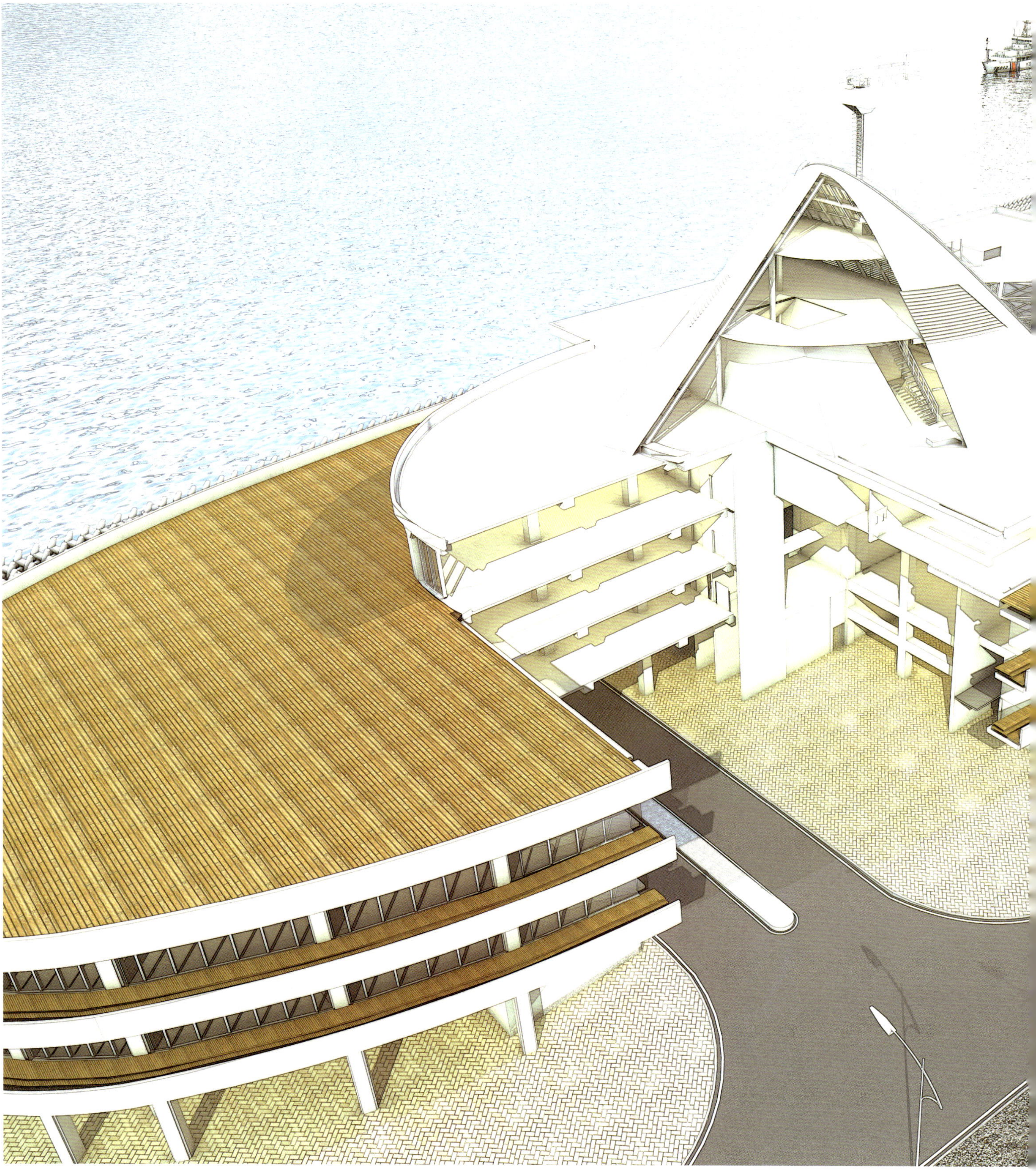

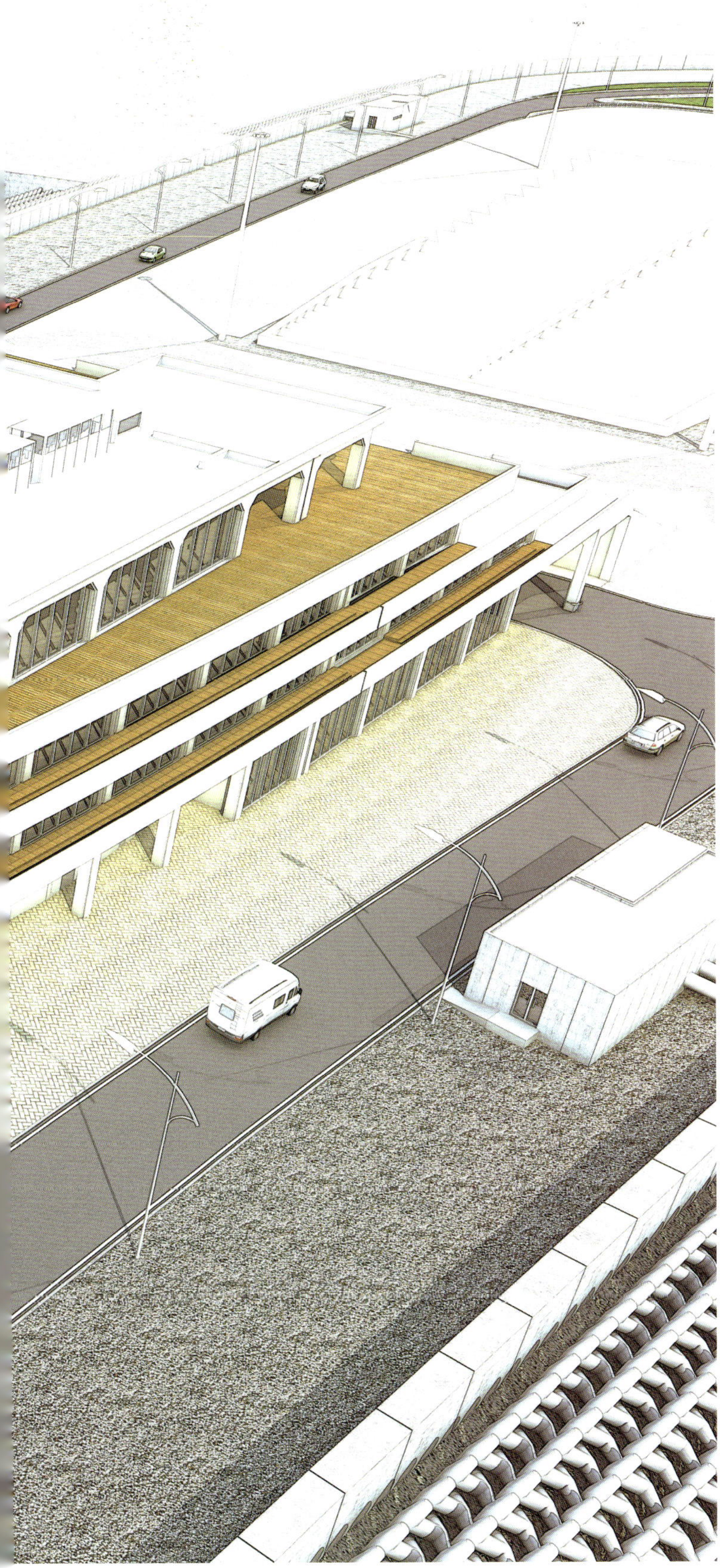

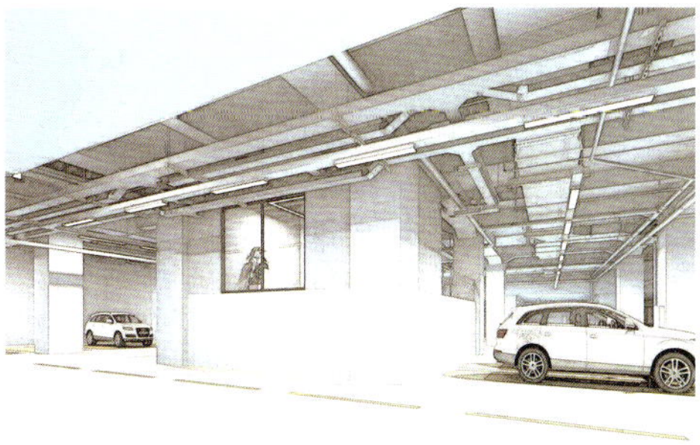

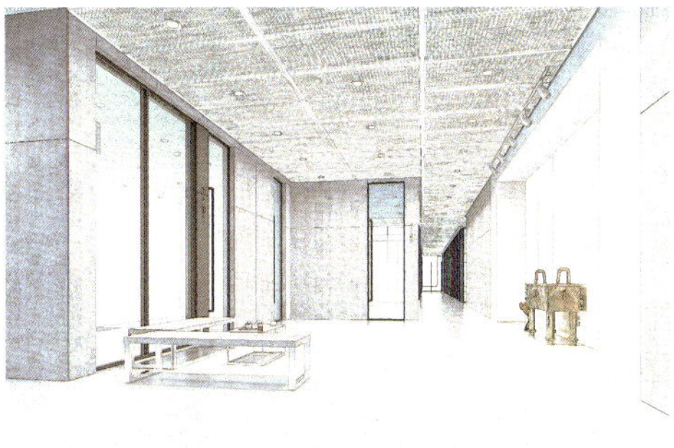

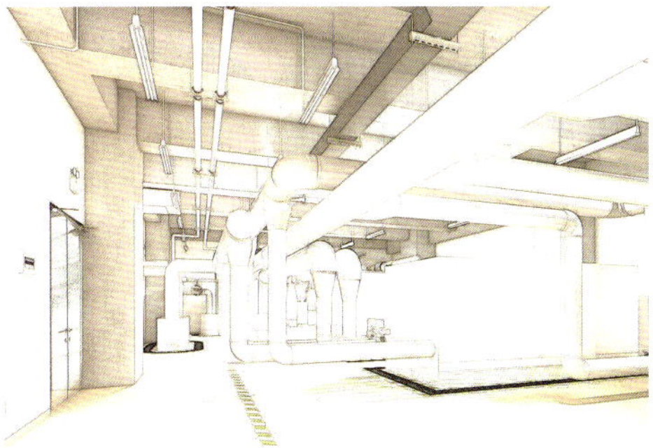

1. 东人工岛岛上主体建筑剖面图
Profile of the Main Building on East Man-Made Island

2—4. 主体建筑室内效果图
Design Sketch of the Interior of the Main Building

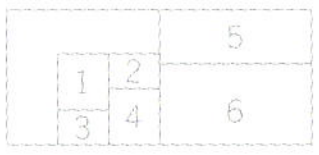

1. 立柱模板拼装
   Assembling of the Column Formwork
2. 立柱钢筋连接
   Connection of the Steel Reinforcement Framework of the Column
3. 立柱钢筋骨架预制
   Fabrication of the Steel Reinforcement Framework of the Column
4. 立柱钢筋笼起吊
   Lifting of the Steel Column Reinforcement Cage
5. 人工岛四层楼板模板安装
   Installation of Fourth-Floor Framework on the Man-Made Island
6. 人工岛主体建筑封顶
   Topping-out of the Main Building on the Man-Made Island

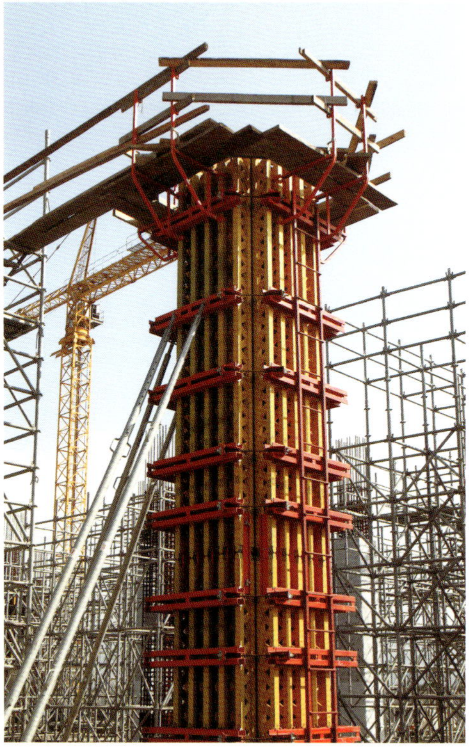

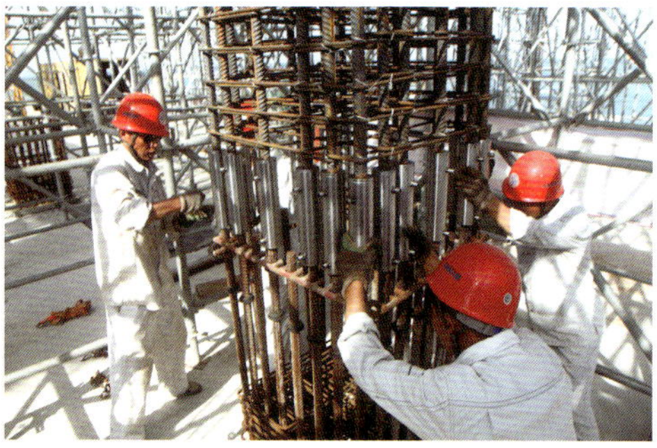

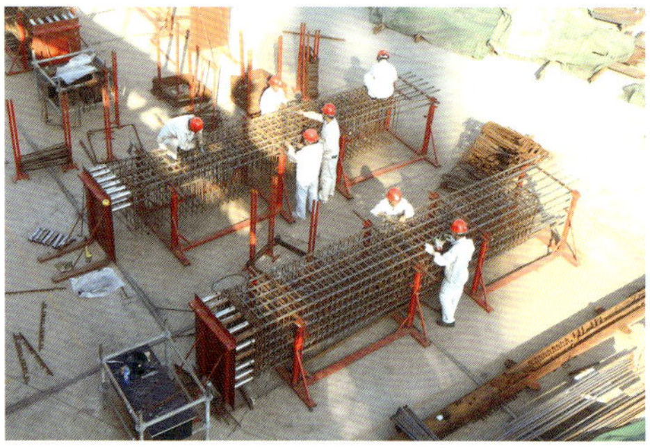

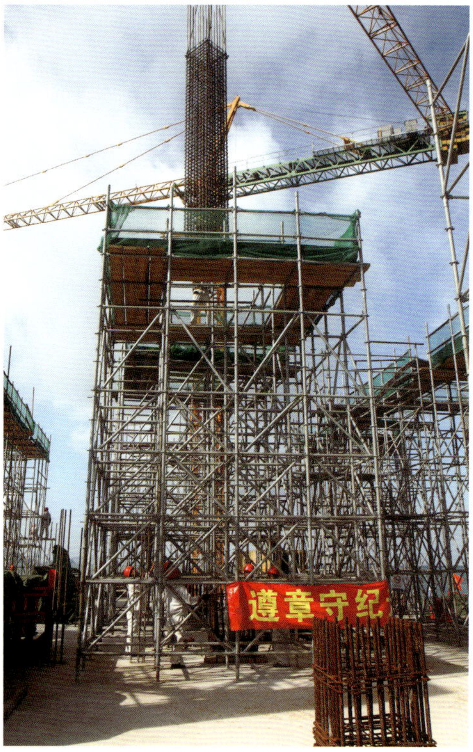

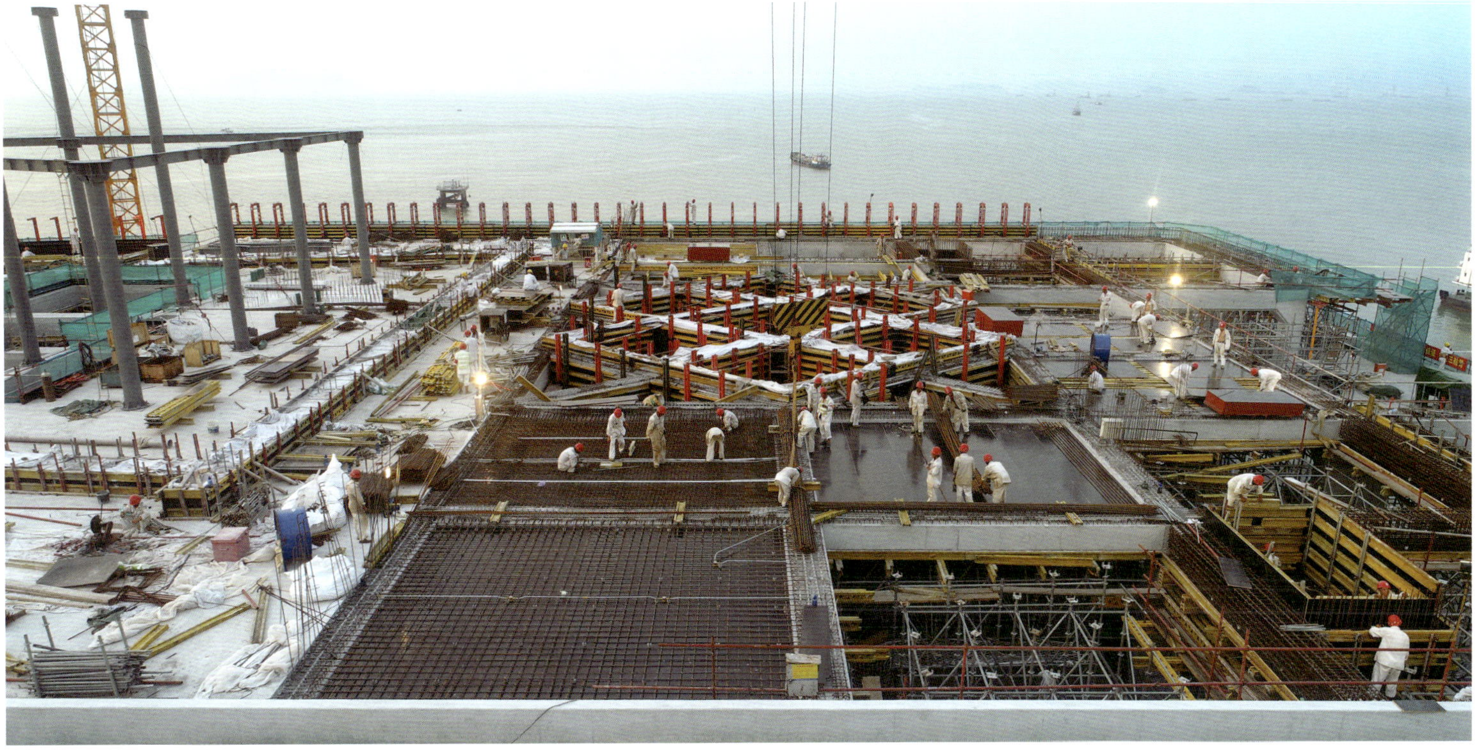

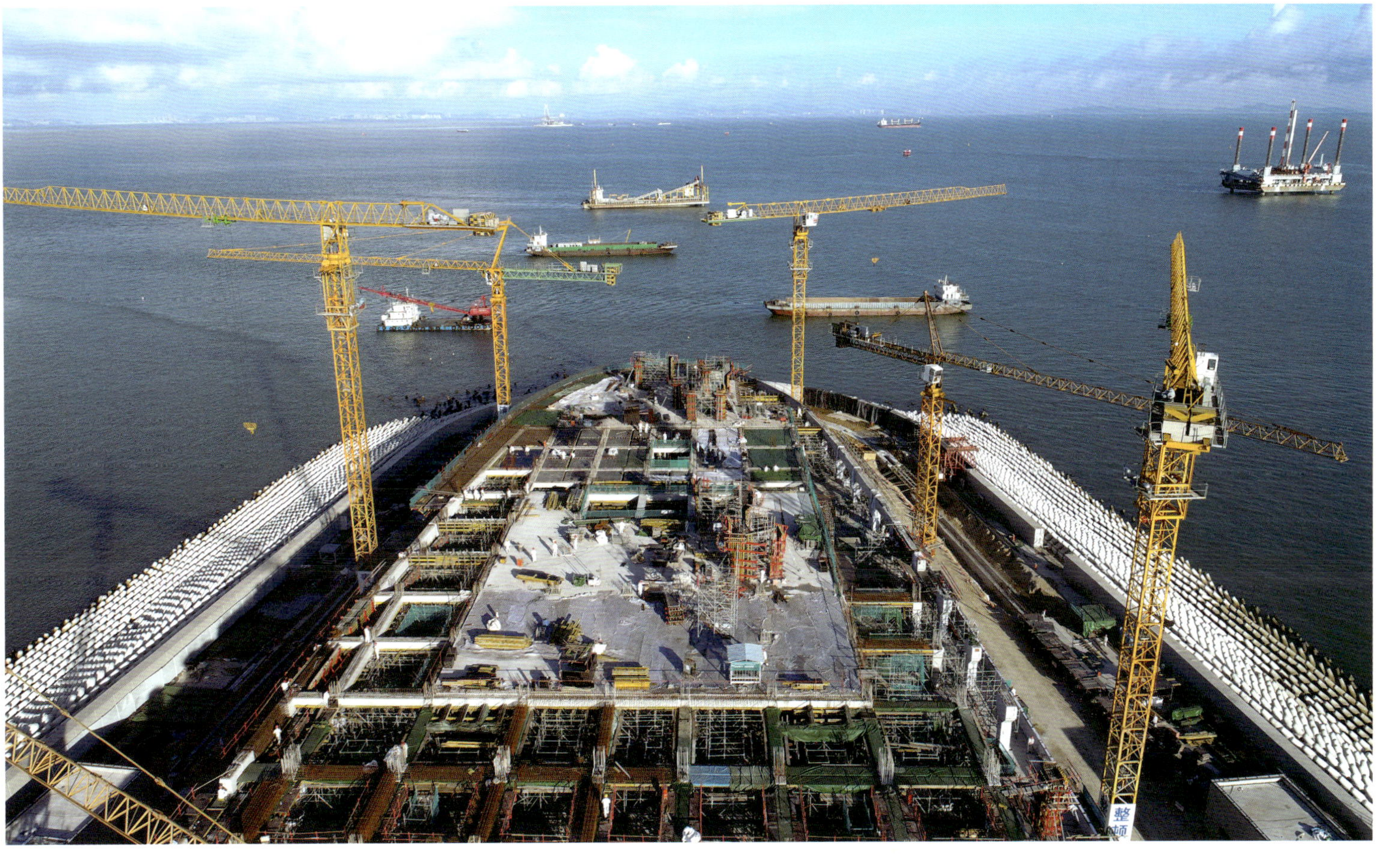
整
顿

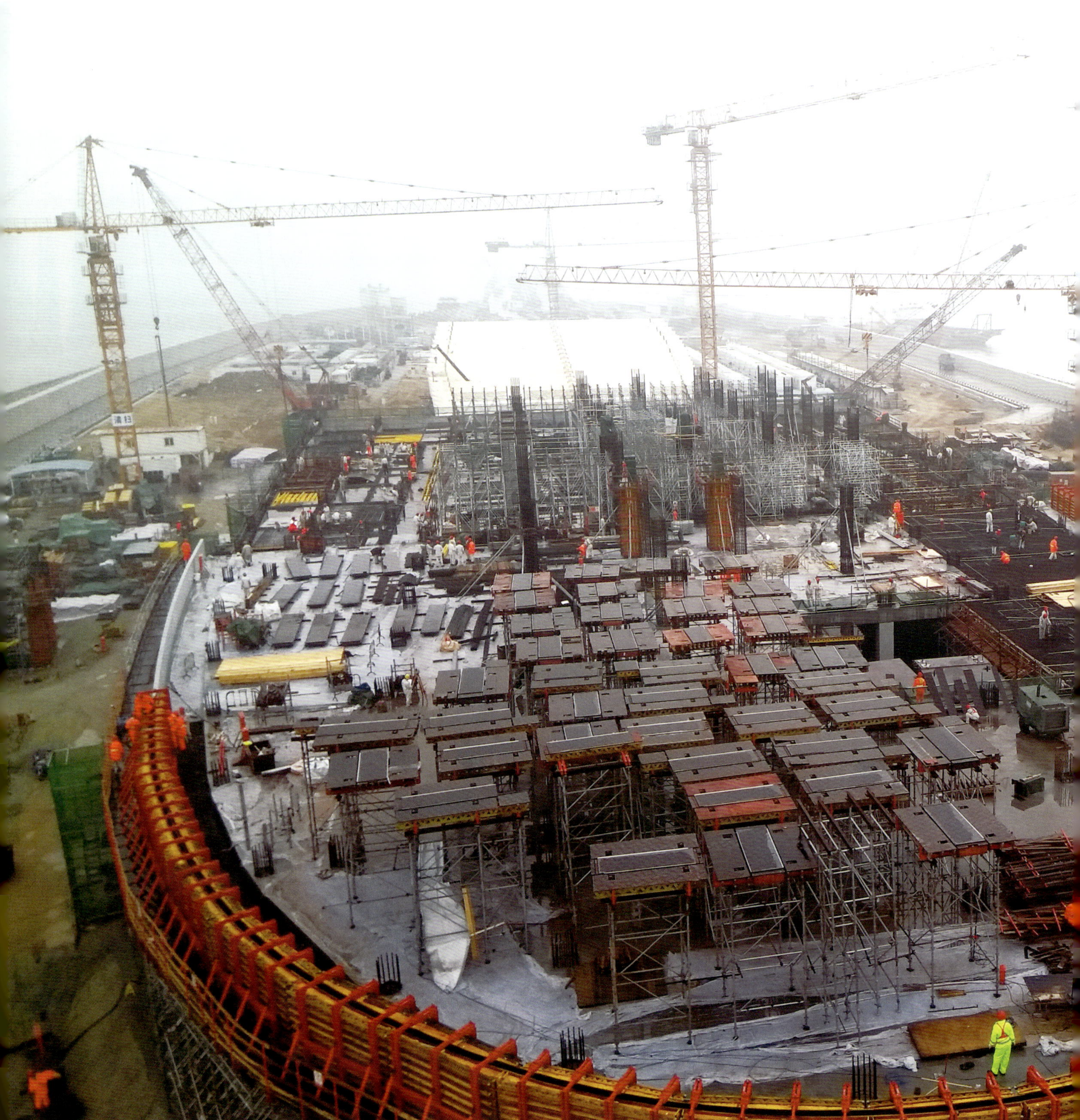
清扫

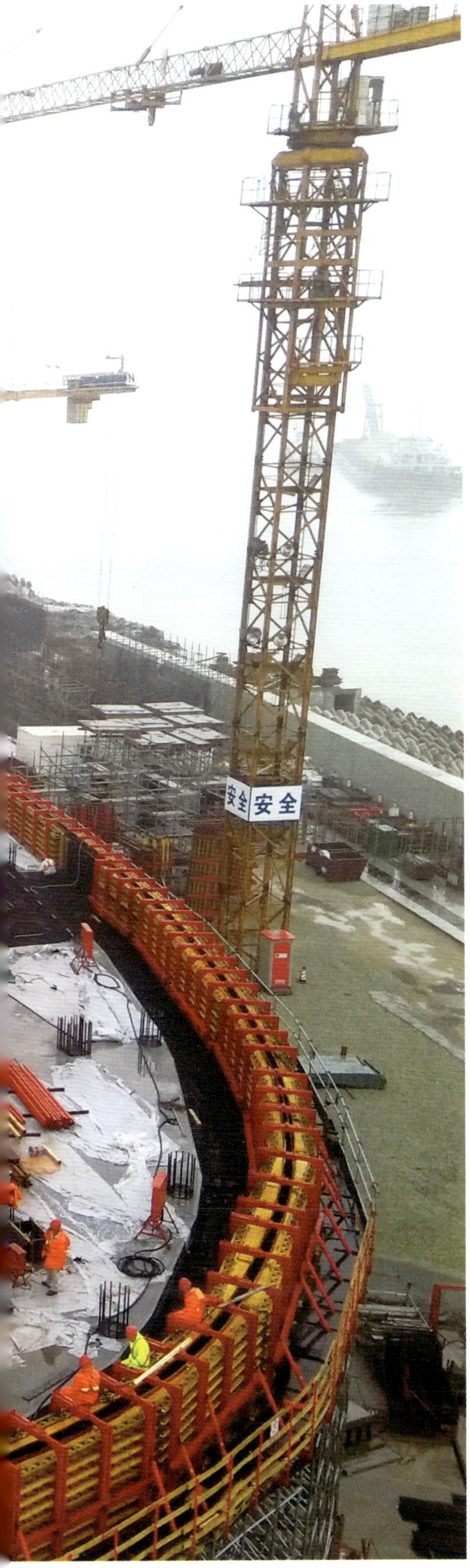

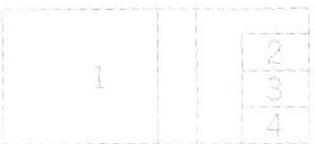

1. 人工岛主体建筑楼板模板、圈型梁模板安装
Floor Framework of the Main Building on the Man-Made Island, and Installation of the Ring Beam Framework

2. 曲线梁钢筋绑扎
Steel Bar Binding for the Curved Beam

3. 圈型梁模板安装
Installation of the Ring Beam Formwork

4. 模板安装完成
Formwork Installation Completed

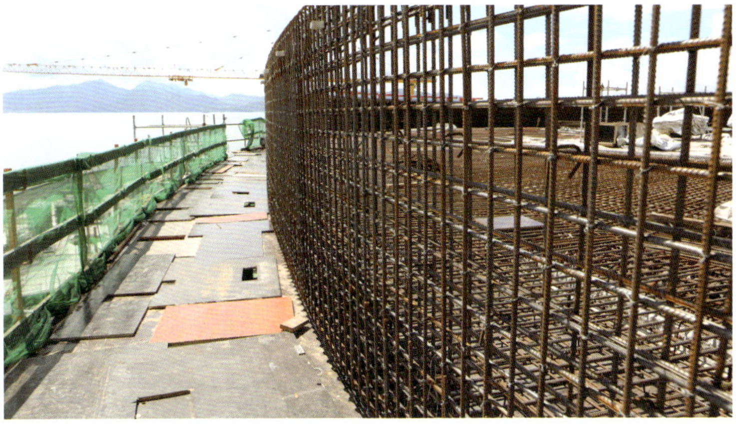

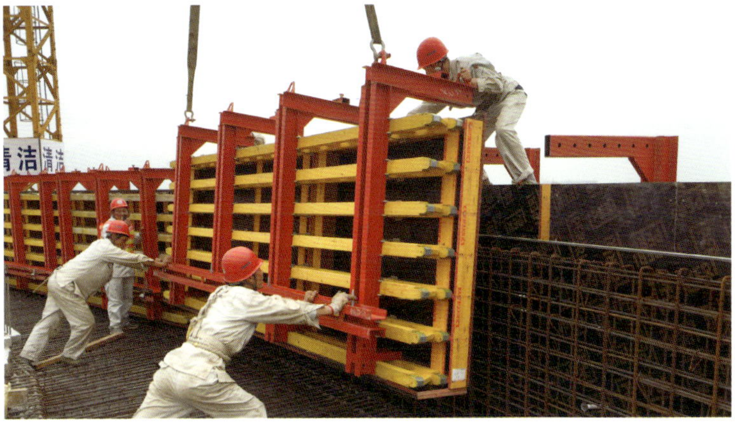

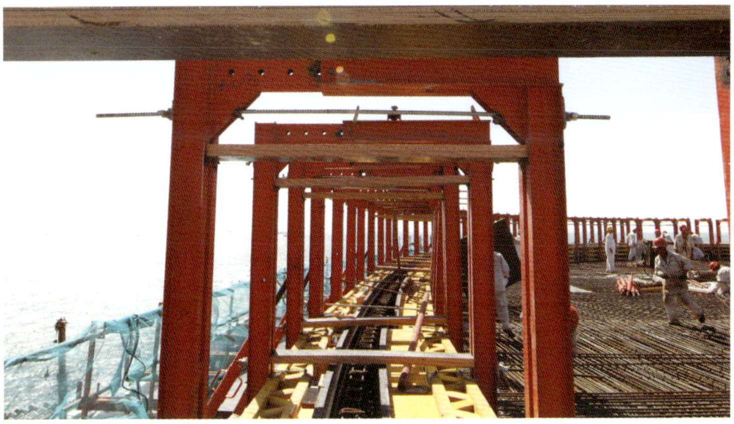

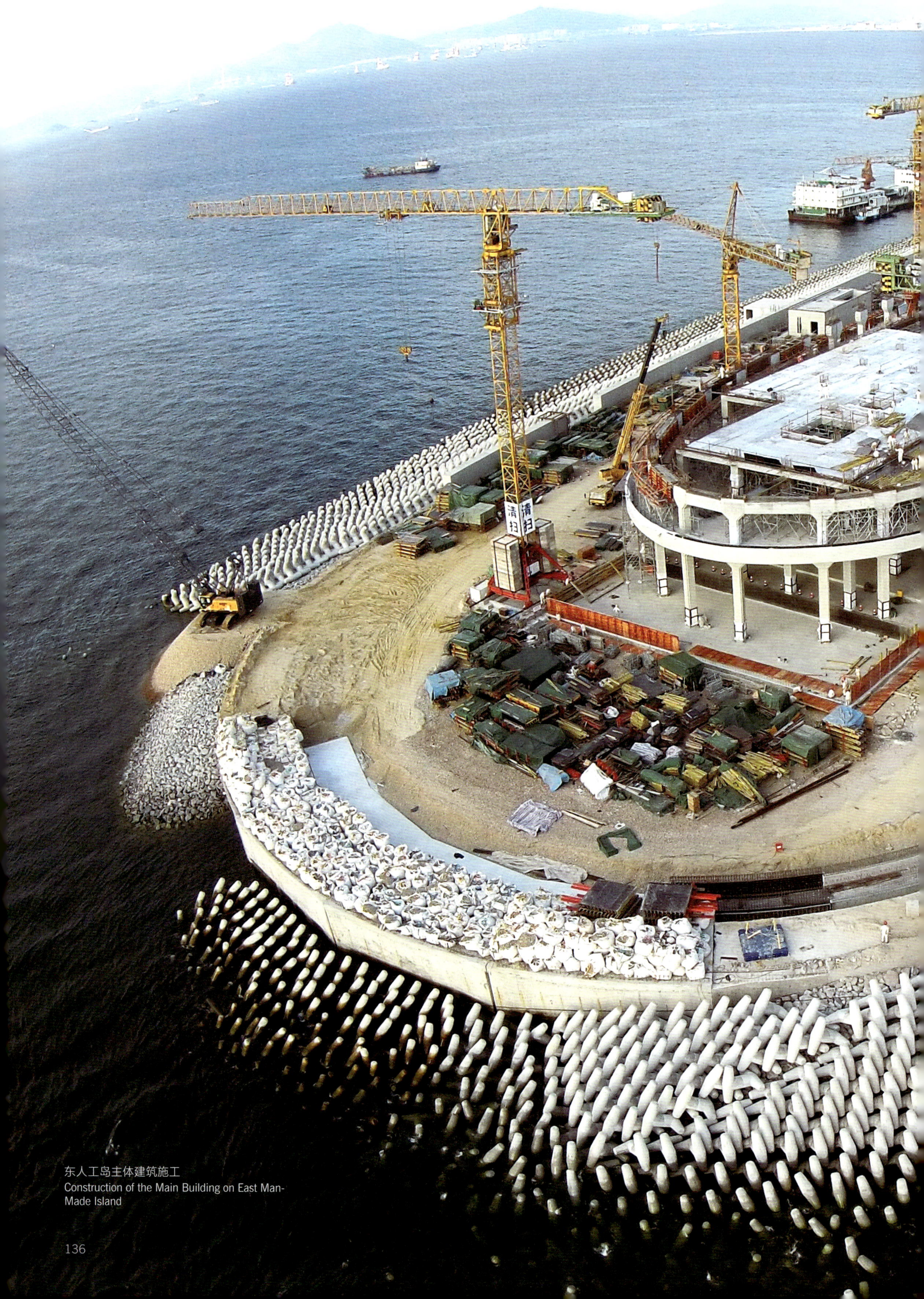

东人工岛主体建筑施工
Construction of the Main Building on East Man-Made Island

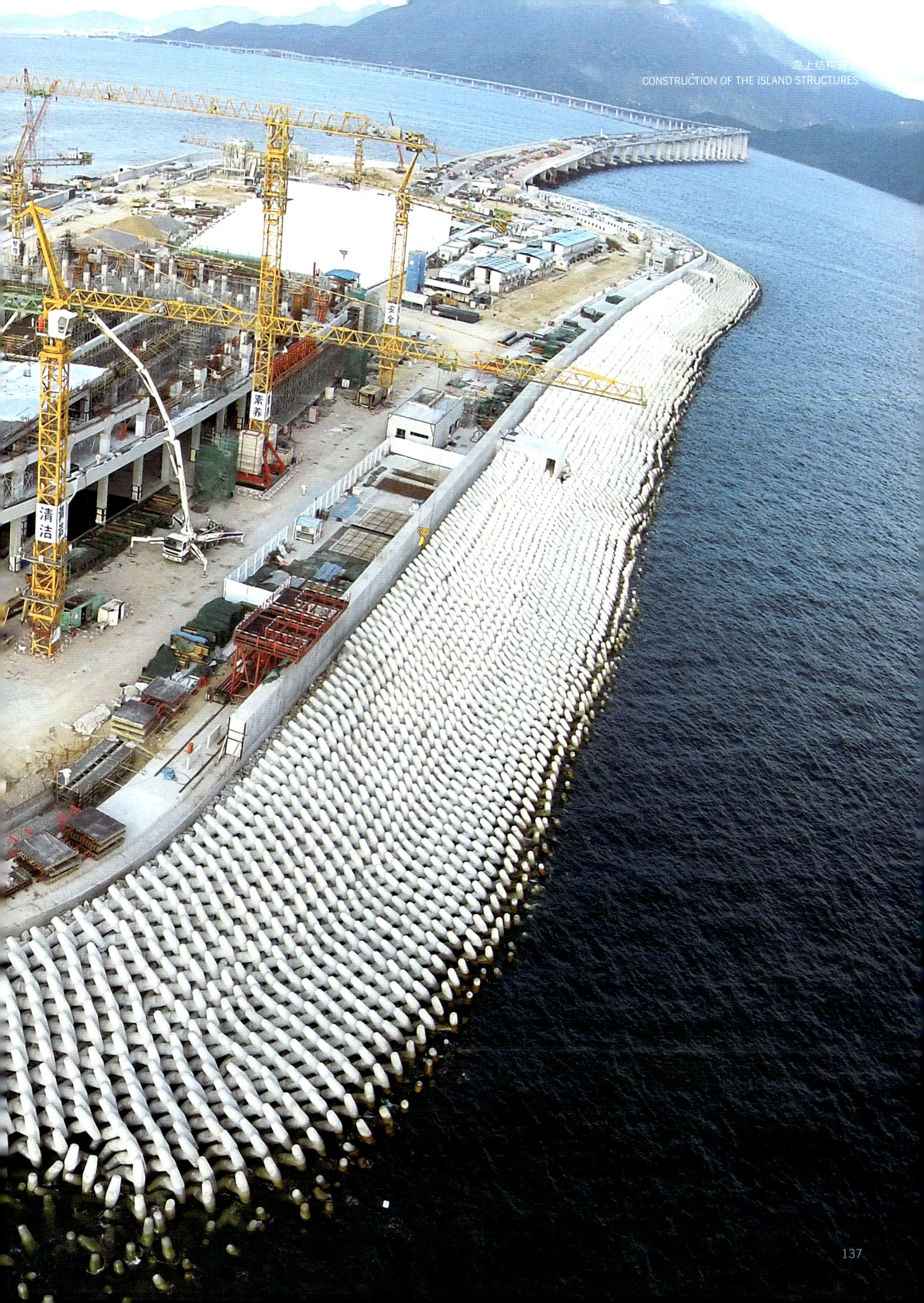
清洁
素养
安全

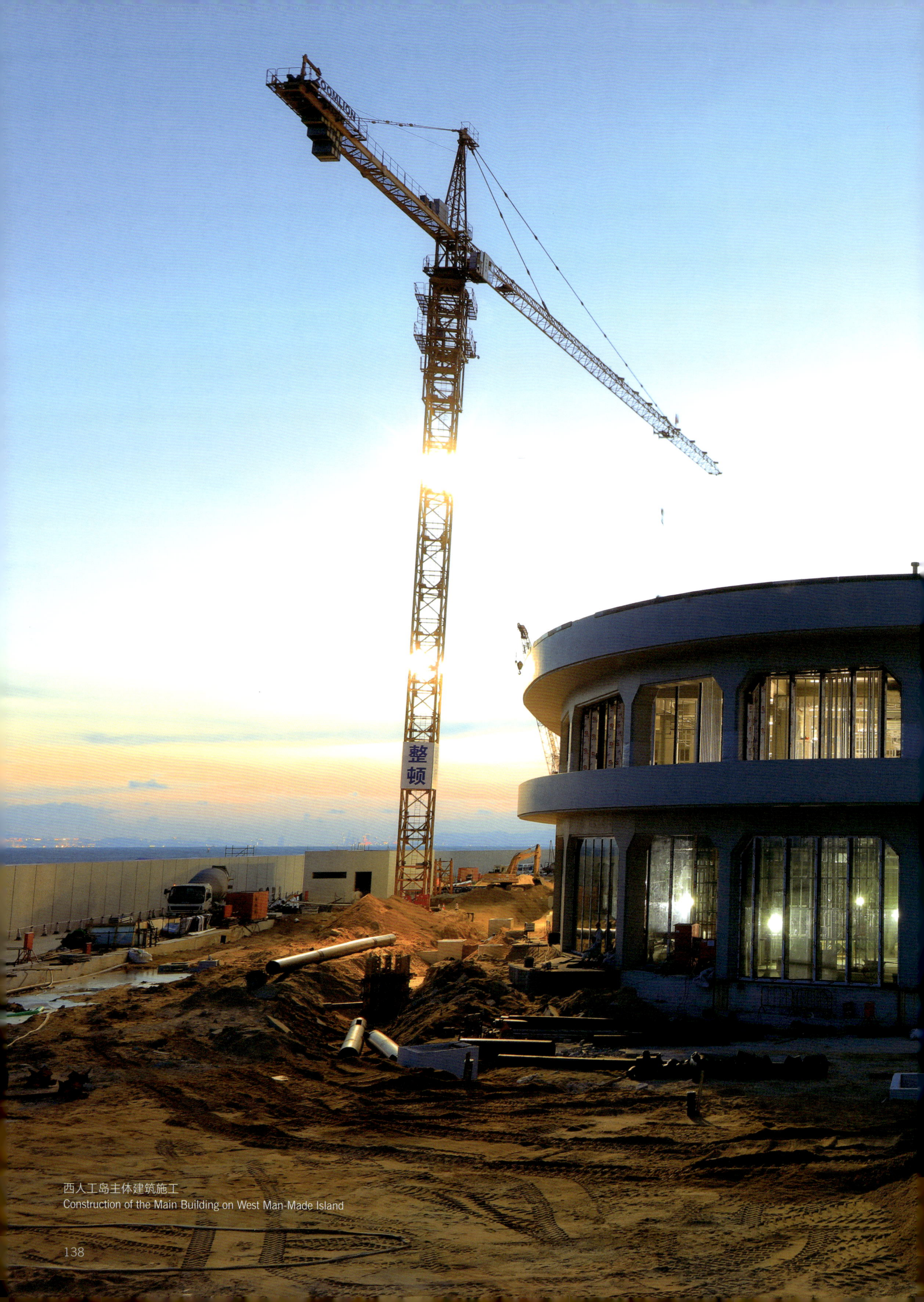

西人工岛主体建筑施工
Construction of the Main Building on West Man-Made Island

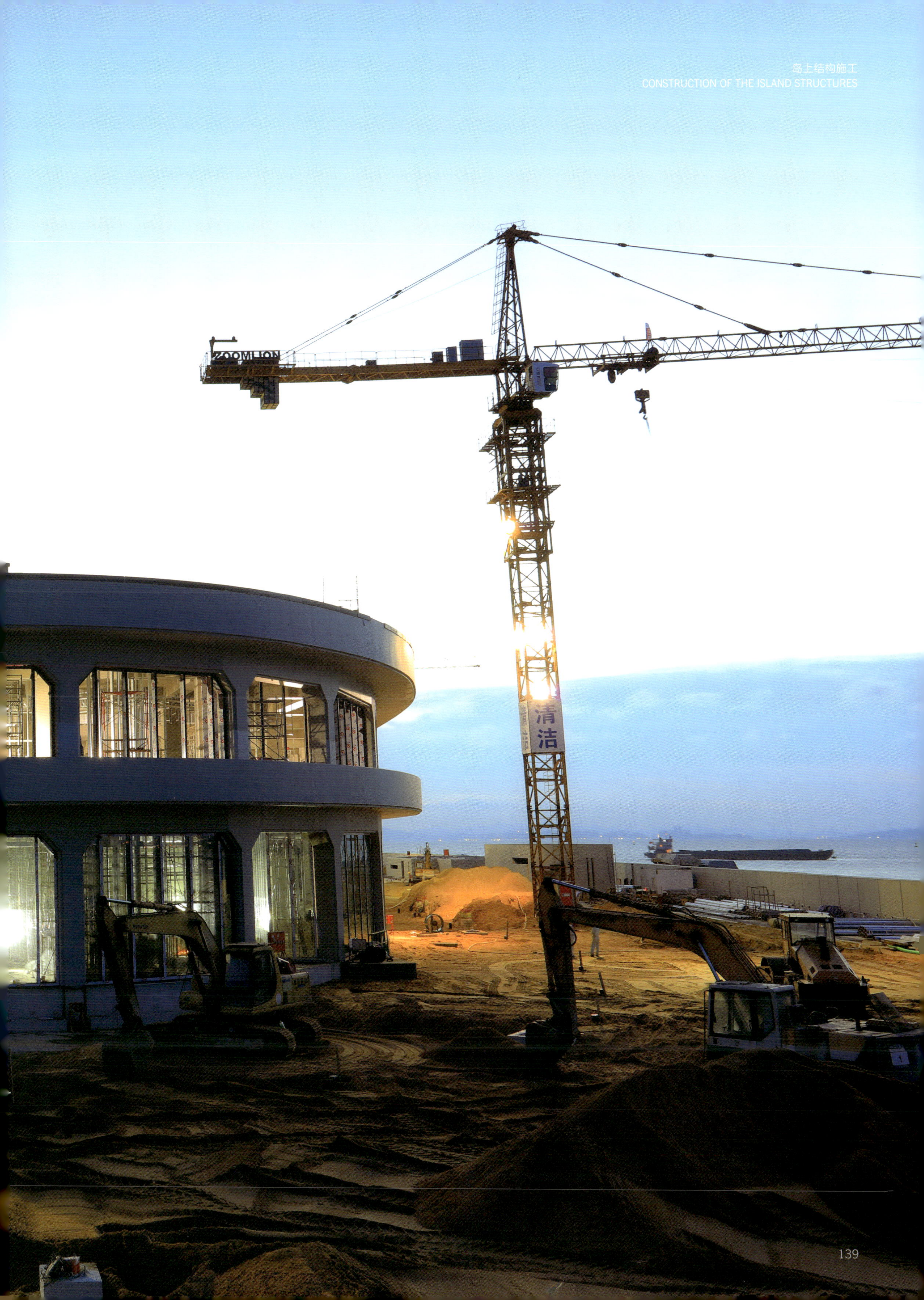
ZOOMLION
清洁

大台阶安装
INSTALLATION OF THE GRAND STEP

东、西人工岛大台阶、大斜板面层采用工厂法预制、现场标准化安装的装配式施工理念，全部构件采用清水混凝土，在牛头岛小构件预制车间生产完成后运输至现场安装，实现成品视觉整洁白净、触觉光滑细腻、线性过渡平滑柔和的整体效果。

The grand steps and the large inclined panels on the East and West Man-Made islands were prefabricated in the factory and installed on site in a standardized way. All the components were made of fair-faced concrete and transported to the site for installation after they were precast in the small component prefabrication workshop of Niutou Island. All the well-done products were characterized by their neat and clean surface, smooth and delicate touch, and their smooth and soft lines and curves.

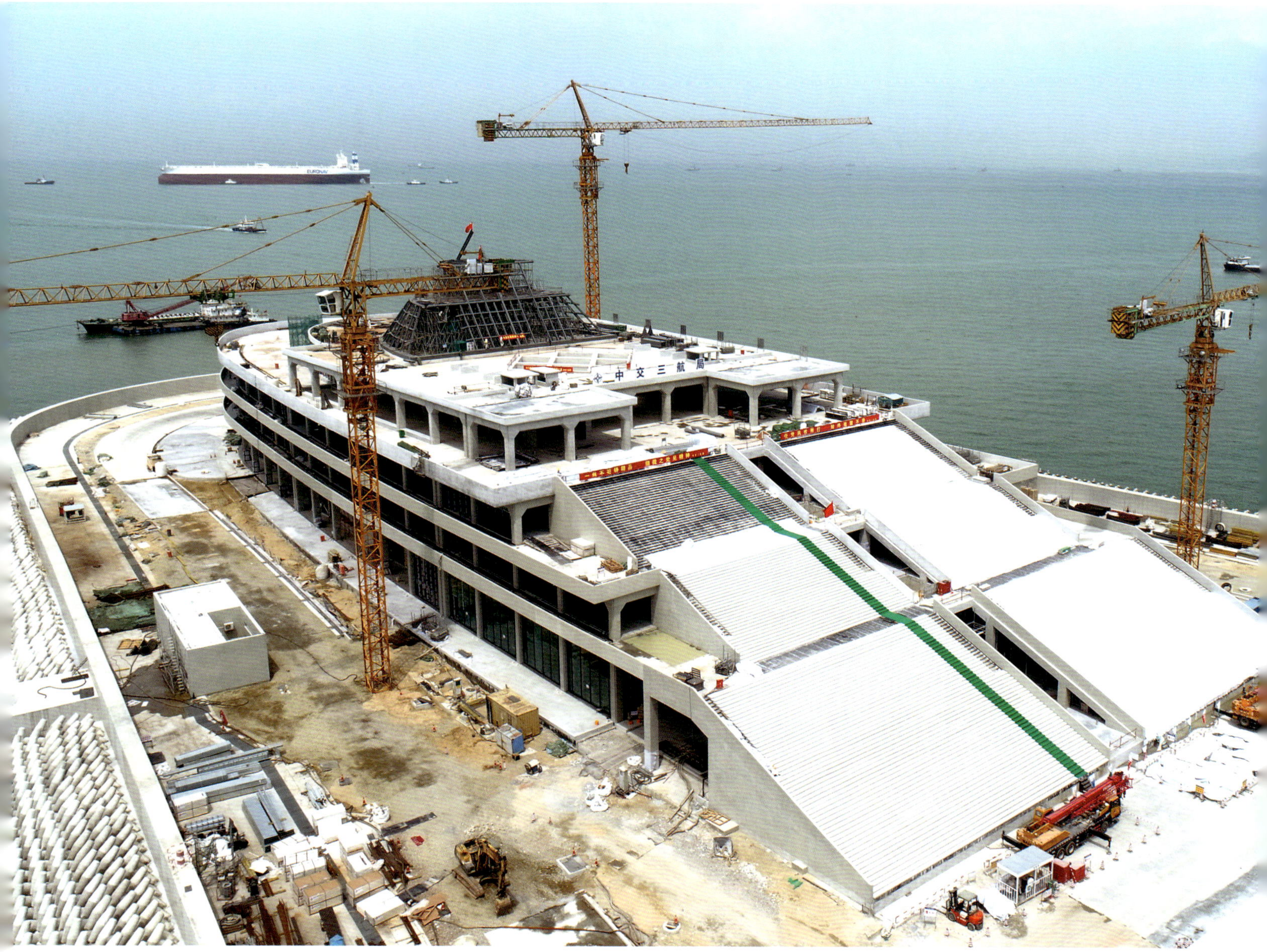

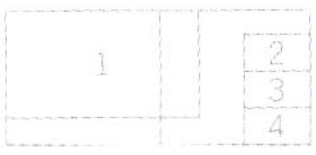

1. 东人工岛主体建筑大台阶安装
   Installation of the Grand Step of the Main Building on East Man-Made Island
2. 东、西人工岛主体建筑铺面预制构件
   Prefabricated Pavement Components of the Main Building on the East and the West Man-Made Islands
3. 台阶铺设
   Construction of the Steps
4. 构件预制场地
   Component Prefabrication Base

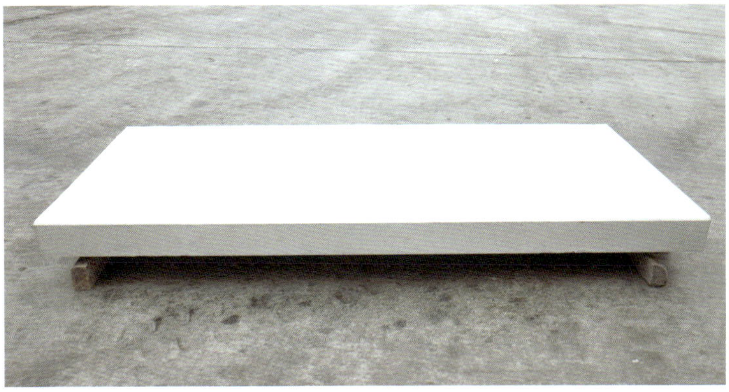

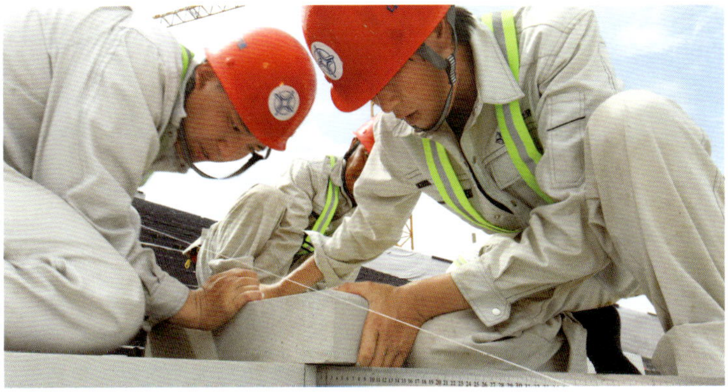

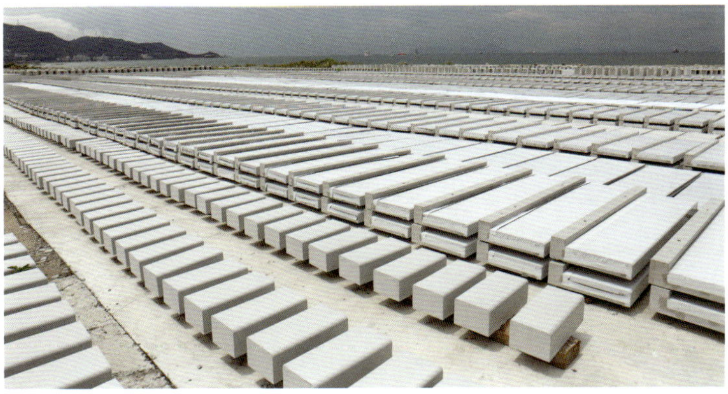

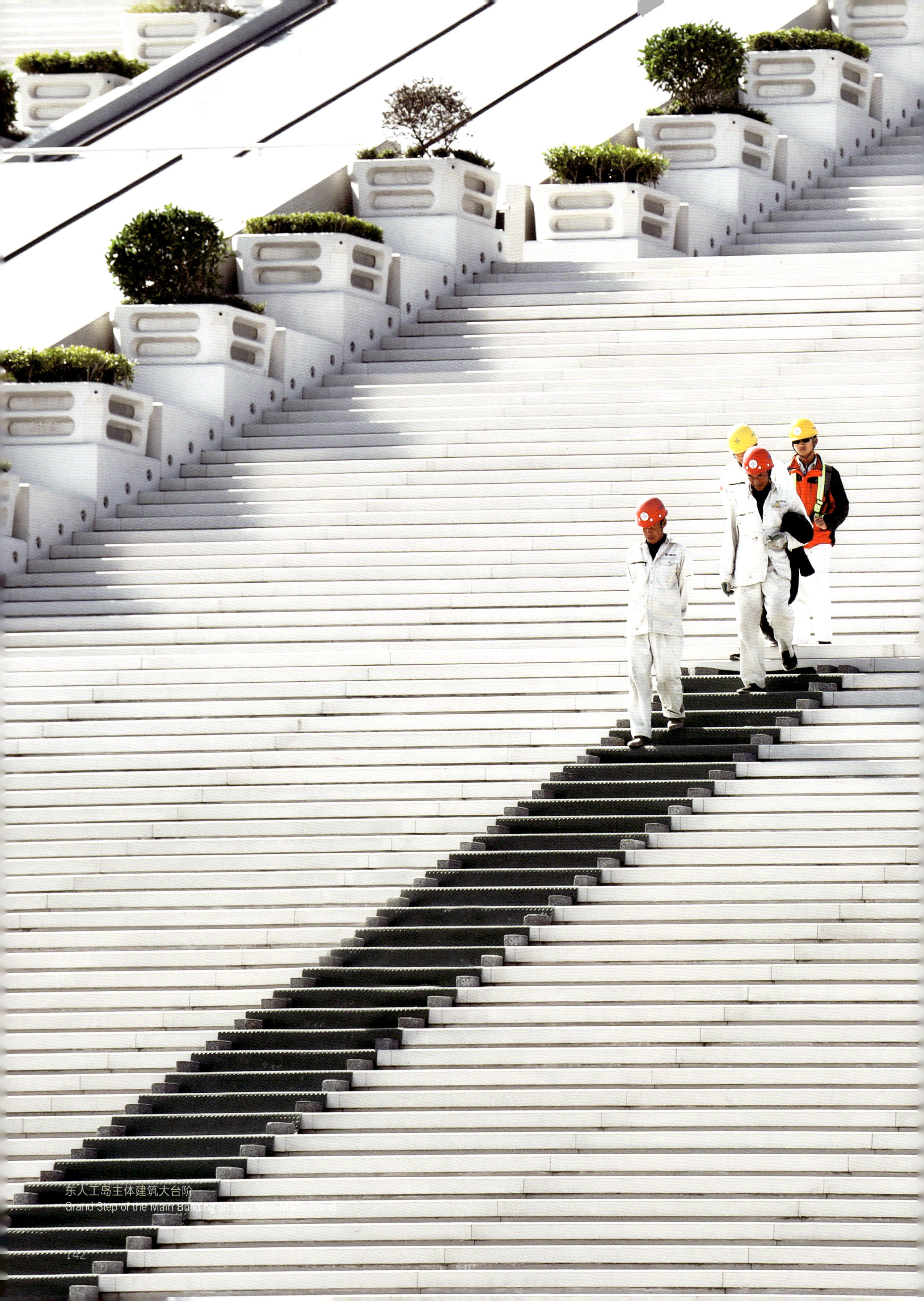

东人工岛主体建筑大台阶
Grand Step of the Main Building on East Man-Made Island

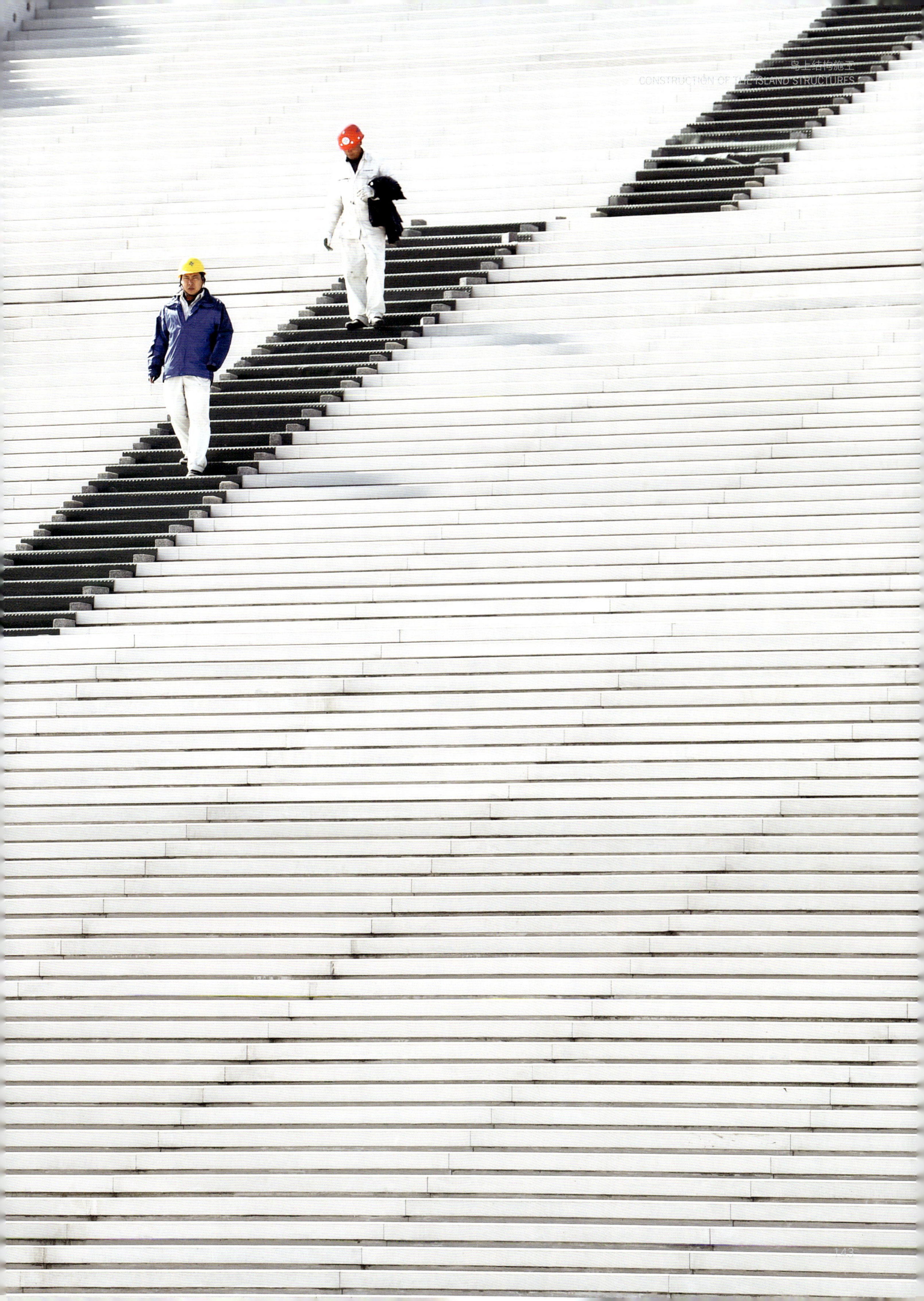

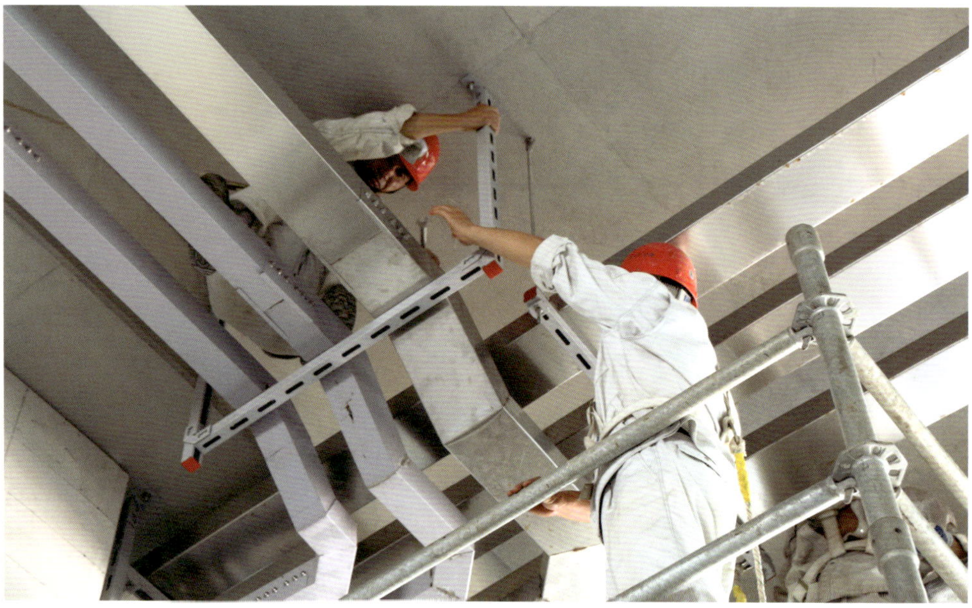

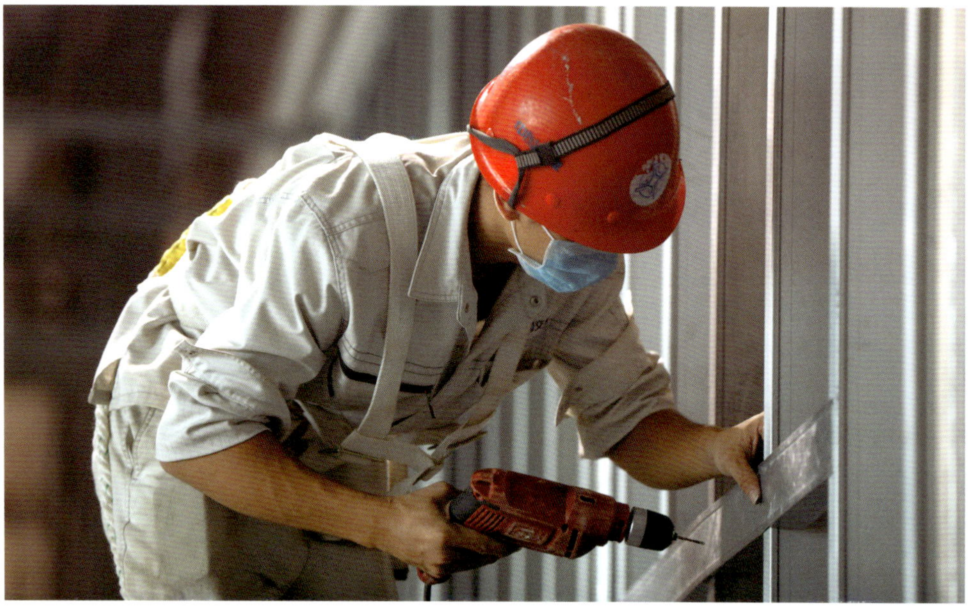

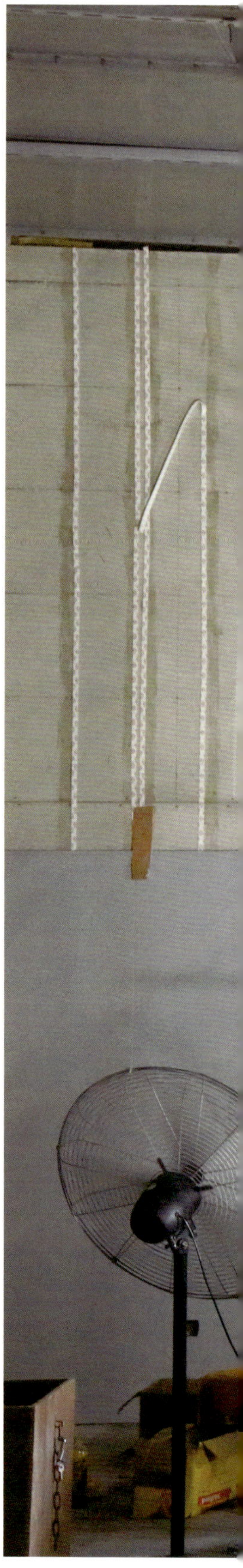

1. 管线吊架安装
   Installation of the Pipeline Hanger
2. 室内轻质隔墙骨架安装
   Installation of the In-Door Light-Weight Partition Wall Framework
3. 室内轻质隔墙装饰板安装
   Installation of In-Door Light-Weight Decorative Plates on the Partition Wall

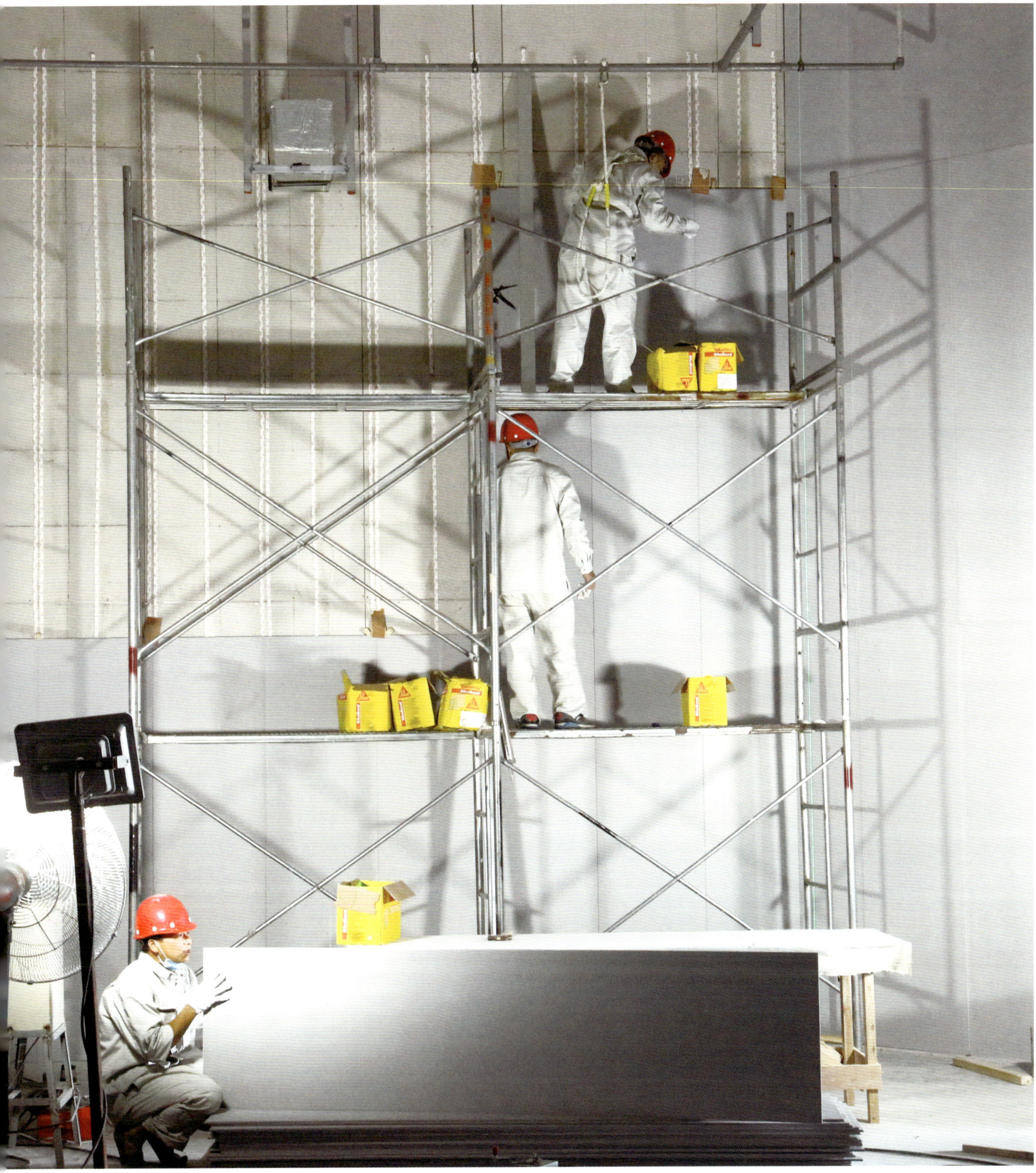

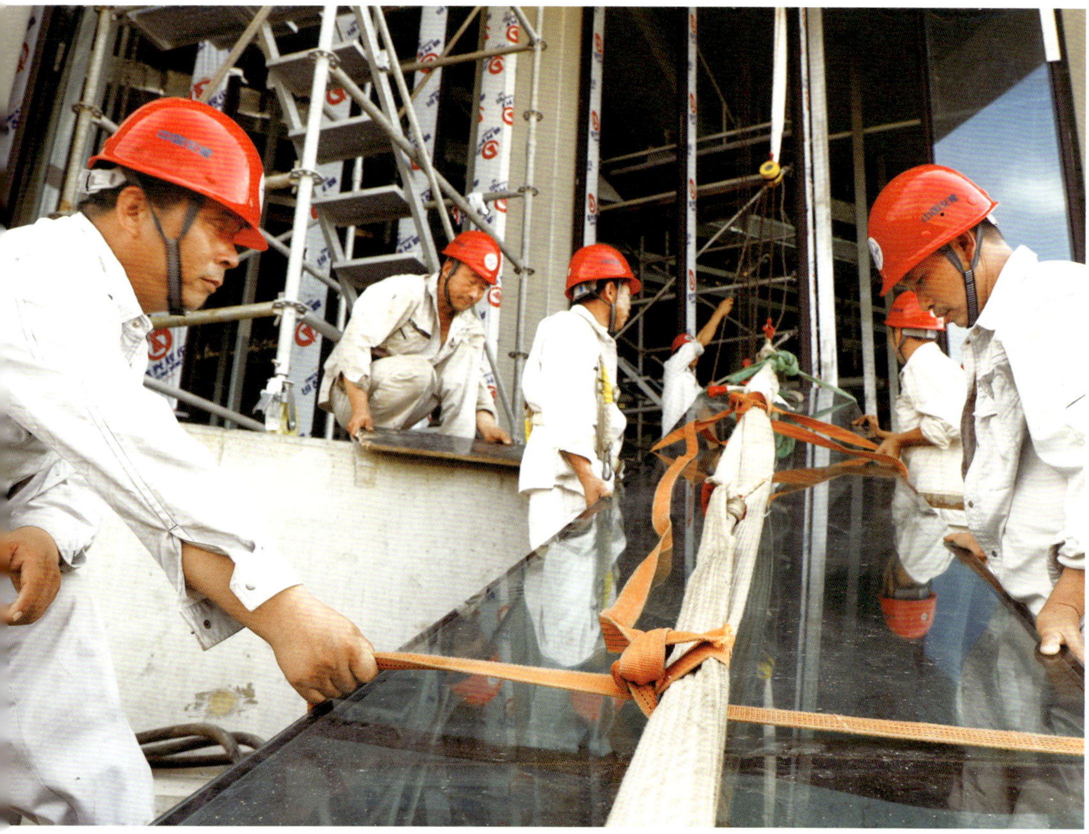

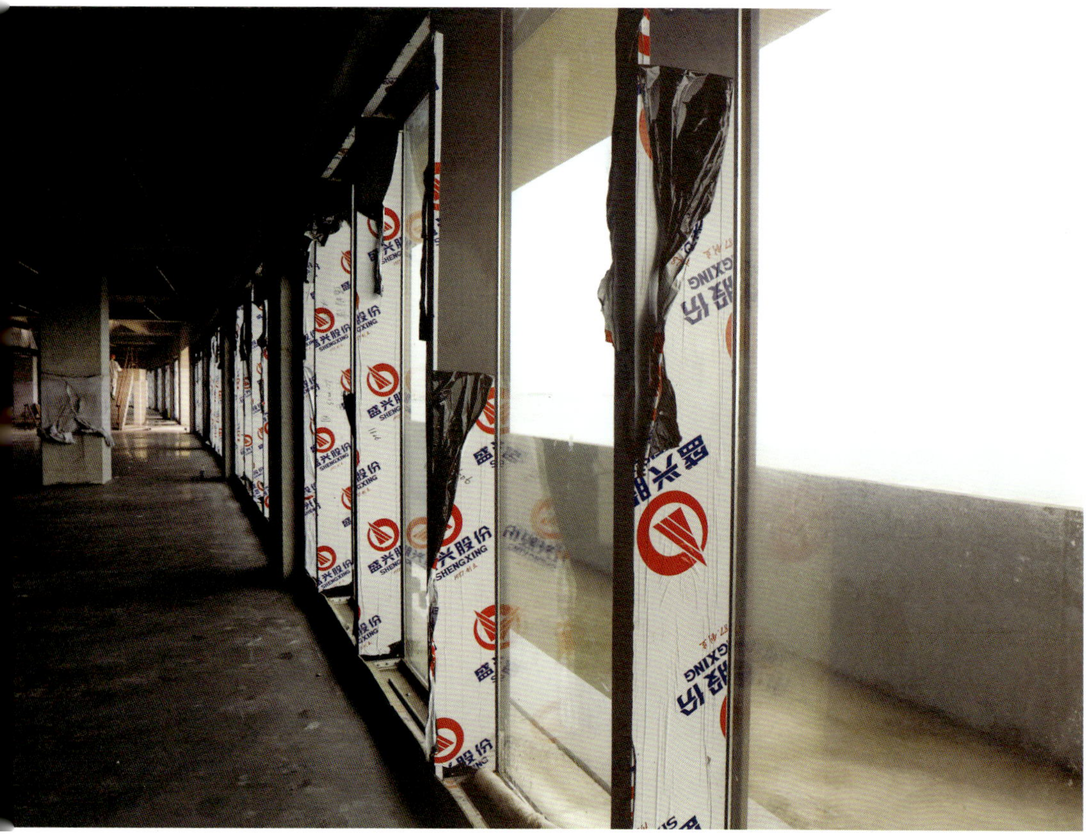

1. 玻璃幕墙安装
Installation of the Glass Wall

2. 玻璃幕墙骨架安装
Installation of the Glass Wall Framework

3. 玻璃幕墙密封
Glass Wall Sealing

4. 主体建筑大台阶玻璃幕墙骨架安装
Installation of the Glass Wall Framework for the Grand Step of the Main Building

5. 安装完成后的玻璃幕墙
Glass Wall Completed

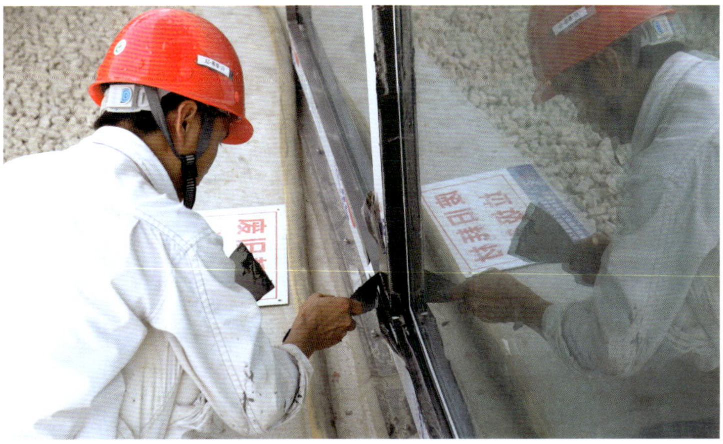

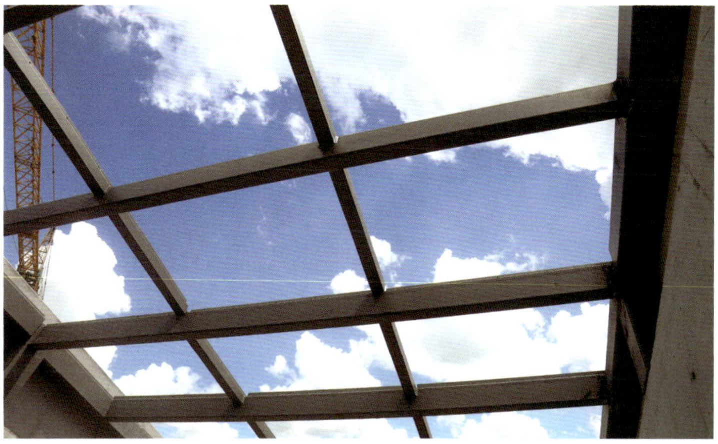

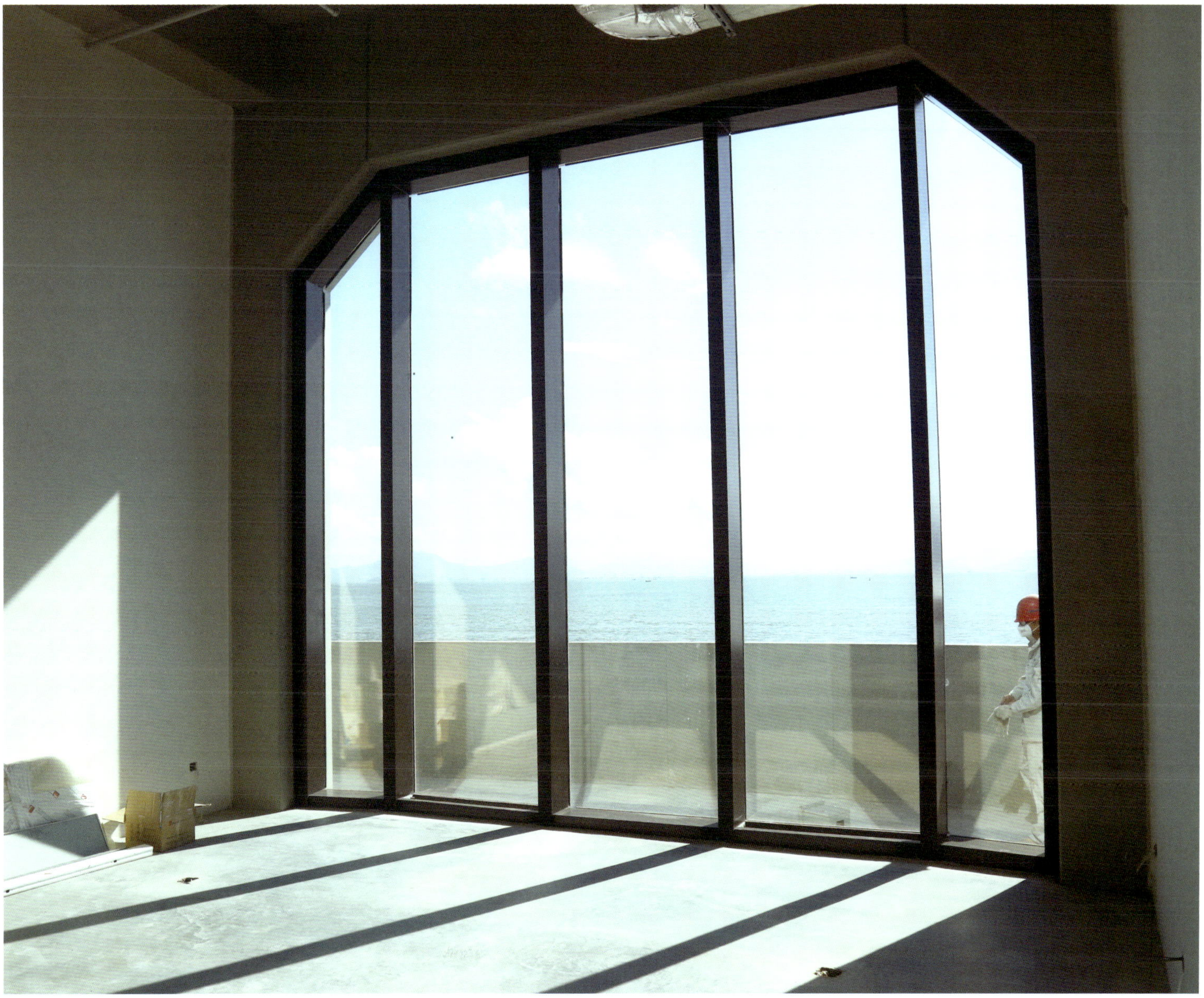

1	2	3
	4	5

1. 装饰装修完成后的东人工岛展厅
Exhibition Hall after Decoration on East Man-Made Island

2—5. 西人工岛主体建筑办公区
Office Area of the Main Building on West Man-Made Island

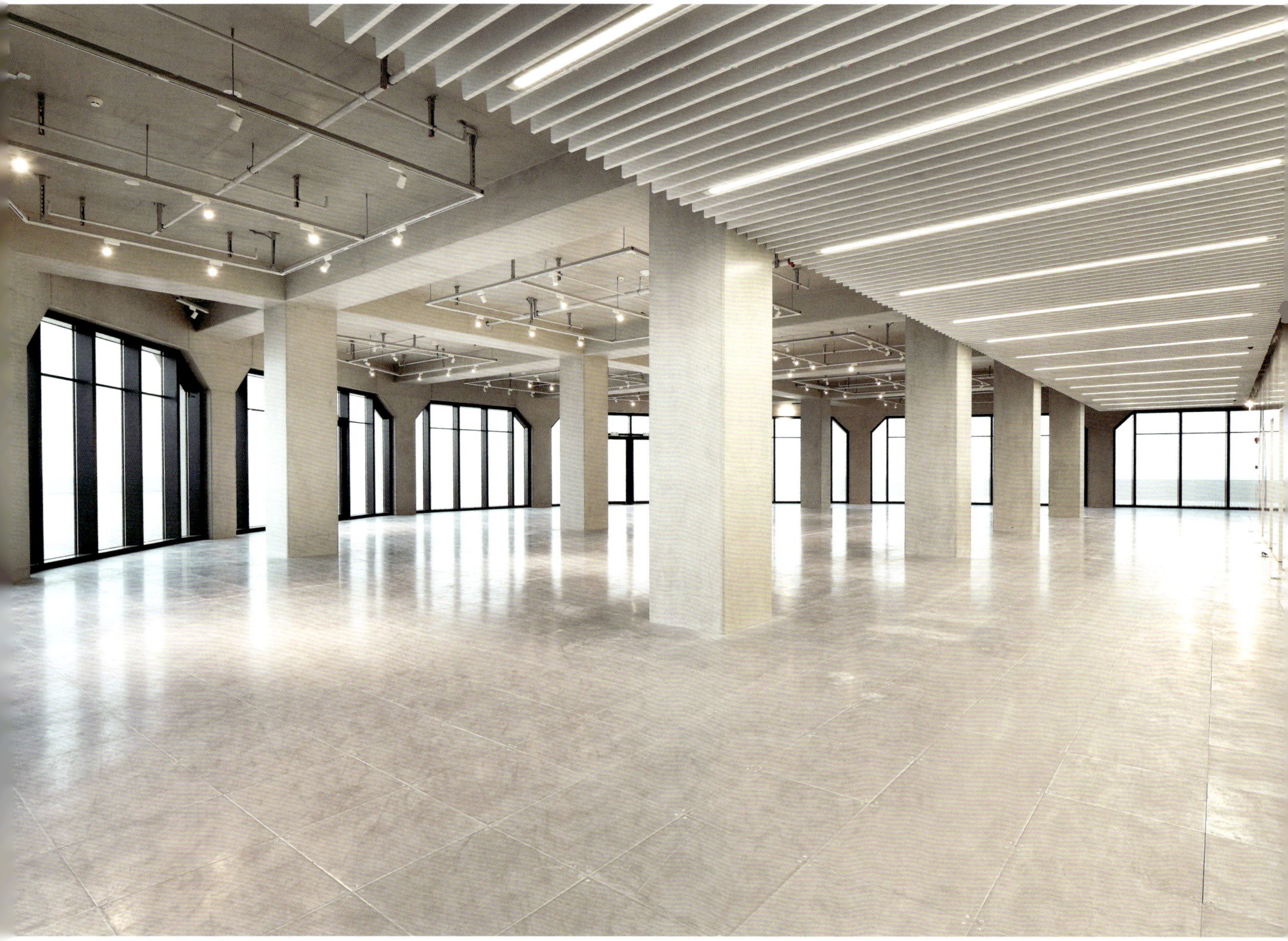

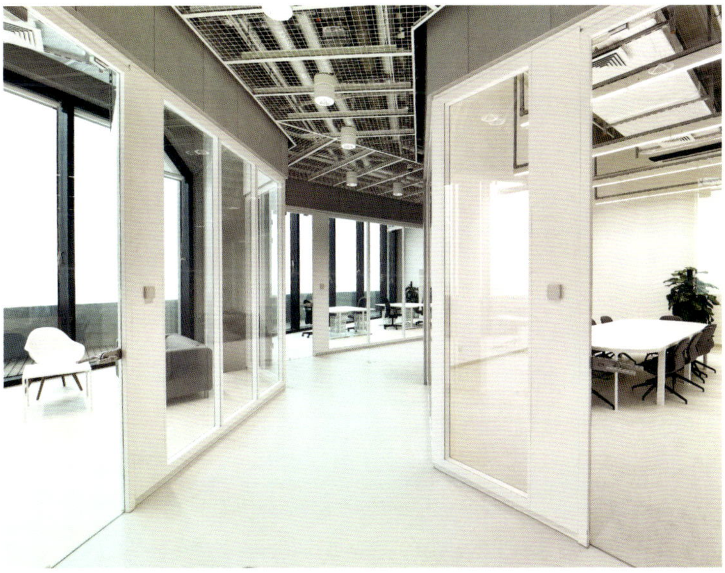

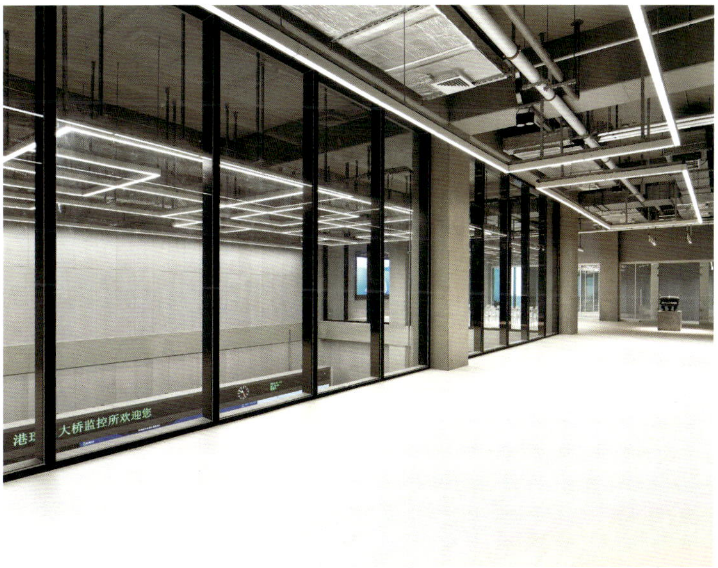
港
大桥监控所欢迎您

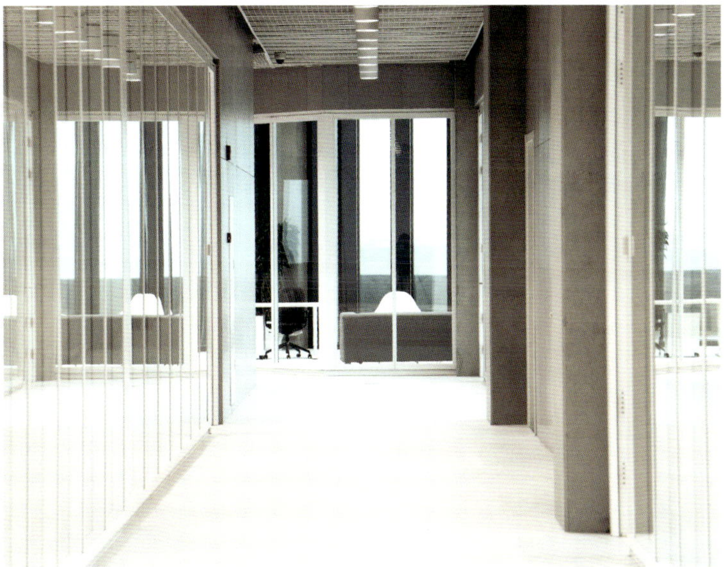

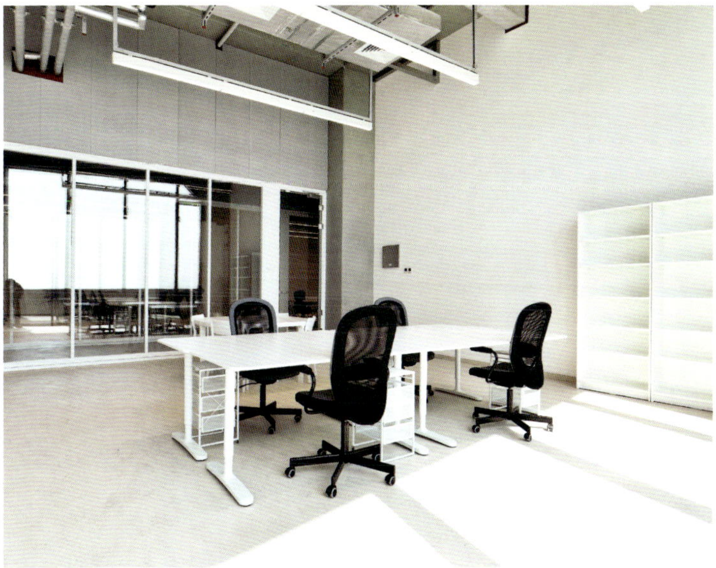

风帽
WIND CAP

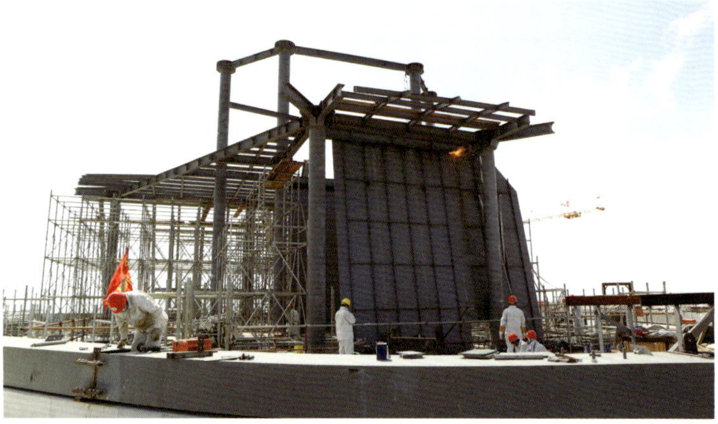

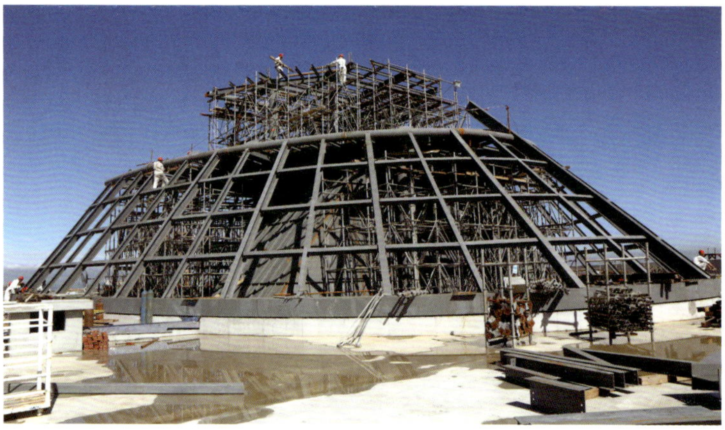

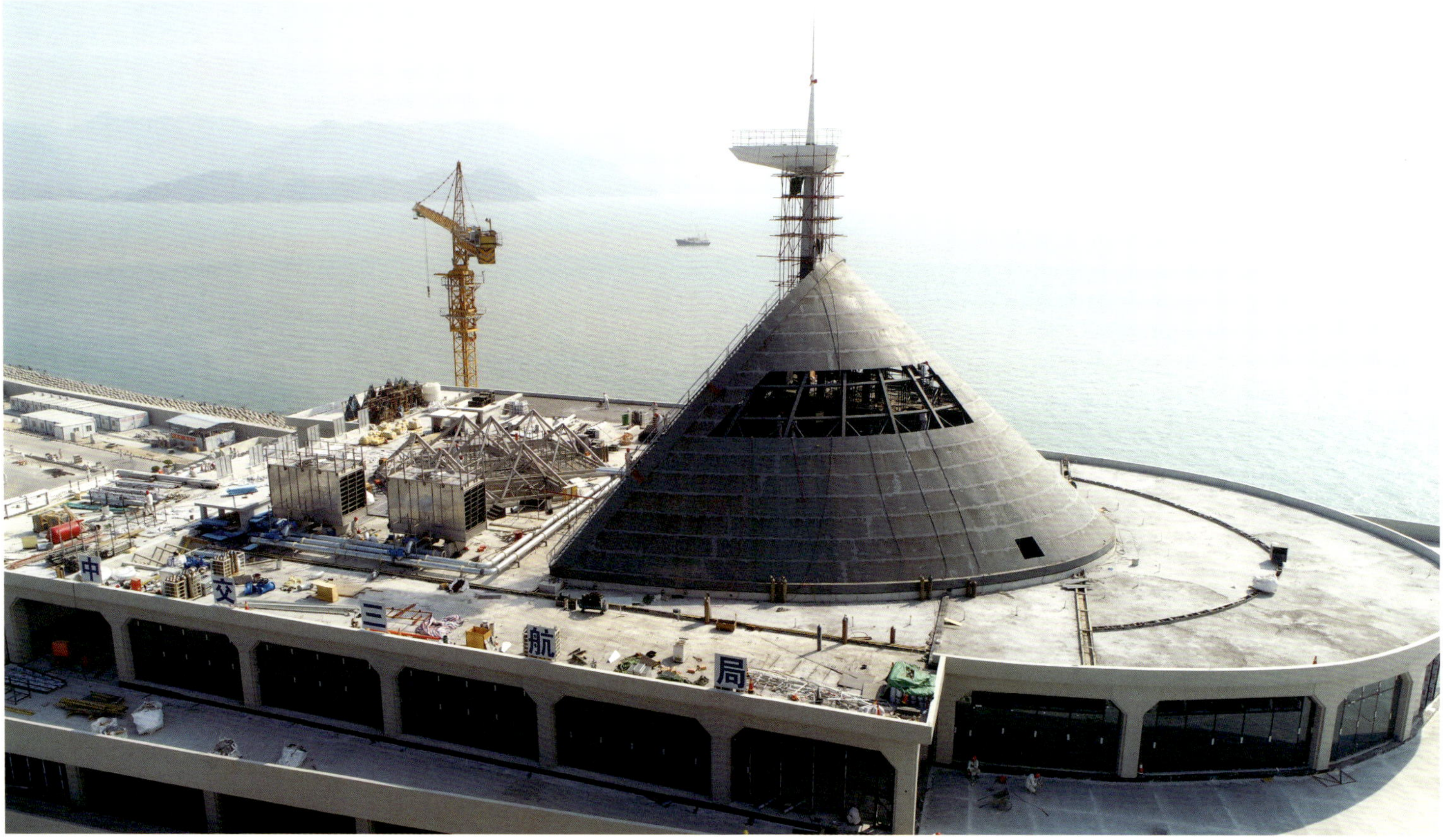

1 2
3 4

1—3. 风帽结构安装
Installation of the Wind Cap

2. 西人工岛风帽
Wind Cap on West Man-Made Island

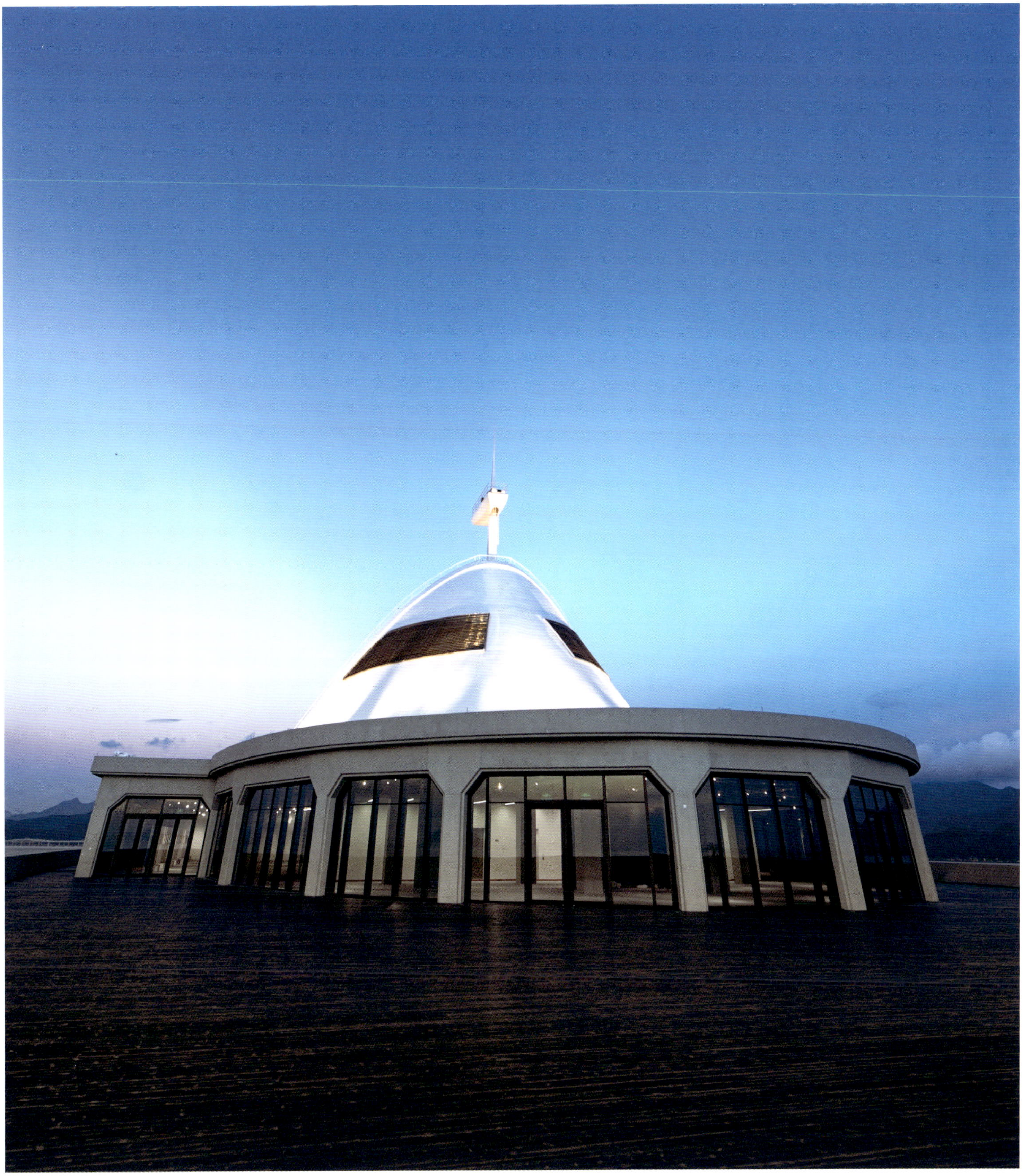

路缘石、透水路砖安装
INSTALLATION OF THE CURBSTONES AND PERMEABLE ROAD BRICKS

1. 路缘石安装
   Installation of the Curbstones
2. 路缘石安装精度控制 1mm
   Curbstone Installation Accuracy within the Limit of 1 millimeter
3. 安装完成后的路缘石
   Curbstones Installed
4. 透水路砖铺装
   Paving of the Permeable Road Bricks
5. 完成铺装的西人工岛广场
   West Man-Made Island Square Completed

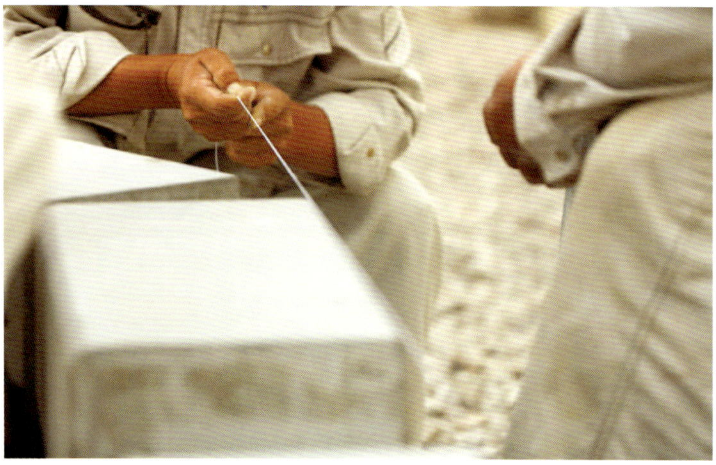

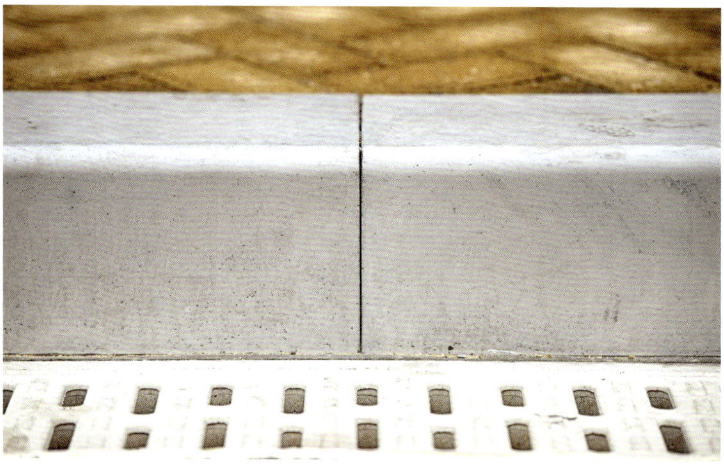

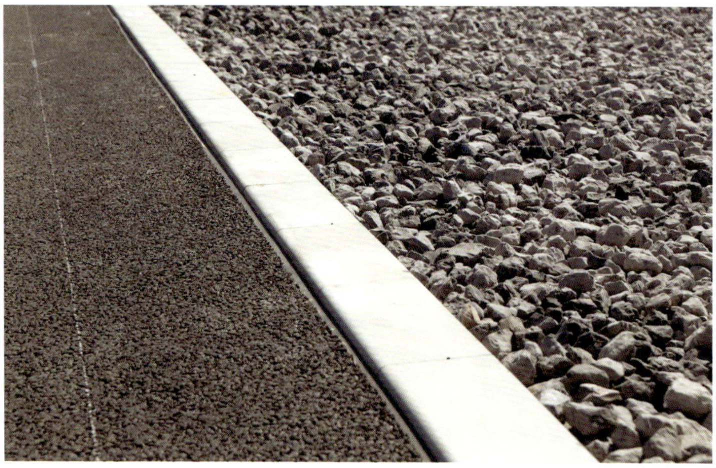

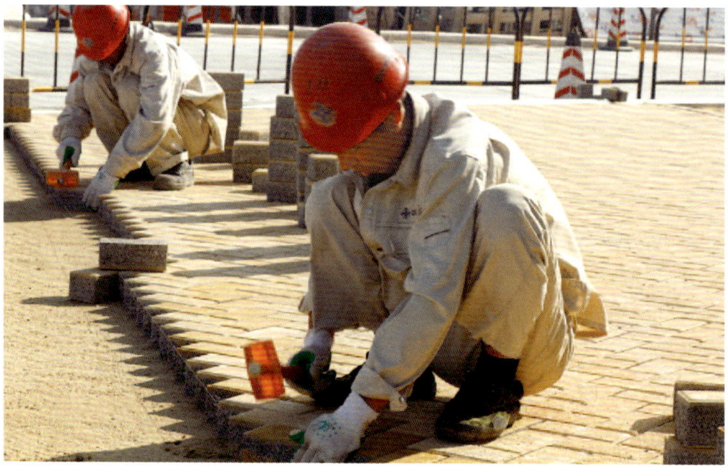

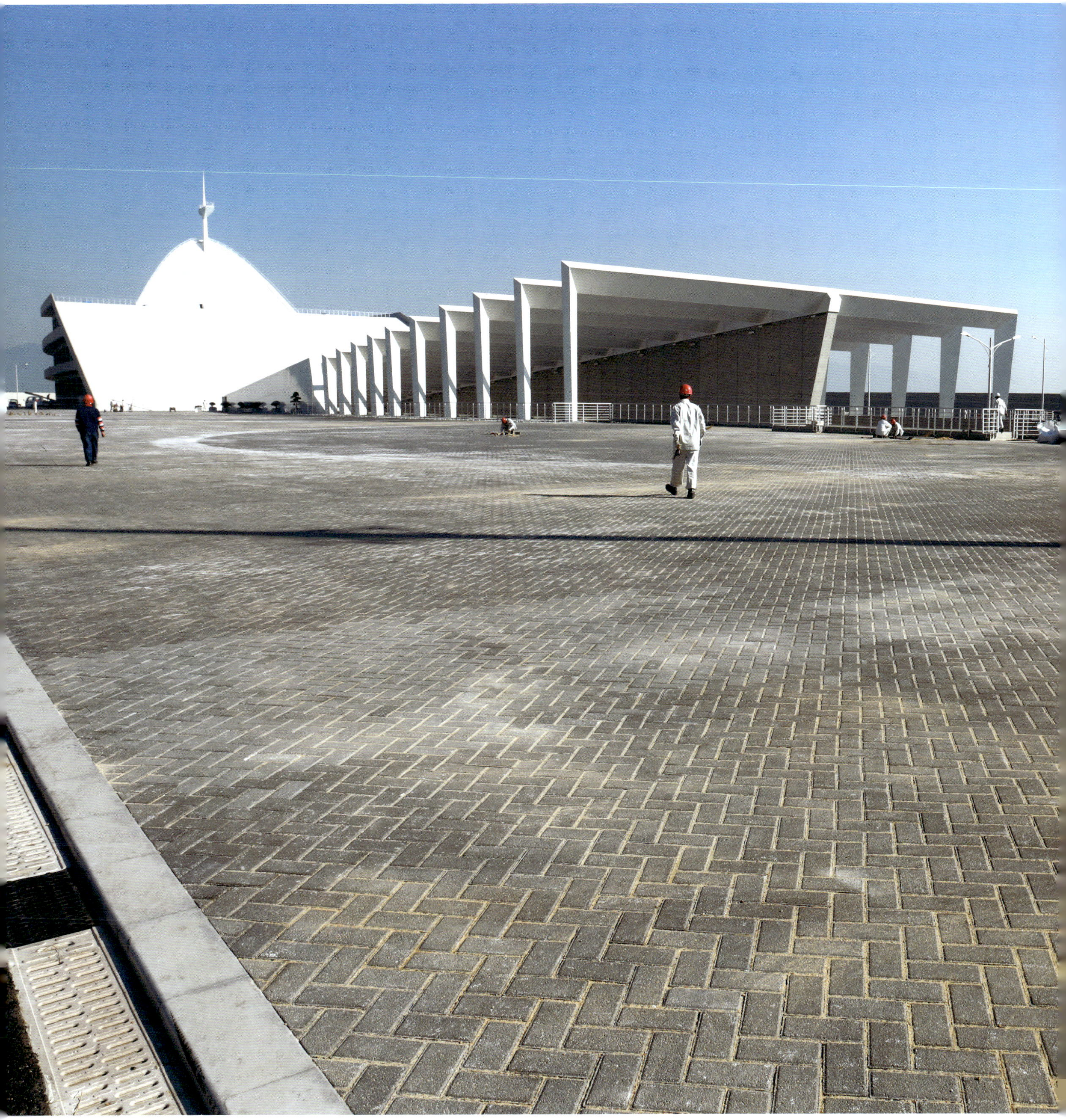

清水混凝土应用
APPLICATION OF FAIR-FACED CONCRETE

人工岛处于高盐雾、多风雨的外海环境，所有装修材料都会被快速消蚀损坏，从而导致无休止的重复装修，从使用寿命、视觉效果和总体成本来看，清水混凝土是最佳的选择。

虽然从 20 世纪 20 年代开始，国际上采用清水混凝土技术，一些大型的公共建筑都采用这种工艺，但是在中国还是很少如此大规模地使用，原因就在于其对施工的过程控制、现场管理、员工素质都有很高的要求。

清水混凝土标准有四个等级。岛隧工程东西人工岛敞开段、挡浪墙、岛上建筑均采用了Ⅲ级、Ⅳ级标准，整体表面清洁，色泽自然，线条符合设计韵律。

岛隧工程的清水混凝土从设计出发，在考虑到大面积效果的同时，兼顾结构造型和景观融合，从本质奠定清水的基调。模板设计模块化，明缝分块，蝉缝划线，对拉螺杆孔眼装饰。通过混凝土现场试验及典型施工形成工法工艺，规定了清水混凝土施工过程中关于施工组织管理、原材料的品质、清水混凝土配合比、混凝土生产和运输、模板的制作和安装、混凝土垫块、钢筋和预埋件的处理、浇筑和振捣、拆模和养护、成品保护等影响混凝土外观的工艺要求和技术措施。

The man-made islands were located in the open sea with high salt fog and windy and rainy weather. All decoration materials would be easily eroded and damaged, resulting in endlessly repeated decoration and restoration. Therefore, fair-faced concrete was the best choice in terms of its life span, visual effects and overall costs.

Although fair-faced concrete technology had been adopted in the world since the 1920s and some large public buildings adopted this technology, it was rarely used on such a large-scale project in China because of the strict requirements for construction process control, site management and staff quality.

There are four fair-faced concrete standards. The open section of the tunnel, the wave-blocking walls and the buildings on the east and west man-made islands all adopted Grade III and IV standards. Its clean surface, the natural color and the lines and curves all exhibit the beauty of the design.

The fair-faced concrete designed for the island-tunnel project suited the special structural and visual effect of the building on large surfaces while keeping its basic tone. The modularized design of the templates, visible seams in blocks, thin seam lines and pulling-screw holes were also used for decoration. By on-the-site tests and typical construction, the technical requirements and measures affecting the appearance of concrete were provided for the operation of fair-faced concrete, such as construction organization and management, quality of raw materials, mixture ratio, concrete production and transportation, fabrication and installation of the templates, concrete cushion blocks, management of reinforcing steel bars and embedded parts, casting and vibratory driving, template removal and maintenance, and finished product protection.

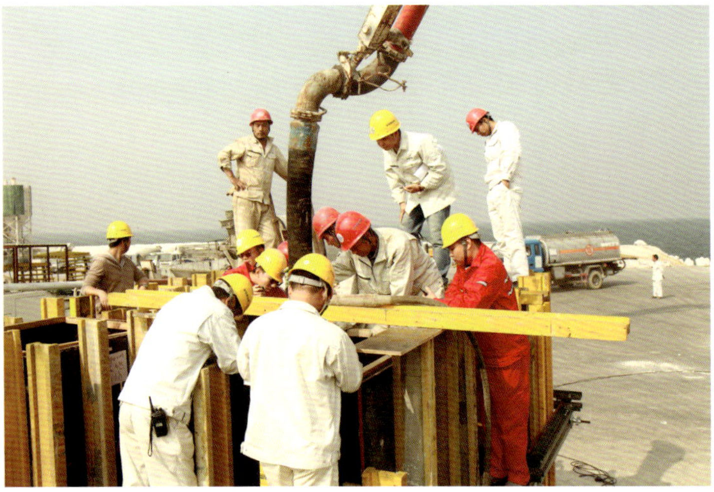

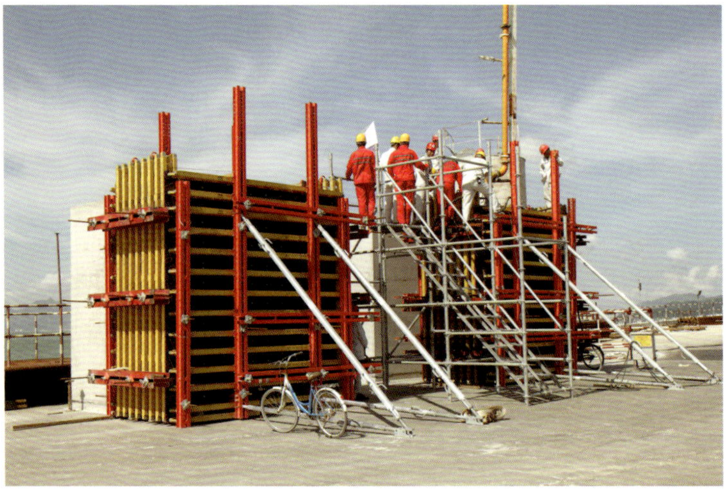

1. 人工岛清水混凝土试验
Fair-Faced Concrete Test on the Man-Made Islands
2. 人工岛清水混凝土配合比优化
Optimization of the Mixture Ratio of Fair-Faced Concrete for the Man-Made Islands
3. 清水混凝土挡浪墙
Wave-Blocking Wall Cast with Fair-Faced Concrete

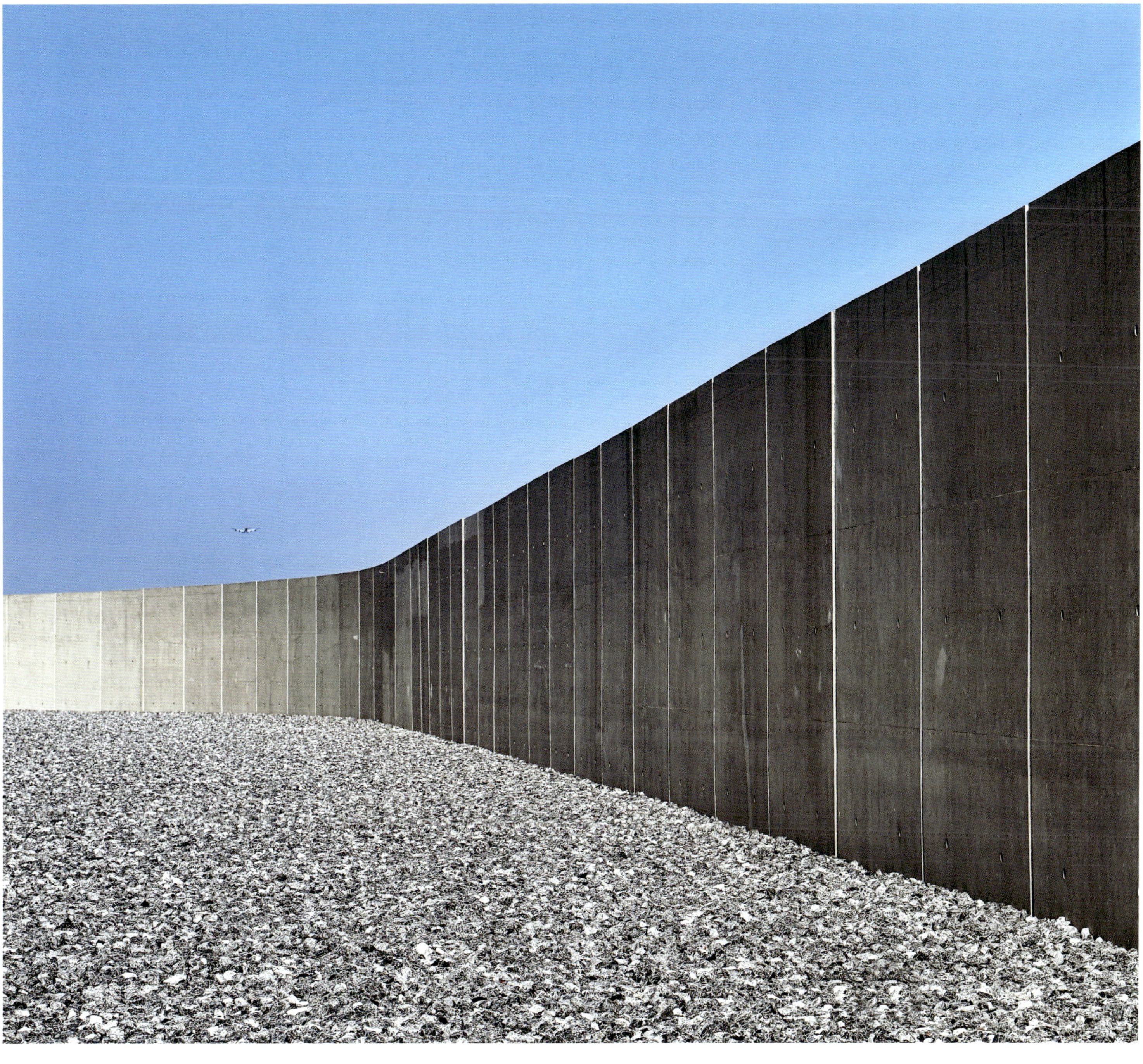

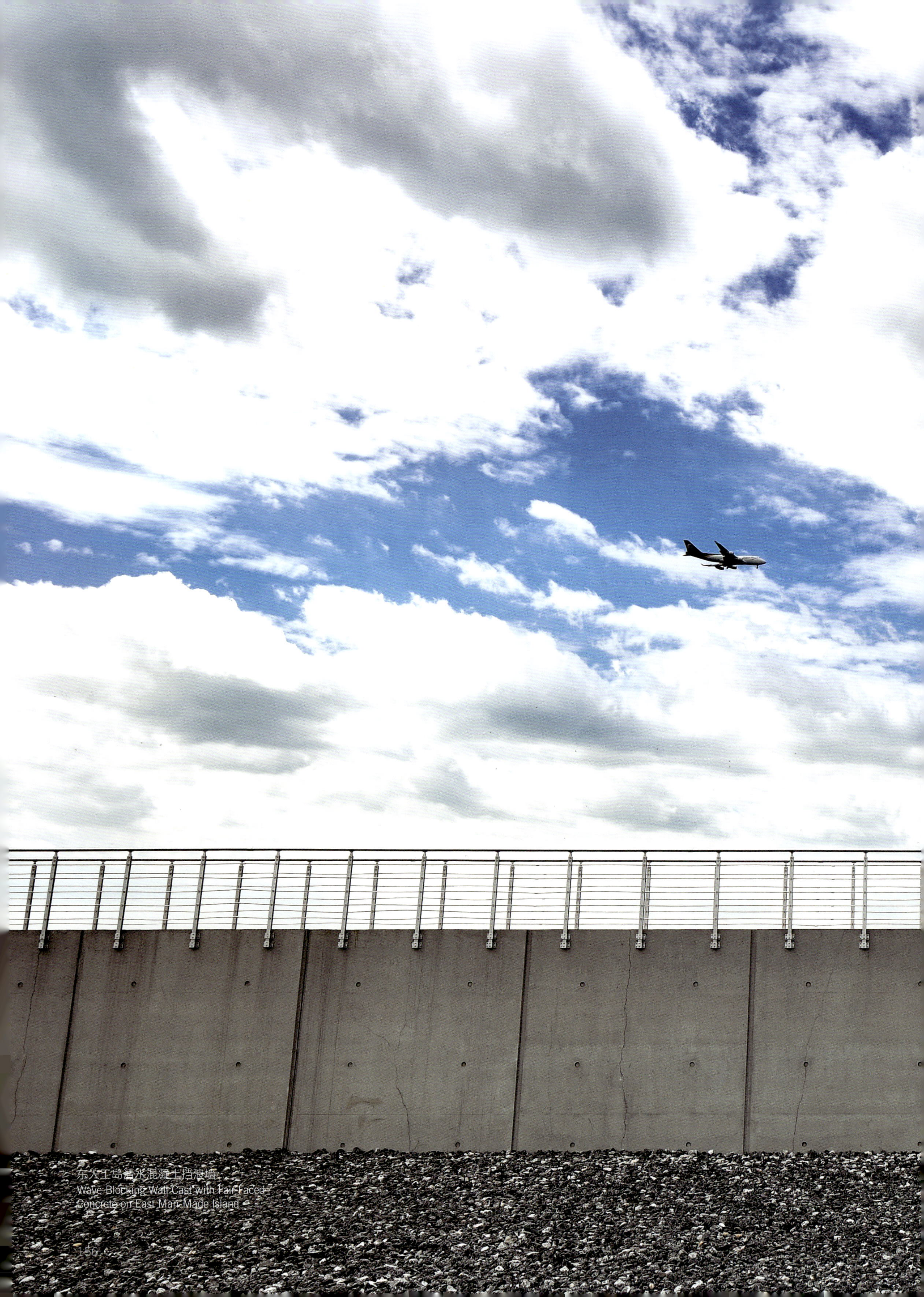

东人工岛清水混凝土挡浪墙
Wave-Blocking Wall Cast with Fair-Faced Concrete on East Man-Made Island

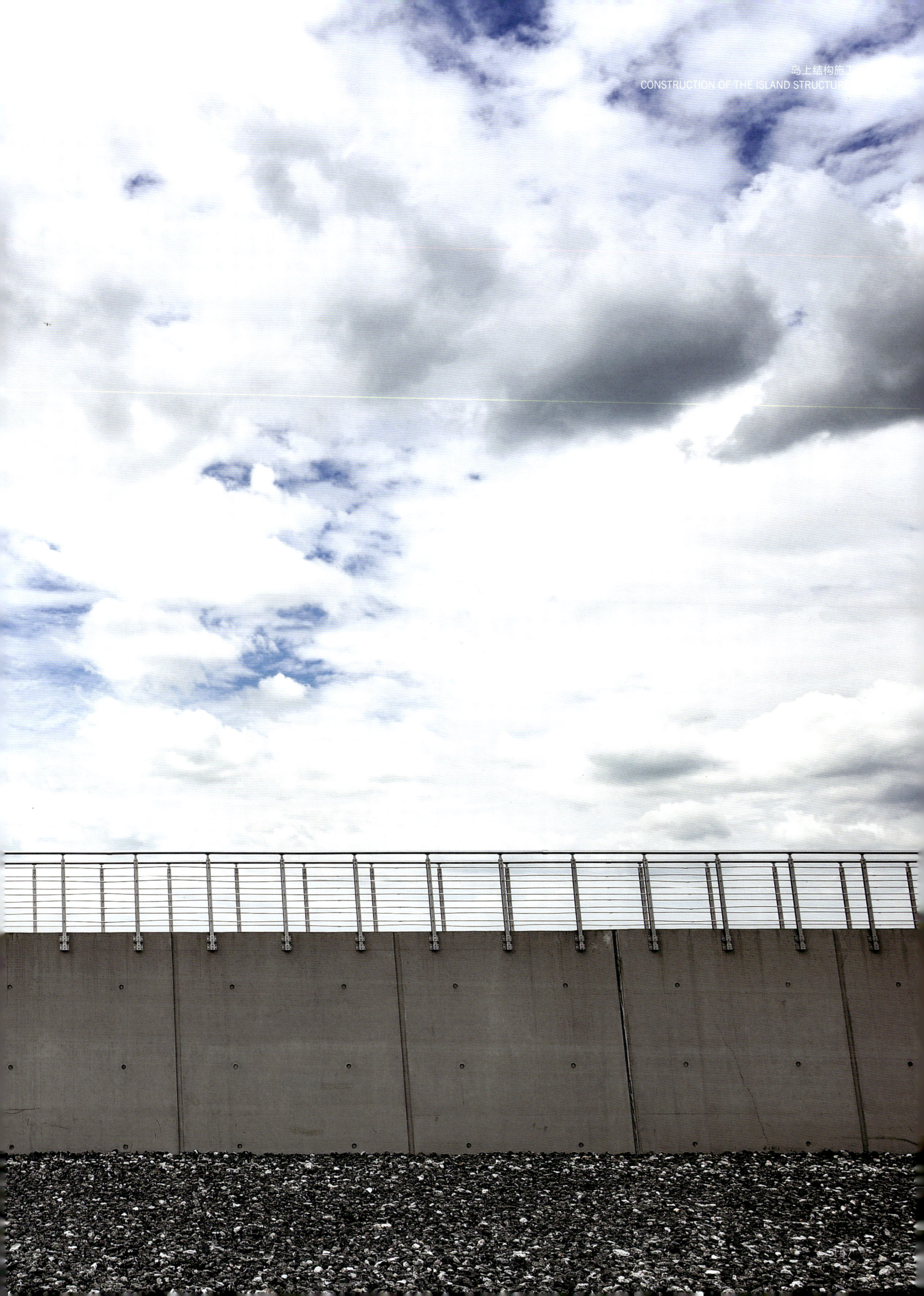

1. 人工岛主体建筑首层清水混凝土结构
Fair-Faced Concrete Structure on the First Floor of the Main Building of the Man-Made Islands

2—4. 清水混凝土立柱和楼板
Fair-Faced Concrete Column and Floor

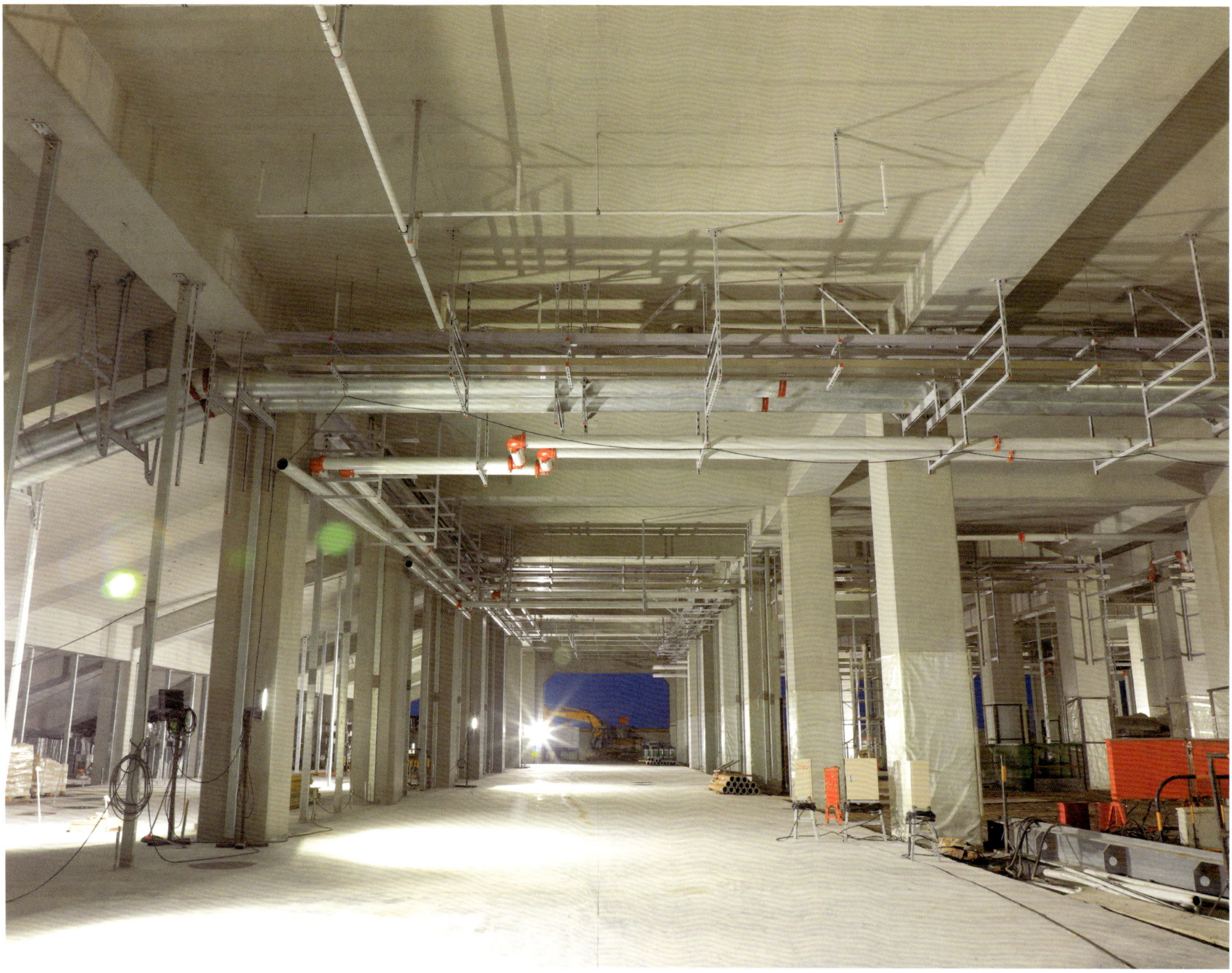

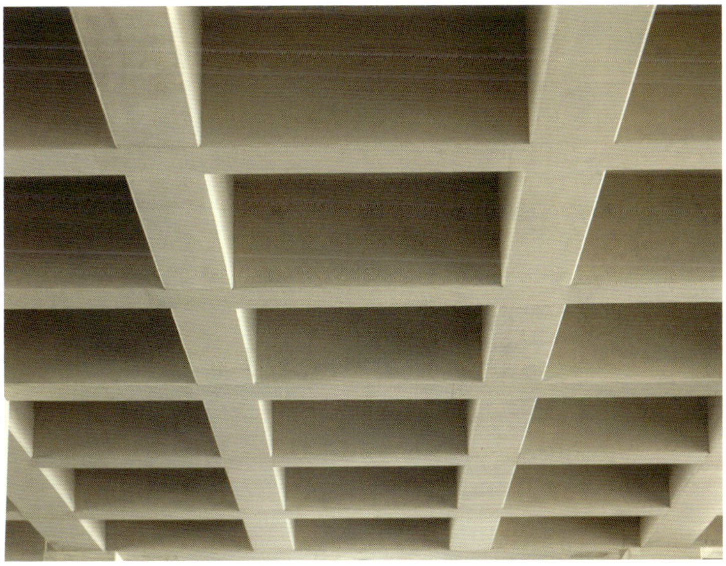

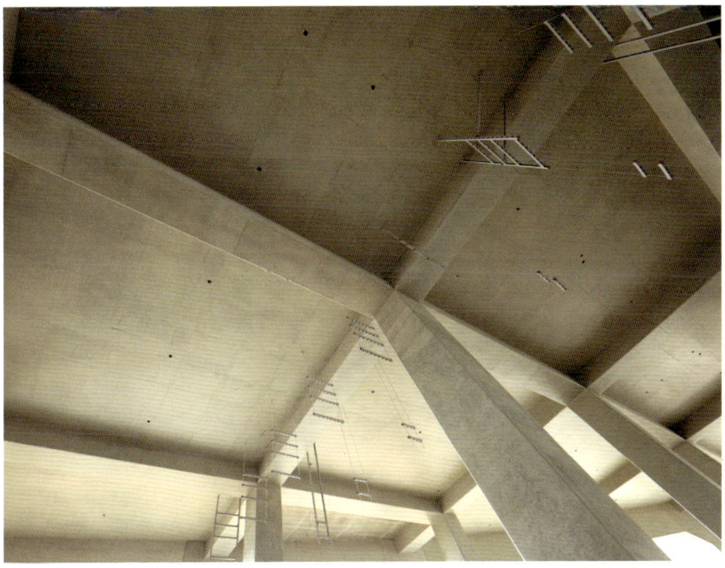

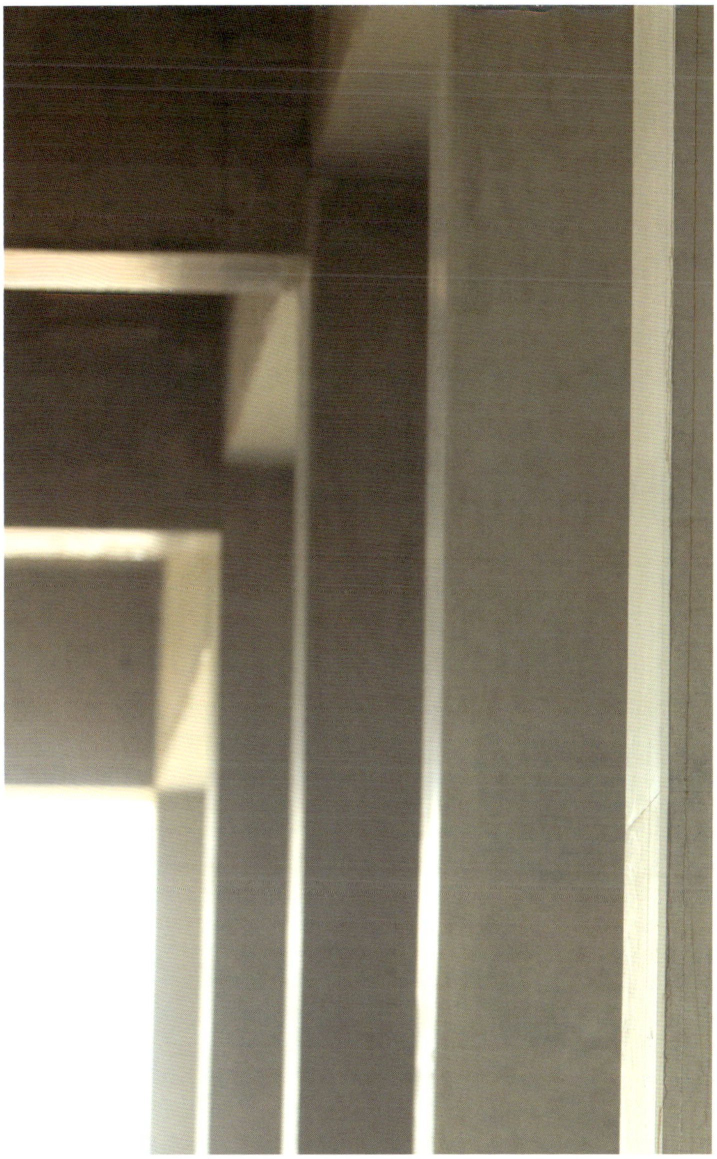

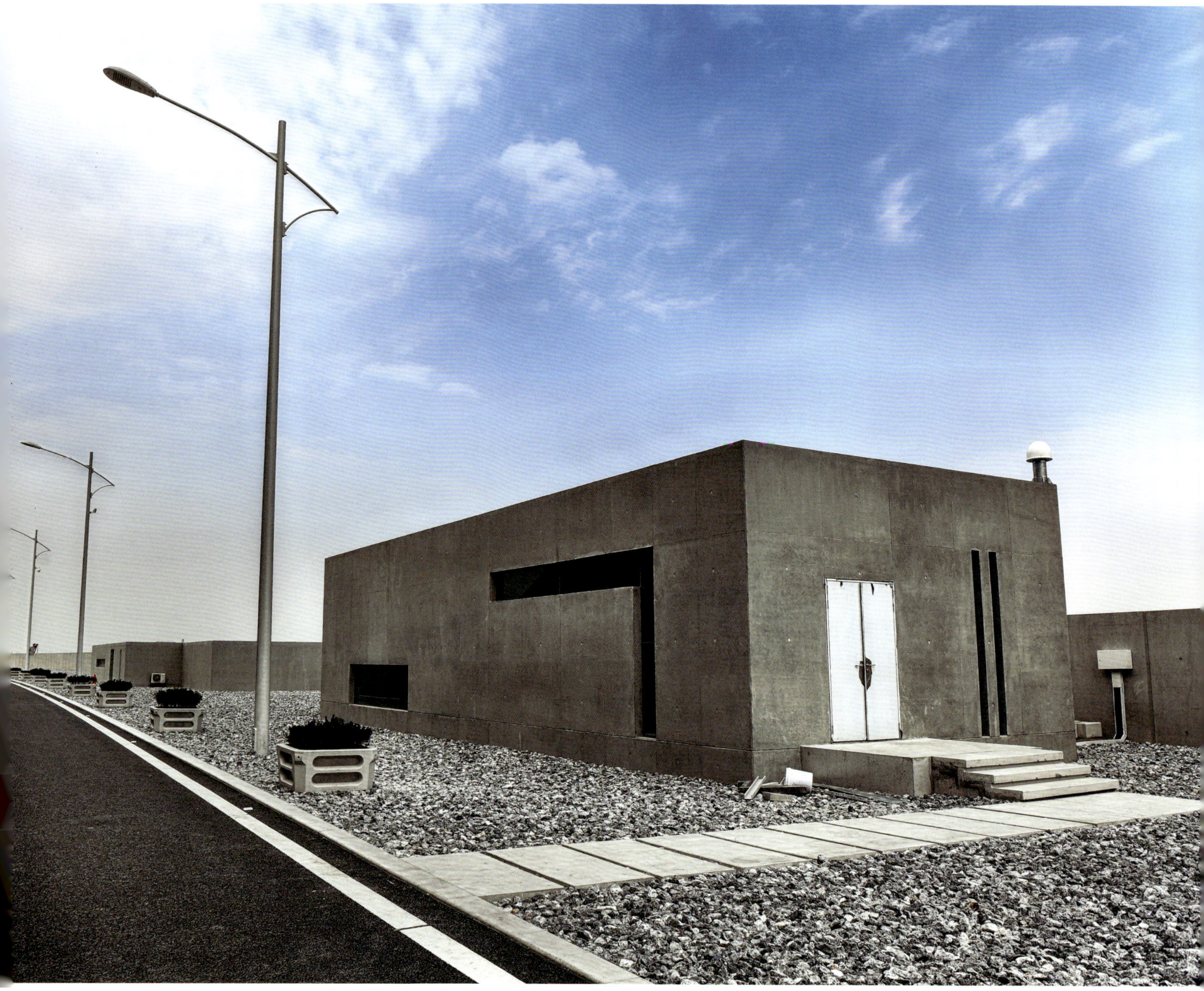

1. 人工岛清水混凝土越浪泵房
Striding Wave Drainage Pump Station Cast with Fair-Faced Concrete on the Man-Made Islands
2. 敞开段清水混凝土排水沟
Fair-Faced Concrete Drainage Ditch at the Open Section

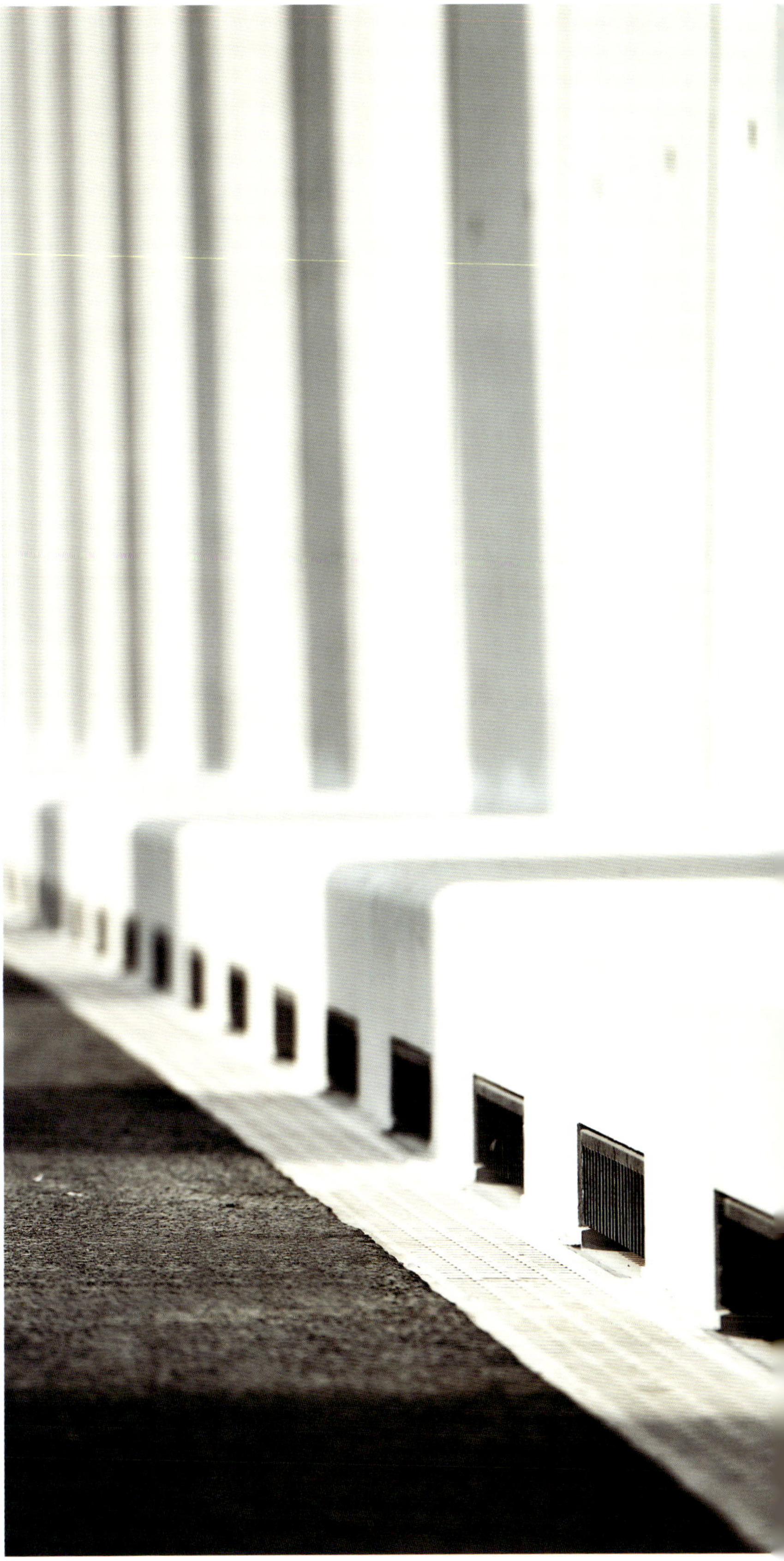

东西人工岛越浪泵房、检修道盖板、路缘石、花盆、台阶等结构物均采用清水混凝土建造。项目总经理部优化清水混凝土配合比，建成了专业预制工厂，实现了小构件工厂法预制、装配化安装目标。

Many structures on the east and west man-made islands were constructed with fair-faced concrete, such as pump station to drain the striding waves, maintenance trail cover plate, curbstones, flowerpots, steps, etc. The project management center optimized the mixture ratio of the fair-faced concrete and set up a professional fabrication factory to precast, assemble and install small components.

非通航孔桥

NON-NAVIGATION CHANNEL BRIDGE

东、西人工岛非通航孔桥为现浇预应力混凝土连续箱梁，分别按照跨径5×49.8米、4×55米+3×55米布置，全长639.75米。其基础采用嵌岩钻孔灌注桩，桩基采用栈桥配合水上平台进行施工，上部箱梁采用少支架施工。

The non-navigation channel bridges on the two man-made islands were continuous structures of cast-on-site pre-stressed concrete box girders with the span length of 5 × 49.8 meters or 4 × 55 meters + 3 × 55 meters respectively and the total length of 639.75 meters. The base poles were made by pouring concrete into the sockets holed in the rock, the foundation of the poles was constructed by operation on the overwater platform and trestle, and the top box girders were built by operation on supporting scaffolds.

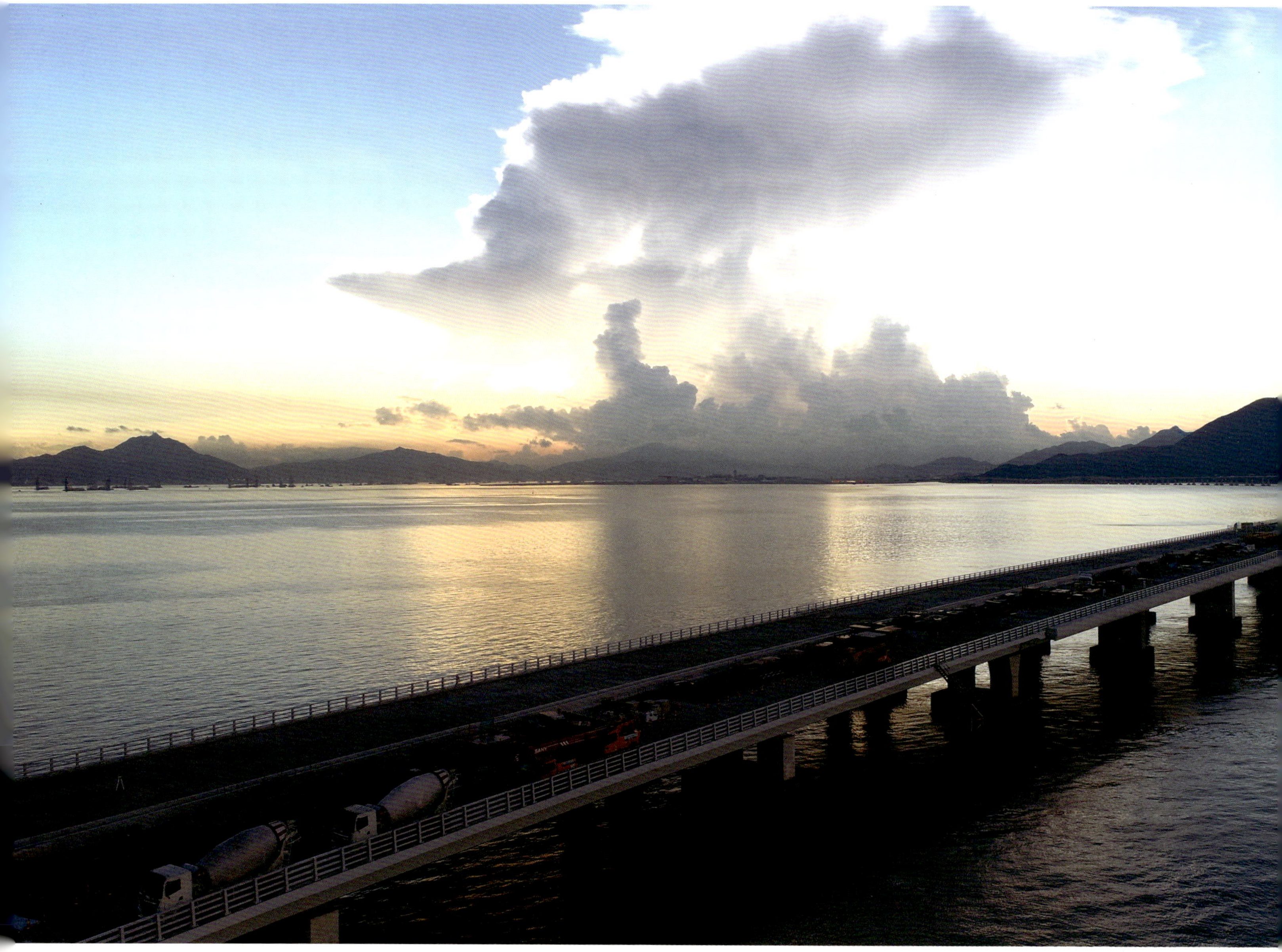

1. 东人工岛非通航孔桥
Non-navigation Channel Bridge on East Man-Made Island
2. 非通航孔桥跨箱梁浇筑施工
Casting of the Spanning Box Girder on the Non-navigation Channel Bridge
3. 西人工岛非通航孔桥与主体桥梁对接
Butt Joint between the Non-Navigation Channel Bridge and the Main Bridge on West Man-Made Island
4. 东人工岛非通航孔桥管线槽
Pipeline Rack of Non-Navigation Channel Bridge on East Man-Made Island

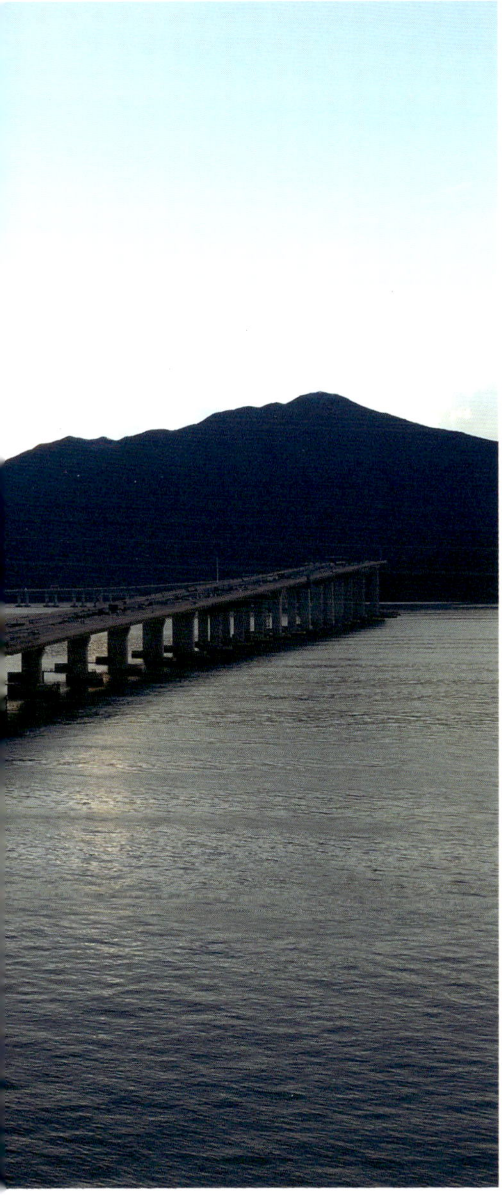

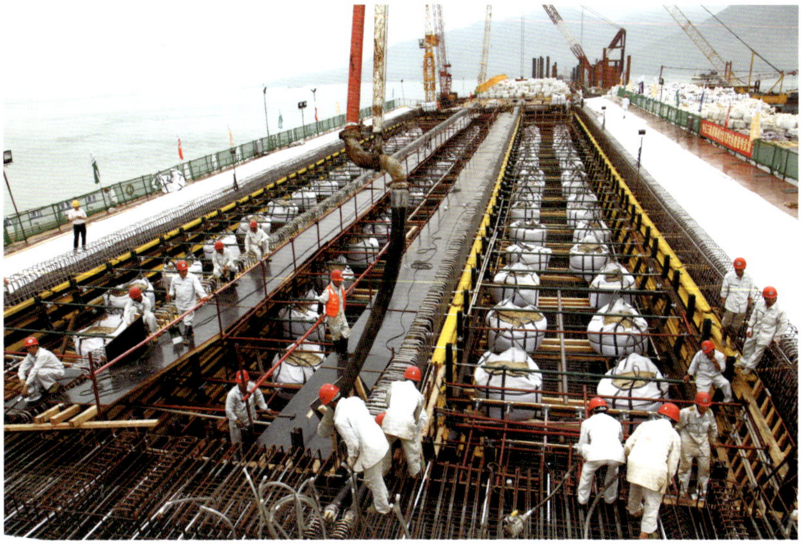

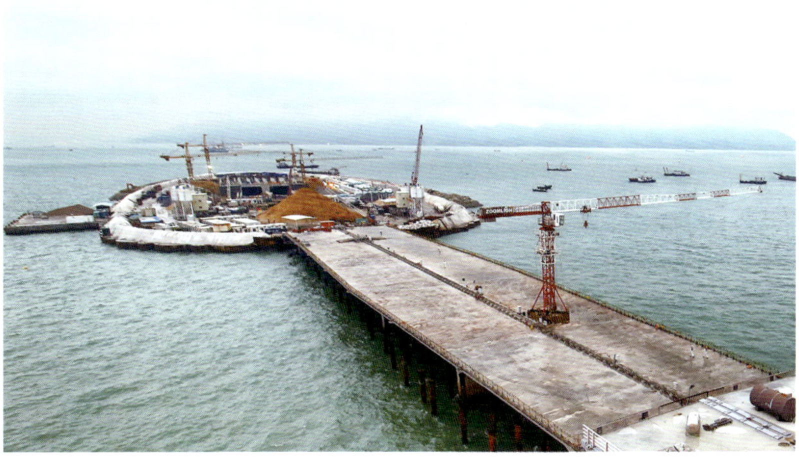

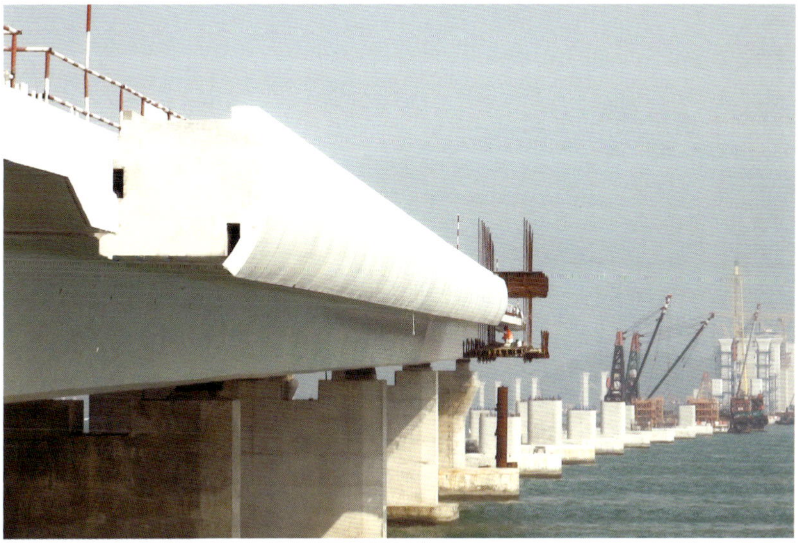

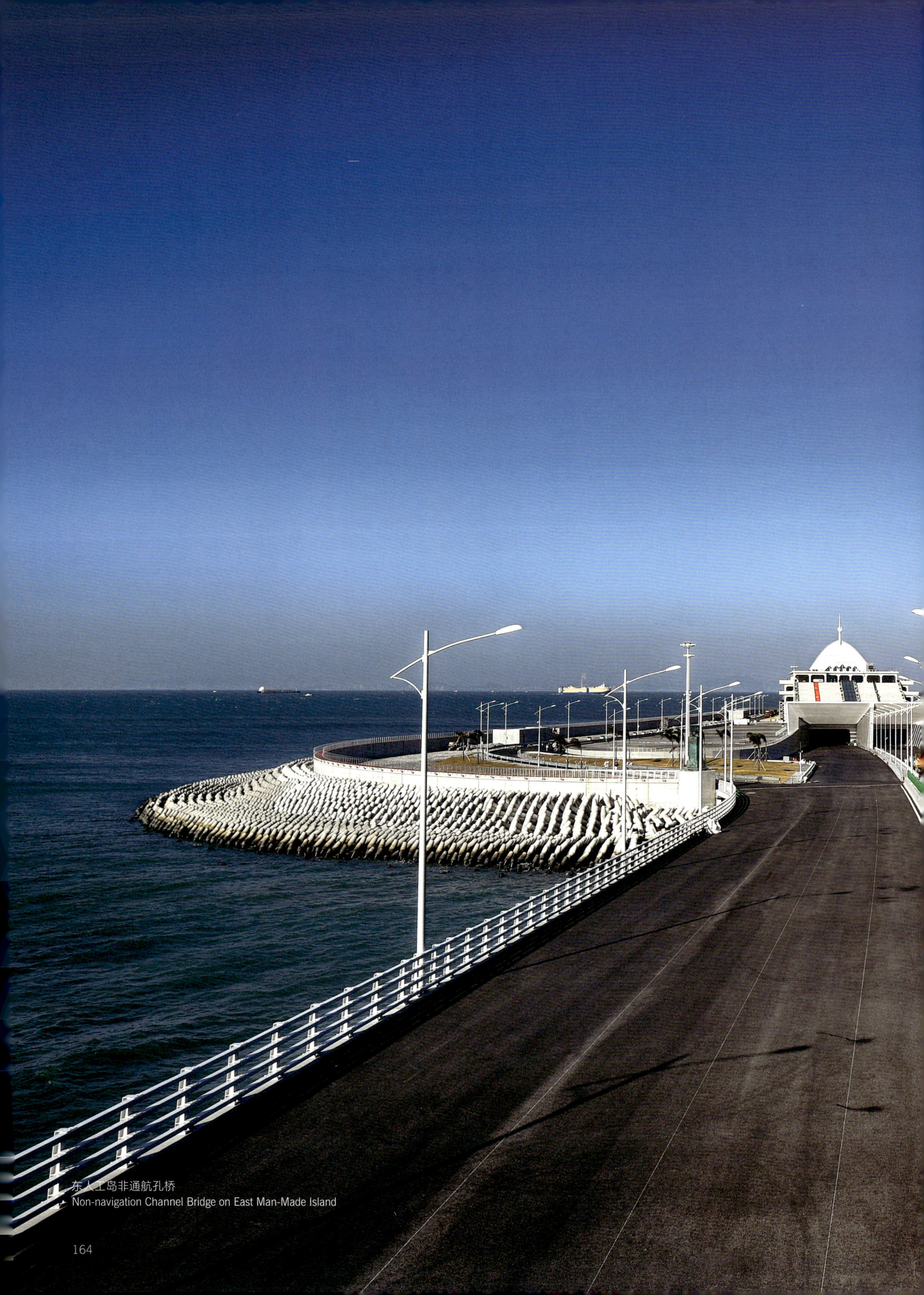

东人工岛非通航孔桥
Non-navigation Channel Bridge on East Man-Made Island

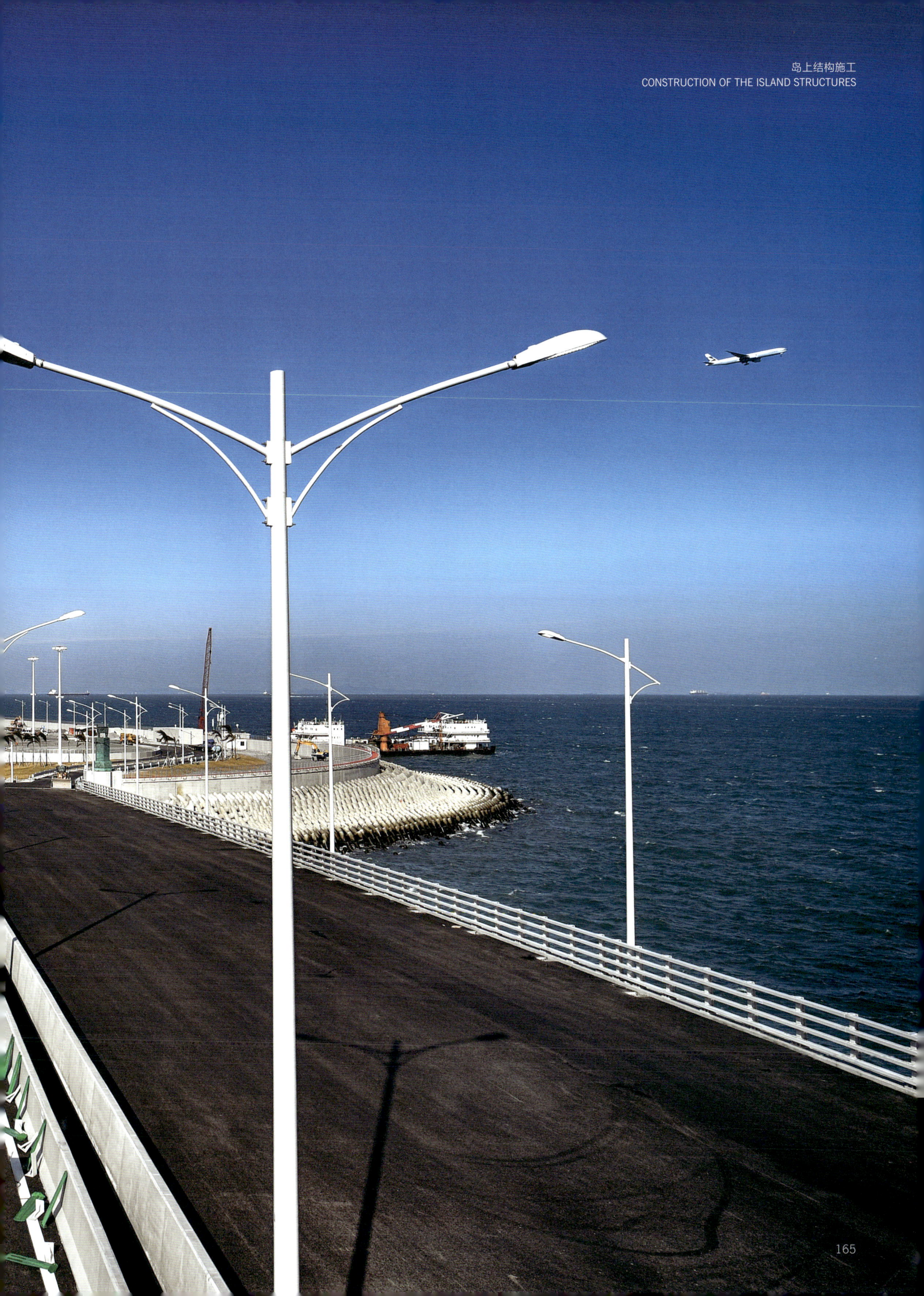

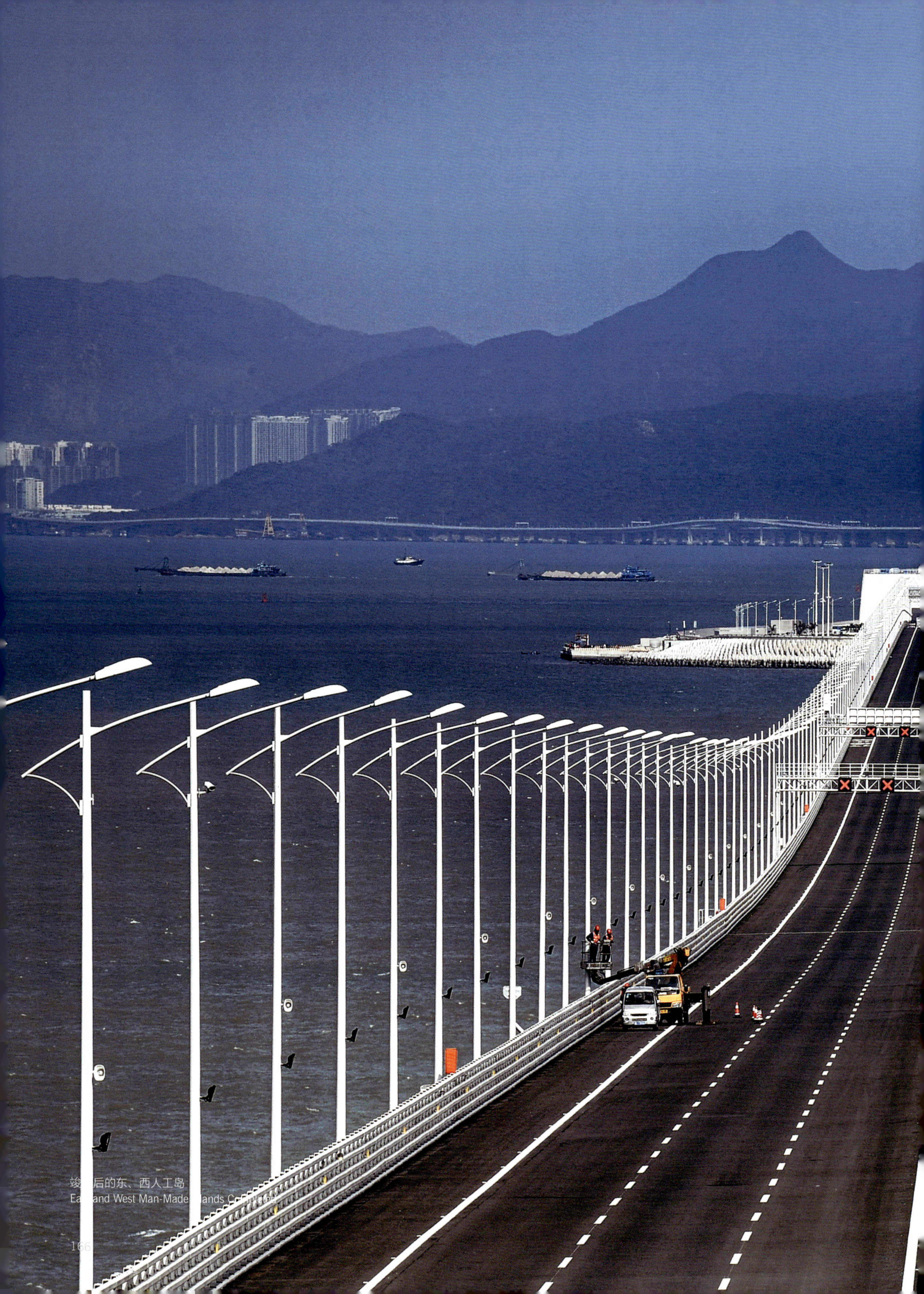

竣工后的东、西人工岛
East and West Man-Made Islands Completed

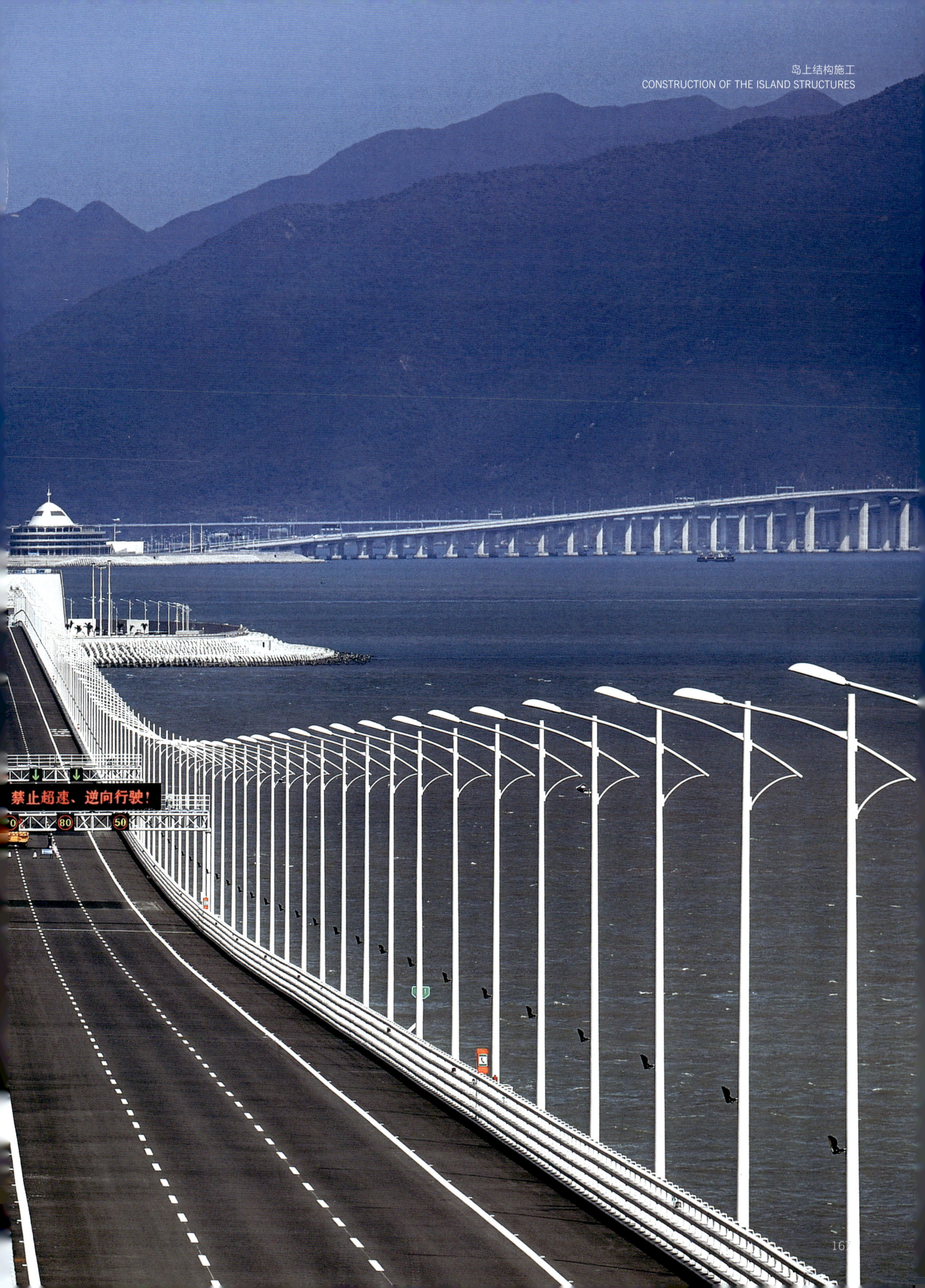
禁止超速、逆向行驶！
80
50

画册索引
ALBUM INDEX

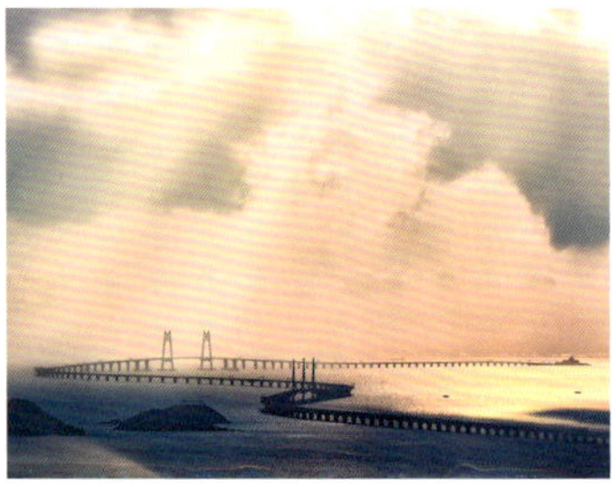

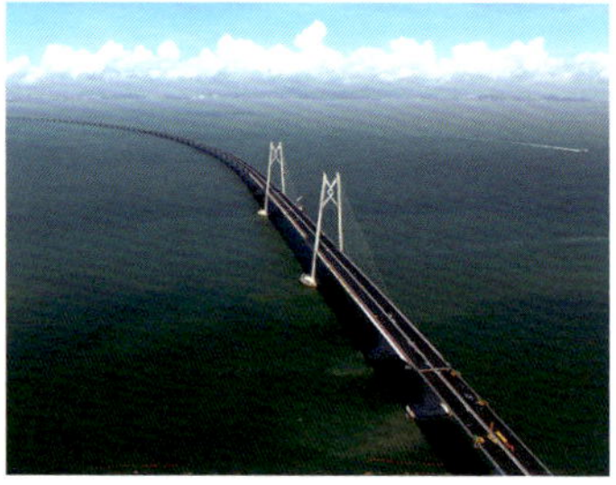

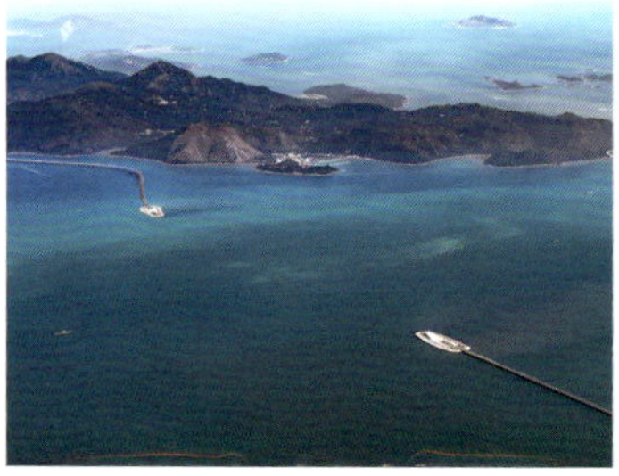

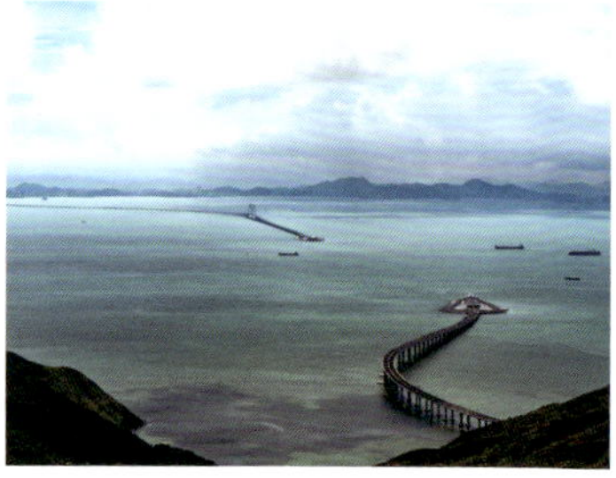

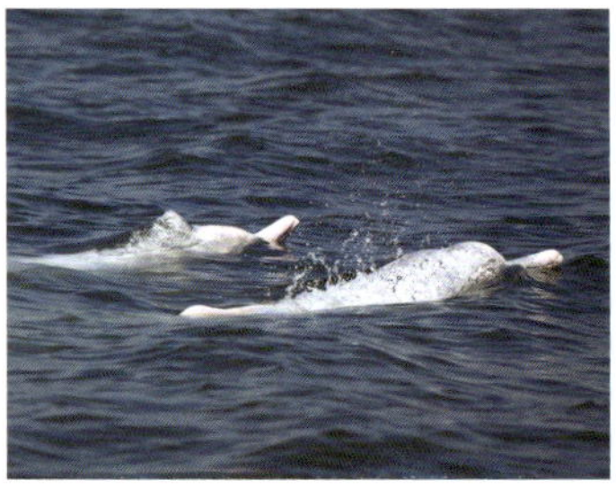

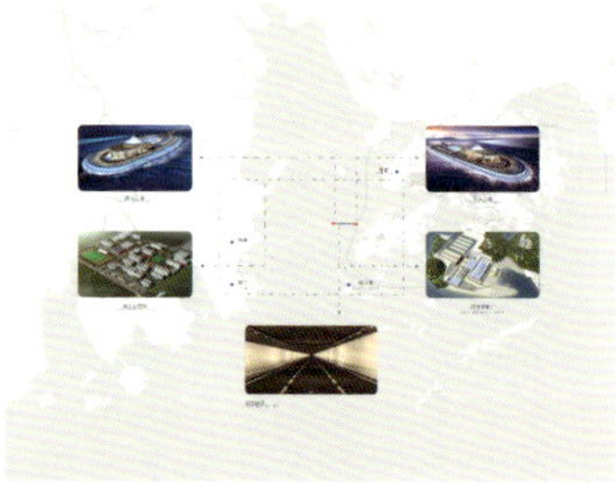

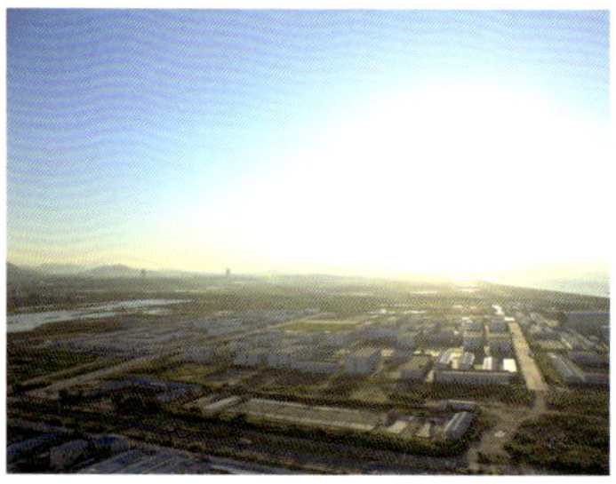

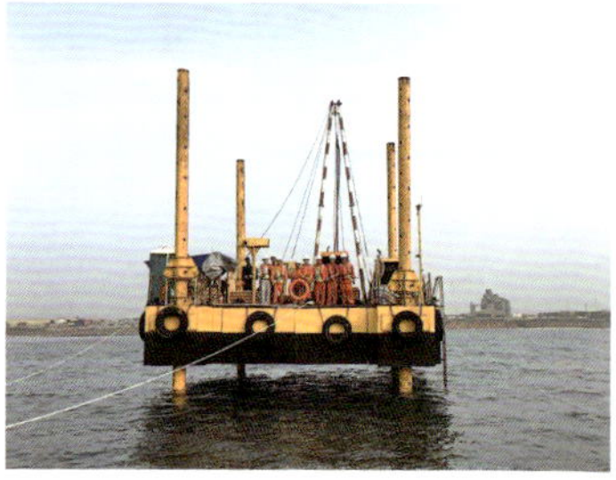

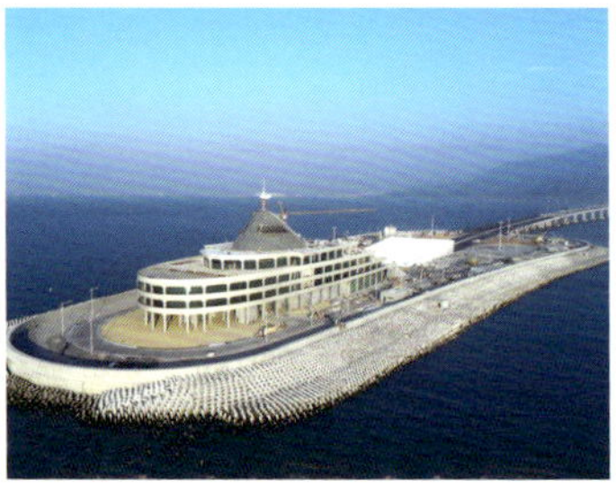

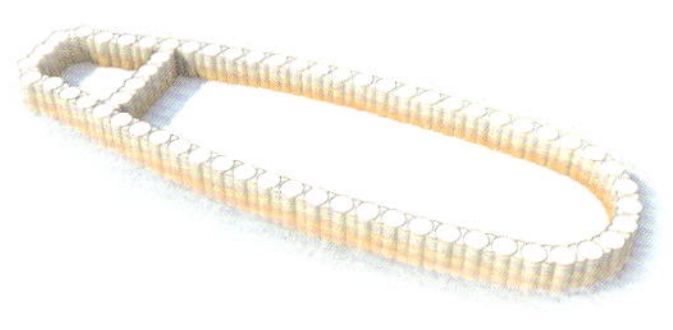

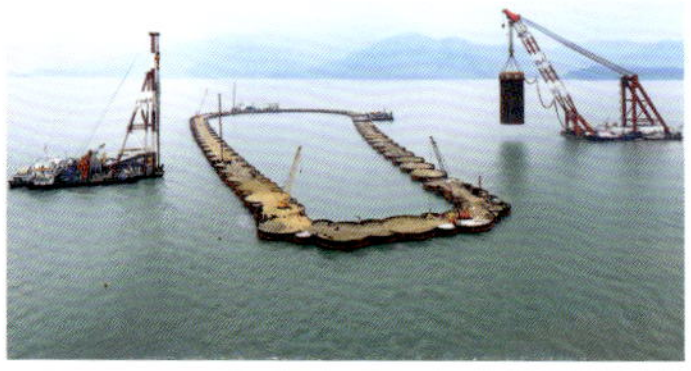

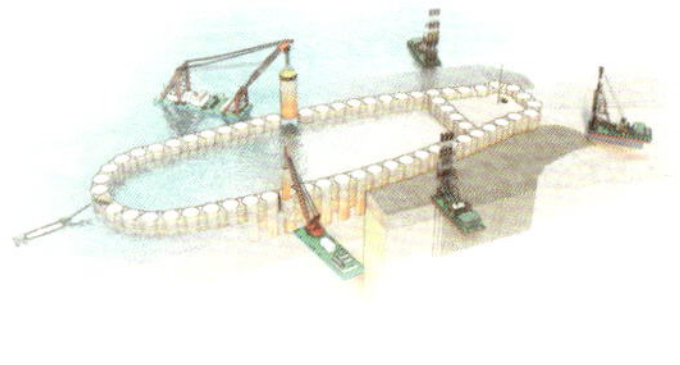

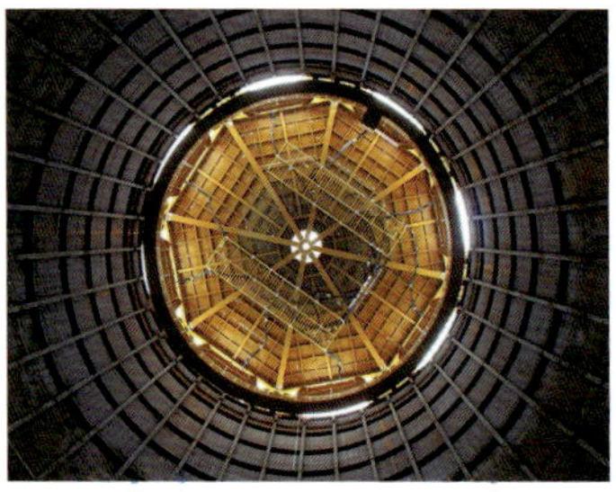

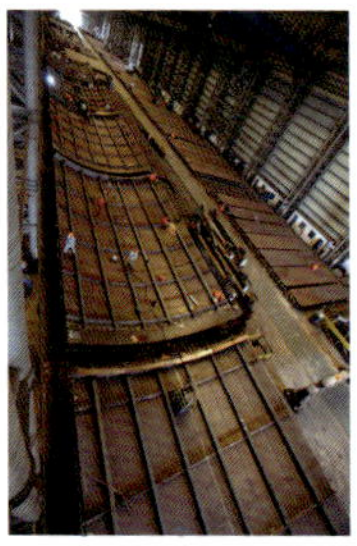

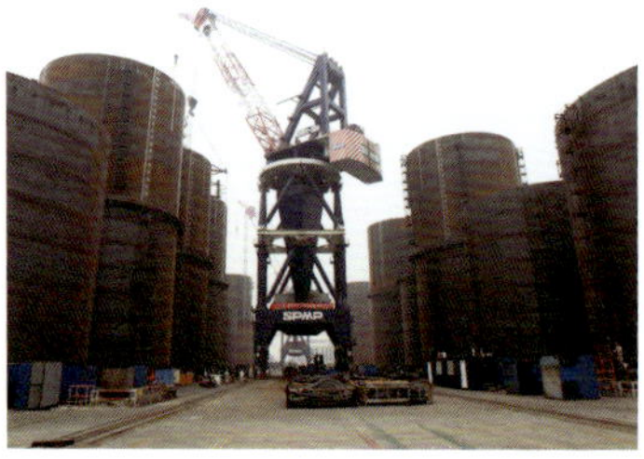

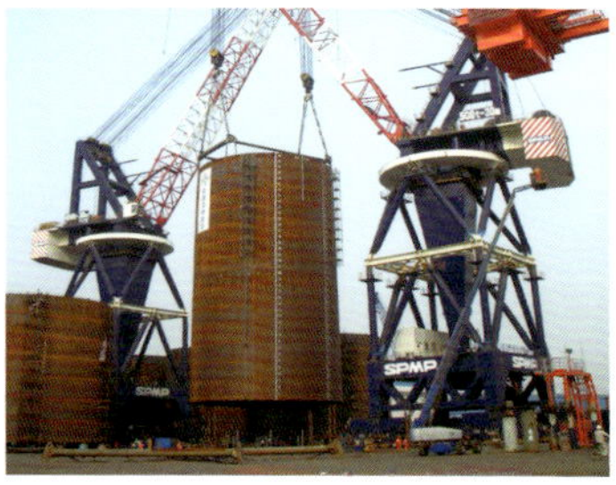

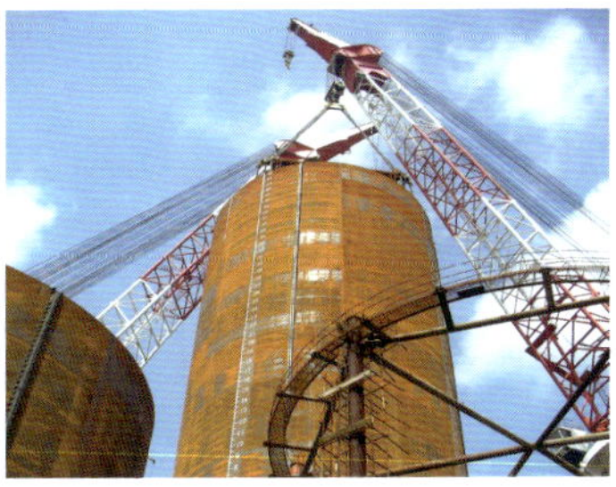

钢圆筒转运
Transportation of the Steel Cylinders
036

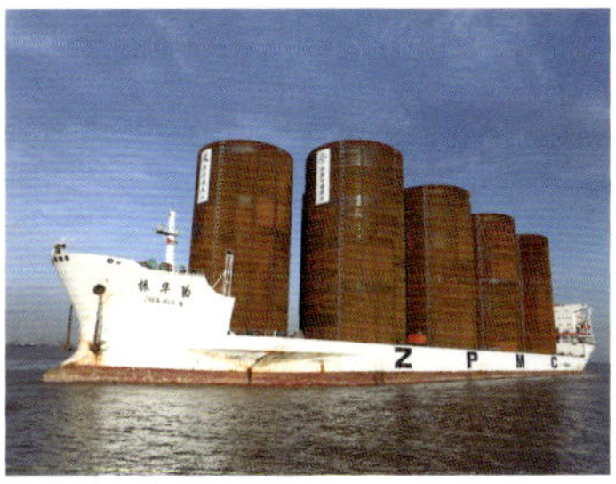

钢圆筒启运
Steel Cylinders Starting Sailing
039

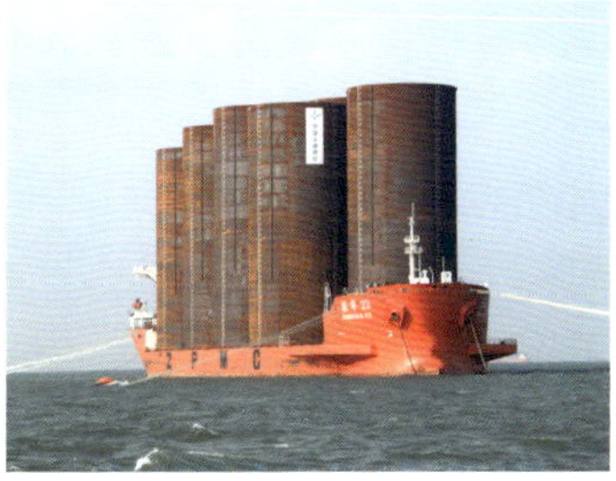

钢圆筒运输船系泊
Anchoring of the Steel Cylinder Shipping Barge
040

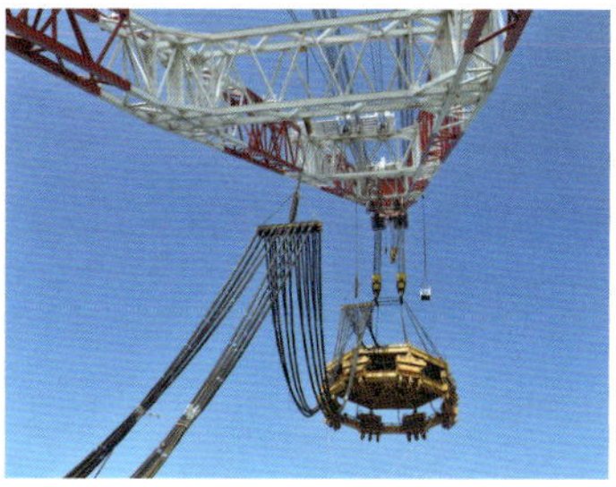

八锤联动振沉系统
Eight-Hammer Vibratory Driving System
042

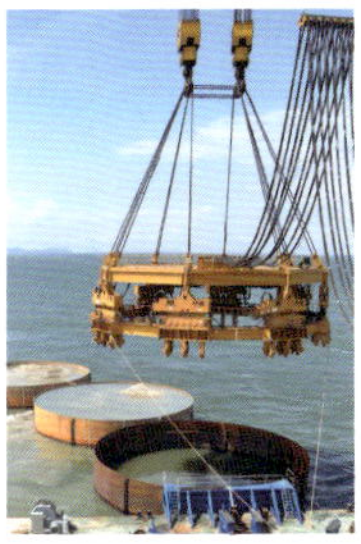

施工中的八锤联动振沉系统
Eight-Hammer Vibratory Driving System in Operation
045

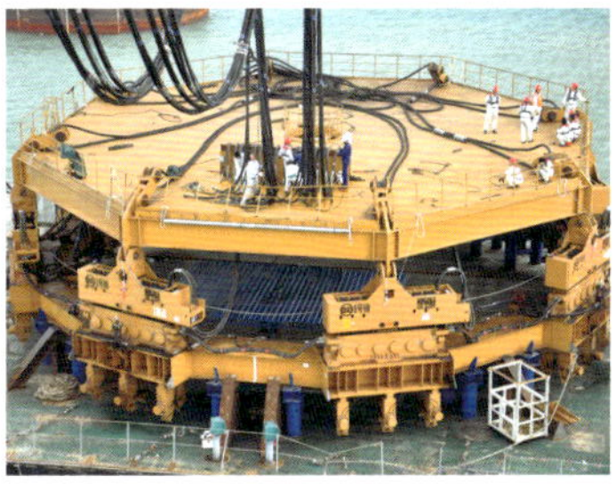

八锤联动系统调试
Adjustment of the Eight-Hammer Driving System
046

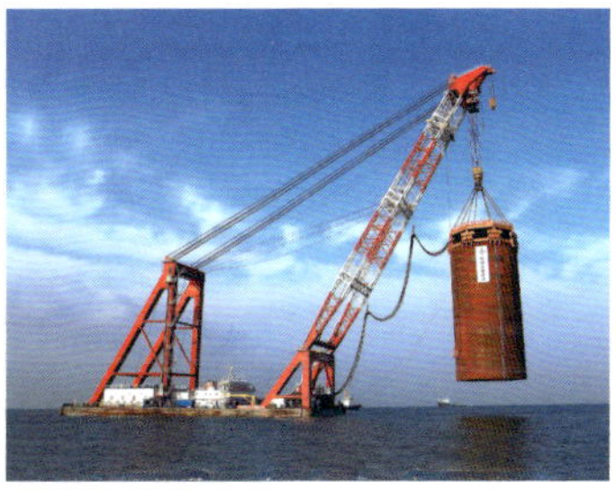

钢圆筒起吊
Steel Cylinder Lifting
049

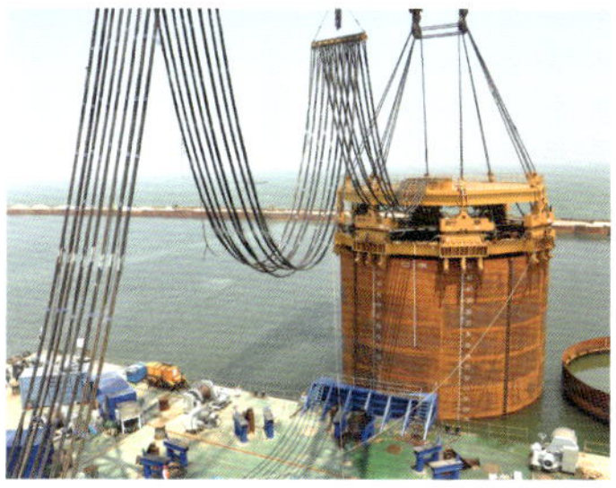

钢圆筒自沉
Automatic Sinking of the Steel Cylinder
051

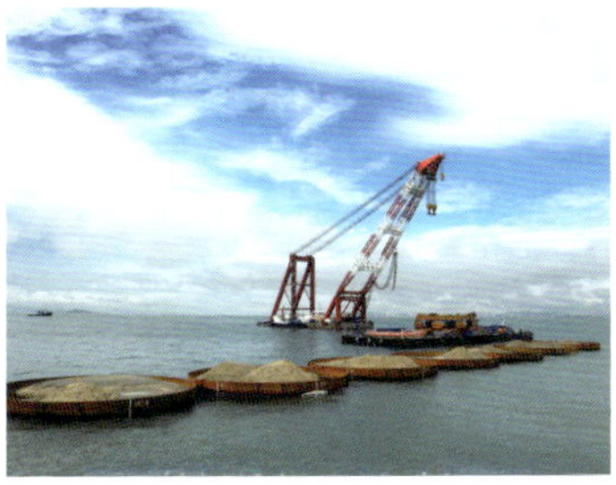

振沉完成的钢圆筒岛壁结构
Steel Cylinder Walls of the Island after Vibratory Driving Completed
053

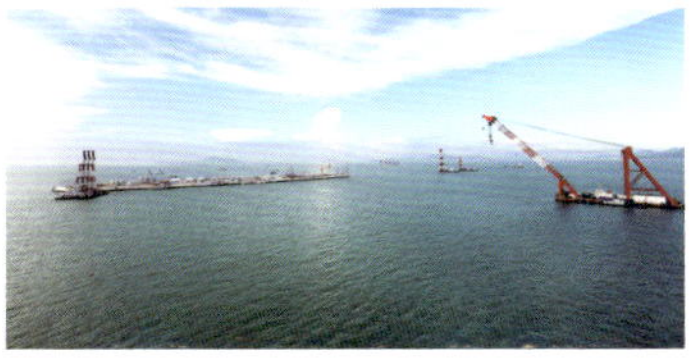

成岛后的东人工岛
East Man-Made Island Completed
054

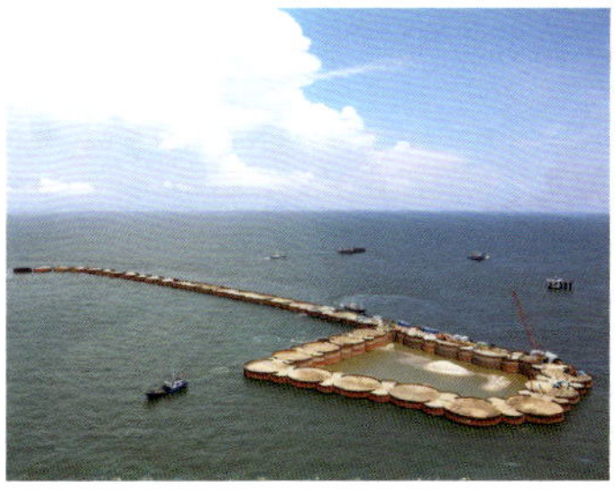

西人工岛成岛过程
Process of West Man-Made Island Reclamation
057

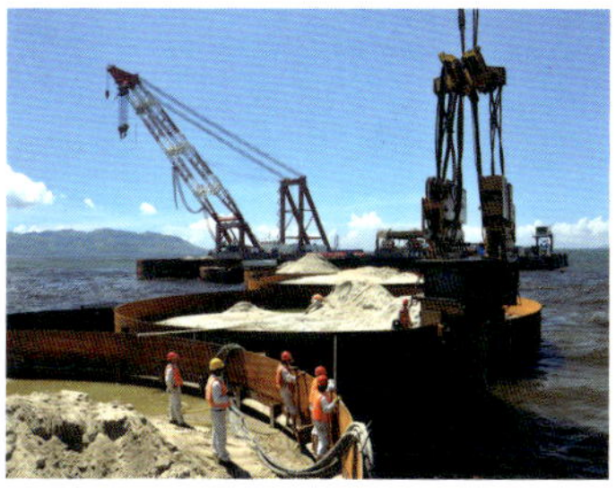

副格打设
Installation of the Connecting Rails
058

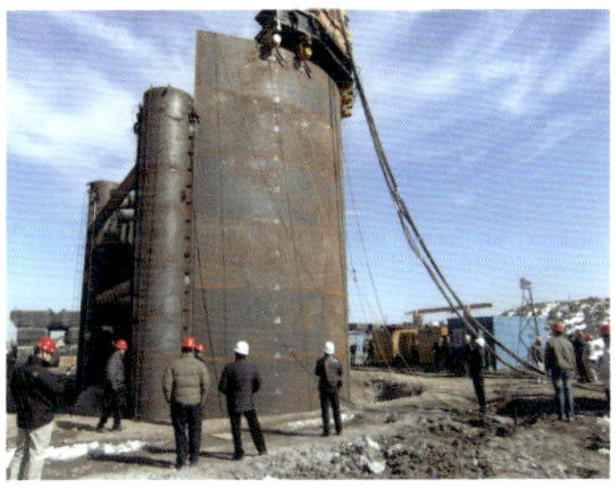

天津副格试验
Connecting Rail Test in Tianjin
060

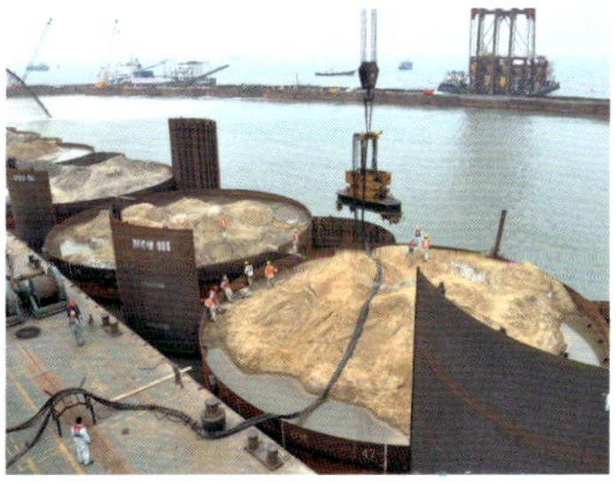

东人工岛副格振沉
Vibratory Driving of the Connecting Rail in East Man-Made Island
063

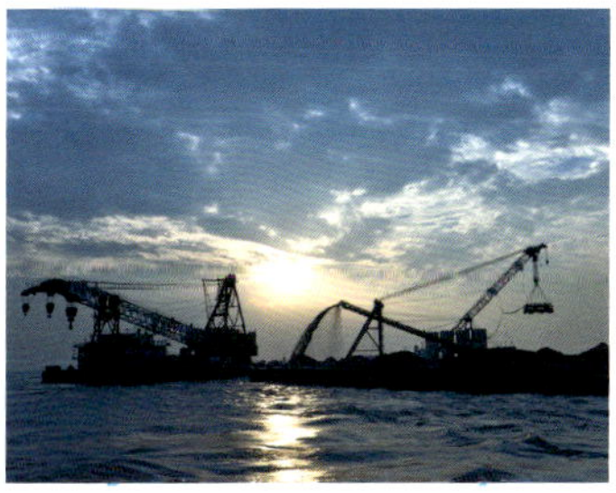

东人工岛回填
Backfilling on East Man-Made Island
064

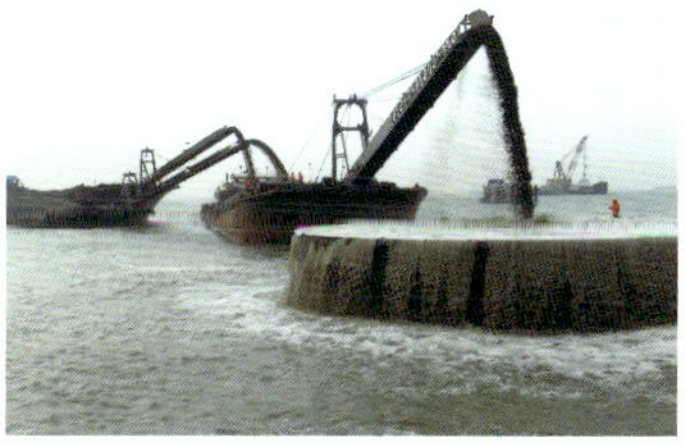

西人工岛首个钢圆筒回填砂
Sand Backfilling of the First Steel Cylinder in West Man-Made Island
067

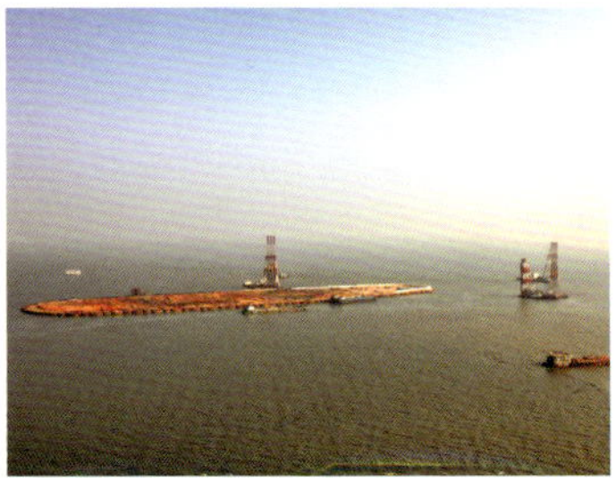
回填完毕的东人工岛
East Man-Made Island with Backfilling Completed
068

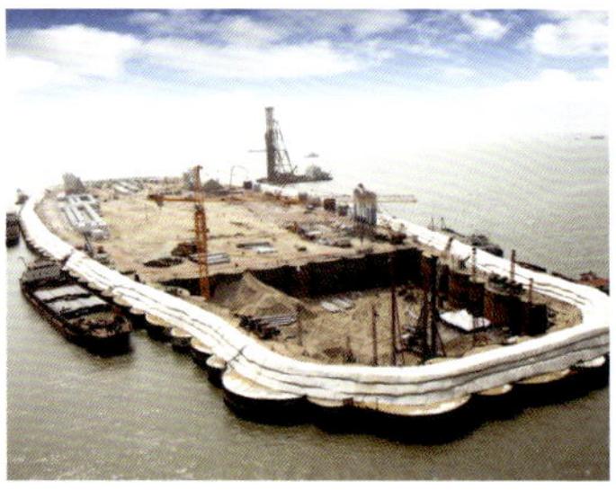
西人工岛深基坑施工
Deep Foundation Trench Construction on West Man-Made Island
072

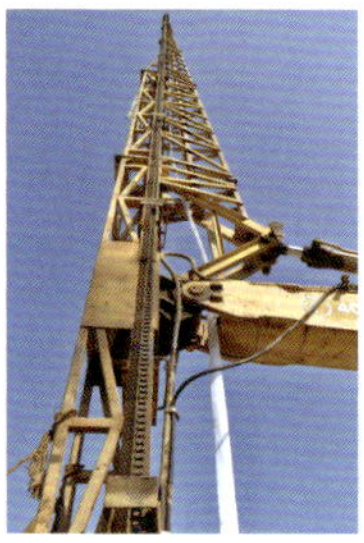
人工岛塑料排水板打设
Sinking of the Plastic Drainage Board on the Man-Made Islands
075

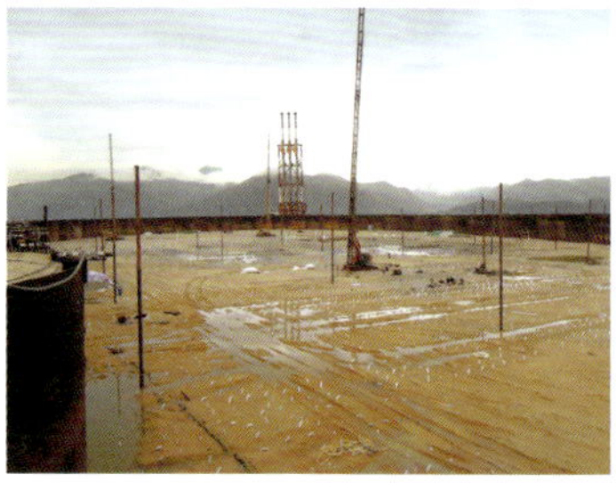
人工岛塑料排水板、降水井打设
Sinking of the Plastic Drainage Boards and the Construction of Dewatering Well on the Man-Made Islands
077

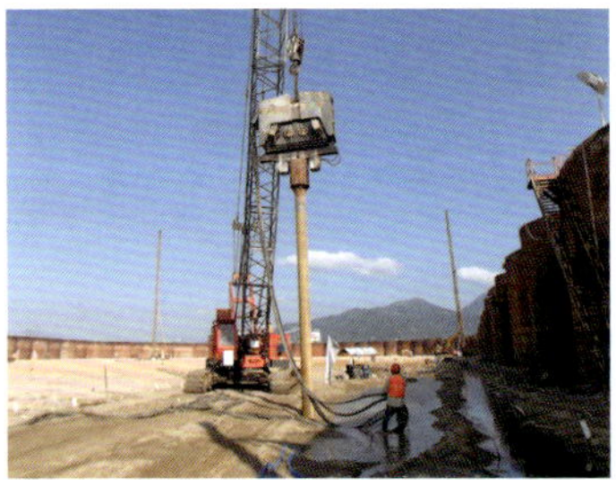
降水井打设
Construction of Dewatering Well
078

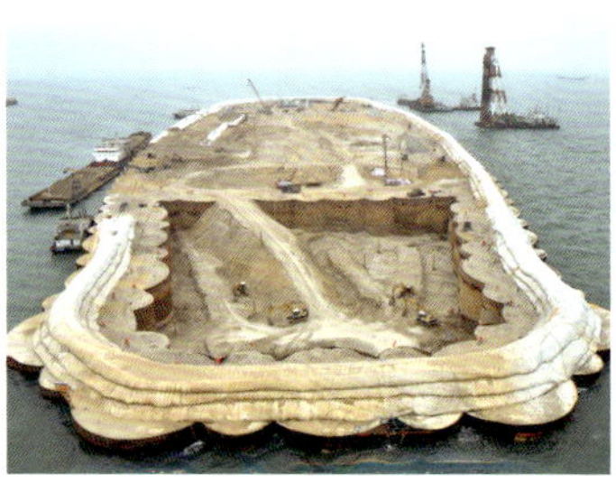
西人工岛岛壁围堰结构
Cofferdam on West Man-Made Island
081

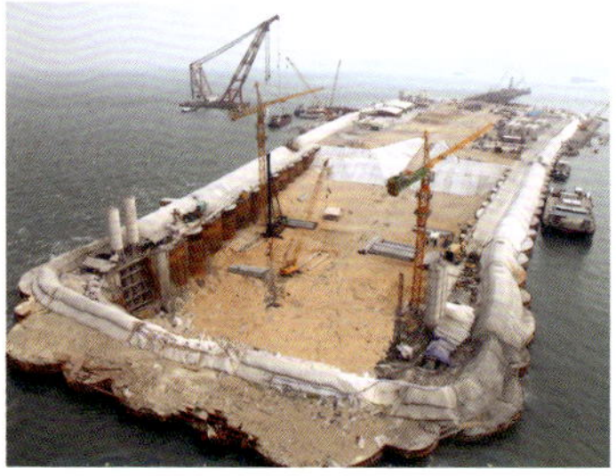
东人工岛深基坑开挖施工
Deep Foundation Trench Dredging on East Man-Made Island
083

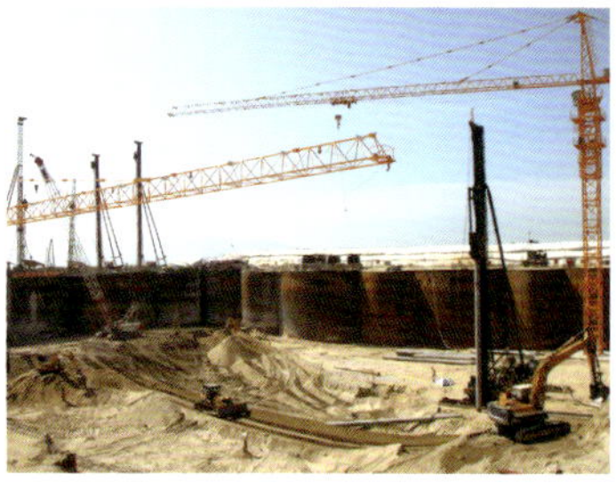
西人工岛深基坑开挖
Deep Foundation Trench Dredging on West Man-Made Island
084

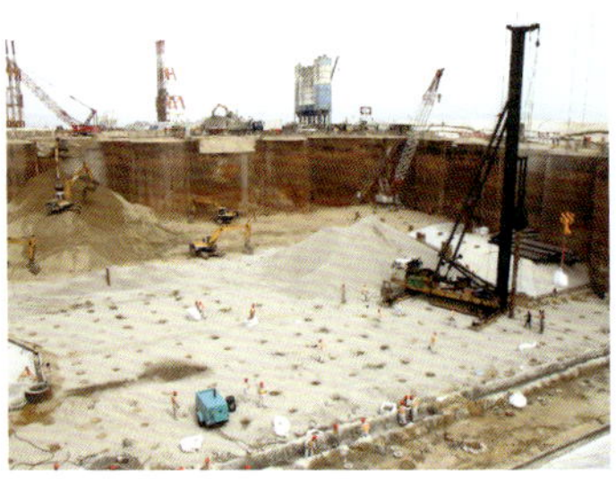
西小岛 PHC 桩打设
PHC Pile Sinking on the Minor West Island
087

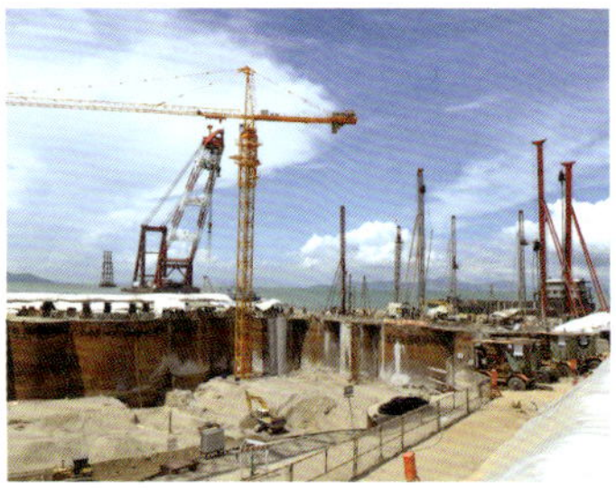
PHC 桩打设及旋喷桩施工
PHC Pile Sinking and Construction of the High Pressure Jet Grouting Piles
088

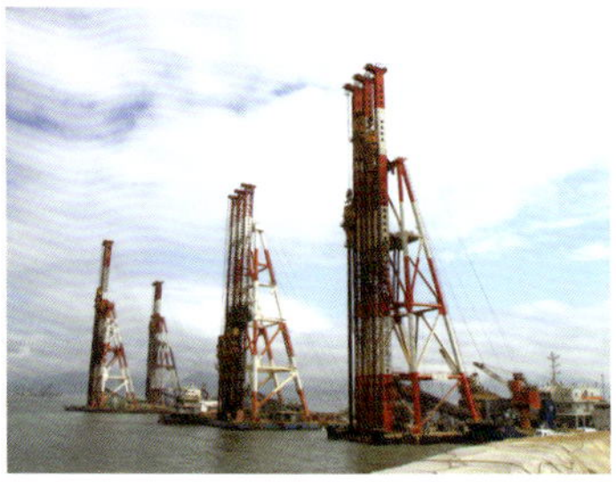
过渡段挤密砂桩打设
Sand Compaction Pile Sinking in the Transitional Section of the Tunnel
091

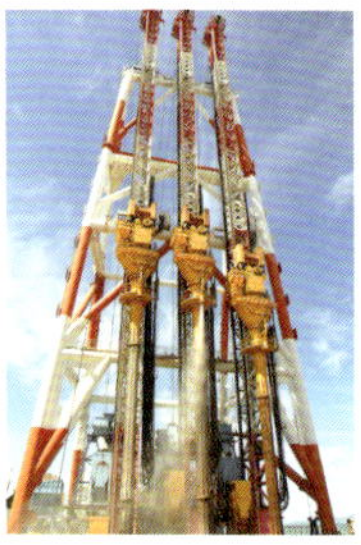
挤密砂桩打设
Sand Compaction Pile Sinking
093

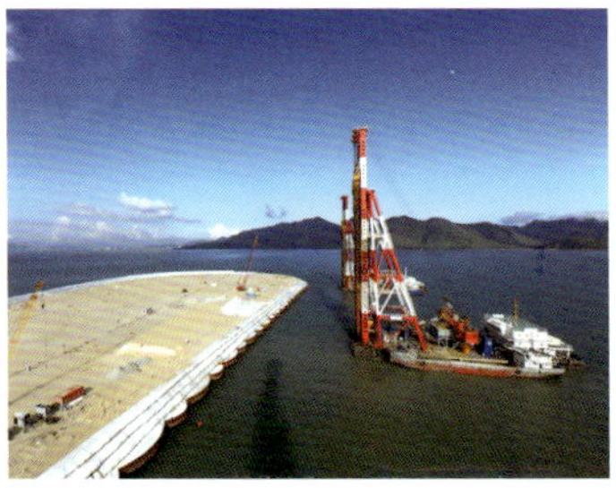
东人工岛岛壁区挤密砂桩打设
Sand Compaction Pile Sinking in the Island Wall Area on East Man-Made Island
094

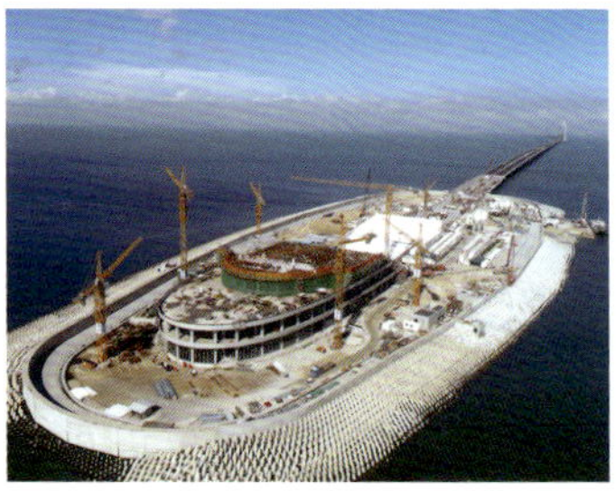
建设中的西人工岛
West Man-Made Island under Construction
098

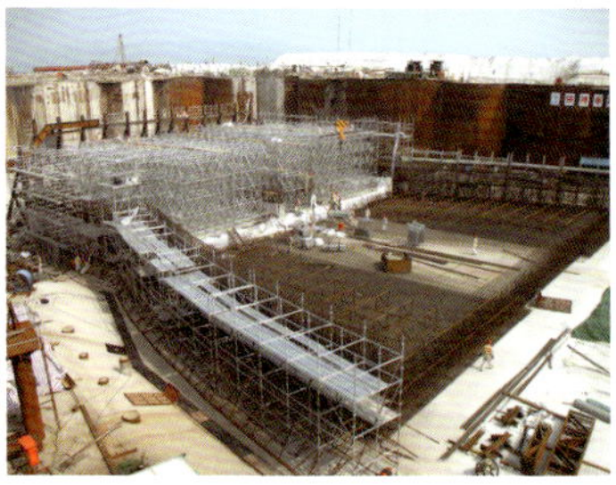
西人工岛现浇段支架搭设
Installation of the Scaffolds in the Cast-on-Site Section on West Man-Made Island
101

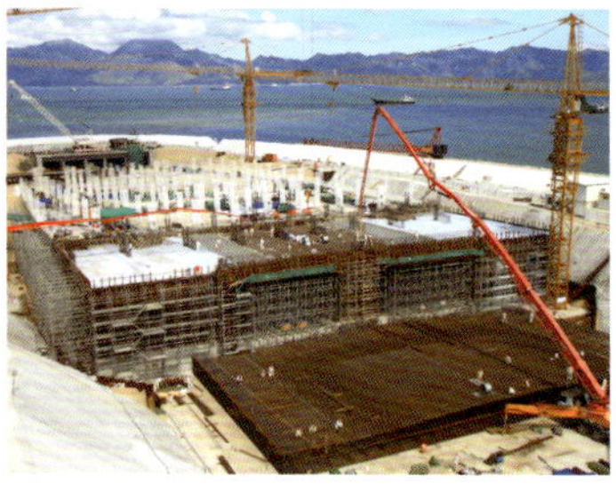
东人工岛暗埋段混凝土浇筑
Concrete Placement in the Buried Section on East Man-Made Island
102

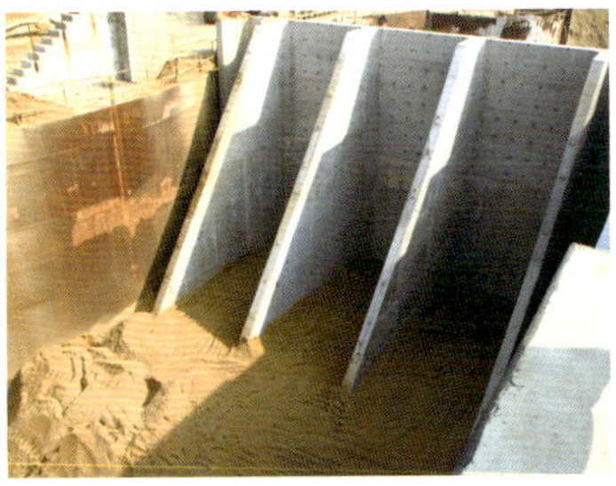

西人工岛暗埋段二次止水墙回填
Secondary Water-Stop Wall Backfilling in the Buried Section of West Man-Made Island
105

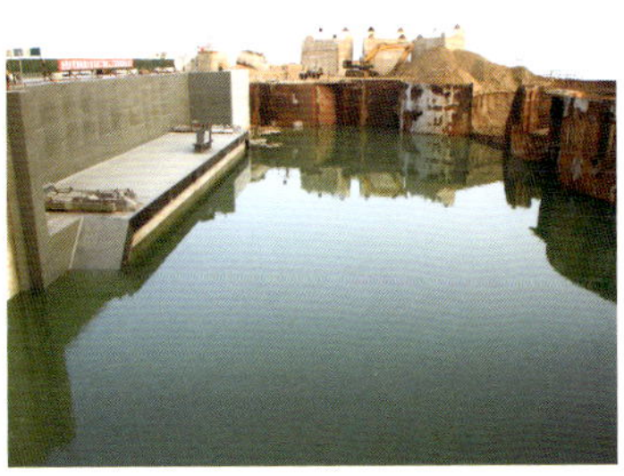

东人工岛暗埋段钢封门回水试验
Backwater Test on the Steel Sealing Devices in the Buried Section on East Man-Made Island
107

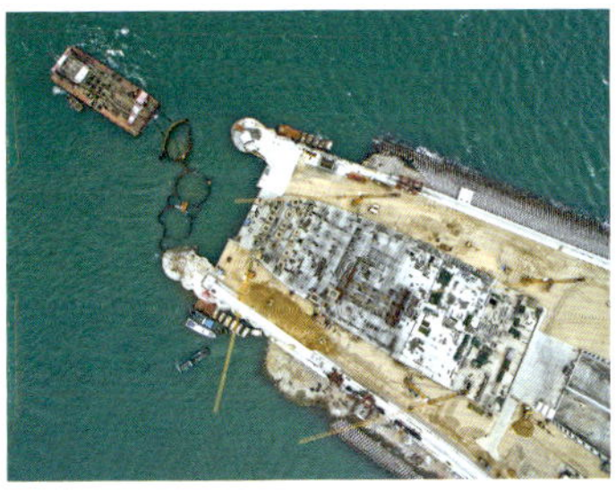

东人工岛岛头钢圆筒拆除
Removal of the Steel Cylinder at the Head Part of East Man-Made Island
108

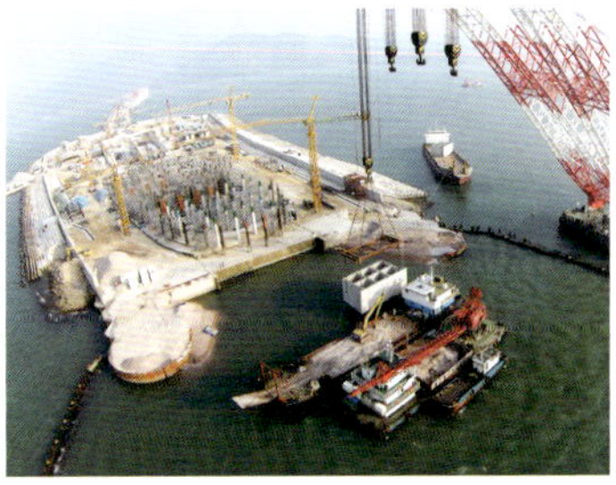

东人工岛减载沉箱安装
Load-Shedding Caisson Installation on East Man-Made Island
110

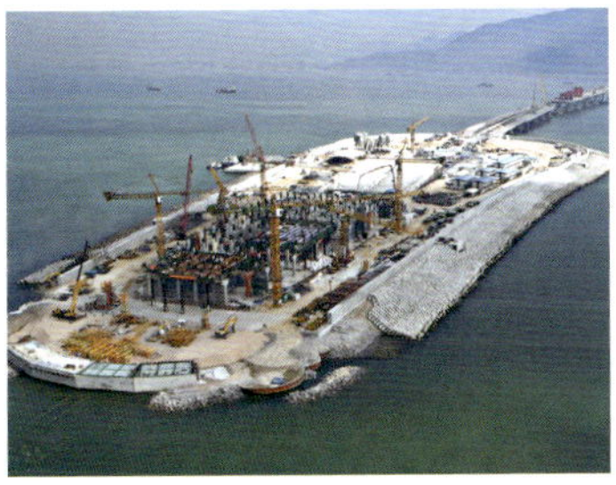

减载沉箱安装完成的东人工岛
East Man-Made Island after Load-Shedding Caissons Installation
112

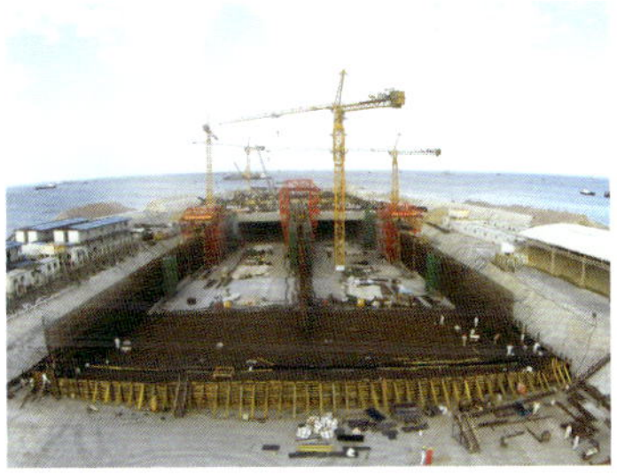

隧道敞开段底板、中隔墙钢筋笼绑扎
Steel Cage Binding for the Bottom Plate and the Partition Wall in the Open Section of the Tunnel
115

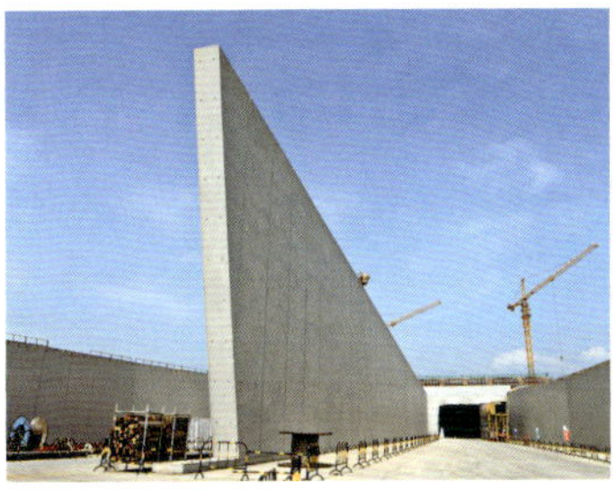

浇筑成型的敞开段
Well-Cast Open Section
116

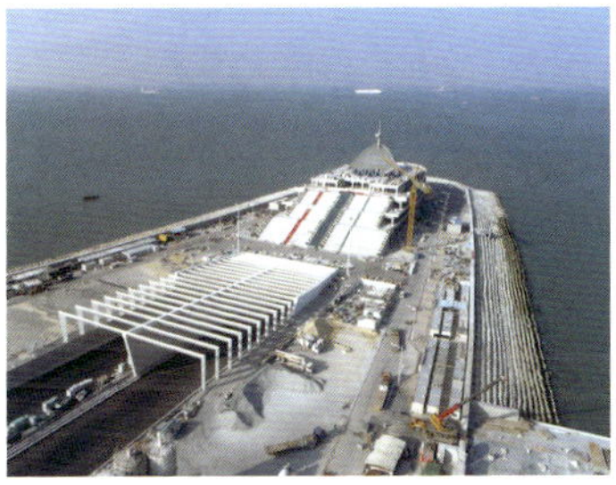

东人工岛减光罩
Light-Reducing Grating on East Man-Made Island
118

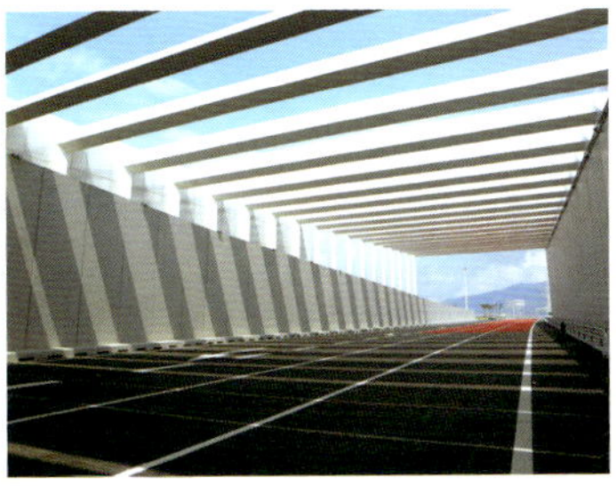

东人工岛隧道口减光罩
Light-Reducing Grating at the Tunnel Entrance on East Man-Made Island
120

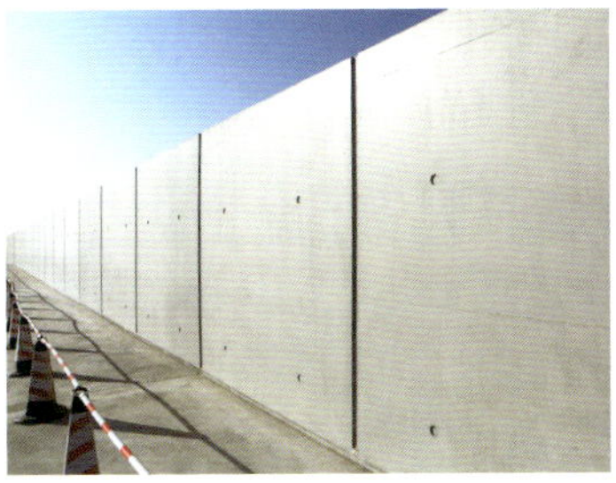

东人工岛挡浪墙
Wave-Blocking Wall of East Man-Made Island
123

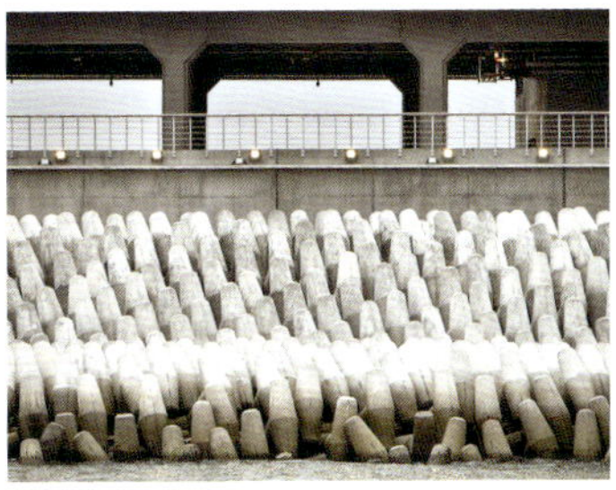

西人工岛岛壁结构
Fending Wall of West Man-Made Island
124

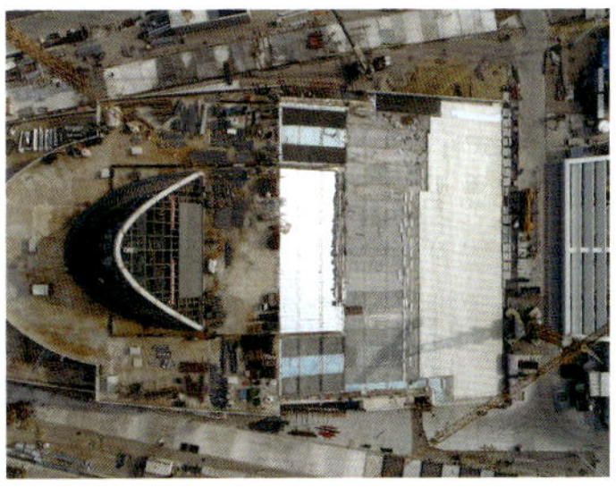

施工中的西人工岛岛上建筑
Buildings under Construction on West Man-Made Island
126

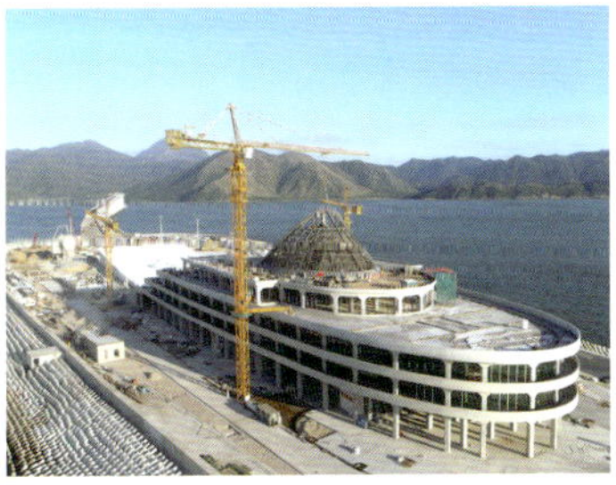

封顶后的东人工岛岛上主体建筑
Topped out Main Building on East Man-Made Island
129

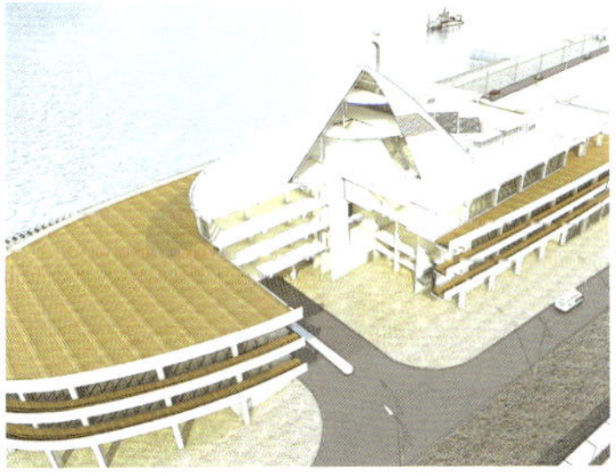

东人工岛岛上主体建筑剖面图
Profile of the Main Building on East Man-Made Island
130

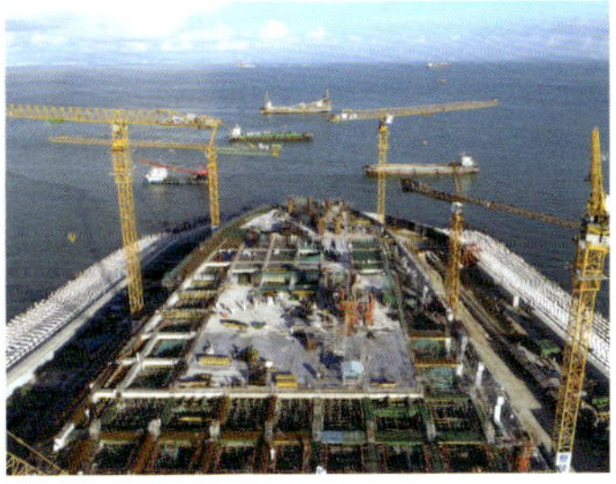

人工岛主体建筑封顶
Topping-out of the Main Building on the Man-Made Island
133

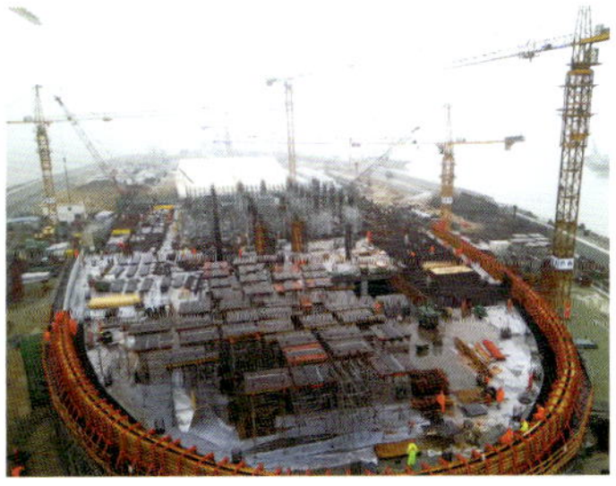

人工岛主体建筑楼板模板、圈型梁模板安装
Floor Framework of the Main Building on the Man-Made Island, and Installation of the Ring Beam Framework
134

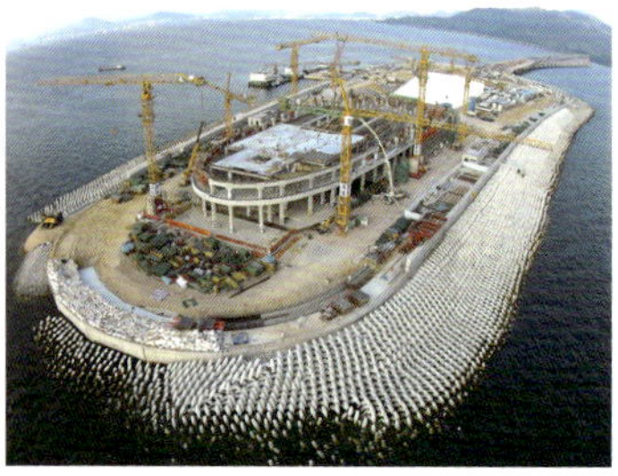

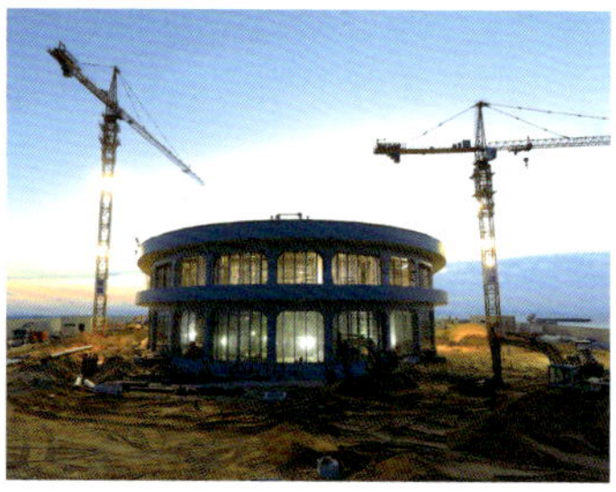

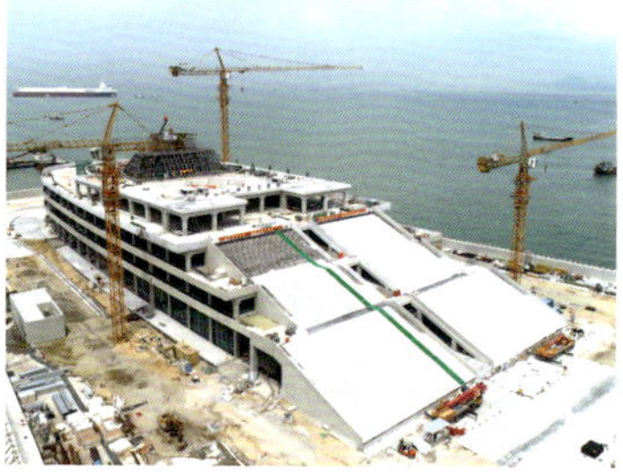

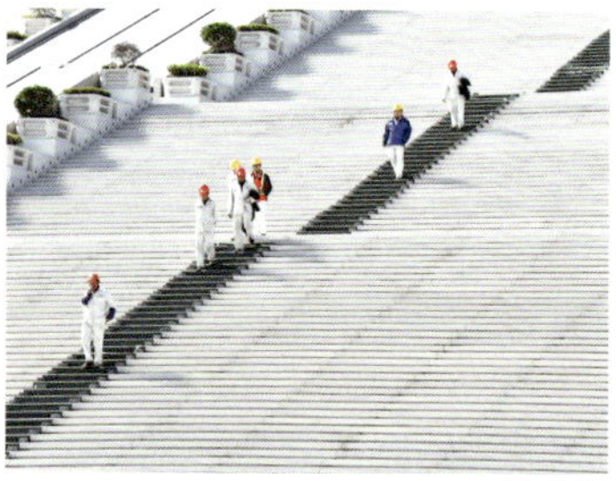

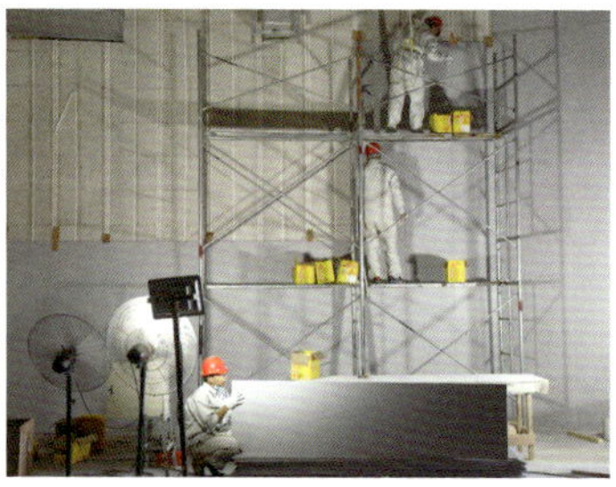

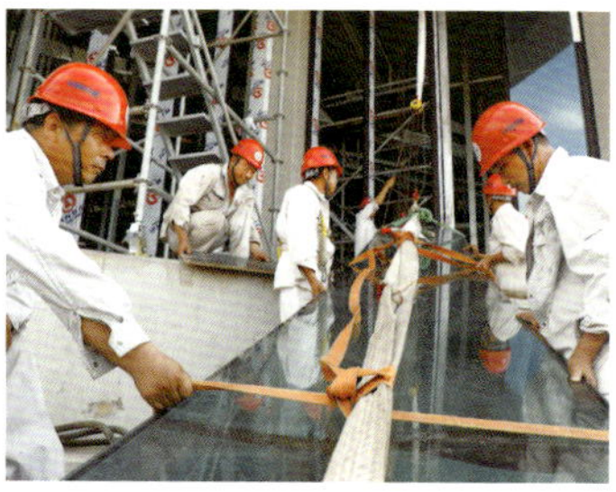

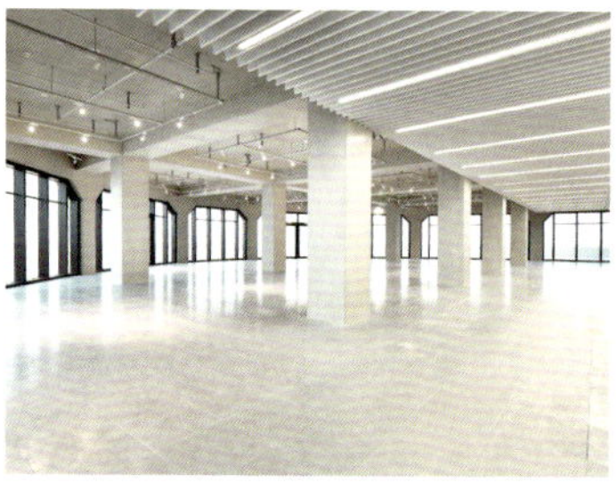

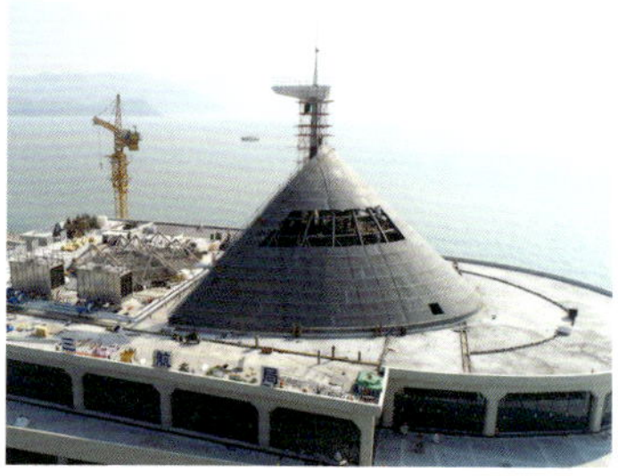

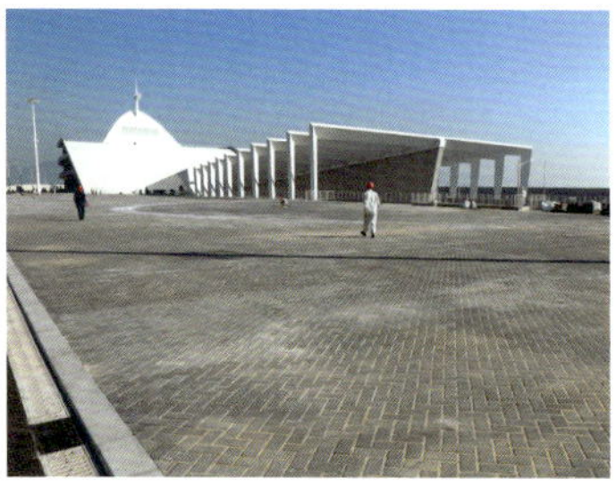

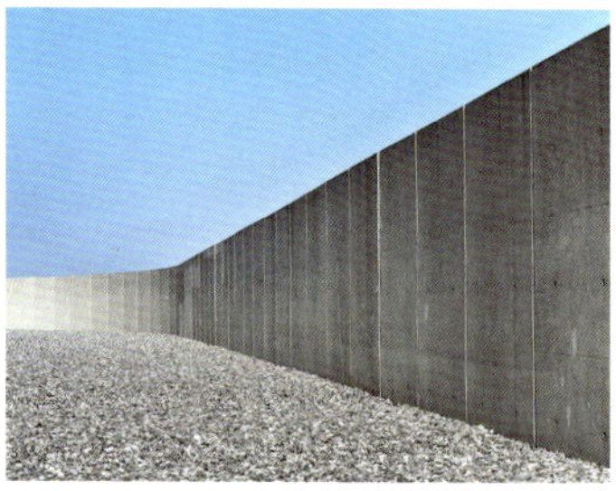

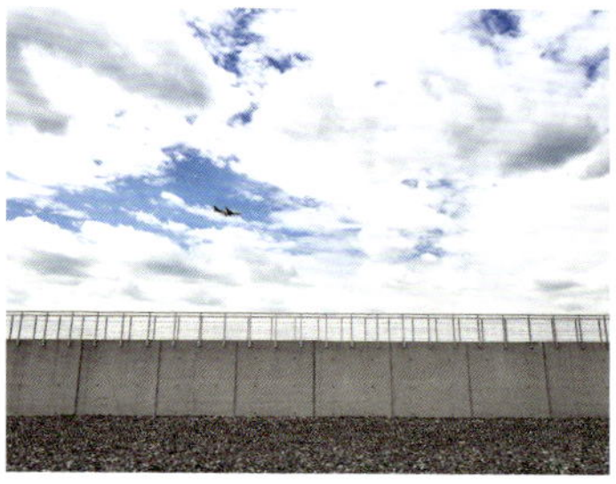

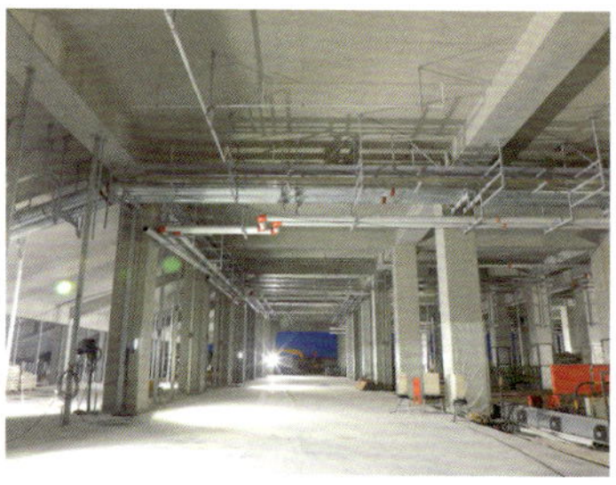

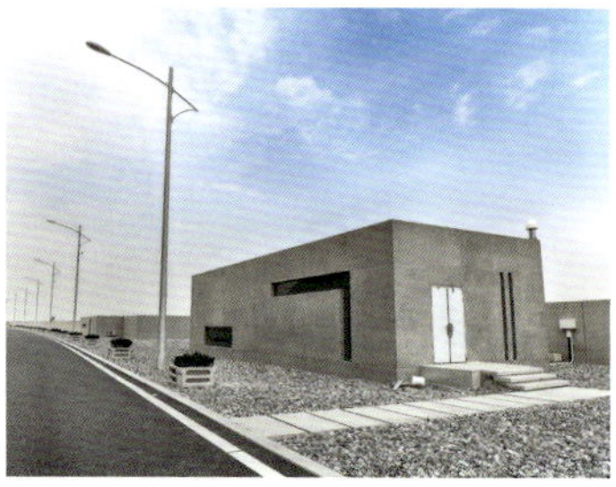

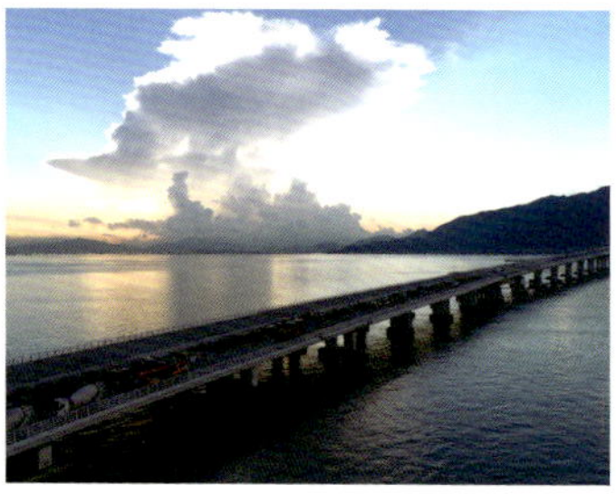

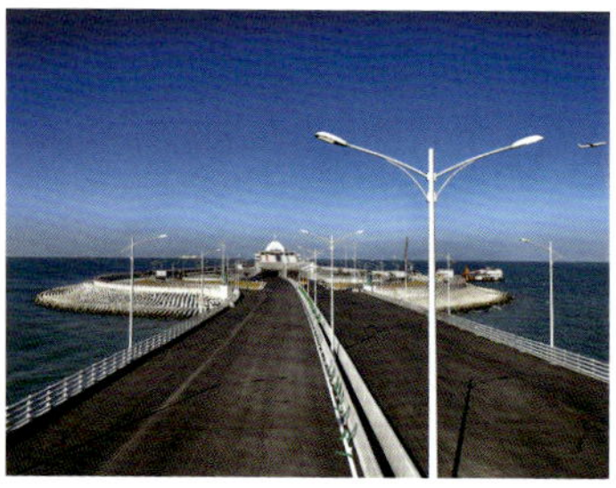

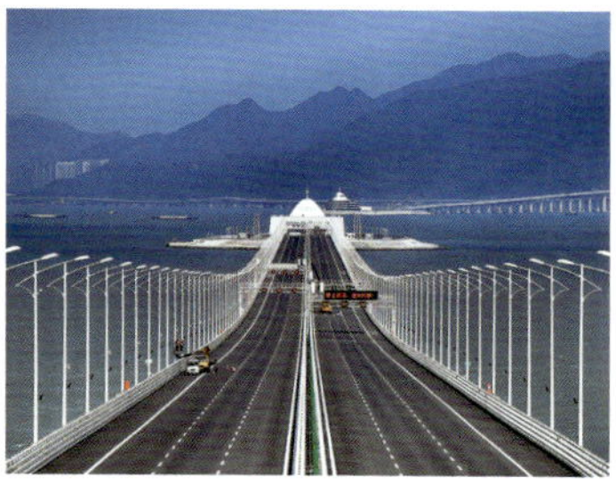